Programming .NET
Windows Applications

Jesse Liberty and Dan Hurwitz

O'REILLY®

Beijing · Cambridge · Farnham · Köln · Paris · Sebastopol · Taipei · Tokyo

Programming .NET Windows Applications
by Jesse Liberty and Dan Hurwitz

Copyright © 2004 O'Reilly & Associates, Inc. All rights reserved.
Printed in the United States of America.

Published by O'Reilly & Associates, Inc., 1005 Gravenstein Highway North, Sebastopol, CA 95472.

O'Reilly & Associates books may be purchased for educational, business, or sales promotional use. Online editions are also available for most titles (*safari.oreilly.com*). For more information, contact our corporate/institutional sales department: (800) 998-9938 or *corporate@oreilly.com*.

Editors:	Tatiana Apandi Diaz and Val Quercia
Production Editor:	Mary Brady
Cover Designer:	Ellie Volckhausen
Interior Designer:	David Futato

Printing History:

October 2003:	First Edition.

ISBN: 0-596-00321-8

[M]

Table of Contents

Preface

Windows Forms represents the third generation of Windows development. When Microsoft first released Windows in 1985, programmers built applications using the Windows API, typically in C. Many of us learned how to build these applications from Charles Petzold, and this is a good place to thank him for his seminal book on Windows programming.

By 1992, many programmers were building Windows applications in C++ using the Microsoft Foundation Classes (MFC). Mike Blaszcack wrote a killer book on this topic, and it remains a classic. In essence, the MFC represented an object-oriented wrapper on the more procedural API.

In the 1990s, the alternative to building C++/MFC applications was using VB and its Rapid Application Development environment.

Microsoft first announced the third generation of Windows development, Windows Forms, and the .NET platform in July 2000. In short, C# (and Visual Basic .NET) and Windows Forms replace C++ and the MFC as well as classic VB. This book aims to provide a complete tutorial to this new way of creating Windows applications.

On a personal note, having spent nine years building MFC applications in C++ (and having earned much of my livelihood writing books about C++) you might expect me to have a certain resistance to the new paradigm. About an hour after writing my first C#/Windows Forms application, I said to my dog, "I'll never go back, and you can't make me." The improvements were so significant, and the increase in productivity so unmistakable, that there was no doubt in my mind that Windows Forms would totally replace C++/MFC in my development of Windows applications.

About This Book

This book will teach you all you need to know to use Windows Forms effectively. We assume you have some background with either C# or Visual Basic .NET (VB.NET), or sufficient programming experience to pick up what you need to know from the examples shown.

Windows Forms is not difficult. All of its concepts are straightforward, and the Visual Studio .NET environment makes building powerful applications much simpler than writing code by hand. The only difficulty of Windows Forms is that many pieces must be woven together to build a robust, scalable, and efficient application.

You will find two authors' names on this book. Each chapter was written initially by one or the other author, but all chapters were then edited by both authors. Jesse Liberty then extensively edited and rewrote every chapter to give the book a more unified voice. The chapters were subsequently edited by the O'Reilly editors and then again by the authors. The bottom line is that although two authors wrote this book, it should read as if it were written by a single author.

How the Book Is Organized

Chapter 1, *Windows Forms and the .NET Framework*, is an introduction to Windows Forms and the .NET Framework, and is compatible with .NET 1.1 and Visual Studio 2003.

Chapter 2, *Getting Started*, covers system requirements and walks you through the creation of several simple "Hello World" applications, using both a text editor and Visual Studio .NET.

Chapter 3, *Visual Studio .NET*, gives a thorough review of the Integrated Development Environment (IDE) that is provided by Microsoft for developing .NET applications.

Chapter 4, *Events*, covers the use of events in .NET Forms applications, and includes extensive examples involving keyboard events and text box validation.

Chapter 5, *Windows Forms*, covers topics common to all .NET Forms applications, including the Form class and the Control class, as well as a discussion of forms inheritance and user interface design.

Chapter 6, *Dialog Boxes*, describes the different types of dialog boxes, including those you can create from scratch and those provided as part of the CommonDialog classes.

Chapter 7, *Controls: The Base Class*, covers the features common to all controls in .NET Forms, including such things as parent/child relationships, ambient properties, size and location, anchoring and docking, and keyboard interaction. It also describes image lists.

Chapter 8, *Mouse Interaction*, covers the use of the mouse with .NET Windows applications, including mouse events and properties.

Chapter 9, *Text and Fonts*, discusses the use of the written word as part of Windows applications, including the Font class and techniques for drawing and measuring text strings.

Chapter 10, *Drawing and GDI+*, covers the Drawing namespace, which provides support for rendering graphics as part of a .NET application. It also includes a sample project, which creates a wicked cool analog clock on your screen.

Chapter 11, *Labels and Buttons*, begins the detailed coverage of the native controls available to the .NET developer. This chapter covers labels, link labels, buttons, checkboxes, and radio buttons.

Chapter 12, *Text Controls*, continues the discussion of native controls, with descriptions of the editable text controls, including the text box and rich text box.

Chapter 13, *Other Basic Controls* covers the rest of the native basic controls, including containers such as the panel and the group box, tabbed pages, the picture box, scrollbars and trackbars, up-down controls (sometimes known as spinners), and the progress bar.

Chapter 14, *TreeView and ListView*, describes the controls necessary to create hierarchical user interfaces as typified by Windows Explorer. A clone of Windows Explorer is developed as an exercise.

Chapter 15, *List Controls*, describes native controls used for presenting lists, including the listbox, the checked listbox, and the combo box.

Chapter 16, *Date and Time Controls*, starts with the techniques that deal with date and time values in .NET, including the DateTime and TimeSpan structures. It then describes the DateTimePicker and MonthCalendar controls and the Timer component.

Chapter 17, *Custom Controls*, describes how you can create your own controls to use when the native controls don't do what your application needs. These custom controls can extend or combine existing controls or can be built entirely from scratch.

Chapter 18, *Menus and Bars*, describes the provisions for creating menus, toolbars, and status bars in .NET Forms applications.

Chapter 19, *ADO.NET*, covers the .NET database technology and how to use databases in your applications.

Chapter 20, *Updating ADO.NET*, describes how to update the data in your database, including the use of transactions and multiuser updates.

Chapter 21, *Exceptions and Debugging*, describes error handling and debugging in the .NET Framework, including the debugger included as part of Visual Studio .NET.

Chapter 22, *Configuration and Deployment*, describes how to configure and deploy .NET Windows applications. It also includes a description of .NET assemblies.

The *Appendix* lists several tables of data useful to .NET programmers, including the ASCII character set, members of the KeyCode enumeration for mapping keyboard keys, and standard and system color names.

Who This Book Is for

This book was written for programmers and web developers who want to build desktop applications using Microsoft's powerful new .NET platform. Many readers will have experience with the Microsoft Foundation Classes or writing to the Windows API, but they may find that while the Windows Forms applications accomplish the same tasks, the approach is often quite different.

It might be helpful to first read a primer on C# or VB.NET (see Jesse Liberty's *Programming C#* (O'Reilly) or *Programming Visual Basic .NET* (O'Reilly)), but this is not required. Experienced VB, Java, or C++ developers may decide that they can pick up what they need to know about the languages just by working through the exercises in this book.

Conventions Used in This Book

The following font conventions are used in this book:

Italic is used for:

- Pathnames, filenames, and program names.
- Internet addresses, such as domain names and URLs.
- New terms where they are defined.

Constant Width is used for:

- Command lines and options that should be typed verbatim.

Constant-Width Italic is used for replaceable items, such as variables or optional elements, within syntax lines or code.

Constant-Width Bold is used for emphasis within program code.

C#   Indicates C# code.

VB   Indicates VB.NET code.

Pay special attention to notes set apart from the text with the following icons:

 This is a tip. It contains useful supplementary information about the topic at hand.

This is a warning. It helps you solve and avoid annoying problems.

Version Support

All code in this book was tested both with Version 1.0 and 1.1 of the .NET Framework and Visual Studio .NET.

Support: A Note From Jesse Liberty

As part of my responsibilities as an author, I provide ongoing support for my books through my web site. You can also obtain the source code for all examples in *Programming .NET Windows Applications* at my site, *http://www.LibertyAssociates.com*.

From my web site, you can access a dedicated book-support discussion forum with a section set aside for questions about *Programming .NET Windows Applications*. Before you post a question, however, please check my web site to see if there is a Frequently Asked Questions list or an errata file. If you check these files and still have a question, then please post to the discussion center.

The most effective way to get help on the discussion forum is to ask a very precise question or to create a very small program that illustrates your area of concern or confusion. You may also want to check the various newsgroups and discussion centers on the Internet. Microsoft offers a wide array of newsgroups, and Developmentor (*http:/discuss.develop.com*) has a wonderful .NET email discussion list.

We have tested and verified the information in this book to the best of our ability, but you may find that features have changed (or even that we have made mistakes!). Please let us know about any errors you find, as well as your suggestions for future editions, by posting to my discussion forum.

We'd Like to Hear from You

If you would like to provide feedback or suggestions to the editors, please write to:

O'Reilly & Associates, Inc.
1005 Gravenstein Highway North
Sebastopol, CA 95472
(800) 998-9938 (in the United States or Canada)
(707) 829-0515 (international/local)
(707) 829-0104 (fax)

There is a web page for this book, which lists errata, examples, or any additional information. You can access this page at:

http://www.oreilly.com/catalog/pnetwinaps

To comment or ask technical questions about this book, send email to:

bookquestions@oreilly.com

You can also send messages electronically. To be put on the mailing list or request a catalog, send email to:

info@oreilly.com

For more information about this book and others, as well as additional technical articles and discussion on Windows Forms and the .NET Framework, see the O'Reilly & Associates web site:

http://www.oreilly.com

and the O'Reilly .NET DevCenter:

http://www.oreillynet.com/dotnet

Acknowledgments

From Jesse Liberty:

John Osborn signed me to O'Reilly, and has nurtured my work and created a special niche for my books, for which I will be forever be in his debt. Valerie Quercia continues to be a phenomenal editor who adds tremendous value to my books.

This book would not be nearly as complete were it not for the extraordinary skills of Dan Hurwitz. He literally made this project possible, and I am grateful to him for both his ongoing contributions and his friendship.

Seth Weiss provides perspective and support, and Mike Kraley is like a tiny thruster rocket on the side of a lumbering ship—providing intermittent abrupt nudges in the right direction.

Stacey, Robin, and Rachel offer the love and support that make writing possible and worthwhile.

This book is dedicated to my mom, Edythe Levine, who has set a very high standard for courage and responsibility.

From Dan Hurwitz:

First and foremost I would like to thank my wife Jennifer, for her love, tolerance, and unwavering support. It sounds like a cliché, but without her help, it would not have been possible for me to put in the tremendous amount of work required to write this book. I would also like to thank my father, brothers Marvin and David, and good friends Joe, Tom, Peter, David, Grover, and Ann, who, along with Jennifer and many others, have helped me get through a very difficult period of my life. Finally, I would like to thank Jesse, my very good friend and coauthor, for providing the opportunity, again, for us to work together.

From both authors:

We would like to thank Ian Griffiths for his extraordinary technical editing of this manuscript, his expertise, and his advice. In addition, we'd like to thank Tatiana Diaz, who stitched together our otherwise disparate pieces into a single coherent work. Ian, Tatiana, Weimeng Lee, and others at O'Reilly, contributed to making this book far better than it otherwise would have been.

CHAPTER 1

Windows Forms and the .NET Framework

.NET is a new development framework that provides a fresh application programming interface to the services and APIs of classic Windows operating systems and brings together several disparate technologies that emerged from Microsoft during the late 1990s. These new technologies include COM+ component services, a commitment to XML and object-oriented design, and a clean interface to the Internet.

To lay the foundation for a full understanding of Windows Forms, this chapter begins with an introduction to the .NET platform and a focus on the .NET Framework.

The .NET Framework

Microsoft .NET supports a Common Type Specification (CTS) that lets you choose the syntax with which you are most comfortable. You can write classes in C# and derive from them in VB.NET. You can throw an exception in VB.NET and catch it in a C# class. Suddenly the choice of language is a personal preference rather than a limiting factor in your application's development.

The .NET Framework sits on top of the operating system, which can be any modern flavor of Windows,* and consists of multiple components. Currently, the .NET Framework contains:

- An expanding list of official languages (e.g., C#, VB.NET, and JScript .NET)
- The Common Language Runtime (CLR), an object-oriented platform for Windows and web development that all these languages share
- A number of related class libraries, collectively known as the Framework Class Library (FCL).

---

* Because of the Common Language Runtime architecture, in theory the operating system can be any OS, including Unix.

Figure 1-1 more fully breaks down the .NET Framework into its system architectural components.

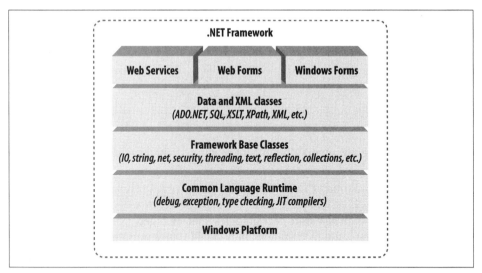

Figure 1-1. .NET Framework architecture

The CLR executes your program; it activates objects, performs security checks on your code, lays your objects out in memory, executes them, and handles garbage collection.

In Figure 1-1, the layer on top of the CLR is a set of framework base classes, followed by an additional layer of data and XML classes, plus another layer of classes intended for applications based on Windows Forms, Web Forms, or web services. Collectively, these classes are known as the Framework Class Library (FCL). With more than 5,000 classes, the FCL facilitates rapid development of applications for either the desktop or the Web.

The set of framework base classes support rudimentary input and output, string manipulation, security management, network communication, thread management, text manipulation, reflection, and collections functionality.

Above the base class level are classes that support data management and XML manipulation. The data classes support persistent management of data that is maintained on backend databases. These classes together are referred to as ADO.NET. Some classes are optimized for Microsoft SQL Server relational database, and some are generic classes that interact with OLE DB–compliant databases. The .NET Framework also supports classes that let you manipulate XML data and perform XML searching and translations. The data handling aspects of the .NET Framework are covered in Chapter 19.

Going beyond the framework base classes and the data and XML classes (and to some extent, building on their technology) are yet another tier of classes geared toward three different technologies:

Windows Forms
> Allows the development of Windows desktop applications with rich and flexible user interfaces. These desktop applications can interact with other computers on the local network or over the Internet through the use of web services.

Web Forms
> Allows the development of robust, scalable web pages and web sites.

Web services
> Allows the development of applications that provide method calls over the Internet.

To learn more about Web Forms and web services, please see *Programming ASP.NET*, Second Edition, by Jesse Liberty and Dan Hurwitz (O'Reilly).

Windows Forms

Windows Forms is the name Microsoft gave to its desktop development technology. Using Windows Forms, it is easier than ever to create applications that are dynamic and data-driven, and that scale well. Used in conjunction with Visual Studio .NET, Windows Forms technology allows you to apply Rapid Application Development (RAD) techniques to building Windows applications. Simply drag and drop controls onto your form, double-click on a control, and write the code to respond to the associated event. In short, the RAD techniques previously available only to VB.NET programmers is now fully realized for all .NET languages.

Languages: C# and VB.NET

You can program Windows Forms in any language that supports the .NET Common Language Specification (CLS). The examples in this book will be given in C# and VB.NET. We believe that C# and VB.NET are very similar, and if you know one you will have no problem with examples shown in the other. That said, we offer the examples in both languages to simplify the process of learning the technology.

Visual Studio .NET

Since all Windows Forms source files are plain text, you can develop all your applications by using your favorite text editor (e.g., Notepad). In fact, many examples in this book are presented just that way. However, Visual Studio .NET offers many advantages and productivity gains. These include the items listed next.

- Visual development of Windows Forms
- Drag-and-drop Windows controls
- IntelliSense and automatic code completion
- Integrated debugging
- Automated build and compile
- Integration with the Visual SourceSafe source control program
- Fully integrated and dynamic help

CHAPTER 2

Getting Started

The start of any journey is often the hardest part, especially if the goal is unclear or seems daunting. So too with learning a new computer technology. One way to alleviate this difficulty is to present, right up front, a clear idea of what is needed to start the journey and examples that demonstrate the possibilities that lie at the end of the road.

The previous chapter introduced the .NET Framework and overall architecture. In later chapters, you will learn how to create Windows applications using .NET and the Windows Forms technology.

This chapter will cover what software you need on your computer to develop applications using the .NET Framework. Then it will show you what a Windows Forms application looks like. It will do this using the traditional route of a simple program to say "Hello World." In this case, there will actually be three successive Hello World programs, each showing progressively more capability. Each of the three programs will be developed twice—once in Notepad and again in Visual Studio .NET— to show the advantages of a good development environment.

System Requirements

This being the new millennium, you need a lot of horsepower to develop and run any modern Windows application, no less so for .NET. Fortunately, memory and disk space are modestly priced commodities these days.

Microsoft officially recommends a 600 MHz Pentium III–class processor or better for developing .NET applications, and RAM ranging from 96 to 256 MB, depending on the operating system. The application will run fine, if slowly, on a 300 MHz machine with 512 MB of RAM. However, as with money and brains, you can never have too much memory, and we recommend the biggest, fastest machine you can afford with at least 512 MB of RAM if at all possible.

Visual Studio .NET is a program that benefits from a lot of screen real estate, so a large, high-resolution monitor makes the development experience much more productive. You should consider a screen resolution of 1024 × 768 to be the minimum. Both authors of this book use high-speed Pentium machines with 512 MB of RAM and two large monitors running at 1280 × 1024, powered by an Appian (*http://www.apian.com*) dual-headed graphics adapter.

To develop .NET applications, the minimum you will need to install is a supported version of Windows (NT 4 Workstation or Server, 2000 Professional or Server, XP Professional, or .NET Server) and the .NET Software Development Kit (SDK) (downloadable from Microsoft). This software will provide all necessary documentation, compilers and tools, the .NET Framework, and the CLR. You will have to write all your code in a text editor, such as Notepad, or a third party tool.

To be most productive with .NET, we recommend you purchase Visual Studio .NET. Visual Studio .NET includes the SDK and documentation, along with an integrated editor, debugger and other useful tools. Some examples in this book will be developed using only a text editor, but most will be developed in Visual Studio .NET. You can save money by buying the C#- or VB.NET-only version

To run an application developed by .NET on a client machine, i.e., a machine without an installed development environment, the .NET Framework Redistributable Package must be downloaded from Microsoft and installed on each client machine. This is possible on all the versions of Windows, mentioned earlier, plus Windows 98 and Windows Me. Deployment is covered in Chapter 22.

If you plan on doing any development that uses the Internet, such as ASP.NET projects, Internet deployment of Windows desktop applications, or the creation or consumption of web services, use an Internet connection for your final testing. For all these activities except the consumption of web services, you also need to install Internet Information Services (IIS) on your development machine. After IIS is installed, you will need to reinstall your .NET product. Bummer, eh? The best solution is to install IIS *first*, and *then* the .NET product.

Actually, it is possible to configure IIS after installing .NET by running the `aspnet_regiis.exe` command-line utility. From a command prompt enter `aspnet_regiis -i`.

This utility can also enable different web applications to run with different versions of the CLR on the same machine.

IIS is not installed by default with any of these operating systems but can be added easily after the OS is installed, if necessary. To add IIS to Windows 2000 or XP, go to the Control Panel, choose Add/Remove Programs, and then Add/Remove Windows Components. Select and install IIS. You will probably need to provide a Windows installation CD as part of the process. To add IIS to NT, install the Windows NT4

Option pack, downloadable from Microsoft over the Internet, and install Internet Information Server 4.0. Don't forget to reinstall any .NET development products after installing IIS.

 If you are installing IIS on a system using either the FAT16 or FAT32 filesystems, then manually configure the FrontPage 2000 Server Extensions. To do this, go to Control Panel, then Administrative Tools, and then Computer Management. Open the Computer Management dialog box and drill down to Internet Information Services (IIS). Right-click on Default web site or web sites (depending on the operating system), and select Configure Server Extensions. Follow the wizard. If the Configure Server Extensions menu item is missing, then the server extensions are already installed.

If you are planning any development that uses database access, you need to install a database. ADO.NET, the database-enabling technology within the .NET Framework, works with any OLE DB–compliant database, although it works best (of course) with Microsoft SQL Server. If you don't have Microsoft SQL Server, Microsoft Access, or another ODBC compliant database installed on your development machine, install the Microsoft SQL Server Desktop Engine (MSDE). This can either be done directly when the .NET product is installed, or the MSDE installation files can be copied to the machine as part of the .NET setup, and then the MSDE installed later.

 Some examples in this book assume that you have installed either SQL Server or MSDE.

Hello World

A long-standing tradition among programmers is to begin study of any new language by writing a program that prints "Hello World" to the screen. In deference to tradition, the first windows applications you create will do just that.

In this section, you will create three progressively more interesting versions of the venerable Hello World program. These versions will demonstrate some of the fundamental features of a Windows application. The first version will be a console application that writes a line of text to the system console (also known as a Command Prompt Window. Some old-timers still call it a DOS box, which is technically no longer accurate.). The next version will be a true Windows application, even if it is somewhat limited. The final version will add a button to demonstrate event handling. (Chapter 4 will cover events in detail.)

Using a Text Editor

The tool you are most likely to use when developing Windows applications is Visual Studio .NET. You may use any editor you like, however. All source code and configuration files for all .NET applications (Windows and web) are flat ASCII text files—easily created, read, and modified using any text editor, ranging from Notepad or WordPad (included with Windows) to powerful third-party code editors and development environments.

 Both Visual Studio .NET and the C# command-line compilers support different language encodings. In Visual Studio .NET, encoding is accessed under File → Advanced Save Options. The C# command-line compiler has a /codepage option to specify the codepage. The VB.NET command-line compiler does not support alternative encodings. In any case, the default code page is UTF8, which is a superset of flat ASCII.

Using Visual Studio .NET has several advantages. The code editor provides indentation and color coding of your source code, the IntelliSense feature helps you choose and enter the right commands and attributes, and the integrated debugger helps you find and fix errors in your code.

The disadvantage of using Visual Studio .NET, however, is that it automatically generates copious amounts of boilerplate code and default object names. As a beginner, you may be better off doing more of the work yourself, giving up the support of the IDE in exchange for the opportunity to see how things really work.

You enhance the clarity, readability, and maintainability of your program by using your own names for namespaces, classes, methods, and functions, rather than using the default names provided by Visual Studio .NET.

Each of the three versions of Hello World mentioned above will first be developed by using a simple text editor to create the source code. The same three versions will then be created using Visual Studio .NET.

All code examples will be presented in both VB.NET and C#, unless both language versions are nearly identical.

Hello World as a console application

The first version of the Hello World program created here will be a *console application*. A console application has no user interface (UI) other than a command prompt. It has no windows, buttons, menus, listboxes, or other graphical elements. All it can do is execute program code, accept input, and display text.

For most purposes, the input console is the keyboard and the output console is the command prompt window. The Console class of the .NET Framework encapsulates both the input and output console, and provides properties and methods for communicating with the console. Text written to (or read from) the console can also be directed to or from other devices or files using streams. The Hello World program shown here will just send some characters to the screen.

If a console application EXE file is double clicked in Windows Explorer, the console application will open its own command prompt window, execute, and close the window. For a quickly running program like Hello World, it all happens so fast that you barely see the screen flicker.

To execute a console application and actually see the results, open a command prompt and run the program by typing the executable name from the command line.

Using the Command Line in .NET

For any of the tools or utilities provided as part of the .NET SDK to run from a command line, the Path property of the operating system environment for that command window must include the correct location of the tool or utility executable. The easiest way to ensure that the Path is set correctly is to not open a normal Command window (Start → Programs → Accessories → Command Prompt), but instead to open a special command prompt window provided as part of .NET. This command window has the Path correctly set to include the locations of all the .NET tools and utilities.

Click on the Start button, and then Programs → Microsoft Visual Studio .NET 2003 → Visual Studio .NET Tools → Visual Studio .NET 2003 Command Prompt. You will probably want to copy this shortcut to someplace more accessible, such as the Windows desktop or a quick launch toolbar.

To execute a console application, either navigate to the directory where the console application lives (using the cd command) and then type the name of the program, or enter the full path to the program as part of the name.

The code listings shown in Example 2-1 and Example 2-2 are the Hello World console applications in C# and VB.NET, respectively. These programs use the WriteLine method to output a line of text to the system console, which is your computer screen.

This book is not a primer on C#, VB.NET, or the .NET framework. We assume you are familiar with this material, and we will not explain the language fundamentals. For a full exploration of VB.NET, see Jesse Liberty's *Programming Visual Basic .NET*, and for C#, see his book *Programming C#* (both from O'Reilly).

A significant theme of this book is that the choice between C# and VB.NET is purely syntactic: you can express almost any programming idea in either language. Write in whichever language is more comfortable for you. The transition from VB.NET or VBScript to VB.NET may be slightly easier than to C#, but much of the Microsoft and third-party documentation is in C#.

This book shows most examples in both languages, with a slight preference for C# because it is a bit more terse. In any case, you will notice that in most cases, the differences between the languages are small and easily understood.

Open a text editor, such as Notepad, and enter the code shown in Example 2-1 or Example 2-2. Save the file to the name shown in the caption for each code listing.

Example 2-1. Hello World console application in C# (HelloWorld-console.cs)

```csharp
namespace ProgrammingWinForms
{
    public class HelloWorld
    {
        static void Main( )
        {
            System.Console.WriteLine("Hello World");
        }
    }
}
```

Example 2-2. Hello World console application in VB.NET (HelloWorld-console.vb)

```vb
namespace ProgrammingWinForms
    public class HelloWorld
        shared sub Main( )
            System.Console.WriteLine("Hello World")
        end sub
    end class
end namespace
```

 The principal differences between C# and VB.NET are that C# is case sensitive, statements in C# are terminated with a semicolon, and namespaces, classes, and methods in C# are contained within curly braces, whereas VB.NET uses the keyword end.

Although VB.NET is not case sensitive, Visual Studio .NET does impose its own casing rules on VB.NET source code (something that is lacking in C#). Since many of the examples in this book were created outside Visual Studio .NET, the VB.NET code in those examples does not necessarily follow the standard casing. It still compiles fine.

Compiling the program

To convert your source code to an executable program, it must be compiled. When working outside Visual Studio .NET, this is done using a command-line compiler. The SDK provides compilers for each supported language. This book uses both the C# and the VB.NET compilers.

Open the Visual Studio .NET command prompt, as discussed in the earlier sidebar "Using the Command Line in .NET." This will ensure that the proper path is set. Navigate to the directory where the source file is saved, using the cd command.

To compile the C# version of the Hello World program (the code shown in Example 2-1), use the following command (assuming you have saved the source file with the name *HelloWorld-console.cs*, as shown in the caption of Example 2-1):

C#
```
csc HelloWorld-console.cs
```

To compile the VB.NET version, use the following command (again assuming the source file was saved with the name *HelloWorld-console.vb* as shown in the caption in Example 2-2):

VB
```
vbc HelloWorld-console.vb
```

In either case, the source file will be processed by the compiler and an EXE file will be created in the current directory. The name of the EXE file will be the same as the source code, without the extension (*HelloWorld-console*) followed by the extension *.exe*. Thus, *HelloWorld-console.exe*.

You can execute the program by typing its name on the command line. Figure 2-1 shows the results of opening a Visual Studio .NET command prompt window, navigating to the proper directory, compiling, and running Hello World for the console in C#.

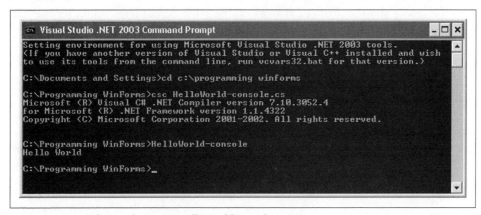

Figure 2-1. Compiling and running HelloWorld-console in C#

This was the simplest kind of compilation. Often, however, you will want the output name to be different from the input name, and for all but the simplest programs, there may be other files that must be referenced as part of the compilation. You control these aspects of command-line compiling with command-line switches. A command-line switch begins with a forward slash. To see all the available options available to the compiler, look in the SDK documentation or enter the appropriate commands:

C#
```
csc /?
```

VB
```
vbc /?
```

Compile the programs again, this time explicitly specifying the name of the output file and the type of executable (console application). To do so, use the appropriate command line:

C#
```
csc /out:csHelloWorld-console.exe /target:exe HelloWorld-console.cs
```

VB
```
vbc /out:vbHelloWorld-console.exe /target:exe HelloWorld-console.vb
```

The /out parameter specifies the output filename. If no /out parameter is specified, the output file will take its name from the source file that contains the Main procedure (in the case of EXE outputs) or the first source file specified (for non-EXE outputs). If there is no path information as part of the /out parameter, then the output file will be created in the current directory. You can qualify the filename with a path, either absolute or relative, to specify the output file location.

The /target parameter specifies the type of executable that will be created. You may also use /t as a shortcut form of /target. Table 2-1 lists four legal values for the /target parameter.

Table 2-1. Legal values of the /target parameter

Value	Short form	Description
/target:exe	/t:exe	Generates a console application with an extension of *.exe*. This is the default if no target option is specified. A Main procedure is required in at least one source file.
/target:library	/t:library	Generates a dynamic-link library (DLL). No Main procedure is required in any source file. If no /out parameter is specified, the output file will have an extension of *.dll*.
/target:module	/t:module	Generates a module that can be added to an assembly. If no out parameter is specified, the output file will have an extension of *.netmodule*. This option is available only via the command line; it is not available from within Visual Studio .NET.
/target:winexe	/t:winexe	Generates an executable Windows program, with an extension of *.exe*. A Main procedure is required in at least one source file.

One of the most commonly used compiler options (in VB.NET compilations, especially) is /reference (the short form is /r). This parameter specifies a file that contains an assembly manifest. The manifest exposes the assembly metadata. This allows other parts of the project to learn about and use any types (classes, member variables, methods, etc.) contained in the referenced file(s). If these types have public accessibility, then they will be available to the project being compiled.

Typically, the referenced files are DLLs that contain the .NET Framework class libraries, although you may also reference class libraries developed by yourself or others.

C# does not need the references in the command-line compile because a file called *csc.rsp* contains "default" references for the C# compiler. There is no equivalent in VB.NET, so the references must be included in the command line.

You can reference multiple files either by using multiple /reference parameters or by using a single parameter with a comma-separated list of filenames. Be certain not to include any spaces between the filenames if referencing multiple files with a single /r. The following two commands are equivalent:

```
vbc /out:bin\vbStockTickerCodeBehind.dll /t:library /r:system.dll,system.web.
dll,system.web.services.dll,
system.data.dll,system.xml.dll StockTickerCodebehind.vb

vbc /out:bin\vbStockTickerCodeBehind.dll /t:library
/r:system.dll /r:system.web.dll /r:system.web.services.dll
/r:system.data.dll /r:system.xml.dll StockTickerCodebehind.vb
```

In these command-line compilations, the VB.NET compiler is executed to compile a source code file named *StockTickerCodebehind.vb*. The output file, *vbStockTicker-CodeBehind.dll*, is a library file located in the *bin* subdirectory under the current directory. Five other DLL's are referenced: *system.dll*, *system.web.dll*, *system.web.services.dll*, *system.data.dll*, and *system.xml.dll*.

Sometimes you need to reference an assembly that is not located in either the CLR's system directory or the current directory of the command prompt window. In this case, use the /lib (with C#) or /libpath (with VB.NET) option to specify a directory to search in. You can search multiple directories by passing in a comma-separated list of directories. The compiler will first search the current directory of the command window, then the CLR system directory, and finally the directories specified in the /lib or /libpath options.

The /bugreport option aids in debugging compile problems. This option opens a text file and causes the compiler to put into it a copy of all the source files used in the compilation (you will probably want to condense and isolate the problem area), all the version information and compiler options, and the compiler output, if any. It will also prompt you for a description of the problem and how you think it should be fixed. These descriptions will accept carriage returns, so you can write a multiline description. The /bugreport option takes a fully qualified filename as its value.

The @ option allows you to specify a file, called a *response file*, which contains compiler options and source code files, just as if they had been entered manually from the command line. Use multiple @ options to specify multiple response files. Response files can have multiple lines, but each compiler option must be on a single line with no line break. The # symbol can be used in response files to comment lines.

When compiling EXE files, the source code must have at least one Main( ) method as an entry point for the program. This entry point must be static in C# or Shared in VB.NET. It can return either void (a sub in VB.NET) or an integer. If there are multiple Main( ) methods in the application, use the /main option to specify the *class* that contains the Main( ) method you will use as the entry point.

You can tell the compiler to search for source code files either in the current directory or in a specified directory. To do so, include an optional path name (absolute or relative) or a wildcard as part of the input file. For example, the following command line compiles a Windows application called *HelloWorld.exe*, using all the C# files in the current directory beginning with the characters HelloWorld:

```
C#    csc /out:HelloWorld.exe /t:winexe HelloWorld*.cs
```

The following command line will search for all similarly named source files in the *c:\ projects* directory:

```
C#    csc /out:HelloWorld.exe /t:winexe c:\projects\HelloWorld*.cs
```

You can also search for source files in the current or specified directory, plus all of their subdirectories, using the /recurse option. For example, the following command line will use all C# source code files in the current directory and all its subdirectories:

```
C#    csc /out:HelloWorld.exe /t:winexe /recurse:*.cs
```

This command line will search for all the C# source code files in the *deploy* subdirectory under the current directory, plus all subdirectories under *deploy*:

```
C#    csc /out:HelloWorld.exe /t:winexe /recurse:deploy\*.cs
```

Hello World as a Windows application

The next version of Hello World you create will be a very simple Windows application. Example 2-3 shows the code for this program in C# and Example 2-4 shows it in VB.NET. In both versions, a Windows Form is created with the text on the title-bar set to Hello World.

Example 2-3. Hello World Windows application in C# (HelloWorld-win.cs)

```
C#  using System.Windows.Forms;

namespace ProgrammingWinForms
{
   public class HelloWorld : System.Windows.Forms.Form
   {
      public HelloWorld( )
      {
         Text = "Hello World";
      }

      static void Main( )
      {
```

Example 2-3. Hello World Windows application in C# (HelloWorld-win.cs) (continued)

```
        Application.Run(new HelloWorld( ));
    }
  }
}
```

Example 2-4. Hello World Windows application in VB.NET (HelloWorld-win.vb)

```
imports System.Windows.Forms

namespace ProgrammingWinForms
   public class HelloWorld : inherits System.Windows.Forms.Form
      public sub New( )
         Text = "Hello World"
      end sub

      shared sub Main( )
         Application.Run(new HelloWorld( ))
      end sub
   end class
end namespace
```

The first line of Example 2-3 and Example 2-4 imports the System.Windows.Forms namespace:

```
using System.Windows.Forms;
```

```
imports System.Windows.Forms
```

This example lets you refer to objects in this namespace without the full qualification. When you declare the form, you are then free to refer to the base class as either System.Windows.Forms.Form or simply as Form.

The third line declares the Form class HelloWorld:

```
public class HelloWorld : System.Windows.Forms.Form
```

```
public class HelloWorld : inherits System.Windows.Forms.Form
```

The VB.NET version can be written equivalently as:

```
public class HelloWorld
inherits System.Windows.Forms.Form
```

Notice that the latter version is on two lines, and that it has neither a colon nor the VB.NET line-continuation character.

However you mark the derivation, the fact that your new class derives from Windows.Forms.Form makes it a Windows Form application.

The next several lines contain the constructor for the HelloWorld class. In this example, you will set the window caption from within the form's constructor by assigning a string to the form's Text property:

C#
```
public HelloWorld( )
{
    Text = "Hello World";
}
```

VB
```
public sub New( )
    Text = "Hello World"
end sub
```

Once again, the Main( ) method is the entry point to the program:

C#
```
static void Main( )
{
    Application.Run(new HelloWorld( ));
}
```

VB
```
shared sub Main( )
    Application.Run(new HelloWorld( ))
end sub
```

The Application class is contained within the System.Windows.Forms namespace. Launch a Windows application by calling the static Run method of the Application class.

As always, the source code must be compiled to create an executable program. The command line for compiling the program is:

C#
```
csc /out:csHelloWorld-win.exe /t:winexe HelloWorld-win.cs
```

VB
```
vbc /out:vbHelloWorld-win.exe /t:winexe /r:system.dll,system.windows.forms.dll
HelloWorld-win.vb
```

In the C# compilation, the output file is called *csHelloWorld-win.exe*, and in the VB.NET compilation it is *vbHelloWorld-win.exe*. Both files are located in the current directory. In both cases, the target output type is a Windows application. The VB.NET command line also includes references to several .NET class libraries.

When either output EXE file is executed, the results will look like that shown in Figure 2-2. Notice that the title of the form was set to Hello World. The form has all the functionality one would expect of a rudimentary Windows application: the window can be moved or resized using standard Windows techniques; clicking on the icon in the upper-left corner of the window drops down the standard window menu; and the minimize, maximize, and close window buttons are present and functional in the upper-righthand corner. Not bad for a very small amount of code.

Figure 2-2. Hello World as a Windows application

Notice the correlation, if only by convention, between the namespace referenced in the source code and the files referenced in the compile command. Namespaces are referenced in the source code with using statements in C# and Imports statements in VB.NET. These namespaces are themselves contained within assembly files, most typically DLLs. Table 2-2 shows the correspondence between some of the commonly used namespaces and the assemblies in which they are contained.

Table 2-2. Correspondence of source code and compiler references

Source-code reference	Compiler reference	Comment
-	*system.dll*	Supplies fundamental classes and base classes. Not necessary in the source code because it is referenced by default.
System.Windows.Forms	*system.windows.forms.dll*	Contains classes necessary to instantiate form objects.
System.Collections	-	Provides classes and interfaces used by various collections, including Arrays and ArrayLists. Not necessary in the compiler reference because it is included in *mscorlib.dll*, which is referenced by default.
System.Drawing	*system.drawing.dll*	Supplies basic drawing capabilities, including Font and Pen classes, and Color, Point, and Rectangle structures.

Hello World Windows application with a button

The final step in the evolution of this Hello World application will be the addition of a control that generates an event in response to a user action. For this example, you will add a button control that raises the click event when a user clicks on the button. An event handler will handle this click event. Chapter 4 discusses events in detail.

The code in Example 2-5 adds a button control and the click-event handler to the previous example in C#. The additional lines of code are shown in boldface. Example 2-6 shows the equivalent example in VB.NET.

Example 2-5. Hello World Windows application with button control in C#
(HelloWorld-win-button.cs)

```
using System;
using System.Drawing;
using System.Windows.Forms;

namespace ProgrammingWinForms
```

Example 2-5. Hello World Windows application with button control in C#
(HelloWorld-win-button.cs) (continued)

```csharp
{
    public class HelloWorld : System.Windows.Forms.Form
    {
        private Button btn;

        public HelloWorld( )
        {
            Text = "Hello World";
            btn = new Button( );
            btn.Location = new Point(50,50);
            btn.Text = "Goodbye";
            btn.Click += new System.EventHandler(btn_Click);

            Controls.Add(btn);
        }

        static void Main( )
        {
            Application.Run(new HelloWorld( ));
        }

        private void btn_Click(object sender, EventArgs e)
        {
            Application.Exit( );
        }

    }
}
```

Example 2-6. Hello World Windows application with button control in VB.NET
(HelloWorld-win-button.vb)

```vbnet
imports System
imports System.Drawing
imports System.Windows.Forms

namespace ProgrammingWinForms
    public class HelloWorld : inherits System.Windows.Forms.Form

        Private WithEvents btn as Button

        public sub New( )
            Text = "Hello World"
            btn = new Button( )
            btn.Location = new Point(50,50)
            btn.Text = "Goodbye"

            Controls.Add(btn)
        end sub

        public shared sub Main( )
```

Example 2-6. Hello World Windows application with button control in VB.NET (HelloWorld-win-button.vb) (continued)

```
        Application.Run(new HelloWorld( ))
    end sub

    private sub btn_Click(ByVal sender as object, _
        ByVal e as EventArgs) _
        Handles btn.Click
    Application.Exit( )
    end sub

  end class
end namespace
```

The C# code from Example 2-5 is compiled with the following command line:

```
    csc /out:HelloWorld-Win-Button.exe /t:winexe HelloWorld-Win-Button.cs
```

The VB.NET code from Example 2-6 is compiled with this command line:

```
    vbc /out:vbHelloWorld-win-Button.exe /t:winexe /r:system.dll,system.windows.forms.
    dll,system.drawing.dll HelloWorld-win-Button.vb
```

As above, the VB.NET compiler does not reference any assemblies by default, so they must be explicitly included in the command line.

When the code from Example 2-5 or Example 2-6 is compiled and run, the results look like Figure 2-3.

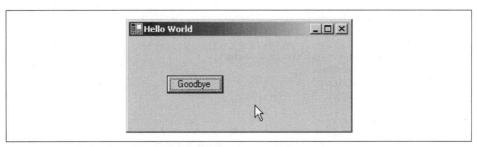

Figure 2-3. Hello World with a button control

In the code that created this application, a private member variable was declared to represent the button:

```
    private Button btn;
```

```
    Private WithEvents btn as Button
```

The WithEvents keyword in the VB.NET code is required for event handling and will be explained in Chapter 4.

Inside the HelloWorld() constructor, the button variable btn is instantiated as a new instance of the Button class and the Location property is specified as a Point:

```
btn = new Button( );
btn.Location = new Point(50,50);
```

```
btn = new Button( )
btn.Location = new Point(50,50)
```

In the C# version, the event handler for the Click event is added.

```
btn.Click += new System.EventHandler(btn_Click);
```

In the VB.NET version, the event handler is hooked up by the combination of the WithEvents keyword in the btn declaration and the Handles keyword in the event-handler method declaration, as you will see momentarily.

Finally in the constructor, the button is added to the Controls collection on the form:

```
Controls.Add(btn);
```

```
Controls.Add(btn)
```

The btn_Click method responds to the button Click event:

```
private void btn_Click(object sender, EventArgs e)
{
    Application.Exit( );
}
```

```
private sub btn_Click(ByVal sender as object, _
        ByVal e as EventArgs) _
        Handles btn.Click
    Application.Exit( )
end sub
```

 Unlike in VB6, the name of the event handler is insignificant. The Handles keyword determines the events handled by each event-handler method.

Chapter 4 will describe the event handler methods in detail. For now, suffice it to say that when the button is clicked, the Exit() method of the Application class is called, which closes the application.

Using Visual Studio .NET

Now that you have created the three Hello World programs using a text editor, you will make the same three programs using Visual Studio .NET. This chapter offers a whirlwind tour of the IDE to show how easy it is to create applications. The next chapter covers Visual Studio .NET in greater detail.

Hello World as a console application

Open Visual Studio .NET. You will see a Start page with a list of your previous projects, if any, an Open Project button, and a New Project button. Click on the New Project button.

You will be presented with the New Project dialog box. You will see a list of Project Types in the left pane and a list of Templates in the right pane.

In the left pane, click on either Visual Basic Projects or Visual C# projects, depending on which language you wish to use.

In the right pane, click on Console Application.

The name will default to *ConsoleApplication1* and the Location will be the default project directory for your system.

 You can change the default Location by clicking Tools → Options. In the tree control on the left, click on Environment → Projects and Solutions. You will see an edit field on the right labeled Visual Studio projects location, along with a Browse button. Either type or browse to the new default directory.

Change the name of the project to *csHelloWorld-Console* or *vbHelloWorld-Console*, depending on which language you are using. The dialog box will look like Figure 2-4.

As indicated by the label below the Location edit field, Visual Studio .NET will create a project in a subdirectory with the same name as the project, located under the default location.

Click OK to create the new project.

Visual Studio .NET will cook for a few moments, and then present a code-editing screen, along with menus and toolbars along the top and information windows along the right edge. If you are using C#, it will look something like Figure 2-5.

If you are using VB.NET, it will look like Figure 2-6.

The next chapter will cover Visual Studio .NET in detail. For now, focus on the code windows.

If you are using C#, notice the commented lines inside the Main() method. Place your mouse cursor at the end of the last commented line and press Enter. This will put the cursor on the next line, properly indented and ready to enter code.

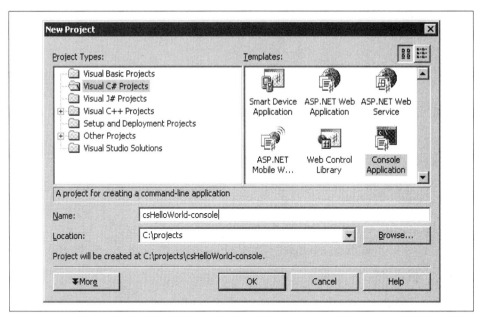

Figure 2-4. New Project dialog box

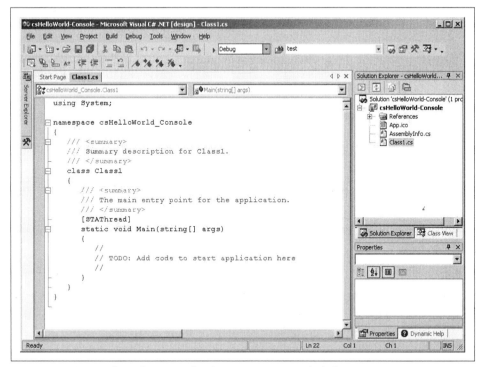

Figure 2-5. C# Console application code-editing screen in Visual Studio .NET

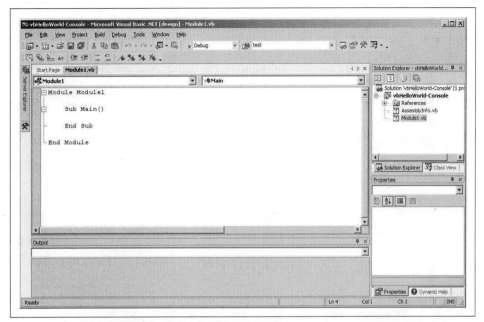

Figure 2-6. VB.NET Console application code-editing screen in Visual Studio .NET

If you are using VB.NET, put your cursor inside the Main( ) method and tab to get the proper indentation.

Type in the appropriate line of code:

```
Console.WriteLine("Hello World");
```

```
Console.WriteLine("Hello World")
```

As soon as you type the period after the word Console, IntelliSense will display a list of all the possible methods and properties available to the Console class. (Remember that C# is case sensitive.)

You can use the arrow key or the mouse to select one of the methods or properties. Alternatively, just start typing. As you do, the first available selection starting with that character will be highlighted. Successive characters will refine the selection. When the desired method or property is highlighted, press Tab or any other key on the keyboard.

If you press Tab, the selection will be entered in the line of code. If you press any other key, the selection will be entered in the line of code, and that key character will also be entered. When you get to the point of entering arguments for the method, a tool tip will pop up showing all the different valid signatures. The next chapter will explore the IntelliSense feature in more detail.

The behavior of C# and VB.NET differ here. In C#, pressing Enter will insert the selected item without adding a new line, while in VB.NET, Enter will add a new line. Tab works the same in either language, inserting the selection with no additional characters or new lines.

Normally you would press F5 to start a program. However, if you do this for a console application, it will go by too fast to see.

Press Ctrl-F5 to run the program without debugging. A console window, similar to a command prompt window, will appear with the output of your program. It will look something like Figure 2-7.

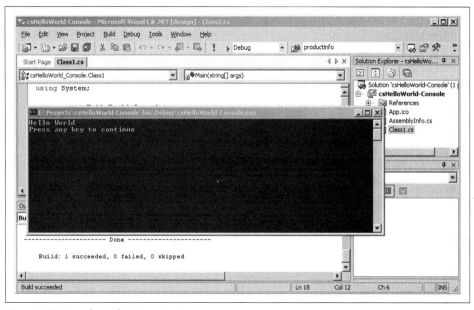

Figure 2-7. Console application output

As you may recall, when you created the console application using a text editor, the relevant line of code had the class System prepended to it, as in:

```
System.Console.WriteLine("Hello World");
```

That is not necessary here because Visual Studio .NET automatically included a reference to the System namespace. In C#, this is immediately apparent from the first line in the code editor:

```
using System;
```

In VB.NET, it is less obvious, but several namespaces are imported by default, rather than with explicit Imports statements. You can see them by right-clicking on the solution in Solution Explorer and selecting Properties, to display the Property Pages for the project (not to be confused with the Properties window). Under Common Properties, click on Imports to see the namespaces imported by default.

Unlike C#, Visual Studio .NET:

- Automatically provides the boilerplate code to create the skeleton of a program
- Automatically provides default namespace references
- Automatically provides default assembly references
- Provides IntelliSense to minimize typing and coding errors
- Automatically compiles the program when you run the application

Hello World as a Windows application

As you did with the text-editor versions of Hello World, now create a new version of the Hello World program as a Windows application—this time using Visual Studio .NET.

Open Visual Studio .NET and click on the New Project button on the Start page. In the left side of the New Project dialog box, select either Visual Basic Projects or Visual C# Projects, depending on the language you want to use.

In the right side of the dialog box, select Windows Application. The default name of the project will be *WindowsApplication1*. Change this name to either *csHelloWorld-Win* or *vbHelloWorld-Win*, depending on which language you are using. The New Project dialog should look like Figure 2-8.

The project will be created in a subdirectory with the same name as the project, located under the default location, as indicated by the label under the Location edit field.

After clicking OK on the dialog box, you will be presented with the Visual Studio .NET design page, similar to Figure 2-9.

Figure 2-9 is similar to the console application screen shown in Figure 2-5, except the main design view contains a visual representation of a Windows Form, rather than a code-editing window, and the Properties window along the lower-right side of the screen now shows properties for the *Form1.cs* file, which is currently highlighted in the Solution Explorer.

Click on the form on the design surface. The Properties window will display the properties of the current control, which in this case is the form. Slide down the Properties window until you see the Text property. It currently has the value Form1. Change the value to Hello World. You will see the titlebar of the form change to say Hello World.

To differentiate it even more from the console version, add a label to the form. Click on the View menu item, then ToolBox. The Toolbox will appear on the screen. Click

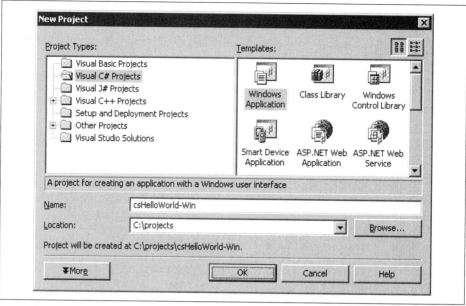

Figure 2-8. New Project Dialog for Hello World Windows application

on the Label control and drag it onto the form. Grab the label control (by clicking on it and dragging) and move it to a suitable location. While the label control is selected, look at the Properties window. It will show the properties for the label. Change the Text property to Visual Studio .NET Version. If necessary, resize the label by clicking on one of the resizing handles and dragging it to enlarge the label until the text no longer wraps. Visual Studio .NET should look something like Figure 2-10.

Run the program by pressing F5 or clicking on the Start icon (▶) on the toolbar. When you do, the window shown in Figure 2-11 will open.

As with the manually coded version, this is a full-fledged Windows application, which can be moved and resized, opens a fully functional window menu once you click the icon in the upper-left corner, and minimize, maximize and close window buttons in the upper-right corner.

Hello World Windows application with a button

The final step in the evolution of this Hello World program is the addition of a button that can respond to a user action. As with the hand-coded version, the button will raise a click event that the program will handle. However, as you will see, Visual Studio .NET will write most of the code for you.

Open the Toolbox once again. You can open it by either hovering the mouse cursor over Toolbox tab on the left edge of the design surface or clicking on View → Toolbox from the menu.

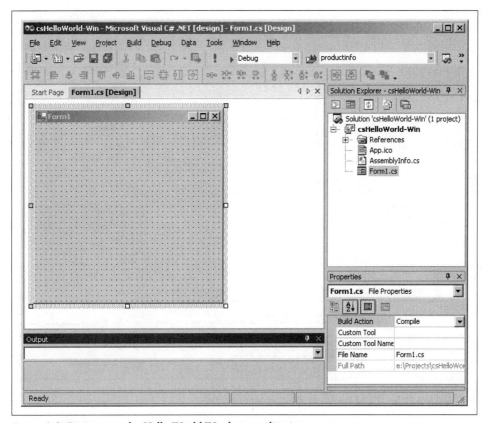

Figure 2-9. Design page for Hello World Windows application

By default, the Toolbox will auto-hide, disappearing from view when the cursor is not over it. It will pop out when the cursor is placed on the Toolbox tab. You can turn this feature off by clicking on the push-pin icon at the top of the Toolbox. The pushpin will be vertical when Auto-Hide is off and sideways when it is on.

Click on the Button control and drag it to a suitable location on the form, or double-click it in the Toolbox to add it to the form and then drag it into position.

While the button is highlighted, go to the Properties window and change the text property to Goodbye. The text written on the button will change accordingly.

Now create and hook up the default event handler by double-clicking the button.

A code window will open up with an event handler method skeleton already created. The cursor will be inside the method, ready to type. Enter the appropriate line of code:

```
Application.Exit();
```

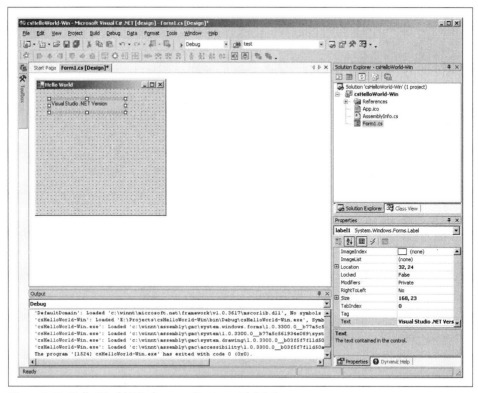

Figure 2-10. Hello World Windows application with label

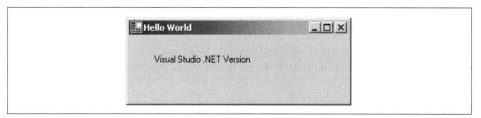

Figure 2-11. Hello World Windows application

VB   Application.Exit( )

As you saw when entering the code for the Windows version of the console application above, IntelliSense will pop up all the available methods and properties of the Application class as soon as you type the period.

The screen should look like Figure 2-12 if you are using C# or Figure 2-13 if you are using VB.NET.

Run the program by pressing F5 or clicking on the Start icon (▶) on the toolbar. When you do, the window shown in Figure 2-14 will open.

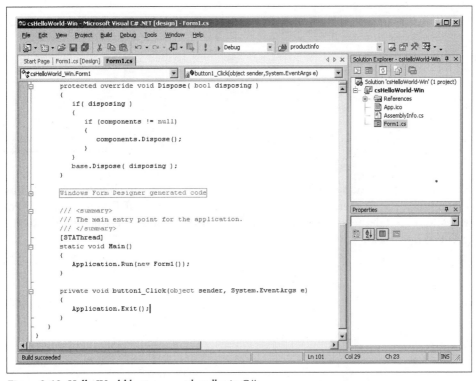

Figure 2-12. Hello World button event handler in C#

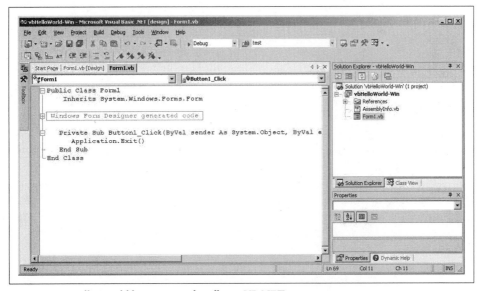

Figure 2-13. Hello World button event handler in VB.NET

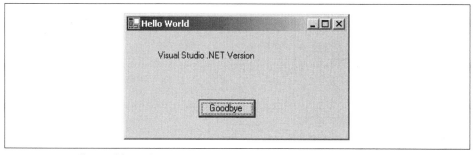

Figure 2-14. Hello World Windows application with button

Clicking on the Goodbye button will raise the click event, which will be handled by the Button1_Click event handler method. Visual Studio .NET automatically provides all the code necessary for creating that event handler and hooking it to the event, greatly easing your programming chores.

CHAPTER 3

Visual Studio .NET

Overview

If your goal is to produce significant, robust, and elegant applications with few bugs in a minimum amount of time, then a modern integrated development environment (IDE) such as Microsoft Visual Studio .NET is an invaluable tool. Visual Studio .NET offers many advantages to the .NET developer:

- A modern interface using a tabbed document metaphor for code and layout screens, and dockable toolbars and informational windows.
- Convenient access to multiple design and code windows.
- What You See Is What You Get (WYSIWYG) visual design of Windows and Web Forms.
- Code completion that allows you to enter code with fewer errors and less typing.
- IntelliSense pop-up help on every method and function call as you type, providing and types of all parameters and the return type.
- Dynamic, context sensitive help that lets you view topics and samples relevant to the code you are writing at the moment. You can also search the complete SDK library from within the IDE.
- Syntax errors are flagged immediately, allowing you to fix problems as they are entered.
- A Start Page that provides easy access to new and existing projects.
- .NET languages that use the same code editor, shortening the learning curve. Each language can have specialized aspects, but all benefit from shared features such as incremental search, code outlining, collapsing text, line numbering, and color coded keywords.
- An HTML editor that provides Design and HTML views that update each other in real time.
- A Solution Explorer that displays all the files comprising your solution (which is a collection of projects) in a hierarchical, outline.

- A Server Explorer that allows you to log on to servers to which you have network access, access the data and services on those servers, and perform a variety of other chores.

- An integrated Debugger that allows you to step through code, observe program run-time behavior, and set breakpoints, even across multiple languages and processes.

- Customization that allows you to set user preferences for IDE appearance and behavior.

- Integrated build and compile support.

- Integrated support for source control software.

- A built-in task list.

On the negative side, Visual Studio .NET can be a black box and thus inscrutable. It is sometimes difficult to know how Visual Studio .NET accomplishes its legerdemain. While Visual Studio .NET can save you a lot of grunt typing, the automatically generated code can obscure what is really necessary to create good working programs. The proliferation of mysteriously named files across your filesystem can be disconcerting when all you want is a simple housekeeping chore, like renaming a minor part of the project. Worst of all, it occasionally decides to reformat all your carefully constructed code, mashing indents and line breaks like a malevolent typist drunk on too much coffee.

Visual Studio .NET is a large and complex program in it's own right, so it is impossible to explore all the possible nooks and crannies in this book. This chapter will lay the foundation for understanding and using Visual Studio .NET and point out traps along the way.

 For a thorough coverage of Visual Studio .NET, please see *Mastering Visual Studio .NET*, by Jon Flanders, Ian Griffiths, and Chris Sells (O'Reilly).

Start Page

The Start Page is what you will see first when you open Visual Studio .NET (unless you configure it otherwise). A typical Start Page is shown in Figure 3-1.

Along the top of the application window is a typical set of menus and buttons. These menus and buttons are context sensitive and will change as the current window changes.

You will see three tabs: Projects, Online Resources, and My Profile. The Projects tab shows the list of existing projects and lets you open a new project. The Online Resources shows a series of links that include:

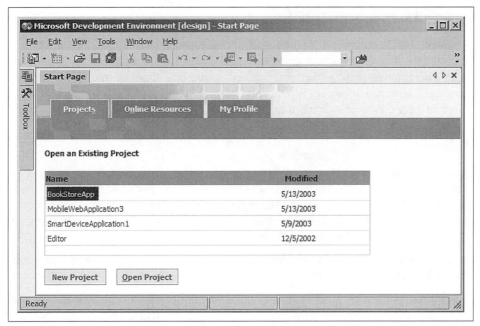

Figure 3-1. Visual Studio .NET Start Page

Get Started

    The default selection, provides a means of finding sample code.

What's New

    Links to new developments in the .NET world, training and events, and tips.

Online Community

    More links to the .NET community, including web sites, newsgroups, tech support resources, code examples, and component sources.

Headlines

    Links to news stories about .NET and specific topics such as XML web services.

Search Online

    A form for searching the MSDN online library.

Downloads

    Links to free and subscriber downloads, including sample applications.

XML Web Services

    Forms to search for or register web services.

Web Hosting

    Links to hosting providers.

The My Profile tab allows configuration of high-level Visual Studio .NET settings.

Projects and Solutions

A typical .NET application is comprised of many items: source files, assembly information files, references, icons, and other files and folders. Visual Studio .NET organizes these items into a container called a *project*. One or more projects are contained within a *solution*. When you create a new project, Visual Studio .NET automatically creates the containing solution.

Solutions

Solutions typically contain one or more project. They may contain other independent items as well. These independent *solution items* are not specific to any particular project, but apply, or *scope*, to the entire solution. The solution items are not an integral part of the application, in that they can be removed without changing the compiled output. You can manage them with source control.

It is also possible to have a solution that does not contain any projects—just solution or miscellaneous files that can be edited using Visual Studio .NET.

Miscellaneous files are independent of the solution or project, but they may be useful. They are not included in a build or compile, but will display in the Solution Explorer (described below) and may be edited there. Typical miscellaneous files include project notes, database schemas, or sample code files.

Solutions are defined within a file named for the solution and have the extension *.sln*. The *.sln* file contains a list of the projects that comprise the solution, the location of any solution-scoped items, and solution-scoped build configurations. Visual Studio .NET also creates a *.suo* file with the same name as the *.sln* file (e.g., *mySolution.sln* and *mySolution.suo*). The *.sou* file contains data used to customize the IDE on a per-user and per-solution basis.

You can open a solution by double-clicking the *.sln* file in Windows Explorer. If the *.sln* file is missing, then recreate that solution from scratch by adding projects into the solution. On the other hand, if the *.suo* file is missing, it will be recreated automatically the next time the solution is opened.

Projects

A project contains source files and other content. Typically, the build process results in the contents of a project being compiled into an assembly—e.g., an executable file (EXE) or a dynamic link library (DLL).

The data describing the project is contained in a project file named after the project name with a language-specific extension. For VB.NET and C#, the extensions are *.vbproj* and *.csproj*, respectively. The project file contains version information, build settings, references to other assemblies (typically members of the CLR, but also custom developed and third-party components), and source files to include as part of the project.

Templates

When you create a new project by clicking the New Project button on the Start Page (shown in Figure 3-1), you get the New Project dialog box, shown in Figure 3-2.

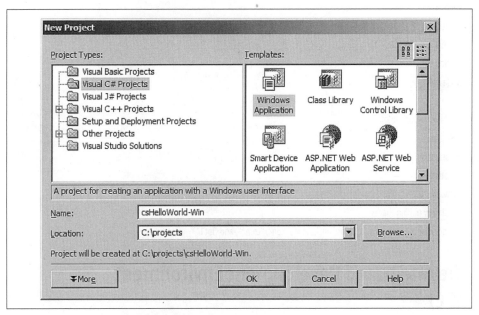

Figure 3-2. New Project dialog box

Select the Project Type and the Template. You will find several templates for each project type. For example, the templates for Visual C# Projects, shown in Figure 3-2, are different from the templates available to Setup and Deployment Projects. By selecting a Visual Studio Solutions project type, you can create an empty solution that is ready to receive whatever items you wish to add.

The template controls what items will be automatically created and included in the project, as well as default project settings. For example, if the project is a C# Windows application, such as the Hello World programs created in Chapter 2, then language-specific *.csproj*, *.csprojusers*, and *.cs* files will be created as part of the project. If the project were a VB.NET project, then the corresponding *.vbproj*, *.vbprojusers*, and *.vb* files would be created instead. If a different template were selected, then an entirely different set of files would be created.

Project names

Project names may consist of any standard ASCII characters, except for those shown in Table 3-1.

Table 3-1. Forbidden project name characters

Project name	Ascii character
Pound	#
Percent	%
Ampersand	&
Asterisk	*
Vertical bar	|
Backslash	\
Colon	:
Double quotation mark	"
Less than	<
Greater than	>
Question mark	?
Forward slash	/
Leading or trailing spaces	
Windows or DOS keywords, such as "nul", "aux", "con", "com1", and "lpt1"	

The Integrated Development Environment (IDE)

The Visual Studio .NET Integrated Development Environment (IDE) consists of windows for visual design of forms; code-editing windows, menus and toolbars providing access to commands and features; toolboxes containing controls for use on the forms; and windows providing properties and information about forms, controls, projects and the solution.

Layout

Visual Studio .NET is a Multiple Document Interface (MDI) application. It consists of a single parent window, which contains multiple other windows. All menus, toolbars, design and editing windows, and miscellaneous other windows are associated with the single parent window.

Figure 3-3 shows a typical layout of the IDE. This section will cover the overall layout and many of the features that make working with the IDE so productive.

The Visual Studio .NET window has a titlebar across the top, with menus below. Under the menus are toolbars with buttons that duplicate many common menu commands. Nearly everything that can be done through menus can also be done with context sensitive pop-up menus, as described below. You can customize the menu and toolbars easily by clicking on Tools → Customize.

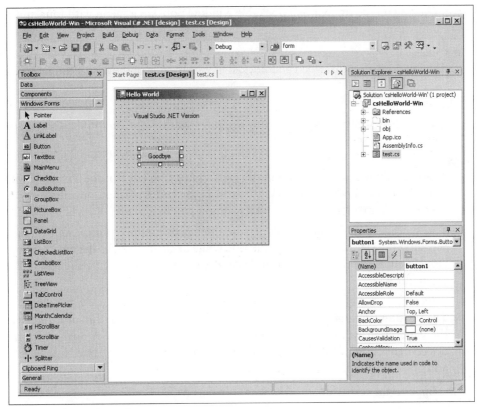

Figure 3-3. Typical IDE layout

The toolbars are docked along the top of the window by default. As with many Windows applications, they can be undocked and moved to other locations, either free-floating or docked along other window edges. Move the toolbars by grabbing them with the mouse and dragging them where you want.

Figure 3-3 shows a design view of a Windows Form, with the design window occupying the main area in the center of the screen. This position allows you to create a visual design by dragging and dropping components from the Toolbox along the left side of the screen.

Along the right side of the screen are two windows, both of which will be covered in more detail below. The upper window is the Solution Explorer. Below it is the Properties window. Many other, similar windows, are available to you, as described later.

All of these windows, plus the Toolbox, are resizable and dockable. You can resize them by placing the mouse cursor over the edge you wish to move. The cursor will change to a double arrow resizing cursor, at which point you can drag the window edge one way or the other.

Right-clicking on the titlebar of a dockable window pops up a menu with four mutually exclusive check items:

Dockable

The window can be dragged and docked along any side of the Visual Studio .NET window.

Hide

The window disappears. To see the window again—i.e., to unhide it—use the View main menu item.

Floating

The window will not dock when dragged against the edge of the Visual Studio .NET window. The floating window can be placed anywhere on the desktop, even outside the Visual Studio .NET window.

You can also double-click on either the titlebar or the tab to dock and undock the window. Double-clicking on the title while docked undocks the entire group. Double-clicking on the tab just undocks the one window, leaving the rest of the group docked.

Auto Hide

The window will disappear, indicated only by a tab, when the cursor is not over the window. It will reappear when the cursor is over the tab. A pushpin in the upper-right corner of the window will point down when Auto Hide is turned off and point sideways when it is turned on.

In the upper-right corner of the window are two icons:

Pushpin

This icon toggles the AutoHide property of the window.

When the pushpin points down, the window is pinned in place; AutoHide is turned off. Moving the cursor off the window will not affect its visibility.

When the pushpin points sideways, AutoHide is turned on. Moving the cursor off the window hides the window. To see the window again, click on the tab, which is now visible along the edge where the window had been docked.

X

The standard close window icon.

The main design window uses a tabbed metaphor—i.e., the tabs along the top edge of that window indicate there are other windows below it. (You can change to an MDI style, if you prefer, in Tools → Options.) Clicking on the tab labeled *test.cs* in Figure 3-3, for example, will bring up the screen shown in Figure 3-4, which contains a code window.

When you switch from a design window to a code window, the menu items, toolbars, and Toolbox change in a context-sensitive manner.

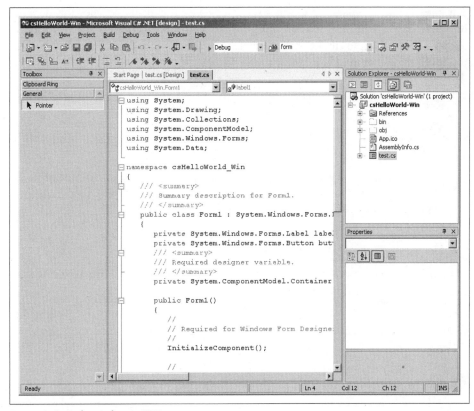

Figure 3-4. Code window in IDE

The code window has drop-down lists at the top of the screen for navigating around the application. The left drop-down contains a list of all the classes in the code and the right drop-down has a list of all objects in the current class. In VB.NET you can also use these drop-downs to select event sources (from the lefthand drop-down) and add event handlers (from the righthand drop-down). This also works in the HTML editor.

Along the bottom edge of the IDE window is a status bar, which shows such information as the current cursor position (when a code window is visible), the status of the Insert key, and any pending shortcut key combinations.

Menus and Toolbars

The menus provide access to many of Visual Studio .NET's commands and capabilities. The most commonly used menu commands are duplicated with toolbar buttons for ease of use.

The menus and toolbars are context sensitive—i.e., the available selection depends on what part of the IDE is currently selected and what activities are expected or allowed. For example, if the current active window is a code-editing window, the top-level menu commands are:

- File
- Edit
- View
- Project
- Build
- Debug
- Tools
- Window
- Help

If the current window is a design window, then the Data and Format menu commands also become available.

The following sections will describe some of the menu items and their submenus, focusing on the aspects that are interesting and different from common Windows commands.

File menu

The File menu provides access to a number of file, project, and solution-related commands. Many of these commands are content sensitive. Below are descriptions of those commands that are not self-explanatory.

New... As in most Windows applications, the New menu item creates new items to be worked on by the application. In Visual Studio .NET, the New menu item has three submenu items to handle the different possibilities:

Project...(Ctrl+Shift+N)
> The Project command brings up the New Project dialog, which is context sensitive. If no project is currently open, as is sometimes the case when Visual Studio .NET is just opened, you will see the dialog box shown in Figure 3-2.
>
> If there is already a project open, then you will get the New Project dialog box shown in Figure 3-5. This dialog box adds radio buttons to give you the choice of adding the new project to the solution or closing the existing solution and creating a new one to hold the new project.

File...(Ctrl+ N)
> The File command brings up a New File dialog box, as shown in Figure 3-6. It offers three different categories of files and many different types of files (templates) within each category. Files created this way are located by default in the

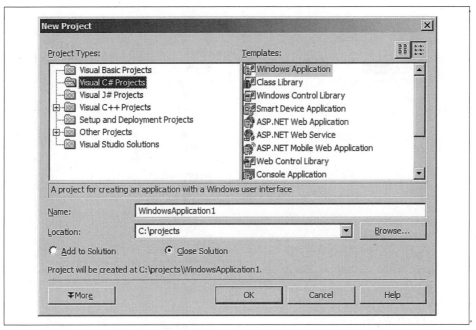

Figure 3-5. New Project dialog box from menu

project directory (although you can browse for a different location). They are displayed in the Solution Explorer if the Show All button is toggled, but are not actually part of the solution unless explicitly added using one of the Add menu items described below. In other words, they are the miscellaneous files described above in the section on Solutions.

Blank Solution...

The Blank Solution command also brings up a New Project dialog similar to that shown in Figure 3-5, with the Add to Solution radio button grayed out, the default Project Type set to Visual Studio Solutions, and the Template set to Blank Solution. When a blank solution is created, it contains no items. Add items by using one of the Add menu items described below.

The New command has an equivalent button in the Standard Toolbar that exposes the New Project and Blank Solution commands.

Open... The Open menu item opens pre-existing items. It has four submenu items:

Project...(Ctrl+Shift+O)

Opens a previously existing project. The currently opened solution is closed before the new project is opened.

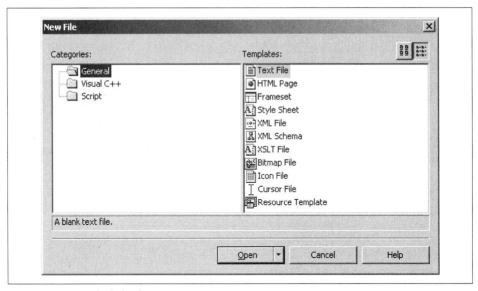

Figure 3-6. New File dialog box

Project From Web...
An Open Project From Web dialog box is presented, and it accepts a URL pointing to the project to open. As with Open Project, the currently opened solution is closed before the new project is opened.

File...(Ctrl+O)
Presents a standard Open File dialog box, allowing you to browse to and open any file accessible on your network. Opened files are visible and editable in Visual Studio .NET, but are not part of the project. To make a file part of the project, use one of the Add menu commands described below. The Open File command has an equivalent button on the Standard Toolbar.

File From Web...
An Open File From Web dialog box is presented and accepts a URL pointing to the file to open. As with Open File, the selected file is not made part of the project.

Add New Item...(Ctrl+Shift+A). Add New Item lets you add a new item to the current project. It presents the Add New Item dialog box shown in Figure 3-7. Expanding the nodes in the Categories pane on the left side of the dialog box narrows the list of Templates shown on the right side.

Use this menu item if you want to add new files to your project, including new source code files. For source code, you would typically add a new Class file, which automatically would have the language-specific filename extension.

This command has an equivalent button in the Standard Toolbar. It is also accessible from the context menu in the Solution Explorer.

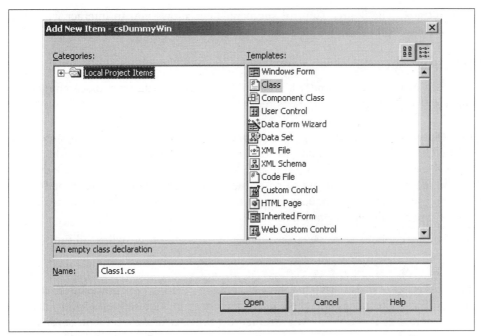

Figure 3-7. Add New Item dialog box

Add Existing Item...(Shift+Alt+A). Add Existing Item is very similar to the Add New Item menu item just described, except that it adds already existing items to the current project. If the item added resides outside the project directory, a copy is made and placed in the project directory.

This menu option is also available from the Solution Explorer context menus.

Add Project. Add Project has three submenus. The first two, New Project and Existing Project, let you add either a new or pre-existing project to the solution. The third, Existing Project From Web, presents a dialog box that accepts the URL of the project to be added.

Open Solution. Clicking on this menu item brings up the Open Solution dialog box, which allows you to browse for the solution to open. The currently open solution will be closed before the new solution is opened.

Close Solution. This menu item is only available if there a solution is currently open. If this menu item is selected, the currently open solution will be closed.

Advanced Save Options... Advanced Save Options is a context-sensitive submenu that is only visible when editing in a code window. It presents a dialog box that lets you set the encoding option and line ending character(s) for the file.

Source Control. The Source Control submenu item allows you to interact with your source control program.

Edit menu

The Edit menu is fairly standard, containing the typical editing and searching commands. It also has some very interesting capabilities.

Cycle Clipboard Ring (Ctrl+Shift+V). The Clipboard Ring is like copy and paste on steroids. Copy different selections to the Windows clipboard, using the Edit → Cut (Ctrl-X) or Edit → Copy (Ctrl-C) commands. Then use Ctrl+Shift+V to cycle through all the selections, allowing you to paste the correct one when it comes around. You can also see the whole clipboard ring in the Toolbox—it's one of the panes that is visible when you're editing a text file.

This submenu item is context sensitive and is visible only when editing a code window.

Find and Replace → Find in Files (Ctrl+Shift+F). Find in Files is a very powerful search utility that finds text strings anywhere in a directory or in subdirectories (subfolders). It presents the dialog box shown in Figure 3-8. Checkboxes present several self-explanatory options, including the ability to search using either wildcards or regular expressions.

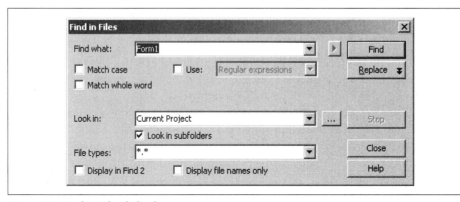

Figure 3-8. Find in Files dialog box

Regular Expressions

Regular expressions are a language unto themselves, expressly designed for incredibly powerful and sophisticated searches. A full explanation of regular expressions is beyond the scope of this book. For a complete discussion of regular expressions, see the SDK documentation or *Mastering Regular Expressions*, by Jeffrey E. F. Friedl (O'Reilly).

If you click on the Replace button in the Find in Files dialog box, you will get the Replace in Files dialog box shown in Figure 3-9 and described next.

Find and Replace → Replace in Files (Ctrl+Shift+H). Replace in Files is identical to the Find in Files command, just described, except that it also allows you to replace the target text string with a replacement text string.

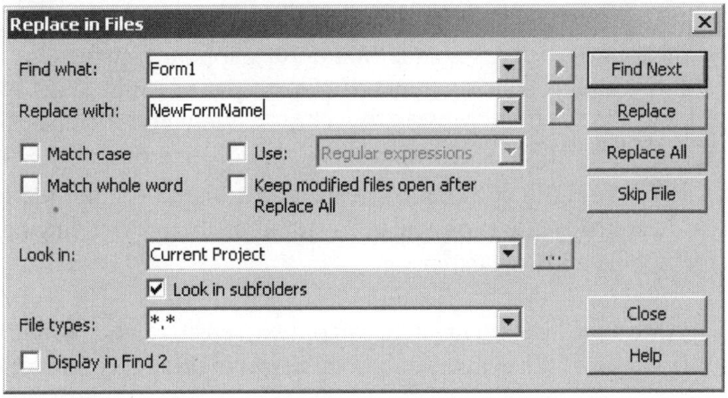

Figure 3-9. Replace in Files dialog box

This command is extremely useful for renaming forms, classes, namespaces, and projects. Renaming objects is a very common requirement, and it is wise—you don't want to be saddled with the default names assigned by Visual Studio .NET.

Renaming should not be difficult, but it can be. Object names are spread throughout a project, often hidden in obscure locations such as solution or project files, and throughout source code files. Although all of these files are text files that can be searched and edited, the task can be tedious and error-prone. The Replace in Files command makes it simple, thorough, and reasonably safe.

Find and Replace → Find Symbol (Alt+F12). Clicking on this submenu item brings up the Find Symbol dialog box shown in Figure 3-10. This allows you to search for symbols such as namespaces, classes, and interfaces, and their members such as properties, methods, events, and variables.

The search results will be displayed in a window labeled Find Symbol Results. From there, you can move to each location in the code by double-clicking on each result.

Go To... This submenu item brings up the Go To Line dialog box, which allows you to enter a line number and immediately go to that line. It is context sensitive and visible only when editing a text window.

Insert File As Text... This submenu item allows you to insert the contents of any file into your source code as though you had typed it in. It is context sensitive and visible only when editing a text window.

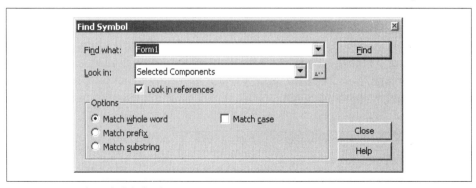

Figure 3-10. Find Symbol dialog box

A standard file browsing dialog box is presented to search for the file that will be inserted. The default file extension will correspond to the project language, but you can search for any file with any extension.

Advanced. The Advanced submenu item is context sensitive and visible only when you edit a code window. It has many submenu items, including commands for:

- Creating or removing tabs in a selection (converting spaces to tabs and vice versa)
- Forcing selected text to uppercase or lowercase
- Deleting horizontal whitespace
- Viewing whitespace (make tabs and space characters visible on the screen)
- Toggling word wrap
- Commenting and uncommenting blocks of text
- Increasing and decreasing line indenting
- Incremental search (described below)

Incremental search (Ctrl+I). Incremental search lets you search an editing window by entering the search string character by character. As each character is entered, the cursor moves to the first occurrence of matching text.

To use incremental search in a window, select the menu item or press Ctrl+I. The cursor icon will change to a binocular with an arrow indicating the direction of search. Begin typing the text string you want to search for.

The case sensitivity of an incremental search will come from the previous Find, Replace, Find in Files, or Replace in Files search (described above).

The search will proceed downward and left to right from the current location. To search backward, use Ctrl+Shift+I.

The key combinations listed in Table 3-2 apply to incremental searching:

Table 3-2. Incremental searching

Key combination	Description
Esc	Stop the search
Backspace	Remove a character from the search text
Ctrl+Shift+I	Change the direction of the search
Ctrl+I	Move to the next occurrence in the file for the current search text

Bookmarks. Bookmarks are useful for marking spots in your code and easily navigating from marked spot to marked spot. Table 3-3 lists five bookmark commands, along with their shortcut key combinations.

This menu item appears only when a code window is the current window.

Table 3-3. Bookmark commands

Command	Key Combination	Description
Toggle Bookmark	Ctrl+K, Ctrl+K	Place or remove a bookmark at the current line. When a bookmark is set, a blue rectangular icon will appear in the column along the left edge of the code window.
Next Bookmark	Ctrl+K, Ctrl+N	Move to the next bookmark.
Previous Bookmark	Ctrl+K, Ctrl+P	Move to the previous bookmark.
Clear Bookmark	Ctrl+K, Ctrl+L	Clear all the bookmarks.
Add Task List Shortcut	Ctrl+K, Ctrl+H	Add an entry to the Task List (described below under the View menu item) for the current line. When a task list entry is set, a curved arrow icon ( ) will appear in the column along the left edge of the code window.

Outlining. Visual Studio .NET allows you to *outline*, or collapse and expand sections of your code, to make it easier to view the overall structure. When a section is collapsed, it appears with a plus sign in a box along the left edge of the code window ( ). Clicking on the plus sign expands the region.

You can nest the outlined regions so that one section can contain one or more other collapsed sections. Several commands that facilitate outlining are shown in Table 3-4.

Table 3-4. Outlining commands

Command	Key combination	Description
Hide Selection	Ctrl+M, Ctrl+H	Collapses currently selected text. In C# only, this command is visible only when automatic outlining is turned off or the Stop Outlining command is selected.
Toggle Outlining Expansion	Ctrl+M, Ctrl+M	Reverses the current outlining state of the innermost section in which the cursor lies.
Toggle All Outlining	Ctrl+M, Ctrl+L	Sets all sections to the same outlining state. If some sections are expanded and some collapsed, then all become collapsed.

Table 3-4. Outlining commands (continued)

Command	Key combination	Description
Stop Outlining	Ctrl+M, Ctrl+P	Expands all sections. Removes the outlining symbols from view.
Stop Hiding Current	Ctrl+M, Ctrl+U	Removes outlining information for the currently selected section. In C# only, this command is visible only when automatic outlining is turned off or the Stop Outlining command is selected.
Collapse to Definitions	Ctrl+M, Ctrl+O	Automatically creates sections for each procedure in the code window and collapses them all.
Start Automatic Outlining	N.A.	Restarts automatic outlining after it is stopped.
Collapse Block	N.A.	In C++ only. Similar to Collapse to Definitions, except it applies only to the region of code containing the cursor.
Collapse All In	N.A.	In C++ only. Same as Collapse Block, except it recursively collapses all logical structures in a function in a single step.

The default behavior of Outlining can be set using the Tools → Options menu item. Go to Text Editor, then indicate the specific language for which you wish to set the options. The outlining options can be set for VB.NET under Basic → VB Specific, for C# under C# → Formatting, and for C++ under C/C++ → Formatting.

IntelliSense. Microsoft IntelliSense technology makes programmers' lives much easier. It has real-time, context-sensitive help available that appears right under your cursor. Code completion automatically completes your thoughts for you, drastically reducing your need to type. Drop-down-lists provide all methods and properties possible in the current context, and are available at a keystroke or mouseclick.

What's not to love? IntelliSense makes up for a lot of Visual Studio .NET's more, shall we say, exasperating traits.

The default IntelliSense features can be configured by going to Tools → Options, and then the language-specific pages under Text Editor.

Most IntelliSense features appear as you type inside a code window, or allow the mouse to hover over a portion of the code. In addition, the Edit → IntelliSense menu item offers the commands shown in Table 3-5.

Table 3-5. IntelliSense commands

Command	Key combination	Description
List Members	Ctrl+J	Displays a list of all possible members available for the current context. Keystrokes incrementally search the list. Press any key to insert the highlighted selection into your code; that key becomes the next character after the inserted name. Use the Tab key to select without entering any additional characters.
		This command can also be accessed by right-clicking and selecting List Member from the context-sensitive menu.

Table 3-5. IntelliSense commands (continued)

Command	Key combination	Description
Parameter Info	Ctrl+Shift+Space	Displays a list of number, names, and types of parameters required for a method, sub, function, or attribute.
Quick Info	Ctrl+K, Ctrl+I	Displays the complete declaration for any identifier, e.g., variable name or class name, in your code. It is also enabled by hovering the mouse cursor over any identifier.
Complete Word	Alt+Right Arrow or Ctrl+Space	Automatically completes the typing of any identifier once you type in enough characters to uniquely identify it. This only works if the identifier is entered in a valid location in the code.

The member list presents itself when you type the dot following any class or member name.

Every member of the class is listed, and each member's type is indicated by an icon. You can find icons for methods, fields, properties, events and so forth. In addition, each icon may have a second icon overlaid to indicate the accessibility of the member: public, private, protected, and so on. If there is no accessibility icon, then the member is public.

> If the member list does not appear, you should ensure that you have added all the necessary using (or imports) statements. Also remember that IntelliSense is case-sensitive in C#. Also, sometimes C# needs a rebuild before it will reflect the most recent changes.

Table 3-6 lists all the different icons used in the member lists and other windows throughout the IDE. Table 3-7 lists the accessibility icons.

Table 3-6. Object icons

Icon	Member type
	Class
	Constant
	Delegate
	Enum
	Enum item
	Event
	Exception
	Global
	Interface
	Intrinsic
	Macro
	Map

Table 3-6. Object icons (continued)

Icon	Member type
	Map item
	Method or function
	Module
{ }	Namespace
	Operator
	Property
	Structure
⟨T⟩	Template
	TypeDef
	Union
	Unknown or error
	Variable or field

Table 3-7. Object accessibility icons

Icon	Accessibility
	Shortcut
	Friend
	Internal
	Private
	Protected

View menu

The View menu is a context-sensitive menu that provides access to the myriad windows available in the Visual Studio .NET IDE. You will probably keep many of these windows open all the time; you will use others rarely, if at all.

The View menu is context sensitive. For example, if your form has no controls on it, the Tab Order submenu will be grayed out.

When the application is running, a number of other windows become visible or available. These windows are accessed via the Debug → Windows menu item, not from the View menu item.

Visual Studio .NET can store several different window layouts. In particular, it remembers a completely different set of open windows during debug sessions than it does during normal editing. These layouts are stored per-user and not per-project or per-solution.

This section covers the areas that may not be self-explanatory.

Open/Open With... This menu item lets you open the current item—i.e., the item currently selected in the Solution Explorer (described below)—in the program of your choice. Open uses the default editor, and Open With allows you to pick from a list of programs. You can add other programs to the list.

The Open With command also lets you open an item with the editor of your choice in Visual Studio .NET. For example, you can open a file in the binary viewer when you might normally get the resource viewer. Perhaps most usefully, you can also specify the default editor for an item. For example, you can make a Windows Form open in code view rather than design view by default.

Solution Explorer (Ctrl+Alt+L). Projects and solutions are managed using the Solution Explorer, which presents the solution and projects, as well as all the files, folders, and items contained within them, hierarchically and visibly. The Solution Explorer is typically visible in a window along the upper-right side of the Visual Studio .NET screen, although the Solution Explorer window can be closed or undocked and moved to other locations.

To view the Solution Explorer if it is not already visible, select View → Solution Explorer from the Visual Studio .NET menu. Alternatively, press the Ctrl+Alt+L keys simultaneously. Figure 3-11 shows a typical Solution Explorer.

Figure 3-11. Solution Explorer

There are several menu buttons along the top of the Solution Explorer window. These buttons are context sensitive (i.e., they may or may not appear, depending on the currently selected item in the Solution Explorer). Table 3-8 details the purpose of each button.

Table 3-8. Solution Explorer buttons

Button	Name	Shortcut keys	Description
	View Code	F7	Displays code in main window. Only visible for source files.
	View Designer	Shift +F7	Displays visual designer in main window. Only visible for items with visual components.

Table 3-8. Solution Explorer buttons (continued)

Button	Name	Shortcut keys	Description
	Refresh	none	Refreshes the Solution Explorer display.
	Show All Files	none	Toggles display of all files in the Solution Explorer. By default, many files are not shown. If Show All Files is clicked, the solution shown in Figure 3-9 will look like Figure 3-12 after several of the nodes are expanded.
	Properties	Alt+Enter	If the currently highlighted item is a solution or a project, it displays the Properties page for that item. Otherwise, moves the cursor to the Properties window for that item.

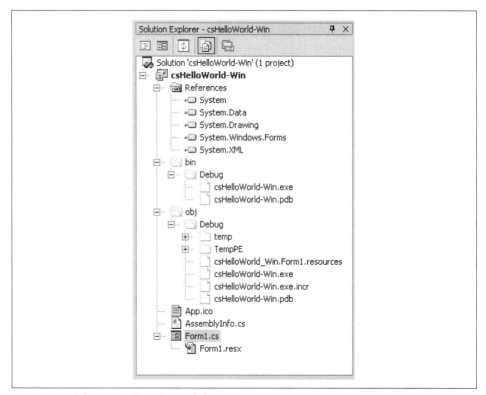

Figure 3-12. Solution Explorer (expanded)

You can also display miscellaneous files in the Solution Explorer. To do so, go to Tools → Options... and then Environment → Documents. Check the checkbox labeled Show Miscellaneous files in Solution Explorer.

Most of the functionality of the Solution Explorer is redundant with the Visual Studio .NET menu items, although it is often easier and more intuitive to perform a given chore in Solution Explorer than in the menus. Right-clicking on any item in the Solution Explorer pops up a context-sensitive menu. Three different pop-up menus from Solution Explorer are shown in Figure 3-13. From left to right, they are for a solution, a project, and a source-code file.

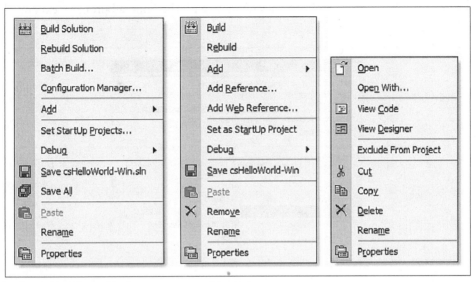

Figure 3-13. Solution Explorer context-sensitive menus

Several points bear mention:

- The Add pop-up menu item for solutions and projects offers submenus that allow new or existing items to be added. This item replicates items contained under the main Project menu.

  Set Startup Projects and Exclude From Project are also replicated under the main Project menu.

- The Build and Rebuild pop-up menu items replicate items contained under the main Build menu.

- The Debug pop-up menu item replicates two items from the main Debug menu.

- If the Properties item is clicked for a source file, the cursor moves to the Properties window. If the Properties item is clicked for a solution or project, the Properties page for that item is opened.

Properties Windows (F4).   The Properties window displays all the properties for the currently selected item. Some of the properties, such as Font and Location, have subproperties, indicated by a plus sign next to their entry in the window. The property values on the right side of the window are editable.

One possible source of confusion is that certain items have more than one set of properties. For example, a Form source file can show two different sets of properties, depending on whether you select the source file in the Solution Explorer or the form as shown in the Design view.

Figure 3-14 shows a typical Properties window with the Font subproperty expanded out.

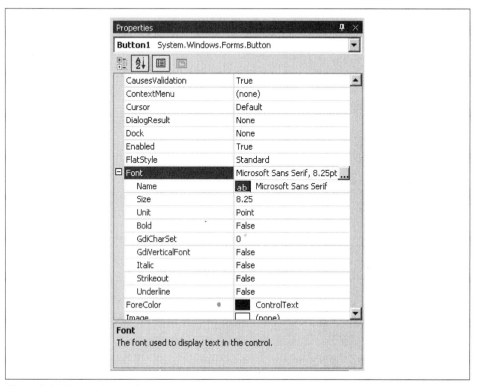

Figure 3-14. Properties window

The name and type of the current object is displayed in the field at the top of the window. In Figure 3-14, it is an object named Button1 of type Button, contained in the System.Windows.Forms namespace.

The Font property has subproperties that may be set either directly in the window or by clicking on the button with three dots on it, which brings up a standard font dialog box. Other properties with subproperties may or may not have a dialog box associated with them, as need be. Other properties, such as the Font Name property, may have drop-downs in the property grid itself.

The property window has several buttons just below the name and type of the object. The first two buttons on the left toggle the list by category or alphabetically. The next button from the left displays properties for an object. The right-most button displays property pages for the object, if there are any.

Some objects have both a Properties window and Properties pages. The Property pages display additional properties from those shown in the Properties window.

If the project is in C#, then an additional lighting bolt button ($\mathcal{G}$) is used to create event handlers for an item. Events are covered in Chapter 4.

For some controls, such as TabControl, an additional panel is part of the Properties window with verbs, such as Add Tab and Remove Tab.

The box below the list has a brief description of the selected property.

Server Explorer (Ctrl+Alt+S). The Server Explorer allows you to access any server to which you have network access. If you have sufficient permissions, you can log on, access system services, open data connections, access and edit database information, and access message queues and performance counters. You can also drag nodes from the Server Explorer onto Visual Studio .NET projects, creating components that reference the data source.

Figure 3-15 shows a typical Server Explorer. It is a hierarchical view of the available servers. In this figure, only one server is available, ATH13T. The figure shows a drill-down into SQL Server, with the tables in the Northwind database. These tables, and all other objects in this tree view, are directly accessible and editable from the window.

Class View (Ctrl+Shift+C). The Class View shows all the classes in the solution hierarchically. A typical Class View, somewhat expanded, is shown in Figure 3-16. The icons used in this window are listed in Table 3-6 and Table 3-7.

As with the Solution Explorer, any item in the class view can be right-clicked, which exposes a pop-up menu with context-sensitive menu items. This provides a convenient way to sort the display of classes in a project or solution, or to add a method, property, or field to a class.

The button on the left above the class list lets you sort the listed classes, either alphabetically, by type, by access, or grouped by type. Clicking on the button itself sorts by the current sort mode, while clicking on the down arrow next to it presents the other sort buttons and changes the sort mode.

The button on the right above the class list allows you to create virtual folders for organizing the listed classes. These folders are saved as part of the solution in the *.suo* file.

These folders are virtual (i.e., they are illusory). They are used only for viewing the list, and as such they have no effect on the actual items. Items copied to the folder are not physically moved, and if the folders are deleted, the items in them are not lost. If you rename or delete an object from the code that is in a folder, you may need to manually drag the item into the folder again to clear the error node.

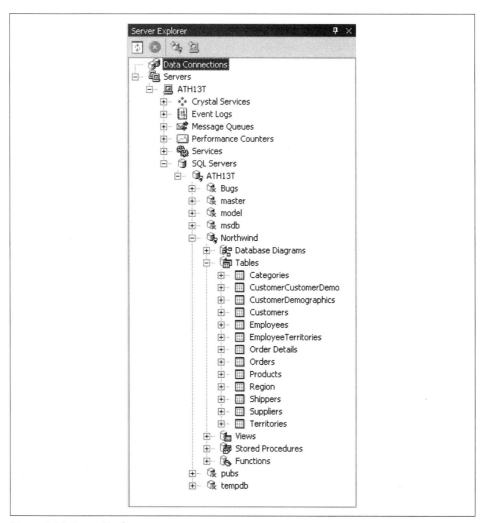

Figure 3-15. Server Explorer

Object Browser (Ctrl+Alt+J)

The Object Browser is a tool for examining objects such as namespaces, classes, and interfaces, and their members, such as methods, properties, variables, and events. Figure 3-17 shows a typical Object Browser window.

The objects are listed in the pane on the left side of the window, and members of the object, if any, are listed in the right pane. The objects are listed hierarchically, with the ability to drill down through the tree structure. The icons used in this window are listed in Table 3-6 and Table 3-7.

Right-clicking on either an object or a member brings up a context-sensitive pop-up menu with a variety of menu options.

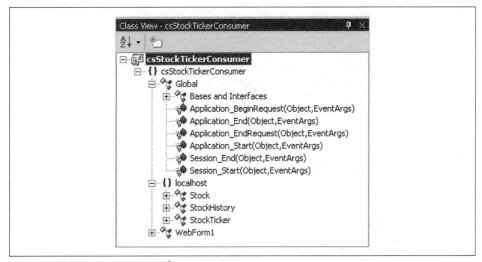

Figure 3-16. Class View

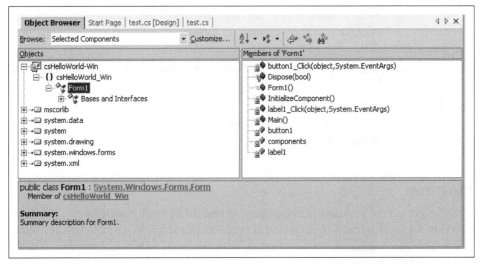

Figure 3-17. Object Browser

Other Windows. Several other windows have been relegated to a submenu called Other Windows:

Macro Explorer (Alt+F8)

Visual Studio .NET offers the ability to automate repetitive chores with macros. A macro is a set of instructions written in VB.NET, either created manually or recorded by the IDE, saved in a file. The Macro Explorer is one of the main tools for viewing, managing, and executing macros. It provides access into the Macro IDE.

Macros are described further in the section below on the Tools → Macro menu command.

Document Outline (Ctrl+Alt+T)

When you design Web Forms, the Document Outline window is used to provide an outline view of the HTML document.

Task List (Ctrl+Alt+K)

In large applications, keeping a to-do list can be quite helpful. Visual Studio .NET provides this functionality with the Task List window. You can also provide shortcuts to comments in the Task List along with token strings, such as TODO, HACK, or UNDONE. The compiler also populates the Task List with compile errors.

Command Window (Ctrl+Alt+A)

The Command window has two modes: Command and Immediate.

Command mode enters commands directly, either bypassing the menu system or executing commands that are not contained in the menu system. (You can add any command to the menu or a toolbar button by using Tools → Customize.)

Immediate mode is used when debugging to evaluate expressions, view and modify variables, and other debugging tasks. The Immediate window and debugging will be covered further in Chapter 21.

For a complete discussion of command window usage, consult the SDK documentation.

Output (Ctrl+Alt+O)

The Output window displays status messages from the IDE to the developer, including debugger messages, compiler messages, and output from stored procedures.

Project menu

The Project menu provides functionality related to project management. All functionality exposed by the Project menu is available in the Solution Explorer. It is often easier and more intuitive to accomplish your goals in Solution Explorer, but the menus lend themselves to keyboard use.

Each command under this menu pertains to the object currently highlighted in the Solution Explorer.

Add... Menu Items. Several menu items allow you to add either an existing or a new item to a project. They are self-explanatory, offering the same functionality as the equivalent items described previously under the File command.

They include:

Add Windows Form
Add Inherited Form

Add User Control
Add Inherited Control
Add Component
Add Class
Add New Item (*Ctrl+Shift+A*)
Add Existing Item (*Shift+Alt+A*)

Exclude From Project. Exclude From Project removes the file from the project but leaves the file intact on the hard drive. This is in contrast with the Delete popup menu item in the Solution Explorer. That will remove the file from the project *and* delete it from the hard drive (actually into the Recycle Bin). If a resource file is associated with the file, it will also be excluded or deleted, respectively.

The Exclude From Project command is also made available in the Solution Explorer by right-clicking on a file.

Add Reference... The Add Reference command is available in the Solution Explorer by right-clicking on a project. In either case, you will get the Add Reference dialog box shown in Figure 3-18. This dialog box allows you to reference assemblies or DLL's external to your application, making the public classes, methods, and members contained in the referenced resource available to your application.

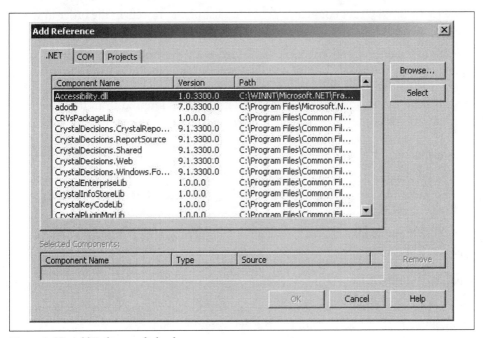

Figure 3-18. Add Reference dialog box

Add Web Reference… The Add Web Reference command, also available in the Solution Explorer by right-clicking a project, allows you to add a web reference to your project, thereby becoming a consuming web service application.

 Web services are covered in *Programming ASP.NET*, Second Edition, by Jesse Liberty and Dan Hurwitz (O'Reilly).

Set as StartUp Project. If there is more than one project in a solution, specify the startup project. This command, also available in the Solution Explorer by right-clicking a project, allows you to make that specification. The project highlighted in Solution Explorer when this command is executed will become the startup project.

Project Dependencies… / Project Build Order… These commands, visible only when a solution contains multiple projects, also available in the Solution Explorer by right-clicking a project, presents a dialog box that allows you to control the build order of the projects in a solution. It presents a dialog box with two tabs: one for Dependencies and one for the Build Order.

The Project Dependencies command allows you to specify, for each project in the solution, which projects it depends upon. The dependent projects will be built first.

The Project Build Order command presents a list of all projects in the order in which they will be built.

If you are using Project References (as added with the Add Reference dialog mentioned above), you won't be able to edit either command. Project Dependencies are inferred when there are references between projects in the same solution. Also, you can't change the Build Order in any case—it is always inferred from the dependencies, whether or not those dependencies were automatically inferred.

Build menu

The Build menu offers menu items for building the current project (highlighted in Solution Explorer) or the solution. It also exposes the Configuration Manager for configuring the build process.

The Build menu will be covered in detail in Chapter 22, which discusses deployment and configuration.

Debug menu

The Debug menu allows you to start an application with or without debugging, set breakpoints in the code, and control the debugging session.

The Debug menu item will be covered, along with debugging, in Chapter 21.

Data menu

This context-sensitive menu is visible only in the design mode. It is not available when editing code pages. The commands under it are available only when there are appropriate data controls on the form.

Chapters 19 through 21 cover data controls and data binding.

Format menu

The Format menu is visible only when in design mode, and the commands under it are available only when one or more controls on the form are selected.

This menu offers the ability to control the size and layout of controls. You can:

- Align controls with a grid or with other controls six different ways
- Change the size of one or more controls to be bigger or smaller (or all be the same)
- Control the spacing horizontally and vertically
- Move controls forward or back in the vertical plane (z-order) of the form
- Lock a control so its size or position cannot be changed

To operate on more than one control, select the controls in one of several ways:

- Hold down Shift or Ctrl while clicking on controls you wish to select.
- Use the mouse to click and drag a selection box around all the controls to be selected. If any part of a control falls within the selection box, then that control will be included.
- To unselect one control, hold down Shift or Ctrl while clicking that control.
- To unselect all the controls, select a different control or press Esc.

When operating on more than one control, the last selected control will be the baseline. In other words, if you are making all the controls the same size, they will all become the same size as the last selected control. Likewise, if aligning a group of controls, they will all align with the last selected control.

As controls are selected, they will display eight resizing handles. These resizing handles will be white for all the selected controls except the baseline, or last control, which will have black handles.

With that in mind, all the commands under the Format menu are fairly self-explanatory.

Tools menu

The Tools menu presents commands that access a wide range of functionality, ranging from connecting to databases, to accessing external tools, to setting IDE options. Some of the most useful commands are described next.

Connect to Device... The Connect to Device command brings up a dialog box that allows you to connect to either a physical mobile device or an emulator.

Connect to Database... The Connect To Database command brings up the dialog box that allows you to select a server, log in to that server, and connect to the database on the server. Microsoft SQL Server is the default database (surprise!), but the Provider tab lets you connect to any number of other databases, including any for which there are Oracle, ODBC, or OLE DB providers.

Connect to Server... The Connect to Server command brings up the dialog box that lets you specify a server to connect to, either by name or by IP address. It also lets you connect by using a different username and password.

This same dialog box can be exposed by right-clicking on Servers in the Server Explorer and selecting Add Server... from the pop-up menu.

Add/Remove Toolbox Items... The Add/Remove Toolbox Items command brings up the Customize Toolbox dialog box shown in Figure 3-19. The dialog box has two tabs: one for adding (legacy) COM components and one for adding .NET CLR–compliant components. All the components available on your machine (including registered COM components and .NET components in specific directories; you can browse for .NET components if they are not listed) are listed in one or the other. In either case, check or uncheck the line in front of the component to include the desired component.

 For adding .NET components to the Toolbox, just drag it from Windows Explorer onto the Toolbox.

It is also possible to add other tabbed lists to this dialog box, although the details for doing so are beyond the scope of this book.

You can sort the components listed in the dialog box by clicking on the column head by which you wish to sort.

Build Comment Web Pages... This menu command brings up a dialog box that allows you to document your application via HTML pages. These HTML pages automatically display the code structure of your application. Projects are listed as hyperlinks. Clicking on a project brings up a page that shows all the classes as hyperlinks on the left side of the page. Clicking on any class lists all the class members, with descriptions, on the right side of the page.

If your language supports XML code comments (as does C#, but VB.NET does not), then you can add your own comments to your source code, and those comments will display in these web pages.

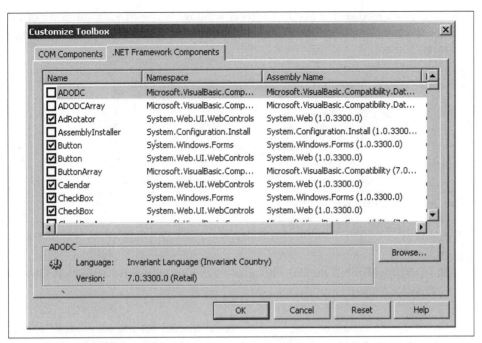

Figure 3-19. Customize Toolbox dialog box

Comment web pages are created by default in a subdirectory of the project called *CodeCommentReport*.

Macros. Macros are a wonderful feature that allows you to automate tasks in the IDE. Macros can either be coded by hand or recorded as you perform the desired task. If you allow the IDE to record the macro for you, then you can subsequently examine and edit the macro code it creates. This is similar to the macro functionality provided as part of Microsoft Word or Excel.

 Be aware that macro recording doesn't work for anything inside a dialog box. For example, if you record the changing of property in a project's Property Pages, the recorded macro will open the Property Pages but won't do anything in there!

You can easily record a temporary macro by using the Macros → Record Temporary-Macro command, or by pressing Ctrl+Shift+R. This temporary macro can then be played back using the Macros → Run TemporaryMacro command, or by pressing Ctrl+Shift+P. It can be saved using the Macros → Save TemporaryMacro command, which will automatically bring up the Macro Explorer, described next.

Macros are managed with a Macro Explorer window, accessed via a submenu of the Macros command, or by pressing Alt+F8, as shown in Figure 3-20 after recording a temporary macro.

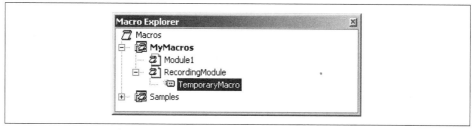

Figure 3-20. Macro Explorer

Right-clicking on a macro in the Macro Explorer pops up a menu with four items:

Run

> Runs the highlighted macro. The macro can also be run by double-clicking on the macro name.

Edit

> Brings up the macro editing IDE, where all macros for the user can be edited. The macro language is VB.NET, irrespective of the language used for the project. The macro editing IDE can also be invoked using the Macros → Macro IDE command, or by pressing Alt+F11.

Rename

> Allows the macro to be renamed.

Delete

> Deletes the macro from the macro file.

All macros are contained in a *macro project* called, by default, MyMacros. This project is comprised of a binary file called *MyMacros.vsmacros* (unless you have elected to convert it to the multiple files format), which is physically located in the *Documents and Settings* directory for each user. You can create a new macro project by using the Macros → New Macro Project command or by right-clicking on the root object in the Macro Explorer and selecting New Macro Project. In either case, you will get the New Macro Project dialog box, which lets you specify the name and location of the new macro project file.

Macro projects contain modules, which are units of code. Each module contains subroutines, which correspond to the macros. For example, the macro called TemporaryMacro, shown in Figure 3-20 is the TemporaryMacros subroutine contained in the module named RecordingModule, which is part of the MyMacros project.

External Tools... Depending on the options selected at the time Visual Studio .NET was installed on your machine, you may have one or more external tools available on the Tools menu. The tools might include Create GUID, ATL/MFC Trace Tool, or Spy++. (Use of these tools is beyond the scope of this book.)

The Tools → External Tools... command allows you to add additional external tools to the Tools menu. When selected, you are presented with the External Tools dialog box. This dialog box has fields for the tool title, the command to execute the tool, any arguments and the initial directory, as well as several checkboxes for different behaviors.

Customize... The Customize... command allows you to customize many aspects of the IDE user interface. (The Options... command, described in the following section, lets you set a variety of other program options.) It brings up the Customize dialog box, which has three different tabs, plus one additional button, allowing customization in four different areas.

Toolbars

This tab, shown in Figure 3-21, presents a checkbox list of all available toolbars, with checkmarks indicating currently visible toolbars. You can control the visibility of specific toolbars by checking or unchecking them in this list, or alternatively, use the View → Toolbars command.

You can also create new toolbars, rename or delete existing toolbars, or reset all the toolbars back to the original installation version on this tab.

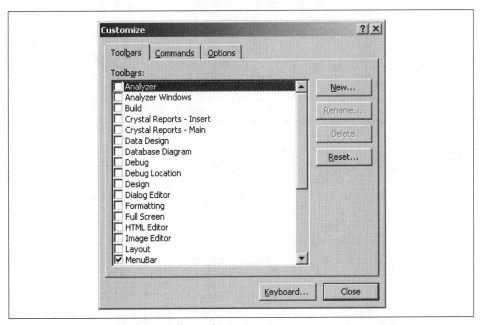

Figure 3-21. Customize dialog (Toolbars tab)

Commands

> The Commands tab, shown in Figure 3-22, allows you to add or remove commands from a toolbar or modify buttons already on the toolbar.
>
> To add a command to a toolbar, select the category and command from the lists in the dialog box, and then use the mouse to drag the command to the desired toolbar.
>
> To remove a command from a toolbar, drag it from the toolbar to anywhere in the IDE while the Customize Commands dialog is showing.
>
> The Modify Selection button is active only when a button on an existing toolbar is selected. It allows you to perform such chores as renaming or deleting the button, changing the image displayed on the button, changing the display style of the button (image only, text only, etc.), and organizing buttons into groups.

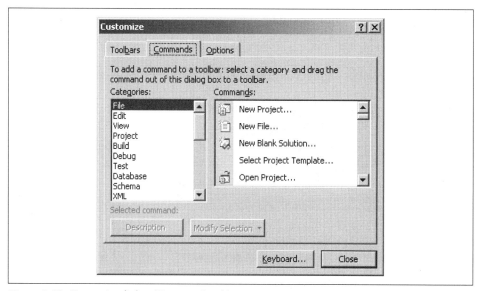

Figure 3-22. Customize dialog (Commands tab)

Options

> The Options tab, shown in Figure 3-23, allows you to change the toolbar's appearance.
>
> The personalized Menus and Toolbars checkboxes are always unavailable and grayed out.
>
> The Other checkboxes allow selection of icon size on buttons, control of tool tips, and the way the menus come in to view (Menu animations).

Keyboard…

> The Keyboard… button brings up the Environment → Keyboard page, shown in Figure 3-24, also accessible under the Tools → Options command described below. This page allows you to define and change keyboard shortcuts for commands.

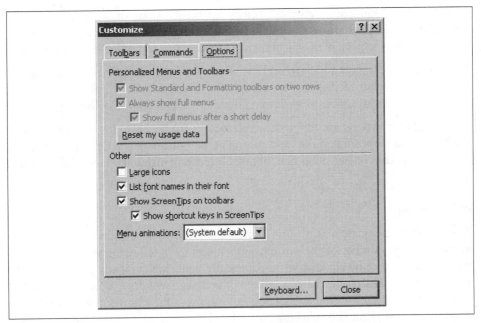

Figure 3-23. Customize dialog (Options tab)

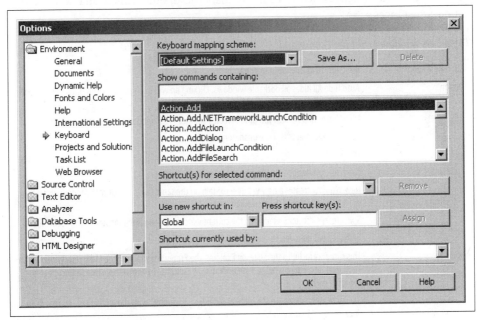

Figure 3-24. Customize dialog (Keyboard button)

Options... The Options... command brings up the Options dialog box, shown in Figure 3-24. This dialog box lets you set a wide range of options, ranging from the number of items to display in lists of recently used items, to XML Designer options.

The dialog box displays a hierarchical list of categories on the left side. Selecting any category allows you to drill down through the tree structure. Clicking on a detail item brings up the available properties on the right side of the dialog box.

Most available options are fairly self-explanatory. If you have any questions about specific settings, clicking on the Help button at the bottom of the Options dialog box will bring up context-sensitive help about all the properties relevant to the current detail item.

Window menu

The Window menu item is a fairly standard Windows application Window command. It displays a list of the currently open windows, allowing you to bring any window to the fore by clicking on it. All the file windows currently displayed in the IDE also have tabs along the top edge of the design window, below the toolbars (unless you selected MDI mode in Tools → Options → Environment → General), and windows can be selected by clicking on a tab.

This is a context-sensitive menu. Table 3-9 lists the menu items available for different circumstances.

Table 3-9. Window menu item commands

Current window	Description of available commands
Design	Auto Hide All hides all dockable windows. Clicking on window's pushpin icon turns AutoHide off for that window.
	New Horizontal/Vertical Tab Group creates another set of windows with it own set of tabs.
	Close All Documents is self-explanatory.
	Window list.
Code	Same as for a design window plus the following:
	New Window creates a new window containing the same file as the current window. Use it to open two windows to the same source file.
	Split creates a second window in the current window for two different views of the same file.
	Remove Split removes a split window.
Dockable	This category includes the Solution Explorer, the Properties window, the Class View window, the Toolboxes, etc. These windows are dockable, as indicated by the pushpin icon in the upper-right corner of each.
	Available menu items are the same as for a design window, with the addition of commands to dock, hide, or float a window.

Help menu

The Help menu provides access to a number of submenus. Those that are not self-explanatory are described here.

Dynamic Help (Ctrl+F1). If you are developing on a machine with enough horsepower, Dynamic Help is wonderful. Otherwise, it is a performance hog. (It can be disabled by unchecking all the checkboxes under Tools → Options → Environment → Dynamic Help) Alternatively, just closing the window is sufficient to prevent the performance hit, and then it is still available when you need it.

That said, using Dynamic Help is very simple. Open a Dynamic Help window by clicking on this menu item or pressing Ctrl+F1. Then wherever the focus is, whether in a design, code, or dockable window, context-sensitive hyperlinks will appear in the Dynamic Help window. Click on any link to bring up the relevant Help topic in a separate window.

Contents... (Ctrl+Alt+F1)/Index... (Ctrl+Alt+F2)/Search... (Ctrl+Alt+F3). These three commands provide different views into the SDK help system, allowing you to search by a (pseudo) table of contents, an incremental index, or a search phrase, respectively. The first type of search is an indexed search, while the latter two are full-text searches, so you may get different results by using the different search types using the same phrase.

 The Help system exposed by these commands is the same Help system exposed in two other places by the Start button:

- Programs → Microsoft Visual Studio .NET 2003 → Microsoft Visual Studio .NET 2003 Documentation
- Programs → Microsoft .NET Framework SDK v1.1 → Documentation

This Help tool uses a browser-type interface, with Forward and Back navigation and Favorites. The list of topics is displayed in the lefthand pane, and the help topic itself, including hyperlinks, is displayed on the right.

Index Results... (Shift+Alt+F2). When searching for Help topics by Index, you will often find many topics for a given index entry. In these cases, the multiple topics are listed in an Index Results window. This window displays automatically if this is the case. This command lets you view the Index Results window if it has been closed.

Search Results... (Shift+Alt+F3). The Search Results window is analogous to the Index Results window described previously, except it pertains to searching for Help topics by search phrase.

Edit Filters... The SDK Help system is voluminous, with information on the full array of topics that might be found in any .NET installation, as well as a ton of non-.NET stuff as well. The Edit Filters command lets you restrict which Help topics will be searched. For example, if you are working exclusively in C#, you might set the filter to either Visual C# or Visual C# and Related.

Check for Updates. This command checks for service releases for your currently installed version of Visual Studio .NET. For this command to work, your machine must be connected to the Internet. If an update is available, you will be prompted to close the IDE before the service release is installed.

Building and Running

You can run your application at any time by selecting either Start or Start Without Debugging from the Debug menu, or you can accomplish the same results by pressing either F5 or Ctrl+F5, respectively. In addition, you can start the program by clicking the Start icon (▸) on the Standard Toolbar.

The program can be built, i.e., EXE and DLL files generated, by selecting a command under the Build menu. You have the option of building the entire solution or only the currently selected project.

For a full discussion of application deployment, please see Chapter 22.

CHAPTER 4

Events

In the 1950s and 1960s, computer programs allowed for little user interaction. You fed in your data and instructions, and an answer popped out. As computers evolved, simple text-based menus were added. At specified times in the running of the program, the user could make choices and the program would respond accordingly. In the 1980s and 1990s, Graphical User Interfaces (GUIs) were developed, and computer programming was revolutionized.

In a modern Windows program, the user constantly interacts with the system: moving, clicking, and dragging the mouse or entering characters at the keyboard.

In Microsoft Windows the widgets with which the user interacts are called *controls*, and controls are visible on the monitor from the moment a modern program starts. In a Windows application, the user's action completely determines the order of execution of a program. This is called *event-driven* programming.

User actions, such as clicking on a button, generate (or "raise") *events*. Other events are generated by the system itself. For example, your program might raise an event when a file has been read into memory, your battery's power is running low, or a timer indicates that a specified time interval has passed.

Publish and Subscribe

In .NET, controls *publish* a set of events to which other classes can *subscribe*. When the publishing class raises an event, all the subscribed classes are notified.

 This design is similar to the Publish/Subscribe (Observer) Pattern described in the seminal work *Design Patterns* by Gamma, et al. (Addison Wesley). Gamma describes the intent of this pattern, "Define a one to many dependency between objects so that when one object changes state, all its dependents are notified and updated automatically."

With this event mechanism, the control says, "Here are things I can notify you about," and other classes might sign up, saying, "Yes, let me know when that happens." For example, a button might notify any number of interested observers when it is clicked. The button is called the *publisher* because the button publishes the Click event, and the other classes are the *subscribers* because they subscribe to the Click event.

Events and Delegates

Events are implemented with delegates. The publishing class defines a delegate that encapsulates a method that the subscribing classes implement. When the event is raised, the subscribing classes' methods (the event handlers) are invoked through the delegate.

 A *delegate* type defines the signature of methods that can be encapsulated by instances of that delegate type. A delegate can be marked as an event to restrict access to that delegate for use as an event handler.

For more information on the relationship between delegates and events, please see either *Programming VB.NET* or *Programming C#*, by Jesse Liberty (O'Reilly).

When you instantiate a delegate, pass in the name of the method the delegate will encapsulate. Register the event using the += operator (in C#) or the Handles and WithEvents keywords in VB.NET. (VB.NET can alternatively use the AddHandler keyword.) You may register more than one delegate with an event; when the event is raised, each of the delegated methods will be notified.

For example, when declaring an event, the .NET documentation describes the event and delegate used in the Button control's Click event:

```
public delegate void EventHandler(object sender, EventArgs e);
public event EventHandler Click;
```

EventHandler is defined to be a delegate for a method that returns void and takes two arguments: one of type Object and the other of type EventArgs. The Click event is implemented with the EventHandler delegate.

Event Arguments

By convention, event handlers in the .NET Framework are designated in C# to return void, are implemented as a sub in VB.NET, and take two parameters. The first parameter is the "source" of the event: the publishing object. The second parameter is an object derived from EventArgs.

EventArgs is the base class for all event data. Other than its constructor, the EventArgs class inherits all its methods only from Object, though it does add a public static field *empty*, which represents an event with no state (to allow for the efficient use of events with no state).

If an event has no interesting data to pass, then the passed event argument will be of type EventArgs, which has no public properties, being essentially a placeholder. However, if there is interesting data, such as the location of a mouseclick or which key was pressed, then the event argument will be of a type derived from EventArgs, and it will have properties for the data being passed.

The general prototype for an event handler is as follows:

C#
```
private void Handler (object sender, EventArgs e)
```

VB
```
Private Sub Handler (ByVal sender As Object, ByVal e As EventArgs)
```

By convention, the name of the object argument is sender and the name of the EventArgs argument is e.

The ByVal keyword in the VB.NET version indicates that the arguments are passed by value, rather than by reference (ByRef). If neither ByVal nor ByRef is included, the default behavior in VB.NET is by value, so the use of the keyword here is redundant. However, using it explicitly serves as a form of documentation, and since Visual Studio .NET explicitly includes the byVal keyword, you will often see it included in event handlers.

While technically you pass by value, the object passed is itself a reference. A copy of the reference is made, but it refers to the original object, and changes made within the method will affect the original object through that copy of the reference. This book refers to passing a reference by value as "pass by reference."

Some events use the base class EventArgs, but EventArgs objects contain no useful additional information about the event. The controls that do require their event handlers to know additional information about the event will pass in an object of a type derived from EventArgs.

For example, the TreeView AfterCollapse event handler receives an argument of type TreeViewEventArgs, derived from EventArgs. TreeViewEventArgs has the properties Action and Node, each of which has values pertaining to the actual event. The specifics of the event argument for each control are detailed when that control is discussed later in this book.

Control Events

Every form and control used in Windows Forms derives from System.Windows. Forms.Control, so they inherit all of the more than 50 public events contained by the Control object. Some of the most commonly used Control events are listed in

Table 4-1 through Table 4-3. For each (public) event, a protected method handles the event.

Many controls support other events, in addition to the inherited events. For example, the TreeView class exposes several events for handling node expansion and collapse. Control-specific events are detailed in the relevant sections.

Table 4-1. Common Control events

Event	Event argument	Description
Click	EventArgs	Raised when a control is clicked by the mouse.
ControlAdded	ControlEventArgs	Raised when a new control is added to Control.ControlCollection.
ControlRemoved	ControlEventArgs	Raised when a control is removed from Control.ControlCollection.
DockChanged	EventArgs	Raised if the Dock property— i.e., which edge of the parent container the control is docked to—is changed, either by user interaction or program control.
DoubleClick	EventArgs	Raised when a control is double-clicked. If a control has both a Click and DoubleClick event handler, the DoubleClick will be preempted by the Click event.
Enter	EventArgs	Raised when a control receives focus. Suppressed for Form objects. For nested controls, cascades up and down the container hierarchy.
Layout	LayoutEventArgs	Raised when any change occurs that affects the layout of the control (e.g., the control is resized or child controls are added or removed).
Leave	EventArgs	Raised when focus leaves the control.
Move	EventArgs	Raised when a control is moved.
Paint	PaintEventArgs	Raised when a control is redrawn.
ParentChanged	EventArgs	Raised when the parent container of a control changes.
Resize	EventArgs	Raised when a control is resized. Generally preferable to use the Layout event.
SizeChanged	EventArgs	Raised when the Size property is changed, either by user interaction or programmatic control. Generally preferable to use the Layout event.
TextChanged	EventArgs	Raised when the Text property changes, either by user interaction or programmatic control.
Validating	CancelEventArgs	Raised when a control is validating. If CancelEventArgs Cancel property set true, then all subsequent focus events are suppressed. Suppressed if Control.CausesValidation property set false.
Validated	EventArgs	Raised when a control completes validation. Suppressed if the CancelEventArgs.Cancel property passed to the Validating event is set true. Suppressed if Control.CausesValidation property set false.

Although all Forms controls inherit from System.Windows.Forms.Control, not all controls necessarily expose all the events contained in Control. For example, the Windows user interface does not allow you to double-click a button control. Yet the Button class inherits from Control via the ButtonBase class. In fact, even though Visual Studio .NET does not expose a DoubleClick event for a Button control, you can add the event and hook it up manually. Your program will compile and run, but the DoubleClick event will never be raised for a button.

.NET can suppress the Click and DoubleClick events on selected controls by setting the StandardClick and StandardDoubleClick values, respectively, of the ControlStyles enumeration.

The events listed in Table 4-2 implement drag-and-drop.

Table 4-2. Control Drag-and-Drop events

Event	Event argument	Description
DragDrop	DragEventArgs	Raised when a drag-and-drop operation is completed.
DragEnter	DragEventArgs	Raised when an object is dragged onto the control. At the time this event is raised, the drag operation is still in progress (i.e., the user hasn't yet let the mouse button go up).
DragLeave	DragEventArgs	Raised when an object is dragged off of the control.
DragOver	DragEventArgs	Raised when an object is dragged over the control.
GiveFeedback	GiveFeedbackEventArgs	Raised during a drag operation to allow modification to the mouse pointer.

The events listed in Table 4-3 are raised when a mouse interacts with a control. Some of these low-level events, in addition to being raised, are synthesized into the higher-level Click and DoubleClick events.

Table 4-3. Control Mouse events

Event	Event argument	Description
MouseEnter	EventArgs	Raised when mouse pointer enters control.
MouseMove	MouseEventArgs	Raised when mouse pointer moved over control.
MouseHover	EventArgs	Raised when mouse hovers over control.
MouseDown	MouseEventArgs	Raised when mouse button pressed while mouse pointer is over control.
MouseWheel	MouseEventArgs	Raised when mouse wheel moved while control has focus.
MouseUp	MouseEventArgs	Raised when mouse button released while mouse pointer is over control.
MouseLeave	EventArgs	Raised when mouse pointer leaves control.

Web Controls Versus Windows Controls

ASP.NET web applications are also event driven. There are many similarities between web form and Windows Forms events. The main difference is that there are nearly 60 different Windows control events, but only six different Web Control events.

The reason for this is that all web form events are processed on the server, rather than locally on the client. As such, each event must be posted back to the server for processing, necessitating a roundtrip between the server and the client. If Web Forms supported the full complement of user interaction events, such as Mouse or Key events, performance would be severely impacted.

For a complete discussion of web form events, please see *Programming ASP.NET*, Second Edition (O'Reilly).

Implementing an Event

Events were demonstrated back in Chapter 2. There, a Button was added to a form and the Click event for the button was handled. Handling the event was demonstrated both in a text editor and in Visual Studio .NET. Those examples also showed that the syntax and mechanics of handling events is somewhat different in C# and VB.NET, although the underlying fundamentals are the same.

The code samples shown in Example 4-1 (in C#) and Example 4-3 (in VB.NET) are duplicates of those shown in Examples 2-5 and 2-6.

In C#

Example 4-1, reproduced here from Example 2-5, demonstrates the basic principles of implementing an event handler in C# by using a text editor.

Example 4-1. Hello World Windows application with button control in C# (HelloWorld-win-button.cs)

```csharp
using System;
using System.Drawing;
using System.Windows.Forms;

namespace ProgrammingWinApps
{
    public class HelloWorld : System.Windows.Forms.Form
    {

        private Button btn;

        public HelloWorld( )
        {
            Text = "Hello World";
```

```
C#         btn = new Button( );
           btn.Location = new Point(50,50);
           btn.Text = "Goodbye";
           btn.Click += new System.EventHandler(btn_Click);

           Controls.Add(btn);
       }

       static void Main( )
       {
           Application.Run(new HelloWorld( ));
       }

       private void btn_Click(object sender, EventArgs e)
       {
           Application.Exit( );
       }
   }
}
```

Handling an event in C# involves two steps:

Implement the event handler method

The event handler method, highlighted in Example 4-1, is called btn_Click. It has the required signature (two parameters: sender of type object and e of type EventArgs), and, as required, it returns void.

The code in the body of the event handler method performs whatever programming task is required to respond to the event. In this example, the event handler closes the application with the static method Application.Exit( ).

Hook up the event handler method to the event

This is done by instantiating an EventHandler delegate, which encapsulates the btn_Click method, then using the += operator to add that delegate to the button's Click event. This is done in Example 4-1 with the following line of code:

```
C#         btn.Click += new System.EventHandler(btn_Click);
```

As easy as this is, Visual Studio .NET makes it even simpler. The fundamentals in working with events in the IDE will be shown with a simple application.

Open Visual Studio .NET and create a new Visual C# Windows Application project. Name it csEvents. Put a Label and Button control on the form. Using the Properties window, set the control properties to the values listed in Table 4-4.

Table 4-4. HelloWorld-Events Control properties

Control type	Property	Value
Form	(Name)	Form1
	Text	Events Demonstrator
	Size	250,200

Table 4-4. HelloWorld-Events Control properties (continued)

Control type	Property	Value
Label	(Name)	lblTitle
	Text	Events Demonstrator
	Size	150,25
Button	(Name)	btnTest
	Text	Do It!

After the controls are placed and the properties set, Visual Studio .NET should look similar to Figure 4-1.

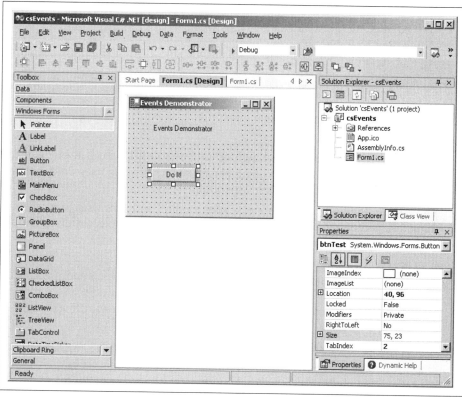

Figure 4-1. csEvents layout in Visual Studio .NET

There are several different ways to implement an event in Visual Studio .NET with C#.

C# and VB.NET differ in the user interface used by Visual Studio .NET to implement events, although the underlying class libraries and technology are the same. These differences are primarily a nod to backward compatibility for VB6 programmers. The VB.NET version will be detailed shortly.

Double-click the control. Double-click the button control. Visual Studio.NET takes this as an indication that you want to implement the default event handler for the button (the click event). Visual Studio.NET creates and registers an event handler, and moves you to the code window with the cursor placed in the body of the event handler:

```csharp
private void btnTest_Click(object sender, System.EventArgs e)
{

}
```

Visual Studio.NET has created a method declaration that follows the event handler prototype exactly. The method name defaults to the name of the control with an underscore character and the default event name concatenated on the end.

> Each control has a default event (whichever event is most commonly used with that control). For many controls, it is the Click event, but not always. The default event for the TreeView control is AfterSelect, although that control does have a Click event. The default event for each control will be detailed when the control is covered.

Enter a line of code to pop up a message box in response to the button click:

```csharp
private void btnTest_Click(object sender, System.EventArgs e)
{
    MessageBox.Show("Click event just handled.","Event Demo");
}
```

Running the form will produce the application shown in Figure 4-2. Clicking the button will pop up a message dialog with the words "Click event just handled," as shown in Figure 4-3.

Figure 4-2. Events Demonstrator application

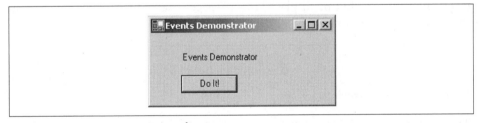

Figure 4-3. Event Demonstrator MessageBox

When you developed Example 4-1 in a text editor, you saw that in addition to implementing the event handler method, you also had to add a delegate encapsulating that method to the event. In Example 4-1, it was done with the following line of code:

```
btn.Click += new System.EventHandler(btn_Click);
```

When using Visual Studio .NET, registering the event is done for you automatically. This can be seen by going to the code window for the form, finding and expanding the region of code labeled Windows Form Designer generated code, and looking for the following section of code inside the InitializeComponent method:

```
//
// btnTest
//
this.btnTest.Location = new System.Drawing.Point(56, 128);
this.btnTest.Name = "btnTest";
this.btnTest.TabIndex = 2;
this.btnTest.Text = "Do It!";
this.btnTest.Click += new System.EventHandler(this.btnTest_Click);
```

The highlighted line of code adds the method to the EventHandler delegate.

Use the lightning bolt icon in the Properties window. Double-clicking on the control only allows you to handle the default event using the default event handler method name. You can also create event handlers for any of a control's events, and name them whatever you like. To do so in C#, highlight the control in the design window and view the Properties window for the control (select View → Properties Window from the menu, press F4, or right-click and select Properties).

At the top of the Properties window is a row of buttons, shown in Figure 4-4. The first two buttons on the left sort the window's contents by category or alphabetically. The right-most button displays Property pages, if any. Of most interest here are the remaining two buttons.

Figure 4-4. Property Window button bar

The Properties button ( ) causes the window to display all the properties for the control, while the Events button ( ) causes the window to display all the supported events for the control. either alphabetically or by category.

If there is an event handler already defined for an event, it will be listed in the column next to the event name. Clicking on that name and pressing the Enter key will take you to that event handler in the code window.

If there is no event handler listed next to an event, highlight the event and press the Enter key to create an event handler with the default name. The method skeleton will be created, the event will be registered, and you will be taken to that method in the code window, where you can enter the body of the method.

Alternatively, you can enter any method name you wish. Pressing Enter will use the name you entered to create a skeleton event handler method and automatically hook up that event handler method to the event.

Finally, when an event is highlighted in the Properties window, a drop-down arrow will appear in the column for the method names. Clicking on the drop-down will display all the methods in the code available to be event handlers. This can be used to assign the same method to many different events, either for the same control or for different controls.

To demonstrate this last point, go to the code window for csEvents. Create a generic event handler method by adding the code shown in Example 4-2 to the Form1 class.

Example 4-2. Generic event handler in C#

```csharp
private void GenericEventHandler(object sender, EventArgs e)
{
    MessageBox.Show("Generic event handler", "Event Demo");
}
```

Now go back to the form designer and highlight the button. If the Events are not visible in the Property window, click on the Events button. Slide down to the Mouse-Enter event and click the drop-down arrow. You will see all the available methods, as shown in Figure 4-5.

Figure 4-5. Event drop-down

Click on GenericEventHandler to hook that handler method to the event.

Now add the same event handler to the Click method of the Label control named lblTitle. Click on the lblTitle control, find the Click event in the list of events in the Property window, click the drop-down arrow, and select GenericEventHandler. Run the program.

You will see that every time the mouse moves over the button, a dialog box similar to that shown in Figure 4-3 appears with the message Generic Event Handler. In fact, it is not possible to click on the button with your mouse because the MouseEnter event occurs before you have the opportunity to click on the button. (You can however click the button by pressing the Enter key once the button has focus.)

Clicking on the label containing the title also brings up the Generic Event Handler message.

Visual Studio .NET does all the work of hooking the GenericEventHandler method to both the lblTitle Click event and the btnTest MouseOver event. You can see how this was done by examining the region of code labeled Windows Form Designer generated code. In the section of code initializing the lblTitle control, the following line hooks the GenericEventHandler method to the Click event:

```C#
this.lblTitle.Click += new System.EventHandler(this.GenericEventHandler);
```

Similarly, the GenericEventHandler method is hooked to the btnTest MouseEnter event with this line of code:

```C#
this.btnTest.MouseEnter +=
        new System.EventHandler(this.GenericEventHandler);
```

 It is very easy to add event handlers to a form by double-clicking on a control. Sometimes adding the handlers is too easy, since accidentally double-clicking on a control will create an empty event handler method for that control, if it does not already have one. You may notice some of these empty methods in your code. These empty methods impose a small performance penalty on your program and clutter your code.

If you simply delete the empty methods, your program will not compile. Remember that the event handler was added to the event delegate in the "hidden" code contained in the InitializeComponent method in the Windows Form Designer generated code region. To manually delete the empty method from your code, you must also delete any references to the method where it is added to an event delegate.

A simple way to delete an event handler is to use the Properties window: highlight the offending event and delete the event handler. This will remove both the method and the registration code.

By the same token, if you rename an event handler method manually, you must find the relevant line in InitializeComponent and rename the method reference there as well, but doing so on the Properties window will update the reference for you.

In the unusual case that you want more than one handler for a single event, you can add as many event handler methods to an event as you wish simply by implementing the event handler methods, and then adding those events to the delegate with additional += statements. (Even in Visual Studio .NET, this requires inserting the lines of code yourself.)

Similarly, you can remove an event handler method by using the -= operator. For example, the following code snippet adds three methods to a delegate for handling the Click event, then removes one of the methods from the delegate. In this way, it is possible to add and remove event handler methods dynamically and thereby start and stop event handling for specific events anywhere in your program:

```C#
btn.Click += new System.EventHandler(GenericEventHandler);
btn.Click += new System.EventHandler(SpecialEventHandler);
btn.Click += new System.EventHandler(ClickEventHandler);
btn.Click -= new System.EventHandler(GenericEventHandler);
```

In VB.NET

Example 4-3, reproduced from Example 2-6, demonstrates the basic principles of implementing an event handler in VB.NET, using a text editor.

Example 4-3. Hello World Windows application with button control in VB.NET (HelloWorld-win-button.vb)

```VB
imports System
imports System.Drawing
imports System.Windows.Forms

namespace ProgrammingWinApps
    public class HelloWorld : inherits System.Windows.Forms.Form

        Private WithEvents btn as Button
        public sub New( )
            Text = "Hello World"

            btn = new Button( )
            btn.Location = new Point(50,50)
            btn.Text = "Goodbye"
            Controls.Add(btn)
        end sub

        public shared sub Main( )
            Application.Run(new HelloWorld( ))
        end sub

        private sub btn_Click(ByVal sender as object, _
                ByVal e as EventArgs) _
                Handles btn.Click
            Application.Exit( )
        end sub
    end class
end namespace
```

As with the C# example shown in Example 4-1, there are two steps to handling an event in VB.NET. However the syntax used in VB.NET is somewhat different than that in C#.

Implement the event handler method

> The event handler method, highlighted in Example 4-3, is called btn_Click. It has the required signature (two objects: sender of type object and e of type EventArgs). Since this method is a subroutine, denoted by the sub keyword, it does not return a value. Event handlers never return a value.

> The Handles keyword specifies which event this method will handle. The identifier following the keyword indicates that this method will handle the Click event for the Button called btn.

> The code in the body of the event handler method performs whatever programming chore is required. In this example, it closes the application with the static method Application.Exit().

Instantiate the control using the WithEvents keyword

> Unlike in C#, there is no code here to explicitly add the method to the delegate. Instead, a Button is declared as a private member variable using the keyword WithEvents. This keyword tells the compiler that this object will raise events:

VB
```
Private WithEvents btn as Button
```

> The compiler automatically creates delegates for any events referred to by a Handles clause and adds the event handler methods to the appropriate delegate.

Implementing events in VB.NET is made even easier when using Visual Studio .NET. To demonstrate this, open Visual Studio .NET and create a new VB.NET Windows application project called vbEvents.

Put a Label control and a Button control on the form. Using the Properties window, set the control properties to the values listed in Table 4-4 (the same values used in the C# example).

You can use VB.NET in several different ways to implement events in Visual Studio .NET.

Double-click the control. Double-click the Button control. You will be brought immediately to the code-editing window for the control, ready to enter code for the default event. The following code skeleton for the event handler method will be in place, with the cursor properly placed for you to commence typing the body of the method:

VB
```
Private Sub btnTest_Click(ByVal sender As System.Object, _
            ByVal e As System.EventArgs) Handles btnTest.Click
End Sub
```

In Visual Studio .NET, the method declaration will be on a single line, not wrapped with a line-continuation character, as printed here.

This method declaration exactly follows the event handler method prototype for VB.NET. The method name defaults to the name of the control with an underscore character and the default event name concatenated on the end. You can, however, use any name you wish, since the actual relationship between the method and the event it handles is dictated by the Handles keyword.

Each control has a default event (whichever event is most commonly used with that control). For many controls, it is the Click event. The default event for the TreeView control, however, is AfterSelect, although that control does have a Click event. The default event for each control will be detailed when the control is covered.

Enter a line of code to pop up a message box so that the btnTest_Click method now looks like:

```
Private Sub btnTest_Click(ByVal sender As System.Object,
            ByVal e As System.EventArgs) Handles btnTest.Click
    MessageBox.Show("Click event just handled.","Event Demo")
End Sub
```

Running the form will produce the same application previously developed in C#, shown in Figure 4-2. Clicking the button will pop up a message dialog with the words "Click event just handled," as shown in Figure 4-3.

In Example 4-3, which was developed in a text editor, you saw that in addition to implementing the event handler method, you must also instantiate the control using the WithEvents keyword. In Example 4-3, that was done with the following line of code:

```
Private WithEvents btn as Button
```

When using Visual Studio .NET, this step is done for you automatically. You can see it by going to the code window for the form, finding and expanding out the region of code labeled Windows Form Designer generated code, and looking for the following line of code:

```
Friend WithEvents btnTest As System.Windows.Forms.Button
```

In Example 4-3, the Private access modifier was used for the object, which restricts access to the object to the class of which it is a member, i.e., HelloWorld. Visual Studio .NET uses the Friend access modifier, which is somewhat more expansive, allowing access from any class within the project in which it is defined.

It is very easy to add event handlers to a form by double-clicking on a control. Sometimes it is too easy, since accidentally double-clicking on a control will create an empty event-handler method for that control, if it does not already have one. You may notice some of these empty methods in your code. In VB.NET applications, they do not usually cause any problems other than clutter.

If you simply delete the empty methods, the VB.NET program will still compile (unlike with C#). This is because there is no explicit connection between the event-handler method and the event in the code. The compiler makes the connection at compile time only if both halves of the connection are present.

If the control itself is deleted from the form designer, the lines of code instantiating the control with the WithEvents keyword will be removed, but the event-handler method will remain. You might want to delete these methods manually if they are no longer used, to minimize clutter and confusion in your code.

Use the drop-down lists at the top of the code window. Double-clicking on the control allows you to add code to the default event only by using the default event-handler method name. You can also create event handlers for any of a control's events. To do so in VB.NET, view the code window. At the top of the window are two drop-down lists, as shown in Figure 4-6. The drop-down on the left lists all the controls on the form, while the drop-down on the right lists all the possible events for each control (plus (Declarations), which moves the cursor to the top of the code window).

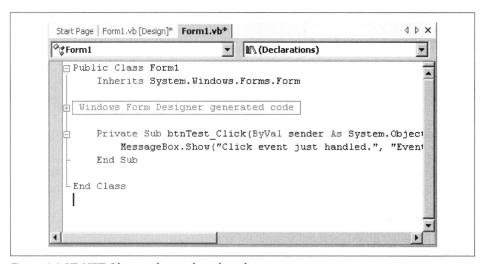

Figure 4-6. VB.NET Object and event drop-down lists

First select the control whose events you wish to handle from the left drop-down. Select the event to handle from the right drop-down. If the event handler already exists, the cursor will move to the subroutine. If the event handler subroutine does not exist, then it will be created, with the cursor located inside the code skeleton, ready to enter your code.

 It is a good idea to use meaningful, nondefault names for all the controls on your form that will be referenced elsewhere in the code to enhance readability and maintainability. Default names of controls are always the name of the control with a number appended, such as Button23, and default event-handler names are the name of the control, with an underscore and the event name, such as Button23_Click. This becomes especially important when assigning events to controls.

An event handler method can easily be renamed simply by editing the method declaration. There is no need to edit any other line of code, since the method name is not associated with the method until compile time.

It is not possible to directly assign the same event handler method to multiple events on a form using this syntax, as can be done in C#. This is because each event-handler method uses the Handles keyword to directly associate the method with a specific event. One way to accomplish this indirectly would be to call the same method from within multiple event handlers.

It is possible, however, to have multiple event-handler methods respond to the same event. This is accomplished by having the Handles keyword on each of the event-handler methods refer to the same event. In this situation, the order in which the multiple events will fire is not defined. If the order is important, then you need to use the dynamic event implementation and the AddHandler statement, described next.

 The drop-down at the top of the code window is somewhat different for the Form than for the controls contained within the Form. When a control other than the Form is selected in the left drop-down, the right drop-down lists all the possible events for that control.

If the Form is selected in the left drop-down menu, the only thing listed besides (Declarations) are existing methods in the Form class plus the protected method Finalize.

There are two other entries in the left drop-down menu that are not objects: (Overrides) and (Base Class Events). (Overrides) causes the right drop-down to display all the virtual methods and properties of the Form class that can be overridden. (Base Class Events) causes the right drop-down to display all the events for the Form class that can be implemented. In either case, selecting an entry from the right drop-down causes Visual Studio .NET to insert the skeleton code for the appropriate property, method, or event to be inserted in the code window. If an event is selected, Visual Studio .NET will also hook the event-handler method to the event.

Dynamic event implementation. In the VB.NET syntax described so far, there is no sign of delegates in the code. The compiler automatically creates the necessary delegates at compile time and adds the methods marked with the Handles keyword to the appropriate delegate for each event.

You can explicitly add the event handler methods to the delegate in VB.NET, as is done in C#, even though it is not the default way in which Visual Studio .NET handles events in VB.NET programs. This is done with the AddHandler statement. AddHandler does not provide any significant performance benefits over the Handles keyword, but does provide greater flexibility. AddHandler and RemoveHandler allow you to add, remove, and change the event handler associated with an event dynamically (in your code at runtime). You can also add multiple event handlers to a single event using AddHandler.

The listing in Example 4-4 shows the modifications to Example 4-3 necessary to use the AddHandler statement rather than the Handles keyword for implementing events. The new or modified lines are highlighted.

Example 4-4. Using AddHandler to implement events

```
imports System
imports System.Drawing
imports System.Windows.Forms

namespace ProgrammingWinApps
    public class EventsDemo : inherits System.Windows.Forms.Form

        Private btn as Button
        public sub New( )
            Text = "Events Demonstration - AddHandler"

            btn = new Button( )
            btn.Location = new Point(50,50)
            btn.Text = "Test"

            Controls.Add(btn)
            AddHandler btn.Click, AddressOf btn_Click
        end sub

        public shared sub Main( )
            Application.Run(new EventsDemo( ))
        end sub

        private sub btn_Click(ByVal sender as object, _
            ByVal e as EventArgs)
            MessageBox.Show("btn_Click method","Events Demonstration")
        end sub
    end class
end namespace
```

Three code changes are necessary to dynamically add event handlers in a VB.NET program.

- The line instantiating the control no longer includes the WithEvents keyword. (This is not mandatory, but the keyword is no longer needed.)
- The event handler method declaration no longer uses the Handles keyword.
- An AddHandler statement is included to add the event-handler method to the delegate that handles the event.

  The AddHandler statement takes two comma-separated arguments. The first argument is the name of the event to be handled, using dot notation. It is a two-part name consisting of the name of the object and the name of the event. The second argument is the AddressOf keyword followed by the name of the method that handles the event.

The RemoveHandler statement uses the same syntax as the AddHandler statement. Together they let you start or stop event handling for any specific event anywhere in the program.

It is possible to use both techniques for event handling in the same program, even for the same event in the same control. Consider the program in Example 4-5, which uses both techniques to handle the Click event for the button.

Example 4-5. Using both AddHandler and Handles to handle events

```
imports System
imports System.Drawing
imports System.Windows.Forms

namespace ProgrammingWinApps
   public class EventsDemo : inherits System.Windows.Forms.Form

      Private WithEvents btn as Button
      public sub New( )
          Text = "Events Demonstration - AddHandler"

         btn = new Button( )
         btn.Location = new Point(50,50)
         btn.Text = "Test"

         Controls.Add(btn)
         AddHandler btn.Click, AddressOf btn_Click
      end sub

      public shared sub Main( )
         Application.Run(new EventsDemo( ))
      end sub

      private sub btn_Click(ByVal sender as object, _
           ByVal e as EventArgs)
         MessageBox.Show("btn_Click method","Events Demonstration")
      end sub

      private sub btn_ClickHandles(ByVal sender as object, _
```

Example 4-5. Using both AddHandler and Handles to handle events (continued)

```
            ByVal e as EventArgs) _
            Handles btn.Click
         MessageBox.Show("btn_ClickHandles method","Events Demonstration")
      end sub
   end class
end namespace
```

The WithEvents keyword was added back to the line instantiating the Button object. It has no effect on the AddHandler statement functionality. However, it does enable the btn_ClickHandles method, which utilizes the Handles keyword, to also handle the button Click event.

When the program is compiled and run, the btnClickHandles method, which the compiler adds to the delegate behind the scenes, is called first. It is followed by the btn_Click method, which is added to the delegate by the AddHandler statement.

The following two statements are equivalent:

```
btn.Click += new System.EventHandler(GenericEventHandler);
```

```
AddHandler btn.Click, AddressOf GenericEventHandler
```

Performance

As mentioned throughout this chapter, events are implemented in the .NET Framework using delegates. This has a performance cost. For most events, especially those involved with user interaction such as Click and MouseOver, the performance hit is negligible. For some events in some applications, such as the Paint event in very high-performance or drawing-intensive applications, the performance penalty may be significant.

Creating a custom control and overriding the protected event method without adding a delegate has many benefits, one of which may be a small reduction in this performance penalty. This technique will be covered in Chapter 17.

Some Examples

In this section, you will see examples of events in use. In the first example, you will use keyboard events to capture keystrokes, showing what information is available about each keystroke. The next example will use keystroke information and the Validating event to control and validate the contents entered into a text box.

Keyboard Events

It is often useful or necessary to capture keystrokes and then take action based on the details related to that keystroke. For example, you may want to disallow certain characters or convert all lowercase characters to uppercase. Keyboard events provide access to this type of functionality.

The three events listed in Table 4-5 are raised when the user presses a key on the keyboard.

Table 4-5. Key Events for all controls

Event	Event data	Description
KeyDown	KeyEventArgs	Raised when a key is pressed. The KeyDown event occurs prior to the KeyPress event.
KeyPress	KeyPressEventArgs	Raised when a character generating key is pressed. The KeyPress event occurs after the KeyDown event and before the KeyUp event.
KeyUp	KeyEventArgs	Raised when a key is released.

The KeyDown and KeyPress events may seem somewhat redundant, but they fire at different points in the keyboard event stream and contain different information in the EventArgs object.

The KeyEventArgs event data associated with the KeyDown and KeyUp events provides low-level information about the keystroke, listed in Table 4-6. This information allows you to determine, for example, if an upper- or lowercase character was pressed. It also tells you if any modifier keys (Alt, Ctrl, or Shift) were pressed and in which combination. (You will also get a KeyDown and a KeyUp event if a modifier key is pressed and released on its own.)

Table 4-6. KeyEventArgs properties (KeyDown and KeyUp)

Property	Data type	Description
Alt	Boolean	Read-only value indicating if the Alt key was pressed. true if pressed, false otherwise.
Control	Boolean	Read-only value indicating if the Ctrl key was pressed. true if pressed, false otherwise.
Shift	Boolean	Read-only value indicating if the Shift key was pressed. true if pressed, false otherwise.
Modifiers	Keys	Read-only flags indicating the combination of modifier keys (Alt, Ctrl, Shift) pressed. Modifier keys can be combined using the bitwise OR operator.
Handled	Boolean	Value indicating if the event was handled. false until set otherwise.
KeyCode	Keys	Read-only value containing the key code for the key pressed. Typical values include the A key, Alt, and BACK (backspace).
KeyData	Keys	Read-only value containing the key code for the key pressed, combined with modifier flags to indicate combination of modifier keys (Alt, Ctrl, Shift).
KeyValue	integer	Key code property expressed as a read-only integer.

The state of the modifier keys can also be retrieved from the read-only Control.ModifierKeys property. This property is static in C# and shared in VB.NET. Like the Modifiers KeyEventArgs property, it is of type Keys.

The Modifiers, KeyCode and KeyData properties are of type Keys. The Keys enumeration, listed in Table A-2 in the Appendix, is comprised of constants identifying all the possible keys on a keyboard. The decimal key code value in Table A-2 corresponds to the virtual-key codes familiar to Windows programmers.

Unicode and ASCII Characters

Each character in the American Standards Committee for Information Interchange (ASCII) character set is represented by a single byte (8 bits) of data, representing 256 characters. The first 128 characters (represented by 7 bits) are standardized and usually referred to as low-order ASCII characters. The upper 128 characters are not standardized, although many well established character sets use all 256 characters. lists the low order ASCII characters.

Unicode characters are a superset of the ASCII character set. They are represented by two bytes, which allows a maximum of 65,536 characters. The Unicode technology was introduced to allow easier representation of languages other than English, especially Asian languages such as Chinese and Japanese, which do not have limited alphabets. Unicode also allows for character sets containing many more characters than an ASCII character set, such as special symbols and stylings of characters.

You can insert Unicode characters or determine the Unicode character code for any character in Windows using the Character Map tool, which is accessible by clicking on the Start menu and then Programs → Accessories → System Tools.

The KeyPress event exposes two properties contained in KeyPressEventArgs, listed in Table 4-7. The KeyChar property is used to retrieve the composed ASCII character. In other words, if an uppercase character is pressed, the KeyChar property tells you that directly, as opposed to telling you a character was pressed in combination with the Shift key.

Table 4-7. KeyPressEventArgs properties (KeyPress)

Property	Description
Handled	Boolean value indicating if the event was handled. `false` until set otherwise. When `true`, the keystroke is not displayed.
KeyChar	Read-only value of type char containing the composed ASCII character.

In the next example, you will create a simple Windows application with a single-line TextBox for entering keystrokes. A larger multiline TextBox will display the keystroke events and event argument properties so that you can see what is going on. Two Labels will simultaneously display the character in both upper- and lowercase, irrespective of how it was entered. Finally, a Reset button will clear all fields. During the course of the example, you will also see how to translate keystrokes from one character to another.

Open Visual Studio .NET and create a new project. Call it KeyEvents. (Since both C# and VB.NET examples are shown here, the examples will be saved as csKeyEvents and vbKeyEvents.)

Drag all the controls listed in Table 4-8 onto the form. Set the properties of the form and the controls to the values shown in Table 4-8. When done, the form should look something like Figure 4-7.

Table 4-8. KeyEvents controls

Control	Name	Property	Value
Form	Form1	Size	425,320
		Text	Key Event Demonstrator
TextBox	txtInput	Location	8,8
		Multiline	False
		Size	100,20
		Text	<blank>
TextBox	txtMsg	Location	8,40
		MultiLine	True
		ScrollBars	Vertical
		Size	304,232
		TabStop	False
		Text	<blank>
Button	btnReset	Location	328,8
		Size	75,23
		Text	Reset
Label	label1	Location	320,104
		Size	40,16
		Text	Lower:
Label	label2	Location	320,56
		Size	40,16
		Text	Upper:
Label	lblUpper	BorderStyle	Fixed3D
		Location	368,56

Table 4-8. KeyEvents controls (continued)

Control	Name	Property	Value
		Size	32,23
		Text	<blank>
Label	lblLower	BorderStyle	Fixed3D
		Location	368,104
		Size	32,23
		Text	<blank>

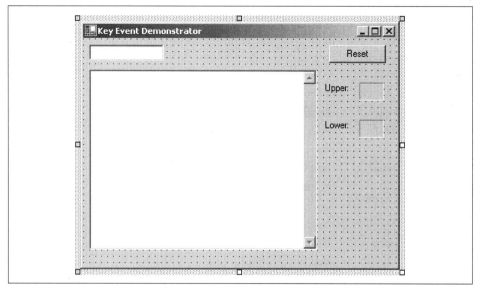

Figure 4-7. KeyEvents form layout

The Reset button will clear the Text properties of the TextBoxes and Labels. To implement this functionality, add an event handler for the Reset button. The easiest way to do this in either C# or VB.NET is to double-click on the control. Alternatively, you could use any of the language-specific techniques described earlier in this chapter. In any case, this will bring up a code window with an empty skeleton for the btnReset_Click event in place and the cursor placed for code entry.

Add the highlighted lines of code shown in Example 4-6 for C# and in Example 4-7 for VB.NET to the event handler skeletons in the code window.

Example 4-6. btnReset Click event handler in C#

```
private void btnReset_Click(object sender, System.EventArgs e)
{
    strMsg = "";
    txtMsg.Text = strMsg;
    txtInput.Text = "";
```

Example 4-6. btnReset Click event handler in C# (continued)

```csharp
        lblUpper.Text = "";
        lblLower.Text = "";
}
```

Example 4-7. btnReset Click event handler in VB.NET

```vbnet
Private Sub btnReset_Click(ByVal sender As System.Object, _
                           ByVal e As System.EventArgs) _
                           Handles btnReset.Click
        strMsg = ""
        txtMsg.Text = strMsg
        txtInput.Text = ""
        lblUpper.Text = ""
        lblLower.Text = ""
End Sub
```

You may notice the variable strMsg underlined in the Visual Studio .NET code window. It is underlined because the editor recognizes that this variable name has not yet been declared. You must declare strMsg as a member variable of the Form1 class so that it is visible to all of the methods of the class. To do this, add the appropriate line of code inside the Form1 class declaration:

```csharp
        private string strMsg = "";
```

```vbnet
        Dim strMsg As String = ""
```

Now you will implement an event handler for the KeyDown event for the TextBox named txtInput. Do *not* double-click on the TextBox control, or an empty code skeleton will be inserted for the TextChanged event, which is the default event for the TextBox control.

Instead, use the techniques described previously in this chapter to insert a code skeleton for a nondefault event, in this case the KeyDown event for txtInput. In C#, highlight the control in the design window, and then click on the Events icon ($\mathscr{J}$) in the Properties window. Scroll down to the KeyDown event, highlight the event, and press Enter. In VB.NET, use the drop-down lists at the top of the code window. In the left drop-down, select the control: txtInput. In the right drop-down, select KeyDown.

To implement the KeyDown event handler, add the highlighted code shown in Example 4-8 (for C#) or in Example 4-9 (for VB.NET) to the empty code skeletons. The KeyDown event handler will get the character from the KeyEventArgs event argument, extract various properties from the event argument, and then append that information to the TextBox txtMsg.

Example 4-8. txtInput KeyDown event in C#

```csharp
private void txtInput_KeyDown(object sender, System.Windows.Forms.KeyEventArgs e)
{
    txtMsg.AppendText("KeyDown event." + "\r\n");
    txtMsg.AppendText("\t" + "KeyCode name: " + e.KeyCode + "\r\n");
    txtMsg.AppendText("\t" + "KeyCode key code: " + ((int)e.KeyCode) +
                "\r\n");
    txtMsg.AppendText("\t" + "KeyData name: " + e.KeyData + "\r\n");
    txtMsg.AppendText("\t" + "KeyData key code: " + ((int)e.KeyData) +
                "\r\n");
    txtMsg.AppendText("\t" + "KeyValue: " + e.KeyValue + "\r\n");
    txtMsg.AppendText("\t" + "Handled: " + e.Handled + "\r\n");
    txtMsg.AppendText("\r\n");
}
```

Example 4-9. txtInput KeyDown event in VB.NET

```vbnet
Private Sub txtInput_KeyDown(ByVal sender As Object, _
                    ByVal e As System.Windows.Forms.KeyEventArgs) _
                    Handles txtInput.KeyDown
    txtMsg.AppendText("KeyDown event." + vbCrLf)
    txtMsg.AppendText(vbTab + "KeyCode name: " + e.KeyCode.ToString() + _
                vbCrLf)
    txtMsg.AppendText(vbTab + "KeyCode key code: " + _
                CInt(e.KeyCode).ToString() + vbCrLf)
    txtMsg.AppendText(vbTab + "KeyData name: " + e.KeyData.ToString() + _
                vbCrLf)
    txtMsg.AppendText(vbTab + "KeyData key code: " + _
                CInt(e.KeyData).ToString() + vbCrLf)
    txtMsg.AppendText(vbTab + "KeyValue: " + e.KeyValue.ToString() + _
                vbCrLf)
    txtMsg.AppendText(vbTab + "Handled: " + e.Handled.ToString() + vbCrLf)
    txtMsg.AppendText(vbCrLf)
End Sub
```

Run the application, make certain the input TextBox has focus, and enter an upper-case G (i.e., a shifted G). The result is shown in Figure 4-8.

Figure 4-8 shows that two KeyDown events were handled. The first was the pressed Shift key; the second was the letter G. The first two lines of data displayed for each event show the contents of the KeyEventArgs.KeyCode property. This is accomplished with the following two lines of code:

```csharp
txtMsg.AppendText("\t" + "KeyCode name: " + e.KeyCode + "\r\n");
txtMsg.AppendText("\t" + "KeyCode key code: " + ((int)e.KeyCode) +
            "\r\n");
```

```vbnet
txtMsg.AppendText(vbTab + "KeyCode name: " + e.KeyCode.ToString() + _
            vbCrLf)
txtMsg.AppendText(vbTab + "KeyCode key code: " + _
            CInt(e.KeyCode).ToString() + vbCrLf)
```

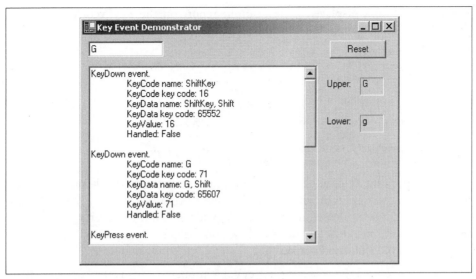

Figure 4-8. KeyEvents application showing a shifted G

The object e refers to the instance of KeyEventArgs passed in as one of the method arguments. It contains the properties listed in Table 4-6. The KeyCode property contains a member of the Keys enumeration (listed in Table A-2 in the Appendix) that identifies which key generated the KeyDown event.

e.KeyCode contains the name of the key. In VB.NET, the ToString() method must be used to include it as part of a string. That is not necessary in C#, although it would not do any harm.

Casting e.KeyCode to an integer returns the KeyCode key code, which corresponds to the virtual-key code familiar to Windows programmers, which itself corresponds (for the lower 127 characters) to the decimal ASCII value for the key. (The ASCII characters are listed in Table A-2.) The cast is done in C# using the cast operator (()) and in VB.NET using the CInt function.

There is another significant difference between the two languages here. The C# version embeds tab characters and new lines using escape sequences in string literals, while the VB.NET version uses VB.NET constants for the purpose. The commonly used VB.NET constants and their C# equivalent are listed in Table 4-9.

Table 4-9. Commonly used VB.NET constants and C# escape sequences

VB.NET constant	C# escape sequence	KeyCode value (decimal)	Meaning
vbCr	\r	13	Carriage return
vbCrLf	\r\n	13 & 10	Carriage return/line-feed combination
vbFormFeed	\f	12	Form feed
vbLf	\n	10	Line feed (new line)
vbTab	\t	9	Tab

The next two lines displayed in the output report on the KeyEventArgs.KeyData property. This is accomplished with the following lines of code:

C#
```
txtMsg.AppendText("\t" + "KeyData name: " + e.KeyData + "\r\n");
txtMsg.AppendText("\t" + "KeyData key code: " + ((int)e.KeyData) +
                "\r\n");
```

VB
```
txtMsg.AppendText(vbTab + "KeyData name: " + e.KeyData.ToString() + _
                vbCrLf)
txtMsg.AppendText(vbTab + "KeyData key code: " + _
                CInt(e.KeyData).ToString() + vbCrLf)
```

The KeyData property returns the same information as the KeyCode property combined with flags to indicate which modifier keys were pressed, if any. In this example, the ShiftKey was pressed in combination with the Shift modifier key (that does seem redundant since they are the same key) and the G key was pressed, also in combination with the Shift modifier key.

The next line reports the value of the KeyValue property. This is the key code corresponding to the key pressed. It is redundant with the KeyCode:

C#
```
txtMsg.AppendText("\t" + "KeyValue: " + e.KeyValue + "\r\n");
```

VB
```
txtMsg.AppendText(vbTab + "KeyValue: " + e.KeyValue.ToString() + _
                vbCrLf)
```

The final line displayed in the KeyDown event handler tells the status of the Handled property, which is false until specifically set otherwise:

C#
```
txtMsg.AppendText("\t" + "Handled: " + e.Handled + "\r\n");
```

VB
```
txtMsg.AppendText(vbTab + "Handled: " + e.Handled.ToString() + vbCrLf)
```

Looking ahead, the KeyUp and the KeyDown events both use the same event argument, KeyEventArgs, so it is reasonable that both event handlers will want to display the same information. To do this, abstract out the contents of the event handler into a helper method, passing the event argument in, and then call the helper method in the event handler. This process is shown in Example 4-10 for C# and in Example 4-11 for VB.NET.

Example 4-10. Handling KeyDown and KeyUp with helper method in C#

C#
```
private void KeyMsgBox(string str, KeyEventArgs e)
{
    txtMsg.AppendText(str + " event." + "\r\n");
    txtMsg.AppendText("\t" + "KeyCode name: " + e.KeyCode + "\r\n");
    txtMsg.AppendText("\t" + "KeyCode key code: " + ((int)e.KeyCode) +
                "\r\n");
    txtMsg.AppendText("\t" + "KeyData name: " + e.KeyData + "\r\n");
    txtMsg.AppendText("\t" + "KeyData key code: " + ((int)e.KeyData) +
                "\r\n");
```

Example 4-10. Handling KeyDown and KeyUp with helper method in C# (continued)

```csharp
    txtMsg.AppendText("\t" + "KeyValue: " + e.KeyValue + "\r\n");
    txtMsg.AppendText("\t" + "Handled: " + e.Handled + "\r\n");
    txtMsg.AppendText("\r\n");
}

private void txtInput_KeyDown(object sender,
                             System.Windows.Forms.KeyEventArgs e)
    KeyMsgBox("KeyDown", e);
```

Example 4-11. Handling KeyUp and KeyDown with helper method in VB.NET

```vbnet
Private Sub KeyMsgBox(ByVal str As String, ByVal e As KeyEventArgs)

    txtMsg.AppendText(str + " event." + vbCrLf)
    txtMsg.AppendText(vbTab + "KeyCode name: " + e.KeyCode.ToString() + _
                    vbCrLf)
    txtMsg.AppendText(vbTab + "KeyCode key code: " + _
                    CInt(e.KeyCode).ToString() + vbCrLf)
    txtMsg.AppendText(vbTab + "KeyData name: " + e.KeyData.ToString() + _
                    vbCrLf)
    txtMsg.AppendText(vbTab + "KeyData key code: " + _
                    CInt(e.KeyData).ToString() + vbCrLf)
    txtMsg.AppendText(vbTab + "KeyValue: " + e.KeyValue.ToString() + _
                    vbCrLf)
    txtMsg.AppendText(vbTab + "Handled: " + e.Handled.ToString() + vbCrLf)
    txtMsg.AppendText(vbCrLf)
End Sub

Private Sub txtInput_KeyDown(ByVal sender As Object, _
                            ByVal e As System.Windows.Forms.KeyEventArgs) _
                            Handles txtInput.KeyDown
    KeyMsgBox("KeyDown", e)
End Sub
```

The helper method is called KeyMsgBox. It takes two arguments: a string which should contain the name of the event and the instance of KeyEventArgs. The first argument is used in the first line in the method to display which event is being handled. e is used just as it was in the actual event handler method, described above.

The call to the helper method is simple; it involves passing in the name of the event and event argument:

```csharp
    KeyMsgBox("KeyDown", e);
```

```vbnet
    KeyMsgBox("KeyDown", e)
```

Now that you have the KeyDown event handler implemented with a helper method to do the work, it is very simple to implement the KeyUp event handler in a similar fashion because both events use the same KeyEventArgs event argument. Again, remember not to double-click on the txtInput control, since that will implement the default event, which is not what you want here. Instead, use the techniques described above for the language you are using. The KeyUp event handler is shown implemented in C# in Example 4-12 and in VB.NET in Example 4-13.

Example 4-12. KeyUp event in C#

```csharp
private void txtInput_KeyUp(object sender,
                           System.Windows.Forms.KeyEventArgs e)
{
    KeyMsgBox("KeyUp", e);
}
```

Example 4-13. KeyUp event in VB.NET

```vbnet
Private Sub txtInput_KeyUp(ByVal sender As Object, _
                           ByVal e As System.Windows.Forms.KeyEventArgs) _
                           Handles txtInput.KeyUp
    KeyMsgBox("KeyUp", e)
End Sub
```

When the application is run with the implemented KeyUp event handler and an uppercase G is again entered in the TextBox, you will get the results shown in Figure 4-9 (scrolling down to the bottom half of the displayed text). The two Key-Down events, for the Shift key and for the G key, are the same as seen previously in Figure 4-8. They are followed by the KeyUp event for the G key, and followed by the KeyUp event for the Shift key. The event data for the KeyUp event is identical to the event data for the KeyDown event.

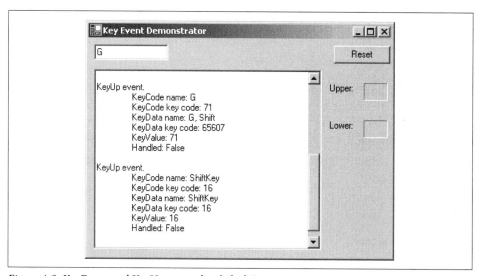

Figure 4-9. KeyDown and KeyUp events for shifted G

The KeyDown and KeyUp events provide a lot of information, but often you really care about the ASCII value of the keystroke—i.e., how the operating system interprets the keystroke, not what key was actually pressed. For example, the G key will result in the same Keys enumeration of G, with a key code value of 71, irrespective of whether the Shift key was pressed (to produce an uppercase G) or not (to produce a lowercase g). To determine the case, you need to process additional properties. Similarly, the number 5 along the top of the keyboard will return a Keys enumeration of D5 with a key code value of 53, while the 5 on the numeric keypad will return a Keys enumeration of NumPad5 with a key code value of 101. In many applications, you won't care which key was pressed, you just want the ASCII value for the number 5, which is 53.

The KeyPress event provides exactly this sort of information. In addition, you can use the KeyPressEventArgs.Handled property to suppress a keystroke from being processed by the operating system. This will be demonstrated later.

To implement the KeyPress event handler, use the described techniques to add a KeyPress code skeleton to the ongoing example. Add the highlighted code shown in Example 4-14 (for C#) or in Example 4-15 (for VB.NET) to the empty code skeletons. This event handler will get the character from the KeyPressEventArgs event argument, and then append various pieces of information about the character to a string displayed in the txtMsg TextBox. It also populates the lblUpper label with an uppercase version of the character and lblLower label with a lowercase version.

Example 4-14. txtInput KeyPress event handler code in C#

```csharp
private void txtInput_KeyPress(object sender,
                        System.Windows.Forms.KeyPressEventArgs e)
{
    char keyChar;
    keyChar = e.KeyChar;

    txtMsg.AppendText("KeyPress event." + "\r\n");
    txtMsg.AppendText("\t" + "KeyChar: " + keyChar + "\r\n");
    txtMsg.AppendText("\t" + "KeyChar Code: " + (int)keyChar + "\r\n");
    txtMsg.AppendText("\t" + "Handled: " + e.Handled + "\r\n");
    txtMsg.AppendText("\r\n");

    // Fill in the Upper and Lower labels
    lblUpper.Text = keyChar.ToString().ToUpper();
    lblLower.Text = keyChar.ToString().ToLower();
}
```

Example 4-15. txtInput KeyPress event handler code in VB.NET

```vbnet
Private Sub txtInput_KeyPress(ByVal sender As Object, _
                    ByVal e As System.Windows.Forms.KeyPressEventArgs) _
                    Handles txtInput.KeyPress
    Dim keyChar As Char
    keyChar = e.KeyChar

    txtMsg.AppendText("KeyPress event." + vbCrLf)
```

Example 4-15. txtInput KeyPress event handler code in VB.NET (continued)

```
txtMsg.AppendText(vbTab + "KeyChar: " + keyChar + vbCrLf)
txtMsg.AppendText(vbTab + "KeyChar Code: " + _
                AscW(keyChar).ToString() + vbCrLf)
txtMsg.AppendText(vbTab + "Handled: " + e.Handled.ToString() + vbCrLf)
txtMsg.AppendText(vbCrLf)

' Fill in the Upper and Lower labels
lblUpper.Text = keyChar.ToString().ToUpper()
lblLower.Text = keyChar.ToString().ToLower()
End Sub
```

Running the application now and entering the letter G without the Shift key produces the results shown in Figure 4-10. Notice that the KeyPress information returns
a lowercase g and a key code of 103, rather than the key code of 71 returned by the
KeyDown event. 103 is the ASCII value for lowercase g while 71 is the ASCII value
for uppercase G.

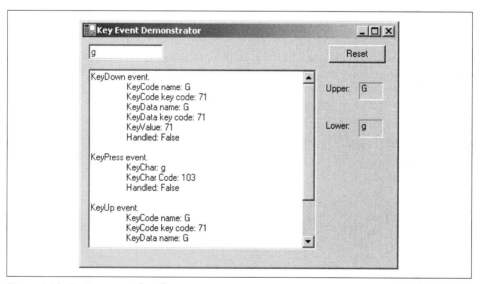

Figure 4-10. KeyPress event handler output

The first two lines in the event handler get the character entered at the keyboard
from the KeyPressEventArgs event argument and assign it to a variable keyChar,
declared as type char, since the KeyPressEventArgs.KeyChar property is of type char
(i.e., it is a Unicode character).

The next several lines in the event handler use the KeyPressEventArgs.KeyChar property to retrieve the composed ASCII character, i.e., already taking into account modifier keys. Both the character name and integer value are displayed:

```
txtMsg.AppendText("\t" + "KeyChar: " + keyChar + "\r\n");
txtMsg.AppendText("\t" + "KeyChar Code: " + (int)keyChar + "\r\n");
```

```
txtMsg.AppendText(vbTab + "KeyChar: " + keyChar + vbCrLf)
txtMsg.AppendText(vbTab + "KeyChar Code: " + _
                 AscW(keyChar).ToString() + vbCrLf)
```

Since the KeyChar property is of type char, there is no need to use the ToString method in either language to concatenate it into a string. The character code value, on the other hand, is an integer and must be cast as such, and then converted to a string using the ToString method.

Objects of type char can implicitly convert to a string, since there is no loss of data in such a conversion. This is true even in VB.NET with the type checking switch on (Option Strict On). You can not implicitly convert from string to char, as information would be lost.

To declare a literal character in C#, enclose it in single quotes:

```
char myChar = 'A';
```

In VB.NET, you append the letter c, as in:

```
Dim myChar as Char = "A"c
```

The VB.NET version uses the AscW method rather than the more common CInt method to cast the value, since Char values in VB.NET cannot be converted to Integer. The AscW method returns an integer value representing the character code of a character.

The final three lines of code in Example 4-14 and Example 4-15 take the character entered, convert it to both upper- and lowercase, and fill in the appropriate labels.

Suppose you want to intercept the keystroke and selectively replace it with a different character. For example, suppose you want to intercept all dollar signs ($) and replace them with a number sign (#). You could do this by handling the Validating event (demonstrated in the next section), but often a better way would be to change the character before it is even displayed on the screen. To do this, modify the Key-Press event-handler method to add the highlighted code shown in Example 4-16 (in C#) and Example 4-17 (in VB.NET).

Example 4-16. Character substitution in KeyPress event in C#

```
private void txtInput_KeyPress(object sender,
                        System.Windows.Forms.KeyPressEventArgs e)
{
    char keyChar;
    keyChar = e.KeyChar;

    txtMsg.AppendText("KeyPress event." + "\r\n");
    txtMsg.AppendText("\t" + "KeyChar: " + keyChar + "\r\n");
    txtMsg.AppendText("\t" + "KeyChar Code: " + (int)keyChar + "\r\n");
    txtMsg.AppendText("\t" + "Handled: " + e.Handled + "\r\n");
    txtMsg.AppendText("\r\n");

    // Fill in the Upper and Lower labels
    lblUpper.Text = keyChar.ToString().ToUpper();
```

Example 4-16. Character substitution in KeyPress event in C# (continued)

```csharp
        lblLower.Text = keyChar.ToString( ).ToLower( );

        // Change $ to #
        if (keyChar.ToString( ) == "$")
        {
            txtInput.AppendText("#");
            e.Handled = true;
        }
}
```

Example 4-17. Character substitution in KeyPress event in VB.NET

```vbnet
Private Sub txtInput_KeyPress(ByVal sender As Object, _
                    ByVal e As System.Windows.Forms.KeyPressEventArgs) _
                    Handles txtInput.KeyPress
    Dim keyChar As Char
    keyChar = e.KeyChar

    txtMsg.AppendText("KeyPress event." + vbCrLf)
    txtMsg.AppendText(vbTab + "KeyChar: " + keyChar + vbCrLf)
    txtMsg.AppendText(vbTab + "KeyChar Code: " + _
                    AscW(keyChar).ToString( ) + vbCrLf)
    txtMsg.AppendText(vbTab + "Handled: " + e.Handled.ToString( ) + vbCrLf)
    txtMsg.AppendText(vbCrLf)

    ' Fill in the Upper and Lower labels
    Dim str As String = e.KeyChar.ToString( )
    lblUpper.Text = keyChar.ToString( ).ToUpper( )
    lblLower.Text = keyChar.ToString( ).ToLower( )

    ' Change $ to #
    If (keyChar.ToString( ) = "$") Then
        txtInput.AppendText("#")
        e.Handled = True
    End If
End Sub
```

When this code is run and a dollar sign (a shifted 4 on a U.S. English keyboard) is entered in the input field, the events displayed are KeyDown for Shift, KeyDown for 4, and KeyPress for $, just as before. The Upper and Lower labels both display $, since that character is unaffected by converting case. Before the event finishes, though, the character is tested to see if it is a $. If so, the AppendText instance method appends the desired character, the # sign, to the text box. Then e.Handled is set to true. This suppresses all further handling of the original keypress.

TextBox Validation

Several events can play a role in validating the contents of a TextBox, including the key events seen in the previous example. The sequence of events that occurs when a TextBox gains and loses focus are:

1. Enter

2. GotFocus

3. Leave

4. Validating

5. Validated

6. LostFocus

Of these, the GotFocus and LostFocus events are low-level events that are not typically used for validation. The Enter event is not useful for validation because it occurs before any data entry can occur. The Leave event is also not usually used for validation because its event argument, EventArgs, does not expose any properties for influencing the event.

Table 4-10 summarizes the most useful events for validating a TextBox.

Table 4-10. TextBox events available for validation

Event name	Event argument	Description
KeyPress	KeyPressEventArgs	Use the KeyPressEventArgs.Handled property to suppress keystrokes.
TextChanged	EventArgs	Raised if the Text property changed, either by user interaction or under programmatic control. Fires with every character entered in a TextBox.
Validating	CancelEventArgs	Raised after focus leaves the control and enters a control that has CausesValidation set to true. If the CancelEventArgs.Cancel property is set to true, then the current event is canceled, the Validated event is suppressed, and the focus is forced to remain in the control.
Validated	EventArgs	Raised after control is finished validating (after the Validating event).

In the following example, you will see the KeyPress and Validating events used to control and validate data entered in a TextBox. The example will allow a user to enter an ISBN number, which will then be validated.

International Standard Book Number (ISBN) numbers are used by the book industry to track and uniquely identify book titles. They are typically found on the back cover of books, often in conjunction with a bar code. There is more to ISBN numbers than the information discussed here (for example, the meaning of the different portions of the number and how they are assigned). All you need to know for this example, however, is that an ISBN number consists of nine digits, called the true number, plus one check digit or the letter X (for check-digit value 10). The digits may be separated into sections separated by hyphens. The hyphens must be allowed but are ignored.

The algorithm for calculating the check digit is as follows: Multiply the first digit in the true number by 10, the next digit by 9, the next by 8, and so on until the last digit is multiplied by 2. Add all these products together. The number needed to increase that sum to the next multiple of 11 is the check digit (that is, the check digit is the sum of the products modulo 11). If the check "digit" turns out to be 10, use the letter X instead.

To demonstrate how this works, open Visual Studio .NET and create a new Windows application project called IsbnValidate. Add the controls and set the properties listed in Table 4-11.

Table 4-11. IsbnValidate controls

Control	Name	Property	Value
Form	Form1	Size	272,320
		Text	ISBN Validation
Label	label1	Location	48,16
		Font	Tahoma, 14.25pt, Bold Italic
		Size	176,23
		Text	ISBN Validation
TextBox	txtInput	Location	72,64
		Size	100,20
		Text	<blank>
Label	label2	Location	24,104
		Size	80,23
		Text	True Number:
Label	label3	Location	32,152
		Size	72,23
		Text	Check Digit:
Label	lblTrue	BorderStyle	Fixed3D
		Location	112,104
		Size	100,23
		Text	<blank>
Label	lblCheck	BorderStyle	Fixed3D
		Location	112,152
		Size	100,23
		Text	<blank>
Label	lblResults	Location	56,192
		Size	152,24
		Text	<blank>
Button	btnClear	Location	88,240
		Size	75,23
		Text	Clear

When all the controls are in place, the form layout should look similar to Figure 4-11.

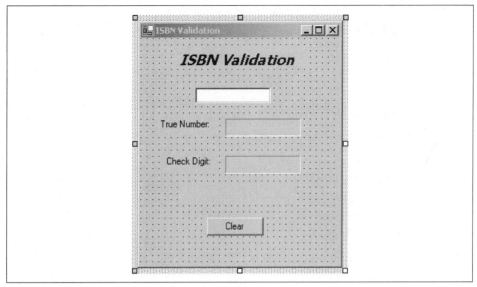

Figure 4-11. ISBN validator design layout

Most validation work will occur in the Validating event of the input TextBox, which takes CancelEventArgs as its event argument. CancelEventArgs has one property: Cancel. When set to true, all events that would normally occur after the Validating event are suppressed. This means that the Validated and LostFocus events do not fire, and the cursor cannot leave the control.

Implement the Validating event handler in C# by highlighting the input TextBox control, clicking on the Events icon (⚡) in the Properties window, scrolling to the Validating event, and entering the event handler method name: IsbnValidate. In VB.NET, go to the code-editing window, select the txtInput control from the drop-down list at the top left of the window, then scroll to the Validating event in the right drop-down. The method skeleton will have the default name of txtInput_Validation. Change it to IsbnValidate.

Enter the highlighted code from Example 4-18 into the C# IsbnValidation code skeleton or the highlighted code from Example 4-19 for into the VB.NET code skeleton.

Example 4-18. IsbnValidation event handler in C#

```
private void IsbnValidate(object sender,
                    System.ComponentModel.CancelEventArgs e)
{
    string strTrue;
    string strCheck;
    string strIsbn = "";
    string strPad;
    int sum = 0;
    int pad;
```

Example 4-18. IsbnValidation event handler in C# (continued)

```csharp
// Get the string from the TextBox
TextBox tb = (TextBox)sender;
string strInput = tb.Text;

try
{
   for (int i = 0; i < strInput.Length; ++i)
   {
      if ( (strInput[i] >= '0' && strInput[i] <= '9') ||
         strInput[i] == 'x' ||
         strInput[i] == 'X' )
         strIsbn += strInput[i];
   }

   if (strIsbn.Length != 10)
      throw new Exception( );

   // extract true number
   strTrue = strIsbn.Substring(0,9);

   // extract check digit
   strCheck = strIsbn.Substring(9,1);

   lblTrue.Text = strTrue;
   lblCheck.Text = strCheck;

   // Calculate the check digit from the true ISBN number.
   // First do the multiplying and add up the products.
   for (int i = 0; i < strTrue.Length; ++i)
   {
      String testString = strTrue.Substring(i,1);
      int testInt = Convert.ToInt32(testString);
      sum += testInt * (10 - i);
   }

   // Calculate the number needed to pad to a multiple of 11
   pad = 11 - (sum % 11);

   // assign digit or X
   strPad = pad == 10 ? "X" : pad.ToString( );


   // Compare the pad w/ strCheck.
   if (strCheck != strPad)
      throw new Exception( );

   lblResults.ForeColor = Color.Green;
   lblResults.Text = "Valid ISBN Number.";
}
catch
{
   e.Cancel = true;
```

Example 4-18. IsbnValidation event handler in C# (continued)

C#

```csharp
        tb.Select(0,tb.Text.Length);
        lblResults.ForeColor = Color.Red;
        lblResults.Text = "Invalid ISBN Number.";
    }
}
```

Example 4-19. IsbnValidation event handler in VB.NET

VB

```vbnet
Private Sub IsbnValidation(ByVal sender As Object, _
                ByVal e As System.ComponentModel.CancelEventArgs) _
                Handles txtInput.Validating

    Dim strTrue As String
    Dim strCheck As String
    Dim strIsbn As String = ""
    Dim strPad As String
    Dim Sum As Integer = 0
    Dim Pad As Integer
    Dim i As Integer

    ' Get the string from the TextBox
    Dim tb As TextBox = CType(sender, TextBox)
    Dim strInput As String = tb.Text

    Try
        For i = 0 To strInput.Length - 1
            If ((strInput.Chars(i) >= "0"c And _
                strInput.Chars(i) <= "9"c) Or _
                strInput.Chars(i) = "x"c Or _
                strInput.Chars(i) = "X"c) Then
                strIsbn += strInput.Chars(i)
            End If
        Next i

        If strIsbn.Length <> 10 Then
            Throw New Exception()
        End If

        strTrue = strIsbn.Substring(0, 9)
        strCheck = strIsbn.Substring(9, 1)

        lblTrue.Text = strTrue
        lblCheck.Text = strCheck

        ' Calculate the check digit from the true ISBN number.
        ' First do the multiplying and add up the products.
        For i = 0 To strTrue.Length - 1
            Dim testString As String = strTrue.Substring(i, 1)
            Dim testInt As Integer = Convert.ToInt32(testString)
            Sum += testInt * (10 - i)
        Next i
```

Example 4-19. IsbnValidation event handler in VB.NET (continued)

```
        ' Calculate the number needed to pad to a multiple of 11
        Pad = 11 - (Sum Mod 11)

        ' assign digit or X
        strPad = CStr(iif(Pad <> 10, Pad.ToString( ), "X"))

        ' Compare the pad w/ strCheck.
        If strCheck <> strPad Then
            Throw New Exception( )
        End If

        lblResults.ForeColor = Color.Green
        lblResults.Text = "Valid ISBN Number."
    Catch
        e.Cancel = True
        tb.Select(0, tb.Text.Length)
        lblResults.ForeColor = Color.Red
        lblResults.Text = "Invalid ISBN Number."
    End Try
End Sub
```

The first several lines in the body of the IsbnValidate method simply declare several member variables for later use. Notice that two of the variables, strIsbn and Sum, are also instantiated at this point. Both variables are used with the += operator; an error will occur if the variable is not instantiated prior to the first use.

The next two lines get the value of the Text property of txtInput:

```
TextBox tb = (TextBox)sender;
string strInput = tb.Text;
```

```
Dim tb As TextBox = CType(sender, TextBox)
Dim strInput As String = tb.Text
```

The sender argument is of type object and so must be cast to type TextBox before the Text property can be retrieved. It would have been equally valid in this example to replace these lines with:

```
string strInput = txtInput.Text;
```

```
Dim strInput As String = txtInput.Text
```

ibut the former syntax is more robust, since it is not tied to a specific control.

A try...catch block is used for the actual validation. The code in the try block is executed. If any errors occur, or if an exception is thrown intentionally, then program execution moves immediately to the catch block and the balance of the code in the try block is never executed. This construct allows a series of tests and an easy and logical way to handle any errors that may arise.

For more on exception handling, see Chapter 21.

The try block first iterates through the input string, filtering out any characters without a valid ISBN number. Remember that ISBN numbers may be printed on books (and entered in this program) with hyphens, which must be removed. The only valid characters are digits or the letter X. In C#, this filtering is accomplished with this code snippet:

```csharp
for (int i = 0; i < strInput.Length; ++i)
{
    if ( (strInput[i] >= '0' && strInput[i] <= '9') ||
        strInput[i] == 'x' ||
        strInput[i] == 'X' )
        strIsbn += strInput[i];
}
```

In C#, the bracket following the string variable name is a zero-based indexer into the string. For example, strInput[2] would refer to the third character in the string. The return type of a string indexer is of type char, i.e., a Unicode character. The characters on the right side of the equality operators (==) are not strings, but chars, as indicated by the single quotes.

In VB.NET, the filtering is accomplished with this code snippet:

```vbnet
For i = 0 To strInput.Length - 1
    If ((strInput.Chars(i) >= "0"c And _
        strInput.Chars(i) <= "9"c) Or _
        strInput.Chars(i) = "x"c Or _
        strInput.Chars(i) = "X"c) Then
        strIsbn += strInput.Chars(i)
    End If
Next i
```

In VB.NET, there is no string indexer, per se, so the String.Chars property is used. This returns a char, so the characters on the right side of the equality operators (=) are chars, as indicated by the trailing cs.

Note that this filtering algorithm allows the X character to be in any position, whereas it is valid only if it is in the final position. You could modify the code to test for the position, but invalid positions will be caught further along in the program.

The next few lines test the length of the string, since a full ISBN number is, by definition, exactly 10 digits long (9 + 1). If the string is not the correct length, an exception is thrown, which stops program execution in the try block and moves it to the catch block:

```csharp
if (strIsbn.Length != 10)
    throw new Exception();
```

```
VB    If strIsbn.Length <> 10 Then
          Throw New Exception( )
      End If
```

The next several lines extract substrings from the full ISBN number (strIsbn) to get the true ISBN number (strTrue) and the check digit (strCheck). These values are then displayed in the lblTrue and lblCheck labels.

Now comes the meat of the matter. A check digit is calculated from the true ISBN number, and then compared to the check digit extracted from the full ISBN number. If the digits are the same, the number is valid, and an appropriate message is displayed in lblResults. If not, then the ISBN number is invalid and an exception is thrown.

First the sum of the products is calculated. In C#, this is done with the following lines of code. Note the use of the Substring method, with the resulting string's conversion to an integer before multiplication and the addition of the product to the integer Sum. You cannot use the string indexer here unless you include a ToString method call because it results in a char. If you convert the char object to an integer, you get the Unicode key code (effectively the character's ASCII value) rather than its numeric value.

```
C#    for (int i = 0; i < strTrue.Length; ++i)
      {
          String testString = strTrue.Substring(i,1);
          int testInt = Convert.ToInt32(testString);
          sum += testInt * (10 - i);
      }
```

In VB.NET, the sum of the products is calculated with these lines of code:

```
VB    For i = 0 To strTrue.Length - 1
          Dim testString As String = strTrue.Substring(i, 1)
          Dim testInt As Integer = Convert.ToInt32(testString)
          sum += testInt * (10 - i)
      Next i
```

The check digit is computed by getting the remainder of the Sum divided by 11 using the modulus operator, and then subtracting that remainder from 11. If the remainder is 10, then the check digit is set to X. In C#, this last test is accomplished with the ternary operator (?):

```
C#    pad = 11 - (sum % 11);
      strPad = pad == 10 ? "X" : pad.ToString( );
```

and in VB.NET, the test is done with the if statement:

```
VB    Pad = 11 - (Sum Mod 11)
      strPad = CStr(iif(Pad <> 10, Pad.ToString( ), "X"))
```

Finally the calculated check digit is compared to the original check digit. If they are not equal, an exception is thrown. Otherwise, a message, in green, is displayed in lblResults.

The catch block first sets the CancelEventArgs.Cancel property to true. This has the effect of suppressing all events further in this event stream, preventing the focus from leaving the field. (As you will see, this causes problems that will be dealt with shortly.) The text in the field is highlighted with the TextBox Select method and a message, in red, is displayed in lblResults. The catch block looks like:

```
catch
{
    e.Cancel = true;
    tb.Select(0,tb.Text.Length);
    lblResults.ForeColor = Color.Red;
    lblResults.Text = "Invalid ISBN Number.";
}
```

```
Catch
    e.Cancel = True
    tb.Select(0, tb.Text.Length)
    lblResults.ForeColor = Color.Red
    lblResults.Text = "Invalid ISBN Number."
End Try
```

Before running the program, implement the Click event for the Clear button. The Clear button will clear the edit field and the three labels that the application fills in. Double-click on the button in design mode to open up a code skeleton for Click, the default event for a button. Then enter the highlighted code in Example 4-20 for the C# version and the highlighted code in Example 4-21 for the VB.NET version.

Example 4-20. IsbnValidate Clear button Click event handler in C#

```
private void btnClear_Click(object sender, System.EventArgs e)
{
    txtInput.Text = "";
    lblResults.Text = "";
    lblTrue.Text = "";
    lblCheck.Text = "";
}
```

Example 4-21. IsbnValidation Clear button Click event handler in VB.NET

```
Private Sub btnClear_Click(ByVal sender As System.Object, _
            ByVal e As System.EventArgs) _
            Handles btnClear.Click
    txtInput.Text = ""
    lblResults.Text = ""
    lblTrue.Text = ""
    lblCheck.Text = ""
End Sub
```

Run the application. After entering a valid ISBN number (from the back of any book) and tabbing out of the TextBox, the window will look like Figure 4-12.

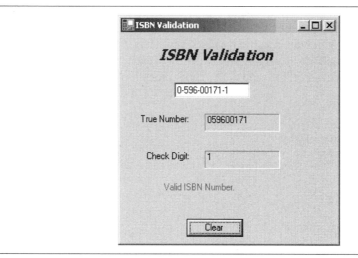

Figure 4-12. IsbnValidate showing a valid ISBN number

Clicking the Clear button will clear all the fields. If you entered an invalid ISBN number, the message will display Invalid ISBN Number, in red. However, entering an invalid number creates a problem: you can't leave the TextBox. You also can't click the Clear button, or even close the window. This is because the catch block sets the CancelEventArgs.Cancel property to true whenever it encounters an invalid number.

 If you ran the program from within Visual Studio .NET, you can kill the program with the Debug → Stop Debugging menu item, or by pressing Shift+F5. If you built an EXE file and ran it outside Visual Studio .NET, you have to use the Windows Task Manager to kill the application.

One solution to this problem is to add a few lines of code to the beginning of the IsbnValidate method to test for an empty TextBox:

C#

```csharp
if (strInput.Length == 0)
    return;
```

VB

```vb
If strInput.Length = 0 Then
    Return
End If
```

This tests the number of characters in the txtInput. If the TextBox is empty, it returns without any further processing. CancelEventArgs.Cancel never gets set, so focus can leave the control.

This validation example is now totally workable. You can enter any characters in the TextBox, and it will be validated. However, you can make one more refinement. Suppose you don't want invalid characters to even display in the input TextBox. The only possible valid characters are the digits, the hyphen, and the upper- and lower-case X. You can suppress every character except for these valid characters from displaying in the control by handling the KeyPress event.

Create a code skeleton for the KeyPress event for the txtInput control with the techniques described above. Then enter the highlighted code in Example 4-22 for the C# version or the highlighted code in Example 4-23 for the VB.NET version.

Example 4-22. txtInput KeyPress event handler in C#

```csharp
private void txtInput_KeyPress(object sender,
                              System.Windows.Forms.KeyPressEventArgs e)
{
    char keyChar;
    keyChar = e.KeyChar;

    // Suppress any keys except digits,X,x,hyphen,Backspace,or Enter
    if(!Char.IsDigit(keyChar)        // 0 - 9
        &&
        keyChar != 8                 // backspace
        &&
        keyChar != 13                // enter
        &&
        keyChar != 'X'
        &&
        keyChar != 'x'
        &&
        keyChar != 45                //  hyphen
        )
    {
        //  Do not display the keystroke
        e.Handled = true;
    }
}
```

Example 4-23. txtInput KeyPress event handler in VB.NET

```vbnet
Private Sub txtInput_KeyPress(ByVal sender As Object, _
        ByVal e As System.Windows.Forms.KeyPressEventArgs) _
        Handles txtInput.KeyPress
    Dim keyChar As Char
    keyChar = e.KeyChar

    ' Suppress any keys except digits,X,x,hyphen (45),Backspace (8),
    '      or Enter (13)
    If ((Not Char.IsDigit(keyChar)) _
        And (AscW(keyChar) <> 8) _
        And (AscW(keyChar) <> 13) _
        And (keyChar <> "X"c) _
        And (keyChar <> "x"c) _
        And (AscW(keyChar) <> 45)) Then
        ' Do not display the keystroke
        e.Handled = True
    End If
End Sub
```

Both versions of the KeyPress event handler assign the key to a variable of type char. Then an if statement tests to see if the character is allowable. If not, then e.Handled is set to true, which suppresses the character from being displayed.

There are some differences in the syntax between C# and VB.NET. In C#, the variable of type char can be compared directly against either the key code value or the string representing the char, indicated by the single quotes around the letters X and x. In VB.NET, by contrast, the key code values can be compared only by using the AscW function, which takes a char as the argument and returns an integer. Also, the syntax in VB.NET for indicating a string is actually a char is that appends the letter c to the string, as in "X"c.

CHAPTER 5

Windows Forms

According to Webster,[*] the noun *form* has nineteen different meanings, none of which is computer related. The closest is definition number ten: "A document with blanks for the insertion of details or information." A Windows Form is a digital analog of a piece of paper used for gathering and displaying information.

A form may be either the main or subsidiary screen of an application, a dialog box, or a display of graphical output. It may be a single document interface (SDI) application or part of a multiple document interface (MDI) application. Forms typically contain controls that the user interacts with, such as buttons, text boxes, scrollbars, labels, and so on.

In the .NET Framework, the form is encapsulated in a Form class. The Form class is at the heart of almost every .NET Windows application.

 The Form object itself is a control that derives from the System. Windows.Forms.Control class (via the classes ScrollableControl and ContainerControl).

This chapter will cover many of the fundamental aspects of Windows Forms, including how to decide between a Windows Forms application and a web application, the different types of available user interfaces and some UI guidelines, how the Forms class is implemented, and how to inherit from forms you create yourself.

 Ultimately, every Windows application is implemented by calls to the Windows Application Programming Interface (API). The API consists of C library calls. The .NET Framework wraps these API calls inside well-encapsulated objects, and provides you with a complete object-oriented, type-safe, garbage-collected, managed environment for indirectly manipulating the Windows API.

---

[*] *Webster's II New College Dictionary* (Houghton Mifflin, 2001)

Web Applications Versus Windows Applications

The choice between creating a web or desktop application is one of the first design decisions made for any project. Previous development technologies had a fairly clear demarcation between the two categories. Web applications run on a web server and receive requests from, and serve web pages to, users running a browser on their local machine. Windows applications, on the other hand, are generally executed independently on the local machine, although there might be network resources brought to bear, such as remote databases.

> This book focuses on Windows applications and rich-client web applications. For a complete discussion of ASP.NET web applications, please see *Programming ASP.NET*, Second Edition (O'Reilly).

With the .NET Framework, this distinction between the two categories is considerably blurred. Rich-client Windows applications may interact with servers using web technology. Web applications may use controls that run on the user's machine. The distinctions between desktop and network and network and Internet, are less crisp than they were a few years ago.

While web applications still run on a web server and Window applications still run on the local machine, many strengths formerly of one modality or the other now apply to both. The "right" decision is not always so clear cut.

You need to consider many issues when deciding whether to build a Windows or a Web application:

Deployment

Web applications are, admittedly, easier to deploy than Windows applications. Update your server, and you're done. On the other hand, .NET desktop applications are far easier to install than previous Windows applications.

There is no need to register applications or DLLs with the local Registry, and all configuration is self-contained within the program's directory. This leads to *XCopy deployment*. To install an application, you only need to copy the directory structure containing the application to the target machine.

> Deployment of Windows applications will be covered in detail in Chapter 22.

It is now possible to have multiple versions of the same DLL on a single machine, with each application using its own version. The same application can even access different versions of the same DLL in the same directory (although we definitely do not encourage this practice).

This means the end of DLL Hell, in which you install a program with a new DLL and an unrelated program breaks. With .NET, DLL Hell should be a thing of the past.

It is even possible to pull the installation of a Windows application across the Internet. Every time your application runs, it will check a web site for updated components, and if any are found, automatically download and install them.

Performance

Windows applications are usually, although not always, faster than web applications. Every request from a browser requires a trip to the server and back. Often this roundtrip occurs over a relatively slow connection. Even DSL (1 MB per second or more) or a T1 (1.544 Mbps) is slow compared to a local network connection (typically 100 Mbps), which itself is slow compared to a local hard drive (up to 100 MB per second, equivalent to 800 Mbps)

ASP.NET improves performance significantly over previous web technologies. It does this by using compiled, rather than interpreted, code modules, and by minimizing the number of roundtrips required. Still, the performance yielded by a web application depends on the speed and condition of the Internet (or intranet) connection and the current load on the server. Even the fastest servers or web farms will bog down if overwhelmed with requests.

In some types of applications, a web application might have a speed advantage over a local application—one with a fast connection, a very fast server, and processing time that is more significant than the access time. For example, suppose you are developing a research application in which a user can make ad hoc queries against a large database. The application could be run either directly from a CD, installed to and run from the local hard drive, or as a web application via a browser. In this situation, it is very possible that a web application, running over a T1, DSL, or cable modem, would be faster than a Windows application running against a database residing on a CD. A web application hitting a very powerful, optimized database server might also be faster than a Windows application installed on the local hard drive if the queries were very complex and time consuming to process.

User interface

User interface is one advantage of using Windows applications over web applications. Let's face it, a browser UI is usually pretty clunky compared to a Windows UI. ASP.NET goes a long way toward improving this situation, and the use of client-side scripting for the browser closes the gap even further. Still, it is much easier to develop a rich, smooth, and satisfying (sounds like a coffee commercial) user experience in a Windows application than in a web application.

This is because web controls are limited to fewer than a dozen events, while Windows Forms controls have access to many times that. Every time an event is raised in a web application, a roundtrip to the server ensues (unless client-side scripting is used). Raising and responding to ubiquitous Windows events such as MouseEnter or TextChanged is too time consuming.

The end result is that Windows applications give the developer the ability to respond more finely to user actions.

Security

Well-designed web applications are very secure, a fact upon which much of the modern economy depends. ASP.NET further improves web security. Still, anytime you send information over the wire, it is at greater risk than data that remains on your computer's internal data bus.

Widespread market penetration

Widespread adoption by users remains one area in which web applications have a clear advantage over Windows applications. Thanks to the ubiquitous web browser, web applications are easily available to anyone with access to an internet connection. Users don't have to decide to install an application, they just use it. With Internet deployment of .Net Windows applications, this gap is narrowed somewhat, but it is still easier to penetrate a mass user base with a web application than with a Windows application.

In addition, even if the .NET Framework were installed on 100 percent of the machines in the world running a Microsoft OS, there would still be many users outside the fold (such as users of Mac, Linux, Sun OS, and countless other platforms, who can access a browser application but not a Windows Forms application). Although it is the stated goal of .NET to be ported to other platforms (rumors of an imminent Linux port abound), this obstacle will always limit the maximum size of the potential user base.

Web services

Web services is a technology that blurs the distinction between web and Windows applications. A web service allows either a web or Windows application to programmatically access a web server, without requiring direct user interaction. This opens up Internet-enabled, wide area access to data and programmatic functionality for Windows applications.

Creating a Windows application that interacts with web services provides worldwide access to data and services coupled with a rich user interface.

For a complete discussion of web services, see *Programming ASP.NET*, Second Edition (O'Reilly).

The Forms Namespace

The System.Windows.Forms namespace is a grouping of classes that comprise the Windows Forms technology. The classes in this namespace provide the ability to create Windows applications, which conform to the standard user interface offered by the Windows operating systems.

The classes contained in the Forms namespace can be grouped into several broad categories.

The Control Class

The System.Windows.Forms.Control class is the base class for all the controls used on a Windows Form. A control is a component that has a visual representation at runtime.

The Control class supplies the basic functionality used by all controls. This basic functionality includes methods, properties, and events to cover:

- User interaction via keyboard and mouse
- Receiving and losing focus
- Size and location
- Appearance (color, backgrounds, etc.)
- Parent-child relationships
- Message routing
- Window handle (hWnd)
- Asynchronous processing
- Security
- Accessibility—making the application usable to everyone, including people with disabilities

Ambient properties

Controls enter into a parent-child relationship on the form. The parent acts as a container for the child control. This relationship should not be confused with the base/derived (generalization/specialization) relationship. For example, a panel may act as a parent control to a button and a listbox, even though button and listbox do not derive from a panel.

Some Control class properties, such as Cursor, Font, BackColor and ForeColor, if not explicitly set for a particular instance of a control, will retrieve the property from their parent controls. They are known as *ambient properties*. Ambient properties allow a control to appear as its parent. If the control does not have a parent and if the property is not set, then a default value is used.

The Control inheritance hierarchy

Each specific control used in Windows Forms will be detailed in Chapters 11 through 17. Figure 5-1 is a list of all the classes that derive from the Control class.

The Form Class

All forms in the .NET Framework are defined in a class, specifically one that inherits from the System.Windows.Forms.Form class. The Form object itself is a control that inherits from the System.Windows.Forms.Control class via the ScrollableControl and ContainerControl classes.

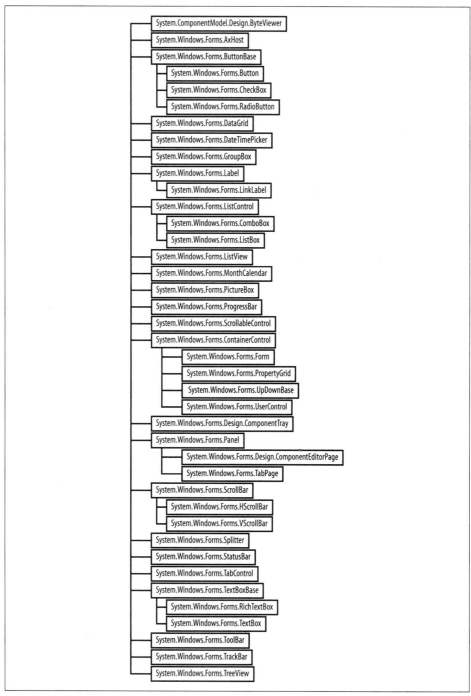

Figure 5-1. Classes derived from Control

Figure 5-2 lists the class hierarchy that contains the Form class and the classes deriving from it.

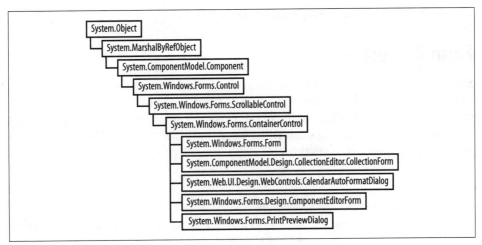

Figure 5-2. Form class hierarchy

Component Classes

Component classes provide features useful to a Windows application but do not derive from the Control class. They include classes such as ToolTip and Error-Provider, which provide additional information to the user; timers; menuing classes such as Menu, MenuItem, and ContextMenu; and classes for providing help information, such as Help and HelpProvider. They enable design-time integration of whatever functionality they contain.

CommonDialog Classes

Many applications perform similar functions, such as opening and saving files or selecting fonts. Ever since Windows 3.1, the Windows API has provided standard dialog boxes to perform many of these common operations. Not only does it save the developer from having to reinvent the wheel, but, more importantly, it also makes applications easier to use. Providing a common dialog used by all applications means that users have to learn how to perform each function only once.

The .NET Framework provides several common dialog boxes in the System.Windows.Forms.CommonDialog class, which is a base class for displaying five commonly used Windows dialog boxes. These common dialogs are as follows:

- FileDialog
- ColorDialog
- FontDialog

- PageSetupDialog
- PrintDialog

Chapter 6 describes the common dialogs more fully.

Form Properties

Since every form is derived from the Form class, which itself is derived from the Control class, they have all the properties of the Control and Form base classes, of which there are about one hundred. Many of the most commonly used properties are listed in Table 5-1. These properties can either be set in Visual Studio .NET at design time or set programmatically at runtime.

Table 5-1. Form properties

Property	Value type	Description
AcceptButton	IButtonControl	Gets or sets the button on a form that is clicked when the user presses Enter, irrespective of which control actually has focus.
ActiveForm	Form	Static property (shared in VB.NET) that gets the currently active form. Returns null (Nothing in VB.NET) if there is no active form.
ActiveMdiChild	Form	Gets currently active MDI child. Returns null (Nothing in VB.NET) if there is no active form. Allows operations on MDI child forms from MDI parent form, or determination if any open MDI child forms.
AutoScroll	Boolean	If set true, the default, scrollbars will automatically display if any controls are outside the form's client region.
BackColor	Color	Gets or sets the background color.
CancelButton	IButtonControl	Gets or sets the button on a form that is clicked when the user presses Escape, irrespective of which control actually has focus.
ClientSize	Size	Gets or sets the size of the area of the form excluding the borders and titlebar.
ControlBox	Boolean	Gets or sets a value indicating if the system menu can be displayed and if the Close button (X) is displayed on the right end of the titlebar. The system menu is exposed by clicking on the titlebar icon if the Icon property is set, or by right-clicking on the titlebar if the Icon property is not set. The default is true.
DesktopBounds	Rectangle	Gets or sets the size and location of the form on the Windows desktop, using pixel-based desktop coordinates.
DesktopLocation	Point	Gets or sets the location of the form on the Windows desktop, using pixel-based desktop coordinates. Differs from the Location property in that it takes into account the taskbar, if any.
DialogResult	DialogResult	Gets or sets the return value from a form or dialog box displayed modally. Legal values are members of the DialogResult enumeration. This is covered in detail in Chapter 6.
FormBorderStyle	FormBorderStyle	Gets or sets the border style. In addition to appearance, the FormBorderStyle dictates whether the form will be resizable. The possible values of the FormBorderStyle enumeration are listed in Table 5-2.
Height	Integer	Gets or sets the height of the form in pixels.

Table 5-1. *Form properties (continued)*

Property	Value type	Description
Icon	Icon	Gets or sets the icon for the form. The icon is displayed in the control box of the form (if ControlBox property is set to `true`) and in the taskbar (if ShowInTaskbar is set to `true`).
MaximizeBox	Boolean	Gets or sets a value indicating if maximize button will be displayed in upper right corner of form on the titlebar. The default is `true`. If true, FormBorderStyle must be either FixedSingle, Sizable, Fixed3D, or FixedDialog. When the form is maximized, the maximize button automatically becomes a restore button.
MinimizeBox	Boolean	Gets or sets a value indicating if minimize button will be displayed in upper right corner of form on the titlebar. Default is `true`. If true, FormBorderStyle must be either FixedSingle, Sizable, Fixed3D or FixedDialog. When the form is maximized, the minimize button automatically becomes a restore button.
Modal	Boolean	Read-only value indicating if form is displayed modally using the ShowDialog method.
Opacity	double	Gets or sets the opacity level of the form, its border, and its controls, which can range between 1.00 (100 percent), the default value, and 0. If value is 0, the form is completely invisible and cannot be clicked on.
ShowInTaskBar	Boolean	Gets or sets value indicating if the form Text property is displayed in the Windows taskbar. Default is `true`.
Size	Size	Gets or sets both the height and width of the form.
SizeGripStyle	SizeGripStyle	Gets or sets one of three possible values that indicate the style of the sizing grip displayed at the lower-right corner of a form. The valid values are `Auto`, which displays the sizing grip as if the form is opened modally, `Hide`, which hides the sizing grip, and `Show`, which always shows the sizing grip.
StartPosition	FormStartPosition	Gets or sets the starting position of the form. Legal values of the FormStartPosition enumeration are listed in Table 5-3.
TopLevel	Boolean	Gets or sets value indicating the form has no parent form (i.e., if `true`, it is either an SDI form or an MDI parent form). The default is `true`. This property works in concert with the Parent property. A non-top-level TopLevel form just disappears if the Parent property is not set to a value. Also, an exception is raised if you try to set TopLevel to `true` without first setting Parent to `null`.
TopMost	Boolean	Gets or sets value indicating that the form is displayed on top of all the other forms, even if it is not the active form. Typically used for modeless dialog boxes that should always be visible, such as alerts.
Width	Integer	Gets or sets the width of the form in pixels.
WindowState	FormWindow-State	Gets or sets value of enumeration that indicates the state of the form. Valid values are `Normal` (the default), `Maximized`, or `Minimized`.

Table 5-2. *FormBorderStyle enumeration values*

Value	Description
Fixed3D	Nonresizeable, 3D border.
FixedDialog	Nonresizeable, dialog-style border.
FixedSingle	Nonresizeable, single line border.
FixedToolWindow	Nonresizeable, tool window border.

Table 5-2. FormBorderStyle enumeration values (continued)

Value	Description
None	No border.
Sizable	Default value. Standard resizable border.
SizableToolWindow	Resizable, tool window border.

Table 5-3. FormStartPosition enumeration values

Value	Description
CenterParent	Center form within parent form.
CenterScreen	Center form within current display.
Manual	Location and size of form dictates its starting position.
WindowsDefaultBounds	Form at Windows default location with bounds determined by Windows default.
WindowsDefaultLocation	Form at Windows default location with dimensions specified in form's constructor.

Forms Inheritance

One of the .NET Framework's powerful features is that it is fully object-oriented, which, among other things, allows class inheritance. Inheritance promotes reuse of objects, potentially saving the developer (and his employer) from a great deal of work. Reusing tested and working code reduces development time and cuts down on the number of bugs.

With inheritance, a class can derive (inherit) from a *base class*. The *derived class* is a specialized case of the base class. For example, if you were modeling the animal kingdom, your Dog class might derive from Mammal, indicating that a Dog is a specialized type of Mammal.

All forms in Windows Forms are members of the Form class. As such, they derive from the System.Windows.Forms class. Any form you create can also be the base class for other forms derived from it. A derived form will have all the properties, controls, and code contained by the base form, plus any additional properties, controls, and code of its own.

This organization provides a powerful way to impose a consistent look and feel across multiple forms. Any changes made in a base form will automatically propagate to all its derived forms when the application is recompiled. In addition, the derived form can override properties and methods. This will be demonstrated in the examples below.

Inheritance also allows controls with common functionality to be placed in a base form and be available to any derived form. By overriding methods in the derived form, the same base control can perform vastly different functions, yet retain a set of common functionality.

For a complete discussion of inheritance and polymorphism, see Jesse Liberty's *Programming C#* or *Programming VB. NET* (O'Reilly).

Programmatic Inheritance

To examine many of the issues relating to forms inheritance without the clutter introduced by Visual Studio .NET, you will create an example using a text editor. This example creates two forms: a base form, called BaseForm, and an inherited form, called InheritedForm, which will derive from BaseForm.

To create the base form, open your favorite text editor and enter the code shown in Example 5-1 for C# or Example 5-2 for VB.NET. Save the source code file with the name indicated in the caption for each example. You will want to save and compile the source code for both BaseForm and InheritedForm in the same directory.

Example 5-1. BaseForm source code in C# (BaseForm.cs)

```
using System;
using System.Drawing;
using System.Windows.Forms;

namespace WinFormsInheritance
{
    public class BaseForm : System.Windows.Forms.Form
    {
        private Button btnClose;
        private Button btnApp;
        protected Label lbl;

        public BaseForm( )
        {
            Text = "Inheritance Base Form";
            BackColor = Color.LightGreen;

            btnClose = new Button( );
            btnClose.Location = new Point(25,100);
            btnClose.Size = new Size(100,25);
            btnClose.Text = "&Close";
            btnClose.Click += new System.EventHandler(btnClose_Click);

            btnApp = new Button( );
            btnApp.Location = new Point(200,100);
            btnApp.Size = new Size(150,25);
            btnApp.Text = "&Base Application";
            btnApp.Click += new System.EventHandler(btnApp_Click);

            lbl = new Label( );
            lbl.Location = new Point(25,25);
            lbl.Size = new Size(100,25);
            lbl.Text = "This label on BaseForm";
```

Example 5-1. BaseForm source code in C# (BaseForm.cs) (continued)

```csharp
         Controls.AddRange(new Control[ ]{lbl, btnClose, btnApp});
      }

      static void Main( )
      {
         Application.Run(new BaseForm( ));
      }

      private void btnClose_Click(object sender, EventArgs e)
      {
         Application.Exit( );
      }

      private void btnApp_Click(object sender, EventArgs e)
      {
         MessageBox.Show("This is the Base application.");
         SomeMethod( );
      }

      protected virtual void SomeMethod( )
      {
         MessageBox.Show("This is SomeMethod called from BaseForm.");
      }
   }
}
```

Example 5-2. BaseForm source code in VB.NET (BaseForm.vb)

```vbnet
imports System
imports System.Drawing
imports System.Windows.Forms

namespace WinFormsInheritance
   public class BaseForm : inherits System.Windows.Forms.Form
      private WithEvents btnClose as Button
      private WithEvents btnApp as Button
      protected lbl as Label

      public Sub New( )
         Text = "Inheritance Base Form"
         BackColor = Color.LightGreen

         btnClose = new Button( )
         btnClose.Location = new Point(25,100)
         btnClose.Size = new Size(100,25)
         btnClose.Text = "&Close"

         btnApp = new Button( )
         btnApp.Location = new Point(200,100)
         btnApp.Size = new Size(150,25)
         btnApp.Text = "&Base Application"

         lbl = new Label( )
         lbl.Location = new Point(25,25)
```

Example 5-2. BaseForm source code in VB.NET (BaseForm.vb) (continued)

```
            lbl.Size = new Size(100,25)
            lbl.Text = "This label on BaseForm"

            Controls.AddRange(new Control( ){lbl, btnClose, btnApp})
        end sub

    Public Shared Sub Main( )
        Application.Run(new BaseForm( ))
    end sub

    private sub btnClose_Click(ByVal sender As Object, _
                               ByVal e As EventArgs) _
                               Handles btnClose.Click
        Application.Exit( )
    end sub

    private sub btnApp_Click(ByVal sender As Object, _
                             ByVal e As EventArgs) _
                             Handles btnApp.Click
        MessageBox.Show("This is the Base application.")
        SomeMethod( )
    end sub

    protected Overridable Sub SomeMethod( )
        MessageBox.Show("This is SomeMethod called from BaseForm.")
    end sub
  end class
end namespace
```

To run either of the forms in Example 5-1 or Example 5-2, the source code must first be compiled to an EXE file. Enter the appropriate line at a command prompt:

```
csc /out:BaseForm.exe /target:winexe BaseForm.cs
```

```
vbc /out:BaseForm.exe /r:system.dll,system.drawing.dll,system.windows.forms.dll /
target:winexe BaseForm.vb
```

Chapter 2 gives a complete discussion of the command-line compiler.

Remember to use a command prompt window with the proper path already set by clicking on Start, and then Programs → Microsoft Visual Studio .NET 2003 → Visual Studio .NET Tools → Visual Studio .NET 2003 Command Prompt.

Any command entered on a command line must be entered without pressing Enter until the command is to be executed. The command will wrap to new lines if it is long enough, but you should not enter any carriage returns.

Notice that the command-line compilation for VB.NET requires explicit referencing of all assemblies, while the C# version requires only "non-default" assemblies.

When BaseForm.exe is run, the result is shown in Figure 5-3. Although you can't see it in the printed book, the background color of the form is light green.

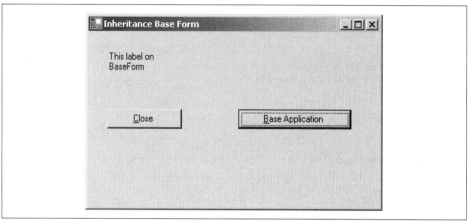

Figure 5-3. BaseForm

BaseForm is a fairly simple and straightforward Windows Form. The first three lines reference namespaces used by the form:

C#
```
using System;
using System.Drawing;
using System.Windows.Forms;
```

VB
```
imports System
imports System.Drawing
imports System.Windows.Forms
```

 System.Drawing is necessary because it contains the Color structure, used in the code to specify the BackColor property.

The namespace of the form itself was set to WinFormsInheritance. The class name for the form is BaseForm, and, like all Windows Forms, it inherits from System.Windows.Forms.Form.

The next three lines declare objects on the form—two buttons and a label:

C#
```
private Button btnClose;
private Button btnApp;
protected Label lbl;
```

VB
```
private WithEvents btnClose as Button
private WithEvents btnApp as Button
protected lbl as Label
```

The two buttons are declared as private, while the label is declared as protected. Objects declared as private cannot be referenced in code in any derived class, while objects declared as protected can be referenced in classes derived from the current class. The upshot is that neither button can be modified by InheritedForm, while the Label control is accessible in InheritedForm.

The constructor is the next section in the code. In C#, it is the method:

```
public BaseForm( )
{
```

and in VB.NET it is:

```
public Sub New( )
```

This is where the Text and BackColor properties of the form are set and the controls are instantiated and fully specified. Notice that event handlers are defined for the Click event for the two buttons in C#, while in VB.NET, this definition is achieved in the control declarations (using the WithEvents keyword) in conjunction with the event-handler method declarations (using the Handles keyword):

```
public BaseForm( )
{
    Text = "Inheritance Base Form";
    BackColor = Color.LightGreen;

    btnClose = new Button( );
    btnClose.Location = new Point(25,100);
    btnClose.Size = new Size(100,25);
    btnClose.Text = "&Close";
    btnClose.Click += new System.EventHandler(btnClose_Click);

    btnApp = new Button( );
    btnApp.Location = new Point(200,100);
    btnApp.Size = new Size(150,25);
    btnApp.Text = "&Base Application";
    btnApp.Click += new System.EventHandler(btnApp_Click);

    lbl = new Label( );
    lbl.Location = new Point(25,25);
    lbl.Size = new Size(100,25);
    lbl.Text = "This label on BaseForm";

    Controls.AddRange(new Control[ ]{lbl, btnClose, btnApp});
}
```

```
public Sub New( )
    Text = "Inheritance Base Form"
    BackColor = Color.LightGreen

    btnClose = new Button( )
    btnClose.Location = new Point(25,100)
```

```
      btnClose.Size = new Size(100,25)
      btnClose.Text = "&Close"

      btnApp = new Button( )
      btnApp.Location = new Point(200,100)
      btnApp.Size = new Size(150,25)
      btnApp.Text = "&Base Application"

      lbl = new Label( )
      lbl.Location = new Point(25,25)
      lbl.Size = new Size(100,25)
      lbl.Text = "This label on BaseForm"

      Controls.AddRange(new Control( ){lbl, btnClose, btnApp})
    end sub
```

The event handler for the btnApp button Click event first puts up a message box ("This is the Base application.") and then calls the method SomeMethod. Notice that SomeMethod is marked virtual in C# and overridable in VB.NET, indicating that the developer expects this method to be overridden in derived classes. SomeMethod puts up a message box with the words "This is SomeMethod called from BaseForm."

To create an inherited form that derives from BaseForm, enter the code from Example 5-3 for C# or Example 5-4 for VB.NET in your text editor and save the files as named in the example captions.

Example 5-3. InheritedForm source code in C# (InheritedForm.cs)

```
using System;
using System.Drawing;
using System.Windows.Forms;

namespace WinFormsInheritance
{
   public class InheritedForm : WinFormsInheritance.BaseForm
   {
      private Button btn;

      public InheritedForm( )
      {
         Text = "Inherited Form";

         btn = new Button( );
         btn.Location = new Point(25,150);
         btn.Size = new Size(125,25);
         btn.Text = "C&lose on Inherited";
         btn.Click += new System.EventHandler(btn_Click);

         Controls.Add(btn);

         lbl.Text = "Now from InheritedForm";
         BackColor = Color.LightBlue;
      }
```

Example 5-3. InheritedForm source code in C# (InheritedForm.cs) (continued)

```csharp
        static void Main( )
        {
            Application.Run(new InheritedForm( ));
        }

        private void btn_Click(object sender, EventArgs e)
        {
            Application.Exit( );
        }

        protected override void SomeMethod( )
        {
            MessageBox.Show("This is the overridden SomeMethod called " +
                        "from InheritedForm.");
        }
    }
}
```

Example 5-4. InheritedForm source code in VB.NET (InheritedForm.vb)

```vbnet
imports System
imports System.Drawing
imports System.Windows.Forms

namespace WinFormsInheritance
    public class InheritedForm : inherits WinFormsInheritance.BaseForm
        private WithEvents btn as Button

        public sub New( )
            Text = "Inherited Form"
            btn = new Button( )
            btn.Location = new Point(25,150)
            btn.Size = new Size(125,25)
            btn.Text = "C&lose on Inherited"

            Controls.Add(btn)

            lbl.Text = "Now from InheritedForm"
            BackColor = Color.LightBlue
        end sub

        Public Shadows Shared Sub Main( )
            Application.Run(new InheritedForm( ))
        end sub

        private sub btn_Click(ByVal sender As Object, _
                            ByVal e As EventArgs) _
                            Handles btn.Click
            Application.Exit( )
        end sub

        protected Overrides Sub SomeMethod( )
```

VB
```
            MessageBox.Show("This is the overridden SomeMethod called " + _
                            "from InheritedForm.")
        end sub
    end class
end namespace
```

InheritedForm is also a straightforward Windows Form. The first thing of note is that it does not inherit directly from System.Windows.Forms.Form, but rather from WinFormsInheritance.BaseForm.

Inside the constructor, the Text property of the form is set to "Inherited Form." Also inside the constructor, the Text property of the Label control on the base form is changed and the BackColor property of the base form is set to a different color. This is done with the lines:

C#
```
    lbl.Text = "Now from InheritedForm";
    BackColor = Color.LightBlue;
```

VB
```
    lbl.Text = "Now from InheritedForm"
    BackColor = Color.LightBlue
```

The Label control was declared protected. If it had been private, then InheritedForm would have caused a compiler error when the Label control was referenced; derived classes cannot access private members in the base class.

> The Label control could also have been declared public, but good object-oriented practice dictates using the minimum accessibility necessary.

Recall that the btnApp_Click event handler method in the BaseForm, from Example 5-1 and Example 5-2, calls the method SomeMethod. In BaseForm, SomeMethod was declared as virtual (overridable). In InheritedForm, another version of SomeMethod is provided that does, in fact, override the base version. This is indicated by the override keyword in C# and the Overrides keyword in VB.NET.

> In the VB.NET version, the keyword Shadows is used in the declaration of the Main method. This keyword, which prevents a compiler warning, indicates that an identically named element is in a base class, and the shadowed element, i.e., the method in the derived class, is unavailable to that derived class.

The command line used to compile *InheritedForm.cs* is as follows:

C#
```
    csc /out:InheritedForm.exe /r:BaseForm.exe /target:winexe InheritedForm.cs
```

and to compile *InheritedForm.vb*, use:

```
vbc /out:InheritedForm.exe /r:system.dll,system.drawing.dll,system.windows.forms.
dll,BaseForm.exe /target:winexe InheritedForm.vb
```

> Remember, even though these command lines wrap in the book and probably also on your screen, they are each a single line and must be entered without pressing Enter until you are ready to execute the line.

Note that both versions of these compiler commands now reference the previously compiled BaseForm.exe. This is necessary so that InheritedForm can inherit from BaseForm.

When InheritedForm is executed and the BaseApplication button is clicked, the first message is "This is the Base application." The second is "This is the overridden SomeMethod called from InheritedForm," as shown in Figure 5-4.

Because of the way event handling works, the base class event handler has not been replaced, but rather the new stuff is added on top of it. This often surprises people because it's not how things usually work in derivation; if you implement something in the derived class, it typically replaces the base class implementation unless you explicitly call down to the base class. But events are different.

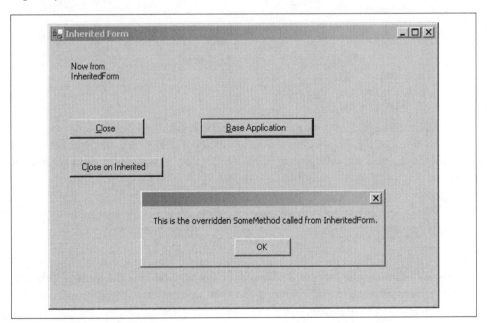

Figure 5-4. InheritedForm with MessageBox

Visual Inheritance

You will now use Visual Studio .NET to create a base form and a form derived from it. Visual Studio .NET provides a means of inheriting forms known as Visual Inheritance. Visual Studio .NET recognizes that a form is inherited and displays the inherited form differently from the base form, indicating which controls are from the base form and which from the derived form. An Inheritance Picker dialog box makes this even easier to accomplish. Visual Inheritance makes deriving forms a very simple task, although there are a few gotchas that we will point out along the way.

Open Visual Studio .NET and create a new Windows Application project named Inheritance in the language of your choice. Add a new form. You'll add several Label controls, some with private accessibility and some with protected accessibility. You will also add a button that, when clicked, will cause the current time to display in one of the Label controls.

When coding a form directly, outside of Visual Studio .NET, the accessibility level of a control is specified with an accessibility keyword (public, private, protected, internal, or protected internal in C#; public, private, protected, friend, or protected friend in VB.NET) as part of the control declaration. For example, the control declarations from Examples 5-1 and 5-2 looked like:

```
private Button btnClose;
private Button btnApp;
protected Label lbl;
```

VB
```
private WithEvents btnClose as Button
private WithEvents btnApp as Button
protected lbl as Label
```

In Visual Studio .NET, it is very easy to set the accessibility level of a control. Select the control in the Design window. In the Property window, set the Modifiers property to the desired accessibility level. You can also set the accessibility in code directly.

 C# and VB.NET diverge here on default-access modifiers for controls placed in Visual Studio .NET. C# defaults to private, while VB.NET defaults to Friend, the equivalent to Internal in C#.

The default name of the form will probably be Form1. Rename the form by selecting it in the Design window and changing the (Name) property in the Properties window from Form1 to BaseForm.

The design view of the form should look like that shown in Figure 5-5. (Note that the project shown in these examples was actually named vbInheritance, to distinguish it from my C# version, csInheritance.)

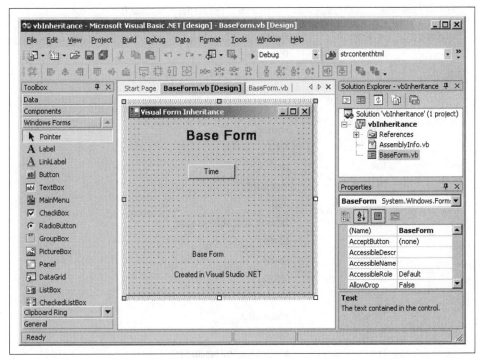

Figure 5-5. BaseForm in Visual Studio .NET

Table 5-4 lists all relevant properties of the controls on BaseForm.

Table 5-4. Inheritance application BaseForm control properties

Control type	Property	Value
Form	(Name)	BaseForm
	Size	300,300
	Text	Visual Form Inheritance
	BackColor	Control (the default color)
Label	(Name)	lblHeading
	Font	Microsoft SansSerif Bold 16 pt.
	Location	24,16
	Modifiers	Protected
	Size	248,23
	Text	Base Form
	TextAlign	MiddleCenter
Button	(Name)	btn
	Location	96,72
	Modifiers	Protected
	Size	75,23

Table 5-4. Inheritance application BaseForm control properties (continued)

Control type	Property	Value
	Text	Time
Label	(Name)	lblOutput
	Font	Microsoft SansSerif Regular 8 pt.
	Location	64,128
	Modifiers	Protected
	Size	136,23
	Text	blank
	TextAlign	MiddleCenter
Label	(Name)	label3
	Font	Microsoft SansSerif Regular 8 pt.
	Location	80,200
	Modifiers	Private
	Size	100,23
	Text	Base Form
	TextAlign	MiddleCenter
Label	(Name)	label2
	Font	Microsoft SansSerif Regular 8 pt.
	Location	40,232
	Modifiers	Private
	Size	216,23
	Text	Created in Visual Studio .NET
	TextAlign	MiddleCenter

If you run the form at this point, there should be no problems if you are working in C#. If you are working in VB.NET, on the other hand, the first gotcha rears its ugly head when the IDE reports build errors. Click on No to stop. The Task List window will open with the following description of an error:

VB
```
'Sub Main' was not found in 'Inheritance.Form1'.
```

Wait a minute, there is no Form1. You renamed the form to BaseForm. What is going on here? The answer is that the IDE is trying to make life easier for VB.NET developers. In doing so, it hides the Main method.

In C#, a static void Main() method is required and is automatically inserted into the code by Visual Studio .NET. In VB.NET, a sub Main is explicitly required when compiling source code with the command-line compiler, but is neither required nor provided by Visual Studio .NET. Instead, the VB.NET compiler working with Visual Studio .NET automatically creates a sub Main and inserts it into the compiled code. Even though you renamed the form legitimately through Visual Studio .NET, once this autogenerated sub Main gets the original form name, it does not let go of it until you explicitly tell it to do so.

> To verify that a Main method is in fact created for your VB.NET program developed in Visual Studio .NET, you can use ILDASM, a tool provided as part of the .NET SDK, to look into the EXE file created by the compiler. Open a .NET command line by clicking the Start button, and then Programs → Microsoft Visual Studio .NET 2003 → Visual Studio .NET Tools → Visual Studio .NET 2003 Command Prompt. Enter the following command line:
>
> ```
> ildasm e:\projects\Inheritance\bin\inheritance.exe
> ```
>
> substituting the actual path to your executable.
>
> Once inside ILDASM, you can drill down through the contents of the file until you see Main::void() as one of the nodes under BaseForm. Double-clicking on any node will display the IL code that comprises the object. Although much of the IL code is cryptic, you will see the name of the Form class in the Main::void() method.

To change the name of the startup form, right-click on the project name in the Solution Explorer and select Properties. This will open a Property Page for the project. (Note that it is distinct from the Properties window that is normally used for object properties.) One of the drop-down fields will be labeled Startup Object. Select Base-Form from this list, and then run the form. It should run with no errors (although it does not do much at this point).

> As an alternative to changing the startup object in the Property Page, you could also double-click on the error message in the Task List window and select BaseForm from the Startup Object dialog box that presents itself.

Add functionality to the button by double-clicking on the button in the Design window. When the event handler code skeleton for the default Click event comes up in the code editor, add the highlighted lines of code from Example 5-5 in C# or from Example 5-6 in VB.NET.

Example 5-5. BaseForm btn_Click in C#

```csharp
protected virtual void  btn_Click(object sender, System.EventArgs e)
{
    lblOutput.Text = "The time is: " + DateTime.Now.ToString("T");
}
```

Example 5-6. Example 5-6. BaseForm btn_Click in VB.NET

```vbnet
Private Sub btn_Click(ByVal sender As System.Object, _
                      ByVal e As System.EventArgs) _
                      Handles btn.Click
```

Example 5-6. Example 5-6. BaseForm btn_Click in VB.NET (continued)

```
lblOutput.Text = "The time is: " + DateTime.Now.ToString("T")
End Sub
```

Running the application and clicking on the button will now display the current time as the Text property of the lblOutput control.

Now add a derived form to the project, using the Inheritance Picker. Right-click on the project name in the Solution Explorer. Select Add, then Add Inherited Form. A familiar Add New Item dialog box will appear. Change the name of the form from *Form2.vb* to *InheritedForm.vb*. The dialog box will look like Figure 5-6.

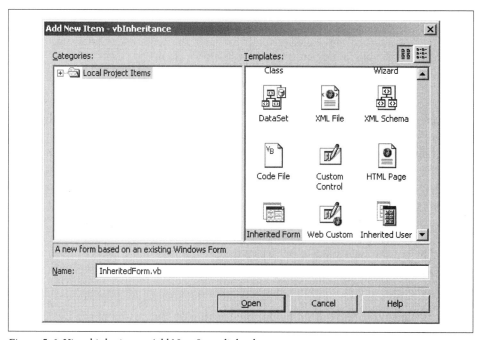

Figure 5-6. Visual inheritance Add New Item dialog box

Clicking on the Open button will present the Inheritance Picker dialog box, shown in Figure 5-7. Select the form to inherit from (in this example, there is only one other form in the project), and then click OK.

A new form, named InheritedForm, derived from BaseForm, will be opened in a new Design window. The source file for the new form, called *InheritanceForm.vb*, will be visible in the Solution Explorer. The IDE will look like Figure 5-8. Although the original form object was renamed to BaseForm, it's source file is still named *Form1.vb*, and appears as such in the Solution Explorer.

All controls inherited from the original base class, i.e., BaseForm, are indicated with a small glyph (⊡) in their upper-lefthand corner.

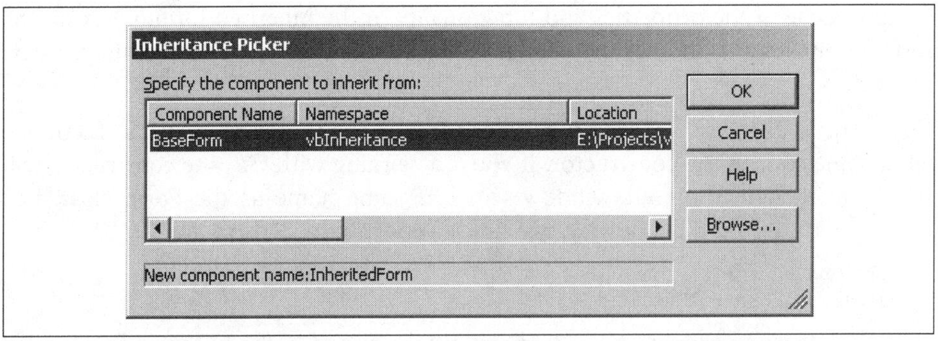

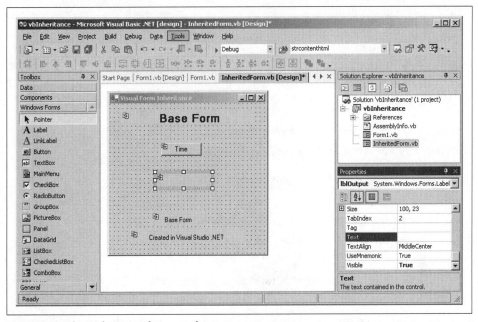

Figure 5-7. Inheritance Picker

Figure 5-8. InheritedForm in design mode

The top three controls on the form, lblHeading, lblOutput, and btn, are protected, while label2 and label3 are private. This means that in the derived form the latter two controls will be visible, but unable to be changed in the IDE or otherwise accessed in code.

You can now see the effects of marking controls in a derived form as protected or private. Click on any of the protected controls. Resizing handles will appear, and you can move or resize the controls. The control properties will be visible and accessible in the Properties window. In contrast, click on one of the private controls. It will have no resizing handles, and cannot be moved or resized. In addition, it's properties are visible in the Properties window, but grayed out and inaccessible.

Change some of the properties and functionality of the inherited form. Click on the form in the Design window, and change its BackColor property to something snazzy, like Yellow.

You want to change the Text property of some of the inherited controls. To do so, enter some code in the constructor. If you are working with C#, the constructor will be the method in the code window with the same name as the Form class, i.e., InheritedForm. Add the following two lines of code in the constructor:

C#
```csharp
btn.Text = "Date";
lblHeading.Text = "Inherited Form";
```

If you are working with VB.NET, first expand the region in the code window labeled Windows Form Designer generated code, and then find the Sub called New( ). Add the following two lines of code:

VB
```vb
btn.Text = "Date"
lblHeading.Text = "Inherited Form"
```

Double-click on the button to bring up the code skeleton for the Click event handler. Enter the highlighted code shown in Example 5-7 for C# and in Example 5-8 for VB.NET.

Example 5-7. InheritedForm btn_Click event handler in C#

C#
```csharp
protected void btn_Click(object sender, System.EventArgs e)
{
    lblOutput.Text = "Today is: " + DateTime.Now.ToString("D");
}
```

Example 5-8. InheritedForm btn_Click event handler in VB.NET

VB
```vb
Private Sub btn_Click(ByVal sender As System.Object, _
                      ByVal e As System.EventArgs) _
                      Handles btn.Click
    lblOutput.Text = "Today is: " + DateTime.Now.ToString("D")
End Sub
```

If you run the program, you will not get the InheritedForm, but rather the Base-Form. There can be only a single entry point into the program, i.e., a single Main method, unless you tell the compiler otherwise and point it in the right direction. You have not yet done this.

If you are handcoding and compiling a project with multiple forms or other classes, and there is more than one Main method, use a /main compiler switch to tell the compiler which class to use as the entry point. (See Chapter 2 for a complete description of command-line compilation.)

Working in Visual Studio .NET, this is accomplished by right-clicking on the project in the Solution Explorer, selecting Properties to get the Property Page for the project, and changing the Startup Object to the desired form.

If you are working in C#, you probably will not see any forms listed other than the first form entered in the project. This is because Visual Studio .NET includes only classes with a Main method in the list of possible startup objects, and it automatically includes a Main method only in the first form. Copy the Main method from the first form to any additional forms, remembering to change the name of the form in the Application.Run statement to the current form, and it will now show up in the list of potential Startup Objects.

Running the program, you will now see the inherited form. Clicking on the button, now labeled Date, you will get something similar to that shown in Figure 5-9. Not only is the form now a garish yellow (at least on the screen, if not in the book) and the button is relabeled and repurposed, but the heading label, lblHeading, now says Inherited Form, while the two labels at the bottom still say Base Form and Created in Visual Studio .NET.

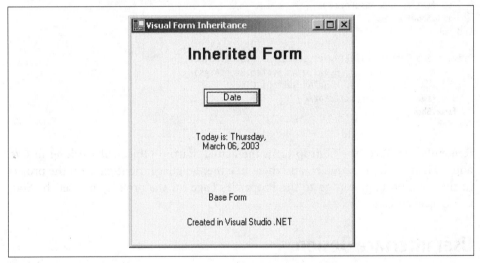

Figure 5-9. InheritedForm

If you want to see either form without having to go through the step of changing the startup object, you need to go through several steps. Add a new form to the project by right-clicking on the project name in the Solution Explorer, selecting Add, then Add Windows Form..., and name it Startup.

Drag two buttons onto the form and change their Text properties to BaseForm and InheritedForm, respectively. Double-click on each button to enter code in their Click event handlers, and enter the code highlighted in Example 5-9 for C# or Example 5-10 for VB.NET.

Example 5-9. Startup form button event handlers in C#

```csharp
private void button1_Click(object sender, System.EventArgs e)
{
   Form frm1 = new BaseForm( );
   frm1.Show( );
}

private void button2_Click(object sender, System.EventArgs e)
{
   Form frm2 = new InheritedForm( );
   frm2.Show( );
}
```

Example 5-10. Startup form button event handlers in VB.NET

```vbnet
Private Sub Button1_Click(ByVal sender As System.Object, _
                          ByVal e As System.EventArgs) _
                          Handles Button1.Click
   dim frm1 as new BaseForm( )
   frm1.Show( )
End Sub

Private Sub Button2_Click(ByVal sender As System.Object, _
                          ByVal e As System.EventArgs) _
                          Handles Button1.Click
   dim frm2 as new InheritedForm( )
   frm2.Show( )
End Sub
```

Remember to make the Startup form the actual Startup Object. If working in C#, add a Main method manually, and then, in either language, right-click on the project in the Solution Explorer, go to the Properties Page for the project, and set the Startup Object accordingly.

User Interface Design

The *user interface* (UI) is one of the keys to a successful application. An application will be a failure if people can't use it easily and effectively, just as surely as if the application were too buggy to run. A good UI is elegant and efficient, exposing the functional requirements to the users clearly and intuitively.

For a program running in the Windows world, the Windows UI provides a foundation of expectations and capability. For example, most people today *expect* their applications to be Windows applications, as opposed to console, or DOS-style, command-line applications. The .NET Framework and the underlying Windows API provide the capability to satisfy these expectations. The Windows environment also shapes the way Windows applications look and feel. Windows applications look and feel different from, for example, Macintosh applications. For that matter, the Windows 98 UI is significantly different from Windows XP. On the other hand, all these graphical user interfaces (GUIs) share common design elements, such as windows, scrollbars, buttons, text boxes, tree views, and hyperlinks.

In a Windows application, you will find several broad categories of UI design: single-document interface (SDI), multiple-document interface (MDI), Explorer-style interface, and dialog boxes. The first three categories will be covered in this chapter. Dialog boxes will be covered in the next chapter.

UI Principles

Good UI design is both an aesthetic and a technical endeavor. Although there is as much art as science in UI design, it is still possible to identify several guidelines for good UI design in the modern era. Entire books can be written on this topic, and many have been. This section mentions several important design considerations to keep in mind.

UI design, like art, politics, and religion, can engender strong opinions on the part of adherents to one philosophy or another. A colleague tells the tale of a seminar in UI design he once attended. Within minutes, the session nearly devolved into violence because so many of the attendees disagreed so strongly with the opinions put forth by the "expert" speaker.

Many software developers believe they are just as capable of coming up with a good UI design as they are of developing the architecture and code to implement the application. This is rarely true. Good design is an art, and good UI designers bring a special talent to bear on the task. Any significant application will almost certainly be improved by adding a UI designer to the team. The earlier in the process this person is brought onboard, the better the end result will be.

Follow standard conventions

Learn once, use everywhere—that is a key feature of any GUI. For example, copy (Ctrl-C) and paste (Ctrl-V) should work the same in all applications as it does in Windows itself. Don't decide that Ctrl-P makes more sense for Paste; you will only confuse users.

Windows provides many common dialog boxes, which will be described in Chapter 6. Use them. Don't create your own File Save dialog box, for example, unless the standard common dialog just won't do.

Be consistent

Be consistent in the design cues you decide to use in the application. For example, if read-only TextBoxes have a gray background color one place in the application, make sure all read-only TextBoxes have the same gray background color. Don't give some read-only TextBoxes a gray background color and others a white background color. If a TextBox changes status from editable to read-only, dynamically change the background color in the program code.

Maximize readability

Text presented in uppercase is not as easy to read as lowercase text with initial uppercase letters. If you want to emphasize some text, use a bold font, underline the text, use a contrasting color, or make the font larger.

Group controls by function

Controls that perform related functions should be grouped together. For example, the OK/Cancel/Apply/Help buttons that are commonly used in dialog boxes should be grouped together, rather than interspersed with other controls in the dialog box.

Arrange controls by importance

Keep in mind that the typical user of left-to-right languages (e.g., English, German, or French) will look first at the upper-left corner of the screen (or piece of paper), then scan across left to right and down the page. Place the most important controls in the upper-left corner and the least important controls in the lower-right corner.

Arrange controls by work flow

Controls should be arranged according to the way users typically work. For example, a form designed for input of biographical information might group all the fields relating to birthplace, then education, and then qualifications, as opposed to interspersing fields about these topics.

Align text and controls

Proper alignment of text and controls enhances the readability of a form. Consider a series of text boxes with labels. They could be arranged in so many ways. Three of those ways are shown in Figure 5-10. In the left-most example, the only alignment is the left edge of the labels. In the middle example, the left edges of both the label and the text box is aligned. In the right example, the right edge of the label is aligned, as are the text boxes.

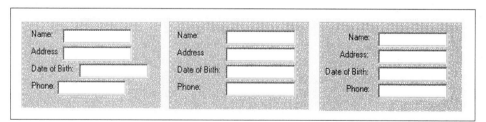

Figure 5-10. Control alignment

Generally, the left example is the least effective. Which of the other two is preferable is a matter of taste. (I prefer the right example.)

Correctly sized text boxes

All the text boxes in Figure 5-10 are the same size. This generally enhances readability. However, if the text to be entered in different fields is of vastly different length, say an email address in one field and a two-character state abbreviation in another, then size the text boxes accordingly.

For potentially large input fields, make the text box resize when the form resizes. In addition, it is best to size a text box to make the entire entry visible at once, if possible.

Use color effectively

You can use color to convey information. For example, consider displaying negative numbers in red and positive numbers in black.

Colors can also enhance, or detract from, readability. Displaying black text on a brown background is very difficult to read, while displaying yellow text on a brown background is easy to read.

However it is good to keep in mind that color can culture-specific; not all cultures interpret the same color scheme the same way. Also, remember that some people are color-blind, so color should not be the only design cue.

Use modal dialogs sparingly

Modal dialogs (dialogs you must deal with before program flow can continue) are often necessary, but should be used as infrequently as possible since they disrupt the flow of the user's experience. Instead, provide modeless forms or dialogs to gather or present the information.

Provide keyboard equivalents

Many users prefer to type rather than use the mouse. Keyboard equivalents for all menu items and access keys for controls allow these people to work without removing their hands from the keyboard.

Get input and feedback from actual users

Talk to end users and get input as early in the design process as possible. Keep them involved, showing them mockups of the UI before all the code is in place.

Error handling

Errors happen. Deal with them so that your end user doesn't have to, or at the very least, receives a clear message describing what the problem is and how to fix it. If a runtime error occurs, whether due to unexpected user input, a dropped network connection, or a failed hard drive, it must be handled.

Specific errors or classes of errors can be handled with specific error-handling routines. Others can be handled with more generic error handlers. If an error is not handled by the application, the CLR will present an ugly error message to the user, a situation you should strive mightily to avoid.

Errors will be covered thoroughly in Chapter 21.

Help

A fully featured application provides Help to end users via a menu item or a hot key. It can be hyperlinked within itself or out to the Internet. It can be monolithic or dynamically context-sensitive. In any case, the development team must decide if and how much Help capability the program warrants or can be provided.

Interface Types

This section will look at four fundamental Windows interface types: SDI, MDI, tabbed interface, and Explorer style interface. The next chapter covers dialog boxes. You will use at least one of these interface types in virtually every Windows application you write.

Many applications, such as Office XP and Visual Studio .NET, mix elements from more than one type of interface. However, these classifications are still useful.

SDI

In a Single Document interface (SDI), an application can open only a single window. A typical SDI application is WordPad (shown in Figure 5-11), installed with most Windows installations.

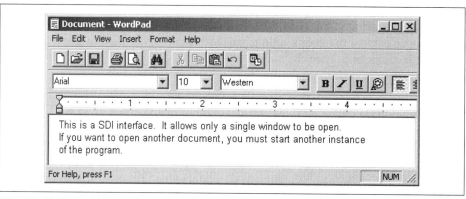

Figure 5-11. Typical SDI application (WordPad)

SDI windows can have all the controls and accouterments of a standard window. It can have menus, toolbars, scrollbars, a titlebar with window control buttons, a status bar, and rulers. It can also contain any control from the .NET Framework or any control derived from a control in the Framework.

The one thing an SDI application cannot have is a Window menu item. The Window menu contains commands for viewing and manipulating the many windows an application may have open. Since SDI applications cannot, by definition, have multiple windows, there is no need for the menu item.

An SDI application can have other forms as part of the application: dialog boxes (described in the next chapter) or standard windows. In any case, functionality provided by other forms generally pertains to the document contained in the main application window, or to the application as a whole.

To create an SDI application, set the IsMdiContainer property for the form to false. This is the default value set by Visual Studio .NET for a new form.

MDI

In a Multiple Document Interface (MDI), the application can have multiple windows open at the same time. As with SDI windows, MDI windows can have the full complement of form features and controls.

MDI applications are easily recognized by the presence of the Window menu item. This item allows you to view or manipulate the several windows, which may be open within the application.

Some MDI applications, such as SQL Server Enterprise Manager (shown in Figure 5-12) and Microsoft Excel, allow you to have several nonmaximized windows open at once, all within a parent, or main, application window.

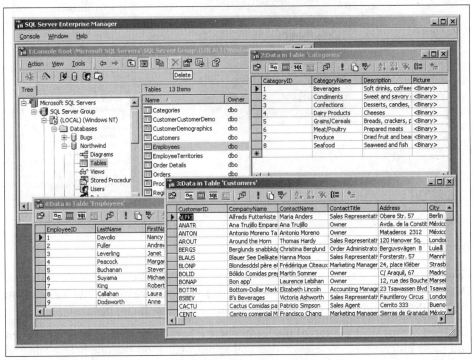

Figure 5-12. Typical MDI application (SQL Server Enterprise Manager)

Other MDI applications, such as Microsoft Word 2000, allow you to split a document into separate panes within the parent window, but each open document is maximized within its own window. Each document has its own parent window, so the application appears to behave similarly to an SDI application. The Window menu command is aware of all the open documents in all the instances of the application, and allows you to switch between them.

Creating an MDI application is fairly straightforward. First, create the parent form, and then create one or more child forms that the parent form can contain.

To demonstrate this, open a new project in Visual Studio .NET. Call it MDIDemo. In the Properties window for the form, change the IsMdiContainer property to true. After changing the Text property, Visual Studio .NET will look like Figure 5-13. Notice that the color of the form will change to a darker gray.

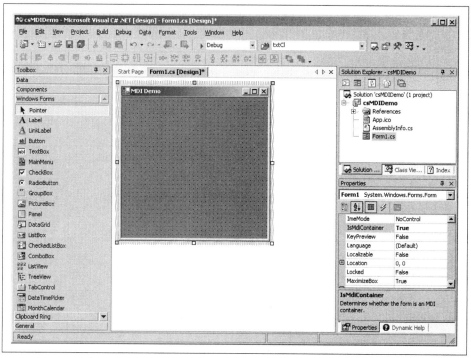

Figure 5-13. MDI form design

Give the parent form a menu by dragging a MainMenu control onto the form. (Menus will be covered in depth in Chapter 18.) You will eventually add a File menu item, with New and Close submenu items, plus a Window menu item.

Click on the menu at the top of the form where it says Type Here. Type File. When you press Enter, two Type Here labels will appear. Click on the one below File and type New. Press Enter, then below New, type Close. Click on the Type Here label to the right of File, and type Window.

Run this form as is and you will get Figure 5-14. The menu items don't do anything yet, but they will soon.

Before adding functionality to the menu items, create a child form that can be instantiated every time the user clicks on the New command. To do this, add a form to the project in one of three ways:

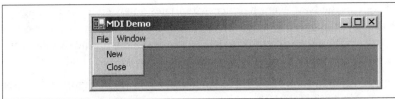

Figure 5-14. MDI sample form

- Select the Project → Add Windows Form... menu item
- Select the Project → Add New Item... menu item
- Right-click on the project name in the Solution Explorer and then click on either Add → Add New Item... or Add → Add Windows Form...

In any case, you will get the Add New Item dialog box, which will let you add a Windows Form to the project. Change the Text property of the new form to MDI Child.

To give the user something to do with this child form, drag a RichTextBox control onto the form. Clear the Text property and set the Dock property of the RichText-Box to Fill by clicking on the center rectangle of the drop-down in the Properties window. This will cause the RichTextBox to fill the child window completely, emulating Notepad or WordPad.

You can also add menus to the child forms. When the child form is activated, menu items on the child forms will automatically display as part of the parent form menu.

Now you can add functionality to the menu items. To do so, create event handlers and add code to each event handler.

Double-click on the New menu item. This will open up an event-handler skeleton for the menuItem2_Click method. Add the highlighted code shown in Example 5-11 (for C#) or in Example 5-12 (for VB.NET).

Example 5-11. File → New menu event handler in C#

```
private void menuItem2_Click(object sender, System.EventArgs e)
{
    Form mdiChild = new Form2( );
    mdiChild.MdiParent = this;
    mdiChild.Show( );
}
```

Example 5-12. File → New menu event handler in VB.NET

```
Private Sub MenuItem2_Click(ByVal sender As System.Object, _
                            ByVal e As System.EventArgs) _
                            Handles MenuItem2.Click
    dim mdiChild as New Form2( )
    mdiChild.MdiParent = me
    mdiChild.Show( )
End Sub
```

The first line of code in the New event handler instantiates a new child form, assigned to the variable mdiChild, using the child form you just created. The next line assigns the child form's parent, i.e., the calling form. In C# this is done with the this keyword and in VB.NET with the me keyword. The last line of code shows the child form.

Running the application now produces the screenshot shown in Figure 5-15 after you click the File → New menu item three times.

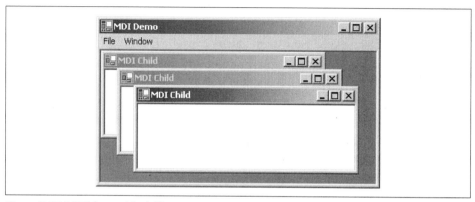

Figure 5-15. MDI form with children

Each child form has full, basic form functionality within the parent window. You can maximize, minimize, or restore the child window, as well as move and resize it. Also, you can type in the window. Anything you type will automatically line wrap, even if you resize the window, courtesy of the RichTextBox control.

You can always close the child form by clicking the X button in the upper-right corner of the window. To implement that functionality in the parent menu, double-click on the Close menu item in the Design view. As before, this will open up a code skeleton for the Close menu event handler. Enter the highlighted code shown in Example 5-13 (for C#) or Example 5-14 (for VB.NET).

Example 5-13. File → Close event handler in C#

```
private void menuItem3_Click(object sender, System.EventArgs e)
{
    Form activeChild = this.ActiveMdiChild;
    activeChild.Close();
}
```

Example 5-14. File → Close event handler in VB.NET

```
Private Sub MenuItem3_Click(ByVal sender As System.Object, _
                            ByVal e As System.EventArgs) _
                            Handles MenuItem3.Click
    dim activeChild as Form = me.ActiveMdiChild
    activeChild.Close()
End Sub
```

The first line of code in the File → Close event handler identifies which child form is active, using the ActiveMdiChild property, and assigns the variable activeChild to that instance of the active form.

The second line closes the active form by using the Close() method of the Form class.

Now when you run the application, you can create multiple instances of the child document, and you can close them from the menu.

Next, program the Window menu item in the parent window to provide the sort of functionality users expect. The Window menu item provides a list of all currently available windows, allowing the user to switch between them by clicking on the list. This functionality is easily implemented by setting the MdiList property to true for the menu item in question. Click on the Window menu item in Design view, and set the MdiList property to true.

Run the application and open several windows in the parent form. Then click on the Window menu item. You will see something similar to Figure 5-16.

A maximum of nine MDI child windows can be listed in the Window menu item. If more than nine child windows need to be displayed, then a "More Windows..." menu item will display at the end of the list and expose a dialog box from which you can select the complete list of child windows.

The only forms that can be listed in the Window menu item are those you can define as MDI child windows by using the MdiParent property, as shown in Example 5-11 and Example 5-12.

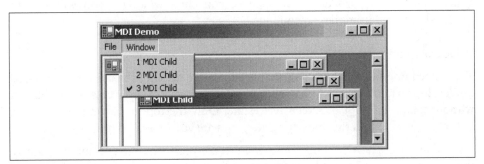

Figure 5-16. Window menu item showing list of child forms

In addition to displaying a list of child windows, the Window menu item often provides window-arrangement commands. Again, the .NET Framework provides an easy way to implement it by using the LayoutMdi method of the Form class. This method takes one of the members of the MdiLayout enumeration, listed in Table 5-5, as an argument.

Table 5-5. MdiLayout enumeration values

Value	Description
ArrangeIcons	Arranges titlebars of minimized MDI child windows along the bottom of the parent window.
Cascade	Cascades all MDI child windows within the parent window.
TileHorizontal	Horizontally tiles all MDI child windows within the parent window.
TileVertical	Vertically tiles all MDI child windows within the parent window.

To demonstrate these different types of window layout, add four submenu items to the parent Form's Window menu item: Arrange Icons, Cascade, Tile Horizontal, and Tile Vertical. Double-click on each submenu item, bringing up the event handler skeleton for that item. Then add the appropriate line of code shown in either Example 5-15 (for C#) or Example 5-16 (for VB.NET).

Example 5-15. LayoutMdi method in C#

```
this.LayoutMdi(System.Windows.Forms.MdiLayout.ArrangeIcons);
this.LayoutMdi(System.Windows.Forms.MdiLayout.Cascade);
this.LayoutMdi(System.Windows.Forms.MdiLayout.TileHorizontal);
this.LayoutMdi(System.Windows.Forms.MdiLayout.TileVertical);
```

Example 5-16. LayoutMdi method in VB.NET

```
me.LayoutMdi(System.Windows.Forms.MdiLayout.ArrangeIcons)
me.LayoutMdi(System.Windows.Forms.MdiLayout.Cascade)
me.LayoutMdi(System.Windows.Forms.MdiLayout.TileHorizontal)
me.LayoutMdi(System.Windows.Forms.MdiLayout.TileVertical)
```

When you run the program and open several child windows, you will see the expected behavior from these menu items.

Tabbed interface

The tabbed interface borrows its metaphor from the divider tabs used in a loose-leaf binder. It provides a means of having multiple windows readily accessible to the user without taking up a lot of screen real estate. Only the top-most window is visible, but tabs identifying all the underlying windows are visible at all times.

Tabbed interfaces have become common in recent years, since they combine many of the best features of SDI and MDI interfaces: the screen is not cluttered with multiple windows and the nonvisible windows are not totally hidden, as with MDI programs, yet multiple windows are readily available, unlike SDI programs.

Perhaps the program that best exhibits a tabbed interface most familiar to .NET developers is Visual Studio .NET. Looking back at Figure 5-13, you'll see two tabs above the design window, labeled Start Page and Form1.cs [Design]. Clicking on any of those tabs brings that window to the top. It is possible to have many tabs across the top. If there are too many to fit in the available space, navigation arrows allow you to scroll back and forth amongst the tabs.

The .NET Framework provides the Windows Forms TabControl control to implement the tabbed interface. The TabControl contains a collection of TabPage objects. Various properties let you control the behavior and appearance of those tab pages.

The TabControl is covered thoroughly in Chapter 13.

Explorer style

The Explorer style interface is named for Windows Explorer, the file and directory management tool included with all versions of Windows since Win95, as shown in Figure 5-17.

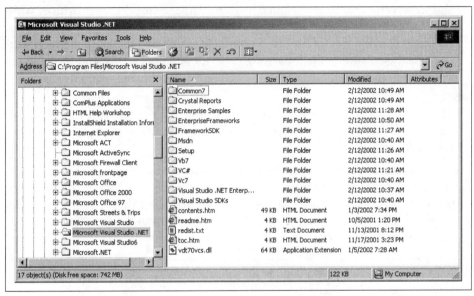

Figure 5-17. Windows Explorer

An Explorer interface is characterized by a two pane window. The left pane displays a list of items graphically and hierarchically. The right pane displays details relevant to the item selected on the left. In the case of Windows Explorer, the items in both panes consist of files and directories. Some icons are associated with each item to provide a visual representation of the item's classification. For example, most directories have the folder icon (📁), the currently selected directory has the open folder icon (📂), and each file with a different extension has its own icon.

Like SDI and MDI windows, an Explorer style window may also have menus, toolbars, and a status bar.

The Explorer interface is minimally constructed from three controls. These controls will be described in detail in Chapter 14. In brief, each Explorer-style window has the features described next.

TreeView

    Occupies the left pane of Windows Explorer. Displays hierarchical data as a series of labeled items called *nodes*. Each node may contain other nodes, called *child nodes*, in which case it is the *parent node* to its child nodes. The nodes are of type *TreeNode* and contained within the *Nodes* collection. The .NET Framework provides properties, methods, and events for managing and manipulating TreeViews and users' interactions with them.

ListView

    Occupies the right pane of Windows Explorer. It is similar to the TreeView, except that it displays a single list of items rather than a hierarchical view. The list items can either be represented by icons (large or small) or text (with or without an icon). Each item can have *subitems*, which are displayed in columns, either with or without a header. As with the TreeView, there are many properties, methods, and events for setting behavior and appearance and for handling events.

Splitter

    The Splitter is an unobtrusive little control used to separate two other controls docked to the Splitter, allowing user to set the relative size of the two docked controls easily.

The next example demonstrates the creation of a simple Explorer style interface, using a hierarchy of motor vehicles. In this example, the TreeView in the left pane displays the different categories of vehicles. Drilling down through the nodes will eventually display a list of specific models in the ListView in the right pane. The finished application looks something like that shown in Figure 5-18.

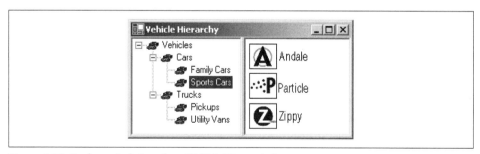

Figure 5-18. Explorer-Style Interface (Vehicle Hierarchy)

Open a new Windows application in Visual Studio .NET using the language of your choice. Name it VehicleHierarchy.

Drag a TreeView control onto the form. Set its Dock property to Left. Next, drag a Splitter control on to the form. It will glom (a technical term meaning to stick on the side of something, as in "my daughter gloms onto my leg when we enter a room full of people.") onto the right edge of the TreeView control.

Drag a ListView control onto the form. Set its Dock property to Fill so that it fills the remaining space on the form between the Splitter and the right edge of the form. Also, change its View property from LargeIcon to List.

While you are at it, change the Text property of the form to Vehicle Hierarchy. At this point, the Visual Studio .NET design will look like Figure 5-19. (Note that the project shown in Figure 5-19 is actually named vbVehicleHierarchy, distinguishing it from csVehicleHierarchy.)

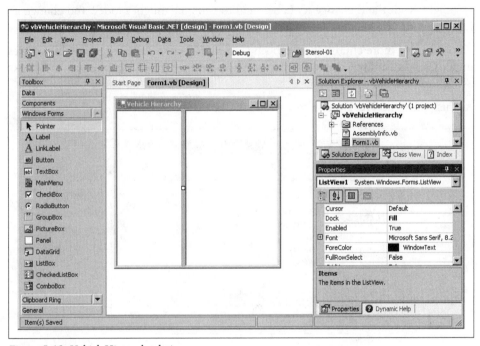

Figure 5-19. VehicleHierarchy design

The next step is to populate the Nodes collection of the TreeView. There are several ways to do this. In many applications, a TreeView or a ListView will be populated dynamically from a database. That technique will be covered fully in Chapter 19.

For this example, select the TreeView control in design view, and then use the Properties window to populate the Nodes collection. The Nodes property in the Properties window has a build button next to it. Click that build button to bring up the Tree-Node Editor dialog box.

 Using this technique, you'll hit the bizarre scrollbar bug if you run the application in Windows XP with themes enabled. If you populate the Nodes collection before the control handle is created, an extraneous (and misthemed) scrollbar that does nothing appears at the bottom of the TreeView. To avoid the problem, populate the Nodes collection in the Form Load event handler.

Use the Add Root button to add all the root-level nodes. In this example, there is only a single root-level node, Vehicles. Click the Add Root button. The Label field will show the default node name, Node0. Replace it with Vehicles.

The Add Child and Delete buttons will now become enabled. With the Vehicles node highlighted, click the Add Child button. A child node named Node1 will appear beneath Vehicles. Highlight Vehicles again, and click the Add Child button again to create another child node named Node2.

Highlight Node1 and change its Label field to Cars. Highlight Node2 and change its Label field to Trucks.

Now add two more child nodes to both Cars and Trucks. Label the two child nodes under Cars as Family Cars and Sports Cars. Label the two child nodes under Trucks as Pickups and Utility Vans.

At this point, the TreeNode editor will look like Figure 5-20.

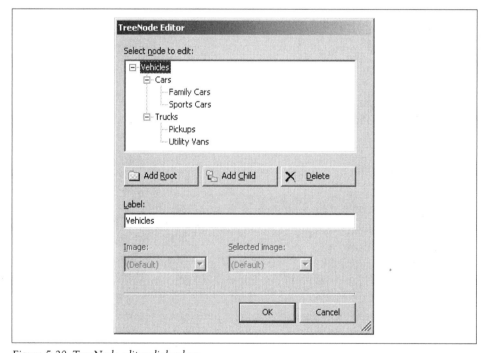

Figure 5-20. TreeNode editor dialog box

You will notice that the finished application shown in Figure 5-18 included small images with each item in the TreeView and the ListView. These images are contained in an ImageList component. A form can have more than one ImageList component, but all the images used in a single TreeView or ListView must come from the same ImageList. For this example, both TreeView and ListView will use the same ImageList. (Chapter 7 will cover the ImageList component in detail.)

To add the ImageList, drag an ImageList control from the Toolbox onto the form. The ImageList component, like all components, will not appear on the form itself, but at the bottom of the Design window, as shown in the screenshot in Figure 5-21.

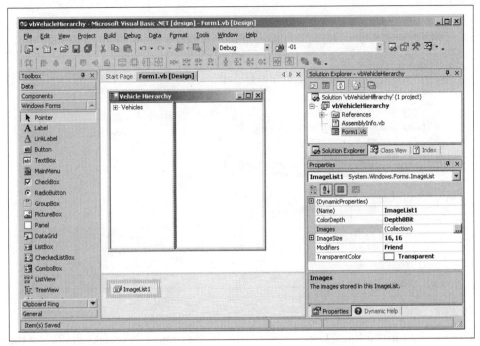

Figure 5-21. ImageList on form

Referring to the Properties window for the ImageList shown in Figure 5-21, you can see that the Images property contains a collection of images. Click on the build button (...) for the Images collection to get the Image Collection Editor dialog box. The Add button will allow you to add images to the ImageList. You can browse to the location of your image files and add them to the Image collection.

The images can be in any of many different bitmap formats (bmp, gif, jpg, jpeg, png, ico). A large number of useful image files are included with Visual Studio .NET, including most of the standard icons and bitmaps from the Windows and Office UI, plus many others of general interest. They can be found, by default, in *C:\Program Files\Microsoft Visual Studio .NET 2003\Common7\Graphics*.

In this example, *cars.ico* will be the generic vehicle icon. To use this image, click on the Add button and browse to the *C:\Program Files\Microsoft Visual Studio .NET 2003\ Common7\Graphics\icons\industry* directory. Select *cars.ico*. It will be added to the collection with an index of zero. The zero-based index identifies the position of the entry in the collection. Once the image is added to the collection, its source file-name is lost.

Images for the manufacturer and model items were clipped from each manufacturer's web site (using an image-editing software package), saved as *.gif* files, and added to the collection. When all the images are added, the dialog box will look like Figure 5-22.

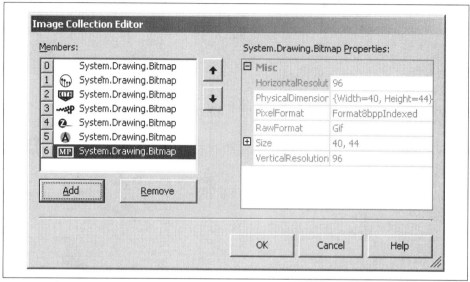

Figure 5-22. Image Collection Editor dialog box

Once you set up an ImageList, other controls in the project can refer to it. Select the TreeView control. There will be an entry with a drop-down for ImageList in the Properties window, as shown in Figure 5-23.

Select the previously created and populated ImageList1. (If the project had more than a single ImageList, all would be listed.) As soon as the ImageList property is assigned, all nodes in the TreeView in Design view will show the image at Index 0.

To assign specific, nondefault images to each item, go to the Nodes property of the TreeView and open the TreeNode Editor, as shown in Figure 5-20. Now, however, as you drill down and select the individual nodes, the Image and Selected Image drop-downs will be enabled. Each will expose all the images contained in the selected ImageList. The Image drop-down selects the image to be used for normal display of the item, and the Selected Image drop-down selects the image to be used when the item is selected. For this example, leave the default image for all the items in the TreeView.

When the TreeView is set, you can add code that will dynamically populate the List-View at runtime, in response to the user's selections. Put this code in the event handler for the TreeView AfterSelect event. This event fires after a tree node has been selected. It is the default event for the control, so all you have to do is double-click on the control and the code skeleton will be created for you.

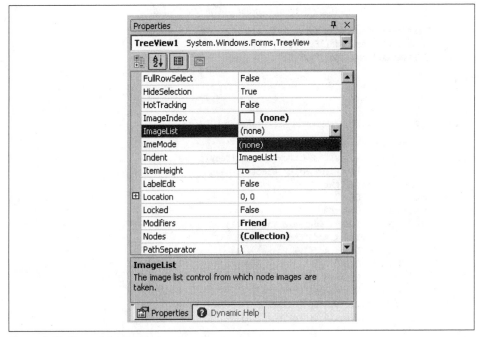

Figure 5-23. ImageList property

Before coding to populate the ListView, set the SmallImageList property of the List-View control to ImageList1, the same ImageList used for the TreeView. This will let you add those images programmatically. (LargeImageList and StateImageList properties will be covered in Chapter 7.)

Double-click on the TreeView control. The code window will open with a code skeleton in place for the AfterSelect event. The cursor will also be properly positioned and ready for typing. Enter the code highlighted in Example 5-17 (for C#) or in Example 5-18 (for VB.NET).

Example 5-17. TreeView AfterSelect event handler in C#

```
private void treeView1_AfterSelect(object sender,
                    System.Windows.Forms.TreeViewEventArgs e)
{
    switch (e.Node.Text)
    {
        case "Family Cars":
            listView1.Clear( );
            listView1.Items.Add("Ford Taurus",3);
            listView1.Items.Add("Chevy Impala", 4);
            listView1.Items.Add("VW Passat", 6);
            break;

        case "Sports Cars":
            listView1.Clear( );
```

Example 5-17. TreeView AfterSelect event handler in C# (continued)

```csharp
            listView1.Items.Add("Corvette", 1);
            listView1.Items.Add("Ferrari", 2);
            listView1.Items.Add("Porsche", 5);
            break;
    }
}
```

Example 5-18. TreeView AfterSelect event handler in VB.NET

```vb
Private Sub TreeView1_AfterSelect(ByVal sender As System.Object, _
            ByVal e As System.Windows.Forms.TreeViewEventArgs) _
            Handles TreeView1.AfterSelect
    select case e.Node.Text
        case "Family Cars"
            listView1.Clear( )
            listView1.Items.Add("Ford Taurus",3)
            listView1.Items.Add("Chevy Impala", 4)
            listView1.Items.Add("VW Passat", 6)
        case "Sports Cars"
            listView1.Clear( )
            listView1.Items.Add("Corvette", 1)
            listView1.Items.Add("Ferrari", 2)
            listView1.Items.Add("Porsche", 5)
    end select
End Sub
```

Chapter 14 will discuss the AfterSelect event and the TreeView and ListView controls in more detail. For now, note that the event argument is of type TreeViewEventArgs. One of the TreeViewEventArgs properties is Node, which contains the tree node that was selected.

A switch (select) case block is used to test the selected node and branch accordingly. In this trivial example, all items are hardcoded using the Add method of the ListViewItemCollection class, after the ListView is first cleared. In a real application, a ListView would often be populated from a data store, such as an XML file or a relational database. (Populating TreeViews and ListViews from a data store will be covered in Chapter 19.)

The Add method of the ListViewItemCollection class is overloaded; the number and type of arguments determine exactly what the method will do. In this example, the first argument is the item to be added to the collection. The second argument is the index into the ImageList associated with this ListView control's SmallImageList property.

If this application is run now, it will look like Figure 5-18. However, nothing will happen if you click on or otherwise select any of the items in the ListView. Many applications will respond to a user clicking on one of the items in the ListView. Do *not* double click on the ListView control. Doing so would insert a code skeleton for the SelectedIndexChanged event, which is the default event for this control. Instead, add a code skeleton for the ItemActivate event of the ListView control. In C#, click on the Events icon in the Property window. In VB.NET, go to the code window, select the control from the left drop-down at the top of the window and the ItemActivate event from the right drop-down. (For more detail on creating event handlers, see Chapter 4.) Then enter the highlighted code shown in Example 5-19 for C# or in Example 5-20 for VB.NET.

Example 5-19. Click event handler and helper method in C#

```
private void listView1_ItemActivate(object sender,
                                    System.EventArgs e)
{
   String strItem = listView1.FocusedItem.Text;
   DisplayCar(strItem);
}

private void DisplayCar(string strCar)
{
   Form frmCar = new Form( );
   frmCar.Text = strCar;

   this.Hide( );
   frmCar.ShowDialog( );
   this.Show( );
}
```

Example 5-20. Click event handler and helper method in VB.NET

```
Private Sub ListView1_ ItemActivate (ByVal sender As Object, _
                                     ByVal e As System.EventArgs) _
                                     Handles ListView1.Click
   dim strItem as String = listView1.FocusedItem.Text
   DisplayCar(strItem)
End Sub

private sub DisplayCar(strCar as String)
   dim frmCar as Form = new Form( )
   frmCar.Text = strCar

   me.Hide( )
   frmCar.ShowDialog( )
   me.Show( )
End Sub
```

The ItemActivate event is raised whenever an item in the ListView is activated. The default way to activate an item at runtime is to either double-click on it or press Enter when the item (or items) is selected. By changing the ListView Activation property from Standard to either OneClick or TwoClick, you can change the activation technique.

- OneClick activates an item as soon as it is clicked. This property value also causes the item to change color as the mouse passes over it.

- TwoClick activates an item when it is clicked twice (not to be confused with double-clicking, in which the two clicks must occur within a short period of time). The first click selects the item, and the second click activates the item. The two clicks can be widely separated in time.

The ItemActivate event handler does not use the event argument at all here. Instead, it gets the Text property of the item that currently has focus using the FocusedItem property of the ListView control, and assigns it to strItem, a string variable. This string variable is passed as an argument to a helper method called DisplayCar, which does the work.

In this example, the "work" consists of creating a new form, setting its Text property to be the same as the item that was clicked, hiding the current form, and displaying the new form modally by using the ShowDialog method of the Form class.

 As discussed in the next chapter on dialog boxes, a modal form is one in which the program flow is halted until the form is dismissed in some manner. Most, but not all, dialog boxes are modal. In contrast, most forms are modeless. With them, the user can move from window to window without first dismissing the previous form. (As you will see in the next chapter, with the exception of the common dialog boxes provided by the Framework, there really is no technical distinction between a form and a dialog box.)

Now when the application is run and the user selects one of the cars in the ListView control, a form specifically for that car is displayed. When the user closes that form by clicking on the Close button (X) in the upper right corner, the original form returns to visibility.

Other approaches could have been used to select items from the ListView. You could have handled either the Click or DoubleClick events, which work well as long as the user selects the list item with a mouseclick. However, they ignore keyboard navigation and activation. Alternatively, you can handle the SelectedIndexChanged event. The problem is that it requires special processing to prevent the event from being processed twice for every change, and it still does not yield the smooth operation expected of an Explorer interface.

This is a very simple example, but it shows the fundamental features of the Explorer interface. In a real application, TreeView and ListView controls might be populated from a database or other data store, and the response to selections might be to display a complex form or start a train of processing.

You can create a knock off of the Windows Explorer similarly, using the same basic controls. This will be demonstrated in Chapter 14, where TreeView, ListView, and Splitter controls are covered in detail.

Input

The primary means of input to a Windows Forms application is either through the mouse or the keyboard. Many other input devices (e.g., speech or bar code readers) use a device driver that translates the input into keyboard equivalents, so that the OS thinks the input is coming from a keyboard.

Mouse input

As a developer, you do not have to do anything for your Windows Forms application to have full-mouse functionality; it is automatically provided by the Control class. However, there are a full range of Mouse events and properties exposed that you can handle or set, respectively, to customize or extend the user's interaction with the mouse. This is covered fully in Chapter 8.

Keyboard input

Windows handles all the plumbing that allows your keyboard to talk to your system. A keyboard device drive mediates between Windows and the physical hardware. As with all hardware device drivers, this software layer abstracts the nitty-gritty details required for a specific hardware device to communicate with a broadly available operating system, providing the OS with a standard interface to deal with.

The KeyEvents example from Chapter 4, demonstrates how to read and process keyboard input in a Windows Forms application. Figure 5-24 shows a screenshot of that application.

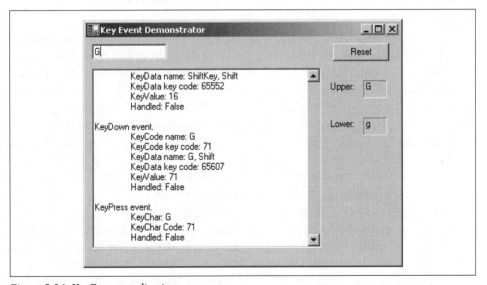

Figure 5-24. KeyEvents application

Each key on a keyboard has unique value assigned to it called a *scan code*. This code is converted by the keyboard device driver into a *virtual-key code*. The virtual-key codes, which identifies the purpose of the key, are listed in as decimal key codes.

An event is raised when the key is pressed down, called the *KeyDown* event, and again when the key is released, called the *KeyUp* event. Neither event is explicitly aware of any other keys being pressed in combination, such as for a Shifted character, or the Alt or Ctrl key being pressed in conjunction with another key. This information is conveyed in the *KeyPress* event as the KeyChar property of KeyPressEventArgs event argument. In Figure 5-24, the user entered an uppercase G, so the KeyPress KeyChar value is G (as is also, confusingly, the KeyDown KeyCode property of the KeyEventArgs event argument). If the user had instead pressed a lowercase g, then the KeyUp and KeyDown event data would have been the same as for the uppercase letter (except there would be no events for a Shift key that was not pressed, of course), but the KeyPress KeyChar value would be a lowercase g.

For a complete discussion of keyboard events, see Chapter 4.

Keyboard shortcuts

Most people would agree that the mouse is a wonderful thing, making modern graphical user interfaces both possible and easy to navigate. Still, many users are loathe to remove a hand from the keyboard any more than is absolutely necessary, since it slows down typing and disturbs the flow of thought and action.

Keyboard shortcuts help you interact with menus without the mouse. There are two different ways to add keyboard equivalents to button or menu selection:

Shortcut Keys
> Special keys or key combinations that may be pressed to invoke a menu item. These keys are typically listed on a menu to the right of the menu item. In the Edit menu from Microsoft Word, shown in Figure 5-25, shortcut keys include Ctrl+Z, Ctrl+V, and Del.

Access Keys
> Also known as keyboard accelerators, these keys allow menu and control navigation when pressed in combination with the Alt key. They are indicated by an underscored letter in a menu item or a control label. In the Edit menu from Microsoft Word, shown in Figure 5-25, access keys include the U in Undo Typing, the R in Repeat Typing, and the S in Paste Special.
>
> The .NET Framework makes it very easy to add access keys to menu items and controls—simply add an ampersand (&) in front of the character in the Text property of the menu item or control that is to be the access letter. For example, suppose you have a button with the Text property set to "Continue." Changing the Text property to "&Continue" will make the button accessible from the keyboard when Alt-C is pressed.

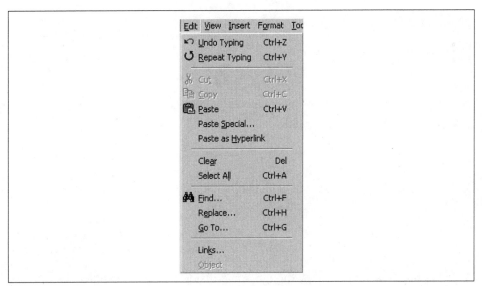

Figure 5-25. Microsoft Word Edit menu

Menus, shortcut keys, and keyboard equivalents are detailed in Chapter 18.

CHAPTER 6
Dialog Boxes

How can I miss you when you won't go away?
—Dan Hicks, "Original Recordings"

A dialog box is a simple form, though some dialog boxes are simpler than others. Typically, a dialog box either displays a message or gathers a bit of information. In either case, the dialog box "pops up" in the middle of your application to serve a specific targeted purpose.

A dialog box is distinguished from a form primarily by appearance (it is typically smaller and simpler than a full-form window) and function (it typically does only one thing), but the truth is there is no hard and fast distinction between a dialog box and a form. Both derive from the Form class.

That said, most dialog boxes have the following traits. They:

- Cannot be resized (although this is changing, thankfully, since many dialog boxes benefit greatly from being resizable)
- Do not appear in the Windows taskbar
- Do not have a control menu in the upper-left corner
- Do not have maximize or minimize buttons in the upper right corner
- Exhibit modal behavior

Modal Versus Modeless

Picture an application comprised of several forms, where one form calls another, which may call yet another. Many MDI applications work this way. Generally speaking, you may keep all the forms open, moving among them as much as you'd like. This is called *modeless* behavior.

In contrast, consider the behavior of most dialog boxes in most applications. A user action causes a dialog box to be displayed, generally for the purpose of presenting information to or gathering input from the user. In the first case, the program cannot proceed until it knows that the information was presented to and acknowledged by the user. In the latter case, the program cannot proceed until either the requisite input has been gathered from the user or the user cancels the dialog. In either case, the program cannot proceed until the user has dismissed the dialog box. This is known as *modal* behavior.

Not all dialog boxes are modal. Common examples of modeless dialog boxes are those found in many word processors and text editors for finding text. As you search for text, the dialog box remains open and you can move freely between the dialog box and the document it is searching.

Even if a modal form or dialog box is opened, the user can still switch focus to other applications. Modal dialog boxes prevent the user from moving around in the current application—i.e., the application that opened the dialog box, using either mouse or keyboard input—but do not prevent the user from working in other applications.

A class of dialog boxes known as *system modal* prohibits moving to another application. These dialog boxes are generally used when Windows has a serious problem that must be addressed before any other activity can occur. The .NET Framework does not inherently support the creation of system modal dialog boxes.

Both forms and dialog boxes can be either modal or modeless, depending on how you invoke them. To make them modeless, call Show(); to make them modal, call ShowDialog().

The following lines of code open a modal dialog:

```
Form frm = new Form( );
frm.ShowDialog( );
```

By changing the method call to Show (rather than ShowDialog), you invoke the same form, but modeless:

```
Form frm = new Form( );
frm.Show ( );
```

Good UI design suggests that you should use modal dialogs only when absolutely necessary.

Form Properties

Every form and dialog box is derived from the Form class, which itself is derived from the Control class. Therefore, they share the approximately 100 properties of the Control and Form base classes. Table 5-1 listed many of the most commonly used form properties.

While all of the form properties can be used with either dialog boxes or normal forms, either modal or modeless, several properties are often used to create the "dialog box" look and otherwise control the appearance and behavior of the form. They include those shown in Table 6-1, extracted from Table 5-1 in Chapter 5.

Table 6-1. Form properties often used with dialog boxes

Property	Type	Description
AcceptButton	IButtonControl	Gets or sets the button on a form that is clicked when the user presses Enter, irrespective of which control actually has focus.
BackColor	Color	Gets or sets the background color.
CancelButton	IButtonControl	Gets or sets the button on a form that is clicked when the user presses Escape, irrespective of which control actually has focus.
ControlBox	Boolean	Gets or sets a value indicating if the system menu can be displayed and if the Close button (X) is displayed on the right end of the titlebar. The system menu is exposed by clicking on the icon in the titlebar if the Icon property is set, or by right-clicking on the titlebar if the Icon property is not set. Default is true.
DialogResult	DialogResult	Gets or sets the return value from a form or dialog box displayed modally. Legal values are members of the DialogResult enumeration. This property is covered in detail in the earlier section "DialogResult."
FormBorderStyle	FormBorderStyle	Gets or sets the border style. In addition to appearance, the FormBorderStyle dictates whether or not the form will be resizable. The possible values of the FormBorderStyle enumeration are listed in Table 6-2.
Icon	Icon	Gets or sets the icon for the form. The icon is displayed in the control box of the form (if the ControlBox property is set to true) and in the taskbar (if the ShowInTaskbar property is set to true).
MaximizeBox	Boolean	Gets or sets a value indicating if a maximize button will be displayed in the upper-right corner of the form on the titlebar. Default is true. If true, FormBorderStyle must be either FixedSingle, Sizable, Fixed3D, or FixedDialog. When the form is maximized, the maximize button automatically becomes a restore button.
MinimizeBox	Boolean	Gets or sets a value indicating if a minimize button will be displayed in the upper-right corner of the form on the titlebar. Default is true. If true, FormBorderStyle must be either FixedSingle, Sizable, Fixed3D, or FixedDialog.
ShowInTaskBar	Boolean	Gets or sets a value indicating if the form Text property is displayed in the Windows taskbar. Default is true.
Size	Size	Gets or sets both the height and width of the form.
StartPosition	FormStartPosition	Gets or sets the starting position of the form. Legal values of the FormStartPosition enumeration are listed in Table 6-3.
TopMost	Boolean	Gets or sets value indicating the form is displayed on top all the other forms, even if it is not the active form. Typically used for modeless dialog boxes, which should always be visible.

Table 6-2. FormBorderStyle enumeration values

Value	Description
Fixed3D	Nonresizable, 3-D border.
FixedDialog	Nonresizable, dialog-style border
FixedSingle	Nonresizable, single line border
FixedToolWindow	Nonresizable, tool window border
None	No border
Sizable	Default value. Standard resizable border
SizableToolWindow	Resizable, tool window border

Table 6-3. FormStartPosition enumeration values

Value	Description
CenterParent	Center form within parent form
CenterScreen	Center form within current display
Manual	Location and size of form dictates its starting position
WindowsDefaultBounds	Form at Windows default location with bounds determined by Windows default
WindowsDefaultLocation	Form at Windows default location with dimensions specified in form's constructor

The following example will demonstrate the creation of a dialog box. This example will consist of a very simple form with only a single button. Clicking the button will open a modal dialog box. The dialog box is a separate form in the project, although many of its properties are set programmatically by the parent form.

> Examples 5-19 and 5-20 in Chapter 5 demonstrated the creation of a modal form dynamically, entirely in code, and based on a user action. This next example creates the basic form to be used as the dialog box in Visual Studio .NET. It then modifies its properties dynamically. Either technique works; the technique you use depends on the requirements of the application.

Create a new project in Visual Studio .NET called DialogDemo.

> In this and all future examples, unless stated otherwise, you are free to use VB.NET or C#. Your choice is entirely a matter of personal preference.

Drag a button onto the form, change the Text property of the button to Create Dialog Box, and resize the button to fit the text. Rename the button to btnCreate.

Add a second form to the project to serve as the dialog box. To do so, either select the menu item Project → Add Windows Form... or right-click on the project name in the Solution Explorer and select Add → Add Windows Form.... When the Add New

Item dialog box comes up, change the default form name to *dlg.cs* or *dlg.vb*, depending on your language. Change the (Name) property of the form to DlgTest.

The new form will show up in the Solution Explorer, along with the original *Form1.cs* or *Form1.vb*. Your screen should look something like Figure 6-1. (Note that this project was actually named vbDialogDemo to distinguish it from the C# version.)

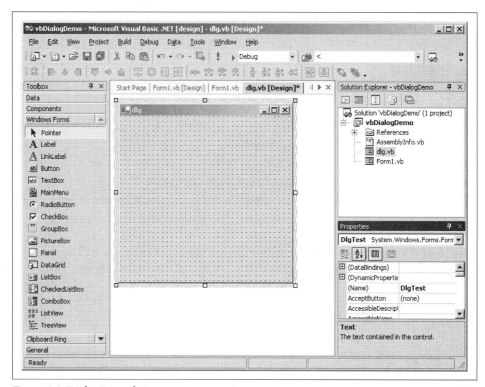

Figure 6-1. DialogDemo design

Click on the Form1.vb[Design] (or Form1.cs[Design]) tab at the top of the design window, and then double-click on the button created previously. This will open a code skeleton for the Click event handler in the code window. The Click event is the default event for a Button control. Enter the highlighted code shown in Example 6-1 (for C#) or in Example 6-2 (for VB.NET).

Example 6-1. Click event handler to show dialog box in C#

```
private void btnCreate_Click(object sender, System.EventArgs e)
{
    Form dlg = new DlgTest();
    dlg.Text = "Dialog Test";
    dlg.FormBorderStyle = FormBorderStyle.FixedDialog;
    dlg.BackColor = Color.Azure;
    dlg.ControlBox = true;
```

Example 6-1. Click event handler to show dialog box in C# (continued)

```csharp
        dlg.MaximizeBox = false;
        dlg.MinimizeBox = false;
        dlg.ShowInTaskbar = false;
        dlg.Icon = new Icon(typeof(csDialogDemo.Form1),"INFO.ICO");
        dlg.Size = new Size(300,300);
        dlg.StartPosition = FormStartPosition.CenterScreen;
        dlg.ShowDialog( );
}
```

Example 6-2. Click event handler to show dialog box in VB.NET

```vbnet
Private Sub btnCreate_Click(ByVal sender As System.Object, _
                            ByVal e As System.EventArgs) _
                            Handles btnCreate.Click
    dim dlg as New DlgTest
    dlg.Text = "Dialog Test"
    dlg.FormBorderStyle = FormBorderStyle.FixedDialog
    dlg.BackColor = Color.Azure
    dlg.ControlBox = true
    dlg.MaximizeBox = false
    dlg.MinimizeBox = false
    dlg.ShowInTaskbar = false
    dim f as New Form1( )
    dlg.Icon = new Icon(f.GetType( ),"INFO.ICO")
    dlg.Size = new Size(300,300)
    dlg.StartPosition = FormStartPosition.CenterScreen
    dlg.ShowDialog( )
End Sub
```

 The *info.ico* icon file used in this example can be found, by default, in *c:\Program Files\Microsoft Visual Studio .NET\Common7\Graphics\ icons\Computer*. You will find many of the standard visual elements used by Windows in this Graphics directory.

Interestingly, *info.icon* displays with unexpected colors in Windows Forms. An alternative file in the same directory, *msgbox04.ico*, displays the correct colors, but may be lost in the blue titlebar of the form.

Before the project will run with this code, the icon file referred to when setting the Icon property needs to be properly located. You could hardwire in a location with a line such as the following:

```vbnet
    dlg.Icon = new Icon("c:\icons\info.ico")
```

but that raises obvious problems for deployment. A slightly better option would be to include the icon file in the same directory as the executable, in which case the following line of code would work:

```vbnet
    dlg.Icon = new Icon("info.ico")
```

Note that in this case, when developing in Visual Studio .NET, the icon file must be included in the proper output directory, typically the *bin\debug* directory located under the project directory when working in C#, or the *bin* directory when working in VB.NET.

In either case, this would require installing the actual icon file as part of the deployment. Instead, use the code shown in Example 6-1 or Example 6-2, which presumes that the icon file is included as an embedded resource in the assembly.

To embed the icon file, add it to the project by right-clicking on the project in the Solution Explorer, selecting Add → Add Existing Item, and navigating to the icon file. This will add a copy of the file to the project directory. Then select the newly added icon file in the Solution Explorer, go to the Properties window, and change the Build action for the file to Embedded Resource, as shown in Figure 6-2. This will cause the icon file to be included automatically in the compiled assembly, eliminating the need for a separate file in the deployment. (All issues concerning deployment of applications are covered in Chapter 22.)

The filenames used in the Icon constructors above are not case sensitive, but the filename used in the Icon constructors used in Example 6-1 and Example 6-2 must match the case of the filename as listed in Windows Explorer. Go figure.

Running the application and clicking on the button will bring up the dialog box shown on top of the parent form in Figure 6-3.

The first line of code in the Click event handler in Figure 6-1 or Figure 6-3 instantiates a new form of type dlgTest, which is the name you gave the form created previously in Visual Studio .NET. The last line of code in the method shows the form modally, using the ShowDialog method. All the lines in between set various properties to control the appearance and behavior of the dialog box. Each property is described in Table 6-1.

DialogResult

While many dialog boxes have the ControlBox, MaximizeBox, MinimizeBox, and ShowInTaskBar properties set to false, the previous example left ControlBox set to the default value of true. The Control box allows the user to close the dialog by clicking on the X in the upper-righthand corner. If the ControlBox is suppressed in a modal dialog box that has no other controls that close the form, then there is no obvious way for the user to close the dialog or end the application, short of killing the application in Task Manager. (The user can press Alt+F4 to close any form or dialog box, or press Escape to close a modal dialog. The developer can always stop debugging.)

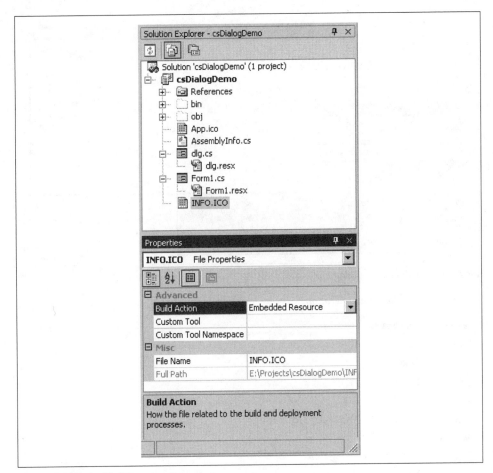

Figure 6-2. Embedded Resource in project

Dialog boxes typically have one or more buttons for accepting the user's interaction and/or terminating itself. These buttons will often be assigned the purpose of causing the dialog box to send a standard message, such as OK, Cancel, Yes, or No. At other times, there may be a custom Text property on the button, such as Update Database. In any case, the Click event for the button can be handled, code can be executed, and a result can be sent to the parent form.

A property of every modal form or dialog called *DialogResult* allows you to set or retrieve a return value when it is closed. The property can be set programmatically at runtime. The valid values of the DialogResult property are members of the Dialog-Result enumeration, detailed in Table 6-4. The value is set programmatically, typically by a button control on the form. This will also have the effect of closing the modal form, unless it is set to None, in which case the form will continue to run.

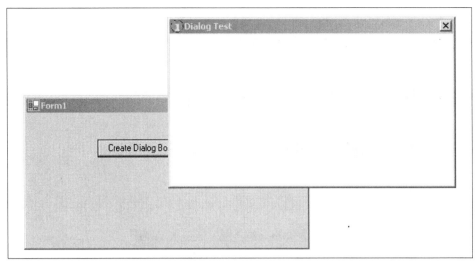

Figure 6-3. DialogDemo dialog box

Table 6-4. DialogResult enumeration

Value	Return value
Abort	Abort
Cancel	Cancel
Ignore	Ignore
No	No
None	Returns nothing. Modal dialog is not terminated.
OK	OK
Retry	Retry
Yes	Yes

To demonstrate terminating a dialog box and passing the return value to the parent form, add some controls and code to the example shown previously. Add a Label control named lblReturn to the parent form. Set its Text property to blank. Go to the code editing window for the parent form and add the highlighted line of code in Example 6-3 (C#) or Example 6-4 (VB.NET) to the event handlers shown previously in Example 6-1 and Example 6-2, respectively.

Example 6-3. Returning DialogResult in C#

```
private void btnCreate_Click(object sender, System.EventArgs e)
{
    Form dlg = new dlgTest( );
    dlg.Text = "Dialog Test";
    dlg.FormBorderStyle=FormBorderStyle.FixedDialog;
    dlg.BackColor = System.Drawing.Color.Azure;
    dlg.ControlBox = true;
```

Example 6-3. Returning DialogResult in C# (continued)

```
dlg.MaximizeBox = false;
dlg.MinimizeBox = false;
dlg.ShowInTaskbar = false;
dlg.Icon = new Icon("info.ico");
dlg.Size = new Size(100,50);
dlg.StartPosition = FormStartPosition.CenterScreen;
dlg.ShowDialog();

// Show the return value
lblReturn.Text = dlg.DialogResult.ToString();
}
```

Example 6-4. Returning DialogResult in VB.NET

```
Private Sub btnCreate_Click(ByVal sender As System.Object, _
                            ByVal e As System.EventArgs) _
                            Handles btnCreate.Click
    dim dlg as New dlgTest
    dlg.Text = "Dialog Test"
    dlg.FormBorderStyle=FormBorderStyle.FixedDialog
    dlg.BackColor = System.Drawing.Color.Azure
    dlg.ControlBox = true
    dlg.MaximizeBox = false
    dlg.MinimizeBox = false
    dlg.ShowInTaskbar = false
    dlg.Icon = new Icon("info.ico")
    dlg.Size = new Size(100,50)
    dlg.StartPosition = FormStartPosition.CenterScreen
    dlg.ShowDialog()

    ' Show the return value
    lblReturn.Text = dlg.DialogResult.ToString()
End Sub
```

As you have seen before, the ShowDialog method displays the dialog box modally. When the dialog box is terminated, it is no longer visible on the screen, but the form object dlg still exists. This allows you to retrieve the DialogResult property from the dialog box.

Move to the design window for the dialog box. Add two buttons, named btnOK and btnCancel. Set their Text properties to Do It! and Cancel, respectively.

Double-click on the Do It! button. This will bring the cursor to a code skeleton for the Button Click event handler. Enter the appropriate line of code:

```
DialogResult = DialogResult.OK;
```

```
DialogResult = DialogResult.OK
```

Double-click on the Cancel button and add the appropriate line:

C#

```
DialogResult = DialogResult.Cancel;
```

VB

```
DialogResult = DialogResult.Cancel
```

When this project is now run, you will see something similar to Figure 6-4.

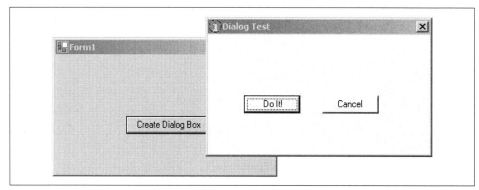

Figure 6-4. Dialog box with buttons

Clicking on the Do It! button will yield the result shown in Figure 6-5.

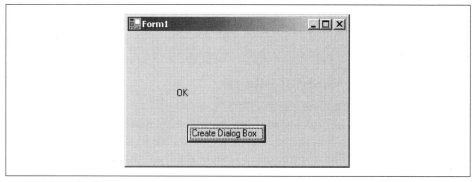

Figure 6-5. Dialog box return value

Clicking on the Cancel button will display Cancel on the parent form. Clicking on the Close button (X) in the upper-right corner of the dialog box, or selecting Close from the system menu exposed by clicking on the icon in the titlebar, or pressing Alt+F4 will return DialogResult.Cancel.

You can combine the call to the ShowDialog method with a test of the DialogResult property. For example, you can combine a call to ShowDialog with a switch block in C#:

C#

```
switch (dlg.ShowDialog())
{
    case DialogResult.Abort:
```

```
            lblReturn.Text = "Abort, Abort";
            break;
        case DialogResult.Cancel:
            lblReturn.Text = "You have cancelled.";
            break;
        case DialogResult.OK:
            lblReturn.Text = "I'm OK, You're OK";
            break;
        default:
            lblReturn.Text = "Whatever...";
            break;
    }
```

or a select case block in VB.NET:

```
    select case dlg.ShowDialog( )
        case DialogResult.Abort
            lblReturn.Text = "Abort, Abort"
        case DialogResult.Cancel
            lblReturn.Text = "You have cancelled."
        case DialogResult.OK
            lblReturn.Text = "I'm OK, You're OK"
        case else
            lblReturn.Text = "Whatever..."
    end select
```

Termination Buttons

Since many dialog boxes are terminated by clicking on a button, the .NET Framework makes this process even easier than shown in the previous examples.

The Button control implements the IButtonControl interface, which provides a DialogResult property. You can assign any valid DialogResult value to any button. The value of this DialogResult property must be one of the members of the same DialogResult enumeration used by the Form.DialogResult property, shown in Table 6-4. When a button in a modal dialog box is clicked, its DialogResult property is assigned to the dialog box. This has the effect of terminating the dialog box with that DialogResult value.

To demonstrate this idea, comment out the Click event handlers for the btnOK and btnCancel buttons in the ongoing example (*dlg.cs* for the C# version, *dlg.vb* for the VB.NET version).

In the C# version, also remember to expand the code in the Windows Form Designer generated code region, find the lines that add the event-handler methods to the Click delegate for each button, and delete them. These lines will look like:

```
        this.btnOK.Click += new
            System.EventHandler(this.btnOK_Click);
        this.btnCancel.Click += new
            System.EventHandler(this.btnCancel_Click);
```

If you run the application now, the only way to close the dialog box is by clicking on the Close button in the upper-right corner, clicking on Close in the system menu, or pressing Alt+F4. The OK and Cancel buttons will have no effect.

Display the dialog box in Design view, select each button in turn, and set the Dialog-Result property for the btnOK and btnCancel buttons to OK and Cancel, respectively, in the Properties window. Now when you run the application, it will behave exactly as it did originally, when the button-click event handlers were in place. However, you did not have to implement any event handlers.

If you are not using Visual Studio .NET, or if you are creating the dialog box entirely in code, you can accomplish the same result by setting the DialogResult property with lines of code similar to the following (the VB.NET version is identical except for the trailing semicolon):

C#

```
btnOK.DialogResult = System.Windows.Forms.DialogResult.OK;
btnCancel.DialogResult =
            System.Windows.Forms.DialogResult.Cancel;
```

Perhaps the two most common actions your user will perform with a dialog box are to either accept the dialog or cancel the dialog. Users expect to be able to press Enter to accept a dialog box, or Escape to cancel a dialog. If a control other than your designated accept or cancel button has focus, then pressing either key will not have the desired effect until the appropriate button has focus.

You can designate a button on the form to always respond to the Enter key by setting the form's AcceptButton property. Likewise, you can designate the form to always respond to the Escape key by setting the form's CancelButton property. The value of each property must be a Button or LinkLabel control—i.e., a control that implements the IButtonControl interface.

You can set the AcceptButton or CancelButton properties of a dialog box in Visual Studio .NET by selecting the form, and then setting the appropriate property in the Properties window. Each property will have a drop-down in the Properties window that displays all the buttons or LinkLabels on the form. Select the button for each property to be the default accept or cancel button.

If you are not using Visual Studio .NET, or if you are creating the dialog box entirely in code, you can set the AcceptButton or Cancel-Button properties with lines of code similar to the following (the VB. NET version is identical except for the trailing semicolon):

C#

```
AcceptButton = btnOK;
CancelButton = btnCancel;
```

Apply Button

All dialog buttons discussed so far set the dialog box's DialogResult property to a value, which not only has the effect of returning that value to the parent form, but also of closing the dialog box. Sometimes you'll want the parent form to process the changes made in the dialog box while leaving the dialog box open. Many programs implement an Apply button for this purpose.

An Apply button typically is disabled, i.e., grayed out, when the dialog first opens. As soon as any change is made in one of the dialog controls, the button is enabled. Clicking the Apply button makes available to the parent form all the changes made in the dialog box, but leaves the dialog box open. The Apply button is then disabled until the next change in the dialog box is made.

You might be tempted to implement the Apply button by creating a public method in the parent Form class that performs whatever work needs to be done when the Apply button is clicked. The Apply button would simply execute that public method when it was clicked, passing any required information as arguments.

This is not a clean way to implement an Apply button, however, because the dialog box class needs to know too much about the parent class. Also, if other classes invoke your dialog box, the dialog box must know their methods as well. This design tightly couples the dialog class to the forms that invoke it, which is generally an indication of poor design.

A preferable design, which decouples the dialog class from the calling class, is to have the Dialog Box raise an event when the Apply button is clicked. The Apply event would be handled by the parent form and any other interested classes. With this event-driven design, the Dialog box and the parent class can be modified independently of one another; they are associated only through the indirection of publishing and subscribing to the Apply event.

The following example demonstrates how to raise and handle an Apply event when the user clicks the Apply button.

Open Visual Studio .NET and create a new Windows Application project called DialogapplyEvent in the language of your choice. Drag a Button control onto the form. Name the button btnCreate and change the Text property to Create Dialog Box. Resize it as necessary to make it look good. Drag a Label control onto the form and name it lblReturn. Blank out its Text property.

 This example creates the dialog box form entirely in code, as opposed to the example shown in Figure 6-1, where the dialog form was created in Visual Studio .NET as part of the project.

Right-click anywhere on the form in the Design window and select View Code. This will open the source code for the Form class. Add the code to create the dialog box class, DialogDemo, shown in Example 6-5 (in C#) or in Example 6-6 (in VB.NET), somewhere inside the Form1 class.

Example 6-5. DialogDemo class using an event in C#

```
// Dialog box class
private class DialogDemo : Form
{
    private Button btnApply;
    private TextBox txt;
    public event EventHandler ClickApply;

    public DialogDemo( )
    {
        Text = "Apply Dialog Demo";
        FormBorderStyle = FormBorderStyle.FixedDialog;
        BackColor = System.Drawing.Color.Aquamarine;
        ControlBox = false;
        MaximizeBox = false;
        MinimizeBox = false;
        ShowInTaskbar = false;
        Size = new Size(400,200);
        StartPosition = FormStartPosition.CenterScreen;

        // Create the OK button
        Button btnOK = new Button( );
        btnOK.Text = "OK";
        btnOK.DialogResult = DialogResult.OK;
        btnOK.Location = new Point(50,50);
        btnOK.TabIndex = 0;
        btnOK.Click += new EventHandler(applyButtonOnClick);
        Controls.Add(btnOK);

        // Create the Apply button
        btnApply = new Button( );
        btnApply.Text = "Apply";
        btnApply.Location = new Point(150,50);
        btnApply.TabIndex = 1;
        btnApply.Enabled = false;
        btnApply.Click += new EventHandler(applyButtonOnClick);
        Controls.Add(btnApply);

        // Create the Cancel button
        Button btnCancel = new Button( );
        btnCancel.Text = "Cancel";
        btnCancel.DialogResult = DialogResult.Cancel;
        btnCancel.Location = new Point(250,50);
        btnCancel.TabIndex = 2;
        Controls.Add(btnCancel);

        // create input text box
```

Example 6-5. DialogDemo class using an event in C# (continued)

C#

```
    txt = new TextBox( );
    txt.Size = new Size(100,15);
    txt.Location = new Point(150,15);
    txt.TextChanged += new EventHandler(TextBoxChanged);
    Controls.Add(txt);

}  // close DialogDemo constructor

private void TextBoxChanged(object sender, EventArgs e)
{
    TextBox txt = (TextBox)sender;
    DialogDemo dlg = (DialogDemo)txt.Parent;
    dlg.EnableapplyButton = true;
}

public bool EnableapplyButton
{
    get {return btnApply.Enabled; }
    set {btnApply.Enabled = value; }
}

public string TextOut
{
    get {return txt.Text; }
}

private void applyButtonOnClick (object sender, EventArgs e)
{
    if (ClickApply != null)
        ClickApply(this, new EventArgs( ));
}
}    //  close for DialogDemo class
```

Example 6-6. DialogDemo class using an event in VB.NET

VB

```
'  Dialog box class
private class DialogDemo
        inherits Form
    dim btnApply as Button
    dim txt as TextBox
    public event ClickApply as EventHandler

    public sub new ( )
            myBase.New
        Text = "Apply Dialog Demo"
        FormBorderStyle = FormBorderStyle.FixedDialog
        BackColor = System.Drawing.Color.Aquamarine
        ControlBox = false
        MaximizeBox = false
        MinimizeBox = false
        ShowInTaskbar = false
        Size = new Size(400,200)
        StartPosition = FormStartPosition.CenterScreen
```

Example 6-6. DialogDemo class using an event in VB.NET (continued)

```
VB
      '  Create the OK button
      dim btnOK as New Button
      btnOK.Text = "OK"
      btnOK.DialogResult = DialogResult.OK
      btnOK.Location = new Point(50,50)
      btnOK.TabIndex = 0
      AddHandler btnOK.Click, AddressOf applyButtonOnClick
      Controls.Add(btnOK)

      '  Create the Apply button
      btnApply = new Button( )
      btnApply.Text = "Apply"
      btnApply.Location = new Point(150,50)
      btnApply.TabIndex = 1
      btnApply.Enabled = false
      AddHandler btnApply.Click, AddressOf applyButtonOnClick
      Controls.Add(btnApply)

      '  Create the Cancel button
      dim btnCancel as new Button( )
      btnCancel.Text = "Cancel"
      btnCancel.DialogResult = DialogResult.Cancel
      btnCancel.Location = new Point(250,50)
      btnCancel.TabIndex = 2
      Controls.Add(btnCancel)

      '  create input text box
      txt = new TextBox( )
      txt.Size = new Size(100,15)
      txt.Location = new Point(150,15)
      AddHandler txt.TextChanged, AddressOf TextBoxChanged
      Controls.Add(txt)

   end sub    ' close DialogDemo constructor

   private sub applyButtonOnClick(sender as Object, e as EventArgs)
      RaiseEvent ClickApply(me, new EventArgs( ))
   end sub

   private sub TextBoxChanged(sender as Object, e as EventArgs)
      dim txt as TextBox = CType(sender,TextBox)
      dim dlg as DialogDemo = CType(txt.Parent,DialogDemo)
      dlg.EnableapplyButton = true
   end sub

   public property EnableapplyButton as Boolean
      get
         return btnApply.Enabled
      end get
      set
         btnApply.Enabled = value
      end set
```

Example 6-6. DialogDemo class using an event in VB.NET (continued)

```
VB    end property

      public ReadOnly property TextOut as string
        get
            return txt.Text
        end get
      end property

  end class     '  close DialogDemo class
```

The first thing to note about the DialogDemo class is that it is nested inside the class of the parent form. This design implicitly makes the dialog box available to the Form1 class, but not to any other form. If you want to create a dialog box that will be accessible to different parent forms, then it needs public exposure, probably in a class by itself, or perhaps in a class that also contains other dialog box classes used by your application.

The next thing to note about the DialogDemo class is that it inherits from the Form class. The dialog box being created is just a form, like any other form. What makes it modal is the way it is called from the parent form. When the btnCreate button is clicked, the btnCreate_Click event handler method, shown in C# in Example 6-7 and in VB.NET in Example 6-8, is fired. The ShowDialog() method displays the form modally. If the Show() method of the Form class were used to display the dialog box rather than ShowDialog(), it would be a modeless dialog.

Create the event handler for the Click event for the btnCreate button by going to the Design view and double-clicking on the button. Add the code highlighted in Example 6-7 (in C#) or in Example 6-8 (in VB.NET) to the code skeleton for the btnCreate Click event-handler method.

Example 6-7. btnCreate event handler using the ClickApply event in C#

```
C#  private void btnCreate_Click(object sender, System.EventArgs e)
    {
        DialogDemo dlg = new DialogDemo();
        dlg.EnableapplyButton = false;

        // Add the event handler
        dlg.ClickApply += new EventHandler(DialogDemoOnApply);

        // Show the dialog modally
        dlg.ShowDialog();

        if (dlg.DialogResult == DialogResult.OK)
            {lblReturn.Text = dlg.TextOut;}
        else
            {lblReturn.Text = dlg.DialogResult.ToString();}
    }
```

Example 6-8. btnCreate event handler using the ClickApply event in VB.NET

```
Private Sub btnCreate_Click(ByVal sender As System.Object, _
                            ByVal e As System.EventArgs) _
                            Handles btnCreate.Click
   dim dlg as new DialogDemo()
   dlg.EnableapplyButton = false

   ' Add the event handler
   AddHandler dlg.ClickApply, AddressOf DialogDemoOnApply

   ' Show the dialog modally
   dlg.ShowDialog()

   if dlg.DialogResult = DialogResult.OK then
      lblReturn.Text = dlg.TextOut
   else
      lblReturn.Text = dlg.DialogResult.ToString()
   end if
End Sub
```

Before the ShowDialog() method can be called, the dialog box must be created. The first line of code in the btnCreate_Click method instantiates a new object of type DialogDemo. The instantiation of the dialog box looks like the following:

```
DialogDemo dlg = new DialogDemo();
```

```
dim dlg as new DialogDemo()
```

Once the dialog box is instantiated, the EnableapplyButton property is set to false, which disables the Apply button. It will be kept disabled until one of the controls in the dialog box is modified, making the Apply button relevant.

The EnableapplyButton property is of type Boolean. It gets and sets the value of the Enabled property of the Apply button. If the Enabled property of a control is false, then the control is visible, but grayed out, and cannot receive focus. Thus, it cannot be clicked on or otherwise manipulated.

After the dialog box returns from the modal display, the DialogResult property is tested. If the DialogResult is OK, indicating that the dialog box was dismissed with the OK button, then the display label, lblReturn, is populated with the value of the read-only TextOut property of DialogDemo. If the DialogResult value is anything other than OK, which in this example can only be Cancel, then the DialogResult itself is displayed in lblReturn. Depending on the requirements of the application, any of a number of techniques can be used to test the DialogResult return value and process the dialog box control values accordingly.

The DialogDemo class shown in C# in Example 6-5 and in VB.NET in Example 6-6 declares two member variables:

```
C#   private Button btnApply;
     private TextBox txt;
     dim btnApply as Button
     dim txt as TextBox
```

These are member variables, so they are visible to all the methods and properties in the DialogDemo class.

The DialogDemo constructor sets various properties of the dialog box, including FormBorderStyle, BackColor, ControlBox, and MaximizeBox.

The constructor then instantiates and specifies several controls on the dialog box: OK, Apply, Cancel, and a TextBox for accepting typed user input. Each control is added to the Controls collection of the dialog box.

Both OK and Apply have the same event handler, ApplyButtonOnClick, added to the delegate for their Click event. This is because both buttons cause the text entered into the TextBox control to be displayed on the parent form.

The TextBox control raises the TextChanged event whenever the content of the TextBox is changed, either by adding or deleting characters. The event is handled by the TextBoxChanged event handler method. In C#, the event handler is added to the delegate with this line of code:

```
C#   txt.TextChanged += new EventHandler(TextBoxChanged);
```

and the TextBoxChanged method looks like:

```
C#   private void TextBoxChanged(object sender, EventArgs e)
     {
         this.EnableapplyButton = true;
     }
```

In VB.NET, the event handler is added to the delegate with this line of code:

```
VB   AddHandler txt.TextChanged, AddressOf TextBoxChanged
```

and the TextBoxChanged method looks like:

```
VB   private sub TextBoxChanged(sender as Object, e as EventArgs)
         me.EnableapplyButton = true
     end sub
```

An event called ClickApply was declared in the DialogDemo class (Example 6-5 in C#; Example 6-6 in VB.NET). This event will be handled by a method called Dialog-DemoOnApply, shown in Example 6-9 (in C#) or in Example 6-10 (in VB.NET). Enter the code for DialogDemoOnApply somewhere within the Form1 class, but not within the DialogDemo class.

Example 6-9. DialogDemoOnApply method in C#

```
C#   private void DialogDemoOnApply(object sender, System.EventArgs e)
     {
         DialogDemo dlg = (DialogDemo)sender;
         lblReturn.Text = dlg.TextOut;
```

Example 6-9. DialogDemoOnApply method in C# (continued)

```csharp
dlg.EnableapplyButton = false;
}
```

Example 6-10. DialogDemoOnApply method in VB.NET

```vbnet
private sub DialogDemoOnApply(ByVal sender As System.Object, _
                             ByVal e As System.EventArgs)
    dim dlg as DialogDemo = CType(sender, DialogDemo)
    lblReturn.Text = dlg.TextOut
    dlg.EnableapplyButton = false
end sub
```

The Apply button ultimately raises the ClickApply event when it is clicked. It does so through a multistep process. The Apply button Click event has an event handler method called ApplyButtonOnClick added to its delegate. This is done with the following line of code:

```csharp
btnApply.Click += new EventHandler(applyButtonOnClick);
```

```vbnet
AddHandler btnApply.Click, AddressOf applyButtonOnClick
```

The ApplyButtonOnClick method raises the ClickApply method. This method is reproduced here:

```csharp
private void applyButtonOnClick (object sender, EventArgs e)
{
    if (ClickApply != null)
        ClickApply(this, new EventArgs());
}
```

```vbnet
private sub applyButtonOnClick(sender as Object, e as EventArgs)
    RaiseEvent ClickApply(me, new EventArgs())
end sub
```

Since both the OK and Apply buttons perform the same task, with the only difference being that the dialog box closes when the OK button is clicked, they both use the same applyButtonOnClick method as their Click event handler.

 VB.NET and C# differ slightly in raising events. In the C# version, you first test to see if any methods have been registered with the delegate before raising the event. If the ClickApply event has not had any event handlers added, its delegate will be null. Since the btnCreate_Click method added DialogDemoOnApply to the ClickApply delegate, the ClickApply delegate is not null, so the ClickApply event is raised. In the VB.NET version, on the other hand, the compiler does the checking for you. If no methods were added to the delegate, nothing happens; otherwise the event is raised. The resulting intermediate language created by the compiler for these two different language implementations are essentially the same.

The parent form handles this ClickApply event by adding an event-handler method, DialogDemoOnApply, to the ClickApply delegate. This was done in the Click event handler for btnCreate, btnCreate_Click, which was listed in Example 6-7 (in C#) and Example 6-8 (in VB.NET). The method was added to the delegate with the following line of code:

`C#`
```
dlg.ClickApply += new EventHandler(DialogDemoOnApply);
```

`VB`
```
AddHandler dlg.ClickApply, AddressOf DialogDemoOnApply
```

The DialogDemoOnApply method, which handles this event and is shown in Example 6-9 in C# and in Example 6-10 in VB.NET, gets an instance of the dialog box class that raised the event by casting the sender object as type DialogDemo. (Remember, even though sender is already of type DialogDemo, the compiler does not know this.) Once the reference to the DialogDemo dialog box is in hand, the value of the read-only TextOut property can be assigned to the label on the parent form and the EnableapplyButton property can be set to `false`, which disables the Apply button on the dialog box until the TextBox is modified again.

Examine the DialogDemo class more closely. Notice there is no member variable of type Form1 (the parent Form class), and no direct coupling between the dialog box class and the parent class. There is, however, a declared public event delegate called ClickApply:

`C#`
```
public event EventHandler ClickApply;
```

`VB`
```
public event ClickApply as EventHandler
```

This delegate is of type EventHandler, which specifies that the event-handler methods added to the delegate will take two arguments: an object (typically called sender) and an argument of type EventArgs (typically called e).

Looking back at the event handler method added to the ClickApply delegate, you can see that it does in fact correspond to the required signature:

`C#`
```
private void DialogDemoOnApply(object sender, System.EventArgs e)
```

`VB`
```
private sub DialogDemoOnApply(ByVal sender As System.Object, _
                             ByVal e As System.EventArgs)
```

CommonDialog Classes

Many applications perform similar functions, such as opening and saving files, or selecting fonts. Ever since Windows 3.1, the Windows API has provided standard dialog boxes to perform many of these common operations. Not only does this save the developer from having to reinvent the wheel, but, more importantly. Providing a common dialog used by all applications means that users have to learn how to perform each function only once.

The .NET Framework provides five common dialog boxes. These dialogs are contained in classes that derive from the System.Windows.Forms.CommonDialog class. They are:

- FileDialog
- ColorDialog
- FontDialog
- PageSetupDialog
- PrintDialog

The common dialogs share many properties, methods and events, some of which are listed in Table 6-5.

Table 6-5. CommonDialog common properties, methods, and events

Member	Type	Description
Container	Public Property	Returns the IContainer that contains the dialog box.
Reset	Public Method	Resets the properties of the dialog box to its default values.
ShowDialog	Public Method	Runs the common dialog box.
HelpRequest	Public Event	Raised when user clicks the Help button of a common dialog box.

The following sections describe each of the common dialogs provided in the CommonDialog class. A single example is used to demonstrate all of the common dialogs. The example consists of a form with a TextBox control for entering and editing text. The form has buttons for opening and loading a file into the TextBox and saving the contents of the TextBox to a file, changing the background color of the TextBox and changing the text color, changing the font, printing the contents of the TextBox, and setting page properties for printing. The completed example with all the buttons is shown in Figure 6-6.

To start this example, open Visual Studio .NET and create a new Windows Application project. Name it CommonDialogs. Drag a TextBox and eight buttons on to the form until it looks like Figure 6-6. Set the properties of the form and the controls to the values shown in Table 6-6.

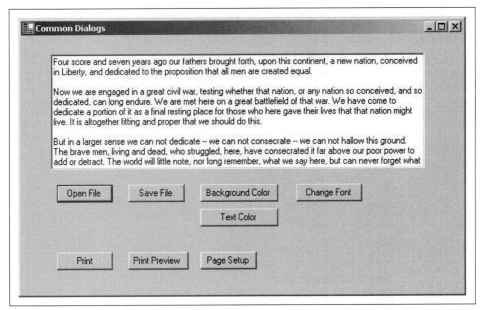

Figure 6-6. CommonDialogs application

Table 6-6. CommonDialogs application control properties

Control type	Property	Value
Form	(Name)	Form1
	Text	Common Dialogs
Textbox	(Name)	txtFile
	Multiline	True
	TabIndex	0
	Text	blank
	Anchor	Top, Bottom, Left, Right
Button	(Name)	btnOpenFile
	TabIndex	1
	Text	Open File
	Anchor	Bottom, Left
Button	(Name)	btnSaveFile
	TabIndex	2
	Text	Save File
	Anchor	Bottom, Left
Button	(Name)	btnBackColor
	TabIndex	3
	Text	Background Color

Table 6-6. CommonDialogs application control properties (continued)

Control type	Property	Value
	Anchor	Bottom, Left
Button	(Name)	btnTextColor
	TabIndex	4
	Text	Text Color
	Anchor	Bottom, Left
Button	(Name)	btnFont
	TabIndex	5
	Text	Change Font
	Anchor	Bottom, Left
Button	(Name)	btnPrint
	TabIndex	6
	Text	Print
	Anchor	Bottom, Left
Button	(Name)	btnPrintPreview
	TabIndex	7
	Text	Print Preview
	Anchor	Bottom, Left
Button	(Name)	btnPageSetup
	TabIndex	8
	Text	Page Setup
	Anchor	Bottom, Left

FileDialog

The FileDialog class is an abstract class, so it cannot be instantiated directly. Instead, you can instantiate one of the two classes derived from this class: OpenFileDialog and SaveFileDialog. Both derived classes will be demonstrated in the Common-Dialogs example.

OpenFileDialog and SaveFileDialog classes are sealed; they cannot be inherited from. In fact, the FileDialog class cannot be inherited from either.

The FileDialog class provides many properties, methods, and events that are common to both the OpenFileDialog and the SaveFileDialog classes. Table 6-7 lists many of the commonly used properties, all of which are read/write.

Table 6-7. *FileDialog common properties*

Property	Type	Description
AddExtension	Boolean	If true (the default), the dialog box adds an extension to the filename if the user omits the extension. If false, no extension is added. The extension added depends on the currently selected file filter and the value of CheckFileExists. If CheckFileExists is true, the extension added is the first extension from the current file filter that matches an existing file. If no files match the current file filter, the extension specified in DefaultExt is used. If CheckFileExists is false, the first valid extension from the current file filter is used. If the current file filter does not contain any valid extensions, the DefaultExt is used.ᵃ
CheckFileExists	Boolean	If true (the default for OpenFileDialog), a warning is displayed if a filename is specified that does not exist. If false (the default for SaveFileDialog), no warning is displayed.
CheckPathExists	Boolean	If true (the default), a warning is displayed if a user-specified path does not exist.
DefaultExt	string	Default filename extension, not including the period (.). The default value is an empty string ("").
FileName	string	The single filename selected, including both the file path and the extension. The default value is an empty string (""). If no file is selected, it returns an empty string.
FileNames	string array	Array of strings containing all the filenames selected, including both the file path and the extension for each filename. If no files are selected, it returns an empty array.
Filter	string	A string that determines the choices available in the File of type: drop-down menu (in the OpenFileDialog) or the Save as type: drop-down menu (in the SaveFileDialog).
		The string consists of filter description text followed by a filter pattern, separated by a vertical bar (|). Multiple descriptions and patterns can be concatenated, separated by a vertical bar (|). Examples will be shown in Example 6-11 and Example 6-12.
FilterIndex	integer	The one-based index of the currently selected filter. Default value is 1.
InitialDirectory	string	Initial directory displayed in the dialog box. Default value is an empty string ("").
RestoreDirectory	Boolean	If true, dialog box restores the current directory to its original value if the user changed the directory while searching for files. Default is false.
ShowHelp	Boolean	If true, the Help button is displayed. Default is false.
Title	string	The dialog box title. Default value is empty string (""). If the value is an empty string, default titles are used: Open for OpenFileDialog or Save As for SaveFileDialog.
ValidateNames	Boolean	If true (the default), the dialog box accepts only valid filenames.

OpenFileDialog

Implement the OpenFileDialog box by double-clicking on the Open File button named btnOpenFile. This will open up the code window with the cursor inside a skeleton for the Click event handler for the button. Insert the highlighted code shown in Example 6-11 for C# or in Example 6-12 for VB.NET. Before doing so, however, you need to reference the System.IO namespace (unless you don't want to do any actual file IO with the selected filename). This is done by adding the following line of code to the very top of the code window:

C#
```
using System.IO;
```

VB
```
imports System.IO
```

Referencing this namespace is not strictly necessary for the operation of the Open-File dialog, if you only wanted to get the name of a file as a string. But if you actually want to do any file IO, then the System.IO namespace must be referenced.

In addition, you must declare two private member variables. The first is a string variable to hold the name of the file that is being opened. It is declared as a member variable, so both the OpenFileDialog and the SaveFileDialog will have access to the same filename. Add the following line of code inside the Form1 class definition:

C#
```
private String strFileName;
```

VB
```
private strFileName as String
```

The second member variable is of type OpenFileDialog:

C#
```
private OpenFileDialog ofd = new OpenFileDialog( );
```

VB
```
dim ofd as new OpenFileDialog( )
```

Instantiating the open file dialog in this manner, rather than inside the button-click event handler, causes the dialog box to remember where it was pointing the last time it was opened, rather than reinitializing to the specified InitialDirectory with every invocation.

 Interestingly, the VB.NET version of the program, shown in Example 6-12, remembers the directory last accessed with the Open File button whether the OpenFileDialog object is instantiated as a member variable or in the event handler method. In fact, it remembers the directory last accessed even from one program execution to the next, ignoring the value of the InitialDirectory property set in the code.

This event handler uses a StreamReader to read the contents of a file and populate the TextBox with those contents. The Stream class allows a program to read and write data, such as a sequence of bytes, from a source to a target. A StreamReader, used here, transfers the data from a text file into a data structure, while a StreamWriter, used shortly in the Save File button, writes the data from a data structure to a file.

Example 6-11. btnOpenFile Click event handler in C#

C#
```
private void btnOpenFile_Click(object sender, System.EventArgs e)
{
    ofd.InitialDirectory = @"c:\";
    ofd.Filter = "Text files (*.txt)|*.txt|" +
            "All files (*.*)|*.*";
    ofd.FilterIndex = 1;                    // 1 based index
```

Example 6-11. btnOpenFile Click event handler in C# (continued)

```csharp
if (ofd.ShowDialog( ) == DialogResult.OK)
{
    StreamReader reader = new StreamReader(ofd.FileName);
    try
    {
        strFileName = ofd.FileName;
        txtFile.Text = reader.ReadToEnd( );
    }
    catch (Exception ex)
    {
        MessageBox.Show(ex.Message);
        return;
    }
    finally
    {
        reader.Close( );
    }
}
}
```

Example 6-12. btnOpenFile Click event handler in VB.NET

```vb
Private Sub btnOpenFile_Click(ByVal sender As System.Object, _
                              ByVal e As System.EventArgs) _
                              Handles btnOpenFile.Click
    ofd.InitialDirectory = "c:\\"
    ofd.Filter = "Text files (*.txt)|*.txt|" + _
                "All files (*.*)|*.*"
    ofd.FilterIndex = 1                      ' 1 based index

    if ofd.ShowDialog( ) = DialogResult.OK then
        dim reader as new StreamReader(ofd.FileName)
        try
            strFileName = ofd.FileName
            txtFile.Text = reader.ReadToEnd( )
        catch ex as Exception
            MessageBox.Show(ex.Message)
            return
        finally
            reader.Close( )
        end try
    end if
End Sub
```

The first several lines of code in the event handler method set three properties of the OpenFileDialog member variable initialized earlier. The InitialDirectory property of the OpenFileDialog is set to the root of Drive C. This looks like the following:

```csharp
ofd.InitialDirectory = @"c:\";
```

In VB.NET, it looks like this:

```
ofd.InitialDirectory = "c:\\"
```

where the backslash must be escaped with a second backslash.

> The @ character is used to create a verbatim string. The code shown is
> equivalent to the following:
>
> ```
> ofd.InitialDirectory = "c:\\";
> ```

The next two lines of code set the Filter property of the OpenFileDialog. This property dictates the contents of the File of type: drop-down menu (or the Save as type: drop-down menu in the SaveFileDialog). It can be confusing. Each line in the drop-down menu requires two entries in the Filter property string, separated by a vertical bar character (|). The first entry contains the descriptive text displayed in the drop-down, and the second entry contains the actual wildcard mask that describes the specified files. Each subsequent line in the drop-down menu gets another two entries. Every entry in the string, except for the very first and very last, is delineated by the vertical bar. Looking at the C# example (the VB.NET is nearly identical), you have:

```
ofd.Filter = "Text files (*.txt)|*.txt|All files (*.*)|*.*";
```

There are two entries in the drop-down menu. The first displays Text files (*.txt), and the wildcard mask that applies is *.txt. The second line of the drop-down menu will be All files (*.*), and the wildcard mask will be *.*.

The next line of code selects the first filter entry as the current filter.

> The index is one-, not zero-based, unlike most indexes in the .NET
> Framework.

The if statement calls the ShowDialog method of the OpenFileDialog class, displaying the instance of the dialog box modally. When the dialog box is terminated, the DialogResult property is tested. If it is OK, then the code in the try/catch/finally block is executed. Otherwise, nothing happens. Try...catch blocks are used to manage exceptions, as described in detail in Chapter 21.

It is wise to put all file operations inside a try/catch/finally block so if any unforeseen problems arise, you can control the error message presented to the user. The StreamReader is instantiated outside the try block, so its scope will span both the try and finally clauses. (Remember that a variable declared inside a try block is scoped only to that try block) If any errors occur, the StreamReader Close method is guaranteed to be called, since it is in the finally block.

A new StreamReader is instantiated, using the selected filename as the input:

```csharp
StreamReader reader = new StreamReader(ofd.FileName);
```

```vbnet
dim reader as new StreamReader(ofd.FileName)
```

Next, the member variable strFileName is assigned the filename. This will be used when saving the file to remember the previously used filename.

The ReadToEnd method of the StreamReader class reads the entire file and assigns the contents to the Text property of the TextBox. Finally, the StreamReader is closed inside the finally block.

When the button is clicked, the dialog box shown in Figure 6-7 is presented. If a file is selected and the Open button clicked, the contents of the file will be displayed in the Form's txtFile TextBox.

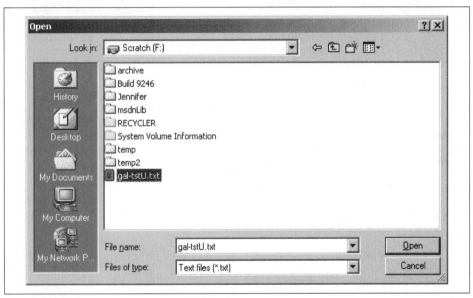

Figure 6-7. OpenFileDialog common dialog box

SaveFileDialog

The SaveFileDialog is similar to the OpenFileDialog. It is shown in Figure 6-8.

To implement this dialog, double-click on the Open File button on the form. This will open the code window with the cursor inside a skeleton for the button's Click event handler. Insert the highlighted code shown in Example 6-13 for C# and in Example 6-14 for VB.NET.

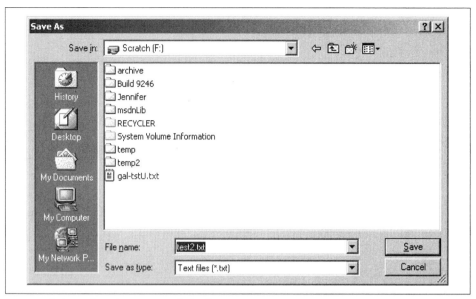

Figure 6-8. SaveFileDialog common dialog box

Example 6-13. btnSaveFile Click event handler in C#

```
private void btnSaveFile_Click(object sender, System.EventArgs e)
{
    SaveFileDialog sfd = new SaveFileDialog( );
    sfd.InitialDirectory = @"c:\";
    sfd.Filter = "Text files (*.txt)|*.txt|" +
                 "All files (*.*)|*.*";
    sfd.FilterIndex = 1;                       //  1 based index

    if (strFileName != null)
        sfd.FileName = strFileName;
    else
        sfd.FileName = "*.txt";

    if (sfd.ShowDialog( ) == DialogResult.OK)
    {
        StreamWriter writer = new StreamWriter(strFileName,false);
        try
        {
            strFileName = sfd.FileName;
            writer.Write(txtFile.Text);
        }
        catch(Exception ex)
        {
            MessageBox.Show(ex.Message);
            return;
        }
        finally
        {
```

Example 6-13. btnSaveFile Click event handler in C# (continued)

```csharp
        writer.Close( );
      }
    }
}
```

Example 6-14. btnSaveFile Click event handler in VB.NET

```vbnet
Private Sub btnSaveFile_Click(ByVal sender As System.Object, _
                        ByVal e As System.EventArgs) _
                        Handles btnSaveFile.Click
   dim sfd as SaveFileDialog = new SaveFileDialog( )
   sfd.InitialDirectory = "c:\\"
   sfd.Filter = "Text files (*.txt)|*.txt|" + _
             "All files (*.*)|*.*"
   sfd.FilterIndex = 1                    ' 1 based index

   if (strFileName <> Nothing) then
      sfd.FileName = strFileName
   else
      sfd.FileName = "*.txt"
   end if

   if sfd.ShowDialog( ) = DialogResult.OK then
      dim writer as new StreamWriter(strFileName,false)
      try
         strFileName = sfd.FileName
         writer.Write(txtFile.Text)
      catch ex as Exception
         MessageBox.Show(ex.Message)
         return
      finally
         writer.Close( )
      end try
   end if
End Sub
```

The code for the SaveFileDialog in Examples 6-13 and 6-14 is similar to that shown previously for the OpenFileDialog. Instead of instantiating a SaveFileDialog object as a member variable, a SaveFileDialog object is instantiated within the event handler. Although this entails a bit of extra overhead, it better encapsulates the logic within the method. Since the dialog box FileName property is initialized with the previously opened or saved filename, as described shortly, there is little functional difference between the two techniques.

The InitialDirectory, Filter, and FilterIndex properties are set the same as before.

The next several lines test to see if the strFileName member variable has been previously assigned a value. If so (i.e., if it is not null in C# or Nothing in VB.NET), then that value is assigned to the FileName property of the SaveFileDialog. If it has not yet been assigned a value, then the FileName property is set to *.txt. In either case, this property will initially be displayed in the dialog box as the selected file. Setting the FileName property in this manner filters the filenames displayed in the dialog box, which, in this example, is the same as one of the filters set with the Filter property.

As with the OpenFileDialog in the previous code examples, the SaveFileDialog is displayed modally using the ShowDialog method and the DialogResult property tested in an if statement. If the user terminated the dialog box by clicking OK, then the code in the try/catch block is executed. This code instantiates a StreamWriter object that writes the contents of the txtFile TextBox out to the specified filename.

ColorDialog

The ColorDialog class opens a common dialog box for selecting colors. The Color-Dialog displays basic system colors, with the optional ability to define custom colors, as shown in Figure 6-9.

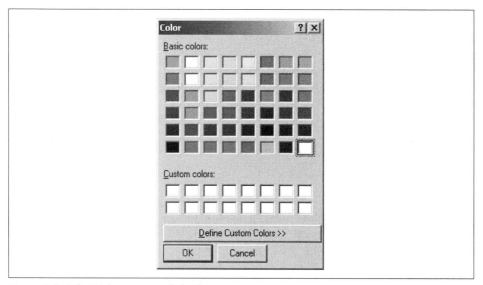

Figure 6-9. ColorDialog common dialog box

The ColorDialog class exposes the read/write properties shown in Table 6-8, which allow you to control the appearance and capabilities of the dialog box.

Table 6-8. ColorDialog initial properties

Property	Type	Description
AllowFullOpen	Boolean	If true (the default value), enables button allowing user to define custom colors.
AnyColor	Boolean	If true, dialog box displays all available colors in the set of basic colors. Default is false.
Color	Color	Color selected by the user. Default value is Color.Black.

Table 6-8. ColorDialog initial properties (continued)

Property	Type	Description
CustomColors	Integer array	An array of integers representing custom colors shown in the dialog box. Each integer contains the alpha, red, green, and blue values to create the color. Custom colors are only available if AllowFullOpen is set `true`. Default value is `null` (in C#) or `Nothing` (in VB.NET)
FullOpen	Boolean	If `true`, dialog box displays custom colors when initially opened. If `false` (the default), user must click Custom Color button to see custom colors. If AllowFullOpen is `false`, then this property has no effect.
ShowHelp	Boolean	If `true`, dialog box displays a Help button. The HelpRequest event must be handled for help to be displayed. Default is `false`.
SolidColorOnly	Boolean	If `true`, dialog box restricts users on systems with 256 or fewer colors to solid colors only. Default is `false`.

The ColorDialog can be used anywhere you need to set a Color. In the example shown in Figure 6-6, this dialog is called by two different buttons: the Background Color button calls the ColorDialog to set the BackColor property of the TextBox and the Text Color button calls it to set the ForeColor property.

To implement these buttons, double-click on each to open a code skeleton for the Click event handler in the code window. Then enter the highlighted code shown in Example 6-15 for C# and in Example 6-16 for VB.NET.

Example 6-15. btnBackColor and btnTextColor Click event handlers in C#

```
private void btnBackColor_Click(object sender, System.EventArgs e)
{
    ColorDialog cd = new ColorDialog();
    cd.AllowFullOpen = true;
    cd.AnyColor = true;
    cd.ShowHelp = false;
    cd.Color = txtFile.BackColor;
    cd.ShowDialog();
    txtFile.BackColor = cd.Color;
}

private void btnTextColor_Click(object sender, System.EventArgs e)
{
    ColorDialog cd = new ColorDialog();
    cd.AllowFullOpen = false;
    cd.ShowHelp = true;
    cd.Color = txtFile.ForeColor;
    cd.ShowDialog();
    txtFile.ForeColor = cd.Color;
}
```

Example 6-16. btnBackColor and btnTextColor Click event handlers in VB.NET

VB
```
Private Sub btnBackColor_Click(ByVal sender As System.Object, _
                               ByVal e As System.EventArgs) _
                               Handles btnBackColor.Click
    dim cd as new ColorDialog( )
    cd.AllowFullOpen = true
    cd.AnyColor = true
    cd.ShowHelp = false
    cd.Color = txtFile.BackColor
    cd.ShowDialog( )
    txtFile.BackColor = cd.Color
End Sub

Private Sub btnTextColor_Click(ByVal sender As System.Object, _
                               ByVal e As System.EventArgs) _
                               Handles btnTextColor.Click
    dim cd as New ColorDialog( )
    cd.AllowFullOpen = false
    cd.ShowHelp = true
    cd.Color = txtFile.ForeColor
    cd.ShowDialog( )
    txtFile.ForeColor = cd.Color
End Sub
```

In each event-handler method, a new ColorDialog is instantiated, and then properties are set to control the dialog box. The default color is set from the current Back-Color or ForeColor of the TextBox, as appropriate, and then the dialog box is displayed modally.

There is no need to test the DialogResult property of the terminated dialog box. If the dialog box is cancelled, nothing changes. If it is terminated with an OK, then the color is automatically set to the current color.

FontDialog

Changing font size, family, style, and effect is a very common occurrence in Windows applications, so there is a CommonDialog to handle that chore for you, shown in Figure 6-10.

 Text and fonts will be covered in detail in Chapter 9.

As with the other members of the CommonDialog class, FontDialog exposes several read/write properties that allow programmatic control of the dialog box. Table 6-9 lists the most commonly used properties.

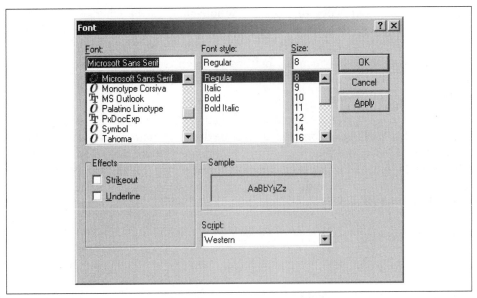

Figure 6-10. FontDialog common dialog box

Table 6-9. FontDialog properties

Property	Type	Description
AllowVectorFonts	Boolean	If `true` (the default), the dialog box allows vector fonts.
AllowVerticalFonts	Boolean	If `true` (the default), the dialog box allows both vertical and horizontal fonts; otherwise, only horizontal fonts are allowed.
AllowScriptChange	Boolean	If `true` (the default), the Script combo box allows the user to change the character set associated with a font. If `false`, the Script combo box is still displayed, but only a single choice is available.
Color	Color	Gets or sets the color of the selected font. The default value is Color.Black.
FixedPitchOnly	Boolean	If `true`, only fixed pitch fonts can be selected. If `false` (the default), both fixed pitch and proportional fonts may be selected.
Font	Font	Gets or sets the font selected by the FontDialog.
MaxSize	integer	The maximum point size a user can select. Default is 0.
MinSize	integer	The minimum point size a user can select. Default is 0.
ShowApply	Boolean	If `true`, the dialog box contains an Apply button. The default is `false`. If the Apply button is clicked, the Apply event is raised, which can be handled, as shown in Example 6-5 through Example 6-10.
ShowColor	Boolean	If `true`, the dialog box displays a color choice. The default is `false`. The color choice is available only if ShowEffects is set to `true`.
ShowEffects	Boolean	If `true` (the default), the dialog box displays strikethrough, underline, and text color options. Text color option is only available if ShowColor is set to `true`.
ShowHelp	Boolean	If `true`, the dialog box displays a Help button. The HelpRequest event must be handled for help to be displayed. The default is `false`.

To implement a FontDialog dialog box, double-click on the Change Font button and add the highlighted code shown in Example 6-17 for C# and in Example 6-18 for VB.NET. Each code listing comprises two methods. The first is the button Click event handler, for which the method skeleton is provided for you by Visual Studio .NET. The second method is the event handler for the Apply button enabled in the FontDialog.

Since the FontDialog is instantiated in one method (btnFont_Click) and referenced in another (fd_Apply), the FontDialog must be declared such that its scope will span both methods. Also, the printing features in this application, described shortly, will need to know what font has been set, so a member variable of type Font must be declared. To accomplish both goals, add the following lines of code somewhere inside the Form1 class definition:

C#

```
private FontDialog fd;
private Font fnt;
```

VB

```
private fd as FontDialog
private fnt as Font = Nothing
```

Example 6-17. btnFont Click event handler in C#

C#

```csharp
private void btnFont_Click(object sender, System.EventArgs e)
{
    fd = new FontDialog();
    fd.ShowHelp = false;
    fd.ShowApply = true;
    fd.Apply += new System.EventHandler(this.fd_Apply);

    if (txtFile.Font != null)
    {
        fd.Font = txtFile.Font;
    }

    if (fd.ShowDialog() == DialogResult.OK)
    {
        txtFile.Font = fd.Font;
        fnt = fd.Font;
    }
}

private void fd_Apply(object sender, System.EventArgs e)
{
    txtFile.Font = fd.Font;
}
```

Example 6-18. btnFont Click event handler in VB.NET

VB

```vbnet
Private Sub btnFont_Click(ByVal sender As System.Object, _
                          ByVal e As System.EventArgs) _
                          Handles btnFont.Click
    fd = new FontDialog()
```

Example 6-18. btnFont Click event handler in VB.NET (continued)

```
VB       fd.ShowHelp = false
         fd.ShowApply = true
         AddHandler fd.Apply, AddressOf fd_Apply

         if not (txtFile.Font is Nothing) then
             fd.Font = txtFile.Font
         End If

         if fd.ShowDialog( ) = DialogResult.OK then
             txtFile.Font = fd.Font
             fnt = fd.Font
         end if
     End Sub

     private sub fd_Apply(ByVal sender As System.Object, _
                          ByVal e As System.EventArgs)
         txtFile.Font = fd.Font
     End Sub
```

The first line of code in the btnFont_Click event handler method instantiates a new
FontDialog object, which was previously declared as a member variable. The
ShowHelp property is set to false to suppress the Help button, and the ShowApply
property is set to true to enable an Apply button.

The next line of code adds the fd_Apply method as an event handler for the Apply
button enabled in the FontDialog.

The last few lines in the Click event handler displays the dialog modally and tests the
DialogResult property in an if statement. If the user clicked OK, then the Font property of the TextBox is set accordingly. Also, the member variable fnt, of type Font, is
set for use by the printing methods, although you could just as easily retrieve the current font from the Font property of the TextBox.

The Apply event handler is very simple: it just changes the Font property of the
TextBox.

PageSetupDialog

Printing is a key aspect of many Windows applications. Setting up the page for printing is a closely related activity. The PageSetupDialog class provides a common dialog to implement this functionality. A typical PageSetupDialog is shown in
Figure 6-11.

Clicking on the Printer... button (enabled with the AllowPrinter property of the Page-
SetupDialog class) brings up a Page Setup Printer dialog box, shown in Figure 6-12.

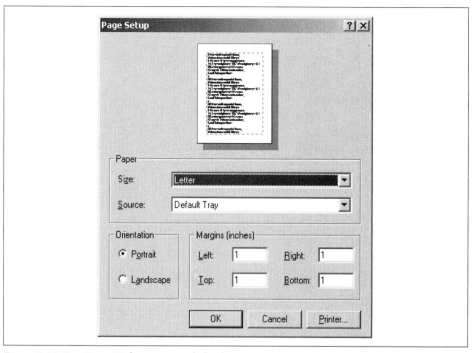

Figure 6-11. PageSetupDialog common dialog box

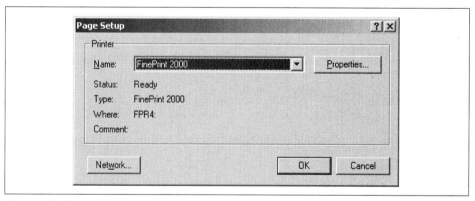

Figure 6-12. PageSetupDialog printer selection dialog box

The FinePrint 2000 printer selected in Figure 6-12 is one of the handiest utilities we've ever used. This shareware installs as a printer on the system and can print any job as one up, two up (two pages per piece of paper), four up, or eight up. It also lets you print or delete selected pages from a print job, although it sometimes acts as a print preview on steroids. You can find out more about FinePrint at *http://www.fineprint.com/*.

Both the PageSetupDialog and the PrintDialog (described in the next section) use a *Document*, which is a property of the PageSetupDialog class. The properties that are set in the PageSetupDialog apply to an instance of a Document. When the Print-Dialog prints that Document, those settings will pertain.

As with the other members of the CommonDialog class, the PageSetupDialog exposes several read/write properties that allow programmatic control of the dialog box. The most commonly used properties are listed in Table 6-10.

Table 6-10. PageSetupDialog properties

Property	Type	Description
AllowMargins	Boolean	If true (the default), the Margins section of the dialog box will be enabled. This allows setting of left, right, top, and bottom margins.
AllowOrientation	Boolean	If true (the default), the Orientation section of the dialog box will be enabled. This allows the selection between landscape or portrait.
AllowPaper	Boolean	If true (the default), the Paper section of the dialog box will be enabled. This allows the selection of paper size and source.
AllowPrinter	Boolean	If true (the default), the Printer button will be enabled, allowing selection of the printer. If false, the printer selection cannot be changed in this dialog box.
Document	PrintDocument	A PrintDocument instance that holds the settings and is subsequently printed by the PrintDialog.
MinMargins	Margins	The minimum margins that can be set. The Margins class contains the properties Left, Right, Top, and Bottom. The default is null in C#, Nothing in VB.NET.
PageSettings	PageSettings	Specifies settings that modify the way a page is printed. Properties include Bounds, Color, Landscape, Margins, PaperSize, PaperSource, PrinterResolution, and PrinterSettings.
PrinterSettings	PrinterSettings	Printer settings that will be modified if the Printer button is clicked. This is typically accessed via PageSettings.PrinterSettings. PrinterName is the most commonly used PrinterSettings property, which specifies printer to print to.
ShowHelp	Boolean	If true, the dialog box displays a Help button. HelpRequest event must be handled for help to be displayed. The default is false.
ShowNetwork	Boolean	If true (the default), the Network button will be enabled when the Printer button is clicked to display the Page Setup Printer dialog box, shown in Figure 6-12.

To implement the PageSetupDialog in the ongoing example, double-click on the Page Setup button to bring up a code skeleton for the button Click event handler. Then enter the code highlighted in Example 6-19 for C# and in Example 6-20 for VB.NET.

Example 6-19. btnPageSetup Click event handler in C#

```csharp
private void btnPageSetup_Click(object sender, System.EventArgs e)
{
    PageSetupDialog psd = new PageSetupDialog();
    psd.Document = pd;
    psd.ShowDialog();
}
```

Example 6-20. btnPageSetup Click event handler in VB.NET

```
Private Sub btnPageSetup_Click(ByVal sender As System.Object, _
                               ByVal e As System.EventArgs) _
                               Handles btnPageSetup.Click
    dim psd as New PageSetupDialog( )
    psd.Document = pd
    psd.ShowDialog( )
End Sub
```

Even with this code entered, the button still will not work correctly. To complete the implementation, a few more lines of code are needed. Notice that the second line of code in the btnPageSetup_Click method assigns a variable named pd, which is not declared in the method, to the PageSetupDialog.Document property. This variable must be a member variable so that it's scope will cover the Print button Click event handler as well as the Page Setup Click event handler. But before you can declare an object of type PrintDocument, the System.Drawing.Printing namespace must be referenced. Add the following line of code at the very top of the code window:

```
using System.Drawing.Printing;
```

```
imports System.Drawing.Printing
```

Now declare and initialize the PrintDocument object as a member variable by including one of the following lines of code inside the Form1 class definition:

```
private PrintDocument pd = new PrintDocument( );
```

```
dim pd as new PrintDocument( )
```

The Page Setup button is now complete.

PrintDialog

The PrintDialog common dialog box provides a standard printing UI for the user. However, it does not make the printing process easy for the developer, as you will see in the next example.

Implement printing in the CommonDialogs application by adding code to the Print button Click event handler. In addition, implement an event handler for the Print-Page event, which is raised every time a page is sent to the printer. The PrintPage event handler must keep track of how many lines have been printed on the page and compute the distance down the page for each line to begin. It then prints each line. If the example were more sophisticated, it would also keep track of the length of each line and handle line wrapping. As it is, long lines in this example will truncate at the right margin.

Figure 6-13 shows a typical PrintDialog common dialog box.

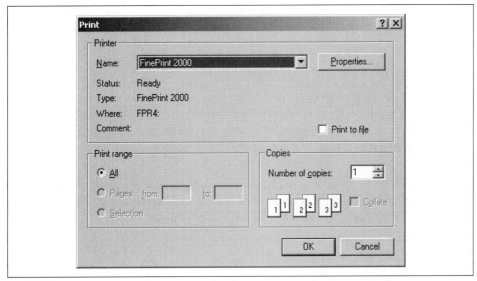

Figure 6-13. PrintDialog common dialog box

This example uses Streams, which were used previously in the OpenFileDialog example. Consequently, your code should already have a reference to the System.IO namespace:

```
using System.IO;
```

```
imports System.IO
```

 There are other techniques for feeding the text to the PrintPage event handler, such as passing the entire string as a whole, keeping track of what actually got printed (knowing the size of the font), and using substrings to print the remainder, or using the Lines property of the TextBox.

Specifically, this example uses the StringReader class derived from the TextReader class. A TextReader is used for character input, which suits the contents of the Text-Box. A StreamReader object is used for generalized byte input, and a BinaryReader object is used for reading binary data.

Since the StringReader object must be referenced by the Print button, the Print Preview button Click event handlers, and the PrintPage event handler, it should be declared as a Form1 class member variable. Insert the following line of code inside the Form1 class definition:

```
private StringReader sr;
```

```
private sr as StringReader
```

If you wanted to print a file rather than the contents of a TextBox, you would use a StreamReader object. In that case, the C# member variable would be:

```
[C#]   private StreamReader sr;
```

and the VB.NET declaration would be:

```
[VB]   private sr as StreamReader
```

The btnPrint_Click event handler calls the Print( ) method on the print document pd declared earlier. This raises a PrintPage event for every page sent to the printer. To print something, you must put the print code into the PrintPage event handler, which in this example is called pdPrintPage.

pdPrintPage must be registered with the event delegate as an event handler method for the PrintPage event. This is done once, in the form constructor. The event handler is added to the delegate with the following line of code:

```
[C#]   pd.PrintPage += new PrintPageEventHandler(pdPrintPage);
```

```
[VB]   AddHandler pd.PrintPage, AddressOf pdPrintPage
```

The StringReader is used in pdPrintPage, the PrintPage event handler, but it must be instantiated before that method is entered. The fundamental reason is that for multi-page print jobs, you want only one StringReader, or else you will just get infinite copies of the first page. You could just instantiate the StringReader in the btnPrint_Click event handler, except that it will also be used by the Print Preview dialog box, described shortly.

To accomplish this, you will use two events of the PrintDocument class: BeginPrint and EndPrint. As their names suggest, they are raised at the beginning and end of the print job, respectively. Both take an event argument of type PrintEventArgs. This event argument offers a Cancel property, which allows the print job to be cancelled. Event handlers for these two events will also be registered in the form constructor:

```
[C#]   pd.BeginPrint += new PrintEventHandler(pdBeginPrint);
       pd.EndPrint += new PrintEventHandler(pdEndPrint);
```

```
[VB]   AddHandler pd.BeginPrint, AddressOf pdBeginPrint
       AddHandler pd.EndPrint, AddressOf pdEndPrint
```

Implement the Print button Click event handler by double-clicking on the Print button and entering the highlighted code from Example 6-21 for C# and Example 6-22 for VB.NET. Notice that these code examples include both the code for the btnPrint_Click event handler and the separate PrintPage event-handler method, pdPrintPage, just described.

Example 6-21. btnPrint Click, PrintPage, BeginPrint, and EndPrint event handlers in C#

```
[C#]  private void btnPrint_Click(object sender, System.EventArgs e)
      {
```

```csharp
PrintDialog pdlg = new PrintDialog( );
pdlg.Document=pd;

if (pdlg.ShowDialog( ) == DialogResult.OK)
{
    try
    {
        pd.Print( );
    }
    catch(Exception ex)
    {
        MessageBox.Show("Print error: " + ex.Message);
    }
}
}

private void pdPrintPage(object sender, PrintPageEventArgs e)
{
    float linesPerPage = 0;
    float verticalOffset = 0;
    float leftMargin = e.MarginBounds.Left;
    float topMargin = e.MarginBounds.Top;
    int linesPrinted = 0;
    String strLine = null;

    linesPerPage = e.MarginBounds.Height / fnt.GetHeight(e.Graphics);

    while (linesPrinted < linesPerPage &&
            ((strLine = sr.ReadLine( ))!= null ))
    {
        verticalOffset = topMargin + (linesPrinted * fnt.GetHeight(e.Graphics));
        e.Graphics.DrawString(strLine, fnt, Brushes.Black, leftMargin,
                                verticalOffset);
        linesPrinted++;
    }

    if (strLine != null)
        e.HasMorePages = true;
    else
        e.HasMorePages = false;
}   //  close pdPrintPage

private void pdBeginPrint(object sender, PrintEventArgs e)
{
    //  Use the following line to print the contents of a TextBox
    sr = new StringReader(txtFile.Text);

    //  Use the following line to print a file
    //   sr = new StreamReader("c:\\test.txt");

    fnt = txtFile.Font;
}
```

Example 6-21. btnPrint Click, PrintPage, BeginPrint, and EndPrint event handlers in C# (continued)

C#
```csharp
private void pdEndPrint(object sender, PrintEventArgs e)
{
    sr.Close();
    MessageBox.Show("Done printing.");
}
```

Example 6-22. btnPrint Click, PrintPage, BeginPrint, and EndPrint event handlers in VB.NET

VB
```vbnet
    Private Sub btnPrint_Click(ByVal sender As System.Object, _
                               ByVal e As System.EventArgs) _
                               Handles btnPrint.Click
        dim pdlg as New PrintDialog()
        pdlg.Document=pd

        if pdlg.ShowDialog() = DialogResult.OK then
            try
                ' Set the font from the current font of the TextBox
                fnt = txtFile.Font

                pd.Print()
            catch ex as Exception
                MessageBox.Show("Print error: " + ex.Message)
            end try
        end if
    End Sub

private sub pdPrintPage(ByVal sender As System.Object, _
                        ByVal e As PrintPageEventArgs)
    dim linesPerPage as single = 0
    dim verticalOffset as Single = 0
    dim leftMargin as Single = e.MarginBounds.Left
    dim topMargin as Single = e.MarginBounds.Top
    dim linesPrinted as Integer = 0
    dim strLine as String = Nothing

    linesPerPage = e.MarginBounds.Height / fnt.GetHeight(e.Graphics)

    strLine = sr.ReadLine()
    dim boolDone as Boolean = false
        while ((linesPrinted < linesPerPage) and not boolDone)
            try
                if strLine.Length >= 0 then
                    verticalOffset = topMargin + (linesPrinted * _
                        fnt.GetHeight(e.Graphics))
                    e.Graphics.DrawString(strLine, fnt, Brushes.Black, _
                        leftMargin, verticalOffset)
                    linesPrinted += 1
                    strLine = sr.ReadLine()
                end if
            catch
                boolDone = true
```

```
VB              end try
            end while

        if strLine <> Nothing then
            e.HasMorePages = true
        else
            e.HasMorePages = false
        end if
end sub     '   close pdPrintPage

private sub pdBeginPrint(ByVal sender As System.Object, _
                         ByVal e As PrintEventArgs)
    '   Use the following line to print the contents of a TextBox
    sr = new StringReader(txtFile.Text)

    '   Use the following line to print a file
    'sr = new StreamReader("c:\test.txt")

    '   Set the font from the current font of the TextBox
    fnt = txtFile.Font
End Sub

private sub pdEndPrint(ByVal sender As System.Object, _
                       ByVal e As PrintEventArgs)
    sr.Close( )
    MessageBox.Show("Done printing.")
End Sub
```

The first two lines of code in the btnPrint_Click method instantiates a new Print-Dialog common dialog box and assigns the already declared PrintDocument pd to its Document property. (The PrintDocument was instantiated as a form member variable and used as part of the PageSetupDialog example in the previous section.) If the PageSetupDialog had been called from the Page Setup button, then any changes made to the page setup would be contained in the PrintDocument and therefore applied to the current print job.

The next line is an if statement that displays the dialog box modally and tests the DialogResult property to see if the user terminated the dialog by clicking OK. If so, then the code inside the if block is executed, which is the single line of code that actually performs the printing:

```
pd.Print( )
```

This line is wrapped in a try/catch block. This way, if any problems arise during the printing process, say because the printer is not available, they can be handled gracefully.

The PageDocument Print() method is called to print the document. However, the fun is just beginning. Before the print job actually begins, the PageDocument Begin-Print event is raised, which causes the event handler, pdBeginPrint, to execute. The

StringReader is instantiated here. (There is also a commented-out line of code that could be used instead of the StringReader if you wanted to print the contents of a file, rather than a text box.) The font is set based on the current Font property of TextBox.

As each page is printed, the PrintPage event is raised, which is handled by the event handler method pdPrintPage. This event handler is passed an event argument of type PrintPageEventArgs, which has the properties (read/write, except where noted) listed in Table 6-11.

Table 6-11. PrintPageEventArgs properties

Property	Type	Description
Cancel	Boolean	If `true`, the print job should be canceled.
Graphics	Graphics	Gets the Graphics to paint the page. Read-only.
HasMorePages	Boolean	If `true`, indicates an additional page should be printed. The default is `false`.
MarginBounds	Rectangle	The rectangular area inside the page margins. Read-only.
PageBounds	Rectangle	The rectangular area representing the entire page. Read-only. Note that most printers cannot print to the edge of the page.
PageSettings	PageSettings	Page settings for the current page. Read-only.

The first several lines of code in the pdPrintPage method declare and instantiate variables for use in the method.

linesPerPage is a calculated floating-point number (single in VB.NET) which indicates the number of lines of text on the page, based on the heights of the page and the current font. This calculation is:

```
linesPerPage = e.MarginBounds.Height / fnt.GetHeight(e.Graphics);
```

As shown in Table 6-11, MarginBounds is a property of the PrintPageEventArgs event argument. As an object of type Rectangle, it has the properties shown in Table 6-12 (read/write, except where noted). Thus, the linesPerPage is calculated by dividing the height of the page inside the margins by the height of the current font.

Table 6-12. Rectangle properties

Property	Type	Access	Description
Height	integer		Height of this Rectangle.
Width	integer		Width of this Rectangle.
X	integer		X-coordinate of the upper-left corner of this Rectangle.
Y	integer		Y-coordinate of the upper-left corner of this Rectangle.
Location	Point		Upper-left corner of this Rectangle.
Bottom	integer	Read-only	Y-coordinate of the bottom of this Rectangle.
Top	integer	Read-only	Y-coordinate of the top edge of this Rectangle.
Left	integer	Read-only	X-coordinate of the left edge of this Rectangle.

Table 6-12. Rectangle properties (continued)

Property	Type	Access	Description
Right	integer	Read-only	X-coordinate of the right edge of this Rectangle.
Size	Size		Width and height of this Rectangle.
IsEmpty	Boolean	Read-only	Returns true if Height, Width, X, and Y properties all have values of zero.

The next several lines are the meat of the method, reproduced here:

```csharp
while (linesPrinted < linesPerPage &&
      ((strLine = sr.ReadLine())!= null ))
{
    verticalOffset = topMargin + (linesPrinted * fnt.GetHeight(e.Graphics));
    e.Graphics.DrawString(strLine, fnt, Brushes.Black, leftMargin,
                        verticalOffset);
    linesPrinted++;
}
```

```vbnet
strLine = sr.ReadLine()
dim boolDone as Boolean = false
while ((linesPrinted < linesPerPage) and not boolDone)
    try
        if strLine.Length >= 0 then
            verticalOffset = topMargin + (linesPrinted * _
                fnt.GetHeight(e.Graphics))
            e.Graphics.DrawString(strLine, fnt, Brushes.Black, _
                leftMargin, verticalOffset)
            linesPrinted += 1
            strLine = sr.ReadLine()
        end if
    catch
        boolDone = true
    end try
end while
```

The code here is somewhat different in the two languages. In either case, a while loop tests if the number of lines printed exceeds the number of lines previously calculated per page.

The C# version also tests if the current line is null, indicating that it has read past the end of the StringReader. The C# version is able to assign the string value to strLine from the StringReader in-line with the latter test because the assignment operator (=) in C# is distinct from the equality operator (= =).

In the VB.NET version, the assignment is initially done outside the while loop, and again at the end of each iteration through the while loop. However, a simple test to see if the string strLine is Nothing returns false if the string consists only of a carriage return/line feed, as well as if the string is truly Nothing. This causes the print job to end prematurely if there are any empty lines in the text file being printed. To work around this problem, the Length property of the string is tested in an if statement. If the string is truly Nothing, an exception will be raised, which is trapped by the try/catch block, setting a flag.

If there is something to print, then the vertical offset from the top of the page is calculated based on the Top property of the MarginsBounds property of the PrintPageEventArgs event argument, plus the product of the font height times the number of lines already printed. Then the DrawString method of the Graphics class is called to actually print the line of text. This version of the overloaded method takes five arguments: the string to print, the font, a Brush color, the left margin, and the vertical offset.

 Printing of text will be further detailed in Chapter 10.

Once the line of text is printed, the linesPrinted counter is incremented. In the VB.NET version only, the next string to be printed is fetched from the StringReader, and the while loop is traversed again if the test still passes.

Once the page is printed—i.e., the test in the while loop fails—then the code tests to see if there is still more to print. This is reproduced here:

```
if (strLine != null)
    e.HasMorePages = true;
else
    e.HasMorePages = false;
```

```
if strLine <> Nothing then
    e.HasMorePages = true
else
    e.HasMorePages = false
end if
```

If there is nothing more to print, then strLine will be empty and the HasMorePages property of the PrintPageEventArgs event argument will be set to false; otherwise it will be set true. As long as it is true, the PrintPage event will be raised at the conclusion of each page and pdPrintPage, the PrintPage event handler, will be called again.

When the print job is complete, the PrintDocument EndPrint event is raised, invoking the pdEndPrint event handler. This method closes the StringReader and puts a message up for the user.

Print Preview Dialog

In addition to the common dialogs discussed so far, all of which are derived from the CommonDialog class, the framework includes a PrintPreviewDialog that derives from System.Windows.Forms.Form. This class contains a PrintPreview control, which you could also place directly on a form.

The PrintPreviewDialog, shown in Figure 6-14, uses the same PrintDocument used previously in this example by the PageSetup and Print dialogs. Any changes made to the print document in the PageSetup dialog are reflected in the print preview. The Preview dialog allows the user to zoom in on previewed page, set the number of pages displayed at one time (1, 2, 3, 4, or 6), and to print directly from this dialog.

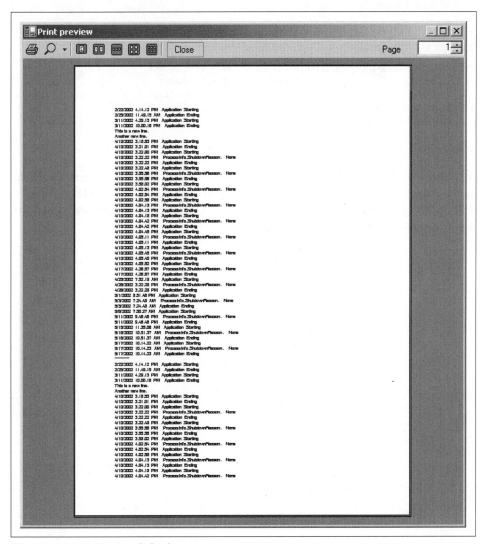

Figure 6-14. PrintPreview dialog box

This dialog is called using the btnPrintPreview button. The Click event handler for the button is shown in Example 6-23 in C# and in Example 6-24 in VB.NET.

Example 6-23. btnPrintPreview Click event handler in C#

```
private void btnPrintPreview_Click(object sender, System.EventArgs e)
{
    PrintPreviewDialog ppdlg = new PrintPreviewDialog();
    ppdlg.Document = pd;
    ppdlg.ShowDialog();
}
```

Example 6-24. btnPrintPreview Click event handler in VB.NET

```
Private Sub btnPrintPreview_Click(ByVal sender As System.Object, _
                                  ByVal e As System.EventArgs) _
                                  Handles btnPrintPreview.Click
    dim ppdlg as New PrintPreviewDialog()
    ppdlg.Document = pd
    ppdlg.ShowDialog()
End Sub
```

This event handler instantiates the PrintPreview dialog box and assigns the Document property. Then a single line of code displays the dialog box modally. All work of displaying the preview is handled by the PageDocument PrintPage event handler, already implemented for the Print dialog.

CHAPTER 7

Controls: The Base Class

A *control* is an object with a visual interface that appears on a form and that displays information to the user. Examples of controls include buttons, labels and listboxes. Controls are also used to gather input from the user, either from the keyboard or from a pointing device such as the mouse.

There are nearly forty different controls included with the .NET Framework (not to mention numerous other components and related objects), providing a wide range of functionality. You can also derive from most controls to create specialized versions of the standard controls, or you can combine controls and even create entirely new controls. The creation of custom controls is covered in Chapter 17.

Control Class

All controls are derived from the System.Windows.Forms.Control base class, which provides an extensive set of properties, methods, and events for all controls, giving the controls their basic functionality. Many of the most common and useful members will be described in this and subsequent chapters.

Class Hierarchy

The Control class is not instantiated directly; only derived classes are instantiated. Figure 7-1 shows the class hierarchy for the Control classes.

System.Object is the ultimate base class of all controls (as well as all classes in the .NET Framework). The Object class provides low-level services to all classes through methods such as ToString (which returns a String that represents the Object in a culture-sensitive, human-readable format). It is very common for classes to override the Object methods.

The next level in the class hierarchy is System.MarshalByRefObject, which provides services to applications that support remoting.

Remoting, the process of moving objects across application domain or machine boundaries, is beyond the scope of this book but is discussed in Jesse Liberty's *Programming C#* (O'Reilly).

The System.ComponentModel.Component class provides an implementation of the IComponent interface, which enables the logical containment of components in a container. It provides the Container, Events, and other properties, as well as the Dispose method (which releases resources used by a component), all of which are important to the implementation of controls. In addition to controls, the Component class is also the base class for such objects as the Timer, the HelpProvider, and the Tool-Tip. Specific components will be discussed throughout the book, where relevant.

Finally we get to the System.Windows.Forms.Control class. Components that have a visual representation are derived from the Control class. As such, they have properties such as BackColor, Location, Size, and Text; methods such as Hide, Show, and Focus; and events such as Click, GotFocus, and Paint.

Note that the Form itself is a Control, derived from the Control class via the ScrollableControl and ContainerControl classes.

Common Features

Since all controls are derived from a common class, it stands to reason that they will have a common set of features and functionality. The rest of this chapter will explore the aspects common to all controls.

Parent/child relationship

All controls can take part in parent/child relationships. A *parent* control can contain one or more *child* controls. Those child controls are contained within the Controls collection of the parent. Every control, except the top-level form, has a *Parent* property, of type Control, which is used to get or set the parent control, which contains the control. If the Parent property is null (Nothing in VB.NET)—i.e., the control does not have a parent control—then the control will not be visible or accessible unless it is the top-level control. These relationships are defined by the values of the Control properties listed in Table 7-1.

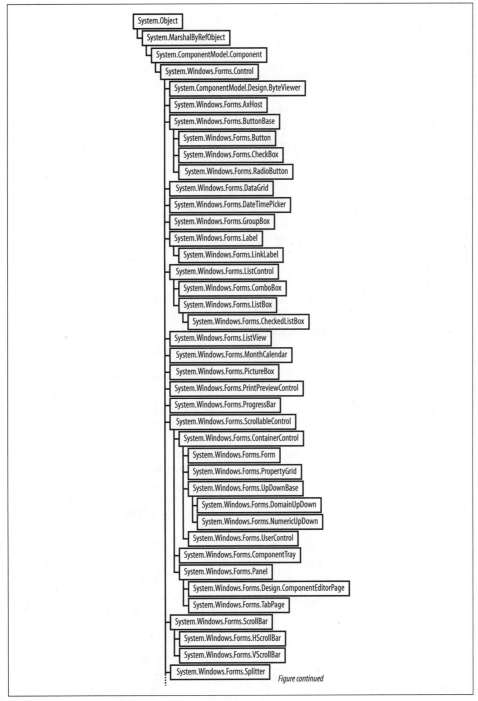

Figure 7-1. Control class hierarchy

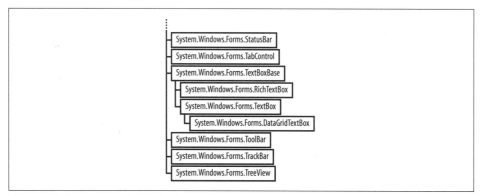

Figure 7-1. Control class hierarchy (continued)

Table 7-1. Control properties relevant to parent/child relationships

Property	Value type	Description
Container	IContainer	Read-only. An object that implements the IContainer interface.
ContainsFocus	Boolean	Read-only. Returns true if the control or one of its children has focus.
Controls	Control.ControlCollection	Read-only. Returns a collection of all the child controls.
HasChildren	Boolean	Read-only. Returns true if the control has one or more child controls—i.e., if the Count property of the Controls collection is greater than zero.
Parent	Control	Read/write. The control object that contains this control. If null (Nothing in VB.NET), then this control is removed from the Controls collection and will not be displayed or accessible.
TopLevelControl	Control	Read-only. Returns the control at the very top of the control hierarchy—i.e., the control with no parent.
		The TopLevelControl will be the Form. In the case of MDI child forms and their children, the TopLevelControl will be the containing MDI parent form.

The source code shown in Example 7-1 (in C#) and in Example 7-2 (in VB.NET) demonstrate several of the properties listed in Table 7-1. In these examples, a button control is instantiated, has several properties set, and has a method added to the Click event delegate. The highlighted lines of code demonstrate two equivalent ways (one of which is commented out) to add the Button control to the ControlParent's controls collection.

Example 7-1. Control parent/child properties in C# (ControlParent.cs)

```csharp
using System;
using System.Drawing;
using System.Windows.Forms;
```

```csharp
namespace ProgrammingWinApps
{
   public class ControlParent : Form
   {

      private Button btn;

      public ControlParent( )
      {
         Text = "Control Parent";

         btn = new Button( );
         btn.Location = new Point(50,50);
         btn.Size = new Size(100,23);
         btn.Text = "Relationships";
         btn.Click += new System.EventHandler(btn_Click);

         // Use one of the following lines to add the Button control
         //   to the Controls collection.
         // Controls.Add(btn);
         btn.Parent = this;
      }

      static void Main( )
      {
         Application.Run(new ControlParent( ));
      }

      private void btn_Click(object sender, EventArgs e)
      {
         MessageBox.Show("Button Parent:  " + btn.Parent.ToString( ) + "\n" +
            "Button HasChildren:  " + btn.HasChildren.ToString( ) + "\n" +
            "TopLevelControl:  " + btn.TopLevelControl.ToString( ) + "\n" +
            "Form HasChildren:  " + this.HasChildren.ToString( ) + "\n" +
            "Form Controls Count:  " + this.Controls.Count.ToString( ),
            "Button Relationships");        }
   }
}
```

Example 7-2. Control parent/child properties in VB.NET (ControlParent.vb)

```vbnet
imports System
imports System.Drawing
imports System.Windows.Forms

namespace ProgrammingWinApps
   public class ControlParent : inherits Form

      Private WithEvents btn as Button
```

Example 7-2. Control parent/child properties in VB.NET (ControlParent.vb) (continued)

VB

```
    public sub New( )
        Text = "Control Parent"

        btn = new Button( )
        btn.Location = new Point(50,50)
        btn.Size = new Size(100,23)
        btn.Text = "Relationships"

        ' Use one of the following lines to add the Button control
        '    to the Controls collection.
        ' Controls.Add(btn)
        btn.Parent = me
    end sub

    public shared sub Main( )
        Application.Run(new ControlParent( ))
    end sub

    private sub btn_Click(ByVal sender as object, _
            ByVal e as EventArgs) _
            Handles btn.Click
        MessageBox.Show("Button Parent:    " + btn.Parent.ToString( ) + vbLf + _
            "Button HasChildren:   " + btn.HasChildren.ToString( ) + vbLf + _
            "TopLevelControl:   " + btn.TopLevelControl.ToString( ) + vbLf + _
            "Form HasChildren:   " + me.HasChildren.ToString( ) + vbLf + _
            "Form Controls Count:   " + me.Controls.Count.ToString( ), _
            "Button Relationships")
    end sub
  end class
end namespace
```

The code in Examples 7-1 and 7-2 is handcoded in a text editor, as will be many of the examples in the chapters covering controls, to avoid the clutter introduced by Visual Studio .NET. As with all source code files created outside Visual Studio .NET, they must be compiled from a command line to generate the executable file, as described in Chapter 2. Remember to use the command prompt found at Start Button → Programs → Microsoft Visual Studio .NET 2003 → Visual Studio .NET Tools → Visual Studio .NET 2003 Command Prompt.

To compile the code, use the appropriate following command:

C#

```
csc /out:ControlParent.exe /t:winexe ControlParent.cs
```

VB

```
vbc /out:ControlParent.exe /t:winexe /r:system.dll,system.drawing.dll,system.windows.
forms.dll,system.data.dll /imports:Microsoft.VisualBasic ControlParent.vb
```

C# doesn't need the references in the command line because a file called *csc.rsp* contains "default" references for the C# compiler. VB.NET has no equivalent, so the references must be included in the command line.

In addition to the "default" references, this VB.NET example imports the Microsoft.VisualBasic namespace to enable use of the vbCrLf Visual Basic intrinsic constant. When VB.NET programs are compiled in Visual Studio .NET, that namespace is automatically and invisibly included.

In the code in Examples 7-1 and 7-2, a Button control named btn is declared as a member variable. It is instantiated and has several properties set in the constructor. Of particular interest here are the two highlighted lines of code in each example:

C#
```
// Controls.Add(btn);
btn.Parent = this;
```

VB
```
' Controls.Add(btn)
btn.Parent = me
```

These two lines of code accomplish the same task: they define the parent control for the button, and they add the button to the parent's Controls collection.

The first line (commented out) explicitly adds the button to the Controls collection and implicitly makes the current object the parent of the button. The second line explicitly assigns the parent/child relation and implicitly adds the button to the Controls collection. Which way you accomplish this task is entirely up to you; the end result is the same.

You can add multiple controls to the Controls collection using the AddRange method of the Control.ControlCollection class. This method takes an array of Controls as an argument. So, for example, suppose you had a form with three buttons named btn1, btn2, and btn3. Rather than having three individual statements declaring the Parent property for each control, you could use a single AddRange statement. This would look like:

C#
```
this.Controls.AddRange(new Control[] {btn1, btn2, btn3})
```

VB
```
me.Controls.AddRange(new Control() {btn1, btn2, btn3})
```

Visual Studio .NET always adds controls to the Controls collection using the AddRange method, even if only a single control is being added.

The Button Click event handler puts up a MessageBox that concatenates and displays several Control properties. Notice that the C# version of the program uses the

NewLine escape sequence (\n) directly, while the VB.NET version uses the equivalent VB.NET intrinsic constant vbLf.

 Common C# escape sequences and the equivalent VB.NET constants are listed in Table 4-9 in Chapter 4.

When the program is compiled, run, and the button is clicked, the MessageBox shown in Figure 7-2 is displayed.

Figure 7-2. ControlParent MessageBox

Z-order

It is possible for two or more controls to occupy the same piece of screen real estate. In fact, by definition, every child control overlays part of its parent control. Controls can partly obscure underlying controls, even without a parent/child relationship. In these situations, one of the controls is "on top" and one of the controls is "on the bottom." Other controls are in between, one above, or below the other. This vertical relationship is quantified in the *z-order*.

The z-order is named after the Z-axis in a three-dimensional Cartesian coordinate system. The X and Y axes represent the horizontal and vertical directions in the plane of the video screen. The Z-axis represents the direction perpendicular to the screen— i.e., the depth of the image.

The z-order of a control can only be set programmatically or at design time. It cannot be changed by the user at runtime, other than forms in an MDI application, except under program control. Clicking on a control or otherwise giving it focus does not change its z-order (unless you write code to make it change).

The z-order is initially determined by the order in which a control is assigned to the Parent's Controls collection. The first control added to the collection (index 0) is at the top of the z-order for that Parent. Each subsequent control added to the Controls collection is placed just below the controls previously added. The child control with an index of Controls.Count -1 is at the bottom of the z-order.

When you click the mouse or otherwise raise a mouse event, the event is directed to the control under the mouse. If there is more than one control directly under the mouse, the event is directed to the control at the top of the z-order—i.e., the visible control. (For a complete discussion of mouse events, see Chapter 8.) So if the mouse is clicked when the mouse cursor is over the parent Form, the Form handles the mouseclick. If the mouse cursor moves over a Panel control on the Form, the Panel handles the mouseclick. If the mouse cursor is over a Button on the Panel which is on the Form, the Button handles the mouseclick.

If multiple controls are docked against the same edge of a container, the docked control with the higher z-order is located closer to the center of the client area. The docked control with the lowest z-order is immediately adjacent to the edge of the container. (See the section "Docking" later in this chapter.)

Changing the z-order

In Visual Studio .NET you can easily change the z-order of a control by selecting the control in design view, and then using the Format → Order menu command to select either Bring to Front or Send To Back. You can also change it by expanding the region of code labeled Windows Form Designer generated code, finding the AddRange statement that adds all the controls to the Controls collection, and editing the order in which those controls are listed in the statement. The first control in the list will be at the top of the z-order, and the last control in the list will be at the bottom.

The boilerplate comment in the code warns against editing the code in the auto-generated region, although it does work if you are careful. Any code in this region not understood by VS.NET will be discarded.

Two methods of the Control class allow you to change the z-order programmatically: BringToFront and SendToBack, neither of which takes any argument or returns any value. So, for example, the following line of code will bring a button called Button1 to the top of the z-order (identical in both languages except for the semicolon):

```
Button1.BringToFront( );
```

while the following line will send it to the bottom of the z-order:

```
Button1.SendToBack( );
```

Ambient properties

If you do not set a property on a control, it might inherit the setting for that property from its container (parent control). Properties that can be inherited by contained controls are called *ambient properties*. Ambient properties allow a control to assume the appearance of its surrounding environment. Table 7-2 lists the ambient properties and their default values.

Table 7-2. Ambient properties

Property	Default value
BackColor	Color.Empty
Cursor	null in C#, Nothing in VB.NET
Font	null in C#, Nothing in VB.NET
ForeColor	Color.Empty

If the control does not have a parent and an ambient property is not set, then the control will use a default value for the ambient property.

The use of ambient properties can be illustrated by modifying the code from Figures 7-1 and 7-2 to add a Label control, setting the BackColor and ForeColor properties of the Form, and observing the effect on both the Button and Label controls. The C# code is shown in Example 7-3 and the VB.NET code is shown in Example 7-4. In both examples, the added lines of code are highlighted.

When the program is compiled and run, both the Button and the Label have a Green background color and a Yellow foreground color, matching the form.

Example 7-3. Ambient property in C# (ControlAmbientProperty.cs)

```
using System;
using System.Drawing;
using System.Windows.Forms;

namespace ProgrammingWinApps
{
   public class ControlAmbientProperties : Form
   {

      private Button btn;
      private Label lbl;
      public ControlAmbientProperties()
      {
         Text = "Control Parent";
         BackColor = Color.Green;
         ForeColor = Color.Yellow;
         btn = new Button();
         btn.Location = new Point(50,50);
         btn.Size = new Size(100,23);
         btn.Text = "Relationships";
         btn.Click += new System.EventHandler(btn_Click);
         btn.Parent = this;

         lbl = new Label();
         lbl.Text = "Ambient Properties";
         lbl.Parent = this;
      }

      static void Main()
      {
```

Example 7-3. Ambient property in C# (ControlAmbientProperty.cs) (continued)

```csharp
        Application.Run(new ControlAmbientProperties());
    }

    private void btn_Click(object sender, EventArgs e)
    {
        MessageBox.Show("Button Parent:  " + btn.Parent.ToString() + "\n" +
            "Button HasChildren:  " + btn.HasChildren.ToString() + "\n" +
            "TopLevelControl:  " + btn.TopLevelControl.ToString() + "\n" +
            "Form HasChildren:  " + this.HasChildren.ToString() + "\n" +
            "Form Controls Count:  " + this.Controls.Count.ToString(),
            "Button Relationships");
    }
  }
}
```

Example 7-4. Ambient property in VB.NET (ControlAmbientProperty.vb)

```vbnet
imports System
imports System.Drawing
imports System.Windows.Forms

namespace ProgrammingWinApps
   public class ControlParent : inherits Form

      Private WithEvents btn as Button
      private lbl as Label
      public sub New()
         Text = "Control Parent"
         BackColor = Color.Green
         ForeColor = Color.Yellow
         btn = new Button()
         btn.Location = new Point(50,50)
         btn.Size = new Size(100,23)
         btn.Text = "Relationships"
         btn.Parent = me

         lbl = new Label()
         lbl.Text = "Ambient Properties"
         lbl.Parent = me
      end sub

      public shared sub Main()
         Application.Run(new ControlParent())
      end sub

      private sub btn_Click(ByVal sender as object, _
            ByVal e as EventArgs) _
            Handles btn.Click
         MessageBox.Show("Button Parent:  " + btn.Parent.ToString() + vbCrLf + _
            "Button HasChildren:  " + btn.HasChildren.ToString() + vbCrLf + _
            "TopLevelControl:  " + btn.TopLevelControl.ToString() + vbCrLf + _
            "Form HasChildren:  " + me.HasChildren.ToString() + vbCrLf + _
```

Example 7-4. Ambient property in VB.NET (ControlAmbientProperty.vb) (continued)

```
            "Form Controls Count:  " + me.Controls.Count.ToString( ), _
            "Button Relationships")
      end sub
   end class
end namespace
```

Font

All controls have a Font property, of type Font. The Font property specifies the type-face or design, size, and style, for any text displayed by the control. Fonts and their properties are covered in detail in Chapter 9.

Size and location

The size and location of controls can be set either interactively using Visual Studio .NET, programmatically at design time, or programmatically at runtime. The control properties that pertain to size and location are listed in Table 7-3.

You have already seen the size and location for a Button control set in Example 7-3 (in C#) and in Example 7-4 (in VB.NET):

```
btn.Location = new Point(50,75)
btn.Size = new Size(100,23)
```

The Location property, of type Point, specifies the top-left corner of the control relative to the top-left corner of its container control, expressed as an instance of Point. Point is a structure (struct in C#) that provides an ordered pair of integer X,Y coordinates. In the code snippet shown above, the btn control is located 50 pixels to the right and 75 pixels down from the upper-left corner of its container (the form).

 The units can be pixels, inches, millimeters, etc., contained in the GraphicsUnits enumeration, listed in Table 10-3 in Chapter 10. For more on the scale units used by Location and Size, see Chapter 10.

The Label control does not have a set Location property; it defaults to a location of (0,0): the upper-left corner of the containing form.

The Size property of the Control class is of type Size. The Size value is a structure that contains an ordered pair of integers specifying the width and height of the control. In the code snippet above, btn is 100 pixels wide and 23 pixels high.

Both the Size and Point objects are value types, rather than reference types. This means that when these properties are returned, a copy of the original is returned, not a reference to the original value. If you change the value, it will not have any effect on the control. Instead, to change the size or location of a control, you must assign a new Point or Size object to the Location or Size properties, respectively, as shown in the code snippet above.

Alternatively, you can change the Location of a control by setting the Left or Top properties (the Right and Bottom properties are read-only) of the control and you can change the Size of a control by setting the Width or Height property of the control.

Several of the properties listed in Table 7-3 distinguish between the area and the client area of a control. For most controls, they are the same. For forms, however, the *client area* refers to the entire control minus the scrollbars, borders, titlebars and menus.

These properties, as well as several others listed in Table 7-3 are demonstrated in Example 7-5 in C# and in Example 7-6 in VB.NET.

Table 7-3. Control Size and location properties

Property	Value type	Description
Bottom	integer	Read-only. Returns the distance, in pixels, from control's bottom edge to the top edge of its container client area.
Bounds	Rectangle	Read/write. The size and location of the control.
ClientRectangle	Rectangle	Read-only. Returns the rectangle representing the client area of the control.
ClientSize	Size	Read/write. The size of the client area of a control. Requires the System.Drawing namespace.
DisplayRectangle	Rectangle	Read-only. Returns a rectangle representing the display area of a control—i.e., the smallest rectangle that encloses the control. For most controls, this corresponds to the ClientRectangle. It is useful primarily for scrollable controls, since it includes the entire control, including any part of the control not currently scrolled into view.
Height	integer	Read/write. The height of the control, in pixels.
Left	integer	Read/write. The x-coordinate, in pixels, of the left edge of the control. It is equivalent to the Point.X property of the Location property value.
Location	Point	Read/write. The upper-left corner of a control relative to the upper-left corner of its container. If the control is a Form, it is the upper-left corner of the Form in screen coordinates. Requires the System.Drawing namespace.
Right	integer	Read-only. Returns the distance, in pixels, from the control's right edge to the left edge of its container.
Size	Size	Read/write. An ordered pair of width and height properties specifying the size of a rectangular region which contains the control. Requires the System.Drawing namespace.
Top	integer	Read/write. The y-coordinate, in pixels, of the top edge of the control. This is equivalent to the Point.Y property of the Location property value.
Width	integer	Read/write. The width of the control, in pixels.

Example 7-5. Control size and location in C# (ControlSizeLocation.cs)

```
using System;
using System.Drawing;
using System.Windows.Forms;
```

Example 7-5. Control size and location in C# (ControlSizeLocation.cs) (continued)

```csharp
namespace ProgrammingWinApps
{
    public class ControlSizeLocation : Form
    {

        private Button btnShow;
        private Button btnChange;
        private Label lbl;

        public ControlSizeLocation( )
        {
            Text = "Control Parent";
            BackColor = Color.LightBlue;
            ForeColor = Color.DarkBlue;
            Size = new Size(350,200);

            btnShow = new Button( );
            btnShow.Location = new Point(50,50);
            btnShow.Size = new Size(100,23);
            btnShow.Text = "Show";
            btnShow.Click += new System.EventHandler(btnShow_Click);
            btnShow.Parent = this;

            btnChange = new Button( );
            btnChange.Location = new Point(200,50);
            btnChange.Size = new Size(100,23);
            btnChange.Text = "Change";
            btnChange.Click += new System.EventHandler(btnChange_Click);
            btnChange.Parent = this;

            lbl = new Label( );
            lbl.Text = "Control Size and Location";
            lbl.Size = new Size(400,25);
            lbl.Parent = this;
        }

        static void Main( )
        {
            Application.Run(new ControlSizeLocation( ));
        }

        private void btnShow_Click(object sender, EventArgs e)
        {
            MessageBox.Show("Button Bottom: \t" +
                    btnShow.Bottom.ToString( ) + "\n" +
                "Button Top:   \t" + btnShow.Top.ToString( ) + "\n" +
                "Button Left:  \t" + btnShow.Left.ToString( ) + "\n" +
                "Button Right: \t" + btnShow.Right.ToString( ) + "\n" +
                "Button Location: \t" + btnShow.Location.ToString( ) + "\n" +
                "Button Width:  \t" + btnShow.Width.ToString( ) + "\n" +
                "Button Height: \t" + btnShow.Height.ToString( ) + "\n" +
```

Example 7-5. Control size and location in C# (ControlSizeLocation.cs) (continued)

```
                "Button Size: \t" + btnShow.Size.ToString() + "\n" +
                "Button ClientSize: \t" + btnShow.ClientSize.ToString() + "\n" +
                "Form Size: \t" + this.Size.ToString() + "\n" +
                "Form ClientSize: \t " + this.ClientSize.ToString(),
                "Size & Location");
        }

        private void btnChange_Click(object sender, EventArgs e)
        {
            this.Size = new Size(800,200);
        }

    }
}
```

Example 7-6. Control size and location in VB.NET (ControlSizeLocation.vb)

```
imports System
imports System.Drawing
imports System.Windows.Forms

namespace ProgrammingWinApps
    public class ControlSizeLocation : inherits Form

        Private WithEvents btnShow as Button
        Private WithEvents btnChange as Button
        private lbl as Label

        public sub New()
            Text = "Control Parent"
            BackColor = Color.LightBlue
            ForeColor = Color.DarkBlue
            Size = new Size(350,200)

            btnShow = new Button()
            btnShow.Location = new Point(50,50)
            btnShow.Size = new Size(100,23)
            btnShow.Text = "Show"
            btnShow.Parent = me

            btnChange = new Button()
            btnChange.Location = new Point(200,50)
            btnChange.Size = new Size(100,23)
            btnChange.Text = "Change"
            btnChange.Parent = me

            lbl = new Label()
            lbl.Text = "Control Size and Location"
            lbl.Size = new Size(400,25)
```

```
VB        lbl.Parent = me
      end sub

      public shared sub Main( )
         Application.Run(new ControlSizeLocation( ))
      end sub

      private sub btnShow_Click(ByVal sender as object, _
            ByVal e as EventArgs) _
            Handles btnShow.Click
         MessageBox.Show("Button Bottom:  " + _
               vbTab + btnShow.Bottom.ToString( ) + vbLf + _
            "Button Top:   " + vbTab + _
               btnShow.Top.ToString( ) + vbLf + _
            "Button Left:   " + vbTab + _
               btnShow.Left.ToString( ) + vbLf + _
            "Button Right:  " + vbTab + _
               btnShow.Right.ToString( ) + vbLf + _
            "Button Location: " + vbTab + _
               btnShow.Location.ToString( ) + vbLf + _
            "Button Width:   " + vbTab + _
               btnShow.Width.ToString( ) + vbLf + _
            "Button Height:  " + vbTab + _
               btnShow.Height.ToString( ) + vbLf + _
            "Button Size:   " + vbTab + _
               btnShow.Size.ToString( ) + vbLf + _
            "Button ClientSize:  " + vbTab + _
               btnShow.ClientSize.ToString( ) + vbLf + _
            "Form Size:   " + vbTab + me.Size.ToString( ) + vbLf + _
            "Form ClientSize: " + vbTab + me.ClientSize.ToString( ), _
            "Size & Location")
      end sub

      private sub btnChange_Click(ByVal sender as object, _
            ByVal e as EventArgs) _
            Handles btnChange.Click
         me.Size = new Size(800,200)
      end sub
   end class
end namespace
```

The program shown in Examples 7-5 and 7-6 puts up a form 350 pixels wide and 200 pixels high, as indicated by the following line of code (identical in both languages except for the trailing semicolon):

```
Size = new Size(350,200);
```

Another way to accomplish this would be use these two lines:

```
Width = 350;
Height = 200;
```

The SDK documentation suggests that an application will have better performance if the Size property of a control is not set in its constructor. Instead, it recommends overriding the protected property Default-Size. If this performance improvement is significant to your application, you can add the following property to the class in C#:

```
protected override Size DefaultSize
{
    get
    {
        return new Size(400,400);
    }
}
```

or this code in VB.NET:

```
protected ReadOnly overrides Property DefaultSize as Size
    get
        return new Size(400,400)
    end get
end property
```

These code snippets will change the form size to 400 × 400 (intentionally different from inside the constructor so the difference is apparent). If you are overriding the DefaultSize property, do not set the Size, ClientSize, Height, or Width properties in the constructor.

There are two buttons on the form: one marked Show, named btnShow, and the other marked Change, named btnChange. Both buttons have their Location and Size properties set so that they will be aligned with each other and centered in the form, and their Text and Parent properties are set appropriately.

The event handler for the Show button Click event (btnShow_Click) displays the value of the Size and Location properties for the button and the form.

Note that this MessageBox uses both tab characters (\t in C# and vbTab in VB.NET) and line feeds (\n in C# and vbLf in VB.NET) to control the formatting of the displayed text.

When you run the program and click on the Show button, the message box will be displayed, as shown in Figure 7-3.

The event handler for the Change button (btnChange_Change) changes the size of the form to 800 pixels wide × 200 pixels high:

```
this.Size = new Size(800,200);
```

```
me.Size = new Size(800,200)
```

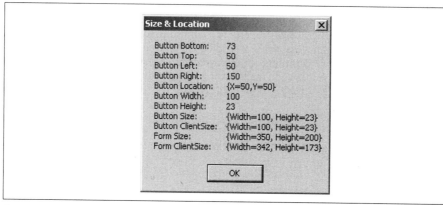

Figure 7-3. Control size and location

Dynamically setting size and location

The programs shown in Examples 7-5 and 7-6 work fine, but they have several short-comings. First of all, the size of the buttons are hardcoded. If the Button Text property changes, you may have to change the width of the button, and if the system running the program uses a different font size, the button may be sized incorrectly. The second shortcoming has to do with the location. The button is centered when the form first displays, but if the user resizes the form, then the button no longer will be centered.

The programs shown in Example 7-7 (in C#) and in Example 7-8 (in VB.NET) address these issues. The lines of code that differ from Examples 7-5 and 7-6 are highlighted. An analysis follows the code listings.

Example 7-7. Dynamic control size and location in C#
(ControlDynamicSizeLocation.cs)

```csharp
using System;
using System.Drawing;
using System.Windows.Forms;

namespace ProgrammingWinApps
{
    public class ControlDynamicSizeLocation : Form
    {
        private Button btnShow;
        private Label lbl;
        int xButtonSize, yButtonSize;

        public ControlDynamicSizeLocation()
        {
            Text = "Control Parent";
```

Example 7-7. Dynamic control size and location in C#
(ControlDynamicSizeLocation.cs) (continued)

```csharp
    btnShow = new Button( );
    btnShow.Parent = this;
    btnShow.Text = "Show Button Properties";
    //  move Size to after instantiation of btnShow so OnResize will work.
    Size = new Size(350,400);

    xButtonSize = (int)(Font.Height * .75) * btnShow.Text.Length;
    yButtonSize = Font.Height * 2;
    btnShow.Size = new Size(xButtonSize, yButtonSize);
    btnShow.Click += new System.EventHandler(btnShow_Click);

    lbl = new Label( );
    lbl.Text = "Control Size and Location - Dynamic";
    lbl.AutoSize = true;
    lbl.Parent = this;

    OnResize(EventArgs.Empty);
}

protected override void OnResize(EventArgs e)
{
    base.OnResize(e);

    //  Reposition btnShow based on new form size.
    int xPosition = (int)(this.ClientSize.Width / 2) -
                        (int)(xButtonSize / 2);
    int yPosition = (int)(this.ClientSize.Height / 2) -
                        (int)(yButtonSize / 2);
    btnShow.Location = new Point(xPosition, yPosition);
}

static void Main( )
{
    Application.Run(new ControlDynamicSizeLocation( ));
}

private void btnShow_Click(object sender, EventArgs e)
{
    MessageBox.Show("Button Bottom:  \t" +
        btnShow.Bottom.ToString( ) + "\n" +
      "Button Top:  \t" + btnShow.Top.ToString( ) + "\n" +
      "Button Left:  \t" + btnShow.Left.ToString( ) + "\n" +
      "Button Right:  \t" + btnShow.Right.ToString( ) + "\n" +
      "Button Location: \t" + btnShow.Location.ToString( ) + "\n" +
      "Button Width:  \t" + btnShow.Width.ToString( ) + "\n" +
      "Button Height:  \t" + btnShow.Height.ToString( ) + "\n" +
      "Button Size:  \t" + btnShow.Size.ToString( ) + "\n" +
      "Button ClientSize:  \t" + btnShow.ClientSize.ToString( ) + "\n" +
      "Font:\t" + btnShow.Font.ToString( ) + "\n" +
      "Font Family:\t" + btnShow.Font.FontFamily.ToString( ) + "\n" +
      "Font Style:\t" + btnShow.Font.Style.ToString( ) + "\n" +
```

Example 7-7. Dynamic control size and location in C#
(ControlDynamicSizeLocation.cs) (continued)

C#

```
            "Font Unit:\t" + btnShow.Font.Unit.ToString( ) + "\n" +
            "Form ClientSize: \t " + this.ClientSize.ToString( ),
            "Size & Location");
    }
  }
}
```

Example 7-8. Dynamic control size and location in VB.NET
(ControlDynamicSizeLocation.vb)

VB

```
imports System
imports System.Drawing
imports System.Windows.Forms

namespace ProgrammingWinApps
   public class ControlDynamicSizeLocation : inherits Form

      Private WithEvents btnShow as Button
      private lbl as Label
      private xButtonSize as integer
      private ybuttonSize as integer

      public sub New( )
         Text = "Control Parent"

         btnShow = new Button( )
         btnShow.Parent = me
         btnShow.Text = "Show Button Properties"

         '  move Size to after instantiation of btnShow so OnResize will work.
         Size = new Size(350,400)

         xButtonSize = Cint(Font.Height * .75) * btnShow.Text.Length
         yButtonSize = Font.Height * 2
         btnShow.Size = new Size(xButtonSize, yButtonSize)

         lbl = new Label( )
         lbl.Text = "Control Size and Location - Dynamic"
         lbl.AutoSize = true
         lbl.Parent = me

         OnResize(EventArgs.Empty)
      end sub


      protected overrides sub OnResize(ByVal e as EventArgs)
         MyBase.OnResize(e)

         '  Reposition btnShow based on new form size.
         dim xPosition as integer = Cint(me.ClientSize.Width / 2) - _
                               Cint(xButtonSize / 2)
         dim yPosition as integer = Cint(me.ClientSize.Height / 2) - _
```

```
VB                                    Cint(yButtonSize / 2)
            btnShow.Location = new Point(xPosition, yPosition)
         end sub

         public shared sub Main( )
             Application.Run(new ControlDynamicSizeLocation( ))
         end sub

         private sub btnShow_Click(ByVal sender as object, _
               ByVal e as EventArgs) _
               Handles btnShow.Click
             MessageBox.Show("Button Bottom:   " + _
                 vbTab + btnShow.Bottom.ToString( ) + vbLf + _
                 "Button Top:    " + vbTab + _
                 btnShow.Top.ToString( ) + vbLf + _
                 "Button Left:   " + vbTab + _
                 btnShow.Left.ToString( ) + vbLf + _
                 "Button Right:   " + vbTab + _
                 btnShow.Right.ToString( ) + vbLf + _
                 "Button Location: " + vbTab + _
                 btnShow.Location.ToString( ) + vbLf + _
                 "Button Width:   " + vbTab + _
                 btnShow.Width.ToString( ) + vbLf + _
                 "Button Height:   " + vbTab + _
                 btnShow.Height.ToString( ) + vbLf + _
                 "Button Size:   " + vbTab + _
                 btnShow.Size.ToString( ) + vbLf + _
                 "Button ClientSize:   " + vbTab + _
                 btnShow.ClientSize.ToString( ) + vbLf + _
                 "Font:" + vbTab + btnShow.Font.ToString( ), _
                 "Size & Location")
         end sub
      end class
   end namespace
```

Two main issues are addressed in Examples 7-7 and 7-8: the size of the control and the location of the control.

Dynamically controlling size. The size of the Button control, btnShow, is determined by the number of characters in the btnShow.Text property and the size of the Font. Two member variables, xButtonSize and yButtonSize, are declared. They need to be scoped for the entire class because they will be referenced in two different methods (discussed later).

The btnShow.Text.Length property determines the number of characters. The width of the button is calculated by multiplying the number of characters in the Text property by a width factor for each character. Three-quarters of the Height of the Font is used for the width factor. This width factor works well for most fonts, including proportional (variable pitch) and fixed pitch fonts.

You might think you could use the Size property of the Font for the width factor. This property is actually the em-size of the font, the width of the letter M. However, when changing the default Windows display font from Small to Large, the em-size actually decreases, although the Font.Height does increase correctly. Windows applies a scaling factor to the font to display the desired size, even though the reported em-size is counterintuitive.

You could accomplish the same goal by measuring the size of the string using the Graphics class method MeasureString, as shown in Chapter 10.

The line of code that calculates the width of the button is as follows:

C#
```
xButtonSize = (int)( Font.Height * .75) * btnShow.Text.Length;
```

VB
```
xButtonSize = Cint(Font.Height * .75) * btnShow.Text.Length
```

The product of the Font.Height property, of type float in C# (single in VB.NET), and a numeric constant must be cast to an integer, since xButtonSize is of type integer. The Length property is already an integer.

The Height of the Font determines the Height of the Button. This is done in the following line of code:

```
yButtonSize = Font.Height * 2
```

Multiplying the Font.Height by 2 just makes the button less visually crowded. It turns out that the button has an internal border of 4 pixels around each edge. If you made the Button height the same as Font.Height, then 8 pixels would be clipped from the characters. If you are really tight on form real estate, you could use the following line of code to set the button height, making the button equal to Font.Height plus 8 pixels:

```
yButtonSize = Font.Height + 8
```

These two dimensions come together when the button's Size property is set in the following line of code:

```
btnShow.Size = new Size(xButtonSize, yButtonSize)
```

Now no matter what font is used for the Form, the button will be sized correctly. (If you are setting the Font for the Form, do so in the constructor before the Button size is calculated.) Also, you will not have to rejigger the size of the button if you change the Text property.

Dynamically controlling location. There are two situations to consider when controlling the location of the Button control. The first is when the form initially loads, and the second is when the form is resized by the user. Considering the latter situation first, all members of the Control class, including the Form, raise a Resize event whenever they are resized, whether by the user or programmatically. This Resize event is handled by the .NET Framework using the OnResize event handler.

For a complete discussion of events, see Chapter 4.

In Examples 7-7 and 7-8, the OnResize method is overridden to dynamically recalculate the correct button Location based on the new Form dimensions. The overridden OnResize event handler is reproduced here:

C#
```csharp
protected override void OnResize(EventArgs e)
{
    base.OnResize(e);

    // Reposition btnShow based on new form size.
    int xPosition = (int)(this.ClientSize.Width / 2) -
                    (int)(xButtonSize / 2);
    int yPosition = (int)(this.ClientSize.Height / 2) -
                    (int)(yButtonSize / 2);
    btnShow.Location = new Point(xPosition, yPosition);
}
```

VB
```vb
protected overrides sub OnResize(ByVal e as EventArgs)
    MyBase.OnResize(e)

    ' Reposition btnShow based on new form size.
    dim xPosition as integer = Cint(me.ClientSize.Width / 2) - _
                               Cint(xButtonSize / 2)
    dim yPosition as integer = Cint(me.ClientSize.Height / 2) - _
                               Cint(yButtonSize / 2)
    btnShow.Location = new Point(xPosition, yPosition)
end sub
```

You can accomplish the same effect as these examples with a lot less effort using the Anchor property, as discussed later in this chapter in the section "Anchoring." However, this technique can accomplish things not possible with Anchor, such as forcing columns of controls to dynamically reposition in response to user resizing the form.

The override keyword (in VB.NET it is overrides) indicates to the compiler that this method is overriding a virtual OnResize method (overridable in VB.NET). The OnResize method takes a single argument, of type EventArgs.

The first line in the method calls the OnResize method from the base class. This ensures that any functionality contained in the base method is not omitted and any other methods registered with the event delegate are notified. This *chaining up* to the base method is done with the following line of code:

C#
```csharp
base.OnResize(e);
```

VB
```vb
MyBase.OnResize(e)
```

Next, two integer variables are declared and instantiated to hold the X and Y coordinates of the button, xPosition and yPosition, respectively. These coordinates are calculated based on the ClientSize of the Form (the size of the entire Form window minus the titlebar, menu and toolbar, status bar, and any scrollbars) and the size of the Button. All size terms are cast as integers, since xPosition and yPosition are integers.

Finally, the Location property of btnShow is set using xPosition and yPosition.

Once the OnResize method is overridden, it can be called in the constructor with the following line of code (identical in both languages except for the semicolon):

```
OnResize(EventArgs.Empty)
```

The EventArgs.Empty argument is an empty placeholder, of type EventArgs.

Now the button is located correctly when the form is first opened, and upon any subsequent resizing.

 When this program was originally coded, all the Form properties were grouped in the constructor, followed by the Button properties, as in:

```
Text = "Control Parent";
Size = new Size(350,200);
btnShow = new Button( );
btnShow.Parent = this;
btnShow.Text = "Show";
```

This caused the following runtime error: "Object reference not set to an instance of an object."

This was caused by the Form Size property raising the Resize event, which invoked OnResize. The overridden OnResize method references btnShow, but btnShow had not yet been instantiated.

Moving the Form Size statement to a location in the code after btnShow had been instantiated solved the problem.

When the program shown in Examples 7-7 and 7-8 is run on a system with the default Windows font set to Small Font, the result of clicking the Show Button Properties button is shown in Figure 7-4.

AutoScale

In the ControlDynamicSizeLocation examples shown above (Examples 7-7 and 7-8), an algorithm was handcoded to dynamically determine the size and location of the Button control based on the Font property of the Form.

When using Visual Studio .NET, however, the size and location of controls is hardcoded, like the ControlSizeLocation examples shown above (Example 7-5 and Example 7-6). As you have seen, this can lead to problems if the user changes fonts for Windows or the form, or resizes the form.

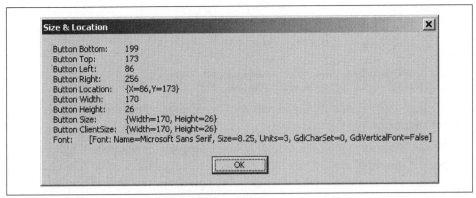

Figure 7-4. Dynamic control size and location (small font)

Visual Studio .NET uses a .NET Framework feature called *AutoScale* to handle this scaling without having to explicitly code for it.

To see AutoScale in action, create a new Windows Application project in Visual Studio .NET in the language of your choice. Drag a single Button control onto the form and resize the button by dragging on one of the resizing handles.

Right-click on the form and select View Code to see the source code for the form. Click on the plus sign next to the line in the code that says Windows Form Designer generated code to expand the autogenerated code. You will see a method named InitializeComponent, which is called from the constructor to initialize all the controls and components on the form. Within InitializeComponent are lines of code similar to the following:

C#

```
//
// button1
//
this.button1.Location = new System.Drawing.Point(88, 80);
this.button1.Name = "button1";
this.button1.Size = new System.Drawing.Size(104, 23);
this.button1.TabIndex = 0;
this.button1.Text = "button1";
//
// Form1
//
this.AutoScaleBaseSize = new System.Drawing.Size(5, 13);
this.ClientSize = new System.Drawing.Size(292, 272);
```

VB

```
'
'Button1
'
Me.Button1.Location = New System.Drawing.Point(80, 64)
Me.Button1.Name = "Button1"
Me.Button1.Size = New System.Drawing.Size(128, 23)
```

```
Me.Button1.TabIndex = 0
Me.Button1.Text = "Button1"
'
'Form1
'
Me.AutoScaleBaseSize = New System.Drawing.Size(5, 13)
Me.ClientSize = New System.Drawing.Size(292, 272)
```

The highlighted lines of code above include the seemingly hardcoded sizes and locations of the Button and Form controls.

The key to autoscaling is the AutoScaleBaseSize property of the form. This property, of type Size, gets and sets the base size used in autoscaling the form and its child controls. This size is compared with the size of the current system font at display time to calculate scaling factors in both the horizontal and vertical directions.

It turns out that when the system font size is Small Fonts (set by going to Control Panel and then Display, selecting Properties, and then the Settings tab), the size of the font is 5 × 13 pixels. Large Fonts have a size of 6 × 15 pixels.

If the form is designed on a machine set to Small Fonts and then run on a machine also set to Small Fonts, the scaling factor in the X direction is 5/5 or 1, so no scaling takes place. The Y scaling is similar. However, if the form is run on a machine set to Large Fonts, the form and its controls are scaled in the X direction by a factor of 5/6 and in the Y direction by a factor of 13/15. The result is that the form and all the controls are scaled in both size and location so that the appearance looks the same no matter which system font is used.

Since the AutoScaleBaseSize property is of type Size, it can also be used to obtain the width and height of the current system font with the following lines of code:

```
int x = AutoScaleBaseSize.Width;
int y = AutoScaleBaseSize.Height;
```

Anchoring

The programs coded in Examples 7-7 and 7-8 dynamically positioned a control by overriding the OnResize event handler. The Anchor property provides an alternative, and much easier, technique to dynamically position a control.

The Anchor property positions a control relative to the edge (or edges) of its container. As the container, say a form, is resized, the anchored control retains the same position relative to the specified edge (or edges).

The property can have one or more of the values shown Table 7-4, combined in a bitwise fashion using the logical OR operator. The default value is a combination of Top and Left. If a value of None is used, then the anchored control will retain its position in the client area relative to the size of the client area.

Table 7-4. Anchor property values

Value
Bottom
Left
None
Right
Top

The programs listed in Examples 7-9 and 7-10 demonstrate the use of anchoring controls. These programs each have five buttons (which don't really do anything except look pretty), one anchored to each of the corners of the form and one that spans the middle of the form. Each button has a margin between it and the edge of the form client area. As you resize the form, the four corner buttons retain the same relative positions in their corners and the middle button changes width to match the client area of the form. The end result is shown in Figure 7-5.

Example 7-9. Control anchoring in C# (ControlAnchor.cs)

```
using System;
using System.Drawing;
using System.Windows.Forms;

namespace ProgrammingWinApps
{
    public class ControlAnchor : Form
    {
        public ControlAnchor( )
        {
            Text = "Control Anchoring";
            Size = new Size(350,400);

            int xButtonSize, yButtonSize;

            // All the buttons will have the same height.
            yButtonSize = Font.Height * 2;

            // All the buttons will be the same distance from the
            //    edge of the form.
            int xMargin, yMargin;
            xMargin = yMargin = Font.Height * 2;

            // Upper Left Button
            Button btn = new Button( );
            btn.Parent = this;
            btn.Text = "Upper Left";
            xButtonSize = (int)(Font.Height * .75) * btn.Text.Length;
            btn.Size = new Size(xButtonSize, yButtonSize);
            btn.Location = new Point(xMargin, yMargin);
```

Example 7-9. Control anchoring in C# (ControlAnchor.cs) (continued)

```csharp
            // Lower Left Button
            btn = new Button( );
            btn.Parent = this;
            btn.Text = "Lower Left";
            xButtonSize = (int)(Font.Height * .75) * btn.Text.Length;
            btn.Size = new Size(xButtonSize, yButtonSize);
            btn.Location = new Point(xMargin,
                                this.ClientSize.Height -
                                    yMargin - yButtonSize);
            btn.Anchor = AnchorStyles.Bottom | AnchorStyles.Left;

            // Upper Right Button
            btn = new Button( );
            btn.Parent = this;
            btn.Text = "Upper Right";
            xButtonSize = (int)(Font.Height * .75) * btn.Text.Length;
            btn.Size = new Size(xButtonSize, yButtonSize);
            btn.Location = new Point(this.ClientSize.Width -
                                        xMargin - xButtonSize, yMargin);
            btn.Anchor = AnchorStyles.Top | AnchorStyles.Right;

            // Lower Right Button
            btn = new Button( );
            btn.Parent = this;
            btn.Text = "Lower Right";
            xButtonSize = (int)(Font.Height * .75) * btn.Text.Length;
            btn.Size = new Size(xButtonSize, yButtonSize);
            btn.Location = new Point(this.ClientSize.Width - xMargin -
                                        xButtonSize,
                                    this.ClientSize.Height - yMargin -
                                        yButtonSize);
            btn.Anchor = AnchorStyles.Bottom | AnchorStyles.Right;

            // Middle spanning Button
            btn = new Button( );
            btn.Parent = this;
            btn.Text = "Middle Span";
            xButtonSize = this.ClientSize.Width - (2 * xMargin);
            btn.Size = new Size(xButtonSize, yButtonSize);
            btn.Location = new Point(xMargin,
                                (int)(this.ClientSize.Height / 2) -
                                    yButtonSize);
            btn.Anchor = AnchorStyles.Left | AnchorStyles.Right;
        }

        static void Main( )
        {
            Application.Run(new ControlAnchor( ));
        }
    }
}
```

Example 7-10. Control anchoring in VB.NET (ControlAnchor.vb)

```
imports System
imports System.Drawing
imports System.Windows.Forms

namespace ProgrammingWinApps
   public class ControlAnchor : inherits Form

      public sub New( )
         Text = "Control Anchoring"
         Size = new Size(350,400)

         dim xButtonSize, yButtonSize as integer

         ' All the buttons will have the same height.
         yButtonSize = Font.Height * 2

         ' All the buttons will be the same distance from the
         '    edge of the form.
         dim xMargin, yMargin  as integer
         xMargin = Font.Height * 2
         yMargin = Font.Height * 2

         ' Upper Left Button
         dim btn as new Button( )
         btn.Parent = me
         btn.Text = "Upper Left"
         xButtonSize = Cint(Font.Height * .75) * btn.Text.Length
         btn.Size = new Size(xButtonSize, yButtonSize)
         btn.Location = new Point(xMargin, yMargin)

         ' Lower Left Button
         btn = new Button( )
         btn.Parent = me
         btn.Text = "Lower Left"
         xButtonSize = Cint(Font.Height * .75) * btn.Text.Length
         btn.Size = new Size(xButtonSize, yButtonSize)
         btn.Location = new Point(xMargin, _
                        me.ClientSize.Height - yMargin - _
                           yButtonSize)
         btn.Anchor = AnchorStyles.Bottom Or AnchorStyles.Left

         ' Upper Right Button
         btn = new Button( )
         btn.Parent = me
         btn.Text = "Upper Right"
         xButtonSize = Cint(Font.Height * .75) * btn.Text.Length
         btn.Size = new Size(xButtonSize, yButtonSize)
         btn.Location = new Point(me.ClientSize.Width - xMargin - _
                        xButtonSize, _
                           yMargin)
         btn.Anchor = AnchorStyles.Top Or AnchorStyles.Right
```

Example 7-10. Control anchoring in VB.NET (ControlAnchor.vb) (continued)

```
           ' Lower Right Button
           btn = new Button( )
           btn.Parent = me
           btn.Text = "Lower Right"
           xButtonSize = Cint(Font.Height * .75) * btn.Text.Length
           btn.Size = new Size(xButtonSize, yButtonSize)
           btn.Location = new Point(me.ClientSize.Width - xMargin - _
                          xButtonSize, _
                          me.ClientSize.Height - yMargin - _
                          yButtonSize)
           btn.Anchor = AnchorStyles.Bottom Or AnchorStyles.Right

           ' Middle spanning Button
           btn = new Button( )
           btn.Parent = me
           btn.Text = "Middle Span"
           xButtonSize = me.ClientSize.Width - (2 * xMargin)
           btn.Size = new Size(xButtonSize, yButtonSize)
           btn.Location = new Point(xMargin, _
                          Cint(me.ClientSize.Height / 2) - _
                          yButtonSize)
           btn.Anchor = AnchorStyles.Left Or AnchorStyles.Right
        end sub

        public shared sub Main( )
           Application.Run(new ControlAnchor( ))
        end sub
   end class
end namespace
```

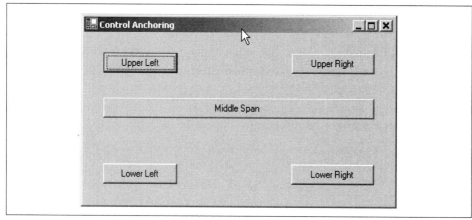

Figure 7-5. Control anchoring

In this example, there are no member variables; all the variables and controls are declared and instantiated inside the constructor of the Form. A pair of integers are declared to hold the dimensions of each Button, and then the common Button height is calculated based on the Height property of the current Font:

```
int xButtonSize, yButtonSize;
yButtonSize = Font.Height * 2;
```

```
dim xButtonSize, yButtonSize as integer
yButtonSize = Font.Height * 2
```

The margin between each of the buttons and the edge of the form is also calculated based on the Height property of the current Font. All the buttons will have the same margin:

```
int xMargin, yMargin;
xMargin = yMargin = Font.Height * 2;
```

```
dim xMargin, yMargin  as integer
xMargin = Font.Height * 2
yMargin = Font.Height * 2
```

Each button is instantiated and specified in a manner similar to each other. A typical corner button looks like the following:

```
//  Lower Left Button
btn = new Button( );
btn.Parent = this;
btn.Text = "Lower Left";
xButtonSize = (int)(Font.Height * .75) * btn.Text.Length;
btn.Size = new Size(xButtonSize, yButtonSize);
btn.Location = new Point(xMargin,
                    this.ClientSize.Height -
                        yMargin - yButtonSize);
btn.Anchor = AnchorStyles.Bottom | AnchorStyles.Left;
```

```
'  Lower Left Button
btn = new Button( )
btn.Parent = me
btn.Text = "Lower Left"
xButtonSize = Cint(Font.Height * .75) * btn.Text.Length
btn.Size = new Size(xButtonSize, yButtonSize)
btn.Location = new Point(xMargin, _
                    me.ClientSize.Height - yMargin - _
                        yButtonSize)
btn.Anchor = AnchorStyles.Bottom Or AnchorStyles.Left
```

The width of each button, contained in the variable xButtonSize, is based on the current Font Height and the number of characters in the Font Text property. The height of each button, contained in the variable yButtonSize, was defined previously for all buttons.

The Location property for each button is calculated by the xMargin and yMargin, defined above, and the size of the client area of the form.

Finally, the Anchor property is set for each button except for the upper-left button. The default Anchor property is equivalent to:

```
AnchorStyles.Top | AnchorStyles.Left
```

```
AnchorStyles.Top Or AnchorStyles.Left
```

where the logical OR operator is used to combine more than one Anchor properties.

The important thing to note about this example is that there is no OnResize method. The size and location of each of the five buttons is not recalculated outside of the constructor. You can verify this for yourself by modifying the line of code that specifies the width of the middle button, replacing the reference to the ClientSize.Width with a hardcoded number, and observing the behavior. For example, replace this line:

```
xButtonSize = me.ClientSize.Width - (2 * xMargin)
```

with this line:

```
xButtonSize = 300
```

When you resize the resulting form, the middle button will continue to dynamically resize itself because it is anchored to both the left and right edges of the container.

The middle button has its width calculated based on the client size of the form minus the margin on either side:

```
xButtonSize = me.ClientSize.Width - (2 * xMargin)
```

and then it is anchored to both the left and right sides of the container:

```
btnMid.Anchor = AnchorStyles.Left Or AnchorStyles.Right
```

This causes the button to automatically resize itself as the form width is changed.

Docking

The Dock property is similar to the Anchor property because it associates a control with an edge of its container. However, rather than maintain a relative position near the edge, it butts right up against the edge, extending from one side of the container to the other. For example, if a control is docked along the top edge, it will extend from the left edge to the right.

Docking is often used for toolbars (docked along the top edge) or status bars (docked along the bottom edge). It is also used with TreeView controls to create Explorer type interfaces, as described in Chapter 5.

The Dock property can have any of the values contained in the DockStyle enumeration, listed in Table 7-5. Unlike the Anchor property values, the DockStyle values cannot be combined; a control can have only a single DockStyle.

If the Fill value is used, the control will dock to all four edges of its container and totally fill it. If a value of None is used, the control will not be docked.

Docking and anchoring are mutually exclusive. A control cannot be both docked and anchored—i.e., the value of one of those properties must be set to None.

Table 7-5. DockStyle values

Value
Bottom
Fill
Left
None
Right
Top

The programs shown in Examples 7-11 and 7-12 demonstrate two docked buttons, one to the top of the form client area and one to the bottom. You will see that as you resize the form, the buttons resize to fill the edge automatically. When the program is compiled and run, it will look something like that shown in Figure 7-6.

Notice in these examples that although a Height property is defined for the buttons, there is no Width or Size property. Also, there is no Location property defined. The Dock property makes all of those properties superfluous.

If multiple controls are docked against the same edge of a container, the docked control with the higher z-order is located closer to the center of the client area. The docked control with the lowest z-order is immediately adjacent to the edge of the container. (Z-order was discussed earlier in this chapter.) You can verify this by modifying the code in Example 7-11 or Example 7-12 to make both buttons dock against the same edge.

Example 7-11. Docking in C# (ControlDock.cs)

```
using System;
using System.Drawing;
using System.Windows.Forms;

namespace ProgrammingWinApps
{
   public class ControlDock : Form
   {
      public ControlDock( )
      {
            Text = "Control Docking";
         Size = new Size(350,400);

         //  Both buttons will have the same height.
         int yButtonSize = Font.Height * 2;

         //  First Button
         Button btn = new Button( );
```

Example 7-11. Docking in C# (ControlDock.cs) (continued)

```csharp
         btn.Parent = this;
         btn.Text = "First Button";
         btn.Height = yButtonSize;
         btn.Dock = DockStyle.Top;

         //  Second Button
         btn = new Button( );
         btn.Parent = this;
         btn.Text = "Second Button";
         btn.Height = yButtonSize;
         btn.Dock = DockStyle.Bottom;
      }

      static void Main( )
      {
         Application.Run(new ControlDock( ));
      }
   }
}
```

Example 7-12. Docking in VB.NET (ControlDock.vb)

```vb
imports System
imports System.Drawing
imports System.Windows.Forms

namespace ProgrammingWinApps
   public class ControlDock : inherits Form

      public sub New( )
            Text = "Control Docking"
         Size = new Size(350,400)

         '  Both buttons will have the same height.
         dim yButtonSize as integer = Font.Height * 2

         '  First Button
         dim btnFirst as new Button( )
         btnFirst.Parent = me
         btnFirst.Text = "First Button"
         btnFirst.Height = yButtonSize
         btnFirst.Dock = DockStyle.Top
         '  Second Button
         dim btnSecond as new Button( )
         btnSecond.Parent = me
         btnSecond.Text = "Second Button"
         btnSecond.Height = yButtonSize
         btnSecond.Dock = DockStyle.Bottom
      end sub

      public shared sub Main( )
         Application.Run(new ControlDock( ))
```

Example 7-12. Docking in VB.NET (ControlDock.vb) (continued)

```
      end sub
    end class
end namespace
```

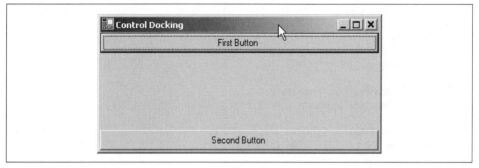

Figure 7-6. Control docking

Painting the control

All controls have a Paint event, which is raised when the control is about to be drawn. You can add an event handler to the Paint event delegate to dictate how the control gets drawn. This allows you to draw text and graphics directly on the client area of a form, for example, or change the appearance of a button.

 For a complete discussion of delegates and events, see Chapter 4.

The Paint event, drawing, and graphics will be covered in detail in Chapter 10.

Tag property

It is often useful to be able to associate some data with a control. This can be done using the Tag property.

This property can be of any type, not just a string. In the programs shown in Examples 7-13 and 7-14, the Tag property is of type FontStyle. But it could also be of type Color, Location, or Size, to name a few, or of a type defined in your program, or it can even be a DataSet, so that the data associated with a control will be readily available.

The programs shown in Examples 7-13 and 7-14 present several buttons, one for each member of the FontStyle enumeration. The contents of the FontStyle enumeration are put into an array of FontStyle's, which is then iterated through using a foreach loop. On each iteration, a new button is created. Clicking on one of these buttons applies that FontStyle to the Label control on the form.

Example 7-13. Control Tag property in C# (Tags.cs)

```
using System;
using System.Drawing;
```

Example 7-13. Control Tag property in C# (Tags.cs) (continued)

```csharp
using System.Windows.Forms;

namespace ProgrammingWinApps
{
   public class Tags : Form
   {
      Label lbl;

      public Tags( )
      {
         Text = "Control Tag Property";
         Size = new Size(300,200);

         lbl = new Label( );
         lbl.Text = "The quick brown fox...";
         lbl.AutoSize = true;
         lbl.Parent = this;
         lbl.Location = new Point(0,0);

         FontStyle theEnum = new FontStyle( );
         FontStyle[ ] theStyles =
             (FontStyle[ ])Enum.GetValues(theEnum.GetType( ));

         int i = 1;
         foreach (FontStyle style in theStyles)
         {
            Button btn = new Button( );
            btn.Parent = this;
            btn.Location = new Point(25,25 * i);
            btn.Size = new Size(75,20);
            btn.Text = style.ToString( );
            btn.Tag = style;
            btn.Click += new System.EventHandler(btn_Click);
            i++;
         }
      }

      static void Main( )
      {
         Application.Run(new Tags( ));
      }

      private void btn_Click(object sender, EventArgs e)
      {
         Button btn = (Button)sender;
         FontStyle fs = (FontStyle)btn.Tag;
         lbl.Font = new Font(lbl.Font, fs);
      }
   }
}
```

Example 7-14. Control Tag property in VB.NET (Tags.vb)

```vb
imports System
imports System.Drawing
imports System.Windows.Forms

namespace ProgrammingWinApps
   public class Tags : inherits Form

      private lbl as Label

      public sub New()
         Text = "Control Tag Property"
         Size = new Size(300,200)

         lbl = new Label()
         lbl.Text = "The quick brown fox..."
         lbl.AutoSize = true
         lbl.Parent = me
         lbl.Location = new Point(0,0)

         dim theEnum as new FontStyle()
         dim theStyles as FontStyle() = CType([Enum].GetValues( _
                     theEnum.GetType()), FontStyle())

         dim i as integer = 1
         dim style as FontStyle
         for each style in theStyles
            dim btn as new Button()
            btn.Parent = me
            btn.Location = new Point(25,25 * i)
            btn.Size = new Size(75,20)
            btn.Text = style.ToString()
            btn.Tag = style
            AddHandler btn.Click, AddressOf btn_Click
            i += 1
         next
      end sub

      public shared sub Main()
         Application.Run(new Tags())
      end sub

      private sub btn_Click(ByVal sender as object, _
            ByVal e as EventArgs)
         dim btn as Button = CType(sender, Button)
         dim fs as FontStyle = CType(btn.Tag, FontStyle)
         lbl.Font = new Font(lbl.Font, fs)
      end sub

   end class
end namespace
```

In the constructor for the Form, the Text and Size properties of the Form are set and the Label control is instantiated and specified.

The next two lines in the code are both crucial and dense. They get the contents of the FontStyle enumeration and, using reflection, put the values into an array of Font-Styles:

```
FontStyle theEnum = new FontStyle();
FontStyle[] theStyles = (FontStyle[])Enum.GetValues(theEnum.GetType());
```

```
dim theEnum as new FontStyle()
dim theStyles as FontStyle() = CType((Enum).GetValues( _
                theEnum.GetType()), FontStyle())
```

This convolution is necessary because the foreach loop used further on in the program can loop through an array, but cannot loop through an enumeration since an enumeration is not a collection.

The Enum class provides a number of methods for handling enumerations. Since the goal is to get the contents of the enumeration into an array, the static method Enum.GetValues serves the purpose. It takes the type of the enumeration as a parameter.

The type of the enumeration can be obtained from the GetType method, but this is not static—it requires an instance of the enumeration in question. Hence, the first line in this code snippet instantiates a new instance of the FontStyle enumeration, called theEnum. This instance is then used to call GetType, which returns the type of the enumeration to GetValues, which returns an array of values. The array of values is cast to an array of FontStyle's called theStyles.

The C# version can be simplified down to a single line of code using the typeof operator, which returns the type of a class. There is no need to create an instance of type FontStyle. Thus, the following line will return an array of FontStyles:

```
FontStyle[ ] theStyles = (FontStyle[ ])Enum.
GetValues(typeof(FontStyle));
```

There is no corresponding operator in VB.NET.

For a complete discussion of reflection, see *Programming C#* by Jesse Liberty (O'Reilly).

Next comes the foreach loop (for each in VB.NET), which iterates through the array of each FontStyle, creating a Button for each one:

```
int i = 1;
foreach (FontStyle style in theStyles)
{
```

```
        Button btn = new Button( );
        btn.Parent = this;
        btn.Location = new Point(25,25 * i);
        btn.Size = new Size(75,20);
        btn.Text = style.ToString( );
        btn.Tag = style;
        btn.Click += new System.EventHandler(btn_Click);
        i++;
    }
```

```
    dim i as integer = 1
    dim style as FontStyle
    for each style in theStyles
        dim btn as new Button( )
        btn.Parent = me
        btn.Location = new Point(25,25 * i)
        btn.Size = new Size(75,20)
        btn.Text = style.ToString( )
        btn.Tag = style
        AddHandler btn.Click, AddressOf btn_Click
        i += 1
    next
```

The integer counter i is declared and initialized to increment the Location property of each button. For each member of the theStyles array, a new Button control is declared and instantiated and a number of properties set. Notice that the Text property is set to the string representation of the current FontStyle. The advantage of using the Tag property is that it retains the type of the array. This will be useful shortly. Also notice that all the Buttons use the same event-handler method to respond to the Click event.

The resulting form is shown in Figure 7-7.

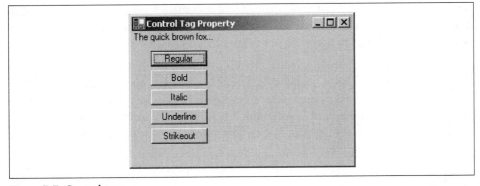

Figure 7-7. Control tags

The Click event handler does the work of determining which Button has been clicked, what FontStyle is associated with that button, and applying that FontStyle to the Label control.

```csharp
private void btn_Click(object sender, EventArgs e)
{
    Button btn = (Button)sender;
    FontStyle fs = (FontStyle)btn.Tag;
    lbl.Font = new Font(lbl.Font, fs);
}
```

```vb
private sub btn_Click(ByVal sender as object, _
        ByVal e as EventArgs)
    dim btn as Button = CType(sender, Button)
    dim fs as FontStyle = CType(btn.Tag, FontStyle)
    lbl.Font = new Font(lbl.Font, fs)
end sub
```

The first line in the method handles the job of determining which Button raised the Click event. The sender argument is cast to a Button type and assigned to a local variable btn. This btn variable is independent from the btn variable referred to in the foreach loop above; they just happen to have the same name, but a different scope.

The next line in the method gets the Tag property from the Button and casts it to an object of type FontStyle. Although it may seem that you could just as easily use the Text property and cast it to type FontStyle, this will not work. If you try substituting this line:

```csharp
FontStyle fs = (FontStyle)btn.Text;
```

```vb
dim fs as FontStyle = CType(btn.Text, FontStyle)
```

you will get the following compile error:

```
Cannot convert type 'string' to 'System.Drawing.FontStyle'
```

Finally, the FontStyle is applied to the Label control. This too is not as simple as you might think, since the Font.Style property of a control's font is read-only. In fact, since the Font object is immutable, i.e., all of its properties are read-only, the only way to change a Font property is to assign a new Font object based on the existing Font.

The Font object has over a dozen different overloaded constructors, covered in Chapter 9. The one used here takes an existing Font object as a prototype from which to create the new Font object, and a member of the FontStyle enumeration to apply to the new Font. (Multiple FontStyle enumeration values could be combined using the OR operator.)

Tabbing

The user can shift focus from one control to the next on a form by pressing the Tab key. (The arrow keys also shift focus until the focus arrives at a control such as a

---

TextBox, where the arrow keys have functionality within the control.) When tabbing among controls, the order in which the controls get focus is known as the *tab order*. You can traverse the tab order in reverse by pressing Shift-Tab.

Two properties of Control that affect tabbing are listed in Table 7-6.

Table 7-6. Tabbing properties

Property	Type	Description
TabStop	Boolean	If true, the default, the control can get focus while participating in the tab order.
TabIndex	integer	The index of a control in the tab order. Lower values are earlier in the tab order. If two or more controls have the same TabIndex, the control with the lower z-order will get focus first.

 Some controls, such as the Label, participate in the tab order, but their TabStop property is false, so they cannot receive focus. Focus instead goes to the next control in the tab order. Later chapters will cover this topic.

When developing forms in VS.NET, the TabIndex initially tracks the control's z-order. However, you can subsequently change either the TabIndex property or the z-order independently of each other.

Keyboard interaction

Although the keyboard is probably the primary means of user interaction with your application, the Control class provides such seamless keyboard support that you can usually ignore it. That said, a few issues bear further discussion.

A slew of events associated with keyboard interaction allow you to determine which key has been pressed, if any modifier keys (such as Shift, Alt, or Ctrl) have been pressed, and so on. They also allow you to trap key presses, disallow them, or send an alternative key press instead. All key events are covered thoroughly in Chapter 4.

Input focus. When a key is pressed on the keyboard attached to a computer running Windows, the keyboard events are received by the object with *input focus*. This focus may be a specific window or form, or it may be a child control on a form. In any event, Windows handles all the details to ensure that the correct object receives the keyboard input.

The focus can be shifted by the user by clicking the mouse on an object or traversing the tab order with the Tab key, Shift Tab, or one of the arrow keys. You can also set the input focus to a specific control programmatically using the Focus() method.

For a control to be able to receive focus, its ControlStyles.Selectable style bit must be set to true, it must be contained by another control, and all its parent controls must be both visible and enabled. Some controls, including Panel, GroupBox, PictureBox, ProgressBar, Splitter, Label, and LinkLabel (when there is no link in the control) cannot receive focus under any circumstances.

Navigation. One way to use the keyboard to navigate around an application is by tabbing. Tabbing and the tab order were discussed previously in this chapter.

Another way to navigate an application is with the shortcut and access keys, which will be covered more thoroughly in Chapter 18. In brief, *access keys* allow keyboard navigation of menu items by pressing Alt in combination with a character underlined in the menu item. *Shortcut keys* are single keys, typically function keys (F1, F2, etc.), that are associated with a menu item and invoke that menu item.

ImageLists

The ImageList is not really a control, but rather a component that contains an indexed collection of Image objects. These images can then be displayed by any control that has an ImageList property, including Label, LinkLabel, Button, CheckBox, RadioButton, ListView (which actually has two variants of the ImageList property: a SmallImageList and a LargeImageList), TabControl, ToolBar, and TreeView.

The Image objects contained in the Images collection can be members of, or descended from, one of the following classes:

Bitmap
> Contains pixel data for an image and its attributes.

Icon
> A small, transparent bitmap used to represent an object.

 The documentation released with Versions 1 and 1.1 of the .NET Framework SDK states that metafiles, which are used to describe a sequence of graphics operations, may also be added to an image list. However, this is incorrect. If you attempt to add a metafile to an image list, a compiler error will result.

Setting the ImageList property of a control associates an image list with that control. Your code can then dynamically set the image to be displayed on the control at runtime by referencing the zero-based index of the desired image In the Images collection. This will be demonstrated shortly.

Some of the controls (Label, LinkLabel, Button, CheckBox, and RadioButton) that can use the ImageList component also have an Image property, which allows a single image to be associated with the control. If a control has both Image and

ImageList properties, they can not both be set for the same control at the same time. If the Image property is set, then the ImageList property will be set to a null reference (Nothing in VB.NET) and the ImageIndex property will be set to the default value of -1. If the ImageList property is set, then the Image property will be set to a null reference (Nothing in VB.NET).

 It is also possible to use an ImageList to draw images directly on the client area of the form, independently of any controls, using the overloaded Draw method of the ImageList class.

A form can have multiple image lists defined. For example, two buttons on a form can each have a different ImageList properties set, each displaying the images from a different collection of images. Conversely, the same image list can be used by multiple controls on a form. So, for example, both buttons could reference the same image list, and the code that specifies the ImageIndex for each button might select the same image for each button or different images from the same collection for each button. However, each control can reference images only from a single image list.

All images in an image list must be the same size. The size of the images displayed by the image list can be set using the ImageSize property. If an image is added to the Images collection that is not the correct size, it will be scaled to the correct size when it is displayed.

The commonly used properties of the ImageList component are listed in Table 7-7.

Table 7-7. ImageList properties

Property	Value type	Description
ColorDepth	ColorDepth	Read/write. The number of colors available for the image. Values come from the ColorDepth enumeration, which are listed in Table 7-8. The default value is Depth8Bit.
Images	ImageList.ImageCollection	Read/write. A collection of images. The ImageList.ImageCollection class has a number of properties and methods, with the common ones listed in Table 7-9, and Table 7-10.
ImageSize	Size	Read/write. The Height and Width of the images in the image list. The default size is 16 × 16 pixels, and the maximum size is 256 × 256.
Transparent-Color	Color	Read/write. The color to treat as transparent. The default is Color.Transparent.

Table 7-8. ColorDepth enumeration values

Member
Depth4Bit
Depth8Bit
Depth16Bit

Table 7-8. ColorDepth enumeration values (continued)

Member
Depth24Bit
Depth32Bit

Table 7-9. ImageList.ImageCollection properties

Property	Value type	Description
Count	Integer	Returns number of images in the collection. The default is zero.
Empty	Boolean	Returns true if there are no images in the collection. The default is false.
Item	Image	Read/write. The image at the specified index.

Table 7-10. ImageList.ImageCollection methods

Method	Description
Add	Overloaded. Adds a specified icon or image to the ImageList.
AddStrip	Adds one or more images contained in a bitmap to the ImageList.
Clear	Removes all images and masks from the ImageList.
RemoveAt	Removes the image at the specified index from the ImageList.

Only image objects are added to the Images collection, not files or the names of files containing those images. Once an image is added to an image list, the source filename for that image is no longer available from the image list. It may, of course, still be available elsewhere, such as from an array of filenames, as demonstrated in the following example.

 If you are developing your application in Visual Studio .NET and you add the images to the ImageList using the Image Collection Editor, described later in this section, there will be no persistence of the filenames associated with the images.

In Example 7-15 (in C#) and Example 7-16 (in VB.NET), an array is filled with a number of image filenames. (These images are included with a standard Visual Studio .NET installation.) The array is iterated to add all the images to an ImageList. Three controls are added which display an image from the ImageList: a Label, a LinkLabel, and a Button. A NumericUpDown control is provided to allow the user to select the index of the image to display on the controls. The Button control displays a different image from the Label and LinkLabel controls. When either program is compiled and run and the NumericUpDown value is changed, the result is shown in Figure 7-8.

Figure 7-8. Image lists

Example 7-15. ImageList in C# (ImageLists.cs)

```csharp
using System;
using System.Drawing;
using System.Windows.Forms;
using System.Collections;

namespace ProgrammingWinApps
{
    public class ImageLists : Form
    {
        ImageList imgList;
        Label lbl;
        LinkLabel lnk;
        Button btn;
        NumericUpDown nmbrUpDown;

        public ImageLists()
        {
            Text = "ImageLists";
            Size = new Size(300,300);

            imgList = new ImageList();
            Image img;

            // Use an array to add filenames to the ImageList
            String[] arFiles = {
                @"C:\Program Files\Microsoft Visual Studio .NET\Common7\" +
                        @"Graphics\bitmaps\assorted\happy.bmp",
                @"C:\Program Files\Microsoft Visual Studio .NET\Common7\" +
                        @"Graphics\bitmaps\assorted\hand.bmp",
                @"C:\Program Files\Microsoft Visual Studio .NET\Common7\" +
                        @"Graphics\bitmaps\assorted\phone.bmp",
                @"C:\Program Files\Microsoft Visual Studio .NET\Common7\" +
                        @"Graphics\icons\industry\bicycle.ico",
```

Example 7-15. ImageList in C# (ImageLists.cs) (continued)

```csharp
            @"C:\Program Files\Microsoft Visual Studio .NET\Common7\" +
                @"Graphics\icons\industry\hammer.ico",
            @"C:\Program Files\Microsoft Visual Studio .NET\Common7\" +
                @"Graphics\icons\industry\rocket.ico"
        };

    for (int i = 0; i < arFiles.Length; i++)
    {
        img = Image.FromFile(arFiles[i]);
        imgList.Images.Add(img);
    }

    //  Change the size
    imgList.ImageSize = new Size(32, 32);

    //  Replace an image
    img = Image.FromFile(
        "C:\\Program Files\\Microsoft Visual Studio .NET\\Common7\\" +
                "Graphics\\icons\\industry\\wrench.ico");
    imgList.Images[imgList.Images.Count - 1] = img;

    lbl = new Label();
    lbl.Parent = this;
    lbl.Text = "The quick brown fox...";
    lbl.Location = new Point(0,0);
    lbl.Size = new Size(lbl.PreferredWidth + imgList.ImageSize.Width,
    imgList.ImageSize.Height + 10);
    lbl.BorderStyle = BorderStyle.Fixed3D;
    lbl.ImageList = imgList;
    lbl.ImageIndex = 0;
    lbl.ImageAlign = ContentAlignment.MiddleRight;

    int yDelta = lbl.Height + 10;

    lnk = new LinkLabel();
    lnk.Parent = this;
    lnk.Text = "The slow red dog...";
    lnk.Size = new Size(lnk.PreferredWidth + imgList.ImageSize.Width,
                        imgList.ImageSize.Height + 10);
    lnk.Location = new Point(0, yDelta);
    lnk.ImageList = imgList;
    lnk.ImageIndex = 0;
    lnk.ImageAlign = ContentAlignment.MiddleRight;

    btn = new Button();
    btn.Parent = this;
    btn.ImageList = imgList;
    btn.ImageIndex = imgList.Images.Count - 1;
    btn.Location = new Point(0, 2 * yDelta);
    btn.Size = new Size(3 * imgList.ImageSize.Width,
                        2 * imgList.ImageSize.Height);
```

Example 7-15. ImageList in C# (ImageLists.cs) (continued)

```csharp
        // Create numeric updown to select the image
        nmbrUpDown = new NumericUpDown( );
        nmbrUpDown.Parent = this;
        nmbrUpDown.Location = new Point(0, 4 * yDelta);
        nmbrUpDown.Value = 0;
        nmbrUpDown.Minimum = 0;
        nmbrUpDown.Maximum = imgList.Images.Count - 1;
        nmbrUpDown.Width = 50;
        nmbrUpDown.ReadOnly = true;
        nmbrUpDown.ValueChanged +=
            new System.EventHandler(nmbrUpDown_ValueChanged);

    } // close ImageLists constructor

    static void Main( )
    {
        Application.Run(new ImageLists( ));
    }

        private void nmbrUpDown_ValueChanged(object sender, EventArgs e)
        {
            NumericUpDown n = (NumericUpDown)sender;
            lbl.ImageIndex = (int)n.Value;
            lnk.ImageIndex = (int)n.Value;
            btn.ImageIndex = (imgList.Images.Count - 1) - (int)n.Value;
        }
    }
}
```

Example 7-16. ImageList in VB.NET (ImageLists.vb)

```vbnet
imports System
imports System.Drawing
imports System.Windows.Forms

namespace ProgrammingWinApps
   public class ImageLists : inherits Form

      dim imgList as ImageList
         dim lbl as Label
         dim lnk as LinkLabel
         dim btn as Button
         dim nmbrUpDown as NumericUpDown

      public sub New( )
         Text = "ImageLists"
         Size = new Size(300,300)

         imgList = new ImageList( )
         dim img as Image
         dim i as integer

         dim arFiles as string( ) = { _
```

Example 7-16. ImageList in VB.NET (ImageLists.vb) (continued)

```
            "C:\\Program Files\\Microsoft Visual Studio .NET\\Common7\\" + _
                "Graphics\\bitmaps\\assorted\\happy.bmp", _
            "C:\\Program Files\\Microsoft Visual Studio .NET\\Common7\\" + _
                "Graphics\\bitmaps\\assorted\\hand.bmp", _
            "C:\\Program Files\\Microsoft Visual Studio .NET\\Common7\\" + _
                "Graphics\bitmaps\assorted\phone.bmp", _
            "C:\\Program Files\\Microsoft Visual Studio .NET\\Common7\\" + _
                "Graphics\\icons\\industry\\bicycle.ico", _
            "C:\\Program Files\\Microsoft Visual Studio .NET\\Common7\\" + _
                "Graphics\icons\industry\hammer.ico", _
            "C:\\Program Files\\Microsoft Visual Studio .NET\\Common7\\" + _
                "Graphics\\icons\\industry\\rocket.ico" _
        }

    for i = 0 to arFiles.Length - 1
        img = Image.FromFile(arFiles(i))
        imgList.Images.Add(img)
    next

    ' Change the size
    imgList.ImageSize = new Size(32, 32)

    ' Replace an image
    img = Image.FromFile( _
            "C:\\Program Files\\Microsoft Visual Studio .NET\\Common7\\" + _
                "Graphics\\icons\\industry\\wrench.ico")
    imgList.Images(imgList.Images.Count - 1) = img


    lbl = new Label( )
    lbl.Parent = me
    lbl.Text = "The quick brown fox..."
    lbl.Location = new Point(0,0)
    lbl.Size = new Size (lbl.PreferredWidth + imgList.ImageSize.Width, _
                    imgList.ImageSize.Height + 10)
    lbl.BorderStyle = BorderStyle.Fixed3D
    lbl.ImageList = imgList
    lbl.ImageIndex = 0
    lbl.ImageAlign = ContentAlignment.MiddleRight

    dim yDelta as integer = lbl.Height + 10

    lnk = new LinkLabel( )
    lnk.Parent = me
    lnk.Text = "The slow red dog..."
    lnk.Size = new Size( _
                lnk.PreferredWidth + imgList.ImageSize.Width, _
                imgList.ImageSize.Height + 10)
    lnk.Location = new Point(0, yDelta)
    lnk.ImageList = imgList
    lnk.ImageIndex = 0
    lnk.ImageAlign = ContentAlignment.MiddleRight
```

Example 7-16. ImageList in VB.NET (ImageLists.vb) (continued)

```vb
btn = new Button( )
btn.Parent = me
btn.ImageList = imgList
btn.ImageIndex = imgList.Images.Count - 1
btn.Location = new Point(0, 2 * yDelta)
btn.Size = new Size(3 * imgList.ImageSize.Width, _
                2 * imgList.ImageSize.Height)

' Create numeric updown to select the image
nmbrUpDown = new NumericUpDown( )
nmbrUpDown.Parent = me
nmbrUpDown.Location = new Point(0, 4 * yDelta)
nmbrUpDown.Value = 0
nmbrUpDown.Minimum = 0
nmbrUpDown.Maximum = imgList.Images.Count - 1
nmbrUpDown.Width = 50
nmbrUpDown.ReadOnly = true
AddHandler nmbrUpDown.ValueChanged, _
    AddressOf nmbrUpDown_ValueChanged
end sub

public shared sub Main( )
  Application.Run(new ImageLists( ))
end sub

private sub nmbrUpDown_ValueChanged(ByVal sender as object, _
                        ByVal e as EventArgs)
    dim n as NumericUpDown  = CType(sender, NumericUpDown)
    lbl.ImageIndex = CType(n.Value, Integer)
    lnk.ImageIndex = CType(n.Value, Integer)
    btn.ImageIndex = (imgList.Images.Count - 1) - _
                    CType(n.Value, Integer)
end sub
  end class
end namespace
```

In Examples 7-15 and 7-16, the ImageList and the controls on the form are declared as member variables so that they will be visible to all the methods of the form. There is a Label, a LinkLabel, a Button, and a NumericUpDown control. (These controls will be discussed in detail in subsequent chapters.)

In the constructor of the class, the ImageList component is instantiated and a variable of type Image is declared:

```csharp
imgList = new ImageList( );
Image img;
```

```vb
imgList = new ImageList( )
dim img as Image
```

Next a string array is declared, instantiated, and populated with several filenames of image files. (In a real application, you would not distribute image files this way, but embed them as resources in the executable.) The array is then iterated, instantiating an Image object from each filename using the static Images.FromFile method. That Image is then added to the ImageList:

```
for (int i = 0; i < arFiles.Length; i++)
{
    img = Image.FromFile(arFiles[i]);
    imgList.Images.Add(img);
}
```

```
for i = 0 to arFiles.Length - 1
    img = Image.FromFile(arFiles(i))
    imgList.Images.Add(img)
next
```

Next the size of all the images in the ImageList is changed from the default of 16 × 16 to 32 × 32:

```
imgList.ImageSize = new Size(32, 32);
```

The next two statements demonstrate how the Images collection can be treated similarly to an array, with the ImageList.ImageCollection index used as in indexer into the collection. In this code snippet, an image is set (i.e., the last image (*rocket.ico*) is replaced with *wrench.ico*):

```
img = Image.FromFile(
    "C:\\Program Files\\Microsoft Visual Studio .NET\\Common7\\" +
        "Graphics\\icons\\industry\\wrench.ico");
imgList.Images(imgList.Images.Count - 1] = img;
```

```
img = Image.FromFile( _
    "C:\\Program Files\\Microsoft Visual Studio .NET\\Common7\\" + _
        "Graphics\\icons\\industry\\wrench.ico")
imgList.Images(imgList.Images.Count - 1) = img
```

If you try to reference an index higher than what exists in the image list, an exception will be thrown.

As of this writing (Version 1.1), there is some sort of bug at work here. The image contained in wrench.ico is 16 × 16 pixels, and the current size of the ImageList is 32 × 32. The replacement image is overlaid on the original rather than being properly scaled and replacing the original image. Hence, the rocket is visible under the wrench. If the ImageList is not resized, then the wrench image properly replaces the rocket image. If the ImageList is resized after the wrench image replaces the rocket, then all the images in the ImageList are lost (i.e., the Count property goes to 0).

You could also get an image from the image list, with a line of code such as this:

C#

```
img = imgList.Images[2];
```

VB

```
img = imgList.Images(2)
```

Now that the image list is populated, it can be used by the different controls on the form. Each control is declared and specified. The Label control, lbl, has its Size property set based on its own PreferredWidth property (which automatically takes into account the current font and the length of its Text property) and the Width and Height of the ImageSize property of the image list:

```
lbl.Size = new Size (lbl.PreferredWidth + imgList.ImageSize.Width,
                     imgList.ImageSize.Height + 10);
```

The ImageList property is set to the image list created above, the ImageIndex property is set to zero so the control will display the first image in the collection, and the alignment of the image is set using the ImageAlign property:

```
lbl.ImageList = imgList;
lbl.ImageIndex = 0;
lbl.ImageAlign = ContentAlignment.MiddleRight;
```

At this point, now that the Height of lbl is known, an integer, yDelta, is declared based on that dimension, to be used by the other controls on the form to aid in setting the vertical position.

The LinkLabel control is declared and specified very similarly to the Label control.

The Button control is a bit different. Like the Label and LinkLabel on the form, its ImageList property is set:

```
btn.ImageList = imgList;
```

But rather than set the ImageIndex property to point to the first Image in the collection, it is set to point to the last image in the collection:

```
btn.ImageIndex = imgList.Images.Count - 1;
```

The Size property of the Button is derived entirely from the ImageSize property, multiplying both the ImageSize.Width and ImageSize.Height properties by integer factors to give a more pleasing appearance.

The final control on the form is a NumericUpDown control. This control allows the user to cycle through a range of integers. An event is raised every time the integer value of the control is changed. The event handler for this event can then change the image from the Images collection that is displayed on each of the other controls.

The initial value and the minimum value of the NumericUpDown is set to 0, and its maximum value is set to the highest index value of the collection, using the Count property of the collection. Remember that the index of the collection is zero based, so you must subtract 1 from the Count.

```
nmbrUpDown.Value = 0;
nmbrUpDown.Minimum = 0;
nmbrUpDown.Maximum = imgList.Images.Count - 1;
```

The event handler method for the ValueChanged event is added to the event delegate:

```
nmbrUpDown.ValueChanged +=
        new System.EventHandler(nmbrUpDown_ValueChanged);
```

```
AddHandler nmbrUpDown.ValueChanged, _
        AddressOf nmbrUpDown_ValueChanged
```

The event handler method, nmbrUpDown_ValueChanged, is reproduced here:

```
private void nmbrUpDown_ValueChanged(object sender, EventArgs e)
{
    NumericUpDown n = (NumericUpDown)sender;
    lbl.ImageIndex = (int)n.Value;
    lnk.ImageIndex = (int)n.Value;
    btn.ImageIndex = (imgList.Images.Count - 1) - (int)n.Value;
}
```

```
private sub nmbrUpDown_ValueChanged(ByVal sender as object, _
                            ByVal e as EventArgs)
    dim n as NumericUpDown  = CType(sender, NumericUpDown)
    lbl.ImageIndex = CType(n.Value, Integer)
    lnk.ImageIndex = CType(n.Value, Integer)
    btn.ImageIndex = (imgList.Images.Count - 1) - _
                    CType(n.Value, Integer)
end sub
```

The first line of code in the method casts the sender object as a variable of type NumericUpDown. Then the Value property of that object, i.e., the new value, can be cast as an integer and used to set the ImageIndex property for each control, forcing each of the controls to display the appropriate image from the Images collection. Notice how the ImageIndex of the Button control is calculated to go backward through the collection.

As mentioned earlier, when creating an image list in Visual Studio .NET, you can use the Image Collection Editor to add images. To add an image list to a form, drag an ImageList component from the ToolBox anywhere onto the form. It will not be visible on the form itself, but will display at the bottom of the Design window. Click on the ImageList there, and the Properties window will show its properties. (If need be, right-click on the ImageList component on the Design window and select Properties.)

Click on the Images property and a build button will appear (...). Clicking on that button will present the Image Collection Editor, shown in Figure 7-9, after adding two images to the collection. Clicking on the Add button will bring up a standard File Open dialog box, allowing you to browse your system for files.

Notice that the properties displayed for each image on the right side of the dialog box do not include the source filename. The image is essentially copied to the Image-List. If you need to know the name of the image, you will need to use some means other than this collection editor, such as the array used in Examples 7-15 and 7-16.

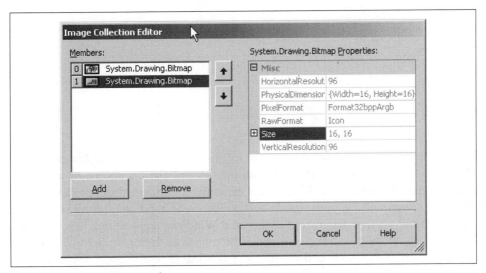

Figure 7-9. Image Collection Editor

If you examine the source code generated by Visual Studio .NET for the ImageList inside the region labeled Windows Form Designer generated code, you will see a line similar to this:

C#
```
this.imageList1.ImageStream =
    ((System.Windows.Forms.ImageListStreamer)(resources.GetObject(
        "imageList1.ImageStream")));
```

VB
```
Me.ImageList1.ImageStream = CType(resources.GetObject( _
    "ImageList1.ImageStream"), System.Windows.Forms.ImageListStreamer)
```

The bitmaps for the images are serialized into a resource file, with an extension of *.resx*. This is an XML file, which you can examine in a text editor. There you will find tags similar to the following:

```
<data name="imageList1.ImageStream" mimetype="application/x-microsoft.net.object.
binary.base64">
    <value>
        AAEAAAD/////AQAAAAAAAAMAgAAAFpTeXN0ZWOuV2luZG93cy5Gb3JtcywgVmVy
        MC4wLCBDdWx0dXJlPW5ldXRyYWwsIFB1YmxpYYotleVRva2VuPWI3N2E1YzU2MTkz
    </value>
```

All the image data from the image list is encoded within the <value> tags.

CHAPTER 8

Mouse Interaction

The example programs presented so far in this book have all been comprised of a Form object, which itself is derived from the Control class, with one or more child Control objects on the form. None of the examples has included any explicit code for implementing mouse support (other than Click event handlers), yet all support the mouse in the manner you would expect of a Windows application. This is because all members of the Control class handle the mouse of their own accord. They also have properties, methods and events for extending mouse support when the standard behavior is insufficient.

SystemInformation Properties

Strictly speaking, it is not necessary to have a mouse or other pointing device installed on a Windows system, although as a practical matter, it is difficult to work with Windows without one, and virtually every modern Windows computer has a mouse or pointer installed. The SystemInformation class provides several read-only static (Shared in VB.NET) properties, listed in Table 8-1, which allow a program to determine if a mouse is connected to the system, and if so, the configuration and capabilities of the mouse. Accessing these properties is demonstrated in the programs listed in Example 8-1 (in C#) and in Example 8-2 (in VB.NET).

Most mice in use today on Windows systems have two buttons: the left button is typically the primary button and the right button is typically the secondary button. The user can swap these preferences in the Control Panel/Mouse applet to allow left-handed users to reverse the buttons. If the primary button is clicked twice in rapid succession without moving more than a certain number of pixels, the action is interpreted as a double-click. Many mice today also have a mouse wheel, which can also be seen by the system as a third button. The last three properties listed in Table 8-1 relate to the wheel.

Table 8-1. SystemInformation mouse properties

Property	Type	Description
DoubleClickSize	Size	Returns dimensions, in pixels, of rectangular area around the first mouse click within which two mouse clicks can be considered a double-click.
DoubleClickTime	Integer	Returns maximum number of milliseconds allowed between two mouse clicks for them to be considered a double-click. Can be set by the user in Control Panel.
MouseButtons	Integer	Returns number of buttons on the mouse. Zero if no mouse is installed.
MouseButtonsSwapped	Boolean	Returns true if the function of the left and right mouse buttons are swapped. Can be set by the user in Control Panel.
MousePresent	Boolean	Returns true if mouse is installed.
MouseWheelPresent	Boolean	Returns true if mouse has a mouse wheel.
MouseWheelScrollLines	Integer	Returns number of lines to scroll when the mouse wheel is rotated one notch, or detent. Used by controls with a scrollbar.
NativeMouseWheelSupport	Boolean	Returns true if the OS supports a mouse wheel natively.

Example 8-1. Accessing SystemInformation in C# (SystemInfo.cs)

```
using System;
using System.Drawing;
using System.Windows.Forms;

namespace ProgrammingWinApps
{
    public class SystemInfo : Form
    {
        string[ ] SysInfoLabels =
            {
                "DoubleClickSize",
                "DoubleClickTime",
                "MouseButtons",
                "MouseButtonsSwapped",
                "MousePresent",
                "MouseWheelPresent",
                "MouseWheelScrollLines",
                "NativeMouseWheelSupport"
            };

        string[ ] SysInfoValues =
            {
                SystemInformation.DoubleClickSize.ToString( ),
                SystemInformation.DoubleClickTime.ToString( ),
                SystemInformation.MouseButtons.ToString( ),
                SystemInformation.MouseButtonsSwapped.ToString( ),
                SystemInformation.MousePresent.ToString( ),
                SystemInformation.MouseWheelPresent.ToString( ),
                SystemInformation.MouseWheelScrollLines.ToString( ),
                SystemInformation.NativeMouseWheelSupport.ToString( )
            };
```

Example 8-1. Accessing SystemInformation in C# (SystemInfo.cs) (continued)

C#

```csharp
    public SystemInfo( )
    {
        Text = "System Information";
        Size = new Size(400,400);
    }

    static void Main( )
    {
        Application.Run(new SystemInfo( ));
    }

    protected override void OnPaint(PaintEventArgs e)
    {
        base.OnPaint(e);
        Graphics g = e.Graphics;
        int y = 0;
        int yDelta = Font.Height;

        for(int i = 0; i < SysInfoLabels.Length; i++)
        {
            string str = SysInfoLabels[i];
            str += ": " + SysInfoValues[i];
            g.DrawString(str, Font, Brushes.Black, 0, y += yDelta);
        }
    }
  }
}
```

Example 8-2. Accessing SystemInformation in VB.NET (SystemInfo.vb)

VB

```vbnet
Option Strict On
imports System
imports System.Drawing
imports System.Windows.Forms

namespace ProgrammingWinApps
    public class SystemInfo : inherits Form

        dim SysInfoLabels( ) as string  = _
            {"DoubleClickSize", _
            "DoubleClickTime", _
            "MouseButtons", _
            "MouseButtonsSwapped", _
            "MousePresent", _
            "MouseWheelPresent", _
            "MouseWheelScrollLines", _
            "NativeMouseWheelSupport"}

        dim SysInfoValues as string( )  = _
            {SystemInformation.DoubleClickSize.ToString( ), _
            SystemInformation.DoubleClickTime.ToString( ), _
```

```
        SystemInformation.MouseButtons.ToString( ), _
        SystemInformation.MouseButtonsSwapped.ToString( ), _
        SystemInformation.MousePresent.ToString( ), _
        SystemInformation.MouseWheelPresent.ToString( ), _
        SystemInformation.MouseWheelScrollLines.ToString( ), _
        SystemInformation.NativeMouseWheelSupport.ToString( ) }

    public sub New( )
        Text = "System Information"
        Size = new Size(400,400)
    end sub

    public shared sub Main( )
        Application.Run(new SystemInfo( ))
    end sub

    protected overrides sub OnPaint(ByVal e as PaintEventArgs)
        myBase.OnPaint(e)
        dim g as Graphics = e.Graphics

        dim y as integer = 0
        dim yDelta as integer = Font.Height
        dim i as integer

        for i = 0 to SysInfoLabels.Length - 1
            dim str as string = SysInfoLabels(i)
            str = str + ":   " + SysInfoValues(i)
            y = y + yDelta
            g.DrawString(str, Font, Brushes.Black, 0, y)
        next
    end sub
  end class
end namespace
```

In the programs listed in Examples 8-1 and 8-2, two string arrays are declared as member variables: one array contains a set of labels to display on the form and the other contains a matching set of SystemInformation property values. Nothing happens in the Form's constructor other than the setting of Text and Size properties of the form.

The real action occurs in the override of the OnPaint method. This method is called every time the form is redrawn. You begin by chaining up to the base class's OnPaint method so that other methods registered with the OnPaint event delegate are notified, and also to insure that no base-class functionality is missed:

```
base.OnPaint(e);
```

```
myBase.OnPaint(e)
```

The contents of the arrays of labels and SystemInformation property values are drawn on the surface of the form using a Graphics object. (Chapter 10 covers graphics in detail.) A Graphics object is instantiated, representing the surface of the form:

C#
```
Graphics g = e.Graphics;
```

VB
```
dim g as Graphics = e.Graphics
```

Then the array of labels, SysInfoLabels, is iterated. For each entry, a string is built up consisting of the label and the corresponding property value. This string is drawn using the DrawString method:

C#
```
g.DrawString(str, Font, Brushes.Black, 0, y += yDelta);
```

VB
```
y = y + yDelta
g.DrawString(str, Font, Brushes.Black, 0, y)
```

Mouse Events

All Control objects support several mouse events, listed in Table 8-2. Three of them—MouseEnter, MouseHover, and MouseLeave—are raised, respectively, every time the mouse cursor goes from being outside to inside the control, stays stationary over a control (or at least does not move outside the control; only a single Mouse-Hover event is raised for every MouseEnter/MouseLeave pair, even if the cursor hovers, moves a bit, then hovers again), or leaves the control's airspace. Each event passes an event argument of type EventArgs, which carries no information about the event. No coordinates are passed, for example. These three events tell you only that the mouse cursor has interacted with a control.

Four low level events, also listed in Table 8-2, pass significant information about the event, in a structure of type MouseEventArgs: MouseDown, MouseMove, Mouse-Wheel, and MouseUp. From the properties of the MouseEventArgs argument, listed in Table 8-3, you can tell which button was pressed on the mouse, and the coordinates of the hot spot of the mouse cursor (relative to the top left corner of the control) when the event was raised, in addition to other information.

Finally, there are two high level events: Click and DoubleClick. These events also take an event argument of type EventArgs, meaning that the event has no additional information. (Additional Control properties, listed in Table 8-5, provide information such as the coordinates and the mouse buttons pressed.) A Click event occurs when there is a single press and release of a mouse button while the mouse cursor is over the Control. A DoubleClick event occurs when the mouse button is clicked twice in succession, with the time interval between the clicks less than the number of milliseconds in SystemInformation.DoubleClickTime and the mouse movement between clicks less than the number of pixels in SystemInformation.DoubleClickSize.

Table 8-2. Mouse-related events

Event	Event argument	Description
Click	EventArgs	Raised when the control is clicked.
DoubleClick	EventArgs	Raised when the control is double-clicked.
MouseEnter	EventArgs	Raised when the mouse cursor enters the control.
MouseHover	EventArgs	Raised when the mouse cursor hovers over the control.
MouseLeave	EventArgs	Raised when the mouse cursor leaves the control.
MouseDown	MouseEventArgs	Raised when the mouse cursor is over the control and a mouse button is pressed.
MouseMove	MouseEventArgs	Raised when the mouse cursor is moved over the control.
MouseWheel	MouseEventArgs	Raised when the control has focus and the mouse wheel is rotated.
MouseUp	MouseEventArgs	Raised when the mouse cursor is over the control and a mouse button is released.

Although all Forms controls inherit from System.Windows.Forms. Control, not all controls necessarily expose all the events contained in Control. For example, the Windows user interface does not support the concept of double-clicking a Button control. Yet the Button class inherits from Control via the ButtonBase class, and thus inherits the DoubleClick event In fact, even though Visual Studio .NET does not expose a DoubleClick event for a Button control in the Properties window (in C#) or the VB.NET drop-down event list, you can hook it up manually. Your program will compile and run, but the DoubleClick event will never be raised because the Windows event model does not raise that event for Buttons.

.NET can suppress the Click and DoubleClick events on selected controls by setting the StandardClick and StandardDoubleClick values, respectively, of the ControlStyles enumeration. For example, if StandardDoubleClick is set to false, the control will not fire Double-click events.

Only one mouse button is represented in each event. If you try pressing two mouse buttons simultaneously, you will get two separate Mouse events. (While the Button property of MouseEventArgs is of type MouseButtons, and while theoretically you can use bit-wise combinations to combine two Button enumerated values, you can have only one mouse button per event.) See Table 8-4 for MouseButtons enumeration values.

Table 8-3. MouseEventArgs properties

Property	Description
Button	Returns the pressed mouse button. Must be one of the members of the MouseButtons enumeration (listed in Table 8-4).
Clicks	Returns the integer number of times the mouse button was pressed and released. Resets after two clicks.

Table 8-3. MouseEventArgs properties (continued)

Property	Description
Delta	Returns the signed integer number of detents the mouse wheel was rotated. A positive value indicates that the wheel was rotated forward, i.e., away from the user, and a negative value indicates the wheel was rotated backward, i.e., toward the user.
X	The X coordinate, in pixels, of the mouse cursor's hot spot when the button was clicked, relative to the top-left corner of the control.
Y	The Y coordinate, in pixels, of the mouse cursor's hot spot when the button was clicked, relative to the top-left corner of the control.

The documentation in both Versions 1 and 1.1 incorrectly says that the X and Y MouseEventArgs properties are relative to the client area of the form.

Table 8-4. MouseButtons enumeration

Member	Description
Left	Left, or primary, mouse button pressed.
Middle	Middle mouse button pressed.
None	No mouse button pressed.
Right	Right, or secondary, mouse button pressed.
Xbutton1	First XButton of five button Microsoft IntelliMouse Explorer pressed.
Xbutton2	Second XButton of five button Microsoft IntelliMouse Explorer pressed.

The programs listed in Example 8-3 (in C#) and in Example 8-4 (in VB.NET) demonstrate the MouseEnter, MouseHover, and MouseLeave events. These events are handled both for a Button control (which performs no other function in these programs other than acting as a typical control) and for the form. When the mouse cursor enters, hovers over, or leaves either the button or the form, a text string is painted on the form client area with that information. In addition, if the button raises any of these three events, the Text property of the button is changed.

Example 8-3. MouseEnter, MouseHover, and MouseLeave event handling in C# (MouseEnterHoverLeave.cs)

```
using System;
using System.Drawing;
using System.Windows.Forms;

namespace ProgrammingWinApps
{
    public class MouseEnterHoverLeave : Form
    {
        private Button btn;
        string str = "";
```

```csharp
public MouseEnterHoverLeave()
{
    Text = "Mouse Enter / Hover / Leave";
    Size = new Size(400,400);

    btn = new Button();
    btn.Parent = this;
    btn.Location = new Point(50,50);
    btn.Size = new Size(150,25);
    btn.MouseEnter += new System.EventHandler(btn_MouseEnter);
    btn.MouseHover += new System.EventHandler(btn_MouseHover);
    btn.MouseLeave += new System.EventHandler(btn_MouseLeave);
}

static void Main()
{
    Application.Run(new MouseEnterHoverLeave());
}

private void btn_MouseEnter(object sender, EventArgs e)
{
    btn.Text = "MouseEnter";
    str += "\nButton MouseEnter";
    Invalidate();
}

private void btn_MouseHover(object sender, EventArgs e)
{
    btn.Text = "MouseHover";
    str += "\nButton MouseHover";
    Invalidate();
}

private void btn_MouseLeave(object sender, EventArgs e)
{
    btn.Text = "MouseLeave";
    str += "\nButton MouseLeave";
    Invalidate();
}

protected override void OnMouseEnter(EventArgs e)
{
    base.OnMouseEnter(e);
    str += "\nForm MouseEnter";
    Invalidate();
}

protected override void OnMouseHover(EventArgs e)
{
    base.OnMouseHover(e);
    str += "\nForm MouseHover";
```

Example 8-3. MouseEnter, MouseHover, and MouseLeave event handling in C#
(MouseEnterHoverLeave.cs) (continued)

```csharp
            Invalidate();
        }

        protected override void OnMouseLeave(EventArgs e)
        {
            base.OnMouseLeave(e);
            str += "\nForm MouseLeave";
            Invalidate();
        }

        protected override void OnPaint(PaintEventArgs e)
        {
            base.OnPaint(e);
            Graphics g = e.Graphics;
            g.DrawString(str, Font, Brushes.Black, 50, 75);
        }
    }
}
```

Example 8-4. MouseEnter, MouseHover, and MouseLeave in VB.NET
(MouseEnterHoverLeave.vb)

```vbnet
Option Strict On
imports System
imports System.Drawing
imports System.Windows.Forms

namespace ProgrammingWinApps
    public class MouseEnterHoverLeave : inherits Form

        private btn as Button
        dim str as string = ""

        public sub New()
            Text = "Mouse Enter / Hover / Leave"
            Size = new Size(400,400)

            btn = new Button()
            btn.Parent = me
            btn.Location = new Point(50,50)
            btn.Size = new Size(150,25)
            AddHandler btn.MouseEnter, AddressOf btn_MouseEnter
            AddHandler btn.MouseHover, AddressOf btn_MouseHover
            AddHandler btn.MouseLeave, AddressOf btn_MouseLeave
        end sub

        public shared sub Main()
            Application.Run(new MouseEnterHoverLeave())
        end sub

        private sub btn_MouseEnter(ByVal sender as object, _
```

```
[VB]              ByVal e as EventArgs)
             btn.Text = "MouseEnter"
             str = str + vbNewLine + "Button MouseEnter"
             Invalidate()
         end sub

         private sub btn_MouseHover(ByVal sender as object, _
             ByVal e as EventArgs)
             btn.Text = "MouseHover"
             str = str + vbNewLine + "Button MouseHover"
             Invalidate()
         end sub

         private sub btn_MouseLeave(ByVal sender as object, _
             ByVal e as EventArgs)
             btn.Text = "MouseLeave"
             str = str + vbNewLine + "Button MouseLeave"
             Invalidate()
         end sub

         protected overrides sub OnMouseEnter(ByVal e as EventArgs)
             myBase.OnMouseEnter(e)
             str = str + vbNewLine + "Form MouseEnter"
             Invalidate()
         end sub

         protected overrides sub OnMouseHover(ByVal e as EventArgs)
             myBase.OnMouseHover(e)
             str = str + vbNewLine + "Form MouseHover"
             Invalidate()
         end sub

         protected overrides sub OnMouseLeave(ByVal e as EventArgs)
             myBase.OnMouseLeave(e)
             str = str + vbNewLine + "Form MouseLeave"
             Invalidate()
         end sub

         protected overrides sub OnPaint(ByVal e as PaintEventArgs)
             myBase.OnPaint(e)
             dim g as Graphics = e.Graphics
             g.DrawString(str, Font, Brushes.Black, 50, 75)
         end sub
     end class
end namespace
```

In the constructor of the programs in Example 8-3 and Example 8-4, in addition to setting the Form Text and Size properties, the Button control is instantiated and specified, including the addition of event handlers for the MouseEnter, Mouse-Hover, and MouseLeave events.

```
C#  btn.MouseEnter += new System.EventHandler(btn_MouseEnter);
    btn.MouseHover += new System.EventHandler(btn_MouseHover);
    btn.MouseLeave += new System.EventHandler(btn_MouseLeave);
```

```
VB  AddHandler btn.MouseEnter, AddressOf btn_MouseEnter
    AddHandler btn.MouseHover, AddressOf btn_MouseHover
    AddHandler btn.MouseLeave, AddressOf btn_MouseLeave
```

Each event handler changes the Text property of the button and then concatenates a new line character and some appropriate text to the member string variable *str*. The Invalidate method is called, which causes a Paint event to be raised for the Form. The btn_MouseEnter looks like:

```
C#  private void btn_MouseEnter(object sender, EventArgs e)
    {
        btn.Text = "MouseEnter";
        str += "\nButton MouseEnter";
        Invalidate();
    }
```

```
VB  private sub btn_MouseEnter(ByVal sender as object, _
                               ByVal e as EventArgs)
        btn.Text = "MouseEnter"
        str = str + vbNewLine + "Button MouseEnter"
        Invalidate()
    end sub
```

When the Form's Paint event is raised, the OnPaint method is invoked. This is overridden by a method that first chains up to the base method, ensuring that any other methods registered with the delegate will be invoked. The overridden OnPaint method then instantiates a Graphics object and draws the str text string. This overridden OnPaint method looks like:

```
C#  protected override void OnPaint(PaintEventArgs e)
    {
        base.OnPaint(e);
        Graphics g = e.Graphics;
        g.DrawString(str, Font, Brushes.Black, 50, 75);
    }
```

```
VB  protected overrides sub OnPaint(ByVal e as PaintEventArgs)
        myBase.OnPaint(e)
        dim g as Graphics = e.Graphics
        g.DrawString(str, Font, Brushes.Black, 50, 75)
    end sub
```

Notice that there is only a single string being drawn, which is built up of all the event messages. This obviates the need to keep track of the vertical coordinate, as was done in Examples 8-1 and 8-2.

Compiling and running the program, and then moving the mouse over the button, hovering a bit, and moving the mouse off of the form results in the screenshot shown in Figure 8-1.

The sequence of events is interesting. The cursor first enters the Form, and then leaves the Form as it enters the Button. Next, the cursor hovers over the Button, and then leaves the Button and enters the Form once again. It finally leaves the Form for good, moving onto the desktop.

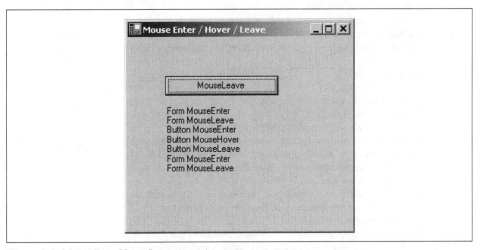

Figure 8-1. MouseEnterHoverLeave in action

The programs in Example 8-5 (in C#) and Example 8-6 (in VB.NET) demonstrate *all* mouse events, including MouseEnter, MouseHover, MouseLeave, MouseDown, MouseMove, MouseUp, MouseWheel, Click, and DoubleClick.

> Examples 8-5 and 8-6 use a label (rather than a Button), and the event logging strings are displayed in a TextBox, rather than on the client area of the Form. These changes were implemented to facilitate scrolling through the log of events.

The code that differs from the previous example is highlighted.

Example 8-5. Mouse events in C# (MouseEvents.cs)

```
using System;
using System.Drawing;
using System.Windows.Forms;

namespace ProgrammingWinApps
{
    public class MouseEvents : Form
    {
        private Label lbl;
        private Button btnReset;
```

Example 8-5. Mouse events in C# (MouseEvents.cs) (continued)

```csharp
    private TextBox txt;

public MouseEvents( )
{
    Text = "Mouse Events";
    Size = new Size(400,600);

    btnReset = new Button( );
    btnReset.Parent = this;
    btnReset.Location = new Point(250,50);
    btnReset.Text = "Reset";
    btnReset.Click += new System.EventHandler(btnReset_Click);

    lbl = new Label( );
    lbl.Parent = this;
    lbl.Location = new Point(50,50);
    lbl.Size = new Size(150,25);
    lbl.BorderStyle = BorderStyle.Fixed3D;
    lbl.MouseEnter += new System.EventHandler(lbl_MouseEnter);
    lbl.MouseHover += new System.EventHandler(lbl_MouseHover);
    lbl.MouseLeave += new System.EventHandler(lbl_MouseLeave);
    lbl.MouseDown += new
        System.Windows.Forms.MouseEventHandler(lbl_MouseDown);
    // Comment out to reduce quantity of text generated.
    // lbl.MouseMove += new
    //     System.Windows.Forms.MouseEventHandler(lbl_MouseMove);
    lbl.MouseUp += new System.Windows.Forms.MouseEventHandler(lbl_MouseUp);
    lbl.MouseWheel += new
        System.Windows.Forms.MouseEventHandler(lbl_MouseWheel);
    lbl.Click += new System.EventHandler(lbl_Click);
    lbl.DoubleClick += new System.EventHandler(lbl_DoubleClick);

    txt = new TextBox( );
    txt.Parent = this;
    txt.Location = new Point(50,90);
    txt.Size = new Size(300,475);
    txt.BorderStyle = BorderStyle.FixedSingle;
    txt.Multiline = true;
    txt.ScrollBars = ScrollBars.Vertical;
}

static void Main( )
{
    Application.Run(new MouseEvents( ));
}

private void btnReset_Click(object sender, EventArgs e)
{
    lbl.Text = "";
    txt.Text = "";
}
```

Example 8-5. Mouse events in C# (MouseEvents.cs) (continued)

```csharp
private void lbl_MouseEnter(object sender, EventArgs e)
{
    lbl.Text = "MouseEnter";
    TextBoxDraw("Label MouseEnter");
}

private void lbl_MouseHover(object sender, EventArgs e)
{
    lbl.Text = "MouseHover";
    TextBoxDraw("Label MouseHover");
}

private void lbl_MouseLeave(object sender, EventArgs e)
{
    lbl.Text = "MouseLeave";
    TextBoxDraw("Label MouseLeave");
}

private void lbl_MouseDown(object sender, MouseEventArgs e)
{
    lbl.Text = "MouseDown";
    string str;
    str = "Label MouseDown";
    str += "\r\n\tButton:  " + e.Button.ToString( );
    str += "\r\n\tClicks:  " + e.Clicks.ToString( );
    str += "\r\n\tDelta:   " + e.Delta.ToString( );
    str += "\r\n\tX:   " + e.X.ToString( );
    str += "\r\n\tY:   " + e.Y.ToString( );
    TextBoxDraw(str);
}

private void lbl_MouseMove(object sender, MouseEventArgs e)
{
    lbl.Text = "MouseMove";
    string str;
    str = "Label MouseMove";
    str += "\r\n\tButton:  " + e.Button.ToString( );
    str += "\r\n\tClicks:  " + e.Clicks.ToString( );
    str += "\r\n\tDelta:   " + e.Delta.ToString( );
    str += "\r\n\tX:   " + e.X.ToString( );
    str += "\r\n\tY:   " + e.Y.ToString( );
    TextBoxDraw(str);
}

private void lbl_MouseUp(object sender, MouseEventArgs e)
{
    lbl.Text = "MouseUp";
    string str;
    str = "Label MouseUp";
    str += "\r\n\tButton:  " + e.Button.ToString( );
    str += "\r\n\tClicks:  " + e.Clicks.ToString( );
    str += "\r\n\tDelta:   " + e.Delta.ToString( );
    str += "\r\n\tX:   " + e.X.ToString( );
```

Example 8-5. Mouse events in C# (MouseEvents.cs) (continued)

```csharp
        str += "\r\n\tY:   " + e.Y.ToString();
        TextBoxDraw(str);
    }

    private void lbl_MouseWheel(object sender, MouseEventArgs e)
    {
        lbl.Text = "MouseWheel";
        string str;
        str = "Label MouseWheel";
        str += "\r\n\tButton:  " + e.Button.ToString();
        str += "\r\n\tClicks:  " + e.Clicks.ToString();
        str += "\r\n\tDelta:   " + e.Delta.ToString();
        str += "\r\n\tX:   " + e.X.ToString();
        str += "\r\n\tY:   " + e.Y.ToString();
        TextBoxDraw(str);
    }

    private void lbl_Click(object sender, EventArgs e)
    {
        lbl.Text = "Click";
        TextBoxDraw("Label Click");
    }

    private void lbl_DoubleClick(object sender, EventArgs e)
    {
        lbl.Text = "DoubleClick";
        TextBoxDraw("Label DoubleClick");
    }

    protected override void OnMouseEnter(EventArgs e)
    {
        base.OnMouseEnter(e);
        TextBoxDraw("Form MouseEnter");
    }

    protected override void OnMouseHover(EventArgs e)
    {
        base.OnMouseHover(e);
        TextBoxDraw("Form MouseHover");
    }

    protected override void OnMouseLeave(EventArgs e)
    {
        base.OnMouseLeave(e);
        TextBoxDraw("Form MouseLeave");
    }

    private void TextBoxDraw(String str)
    {
        txt.AppendText("\r\n" + str);
    }
  }
}
```

Example 8-6. Mouse events in VB.NET (MouseEvents.vb)

```
Option Strict On
imports System
imports System.Drawing
imports System.Windows.Forms

namespace ProgrammingWinApps
    public class MouseEvents : inherits Form

        private lbl as Label
        private txt as TextBox
        private WithEvents btnReset as Button

        public sub New( )
            Text = "Mouse Events"
            Size = new Size(400,600)

            btnReset = new Button( )
            btnReset.Parent = me
            btnReset.Location = new Point(250,50)
            btnReset.Text = "Reset"

            lbl = new Label( )
            lbl.Parent = me
            lbl.Location = new Point(50,50)
            lbl.Size = new Size(150,25)
            lbl.BorderStyle = BorderStyle.Fixed3D
            AddHandler lbl.MouseEnter, AddressOf lbl_MouseEnter
            AddHandler lbl.MouseHover, AddressOf lbl_MouseHover
            AddHandler lbl.MouseLeave, AddressOf lbl_MouseLeave
            AddHandler lbl.MouseDown, AddressOf lbl_MouseDown
            ' Comment out to reduce quantity of text generated.
            ' AddHandler lbl.MouseMove, AddressOf lbl_MouseMove
            AddHandler lbl.MouseUp, AddressOf lbl_MouseUp
            AddHandler lbl.MouseWheel, AddressOf lbl_MouseWheel
            AddHandler lbl.Click, AddressOf lbl_Click
            AddHandler lbl.DoubleClick, AddressOf lbl_DoubleClick

            txt = new TextBox( )
            txt.Parent = me
            txt.Location = new Point(50,90)
            txt.Size = new Size(300,475)
            txt.BorderStyle = BorderStyle.FixedSingle
            txt.Multiline = true
            txt.ScrollBars = ScrollBars.Vertical
        end sub

        public shared sub Main( )
            Application.Run(new MouseEvents( ))
        end sub

        private sub btnReset_Click(ByVal sender as object, _
                                   ByVal e as EventArgs) _
                                   Handles btnReset.Click
```

Example 8-6. Mouse events in VB.NET (MouseEvents.vb) (continued)

VB

```
            lbl.Text = ""
            txt.Text = ""
        end sub

        private sub lbl_MouseEnter(ByVal sender as object, _
                                   ByVal e as EventArgs)
            lbl.Text = "MouseEnter"
            TextBoxDraw("Label MouseEnter")
        end sub

        private sub lbl_MouseHover(ByVal sender as object, _
                                   ByVal e as EventArgs)
            lbl.Text = "MouseHover"
            TextBoxDraw("Label MouseHover")
        end sub

        private sub lbl_MouseLeave(ByVal sender as object, _
                                   ByVal e as EventArgs)
            lbl.Text = "MouseLeave"
            TextBoxDraw("Label MouseLeave")
        end sub

        private sub lbl_MouseDown(ByVal sender as object, _
                                  ByVal e as MouseEventArgs)
            lbl.Text = "MouseDown"
            dim str as string
            str = "Label MouseDown"
            str = str + vbNewLine + vbTab + "Button:  " + e.Button.ToString()
            str = str + vbNewLine + vbTab + "Clicks:  " + e.Clicks.ToString()
            str = str + vbNewLine + vbTab + "Delta:   " + e.Delta.ToString()
            str = str + vbNewLine + vbTab + "X:   " + e.X.ToString()
            str = str + vbNewLine + vbTab + "Y:   " + e.Y.ToString()
            TextBoxDraw(str)
        end sub

        private sub lbl_MouseMove(ByVal sender as object, _
                                  ByVal e as MouseEventArgs)
            lbl.Text = "MouseMove"
            dim str as string
            str = "Label MouseMove"
            str = str + vbNewLine + vbTab + "Button:  " + e.Button.ToString()
            str = str + vbNewLine + vbTab + "Clicks:  " + e.Clicks.ToString()
            str = str + vbNewLine + vbTab + "Delta:   " + e.Delta.ToString()
            str = str + vbNewLine + vbTab + "X:   " + e.X.ToString()
            str = str + vbNewLine + vbTab + "Y:   " + e.Y.ToString()
            TextBoxDraw(str)
        end sub

        private sub lbl_MouseUp(ByVal sender as object, _
                                ByVal e as MouseEventArgs)
            lbl.Text = "MouseUp"
            dim str as string
```

Example 8-6. Mouse events in VB.NET (MouseEvents.vb) (continued)

```
VB              str = "Label MouseUp"
                str = str + vbNewLine + vbTab + "Button:  " + e.Button.ToString()
                str = str + vbNewLine + vbTab + "Clicks:  " + e.Clicks.ToString()
                str = str + vbNewLine + vbTab + "Delta:   " + e.Delta.ToString()
                str = str + vbNewLine + vbTab + "X:   " + e.X.ToString()
                str = str + vbNewLine + vbTab + "Y:   " + e.Y.ToString()
                TextBoxDraw(str)
            end sub


            private sub lbl_MouseWheel(ByVal sender as object, _
                                       ByVal e as MouseEventArgs)
                lbl.Text = "MouseWheel"
                dim str as string
                str = "Label MouseWheel"
                str = str + vbNewLine + vbTab + "Button:  " + e.Button.ToString()
                str = str + vbNewLine + vbTab + "Clicks:  " + e.Clicks.ToString()
                str = str + vbNewLine + vbTab + "Delta:  " + e.Delta.ToString()
                str = str + vbNewLine + vbTab + "X:   " + e.X.ToString()
                str = str + vbNewLine + vbTab + "Y:   " + e.Y.ToString()
                TextBoxDraw(str)
            end sub


            private sub lbl_Click(ByVal sender as object, _
                                  ByVal e as EventArgs)
                lbl.Text = "Click"
                TextBoxDraw("Label Click")
            end sub


            private sub lbl_DoubleClick(ByVal sender as object, _
                                        ByVal e as EventArgs)
                lbl.Text = "DoubleClick"
                TextBoxDraw("Label DoubleClick")
            end sub

        protected overrides sub OnMouseEnter(ByVal e as EventArgs)
                TextBoxDraw("Form MouseEnter")
            end sub

        protected overrides sub OnMouseHover(ByVal e as EventArgs)
                TextBoxDraw("Form MouseHover")
            end sub

        protected overrides sub OnMouseLeave(ByVal e as EventArgs)
                TextBoxDraw("Form MouseLeave")
            end sub

            private sub TextBoxDraw(str as string)
                txt.AppendText(vbNewLine + str)
            end sub
      end class
end namespace
```

Figure 8-2 illustrates the output from Example 8-5 and Example 8-6. As the mouse interacts with either the Form or the Label control, the log of mouse events, including the MouseEventArgs property values, is displayed in the TextBox. Clicking the Reset button clears the TextBox and the Label.

When the mouse cursor is moved from a position over the Form (but not over any child controls) to a position over any of the child controls, a Form MouseLeave event is raised. If this program were tracking the mouse events for the child control (as it is for the Label control), then you would see a concomitant MouseEnter for the child control that the cursor just passed over. This is an effect of the z-order of the controls, a topic covered in Chapter 7. In short, the control on top receives the mouse events.

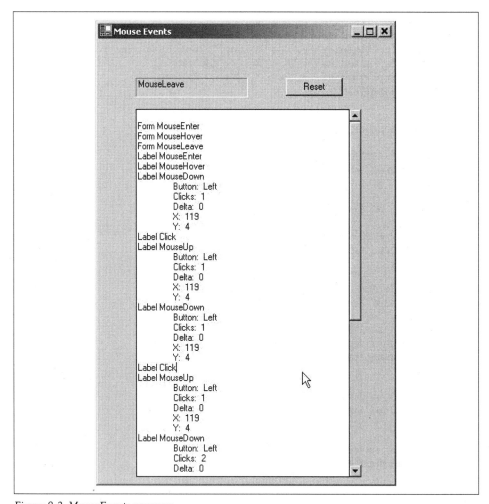

Figure 8-2. MouseEvents program

The code in this example is very straightforward. The Reset button adds a method called btnReset_Click to the Click event delegate, which sets the values of the Label and TextBox controls to empty strings.

As with the previous example, the Form MouseEnter, MouseHover, and Mouse-Leave events are overridden. Similar to before, each overridden method appends a string onto the output TextBox. Now, however, rather than call the Invalidate method, which raises a Paint event for the Form, the method TextBoxDraw is called.

TextBoxDraw is a simple method that takes a string as an argument and appends that string to the Text property of the TextBox using the TextBox AppendText method. It is:

C#
```
private void TextBoxDraw(string str)
{
    txt.AppendText("\r\n" + str);
}
```

VB
```
private sub TextBoxDraw(str as string)
    txt.AppendText(vbNewLine + str)
end sub
```

The C# code requires both a carriage return escape character (\r) and a new line escape character (\n) to force a new line in a TextBox control. (Most other controls require only a \n.)

To track these events, begin by instantiating the Label control lbl:

C#
```
lbl = new Label();
lbl.Parent = this;
lbl.Location = new Point(50,50);
lbl.Size = new Size(150,25);
lbl.BorderStyle = BorderStyle.Fixed3D;
```

VB
```
lbl = new Label()
lbl.Parent = me
lbl.Location = new Point(50,50)
lbl.Size = new Size(150,25)
lbl.BorderStyle = BorderStyle.Fixed3D
```

Then add event handlers to the relevant delegates for all the different mouse events. In C#, the type of event argument is indicated by the name of the event handler delegate to which the event handler method is added (in this example, System.EventHandler and System.Windows.Forms.MouseEventHandler are the delegates).

C#
```
lbl.MouseEnter += new System.EventHandler(lbl_MouseEnter);
lbl.MouseHover += new System.EventHandler(lbl_MouseHover);
lbl.MouseLeave += new System.EventHandler(lbl_MouseLeave);
```

```csharp
lbl.MouseDown += new
    System.Windows.Forms.MouseEventHandler(lbl_MouseDown);
// Comment out to reduce quantity of text generated.
// lbl.MouseMove += new
//    System.Windows.Forms.MouseEventHandler(lbl_MouseMove);
lbl.MouseUp += new System.Windows.Forms.MouseEventHandler(lbl_MouseUp);
lbl.MouseWheel += new
    System.Windows.Forms.MouseEventHandler(lbl_MouseWheel);
lbl.Click += new System.EventHandler(lbl_Click);
lbl.DoubleClick += new System.EventHandler(lbl_DoubleClick);
```

In VB.NET, the AddHandler syntax is used:

```
AddHandler lbl.MouseEnter, AddressOf lbl_MouseEnter
AddHandler lbl.MouseHover, AddressOf lbl_MouseHover
AddHandler lbl.MouseLeave, AddressOf lbl_MouseLeave
AddHandler lbl.MouseDown, AddressOf lbl_MouseDown
' Comment out to reduce quantity of text generated.
' AddHandler lbl.MouseMove, AddressOf lbl_MouseMove
AddHandler lbl.MouseUp, AddressOf lbl_MouseUp
AddHandler lbl.MouseWheel, AddressOf lbl_MouseWheel
AddHandler lbl.Click, AddressOf lbl_Click
AddHandler lbl.DoubleClick, AddressOf lbl_DoubleClick
```

> Notice that the event handler for the MouseMove event is commented out. MouseMove events fire every time the mouse moves at all. This generates a lot of output. To see this, uncomment the MouseMove event and rebuild the application.

In the instantiation and specification of the output TextBox, the BorderStyle is set to the FixedSingle BorderStyle enumeration, the Multiline property is set to true, and a vertical scrollbar is added. Here is the code:

```
txt.BorderStyle = BorderStyle.FixedSingle
txt.Multiline = true
txt.ScrollBars = ScrollBars.Vertical
```

The MouseEnter, MouseHover, and MouseLeave event handlers are essentially the same as in the previous example. The events that take an event argument of type MouseEventArgs (MouseDown, MouseMove, MouseUp, and MouseWheel) each output text that displays the values of the event argument properties. The tab character escape sequence (\t) enhances the output.

```csharp
private void lbl_MouseDown(object sender, MouseEventArgs e)
{
    lbl.Text = "MouseDown";
    string str;
    str = "Label MouseDown";
    str += "\r\n\tButton:  " + e.Button.ToString();
    str += "\r\n\tClicks:  " + e.Clicks.ToString();
```

```
    str += "\r\n\tDelta:  " + e.Delta.ToString( );
    str += "\r\n\tX:   " + e.X.ToString( );
    str += "\r\n\tY:   " + e.Y.ToString( );
    TextBoxDraw(str);
}
```

The VB.NET event handler uses VB.NET constants to achieve the same effects.

```
private sub lbl_MouseDown(ByVal sender as object, _
                          ByVal e as MouseEventArgs)
    lbl.Text = "MouseDown"
    dim str as string
    str = "Label MouseDown"
    str = str + vbNewLine + vbTab + "Button:  " + e.Button.ToString( )
    str = str + vbNewLine + vbTab + "Clicks:  " + e.Clicks.ToString( )
    str = str + vbNewLine + vbTab + "Delta:  " + e.Delta.ToString( )
    str = str + vbNewLine + vbTab + "X:  " + e.X.ToString( )
    str = str + vbNewLine + vbTab + "Y:  " + e.Y.ToString( )
    TextBoxDraw(str)
end sub
```

Experimenting with the program coded in this example and shown in Figure 8-2, you can see that the low-level mouse events occur in the following order for any given control:

- MouseEnter
- MouseMove
- MouseHover/MouseDown/MouseWheel
- MouseUp
- MouseLeave

The MouseDown and MouseUp events are rolled up into a Click or DoubleClick event. A Click event comes after the MouseDown but before the Mouse Up. A DoubleClick first registers a Click event (with its surrounding MouseDown and MouseUp), followed by a second MouseDown and MouseUp. The events and MouseEventArgs.Click property for a DoubleClick are shown in Figure 8-3. Notice that the Clicks property shows 2 only for the second MouseDown event; the first Mouse-Down Clicks property value is 1.

Mouse Properties

In addition to the mouse events described earlier, several useful mouse related properties of the Control class are listed in Table 8-5.

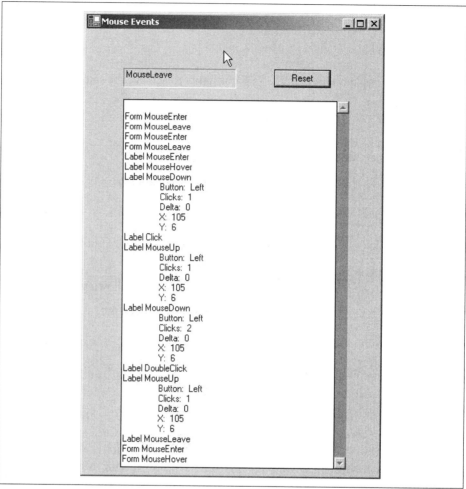

Figure 8-3. DoubleClick constituent events

Table 8-5. Mouse related Control properties

Property	Type	Description
Capture	Boolean	Read/write. true if the control has captured the mouse. When captured, the control receives mouse input even if the mouse is not within the borders of the control. Typically the mouse is captured for you automatically while a mouse button is depressed (e.g., during drag operations).
Cursor	Cursor	Read/write. The Cursor object to display when the mouse is over the control. The Cursor object is a member of the Cursors class, which provides a collection of Cursor objects (listed in Table 8-6).
MouseButtons	MouseButtons	Read-only. Static (Shared in VB.NET) bitwise combination of values from MouseButtons enumeration (listed in Table 8-4).

Table 8-5. Mouse related Control properties (continued)

Property	Type	Description
MousePosition	Point	Read-only. Static (Shared in VB.NET) point that contains the screen coordinates of the mouse cursor relative to the upper-left corner of the screen. Can use the Control PointToClient method to convert to client coordinates.
ModifierKeys	Keys	Read-only. Static (shared in VB.NET) bitwise combination of Keys values, indicating status of Shift, Ctrl, and Alt keys.

Many controls automatically change the mouse cursor as necessary. For example, when the cursor hovers over a Splitter control, the cursor changes to either the horizontal or vertical splitter symbol, as appropriate. If the mouse cursor hovers over any border of a Form, it will change to the appropriate resizing symbol.

You can use the Cursor property to control the mouse cursor that displays when the mouse cursor hot spot is over a control. The Cursor property is of type Cursor. The Cursor objects are provided by the Cursors class (note the plural), which contains a collection of Cursor objects. The members of the Cursors class are listed in Table 8-6. All Cursors except the panning and no-move cursors can have their appearance modified systemwide by going to Control Panel → Mouse → Pointers.

Table 8-6. Cursors members

Member	Default Appearance	Description
AppStarting	▷⧖	Cursor that appears when an application starts, typically a combination of an arrow and an hourglass.
Arrow	▷	Arrow cursor.
Cross	+	Crosshair cursor.
Default	▷	Default cursor, usually an arrow cursor.
Hand	✋	Hand cursor, typically used when hovering over a link.
Help	▷?	Help cursor.
HSplit	⬍	Horizontal splitter cursor.
IBeam	I	I-beam cursor, usually used to represent a text cursor.
No	⊘	Cursor that indicates current region is invalid for current operation.
NoMove2D	◆	Cursor used during wheel button operations when the mouse is not moving but the window can be scrolled both horizontally and vertically.
NoMoveHoriz	◀•▶	Cursor used during wheel operations when the mouse is not moving but the window can be scrolled horizontally.

Table 8-6. Cursors members (continued)

Member	Default Appearance	Description
NoMoveVert		Cursor used during wheel operations when the mouse is not moving but the window can be scrolled vertically.
PanEast		Cursor used during wheel operations when the mouse is moving and the window is scrolling horizontally to the right.
PanNE		Cursor used during wheel operations when the mouse is moving and the window is scrolling horizontally and vertically upward to the right.
PanNorth		Cursor used during wheel operations when the mouse is moving and the window is scrolling vertically upward.
PanNW		Cursor used during wheel operations when the mouse is moving and the window is scrolling horizontally and vertically upward to the left.
PanSE		Cursor used during wheel operations when the mouse is moving and the window is scrolling horizontally and vertically downward to the right.
PanSouth		Cursor used during wheel operations when the mouse is moving and the window is scrolling vertically downward.
PanSW		Cursor used during wheel operations when the mouse is moving and the window is scrolling horizontally and vertically downward to the left.
PanWest		Cursor used during wheel operations when the mouse is moving and the window is scrolling horizontally to the left.
SizeAll		Four-headed sizing cursor.
SizeNESW		Two-headed diagonal (northeast/southwest) sizing cursor.
SizeNS		Two-headed diagonal (north/south) sizing cursor.
SizeNWSE		Two-headed diagonal (northwest/southeast) sizing cursor.
SizeWE		Two-headed diagonal (west/east) sizing cursor.
UpArrow		UpArrow cursor, typically used to indicate an insertion point.
VSplit		Vertical splitter cursor.
WaitCursor		Wait cursor, typically an hourglass.

The mouse properties are demonstrated in the MouseProperties program, listed in Example 8-7 (in C#) and in Example 8-8 (in VB.NET). The code that is different from the previous example is highlighted. When these examples are run, they look similar to the program shown previously in Figure 8-2.

Example 8-7. Mouse properties in C# (MouseProperties.cs)

```
using System;
using System.Drawing;
```

Example 8-7. Mouse properties in C# (MouseProperties.cs) (continued)

```csharp
using System.Windows.Forms;

namespace ProgrammingWinApps
{
    public class MouseProperties : Form
    {
        private Label lbl;
        private Button btnReset;
        private TextBox txt;
        int i = 0;

        Cursor[ ] theCursors = {Cursors.AppStarting,
                                Cursors.Arrow,
                                Cursors.Hand,
                                Cursors.Help,
                                Cursors.No};

        public MouseProperties( )
        {
            Text = "Mouse Properties";
            Size = new Size(400,600);

            btnReset = new Button( );
            btnReset.Parent = this;
            btnReset.Location = new Point(250,50);
            btnReset.Text = "Reset";
            btnReset.Click += new System.EventHandler(btnReset_Click);

            lbl = new Label( );
            lbl.Parent = this;
            lbl.Location = new Point(50,50);
            lbl.Size = new Size(150,25);
            lbl.BorderStyle = BorderStyle.Fixed3D;
            lbl.MouseEnter += new System.EventHandler(lbl_MouseEnter);
            lbl.MouseHover += new System.EventHandler(lbl_MouseHover);
            lbl.MouseLeave += new System.EventHandler(lbl_MouseLeave);
            lbl.MouseDown += new
                    System.Windows.Forms.MouseEventHandler(lbl_MouseDown);
            //   Comment out to reduce quantity of text generated.
            //    lbl.MouseMove += new
            //       System.Windows.Forms.MouseEventHandler(lbl_MouseMove);
            lbl.MouseUp += new System.Windows.Forms.MouseEventHandler(lbl_MouseUp);
            lbl.MouseWheel += new
                    System.Windows.Forms.MouseEventHandler(lbl_MouseWheel);
            lbl.Click += new System.EventHandler(lbl_Click);
            lbl.DoubleClick += new System.EventHandler(lbl_DoubleClick);

            txt = new TextBox( );
            txt.Parent = this;
            txt.Location = new Point(50,90);
            txt.Size = new Size(300,475);
            txt.BorderStyle = BorderStyle.FixedSingle;
```

Example 8-7. Mouse properties in C# (MouseProperties.cs) (continued)

C#

```csharp
        txt.Multiline = true;
        txt.ScrollBars = ScrollBars.Vertical;
    }

    static void Main( )
    {
        Application.Run(new MouseProperties( ));
    }

    private void btnReset_Click(object sender, EventArgs e)
    {
        lbl.Text = "";
        txt.Text = "";
    }

    private void lbl_MouseEnter(object sender, EventArgs e)
    {
        lbl.Text = "MouseEnter";
        EventArgsStrings( );
        TextBoxDraw("Label MouseEnter");

        lbl.Cursor = Cursors.WaitCursor;
    }

    private void lbl_MouseHover(object sender, EventArgs e)
    {
        lbl.Cursor = theCursors[i % 5];
        i++;
        lbl.Text = "MouseHover";
        EventArgsStrings( );
        TextBoxDraw("Label MouseHover");
    }

    private void lbl_MouseLeave(object sender, EventArgs e)
    {
        lbl.Text = "MouseLeave";
        EventArgsStrings( );
        TextBoxDraw("Label MouseLeave");
    }

    private void lbl_MouseDown(object sender, MouseEventArgs e)
    {
        lbl.Text = "MouseDown";
        MouseEventArgsStrings(e);
        TextBoxDraw("Label MouseDown");
    }

    private void lbl_MouseMove(object sender, MouseEventArgs e)
    {
        lbl.Text = "MouseMove";
        MouseEventArgsStrings(e);
        TextBoxDraw("Label MouseMove");
    }
```

Example 8-7. Mouse properties in C# (MouseProperties.cs) (continued)

```
private void lbl_MouseUp(object sender, MouseEventArgs e)
{
   lbl.Text = "MouseUp";
   MouseEventArgsStrings(e);
   TextBoxDraw("Label MouseUp");
}

private void lbl_MouseWheel(object sender, MouseEventArgs e)
{
   lbl.Text = "MouseWheel";
   MouseEventArgsStrings(e);
   TextBoxDraw("Label MouseWheel");
}

private void lbl_Click(object sender, EventArgs e)
{
   lbl.Text = "Click";
   EventArgsStrings();
   TextBoxDraw("Label Click");
}

private void lbl_DoubleClick(object sender, EventArgs e)
{
   lbl.Text = "DoubleClick";
   EventArgsStrings();
   TextBoxDraw("Label DoubleClick");
}

private void EventArgsStrings()
{
   string str;
   str = "\tCursor:   " + lbl.Cursor.ToString();
   str += "\r\n\tCapture:  " + lbl.Capture.ToString();
   str += "\r\n\tMouseButtons:  " + MouseButtons.ToString();
   str += "\r\n\tMousePosition:  " + MousePosition.ToString();
   str += "\r\n\tModifierKeys:  " + ModifierKeys.ToString();
   TextBoxDraw(str);
}

private void MouseEventArgsStrings(MouseEventArgs e)
{
   string str;
   str = "\tButton:   " + e.Button.ToString();
   str += "\r\n\tClicks:   " + e.Clicks.ToString();
   str += "\r\n\tDelta:   " + e.Delta.ToString();
   str += "\r\n\tX:   " + e.X.ToString();
   str += "\r\n\tY:   " + e.Y.ToString();
   TextBoxDraw(str);
   EventArgsStrings();
}

private void TextBoxDraw(string str)
```

Example 8-7. Mouse properties in C# (MouseProperties.cs) (continued)

```csharp
        {
            txt.AppendText(str);
        }
    }
}
```

Example 8-8. Mouse properties in VB.NET (MouseProperties.vb)

```vbnet
Option Strict On
imports System
imports System.Drawing
imports System.Windows.Forms

namespace ProgrammingWinApps
    public class MouseProperties : inherits Form

        private lbl as Label
        private WithEvents btnReset as Button
        private txt as TextBox
        dim i as integer = 0

        dim theCursors as Cursor() = {Cursors.AppStarting, _
                                      Cursors.Arrow, _
                                      Cursors.Hand, _
                                      Cursors.Help, _
                                      Cursors.No}

        public sub New()
            Text = "Mouse Properties"
            Size = new Size(400,600)

            btnReset = new Button()
            btnReset.Parent = me
            btnReset.Location = new Point(250,50)
            btnReset.Text = "Reset"

            lbl = new Label()
            lbl.Parent = me
            lbl.Location = new Point(50,50)
            lbl.Size = new Size(150,25)
            lbl.BorderStyle = BorderStyle.Fixed3D
            AddHandler lbl.MouseEnter, AddressOf lbl_MouseEnter
            AddHandler lbl.MouseHover, AddressOf lbl_MouseHover
            AddHandler lbl.MouseLeave, AddressOf lbl_MouseLeave
            AddHandler lbl.MouseDown, AddressOf lbl_MouseDown
            '  Comment out to reduce quantity of text generated.
            '  AddHandler lbl.MouseMove, AddressOf lbl_MouseMove
            AddHandler lbl.MouseUp, AddressOf lbl_MouseUp
            AddHandler lbl.MouseWheel, AddressOf lbl_MouseWheel
            AddHandler lbl.Click, AddressOf lbl_Click
            AddHandler lbl.DoubleClick, AddressOf lbl_DoubleClick
```

Example 8-8. Mouse properties in VB.NET (MouseProperties.vb) (continued)

```
         txt = new TextBox( )
         txt.Parent = me
         txt.Location = new Point(50,90)
         txt.Size = new Size(300,475)
         txt.BorderStyle = BorderStyle.FixedSingle
         txt.Multiline = true
         txt.ScrollBars = ScrollBars.Vertical
    end sub

    public shared sub Main( )
         Application.Run(new MouseProperties( ))
    end sub

    private sub btnReset_Click(ByVal sender as object, _
                               ByVal e as EventArgs) _
                               Handles btnReset.Click
         lbl.Text = ""
         txt.Text = ""
    end sub

    private sub lbl_MouseEnter(ByVal sender as object, _
                               ByVal e as EventArgs)
         lbl.Text = "MouseEnter"
         EventArgsStrings( )
         TextBoxDraw("Label MouseEnter")
    end sub

    private sub lbl_MouseHover(ByVal sender as object, _
                               ByVal e as EventArgs)
         lbl.Cursor = theCursors(i mod 5)
         i = i + 1

         lbl.Text = "MouseHover"
         EventArgsStrings( )
         TextBoxDraw("Label MouseHover")
    end sub

    private sub lbl_MouseLeave(ByVal sender as object, _
                               ByVal e as EventArgs)
         lbl.Text = "MouseLeave"
         EventArgsStrings( )
         TextBoxDraw("Label MouseLeave")
    end sub

    private sub lbl_MouseDown(ByVal sender as object, _
                              ByVal e as MouseEventArgs)
         lbl.Text = "MouseDown"
         MouseEventArgsStrings(e)
         TextBoxDraw("Label MouseDown")
    end sub

    private sub lbl_MouseMove(ByVal sender as object, _
                              ByVal e as MouseEventArgs)
```

Example 8-8. Mouse properties in VB.NET (MouseProperties.vb) (continued)

VB

```
      lbl.Text = "MouseMove"
      MouseEventArgsStrings(e)
      TextBoxDraw("Label MouseMove")
   end sub

   private sub lbl_MouseUp(ByVal sender as object, _
                          ByVal e as MouseEventArgs)
      lbl.Text = "MouseUp"
      MouseEventArgsStrings(e)
      TextBoxDraw("Label MouseUp")
   end sub

   private sub lbl_MouseWheel(ByVal sender as object, _
                             ByVal e as MouseEventArgs)
      lbl.Text = "MouseWheel"
      MouseEventArgsStrings(e)
      TextBoxDraw("Label MouseWheel")
   end sub

   private sub lbl_Click(ByVal sender as object, _
                        ByVal e as EventArgs)
      lbl.Text = "Click"
      EventArgsStrings()
      TextBoxDraw("Label Click")
   end sub

   private sub lbl_DoubleClick(ByVal sender as object, _
                              ByVal e as EventArgs)
      lbl.Text = "DoubleClick"
      EventArgsStrings()
      TextBoxDraw("Label DoubleClick")
   end sub

   private sub EventArgsStrings()
      dim str as string
      str = vbTab + "Cursor:   " + _
            lbl.Cursor.ToString()
      str = str + vbNewLine + vbTab + "Capture:   " + _
            lbl.Capture.ToString()
      str = str + vbNewLine + vbTab + "MouseButtons:   " + _
            MouseButtons.ToString()
      str = str + vbNewLine + vbTab + "MousePosition:   " + _
            MousePosition.ToString()
      str = str + vbNewLine + vbTab + "ModifierKeys:   " + _
            ModifierKeys.ToString()
      TextBoxDraw(str)
   end sub

   private sub MouseEventArgsStrings(ByVal e as MouseEventArgs)
      dim str as string
      str = vbTab + "Button:   " + e.Button.ToString()
      str = str + vbNewLine + vbTab + "Clicks:   " + e.Clicks.ToString()
      str = str + vbNewLine + vbTab + "Delta:   " + e.Delta.ToString()
```

Example 8-8. Mouse properties in VB.NET (MouseProperties.vb) (continued)

```vb
            str = str + vbNewLine + vbTab + "X:  " + e.X.ToString()
            str = str + vbNewLine + vbTab + "Y:  " + e.Y.ToString()
            TextBoxDraw(str)
            EventArgsStrings()
        end sub

        private sub TextBoxDraw(str as string)
            txt.AppendText(vbNewLine + str)
        end sub
    end class
end namespace
```

In the code in Examples 8-7 and 8-8, the program creates a member array of Cursor objects:

```csharp
Cursor[] theCursors = {Cursors.AppStarting,
                       Cursors.Arrow,
                       Cursors.Hand,
                       Cursors.Help,
                       Cursors.No};
```

```vb
dim theCursors as Cursor() = {Cursors.AppStarting, _
                             Cursors.Arrow, _
                             Cursors.Hand, _
                             Cursors.Help, _
                             Cursors.No}
```

This program uses only five different Cursor objects in the array. They are displayed in succession in the MouseHover event, using the member variable i as a counter, in conjunction with the modulus operator, to index into the array:

```csharp
private void lbl_MouseHover(object sender, EventArgs e)
{
    lbl.Cursor = theCursors[i % 5];
    i++;
    lbl.Text = "MouseHover";
    EventArgsStrings();
    TextBoxDraw("Label MouseHover");
}
```

```vb
private sub lbl_MouseHover(ByVal sender as object, _
                          ByVal e as EventArgs)
    lbl.Cursor = theCursors(i mod 5)
    i = i + 1
    lbl.Text = "MouseHover"
    EventArgsStrings()
    TextBoxDraw("Label MouseHover")
end sub
```

Each event trapped in this program displays the same information as in the previous example, plus the values of the mouse properties. This example is refined a bit from the previous example by moving all the common code for constructing the display string into helper methods. There are two of these helper methods: Event-ArgsStrings, which takes no arguments, and MouseEventArgsStrings, which takes the MouseEventArgs as an argument. Here are these two methods:

```
private void EventArgsStrings()
{
    string str;
    str = "\tCursor:   " + lbl.Cursor.ToString();
    str += "\r\n\tCapture:   " + lbl.Capture.ToString();
    str += "\r\n\tMouseButtons:   " + MouseButtons.ToString();
    str += "\r\n\tMousePosition:   " + MousePosition.ToString();
    str += "\r\n\tModifierKeys:   " + ModifierKeys.ToString();
    TextBoxDraw(str);
}

private void MouseEventArgsStrings(MouseEventArgs e)
{
    string str;
    str = "\tButton:   " + e.Button.ToString();
    str += "\r\n\tClicks:   " + e.Clicks.ToString();
    str += "\r\n\tDelta:   " + e.Delta.ToString();
    str += "\r\n\tX:   " + e.X.ToString();
    str += "\r\n\tY:   " + e.Y.ToString();
    TextBoxDraw(str);
    EventArgsStrings();
}
```

```
private sub EventArgsStrings()
    dim str as string
    str = vbTab + "Cursor:   " + _
            lbl.Cursor.ToString()
    str = str + vbNewLine + vbTab + "Capture:   " + _
            lbl.Capture.ToString()
    str = str + vbNewLine + vbTab + "MouseButtons:   " + _
            MouseButtons.ToString()
    str = str + vbNewLine + vbTab + "MousePosition:   " + _
            MousePosition.ToString()
    str = str + vbNewLine + vbTab + "ModifierKeys:   " + _
            ModifierKeys.ToString()
    TextBoxDraw(str)
end sub

private sub MouseEventArgsStrings(ByVal e as MouseEventArgs)
    dim str as string
    str = vbTab + "Button:   " + e.Button.ToString()
    str = str + vbNewLine + vbTab + "Clicks:   " + e.Clicks.ToString()
    str = str + vbNewLine + vbTab + "Delta:   " + e.Delta.ToString()
    str = str + vbNewLine + vbTab + "X:   " + e.X.ToString()
    str = str + vbNewLine + vbTab + "Y:   " + e.Y.ToString()
    TextBoxDraw(str)
    EventArgsStrings()
end sub
```

CHAPTER 9

Text and Fonts

The well-made page is now what it was then ...
—Robert Bringhurst
The Elements of Typographic Style

People have been writing for millennia, starting with styli on clay tablets, moving to ink on paper, and now using pixels on monitors and laser printers. Writing on a computer is accomplished with *text*, the characters that make up the content, and *fonts*, which provide the visual aspect to the characters, such as typestyle and size.*

Text is ubiquitous. All the examples in this book have used text. Every control has a Text property. The contents of this Text property generally must be rendered (some controls do not render their Text property) on the screen or on a piece of paper. Many controls, such as the Label, TextBox, and RichTextBox, exist primarily to display text. Furthermore, many applications draw text directly on the client area of the form.

This chapter shows how text and fonts are handled in .NET applications.

Text

Text can be thought of as the output from a typewriter (remember typewriters?). That is, text is just characters, with no special formatting other than spaces, tabs, and newlines. Text is typically saved to a file (often called a flat file or an ASCII file).

On most Windows systems, text files commonly (but not always) have the file extension *.txt*. Double-click on a file with that extension in Windows Explorer, and Notepad, the default application for *.txt* files, will open. .NET programs can capture text in String objects.

---

* This chapter deals only with western-style text and not with ideograms as used in Chinese and Japanese text.

In a single-byte character set, each text character is defined by one byte of data. The maximum one byte number in hexadecimal is FF, or 255 in decimal. Thus, using a zero-based index, a maximum of 256 different characters can be represented in a single byte character set, since each character must be uniquely indexed. The index assigned to a character is called the *code point* or *character code*.

The most commonly used single byte character set in the PC world is the American Standards Committee for Information Interchange (ASCII) character set. The first 128 characters, corresponding to seven bit bytes (maximum hex value of 7F), are more or less standardized and are usually considered low-order ASCII characters. The upper 128 characters are not part of the ASCII standard, although many well established character sets use all 256 characters.

The mainframe world often uses a similar, but incompatible, single byte character set called Extended Binary Coded Decimal Interchange Code, (EBCDIC), which was originally developed by IBM for the System/360.

The low-order ASCII characters are listed in .

An alternative to a single-byte character set is a two-byte character set. Two-byte character sets can provide up to 65,536 characters. The most common two-byte character set is the Unicode character set, which is a superset of the ASCII character set.

The Unicode technology was introduced to allow easier representation of languages other than English, especially Asian languages such as Chinese and Japanese, which may not have limited alphabets. Unicode also allows character sets of Western languages, such as Spanish, that have a wide range of styles and special characters within a single character set.

To enter any character from the keyboard, either ASCII or Unicode, press and hold the Alt key while pressing the four digits of the decimal value on the numeric keypad (not the number keys at the top of the keyboard). Pad the beginning of the decimal value with zeros to make four digits. So, for example, to enter a backslash character, which is hex 5C or decimal 92, press Alt 0092.

You can view and place any character, either ASCII or Unicode, from any character set loaded in your system, into any Windows application. To do so, use the Windows-provided Character Map applet accessible from the Start button, and then Programs → Accessories → System Tools → Character Map.

You can convert back and forth between the hex value of a character and the character it represents. This is done somewhat differently in C# and VB.NET.

In C#, you cast from one representation to another, as in the following line of code from Example 9-14 in Chapter 4.

```
strMsg += "\t" + "KeyChar Code: " + ((int)keyChar).ToString() + "\r\n";
```

where keyChar is an object of type char. This char is converted to an int, and then that int is appended to the string using the static ToString method (which is actually not necessary here, since C# will automatically convert to a string any expression appended to a string with the + operator).

The equivalent line of code in VB.NET is as follows:

```
strMsg += vbTab + "KeyChar Code: " + AscW(keyChar).ToString( ) + vbCrLf
```

where the AscW function converts the character code into its integer value, for it to be then converted to a string. AscW returns an integer representing a Unicode character code between 0 and 65535. The similar function Asc returns a value between 0 and 255 for single byte character sets, and between -32768 and 32767 for double byte character sets. For the low-order characters, they are equivalent.

To convert in the opposite direction in C#, cast an integer to a char. For example:

```
(char)65
```

would return an "A".

In VB.NET, use the Chr and ChrW functions, which both take integer arguments representing a character code and return a char. ChrW takes a Unicode character code as an argument, while Chr takes either a single- or double-byte character code.

Several sample programs in Chapter 4 demonstrate working with characters, character codes, keystrokes, and key codes.

Fonts

Fonts provide control over the visual aspect of text. They define the style of the characters, the size, and any attributes such as bold or italic.

Typographical Stuff

There is a considerable difference between the way a computer user thinks of fonts and the way a traditional typographer thinks of fonts, even if that typographer uses a computer for her font design work. This section looks at fonts from the typical computer user's point of view.

To learn more about traditional typography, several good books are available, such as *The Elements of Typographic Style* by Robert Bringhurst (Hartley & Marks).

Before delving into the properties, methods, and events provided by the Font class, let's review the most common typographic conventions, especially as they apply to .NET applications.

Fonts are classified according to common stylistic features. The broadest classification, is that of serif fonts versus sans serif. A *serif* is the little frill found at the bottom of the character strokes. Commonly used serif font families include Times New Roman, Garamond, and Palatino. Serif fonts are often referred to as *roman* fonts (notice the lower case). A *sans serif* font (Latin for "without serif") does not have these embellishments. The commonly used sans serif fonts include Arial, Tahoma, Verdana, and Helvetica.

Most Windows systems also include one or more fonts, such as Symbols and Dingbats, that don't fall into either category, since they contain mostly non-alphabetic characters (●❄□◆✠✢). Many fonts are also alphabetic but not classifiable as either serif or sans serif because they are so stylized.

Serifs can improve the readability of blocks of printed text. Most newspapers, including The Times of London (which commissioned the original version of the Times font) and the New York Times, as well as most books and magazines use a serif font for body text. Sans-serif fonts are used for body text as well, but especially for headings, captions, and titles. Since they are more compact than the equivalently sized serif font, and also because they tend to look better at low and moderate resolutions than serif fonts, they find common use on computer screens. The default Windows font is called Microsoft Sans Serif.

The next broadest font classification is *families*. The members of a *font family* share many design features and are easily recognized as being related. Most (but not all) font families have a base, or regular style. If the character strokes are made heavier, then the font becomes *bold*. If the characters are slanted to the right and given an extra bit of filigree, then the font becomes *italic*, or italicized. If slanted only, and not stylized, it is *oblique*. So, for example, *Times New Roman Italic* is clearly the italicized version of Times New Roman and Arial Bold is the bold version of Arial.

Strictly speaking, the bold member of a font family has a distinctly different font from the regular member, likewise for the italic and bold italic versions. However, as a practical matter, font users on computers think of the font family as the font, with bold and italic applied as attributes, although there may be additional font families that differ primarily by attribute, such as Arial, Arial Black, and Arial Narrow. The common font dialog supports this viewpoint, as do the constructors of the Font class, as you will see shortly. Windows and the .NET framework also support adding underline and ~~strikethrough~~ effects.

The appearance of a font is often called the *typeface*, or simply *face*. Technically, it refers to a specific font, such as Times New Roman Bold. But in the common usage of today, it refers more to the font family, e.g., Times New Roman, which then has style attributes applied.

Each unique font, as distinct from font family, is provided in a separate file on the computer. For example, a standard Windows installation includes Arial.ttf, Arial

Bold.ttf, Arial Italic.ttf, and Arial Bold Italic.ttf. The common font dialog sorts the related font files into families and presents the family, Arial in this example, along with the possible styles: regular, bold, italic, and bold italic.

Font sizes are measured in units of points. A *point* is about 1/72 of an inch. The equivocation is necessary because font metrics in the real world are a non-standard art. Different fonts measure themselves differently. Generally, the point size is measured from the bottom of the descenders, i.e., that part of the characters such as g or y that extend below the baseline, to the top of the ascenders, i.e., that part of the character that extends above the baseline, including the space allowed for diacritical marks. (Diacritical marks added above a character to indicate a special phonetic value, such as the acute [for example, é] and grave [for example, è] accents and the umlaut [for example, ü].)

In the early days of computers, all fonts were rendered from bitmaps. These bitmaps were carefully tweaked by typographers to present the best possible appearance for each font in each available size. A 12-point font was a distinctly different file from a 14-point font, and a bold font was different from a regular font. If you wanted a 14-point font and your system did not have a 14-point version of the font you wanted, you were out of luck. Windows 3.1 changed that for Windows users with the advent of TrueType fonts.

TrueType fonts are scalable outline fonts that make it possible to render any size font from a single font file. The file does not contain a bitmap, but rather instructions for creating the bitmap (many fonts still contain hand-tweaked bitmaps for the smaller sizes). These instructions include hints for optimizing the appearance over a wide range of sizes. Windows 2000 added support for OpenType fonts, an extension of TrueType technology that adds extended font-specific information.

Windows still supports the old-style bitmap fonts (designated with an A icon in the Fonts applet of Control Panel), but the .NET Framework does not provide access to them.

With TrueType and OpenType fonts, you can specify any size font for either screen display or printer output, and the operating system will generate the correct bitmap. You can see which fonts are installed on a computer by going to Control Panel → Fonts. The TrueType and OpenType fonts have a TT or O icon, respectively, and a file extension of TTF. Double-clicking on any font will open a sample page showing the font in a range of sizes, along with other information.

Another way to classify fonts is by character width. In *fixed pitch* fonts, all characters, from the period to the lowercase i to the uppercase W, are the same width. These are the fonts of the typewriter and early impact printers. They are rarely used today, except for in the command line and for code listings. Fixed pitch fonts commonly found on Windows systems include Courier and Lucida Console.

The most commonly used fonts, both in the computer world and the real world, are *proportional* fonts. The lowercase i takes less horizontal space than the uppercase W. Typographers take great care to design proportional fonts to ensure that the characters flow smoothly. *Kerning*, the process of adjusting the whitespace between the characters, may vary depending on which letters are adjacent to one another. All this makes for easy reading and beautiful looking text, but it makes life difficult for the software developer who must know exactly how long a text string is so that subsequent characters or other graphic elements can be placed correctly. As you will see shortly, the .NET Framework solves this problem by providing the MeasureString method.

Font Class

Instances of the Font class define a specific font to be used for some text. This font definition includes the font family or typeface, such as Times New Roman or Arial, any style attributes, and the size.

Font properties

The Font object is immutable: all Font properties are read-only. If you want to change any of the properties of a Font object, then you must create a new Font object, using one of the thirteen available constructors and described shortly. However, one of the constructors lets you create a new Font object from an existing Font object while using a different set of styles.

Table 9-1 lists the commonly used properties of the Font class, all of which are read-only.

Table 9-1. Font properties

Property	Value type	Description
Bold	Boolean	Returns true if this font is bold.
FontFamily	FontFamily	Returns a FontFamily object, i.e., a group of typefaces having a similar design.
GdiCharSet	Byte	Returns the GDI character set for this font.
GdiVerticalFont	Boolean	Returns true if this font derives from a GDI vertical font.
Height	Integer	Returns the height of this font, in current graphics units. This is the recommended line spacing for the font for display on the video monitor.
Italic	Boolean	Returns true if this font is italic.
Name	String	Returns the name of the typeface for this font.
Size	Float (C#) Single (VB.NET)	Returns the em size for this font, defined as the horizontal size equivalent to the point size of the font, in current design units.
SizeInPoints	Float /single	Returns the size of this font, in points.
Strikeout	Boolean	Returns true if this font has a horizontal line through it.

Table 9-1. Font properties (continued)

Property	Value type	Description
Style	FontStyle	Returns one or more members of the FontStyle enumeration for this font. Members of the FontStyle enumeration are listed in Table 9-3. The values may be combined in a bitwise manner using the logical OR operator.
Underline	Boolean	Returns true if this font is underlined.
Unit	GraphicsUnit	Returns a member of the GraphicsUnit enumeration. Possible values are listed in Table 9-4.

All controls have a Font property, of type Font, that specifies the typeface or design, size, and style, for any text displayed by the control.

Since the Font property is an ambient property, the current font for any child control is the same as the current font for the parent control, unless the child control explicitly sets it.

The default font for any form is determined by the Windows default font, which is set by going to Control Panel, and then the Display, selecting Properties and then the Settings tab. (You can get to the same Display dialog by right-clicking on the desktop and selecting Properties.) The specifics of each tab depend on the video driver installed on that system.

If the Font property of a control has been changed to something other than default, it can be set back to default in one of two ways: by setting the font equal to the static Control property DefaultFont or using the static Control method ResetFont.

The programs listed in Example 9-1 (in C#) and in Example 9-2 (in VB.NET) demonstrate many Font properties. They display a form with a label in one corner. A button captioned Show pops up a message box displaying various font properties of the Show button and the label. A second button, labeled Change, opens the Font common dialog box (covered in detail in Chapter 6) to let you change the font of the label.

Example 9-1. Font properties in C# (FontProperties.cs)

```
using System;
using System.Drawing;
using System.Windows.Forms;

namespace ProgrammingWinApps
{
    public class FontProperties : Form
    {

        private Button btnShow;
        private Button btnChange;
        private Label lbl;
        private FontDialog fd;
```

Example 9-1. Font properties in C# (FontProperties.cs) (continued)

```csharp
public FontProperties( )
{
   Text = "Font Properties";
   Size = new Size(350,200);

   btnShow = new Button( );
   btnShow.Location = new Point(50,50);
   btnShow.Size = new Size(100,23);
   btnShow.Text = "Show";
   btnShow.Click += new System.EventHandler(btnShow_Click);
   btnShow.Parent = this;

   btnChange = new Button( );
   btnChange.Location = new Point(200,50);
   btnChange.Size = new Size(100,23);
   btnChange.Text = "Change";
   btnChange.Click += new System.EventHandler(btnChange_Click);
   btnChange.Parent = this;

   lbl = new Label( );
   lbl.Text = "The quick brown fox...";
   lbl.AutoSize = true;
   lbl.Parent = this;
}

static void Main( )
{
   Application.Run(new FontProperties( ));
}

private void btnShow_Click(object sender, EventArgs e)
{
   MessageBox.Show("Button Font:\t" + btnShow.Font.ToString( ) + "\n" +
      "Button Font Family:\t" + btnShow.Font.FontFamily.ToString( ) + "\n" +
      "Button Font Style:\t" + btnShow.Font.Style.ToString( ) + "\n" +
      "Button Font Unit:\t" + btnShow.Font.Unit.ToString( ) + "\n" +
      "Button Font Height:\t" + btnShow.Font.Height.ToString( ) + "\n" +
      "Label Font:\t" + lbl.Font.ToString( ) + "\n" +
      "Label Font Family:\t" + lbl.Font.FontFamily.ToString( ) + "\n" +
      "Label Font Style:\t" + lbl.Font.Style.ToString( ) + "\n" +
      "Label Font Unit:\t" + lbl.Font.Unit.ToString( ) + "\n" +
      "Label Font Height:\t" + lbl.Font.Height.ToString( ) + "\n",
      "Font Properties");
}

private void btnChange_Click(object sender, EventArgs e)
{
   fd = new FontDialog( );
   fd.ShowHelp = false;
   fd.ShowApply = true;

   fd.Apply += new System.EventHandler(this.fd_Apply);
```

Example 9-1. Font properties in C# (FontProperties.cs) (continued)

```csharp
        if (fd.ShowDialog( ) == DialogResult.OK)
            lbl.Font = fd.Font;
    }

    private void fd_Apply(object sender, System.EventArgs e)
    {
        lbl.Font = fd.Font;
    }
  }
}
```

Example 9-2. Font properties in VB.NET (FontProperties.vb)

```vb
Option Strict On
imports System
imports System.Drawing
imports System.Windows.Forms

namespace ProgrammingWinApps
   public class FontProperties : inherits Form

      Private WithEvents btnShow as Button
      Private WithEvents btnChange as Button
      private lbl as Label
      private fd as FontDialog

      public sub New( )
         Text = "Font Properties"
         Size = new Size(350,200)

         btnShow = new Button( )
         btnShow.Location = new Point(50,50)
         btnShow.Size = new Size(100,23)
         btnShow.Text = "Show"
         btnShow.Parent = me

         btnChange = new Button( )
         btnChange.Location = new Point(200,50)
         btnChange.Size = new Size(100,23)
         btnChange.Text = "Change"
         btnChange.Parent = me

         lbl = new Label( )
         lbl.Text = "The quick brown fox..."
         lbl.AutoSize = true
         lbl.Parent = me
      end sub

      public shared sub Main( )
         Application.Run(new FontProperties( ))
      end sub
```

Example 9-2. Font properties in VB.NET (FontProperties.vb) (continued)

VB

```
    private sub btnShow_Click(ByVal sender as object, _
        ByVal e as EventArgs) _
        Handles btnShow.Click
      MessageBox.Show("Button Font:   " + _
          vbTab + btnShow.Font.ToString() + vbCrLf + _
          "Button Font Family:   " + vbTab + _
          btnShow.Font.FontFamily.ToString() + vbCrLf + _
          "Button Font Style:   " + vbTab + _
          btnShow.Font.Style.ToString() + vbCrLf + _
          "Button Font Unit:   " + vbTab + _
          btnShow.Font.Unit.ToString() + vbCrLf + _
          "Button Font Height:   " + vbTab + _
          btnShow.Font.Height.ToString() + vbCrLf + _
          "Label Font:   " + vbTab + _
          lbl.Font.ToString() + vbCrLf + _
          "Label Font Family:   " + vbTab + _
          lbl.Font.FontFamily.ToString() + vbCrLf + _
          "Label Font Style:   " + vbTab + _
          lbl.Font.Style.ToString() + vbCrLf + _
          "Label Font Unit:   " + vbTab + _
          lbl.Font.Unit.ToString() + vbCrLf + _
          "Label Font Height:   " + vbTab + _
          lbl.Font.Height.ToString() + vbCrLf, _
          "Font Properties")
    end sub

    private sub btnChange_Click(ByVal sender as object, _
        ByVal e as EventArgs) _
        Handles btnChange.Click
      fd = new FontDialog()
      fd.ShowHelp = false
      fd.ShowApply = true

      AddHandler fd.Apply, AddressOf fd_Apply

      if fd.ShowDialog() = DialogResult.OK then
        lbl.Font = fd.Font
      end if
    end sub

    private sub fd_Apply(ByVal sender As System.Object, _
                    ByVal e As System.EventArgs)
      lbl.Font = fd.Font
    End Sub
  end class
end namespace
```

Class member variables are declared for each control on the form as well as the font common dialog. The label and button controls are instantiated and specified inside the constructor. No Size property is specified for the Label control; instead the Auto-Size property is set to true. This will cause the Label to size itself automatically to accommodate its Text property.

When the Show button is clicked, the btnShow_Click event handler method is executed, which invokes a MessageBox that displays a variety of Font properties btn-Show and the Label control.

Clicking on the Change button fires the btnChange_Click event handler, which displays the Font common dialog box. (Chapter 6 covers this dialog box in detail.) Since the ShowApply property of the dialog box is set to true, the Apply button is visible and operative on the dialog box. The Apply event raised by this button is handled by fd_Apply. The following appropriate line adds that method to the event delegate:

C#
```
fd.Apply += new System.EventHandler(this.fd_Apply);
```

VB
```
AddHandler fd.Apply, AddressOf fd_Apply
```

Running either program and changing the font to 16-point bold italic Comic Sans MS produces the form shown in Figure 9-1. Clicking on the Show button brings up the dialog shown in Figure 9-2.

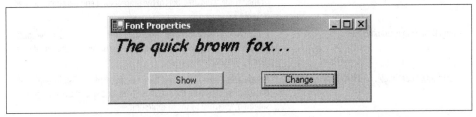

Figure 9-1. Font Properties program

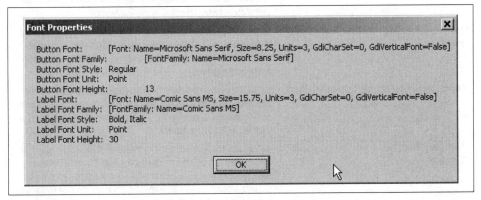

Figure 9-2. Font Properties dialog box

Constructors

There are 13 overloaded constructors for the Font class, the arguments of which are listed in Table 9-2, allowing for a wide range of needs. The simplest constructor lets you take an existing Font object and apply different styles. The remaining constructors are based on either a FontFamily object or a string representing a font family.

Table 9-2. Font class constructor argument lists

Constructor argument list	Description
Font, FontStyle	Instantiates a new font object, applying the specified styles from the FontStyle enumeration to an existing font object. Members of the Font-Style enumeration, which may be combined in a bitwise manner, are listed in Table 9-3.
FontFamily, float (Single in VB.NET)	Instantiates a new font object from the specified FontFamily object and of the specified size in points.
string, float/Single	Instantiates a new font object from the FontFamily named in the specified string and of the specified size in points.
FontFamily, float/Single, FontStyle	Instantiates a new font object from the specified FontFamily object, of the specified size in points, and with specified styles.
string, float/Single, FontStyle	Instantiates a new font object from the FontFamily named in the specified string, of the specified size in points, and with the specified styles.
FontFamily, float/Single, GraphicsUnit	Instantiates a new Font object from the specified FontFamily object, of the specified size, and with the unit of measurement specified by the GraphicsUnit. Valid members of the GraphicsUnit enumeration are listed in Table 9-4.
string, float/Single, GraphicsUnit	Instantiates a new Font object from the FontFamily named in the specified string, of the specified size, and with the unit of measurement specified by the GraphicsUnit.
FontFamily, float/Single, FontStyle, GraphicsUnit	Instantiates a new Font object from the specified FontFamily object, of the specified size, with the specified styles, and with the unit of measurement specified by the GraphicsUnit.
string, float/Single, FontStyle, GraphicsUnit	Instantiates a new Font object from the FontFamily named in the specified string, of the specified size, with the specified styles, and with the unit of measurement specified by the GraphicsUnit.
FontFamily, float/Single, FontStyle, GraphicsUnit, byte	Instantiates a new Font object from the specified FontFamily object, of the specified size, with the specified styles, with the unit of measurement specified by the GraphicsUnit, and the GDI character set specified by the byte argument.
string, float/Single, FontStyle, GraphicsUnit, byte	Instantiates a new Font object from the FontFamily named in the specified string, of the specified size, with the specified styles, with the unit of measurement specified by the GraphicsUnit, and the GDI character set specified by the byte argument.
FontFamily, float/Single, FontStyle, GraphicsUnit, byte, bool	Instantiates a new Font object from the specified FontFamily object, of the specified size, with the specified styles, with the unit of measurement specified by the GraphicsUnit, the GDI character set specified by the byte argument, and a Boolean value of `true` if the new Font object is derived from a GDI vertical font.
string, float/Single, FontStyle, GraphicsUnit, byte, bool	Instantiates a new Font object from the FontFamily named in the specified string, of the specified size, with the specified styles, with the unit of measurement specified by the GraphicsUnit, the GDI character set specified by the byte argument, and a Boolean value of `true` if the new Font object is derived from a GDI vertical font.

The members of the FontStyle enumeration may be combined in a bitwise manner using the logical OR operator.

Table 9-3. FontStyle enumeration members

Member
Value
Regular
Bold
Italic
Strikeout
Underline

Table 9-4. GraphicsUnit enumeration members

Member	Unit of measure
Display	1/75 inch (raises an exception when used with Font)
Document	1/300 inch
Inch	1 inch
Millimeter	1 millimeter
Pixel	1 device pixel
Point	1/72 inch
World	world unit

The next several examples demonstrate some commonly used constructors. All the constructor examples will be based on the same simple form. It displays a multiline text string in the Text property of a RichTextBox control. (RichTextBox controls are covered in detail in Chapter 12.) Since the Font property of a control is an ambient property, the RichTextBox will inherit its Font property from the form. In the form constructor, the Font constructor will set the current font for the form.

The rich text box control in these examples displays two lines of static text followed by several lines displaying current font properties.

The following line of text is traditionally used by typographers to sample fonts because it uses every letter of the alphabet concisely: "The quick brown fox jumps over the lazy dog."

Constructor based on existing font and FontStyles. Example 9-3 (in C#) and Example 9-4 (in VB.NET) use the font constructor based on an existing Font object. The highlighted lines of code show the usage of the font constructor. Since this form of the constructor needs to base itself on an existing Font object, the first line of highlighted code creates that object from the default font of the form.

Example 9-3. Font constructor based on existing font in C# (FontConstructor1.cs)

```
using System;
using System.Drawing;
using System.Windows.Forms;

namespace ProgrammingWinApps
{
    public class FontConstructor1 : Form
    {
        public FontConstructor1( )
        {
            Text = "Font Constructor";
            Size = new Size(350,200);

            //  Font constructor stuff
            Font fnt = Font;
            fnt = new Font(fnt, FontStyle.Bold | FontStyle.Italic);
            Font = fnt;
            //  End of font constructor stuff

            RichTextBox rtxt = new RichTextBox( );
            rtxt.Text = "The quick brown fox jumps over the lazy dog.\n" +
                    "This is a second line of text.";
            rtxt.Text += "\nFont Name:\t" + Font.Name;
            rtxt.Text += "\nFont Family:\t" + Font.FontFamily;
            rtxt.Text += "\nFont Styles:\t" + Font.Style;
            rtxt.Text += "\nFont Size:\t" + Font.Size;
            rtxt.Text += "\nFont Height:\t" + Font.Height;
            rtxt.Text += "\nFont Units:\t" + Font.Unit;
            rtxt.Multiline = true;
            rtxt.Dock = DockStyle.Fill;
            rtxt.Parent = this;
        }

        static void Main( )
        {
            Application.Run(new FontConstructor1( ));
        }

    }
}
```

Example 9-4. Font constructor based on existing font in VB.NET (FontConstructor1.vb)

```
Option Strict On
imports System
imports System.Drawing
imports System.Windows.Forms

namespace ProgrammingWinApps
    public class FontConstructor1 : inherits Form

        public sub New( )
```

Example 9-4. Font constructor based on existing font in VB.NET (FontConstructor1.vb) (continued)

```
Text = "Font Constructor"
Size = new Size(350,200)

'  Font constructor stuff
dim fnt as Font = Font
fnt = new Font(fnt, FontStyle.Bold or FontStyle.Italic)
Font = fnt
'  End of font constructor stuff

dim rtxt as new RichTextBox( )
rtxt.Text = "The quick brown fox jumps over the lazy dog." + vbCrLf + _
        "This is a second line of text."
rtxt.Text += vbCrLf + "Font Name:" + vbTab + Font.Name
rtxt.Text += vbCrLf + "Font Family:" + vbTab + _
                Font.FontFamily.ToString( )
rtxt.Text += vbCrLf + "Font Styles:" + vbTab + Font.Style.ToString
rtxt.Text += vbCrLf + "Font Size:" + vbTab + Font.Size.ToString( )
rtxt.Text += vbCrLf + "Font Height:" + vbTab + Font.Height.ToString( )
rtxt.Text += vbCrLf + "Font Units:" + vbTab + Font.Unit.ToString( )
rtxt.Multiline = true
rtxt.Dock = DockStyle.Fill
rtxt.Parent = me
end sub

public shared sub Main( )
    Application.Run(new FontConstructor1( ))
end sub

    end class
end namespace
```

The middle highlighted line of code is the actual Font constructor. It takes two arguments: an existing Font object and one or more FontStyles. The FontStyles are combined in a bitwise manner using the logical OR operator. The third line of highlighted code then assigns the new Font object back to the Form's current font.

When this example is compiled and run, it results in the form shown in Figure 9-3.

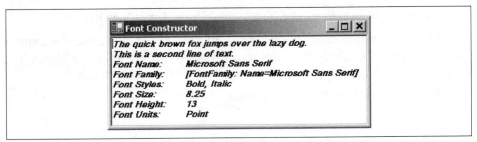

Figure 9-3. Font constructor based on existing font.

Constructor based on FontFamily and size. The next several code snippets demonstrate two different constructors based on the font family name and a font size. The first version takes a string containing the name of a font family as an argument, along with the size of the font in points.

The font family name must correspond exactly to one of the installed font families on your system. The easiest way to see what font families are on a machine is to open a font dialog from WordPad and look through the font drop-down list. (An example presented shortly will show how to find all the font families installed on a system programmatically.)

If the font family is not installed on the system or the name is misspelled, no exception will be thrown, but the font will revert to the default Windows font, Microsoft Sans Serif. The font name string is not case sensitive. Even in C# "times new roman" is the same as "Times New Roman."

To use this constructor, replace the highlighted lines of C# code in Example 9-3, reproduced here:

```
Font fnt = Font;
fnt = new Font(fnt, FontStyle.Bold | FontStyle.Italic);
Font = fnt;
```

with the following lines of code:

```
Font fnt = new Font("Times New Roman", 10);
fnt = new Font(fnt, FontStyle.Bold | FontStyle.Italic);
Font = fnt;
```

or the highlighted VB.NET lines in Example 9-4, reproduced here:

```
dim fnt as Font = Font
fnt = new Font(fnt, FontStyle.Bold or FontStyle.Italic)
Font = fnt
```

with these lines:

```
dim fnt as new Font("Times New Roman", 10)
fnt = new Font(fnt, FontStyle.Bold or FontStyle.Italic)
Font = fnt
```

This will cause the form font to be 10-point Bold Italic Times New Roman.

Another version of the constructor takes a FontFamily object rather than the name of the font family in a string. There are several ways to get a FontFamily object. The simplest FontFamily constructor takes a string with the name of the family:

```
FontFamily ffTNR = new FontFamily("Times New Roman");
```

```
dim ffTNR as new FontFamily("Times New Roman")
```

You can create generic font families by using members of the GenericFontFamilies enumeration, listed in Table 9-5, as the argument to the FontFamily constructor.

Table 9-5. GenericFontFamilies enumeration

Value	Description
Monospace	Generic fixed-pitch FontFamily object
SansSerif	Generic sans serif FontFamily object
Serif	Generic serif FontFamily object

The programs listed in Examples 9-5 and 9-6 each use the same form as the previous example, but here the rich text box is populated with a list of all the font families installed on the system that have a regular font.

Example 9-5. Font families in C# (FontFamiles.cs)

```
using System;
using System.Drawing;
using System.Windows.Forms;

namespace ProgrammingWinApps
{
    public class FontFamilies : Form
    {
        public FontFamilies()
        {
            Text = "Font Families";
            Size = new Size(350,200);

            RichTextBox rtxt = new RichTextBox();
            rtxt.Multiline = true;
            rtxt.Dock = DockStyle.Fill;
            rtxt.Parent = this;

            FontFamily[] ffArray = FontFamily.Families;
            foreach( FontFamily ff in ffArray )
            {
                if (ff.IsStyleAvailable(FontStyle.Regular))
                {
                    rtxt.Text += ff.Name + "\n";
                }
            }
        }

        static void Main()
        {
            Application.Run(new FontFamilies());
        }
    }
}
```

Example 9-6. Font families in VB.NET (FontFamiles.vb)

```
Option Strict On
imports System
imports System.Drawing
```

Example 9-6. Font families in VB.NET (FontFamiles.vb) (continued)

```vb
imports System.Windows.Forms

namespace ProgrammingWinApps
    public class FontFamilies : inherits Form

        public sub New( )
            Text = "Font Families"
            Size = new Size(350,200)

            dim rtxt as new RichTextBox( )
            rtxt.Multiline = true
            rtxt.Dock = DockStyle.Fill
            rtxt.Parent = me

            dim  ffArray as FontFamily( ) = FontFamily.Families
            dim ff as FontFamily

            for each ff in ffArray
               if ff.IsStyleAvailable(FontStyle.Regular) then
                  rtxt.Text += ff.Name + vbCrLf
               end if
            next
        end sub

        public shared sub Main( )
            Application.Run(new FontFamilies( ))
        end sub

    end class
end namespace
```

In Examples 9-5 and 9-6, after the RichTextBox object is instantiated, an array of FontFamily objects is created using the static property Families of the FontFamily class.

The array is iterated using a foreach loop (For Each in VB.NET), adding each Font-Family name to the Text property of the rich text box.

Here is the tricky part: you must verify that a FontFamily has a *regular* member—i.e., a member that is neither bold nor italic—before trying to create it. The style verification is performed using the IsStyleAvailable method of the FontFamily class. This is necessary because the default font style is FontStyle.Regular. Therefore, the Font constructor using the FontFamily object will try to create a regular font. If a regular member of the font family does not exist, an exception is thrown.

On my system, Monotype Corsiva did not have a regular style. However, the font dialog box in Microsoft Word lists the two available styles for that font as Regular and Bold Italic. In actuality, the two styles available for that font are Italic and Bold Italic.

Assuming a regular style exists for the family, a new 10-point Font object is instantiated in that font family and it's Name property is added to the rich text box's Text property.

The result is shown in Figure 9-4.

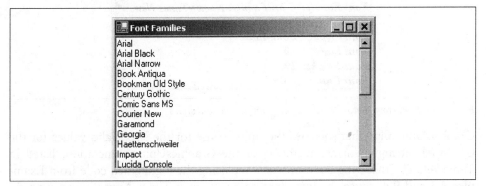

Figure 9-4. Font families

Constructor based on FontFamily, size, and FontStyles. Two Font constructors take three arguments: a font family, the size in points, and a bitwise combination of FontStyles. The font family can be either a FontFamily object or a string representing a font family.

Using the programs listed in Examples 9-3 and 9-4 as test beds, replace the highlighted code with this code snippet:

```
FontFamily ff = new FontFamily("Times New Roman");
Font fnt = new Font(ff, 12, FontStyle.Bold | FontStyle.Italic);
Font = fnt;
```

```
dim ff as new FontFamily("Times New Roman")
dim fnt as new Font(ff, 12, FontStyle.Bold or FontStyle.Italic)
Font = fnt
```

These code snippets declare a FontFamily object representing Times New Roman. The Font constructor is then invoked, passing that FontFamily object, the size (12 points), and a combination of Bold and Italic FontStyles. The result is shown in Figure 9-5.

An alternative form of the font constructor takes a string representing the font family rather than a FontFamily object. Thus, the following C# code snippet would have the same results (VB.NET is analogous):

```
Font fnt = new Font("Times New Roman", 12, FontStyle.Bold | FontStyle.Italic);
Font = fnt;
```

Constructor based on FontFamily, size, and GraphicsUnit. Another pair of Font constructors takes three arguments: a font family (either an object or a string), a size, and a

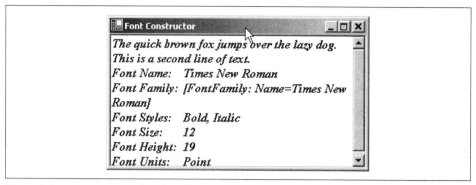

Figure 9-5. Font constructor based on font family, size, and styles

GraphicsUnit value that specifies the units to use for the size. Valid values for the GraphicsUnit argument are members of the GraphicsUnit enumeration, listed in Table 9-4. The following code snippets, replacing the highlighted code from Examples 9-3 and 9-4, cause the form font to be 1/4-inch Times New Roman approximately equivalent to 18 point:

```
FontFamily ff = new FontFamily("Times New Roman");
Font fnt = new Font(ff, .25f, GraphicsUnit.Inch);
Font = fnt;
```

```
dim ff as new FontFamily("Times New Roman")
dim fnt as new Font(ff, .25f, GraphicsUnit.Inch)
Font = fnt
```

The resulting form, resized to fit all the text, is shown in Figure 9-6.

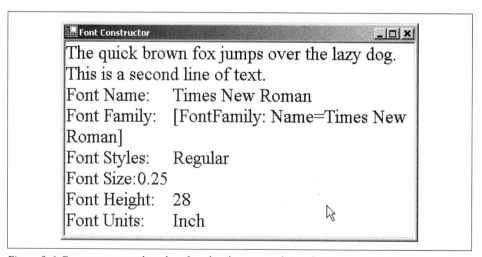

Figure 9-6. Font constructor based on font family, size, and GraphicUnit

Constructor based on FontFamily, size, FontStyles, and GraphicsUnit. The final pair of Font constructors examined in detail is similar to the previous two pairs, except they take both a FontStyles argument and a GraphicsUnit argument to specify the units for the size.

The following code snippets would create an Arial Bold Italic font, 1/2-inch in size:

```C#
FontFamily ff = new FontFamily("Arial");
Font fnt = new Font(ff, .5f, FontStyle.Bold | FontStyle.Italic,
                    GraphicsUnit.Inch);
Font = fnt;
```

```VB
dim ff as new FontFamily("Arial")
dim fnt as new Font(ff, .5f, FontStyle.Bold or FontStyle.Italic, _
                    GraphicsUnit.Inch)
Font = fnt
```

Line spacing

The vertical space between lines of text is called *leading* (in the old days of physical type, you would put extra space between lines by adding a plain piece of lead). If two lines of 12-point text are spaced 12 points apart, then there is no leading. Text set this way will appear dense and difficult to read. This is especially true if there are a lot of upper case letters and/or diacritical marks.

Typographers note the size of the text and the leading together, so the earlier example would be written as 12/12. If two points of space are added between the lines, then it would become 12/14. Typographers, graphic artists, and page layout editors put a great deal of effort into adjusting the vertical spacing of lines of text to suit the material being displayed.

The .NET Framework provides two different techniques for determining the vertical line spacing of a font. There are no Font properties or methods provided to set the line spacing explicitly. In multiline text box controls, the line spacing is automatically set by the font and the control. You *can* control the line spacing if you draw the text strings directly to a graphics object (discussed later in Chapter 10).

Both the Height property and the GetHeight method return the recommended line spacing, in current units, of the Font object. The value returned by the Height property is applicable only when using the default page transform on the video display. The GetHeight method, on the other hand, has one overloaded form (out of three) that takes a Graphics object as an argument. By knowing the Graphics object, it also knows the current page transform and the device resolution, so it is able to give the correct line spacing for all situations, both on the video display and the printer.

See Chapter 10 for a discussion of page transforms and Graphics objects.

Drawing Strings

All the examples so far in this chapter have displayed text by using a control's Text property. You can also draw strings directly onto the client area of a form or other control by using a Graphics object and the Paint event.

Chapter 10 will cover graphics and drawing more thoroughly. This section only introduces enough about the Graphics object in order to explain how to draw and use strings.

A Graphics object provides a surface to draw on. There are several ways to obtain a Graphics object. The technique used in this section adds an event handler to the Paint event delegate and then extracts the Graphics object from the PaintEventArgs event argument that is passed to the handler when the event is raised. This will be clarified shortly with an example.

DrawString( )

The DrawString method of the Graphics class draws text strings. It has six over-loaded forms, the arguments of which are listed in Table 9-6.

Table 9-6. DrawString() arguments

Arguments	Description
string, Font, Brush, float (Single in VB.NET), float/Single	Draw the specified string, using the specified Font and Brush objects, located such that the upper-left corner of the text is located at the X and Y coordinates indicated by the two numbers, respectively.
string, Font, Brush, PointF	Draw the specified string, using the specified Font and Brush objects, located such that the upper-left corner of the text is located at the specified PointF coordinates.
string, Font, Brush, RectangleF	Draw the specified string, using the specified Font and Brush objects, in the specified RectangleF object.
string, Font, Brush, float/Single, float/Single, StringFormat	Draw the specified string, using the specified Font and Brush objects, at a location indicated by X and Y coordinates of the upper-left corner of the text, using the specified StringFormat object (described later in this chapter in the section "Brush and brushes").
string, Font, Brush, PointF, StringFormat	Draw the specified string, using the specified Font and Brush objects at the specified PointF coordinates, using the specified StringFormat object (described later in this chapter in the section "Brush and brushes").
string, Font, Brush, RectangleF, StringFormat	Draw the specified string, using the specified Font and Brush objects in the specified RectangleF object, using the specified StringFormat object (described later in this chapter in the section "Brush and brushes").

The programs listed in Examples 9-7 and 9-8 demonstrate how to use the Draw-String method to draw on the client area of the form the name of each font family that has a regular style installed on the system. Examples 9-7 and 9-8 are similar to Examples 9-5 and 9-6, except that the text is drawn directly on the form; there is no rich text box control. Creating the form is the only work done in the constructor of the form. All the heavy lifting occurs in the overridden OnPaint event handler method.

Example 9-7. Drawing FontFamilies in C# (DrawFontFamilies.cs)

```csharp
using System;
using System.Drawing;
using System.Windows.Forms;

namespace ProgrammingWinApps
{
    public class DrawFontFamilies : Form
    {
        public DrawFontFamilies()
        {
            Text = "Drawn Font Families";
            Size = new Size(350,200);
        }

        protected override void OnPaint(PaintEventArgs e)
        {
            base.OnPaint(e);
            float x= 10;
            float y= 10;
            Font fnt;
            Graphics g = e.Graphics;

            FontFamily[ ] ffArray = FontFamily.Families;
            foreach( FontFamily ff in ffArray )
            {
                if (ff.IsStyleAvailable(FontStyle.Regular))
                {
                    fnt = new Font(ff, 10);
                    g.DrawString(ff.Name, fnt, Brushes.Black, x, y);
                    y += fnt.GetHeight( );
                }
            }
        }

        static void Main( )
        {
            Application.Run(new DrawFontFamilies( ));
        }
    }
}
```

Example 9-8. Drawing FontFamilies in VB.NET (DrawFontFamilies.vb)

```
Option Strict On
imports System
imports System.Drawing
imports System.Windows.Forms

namespace ProgrammingWinApps
   public class DrawFontFamilies : inherits Form

      public sub New( )
         Text = " Drawn Font Families"
         Size = new Size(350,200)
      end sub

      protected overrides sub OnPaint(ByVal e as PaintEventArgs)
         myBase.OnPaint(e)
         dim x as single = 10
         dim y as single = 10
         dim fnt as Font
         dim g as Graphics = e.Graphics

         dim ffArray as FontFamily( ) = FontFamily.Families
         dim ff as FontFamily
         for each ff in ffArray
            if ff.IsStyleAvailable(FontStyle.Regular) then
               fnt = new Font(ff, 10)
               g.DrawString(ff.Name, fnt, Brushes.Black, x, y)
               y += fnt.GetHeight( )
            end if
         next
      end sub

      public shared sub Main( )
         Application.Run(new DrawFontFamilies( ))
      end sub

   end class
end namespace
```

The overridden OnPaintevent handler method has an event argument of type Paint-
EventArgs, which has two read-only properties: ClipRectangle and Graphics. Clip-
Rectangle defines a rectangle in which to paint. The Graphics property returns a
Graphics object, which in turn exposes the DrawString method.

Within OnPaint, several objects are initialized, including:

- Two numbers (float in C#, Single in VB.NET), which will be used to locate the
  text strings on the drawing surface

- A Font object

- A Graphics object

An array of font families is instantiated and iterated as shown in Examples 9-5 and 9-6, except that the text string buildup is replaced with a call to DrawString and the vertical coordinate is incremented by the preferred line spacing returned from the GetHeight() method.

When the program is compiled and run, you will get something similar to Figure 9-7, after the form is resized to eliminate the vertical scrollbar.

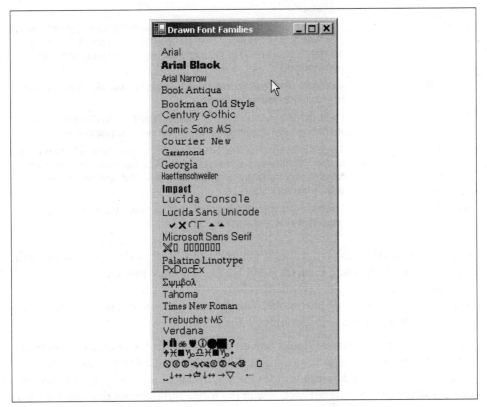

Figure 9-7. Drawn font families

The call to DrawString takes five arguments:

```csharp
g.DrawString(ff.Name, fnt, Brushes.Black, x, y);
```

The first argument is the text string to draw, in this case the name of the FontFamily. The second argument is a Font object to use for the text string. On each iteration through the loop, the Font object is reset to the next available font family at 10 points. The next argument is a Brush object, which will be covered shortly. The final two arguments are the horizontal and vertical coordinates, in current units, of the top-left corner of the text string.

Brush and brushes

Brush is an abstract (MustInherit in VB.NET) class in the System.Drawing namespace. A Brush object fills the interior spaces of graphical shapes. Five different classes are derived from Brush, as listed in Table 9-7.

Table 9-7. Brush-derived classes

Class	Description
HatchBrush	A brush that fills a graphical shape with a hatch style from the HatchStyle enumeration, such as BackwardDiagonal, DarkVertical, Divot, and Percent60. The ForegroundColor property gets the color of the lines and the BackgroundColor property gets the color of the space behind the lines.
LinearGradientBrush	A brush with a linear gradient. Properties such as Blend, GammaCorrection, and Transform let you control the resulting appearance.
PathGradientBrush	A brush that fills a graphical shape with a gradient. Properties such as Blend, CenterColor, and Transform allow programmatic interaction with the resulting appearance.
SolidBrush	A brush that fills a graphical shape with a color. Valid colors are either members of the Color structure, which has members such as Color.Brown, Color.Crimson, and Color.PaleGolden-rod, or a custom color you create. contains the complete list of standard colors. Chapter 10 describes the Color structure.
TextureBrush	A brush that fills a graphical shape with a texture. The texture can come from an Image object, either a bitmap or a metafile.

For easy access to the colored brushes, you can use a Brushes class (note the plural), which contains only static (Shared in VB.NET), read-only properties of type Brush corresponding to each of the standard colors, such as Brushes.Black, Brushes.Dark-Goldenrod, and Brushes.WhiteSmoke. This Brushes class provides the Brush object used in the DrawString call in Examples 9-7 and 9-8.

The form shown in Figure 9-7 looks fine on my system, and may look fine on yours, but what happens if the user has changed the Windows color scheme so that the form has a dark or black background? One way to avoid this problem is to set your SolidBrush to use the current ForeColor of the form, and then use that SolidBrush as the Brush object in the call to DrawString, as in:

C#

```
Brush b = new SolidBrush(ForeColor);
g.DrawString(ff.Name, fnt, b, (int)x, (int)y);
```

VB

```
dim b as Brush = new SolidBrush(ForeColor)
g.DrawString(ff.Name, fnt, b, CInt(x), CInt(y))
```

Formatting and alignment

Several overloaded versions of the DrawString method take an object of type String-Format as one of the arguments. The StringFormat class has properties that provide horizontal and vertical text alignment, automatic insertion of ellipsis characters if the string exceeds its allotted space, and other formatting features. Commonly used StringFormat properties are listed in Table 9-8.

Table 9-8. StringFormat properties

Property	Type	Description
Alignment	StringAlignment	Read/write. Provides horizontal alignment of text strings relative to the location point of the string or the containing rectangle. Valid values are members of the StringAlignment enumeration, listed in Table 9-9.
FormatFlags	StringFormatFlags	Read/write. Valid values are a bitwise combination of members of the StringFormatFlags enumeration, listed in Table 9-10.
HotkeyPrefix	HotkeyPrefix	Read/write. Controls underline mode of characters following an ampersand (&) character. Valid values are members of HotkeyPrefix enumeration: if Hide, the character following the ampersand is not underlined and the ampersand is not displayed; if Show, the character after the ampersand is underlined; if None, the ampersand is displayed and nothing is underlined. If set to HotkeyPrefix.Show, you must still provide an event handler to implement the keyboard shortcut.
LineAlignment	StringAlignment	Read/write. Provides vertical alignment of text strings relative to the location point of the string or the containing rectangle. Valid values are members of the StringAlignment enumeration, listed in Table 9-9.
Trimming	StringTrimming	Read/write. Specifies how to trim characters if the text exceeds the bounds of the layout rectangle. Valid values are members of the String-Trimming enumeration, listed in Table 9-11.

Table 9-9. StringAlignment enumeration

Value	Description
Center	Text is center-aligned. For both horizontal alignment (Alignment property) and vertical alignment (LineAlignment property), the center of the string will be at the location point or in the center of the layout rectangle.
Near	For horizontal alignment of left-to-right text, this value will be left-aligned relative to the location point or rectangle. For right-to-left text, it will be right-aligned. For vertical alignment, it will be bottom-aligned relative to the location point or rectangle.
Far	For horizontal alignment of left-to-right text, it will be right-aligned relative to the location point or rectangle. For right-to-left text, it will be left-aligned. For vertical alignment, the value will be top-aligned relative to the location point or rectangle.

Table 9-10. StringFormatFlags enumeration

Value	Description
DirectionRightToLeft	Text is right to left.
DirectionVertical	Text is vertical.
DisplayFormatControl	Displays control characters in the output.
FitBlackBox	None of the characters overhang the bounding rectangle.
LineLimit	Only entire lines are visible.

Table 9-10. StringFormatFlags enumeration (continued)

Value	Description
MeasureTrailing-Spaces	Forces MeasureString method to include trailing spaces.
NoClip	Characters and unwrapped text may exceed the bounding rectangle.
NoFontFallback	Disables display of alternate font if the requested font is not available.
NoWrap	Disables line wrapping.

Table 9-11. StringTrimming enumeration

Value	Description
Character	Text is trimmed to the nearest character.
EllipsisCharacter	Text is trimmed to the nearest character and an ellipsis is inserted the end of the trimmed line.
EllipsisPath	The center of the trimmed line is removed and replace by an ellipsis. If the text includes a path, as much of the last slash-delimited segment is retained as possible.
EllipsisWord	Text is trimmed to the nearest word and an ellipsis is inserted the end of the trimmed line.
None	No trimming occurs.
Word	Text is trimmed to nearest word.

The programs listed in Examples 9-9 and 9-10 demonstrate the use of the Alignment StringFormat property. In these code listings, the Alignment value of the StringFormat property is set to Center. The result can be seen in the middle image in Figure 9-8. If the value had been set to Near, the text strings would have been left justified against the location point, as seen in the left-most image in Figure 9-8, and if the value had been set to Far, the text strings would have been right justified against the location point, as seen in the right-most image in Figure 9-8.

 Near and far are used rather than right and left to let you use languages that are not written from right to left (e.g., Hebrew or Chinese). They are also used for vertical alignment.

Example 9-9. DrawString method with Alignment in C# (DrawFontFamiliesFormatted.cs)

```csharp
using System;
using System.Drawing;
using System.Windows.Forms;

namespace ProgrammingWinApps
{
    public class DrawFontFamiliesFormatted : Form
    {
        public DrawFontFamiliesFormatted()
        {
            Text = "Drawn Font Families Formatted";
            Size = new Size(350,200);
```

Example 9-9. DrawString method with Alignment in C#
(DrawFontFamiliesFormatted.cs) (continued)

```csharp
        ResizeRedraw = true;
    }

    protected override void OnPaint(PaintEventArgs e)
    {
        base.OnPaint(e);
        float y= 10;
        Font fnt;
        Graphics g = e.Graphics;
        StringFormat fmt = new StringFormat();
        fmt.Alignment = StringAlignment.Center;

        FontFamily[ ] ffArray = FontFamily.Families;
        foreach( FontFamily ff in ffArray )
        {
            if (ff.IsStyleAvailable(FontStyle.Regular))
            {
                fnt = new Font(ff, 10);
                Brush b = new SolidBrush(ForeColor);
                g.DrawString(ff.Name, fnt, b, ClientSize.Width / 2, (int)y, fmt);
                y += fnt.GetHeight( );
            }
        }
    }

    static void Main( )
    {
        Application.Run(new DrawFontFamiliesFormatted( ));
    }
  }
}
```

Example 9-10. DrawString method with Alignment in VB.NET
(DrawFontFamiliesFormatted.vb)

```vbnet
Option Strict On
imports System
imports System.Drawing
imports System.Windows.Forms

namespace ProgrammingWinApps
   public class DrawFontFamiliesFormatted : inherits Form

      public sub New( )
         Text = "Drawn Font Families Formatted"
         Size = new Size(350,200)
         ResizeRedraw = true
      end sub

      protected overrides sub OnPaint(ByVal e as PaintEventArgs)
         myBase.OnPaint(e)
         dim y as single = 10
```

Example 9-10. DrawString method with Alignment in VB.NET (DrawFontFamiliesFormatted.vb) (continued)

```
        dim fnt as Font
        dim g as Graphics = e.Graphics
        dim fmt as new StringFormat( )
        fmt.Alignment = StringAlignment.Center

        dim ffArray as FontFamily( ) = FontFamily.Families
        dim ff as FontFamily
        for each ff in ffArray
           if ff.IsStyleAvailable(FontStyle.Regular) then
              fnt = new Font(ff, 10)
              dim b as Brush = new SolidBrush(ForeColor)
              g.DrawString(ff.Name,fnt,b,CInt(ClientSize.Width / 2),CInt(y),fmt)
              y += fnt.GetHeight( )
           end if
        next
     end sub

     public shared sub Main( )
        Application.Run(new DrawFontFamiliesFormatted( ))
     end sub

   end class
end namespace
```

Figure 9-8. Alignment StringFormat property: Near, Center, and Far (left to right)

In Examples 9-9 and 9-10, the Brush object is instantiated as a SolidBrush by using the ForeColor property, so it will be visible irrespective of the color scheme chosen by the user.

In the call to the DrawString method, the horizontal location of the string is set to one half of the width of the client area of the form; this allows you to center the strings in the center of the form.

Inside the constructor you set the ResizeRedraw property to true. Doing so forces the form to invalidate and redraw the client area every time the form is resized by the user, eliminating artifacts left behind when the form is resized.

In Examples 9-11 and 9-12, a simple form is created with a button and a text string drawn on the client area. The button is labeled "Do It!" The Alt-D keyboard short-cut is implemented by adding an ampersand to the Text property of the button. The resulting form is shown in Figure 9-9.

Example 9-11. DrawString with HotkeyPrefix StringFormat property in C#
(DrawStringHotkey.cs)

```csharp
using System;
using System.Drawing;
using System.Windows.Forms;
using System.Drawing.Text;        //  necessary for HotkeyPrefix

namespace ProgrammingWinApps
{
    public class DrawStringHotkey : Form
    {
        public DrawStringHotkey( )
        {
            Text = "DrawString Hotkey";
            Size = new Size(350,200);
            ResizeRedraw = true;

            Button btn = new Button( );
            btn.Parent = this;
            btn.Text = "&Do It!";
            btn.Location = new Point((ClientSize.Width / 2) - (btn.Width / 2),
                                ClientSize.Height / 2);
            btn.Click += new EventHandler(btn_Click);
        }

        protected override void OnPaint(PaintEventArgs e)
        {
            base.OnPaint(e);
            Graphics g = e.Graphics;
            StringFormat fmt = new StringFormat( );
            fmt.Alignment = StringAlignment.Center;
            fmt.HotkeyPrefix = HotkeyPrefix.Show;

            Brush b = new SolidBrush(ForeColor);
            g.DrawString("&Do It!", Font, b, ClientSize.Width / 2, 50, fmt);
        }

        private void btn_Click(object sender, EventArgs e)
        {
            MessageBox.Show("Now you've done it.");
        }

        static void Main( )
        {
            Application.Run(new DrawStringHotkey( ));
        }
    }
}
```

Example 9-12. DrawString with HotkeyPrefix StringFormat property in VB.NET
(DrawStringHotkey.vb)

```vbnet
Option Strict On
imports System
```

Example 9-12. DrawString with HotkeyPrefix StringFormat property in VB.NET (DrawStringHotkey.vb) (continued)

```
imports System.Drawing
imports System.Windows.Forms
imports System.Drawing.Text            '  necessary for HotkeyPrefix

namespace ProgrammingWinApps
   public class DrawStringHotkey : inherits Form

      public sub New()
         Text = "Drawn Font Families Formatted"
         Size = new Size(350,200)
         ResizeRedraw = true

         dim btn as new Button()
         btn.Parent = me
         btn.Text = "&Do It!"
         btn.Location = new Point(CInt((ClientSize.Width / 2)) - _
                    CInt((btn.Width / 2)), _
                  CInt(ClientSize.Height / 2))
         AddHandler btn.Click, AddressOf btn_Click
      end sub

      protected overrides sub OnPaint(ByVal e as PaintEventArgs)
         myBase.OnPaint(e)
         dim g as Graphics = e.Graphics
         dim fmt as new StringFormat()
         fmt.Alignment = StringAlignment.Center
         fmt.HotkeyPrefix = HotkeyPrefix.Show

         dim b as Brush = new SolidBrush(ForeColor)
         g.DrawString("&Do It!", Font, b, Cint(ClientSize.Width / 2), 50, fmt)
      end sub

      private sub btn_Click(ByVal sender as object, _
                        ByVal e as EventArgs)
         MessageBox.Show("Now you've done it.")
      end sub

      public shared sub Main()
         Application.Run(new DrawStringHotkey())
      end sub

   end class
end namespace
```

First, note that you must add a reference to the System.Drawing.Text namespace for the HotkeyPrefix to work:

```
using System.Drawing.Text;
```

```
imports System.Drawing.Text
```

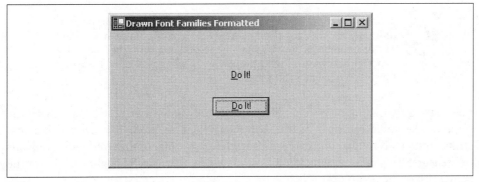

Figure 9-9. HotkeyPrefix StringFormat property

The button control is instantiated in the constructor and its Location property is set so that it is centered in the form. The Text property has an ampersand before the D; this causes the D to be underlined and automatically implements the keyboard shortcut. An event handler is added for the Click event. The event handler method in this example simply puts up a message box.

In the PaintHandler method, two properties are set for the StringFormat object: the Alignment property is set to Center and the HotkeyPrefix property is set to Show. Then in the string argument of DrawString, an ampersand is inserted just before the D, causing that character to be underlined.

Underlining the character via the DrawString method does not implement any keyboard shortcuts or key event handling. That must be done using other techniques. This example uses the Button keyboard shortcut. You could also use key event handling described in Chapter 4 or the menu keyboard shortcuts described in Chapter 18.

Measuring Strings

In Chapter 7, several examples were presented that sized a control based on the estimated size of its Text property. This estimate was arrived at by multiplying the number of characters in the string by the Font.Height property and by an arbitrary "fudge factor." The MeasureString method of the Graphics class provides a much more elegant and precise (although it will not be perfectly precise unless using anti-aliased text) way of measuring the length and height of a text string, taking into account the actual Font object used to draw the string.

The MeasureString method has several overloaded forms. All the forms return a SizeF structure that represents the size of the string in pixels. The basic form takes two arguments: the string to measure and the Font object with which to draw the string. All the other forms take those same two arguments, plus additional arguments that force line wrapping, take formatting into account, and so on.

A SizeF structure represents the size of a rectangular region with an ordered pair of floating-point numbers (float in C#, Single in VB.NET). The first number is the width and the second number is the height. The structure has two read/write properties: Height and Width. This structure is described more fully in Chapter 10.

For a string consisting of a single line of text, the value of SizeF.Height will be the same as the value returned by the Font.GetHeight method. However, if the text string contains NewLine or LineFeed characters, or if one of the overloaded versions of MeasureString is used, which forces a line wrap, then SizeF.Height will reflect the actual size of the text block.

Table 9-12 lists the argument lists for each overloaded form.

Table 9-12. MeasureString() arguments

Arguments	Description
string, Font	Returns SizeF structure, in pixels, of the specified string drawn with the specified Font object.
string, Font, integer	Returns SizeF structure, in pixels, of the specified string drawn with the specified Font object. Integer is the maximum width of the SizeF structure, in pixels; if the string will not fit within this width, it will wrap and the height of the returned SizeF structure will reflect the size with the actual number of lines.
string, Font, SizeF	Returns SizeF structure, in pixels, of the specified string drawn with the specified Font object. SizeF structure is the maximum size, in pixels, of the string's layout area.
string, Font, integer, StringFormat	Returns SizeF structure, in pixels, of the specified string drawn with the specified Font object, using specified StringFormat properties. Integer is the maximum width of the SizeF structure, in pixels; if the string will not fit within this width, it will wrap and the height of the returned SizeF structure will reflect the size with the actual number of lines.
string, Font, PointF, StringFormat	Returns SizeF structure, in pixels, of the specified string drawn with the specified Font object, with its upper-left corner located at the point described by the PointF structure, using the specified StringFormat properties.
string, Font, SizeF, StringFormat	Returns SizeF structure, in pixels, of the specified string drawn with the specified Font object, using the specified StringFormat properties. SizeF structure is the maximum size, in pixels, of the string's layout area.
string, Font, SizeF, StringFormat, integer, integer	Returns SizeF structure, in pixels, of the specified string drawn with the specified Font object, using the specified StringFormat properties. SizeF structure is the maximum size, in pixels, of the string's layout area. The first integer argument is the number of characters in the string, and the second integer argument is the number of lines of text.

The examples listed in Examples 9-13 and 9-14, based on the previous examples, demonstrate the use of the MeasureString method. In these examples, a button displays the results of measuring a sample string drawn on the form. MeasureString is also used in the Analog Clock project shown in Chapter 10.

Example 9-13. MeasureString method in C# (StringMeasure.cs)

```csharp
using System;
using System.Drawing;
using System.Windows.Forms;

namespace ProgrammingWinApps
{
   public class StringMeasure : Form
   {
      SizeF sz = new SizeF();

      public StringMeasure()
      {
         Text = "Measure String";
         Size = new Size(350,200);

         Button btn = new Button();
         btn.Parent = this;
         btn.Text = "&Measure";
         btn.Location = new Point((ClientSize.Width / 2) - (btn.Width / 2),
                          ClientSize.Height / 2);
         btn.Click += new EventHandler(btn_Click);
      }

      protected override void OnPaint(PaintEventArgs e)
      {
         base.OnPaint(e);
         string str = "The quick brown fox jumped...";
         PointF pt = new PointF(ClientSize.Width / 2, 50);
         Graphics g = e.Graphics;
         StringFormat fmt = new StringFormat();
         fmt.Alignment = StringAlignment.Center;

         Brush b = new SolidBrush(ForeColor);
         g.DrawString(str, Font, b, pt, fmt);
         sz = g.MeasureString(str,Font, pt, fmt);
      }

      private void btn_Click(object sender, EventArgs e)
      {
         MessageBox.Show("The string size is " + sz.ToString());
      }

      static void Main()
      {
         Application.Run(new StringMeasure());
      }
   }
}
```

Example 9-14. MeasureString method in VB.NET (StringMeasure.cs)

```
Option Strict On
imports System
imports System.Drawing
imports System.Windows.Forms

namespace ProgrammingWinApps
    public class StringMeasure : inherits Form

        dim sz as new SizeF( )

        public sub New( )
            Text = "Drawn Font Families Formatted"
            Size = new Size(350,200)

            dim btn as new Button( )
            btn.Parent = me
            btn.Text = "&Measure"
            btn.Location = new Point(CInt((ClientSize.Width / 2)) - _
                           CInt((btn.Width / 2)), _
                        CInt(ClientSize.Height / 2))
            AddHandler btn.Click, AddressOf btn_Click
        end sub

        protected overrides sub OnPaint(ByVal e as PaintEventArgs)
            myBase.OnPaint(e)
            dim str as String = "The quick brown fox jumped..."
            dim pt as new PointF(CInt(ClientSize.Width / 2), 50)
            dim g as Graphics = e.Graphics
            dim fmt as new StringFormat( )
            fmt.Alignment = StringAlignment.Center

            dim b as Brush = new SolidBrush(ForeColor)
            g.DrawString(str, Font, b, pt, fmt)
            sz = g.MeasureString(str,Font, pt, fmt)
        end sub

        private sub btn_Click(ByVal sender as object, _
                            ByVal e as EventArgs)
            MessageBox.Show("The string size is " + sz.ToString( ))
        end sub

        public shared sub Main( )
            Application.Run(new StringMeasure( ))
        end sub

    end class
end namespace
```

In the programs listed in Examples 9-13 and 9-14, a class member variable of type SizeF is declared. This variable will store the return value of the MeasureString method in the PaintHandler method, and then display the size in the btn_Click method.

In the PaintHandler method, two additional variables are declared: a string that draws and measures, and a PointF variable that holds the location of the text string on the graphics surface. The latter variable is necessary because the only variants of the MeasureString method that take a StringFormat argument also require either some sort of size indicator or a location parameter, hence the PointF. If your Draw-String method uses a StringFormat argument, it is wise to use the same StringFormat argument when measuring the string.

CHAPTER 10

Drawing and GDI+

The designers of .NET, and especially of Visual Studio .NET, clearly had in mind a model in which you could write sophisticated Windows Applications using only the controls available in the Toolbox. This approach is very successful, and many Windows programmers will never need to go beyond the Toolbox and forms model for building powerful user interfaces.

As discussed elsewhere in this book, the Toolbox includes controls for displaying data (labels, DataGrids, Calendars, listboxes, etc.) as well as for offering the user choices (radio buttons, checkboxes, listboxes, etc.) and for gathering data (text boxes, etc.) In addition, several controls and components manage date and time (Timer, etc.) or the form itself (splitter, etc.).

From time to time, however, you will want to display data in a way that is not possible with just the controls offered in the Toolbox. You might wish to draw on a control, or directly on the form itself, and for that you'll need the tools made available through GDI+ and the Graphics object.

To get an idea of what you can accomplish with these tools, this chapter first covers the basics with simple demonstration programs. It then focuses on a small but complete project, in which you will create an analog clock.

The Drawing Namespace

The System.Drawing namespace includes several classes and structures. The most important of them are summarized, briefly, in Table 10-1.

Table 10-1. Drawing namespace classes and structures

Class	Description
Bitmap	Encapsulates a GDI+ bitmap, i.e., pixel data representing an image.
Brush	Abstract base class. Used to fill the interiors of graphical shapes.
Brushes	Provides static brush definitions for all standard colors.

Table 10-1. Drawing namespace classes and structures (continued)

Class	Description
Color	Structure representing colors, e.g., Color.Green.
Font	Defines a format for text, including font face, and sizeEncapsulates a typeface, size, style, and effects.
FontFamily	Group of type faces with the same basic design.
Graphics	Encapsulates a GDI+ drawing surface.
Icon	Transparent bitmaps used for Windows icons.
Image	Abstract base class common to the Bitmap, Icon, and Metafile classes.
Pen	Defines an object used to draw lines and curves.
Pens	Provides static Pen definitions for all the standard colors.
Point	Structure used to represent an ordered pair of integers. Typically used to specify two-dimensional Cartesian coordinates.
PointF	Same as Point, but uses a floating-point number (float in C#, Single in VB.NET) rather than an integer.
Rectangle	Structure that represents the location and size of a rectangular region.
RectangleF	Same as Rectangle, but uses floating-point values (float in C#, single in VB.NET) rather than integers.
Size	Structure that represents the size of a rectangular region as an order pair (Point) representing width and height.
SizeF	Same as Size, but uses PointF rather than Point.
SystemBrushes	A utility class with 21 static, read-only properties that return objects of type Brush (each of a different color).
SystemPens	A utility class with 15 static, read-only properties that return objects of type Pen (each of a different color).

Arguably the most important class for graphics programming is (surprise!) the Graphics class. The other classes will be described as they are encountered, but before proceeding, let's examine the Graphics class in detail.

The Graphics Class

The Graphics class represents a GDI+ drawing surface. A Graphics object maintains the state of the drawing surface, including the scale and units, as well as the orientation of the drawing surface.

The Graphics class provides many properties. The most commonly used properties are listed in Table 10-2, most of which will be demonstrated later in this chapter.

Table 10-2. Graphics properties

Property	Type	Description
Clip	Region	Read/write. Specifies the area available for drawing.
DpiX / DpiY	Float / single	Read/write. The horizontal and vertical resolution (respectively) of the Graphics object in dots per inch.

Table 10-2. Graphics properties (continued)

Property	Type	Description
PageScale	Float / single	Read/write. The scaling between world units and page units for this Graphics object.
PageUnit	GraphicsUnit	Read/write. The unit of measure for page coordinates. Valid values are members of the GraphicsUnit enumeration, listed in Table 10-3.

The PageScale sets the scaling between the world units and the page units. To understand these concepts, you must first understand coordinates.

Coordinates

The French philosopher René Descartes (1596-1650) is best known today for stating that while he may doubt, he can not doubt that he exists. This is summarized in his oft-quoted statement *Cogito Ergo Sum* (I think, therefore I am).*

Among mathematicians, Descartes may be best known for inventing Analytical Geometry and what are now called Cartesian coordinates. In a classic Cartesian coordinate system, you envision an x axis and a y axis, as shown in Figure 10-1, with the origin (0,0) at the center. The values to the right of the origin and above the origin are positive, and the values to the left and below are negative.

In most graphical programming environments, like in Windows, the coordinate system has its origin at the upper-lefthand corner, rather than in the center, and you count upward to the right and *down*, as shown in Figure 10-2. The coordinates you pass to the various drawing methods of the Graphics class are called *world coordinates*.

Transforms introduced

These world coordinates are transformed into *page coordinates* by *world transformations*. You'll use these world transformations (e.g., TranslateTransform, ScaleTransform, and RotateTransform) later in this chapter to set the center and the orientation of your coordinate system. When drawing a clock face, for example, setting the origin (0,0) to the center of the clock is more convenient.

Page transforms convert page coordinates into device coordinates: pixels relative to the upper-lefthand corner of the client area on your monitor, bitmap, page, etc. The page transforms are the PageUnit and PageScale properties of the Graphics object, which were listed in Table 10-2.

The PageUnit property chooses the unit in which you will make your transformations and scale your drawings. These Units are one of the GraphicsUnits-enumerated values shown in Table 10-3.

---

* Philosopher joke: Rene Descartes goes into McDonald's and orders a Big Mac. The person behind the counter asks, "You want fries with that?" Descartes replies "I think not," and immediately disappears.

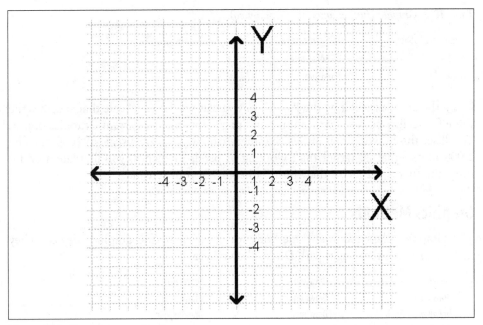

Figure 10-1. Cartesian coordinates

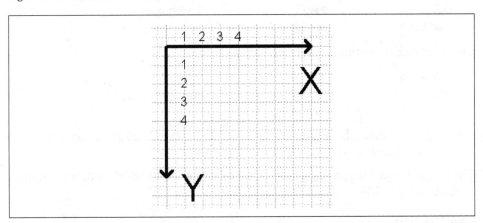

Figure 10-2. World coordinates

Table 10-3. GraphicsUnits enumeration

Enumerated value	Unit of measure
Display	1/75 of an inch
Document	1/300 of an inch
Inch	1 inch
Millimeter	1 millimeter
Pixel	1 Pixel

Table 10-3. GraphicsUnits enumeration (continued)

Enumerated value	Unit of measure
Point	1/72 of an inch
World	World unit

Using the unit described by the PageUnit, you can set the PageScale that specifies the value for scaling between world units and page units for the current Graphics object. You'll see this at work later in this chapter when you'll create a scale of 2000 units by 2,000 units—that is, rather than working in pixels or inches, you'll create an arbitrary unit that is 1/2000 of the width (or height) of your screen.

Graphics Methods

The Graphics class has many methods for drawing to the graphics device. They include methods that begin with *Draw*, shown here:

DrawArc	DrawIcon	DrawPath
DrawBezier	DrawIconUnstretched	DrawPie
DrawBeziers	DrawImage	DrawPolygon
DrawClosedCurve	DrawImageUnscaled	DrawRectangle
DrawCurve	DrawLine	DrawRectangles
DrawEllipse	DrawLines	DrawString

They also include methods that begin with *Fill*, shown here:

FillClosedCurve	FillPie	FillRectangles
FillEllipse	FillPolygon	FillRegion
FillPath	FillRectangle	

(Draw methods draw the outline of the figure; Fill methods fill the interior with the color of the current brush).

The methods you'll use in this chapter, and other commonly used methods, are summarized in Table 10-4.

Table 10-4. Graphics methods

Method	Description
Clear	Clear the drawing area and fill it with the specified color.
DrawString	Draw a string at a particular location using a particular brush and font.
DrawLine	Draw a line connecting two points.
FillEllipse	Fill an ellipse defined by a bounding rectangle.
MeasureString	Return the size of a string when drawn with a specific font within the context of the current Graphics object.
Restore	Restore the state of a Graphics object (see Save, below).

Table 10-4. Graphics methods (continued)

Method	Description
RotateTransform	Apply a rotation to the transformation matrix of a Graphics object.
Save	Save the state of a Graphics object.
ScaleTransform	Apply a scaling operation to the transformation matrix of a Graphics object.
TransformPoints	Transform an array of points from one coordinate space to another, using the current world and page transformations.
TranslateTransform	Apply a translation operation on the transformation matrix.

Create the second hand dot shown in Figure 10-5 using the FillEllipse method, and create the clock hands using the DrawLine method. Write characters using the DrawString method. You can learn more about this process below.

Save and Restore are two important methods in the Graphics class. The Save method saves the current state of the Graphics class and returns that state in a GraphicsState object. You do not need to know anything about the internal mechanism of the GraphicsState object. It can be treated as a token that you pass into Restore, which restores the saved state of the Graphics object. Thus, you might write code that looks like this:

```
GraphicsState state = myGraphicsObject.Save( );
// make transformations here
myGraphicsObject.Restore(state);
```

```
dim state as GraphicsState = myGraphicsObject.Save( )
'' make transformations here
myGraphicsObject.Restore(state)
```

Using Save and Restore allows you to change the scale or orientation of your Graphics object, and then set it back to the way it was before you transformed it.

The transformation methods are detailed later in this chapter.

Obtaining a Graphics Object

You can obtain a Graphics object in many different ways. Two of the ways involve the Paint event, which is described in detail in the next section. You can add an event handler to the Paint event delegate or override the OnPaint event handler method. In either case, the event handler method takes a PaintEventArgs parameter, which has a property that returns a Graphics object.

```
protected override void OnPaint ( PaintEventArgs e )
{
    Graphics g = e.Graphics;
```

```
protected override sub OnPaint (e as PaintEventArgs)
    dim g as Graphics = e.Graphics
```

If you override the OnPaint method, you should always finish by chaining up to the base class, forcing it to be invoked. To do so, use the following line of code:

C#
```
base.OnPaint(e);
```

VB
```
myBase.OnPaint(e)
```

Another way to obtain a Graphics object is to call the CreateGraphics method on a control or form:

C#
```
Graphics g = this.CreateGraphics();
```

VB
```
dim g as Graphics = me.CreateGraphics()
```

If you do create a Graphics object using CreateGraphics, be sure to call the Dispose method of the Graphics object when you are done with it. Never store a Graphics object as a member variable of your own class. Create or obtain the Graphics object when you need it and then dispose of it properly. The C# using keyword can help automate this process for you.

Color Structure

The System.Drawing namespace provides a Color structure to represent standard system-defined colors. Whenever a color is needed, you can use any of the 141 public static properties of the Color structure. These properties include such standbys as Red, Blue, Green, Gray, and Black; variations on the standards such as LightBlue, LightGreen, LightPink, and DarkOrange; and gems such as LightGoldenRodYellow, MediumSlateBlue, and PapayaWhip. The complete list of standard colors is provided in the Appendix.

In addition to the standard colors, 26 members of the SystemColor enumeration represent the colors used for various elements of the Windows desktop. They include such items as ActiveBorder, Desktop, and WindowFrame. The complete System-Color enumeration is also shown in the Appendix.

The combination of the standard colors and the SystemColors comprise the Known-Color enumeration.

The color system is based on the ARGB model, where A stands for Alpha, or the transparency of the color, and RGB stands for Red-Green Blue. One byte is allocated each for the Alpha and the three primary colors. An Alpha value of 0 is transparent and FF is opaque. Likewise, a zero value for a color (R, G, or B) indicates that none of that color is present, while a value of FF indicates that the color is full on.

In addition to the static properties representing the standard colors, several commonly used instance properties of the Color structure are listed in Table 10-5.

Table 10-5. Color structure instance properties

Value	Description
A	Returns byte value of Alpha component
R	Returns byte value of red component
G	Returns byte value of green component
B	Returns byte value of blue component
Name	Returns the name of the color, either user-defined, a known color, or an RGB value

Geometric Structures—Points, Rectangles, and Sizes

The System.Drawing namespace provides several structures for representing a location (Point and PointF), a rectangular area (Rectangle and RectangleF), and a size (Size and SizeF).

All of these structures consist of a pair of read/write ordered pair of numbers. The versions *without* the trailing F in the name take an ordered pair of ordered pairs of integers (four integers in total) and the versions with the trailing F take an ordered pair of ordered pairs of floating-point numbers (float in C# or single in VB.NET). The numbers typically represent pixels. They can also represent other units, such as Inch or Millimeter, hence the need for floating-point as well as integer values.

The integer versions of these structures can be cast to the floating-point version:

C#
```
PointF ptf;
Point pt = null;
ptf = pt;
```

VB
```
dim ptf as PointF
dim pt as Point
ptf = pt
```

You cannot cast in the opposite direction, since information may be lost. However, all three integer versions provide static methods (Ceiling, Round, and Truncate) for converting from the floating-point version to the integer version.

In the Point/PointF structure, the first number represents the x, or horizontal coordinate in a two-dimensional Cartesian coordinate system. The second number represents the y, or vertical coordinate.

The Size/SizeF structures are similar to the Point/PointF structures, except that the ordered pair of numbers represent the Width and Height properties of a rectangular region.

The Rectangle and RectangleF structures represent a rectangular region. Each has two constructors, listed in Table 10-6. The first constructor takes a Point (or PointF) structure and a Size (or SizeF) structure. The second constructor takes four numbers, either integers or float/singles. The first two numbers represent the x and y coordinates of the upper-left corner of the rectangle, and the second two numbers represent the width and height of the rectangle.

Table 10-6. Rectangle and RectangleF constructors

Rectangle	Point, Size
	Integer, Integer, Integer, Integer
RectangleF	PointF, SizeF
	Integer, Integer, Integer, Integer

The Rectangle and RectangleF structures also provide several properties for either getting information about the rectangle or setting properties. These properties are listed in Table 10-7.

Table 10-7. Rectangle and RectangleF properties

Property	Type	Description
Bottom	Integer Float/single	Read-only. Returns the y coordinate of the bottom edge of the rectangle.
Height	Integer Float/single	Read/write. The height of the rectangle.
IsEmpty	Boolean	Read-only. Returns true if all numeric properties have a value of zero.
Left	Integer Float/single	Read-only. Returns the x coordinate of the left edge of the rectangle.
Location	Point/PointF	Read/write. The point at the upper-left corner of the rectangle.
Right	Integer Float/single	Read-only. Returns the x coordinate of the right edge of the rectangle.
Size	Size/SizeF	Read/write. The size of the rectangle.
Top	Integer Float/single	Read-only. Returns the y coordinate of the top edge of the rectangle.
Width	Integer Float/single	Read/write. The width of the rectangle.
X	Integer Float/single	Read/write. The x coordinate of the upper-left corner of the rectangle.
Y	Integer Float/single	Read/write. The y coordinate of the upper-left corner of the rectangle.

Brush and Brushes

A *Brush* object is used to fill the interior spaces of graphical shapes. The Brush class is abstract (MustInherit), and five different classes are derived from Brush, listed in Table 10-8.

Table 10-8. Brush-derived classes

Class	Description
HatchBrush	A rectangular brush with a hatch style from the HatchStyle enumeration, such as BackwardDiagonal, DarkVertical, Divot, and Percent60. The ForegroundColor property gets the color of the lines and the BackgroundColor property gets the color of the space behind the lines.
LinearGradientBrush	A brush with a linear gradient. Properties such as Blend, GammaCorrection, and Transform allow you to change the appearance programatically.
PathGradientBrush	A brush that fills a graphical shape with a gradient. Properties such as Blend, CenterColor, and Transform allow you to change the appearance programatically.
SolidBrush	A brush that fills a graphical shape with a color. Valid colors are members of the Color structure.
TextureBrush	A brush that fills a graphical shape with a texture. The texture can come from an Image object, either a bitmap or a metafile.

For easy access to the colored brushes, a Brushes class (note the plural) contains only static (shared), read-only properties of type Brush corresponding to each standard color. This Brushes class often provides the Brush object used in calls to the Draw-String method.

 If you explicitly create a Brush (or Pen), you must explicitly dispose of it, but you must *not* dispose of any brushes returned to you by Brushes, SystemBrushes, Pens, or SystemPens.

Pen and Pens

The Pen and Pens classes are similar to the Brush and Brushes classes, except they are used for drawing lines and curves rather than filling graphical shapes. The constructors of the Pen class take either a Brush object or a Color as an argument. Additionally, you can pass in a floating-point number (float in C#, single in VB.NET) that specifies the width of the Pen object.

As with the Brushes class, there is a Pens class (note the plural) for easy access to a Pen object of a standard color. The Pens class contains static members corresponding to each standard color. The following code snippet demonstrates one way to instantiate and use a Pen object.

```
Pen pn = Pens.LimeGreen;
pn.EndCap = LineCap.ArrowAnchor;
pn.Width = 20;
g.DrawLine(pn,0,0,0,50);
```

```
Dim pn as Pen = Pens.LimeGreen
pn.EndCap = LineCap.ArrowAnchor
pn.Width = 20
g.DrawLine(pn, 0, 0, 0, 50)
```

Table 10-9 lists many of the most commonly used properties of the Pen class. Many of them will be demonstrated in the Analog Clock project later in this chapter.

Table 10-9. Pen properties

Property	Type	Description
Alignment	PenAlignment	Read/write. Specifies the alignment for this Pen object relative to a theoretical line. Valid values are members of the PenAlignment enumeration, listed in Table 10-10.
Brush	Brush	Read/write. The Brush object that controls attributes of the pen (e.g., does the pen draw a solid or a pattern?).
Color	Color	Read/write. The color of the Pen. Legal values are members of the Color structure, e.g., Color.DarkGoldenrod.
DashCap	DashCap	Read/write. The cap style used at the beginning and end of the dashes that comprise a dashed line. Valid values are Flat, Round, and Triangle.
DashPattern	float[ ] / single( )	Read/write. An array of numbers specifying the lengths of alternating dashes and spaces.
DashStyle	DashStyle	Read/write. The style used for dashed lines. Valid values are members of the DashStyle enumeration, listed in Table 10-11.
EndCap	LineCap	Read/write. The enumerated arrow type. Valid values are members of the LineCap enumeration, listed in Table 10-12.
StartCap	LineCap	Read/write. The enumerated arrow type. Valid values are members of the LineCap enumeration, listed in Table 10-12.
Width	Float	The thickness of the drawn line.

Table 10-10. PenAlignment enumeration values

Value	Description
Center	Centered over the theoretical line
Inset	Positioned to the inside of the theoretical line
Left	Positioned to the left of the theoretical line
Outset	Positioned to the outside of the theoretical line
Right	Positioned to the right of the theoretical line

Table 10-11. DashStyle enumeration values

Value	Description
Custom	Custom style
Dash	Dashes
DashDot	Repeating pattern of dash-dot
DashDotDot	Repeating pattern of dash-dot-dot

Table 10-11. DashStyle enumeration values (continued)

Value	Description
Dot	Dots
Solid	Solid line

Table 10-12. LineCap enumeration values

Value	Description
AnchorMask	Mask to check if cap is an anchor cap
ArrowAnchor	Arrow-shaped anchor cap
Custom	Custom line cap
DiamondAnchor	Diamond-shaped anchor cap
Flat	Flat line cap
NoAnchor	No anchor
Round	Round line cap
RoundAnchor	Round anchor cap
Square	Square cap
SquareAnchor	Square anchor cap
Triangle	Triangular line cap

Paint Event

All controls have a Paint event, which is raised when the control is about to be drawn. You can add an event handler to the Paint event delegate to dictate how the control is drawn. Using the Paint event, for example, you can draw a string of text directly onto the client area of a form, as shown in Example 10-1 (in C#) and in Example 10-2 (in VB.NET).

For a complete discussion of delegates and events, see Chapter 4.

Example 10-1. Drawing a string with Paint event using C# (PaintDemo.cs)

```csharp
using System;
using System.Drawing;
using System.Windows.Forms;

namespace ProgrammingWinApps
{
    public class PaintDemo : Form
    {

        public PaintDemo( )
        {
            Text = "Paint Demonstration";
```

Example 10-1. Drawing a string with Paint event using C# (PaintDemo.cs) (continued)

```
        Size = new Size(300,200);
        Paint += new PaintEventHandler(PaintHandler);
    }

    static void Main( )
    {
        Application.Run(new PaintDemo( ));
    }

    private void PaintHandler(object sender, PaintEventArgs e)
    {
        Graphics g = e.Graphics;
        g.DrawString("Look Ma, no label!", Font, Brushes.Black, 50, 75);
    }
  }
}
```

Example 10-2. Drawing a string with Paint event using VB.NET (PaintDemo.vb)

```
imports System
imports System.Drawing
imports System.Windows.Forms

namespace ProgrammingWinApps
    public class PaintDemo : inherits Form

        public sub New( )
            Text = "Paint Demonstration"
            Size = new Size(300,200)
            AddHandler Paint, AddressOf PaintHandler
        end sub

        public shared sub Main( )
            Application.Run(new PaintDemo( ))
        end sub

        private sub PaintHandler(ByVal sender as object, _
                            ByVal e as PaintEventArgs)
            dim g as Graphics = e.Graphics
            g.DrawString("Look Ma, no label!", Font, Brushes.Black, 50, 75)
        end sub
    end class
end namespace
```

When either program in Example 10-1 or Example 10-2 is compiled and run, you will get the form shown in Figure 10-3.

Both versions of the PaintDemo program start by referencing the required namespaces: System, System.Drawing, and System.Windows.Forms. Inside the constructor of each program, the Text and Size properties are set, and the PaintHandler method is added to the delegate for the Paint event:

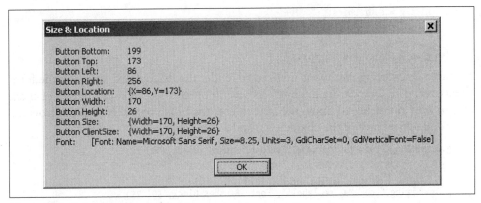

Figure 10-3. Paint event demonstration

C#
```
Text = "Paint Demonstration";
Size = new Size(300,200);
Paint += new PaintEventHandler(PaintHandler);
```

VB
```
Text = "Paint Demonstration"
Size = new Size(300,200)
AddHandler Paint, AddressOf PaintHandler
```

Remember that all of these properties (and events) are implicitly members of the class—i.e., the PaintDemo form. You can make this explicit by using the appropriate lines of code:

C#
```
this.Text = "Paint Demonstration";
this.Size = new Size(300,200);
this.Paint += new PaintEventHandler(PaintHandler);
```

VB
```
Me.Text = "Paint Demonstration"
Me.Size = new Size(300,200)
Me.AddHandler Paint, AddressOf PaintHandler
```

The PaintHandler method is a typical event handler, taking two arguments. The first is of type object and the second is of type PaintEventArgs, which has the two read-only properties listed in Table 10-13.

Table 10-13. PaintEventArgs properties

Property	Type	Description
ClipRectangle	Rectangle	The rectangle to paint
Graphics	Graphics	The Graphics object used to paint

A new Graphics object is instantiated from the PaintEventArgs argument.

`C#`   Graphics g = e.Graphics;

`VB`   dim g as Graphics = e.Graphics

Then the DrawString method is invoked to render the desired text string on the form client area. The DrawString method has several overloaded versions, but all of them take at least the string to draw, the font to use, the brush to use (which controls the color and appearance of the characters), and a location:

`C#`   g.DrawString("Look Ma, no label!", Font, Brushes.Black, 50, 75);

`VB`   g.DrawString("Look Ma, no label!", Font, Brushes.Black, 50, 75)

In this example, the font used is the current font for the form (it also could have been written as this.Font in C# or me.Font in VB.NET), the brush is Black, and the location of the upper-left corner of the text string is 50 units in from the left edge of the client area and 75 units down from the top.

Overriding the OnPaint method

The programs shown in Examples 10-1 and 10-2 worked by adding an event handler method to the Paint event. You can accomplish the same outcome by overriding the OnPaint event directly just as you might override any virtual method. The Control class defines the OnPaint method as follows:

`C#`   protected virtual void OnPaint(PaintEventArgs e);

`VB`   Overridable Protected Sub OnPaint(ByVal e As PaintEventArgs)

Example 10-3 (in C#) and in Example 10-4 (in VB.NET) demonstrate how to override the OnPaint event. The differences from the previous examples are highlighted.

Example 10-3. Overriding the OnPaint event in C# (PaintOverride.cs)

`C#`
```
using System;
using System.Drawing;
using System.Windows.Forms;

namespace ProgrammingWinApps
{
   public class PaintOverride : Form
   {

      public PaintOverride( )
      {
         Text = "Paint Demonstration";
```

`C#`

```csharp
        Size = new Size(300,200);
    }

    static void Main( )
    {
        Application.Run(new PaintOverride( ));
    }

    protected override void OnPaint(PaintEventArgs e)
    {
        Graphics g = e.Graphics;
        g.DrawString("Look Ma, I'm overridden!", Font, Brushes.Black, 50, 75);
        base.OnPaint(e);
    }
  }
}
```

Example 10-4. Overriding the OnPaint event in VB.NET (PaintOverride.vb)

`VB`

```vbnet
imports System
imports System.Drawing
imports System.Windows.Forms

namespace ProgrammingWinApps
   public class PaintOverride : inherits Form

      public sub New( )
         Text = "Paint Demonstration"
         Size = new Size(300,200)
      end sub

      public shared sub Main( )
         Application.Run(new PaintOverride( ))
      end sub

      protected overrides sub OnPaint(ByVal e as PaintEventArgs)
         myBase.OnPaint(e)
         dim g as Graphics = e.Graphics
         g.DrawString("Look Ma, I'm overridden!", _
             Font, Brushes.Black, 50, 75)
      end sub
   end class
end namespace
```

In Examples 10-3 and 10-4, no methods are added to any event delegates. Instead, the protected OnPaint method is overridden. When overriding an event handler, the only required argument is the event argument—in this case, PaintEventArgs.

The last line in the overridden method *chains up* to the base method (invokes the base method) to ensure that all the base class functionality will be implemented and that any other methods registered with the delegate will be notified. This is done with the line:

`C#`
```
base.OnPaint(e);
```

`VB`
```
myBase.OnPaint(e)
```

The remaining two lines in the overridden method are the same as in the previous examples.

Forcing a paint event—the Invalidate method

You can force a region to redraw by calling the Invalidate method on a control. This method does not actually raise the Paint event, but invalidates the area of the control or a region within the control. Once an area or region has been invalidated, it will be redrawn. This will occur when all current events are finished processing. If you want the redraw to occur immediately, call the Update method after calling the Invalidate method.

The Invalidate method is overloaded with six different versions. The parameters supplied to the method dictate exactly what part of the control will be invalidated. The overloaded versions are listed in Table 10-14.

Table 10-14. Invalidate methods

Method Call	Description
Invalidate( )	Invalidates the region of the control
Invalidate(Boolean)	If Boolean is `true`, invalidates the child controls
Invalidate(Rectangle)	Invalidates the region specified by the Rectangle
Invalidate(Region)	Invalidates the specified Region
Invalidate(Rectangle, Boolean)	Invalidates the region specified by the Rectangle, and if Boolean is `true`, invalidates the child controls
Invalidate(Region, Boolean)	Invalidates the specified Region, and if Boolean is `true`, invalidates the child controls

Use of the Invalidate method is shown in Example 10-5 (in C#) and in Example 10-6 (in VB.NET). The lines of code differing from the basic examples in Examples 10-1 and 10-2 are highlighted.

Example 10-5. Invalidate method in C# (PaintInvalidate.cs)

`C#`
```
using System;
using System.Drawing;
using System.Windows.Forms;

namespace ProgrammingWinApps
```

Example 10-5. Invalidate method in C# (PaintInvalidate.cs) (continued)

```csharp
{
    public class PaintInvalidate : Form
    {
        private Button btn;

        public PaintInvalidate()
        {
            Text = "Paint Invalidate Demonstration";
            Size = new Size(300,200);

            btn = new Button();
            btn.Parent = this;
            btn.Location = new Point(25,25);
            btn.Text = "Update";
            btn.Click += new System.EventHandler(btn_Click);
        }

        static void Main()
        {
            Application.Run(new PaintInvalidate());
        }

        protected override void OnPaint(PaintEventArgs e)
        {
            base.OnPaint(e);
            Graphics g = e.Graphics;
            String str = "Look Ma, I'm overridden!";
            str += "\nThe time is " + DateTime.Now.ToLongTimeString();
            g.DrawString(str, Font, Brushes.Black, 50, 75);
        }

        private void btn_Click(object sender, EventArgs e)
        {
            Invalidate();
        }
    }
}
```

Example 10-6. Invalidate method in VB.NET (PaintInvalidate.vb)

```vbnet
imports System
imports System.Drawing
imports System.Windows.Forms

namespace ProgrammingWinApps
    public class PaintInvalidate : inherits Form

        private WithEvents btn as Button

        public sub New()
```

Example 10-6. Invalidate method in VB.NET (PaintInvalidate.vb) (continued)

```
            Text = "Paint Invalidate Demonstration"
            Size = new Size(300,200)

            btn = new Button( )
            btn.Parent = me
            btn.Location = new Point(25,25)
            btn.Text = "Update"
        end sub

        public shared sub Main( )
            Application.Run(new PaintInvalidate( ))
        end sub

        protected overrides sub OnPaint(ByVal e as PaintEventArgs)
            myBase.OnPaint(e)
            dim g as Graphics = e.Graphics
            dim str as string = "Look Ma, I'm overridden!"
            str += vbCrLf + "The time is " + DateTime.Now.ToLongTimeString( )
            g.DrawString(str, Font, Brushes.Black, 50, 75)
        end sub

        private sub btn_Click(ByVal sender as object, _
                ByVal e as EventArgs) _
                Handles btn.Click
            Invalidate( )
        end sub
    end class
end namespace
```

When either program is compiled and run, you get something similar to that shown in Figure 10-4. Clicking on the button updates the time displayed in the client area of the form.

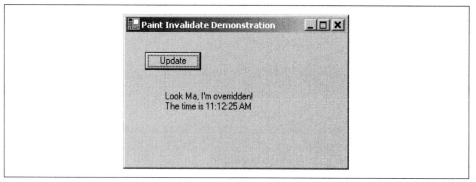

Figure 10-4. Paint Invalidate program

The Invalidate method is called against the Form object. The line:

```
    Invalidate( )
```

is implicitly the same as:

```
this.Invalidate( );
```

```
me.Invalidate( )
```

Another way to force a Form to invalidate itself and cause the Paint event to be raised is to set the ResizeRedraw property to true. This will cause the object, the Form in this case, to redraw itself every time the object is resized. In fact, if an application is not behaving the way you might expect when resizing, then setting this property to true might alleviate the problem.

The Analog Clock Project

To illustrate the use of the Graphics object and GDI+ methods, you'll create a clock face with conventional hour and minute hands and a green dot in lieu of a second hand. You will also display the date rotating around the clock face, as shown in Figure 10-5. (If your copy of the book does not display the moving text, you may need to run the program itself, which you will find in Examples 10-11 or 10-12).

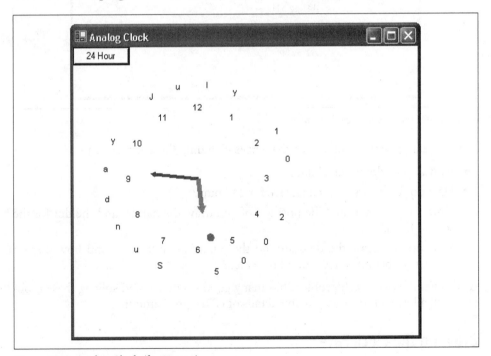

Figure 10-5. Analog Clock (first image)

Notice the button marked "24 Hours" in the upper-lefthand corner. Clicking that button changes the clock to a 24 hour display, as shown in Figure 10-6. Notice that in 24 hour mode, the minute hand maintains its position, but the hour hand must be adjusted.

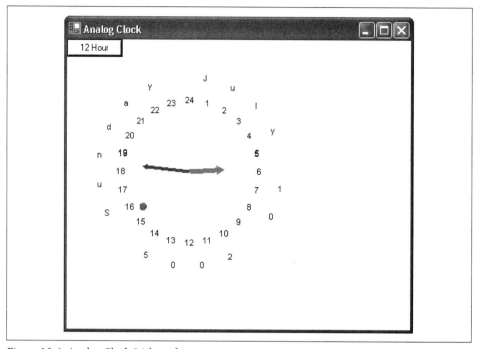

Figure 10-6. Analog Clock 24-hour face

This project presents a number of challenges including those listed next.

- How do you draw a clock face?
- How do you redraw the clock face for 24 hours?
- How do you determine the position of and draw the hands (and the dot for the second hand?)
- How do you draw the date around the outer circumference, and how do you move it so that it rotates around the clock?

As is often the case, each problem has many good solutions, and solving these problems will allow you to explore many details of GDI+ programming.

Drawing the Clock Face

In the first iteration of the clock program, you'll just draw the clock face, as shown in Figure 10-7. The complete source code is shown in Examples 10-7 and 10-8. Detailed analysis follows.

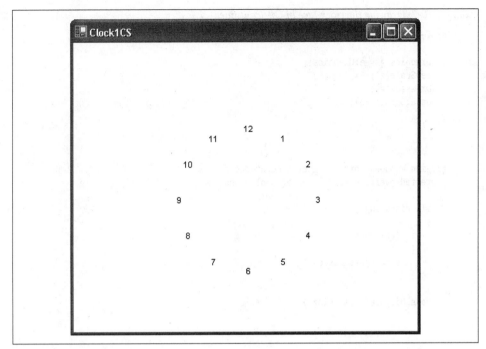

Figure 10-7. Simple clock face

Example 10-7. Drawing the clock face in C#

```csharp
using System;
using System.Drawing;
using System.Collections;
using System.ComponentModel;
using System.Windows.Forms;
using System.Data;

namespace Clock1CS
{
    // Summary description for Form1.
    public class Form1 : System.Windows.Forms.Form
    {
        // Required designer variable.
        private System.ComponentModel.Container components = null;

        public Form1( )
        {
            // Required for Windows Form Designer support
            InitializeComponent( );

            // use the user's choice of colors
            BackColor = SystemColors.Window;
            ForeColor = SystemColors.WindowText;

        }
```

Example 10-7. Drawing the clock face in C# (continued)

```csharp
protected override void OnPaint ( PaintEventArgs e )
{
   Graphics g = e.Graphics;
   SetScale(g);
   DrawFace(g);
   base.OnPaint(e);
}



#region Windows Form Designer generated code
protected override void Dispose( bool disposing )
{
   if( disposing )
   {
      if (components != null)
      {
         components.Dispose( );
      }
   }
   base.Dispose( disposing );
}


/// <summary>
/// Required method for Designer support - do not modify
/// the contents of this method with the code editor.
/// </summary>
private void InitializeComponent( )
{
   //
   // Form1
   //
   this.AutoScaleBaseSize = new System.Drawing.Size(5, 13);
   this.ClientSize = new System.Drawing.Size(292, 266);
   this.Name = "Form1";
   this.Text = "Clock1CS";

}
#endregion

[STAThread]
static void Main( )
{
   Application.Run(new Form1( ));
}

private void SetScale(Graphics g)
{
   // if the form is too small, do nothing
   if ( Width == 0 || Height == 0 )
      return;
```

Example 10-7. Drawing the clock face in C# (continued)

```csharp
    // set the origin at the center
    g.TranslateTransform(Width/2, Height/2);

    // set inches to the minimum of the width
    // or height dividedby the dots per inch
    float inches = Math.Min(Width / g.DpiX, Height / g.DpiX);

    // set the scale to a grid of 2000 by 2000 units
    g.ScaleTransform(
        inches * g.DpiX / 2000, inches * g.DpiY / 2000);
}

private void DrawFace(Graphics g)
{
    // numbers are in forecolor except flash number in green
    // as the seconds go by.

    Brush brush = new SolidBrush(ForeColor);
    Font font = new Font("Arial", 40);

    float x, y;

    const int numHours = 12;
    const int deg = 360 / numHours;
    const int FaceRadius = 450;

    // for each of the hours on the clock face
    for (int i = 1; i <= numHours; i++)
    {

        // two ways to do alignment.

        /*
        // 1. figure out size of the string and then
        // offset by half the height and half the width

        // measure the string you're going to draw given
        // the current font
        SizeF stringSize =
            g.MeasureString(i.ToString( ),font);

        x = GetCos(i*deg + 90) * FaceRadius;
        x += stringSize.Width / 2;
        y = GetSin(i*deg + 90) * FaceRadius;
        y += stringSize.Height / 2;

        g.DrawString(i.ToString( ), font, brush, -x, -y);

        */

        // 2. use a StringFormat object and set
        // its alignment to center
```

Example 10-7. Drawing the clock face in C# (continued)

```csharp
            // i = hour  30 degrees = offset per hour
            // +90 to make 12 straight up
            x = GetCos(i*deg + 90) * FaceRadius;
            y = GetSin(i*deg + 90) * FaceRadius;

            StringFormat format = new StringFormat( );
            format.Alignment = StringAlignment.Center;
            format.LineAlignment = StringAlignment.Center;

            g.DrawString(
               i.ToString( ), font, brush, -x, -y,format);

         }   // end for loop
         brush.Dispose( );
         font.Dispose( );
      }       // end drawFace

   private static float GetSin(float degAngle)
   {
      return (float) Math.Sin(Math.PI * degAngle / 180f);
   }

   private static float GetCos(float degAngle)
   {
      return (float) Math.Cos(Math.PI * degAngle / 180f);
   }

   }   // end class
}       // end namespace
```

Example 10-8. Drawing the clock face in VB.NET

```vbnet
Imports System
Imports System.Drawing
Imports System.Collections
Imports System.ComponentModel
Imports System.Windows.Forms
Imports System.Data

Namespace ClockFace1



   Public Class Form1
       Inherits System.Windows.Forms.Form


#Region " Windows Form Designer generated code "
#End Region

       Protected Overrides Sub OnPaint(ByVal e As PaintEventArgs)
           MyBase.OnPaint(e)
```

Example 10-8. Drawing the clock face in VB.NET (continued)

```vb
        Dim g As Graphics = e.Graphics
        SetScale(g)
        DrawFace(g)
End Sub 'OnPaint




Private Sub SetScale(ByVal g As Graphics)
    ' if the form is too small, do nothing
    If Width = 0 Or Height = 0 Then
        Return
    End If
    ' set the origin at the center
    g.TranslateTransform(Width/2, Height/2)

    ' set inches to the minimum of the width or height divided
    ' by the dots per inch
    Dim inches As Single = _
        Math.Min(Width / g.DpiX, Height / g.DpiX)

    ' set the scale to a grid of 2000 by 2000 units
    g.ScaleTransform( _
        inches * g.DpiX / 2000, inches * g.DpiY / 2000)
End Sub 'SetScale


Private Sub DrawFace(ByVal g As Graphics)
    ' numbers are in forecolor except flash number in green
    ' as the seconds go by.
    Dim myBrush = New SolidBrush(ForeColor)
    Dim greenBrush = New SolidBrush(Color.Green)
    Dim myFont As New Font("Arial", 40)
    Dim x, y As Single

    Const numHours As Integer = 12
    Const deg As Integer = 30
    Const FaceRadius As Integer = 450

    ' for each of the hours on the clock face
    Dim i As Integer
    For i = 1 To numHours

        ' two ways to do alignment.
        ' 1. figure out size of the string and then offset by half
        ' the height and half the width
        ' measure the string you're going to draw given
        ' the current font

        ''Dim stringSize As SizeF = _
            g.MeasureString(i.ToString( ), font)
```

Example 10-8. Drawing the clock face in VB.NET (continued)

```
            ''x = GetCos(i * deg + 90) * FaceRadius
            ''x += stringSize.Width / 2
            ''y = GetSin(i * deg + 90) * FaceRadius
            ''y += stringSize.Height / 2
            ''g.DrawString(i.ToString( ), font, brush, -x, -y)


            ' 2. use a StringFormat object and set its
            ' alignment to center
            ' i = hour   30 degrees = offset per hour
            ' +90 to make 12 straight up
            x = GetCos((i * deg + 90)) * FaceRadius
            y = GetSin((i * deg + 90)) * FaceRadius

            Dim format As New StringFormat( )
            format.Alignment = StringAlignment.Center
            format.LineAlignment = StringAlignment.Center

            g.DrawString(i.ToString( ), myFont, myBrush, -x, -y, format)
        Next i
    End Sub 'DrawFace

    Private Shared Function GetSin(ByVal degAngle As Single) As Single
        Return CSng(Math.Sin((Math.PI * degAngle / 180.0F)))
    End Function 'GetSin


    Private Shared Function GetCos(ByVal degAngle As Single) As Single
        Return CSng(Math.Cos((Math.PI * degAngle / 180.0F)))
    End Function 'GetCos
  End Class 'Form1
End Namespace
```

Color

When you draw the clock face, you'll need to tell the CLR what color to use for the numbers. You might be tempted to use black, which is perfectly appropriate, but it does raise a problem. As noted in Chapter 9, however, the user may have changed the color scheme to a very dark background (even to black), which would make your clock face invisible.

A better alternative is to set the BackColor and ForeColor for your form based on the Window and WindowText colors the user has chosen. You can do so in the constructor for the form:

```
BackColor = SystemColors.Window;
ForeColor = SystemColors.WindowText;
```

You can now set the brush color to the foreground color and feel comfortable with your choice.

OnPaint

Each time the form is created or invalidated, its OnPaint method is called. You can override the OnPaint method to get a Graphics object to work with and paint the control as you wish.

Your override will extract the Graphics object from the PaintEventArgs object passed in as a parameter. It will then pass that Graphics object to two methods: SetScale and DrawFace, described below:

```csharp
protected override void OnPaint ( PaintEventArgs e )
{
    Graphics g = e.Graphics;
    SetScale(g);
    DrawFace(g);
    base.OnPaint(e);
}
```

```vb
Protected Overrides Sub OnPaint(ByVal e As PaintEventArgs)
    Dim g As Graphics = e.Graphics
    SetScale(g)
    DrawFace(g)
End Sub 'OnPaint
```

Transforming the coordinates

The job of the SetScale method is to make the world transformations to set the origin at the center of the form, and to set the scale to an arbitrary grid of 1,000 units in each of the four directions from the center:

```csharp
private void SetScale(Graphics g)
{
```

```vb
Private Sub SetScale(ByVal g As Graphics)
```

Start by making sure that the form has at least some width or height:

```csharp
if ( Width == 0 || Height == 0 )
    return;
```

```vb
If Width = 0 Or Height = 0 Then
    Return
End If
```

That done, you are ready to set the origin to the center. To do so, call Translate-Transform on the Graphics object received as a parameter to the method.

The TranslateTransform method is overloaded; the version you'll use takes two floating-point numbers (float in C#, single in VB.NET) as parameters: the x-component of the translation and the y-component. You want to move the origin from the upper left halfway across the form in the x-direction and halfway down the form in the y-direction.

 World translations are implemented with matrices. This mathematical concept is beyond the scope of this book, and you do not need to understand the matrices to use the transformations. For more information, however, please either consult the SDK documentation or look at Charles Petzold's excellent book *Programming Microsoft Windows With C#* (Microsoft Press).

The form inherits two properties from Control that you'll use: Width and Height. Each returns its value in pixels:

C#
```
g.TranslateTransform(Width/2, Height/2);
```

The effect is to transform the origin (0,0) to the center both horizontally and vertically.

You are now set to transform the scale from its current units (pixels by default) to an arbitrary unit. Don't worry about how large each unit is, but you do want 1,000 units in each direction from the origin, no matter what the screen resolution is. Unfortunately, the size of the units must be equal both horizontally and vertically, so you'll need to choose a size. You will thus compute which size is smaller in inches: the width or the height of the device:

C#
```
float inches = Math.Min(Width/g.DpiX, Height/g.DpiX);
```

VB
```
Dim inches As Single = Math.Min(Width/g.DpiX, Height/g.DpiX)
```

The variable *inches* now has the smaller of the width or height of the device measured in inches. Multiply that many inches times the dots per inch on the x axis to get the number of dots in the width, and divide by 2,000 to create a unit that is 1/2000th of the width of the form You'll then do the same for the y axis. If you pass these values to ScaleTransform, you'll create an arbitrary scale 2,000 units on the x axis and 2,000 units on the y axis, or 1,000 units in each direction from the center.

C#
```
g.ScaleTransform(
    inches * g.DpiX/2000, inches * g.DpiY/2000);
```

 To see this computation for ScaleTransform more clearly, you might use interim variables:
```
totalDotsX = inches * g.DpiX;
numDotsIn2000UnitsX = totalDotsX / 2000;

totalDotsY = inches * g.DpiY;
numDotsIn2000UnitsY = totalDotsY / 2000;

g.ScaleTransform(numDotsIn2000UnitsX, numDotsIn2000UnitsY);
```

When this method ends, you have the grid you need to draw the clock face. The DrawFace method actually does the work.

World transforms

To draw this clock, write the strings 1 through 12 in the appropriate location. Specify the location as x,y coordinates, and these coordinates must be on the circumference of an imaginary circle.

To compute the x coordinate, take the hour and multiply it by 30, add 90, convert this value from degrees to radians, take the cosine, and then multiply that result by the radius. The formula for the y coordinate is identical, except that you use the sin rather than the cosine:

```
x = GetCos(i*deg + 90) * FaceRadius;
```

To understand why this formula works, see the sidebar "Computing the x,y Coordinates" in this chapter.

Computing the x,y Coordinates

Compute the x coordinate of a point on a circle by multiplying the cosine of the angle by the radius and you compute the y coordinate of a point on a circle by multiplying the sin of the angle by the radius. (see *PreCalculus with Unit Circle Trigonometry* by David Cohn [West Wadsworth]).

These formulae assume that the center of the circle is the origin of your coordinate system, and that the angle is measured counter clockwise from the positive x axis. They also assume that the y axis is positive above the origin and negative below.

A circle is 360 degrees; to evenly space 12 numbers around the face, each number must be 30 degrees from the previous number. The C# Cosine and Sin functions take their parameters in radians, however, not degrees. You'll need to convert degrees to radians using a simple formula: radians equal degrees times pi, divided by 180.

When creating a clock face, it is convenient to measure the degrees offset from the y axis (aligned with 12 o'clock) rather than the x axis, and to increase the angle as you move clockwise (hence the name) rather than the mathematically traditional counterclockwise. In addition, the coordinate system you'll be using has y values that are negative above the origin, rather than positive.

You solve all three conversions (using the y axis as the zero angle, moving clockwise, and the required coordinate system) by taking advantage of the fact that the cosine of 90 plus an angle is equal to the opposite of the cosine of 90 minus the angle. Thus, to compute 2 o'clock in this system, you compute that 2 is 60 degrees *clockwise* from 12, add 90, and convert the resulting angle (150) to radians and take the cosine of that value. You can then multiply the result times the radius of the circle and you'll get x,y coordinates that match your coordinate system.

Draw each number on the clock face with the overloaded DrawString method of the Graphics object. Table 10-15 lists the overloaded forms of the DrawString method.

Table 10-15. DrawString method overload list (C# and VB.NET)

Method	Description
`void DrawString(string, Font, Brush, PointF);` `sub DrawString(string, Font, Brush, PointF)`	Draw the specified string using the specified font and brush at the specified point.
`void DrawString(string, Font, Brush, RectangleF);` `sub DrawString(string, Font, Brush, RectangleF)`	Draw the specified string using the specified font and brush in the specified rectangle.

`void DrawString(string, Font, Brush, PointF,`
`    StringFormat);`
`sub DrawString(string, Font, Brush, PointF, _`
`    StringFormat)`
	Draw the specified string using the specified font and brush at the specified point using the specified StringFormat.

`void DrawString(string, Font, Brush, RectangleF,`
`    StringFormat);`
`sub DrawString(string, Font, Brush, RectangleF, _`
`    StringFormat)`
	Draw the specified string using the specified font and brush in the specified rectangle using the specified StringFormat.

`void DrawString(string, Font, Brush, float, float);` `sub DrawString(string, Font, Brush, float, float)`	Draw the specified string using the specified font and brush at the specified x and y coordinates.

`void DrawString(string, Font, Brush, float, float,`
`    StringFormat);`
`sub DrawString(string, Font, Brush, float, float, _`
`    StringFormat)`
	Draw the specified string using the specified font and brush at the specified x and y coordinates using the specified StringFormat.

The version of DrawString you'll use in this example will take five parameters:

- The string to draw (the numbers 1 through 12)
- The font to draw in (e.g., Arial 8)
- A brush to determine the color and texture of the text
- The x coordinate of the upper-lefthand corner of the text
- The y coordinate of the upper-lefthand corner of the text

You know you'll need a brush, and you know you want to draw in the foreground color determined by the user, so create an instance of a SolidBrush, passing in the ForeColor property of the form:

C#
```
Brush brush = new SolidBrush(ForeColor);
```

VB
```
Dim brush = New SolidBrush(ForeColor)
```

You also need a Font object. You'll create a font to represent the font face Arial and the size 40. This size will be relative to your new arbitrary scale, so it is arrived at by trial and error:

C#
```
Font font = new Font("Arial", 40);
```

VB
```
Dim font As New Font("Arial", 40)
```

Next, declare two float variables to hold the x and y coordinates that you will compute using the formula discussed earlier (see "Computing the x,y Coordinates"), as well as a few useful constants:

C#
```
float x, y;
const int numHours = 12;
const int deg = 360 / numHours;
const int FaceRadius = 450;
```

VB
```
Dim x, y As Single
Const numHours As Integer = 12
Const deg As Integer = 360 / numHours
Const FaceRadius As Integer = 450
```

Create the string to draw by creating a for loop:

C#
```
for (int i = 1; i <= numHours; i++)
{
```

VB
```
Dim i As Integer
For i = 1 To numHours
```

Within that loop, draw each number in turn. The first task is to compute the x,y coordinates on the circle:

```
x = GetCos(i*deg + 90) * FaceRadius;
y = GetSin(i*deg + 90) * FaceRadius;
```

The GetCos and GetSin methods convert the degrees to radians:

C#
```
private static float GetSin(float degAngle)
{
    return (float) Math.Sin(Math.PI * degAngle / 180f);
}

private static float GetCos(float degAngle)
{
    return (float) Math.Cos(Math.PI * degAngle / 180f);
}
```

VB
```
Private Shared Function GetSin(ByVal degAngle As Single) As Single
    Return CSng(Math.Sin((Math.PI * degAngle / 180.0F)))
End Function 'GetSin

Private Shared Function GetCos(ByVal degAngle As Single) As Single
    Return CSng(Math.Cos((Math.PI * degAngle / 180.0F)))
End Function 'GetCos
```

Once you have the coordinates, you are ready to draw the numbers. The problem, however, is that the x,y coordinates you've computed will be the location of the upper-lefthand corner of the numbers you draw. This will result in a slightly lopsided clock.

To fix this, center the string around the point determined by your location formula. You can do this in two ways. In the first approach, measure the string, and then subtract half the width and height from the location. Begin by calling the MeasureString method on the Graphics object, passing in the string (the number you want to display) and the font in which you want to display it:

C#
```
SizeF stringSize =
    g.MeasureString(i.ToString(),font);
```

VB
```
Dim stringSize As SizeF = _
    g.MeasureString(i.ToString(), font)
```

You get back an object of type SizeF. SizeF is a struct, described earlier, that has two important properties: Width and Height. You can now compute the location of the object, and then offset the x location by half the width and the y location by half the height.

C#
```
x = GetCos(i*deg + 90) * FaceRadius;
x += stringSize.Width / 2;
y = GetSin(i*deg + 90) * FaceRadius;
y += stringSize.Height / 2;
```

This works perfectly, but .NET is willing to do a lot of the work for you. The trick of the second approach is to call an overloaded version of the DrawString method that takes an additional (sixth) parameter: an object of type StringFormat:

C#
```
StringFormat format = new StringFormat();
```

VB
```
Dim format As New StringFormat()
```

You now set the Alignment and LineAlignment properties of the StringFormat object to set the horizontal and vertical alignment of the text you will display. These properties take one of the StringAlignment enumerated values: Center, Far, and Near. Center will center the text as you'd expect. The Near value specifies that the text is aligned near the origin, while the far value specifies that the text is displayed far from the origin. In a left-to-right layout, the near position is left and the far position is right.

```
format.Alignment = StringAlignment.Center;
format.LineAlignment = StringAlignment.Center;
```

You are now ready to display the string:

```
g.DrawString(i.ToString(), font, brush, -x, -y,format);
```

The StringFormat object takes care of aligning your characters, and your clock face is no longer lopsided.

Adding the Hands

Now it's time to add the hour and minute hands to the clock. You will also implement the second "hand" as a ball that will rotate around the circumference of the clock. To see this work, add a timer to update the time every second. Also add the button that switches between the 24- and 12-hour clock.

The complete source code is provided in Examples 10-9 and 10-10. A detailed analysis follows.

Example 10-9. Clock face 2 in C#

```
using System;
using System.Collections;
using System.ComponentModel;
using System.Data;
using System.Drawing;
using System.Drawing.Drawing2D;
using System.Timers;
using System.Windows.Forms;


namespace Clock2CS
{
    // Summary description for Form1.
    public class Form1 : System.Windows.Forms.Form
    {
        // Required designer variable.
        private System.ComponentModel.Container components = null;

        private int FaceRadius = 450;    // size of the clock face
        private bool b24Hours = false;   // 24 hour clock face?

        private System.Windows.Forms.Button btnClockFormat;
        private DateTime currentTime;       // used in more than one method

        public Form1( )
        {
            // Required for Windows Form Designer support
            InitializeComponent( );

            // use the user's choice of colors
            BackColor = SystemColors.Window;
            ForeColor = SystemColors.WindowText;

            // update the clock by timer
            System.Timers.Timer timer = new System.Timers.Timer( );
            timer.Elapsed += new System.Timers.ElapsedEventHandler(OnTimer);
            timer.Interval = 500;
            timer.Enabled = true;
        }

        protected override void OnPaint ( PaintEventArgs e )
        {
            base.OnPaint(e);
            Graphics g = e.Graphics;
            SetScale(g);
            DrawFace(g);
```

Example 10-9. Clock face 2 in C# (continued)

```
       DrawTime(g,true);    // force an update
    }

    // every time the timer event fires, update the clock
    public void OnTimer(Object source, ElapsedEventArgs e)
    {
       Graphics g = this.CreateGraphics( );

       SetScale(g);
       DrawFace(g);
       DrawTime(g,false);
       g.Dispose( );

    }


    #region Windows Form Designer generated code
    #endregion

    [STAThread]
    static void Main( )
    {
       Application.Run(new Form1( ));
    }

    private void SetScale(Graphics g)
    {
       // if the form is too small, do nothing
       if ( Width == 0 || Height == 0 )
          return;

       // set the origin at the center
       g.TranslateTransform(Width/2, Height/2);

       // set inches to the minimum of the width
       // or height dividedby the dots per inch
       float inches = Math.Min(Width / g.DpiX, Height / g.DpiX);

       // set the scale to a grid of 2000 by 2000 units
       g.ScaleTransform(
          inches * g.DpiX / 2000, inches * g.DpiY / 2000);
    }

    private void DrawFace(Graphics g)
    {
       // numbers are in forecolor except flash number in green
       // as the seconds go by.
       Brush brush = new SolidBrush(ForeColor);
       Font font = new Font("Arial", 40);
       float x, y;

       // new code
       int numHours = b24Hours ? 24 : 12;
```

Example 10-9. Clock face 2 in C# (continued)

```
        int deg = 360 / numHours;

        // for each of the hours on the clock face
        for (int i = 1; i <= numHours; i++)
        {
            // i = hour  30 degrees = offset per hour
            // +90 to make 12 straight up
            x = GetCos(i*deg + 90) * FaceRadius;
            y = GetSin(i*deg + 90) * FaceRadius;

            StringFormat format = new StringFormat( );
            format.Alignment = StringAlignment.Center;
            format.LineAlignment = StringAlignment.Center;

            g.DrawString(
                i.ToString( ), font, brush, -x, -y,format);

        }   // end for loop
    }       // end drawFace


    private void DrawTime(Graphics g, bool forceDraw)
    {

        //  length of the hands
        float hourLength = FaceRadius * 0.5f;
        float minuteLength = FaceRadius * 0.7f;
        float secondLength = FaceRadius * 0.9f;

        // set to back color to erase old hands first
        Pen hourPen = new Pen(BackColor);
        Pen minutePen = new Pen(BackColor);
        Pen secondPen = new Pen(BackColor);

        // set the arrow heads
        hourPen.EndCap = LineCap.ArrowAnchor;
        minutePen.EndCap = LineCap.ArrowAnchor;

        // hour hand is thicker
        hourPen.Width = 30;
        minutePen.Width = 20;

        // second hand
        Brush secondBrush = new SolidBrush(BackColor);
        const int EllipseSize = 50;

        GraphicsState state;    // to protect and to serve


        // Step 1.  Delete the old time

        // delete the old second hand
        // figure out how far around to rotate to draw the second hand
```

Example 10-9. Clock face 2 in C# (continued)

```csharp
// save the current state, rotate, draw and then restore the
// state
float rotation = GetSecondRotation();
state = g.Save();
g.RotateTransform(rotation);
g.FillEllipse(
   secondBrush,
   -(EllipseSize/2),
   -secondLength,
   EllipseSize,
   EllipseSize);
g.Restore(state);

DateTime newTime = DateTime.Now;
bool newMin = false;    // has the minute changed?

// if the minute has changed, set the flag
if ( newTime.Minute != currentTime.Minute )
   newMin = true;


// if the minute has changed or you must draw anyway then you
// must first delete the old minute and hour hand
if ( newMin  || forceDraw )
{

   // figure out how far around to rotate to draw the minute hand
   // save the current state, rotate, draw and then
   // restore the state
   rotation = GetMinuteRotation();
   state = g.Save();
   g.RotateTransform(rotation);
   g.DrawLine(minutePen,0,0,0,-minuteLength);
   g.Restore(state);

   // figure out how far around to rotate to draw the hour hand
   // save the current state, rotate, draw and then
   // restore the state
   rotation = GetHourRotation();
   state = g.Save();
   g.RotateTransform(rotation);
   g.DrawLine(hourPen,0,0,0,-hourLength);
   g.Restore(state);
}

// step 2 - draw the new time
currentTime = newTime;

hourPen.Color = Color.Red;
minutePen.Color = Color.Blue;
secondPen.Color = Color.Green;
secondBrush = new SolidBrush(Color.Green);
```

Example 10-9. Clock face 2 in C# (continued)

```csharp
            // draw the new second hand
            // figure out how far around to rotate to draw the second hand
            // save the current state, rotate, draw and then restore the
            // state
            state = g.Save( );
            rotation = GetSecondRotation( );
            g.RotateTransform(rotation);
            g.FillEllipse(
                secondBrush,
                -(EllipseSize/2),
                -secondLength,
                EllipseSize,
                EllipseSize);
            g.Restore(state);

            // if the minute has changed or you must draw anyway then you
            // must draw the new minute and hour hand
            if ( newMin || forceDraw )
            {

                // figure out how far around to rotate to draw the minute hand
                // save the current state, rotate, draw and then
                // restore the state
                state = g.Save( );
                rotation = GetMinuteRotation( );
                g.RotateTransform(rotation);
                g.DrawLine(minutePen,0,0,0,-minuteLength);
                g.Restore(state);

                // figure out how far around to rotate to draw the hour hand
                // save the current state, rotate, draw and then
                // restore the state
                state = g.Save( );
                rotation = GetHourRotation( );
                g.RotateTransform(rotation);
                g.DrawLine(hourPen,0,0,0,-hourLength);
                g.Restore(state);
            }
        }

        // determine the rotation to draw the hour hand
        private float GetHourRotation( )
        {
            // degrees depend on 24 vs. 12 hour clock
            float deg = b24Hours ? 15 : 30;
            float numHours = b24Hours ? 24 : 12;
            return( 360f * currentTime.Hour / numHours +
                deg * currentTime.Minute / 60f);
        }

        private float GetMinuteRotation( )
        {
```

Example 10-9. Clock face 2 in C# (continued)

```csharp
            return( 360f * currentTime.Minute / 60f );
        }

        private float GetSecondRotation( )
        {
            return(360f * currentTime.Second / 60f);
        }

        private static float GetSin(float degAngle)
        {
            return (float) Math.Sin(Math.PI * degAngle / 180f);
        }

        private static float GetCos(float degAngle)
        {
            return (float) Math.Cos(Math.PI * degAngle / 180f);
        }

        private void btnClockFormat_Click(object sender, System.EventArgs e)
        {
            btnClockFormat.Text = b24Hours ? "24 Hour" : "12 Hour";
            b24Hours = ! b24Hours;
            this.Invalidate( );

        }

    }   // end class
}       // end namespace
```

Example 10-10. Clock face 2 in VB.NET

```vbnet
Imports System
Imports System.Collections
Imports System.ComponentModel
Imports System.Data
Imports System.Drawing
Imports System.Drawing.Drawing2D
Imports System.Timers
Imports System.Windows.Forms

Namespace ClockFace1


    Public Class Form1
        Inherits System.Windows.Forms.Form

        Private FaceRadius As Integer = 450 ' size of the clock face
        Private b24Hours As Boolean = False ' 24 hour clock face?
        Private currentTime As DateTime
        Private WithEvents btnClockFormat as Button
```

Example 10-10. Clock face 2 in VB.NET (continued)

```vb
Public Sub New( )
    MyBase.New( )

    'This call is required by the Windows Form Designer.
    InitializeComponent( )
    ' use the user's choice of colors
    BackColor = SystemColors.Window
    ForeColor = SystemColors.WindowText

    ' redraw when resized
    Me.ResizeRedraw = True

    ' update the clock by timer
    Dim timer As New System.Timers.Timer( )
    AddHandler timer.Elapsed, AddressOf OnTimer
    timer.Interval = 500
    timer.Enabled = True
End Sub


' every time the timer event fires, update the clock
Public Sub OnTimer( _
   ByVal source As Object, ByVal e As ElapsedEventArgs)
    Dim g As Graphics = Me.CreateGraphics( )

    SetScale(g)
    DrawFace(g)
    DrawTime(g, False)
    g.Dispose( )
End Sub 'OnTimer

#Region " Windows Form Designer generated code "
#End Region

Protected Overrides Sub OnPaint(ByVal e As PaintEventArgs)
    MyBase.OnPaint(e)
    Dim g As Graphics = e.Graphics
    SetScale(g)
    DrawFace(g)
    DrawTime(g, True) ' force an update
End Sub 'OnPaint

Private Sub SetScale(ByVal g As Graphics)
    ' if the form is too small, do nothing
    If Width = 0 Or Height = 0 Then
        Return
    End If
    ' set the origin at the center
    g.TranslateTransform(Width / 2, Height / 2)

    ' set inches to the minimum of the width or height divided
    ' by the dots per inch
```

Example 10-10. Clock face 2 in VB.NET (continued)

```vb
            Dim inches As Single = _
              Math.Min(Width / g.DpiX, Height / g.DpiX)

            ' set the scale to a grid of 2000 by 2000 units
            g.ScaleTransform(inches * g.DpiX / 2000, _
                  inches * g.DpiY / 2000)
        End Sub 'SetScale


        Private Sub DrawFace(ByVal g As Graphics)
            ' numbers are in forecolor except flash number in green
            ' as the seconds go by.
            Dim brush = New SolidBrush(ForeColor)
            Dim font As New Font("Arial", 40)
            Dim x, y As Single

            Dim numHours As Integer
            If b24Hours Then
                numHours = 24
            Else
                numHours = 12
            End If
            Dim deg As Integer = 360 / numHours
            Const FaceRadius As Integer = 450

            ' for each of the hours on the clock face
            Dim i As Integer
            For i = 1 To numHours
                ' i = hour  30 degrees = offset per hour
                ' +90 to make 12 straight up
                x = GetCos((i * deg + 90)) * FaceRadius
                y = GetSin((i * deg + 90)) * FaceRadius

                Dim format As New StringFormat( )
                format.Alignment = StringAlignment.Center
                format.LineAlignment = StringAlignment.Center

                g.DrawString(i.ToString( ), font, brush, -x, -y, format)
            Next i
        End Sub 'DrawFace

        Private Sub DrawTime( _
            ByVal g As Graphics, ByVal forceDraw As Boolean)

            ' length of the hands
            Dim hourLength As Single = FaceRadius * 0.5F
            Dim minuteLength As Single = FaceRadius * 0.7F
            Dim secondLength As Single = FaceRadius * 0.9F

            ' set to back color to erase old hands first
            Dim hourPen As New Pen(BackColor)
```

Example 10-10. Clock face 2 in VB.NET (continued)

VB

```
Dim minutePen As New Pen(BackColor)
Dim secondPen As New Pen(BackColor)

' set the arrow heads
hourPen.EndCap = LineCap.ArrowAnchor
minutePen.EndCap = LineCap.ArrowAnchor

' hour hand is thicker
hourPen.Width = 30
minutePen.Width = 20

' second hand is in green
Dim secondBrush = New SolidBrush(BackColor)
Const EllipseSize As Single = 50

Dim rotation As Single ' how far around the circle?
Dim state As GraphicsState ' to to protect and to serve
Dim newTime As DateTime = DateTime.Now
Dim newMin As Boolean = False ' has the minute changed?
' if the minute has changed, set the flag
If newTime.Minute <> currentTime.Minute Then
    newMin = True
End If
' 1 - delete the old time
' delete the old second hand
' figure out how far around to rotate to draw the second hand
' save the current state, rotate, draw and then
' restore the state
rotation = GetSecondRotation()
state = g.Save()
g.RotateTransform(rotation)
g.FillEllipse( _
    secondBrush, _
    -(EllipseSize / 2), _
    -secondLength, _
    EllipseSize, _
    EllipseSize)
g.Restore(state)

' if the minute has changed or you must draw anyway then you
' must first delete the old minute and hour hand
If newMin Or forceDraw Then

    ' how far around to rotate to draw the minute hand
    ' save the current state, rotate, draw and then
    ' restore the state
    rotation = GetMinuteRotation()
    state = g.Save()
    g.RotateTransform(rotation)
    g.DrawLine(minutePen, 0, 0, 0, -minuteLength)
    g.Restore(state)
```

Example 10-10. Clock face 2 in VB.NET (continued)

```
                    ' figure out how far around to rotate to draw the
                    ' hour hand save the current state, rotate, draw and then
                    ' restore the state
                    rotation = GetHourRotation( )
                    state = g.Save( )
                    g.RotateTransform(rotation)
                    g.DrawLine(hourPen, 0, 0, 0, -hourLength)
                    g.Restore(state)
            End If

            ' step 2 - draw the new time
            currentTime = newTime

            hourPen.Color = Color.Red
            minutePen.Color = Color.Blue
            secondPen.Color = Color.Green
            secondBrush = New SolidBrush(Color.Green)

            ' draw the new second hand
            ' figure out how far around to rotate to draw the second hand
                ' save the current state, rotate, draw and then
                ' restore the state
            state = g.Save( )
            rotation = GetSecondRotation( )
            g.RotateTransform(rotation)
            g.FillEllipse( _
                secondBrush, _
                -(EllipseSize / 2), _
                -secondLength, _
                EllipseSize, _
                EllipseSize)
            g.Restore(state)

            ' if the minute has changed or you must draw anyway then you
            ' must draw the new minute and hour hand
            If newMin Or forceDraw Then

                ' how far around to rotate to draw the minute hand
                ' save the current state, rotate, draw and then
                ' restore the state
                state = g.Save( )
                rotation = GetMinuteRotation( )
                g.RotateTransform(rotation)
                g.DrawLine(minutePen, 0, 0, 0, -minuteLength)
                g.Restore(state)

                ' figure out how far around to rotate to draw the hour hand
                ' save the current state, rotate, draw and then
                ' restore the state
                state = g.Save( )
                rotation = GetHourRotation( )
                g.RotateTransform(rotation)
```

Example 10-10. Clock face 2 in VB.NET (continued)

```
VB
                g.DrawLine(hourPen, 0, 0, 0, -hourLength)
                g.Restore(state)
            End If
    End Sub 'DrawTime


    ' determine the rotation to draw the hour hand
    Private Function GetHourRotation( ) As Single
        ' degrees depend on 24 vs. 12 hour clock
        Dim deg As Single
        Dim numHours As Single
        If b24Hours Then
            deg = 15
            numHours = 24
        Else
            deg = 30
            numHours = 12
        End If

        Return 360.0F * currentTime.Hour / _
          numHours + deg * currentTime.Minute / 60.0F
    End Function 'GetHourRotation


    Private Function GetMinuteRotation( ) As Single
        Return 360.0F * currentTime.Minute / 60.0F
    End Function 'GetMinuteRotation


    Private Function GetSecondRotation( ) As Single
        Return 360.0F * currentTime.Second / 60.0F
    End Function 'GetSecondRotation


    Private Shared Function GetSin(ByVal degAngle As Single) As Single
        Return CSng(Math.Sin((Math.PI * degAngle / 180.0F)))
    End Function 'GetSin


    Private Shared Function GetCos(ByVal degAngle As Single) As Single
        Return CSng(Math.Cos((Math.PI * degAngle / 180.0F)))
    End Function 'GetCos

    Private Sub btnClockFormat_Click( _
      ByVal sender As System.Object, _
      ByVal e As System.EventArgs) _
      Handles btnClockFormat.Click

        If b24Hours Then
            btnClockFormat.Text = "24 Hours"
            b24Hours = False
        Else
```

Example 10-10. Clock face 2 in VB.NET (continued)

```
                btnClockFormat.Text = "12 Hours"
                b24Hours = True
            End If

        Me.Invalidate()

    End Sub
    End Class 'Form1
End Namespace
```

Creating the timer

One of the most significant changes in this version of the program is the use of a timer to tick off the seconds. You instantiate the timer in the constructor:

```
    System.Timers.Timer timer = new System.Timers.Timer();
```

```
    Dim timer As New System.Timers.Timer()
```

Set its event handler by passing in the name of the method you want called when the interval you'll specify has elapsed:

```
    timer.Elapsed += new System.Timers.ElapsedEventHandler(OnTimer);
```

```
    AddHandler timer.Elapsed, AddressOf OnTimer
```

The interval is set in milliseconds; in this case you'll update the timer every 500 milliseconds (every half second):

```
    timer.Interval = 500;
```

Finally, kick off the timer by enabling it:

```
    timer.Enabled = true;
```

Implementing OnTimer. The event handler you've passed to the timer's Elapsed event is OnTimer(). The implementation of OnTimer is similar to that of OnPaint: set the scale, draw the face, and then draw the hands. The latter operation occurs in a new method named DrawTime, discussed next:

```
    public void OnTimer(Object source, ElapsedEventArgs e)
    {
        Graphics g = this.CreateGraphics();

        SetScale(g);
        DrawFace(g);
        DrawTime(g,false);

        g.Dispose();
    }
```

```
Public Sub OnTimer( _
    ByVal source As Object, ByVal e As ElapsedEventArgs)
    Dim g As Graphics = Me.CreateGraphics( )

    SetScale(g)
    DrawFace(g)
    DrawTime(g, False)

    g.Dispose( )
End Sub 'OnTimer
```

The key difference between OnTimer and OnPaint is that the EventArgs structure passed to OnTimer does not have a Graphics object. You'll get one from the form by calling CreateGraphics (highlighted in the code snippet).

This Graphics object then invokes the same methods invoked in OnPaint. When you are done with the Graphics object obtained by CreateGraphics, you must dispose of it through a call to its Dispose method (also highlighted in the snippet).

DrawTime method

After OnTimer calls DrawFace, it calls DrawTime (OnPaint has been modified to call DrawTime as well). DrawTime is responsible for drawing the hands on the clock to correspond to the current time.

In the DrawTime method, you will first delete the hands from their current positions and then draw them in their new positions. You will draw the hands as lines and put an arrow at the end of the line to simulate an old fashioned clock's hand. Deleting the hands is accomplished by drawing the hands with a brush set to the color of the background (thus making them invisible).

Drawing the hands

You will draw the hands of the clock with a Pen object. The Pen class has properties and methods, described previously in Table 10-9.

Pass the pen to a drawing method, and that method determines how long a line to draw and what direction to draw in. The line you draw will have the Color, Width, and other characteristics you set with the Pen's properties.

The EndCap property is of type LineCap, an enumeration listed in Table 10-12. In addition to the ArrowAnchor used in these examples, you can chose to create a Round, Square, Triangle, or Flat line cap, or you can create a RoundAnchor, Square-Anchor, or NoAnchor.

You instantiate a Pen with a color as follows:

```
Pen myPen = new Pen(Color.Red);
```

```
dim myPen as new Pen(Color.Red)
```

Deleting the existing line. Now that you have the necessary tools in hand, it is time to update the clock face. First, delete the hands from their old position. Start by creating three pens, one each to draw the hour, minute, and second hands. Each pen will use the background color:

```
Pen hourPen = new Pen(BackColor);
Pen minutePen = new Pen(BackColor);
Pen secondPen = new Pen(BackColor);
```

```
Dim hourPen As New Pen(BackColor)
Dim minutePen As New Pen(BackColor)
Dim secondPen As New Pen(BackColor)
```

Next, set the hour and minute pen to use an ArrowAnchor:

```
hourPen.EndCap = LineCap.ArrowAnchor;
minutePen.EndCap = LineCap.ArrowAnchor;
```

and set the width of the hour and minute pens:

```
hourPen.Width = 30;
minutePen.Width = 20;
```

You do not need to set the EndCap or Width of the second hand because you'll just draw a dot for the second hand (shown below). What you do need for drawing the second hand, however, is a brush:

```
Brush secondBrush = new SolidBrush(BackColor);
```

```
Dim secondBrush = New SolidBrush(BackColor)
```

Begin by deleting the second hand. To do so, you must determine the position in which to draw the second hand. Here you'll use an interesting approach. Rather than computing the x,y location of the second hand, assume that the second hand is always at 12 o'clock. How can this work? The answer is to rotate the world around the center of the clock face.

Picture a simple clock face with an x,y grid superimposed on it, as shown in Figure 10-8.

One way to draw a second hand at 2 o'clock is to compute the x,y coordinates of 2 o'clock (as you did when drawing the clock face). An alternative approach is to rotate the clock the appropriate number of degrees, and then draw the second hand straight up.

One way to think about this is to picture the clock face and a ruler, as shown in Figure 10-9. You can move the ruler to the right angle, or you can keep the ruler straight up and down and rotate the clock face under it. In the next example, use this second technique to draw the hands of the clock.

Create a method GetSecondRotation() to return a floating-point number, indicating how much the "paper" should be turned.

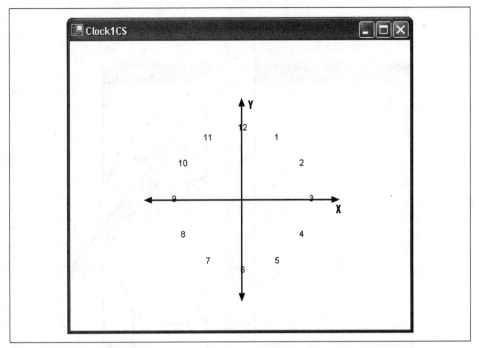

Figure 10-8. Drawing the clock face

```
float rotation = GetSecondRotation();
```

```
Dim rotation As Single
rotation = GetSecondRotation()
```

The helper method GetSecondRotation uses the current time member field. Notice that the currentTime field has not yet been updated, so it has the same "current time" that you had when you drew the hands.

Divide the current second by 60 (60 seconds per minute), and then multiply by 360 (360 degrees in a circle). For example, at 15 seconds past the minute, GetSecondRotation() will return 90 because 360 * 15 / 60 = 90.

```
private float GetSecondRotation()
{
    return(360f * currentTime.Second / 60f);
}
```

```
Private Function GetSecondRotation() As Single
    Return 360.0F * currentTime.Second / 60.0F
End Function 'GetSecondRotation
```

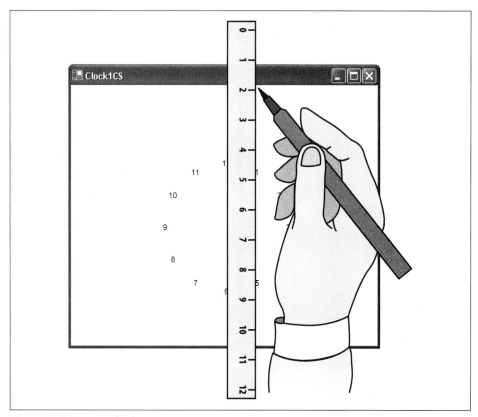

Figure 10-9. Paper and ruler

RotateTransform

You now know how much you want to rotate the world (i.e., rotate the paper under the ruler) to draw the second hand. The steps are:

1. Save the current state of the Graphics object

2. Rotate the world

3. Draw the second hand

4. Restore the state of the Graphics object

It is as if you spin your paper, draw the dot, and then spit it back to the way it was. The code snippet you need to accomplish this is (the VB.NET is virtually identical):

```
state = g.Save();
g.RotateTransform(rotation);
//...do stuff here
g.Restore(state);
```

The transform method for rotating the world is called RotateTransform, and it takes a single argument: the number of degrees to rotate.

FillElipse

The method you'll use to draw the dot representing the second hand is *FillElipse*. This method of the Graphics object is overloaded; the version used here takes five parameters:

- The brush that will determine the color and texture of the ellipse
- The x coordinate of the upper-lefthand corner of the bounding rectangle
- The y coordinate of the upper-lefthand corner of the bounding rectangle
- The width of the bounding rectangle
- The height of the bounding rectangle

You'll use the brush you created earlier, named *secondBrush*. When you are deleting, secondBrush will be set to the background color. When you are drawing the second hand, it will be set to green.

The x and y coordinates of the second hand are determined so that the second hand is straight up from the origin, centered on the y axis (remember, you've turned the paper under the ruler. Now you should draw along the ruler).

The y coordinate is easy; you'll use the constant you've defined for the length of the second hand. Remember, however, that in this world, the y coordinates are negative above the origin, and since you want to draw straight up to 12 o'clock, you must use a negative value.

The x coordinate is just a bit trickier. The premise was that you'd just draw straight up, along the y axis. Unfortunately, this will place the upper-lefthand corner of the bounding rectangle along the y axis, and you'll want to center the ellipse on the y axis. You thus pass an x coordinate that is half the size of the bounding rectangle (e.g., 25) and set that negative so that the ball will be centered on the y axis.

Since you want your ellipse to be circular, the bounding rectangle will be square, with each side set to 50:

```csharp
const int EllipseSize = 50;
state = g.Save( );
rotation = GetSecondRotation( );
g.RotateTransform(rotation);
g.FillEllipse(
    secondBrush,
    -(EllipseSize/2),
    -secondLength,
    EllipseSize,
    EllipseSize);
g.Restore(state);
```

```vbnet
Const EllipseSize As Single = 50
state = g.Save( )
rotation = GetSecondRotation( )
```

```vb
        g.RotateTransform(rotation)
        g.FillEllipse( _
            secondBrush, _
            -(EllipseSize / 2), _
            -secondLength, _
            EllipseSize, _
            EllipseSize)
        g.Restore(state)
```

Having drawn the second hand, go on to draw the minute and hour hand. If you redraw them both every second, however, the clock face flickers annoyingly. Therefore, redraw these two hands only if the minute has changed. To test this, compare the new time with the old time and determine whether the minute value has changed:

```csharp
        DateTime newTime = DateTime.Now;
        bool newMin = false;   // has the minute changed?

        if ( newTime.Minute != currentTime.Minute )
            newMin = true;
```

```vb
        Dim newTime As DateTime = DateTime.Now
        Dim newMin As Boolean = False ' has the minute changed?

        If newTime.Minute <> currentTime.Minute Then
            newMin = True
        End If
```

You can then test the newMin Boolean value before updating the minute and hour hands:

```csharp
        if ( newMin  || forceDraw )
        {
            // draw the minute and hour hands
        }
```

```vb
        If newMin Or forceDraw Then
            ' draw the minute and hour hands
        End If
```

The test is that *either* the minute has changed or the forceDraw parameter passed into the DrawTime method is true. This allows onPaint to ensure that the hands are drawn on a repaint by calling DrawTime and passing in true for the Boolean value.

The implementation of drawing the minute and hour hands is nearly identical to that for drawing the second hand. This time, however, rather than drawing an ellipse, you actually draw a line. You do so with the DrawLine method of the Graphics object, passing in a pen and four integer values.

The first two values represent the x,y coordinates of the origin of the line, and the second set of two values represent the x,y coordinates of the end of the line. In each

---

case, the origin of the line will be the center of the clock face, 0,0. The x coordinate of the end of the line will be 0 because you'll draw along the y axis. The y coordinate of the end of the line will be the length of the hour hand. Once again, because the y coordinates are negative above the origin, you'll pass it as a negative number.

The length of the hour and minute hands are defined at the top of the method, as is the distance from the origin for the ellipse representing the second hand:

```
float hourLength = FaceRadius * 0.5f;
float minuteLength = FaceRadius * 0.7f;
float secondLength = FaceRadius * 0.9f;
```

 You may notice that you are drawing the line along the y axis (as you might run a pen along a ruler) rather than centered on the y axis. This keeps the code a bit simpler, but you are free to determine the width of the line and then to offset the drawing by that amount. This is left as an exercise for the obsessive-compulsive reader.

If the minute has advanced (or if forceDraw is true), you will determine the rotation for the minute, save the state of the Graphics object, rotate the world, draw the line, and restore the state of the Graphics object. You can then do the same thing for the hour hand:

```
if ( newMin  || forceDraw )
{
    rotation = GetMinuteRotation( );
    state = g.Save( );
    g.RotateTransform(rotation);
    g.DrawLine(minutePen,0,0,0,-minuteLength);
    g.Restore(state);

    rotation = GetHourRotation( );
    state = g.Save( );
    g.RotateTransform(rotation);
    g.DrawLine(hourPen,0,0,0,-hourLength);
    g.Restore(state);
}
```

```
If newMin Or forceDraw Then
    rotation = GetMinuteRotation( )
    state = g.Save( )
    g.RotateTransform(rotation)
    g.DrawLine(minutePen, 0, 0, 0, -minuteLength)
    g.Restore(state)

    rotation = GetHourRotation( )
    state = g.Save( )
    g.RotateTransform(rotation)
    g.DrawLine(hourPen, 0, 0, 0, -hourLength)
    g.Restore(state)
End If
```

The two helper methods, GetMinuteRotation and GetHourRotation, simply determine the degrees to rotate the world for the current minute and hour. GetMinuteRotation is simple, it multiplies the 360 degrees of the clock by the current minute and divides by 60 (60 minutes in an hour):

C#
```
private float GetMinuteRotation()
{
   return( 360f * currentTime.Minute / 60f );
}
```

VB
```
Private Function GetMinuteRotation() As Single
      Return 360.0F * currentTime.Minute / 60.0F
End Function
```

The GetHourRotation method is more complicated because in this version you may have set the face to 24 hour mode, and the angle for the hour hand will be different if there are 24 hours around the clock face rather than 12.

Each hour will be 30 degrees from the previous hour if the clock face has 12 hours, or 15 degrees if the clock face has 24. To get the angle for the hour, multiply 360 by the current hour and divide by the number of hours (12 or 24) on the clock face.

You should also move the hour hand a bit more to allow for the number of minutes past the hour. For example, at 12:30 the hour hand should be halfway between the 12 and the 1.

To accomplish this adjustment, add another rotation computed by multiplying the number of degrees between hours (15 or 30) by the current number of minutes past the hour and dividing by 60:

C#
```
private float GetHourRotation()
{
   float deg = b24Hours ? 15 : 30;
   float numHours = b24Hours ? 24 : 12;
   return( 360f * currentTime.Hour / numHours +
      deg * currentTime.Minute / 60f);
}
```

VB
```
Private Function GetHourRotation() As Single
      Dim deg As Single
      Dim numHours As Single
      If b24Hours Then
            deg = 15
            numHours = 24
      Else
            deg = 30
            numHours = 12
      End If

      Return 360.0F * currentTime.Hour / _
         numHours + deg * currentTime.Minute / 60.0F
End Function 'GetHourRotation
```

Drawing the new time

Once you've done all the work shown so far, you've drawn the second hand, the minute hand, and the hour hand in the background color, effectively erasing them. Next, set the currentTime variable to the new time, and set the pen and brush colors to the colors you want to draw:

```
currentTime = newTime

hourPen.Color = Color.Red
minutePen.Color = Color.Blue
secondPen.Color = Color.Green
secondBrush = New SolidBrush(Color.Green)
```

You are now ready to redraw these hands using the same technique shown above: save the state, rotate, draw the hand, and restore the state.

Notice the use of the Boolean variable newMin. Here's why it is required.

Imagine that you test the time when you are ready to erase the hands, but it is not a new minute. You thus do not erase the minute and hour hands, but test the time again when it is time to draw the hands with their correct colors. You might have just passed the minute mark, and now the minute values for current time and new time would be different, and you would draw the new hands without having erased them first. Suddenly the minute and hour hands get fatter.

You can avoid this bug by setting the newMin Boolean variable before erasing, and then using that Boolean when redrawing.

Implementing the 24 hour clock button

The event handler for the 24 hour clock button is straightforward: it toggles the b24Hour Boolean member variable and toggles the text. Finally, it invalidates the form so the clock is redrawn:

```
private void btnClockFormat_Click(object sender, System.EventArgs e)
{
    btnClockFormat.Text = b24Hours ? "24 Hour" : "12 Hour";
    b24Hours = ! b24Hours;
    this.Invalidate( );
}
```

```
Private Sub btnClockFormat_Click( _
    ByVal sender As System.Object, _
    ByVal e As System.EventArgs) _
    Handles btnClockFormat.Click

    If b24Hours Then
        btnClockFormat.Text = "24 Hours"
        b24Hours = False
```

```
        Else
            btnClockFormat.Text = "12 Hours"
            b24Hours = True
        End If

        Me.Invalidate()

    End Sub
```

The only remaining change you need to make to the code is to update the DrawFace method to draw either the 24 hour or the 12 hour clock face:

```csharp
private void DrawFace(Graphics g)
{
    Brush brush = new SolidBrush(ForeColor);
    Font font = new Font("Arial", 40);
    float x, y;

    int numHours = b24Hours ? 24 : 12;
    int deg = 360 / numHours;

    for (int i = 1; i <= numHours; i++)
    {
        x = GetCos(i*deg + 90) * FaceRadius;
        y = GetSin(i*deg + 90) * FaceRadius;

        StringFormat format = new StringFormat();
        format.Alignment = StringAlignment.Center;
        format.LineAlignment = StringAlignment.Center;

        g.DrawString(
            i.ToString(), font, brush, -x, -y,format);

    }
}
```

```vb
Private Sub DrawFace(ByVal g As Graphics)
    Dim brush = New SolidBrush(ForeColor)
    Dim font As New Font("Arial", 40)
    Dim x, y As Single

    Dim numHours As Integer
    If b24Hours Then
        numHours = 24
    Else
        numHours = 12
    End If
    Dim deg As Integer = 360 / numHours
    Const FaceRadius As Integer = 450

    ' for each of the hours on the clock face
    Dim i As Integer
    For i = 1 To numHours
```

```
        x = GetCos((i * deg + 90)) * FaceRadius
        y = GetSin((i * deg + 90)) * FaceRadius

        Dim format As New StringFormat( )
        format.Alignment = StringAlignment.Center
        format.LineAlignment = StringAlignment.Center

        g.DrawString(i.ToString( ), font, brush, -x, -y, format)
    Next i
End Sub 'DrawFace
```

The new code is shown in bold. The trick is to set the numHours variable to 12 or 24, based on the value of the member variable b24Hours. You then set the deg variable based on dividing the 360 degrees in the circle by the number of hours you are showing on the clock face. Then compute the Sin and Cosine value accordingly.

Drawing the Animated Date

In the third and final version of the program, you will add code to draw the date around the clock face and animate it. While you're at it, you'll also let the user click on the form to create a new center: by moving the clock's center to the location of the mouse when the user left-clicks. The complete source is shown in Examples 10-11 and 10-12.

Example 10-11. Final version clock face (CS)

```
using System;
using System.Collections;
using System.ComponentModel;
using System.Data;
using System.Drawing;
using System.Drawing.Drawing2D;
using System.Timers;
using System.Windows.Forms;


namespace Clock3CS
{
    // Rename the class
    public class ClockFace : System.Windows.Forms.Form
    {
        // Required designer variable.
        private System.ComponentModel.Container components = null;

        private int FaceRadius = 450;        // size of the clock face
        private bool b24Hours = false;        // 24 hour clock face?
        private System.Windows.Forms.Button btnClockFormat;
        private DateTime currentTime;        // used in more than one method

        // new
        private int xCenter;                 // center of the clock
        private int yCenter;
        private static int DateRadius = 600; // outer circumference for date
```

Example 10-11. Final version clock face (CS) (continued)

```
private static int Offset = 0;        // for moving the text
Font font = new Font("Arial", 40);    // use the same font throughout
private StringDraw sdToday;           // the text to animate

public ClockFace( )
{
    // Required for Windows Form Designer support
    InitializeComponent( );

    // use the user's choice of colors
    BackColor = SystemColors.Window;
    ForeColor = SystemColors.WindowText;


    // *** begin new
    string today = System.DateTime.Now.ToLongDateString( );
    today = " " + today.Replace(",","");

    // create a new stringdraw object with today's date
    sdToday = new StringDraw(today,this);
    currentTime = DateTime.Now;


    // set the current center based on the
    // client area
    xCenter = Width / 2;
    yCenter = Height / 2;


    // *** end new


    // update the clock by timer
    System.Timers.Timer timer = new System.Timers.Timer( );
    timer.Elapsed += new System.Timers.ElapsedEventHandler(OnTimer);
    timer.Interval = 5;  // shorter interval - more movement
    timer.Enabled = true;


}

protected override void OnPaint ( PaintEventArgs e )
{
    base.OnPaint(e);
    Graphics g = e.Graphics;
    SetScale(g);
    DrawFace(g);
    DrawTime(g,true);    // force an update
}

// every time the timer event fires, update the clock
public void OnTimer(Object source, ElapsedEventArgs e)
```

Example 10-11. Final version clock face (CS) (continued)

C#

```
    {
        Graphics g = this.CreateGraphics();

        SetScale(g);
        DrawFace(g);
        DrawTime(g,false);
        DrawDate(g);
        g.Dispose();

    }


    #region Windows Form Designer generated code
    #endregion

    [STAThread]
    static void Main()
    {
        Application.Run(new ClockFace());
    }

    private void SetScale(Graphics g)
    {
        // if the form is too small, do nothing
        if ( Width == 0 || Height == 0 )
            return;

        // set the origin at the center
        g.TranslateTransform(xCenter, yCenter);   // use the members vars

        // set inches to the minimum of the width
        // or height dividedby the dots per inch
        float inches = Math.Min(Width / g.DpiX, Height / g.DpiX);

        // set the scale to a grid of 2000 by 2000 units
        g.ScaleTransform(
            inches * g.DpiX / 2000, inches * g.DpiY / 2000);
    }

    private void DrawFace(Graphics g)
    {
        // numbers are in forecolor except flash number in green
        // as the seconds go by.
        Brush brush = new SolidBrush(ForeColor);
        float x, y;

        // new code
        int numHours = b24Hours ? 24 : 12;
        int deg = 360 / numHours;

        // for each of the hours on the clock face
        for (int i = 1; i <= numHours; i++)
```

Example 10-11. Final version clock face (CS) (continued)

```csharp
    {
        // i = hour  30 degrees = offset per hour
        // +90 to make 12 straight up
        x = GetCos(i*deg + 90) * FaceRadius;
        y = GetSin(i*deg + 90) * FaceRadius;

        StringFormat format = new StringFormat( );
        format.Alignment = StringAlignment.Center;
        format.LineAlignment = StringAlignment.Center;

        g.DrawString(
            i.ToString( ), font, brush, -x, -y,format);

    }    // end for loop
}        // end drawFace


private void DrawTime(Graphics g, bool forceDraw)
{

    //  length of the hands
    float hourLength = FaceRadius * 0.5f;
    float minuteLength = FaceRadius * 0.7f;
    float secondLength = FaceRadius * 0.9f;

    // set to back color to erase old hands first
    Pen hourPen = new Pen(BackColor);
    Pen minutePen = new Pen(BackColor);
    Pen secondPen = new Pen(BackColor);

    // set the arrow heads
    hourPen.EndCap = LineCap.ArrowAnchor;
    minutePen.EndCap = LineCap.ArrowAnchor;

    // hour hand is thicker
    hourPen.Width = 30;
    minutePen.Width = 20;

    // second hand
    Brush secondBrush = new SolidBrush(BackColor);
    const int EllipseSize = 50;

    GraphicsState state;    // to to protect and to serve


    // 1 - delete the old time

    // delete the old second hand
    // figure out how far around to rotate to draw the second hand
    // save the current state, rotate, draw and then restore the state
    float rotation = GetSecondRotation( );
    state = g.Save( );
```

Example 10-11. Final version clock face (CS) (continued)

```csharp
                g.RotateTransform(rotation);
                g.FillEllipse(
                    secondBrush,
                    -(EllipseSize/2),
                    -secondLength,
                    EllipseSize,
                    EllipseSize);
                g.Restore(state);

                DateTime newTime = DateTime.Now;
                bool newMin = false;    // has the minute changed?

                // if the minute has changed, set the flag
                if ( newTime.Minute != currentTime.Minute )
                    newMin = true;


                // if the minute has changed or you must draw anyway then you
                // must first delete the old minute and hour hand
                if ( newMin  || forceDraw )
                {

                    // figure out how far around to rotate to draw the minute hand
                    // save the current state, rotate, draw and
                    // then restore the state
                    rotation = GetMinuteRotation( );
                    state = g.Save( );
                    g.RotateTransform(rotation);
                    g.DrawLine(minutePen,0,0,0,-minuteLength);
                    g.Restore(state);

                    // figure out how far around to rotate to draw the hour hand
                    // save the current state, rotate, draw and
                    // then restore the state
                    rotation = GetHourRotation( );
                    state = g.Save( );
                    g.RotateTransform(rotation);
                    g.DrawLine(hourPen,0,0,0,-hourLength);
                    g.Restore(state);
                }

                // step 2 - draw the new time
                currentTime = newTime;

                hourPen.Color = Color.Red;
                minutePen.Color = Color.Blue;
                secondPen.Color = Color.Green;
                secondBrush = new SolidBrush(Color.Green);

                // draw the new second hand
                // figure out how far around to rotate to draw the second hand
                // save the current state, rotate, draw and then restore the state
```

Example 10-11. Final version clock face (CS) (continued)

```
         state = g.Save( );
         rotation = GetSecondRotation( );
         g.RotateTransform(rotation);
         g.FillEllipse(
            secondBrush,
            -(EllipseSize/2),
            -secondLength,
            EllipseSize,
            EllipseSize);
         g.Restore(state);

         // if the minute has changed or you must draw anyway then you
         // must draw the new minute and hour hand
         if ( newMin || forceDraw )
         {

            // figure out how far around to rotate to draw the minute hand
            // save the current state, rotate, draw and
            // then restore the state
            state = g.Save( );
            rotation = GetMinuteRotation( );
            g.RotateTransform(rotation);
            g.DrawLine(minutePen,0,0,0,-minuteLength);
            g.Restore(state);

            // figure out how far around to rotate to draw the hour hand
            // save the current state, rotate, draw and
            // then restore the state
            state = g.Save( );
            rotation = GetHourRotation( );
            g.RotateTransform(rotation);
            g.DrawLine(hourPen,0,0,0,-hourLength);
            g.Restore(state);
         }
      }

      // determine the rotation to draw the hour hand
      private float GetHourRotation( )
      {
         // degrees depend on 24 vs. 12 hour clock
         float deg = b24Hours ? 15 : 30;
         float numHours = b24Hours ? 24 : 12;
         return( 360f * currentTime.Hour / numHours +
            deg * currentTime.Minute / 60f);
      }

      private float GetMinuteRotation( )
      {
         return( 360f * currentTime.Minute / 60f );
      }

      private float GetSecondRotation( )
      {
```

Example 10-11. Final version clock face (CS) (continued)

```
                return(360f * currentTime.Second / 60f);
             }

        private static float GetSin(float degAngle)
        {
            return (float) Math.Sin(Math.PI * degAngle / 180f);
        }

        private static float GetCos(float degAngle)
        {
            return (float) Math.Cos(Math.PI * degAngle / 180f);
        }

        private void btnClockFormat_Click(object sender, System.EventArgs e)
        {
            btnClockFormat.Text = b24Hours ? "24 Hour" : "12 Hour";
            b24Hours = ! b24Hours;
            this.Invalidate();
        }

        private void DrawDate(Graphics g)
        {
            Brush brush = new SolidBrush(ForeColor);
            sdToday.DrawString(g,brush);
        }

        private void ClockFace_MouseDown(
            object sender, System.Windows.Forms.MouseEventArgs e)
        {
            xCenter = e.X;
            yCenter = e.Y;
            this.Invalidate();


        }


        // each letter in the outer string knows how to draw itself
        private class LtrDraw
        {
            char myChar;        // the actual letter i draw
            float x;            // current x coordinate
            float y;            // current y coordinate
            float oldx;          // old x coordinate (to delete)
            float oldy;          // old y coordinate (to delete)


            // constructor
            public LtrDraw(char c)
            {
                myChar = c;
            }
```

Example 10-11. Final version clock face (CS) (continued)

```
       // property for X coordinate
       public float X
       {
          get { return x; }
          set { oldx = x; x = value; }
       }

       // property for Y coordinate
       public float Y
       {
          get { return y; }
          set { oldy = y; y = value; }
       }

       // get total width of the string
       public float GetWidth(Graphics g, Font font)
       {
          SizeF stringSize = g.MeasureString(myChar.ToString( ),font);
          return stringSize.Width;
       }

       // get total height of the string
       public float GetHeight(Graphics g, Font font)
       {
          SizeF stringSize = g.MeasureString(myChar.ToString( ),font);
          return stringSize.Height;
       }


       // get the font from the control and draw the current character
       // First delete the old and then draw the new
       public void DrawString(Graphics g, Brush brush, ClockFace cf)
       {
          Font font = cf.font;
          Brush blankBrush = new SolidBrush(cf.BackColor);
          g.DrawString(myChar.ToString( ),font,blankBrush,oldx,oldy);
          g.DrawString(myChar.ToString( ),font,brush,x,y);
       }

    }

    // holds an array of LtrDraw objects
    // and knows how to tell them to draw
    private class StringDraw
    {
       ArrayList theString = new ArrayList( );
       LtrDraw l;
       ClockFace theControl;

       // constructor takes a string, populates the array
       // and stashes away the calling control (ClockFace)
       public StringDraw(string s, ClockFace theControl)
```

Example 10-11. Final version clock face (CS) (continued)

```csharp
        {
            this.theControl = theControl;
            foreach (char c in s)
            {
                l = new LtrDraw(c);
                theString.Add(l);
            }
        }

        // divide the circle by the number of letters
        // and draw each letter in position
        public void DrawString(Graphics g, Brush brush)
        {
            int angle = 360 / theString.Count;
            int counter = 0;

            foreach (LtrDraw theLtr in theString)
            {
                // 1. To find the X coordinate, take the Cosine of the angle
                // and multiply by the radius.
                // 2. To compute the angle, start with the base angle
                // (360 divided by the number of letters)
                // and multiply by letter position.
                // Thus if each letter is 10 degrees, and this is the third
                // letter, you get 30 degrees.
                // Add 90 to start at 12 O'clock.
                // Each time through, subtract the clockFace offset to move
                // the entire string around the clock on each timer call
                float newX = GetCos(
                    angle  * counter + 90 -
                        ClockFace.Offset) * ClockFace.DateRadius ;
                float newY = GetSin(
                    angle * counter + 90 -
                    ClockFace.Offset) * ClockFace.DateRadius ;
                theLtr.X =
                    newX - (theLtr.GetWidth(g,theControl.font) / 2);
                theLtr.Y =
                    newY - (theLtr.GetHeight(g,theControl.font) / 2);
                counter++;
                theLtr.DrawString(g,brush,theControl);
            }
            ClockFace.Offset += 1;  // rotate the entire string
        }
    }
}   // end class
}       // end namespace
```

Example 10-12. Final version clock face (VB.NET)

```vbnet
Imports System
Imports System.Collections
Imports System.ComponentModel
Imports System.Data
```

Example 10-12. Final version clock face (VB.NET) (continued)

```vb
Imports System.Drawing
Imports System.Drawing.Drawing2D
Imports System.Timers
Imports System.Windows.Forms

Namespace Clock3VB

    Public Class ClockFace
        Inherits System.Windows.Forms.Form

        Private FaceRadius As Integer = 450 ' size of the clock face
        Private b24Hours As Boolean = False ' 24 hour clock face?
        Private currentTime As DateTime ' used in more than one method
        ' new
        Private xCenter As Integer ' center of the clock
        Private yCenter As Integer
        ' outer circumference for date
        Private Shared DateRadius As Integer = 600
        Private Shared offset As Integer = 0 ' for moving the text
        ' use the same font throughout
        Private myFont As New font("Arial", 40)
        Private sdToday As StringDraw

        Public Sub New()
            ' Required for Windows Form Designer support
            InitializeComponent()

            ' use the user's choice of colors
            BackColor = SystemColors.Window
            ForeColor = SystemColors.WindowText


            ' *** begin new code
            Dim today As String = System.DateTime.Now.ToLongDateString()
            today = " " + today.Replace(",", "")

            ' create a new stringdraw object with today's date
            sdToday = New StringDraw(today, Me)
            currentTime = DateTime.Now


            ' set the current center based on the
            ' client area
            xCenter = Width / 2
            yCenter = Height / 2


            ' *** end new code

            ' update the clock by timer
            Dim timer As New System.Timers.Timer()
            AddHandler timer.Elapsed, AddressOf OnTimer
```

Example 10-12. Final version clock face (VB.NET) (continued)

```vbnet
        timer.Interval = 5 ' shorter interval - more movement
        timer.Enabled = True
    End Sub 'New



    ' every time the timer event fires, update the clock
    Public Sub OnTimer( _
      ByVal source As Object, ByVal e As ElapsedEventArgs)
        Dim g As Graphics = Me.CreateGraphics( )

        SetScale(g)
        DrawFace(g)
        DrawTime(g, False)
        DrawDate(g)
        g.Dispose( )
    End Sub 'OnTimer

#Region " Windows Form Designer generated code "

#End Region
    Protected Overrides Sub OnPaint(ByVal e As PaintEventArgs)
        myBase.OnPaint(e)
        Dim g As Graphics = e.Graphics
        SetScale(g)
        DrawFace(g)
        DrawTime(g, True) ' force an update
    End Sub 'OnPaint

    Private Sub SetScale(ByVal g As Graphics)
        ' if the form is too small, do nothing
        If Width = 0 Or Height = 0 Then
            Return
        End If
        ' set the origin at the center
        g.TranslateTransform(xCenter, yCenter) ' use the members vars
        ' set inches to the minimum of the width
        ' or height dividedby the dots per inch
        Dim inches As Single = _
          Math.Min(Width / g.DpiX, Height / g.DpiX)

        ' set the scale to a grid of 2000 by 2000 units
        g.ScaleTransform( _
          inches * g.DpiX / 2000, inches * g.DpiY / 2000)
    End Sub 'SetScale


    Private Sub DrawFace(ByVal g As Graphics)
        ' numbers are in forecolor except flash number in green
        ' as the seconds go by.
```

Example 10-12. Final version clock face (VB.NET) (continued)

```vb
            Dim brush = New SolidBrush(ForeColor)
            Dim x, y As Single

            ' new code

            Dim numHours As Integer
            If (b24Hours) Then
                numHours = 24
            Else
                numHours = 12
            End If

            Dim deg As Integer = 360 / numHours

            ' for each of the hours on the clock face
            Dim i As Integer
            For i = 1 To numHours
                ' i = hour  30 degrees = offset per hour
                ' +90 to make 12 straight up
                x = GetCos((i * deg + 90)) * FaceRadius
                y = GetSin((i * deg + 90)) * FaceRadius

                Dim format As New StringFormat( )
                format.Alignment = StringAlignment.Center
                format.LineAlignment = StringAlignment.Center

                g.DrawString(i.ToString( ), myFont, brush, -x, -y, format)
            Next i
    End Sub 'DrawFace

    ' end for loop
    ' end drawFace

    Private Sub DrawTime( _
        ByVal g As Graphics, ByVal forceDraw As Boolean)

        ' length of the hands
        Dim hourLength As Single = FaceRadius * 0.5F
        Dim minuteLength As Single = FaceRadius * 0.7F
        Dim secondLength As Single = FaceRadius * 0.9F

        ' set to back color to erase old hands first
        Dim hourPen As New Pen(BackColor)
        Dim minutePen As New Pen(BackColor)
        Dim secondPen As New Pen(BackColor)

        ' set the arrow heads
        hourPen.EndCap = LineCap.ArrowAnchor
        minutePen.EndCap = LineCap.ArrowAnchor

        ' hour hand is thicker
        hourPen.Width = 30
        minutePen.Width = 20
```

Example 10-12. Final version clock face (VB.NET) (continued)

```
' second hand
Dim secondBrush = New SolidBrush(BackColor)
Const EllipseSize As Integer = 50
Dim halfEllipseSize As Integer = EllipseSize / 2

Dim state As GraphicsState ' to to protect and to serve

' 1 - delete the old time
' delete the old second hand
' figure out how far around to rotate to draw the second hand
' save the current state, rotate, draw
' and then restore the state
Dim rotation As Single = GetSecondRotation()
state = g.Save()
g.RotateTransform(rotation)

g.FillEllipse( _
     secondBrush, -(halfEllipseSize), _
     -secondLength, EllipseSize, EllipseSize)
g.Restore(state)

Dim newTime As DateTime = DateTime.Now
Dim newMin As Boolean = False ' has the minute changed?
' if the minute has changed, set the flag
If newTime.Minute <> currentTime.Minute Then
    newMin = True
End If

' if the minute has changed or you must draw anyway then you
' must first delete the old minute and hour hand
If newMin Or forceDraw Then

    ' figure out how far around to rotate to
    ' draw the minute hand
    ' save the current state, rotate, draw
    ' and then restore the state
    rotation = GetMinuteRotation()
    state = g.Save()
    g.RotateTransform(rotation)
    g.DrawLine(minutePen, 0, 0, 0, -minuteLength)
    g.Restore(state)

    ' figure out how far around to rotate to draw the hour hand
    ' save the current state, rotate, draw
    ' and then restore the state
    rotation = GetHourRotation()
    state = g.Save()
    g.RotateTransform(rotation)
    g.DrawLine(hourPen, 0, 0, 0, -hourLength)
    g.Restore(state)
End If
```

Example 10-12. Final version clock face (VB.NET) (continued)

```vb
        ' step 2 - draw the new time
        currentTime = newTime

        hourPen.Color = Color.Red
        minutePen.Color = Color.Blue
        secondPen.Color = Color.Green
        secondBrush = New SolidBrush(Color.Green)

        ' draw the new second hand
        ' figure out how far around to rotate to draw the second hand
        ' save the current state, rotate, draw
        ' and then restore the state
        state = g.Save()
        rotation = GetSecondRotation()
        g.RotateTransform(rotation)
        g.FillEllipse( _
          secondBrush, -(halfEllipseSize), _
          -secondLength, EllipseSize, EllipseSize)
        g.Restore(state)

        ' if the minute has changed or you must draw anyway then you
        ' must draw the new minute and hour hand
        If newMin Or forceDraw Then

            ' figure out how far around to rotate to
            ' draw the minute hand
            ' save the current state, rotate, draw
            ' and then restore the state
            state = g.Save()
            rotation = GetMinuteRotation()
            g.RotateTransform(rotation)
            g.DrawLine(minutePen, 0, 0, 0, -minuteLength)
            g.Restore(state)

            ' figure out how far around to rotate to draw the hour hand
            ' save the current state, rotate, draw
            ' and then restore the state
            state = g.Save()
            rotation = GetHourRotation()
            g.RotateTransform(rotation)
            g.DrawLine(hourPen, 0, 0, 0, -hourLength)
            g.Restore(state)
        End If
    End Sub 'DrawTime


    ' determine the rotation to draw the hour hand
    Private Function GetHourRotation() As Single
        ' degrees depend on 24 vs. 12 hour clock
        Dim deg As Single
        Dim numHours As Single
        If (b24Hours) Then
```

Example 10-12. Final version clock face (VB.NET) (continued)

`VB`

```
            deg = 15
            numHours = 24
        Else
            deg = 30
            numHours = 12
        End If
        Return 360.0F * currentTime.Hour / _
          numHours + deg * currentTime.Minute / 60.0F
    End Function 'GetHourRotation


    Private Function GetMinuteRotation( ) As Single
        Return 360.0F * currentTime.Minute / 60.0F
    End Function 'GetMinuteRotation


    Private Function GetSecondRotation( ) As Single
        Return 360.0F * currentTime.Second / 60.0F
    End Function 'GetSecondRotation


    Private Shared Function GetSin(ByVal degAngle As Single) As Single
        Return CSng(Math.Sin((Math.PI * degAngle / 180.0F)))
    End Function 'GetSin


    Private Shared Function GetCos(ByVal degAngle As Single) As Single
        Return CSng(Math.Cos((Math.PI * degAngle / 180.0F)))
    End Function 'GetCos


    Private Sub btnClockFormat_Click( _
        ByVal sender As System.Object, _
        ByVal e As System.EventArgs) _
        Handles btnClockFormat.Click
        If (b24Hours) Then
            btnClockFormat.Text = "24 Hour"
        Else
            btnClockFormat.Text = "12 Hour"
        End If
        b24Hours = Not b24Hours
        Me.Invalidate( )
    End Sub 'btnClockFormat_Click


    Private Sub DrawDate(ByVal g As Graphics)
        Dim brush = New SolidBrush(ForeColor)
        sdToday.DrawString(g, brush)
    End Sub 'DrawDate
```

Example 10-12. Final version clock face (VB.NET) (continued)

```vb
Private Sub ClockFace_MouseDown( _
  ByVal sender As Object, _
  ByVal e As System.Windows.Forms.MouseEventArgs) _
  Handles MyBase.MouseDown
    xCenter = e.X
    yCenter = e.Y
    Me.Invalidate( )
End Sub 'ClockFace_MouseDown

  _


' each letter in the outer string knows how to draw itself
Private Class LtrDraw
    Private myChar As Char ' the actual letter i draw
    Private _x As Single ' current x coordinate
    Private _y As Single ' current y coordinate
    Private oldx As Single ' old x coordinate (to delete)
    Private oldy As Single
    ' old y coordinate (to delete)

    ' constructor
    Public Sub New(ByVal c As Char)
        myChar = c
    End Sub 'New

    ' property for X coordinate

    Public Property X( ) As Single
        Get
            Return _x
        End Get
        Set(ByVal Value As Single)
            oldx = _x
            _x = Value
        End Set
    End Property
    ' property for Y coordinate

    Public Property Y( ) As Single
        Get
            Return _y
        End Get
        Set(ByVal Value As Single)
            oldy = _y
            _y = Value
        End Set
    End Property

    ' get total width of the string
    Public Function GetWidth( _
        ByVal g As Graphics, ByVal myFont As Font) As Single
        Dim stringSize As SizeF = _
```

Example 10-12. Final version clock face (VB.NET) (continued)

```
                    g.MeasureString(myChar.ToString( ), myFont)
              Return stringSize.Width
        End Function 'GetWidth



         ' get total height of the string
         Public Function GetHeight( _
             ByVal g As Graphics, ByVal myFont As Font) As Single
             Dim stringSize As SizeF = _
                g.MeasureString(myChar.ToString( ), myFont)
             Return stringSize.Height
         End Function 'GetHeight



         ' get the font from the control and draw the current character
         ' First delete the old and then draw the new
         Public Sub DrawString( _
           ByVal g As Graphics, ByVal brush As Brush, _
           ByVal ctrl As ClockFace)
             Dim myFont As Font = ctrl.myFont
             Dim blankBrush = New SolidBrush(ctrl.BackColor)
             g.DrawString( _
                myChar.ToString( ), myFont, blankBrush, oldx, oldy)
             g.DrawString(myChar.ToString( ), myFont, brush, X, Y)
        End Sub 'DrawString
     End Class 'LtrDraw

     _

     ' holds an array of LtrDraw objects
     ' and knows how to tell them to draw
     Private Class StringDraw
         Private theString As New ArrayList( )
         Private l As LtrDraw
         Private theControl As ClockFace



         ' constructor takes a string, populates the array
         ' and stashes away the calling control (ClockFace)
         Public Sub New( _
             ByVal s As String, ByVal theControl As ClockFace)
             Me.theControl = theControl
             Dim c As Char
             For Each c In s
                 l = New LtrDraw(c)
                 theString.Add(l)
             Next c
         End Sub 'New



         ' divide the circle by the number of letters
         ' and draw each letter in position
```

Example 10-12. Final version clock face (VB.NET) (continued)

```
Public Sub DrawString( _
    ByVal g As Graphics, ByVal brush As Brush)
    Dim angle As Integer = 360 / theString.Count
    Dim counter As Integer = 0

    Dim theLtr As LtrDraw
    For Each theLtr In theString
        ' 1. To find the X coordinate,
        ' take the Cosine of the angle
        ' and multiply by the radius.
        ' 2. To compute the angle, start with the base angle
        ' (360 divided by the number of letters)
        ' and multiply by letter position.
        ' Thus if each letter is 10 degrees,
        ' and this is the third
        ' letter, you get 30 degrees.
        ' Add 90 to start at 12 O'clock.
        ' Each time through, subtract the clockFace
        ' offset to move the entire string around
        ' the clock on each timer call
        Dim newX As Single = _
            GetCos((angle * counter + 90 - ClockFace.offset)) _
            * ClockFace.DateRadius
        Dim newY As Single = _
            GetSin((angle * counter + 90 - ClockFace.offset)) _
            * ClockFace.DateRadius
        theLtr.X = newX - _
            theLtr.GetWidth(g, theControl.myFont) / 2
        theLtr.Y = newY - _
            theLtr.GetHeight(g, theControl.myFont) / 2
        counter += 1
        theLtr.DrawString(g, brush, theControl)
    Next theLtr
    ClockFace.offset += 1 ' rotate the entire string
End Sub 'DrawString
        End Class 'StringDraw
    End Class 'ClockFace
End Namespace 'Clock3CS ' end class
```

Animating the string

In the previous examples, you saw two ways to manage drawing text at a specific location. In the first, you determined the x,y coordinates and then used the Draw-String method to draw the characters at that location (clock face). In the second, you rotated the world a set rotation, and then used DrawString to draw each text character to a specific location (e.g., centered on the y axis, a fixed distance from the origin, as seen when using DrawTime).

In the next example, however, you want the date to move around the clock face, and more importantly, you want the letters to act as cars on a Ferris Wheel, maintaining their up-down orientation as they rotate around the center.

Ferris Wheel

The Ferris Wheel was invented by George W. Ferris, a bridge builder from Pittsburgh, Pennsylvania, and shown at the 1893 World's Columbian Exposition in Chicago. The original wheel was supported by twin steel towers, each standing 140 feet tall; its 45 foot axel was the largest piece of forged steel in the world. The wheel was 250 feet in diameter, and its circumference was 825 feet. It stood 264 feet in the air and was powered by two 1,000 horsepower engines. The wheel had 36 wooden cars, each capable of holding 60 people, keeping them upright at all times. Over 1.5 million people rode the original Ferris Wheel at the Chicago fair.

The LtrDraw class. To accomplish this design goal, each letter in the date will be encapsulated by an instance of the LtrDraw class that you will define. The LtrDraw class will be used only by methods of ClockFace, so LtrDraw will be declared as a nested class within the ClockFace class.

```
public class ClockFace : System.Windows.Forms.Form
{
    //…
    private class LtrDraw
    {
        // …
    }           // end nested class
}               // end outer class
```

This class will have, as member variables, both the character you want to draw and the x,y coordinates of where to draw it. In fact, the LtrDraw instance will know two sets of x,y coordinates: where the letter was (so you can erase the old letter) and where it is (so you can draw the letter in its new location):

```
private class LtrDraw
{
    char myChar;
    float x;
    float y;
    float oldx;
    float oldy;
```

```
Private Class LtrDraw
    Private myChar As Char
    Private _x As Single
    Private _y As Single
    Private oldx As Single
    Private oldy As Single
```

The LtrDraw constructor initializes the myChar member variable:

C#
```csharp
public LtrDraw(char c)
{
   myChar = c;
}
```

VB
```vb
Public Sub New(ByVal c As Char)
      myChar = c
End Sub 'New
```

The x,y coordinates are accessed through properties. The get accessor just returns the member variable's value, but the set accessor first stores the current value in the oldx/oldy members:

C#
```csharp
public float X
{
   get { return x; }
   set { oldx = x; x = value; }
}

public float Y
{
   get { return y; }
   set { oldy = y; y = value; }
}
```

VB
```vb
Public Property X() As Single
      Get
            Return _x
      End Get
      Set(ByVal Value As Single)
            oldx = _x
            _x = Value
      End Set
End Property

Public Property Y() As Single
      Get
            Return _y
      End Get
      Set(ByVal Value As Single)
            oldy = _y
            _y = Value
      End Set
End Property
```

The LtrDraw class also provides methods that return the letter's Width and Height. These two methods delegate the actual measurement to the MeasureString method of the Graphics object, passing in the character the object holds in the myChar member variable and the font that is passed in to the method:

```
public float GetWidth(Graphics g, Font font)
{
    SizeF stringSize = g.MeasureString(myChar.ToString(),font);
    return stringSize.Width;
}
public float GetHeight(Graphics g, Font font)
{
    SizeF stringSize = g.MeasureString(myChar.ToString(),font);
    return stringSize.Height;
}
```

```
Public Function GetWidth( _
    ByVal g As Graphics, ByVal myFont As Font) As Single
    Dim stringSize As SizeF = _
        g.MeasureString(myChar.ToString( ), myFont)
    Return stringSize.Width
End Function 'GetWidth


' get total height of the string
Public Function GetHeight( _
    ByVal g As Graphics, ByVal myFont As Font) As Single
    Dim stringSize As SizeF = _
        g.MeasureString(myChar.ToString( ), myFont)
    Return stringSize.Height
End Function 'GetHeight
```

Finally, the LtrDraw class knows how to draw the letter via the DrawString method, given a Brush and a reference to the ClockFace object:

```
public void DrawString(Graphics g, Brush brush, ClockFace cf)
{
```

The first task is to get a reference to the font held by the ClockFace as a member variable:

```
Font font = cf.font;
```

Next, create a blank brush and use it to delete the character from its old position:

```
Brush blankBrush = new SolidBrush(cf.BackColor);
g.DrawString(myChar.ToString( ),font,blankBrush,oldx,oldy);
```

Finally, you are ready to draw the character in the new position, using the font you've extracted from the ClockFace and the brush you were given:

```
g.DrawString(myChar.ToString( ),font,brush,x,y);
}
```

```
Public Sub DrawString( _
    ByVal g As Graphics, ByVal brush As Brush, ByVal ctrl As ClockFace)
    Dim myFont As Font = ctrl.myFont
    Dim blankBrush = New SolidBrush(ctrl.BackColor)
```

```
VB        g.DrawString(myChar.ToString( ), myFont, blankBrush, oldx, oldy)
          g.DrawString(myChar.ToString( ), myFont, brush, X, Y)
      End Sub 'DrawString
```

The StringDraw class. The LtrDraw class encapsulates a single letter. For the entire
string, create a collection class to hold an array of LtrDraw objects. The StringDraw
class uses an ArrayList to allow you to build up an array of LtrDraw objects and it
holds a reference to the ClockFace object. StringDraw will be a nested class within
ClockFace as well:

```
C#    private class StringDraw
      {
          ArrayList theString = new ArrayList( );
          LtrDraw l;
          ClockFace theControl;
```

```
VB        Private Class StringDraw
              Private theString As New ArrayList( )
              Private l As LtrDraw
              Private theControl As ClockFace
```

Use the member variable l, the reference to a LtrDraw object, in the constructor to
create instances of LtrDraw that you can add to the collection:

```
C#    public StringDraw(string s, ClockFace theControl)
      {
          this.theControl = theControl;
          foreach (char c in s)
          {
            l = new LtrDraw(c);
            theString.Add(l);
          }
      }
```

```
VB    Public Sub New(ByVal s As String, ByVal theControl As ClockFace)
          Me.theControl = theControl
          Dim c As Char
          For Each c In s
              l = New LtrDraw(c)
              theString.Add(l)
          Next c
      End Sub 'New
```

You are passed a string and a reference to a ClockFace object. Stash the reference in
the member variable theControl. Then treat the string as an array of characters, and
iterate through the array using the foreach (for each) construct. For each letter you
retrieve from the string, create an instance of the LtrDraw class, and then add that
instance to the ArrayList member.

Reusing the LtrDraw reference (l) is safe because a reference to the new object is kept in the ArrayList.

The only method in the StringDraw class is cleverly named DrawString. This method takes two arguments: a Graphics object and a Brush.

C#
```
public void DrawString(Graphics g, Brush brush)
{
```

VB
```
Public Sub DrawString(ByVal g As Graphics, ByVal brush As Brush)
```

This method first sets the angle by which each letter will be separated. Ask the string for the count of characters and use that value to divide the 360 degrees of the circle into equal increments:

C#
```
int angle = 360 / theString.Count;
```

VB
```
Dim angle As Integer = 360 / theString.Count
```

Your job now is to iterate through the members of the ArrayList. For each LtrDraw object, compute the new x and y coordinates.

Do so by multiplying the angle value computed above by what amounts to the i-based index of the letter (that is, 1 for the second letter, 2 for the third, and so forth). Then add 90 to start the string at 12 o'clock (this is not strictly necessary, since the string will rotate around the clock face). Take the cosine of this value (using your old friend GetCos, which converts the angle to radians and then returns the cosine of that angle), and multiply by the constant DateRadius defined in the ClockFace class:

C#
```
float newX =
    GetCos(angle  * counter + 90) * ClockFace.DateRadius ;
```

To make the string move, however, you have one more task. In the ClockFace class, declare a static (shared) member variable named offset. Modify your computation of the angle to subtract this value from the computed angle:

C#
```
float newX =
    GetCos(angle  * counter + 90 - ClockFace.Offset) * ClockFace.DateRadius ;
```

Each time this method is invoked, you'll increment the offset value so that each time you run this method, the string will be drawn using an angle one degree less than the previous time.

You can compute the new y coordinate in much the same way:

C#
```
float newY =
    GetSin(angle * counter + 90 - ClockFace.Offset) * ClockFace.DateRadius ;
```

```vb
Dim newX As Single = _
    GetCos((angle * counter + 90 - ClockFace.offset)) _
    * ClockFace.DateRadius
Dim newY As Single = _
    GetSin((angle * counter + 90 - ClockFace.offset)) _
    * ClockFace.DateRadius
```

Once again, however, you've computed the upper-lefthand corner of the bounding rectangle for the character you are going to draw. To center the character at this location, you must compute the width and height of the character and adjust your coordinates accordingly:

C#

```csharp
theLtr.X =
    newX - (theLtr.GetWidth(g,theControl.font) / 2);
theLtr.Y =
    newY - (theLtr.GetHeight(g,theControl.font) / 2);
```

That accomplished, increment the counter:

C#

```csharp
counter++;
```

VB

```vb
counter += 1
```

and you are ready to tell the LtrDraw object to draw itself:

```csharp
theLtr.DrawString(g,brush,theControl);
```

Once the loop is completed, increment the static Offset member of the ClockFace:

C#

```csharp
ClockFace.Offset += 1;
```

To encourage the date to move around the clock face quickly and smoothly, change the timer interval from 500 milliseconds to 50 milliseconds. Do this in the constructor, where you'll make a few other changes as well, shown below.

New member variables. Before examining the constructor, you'll need to add six new member variables.

The xCenter and yCenter variables will hold the x and y coordinates of the center of the clock.

C#

```csharp
private int xCenter;
private int yCenter;
```

You previously computed these values by dividing the width and height of the form by 2 (dividing in half), and that is how you'll compute the initial values for xCenter and yCenter as well, as you'll see in the new code in the constructor, below.

You'll add a new static value for the radius of the date string and add the static value Offset, discussed above:

C#

```csharp
private static int DateRadius = 600;
private static int Offset = 0;
```

Because you want to use the same font in many places, make the font a member variable of the ClockFace class:

```
C#   Font font = new Font("Arial", 40);
```

Finally, give your ClockFace class an instance of the nested class StringDraw:

```
C#   private StringDraw sdToday;
```

```
VB   Private xCenter As Integer
     Private yCenter As Integer
     Private Shared DateRadius As Integer = 600
     Private Shared offset As Integer = 0
     Private myFont As New font("Arial", 40)
     Private sdToday As StringDraw
```

Modifying the constructor. You are now ready to implement the changes to the Clock-Face constructor. You will instantiate the StringDraw object by passing in two parameters: a string representing the current date and a reference to the current ClockFace object:

```
C#   sdToday = new StringDraw(today,this);
```

```
VB   sdToday = New StringDraw(today, Me)
```

You create the today string by getting the current date from the System.DateTime. Now property, calling the ToLongDateString() method.

```
C#   string today = System.DateTime.Now.ToLongDateString();
```

```
VB   Dim today As String = System.DateTime.Now.ToLongDateString()
```

For aesthetic reasons, remove commas from this string by calling the Replace() method of String:

```
C#   today = " " + today.Replace(",","");
```

The only other changes in the constructor initialize the current time and the x,y coordinates:

```
C#   currentTime = DateTime.Now;
     xCenter = Width / 2;
     yCenter = Height / 2;
```

Resetting the center

You want the user to be able to move the clock by clicking on the form. Use the xCenter and yCenter member variables to change the center of the clock, in response to a mousedown. The event handler will readjust the xCenter and yCenter to the values returned by the X and Y properties of the MouseEventArgs object passed in to the handler:

```
private void ClockFace_MouseDown(
    object sender, System.Windows.Forms.MouseEventArgs e)
{
    xCenter = e.X;
    yCenter = e.Y;
```

Once this is done, call Invalidate() to force a call to Paint():

```
    this.Invalidate();

}
```

```
Private Sub ClockFace_MouseDown( _
    ByVal sender As Object, _
    ByVal e As System.Windows.Forms.MouseEventArgs) _
    Handles MyBase.MouseDown
        xCenter = e.X
        yCenter = e.Y
        Me.Invalidate()
End Sub 'ClockFace_MouseDown
```

CHAPTER 11

Labels and Buttons

Controls are Windows Forms widgets: listboxes, buttons, checkboxes, labels, text boxes, and so forth, that provide a visual user interface for a Windows application.

Previous chapters covered many of the features common to all Windows Forms controls—all members of the System.Windows.Forms.Control class and all objects derived from that class. These features provide all controls with a basic level of functionality, including size, location, appearance, and mouse and keyboard support.

This chapter will describe two of the most basic classes of controls provided as part of the .NET Framework: Label and Button. Virtually all applications use both types of controls. Although they look simple and one dimensional, both classes offer surprising depth and versatility.

Label

A Label control, of the class System.Windows.Forms.Label, displays read-only text on a form. Text controls that provide read/write capability, such as the TextBox and RichTextBox, are described in Chapter 12.

Labels serve several different functions. At the most basic level, they display text on the client area of a form, such as titles, paragraphs, or captions for other controls. The text displayed by a Label is contained in its Text property. The Text property can be either hardcoded (set at design time) or dynamic (set programmatically at runtime).

Several examples presented in Chapter 7 dynamically control the size of a control (a button was used in the examples), based on the Text property of the control and the size of the font for that control. The Label control eases this chore with the AutoSize property. When set to true, the control is automatically resized to display the entire contents of the Text property.

In addition to the properties just mentioned, the Label control has many other properties, the most commonly used of which are listed in Table 11-1.

Table 11-1. Label properties

Property	Value type	Description
AutoSize	Boolean	Read/write. Value indicating that the label will automatically resize to display the entire Text property. Default is `false`. Using both PreferredWidth and PreferredHeight yields the same label size as AutoSize set to `true`.
BackgroundImage	Image	Read/write. The background image displayed on the label.
BorderStyle	BorderStyle	Read/write. The border style for the label. Values are members of the BorderStyle enumeration, listed in Table 11-2. The default value is BorderStyle.None.
FlatStyle	FlatStyle	Read/write. The flat style appearance of the label. Values are members of the FlatStyle enumeration, listed in Table 11-10. The default value is FlatStyle.Standard.
Image	Image	Read/write. The image displayed on the label. Cannot be used for the same control at the same time as the ImageList or ImageIndex properties.
ImageAlign	ContentAlignment	Read/write. Aligns image displayed in the label. Values are members of the ContentAlignment enumeration, listed in Table 11-3. The default value is ContentAlignment.MiddleCenter.
ImageIndex	Integer	Read/write. Zero-based index value of the Image object contained in the ImageList.
ImageList	ImageList	Read/write. The image list that contains the images displayed in the label control. One image is displayed at a time, selected by the ImageIndex property. The ImageList stores a collection of Image objects.
		The ImageList component is described fully in Chapter 7.
PreferredHeight	Integer	Read-only. Returns the height of the label, in pixels, if a single line of text were displayed. The value returned reflects the current font for the label.
PreferredWidth	Integer	Read-only. Returns the width of the label, in pixels, if a single line of text were displayed, assuming no line wrapping. The returned value reflects the current font for the label.
TextAlign	ContentAlignment	Read/write. Aligns text displayed in the label. Values are members of the ContentAlignment enumeration, listed in Table 11-3. The default value is ContentAlignment.TopLeft.
UseMnemonic	Boolean	Read/write. Value indicating if an ampersand (&) character in the label's Text property will be interpreted as an access key character. If `true` (the default), the user can move focus to the control following in the tab order by pressing the Alt key in combination with the access key.

Table 11-2. BorderStyle enumeration values

Value	Description
Fixed3D	3-D border.
FixedSingle	Single-line border.
None	No border.

Table 11-3. ContentAlignment enumeration values

Value	Vertical alignment	Horizontal alignment
BottomCenter	Bottom	Center
BottomLeft	Bottom	Left
BottomRight	Bottom	Right
MiddleCenter	Middle	Center
MiddleLeft	Middle	Left
MiddleRight	Middle	Right
TopCenter	Top	Center
TopLeft	Top	Left
TopRight	Top	Right

Using labels to provide access keys

A Label control also helps provide keyboard navigation through the use of *access keys*. An access key lets you press, for example, Alt-A to go to a control, such as a button, with an underlined A on it. Using a label to create an access key is useful when you need to navigate to a control, such as text box, that does not provide its own access key.

To create an access key, add a Label control to the form, setting its Text property with an ampersand (&) in front of the character to be used as the access key. Set the UseMnemonic property of the Label to true (the default value). Create the target control to which the access key should send focus to, such as a text box. Now set the TabIndex property of Label and its associated target control so that the TabIndex of the target control is one greater than the TabIndex of the Label. This latter step can be done by either setting the TabIndex properties explicitly or creating and adding the Label control to the Controls collection first, immediately followed by the target control.

When the user presses the Alt key in combination with the key after the ampersand, focus will shift to the target control. Examples 11-1 and 11-2 will demonstrate this concept.

Many of the examples used in the book so far have included Label controls; they are rather ubiquitous. The program listed in Example 11-1 (in C#) and Example 11-2 (in VB.NET) demonstrates many of the common uses and properties of labels, borrowing several techniques from previous examples. In these examples, a form is created with three different labels: one is a caption to a TextBox (which gathers user input), the second dynamically displays the contents of that TextBox, and the third displays an image. Also, a set of RadioButtons change the font style of Label, echoing the contents of the TextBox. (Radio buttons are discussed later in this chapter.)

Example 11-1. Label demonstration in C# (labels.cs)

```
using System;
using System.Drawing;
using System.Windows.Forms;

namespace ProgrammingWinApps
{
    public class Labels : Form
    {
        Label lblEcho;
        TextBox txt;

        public Labels( )
        {
            Text = "Labels";
            Size = new Size(300,250);

            lblEcho = new Label( );
            lblEcho.Parent = this;
            lblEcho.Text = "The quick brown fox...";
            lblEcho.Location = new Point(0,0);
            lblEcho.AutoSize = true;
            lblEcho.BorderStyle = BorderStyle.Fixed3D;
            int yDelta = lblEcho.Height + 10;

            Image img = Image.FromFile(
                @"C:\Program Files\Microsoft Visual Studio .NET 2003\Common7\" +
                @"Graphics\bitmaps\assorted\happy.bmp");
            Label lblImage = new Label( );
            lblImage.Parent = this;
            lblImage.Location = new Point(250, 0);
            lblImage.Image = img;
            lblImage.Anchor = AnchorStyles.Top | AnchorStyles.Right;
            lblImage.Size = new Size(img.Width, img.Height);

            Label lblCaption = new Label( );
            lblCaption.Parent = this;
            lblCaption.Text = "&Enter Text Here:";
            lblCaption.Size = new Size(lblCaption.PreferredWidth,
                                       lblCaption.PreferredHeight);
            lblCaption.Location = new Point(0, yDelta);
//   Commented out so border will not hide the underscore
//          lblCaption.BorderStyle = BorderStyle.FixedSingle;

            txt = new TextBox( );
            txt.Parent = this;
            txt.Size = new Size(100,23);
            txt.Location = new Point(lblCaption.Width + 5, yDelta);
            txt.TextChanged += new System.EventHandler(txt_TextChanged);

            FontStyle theEnum = new FontStyle( );
            FontStyle[ ] theStyles =
                (FontStyle[ ])Enum.GetValues(theEnum.GetType( ));
```

Example 11-1. Label demonstration in C# (labels.cs) (continued)

```csharp
        int i = 1;
        foreach (FontStyle style in theStyles)
        {
            RadioButton rdo = new RadioButton( );
            rdo.Parent = this;
            rdo.Location = new Point(25, yDelta * (i + 1));
            rdo.Size = new Size(75,20);
            rdo.Text = style.ToString( );
            rdo.Tag = style;
            rdo.CheckedChanged += new
                System.EventHandler(rdo_CheckedChanged);
            if (rdo.Text == "Regular")
                rdo.Checked = true;
            i++;
        }
    }

    static void Main( )
    {
        Application.Run(new Labels( ));
    }

    private void txt_TextChanged(object sender, EventArgs e)
    {
        lblEcho.Text = txt.Text;
    }

    private void rdo_CheckedChanged(object sender, EventArgs e)
    {
        RadioButton rdo = (RadioButton)sender;
        FontStyle fs = (FontStyle)rdo.Tag;
        lblEcho.Font = new Font(lblEcho.Font, fs);
    }
    }
}
```

Example 11-2. Label demonstration in VB.NET (labels.vb)

```vbnet
Option Strict On
imports System
imports System.Drawing
imports System.Windows.Forms

namespace ProgrammingWinApps
    public class Labels : inherits Form
        dim lblEcho as Label
        dim txt as TextBox

        public sub New( )
            Text = "Labels"
            Size = new Size(300,250)
```

Example 11-2. Label demonstration in VB.NET (labels.vb) (continued)

```VB
        lblEcho = new Label( )
        lblEcho.Parent = me
        lblEcho.Text = "The quick brown fox..."
        lblEcho.Location = new Point(0,0)
        lblEcho.AutoSize = true
        lblEcho.BorderStyle = BorderStyle.Fixed3D
        dim yDelta as integer = lblEcho.Height + 10

        dim img as Image = Image.FromFile( _
          "C:\\Program Files\\Microsoft Visual Studio .NET 2003\\" + _
          "Common7\\Graphics\\bitmaps\\assorted\\happy.bmp")
        dim lblImage as Label = new Label( )
        lblImage.Parent = me
        lblImage.Location = new Point(250, 0)
        lblImage.Image = img
        lblImage.Anchor = AnchorStyles.Top or AnchorStyles.Right
        lblImage.Size = new Size(img.Width, img.Height)

        dim lblCaption as Label = new Label( )
        lblCaption.Parent = me
        lblCaption.Text = "&Enter Text Here:"
        lblCaption.Size = new Size(lblCaption.PreferredWidth, _
                                   lblCaption.PreferredHeight)
        lblCaption.Location = new Point(0, yDelta)
' Commented out so border will not hide the underscore
'
        lblCaption.BorderStyle = BorderStyle.FixedSingle

        txt = new TextBox( )
        txt.Parent = me
        txt.Size = new Size(100,23)
        txt.Location = new Point(lblCaption.Width + 5, yDelta)
        AddHandler txt.TextChanged, AddressOf txt_TextChanged

        dim theEnum as new FontStyle( )
        dim theStyles as FontStyle( ) = CType([Enum].GetValues( _
                     theEnum.GetType( )), FontStyle( ))

        dim i as integer = 1
        dim style as FontStyle
        for each style in theStyles
           dim rdo as RadioButton = new RadioButton( )
           rdo.Parent = me
           rdo.Location = new Point(25, yDelta * (i + 1))
           rdo.Size = new Size(75,20)
           rdo.Text = style.ToString( )
           rdo.Tag = style
           AddHandler rdo.CheckedChanged, AddressOf rdo_CheckedChanged
           if rdo.Text = "Regular" then
              rdo.Checked = true
           end if
           i = i + 1
        next
```

Example 11-2. Label demonstration in VB.NET (labels.vb) (continued)

```vb
        end sub

        public shared sub Main( )
            Application.Run(new Labels( ))
        end sub

        private sub txt_TextChanged(ByVal sender as object, _
                            ByVal e as EventArgs)
            lblEcho.Text = txt.Text
        end sub

        private sub rdo_CheckedChanged(ByVal sender as object, _
                            ByVal e as EventArgs)
            dim rdo as RadioButton  = CType(sender, RadioButton)
            dim fs as FontStyle = CType(rdo.Tag, FontStyle)
            lblEcho.Font = new Font(lblEcho.Font, fs)
        end sub
    end class
end namespace
```

When either program is compiled and run, you get the form shown in Figure 11-1. After entering some text in the TextBox and changing the font style to bold, the form will look like Figure 11-2.

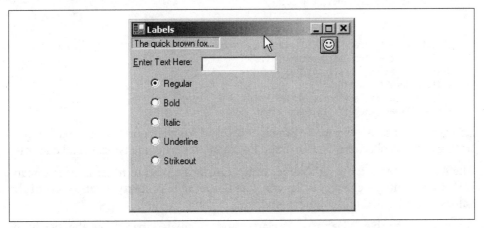

Figure 11-1. Labels program on startup

The first label created in the constructor of the form, lblEcho, echoes the text entered in the TextBox. It and the Textbox are declared as form member variables, and thus can be accessed from any method of the Form class:

```csharp
Label lblEcho;
TextBox txt;
```

```vb
dim lblEcho as Label
dim txt as TextBox
```

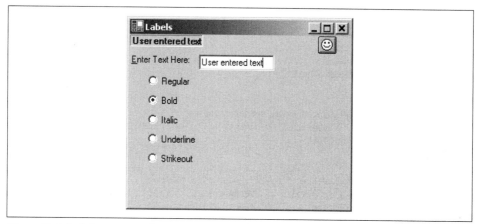

Figure 11-2. Labels program after entering text and changing font style

lblEcho is instantiated in the constructor and its properties are set:

C#
```
lblEcho.Parent = this;
lblEcho.Text = "The quick brown fox...";
lblEcho.Location = new Point(0,0);
lblEcho.AutoSize = true;
lblEcho.BorderStyle = BorderStyle.Fixed3D;
int yDelta = lblEcho.Height + 10;
```

VB
```
lblEcho.Parent = me
lblEcho.Text = "The quick brown fox..."
lblEcho.Location = new Point(0,0)
lblEcho.AutoSize = true
lblEcho.BorderStyle = BorderStyle.Fixed3D
dim yDelta as integer = lblEcho.Height + 10
```

As with all controls, setting the parent property adds the control to the parent control's Controls collection. The Text and Location properties are typical of all controls.

The AutoSize property is set to true, which causes the label to resize itself automatically as its contents changes in length. The BorderStyle property is set to one of the values of the BorderStyle enumeration listed in Table 11-2.

An integer variable, yDelta, is declared and calculated based on the height of lblEcho. This variable will be used later in the program to calculate the vertical position of the other controls.

The next control to be created is lblImage, whose sole purpose here is to display an image. The Image object is created using the FromFile static method of the Image class. The file containing the image used here is hardcoded; it is one of many images that ship with Visual Studio .NET:

C#
```
Image img = Image.FromFile(
    @"C:\Program Files\Microsoft Visual Studio .NET 2003\Common7\" +
    @"Graphics\bitmaps\assorted\happy.bmp");
```

```VB
dim img as Image = Image.FromFile( _
    "C:\\Program Files\\Microsoft Visual Studio .NET 2003\\Common7\\" + _
    "Graphics\\bitmaps\\assorted\\happy.bmp")
```

Notice how a literal string (using the @ sign) is used in the C# version to eliminate the requirement of escaping the backslash characters with a second backslash. This feature is not supported in VB.NET.

The Image property is then set to that Image object:

```VB
lblImage.Image = img
```

The Anchor property is set to a bitwise combination of Top and Right. This keeps the location of the control constant relative to the top and right edges of the form, even if the form is resized by the user. (Anchoring was covered in Chapter 7.)

The Size property of the control is set based on the Width and Height of the Image object it contains.

```VB
lblImage.Size = new Size(img.Width, img.Height)
```

The next control to be declared, instantiated, and have its properties set is lblCaption, a Label control used as a caption for the TextBox that will be created shortly. Notice that the Text property has an ampersand character in front of the letter E. This will cause that letter E to be underlined when the form is displayed, indicating that it is an access key.

```VB
lblCaption.Text = "&Enter Text Here:"
```

When the user presses Alt + E, focus will move to the control immediately following the label in the tab order. In this case, the control would be the TextBox, since it is added to the Controls collection immediately after lblCaption.

If you need to include an ampersand as part of the displayed text, use a second ampersand character to *escape* the first. For example, if the text to be displayed in a label is Cut & Paste, use the following line of code:

```VB
lblCaption.Text = "&Cut && Paste"
```

The Size property is set using the PreferredWidth and PreferredHeight properties of the Label control for the width and height, respectively.

```VB
lblCaption.Size = new Size(lblCaption.PreferredWidth, _
                           lblCaption.PreferredHeight)
```

The Location property uses the yDelta variable calculated earlier for its vertical offset from the upper edge of the form client area.

```VB
lblCaption.Location = new Point(0, yDelta)
```

The BorderStyle property of lblCaption is set to FixedSingle, but commented out. Uncommenting this line of code will show the size of the label clearly and demonstrate what this border looks like. However, it will also hide the underscore character beneath the access key, although the access key will still work as expected.

A TextBox called txt is created next. Chapter 12 will cover TextBoxes in detail. For now, note that the Location property uses the width of lblCaption and the previously calculated value yDelta to correctly place the control relative to the other controls, and an event handler is created to handle the TextChanged event. This latter feature will cause the contents of the TextBox to be echoed by lblEcho:

C#
```
txt.Location = new Point(lblCaption.Width + 5, yDelta);
txt.TextChanged += new System.EventHandler(txt_TextChanged);
```

VB
```
txt.Location = new Point(lblCaption.Width + 5, yDelta)
AddHandler txt.TextChanged, AddressOf txt_TextChanged
```

The event handler method itself is very simple, containing a single line of code that assigns the Text property of the TextBox to the Text property of lblEcho.

VB
```
lblEcho.Text = txt.Text
```

The next section of code is similar to the examples from Chapter 7 that demonstrated the use of the Tag property. In this example, an array of FontStyles is created from the FontStyle enumeration:

C#
```
FontStyle theEnum = new FontStyle();
FontStyle[] theStyles = (FontStyle[])Enum.GetValues(theEnum.GetType());
```

VB
```
dim theEnum as new FontStyle()
dim theStyles as FontStyle() = CType([Enum].GetValues( _
                theEnum.GetType()), FontStyle())
```

This array is then looped through using a foreach (For Each in VB.NET) loop, creating a RadioButton for each member of the enumeration.

You converted the enumeration to an array so you could call foreach on that array. You can iterate through an array, but not through an enumeration.

When the RadioButton is changed, the CheckedChanged event is fired, which is handled by the rdo_CheckedChanged method. This loop and event handler is very similar to Examples 7-13 and 7-14, so the analysis will not be repeated here.

Pay attention to how the FontStyle of the lblEcho label is changed.

VB
```
lblEcho.Font = new Font(lblEcho.Font, fs)
```

The Font.Style property is read-only. In fact, since the Font object is immutable (all of its properties are read-only), the only way to change a Font property is to assign a new Font object based on the existing Font. The Font object has over a dozen different overloaded constructors, which are covered in Chapter 9. The one used here takes an existing Font object as a prototype from which to create the new Font object and a member of the FontStyle enumeration to apply to the new Font.

LinkLabel

Closely related to and derived from the Label control is the LinkLabel control, of the class System.Windows.Forms.LinkLabel, which displays one or more hyperlinks. In addition to the properties and features discussed above for the Label control, the LinkLabel has the properties listed in Table 11-4.

The LinkLabel control does not automatically provide actual linkage to anything, nor, by default, does it change the color of the link once it has been visited, as is done in most browsers. It is easy to add these features, however, with the properties and events of the LinkLabel class, as demonstrated next.

Table 11-4. LinkLabel properties

Property	Value type	Description
ActiveLinkColor	Color	Read/write. The color to display an active link. A link is active while it is clicked. The default color is specified by the system, typically Color.Red.
DisabledLinkColor	Color	Read/write. The color to display a disabled link. Disabled links do not raise the LinkClicked event.
LinkArea	LinkArea	Read/write. The area within the LinkLabel control that represents a hyperlink.
		The Start property of the LinkArea structure is the zero-based index of the character in the LinkLabel Text property representing the start of the link.
		The Length property of the LinkArea structure is the number of characters, including the starting character, comprising the link.
LinkBehavior	LinkBehavior	Read/write. The behavior of the link. The values must be a member of the LinkBehavior enumeration, listed in Table 11-5.
LinkColor	Color	Read/write. The color to display a normal link. The default color is specified by the system, typically Color.Blue.
Links	LinkLabel.LinkCollection	Read-only. Returns the collection of links contained within the LinkLabel.
LinkVisited	Boolean	Read/write. Value indicating if the link should display as though it were visited. Default is false. Does not automatically get set to true; this must be done by code in the LinkClicked event handler.
		Only applies to the first link defined for the control. Use the Visited property of the LinkLabel.Link class for multiple links in a control.
VisitedLinkColor	Color	Read/write. The color to display a link that has been visited previously. The default color is specified by the system, typically Color.Purple.

Table 11-5. LinkBehavior enumeration values

Value	Description
AlwaysUnderline	The link is always displayed with underlined text.
HoverUnderline	The link is displayed with underlined text only when the mouse is hovering over the link.
NeverUnderline	The link text is never underlined. It can be distinguished by using the LinkColor property.
SystemDefault	The link is displayed using the system default.

When a LinkLabel control is clicked, it raises an event called LinkClicked, which has an event argument of type LinkLabelLinkClickedEventArgs. This event argument exposes a single read-only property called Link, which returns the link that was clicked. Several different ways of handling this event will be demonstrated in Example 11-3 (using C#) and Example 11-4 (using VB.NET).

A Links property of the LinkLabel, listed in Table 11-4, is of type LinkLabel.LinkCollection, a sub-class of LinkLabel. This is a collection of all the links contained by the LinkLabel control. As a class in its own right, it exposes several useful properties (listed in Table 11-6) and methods (listed in Table 11-7).

Table 11-6. LinkLabel.LinkCollection properties

Property	Value type	Description
Count	Integer	Read-only property that returns the number of links in the collection.
Item	LinkLabel.Link	Read/write. The link at the specified index.

Table 11-7. LinkLabel.LinkCollection methods

Method	Description
Add	Adds a link to the collection. Overloaded.
Clear	Removes all the links from the collection.
Contains	Returns true if the specified link is contained in the collection.
GetEnumerator	Returns an enumerator used to iterate through the collection.
IndexOf	Returns index of the specified link in the collection.
Remove	Removes the specified link from the collection.
RemoveAt	Removes the link with the specified zero-based index from the collection.

Each link within a LinkLabel control is represented by a member of the LinkLabel.Link class. Each Link has the properties listed in Table 11-8.

Table 11-8. LinkLabel.Link properties

Property	Value type	Description
Enabled	Boolean	Read/write. Value indicating if the link is enabled. If disabled, then clicking on the link does not raise the LinkClicked event, and the link will appear in the color specified by the DisabledLinkColor property.
Length	Integer	Read/write. The number of characters in the link text.
LinkData	Object	Read/write. Data associated with the link.
Start	Integer	Read/write. The zero-based starting location of the link within the Text of the LinkLabel.
Visited	Boolean	Read/write. The value indicating whether the link should display as though it were visited. Default is false. Does not automatically get set to true; this must be done by code in the LinkClicked event handler.
		Used for multiple links in a control.

Example 11-3 (in C#) and Example 11-4 (in VB.NET) demonstrate many features of the LinkLabel control. These examples show five different LinkLabel controls, each configured differently. The first three LinkLabels are single links to web pages, the next is a LinkLabel containing four different links, and the last links to a text file that automatically opens up Notepad (or whichever application on the user system is the default application for files with a *.txt* extension). A full analysis follows the code listings.

Example 11-3. LinkLabels in C# (LinkLabels.cs)

```csharp
using System;
using System.Drawing;
using System.Windows.Forms;

namespace ProgrammingWinApps
{
    public class LinkLabels : Form
    {
        LinkLabel lnkMsft;
        LinkLabel lnkLA;

        public LinkLabels()
        {
            Text = "LinkLabels";
            Size = new Size(300,250);

            // use Text property & LinkArea
            lnkMsft = new LinkLabel();
            lnkMsft.Parent = this;
            lnkMsft.Text = "www.microsoft.com";
            lnkMsft.Location = new Point(0,0);
            lnkMsft.AutoSize = true;
            lnkMsft.BorderStyle = BorderStyle.None;
            lnkMsft.LinkArea = new LinkArea(4,9);
            lnkMsft.LinkClicked +=
                new System.Windows.Forms.LinkLabelLinkClickedEventHandler(
                    lnkMsft_LinkClicked);

            // use Add
            lnkLA = new LinkLabel();
            lnkLA.Parent = this;
            lnkLA.Text = "Liberty Associates";
            lnkLA.Location = new Point(0,25);
            lnkLA.AutoSize = true;
            lnkLA.BorderStyle = BorderStyle.None;
            lnkLA.Links.Add(0,7,"www.LibertyAssociates.com");
            lnkLA.LinkClicked +=
                new System.Windows.Forms.LinkLabelLinkClickedEventHandler(
                    lnkLA_LinkClicked);

            // use generic Add & generic handler
            LinkLabel lnkSterSol = new LinkLabel();
            lnkSterSol.Parent = this;
```

Example 11-3. LinkLabels in C# (LinkLabels.cs) (continued)

```csharp
      lnkSterSol.Text = "Sterling Solutions";
      lnkSterSol.Location = new Point(0,50);
      lnkSterSol.AutoSize = true;
      lnkSterSol.BorderStyle = BorderStyle.None;
      lnkSterSol.Links.Add(0,lnkSterSol.Text.ToString( ).Length,
                        "www.SterSol.com");
      lnkSterSol.LinkClicked +=
         new System.Windows.Forms.LinkLabelLinkClickedEventHandler(
            lnkGeneric_LinkClicked);

      //  multiple links & generic handler
      LinkLabel lnkMulti = new LinkLabel( );
      lnkMulti.Parent = this;
      lnkMulti.Text = "Ford  Chevy  VW  Porsche";
      lnkMulti.Location = new Point(0,75);
      lnkMulti.AutoSize = true;
      lnkMulti.BorderStyle = BorderStyle.None;
      lnkMulti.LinkBehavior = LinkBehavior.HoverUnderline;
      lnkMulti.Links.Add(0,4,"www.Ford.com");
      lnkMulti.Links.Add(6,5,"www.chevrolet.com");
      lnkMulti.Links.Add(13,2, "www.vw.com");
      lnkMulti.Links.Add(17,7,"www.porsche.com");
      lnkMulti.LinkClicked +=
         new System.Windows.Forms.LinkLabelLinkClickedEventHandler(
            lnkGeneric_LinkClicked);

      //  link to text file
      LinkLabel lnkTxtFile = new LinkLabel( );
      lnkTxtFile.Parent = this;
      lnkTxtFile.Text = "Gettysburg Address";
      lnkTxtFile.Location = new Point(0,100);
      lnkTxtFile.AutoSize = true;
      lnkTxtFile.BorderStyle = BorderStyle.None;
      lnkTxtFile.LinkBehavior = LinkBehavior.NeverUnderline;
      lnkTxtFile.ActiveLinkColor = Color.Green;
      lnkTxtFile.LinkColor = Color.Red;
      lnkTxtFile.VisitedLinkColor = Color.Orange;
      lnkTxtFile.Links.Add(0,lnkTxtFile.Text.ToString( ).Length,
                        @"c:\GettysburgAddress.txt");
      lnkTxtFile.LinkClicked +=
         new System.Windows.Forms.LinkLabelLinkClickedEventHandler(
            lnkGeneric_LinkClicked);
   }

   static void Main( )
   {
      Application.Run(new LinkLabels( ));
   }

   private void lnkMsft_LinkClicked(object sender,
                        LinkLabelLinkClickedEventArgs e)
   {
```

Example 11-3. LinkLabels in C# (LinkLabels.cs) (continued)

```
            lnkMsft.Links[lnkMsft.Links.IndexOf(e.Link)].Visited = true;
            System.Diagnostics.Process.Start(lnkMsft.Text);
         }

         private void lnkLA_LinkClicked(object sender,
                                LinkLabelLinkClickedEventArgs e)
         {
            lnkLA.LinkVisited = true;
            System.Diagnostics.Process.Start(e.Link.LinkData.ToString( ));
         }

         private void lnkGeneric_LinkClicked(object sender,
                                LinkLabelLinkClickedEventArgs e)
         {
            LinkLabel lnk = new LinkLabel( );
            lnk = (LinkLabel)sender;
            lnk.Links[lnk.Links.IndexOf(e.Link)].Visited = true;
            System.Diagnostics.Process.Start(e.Link.LinkData.ToString( ));
         }
      }
   }
}
```

Example 11-4. LinkLabels in VB.NET (LinkLabels.vb)

```
Option Strict On
imports System
imports System.Drawing
imports System.Windows.Forms

namespace ProgrammingWinApps
   public class LinkLabels : inherits Form
      dim lnkMsft as LinkLabel
      dim lnkLA as LinkLabel

      public sub New( )
         Text = "LinkLabels"
         Size = new Size(300,250)

         ' use Text property & LinkArea
         lnkMsft = new LinkLabel( )
         lnkMsft.Parent = me
         lnkMsft.Text = "www.microsoft.com"
         lnkMsft.Location = new Point(0,0)
         lnkMsft.AutoSize = true
         lnkMsft.BorderStyle = BorderStyle.None
         lnkMsft.LinkArea = new LinkArea(4,9)
         AddHandler lnkMsft.LinkClicked, AddressOf lnkMsft_LinkClicked

         ' use Add
         lnkLA = new LinkLabel( )
         lnkLA.Parent = me
         lnkLA.Text = "Liberty Associates"
```

Example 11-4. LinkLabels in VB.NET (LinkLabels.vb) (continued)

```
        lnkLA.Location = new Point(0,25)
        lnkLA.AutoSize = true
        lnkLA.BorderStyle = BorderStyle.None
        lnkLA.Links.Add(0,7,"www.LibertyAssociates.com")
        AddHandler lnkLA.LinkClicked, AddressOf lnkLA_LinkClicked

        '  use generic Add & generic handler
        dim lnkSterSol as LinkLabel = new LinkLabel( )
        lnkSterSol.Parent = me
        lnkSterSol.Text = "Sterling Solutions"
        lnkSterSol.Location = new Point(0,50)
        lnkSterSol.AutoSize = true
        lnkSterSol.BorderStyle = BorderStyle.None
        lnkSterSol.Links.Add(0,lnkSterSol.Text.ToString( ).Length, _
                        "www.SterSol.com")
        AddHandler lnkSterSol.LinkClicked, _
                        AddressOf lnkGeneric_LinkClicked

        '  multiple links & generic handler
        dim lnkMulti as LinkLabel = new LinkLabel( )
        lnkMulti.Parent = me
        lnkMulti.Text = "Ford  Chevy  VW  Porsche"
        lnkMulti.Location = new Point(0,75)
        lnkMulti.AutoSize = true
        lnkMulti.BorderStyle = BorderStyle.None
        lnkMulti.LinkBehavior = LinkBehavior.HoverUnderline
        lnkMulti.Links.Add(0,4,"www.Ford.com")
        lnkMulti.Links.Add(6,5,"www.chevrolet.com")
        lnkMulti.Links.Add(13,2, "www.vw.com")
        lnkMulti.Links.Add(17,7,"www.porsche.com")
        AddHandler lnkMulti.LinkClicked, AddressOf lnkGeneric_LinkClicked

        '  link to text file
        dim lnkTxtFile as LinkLabel = new LinkLabel( )
        lnkTxtFile.Parent = me
        lnkTxtFile.Text = "Gettysburg Address"
        lnkTxtFile.Location = new Point(0,100)
        lnkTxtFile.AutoSize = true
        lnkTxtFile.BorderStyle = BorderStyle.None
        lnkTxtFile.LinkBehavior = LinkBehavior.NeverUnderline
        lnkTxtFile.ActiveLinkColor = Color.Green
        lnkTxtFile.LinkColor = Color.Red
        lnkTxtFile.VisitedLinkColor = Color.Orange
        lnkTxtFile.Links.Add(0,lnkTxtFile.Text.ToString( ).Length, _
            "c:\\GettysburgAddress.txt")
        AddHandler lnkTxtFile.LinkClicked, _
                        AddressOf lnkGeneric_LinkClicked
    end sub

    public shared sub Main( )
        Application.Run(new LinkLabels( ))
    end sub
```

Example 11-4. LinkLabels in VB.NET (LinkLabels.vb) (continued)

```
private sub lnkMsft_LinkClicked(ByVal sender as object, _
                        ByVal e as LinkLabelLinkClickedEventArgs)
    lnkMsft.Links(lnkMsft.Links.IndexOf(e.Link)).Visited = true
    System.Diagnostics.Process.Start(lnkMsft.Text)
end sub

private sub lnkLA_LinkClicked(ByVal sender as object, _
                    ByVal e as LinkLabelLinkClickedEventArgs)
    lnkLA.LinkVisited = true
    System.Diagnostics.Process.Start(e.Link.LinkData.ToString())
end sub

private sub lnkGeneric_LinkClicked(ByVal sender as object, _
                    ByVal e as LinkLabelLinkClickedEventArgs)
    dim lnk as LinkLabel = new LinkLabel()
    lnk = CType(sender, LinkLabel)
    lnk.Links(lnk.Links.IndexOf(e.Link)).Visited = true
    System.Diagnostics.Process.Start(e.Link.LinkData.ToString())
end sub
  end class
end namespace
```

When either program is compiled and run, you will get the form shown in Figure 11-3. Although you can't see it in this monochrome image, on the user's screen the underlined links are blue, as is the line showing the four automobile brands, and the Gettysburg Address line is red.

Figure 11-3. LinkLabels

The LinkLabels program starts by declaring two LinkLabel controls as form member variables. These two controls need to be declared this way because they are referenced outside the constructor; the other controls are never referenced outside the constructor and can be local to the constructor method.

```
LinkLabel lnkMsft;
LinkLabel lnkLA;
```

```
dim lnkMsft as LinkLabel
dim lnkLA as LinkLabel
```

The first LinkLabel control to be created, lnkMsft, provides a link to the Microsoft web site. As shown in Figure 11-3, the Text property of the control is the full URL of the web site, but the actual link is comprised only of the word Microsoft. The implementation technique used here dictates that the full URL be used in the Text property, but you can limit the characters comprising the actual link. The code used to implement this LinkLabel in C# follows:

```
lnkMsft = new LinkLabel();
lnkMsft.Parent = this;
lnkMsft.Text = "www.microsoft.com";
lnkMsft.Location = new Point(0,0);
lnkMsft.AutoSize = true;
lnkMsft.BorderStyle = BorderStyle.None;
lnkMsft.LinkArea = new LinkArea(4,9);
lnkMsft.LinkClicked +=
    new System.Windows.Forms.LinkLabelLinkClickedEventHandler(
        lnkMsft_LinkClicked);
```

The VB.NET code is exactly the same, except for the trailing semicolons and the highlighted lines at the end of the snippet that add the event handler method to the LinkClicked event delegate. The VB.NET equivalent for adding the handler to the delegate is as follows:

```
AddHandler lnkMsft.LinkClicked, AddressOf lnkMsft_LinkClicked
```

In this code snippet, all the lines of code are similar to those used for a normal Label control except for the last two statements.

The LinkArea property specifies which characters in the Text property comprise the actual link. The first argument specifies the starting character, zero-based, and the second argument specifies the number of characters, including the starting character, to include in the link.

This control has its own event handler method. (As you will see shortly, some of the LinkLabel controls on this form use a generic event handler.) The event handler method is reproduced here:

```
private void lnkMsft_LinkClicked(object sender,
                                LinkLabelLinkClickedEventArgs e)
{
    lnkMsft.Links[lnkMsft.Links.IndexOf(e.Link)].Visited = true;
    System.Diagnostics.Process.Start(lnkMsft.Text);
}
```

VB
```
private sub lnkMsft_LinkClicked(ByVal sender as object, _
                                ByVal e as LinkLabelLinkClickedEventArgs)
    lnkMsft.Links(lnkMsft.Links.IndexOf(e.Link)).Visited = true
    System.Diagnostics.Process.Start(lnkMsft.Text)
end sub
```

The event argument, of type LinkLabelLinkClickedEventArgs, exposes the link that raised the event in the Link property as e.Link. That property is nested in the first line of code in the method to find the index of the link in the Links collection. This index is then used to set the Visited property of that LinkLabel.Link to true. This has the effect of changing the color of the link to the VisitedLinkColor. Since the VisitedLinkColor property is not set for this control, it defaults to purple.

The second line in the method invokes a static form of the System.Diagnostics.Process.Start method. This method takes a filename (at the minimum), and starts the default application associated with files with that file extension. Notice that in this method, the passed filename in is the Text property of the control. (It is also possible to pass in a filename that is not displayed as the Text property of the control, as you will see on the other LinkLabels in this example.) Since the filename passed in is actually a URL, the default application that runs is a web browser.

The next LinkLabel control on the form, lnkLA, displays a link to *www.LibertyAssociates.com*. This is similar to the Microsoft link, except it adds a link to the Links collection rather than specifying the LinkArea property. This is done with the following lines of code:

C#
```
lnkLA.Text = "Liberty Associates";
lnkLA.Links.Add(0,7,"www.LibertyAssociates.com")
```

The Add method takes three arguments. The first two are the same as for LinkArea—the zero-based starting character and the length of the link. The third argument is the URL it links to. Notice that this LinkLabel displays one text string, specified in the Text property for the control, but links to a URL different from that text string, specified in the Links property.

This LinkLabel control also has its own two-line event handler for the LinkClicked event, reproduced here:

C#
```
private void lnkLA_LinkClicked(object sender,
                               LinkLabelLinkClickedEventArgs e)
{
    lnkLA.LinkVisited = true;
    System.Diagnostics.Process.Start(e.Link.LinkData.ToString());
}
```

C#
```
private sub lnkLA_LinkClicked(ByVal sender as object, _
                             ByVal e as LinkLabelLinkClickedEventArgs)
    lnkLA.LinkVisited = true
    System.Diagnostics.Process.Start(e.Link.LinkData.ToString())
end sub
```

Similar to the previous event handler, the first line sets the LinkVisited property to true so it will display with the color specified by the VisitedLinkColor (which is not set for this control, so it defaults to purple). The LinkVisited property should be used only for a LinkLabel that has a single link. The Microsoft LinkLabel could have also used the simpler LinkVisited property rather than indexing into the Links collection and setting the Visited property; in this case they are equivalent. You will encounter a situation in which the indexing syntax is required shortly.

The Liberty Associates LinkLabel links to the URL specified previously in the Add method.

`VB`

```
System.Diagnostics.Process.Start(e.Link.LinkData.ToString())
```

Here, the LinkData property of the Link contains the URL. It is converted to a string, using the ToString method, which is given to the Start method. Again, since this is a valid URL, a browser will be invoked.

The next LinkLabel control on the form, lnkSterSol, displays a hyperlink to *www. SterSol.com*. This is similar to the Liberty Associates hyperlink, with two changes. First, the Add method uses a dynamic calculation of the length of the Text property to specify the length of the linked characters.

`VB`

```
lnkSterSol.Links.Add(0,lnkSterSol.Text.ToString().Length, _
                "www.SterSol.com")
```

This calculation ensures that the entire Text property displays as a link without having to count the characters manually and hardcode the literal number in the arguments.

The second change is a move to a generic event handler, one that can be used with any number of LinkLabel controls. The line that adds this generic event handler to the LinkClicked event delegate is as follows:

`C#`

```
lnkSterSol.LinkClicked +=
    new System.Windows.Forms.LinkLabelLinkClickedEventHandler(
        lnkGeneric_LinkClicked);
```

`VB`

```
AddHandler lnkSterSol.LinkClicked, AddressOf lnkGeneric_LinkClicked
```

The generic event handler method is called lnkGeneric_LinkClicked. It is reproduced here:

`C#`

```
private void lnkGeneric_LinkClicked(object sender,
                                LinkLabelLinkClickedEventArgs e)
{
    LinkLabel lnk = new LinkLabel();
    lnk = (LinkLabel)sender;
    lnk.Links[lnk.Links.IndexOf(e.Link)].Visited = true;
    System.Diagnostics.Process.Start(e.Link.LinkData.ToString());
}
```

```
private sub lnkGeneric_LinkClicked(ByVal sender as object, _
                            ByVal e as LinkLabelLinkClickedEventArgs)
   dim lnk as LinkLabel = new LinkLabel( )
   lnk = CType(sender, LinkLabel)
   lnk.Links(lnk.Links.IndexOf(e.Link)).Visited = true
   System.Diagnostics.Process.Start(e.Link.LinkData.ToString( ))
end sub
```

The first two lines in the method declare a LinkLabel variable, lnk, and instantiate it with the object, called sender, which raised the event. That object is cast to type LinkLabel in the second line in the method. Then the Visited property of the Link in the Links collection is set to true, as was done for the Microsoft event handler. Finally, the static Process.Start method is called, as was done for the Liberty Associates event handler.

The next LinkLabel on the form demonstrates a control with multiple links in a single control. The Text property contains the text to display for four different links, and four separate Add statements, each of which specifies a starting character, the number of characters in the link, and the URL to which it links.

```
lnkMulti.Text = "Ford  Chevy  VW  Porsche"
lnkMulti.LinkBehavior = LinkBehavior.HoverUnderline
lnkMulti.Links.Add(0,4,"www.Ford.com")
lnkMulti.Links.Add(6,5,"www.chevrolet.com")
lnkMulti.Links.Add(13,2, "www.vw.com")
lnkMulti.Links.Add(17,7,"www.porsche.com")
```

This LinkLabel control also demonstrates the use of the LinkBehavior property, which is why these links did not display as underlined back in Figure 11-3. They do display as underlined when the mouse hovers over each individual link.

The lnkMulti control uses the generic LinkClicked event handler, which uses the indexed Visited property rather than the unitary LinkVisited property. Consequently, each individual link correctly displays if it has been visited. If you had substituted the following line into the generic event handler:

```
lnk.LinkVisited = true
```

then the first link in the collection, such as Ford, would have displayed as visited irrespective of which of the four links was actually clicked.

The final LinkLabel control in the application links to a file on the local hard drive rather than a URL. In this case, a text file contains Lincoln's Gettysburg Address, located in the root of Drive C. The generic event handler is again used. Since the filename has an extension of *.txt*, the default application for that extension is used to open it (typically, Notepad).

If Gettysburg.txt is missing from your hard drive, clicking on this link will throw a file not found exception.

This LinkLabel also sets several of the display properties that change the default colors and behavior of the link. The lines of code that create the control are reproduced here:

```csharp
LinkLabel lnkTxtFile = new LinkLabel();
lnkTxtFile.Parent = this;
lnkTxtFile.Text = "Gettysburg Address";
lnkTxtFile.Location = new Point(0,100);
lnkTxtFile.AutoSize = true;
lnkTxtFile.BorderStyle = BorderStyle.None;
lnkTxtFile.LinkBehavior = LinkBehavior.NeverUnderline;
lnkTxtFile.ActiveLinkColor = Color.Green;
lnkTxtFile.LinkColor = Color.Red;
lnkTxtFile.VisitedLinkColor = Color.Orange;
lnkTxtFile.Links.Add(0,lnkTxtFile.Text.ToString().Length,
                @"c:\GettysburgAddress.txt");
lnkTxtFile.LinkClicked +=
    new System.Windows.Forms.LinkLabelLinkClickedEventHandler(
        lnkGeneric_LinkClicked);
```

```vbnet
dim lnkTxtFile as LinkLabel = new LinkLabel()
lnkTxtFile.Parent = me
lnkTxtFile.Text = "Gettysburg Address"
lnkTxtFile.Location = new Point(0,100)
lnkTxtFile.AutoSize = true
lnkTxtFile.BorderStyle = BorderStyle.None
lnkTxtFile.LinkBehavior = LinkBehavior.NeverUnderline
lnkTxtFile.ActiveLinkColor = Color.Green
lnkTxtFile.LinkColor = Color.Red
lnkTxtFile.VisitedLinkColor = Color.Orange
lnkTxtFile.Links.Add(0,lnkTxtFile.Text.ToString().Length, _
    "c:\\GettysburgAddress.txt")
AddHandler lnkTxtFile.LinkClicked, AddressOf lnkGeneric_LinkClicked
```

The LinkVisited and Visited properties are reset every time the application is run, unlike the default behavior of most browsers. If you want those properties to persist from one program execution to the next, you must save the information somewhere, such as in an XML configuration file.

Button Classes

If labels are the most common control in Windows applications, then buttons must be a close second. A command button tells the application to take some action. In the .NET Framework, the Button control is an instance of the System.Windows. Forms.Button class. It, along with the CheckBox and RadioButton controls, are derived from the ButtonBase class, as shown in Figure 11-4. The CheckBox and RadioButton controls are covered in the next section.

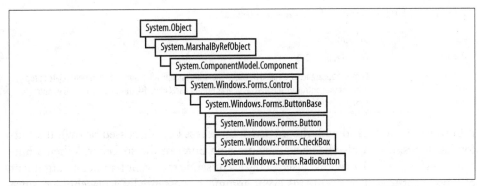

Figure 11-4. Button class hierarchy

The ButtonBase class has several commonly used properties listed in Table 11-9, in addition to those inherited from Control. The ImageList and ImageIndex properties were demonstrated in the section "ImageLists" in Chapter 7. Other common Button-Base properties will be demonstrated with a Button control in Examples 11-5 and 11-6.

Table 11-9. ButtonBase properties

Property	Value type	Description
FlatStyle	FlatStyle	Read/write. The flat-style appearance of the control. Valid values must be a member of the FlatStyle enumeration, listed in Table 11-10. The default value is FlatStyle.Standard.
Image	Image	Read/write. The image displayed on the control. Cannot be used for the same control at the same time as the ImageList or ImageIndex properties.
ImageAlign	ContentAlignment	Read/write. Aligns image displayed in the label. Values are members of the ContentAlignment enumeration, listed in Table 11-3. The default value is ContentAlignment.MiddleCenter.
ImageIndex	Integer	Read/write. Zero-based index value of the Image object contained in the ImageList.
ImageList	ImageList	Read/write. The image list containing the images displayed in the control. One image is displayed at a time, selected by the ImageIndex property. The ImageList stores a collection of Image objects. The ImageList component is described fully in Chapter 7.
TextAlign	ContentAlignment	Aligns text displayed in the control. Values are members of the ContentAlignment enumeration, listed in Table 11-3. The default value is ContentAlignment.MiddleCenter.

Table 11-10. FlatStyle enumeration values

Value	Description
Flat	Control appears flat.
Popup	Control appears 3-D when the mouse cursor is over it, flat otherwise. The 3D appearance is the same as Standard.

Table 11-10. FlatStyle enumeration values (continued)

Value	Description
Standard	Control appears 3-D.
System	Control appearance controlled by user's operating system. All image and alignment related properties of the control are ignored, as well as Button.BackColor. Use this value to force the control to conform to the system's theme.

A Button may be clicked with the mouse or an access key (discussed below). If a Button has focus, it may also be clicked by pressing Enter or the spacebar. When a Button is clicked, a Click event is raised. This event sends the event handler an argument of type EventArgs. The EventArgs event argument is essentially a placeholder, since it exposes no properties or information about the event.

In the programs listed in Example 11-5 (in C#) and Example 11-6 (in VB.NET), a form is created with a single button on it. The Text property of the button displays the value of the button's FlatStyle property. Each time the button is clicked, a new FlatStyle property is applied to the button, the Text property is changed to the current FlatStyle, and the size of the button is adjusted to the reflect the length of the displayed string. A happy face image is also displayed on the button for good measure. The resulting form looks like Figure 11-5.

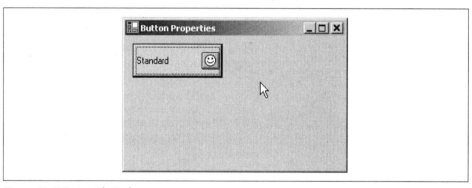

Figure 11-5. ButtonFlatStyle program

 This form would look much nicer if the button were centered. Several examples in Chapter 7 demonstrate how to do this. This example forgoes such niceties for the sake of concision.

Example 11-5. Button demonstration in C# (ButtonFlatStyle.cs)

```csharp
using System;
using System.Drawing;
using System.Windows.Forms;

namespace ProgrammingWinApps
{
```

Example 11-5. Button demonstration in C# (ButtonFlatStyle.cs) (continued)

```csharp
public class ButtonFlatStyle : Form
{
    Button btn;
    int i = 1;
    FlatStyle[ ] theStyles;
    Image img;

    public ButtonFlatStyle( )
    {
        Text = "Button Properties";
        Size = new Size(300,200);

        img = Image.FromFile(
            @"C:\Program Files\Microsoft Visual Studio .NET 2003\" +
            @"Common7\Graphics\bitmaps\assorted\happy.bmp");

        btn = new Button( );
        btn.Parent = this;
        btn.Text = btn.FlatStyle.ToString( );
        btn.Location = new Point(10,10);
        btn.BackColor = Color.LightGreen;
        btn.Click += new System.EventHandler(btn_Click);
        btn.Image = img;
        btn.ImageAlign = ContentAlignment.MiddleRight;
        btn.TextAlign = ContentAlignment.MiddleLeft;

        ButtonSize(btn);

        //  get the FlatStyle values into an array
        FlatStyle theEnum = new FlatStyle( );
        theStyles = (FlatStyle[ ])Enum.GetValues(theEnum.GetType( ));
    }

    static void Main( )
    {
        Application.Run(new ButtonFlatStyle( ));
    }

    private void btn_Click(object sender, EventArgs e)
    {
        Button btn = (Button)sender;
        btn.FlatStyle = theStyles[i];
        btn.Text = btn.FlatStyle.ToString( );
        ButtonSize(btn);

        if (i < theStyles.Length - 1)
            i++;
        else
            i = 0;
    }

    private void ButtonSize(Button btn)
    {
```

Example 11-5. Button demonstration in C# (ButtonFlatStyle.cs) (continued)

```csharp
         int xSize = ((int)(Font.Height * .75) * btn.Text.Length) +
                    (img.Width * 2);
         int ySize = img.Height * 2;
         btn.Size = new Size(xSize, ySize);
      }
   }
}
```

Example 11-6. Button demonstration in VB.NET (ButtonFlatStyle.vb)

```vb
Option Strict On
imports System
imports System.Drawing
imports System.Windows.Forms

namespace ProgrammingWinApps
   public class ButtonFlatStyle : inherits Form

      dim btn as Button
      dim i as integer
      dim theStyles as FlatStyle( )
      dim img as Image

      public sub New( )
         Text = "Button Properties"
         Size = new Size(300,200)

         img = Image.FromFile( _
            "C:\\Program Files\\Microsoft Visual Studio .NET 2003\\" + _
               "Common7\\Graphics\\bitmaps\\assorted\\happy.bmp")
         btn = new Button( )
         btn.Parent = me
         btn.Text = btn.FlatStyle.ToString( )
         btn.Location = new Point(10,10)
         btn.BackColor = Color.LightGreen
         AddHandler btn.Click, AddressOf btn_Click
         btn.Image = img
         btn.ImageAlign = ContentAlignment.MiddleRight
         btn.TextAlign = ContentAlignment.MiddleLeft

         ButtonSize(btn)

          '  get the FlatStyle values into an array
         dim theEnum as new FlatStyle( )
         theStyles = CType([Enum].GetValues( _
                     theEnum.GetType( )), FlatStyle( ))
      end sub

      public shared sub Main( )
         Application.Run(new ButtonFlatStyle( ))
      end sub

      private sub btn_Click(ByVal sender as object, _
```

```
[VB]                          ByVal e as EventArgs)
            Dim btn as Button = CType(sender, Button)
            btn.FlatStyle = theStyles(i)
            btn.Text = btn.FlatStyle.ToString()
            ButtonSize(btn)

            if (i < theStyles.Length - 1) then
                i = i + 1
            else
                i = 0
            end if
        end sub

        private sub ButtonSize(btn as Button)
            dim xSize as integer = (CType(Font.Height * .75, integer) * _
                            btn.Text.Length) + (img.Width * 2)
            dim ySize as integer = img.Height * 2
            btn.Size = new Size(xSize, ySize)
        end sub
    end class
end namespace
```

The programs in Examples 11-5 and 11-6 start off by declaring several class members, including a Button, an Image, an integer, and an array of FlatStyle objects. All of these members will be used throughout the class.

In the constructor, the image is instantiated to the bitmap contained in happy.bmp, a file included with the typical Visual Studio .NET installation. This is done by calling the static FromFile method of the Image class:

```
[C#]    img = Image.FromFile(
            @"C:\Program Files\Microsoft Visual Studio .NET 2003\Common7\" +
                @"Graphics\bitmaps\assorted\happy.bmp");
```

```
[VB]    img = Image.FromFile( _
            "C:\\Program Files\\Microsoft Visual Studio .NET 2003\\" + _
                "Common7\\Graphics\\bitmaps\\assorted\\happy.bmp")
```

The Button control was previously declared a member variable. Here it is instantiated, and its Parent property is set to the form:

```
[C#]    btn = new Button();
        btn.Parent = this;
```

```
[VB]    btn = new Button()
        btn.Parent = me
```

The Text property of the button is set to a string representation of the current value of the button's FlatStyle property.

```
[C#]    btn.Text = btn.FlatStyle.ToString();
```

Since the FlatStyle property for this button has not yet been set, it will default to a value of Standard.

The Location of the button is set so the upper-left corner of the control will be 10 pixels in from the left edge of the form's client area and 10 pixels down from the top of the form's client area.

The background color of the button is set to LightGreen, which will not be obvious in this book, but will be visible on the screen.

The most commonly used event raised by the Button control is the Click event, although it supports all events common to the Control class other than Double-Click. The Click event handler method is added to the event delegate with the appropriate following line of code:

C#
```
btn.Click += new System.EventHandler(btn_Click);
```

VB
```
AddHandler btn.Click, AddressOf btn_Click
```

In either case, the name of the Click event handler method is btn_Click. It will be analyzed shortly.

 .NET can suppress the DoubleClick event on Button controls by setting the StandardDoubleClick value of the ControlStyles enumeration.

The next three statements sets the Image property to the Image object previously instantiated with the happy face. The image is aligned to the middle of the right edge of the button, and the text is aligned to the middle of the button's left edge.

C#
```
btn.Image = img;
btn.ImageAlign = ContentAlignment.MiddleRight;
btn.TextAlign = ContentAlignment.MiddleLeft;
```

Normally the button would be sized in the constructor. As you will soon see, though, you should also resize the button in its Click event handler. Therefore it makes sense to factor out the common code to a ButtonSize helper method, and call that method from both the constructor and the Click event handler.

The ButtonSize method takes an object of type Button as its argument. The passed-in Button object is the button that will be resized. The method is reproduced here:

C#
```
private void ButtonSize(Button btn)
{
    int xSize = ((int)(Font.Height * .75) * btn.Text.Length) +
                (img.Width * 2);
    int ySize = img.Height * 2;
    btn.Size = new Size(xSize, ySize);
}
```

```vb
private sub ButtonSize(btn as Button)
    dim xSize as integer = (CType(Font.Height * .75, integer) * _
                            btn.Text.Length) + (img.Width * 2)
    dim ySize as integer = img.Height * 2
    btn.Size = new Size(xSize, ySize)
end sub
```

The first statement in the method calculates the width of the button, based on multiplying the height of the form's current Font by a factor of 0.75 and adding twice the width of the Image object displayed on the button. The height of the button is calculated as twice the height of the Image object. (All of these factors were determined through trial and error to yield a desirable size.) Once the height and width of the button is calculated, the Size property of btn is set by declaring a new Size structure.

 Several examples in Chapter 7 show different techniques of dynamically setting the size and location of controls.

The Click event handler accomplishes its task of cycling through the values of the FlatStyle enumeration by indexing into an array containing those enumeration values. It is accomplished with the following two statements:

```csharp
FlatStyle theEnum = new FlatStyle();
theStyles = (FlatStyle[ ])Enum.GetValues(theEnum.GetType());
```

```vb
dim theEnum as new FlatStyle()
theStyles = CType([Enum].GetValues(theEnum.GetType()), FlatStyle())
```

You have seen similar statements in other examples in this book, wherever it is necessary to iterate or otherwise treat an enumeration as an indexed collection.

Once the array is in hand, the btn_Click event handler method can use the integer counter i to index into the array, setting the style of the button to the desired value of FlatStyle. The event handler method is reproduced here:

```csharp
private void btn_Click(object sender, EventArgs e)
{
    Button btn = (Button)sender;
    btn.FlatStyle = theStyles[i];
    btn.Text = btn.FlatStyle.ToString();
    ButtonSize(btn);

    if (i < theStyles.Length - 1)
        i++;
    else
        i = 0;
}
```

```
    private sub btn_Click(ByVal sender as object, _
                         ByVal e as EventArgs)
      Dim btn as Button = CType(sender, Button)
      btn.FlatStyle = theStyles(i)
      btn.Text = btn.FlatStyle.ToString( )
      ButtonSize(btn)

      if (i < theStyles.Length - 1) then
         i = i + 1
      else
         i = 0
      end if

    end sub
```

The first statement in the method casts the object that raised the event as a Button and assigns it to a variable, btn, of type Button. Although a button raised the event that invoked the method, the compiler has no way of knowing this, so the explicit cast is necessary. The variable btn used in this method is not the same btn used in the constructor. Although they look the same, they are scoped independently. You could have called the Button variable in this method fred, and the method would still work exactly the same, although it would have been confusing.

The next two statements in the method assign the indexed value of the array of Flat-Styles to the FlatStyle property of the button and assign the string representation of the FlatStyle property to the button's Text property. Then the ButtonSize method is called, as it was in the constructor, to resize the button.

Finally, the method checks the value of the counter and either increments it or resets it to zero.

When the FlatStyle is set to System, the Image and BackColor properties are ignored and the operating system controls the appearance of the button.

Button

The previous section covered features common to all the classes derived from the ButtonBase class, using a Button object as the test case. In this section, each of the derived classes, including Button, will be covered in detail.

DialogResult property

The Button control has one property, DialogResult, that is not derived from either ButtonBase or Control and not shared with CheckBox or RadioButton. The DialogResult property, which was covered in Chapter 6, is used with buttons on dialog boxes, such as a modal child form. The DialogResult property of a button returns a specific value from a dialog box. If a button on a dialog box has its DialogResult property set, the dialog box will be closed when the button is clicked. The value of the button's DialogResult property will be returned to the parent form as the dialog

---

box's DialogResult property. This is all done without the programmer having to hook up events or write extra code.

The valid values of the DialogResult property, for either the button or the dialog box, must be members of the DialogResult enumeration, listed in Table 11-11. The default value is DialogResult.None.

Table 11-11. DialogResult enumeration

Value	Return value
Abort	Abort.
Cancel	Cancel.
Ignore	Ignore.
No	No.
None	Returns nothing. Modal dialog is not terminated.
OK	OK.
Retry	Retry.
Yes	Yes.

Refer to Chapter 6 for examples showing the usage of the DialogResult property.

PerformClick method

The PerformClick method generates a click event for the button. This method, which is not derived from Control but is shared with the RadioButton class, can be useful when you want the functionality contained in a button that will be invoked, without requiring the user to actually click the button.

Consider a form with two buttons, btn1 and btn2. Each has a Click event handler, shown here (the VB.NET versions are nearly identical):

```csharp
private void btn1_Click(object sender, EventArgs e)
{
    MessageBox.Show("Button1 clicked.");
    btn2.PerformClick();
}

private void btn2_Click(object sender, EventArgs e)
{
    MessageBox.Show("Button2 clicked.");
}
```

If the user clicks on btn2, a message box will display saying Button2 clicked. If the user clicks on btn1, the user will see two message boxes: Button1 clicked and Button2 clicked.

Access keys

In addition to clicking with the mouse, a button can be clicked by an access key. An access key is specified by inserting an ampersand in front of the desired character in the button's Text property. That character will be underlined on the button's face. The button can be clicked, even if it does not have focus, by pressing the access key simultaneously with the Alt key.

If the Text property needs to show an ampersand character, escape it by doubling the ampersand.

The following code snippet specifies a button:

```
btn1 = new Button();
btn1.Parent = this;
btn1.Text = "&Cut && Paste";
btn1.Location = new Point(10,10);
btn1.Click += new System.EventHandler(btn1_Click);
```

This would create a button displaying the legend Cut & Paste. Pressing Alt-C would click the button, regardless of which control on the form had focus.

Form Button properties

The Form class provides two properties that allow specified buttons to be clicked using specific keys on the keyboard, even if those buttons do not have focus.

The form AcceptButton property lets you get or set a button that will be clicked if the user presses Enter, even if that button does not have focus. The only time Enter will not click the designated button would be if the currently selected control intercepts the Enter key. For example, a multiline text box will process the Enter key as part of its text, preventing it from triggering AcceptButton.

The form CancelButton property lets you get or set a button that will be clicked if the user presses Escape, even if that button does not have focus.

Consider a form called frmMain with two buttons, btnOK and btnCancel. The following code snippet (in C#) from the constructor of the form sets the AcceptButton and CancelButton properties of the form:

```
frmMain.AcceptButton = btnOK;
frmMain.CancelButton = btnCancel;
```

If the user presses Enter, btnOK will be clicked, and if she presses Escape, btnCancel will be clicked.

CheckBox

The CheckBox control is derived from the ButtonBase class, as are the Button and RadioButton controls. It is typically used to indicate a Boolean such as Yes/No or True/False.

A CheckBox normally consists of a small square with a text string next to it. Clicking on either the square or the associated text string toggles the state of the control. If the square is checked, it becomes unchecked, and vice versa. If the control has focus, the state can also be toggled by pressing the spacebar.

The normal appearance of the CheckBox can be changed to resemble a button by setting the Appearance property. The button appears depressed when checked and raised when unchecked. Unlike a true button control, it retains the depressed appearance until it is clicked again, which causes it to toggle to the raised position.

The most important property of the Checkbox control is the Checked property. It either sets the state of the control or determines whether the control is checked or unchecked. If the AutoCheck property is true (the default value), then the Checked property will be changed automatically when the CheckBox is clicked. If you set the AutoCheck property to false, then you must explicitly set the Checked property in a Click event handler.

The commonly used properties of the CheckBox control are listed in Table 11-12.

Table 11-12. CheckBox properties

Property	Value type	Description
Appearance	Appearance	Read/write. If the value is Appearance.Normal (the default), then the checkbox will have a normal appearance. If the value is Appearance.Button, the checkbox will look like a button that toggles, (either in an up or down state).
AutoCheck	Boolean	Read/write. Value indicating if the Checked or CheckState properties are automatically changed when the Click event is raised. If true (the default), those properties will be automatically changed when the control is clicked.
CheckAlign	ContentAlignment	Read/write. Controls both the horizontal and vertical alignment of the checkbox in a CheckBox control. Valid values must come from the ContentAlignment enumeration, listed in Table 11-3. The default is ContentAlignment.MiddleLeft.
Checked	Boolean	Read/write. Value indicating the state of the checkbox. If true, the checkbox is checked, otherwise false (the default).
CheckState	CheckState	Read/write. The state of the checkbox. The valid values must be members of the CheckState enumeration, listed in Table 11-13. The default value is CheckState.Unchecked.
TextAlign	ContentAlignment	Read/write. Aligns text displayed next to the checkbox. Values are members of the ContentAlignment enumeration, listed in Table 11-3. The default value is ContentAlignment.MiddleLeft.
ThreeState	Boolean	Read/write. Value indicating if the control can display three states or two. If true, the checkbox can display three states, otherwise false (the default).

The CheckBox control has a ThreeState property that, if true, allows it to indicate an indeterminate state in addition to the Boolean values. If the ThreeState property of the control is true, then each time it is clicked, its state cycles through the three values of the CheckState enumeration: Checked, Unchecked, and Indeterminate.

A good example of a CheckBox making use of the ThreeState property can be found in the Font dialog box used in Microsoft Word. This dialog box has several checkboxes, one each for effects such as Strikethrough, Superscript, or Subscript. If you highlight a word with no effects applied to and then open the Font dialog box, none of the checkboxes will be checked. Check the Strikethrough checkbox, and then close the dialog box, and the word will have a line through it. Leaving the word highlighted, open the dialog box again and now the Strikethrough checkbox will be checked. This is typical two-state behavior—the text selection is unambiguously struck through. However, if you highlight the entire line of text with both normal words and struck-through words and then open the Font dialog box, the Strikethrough checkbox will have a checkmark, but the square and the checkmark will be gray. This is the indeterminate state, since the selection has both struck-through and non-struck-through characters.

If the ThreeState property is true, then use the CheckState property rather than the Checked property to get or set the state of the checkbox. The valid values of the CheckState property are members of the CheckState enumeration, listed in Table 11-13.

Table 11-13. CheckState enumeration

Value	Appearance.Normal	Appearance.Button
Checked	Displays checkmark	Button looks depressed
Unchecked	No checkmark	Button looks raised
Indeterminate	Displays checkmark in shaded checkbox	Button looks flat

The CheckBox control has many events, most of which are inherited from the Control class. Table 11-14 lists the most commonly used events. Of those, only the Click event is inherited from Control. If the AutoCheck property is set to its default value of true, then there is rarely any need to handle the Click event.

Table 11-14. CheckBox events

Property	Event argument	Description
AppearanceChanged	EventArgs	Raised when the Appearance property of the control changes
CheckedChanged	EventArgs	Raised when the Checked property of the control changes
CheckStateChanged	EventArgs	Raised when the CheckState property of the control changes
Click	EventArgs	Raised when the control is clicked.

The programs listed in Examples 11-7 and 11-8 demonstrate the basic features of using CheckBox controls. The Appearance, CheckAlign, and TextAlign properties will be demonstrated in Examples 11-9 and 11-10 in the next section, where

RadioButton controls will be used to change these CheckBox properties. In the next example, a checkbox is created for each member of the FontStyle enumeration. Clicking on one or more of the checkboxes applies that font style to the text contained in a label control. The checkboxes are contained in a Panel control to allow easy iteration through the checkboxes in the CheckedChanged event handler. When the examples are compiled and run, the program will look like the screenshot shown in Figure 11-6.

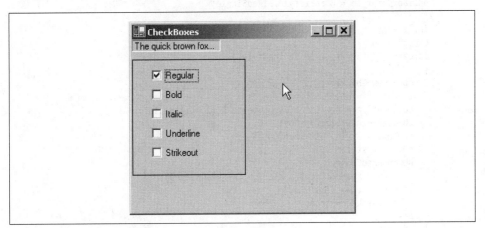

Figure 11-6. CheckBoxes

Example 11-7. CheckBoxes using C# (CheckBoxes.cs)

```csharp
using System;
using System.Drawing;
using System.Windows.Forms;

namespace ProgrammingWinApps
{
    public class CheckBoxes : Form
    {
        Label lbl;
        Panel pnl;
        FontStyle[ ] theStyles;

        public CheckBoxes( )
        {
            Text = "CheckBoxes";
            Size = new Size(300,250);

            lbl = new Label( );
            lbl.Parent = this;
            lbl.Text = "The quick brown fox...";
            lbl.Location = new Point(0,0);
            lbl.AutoSize = true;
            lbl.BorderStyle = BorderStyle.Fixed3D;
            int yDelta = lbl.Height + 10;
```

Example 11-7. CheckBoxes using C# (CheckBoxes.cs) (continued)

```
        FontStyle theEnum = new FontStyle( );
        theStyles = (FontStyle[ ])Enum.GetValues(theEnum.GetType( ));

        pnl = new Panel( );
        pnl.Parent = this;
        pnl.Location = new Point(0, yDelta );
        pnl.Size = new Size(150, (theStyles.Length + 1) * yDelta);
        pnl.BorderStyle = BorderStyle.FixedSingle;

        int i = 1;
        CheckBox cb;
        foreach (FontStyle style in theStyles)
        {
            cb = new CheckBox( );
            cb.Parent = pnl;
            cb.Location = new Point(25, (yDelta * (i - 1)) + 10);
            cb.Size = new Size(75,20);
            cb.Text = style.ToString( );
            cb.Tag = style;
            cb.CheckedChanged +=
                    new System.EventHandler(cb_CheckedChanged);
            if (cb.Text == "Regular")
                cb.Checked = true;
            i++;
        }
    }

    static void Main( )
    {
        Application.Run(new CheckBoxes( ));
    }

    private void cb_CheckedChanged(object sender, EventArgs e)
    {
        FontStyle fs = 0;
        for (int i = 0; i < pnl.Controls.Count; i++)
        {
            CheckBox cb = (CheckBox)pnl.Controls[i];
            if (cb.Checked)
                fs |= (FontStyle)cb.Tag;

// The following lines accomplish the same task in a more condensed way.
//          if (((CheckBox)pnl.Controls[i]).Checked)
//              fs |= (FontStyle)((CheckBox)pnl.Controls[i]).Tag;
        }
        lbl.Font = new Font(lbl.Font, fs);
    }
  }
}
```

Example 11-8. CheckBoxes using VB.NET (CheckBoxes.vb)

```
Option Strict On
imports System
imports System.Drawing
imports System.Windows.Forms

namespace ProgrammingWinApps
    public class CheckBoxes : inherits Form

        dim lbl as Label
        dim pnl as Panel
        dim theStyles as FontStyle( )

        public sub New( )
            Text = "Button Properties"
            Size = new Size(300,250)

            lbl = new Label( )
            lbl.Parent = me
            lbl.Text = "The quick brown fox..."
            lbl.Location = new Point(0,0)
            lbl.AutoSize = true
            lbl.BorderStyle = BorderStyle.Fixed3D

            dim yDelta as integer = lbl.Height + 10

            '  get the FontStyle values into an array
            dim theEnum as new FontStyle( )
            theStyles = CType([Enum].GetValues( _
                        theEnum.GetType( )), FontStyle( ))

            pnl = new Panel( )
            pnl.Parent = me
            pnl.Location = new Point(0, yDelta )
            pnl.Size = new Size(150, (theStyles.Length + 1) * yDelta)
            pnl.BorderStyle = BorderStyle.FixedSingle

            dim i as integer = 1
            dim style as FontStyle
            dim cb as CheckBox
            for each style in theStyles
                cb = new CheckBox( )
                cb.Parent = pnl
                cb.Location = new Point(25, (yDelta * (i - 1)) + 10)
                cb.Size = new Size(75,20)
                cb.Text = style.ToString( )
                cb.Tag = style
                AddHandler cb.CheckedChanged, AddressOf cb_CheckedChanged

                if cb.Text = "Regular" then
                    cb.Checked = true
                end if
                i = i + 1
```

Example 11-8. CheckBoxes using VB.NET (CheckBoxes.vb) (continued)

```
            next
        end sub

        public shared sub Main( )
            Application.Run(new CheckBoxes( ))
        end sub

        private sub cb_CheckedChanged(ByVal sender as object, _
                              ByVal e as EventArgs)
            dim fs as FontStyle = 0
            dim i as integer
            for i = 0 to pnl.Controls.Count    - 1
               dim cb as CheckBox = CType(pnl.Controls(i), CheckBox)
               if cb.Checked then
                  fs  = fs or CType(cb.Tag, FontStyle)
               end if

'  The following lines accomplish the same task in a more condensed way.
'           if (CType(pnl.Controls(i), CheckBox)).Checked then
'              fs  = fs or CType(CType(pnl.Controls(i), _
'                                 CheckBox).Tag, FontStyle)
'           end if
            next

            lbl.Font = new Font(lbl.Font, fs)
        end sub
    end class
end namespace
```

Three member variables are declared, so they will be available to all methods—two controls and an array of FontStyle objects:

```
    Label lbl;
    Panel pnl;
    FontStyle[ ] theStyles;
```

```
    dim lbl as Label
    dim pnl as Panel
    dim theStyles as FontStyle( )
```

In the constructor, the Label control is instantiated and specified with several properties, including a Text property that will be displayed on the form. An integer yDelta is calculated, and will be used soon for positioning other controls.

The next two statements put the contents of the FontStyle enumeration into an array. This is necessary because you cannot iterate through an enumeration directly, and you will need to iterate before creating one checkbox for each member of the enumeration. You have seen similar code in previous examples.

```
    FontStyle theEnum = new FontStyle( );
    theStyles = (FontStyle[ ])Enum.GetValues(theEnum.GetType( ));
```

```vb
dim theEnum as new FontStyle( )
theStyles = CType([Enum].GetValues( _
                    theEnum.GetType( )), FontStyle( ))
```

This array is then looped through using a foreach loop, creating a CheckBox for each member of the enumeration. The Parent property of each CheckBox is set as the Panel control. This setting facilitates iterating through all the checkbox controls in the event handler, since it cleanly encapsulates the collection of checkbox controls within a container control. (The Panel control will be covered in detail in Chapter 13.)

The Tag property of each checkbox control is set to its associated FontStyle. This allows the Tag property to be used in the event handler to set the FontStyle directly without having to cast a text string to a FontStyle.

An event handler method, cb_CheckedChanged, is added to the delegate for the CheckedChanged event. When the CheckBox is changed, the CheckedChanged event is fired, which is then handled by that method:

```csharp
cb.CheckedChanged += new System.EventHandler(cb_CheckedChanged);
```

```vb
AddHandler cb.CheckedChanged, AddressOf cb_CheckedChanged
```

Finally, the Text property of the checkbox is tested. If it is Regular, then the Checked property of that checkbox is set to true so the checkbox will appear checked. Regular is the default value at program initialization.

The cb_CheckedChanged event handler is called every time one of the checkboxes has a changed value. It is not necessary for all checkbox controls in a group to use the same event handler, but in this case it serves the goal of the program, which is to apply one or more FontStyles to the Label control's Text property.

FontStyles can be added together bitwise using the logical OR operator. This is done by iterating through each of the checkbox controls, testing to see if the checkbox is checked, and if it is checked, OR'ing its Tag property to the built-up FontStyle variable.

The method starts by declaring, instantiating, and initializing the FontStyle variable to 0:

```csharp
FontStyle fs = 0;
```

```vb
dim fs as FontStyle = 0
```

Then the Controls collection of the Panel control is iterated. Within the for loop, each member of the Panel's Controls collection is cast to a CheckBox:

```csharp
CheckBox cb = (CheckBox)pnl.Controls[i];
```

```vb
dim cb as CheckBox = CType(pnl.Controls(i), CheckBox)
```

Then the Checked property of that checkbox is tested. If it is checked, the value of its Tag property is OR'ed to the pre-existing FontStyle variable:

```
if (cb.Checked)
    fs |= (FontStyle)cb.Tag;
```

```
if cb.Checked then
    fs = fs or CType(cb.Tag, FontStyle)
end if
```

You can condense the casting of the control into the testing for a gain in code density but a loss of readability. The necessary lines are commented out in the example. It would be:

```
if (((CheckBox)pnl.Controls[i]).Checked)
    fs |= (FontStyle)((CheckBox)pnl.Controls[i]).Tag;
```

```
if (CType(pnl.Controls(i), CheckBox)).Checked then
    fs = fs or CType(CType(pnl.Controls(i), _
                    CheckBox).Tag, FontStyle)
end if
```

Finally, the FontStyle is applied to the Label control by creating a new Font object that uses the current Font property as a template.

```
lbl.Font = new Font(lbl.Font, fs);
```

RadioButton

The RadioButton control, the last of the ButtonBase derived controls, is similar to the CheckBox. The main difference between the RadioButton and the CheckBox is that RadioButton controls are typically grouped with other RadioButtons and only one of the controls in the group can be checked at one time. In other words, if an unchecked radio button in a group is clicked by the user, the currently checked radio button will become unchecked automatically (assuming that the AutoClick property is set to the default value of true).

RadioButtons are typically grouped by a container control. These controls include Panels and GroupBoxes, both of which are described in Chapter 13. If one or more RadioButtons are on the form but not in a container control, then those "freestanding" radio buttons are grouped together.

The essential difference between a Panel control and a GroupBox control is that a Panel control can have scrollbars but no caption, while a GroupBox control can have a Text property that will appear as a caption, but no scrollbars.

If two or more groups of radio buttons are on a form, they will be totally independent of each other. There can be at most one checked radio button in each group, but changing the Checked state of the radio buttons in one group will have no effect on the other group.

The RadioButton control has the same common properties as the CheckBox control, listed in Table 11-12, with the omission of the ThreeState related properties: Check-State and ThreeState. Likewise, it has the same events as the CheckBox events listed in Table 11-14, with the omission of CheckStateChanged.

The RadioButton control has one method not derived from Control (or some other base class), but shared with the Button control: the PerformClick method. It behaves the same as it does with the Button control, described previously in this chapter.

Examples 11-9 and 11-10 build on the examples used to demonstrate CheckBoxes and showing how to use radio buttons to change properties of a CheckBox control. The finished program is shown in Figure 11-7.

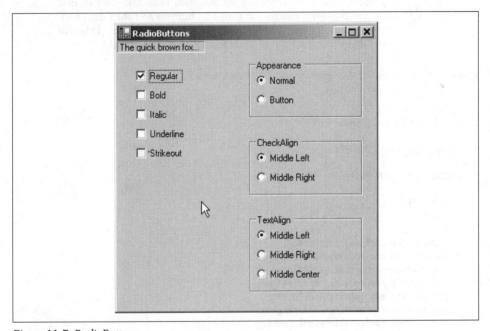

Figure 11-7. RadioButtons

The example programs add three GroupBox controls, each of which contains a group of RadioButton controls. Clicking on any of the radio buttons changes the appearance of the checkboxes. The Appearance group lets you toggle between Normal and Button values for the Appearance property. The CheckAlign group changes the values of the CheckAlign property of the CheckBox control, and the TextAlign group changes the TextAlign property.

Although this program changes the appearance of the CheckBox control, RadioButton controls behave and appear much like the CheckBox control.

When there are only two choices in a radio button group, you can use a single CheckBox instead. For example, you could replace the Appearance radio buttons with a single CheckBox labeled Button. When checked, it would set the Appearance property to Appearance.Button, and when unchecked it would set the value to Appearance.Normal. The main advantage of using a radio button in this case is that both available options are explicitly displayed to the user.

The changes in Examples 11-9 and 11-10 from Examples 11-7 and 11-8 are highlighted. These code listings are long, but there is a fair amount of repetitious code that you can cut and paste with minor changes. If you are developing with Visual Studio .NET, much of this code will be generated for you automatically.

 If you are developing with Visual Studio .NET, dragging and dropping radio buttons into different groups, you must take care to first create the container control for the radio buttons and then drag-and-drop the RadioButton controls onto the container control. This will ensure that the correct parent/child relationships are formed.

Example 11-9. RadioButton controls using C# (RadioButtons.cs)

```csharp
using System;
using System.Drawing;
using System.Windows.Forms;

namespace ProgrammingWinApps
{
    public class RadioButtons : Form
    {
        Label lbl;
        Panel pnl;
        int yDelta;
        RadioButton rdoAppearanceNormal;
        RadioButton rdoAppearanceButton;
        RadioButton rdoCheckAlignMiddleLeft;
        RadioButton rdoCheckAlignMiddleRight;
        RadioButton rdoTextAlignMiddleLeft;
        RadioButton rdoTextAlignMiddleRight;
        RadioButton rdoTextAlignMiddleCenter;
        FontStyle[ ] theStyles;

        public RadioButtons( )
        {
            Text = "RadioButtons";
            Size = new Size(350,375);

            lbl = new Label( );
            lbl.Parent = this;
            lbl.Text = "The quick brown fox...";
            lbl.Location = new Point(0,0);
            lbl.AutoSize = true;
            lbl.BorderStyle = BorderStyle.Fixed3D;
            yDelta = lbl.Height + 10;
```

Example 11-9. RadioButton controls using C# (RadioButtons.cs) (continued)

```csharp
// Get the FontStyles into an array
FontStyle theEnum = new FontStyle();
theStyles = (FontStyle[])Enum.GetValues(theEnum.GetType());

pnl = new Panel();
pnl.Parent = this;
pnl.Location = new Point(0, yDelta);
pnl.Size = new Size(150, (theStyles.Length + 1) * yDelta);
pnl.BorderStyle = BorderStyle.None;

int i = 1;
CheckBox cb;
foreach (FontStyle style in theStyles)
{
    cb = new CheckBox();
    cb.Parent = pnl;
    cb.Location = new Point(25, (yDelta * (i - 1)) + 10);
    cb.Size = new Size(75,20);
    cb.Text = style.ToString();
    cb.Tag = style;
    cb.CheckedChanged +=
        new System.EventHandler(cb_CheckedChanged);
    if (cb.Text == "Regular")
        cb.Checked = true;
    i++;
}

GroupBox grpAppearance = new GroupBox();
grpAppearance.Parent = this;
grpAppearance.Text = "Appearance";
grpAppearance.Location = new Point(175,yDelta);
grpAppearance.Size = new Size(150, yDelta * 3);

rdoAppearanceNormal = new RadioButton();
rdoAppearanceNormal.Parent = grpAppearance;
rdoAppearanceNormal.Text = "Normal";
rdoAppearanceNormal.Location = new Point(10, 15);
rdoAppearanceNormal.Checked = true;
rdoAppearanceNormal.CheckedChanged +=
        new System.EventHandler(rdoAppearance_CheckedChanged);

rdoAppearanceButton = new RadioButton();
rdoAppearanceButton.Parent = grpAppearance;
rdoAppearanceButton.Text = "Button";
rdoAppearanceButton.Location = new Point(10, 15 + yDelta);
rdoAppearanceButton.CheckedChanged +=
        new System.EventHandler(rdoAppearance_CheckedChanged);

GroupBox grpCheckAlign = new GroupBox();
grpCheckAlign.Parent = this;
grpCheckAlign.Text = "CheckAlign";
grpCheckAlign.Location = new Point(175,
```

Example 11-9. RadioButton controls using C# (RadioButtons.cs) (continued)

C#

```
                                grpAppearance.Bottom + 25);
        grpCheckAlign.Size = new Size(150, yDelta * 3);

        rdoCheckAlignMiddleLeft = new RadioButton( );
        rdoCheckAlignMiddleLeft.Parent = grpCheckAlign;
        rdoCheckAlignMiddleLeft.Text = "Middle Left";
        rdoCheckAlignMiddleLeft.Tag = ContentAlignment.MiddleLeft;
        rdoCheckAlignMiddleLeft.Location = new Point(10, 15);
        rdoCheckAlignMiddleLeft.Checked = true;
        rdoCheckAlignMiddleLeft.CheckedChanged +=
            new System.EventHandler(rdoCheckAlign_CheckedChanged);

        rdoCheckAlignMiddleRight = new RadioButton( );
        rdoCheckAlignMiddleRight.Parent = grpCheckAlign;
        rdoCheckAlignMiddleRight.Text = "Middle Right";
        rdoCheckAlignMiddleRight.Tag = ContentAlignment.MiddleRight;
        rdoCheckAlignMiddleRight.Location = new Point(10, 15 + yDelta);
        rdoCheckAlignMiddleRight.CheckedChanged +=
            new System.EventHandler(rdoCheckAlign_CheckedChanged);

        GroupBox grpTextAlign = new GroupBox( );
        grpTextAlign.Parent = this;
        grpTextAlign.Text = "TextAlign";
        grpTextAlign.Location = new Point(175,
                                    grpCheckAlign.Bottom + 25);
        grpTextAlign.Size = new Size(150, yDelta * 4);

        rdoTextAlignMiddleLeft = new RadioButton( );
        rdoTextAlignMiddleLeft.Parent = grpTextAlign;
        rdoTextAlignMiddleLeft.Text = "Middle Left";
        rdoTextAlignMiddleLeft.Tag = ContentAlignment.MiddleLeft;
        rdoTextAlignMiddleLeft.Location = new Point(10, 15);
        rdoTextAlignMiddleLeft.Checked = true;
        rdoTextAlignMiddleLeft.CheckedChanged +=
            new System.EventHandler(rdoTextAlign_CheckedChanged);

        rdoTextAlignMiddleRight = new RadioButton( );
        rdoTextAlignMiddleRight.Parent = grpTextAlign;
        rdoTextAlignMiddleRight.Text = "Middle Right";
        rdoTextAlignMiddleRight.Tag = ContentAlignment.MiddleRight;
        rdoTextAlignMiddleRight.Location = new Point(10, 15 + yDelta);
        rdoTextAlignMiddleRight.CheckedChanged +=
            new System.EventHandler(rdoTextAlign_CheckedChanged);

        rdoTextAlignMiddleCenter = new RadioButton( );
        rdoTextAlignMiddleCenter.Parent = grpTextAlign;
        rdoTextAlignMiddleCenter.Text = "Middle Center";
        rdoTextAlignMiddleCenter.Tag = ContentAlignment.MiddleCenter;
        rdoTextAlignMiddleCenter.Location = new Point(10,
                                            15 + (2 * yDelta));
        rdoTextAlignMiddleCenter.CheckedChanged +=
            new System.EventHandler(rdoTextAlign_CheckedChanged);
```

Example 11-9. RadioButton controls using C# (RadioButtons.cs) (continued)

```csharp
    } // close for constructor

static void Main()
{
    Application.Run(new RadioButtons());
}

private void cb_CheckedChanged(object sender, EventArgs e)
{
    FontStyle fs = 0;
    for (int i = 0; i < pnl.Controls.Count; i++)
    {
        CheckBox cb = (CheckBox)pnl.Controls[i];
        if (cb.Checked)
            fs |= (FontStyle)cb.Tag;
    }
    lbl.Font = new Font(lbl.Font, fs);
}

private void rdoAppearance_CheckedChanged(object sender,
                                          EventArgs e)
{
    if (rdoAppearanceNormal.Checked)
    {
        for (int i = 0; i < pnl.Controls.Count; i++)
        {
            CheckBox cb = (CheckBox)pnl.Controls[i];
            cb.Appearance = Appearance.Normal;
        }
    }
    else
    {
        for (int i = 0; i < pnl.Controls.Count; i++)
        {
            CheckBox cb = (CheckBox)pnl.Controls[i];
            cb.Appearance = Appearance.Button;
        }
    }
}

private void rdoCheckAlign_CheckedChanged(object sender,
                                          EventArgs e)
{
    RadioButton rdo = (RadioButton)sender;
    for (int i = 0; i < pnl.Controls.Count; i++)
    {
        CheckBox cb = (CheckBox)pnl.Controls[i];
        cb.CheckAlign = (ContentAlignment)rdo.Tag;
    }
}

private void rdoTextAlign_CheckedChanged(object sender, EventArgs e)
{
```

Example 11-9. RadioButton controls using C# (RadioButtons.cs) (continued)

C#
```
            RadioButton rdo = (RadioButton)sender;
            for (int i = 0; i < pnl.Controls.Count; i++)
            {
               CheckBox cb = (CheckBox)pnl.Controls[i];
               switch ((int)rdo.Tag)
               {
                  case (int)ContentAlignment.MiddleLeft :
                     cb.TextAlign = ContentAlignment.MiddleLeft;
                     break;
                  case (int)ContentAlignment.MiddleRight :
                     cb.TextAlign = ContentAlignment.MiddleRight;
                     break;
                  case (int)ContentAlignment.MiddleCenter :
                     cb.TextAlign = ContentAlignment.MiddleCenter;
                     break;
               }
            }
         }    //  close for rdoTextAlign_CheckedChanged
      }       //  close for form class
}            //  close form namespace
```

Example 11-10. RadioButton controls using VB.NET (RadioButtons.vb)

VB
```
Option Strict On
imports System
imports System.Drawing
imports System.Windows.Forms

namespace ProgrammingWinApps
   public class RadioButtons : inherits Form

      dim lbl as Label
      dim pnl as Panel
      dim yDelta as integer
      dim rdoAppearanceNormal as RadioButton
      dim rdoAppearanceButton as RadioButton
      dim rdoCheckAlignMiddleLeft as RadioButton
      dim rdoCheckAlignMiddleRight as RadioButton
      dim rdoTextAlignMiddleLeft as RadioButton
      dim rdoTextAlignMiddleRight as RadioButton
      dim rdoTextAlignMiddleCenter as RadioButton
      dim theStyles as FontStyle( )

      public sub New( )
         Text = "RadioButtons"
         Size = new Size(350,375)

         lbl = new Label( )
         lbl.Parent = me
         lbl.Text = "The quick brown fox..."
         lbl.Location = new Point(0,0)
         lbl.AutoSize = true
```

Example 11-10. RadioButton controls using VB.NET (RadioButtons.vb) (continued)

```vb
lbl.BorderStyle = BorderStyle.Fixed3D
yDelta = lbl.Height + 10

' get the FontStyle values into an array
dim theEnum as new FontStyle( )
theStyles = CType([Enum].GetValues( _
               theEnum.GetType( )), FontStyle( ))

pnl = new Panel( )
pnl.Parent = me
pnl.Location = new Point(0, yDelta )
pnl.Size = new Size(150, (theStyles.Length + 1) * yDelta)
pnl.BorderStyle = BorderStyle.None

dim i as integer = 1
dim style as FontStyle
dim cb as CheckBox
for each style in theStyles
   cb = new CheckBox( )
   cb.Parent = pnl
   cb.Location = new Point(25, (yDelta * (i - 1)) + 10)
   cb.Size = new Size(75,20)
   cb.Text = style.ToString( )
   cb.Tag = style
   AddHandler cb.CheckedChanged, AddressOf cb_CheckedChanged

   if cb.Text = "Regular" then
      cb.Checked = true
   end if
   i = i + 1
next

dim grpAppearance as GroupBox = new GroupBox( )
grpAppearance.Parent = me
grpAppearance.Text = "Appearance"
grpAppearance.Location = new Point(175,yDelta)
grpAppearance.Size = new Size(150, yDelta * 3)

rdoAppearanceNormal = new RadioButton( )
rdoAppearanceNormal.Parent = grpAppearance
rdoAppearanceNormal.Text = "Normal"
rdoAppearanceNormal.Location = new Point(10, 15)
rdoAppearanceNormal.Checked = true
AddHandler rdoAppearanceNormal.CheckedChanged, _
      AddressOf rdoAppearance_CheckedChanged

rdoAppearanceButton = new RadioButton( )
rdoAppearanceButton.Parent = grpAppearance
rdoAppearanceButton.Text = "Button"
rdoAppearanceButton.Location = new Point(10, 15 + yDelta)
AddHandler rdoAppearanceButton.CheckedChanged, _
      AddressOf rdoAppearance_CheckedChanged
```

Example 11-10. RadioButton controls using VB.NET (RadioButtons.vb) (continued)

VB

```vb
dim grpCheckAlign as GroupBox = new GroupBox( )
grpCheckAlign.Parent = me
grpCheckAlign.Text = "CheckAlign"
grpCheckAlign.Location = new Point(175, _
                                    grpAppearance.Bottom + 25)
grpCheckAlign.Size = new Size(150, yDelta * 3)

rdoCheckAlignMiddleLeft = new RadioButton( )
rdoCheckAlignMiddleLeft.Parent = grpCheckAlign
rdoCheckAlignMiddleLeft.Text = "Middle Left"
rdoCheckAlignMiddleLeft.Tag = ContentAlignment.MiddleLeft
rdoCheckAlignMiddleLeft.Location = new Point(10, 15)
rdoCheckAlignMiddleLeft.Checked = true
AddHandler rdoCheckAlignMiddleLeft.CheckedChanged, _
    AddressOf rdoCheckAlign_CheckedChanged

rdoCheckAlignMiddleRight = new RadioButton( )
rdoCheckAlignMiddleRight.Parent = grpCheckAlign
rdoCheckAlignMiddleRight.Text = "Middle Right"
rdoCheckAlignMiddleRight.Tag = ContentAlignment.MiddleRight
rdoCheckAlignMiddleRight.Location = new Point(10, 15 + yDelta)
AddHandler rdoCheckAlignMiddleRight.CheckedChanged, _
    AddressOf rdoCheckAlign_CheckedChanged

dim grpTextAlign as GroupBox = new GroupBox( )
grpTextAlign.Parent = me
grpTextAlign.Text = "TextAlign"
grpTextAlign.Location = new Point(175, grpCheckAlign.Bottom + 25)
grpTextAlign.Size = new Size(150, yDelta * 4)

rdoTextAlignMiddleLeft = new RadioButton( )
rdoTextAlignMiddleLeft.Parent = grpTextAlign
rdoTextAlignMiddleLeft.Text = "Middle Left"
rdoTextAlignMiddleLeft.Tag = ContentAlignment.MiddleLeft
rdoTextAlignMiddleLeft.Location = new Point(10, 15)
rdoTextAlignMiddleLeft.Checked = true
AddHandler rdoTextAlignMiddleLeft.CheckedChanged, _
    AddressOf rdoTextAlign_CheckedChanged

rdoTextAlignMiddleRight = new RadioButton( )
rdoTextAlignMiddleRight.Parent = grpTextAlign
rdoTextAlignMiddleRight.Text = "Middle Right"
rdoTextAlignMiddleRight.Tag = ContentAlignment.MiddleRight
rdoTextAlignMiddleRight.Location = new Point(10, 15 + yDelta)
AddHandler rdoTextAlignMiddleRight.CheckedChanged, _
    AddressOf rdoTextAlign_CheckedChanged

rdoTextAlignMiddleCenter = new RadioButton( )
rdoTextAlignMiddleCenter.Parent = grpTextAlign
rdoTextAlignMiddleCenter.Text = "Middle Center"
rdoTextAlignMiddleCenter.Tag = ContentAlignment.MiddleCenter
rdoTextAlignMiddleCenter.Location = new Point(10, _
                                    15 + (2 * yDelta))
```

```
        AddHandler rdoTextAlignMiddleCenter.CheckedChanged, _
            AddressOf rdoTextAlign_CheckedChanged
end sub  '  close for constructor

public shared sub Main( )
    Application.Run(new RadioButtons( ))
end sub

private sub cb_CheckedChanged(ByVal sender as object, _
                        ByVal e as EventArgs)
    dim fs as FontStyle = 0
    dim i as integer
    for i = 0 to pnl.Controls.Count    - 1
        dim cb as CheckBox = CType(pnl.Controls(i), CheckBox)
        if cb.Checked then
            fs   = fs or CType(cb.Tag, FontStyle)
        end if
    next
    lbl.Font = new Font(lbl.Font, fs)
end sub

private sub rdoAppearance_CheckedChanged(ByVal sender as object, _
                        ByVal e as EventArgs)
    dim i as integer
    if rdoAppearanceNormal.Checked then
        for i = 0 to pnl.Controls.Count - 1
            dim cb as CheckBox = CType(pnl.Controls(i), CheckBox)
            cb.Appearance = Appearance.Normal
        next
    else
        for i = 0 to pnl.Controls.Count - 1
            dim cb as CheckBox = CType(pnl.Controls(i), CheckBox)
            cb.Appearance = Appearance.Button
        next
    end if
end sub

private sub rdoCheckAlign_CheckedChanged(ByVal sender as object, _
                        ByVal e as EventArgs)
    dim rdo as RadioButton = CType(sender, RadioButton)
    dim i as integer
    for i = 0 to pnl.Controls.Count - 1
        dim cb as CheckBox = CType(pnl.Controls(i), CheckBox)
        cb.CheckAlign = CType(rdo.Tag, ContentAlignment)
    next
end sub

private sub rdoTextAlign_CheckedChanged(ByVal sender as object, _
                        ByVal e as EventArgs)
    dim rdo as RadioButton = CType(sender, RadioButton)
    dim i as integer
    for i = 0 to pnl.Controls.Count - 1
```

`VB`

```
            dim cb as CheckBox = CType(pnl.Controls(i), CheckBox)
            select case rdo.Tag
                case ContentAlignment.MiddleLeft
                    cb.TextAlign = ContentAlignment.MiddleLeft
                case ContentAlignment.MiddleRight
                    cb.TextAlign = ContentAlignment.MiddleRight
                case ContentAlignment.MiddleCenter
                    cb.TextAlign = ContentAlignment.MiddleCenter
            end select
        next
    end sub
  end class
end namespace
```

The first significant difference in these examples is that the yDelta variable is now a member of the class (and thus available to all the methods of the class).

There are a number of relatively minor changes in the constructor. The Text property and Size of the form has been modified and the instantiation of yDelta now reflects the fact that it is a member variable rather than a local variable. The Border-Style of the Panel control has been set to BorderStyle.None so that it will not be visible on the form, but will still function as a container of the CheckBoxes.

Now comes the meat of the differences in the constructor. There are three new GroupBox controls, each containing several RadioButton controls. Each set of radio buttons within a group box are mutually exclusive: only one radio button in each group can be checked at the same time.

Within each group, the radio button corresponding to the default value has its Checked property set to true so that the form will initialize with the correctly checked radio button. yDelta is used for calculating the Location and Size properties of many of the controls. The Location property of the second and third group boxes are calculated based on the Bottom property of the previous group box. Here are the lines of code that set the Location property for each group box (the same in both languages except for the trailing semicolon):

```
grpAppearance.Location = new Point(175,yDelta);
grpCheckAlign.Location = new Point(175, grpAppearance.Bottom + 25);
grpTextAlign.Location = new Point(175, grpCheckAlign.Bottom + 25);
```

An event handler is added to the CheckedChanged delegate for each RadioButton control, as was done in the CheckBox control. One event handler is used for all the radio buttons in each group box, so there are a total of three event handler methods, one each for grpAppearance, grpCheckAlign, and grpTextAlign.

Each of the three event handlers uses a different technique for implementing the event handler, although in practice you will probably find the middle method, rdoCheckAlign_CheckedChanged, the most efficient.

The first event handler, rdoAppearance_CheckedChanged, capitalizes on the fact that there are only two radio buttons in the group, and therefore only two possible outcomes. This lends itself to a simple if-else (if...then...else) construct. Within each statement block, the Controls collection of the Panel control is iterated to apply the appropriate value of the Appearance property to the checkboxes.

The second event handler, rdoCheckAlign_CheckedChanged, uses the fact that the Tag property of the radio buttons is set to the appropriate value of the ContentAlignment enumeration. The object raising the CheckedChanged event (i.e., the radio button that has been changed) is cast to a variable of type RadioButton, and then in the iteration of the CheckBox controls, that Tag value is cast back to the ContentAlignment type and assigned to the CheckAlign property of each CheckBox control.

The third event handler, rdoTextAlign_CheckedChanged, uses a switch statement (select case in VB.NET) to apply the correct value of the ContentAlignment enumeration to the checkboxes. There is a slight difference here between the C# and VB.NET versions of the code. Since the switch construct in C# requires either an integer or string expression to switch on, it is not possible to switch directly on the Tag value, which is of type ContentAlignment, as is done in the VB.NET code. Instead the C# version must cast the ContentAlignment enumeration to its equivalent integer value and switch on that.

CHAPTER 12

Text Controls

Almost all computer applications display at least some text. Most .NET controls have a Text property that displays a string of text as part of the control (a caption). Text is used for menus; for help systems; to enter, view, and edit data; to label other controls; and to provide direction to the user. In many applications, such as word processors and text editors, text is the *raison d'etre* for the program itself.

In addition to the Text property of most controls, there are also several .NET controls whose primary purpose is to display text. Those controls are the topic of this chapter.

Text

Text has two different components. The first is the content (the actual characters contained in the text string). The content typically consists of ASCII or Unicode characters entered in one of several ways:

- Directly from the keyboard.
- From the keyboard using the Alt key and a four-digit ASCII or Unicode decimal value.
- Programmatically. (In C#, cast an ASCII or Unicode value to a character type [(char)*n*, where *n* is a decimal ASCII or Unicode value] or, in VB.NET, use a function such as Chr( ))

The second component of text is the format or appearance. This component is defined by the font, which dictates how the characters look. There are many different fonts, such as Times New Roman and Arial. In addition, most fonts can have style attributes applied, such as **bold** or *italic*.

 Text and fonts are covered thoroughly in Chapter 9.

Editable Text Controls: TextBoxBase

In addition to all of the controls that have a run-of-the-mill Text property, there are several controls whose sole purpose is to display editable text. The Label control displays text, but is read-only.

The TextBoxBase class provides a base class for three controls that allow the read-write display of text:

TextBox
> Displays text with no formatting other than the current Font of the control. Has a 64K character capacity limit.

DataGridTextBox
> A text box hosted in a DataGridTextBoxColumn control. Derives from TextBox.

RichTextBox
> Displays text with formatting.

Figure 12-1 shows the class hierarchy of the TextBoxBase class.

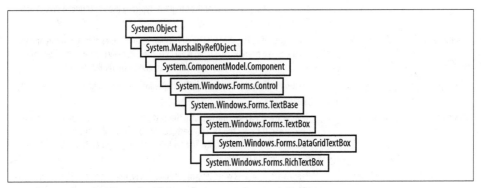

Figure 12-1. TextBoxBase class hierarchy

Properties and Methods

The TextBoxBase class has many properties and methods in addition to those inherited from Control. Many of the properties are listed in Table 12-1 and the methods in Table 12-4. Many of the most commonly used properties and methods are demonstrated in the examples that follow.

Table 12-1. TextBoxBase properties

Property	Value type	Description
AcceptsTab	Boolean	Read/write. Applies to multiline TextBoxes and RichTextBoxes. If true, the Tab key is accepted as part of the text string, otherwise it moves the focus to the next control in the tab order. The default is false.
AutoSize	Boolean	Read/write. If true (the default), the size of control is automatically adjusted when the font changes.

Table 12-1. TextBoxBase properties (continued)

Property	Value type	Description
BackColor	Color	Read/write. The background color of the text box. If set the same as the ForeColor property, the text will not be visible. Overrides the Control base class.
BorderStyle	BorderStyle	Read/write. Border style for the label. Values are members of the BorderStyle enumeration listed in Table 12-2. The default value is BorderStyle.Fixed3D.
CanUndo	Boolean	Read-only. If false (set by ClearUndo method), the user cannot undo the previous operation. If true, the Undo method can be used.
ForeColor	Color	Read/write. The foreground color of the text box—the color of the text Overrides the Control base class. If set the same as the BackColor property, the text will not be visible.
HideSelection	Boolean	Read/write. If true (the default), selected text will cease to be highlighted when the text box loses focus.
Lines	String array	Read/write. An array that contains the text contained in the text box. Each array element corresponds to a line of text.
MaxLength	Integer	Read/write. The maximum number of characters that can be typed into a control.
Modified	Boolean	Read/write. If false (the default), the contents of the text box have not been modified by either the user or the program. Typically used to trigger a save or validation operation.
Multiline	Boolean	Read/write. If true, the text box will display multiple lines of text, interpreting the Enter key as a newline character. If false, the Enter key is disallowed. The default is false for TextBox and DataGridTextBox, and true for RichTextBox.
PreferredHeight	Integer	Read-only. The preferred height of a single-line text box using the current font, in pixels.
ReadOnly	Boolean	Read/write. If false (the default), the Text property can be changed at runtime by the user. If true, the Text property can not be changed by the user, but can still be changed programmatically. The contents of the Text property can be copied by the user despite this value.
ScrollBars	ScrollBars	Read/write. Indicates what type of scrollbar, if any, the text box will have. Valid values must be members of the ScrollBars enumeration, listed in Table 12-3. The default is ScrollBars.None.
SelectedText	String	Read/write. The currently selected text in the text box.
SelectionLength	Integer	Read/write. The length of the SelectedText property.
SelectionStart	Integer	Read/write. The zero-based starting index of the text selected in the text box, if any. If no text is selected, then it is the insertion point for new text. If all the text is selected or if the insertion point is at the beginning of the text box, it returns a value of zero.
Text	String	Read/write. The text displayed by the text box. Overrides the Control base class.
WordWrap	Boolean	Read/write. Applies only when the MultiLine property is true. If true (the default), the contents of the text box will wrap words if the length of a string exceeds the width of the control. If false, the text box will scroll horizontally as the text is entered to display the right end of the text.

Table 12-2. BorderStyle enumeration values

Value	Description
Fixed3D	3-D border
FixedSingle	Single-line border
None	No border

Table 12-3. ScrollBars enumeration

Value	Description
Both	Both horizontal and vertical scrollbars are present. A horizontal scrollbar is present only if the Word-Wrap property is set to `false`.
Horizontal	Only a horizontal scrollbar is present, and then only if the WordWrap property is set to `false`.
None	No scrollbars are present.
Vertical	Only a vertical scrollbar is present.

Table 12-4. TextBoxBase methods

Method	Description
AppendText	Appends text string contained in the argument to the Text property of the text box. Functionally equivalent to using the concatenation operator, although it is actually implemented by setting the selection to the end of the text and then replacing the selection with the text to be appended.
Clear	Empties the Text property of the text box. Equivalent to setting the Text property to an empty string. Cannot be undone by calling the Undo method.
ClearUndo	Removes the information about the most recent operation from the undo buffer so that the undo operation cannot be repeated. Sets the read-only property CanUndo property to `false`.
Copy	Copies the currently selected text in the text box control to the Clipboard. Default functionality provided by Ctrl-C.
Cut	Moves the currently selected text from the text box control to the Clipboard. Default functionality provided by Ctrl-X.
Paste	Replaces the text currently selected in the text box with text currently stored in the Clipboard. Default functionality provided by Ctrl-V.
ScrollToCaret	Scrolls the contents of the text box until the caret (the current text entry point) is visible in the control. If the caret is currently below the visible region, the contents will be scrolled until the caret is at the bottom of the control. If the caret is currently above the visible region, the contents will be scrolled until the caret is at the top of the control. If the caret is currently visible or if the control does not have focus, the method will be have no effect.
Select	Overloaded method for selecting text within a text box control. Takes two integer arguments representing the starting character (zero-based) and the number of characters to be selected.
SelectAll	Selects the entire Text property of a text box control. Default functionality provided by Ctrl-A.
Undo	Undoes the last clipboard or text change operation performed on the contents of the text box control if the CanUndo property is `true`. Default functionality provided by Ctrl-Z.

The program shown in Example 12-1 (in C#) and Example 12-2 (in VB.NET) demonstrates many of the properties and methods of the TextBoxBase class. These examples have two TextBox controls for entering text—one single line and one multiline. A button can display, in another text box, the contents of the Lines array from the multiline text box. A simple menu allows various typical text manipulations, such as copy, cut, paste, and clear all. An analysis of the program follows.

 Many of the methods listed in Table 12-4 are implemented in the base class, so there is no need for you to supply code to provide their functionality. These methods include Copy, Cut, Paste, SelectAll, and Undo.

When the program is compiled and run and some text is entered into the multiline text box, it looks like Figure 12-2.

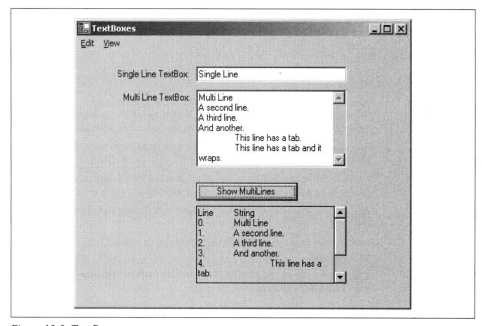

Figure 12-2. TextBoxes

Example 12-1. TextBox control properties and methods in C# (TextBoxes.cs)

```
using System;
using System.Drawing;
using System.Windows.Forms;
using System.Text;

namespace ProgrammingWinApps
{
    public class TextBoxes : Form
    {
```

```csharp
int yDelta;
int yPos = 20;
TextBox txtSingle;
TextBox txtMulti;
TextBox txtDisplay;
Button btn;
TextBox[ ] txtBoxes = new TextBox[2];

public TextBoxes( )
{
   Text = "TextBoxes";
   Size = new Size(450,375);

   Label lblSingle = new Label( );
   lblSingle.Parent = this;
   lblSingle.Text = "Single Line TextBox:";
   lblSingle.Location = new Point(10,yPos);
   lblSingle.Size = new Size(150,20);
   lblSingle.TextAlign = ContentAlignment.MiddleRight;
   yDelta = lblSingle.Height + 10;

   txtSingle = new TextBox( );
   txtSingle.Parent = this;
   txtSingle.Text = "Single Line";
   txtSingle.Size = new Size(200, txtSingle.PreferredHeight);
   txtSingle.Location = new Point(lblSingle.Left +
                              lblSingle.Size.Width, yPos);
   txtSingle.Multiline = false;
   txtSingle.BorderStyle = BorderStyle.Fixed3D;

   Label lblMulti = new Label( );
   lblMulti.Parent = this;
   lblMulti.Text = "Multi Line TextBox:";
   lblMulti.Location = new Point(10, yPos + yDelta);
   lblMulti.Size = new Size(150,20);
   lblMulti.TextAlign = ContentAlignment.MiddleRight;

   txtMulti = new TextBox( );
   txtMulti.Parent = this;
   txtMulti.Text = "Multi Line";
   txtMulti.Size = new Size(200,100);
   txtMulti.Location = new Point(lblMulti.Left +
                              lblMulti.Size.Width,
                              yPos + yDelta);
   txtMulti.AcceptsTab = true;
   txtMulti.Multiline = true;
   txtMulti.BorderStyle = BorderStyle.Fixed3D;
   txtMulti.ScrollBars = ScrollBars.Vertical;

   btn = new Button( );
   btn.Parent = this;
```

```csharp
btn.Text = "Show MultiLines";
btn.Location = new Point(lblMulti.Left + lblMulti.Size.Width,
                 yPos + (5 * yDelta));
btn.Click += new System.EventHandler(btn_Click);
int xSize = ((int)(Font.Height * .75) * btn.Text.Length);
int ySize = Font.Height + 10;
btn.Size = new Size(xSize, ySize);

txtDisplay = new TextBox( );
txtDisplay.Parent = this;
txtDisplay.Text = "";
txtDisplay.Size = new Size(200,100);
txtDisplay.Location = new Point(lblMulti.Left +
                       lblMulti.Size.Width,
                       yPos + (6 * yDelta));
txtDisplay.Multiline = true;
txtDisplay.BorderStyle = BorderStyle.FixedSingle;
txtDisplay.ScrollBars = ScrollBars.Vertical;
txtDisplay.ReadOnly = true;

//  Fill the array of TextBoxes
txtBoxes[0] = txtSingle;
txtBoxes[1] = txtMulti;

//  Menus
//  Edit menu items
MenuItem mnuDash1 = new MenuItem("-");
MenuItem mnuDash2 = new MenuItem("-");
MenuItem mnuUndo = new MenuItem("&Undo",
                 new EventHandler(mnuUndo_Click),
                 Shortcut.CtrlZ);
MenuItem mnuCut = new MenuItem("Cu&t",
                 new EventHandler(mnuCut_Click),
                 Shortcut.CtrlX);
MenuItem mnuCopy = new MenuItem("&Copy",
                 new EventHandler(mnuCopy_Click),
                 Shortcut.CtrlC);
MenuItem mnuPaste = new MenuItem("&Paste",
                 new EventHandler(mnuPaste_Click),
                 Shortcut.CtrlV);
MenuItem mnuDelete = new MenuItem("&Delete",
                 new EventHandler(mnuDelete_Click));
MenuItem mnuSelectAll = new MenuItem("Select &All",
                 new EventHandler(mnuSelectAll_Click),
                 Shortcut.CtrlA);
MenuItem mnuSelect5 = new MenuItem("Select First &5",
                 new EventHandler(mnuSelect5_Click),
                 Shortcut.Ctrl5);
MenuItem mnuClear = new MenuItem("Clea&r",
                 new EventHandler(mnuClear_Click));
MenuItem mnuEdit = new MenuItem("&Edit",
                 new MenuItem[ ] {mnuUndo, mnuDash1, mnuCut,
                 mnuCopy, mnuPaste, mnuDelete, mnuDash2,
```

```
                         mnuSelectAll, mnuSelect5, mnuClear});

    // View Menu items
    MenuItem mnuScrollToCaret = new MenuItem("&Scroll to Caret",
                new EventHandler(mnuScrollToCaret_Click));
    MenuItem mnuShowSelectionStart = new MenuItem(
                "S&how SelectionStart",
                new EventHandler(mnuShowSelectionStart_Click));
    MenuItem mnuView = new MenuItem("&View",
                new MenuItem[ ] {mnuScrollToCaret,
                            mnuShowSelectionStart});

    // Main menu
    Menu = new MainMenu(new MenuItem[ ] {mnuEdit, mnuView});
} // close for constructor

static void Main( )
{
    Application.Run(new TextBoxes( ));
}

private void mnuUndo_Click(object sender, EventArgs e)
{
    for (int i = 0; i < txtBoxes.Length; i++)
    {
        if (txtBoxes[i].Focused)
        {
            TextBox txt = txtBoxes[i];
            if (txt.CanUndo == true)
            {
                txt.Undo( );
                txt.ClearUndo( );
            }
        }
    }
}

private void mnuCut_Click(object sender, EventArgs e)
{
    for (int i = 0; i < txtBoxes.Length; i++)
    {
        if (txtBoxes[i].Focused)
        {
            TextBox txt = txtBoxes[i];
            if (txt.SelectedText != "")
                txt.Cut( );
        }
    }
}

private void mnuCopy_Click(object sender, EventArgs e)
{
    for (int i = 0; i < txtBoxes.Length; i++)
```

```
C#        {
             if (txtBoxes[i].Focused)
             {
                TextBox txt = txtBoxes[i];
                if (txt.SelectionLength > 0)
                   txt.Copy();
             }
          }
       }

       private void mnuPaste_Click(object sender, EventArgs e)
       {
          if (Clipboard.GetDataObject().GetDataPresent(DataFormats.Text)
             == true)
          {
             for (int i = 0; i < txtBoxes.Length; i++)
             {
                if (txtBoxes[i].Focused)
                {
                   TextBox txt = txtBoxes[i];
                   if (txt.SelectionLength > 0)
                   {
                      if (MessageBox.Show(
                         "Do you want to overwrite the currently " +
                         "selected text?",
                         "Cut & Paste", MessageBoxButtons.YesNo) ==
                                  DialogResult.No)
                         txt.SelectionStart =
                                  txt.SelectionStart + txt.SelectionLength;
                   }
                   txt.Paste();
                }
             }
          }
       }

       private void mnuDelete_Click(object sender, EventArgs e)
       {
          for (int i = 0; i < txtBoxes.Length; i++)
          {
             if (txtBoxes[i].Focused)
             {
                TextBox txt = txtBoxes[i];
                if (txt.SelectionLength > 0)
                   txt.SelectedText = "";
             }
          }
       }

       private void mnuClear_Click(object sender, EventArgs e)
       {
          for (int i = 0; i < txtBoxes.Length; i++)
          {
```

```csharp
               if (txtBoxes[i].Focused)
               {
                  TextBox txt = txtBoxes[i];
                  txt.Clear();
               }
            }
        }

        private void mnuSelect5_Click(object sender, EventArgs e)
        {
            for (int i = 0; i < txtBoxes.Length; i++)
            {
               if (txtBoxes[i].Focused)
               {
                  TextBox txt = txtBoxes[i];
                  if (txt.Text.Length >= 5)
                  {
                     txt.Select(0,5);
                  }
                  else
                  {
                     txt.Select(0,txt.Text.Length);
                  }
               }
            }
        }

        private void mnuSelectAll_Click(object sender, EventArgs e)
        {
            for (int i = 0; i < txtBoxes.Length; i++)
            {
               if (txtBoxes[i].Focused)
               {
                  TextBox txt = txtBoxes[i];
                  txt.SelectAll();
               }
            }
        }

        private void mnuScrollToCaret_Click(object sender, EventArgs e)
        {
            for (int i = 0; i < txtBoxes.Length; i++)
            {
               if (txtBoxes[i].Focused)
               {
                  TextBox txt = txtBoxes[i];
                  txt.ScrollToCaret();
               }
            }
        }

        private void mnuShowSelectionStart_Click(object sender, EventArgs e)
```

Example 12-1. TextBox control properties and methods in C# (TextBoxes.cs) (continued)

```csharp
    {
        MessageBox.Show("SelectionStart: " +
                        txtSingle.SelectionStart.ToString( ));
    }

    private void btn_Click(object sender, EventArgs e)
    {
        // Create a string array to hold the Lines property.
        string[ ] arLines = new string [txtMulti.Lines.Length];
        arLines = txtMulti.Lines;

        //  Use stringBuilder for efficiency.
        string str = "Line\tString\r\n";
        StringBuilder sb = new StringBuilder( );
        sb.Append(str);

        // Iterate through the array & display each line.
        for (int i=0; i < arLines.Length; i++)
        {
            str = i.ToString( ) + ".\t" + arLines[i] + "\r\n";
            sb.Append(str);
        }

        txtDisplay.Text = sb.ToString( );
    }

  }         //  close for form class
}           //  close form namespace
```

Example 12-2. TextBox control properties and methods in VB.NET (TextBoxes.vb)

```vbnet
Option Strict On
imports System
imports System.Drawing
imports System.Windows.Forms
imports System.Text

namespace ProgrammingWinApps
   public class TextBoxes : inherits Form

      dim yDelta as integer
      dim yPos as integer = 20
      dim txtSingle as TextBox
      dim txtMulti as TextBox
      dim txtDisplay as TextBox
      dim btn as Button
      dim txtBoxes(1) as TextBox

      public sub New( )
         Text = "TextBoxes"
         Size = new Size(450,375)

         dim lblSingle as new Label( )
```

```vb
lblSingle.Parent = me
lblSingle.Text = "Single Line TextBox:"
lblSingle.Location = new Point(10,yPos)
lblSingle.Size = new Size(150,20)
lblSingle.TextAlign = ContentAlignment.MiddleRight
yDelta = lblSingle.Height + 10

txtSingle = new TextBox( )
txtSingle.Parent = me
txtSingle.Text = "Single Line"
txtSingle.Size = new Size(200, txtSingle.PreferredHeight)
txtSingle.Location = new Point(lblSingle.Left + _
                        lblSingle.Size.Width, yPos)
txtSingle.Multiline = false
txtSingle.BorderStyle = BorderStyle.Fixed3D

dim lblMulti as new Label( )
lblMulti.Parent = me
lblMulti.Text = "Multi Line TextBox:"
lblMulti.Location = new Point(10, yPos + yDelta)
lblMulti.Size = new Size(150,20)
lblMulti.TextAlign = ContentAlignment.MiddleRight

txtMulti = new TextBox( )
txtMulti.Parent = me
txtMulti.Text = "Multi Line"
txtMulti.Size = new Size(200,100)
txtMulti.Location = new Point(lblMulti.Left + _
                lblMulti.Size.Width, yPos + yDelta)
txtMulti.AcceptsTab = true
txtMulti.Multiline = true
txtMulti.BorderStyle = BorderStyle.Fixed3D
txtMulti.ScrollBars = ScrollBars.Vertical

btn = new Button( )
btn.Parent = me
btn.Text = "Show MultiLines"
btn.Location = new Point(lblMulti.Left + _
            lblMulti.Size.Width, yPos + (5 * yDelta))
AddHandler btn.Click, AddressOf btn_Click
dim xSize as integer = CType((Font.Height * .75) * _
            btn.Text.Length, integer)
dim ySize as integer = Font.Height + 10
btn.Size = new Size(xSize, ySize)

txtDisplay = new TextBox( )
txtDisplay.Parent = me
txtDisplay.Text = ""
txtDisplay.Size = new Size(200,100)
txtDisplay.Location = new Point(lblMulti.Left + _
                lblMulti.Size.Width, yPos + (6 * yDelta))
txtDisplay.Multiline = true
txtDisplay.BorderStyle = BorderStyle.FixedSingle
```

VB

```
        txtDisplay.ScrollBars = ScrollBars.Vertical
        txtDisplay.ReadOnly = true

        '  Fill the array of TextBoxes
        txtBoxes(0) = txtSingle
        txtBoxes(1) = txtMulti

        '  Menus
        '  Edit menu items
        dim mnuDash1 as new MenuItem("-")
        dim mnuDash2 as new MenuItem("-")
        dim mnuUndo as new MenuItem("&Undo", _
                     new EventHandler(AddressOf mnuUndo_Click), _
                     Shortcut.CtrlZ)
        dim mnuCut as new MenuItem("Cu&t", _
                    new EventHandler(AddressOf mnuCut_Click), _
                    Shortcut.CtrlX)
        dim mnuCopy as new MenuItem("&Copy", _
                     new EventHandler(AddressOf mnuCopy_Click), _
                     Shortcut.CtrlC)
        dim mnuPaste as new MenuItem("&Paste", _
                      new EventHandler(AddressOf mnuPaste_Click), _
                      Shortcut.CtrlV)
        dim mnuDelete as new MenuItem("&Delete", _
                       new EventHandler(AddressOf mnuDelete_Click))
        dim mnuSelectAll as new MenuItem("Select &All", _
                          new EventHandler(AddressOf mnuSelectAll_Click), _
                          Shortcut.CtrlA)
        dim mnuSelect5 as new MenuItem("Select First &5", _
                        new EventHandler(AddressOf mnuSelect5_Click), _
                        Shortcut.Ctrl5)
        dim mnuClear as new MenuItem("Clea&r", _
                      new EventHandler(AddressOf mnuClear_Click))
        dim mnuEdit as new MenuItem("&Edit", _
                     new MenuItem( ) {mnuUndo, mnuDash1, _
                     mnuCut, mnuCopy, mnuPaste, mnuDelete, mnuDash2, _
                     mnuSelectAll, mnuSelect5, mnuClear})

        '  View Menu items
        dim mnuScrollToCaret as new MenuItem("&Scroll to Caret", _
                     new EventHandler(AddressOf mnuScrollToCaret_Click))
        dim mnuShowSelectionStart as new MenuItem( _
              "&S&how SelectionStart", _
              new EventHandler(AddressOf mnuShowSelectionStart_Click))
        dim mnuView as new MenuItem("&View", _
                     new MenuItem( ) {mnuScrollToCaret, _
                                 mnuShowSelectionStart})

        '  Main menu
        Menu = new MainMenu(new MenuItem( ) {mnuEdit, mnuView})

    end sub  '  close for constructor
```

```
public shared sub Main( )
   Application.Run(new TextBoxes( ))
end sub

private sub mnuUndo_Click(ByVal sender As Object, _
                 ByVal e As EventArgs)
   dim i as integer
   for i = 0 to txtBoxes.Length - 1
      if txtBoxes(i).Focused then
         dim txt as TextBox = txtBoxes(i)
         if txt.CanUndo = true then
            txt.Undo( )
            txt.ClearUndo( )
         end if
      end if
   next
end sub

private sub mnuCut_Click(ByVal sender As Object, _
                 ByVal e As EventArgs)
   dim i as integer
   for i = 0 to txtBoxes.Length - 1
      if txtBoxes(i).Focused then
         dim txt as TextBox = txtBoxes(i)
         if txt.SelectedText <> "" then
            txt.Cut( )
         end if
      end if
   next
end sub

private sub mnuCopy_Click(ByVal sender As Object, _
                 ByVal e As EventArgs)
   dim i as integer
   for i = 0 to txtBoxes.Length - 1
      if txtBoxes(i).Focused then
         dim txt as TextBox = txtBoxes(i)
         if txt.SelectionLength > 0 then
            txt.Copy( )
         end if
      end if
   next
end sub

private sub mnuPaste_Click(ByVal sender As Object, _
                 ByVal e As EventArgs)
   if Clipboard.GetDataObject( ).GetDataPresent(DataFormats.Text) = _
            true then
      dim i as integer
      for i = 0 to txtBoxes.Length - 1
         if txtBoxes(i).Focused then
            dim txt as TextBox = txtBoxes(i)
            if txt.SelectionLength > 0 then
```

Example 12-2. TextBox control properties and methods in VB.NET (TextBoxes.vb) (continued)

```
                    if MessageBox.Show( _
                    "Do you want to overwrite the currently " + _
                        "selected text?", _
                    "Cut & Paste", MessageBoxButtons.YesNo) = _
                        DialogResult.No then
                      txt.SelectionStart = txt.SelectionStart + _
                                    txt.SelectionLength
                    end if
                end if
                txt.Paste( )
            end if
        next
    end if
end sub

private sub mnuDelete_Click(ByVal sender As Object, _
                    ByVal e As EventArgs)
    dim i as integer
    for i = 0 to txtBoxes.Length - 1
        if txtBoxes(i).Focused then
            dim txt as TextBox = txtBoxes(i)
            if txt.SelectionLength > 0 then
                txt.SelectedText = ""
            end if
        end if
    next
end sub

private sub mnuClear_Click(ByVal sender As Object, _
                    ByVal e As EventArgs)
    dim i as integer
    for i = 0 to txtBoxes.Length - 1
        if txtBoxes(i).Focused then
            dim txt as TextBox = txtBoxes(i)
            txt.Clear( )
        end if
    next
end sub

private sub mnuSelect5_Click(ByVal sender As Object, _
                    ByVal e As EventArgs)
    dim i as integer
    for i = 0 to txtBoxes.Length - 1
        if txtBoxes(i).Focused then
            dim txt as TextBox = txtBoxes(i)
            if txt.Text.Length >= 5 then
                txt.Select(0,5)
            else
                txt.Select(0,txt.Text.Length)
            end if
        end if
    next
end sub
```

```vb
private sub mnuSelectAll_Click(ByVal sender As Object, _
                         ByVal e As EventArgs)
   dim i as integer
   for i = 0 to txtBoxes.Length - 1
      if txtBoxes(i).Focused then
         dim txt as TextBox = txtBoxes(i)
         txt.SelectAll()
      end if
   next
end sub

private sub mnuScrollToCaret_Click(ByVal sender As Object, _
                         ByVal e As EventArgs)
   dim i as integer
   for i = 0 to txtBoxes.Length - 1
      if txtBoxes(i).Focused then
         dim txt as TextBox = txtBoxes(i)
         txt.ScrollToCaret()
      end if
   next
end sub

private sub mnuShowSelectionStart_Click(ByVal sender As Object, _
                         ByVal e As EventArgs)
   MessageBox.Show("SelectionStart: " + _
            txtSingle.SelectionStart.ToString())
end sub

private sub btn_Click(ByVal sender as object, _
               ByVal e as EventArgs)
   ' Create a string array to hold the Lines property.
   dim arLines(txtMulti.Lines.Length - 1) as string
   arLines = txtMulti.Lines

   ' Use stringBuilder for efficiency.
   dim str as string = "Line" + vbTab + "String" + vbCrLf
   dim sb as new StringBuilder()
   sb.Append(str)

   ' Iterate through the array & display each line.
   dim i as integer
   for i = 0 to arLines.Length - 1
      str = i.ToString() + "." + vbTab + arLines(i) + vbCrLf
      sb.Append(str)
   next

   txtDisplay.Text = sb.ToString()
end sub

   end class
end namespace
```

The program defines a Form class called TextBoxes, with member variables representing two integers used for calculating the Location property of all the controls, three text boxes, a button, and an array of TextBoxes.

This array of TextBoxes will be used by most menu event handlers when determining which text box should be the target of the pending action. The array declaration looks like this:

C#
```
TextBox[ ] txtBoxes = new TextBox[2];
```

VB
```
dim txtBoxes(1) as TextBox
```

 Remember that arrays in C# are declared with the count of elements, but they are declared with the upper bound in VB.NET. All arrows are zero-indexed in both languages.

Inside the constructor, each control is instantiated and specified with several properties. Labels used for captioning purposes are declared and instantiated here. They are not defined as member variables since they are never referenced outside the constructor. (Had this code been written in Visual Studio .NET, all the controls would be member variables.)

The first TextBox control, txtSingle, is a single line text box: its Multiline property is set to false. The BorderStyle property is set to BorderStyle.Fixed3D to give it a chiseled look.

The second TextBox control, txtMulti, is a multiline text box, since its Multiline property is set to true. In addition to the same BorderStyle setting as the previous control, txtMulti has the AcceptTab property set to true and the ScrollBars property set to ScrollBars.Vertical (see Tables 12-2 and 12-3).

The AcceptTab property causes the Tab key to be entered as a tab character in the text rather than shifting focus to the next control in the tab order. The ScrollBars property displays a vertical scrollbar in the text box. If there is insufficient text to warrant scrolling, the scrollbars are disabled (visible but grayed), otherwise they are enabled.

The button control is straightforward, with it's size based dynamically on the current font and the length of the Text property and an event handler for the Click event.

The final TextBox control, txtDisplay, displays the formatted contents of the Lines array from txtMulti. Since it is for display only, its ReadOnly property is set to true. Setting the ReadOnly property to true also makes the background color light gray without the need to explicitly set the BackColor property. Also, to distinguish the read-only text box visually, the BorderStyle is set to BorderStyle.FixedSingle.

The next two lines of code populate the array of TextBoxes previously declared as a member variable:

```
txtBoxes[0] = txtSingle;
txtBoxes[1] = txtMulti;
```

```
txtBoxes(0) = txtSingle
txtBoxes(1) = txtMulti
```

The next block of code in the constructor creates the menu system. A menu consists of MenuItem objects, which are assembled into higher level MenuItem objects, which are themselves assembled into a main menu. In this example, the main menu consists of two menu items: Edit and View. The Edit menu item has the following menu items: Undo, Cut, Copy, Paste, Delete, Select All, Select First 5, and Clear, along with two separators. The View menu has two menu items: View to Caret and Show SelectionStart.

Menus will be covered in detail in Chapter 18.

All the menu items can have an *accelerator key*, an underlined character that can be pressed in conjunction with the Alt key to effectuate that menu item. Many menu items also have a *shortcut key*, a single key or key combination listed to the right of the menu item, which will effectuate the command.

Menu are typically built backwards—the menu items deepest in the hierarchy are created first, and then they are added to the next level up in the hierarchy. These items are then added to their parent items, and so on up the main menu.

It is not necessary to build the menu backward. You only need to create the children before adding them to the parent. However, you can create the items in any order you wish.

Different menu item constructors are used. All the menu items that actually *do* something have a specified event handler that will be invoked if that menu item is clicked. For example, the Undo menu item is defined in the following code snippet:

```
MenuItem mnuUndo = new MenuItem("&Undo",
                        new EventHandler(mnuUndo_Click),
                        Shortcut.CtrlZ);
```

```
dim mnuUndo as new MenuItem("&Undo", _
                new EventHandler(AddressOf mnuUndo_Click), _
                Shortcut.CtrlZ)
```

The ampersand before the U in Undo causes that letter to appear underlined and indicates that U is an accelerator key. The event handler for this menu item is mnuUndo_Click, and the shortcut key is Ctrl-Z.

Most commands under the Edit menu item have standard Windows shortcut keys: Ctrl-Z for Undo, Ctrl-X for Cut, Ctrl-V for Paste, and so on. Since these are standard shortcuts, they will still work even if they are not explicitly declared when the menu item is created. Explicitly declaring them makes them visible when the menu is displayed, reminding the user that they exist.

There is another, more subtle reason for explicitly declaring the shortcut. The code used here does not exactly duplicate the standard Windows behavior for all operations—for example, Paste asks for user confirmation, while standard Windows Paste just pastes. If the shortcut were not explicitly declared, the user would see standard Windows behavior when using the shortcut and customized behavior when using the menu. Explicitly declaring the shortcut forces both techniques to use your code.

Similarly, in this example the Delete menu item has no declared shortcut key, yet the Delete key works as you would expect. On the other hand, the Select First 5 menu item, which selects the first five characters of the text box, is not a standard Windows command and does not have a standard shortcut. If the shortcut key Ctrl-5 were not explicitly declared in its menu item declaration, there would be no shortcut key.

All menu item event handlers follow the same pattern. The event handler is invoked in response to a menu click; it does not inherently know which text box is the target. Therefore, each method must determine which text box to apply the action to, and whether that action is to undo, cut, copy, or paste. It determines the target text box by iterating through the array of TextBoxes, txtBoxes, testing each one to see if it has focus. If it does, then it applies whatever code is relevant for that event handler. It has the following design pattern:

C#

```csharp
for (int i = 0; i < txtBoxes.Length; i++)
{
    if (txtBoxes[i].Focused)
    {
        // Instantiate variable for the target TextBox
        TextBox txt = txtBoxes[i];

        // Take the action here

    }
}
```

VB

```vb
dim i as integer
for i = 0 to txtBoxes.Length - 1
    if txtBoxes(i).Focused then
        ' Instantiate variable for the target TextBox
        dim txt as TextBox = txtBoxes(i)

        ' Take the action here

    end if
next
```

The highlighted line assigns a reference to the array element that reference is assigned, and the code can then take the appropriate action, typically by calling a TextBoxBase instance method or by setting a TextBoxBase property (treating the TextBox polymorphically).

The Undo menu item event handler, mnuUndo_Click, uses the following lines of code to implement its action:

C#
```
if (txt.CanUndo == true)
{
    txt.Undo( );
    txt.ClearUndo( );
}
```

VB
```
if txt.CanUndo = true then
    txt.Undo( )
    txt.ClearUndo( )
end if
```

First test the CanUndo property to determine if there is anything to undo. If so, the Undo method is called, followed by the ClearUndo method to reset CanUndo to false.

The Cut menu item event handler, mnuCut_Click, uses the following lines of code to implement its action:

C#
```
if (txt.SelectedText != "")
    txt.Cut( );
```

VB
```
if txt.SelectedText <> "" then
    txt.Cut( )
end if
```

This method tests to see whether the SelectedText property is an empty string. If not, then there must be selected text, and the Cut method is called to remove that selection from the text box and place it in the Clipboard.

The Copy menu item event handler, mnuCopy_Click, uses the following lines of code to implement its action:

C#
```
if (txt.SelectionLength > 0)
    txt.Copy( );
```

VB
```
if txt.SelectionLength > 0 then
    txt.Copy( )
end if
```

This method is slightly different from the Cut implementation, testing whether the SelectionLength property is greater than zero. If so, there is some selected text, and the Copy method is called to copy that selection into the Clipboard.

The two different tests used in the Cut and Copy methods are functionally equivalent. Which one you decide to use is a matter of programmer preference.

The Paste menu item event handler, mnuPaste_Click, differs from the standard design pattern in that it wraps the entire thing inside an if statement to test for text data in the Clipboard (see the sidebar "The Windows Clipboard" for an explanation of this):

C#

```
if (Clipboard.GetDataObject( ).GetDataPresent(DataFormats.Text) == true)
{
```

VB

```
if Clipboard.GetDataObject( ).GetDataPresent(DataFormats.Text) _
    = true then
```

If there is text data in the Clipboard, then the Paste operation can proceed, using the same design pattern as the other methods. After iterating through the array of TextBoxes, finding the text box with focus, and getting a reference to that control, the method then implements a slightly more cautious behavior than the standard Windows paste operation. If you currently have text selected, the typical Windows paste operation simply overwrites that selection with the contents of the Clipboard. Here it asks first whether you want to overwrite. If the answer is No, then it uses the current SelectionStart and SelectionLength properties to calculate a new value for SelectionStart before calling the TextBoxBase method Paste. This action pastes the contents of the Clipboard at the end of the currently selected text, rather than replacing the currently selected text:

C#

```
if (txt.SelectionLength > 0)
{
    if (MessageBox.Show(
        "Do you want to overwrite the currently selected text?",
        "Cut & Paste", MessageBoxButtons.YesNo) ==
            DialogResult.No)
        txt.SelectionStart = txt.SelectionStart +
            txt.SelectionLength;
}
txt.Paste( );
```

VB

```
if txt.SelectionLength > 0 then
    if MessageBox.Show( _
    "Do you want to overwrite the currently selected text?", _
    "Cut & Paste", MessageBoxButtons.YesNo) = _
        DialogResult.No then
        txt.SelectionStart = txt.SelectionStart + _
                        txt.SelectionLength
    end if
end if
txt.Paste( )
```

The Windows Clipboard

The Clipboard is a standard Windows system object: a shared chunk of memory used for temporarily storing data used in cut, copy, and paste operations. It is implemented in the .NET Framework through the Clipboard class, which provides two methods: SetDataObject places data in the Clipboard, and GetDataObject retrieves data from the Clipboard.

The overloaded SetDataObject method has two forms. They are:

[C#]
```
public static void SetDataObject(object);
public static void SetDataObject(object, bool);
```

[VB]
```
Overloads Public Shared Sub SetDataObject(object)
Overloads Public Shared Sub SetDataObject(object, Boolean)
```

The first form places the object specified in the argument onto the Clipboard until it is replaced by the next object placed on the Clipboard or the application exits. The second form takes a Boolean value, which if true, persists the object on the Clipboard even after the application exits.

The GetDataObject method retrieves the stored object from the Clipboard. The object can be of many different types. It is returned as an object of type IDataObject, which has predefined data formats. These data formats are contained in the DataFormats class as read-only, static (Shared in VB .NET) public fields, listed in Table 12-5.

To retrieve data from the Clipboard, declare an object of type IDataObject and call the static GetDataObject method:

[C#]
```
IDataObject iData = Clipboard.GetDataObject();
```

[VB]
```
dim iData as IDataObject = Clipboard.GetDataObject()
```

You can then test the IDataObject to determine whether it is a format your application can use, using the GetDataPresent method of the IDataObject class, which returns a Boolean:

[C#]
```
if (iData.GetDataPresent(DataFormats.Text))
```

[VB]
```
if iData.GetDataPresent(DataFormats.Text) then
```

In the Paste method used in Examples 12-1 and 12-2, these two steps were combined into a single line of code:

[C#]
```
if (Clipboard.GetDataObject().GetDataPresent(
   DataFormats.Text) == true)
{
```

[VB]
```
if Clipboard.GetDataObject().GetDataPresent( _
   DataFormats.Text) _= true then
```

Table 12-5. DataFormats Formats (public fields)

Format	Description
Bitmap	Windows bitmap.
CommaSeparatedValue	Comma-separated value (CSV) format used by spreadsheets.
Dib	Windows Device Independent Bitmap (DIB).
Dif	Windows Data Interchange Format (DIF). Not used directly by Windows Forms.
EnhancedMetafile	Windows enhanced metafile format.
FileDrop	Windows file drop format. Not used directly by Windows Forms.
Html	Text consisting of HTML data.
Locale	Windows culture format. Not used directly by Windows Forms.
MetafilePict	Windows metafile format. Not used directly by Windows Forms.
OemText	Windows original equipment manufacturer (OEM) text format.
Palette	Windows palette format.
PenData	Windows pen data format for handwriting software. Not used by Windows Forms.
Riff	Resource Interchange File Format (RIFF) audio format. Not used directly by Windows Forms.
Rtf	Rich Text Format (RTF).
Serializable	A format that encapsulates any type of object.
StringFormat	Windows Forms string object.
SymbolicLink	Windows symbolic link format. Not used directly by Windows Forms.
Text	Standard ANSI text.
Tiff	Tagged Image File Format (TIFF) image. Not used directly by Windows Forms.
UnicodeText	Windows Unicode text format.
WaveAudio	Wave audio format. Not used directly by Windows Forms.

The Delete menu item event handler, mnuDelete_Click, uses the following lines of code to implement its action:

C#
```
if (txt.SelectionLength > 0)
    txt.SelectedText = "";
```

VB
```
if txt.SelectionLength > 0 then
    txt.SelectedText = ""
end if
```

It uses the SelectionLength property to see if anything has been selected. If so, it deletes it by setting the SelectedText property to an empty string.

The Clear menu item event handler, mnuClear_, is very simple. It calls the Clear method to empty the Text property of the text box (the same in both languages except for the trailing semicolon):

C#
```
txt.Clear();
```

The Select First 5 menu item selects the first five characters of the text box. If there are fewer than five characters in the text box, it selects them all:

```
if (txt.Text.Length >= 5)
{
    txt.Select(0,5);
}
else
{
    txt.Select(0,txt.Text.Length);
}
```

```
if txt.Text.Length >= 5 then
    txt.Select(0,5)
else
    txt.Select(0,txt.Text.Length)
end if
```

In either case, it uses the Select method, which takes two integer arguments. The first integer is the zero-based index of the first character to be selected, and the second integer is the number of characters to be selected.

The Select All menu item is implemented using the SelectAll method, which selects the entire contents of the text box.

The Scroll to Caret menu item under the View menu is implemented in the mnuScrollToCaret method, invoking the ScrollToCaret method. To see this item in operation, enter enough lines of text in the multiline text box so that the scrollbar is operative. Then leaving the caret—i.e., the text cursor—near either the top or bottom of the text box, use the scrollbar to scroll away so that the caret is no longer visible. Select the Scroll to Caret menu item. Depending on where the caret was positioned relative to the visible text, the text will be scrolled so that the caret is either the first line in the text box or the last.

The final event handler method implements the Show SelectionStart menu item under the View menu. This menu item displays the current value of the Selection-Start property for the single line text box, txtSingle.

The Click event handler for the button control demonstrates the use of the Lines property of a text box. This is an array of strings whose elements each contain one line of text from the Text property of the text box. This array can be iterated and the lines processed one by one.

In this example, a string array is declared to contain all the elements of the Lines array, and then the Lines array is assigned to that array:

```
string[ ] arLines = new string [txtMulti.Lines.Length];
arLines = txtMulti.Lines;
```

```
dim arLines(txtMulti.Lines.Length - 1) as string
arLines = txtMulti.Lines
```

The StringBuilder class efficiently builds up the string that will be displayed in the display text box, txtDisplay. To use the StringBuilder class, reference the System. Text namespace at the beginning of the program:

C#
```
using System.Text;
```

VB
```
imports System.Text
```

A string variable is declared and instantiated with a string containing a header row. Escape characters are used in C#, while the equivalent VB.NET constants are used in VB.NET. Then the StringBuilder object is instantiated and the string is appended to the StringBuilder:

C#
```
string str = "Line\tString\r\n";
StringBuilder sb = new StringBuilder();
sb.Append(str);
```

VB
```
dim str as string = "Line" + vbTab + "String" + vbCrLf
dim sb as new StringBuilder()
sb.Append(str)
```

Then the array of strings is iterated, and a string is created with information about each line of text, consisting of the index number and the contents of each array element. Each string is appended to the StringBuilder:

C#
```
for (int i=0; i < arLines.Length; i++)
{
    str = i.ToString() + ".\t" + arLines[i] + "\r\n";
    sb.Append(str);
}
```

VB
```
dim i as integer
for i = 0 to arLines.Length - 1
    str = i.ToString() + "." + vbTab + arLines(i) + vbCrLf
    sb.Append(str)
next
```

Finally, the completed StringBuilder object is converted back to a string and displayed in the Text property of the display text box.

VB
```
txtDisplay.Text = sb.ToString()
```

Strictly speaking, it was not necessary to declare and instantiate the intermediate string array, arLines, in this example. That step could have been eliminated by rewriting the iteration, as follows:

C#
```
for (int i=0; i < txtMulti.Lines.Length; i++)
{
    str = i.ToString() + ".\t" + txtMulti.Lines[i] + "\r\n";
    sb.Append(str);
}
```

```
for i = 0 to txtMulti.Lines.Length - 1
   str = i.ToString() + "." + vbTab + txtMulti.Lines(i) + vbCrLf
   sb.Append(str)
next
```

The intermediate string array was created in this example to demonstrate other ways of manipulating the Lines property.

Events

The TextBoxBase class contains a large number of events that are either inherited from Control, or like the Click event, are not inherited but behave as if they were. Some of the most commonly used events are listed in Table 12-6.

Table 12-6. TextBoxBase events

Event	Event argument	Description
Click	EventArgs	Raised when the control is clicked. Not inherited from Control.
DoubleClick	EventArgs	Raised when the control is double-clicked. Inherited from Control.
TextChanged	EventArgs	Raised when the Text property is changed. Inherited from Control.
Validated	EventArgs	Raised when the control is done validating. Inherited from Control.
Validating	CancelEventArgs	Raised while the control is validating. Inherited from Control.

Events are covered thoroughly in Chapter 4. That chapter devotes an entire section to the events common to all controls, including text boxes. It also includes an example that uses the Validating event to validate the contents of a text box.

In Example 12-3, a form contains a text box and a button captioned Save. Clicking the Save button causes the contents of the text box to be saved only if the contents have been changed since the last time the Save button was clicked. (In this example, nothing is actually saved. There is some code that simulates the save operation.) The Modified property is tested to see whether the save operation needs to be performed. The TextChanged event resets the Modified property to false if the changes bring the Text property back to the same value it had the last time it was saved.

The programs listed in Examples 12-3 and 12-4 use some of the techniques described in Chapter 7 to dynamically size and position the text box and button controls on the form. No matter how the form is resized by the user, the text box fills the entire client area, leaving space for the centered button at the bottom.

Example 12-3. TextBoxBase Modified property C# and TextChanged event in C# (TextBoxTextChanged.cs)

```
using System;
using System.Drawing;
using System.Windows.Forms;

namespace ProgrammingWinApps
{
```

```
public class TextBoxTextChanged : Form
{
    TextBox txt;
    Button btn;
    string strOriginal;

    public TextBoxTextChanged( )
    {
        Text = "TextBox Modified and TextChanged";
        Size = new Size(300, 375);

        txt = new TextBox( );
        txt.Parent = this;
        txt.Text = "Enter text here.";
        txt.Size = new Size(ClientSize.Width - 20,
                            ClientSize.Height - 100);
        txt.Location = new Point(10,10);
        txt.TextChanged += new System.EventHandler(txt_TextChanged);
        txt.Multiline = true;
        txt.BorderStyle = BorderStyle.Fixed3D;
        txt.ScrollBars = ScrollBars.Vertical;
        txt.Anchor = AnchorStyles.Left | AnchorStyles.Right |
                    AnchorStyles.Top | AnchorStyles.Bottom;
        strOriginal = txt.Text;

        btn = new Button( );
        btn.Parent = this;
        btn.Text = "Save";
        btn.Location = new Point((ClientSize.Width / 2) -
                                (btn.Width / 2),
                        ClientSize.Height - (btn.Height * 2));
        btn.Click += new System.EventHandler(btn_Click);
        btn.Anchor = AnchorStyles.Bottom;
    } // close for constructor

    static void Main( )
    {
        Application.Run(new TextBoxTextChanged( ));
    }

    private void txt_TextChanged(object sender, EventArgs e)
    {
        if (strOriginal == txt.Text)
            txt.Modified = false;
        else
            txt.Modified = true;
    }

    private void btn_Click(object sender, EventArgs e)
    {
        if (txt.Modified)
        {
```

```
            MessageBox.Show(
                "The contents of the TextBox have been modified.\n\n" +
                "This simulates saving the contents.");
            strOriginal = txt.Text;
            txt.Modified = false;
        }
        else
            MessageBox.Show(
                "The contents of the TextBox have not been modified.\n\n" +
                "It is not being saved.");

    }

    }        //  close for form class
}            //  close form namespace
```

*Example 12-4. TextBoxBase Modified property and TextChanged event in VB.NET
(TextBoxTextChanged.vb)*

```
Option Strict On
imports System
imports System.Drawing
imports System.Windows.Forms

namespace ProgrammingWinApps
   public class TextBoxTextChanged : inherits Form

      dim txt as TextBox
      dim btn as Button
      dim strOriginal as string

      public sub New( )
         Text = "TextBox Modified and TextChanged"
         Size = new Size(300, 375)

         txt = new TextBox( )
         txt.Parent = me
         txt.Text = "Enter text here."
         txt.Size = new Size(ClientSize.Width - 20, _
                             ClientSize.Height - 100)
         txt.Location = new Point(10,10)
         AddHandler txt.TextChanged, AddressOf txt_TextChanged
         txt.Multiline = true
         txt.BorderStyle = BorderStyle.Fixed3D
         txt.ScrollBars = ScrollBars.Vertical
         txt.Anchor = AnchorStyles.Left or AnchorStyles.Right or _
                      AnchorStyles.Top or AnchorStyles.Bottom
         strOriginal = txt.Text

         btn = new Button( )
         btn.Parent = me
         btn.Text = "Save"
         btn.Location = new Point( _
```

```vb
                CInt((ClientSize.Width / 2)) - CInt((btn.Width / 2)), _
                ClientSize.Height - (btn.Height * 2))
        AddHandler btn.Click, AddressOf btn_Click
        btn.Anchor = AnchorStyles.Bottom
    end sub   '  close for constructor

    public shared sub Main( )
        Application.Run(new TextBoxTextChanged( ))
    end sub

    private sub txt_TextChanged(ByVal sender as object, _
                    ByVal e as EventArgs)
        if strOriginal = txt.Text then
            txt.Modified = false
        else
            txt.Modified = true
        end if
    end sub

    private sub btn_Click(ByVal sender as object, _
                    ByVal e as EventArgs)
        if txt.Modified then
            MessageBox.Show( _
                "The contents of the TextBox have been modified." + _
                vbNewLine + vbNewLine + _
                "This simulates saving the contents.")
            strOriginal = txt.Text
            txt.Modified = false
        else
            MessageBox.Show( _
                "The contents of the TextBox have not been modified." + _
                vbNewLine + vbNewLine + _
                "It is not being saved.")
        end if
    end sub

  end class
end namespace
```

The text box Size property is calculated from the size of the form's client area. The width is equal to the width of the client area minus 20 pixels (to allow a 10 pixel margin on either side), and the height is 100 pixels less than the client height, to allow room for the button.

```csharp
    txt.Size = new Size(ClientSize.Width - 20, ClientSize.Height - 100);
```

The text box Location property is hard coded to 10,10. The real work in dynamically positioning the controls is accomplished by setting the Anchor properties of both controls. The text box is anchored to all four sides by OR'ing together the appropriate AnchorStyles values:

```
txt.Anchor = AnchorStyles.Left | AnchorStyles.Right |
             AnchorStyles.Top | AnchorStyles.Bottom;
```

```
txt.Anchor = AnchorStyles.Left or AnchorStyles.Right or _
             AnchorStyles.Top or AnchorStyles.Bottom
```

The button Location is also calculated from the client area size and the size of the button itself.

```
btn.Location = new Point((ClientSize.Width / 2) - (btn.Width / 2),
                         ClientSize.Height - (btn.Height * 2));
```

The button control is anchored only to the bottom of the form.

```
btn.Anchor = AnchorStyles.Bottom;
```

Both controls have event handlers registered with them. The button handles the ubiquitous Click event, while the text box handles the TextChanged event.

```
txt.TextChanged += new System.EventHandler(txt_TextChanged);
```

```
AddHandler txt.TextChanged, AddressOf txt_TextChanged
```

The TextChanged event handler method tests to see if the current contents of the text box differ from the contents the last time the Save button was clicked (or when the form was initialized). The original contents are saved in a string variable called strOriginal, which is originally set in the constructor, and then reset every time the contents are saved.

The Modified property is automatically set to true and the TextChanged event is raised by the CLR as soon as the contents of the text box are changed by the user. Your code, however, is free to set the value to whatever is required to achieve the goals of the program.

RichTextBox

The RichTextBox is similar to the TextBox, but it has additional formatting capabilities. Whereas the TextBox control allows the Font property to be set for the entire control, the RichTextBox allows you to set the Font, as well as other formatting properties, for selections within the text displayed in the control.

When considering the difference between the TextBox and RichTextBox controls, compare Notepad and WordPad, the two text editors that are included with Windows. Notepad, based on the TextBox control, has no formatting applicable to selections within the text. WordPad, on the other hand, is practically a full-fledged word processor, with such features as bullets, hanging indents, fonts, and character styles applicable to selections within the text.

The default file format for the RichTextBox is the Rich Text Format (RTF), a file format that can carry formatting information.

The RichTextBox control inherits all the properties, methods, and events from the TextBoxBase class, so it behaves much like the TextBox control. In addition, it has many properties, methods, and events specific to itself. Many of the most commonly used RichTextBox-specific properties are listed in Table 12-7.

Rich Text Format (RTF)

This format was developed by Microsoft in the mid-1980s to permit easy interchange of formatted text between various applications. RTF Version 1.7, released in August 2001, adds support for features found in Word 2002. The specification can be downloaded as a Word document by going to *http://msdn.microsoft.com/downloads/default. asp*, and then drilling down to Office Solutions Development → Microsoft Word → Rich Text Format Specification, Version 1.7.

Since Microsoft Word can read and write RTF files interchangeably with Word document files, virtually all formatting constructs available to a Word document can be represented in an RTF file. RTF is the native format of WordPad, the lightweight word processor included as part of Windows. If an application needs to read or write a file with formatting, RTF is a relatively convenient (relative to the native Word document format, that is) way to accomplish that task, with a set of features more congruent than HTML with modern word processors.

That said, RTF is difficult to work with, primarily because it is designed to be read by RTF readers (word processors, etc.) and not people. RTF control words are case sensitive. Also, whitespace is strictly controlled, so inadvertent spaces in the wrong place in the file will appear as extra spaces in the displayed text. Just to make life interesting for developers writing an RTF writer, there is no way to comment out part of the file. There is no object model, and constructing or deconstructing RTF files always involves a lot of text parsing and manipulation.

RTF files consist primarily of low-order ASCII characters, although it does support switching code pages to use full Unicode character sets, and you can access the high-order ASCII characters by using escape sequences. The file contains the backslash character used as a control character, control words (a keyword preceded by a backslash), and the text to be displayed. The file also contains control groups enclosed within curly braces ({ }).

—continued—

An RTF file itself is considered a group, so it must be enclosed in curly braces. The file consists of a header and a document. The header tells the reader that this is an RTF file. It may also include control groups describing document wide features, such as tables of fonts, files, colors, stylesheets, or revision markings. The document contains the plain text to be displayed, specific formatting commands, and an information group describing the text. The document is not contained within its own set of curly braces.

A minimal RTF file might look something like this:

```
{\rtf\pard Some RTF text.}
```

The entire file is contained within braces. The header consists of one control word: the \rtf tag tells the reader that this is an RTF file. Often, the \rtf is followed by an integer indicating the major specification revision number, as shown in Example 12-5, which uses Rev. 1. The \pard control word, representing a default paragraph, is the beginning of the document. Some RTF text. is the actual displayed content of the file.

To work with RTF files, use either Word or WordPad to generate sample files and to test your results. Be aware, however, that both programs insert copious quantities of default control words, most of which are unnecessary for an RTF reader to render the document correctly.

Table 12-7. Selected RichTextBox properties

Property	Value type	Description
AllowDrop	Boolean	Read/write. If true, drag-and-drop operations allowed for the control.
AutoWordSelection	Boolean	Read/write. If false (the default), automatic word selection is disabled. If true, selecting any part of a word in the control causes the entire word to be selected. Note: this can be seen when extending a selection from one word to the next with the mouse, but not if extending the selection with the keyboard.
BulletIndent	Integer	Read/write. Number of pixels to indent text after a bullet character when the bullet style is applied. Default is zero.
CanRedo	Boolean	Read-only. If true, the operations that have been undone can be reapplied. Used in conjunction with the Redo method, described in Table 12-11.
DetectUrls	Boolean	Read/write. If true (the default), the control will automatically detect and format URLs as a link when they are entered in the control. The LinkClicked event allows handling of clicks on the link.
RightMargin	Integer	Read/write. Maximum width, in pixels, of each line of text, measured from the left edge of the control (that is correct, the left edge). Text hitting that margin will be treated as though it had hit the right edge of the control.
Rtf	String	Read/write. The text to be displayed by the control in Rich Text Format (RTF). See the sidebar for a description of RTF.

Table 12-7. Selected RichTextBox properties (continued)

Property	Value type	Description
ScrollBars	RichTextBoxScrollBars	Read/write. Specifies which scrollbars are displayed in the control and under what circumstances. Valid values are members of the RichText-BoxScrollBars enumeration, listed in Table 12-10.
SelectedRtf	String	Read/write. The selected text, including the RTF formatting codes.
SelectionAlignment	HorizontalAlignment	Read/write. Valid values are members of the Horizontal-Alignment enumeration listed in Table 12-8.
SelectionBullet	Boolean	Read/write. If `true`, the current selection or insertion point will have the bullet style applied.
SelectionCharOffset	Integer	Read/write. Number of pixels that selected text appears above or below the baseline. Valid values can range from -2000–2000. Positive values raise the text above the baseline; negative values lower the text. Default is zero, which puts the text on the baseline.
SelectionColor	Color	Read/write. The color of the currently selected text or the text on the current line.
SelectionFont	Font	Read/write. The Font of the currently selected text or the text on the current line. If selection contains more than one font, the value is null (in C#) or Nothing (in VB.NET).
SelectionHangingIn-dent	Integer	Read/write. Distance, in pixels, from the left edge of the first line in the paragraph to the left edge of second and subsequent lines in that paragraph.
SelectionIndent	Integer	Read/write. Distance, in pixels, from the left edge of the paragraph to the left edge of the control.
SelectionProtected	Boolean	Read/write. If `false` (the default), the currently selected text or the paragraph containing the insertion point is not protected. If `true`, the Protected event is raised if the user attempts to change the current text selection. Will return `true` only if the entire selection consists of protected text.
SelectionRightIndent	Integer	Read/write. Distance, in pixels, from the right edge of the paragraph to the right edge of the control.
SelectionTabs	Integer array	Read/write. An array of integers in which each member specifies a tab offset, in pixels.
SelectionType	RichTextBoxSelection-Types	Read-only. Bitwise combination of values from the RichTextBoxSelec-tionTypes enumeration, listed in Table 12-9.
ShowSelectionMar-gin	Boolean	Read/write. If `true`, the control contains a selection margin along the left side of the control. Clicking in the selection margin selects the adjacent line of text; double-clicking selects the entire paragraph. Default is `false`.
ZoomFactor	Float / single (VB.NET)	Read-only. Measures how fast the application is. Just kidding. Actually, it is read/write, getting or setting the current zoom level when viewing the control. Legal values range from 0.74 to 64.0. 1.0 indicates that no zoom is applied. Works best with TrueType fonts. Non-TrueType fonts use integer values for ZoomFactor.

Table 12-8. HorizontalAlignment enumeration values

Value	Description
Center	Aligned in the center of the control.
Left	Aligned to the left of the control.
Right	Aligned to the right of the control.

Table 12-9. RichTextBoxSelectionTypes enumeration values

Value	Description
Empty	No text in the current selection.
MultiChar	More than one text character is currently selected.
MultiObject	More than one OLE object is currently selected.
Object	At least one OLE object is currently selected.
Text	Only text is currently selected.

Table 12-10. RichTextBoxScrollBars enumeration values

Value	Description
Both	Displays both horizontal and vertical scrollbars when the text is either wider or longer than the text box.
ForcedBoth	Always displays both horizontal and vertical scrollbars.
ForcedHorizontal	Always displays a horizontal scrollbar, as long as the RichTextBox WordWrap property is set to `false`.
ForcedVertical	Always displays a vertical scrollbar.
Horizontal	Displays a horizontal scrollbar if the text is wider than the text box, as long as the RichTextBox Word-Wrap property is set to `false`.
None	No scrollbars are displayed.
Vertical	Displays a vertical scrollbar if the text is longer than the text box.

The properties listed in Table 12-7 that begin with the word "Selection," such as SelectionAlignment or SelectionBullet, behave similarly: the property applies to the currently selected text. However, if there is currently no selected text, then it will generally apply to the current text insertion point (the caret) and to all text on that line (from the prior new line character to the next new line character). If text is entered after the insertion point, the property will apply to it, until the property is changed. Some selection properties, such as SelectionFont, do not apply to pre-existing but non-selected text, but only to currently selected text, or text entered at the insertion point.

The listing in Example 12-5 demonstrates many RichTextBox properties using C#. Since this program is lengthy and virtually identical in VB.NET (aside from the normal syntactic differences), only the C# version will be presented in its entirety. Sections of code that are significantly different in VB.NET will be shown. The complete VB.NET source code can be downloaded from *http://www.LibertyAssociates.com* (click on Books).

This example creates a stripped-down version of WordPad, with a rich text box that fills the form client area and a truncated menu. (Menus will be covered in detail in Chapter 18.) Many properties and menu items used in this example are the same as those demonstrated for TextBox controls in Examples 12-1 and 12-2. An analysis of the code follows.

When the program is compiled and run, you will get something like Figure 12-3.

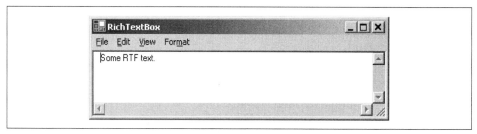

Figure 12-3. RichTextBox

Example 12-5. RichTextBox properties in C# (RichTextBoxes.cs)

```csharp
using System;
using System.Drawing;
using System.Windows.Forms;
using System.IO;

namespace ProgrammingWinApps
{
    public class RichTextBoxes : Form
    {
        RichTextBox rtxt;

        public RichTextBoxes()
        {
            Text = "RichTextBox";
            Size = new Size(400, 500);

            rtxt = new RichTextBox();
            rtxt.Parent = this;
            rtxt.Text = "Enter text here.";
            rtxt.Rtf = "{\\rtf1\\pard Some RTF text.}";
            rtxt.Multiline = true;
            rtxt.BorderStyle = BorderStyle.Fixed3D;
            rtxt.WordWrap = false;
            rtxt.ScrollBars = RichTextBoxScrollBars.ForcedBoth;
            rtxt.Dock = DockStyle.Fill;
            rtxt.DetectUrls = true;        //  true is the default value
            rtxt.AutoWordSelection = true;
            rtxt.BulletIndent = 10;
            rtxt.ShowSelectionMargin = true;

            //  Menus
            //  File menu items
```

Example 12-5. RichTextBox properties in C# (RichTextBoxes.cs) (continued)

C#

```csharp
MenuItem mnuImport = new MenuItem("&Import",
                        new EventHandler(mnuImport_Click));
MenuItem mnuFile = new MenuItem("&File",
                        new MenuItem[ ] {mnuImport});


// Edit menu items
MenuItem mnuDash1 = new MenuItem("-");
MenuItem mnuDash2 = new MenuItem("-");
MenuItem mnuUndo = new MenuItem("&Undo",
                        new EventHandler(mnuUndo_Click),
                        Shortcut.CtrlZ);
MenuItem mnuCut = new MenuItem("Cu&t",
                        new EventHandler(mnuCut_Click),
                        Shortcut.CtrlX);
MenuItem mnuCopy = new MenuItem("&Copy",
                        new EventHandler(mnuCopy_Click),
                        Shortcut.CtrlC);
MenuItem mnuCopyRtf = new MenuItem("Copy &Rtf",
                        new EventHandler(mnuCopyRtf_Click));
MenuItem mnuPaste = new MenuItem("&Paste",
                        new EventHandler(mnuPaste_Click),
                        Shortcut.CtrlV);
MenuItem mnuDelete = new MenuItem("&Delete",
                        new EventHandler(mnuDelete_Click));
MenuItem mnuSelectAll = new MenuItem("Select &All",
                        new EventHandler(mnuSelectAll_Click),
                        Shortcut.CtrlA);
MenuItem mnuSelect5 = new MenuItem("Select First &5",
                        new EventHandler(mnuSelect5_Click),
                        Shortcut.Ctrl5);
MenuItem mnuClear = new MenuItem("Clea&r",
                        new EventHandler(mnuClear_Click));
MenuItem mnuEdit = new MenuItem("&Edit",
                        new MenuItem[ ] {mnuUndo, mnuDash1,
                        mnuCut, mnuCopy, mnuCopyRtf, mnuPaste,
                        mnuDelete, mnuDash2, mnuSelectAll,
                        mnuSelect5, mnuClear});


// View Menu items
MenuItem mnuScrollToCaret = new MenuItem("&Scroll to Caret",
                        new EventHandler(mnuScrollToCaret_Click));
MenuItem mnuView = new MenuItem("&View",
                        new MenuItem[ ] {mnuScrollToCaret});


// Alignment menu items
MenuItem mnuAlignLeft = new MenuItem("Align&Left",
                        new EventHandler(mnuAlignLeft_Click));
MenuItem mnuAlignRight = new MenuItem("Align&Right",
                        new EventHandler(mnuAlignRight_Click));
MenuItem mnuAlignCenter = new MenuItem("Align&Center",
                        new EventHandler(mnuAlignCenter_Click));
```

Example 12-5. RichTextBox properties in C# (RichTextBoxes.cs) (continued)

```
                // Format Menu items
                MenuItem mnuBullet = new MenuItem("&Bullet",
                                    new EventHandler(mnuBullet_Click));
                MenuItem mnuAlign = new MenuItem("&Align",
                                    new MenuItem[ ] {mnuAlignLeft,
                                    mnuAlignRight, mnuAlignCenter});
                MenuItem mnuRed = new MenuItem("&Red",
                                    new EventHandler(mnuRed_Click));
                MenuItem mnuBold = new MenuItem("Bo&ld",
                                    new EventHandler(mnuBold_Click));
                MenuItem mnuHang = new MenuItem("&Hanging Indent",
                                    new EventHandler(mnuHang_Click));
                MenuItem mnuIndent = new MenuItem("&Indent",
                                    new EventHandler(mnuIndent_Click));
                MenuItem mnuRightIndent = new MenuItem("&Right Indent",
                                    new EventHandler(mnuRightIndent_Click));
                MenuItem mnuFormat = new MenuItem("For&mat",
                                    new MenuItem[ ] {mnuBullet, mnuAlign,
                                    mnuRed, mnuBold, mnuHang, mnuIndent,
                                    mnuRightIndent});

                // Main menu
                Menu = new MainMenu(new MenuItem[ ] {mnuFile, mnuEdit,
                                    mnuView, mnuFormat});
            } // close for constructor

            static void Main( )
            {
                Application.Run(new RichTextBoxes( ));
            }

            private void mnuImport_Click(object sender, EventArgs e)
            {
                OpenFileDialog ofd = new OpenFileDialog( );
                ofd.InitialDirectory = @"c:\";
                ofd.Filter = "RTF files (*.rtf)|*.rtf|" +
                            "All files (*.*)|*.*";
                ofd.FilterIndex = 1;                    // 1 based index

                if (ofd.ShowDialog( ) == DialogResult.OK)
                {
                    try
                    {
                        StreamReader reader = new StreamReader(ofd.FileName);
                        rtxt.Rtf = reader.ReadToEnd( );
                        reader.Close( );
                    }
                    catch (Exception ex)
                    {
                        MessageBox.Show(ex.Message);
                        return;
                    }
```

Example 12-5. RichTextBox properties in C# (RichTextBoxes.cs) (continued)

C#

```
      }
   }

   private void mnuUndo_Click(object sender, EventArgs e)
   {
      if (rtxt.CanUndo == true)
      {
         rtxt.Undo( );
         rtxt.ClearUndo( );
      }
   }

   private void mnuCut_Click(object sender, EventArgs e)
   {
      if (rtxt.SelectedText != "")
         rtxt.Cut( );
   }

   private void mnuCopy_Click(object sender, EventArgs e)
   {
      if (rtxt.SelectionLength > 0)
         rtxt.Copy( );
   }

   private void mnuCopyRtf_Click(object sender, EventArgs e)
   {
      if (rtxt.SelectionLength > 0)
      {
         Clipboard.SetDataObject(rtxt.SelectedRtf);
      }
   }

   private void mnuPaste_Click(object sender, EventArgs e)
   {
      if (Clipboard.GetDataObject( ).GetDataPresent(DataFormats.Text)
            == true)
      {
         if (rtxt.CanUndo == true)
         {
            if (rtxt.SelectionLength > 0)
            {
               if (MessageBox.Show(
                  "Do you want to overwrite the currently selected " +
                     "text?",
                  "Cut & Paste", MessageBoxButtons.YesNo) ==
                     DialogResult.No)
                  rtxt.SelectionStart = rtxt.SelectionStart +
                                        rtxt.SelectionLength;
            }
            rtxt.Paste( );
         }
      }
```

Example 12-5. RichTextBox properties in C# (RichTextBoxes.cs) (continued)

C#

```
      }

      private void mnuDelete_Click(object sender, EventArgs e)
      {
         if (rtxt.SelectionLength > 0)
            rtxt.SelectedText = "";
      }

      private void mnuClear_Click(object sender, EventArgs e)
      {
         rtxt.Clear();
      }


      private void mnuSelect5_Click(object sender, EventArgs e)
      {
         if (rtxt.Text.Length >= 5)
         {
            rtxt.Select(0,5);
         }
         else
         {
            rtxt.Select(0,rtxt.Text.Length);
         }
      }

      private void mnuSelectAll_Click(object sender, EventArgs e)
      {
         rtxt.SelectAll();
      }

      private void mnuScrollToCaret_Click(object sender, EventArgs e)
      {
         rtxt.ScrollToCaret();
      }

      private void mnuBullet_Click(object sender, EventArgs e)
      {
         rtxt.SelectionBullet = !rtxt.SelectionBullet;
      }

      private void mnuAlignLeft_Click(object sender, EventArgs e)
      {
         rtxt.SelectionAlignment = HorizontalAlignment.Left;
      }

      private void mnuAlignRight_Click(object sender, EventArgs e)
      {
         rtxt.SelectionAlignment = HorizontalAlignment.Right;
      }

      private void mnuAlignCenter_Click(object sender, EventArgs e)
```

Example 12-5. RichTextBox properties in C# (RichTextBoxes.cs) (continued)

```csharp
      {
         rtxt.SelectionAlignment = HorizontalAlignment.Center;
      }

      private void mnuRed_Click(object sender, EventArgs e)
      {
         if (rtxt.SelectionColor == Color.Red)
            rtxt.SelectionColor = Color.Black;
         else
            rtxt.SelectionColor = Color.Red;
      }

      private void mnuBold_Click(object sender, EventArgs e)
      {
         if (rtxt.SelectionFont.Bold )
            rtxt.SelectionFont =
                new Font(rtxt.SelectionFont, FontStyle.Regular);
         else
            rtxt.SelectionFont =
                new Font(rtxt.SelectionFont, FontStyle.Bold);
      }

      private void mnuHang_Click(object sender, EventArgs e)
      {
         if (rtxt.SelectionHangingIndent == 10 )
            rtxt.SelectionHangingIndent = 0;
         else
            rtxt.SelectionHangingIndent = 10;
      }

      private void mnuIndent_Click(object sender, EventArgs e)
      {
         if (rtxt.SelectionIndent == 10 )
            rtxt.SelectionIndent = 0;
         else
            rtxt.SelectionIndent = 10;
      }

      private void mnuRightIndent_Click(object sender, EventArgs e)
      {
         if (rtxt.SelectionRightIndent == 50 )
            rtxt.SelectionRightIndent = 0;
         else
            rtxt.SelectionRightIndent = 50;
      }

   }     // close for form class
}        // close form namespace
```

The program starts off by declaring a single class member variable, rtxt, representing the RichTextBox control. The equivalent VB.NET line of code would be:

```vbnet
    dim rtxt as RichTextBox
```

In the constructor, both a Text property and an Rtf property are set. However, when you run the program, you will see that only the Rtf property is displayed in the control. If the order of these two lines of code are reversed, then the Text property rather than the Rtf would be visible in the control. Both properties control what is displayed in the control: the Text property assumes plain text and the Rtf property assumes valid RTF formatted text.

Since RTF files use a backslash as a control character, and the backslash character is an escape character in C#, you must double the backslashes before they are properly escaped. Alternatively, you can use an @-quoted string literal in C#, as in:

```
rtxt.Rtf = @"{\rtf1\pard Some RTF text.}";
```

VB.NET does not use the backslash character as an escape character, so the equivalent line of code in VB.NET would be:

```
rtxt.Rtf = "{\rtf1\pard Some RTF text.}"
```

The ScrollBars property is set to ForcedBoth, which causes both a horizontal and vertical scrollbar to be present at all times, even if the contents of the control do not warrant them.

> A horizontal scrollbar will not display unless the WordWrap property is set to false. If, in addition, the ShowSelectionMargin property is set to true (as is the case in Example 12-5), then a horizontal scrollbar will always display when the ScrollBars property is set to Horizontal, even if the text length does not warrant it (as with ForcedHorizontal behavior).

The DockStyle property is set to Fill, which forces the rich text box to fill the client area of the form. The DockStyle property was explained in Chapter 7.

The DetectUrls property is set to true, although the line is not strictly necessary, since this is the default value. However, by changing it to false, you can see the different behavior when you enter any valid URL in the control.

The AutoWordSelection property is set to true. This property causes the entire word to be selected if any part of the word is selected.

> If set to true, the AutoWordSelection property behaves differently when you use the mouse than when you use the keyboard to make the selection. If you select a word with the mouse and extend the selection with the mouse to the next word, the entire word will be selected as soon as the first character is selected. However, if you extend the selection with the keyboard by holding down the Shift key while using the arrow key, the entire word will not be selected. Select a single character in any word with the keyboard and the entire word is not selected.

The BulletIndent and ShowSelectionMargin properties work as described in Table 12-7.

The menus are similar to those used in Examples 12-1 and 12-2, with some additional menu items. The main menu now has File, Edit, View, and Format items. Under File, an Import command lets you import an RTF file. The Edit menu item has an additional command, CopyRtf, which allows you to copy the selected text as RTF rather than plain text. The View menu has only the Scroll To Caret command, while the Format menu is entirely new, demonstrating several of the rich text box formatting capabilities.

The menu item declarations use a different syntax in VB.NET from that in C# for assigning event handlers. A typical menu item declaration looks like:

C#
```
MenuItem mnuUndo = new MenuItem("&Undo",
                   new EventHandler(mnuUndo_Click),
                   Shortcut.CtrlZ);
```

VB
```
dim mnuUndo as new MenuItem("&Undo", _
             new EventHandler(AddressOf mnuUndo_Click), _
             Shortcut.CtrlZ)
```

These menu item declarations were described briefly in conjunction with Examples 12-1 and 12-2 and will be detailed in Chapter 18.

The File → Import menu item is handled by the method mnuImport_Click. This method uses the common dialog OpenFile, described in Chapter 6. The equivalent VB.NET version of this method looks like this:

VB
```
private sub mnuImport_Click(ByVal sender As Object, _
               ByVal e As EventArgs)
    dim ofd as new OpenFileDialog()
    ofd.InitialDirectory = "c:\\"
    ofd.Filter = "RTF files (*.rtf)|*.rtf|" + _
             "All files (*.*)|*.*"
    ofd.FilterIndex = 1                    ' 1 based index

    if ofd.ShowDialog() = DialogResult.OK then
        try
            dim reader as new StreamReader(ofd.FileName)
            rtxt.Rtf = reader.ReadToEnd()
            reader.Close()
        catch ex as Exception
            MessageBox.Show(ex.Message)
            return
        end try
    end if
end sub
```

In either language, a new OpenFileDialog is instantiated and several properties, including InitialDirectory, Filter, and FilterIndex, are set. The dialog is displayed by using the ShowDialog method. If that method returns OK, then the selected file is read into the control by using a StreamReader object. The StreamReader object required that the System.IO namespace be referenced at the beginning of the program:

```
using System.IO;
```

```
imports System.IO
```

> In this example, all the methods implementing the Edit commands are simpler than the equivalent methods shown in Example 12-1 and Example 12-2. The current example has only a single control that might be the target of the action, whereas the previous examples had multiple text boxes and code to determine which text box was the target. In Example 12-5, the target control is hardwired to be rtxt.

The next method of note is mnuCopyRtf_Click, which implements the Edit → Copy Rtf command. This method determines whether anything is selected by testing if the SelectionLength property is greater than zero. If so, it uses the static Clipboard.Set-DataObject method, passing in the SelectedRtf property as an argument. This property includes the RTF formatting codes, so if the contents are pasted into another control or application, the RTF codes are visible. This is in contrast to the Copy method used in mnuCopy_Click, which copies the selection to the Clipboard directly. If the contents of the Clipboard are pasted into Notepad, it is pasted as plain text, but if pasted into WordPad, it is pasted in with the formatting preserved. To see this concept in action, consider the instance of RichTextBoxes shown in Figure 12-4 with some formatted text entered and selected.

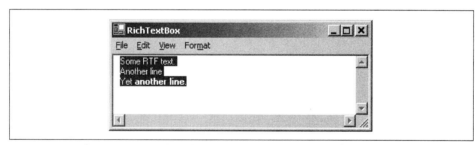

Figure 12-4. RichTextBox with selected text

If the Edit → Copy Rtf command is executed and then pasted in WordPad, and then the Edit → Copy command is executed on the same selection and then pasted into the same WordPad session, the WordPad session will look like Figure 12-5.

The Format menu looks like that shown in Figure 12-6. This is hardly a full-featured format menu, but it demonstrates a representative sampling of properties.

Most of these menu items are simple toggles (e.g., if the selection is not bulleted, then bullet it; otherwise, unbullet it). In the case of the SelectionBullet property, which is a Boolean, a single line of code accomplishes the task:

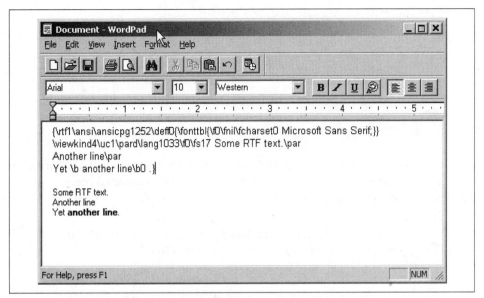

Figure 12-5. WordPad with pasted RTF selections

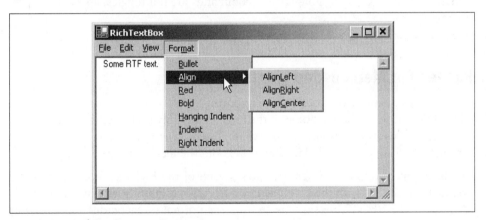

Figure 12-6. RichTextBoxes — Format menu

`C#`

```
rtxt.SelectionBullet = !rtxt.SelectionBullet;
```

`VB`

```
rtxt.SelectionBullet = not rtxt.SelectionBullet
```

The Format → Red command simply toggles the selection between red and black. The code is slightly more complex:

`C#`

```
if (rtxt.SelectionColor == Color.Red)
    rtxt.SelectionColor = Color.Black;
else
    rtxt.SelectionColor = Color.Red;
```

```
if rtxt.SelectionColor.Equals(Color.Red) then
    rtxt.SelectionColor = Color.Black
else
    rtxt.SelectionColor = Color.Red
end if
```

The VB.NET version uses the Equals method rather than the = symbol because VB.NET does not support overloading of operators, except for predefined types, and Color is a class.

The Bold, Hanging Indent, Indent, and Right Indent formatting commands are similar to the Red formatting command (which tests to see if the desired property is current and sets the property accordingly).

In a real-life application, you would probably want to open the Color-Dialog common dialog box and give the user a real choice.

The final formatting commands are the three Align commands: AlignLeft, Align-Center, and AlignRight. Although these commands are not toggles, apply the appropriate property:

```
rtxt.SelectionAlignment = HorizontalAlignment.Center;
```

RichTextBox Methods and Events

As you would expect, the RichTextBox control has several methods and events in addition to those it inherits. Some of the most commonly used methods are listed in Table 12-11, with commonly used events listed in Table 12-16. (Tables 12-12 through 12-15 contain detailed information about the methods.)

The listing in Example 12-6 demonstrates several of the RichTextBox methods and events using C#. As with the previous example, this program is lengthy and virtually identical to the VB.NET version (aside from the normal syntactic differences). Only the C# version is presented in its entirety. Sections of code that are significantly different in VB.NET will be shown. The complete VB.NET source code can be downloaded from *http://www.LibertyAssociates.com* (click on Books).

Table 12-11. RichTextBox methods

Method	Description
CanPaste	Returns `true` if the data in the Clipboard can be pasted to the control in the specified format, `false` otherwise.
Find	Overloaded. Finds text within the control. If found, highlights the text and returns the zero-based index of the search result, or returns −1 if not found. The overloaded forms are listed in Table 12-12.

Table 12-11. RichTextBox methods (continued)

Method	Description
GetCharFromPosition	Takes a point structure as an argument. Returns the character within the control closest to that point.
GetCharIndexFromPosition	Takes a point structure as an argument. Returns the zero-based index of the character within the control closest to that point.
GetLineFromCharIndex	Takes a zero-based character index as an argument. Returns the zero-based line number containing that character.
GetPositionFromCharIndex	Takes a zero-based character index as an argument. Returns the location of that character.
LoadFile	Overloaded. Loads a text file or existing data stream into the control. The overloaded forms are listed in Table 12-14.
Paste	Overloaded. Pastes the contents of the Clipboard into the control. The overloaded form takes a DataFormats.Format as an argument, pasting an object of that format.
Redo	Reapplies the last operation that was undone.
SaveFile	Overloaded. Saves the contents of the control to a file or an existing data stream. The types of files that can be saved are contained in the RichTextBoxStreamType enumeration, listed in Table 12-15.

Table 12-12. RichTextBoxFind method overload argument list

Method	Description
char[ ]	Searches for first occurrence of a character in character array. Case sensitive.
string	Searches for string. Cannot find string if it spans more than one line in the control. Not case sensitive.
char[ ], int	Searches for first occurrence of a character in character array starting at a specified position in the control. If the starting index is zero, it searches from the beginning. Case sensitive.
string, RichTextBoxFinds	Searches for string with options specified by the bitwise combination of RichTextBoxFinds (listed in Table 12-13). Cannot find string if it spans more than one line in the control.
char[ ], int, int	Searches for first occurrence of a character in character array starting at a specified position in the control and ending at a specified position. If the starting index is zero, it searches from the beginning. If the ending index is −1, the search goes to the end. Case sensitive.
string, int, RichTextBoxFinds	Searches for string starting at a specified position in the control with options specified by the bitwise combination of RichTextBoxFinds (listed in Table 12-13). If the starting index is zero, it searches from the beginning. Cannot find string if it spans more than one line in the control.
string, int, int, RichTextBoxFinds	Searches for string starting at a specified position in the control and ending at a specified position with options specified by the bitwise combination of RichTextBoxFinds (listed in Table 12-13). If the starting index is zero, it searches from the beginning. If the ending index is -1, the search goes to the end. Cannot find string if it spans more than one line in the control.

Table 12-13. RichTextBoxFinds enumeration values

Value	Description
MatchCase	Casing must match exactly.
NoHighlight	If found, search text will not be highlighted.

Table 12-13. RichTextBoxFinds enumeration values (continued)

Value	Description
None	Locate all instances, whether whole words or not.
Reverse	Start search at end and search to the beginning.
WholeWord	Locate only whole words.

Table 12-14. RichTextBox LoadFile method overload argument list

Method	Description
string	Loads the RTF file specified in the argument into the control.
stream, RichTextBoxStreamType	Loads an existing data stream into the control. The type of the data stream is specified by the RichTextBoxStreamType argument, whose legal values are listed in Table 12-15.
string, RichTextBoxStreamType	Loads file into the control. The type of the file is specified by the RichTextBoxStreamType argument, whose legal values are listed in Table 12-15.

Table 12-15. RichTextBoxStreamType enumeration values

Value	Description
PlainText	Plain ASCII text stream with no formatting. OLE objects are replaced with spaces.
RichNoOleObjects	RTF stream. OLE objects are replaced with spaces. Only valid for use with the SaveFile method.
RichText	RTF stream.
TextTextOleObjs	Plain text stream. OLE objects are replaced textual representation. Only valid for use with the SaveFile method.
UnicodePlainText	Same as PlainText, except text is encoded as Unicode.

Table 12-16. RichTextBox events

Event	Event argument	Description
HScroll	EventArgs	Raised when the horizontal scrollbar is clicked.
LinkClicked	LinkClickedEventArgs	Raised when user clicks on a link in the control. Event argument provides a LinkText property.
Protected	EventArgs	Raised when the user attempts to modify protected text. Text is protected by setting the SelectionProtected property true for selected text. The program can perform actions such as warning that this is protected text or provide a dialog for specific formatting.
SelectionChanged	EventArgs	Raised when the selection has changed.
VScroll	EventArgs	Raised when the vertical scrollbar is clicked.

Example 12-6. RichTextBox methods and events in C#
(RichTextBoxMethodsEvents.cs)

```
using System;
using System.Drawing;
using System.Windows.Forms;
using System.IO;
```

```
namespace ProgrammingWinApps
{
    public class RichTextBoxMethodsEvents : Form
    {
        RichTextBox rtxt;
        string strFileName;

        public RichTextBoxMethodsEvents()
        {
            Text = "RichTextBox Methods & Events";
            Size = new Size(400, 500);

            rtxt = new RichTextBox();
            rtxt.Parent = this;
            rtxt.Rtf = "{\\rtf1\\pard Some RTF text.}";
            rtxt.Multiline = true;
            rtxt.BorderStyle = BorderStyle.Fixed3D;
            rtxt.ScrollBars = RichTextBoxScrollBars.ForcedVertical;
            rtxt.Dock = DockStyle.Fill;
            rtxt.AutoWordSelection = true;
            rtxt.BulletIndent = 10;
            rtxt.ShowSelectionMargin = true;
            rtxt.LinkClicked += new LinkClickedEventHandler(Link_Click);
            rtxt.SelectionChanged += new EventHandler(Selection_Changed);

            // Menus
            // File menu items
            MenuItem mnuImport = new MenuItem("&Import...",
                                new EventHandler(mnuImport_Click),
                                Shortcut.CtrlI);
            MenuItem mnuLoad = new MenuItem("&Load...",
                                new EventHandler(mnuLoad_Click),
                                Shortcut.CtrlL);
            MenuItem mnuSaveAs = new MenuItem("Save &As...",
                                new EventHandler(mnuSaveAs_Click));
            MenuItem mnuFile = new MenuItem("&File",
                            new MenuItem[] {mnuImport, mnuLoad, mnuSaveAs});

            // Edit menu items
            MenuItem mnuFind = new MenuItem("&Find",
                                new EventHandler(mnuFind_Click),
                                Shortcut.CtrlF);
            MenuItem mnuRedo = new MenuItem("&Redo",
                                new EventHandler(mnuRedo_Click));
            MenuItem mnuEdit = new MenuItem("&Edit",
                                new MenuItem[] {mnuFind, mnuRedo});

            // Main menu
            Menu = new MainMenu(new MenuItem[] {mnuFile, mnuEdit});

        } // close for constructor
```

Example 12-6. RichTextBox methods and events in C#
(RichTextBoxMethodsEvents.cs) (continued)

```
static void Main( )
{
   Application.Run(new RichTextBoxMethodsEvents( ));
}

private void mnuImport_Click(object sender, EventArgs e)
{
   OpenFileDialog ofd = new OpenFileDialog( );
   ofd.InitialDirectory = @"c:\";
   ofd.Filter = "RTF files (*.rtf)|*.rtf|" +
               "All files (*.*)|*.*";
   ofd.FilterIndex = 1;                      //  1 based index

   if (ofd.ShowDialog( ) == DialogResult.OK)
   {
      try
      {
         StreamReader reader = new StreamReader(ofd.FileName);
         rtxt.Rtf = reader.ReadToEnd( );
         reader.Close( );
      }
      catch (Exception ex)
      {
         MessageBox.Show(ex.Message);
         return;
      }
   }
}

private void mnuLoad_Click(object sender, EventArgs e)
{
   OpenFileDialog ofd = new OpenFileDialog( );
   ofd.InitialDirectory = @"c:\";
   ofd.Filter = "RTF files (*.rtf)|*.rtf|" +
               "Text files (*.txt)|*.txt|" +
               "All files (*.*)|*.*";
   ofd.FilterIndex = 1;                      //  1 based index

   if (ofd.ShowDialog( ) == DialogResult.OK)
   {
      try
      {
         //  Determine the file extension
         if (ofd.FileName.EndsWith(".rtf"))
            rtxt.LoadFile(ofd.FileName);
         else
         {
            if (ofd.FileName.EndsWith(".txt"))
               rtxt.LoadFile(ofd.FileName,
                             RichTextBoxStreamType.PlainText);
            else
               MessageBox.Show("Invalid file format.");
```

```
C#
                    }
                }
                catch (Exception ex)
                {
                    MessageBox.Show(ex.Message);
                    return;
                }
            }
        }


        private void mnuSaveAs_Click(object sender, EventArgs e)
        {
            SaveFileDialog sfd = new SaveFileDialog( );
            sfd.InitialDirectory = @"c:\";
            sfd.Filter = "RTF files (*.rtf)|*.rtf|" +
                    "Text files (*.txt)|*.txt|" +
                        "All files (*.*)|*.*";
            sfd.FilterIndex = 1;                        //  1 based index

            if (strFileName != null)
                sfd.FileName = strFileName;
            else
                sfd.FileName = "*.rtf";

            if (sfd.ShowDialog( ) == DialogResult.OK)
            {
                try
                {
                    strFileName = sfd.FileName;

                    //  Determine the file extension
                    if (strFileName.EndsWith(".rtf"))
                        rtxt.SaveFile(strFileName);
                    else
                    {
                        if (strFileName.EndsWith(".txt"))
                            rtxt.SaveFile(strFileName,
                                        RichTextBoxStreamType.PlainText);
                        else
                            MessageBox.Show("Invalid file format.");
                    }
                }
                catch(Exception ex)
                {
                    MessageBox.Show(ex.Message);
                    return;
                }
            }
        }

        private void mnuFind_Click(object sender, EventArgs e)
        {
```

Example 12-6. RichTextBox methods and events in C#
(RichTextBoxMethodsEvents.cs) (continued)

```
            // use the current selection as the string to find.
            if (rtxt.SelectionLength > 0)
            {
                string str = rtxt.SelectedText;
                int intStart = rtxt.Find(str,
                                rtxt.SelectionStart + rtxt.SelectionLength,
                                -1, RichTextBoxFinds.None);
                if (intStart < 0)
                    MessageBox.Show("String not found.");
            }
            else
                MessageBox.Show("Nothing to find.");
        }

        private void mnuRedo_Click(object sender, EventArgs e)
        {
            if (rtxt.CanRedo)
                rtxt.Redo();
        }

        private void Link_Click(object sender, LinkClickedEventArgs e)
        {
            System.Diagnostics.Process.Start(e.LinkText);
        }

        private void Selection_Changed(object sender, EventArgs e)
        {
            if (rtxt.SelectionLength > 0)
                MessageBox.Show("You have changed the selection to \"" +
                    rtxt.SelectedText + "\"");
        }

    }       // close for form class
}           // close form namespace
```

When the program listed in Example 12-6 is compiled and run, it looks similar to that shown for the previous example in Figure 12-3, except that the menu is sparser and there is no horizontal scrollbar.

The code in Example 12-6 is similar to that listed in Example 12-5.

The constructor has two lines that add two event handlers for LinkClicked and SelectionChanged events, respectively:

```
rtxt.LinkClicked += new LinkClickedEventHandler(Link_Click);
rtxt.SelectionChanged += new EventHandler(Selection_Changed);
```

```
AddHandler rtxt.LinkClicked, AddressOf Link_Click
AddHandler rtxt.SelectionChanged, AddressOf Selection_Changed
```

The menu is significantly trimmed down, with only File and Edit top-level menu items, and fewer menu items overall.

As before, most action occurs in the event handler methods. The event handler for importing an RTF file, mnuImport_Click, is unchanged from the previous example. It is left in here simply as a comparison with the Load menu item. The handler for that item, mnuLoad_Click, uses the same OpenFileDialog common dialog, but rather than use a StreamReader to stream the file into the Rtf property of the control, it uses the LoadFile instance method.

Another difference between the Import and Load event handlers is that the Load event handler allows both RTF and text files, reflected in the OpenFileDialog Filter property:

```
ofd.Filter = "RTF files (*.rtf)|*.rtf|" +
             "Text files (*.txt)|*.txt|" +
             "All files (*.*)|*.*";
```

Then within the try block where the selected file is actually loaded, the string Ends-With instance method determines if the selected file is an RTF or a TXT file. If it is the former, the LoadFile method is invoked with only the filename as an argument. If it is the latter, then the LoadFile method is invoked with RichTextBoxStreamType. PlainText passed as an argument:

```
try
{
    // Determine the file extension
    if (ofd.FileName.EndsWith(".rtf"))
        rtxt.LoadFile(ofd.FileName);
    else
    {
        if (ofd.FileName.EndsWith(".txt"))
            rtxt.LoadFile(ofd.FileName,
                          RichTextBoxStreamType.PlainText);
        else
            MessageBox.Show("Invalid file format.");
    }
}
catch (Exception ex)
{
    MessageBox.Show(ex.Message);
    return;
}
```

```
try
    ' Determine the file extension
    if ofd.FileName.EndsWith(".rtf") then
        rtxt.LoadFile(ofd.FileName)
    else
        if (ofd.FileName.EndsWith(".txt"))
            rtxt.LoadFile(ofd.FileName, RichTextBoxStreamType.PlainText)
```

```vb
            else
                MessageBox.Show("Invalid file format.")
            end if
        end if
    catch ex as Exception
        MessageBox.Show(ex.Message)
        return
    end try
```

The File → Save As command is implemented in the mnuSaveAs_Click event handler method. This is analogous to the Load event handler, except that it uses the SaveFileDialog common dialog box and invokes the SaveFile method rather than the LoadFile method. As with the Load event handler, it tests the extension of the specified filename to determine if the file should be saved as RTF or a plain text file, using the same arguments as the LoadFile method.

Most real-world applications implement a Find function by presenting a dialog box for the user to enter the search string. The Edit → Find command implemented in this example forgoes the dialog box and uses the current selection as the search string. If nothing is selected, as determined by testing the SelectionLength property, then the Find method is not invoked.

Assuming there is something selected, the selected text is assigned to a string variable, which is then passed to the Find method, along with several other arguments. Seven overloaded forms of the Find method are listed in Table 12-12, providing the ability to search for either a character or a string, either in the entire control or in a specified range. If it is a string, it uses a combination of RichTextBoxFinds enumeration values, listed in Table 12-13, to refine the search.

In any case, if the search is successful, the Find method returns the zero-based index of the first character of the string that is found. It also highlights the found string. If nothing is found, then the method returns –1.

In this example, four arguments are passed to the Find method: the search string, the starting index, the ending index, and a RichTextBoxFinds enumeration value:

```csharp
int intStart = rtxt.Find(str,
        rtxt.SelectionStart + rtxt.SelectionLength,
        -1, RichTextBoxFinds.None);
```

```vb
    dim intStart as integer = rtxt.Find(str, _
        rtxt.SelectionStart + rtxt.SelectionLength, _
        -1, RichTextBoxFinds.None)
```

Notice that the starting index is set to the index at the start of the selection plus the length of the selection, which effectively starts the search at the end of the selection. If you started the search at the start of the selection, it would just find itself.

The ending index is set to –1, which has the effect of searching to the end of the control contents. The following line would be equivalent to the line used:

```C#
int intStart = rtxt.Find(str,
    rtxt.SelectionStart + rtxt.SelectionLength,
    RichTextBoxFinds.None);
```

Since none of the overloaded forms of the method allows searching for a string from a specified starting point without passing a RichTextBoxFinds parameter, even if there is no refinement to the desired search, the None enumerated value is passed in.

If the search is successful, the found text is highlighted and the character index of the first character of the found string is assigned to the integer intStart. If nothing is found, then –1 would be returned. intStart is tested and if it is negative, a message is displayed.

The Edit → Redo menu item demonstrates the Redo method as invoked in the mnuRedo_Click event handler. It first tests the CanRedo property to see if there is anything to redo. If so, the Redo method is called. This has the effect of reversing the previous Undo operation.

 The Redo command assumes that you have first called Undo to reverse an operation. However, this example does not have an explicit Undo command. The Cut, Copy, Paste, Select All, and Undo commands all work as part of the default behavior of TextBoxBase controls.

Two event handlers in Example 12-6 are not associated with any menu item.

The Link_Click event handler is invoked whenever a URL in the control is clicked. This event handler was assigned to the LinkClicked event back in the constructor with the following line:

```C#
rtxt.LinkClicked += new LinkClickedEventHandler(Link_Click);
```

```VB
AddHandler rtxt.LinkClicked, AddressOf Link_Click
```

This event passes an event argument of type LinkClickedEventArgs, which contains the text of the URL that was clicked. This text is then passed as an argument to the Process.Start method of the System.Diagnostics namespace, which starts an instance of the default application for the passed-in link text, which depends on the link. For example, if the link text is www.LibertyAssociates.com, then a browser will be opened and navigate to that web site. If the link text is file:c:\test.txt, then that file will be opened in Notepad.

The SelectionChanged event is raised every time the selection is changed in the text box. It is assigned to the Selection_Changed event handler method with the appropriate line of code.

```
rtxt.SelectionChanged += new EventHandler(Selection_Changed);
```

```
AddHandler rtxt.SelectionChanged, AddressOf Selection_Changed
```

The Selection_Changed event handler first tests to see if anything is selected (i.e., the selection length is greater than zero) to prevent the message box from popping up every time you deselect. Anything that is selected is displayed in a message box.

CHAPTER 13

Other Basic Controls

The previous two chapters covered many basic controls, such as labels, buttons, and other text controls. Subsequent chapters will cover several more specialized controls, such as list and tree controls and date and time controls.

This chapter covers many of the other basic controls commonly used as part of Windows Forms applications, including:

- Containers such as the Panel and the GroupBox controls
- Tabbed pages
- The PictureBox control
- Scrollbars, the TrackBar control, and the ProgressBar control
- Up-down controls, both numeric and object

The class hierarchy for all controls covered in this chapter is shown in Figure 13-1. You can refer to this figure as you read about each control.

Containers

Many controls can contain other controls, grouping them. The Form control is the ultimate container, but it serves a larger purpose than just containing other controls. The form is the center of Windows Forms-based applications, having many unique properties and methods that empower the Form control to fulfill its role. These include properties such as AcceptButton, Modal, and WindowState, and methods such as Activate and Close. Chapter 5 covers the Form control thoroughly.

Some controls exist only to fill the role of container. They have very few properties, and all their methods are either inherited or overridden from the Control class. They cannot receive focus, although they may play a role in the tab order. Their sole mission is to group other controls to a common purpose. That purpose may be ergonomic, e.g., using a container control to put a border around several labels and text

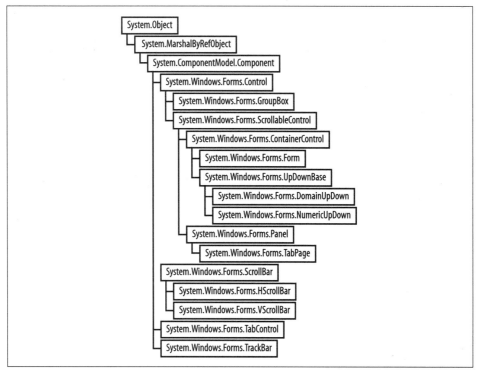

Figure 13-1. Class hierarchy for controls covered in this chapter

boxes used for gathering address information. The purpose may also be directly functional, e.g., grouping several radio buttons so they become mutually exclusive.

The two controls that exist only to be containers are GroupBox and Panel. They are similar in purpose, but have some very different features. In short, the GroupBox displays its Text property as a caption. It cannot scroll. The Panel control, on the other hand, can scroll but does not display its Text property and cannot have a caption.

The class hierarchy shown in Figure 13-1 explains this behavior. The GroupBox class is derived directly from Control, while the Panel control is derived from Control via the ScrollableControl class, thereby gaining the ability to have scrollbars. Neither GroupBox nor Panel are derived from ContainerControl, even though they are containers.

 The ContainerControl class is perhaps misnamed. A control does not have to derive from ContainerControl to be a container, but it has to derive from Control (which has a Controls property that returns a collection of contained controls). The ContainerControl class' main purpose is to deal with focus management.

The Panel class has a read/write Text property that overrides the Control.Text property, but it does not display as part of the control.

If either a GroupBox or Panel control's Enabled property is set to false, then all the controls contained within will also be disabled. Likewise, if a GroupBox or Panel control's Visible property is set to false, then none of its child controls will be visible.

Both the GroupBox and Panel controls were demonstrated in Examples 11-9 and 11-10. Those examples will be reprised here in Example 13-1 (in C#) and Example 13-2 (in VB.NET), with a few minor modifications. The lines of code that differ from the examples in Chapter 11 are highlighted.

When the programs in Examples 13-1 and 13-2 are compiled and run, they yield the form shown in Figure 13-2. This is similar to that shown in Figure 11-7, except that the panel containing the font style checkboxes is intentionally made short to require a vertical scrollbar, and that panel also has a BorderStyle applied to it.

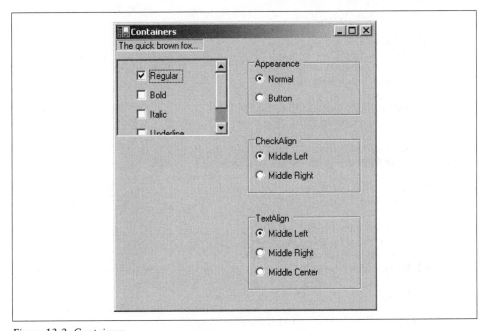

Figure 13-2. Containers

Example 13-1. Containers in C# (Containers.cs)

```
using System;
using System.Drawing;
using System.Windows.Forms;

namespace ProgrammingWinApps
{
```

Example 13-1. Containers in C# (Containers.cs) (continued)

```
public class Containers : Form
{
    Label lbl;
    Panel pnl;
    int yDelta;
    RadioButton rdoAppearanceNormal;
    RadioButton rdoAppearanceButton;
    RadioButton rdoCheckAlignMiddleLeft;
    RadioButton rdoCheckAlignMiddleRight;
    RadioButton rdoTextAlignMiddleLeft;
    RadioButton rdoTextAlignMiddleRight;
    RadioButton rdoTextAlignMiddleCenter;
    FontStyle[ ] theStyles;

    public Containers( )
    {
        Text = "Containers";
        Size = new Size(350,375);

        lbl = new Label( );
        lbl.Parent = this;
        lbl.Text = "The quick brown fox...";
        lbl.Location = new Point(0,0);
        lbl.AutoSize = true;
        lbl.BorderStyle = BorderStyle.Fixed3D;
        yDelta = lbl.Height + 10;

        //  Get the FontStyles into an array
        FontStyle theEnum = new FontStyle( );
        theStyles = (FontStyle[ ])Enum.GetValues(theEnum.GetType( ));

        pnl = new Panel( );
        pnl.Parent = this;
        pnl.Location = new Point(0, yDelta );
        pnl.Size = new Size(150, (theStyles.Length - 1) * yDelta);
        pnl.BorderStyle = BorderStyle.Fixed3D;
        pnl.AutoScroll = true;

        int i = 1;
        CheckBox cb;
        foreach (FontStyle style in theStyles)
        {
            cb = new CheckBox( );
            pnl.Controls.Add(cb);
            cb.Location = new Point(25, (yDelta * (i - 1)) + 10);
            cb.Size = new Size(75,20);
            cb.Text = style.ToString( );
            cb.Tag = style;
            cb.CheckedChanged += new
                System.EventHandler(cb_CheckedChanged);
            if (cb.Text == "Regular")
```

Example 13-1. Containers in C# (Containers.cs) (continued)

```
                cb.Checked = true;
            i++;
        }

        GroupBox grpAppearance = new GroupBox( );
        grpAppearance.Parent = this;
        grpAppearance.Text = "Appearance";
        grpAppearance.Location = new Point(175,yDelta);
        grpAppearance.Size = new Size(150, yDelta * 3);

        rdoAppearanceNormal = new RadioButton( );
        rdoAppearanceNormal.Parent = grpAppearance;
        rdoAppearanceNormal.Text = "Normal";
        rdoAppearanceNormal.Location = new Point(10, 15);
        rdoAppearanceNormal.Checked = true;
        rdoAppearanceNormal.CheckedChanged +=
                new System.EventHandler(rdoAppearance_CheckedChanged);

        rdoAppearanceButton = new RadioButton( );
        rdoAppearanceButton.Parent = grpAppearance;
        rdoAppearanceButton.Text = "Button";
        rdoAppearanceButton.Location = new Point(10, 15 + yDelta);
        rdoAppearanceButton.CheckedChanged +=
                new System.EventHandler(rdoAppearance_CheckedChanged);

        GroupBox grpCheckAlign = new GroupBox( );
        grpCheckAlign.Parent = this;
        grpCheckAlign.Text = "CheckAlign";
        grpCheckAlign.Location = new Point(175,
                                        grpAppearance.Bottom + 25);
        grpCheckAlign.Size = new Size(150, yDelta * 3);

        rdoCheckAlignMiddleLeft = new RadioButton( );
        rdoCheckAlignMiddleLeft.Parent = grpCheckAlign;
        rdoCheckAlignMiddleLeft.Text = "Middle Left";
        rdoCheckAlignMiddleLeft.Tag = ContentAlignment.MiddleLeft;
        rdoCheckAlignMiddleLeft.Location = new Point(10, 15);
        rdoCheckAlignMiddleLeft.Checked = true;
        rdoCheckAlignMiddleLeft.CheckedChanged +=
                new System.EventHandler(rdoCheckAlign_CheckedChanged);

        rdoCheckAlignMiddleRight = new RadioButton( );
        rdoCheckAlignMiddleRight.Parent = grpCheckAlign;
        rdoCheckAlignMiddleRight.Text = "Middle Right";
        rdoCheckAlignMiddleRight.Tag = ContentAlignment.MiddleRight;
        rdoCheckAlignMiddleRight.Location = new Point(10, 15 + yDelta);
        rdoCheckAlignMiddleRight.CheckedChanged +=
                new System.EventHandler(rdoCheckAlign_CheckedChanged);

        GroupBox grpTextAlign = new GroupBox( );
        grpTextAlign.Parent = this;
```

Example 13-1. Containers in C# (Containers.cs) (continued)

```
        grpTextAlign.Text = "TextAlign";
        grpTextAlign.Location = new Point(175,
                                        grpCheckAlign.Bottom + 25);
        grpTextAlign.Size = new Size(150, yDelta * 4);

        rdoTextAlignMiddleLeft = new RadioButton( );
        rdoTextAlignMiddleLeft.Parent = grpTextAlign;
        rdoTextAlignMiddleLeft.Text = "Middle Left";
        rdoTextAlignMiddleLeft.Tag = ContentAlignment.MiddleLeft;
        rdoTextAlignMiddleLeft.Location = new Point(10, 15);
        rdoTextAlignMiddleLeft.Checked = true;
        rdoTextAlignMiddleLeft.CheckedChanged +=
            new System.EventHandler(rdoTextAlign_CheckedChanged);

        rdoTextAlignMiddleRight = new RadioButton( );
        rdoTextAlignMiddleRight.Parent = grpTextAlign;
        rdoTextAlignMiddleRight.Text = "Middle Right";
        rdoTextAlignMiddleRight.Tag = ContentAlignment.MiddleRight;
        rdoTextAlignMiddleRight.Location = new Point(10, 15 + yDelta);
        rdoTextAlignMiddleRight.CheckedChanged +=
            new System.EventHandler(rdoTextAlign_CheckedChanged);

        rdoTextAlignMiddleCenter = new RadioButton( );
        rdoTextAlignMiddleCenter.Parent = grpTextAlign;
        rdoTextAlignMiddleCenter.Text = "Middle Center";
        rdoTextAlignMiddleCenter.Tag = ContentAlignment.MiddleCenter;
        rdoTextAlignMiddleCenter.Location = new Point(10,
                                            15 + (2 * yDelta));
        rdoTextAlignMiddleCenter.CheckedChanged +=
            new System.EventHandler(rdoTextAlign_CheckedChanged);
    } // close for constructor

    static void Main( )
    {
        Application.Run(new Containers( ));
    }

    private void cb_CheckedChanged(object sender, EventArgs e)
    {
        FontStyle fs = 0;
        for (int i = 0; i < pnl.Controls.Count; i++)
        {
            CheckBox cb = (CheckBox)pnl.Controls[i];
            if (cb.Checked)
                fs |= (FontStyle)cb.Tag;
        }
        lbl.Font = new Font(lbl.Font, fs);
    }

    private void rdoAppearance_CheckedChanged(object sender,
                                            EventArgs e)
    {
```

Example 13-1. Containers in C# (Containers.cs) (continued)

```
          if (rdoAppearanceNormal.Checked)
          {
             for (int i = 0; i < pnl.Controls.Count; i++)
             {
                CheckBox cb = (CheckBox)pnl.Controls[i];
                cb.Appearance = Appearance.Normal;
             }
          }
          else
          {
             for (int i = 0; i < pnl.Controls.Count; i++)
             {
                CheckBox cb = (CheckBox)pnl.Controls[i];
                cb.Appearance = Appearance.Button;
             }
          }
       }

       private void rdoCheckAlign_CheckedChanged(object sender,
                                                 EventArgs e)
       {
          RadioButton rdo = (RadioButton)sender;
          for (int i = 0; i < pnl.Controls.Count; i++)
          {
             CheckBox cb = (CheckBox)pnl.Controls[i];
             cb.CheckAlign = (ContentAlignment)rdo.Tag;
          }
       }

       private void rdoTextAlign_CheckedChanged(object sender, EventArgs e)
       {
          RadioButton rdo = (RadioButton)sender;
          for (int i = 0; i < pnl.Controls.Count; i++)
          {
             CheckBox cb = (CheckBox)pnl.Controls[i];
             switch ((int)rdo.Tag)
             {
                case (int)ContentAlignment.MiddleLeft :
                   cb.TextAlign = ContentAlignment.MiddleLeft;
                   break;
                case (int)ContentAlignment.MiddleRight :
                   cb.TextAlign = ContentAlignment.MiddleRight;
                   break;
                case (int)ContentAlignment.MiddleCenter :
                   cb.TextAlign = ContentAlignment.MiddleCenter;
                   break;
             }
          }
       }   // close for rdoTextAlign_CheckedChanged
    }      // close for form class
}          // close form namespace
```

Example 13-2. Containers in VB.NET (Containers.vb)

```vb
Option Strict On
imports System
imports System.Drawing
imports System.Windows.Forms

namespace ProgrammingWinApps
   public class Containers : inherits Form

      dim lbl as Label
      dim pnl as Panel
      dim yDelta as integer
      dim rdoAppearanceNormal as RadioButton
      dim rdoAppearanceButton as RadioButton
      dim rdoCheckAlignMiddleLeft as RadioButton
      dim rdoCheckAlignMiddleRight as RadioButton
      dim rdoTextAlignMiddleLeft as RadioButton
      dim rdoTextAlignMiddleRight as RadioButton
      dim rdoTextAlignMiddleCenter as RadioButton
      dim theStyles as FontStyle( )

      public sub New( )
         Text = "Containers"
         Size = new Size(350,375)

         lbl = new Label( )
         lbl.Parent = me
         lbl.Text = "The quick brown fox..."
         lbl.Location = new Point(0,0)
         lbl.AutoSize = true
         lbl.BorderStyle = BorderStyle.Fixed3D
         yDelta = lbl.Height + 10

         ' get the FontStyle values into an array
         dim theEnum as new FontStyle( )
         theStyles = CType([Enum].GetValues( _
                     theEnum.GetType( )), FontStyle( ))

         pnl = new Panel( )
         pnl.Parent = me
         pnl.Location = new Point(0, yDelta )
         pnl.Size = new Size(150, (theStyles.Length - 1) * yDelta)
         pnl.BorderStyle = BorderStyle.Fixed3D
         pnl.AutoScroll = true

         dim i as integer = 1
         dim style as FontStyle
         dim cb as CheckBox
         for each style in theStyles
            cb = new CheckBox( )
            pnl.Controls.Add(cb)
```

Example 13-2. Containers in VB.NET (Containers.vb) (continued)

VB

```
            cb.Location = new Point(25, (yDelta * (i - 1)) + 10)
            cb.Size = new Size(75,20)
            cb.Text = style.ToString( )
            cb.Tag = style
            AddHandler cb.CheckedChanged, AddressOf cb_CheckedChanged

            if cb.Text = "Regular" then
               cb.Checked = true
            end if
            i = i + 1
         next

         dim grpAppearance as GroupBox = new GroupBox( )
         grpAppearance.Parent = me
         grpAppearance.Text = "Appearance"
         grpAppearance.Location = new Point(175,yDelta)
         grpAppearance.Size = new Size(150, yDelta * 3)

         rdoAppearanceNormal = new RadioButton( )
         rdoAppearanceNormal.Parent = grpAppearance
         rdoAppearanceNormal.Text = "Normal"
         rdoAppearanceNormal.Location = new Point(10, 15)
         rdoAppearanceNormal.Checked = true
         AddHandler rdoAppearanceNormal.CheckedChanged, _
              AddressOf rdoAppearance_CheckedChanged

         rdoAppearanceButton = new RadioButton( )
         rdoAppearanceButton.Parent = grpAppearance
         rdoAppearanceButton.Text = "Button"
         rdoAppearanceButton.Location = new Point(10, 15 + yDelta)
         AddHandler rdoAppearanceButton.CheckedChanged, _
              AddressOf rdoAppearance_CheckedChanged

         dim grpCheckAlign as GroupBox = new GroupBox( )
         grpCheckAlign.Parent = me
         grpCheckAlign.Text = "CheckAlign"
         grpCheckAlign.Location = new Point(175, _
                                       grpAppearance.Bottom + 25)
         grpCheckAlign.Size = new Size(150, yDelta * 3)

         rdoCheckAlignMiddleLeft = new RadioButton( )
         rdoCheckAlignMiddleLeft.Parent = grpCheckAlign
         rdoCheckAlignMiddleLeft.Text = "Middle Left"
         rdoCheckAlignMiddleLeft.Tag = ContentAlignment.MiddleLeft
         rdoCheckAlignMiddleLeft.Location = new Point(10, 15)
         rdoCheckAlignMiddleLeft.Checked = true
         AddHandler rdoCheckAlignMiddleLeft.CheckedChanged, _
              AddressOf rdoCheckAlign_CheckedChanged

         rdoCheckAlignMiddleRight = new RadioButton( )
         rdoCheckAlignMiddleRight.Parent = grpCheckAlign
```

Example 13-2. Containers in VB.NET (Containers.vb) (continued)

```
rdoCheckAlignMiddleRight.Text = "Middle Right"
rdoCheckAlignMiddleRight.Tag = ContentAlignment.MiddleRight
rdoCheckAlignMiddleRight.Location = new Point(10, 15 + yDelta)
AddHandler rdoCheckAlignMiddleRight.CheckedChanged, _
    AddressOf rdoCheckAlign_CheckedChanged

dim grpTextAlign as GroupBox = new GroupBox( )
grpTextAlign.Parent = me
grpTextAlign.Text = "TextAlign"
grpTextAlign.Location = new Point(175, grpCheckAlign.Bottom + 25)
grpTextAlign.Size = new Size(150, yDelta * 4)

rdoTextAlignMiddleLeft = new RadioButton( )
rdoTextAlignMiddleLeft.Parent = grpTextAlign
rdoTextAlignMiddleLeft.Text = "Middle Left"
rdoTextAlignMiddleLeft.Tag = ContentAlignment.MiddleLeft
rdoTextAlignMiddleLeft.Location = new Point(10, 15)
rdoTextAlignMiddleLeft.Checked = true
AddHandler rdoTextAlignMiddleLeft.CheckedChanged, _
    AddressOf rdoTextAlign_CheckedChanged

rdoTextAlignMiddleRight = new RadioButton( )
rdoTextAlignMiddleRight.Parent = grpTextAlign
rdoTextAlignMiddleRight.Text = "Middle Right"
rdoTextAlignMiddleRight.Tag = ContentAlignment.MiddleRight
rdoTextAlignMiddleRight.Location = new Point(10, 15 + yDelta)
AddHandler rdoTextAlignMiddleRight.CheckedChanged, _
    AddressOf rdoTextAlign_CheckedChanged

rdoTextAlignMiddleCenter = new RadioButton( )
rdoTextAlignMiddleCenter.Parent = grpTextAlign
rdoTextAlignMiddleCenter.Text = "Middle Center"
rdoTextAlignMiddleCenter.Tag = ContentAlignment.MiddleCenter
rdoTextAlignMiddleCenter.Location = new Point(10, _
                                    15 + (2 * yDelta))
AddHandler rdoTextAlignMiddleCenter.CheckedChanged, _
    AddressOf rdoTextAlign_CheckedChanged
end sub   '  close for constructor

public shared sub Main( )
   Application.Run(new Containers( ))
end sub

private sub cb_CheckedChanged(ByVal sender as object, _
                    ByVal e as EventArgs)
   dim fs as FontStyle = 0
   dim i as integer
   for i = 0 to pnl.Controls.Count   - 1
      dim cb as CheckBox = CType(pnl.Controls(i), CheckBox)
      if cb.Checked then
```

Example 13-2. Containers in VB.NET (Containers.vb) (continued)

```
                    fs  = fs or CType(cb.Tag, FontStyle)
                end if
            next
            lbl.Font = new Font(lbl.Font, fs)
        end sub

        private sub rdoAppearance_CheckedChanged(ByVal sender as object, _
                            ByVal e as EventArgs)
            dim i as integer
            if rdoAppearanceNormal.Checked then
                for i = 0 to pnl.Controls.Count - 1
                    dim cb as CheckBox = CType(pnl.Controls(i), CheckBox)
                    cb.Appearance = Appearance.Normal
                next
            else
                for i = 0 to pnl.Controls.Count - 1
                    dim cb as CheckBox = CType(pnl.Controls(i), CheckBox)
                    cb.Appearance = Appearance.Button
                next
            end if
        end sub

        private sub rdoCheckAlign_CheckedChanged(ByVal sender as object, _
                            ByVal e as EventArgs)
            dim rdo as RadioButton = CType(sender, RadioButton)
            dim i as integer
            for i = 0 to pnl.Controls.Count - 1
                dim cb as CheckBox = CType(pnl.Controls(i), CheckBox)
                cb.CheckAlign = CType(rdo.Tag, ContentAlignment)
            next
        end sub

        private sub rdoTextAlign_CheckedChanged(ByVal sender as object, _
                            ByVal e as EventArgs)
            dim rdo as RadioButton = CType(sender, RadioButton)
            dim i as integer
            for i = 0 to pnl.Controls.Count - 1
                dim cb as CheckBox = CType(pnl.Controls(i), CheckBox)
                select case rdo.Tag
                    case ContentAlignment.MiddleLeft
                        cb.TextAlign = ContentAlignment.MiddleLeft
                    case ContentAlignment.MiddleRight
                        cb.TextAlign = ContentAlignment.MiddleRight
                    case ContentAlignment.MiddleCenter
                        cb.TextAlign = ContentAlignment.MiddleCenter
                end select
            next
        end sub
    end class
end namespace
```

The Panel control was made too short by modifying the line of code that calculates and sets the Size property. In the version in the previous chapter, the vertical size was based on the Length property of the Styles array plus 1. In the following examples, the vertical size is minus 1. The BorderStyle property is set to Fixed3D, so you can see the outline of the panel, and the AutoScale property is set to true:

```
C#
pnl.Size = new Size(150, (theStyles.Length - 1) * yDelta);
pnl.BorderStyle = BorderStyle.Fixed3D;
pnl.AutoScroll = true;
```

```
VB
pnl.Size = new Size(150, (theStyles.Length - 1) * yDelta)
pnl.BorderStyle = BorderStyle.Fixed3D
pnl.AutoScroll = true
```

By setting the AutoScale property to true, either or both a vertical and horizontal scrollbar will appear, if necessary. In this example, only the vertical scrollbar was necessary.

The other change made in these examples is inside the iteration that generates the CheckBox controls in the panel. The versions of the programs in Chapter 11 added each checkbox to the panel with the following line of code:

```
cb.Parent = pnl
```

These examples use the Add method to add each checkbox to the Controls collection of the Panel control.

```
pnl.Controls.Add(cb)
```

The result is the same either way.

There is no need to repeat how radio buttons and checkboxes work. Note, however, that the group box control makes each set of radio buttons independent and mutually exclusive within its set.

Tabbed Pages

A loose-leaf notebook with tabbed separator pages is an efficient way to organize and present a large amount of information in a compact space. The labeled tab on each separator page clearly separates and identifies the contents of that section. Although you can be in only one section at a time, you can easily see the labels of all available sections and instantly move between them.

This tabbed notebook metaphor, a common user interface design pattern in the Windows world, is implemented in .NET with the TabControl, which contains a collection of TabPage objects. All TabPage objects are layered one on top of another, with only one tab page visible at a time. Select which page to view by clicking on the tab. Each tab page can contain any number of controls.

Referring back to the class hierarchy displayed in Figure 13-1, you can see that the TabControl class is directly derived from the Control class, while the TabPage class is derived from Control via ScrollableControl and Panel. The TabControl control cannot contain other controls, except for TabPage objects. The TabPage objects, on the other hand, can contain other controls and have scrollbars. Unlike the Panel control from which it is derived, the TabPage displays its Text property as the text string on the tab.

The TabControl control has many properties in addition to those inherited from Control. Many are listed in Table 13-1.

Table 13-1. TabControl properties

Property	Value type	Description
Alignment	TabAlignment	Read/write. The edge of the control where the tabs are located. Valid values are members of the TabAlignment enumeration, listed in Table 13-2. The default is TabAlignment.Top.
		If set to Left or Right, the Multiline property is automatically set to true.
Appearance	TabAppearance	Read/write. The visual appearance of the tabs. Valid values are members of the TabAppearance enumeration, listed in Table 13-3. The default is TabAppearance. Normal.
DisplayRectangle	Rectangle	Read-only. Returns a Rectangle representing the display area of the tab pages.
DrawMode	TabDrawMode	Read/write. Allows users to customize how the control is drawn. If it is TabDraw-Mode.Normal, the default, the operating systems draws the tabs. If it is Tab-DrawMode.OwnerDrawFixed, the tabs are drawn by the parent window.
HotTrack	Boolean	Read/write. If false (the default), tabs do not change the appearance when the mouse passes over. If true, the color of the tab text will change.
ImageList	ImageList	Read/write. Specifies the ImageList containing images to be displayed on the tabs. The TabPage.ImageIndex property specifies which image to actually use. (The ImageList is described in Chapter 7.)
ItemSize	Size	Read/write. The size of the tabs. The default size automatically fits images and Text properties.
		The SizeMode property must be set to Fixed to change the ItemSize.Width property.
Multiline	Boolean	Read/write. If false (the default), only one line of tabs will be displayed. If there are more tabs than will fit, arrows will be displayed to allow navigation to undisplayed tabs.
		If false, the Alignment property is automatically set to TabAlignment.Top.
Padding	Point	Read/write. The amount of space around the text on the tab. Default is (6,3).
RowCount	Integer	Read-only. Returns the number of rows of tabs currently displayed.
SelectedIndex	Integer	Read/write. Zero-based index of the currently selected tab page.
ShowToolTips	Boolean	Read/write. If false (the default), ToolTips are not shown for tabs that have them. To create a ToolTip for a tab, set the TabPage.ToolTipText property.

Table 13-1. TabControl properties (continued)

Property	Value type	Description
SizeMode	TabSizeMode	Read/write. Specifies how the tabs are sized. Valid values are members of the TabSizeMode enumeration, listed in Table 13-4. The default is TabSizeMode.Normal.
TabCount	Integer	Read-only. Number of tabs in the TabControl.
TabPages	TabPageCollection	Read-only. The collection of tab pages contained in the control. The TabPageCollection class has properties, listed in Table 13-5, and methods, listed in Table 13-6.
Text	String	Read/write. Overrides Control.Text. Similar to the Panel control—does not display anywhere.

Table 13-2. TabAlignment enumeration

Value	Description
Bottom	Tabs located along the bottom of the control.
Left	Tabs located along the left edge of the control.
Right	Tabs located along the right edge of the control.
Top	Tabs located along the top of the control.

Three of the four possible values of TabAlignment are shown in Figure 13-3. The missing Right value is symmetrical to the Left.

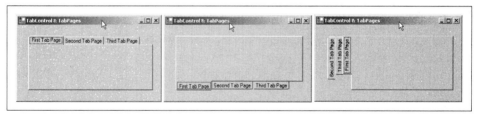

Figure 13-3. TabAlignment

Table 13-3. TabAppearance enumeration

Value	Description
Buttons	Tabs look like 3-D buttons.
FlatButtons	Tabs look like flat buttons.
Normal	Tabs look like standard tabs.

Table 13-4. TabSizeMode enumeration

Value	Description
FillToRight	Tabs are sized so that each row of tabs completely fills the width of the TabControl. Only applicable if Multiline is set to `true` and there is more than one row of tabs.
Fixed	All the tabs are the same width.
Normal	Each tab is sized for the contents of the tab and not adjusted to fill the width of the TabControl.

The Alignment and Appearance properties of the TabControl depend on each other for correct operation. If the Alignment property is set to TabAlignment.Top, then everything works fine regardless of the Appearance property. However, if the Alignment property is set to any value other than Top, the tab pages themselves will appear to be missing unless the Appearance property is set to the default of TabAppearance.Normal. If the Appearance is set to TabAppearance.Buttons or TabAppearance.FlatButtons, the tabs will display as buttons only and events will still fire, but the tab pages themselves will again appear to be missing. Furthermore, the tabs can appear as FlatButtons only if the Alignment is set for Top; if the Alignment is not set for Top, then FlatButtons will appear as Buttons.

The Padding property adds space around the text displayed in the tab. The left image in Figure 13-4 shows tabs using the default value for Padding (6,3) while the right image shows the Padding property set to (20,10). Notice that the Multiline property is set to true for both images: only the right image needed more than one row of tabs. If Multiline had not been set to true, the tabs would display in a single row with a clickable arrow for navigating to the other tabs.

 If the vertical size of the Padding is set larger than default and Multiline is false, the tabs may display with part of the text truncated if there are more tabs than will fit in a one row.

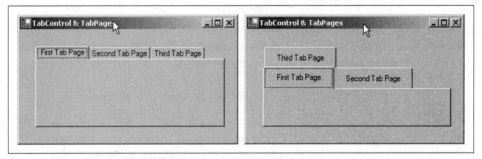

Figure 13-4. TabControl Padding property

All the tab pages contained by the TabControl are members of the TabPageCollection class. The commonly used properties and methods of the TabPageCollection class are listed in Table 13-5 and Table 13-6, respectively.

Table 13-5. TabPageCollection properties

Property	Value type	Description
Count	Integer	Read-only. Returns the number of tab pages in the collection (the number of tab pages in the TabControl).
IsReadOnly	Boolean	Read-only. Always returns `false`.
Item	TabPage	Read/write. The tab page at the zero-based index specified by this property.

Table 13-6. TabPageCollection methods

Method	Description
Add	Adds a TabPage object to the collection.
AddRange	Adds multiple TabPage object to the collection.
Clear	Removes all TabPage objects from the collection.
Contains	Returns true if the specified TabPage is in the collection.
GetEnumerator	Returns an enumerator containing all the TabPage objects. Changing the enumerator changes the collection of TabPages.
IndexOf	Returns the zero-based index of the specified TabPage object or -1 if the object not found.
Remove	Removes the specified TabPage object.
RemoveAt	Removes the TabPage object at the specified zero-based index.

Each tab page in a TabControl can also have properties of its own. The commonly used properties are listed in Table 13-7.

Table 13-7. TabPage properties

Property	Value type	Description
ImageIndex	TabControl.ImageList	Read/write. The index of the image to display on the tab. The zero-based index is in the ImageList specified in the TabControl.ImageList property.
TabIndex	Integer	Read/write. Overridden. The zero-based index of the tab page within the TabPage collection.
Text	String	Read/write. The text displayed on the tab.
ToolTipText	String	Read/write. The text displayed as a ToolTip when the user's mouse passes over the tab, if the TabControl.ShowToolTips property is set to true.

The TabPage TabIndex property is not listed as a member of the TabPage class in the SDK documentation that ships with the .NET Framework (although if you search, it will show up). It also does not show up in the IntelliSense list of all available members for a TabPage object in Visual Studio .NET. However, it will compile and return the value listed in Table 13-7. This functionality is entirely different from the TabIndex property of the Control class.

Its existence can be confirmed by the WinCV class viewer utility, which ships as part of the SDK. To run this utility, open a .NET command prompt (Start → Programs → Microsoft Visual Studio .NET 2003 → Visual Studio .NET Tools → Visual Studio .NET 2003 Command Prompt) and enter the command WINCV.

Other than events inherited from Control, the one commonly used event raised by the TabControl control is SelectedIndexChanged. It is raised whenever a different tab page is selected. Its usage will be demonstrated shortly.

There is actually a second event raised by the TabControl control: DrawItem. It occurs when the tabs are drawn if the DrawMode property was set to TabDrawMode.OwnerDrawFixed. This allows the parent window to draw the tab, giving you control over the appearance of the tabs.

The TabPage class has one method not inherited from the Control or other base class: GetTabPageFromComponent. This static (Shared in VB.NET) method takes a single object as an argument. This method will return the TabPage object containing the component if the component is found; otherwise it will return null (Nothing in VB.NET). For example, if you wanted to find and make current the tab page in a tab control that contains a RichTextBox control called rtxt, you could use a line such as the following:

```
tc.SelectedIndex =
    (TabPage.GetTabPageOfComponent(rtxt)).TabIndex;
```

```
tc.SelectedIndex = _
    TabPage.GetTabPageOfComponent(rtxt).TabIndex
```

The programs listed in Example 13-3 (in C#) and Example 13-4 (in VB.NET) demonstrate many of the features of the TabControl and TabPage classes. In these programs, a tab control is created on a form. This tab control contains four tab pages, three of which actually contain other controls and the fourth of which has a spiffy wrench icon as part of its tab. The look of the tabs is controlled using the Alignment, Appearance (which is set to its default value), Multiline, Padding, and Size-Mode properties. When either program is compiled and run, the first three pages will look like Figure 13-5. The fourth tab page, labeled "A Really Long Tab," contains no controls. It exists mainly to highlight the effects of these properties.

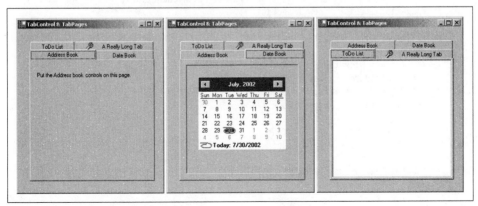

Figure 13-5. TabControl and TabPages

An analysis of Examples 13-3 and 13-4 follows the code listings.

Example 13-3. TabControl and TabPages in C# (TabControls.cs)

```csharp
using System;
using System.Drawing;
using System.Windows.Forms;

namespace ProgrammingWinApps
{
    public class TabControls : Form
    {
        public TabControls()
        {
            Text = "TabControl & TabPages";
            Size = new Size(325,375);

            TabControl tc = new TabControl();
            tc.Parent = this;
            tc.Size = new Size(275,300);
            tc.Location = new Point(25,25);
            tc.Anchor = AnchorStyles.Top | AnchorStyles.Bottom |
                    AnchorStyles.Left | AnchorStyles.Right;
            tc.Alignment = TabAlignment.Top;
            tc.Appearance = TabAppearance.Normal;
            tc.HotTrack = true;
            tc.Multiline = true;
            tc.Padding = new Point(20,3);
            tc.SizeMode = TabSizeMode.FillToRight;
            tc.SelectedIndexChanged += new EventHandler(tc_Changed);
            tc.Text = "Some text";

            //  Get an image for one of the tabs
            Image img = Image.FromFile(
               "C:\\Program Files\\Microsoft Visual Studio .NET 2003\\" +
                    "Common7\\Graphics\\icons\\industry\\wrench.ico");
            ImageList imgList = new ImageList();
            imgList.Images.Add(img);
            tc.ImageList = imgList;

            //  Address book tab
            TabPage tpAddress = new TabPage();
            tpAddress.Parent = tc;
            tpAddress.Text = "Address Book";

            //  Datebook tab
            TabPage tpDates = new TabPage();
            tpDates.Parent = tc;
            tpDates.Text = "Date Book";

            //  ToDo tab
            TabPage tpToDo = new TabPage();
            tpToDo.Parent = tc;
            tpToDo.Text = "ToDo List";
```

Example 13-3. TabControl and TabPages in C# (TabControls.cs) (continued)

```csharp
        // Miscellaneous tab
        TabPage tpMisc = new TabPage( );
        tpMisc.Parent = tc;
        tpMisc.Text = "A Really Long Tab";
        tpMisc.ImageIndex = 0;

        // Address stuff
        Label lbl = new Label( );
        lbl.Parent = tpAddress;
        lbl.Text = "Put the Address book controls on this page.";
        lbl.AutoSize = true;
        lbl.Location = new Point(10,25);

        // Datebook stuff
        Panel pnl = new Panel( );
        pnl.Parent = tpDates;
        pnl.BorderStyle = BorderStyle.Fixed3D;
        pnl.Location = new Point(10,10);
        pnl.Anchor = AnchorStyles.Top | AnchorStyles.Bottom |
                AnchorStyles.Left | AnchorStyles.Right;
        pnl.Size = new Size(tpDates.Width - 20, tpDates.Height - 20);

        MonthCalendar cal = new MonthCalendar( );
        cal.Parent = pnl;
        cal.Location = new Point(25,25);

        // ToDo stuff
        RichTextBox rtxt = new RichTextBox( );
        rtxt.Parent = tpToDo;
        rtxt.Dock = DockStyle.Fill;
        rtxt.BorderStyle = BorderStyle.FixedSingle;
    }  // close for constructor

    static void Main( )
    {
        Application.Run(new TabControls( ));
    }

    private void tc_Changed(object sender, EventArgs e)
    {
        TabControl tc = (TabControl)sender;
        MessageBox.Show("Button " + tc.SelectedIndex.ToString( ));
    }
  }      //  close for form class
}          //  close form namespace
```

Example 13-4. TabControl and TabPages in VB.NET (TabControls.vb)

```vbnet
Option Strict On
imports System
imports System.Drawing
imports System.Windows.Forms
```

```vb
namespace ProgrammingWinApps
    public class TabControls : inherits Form
        public sub New( )
            Text = "TabControl & TabPages"
            Size = new Size(325,375)

            dim tc as new TabControl( )
            tc.Parent = me
            tc.Size = new Size(275,300)
            tc.Location = new Point(25,25)
            tc.Anchor = AnchorStyles.Top or AnchorStyles.Bottom or _
                    AnchorStyles.Left or AnchorStyles.Right
            tc.Alignment = TabAlignment.Top
            tc.Appearance = TabAppearance.Normal
            tc.HotTrack = true
            tc.Multiline = true
            tc.Padding = new Point(20,3)
            tc.SizeMode = TabSizeMode.FillToRight
            AddHandler tc.SelectedIndexChanged, AddressOf tc_Changed
            tc.Text = "Some text"

            ' Get an image for one of the tabs
            dim img as Image = Image.FromFile( _
                "C:\\Program Files\\Microsoft Visual Studio .NET 2003\\" + _
                    "Common7\\Graphics\\icons\\industry\\wrench.ico")
            dim imgList as new ImageList( )
            imgList.Images.Add(img)
            tc.ImageList = imgList

            ' Address book tab
            dim tpAddress as new TabPage( )
            tpAddress.Parent = tc
            tpAddress.Text = "Address Book"

            ' Datebook tab
            dim tpDates as new TabPage( )
            tpDates.Parent = tc
            tpDates.Text = "Date Book"

            ' ToDo tab
            dim tpToDo as new TabPage( )
            tpToDo.Parent = tc
            tpToDo.Text = "ToDo List"

            ' Miscellaneous tab
            dim tpMisc as new TabPage( )
            tpMisc.Parent = tc
            tpMisc.Text = "A Really Long Tab"
            tpMisc.ImageIndex = 0

            ' Address stuff
            dim lbl as new Label( )
            lbl.Parent = tpAddress
```

VB

```
            lbl.Text = "Put the Address book controls on this page."
            lbl.AutoSize = true
            lbl.Location = new Point(10,25)

            ' Datebook stuff
            dim pnl as new Panel( )
            pnl.Parent = tpDates
            pnl.BorderStyle = BorderStyle.Fixed3D
            pnl.Location = new Point(10,10)
            pnl.Anchor = AnchorStyles.Top or AnchorStyles.Bottom or _
                    AnchorStyles.Left or AnchorStyles.Right
            pnl.Size = new Size(tpDates.Width - 20, tpDates.Height - 20)

            dim cal as new MonthCalendar( )
            cal.Parent = pnl
            cal.Location = new Point(25,25)

            ' ToDo stuff
            dim rtxt as new RichTextBox( )
            rtxt.Parent = tpToDo
            rtxt.Dock = DockStyle.Fill
            rtxt.BorderStyle = BorderStyle.FixedSingle
        end sub   ' close for constructor

        public shared sub Main( )
            Application.Run(new TabControls( ))
        end sub

        private sub tc_Changed(ByVal sender as object, _
                        ByVal e as EventArgs)
            dim tc as TabControl = CType(sender,TabControl)
            MessageBox.Show("Button " + tc.SelectedIndex.ToString( ))
        end sub
    end class
end namespace
```

These sample programs don't do much, so almost all of the action occurs inside the constructor. A TabControl object is declared, instantiated, and given a size and location. Its Anchor property is set so the tab control will automatically resize itself if the user resizes the form, retaining the same margins on all four sides with respect to the form.

Several properties of the tab control are set, including Alignment, Appearance (which is set to its default value), Multiline, Padding, and SizeMode. Setting the HotTrack property to true causes the tab text to change color when the mouse moves over the tab.

The SizeMode property, set in these examples to TabSizeMode.FillToRight, profoundly affects the appearance of the tabs if any of the tabs are of significantly different length and/or if there are more tabs than will fit on one row. The valid values of this property are listed in Table 13-4. The effects of each possible value of the property are seen in Figure 13-6.

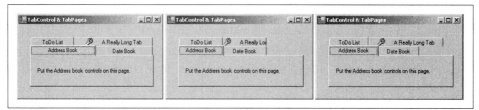

Figure 13-6. TabControl SizeMode property: FillToRight, Fixed, and Normal

An event handler method is added to the delegate for the TabControl SelectedIndex-Changed event:

```
tc.SelectedIndexChanged += new EventHandler(tc_Changed);
```

```
AddHandler tc.SelectedIndexChanged, AddressOf tc_Changed
```

Every time the user selects a new tab, this event will be fired, invoking the event handler method tc_Changed. That event handler puts up a message box in this example, but it could do other useful things, such as logging page hits or updating the database.

The event argument for this event is of type EventArgs, so there is no additional information passed about the event. However, the object named sender can be cast back to a TabControl object (which is safe in this case and will not raise an exception), and then all of the TabControl properties are available to the method, including the SelectedIndex property, as shown in the event handler (reproduced here):

```
private void tc_Changed(object sender, EventArgs e)
{
    TabControl tc = (TabControl)sender;
    MessageBox.Show("Button " + tc.SelectedIndex.ToString());
}
```

```
private sub tc_Changed(ByVal sender as object, _
                    ByVal e as EventArgs)
    dim tc as TabControl = CType(sender,TabControl)
    MessageBox.Show("Button " + tc.SelectedIndex.ToString())
end sub
```

The next several lines of code create an ImageList and populate it with a single image, wrench.ico, which is a standard icon file included with Visual Studio .NET. The ImageList is assigned to the tab control's ImageList property. You need to create the ImageList even though only a single image is used because the TabPage class has an ImageIndex property (listed in Table 13-7) but no Image property, as does the Button class, for example. This image list will be used shortly to put the wrench icon on the fourth tab page.

The four tab pages are instantiated and specified. Each follows the same pattern. The tab page object is instantiated and assigned to a variable. The Parent property of the object is set to the TabControl object, and its Text property is set. The fourth tab page also has its ImageIndex property set to 0 so the wrench icon will display:

```csharp
TabPage tpAddress = new TabPage( );
tpAddress.Parent = tc;
tpAddress.Text = "Address Book";

tpMisc.ImageIndex = 0;
```

```vb
dim tpAddress as new TabPage( )
tpAddress.Parent = tc
tpAddress.Text = "Address Book"

tpMisc.ImageIndex = 0
```

If this project were implemented in Visual Studio .NET, the Parent property would not be set this way. Instead, an array of Control objects would be created by Visual Studio .NET, and the AddRange method used to add the array of TabPage objects to the TabControl object's Controls collection. It would look something like:

```csharp
this.tc.Controls.AddRange(new
    System.Windows.Forms.Control[ ] {
                    this. tpAddress,
                    this. tpDates,
                    this. tpToDo,
                this.tpMisc});
```

```vb
Me.tc.Controls.AddRange( _
    New System.Windows.Forms.Control( ) _
    {Me.tpAddress, Me.tpDates, Me.tpToDo, _
    _Me.tpMisc })
```

which can be seen by expanding the Windows Form Designer generated code.

Each of the first three tabs then has one or more controls added to them. Adding controls to a tab page is the same as adding controls to a form, except that the Parent property of each control is set to the appropriated TabPage object rather than the form.

Referring to the previous note, the Parent property of each control is implicitly set in Visual Studio .NET by using the AddRange method.

Tabbed Pages Using Visual Studio .NET

In Visual Studio .NET, most controls are represented by an icon in the Toolbox, and can be either dragged onto the form or double-clicked to be placed on the form. The TabControl control follows that model: there is an icon for the TabControl in the

Toolbox (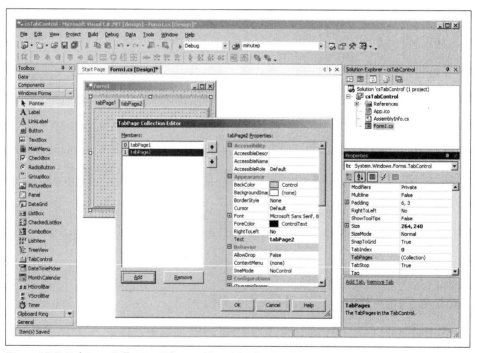 TabControl) that can be either double-clicked or dragged onto a form. However, the TabPage control in the Toolbox has no icon.

There are two different ways to add TabPage objects to a TabControl control, aside from manually coding them as was done earlier in this chapter. The first way is to select and right-click the TabControl control in Design view, and then click on the Add Tab menu item from the pop-up menu. This will add a tab page directly to the tab control, with a default name of tabPage1 (tabPage2, and so on). Once the tab page is added, you can set its properties by selecting it in Design view and editing the properties in the Properties window.

The second way to add tab pages is to select the tab control in Design view, locate the TabPages property in the Properties window, and click on the Build button (...). This will bring up the TabPage Collection Editor dialog box, shown in Figure 13-7. This dialog box has buttons for adding and removing tab pages, as well as a Properties window for setting the properties of the currently selected tab page. It also has buttons for easily changing the order of the tab pages.

No matter which technique you use, you can use either the Properties window—the one in the main Visual Studio .NET window or the one in the TabPage Collection Editor—to edit the properties of the currently selected tab page.

Figure 13-7. TabPage Collection Editor in Visual Studio .NET

PictureBox

The PictureBox control displays an Image object. The Image object to be displayed can be a member of, or descended from, one of the following classes:

Bitmap
> Contains pixel data for an image and its attributes. Typical file types are *jpg*, *gif*, or *bmp*.

Icon
> A small, transparent bitmap used to represent an object. The typical file extension is *ico*.

Metafile
> Contains records that describe a sequence of graphics operations. The typical file extension is *wmf*.

The PictureBox is a relatively simple control, with only three commonly used properties other than those inherited from Control or other base classes. The properties are listed in Table 13-8. The important property is SizeMode, which controls how the image is fit to the PictureBox.

Table 13-8. PictureBox properties

Property	Value type	Description
BorderStyle	BorderStyle	Read/write. Valid values are members of the BorderStyle enumeration, listed in Table 13-9. The default value is BorderStyle.None.
Image	Image	Read/write. The image to display in the control.
SizeMode	PictureBoxSizeMode	Read/write. How the image is displayed. Valid values are members of the PictureBoxSizeMode enumeration, listed in Table 13-10. The default value is PictureBoxSizeMode.Normal.

Table 13-9. BorderStyle enumeration values

Value	Description
Fixed3D	3-D border.
FixedSingle	Single line border.
None	No border.

Table 13-10. PictureBoxSizeMode enumeration values

Value	Description
AutoSize	The PictureBox is automatically sized to fit the image it contains.
CenterImage	The image is centered in the control. If the image is larger than the control, the image is clipped on all four sides.
Normal	The image is placed in the upper-left corner of the control. If the image is larger than the control, the image is clipped.
StretchImage	The image is resized to fit the control.

The programs listed in Example 13-5 (in C#) and in Example 13-6 (in VB.NET) demonstrate the PictureBox control with all four possible values of the SizeMode property. For each possible SizeMode value, two picture boxes are presented: one intentionally larger than the image and one smaller. The image used here is a *gif* file that is 151 pixels wide by 140 pixels high.

Example 13-5. PictureBoxes in C# (PictureBoxes.cs)

```csharp
using System;
using System.Drawing;
using System.Windows.Forms;

namespace ProgrammingWinApps
{
    public class PictureBoxes : Form
    {
        public PictureBoxes()
        {
            Text = "PictureBoxes";
            Size = new Size(550,500);
            AutoScroll = true;

            //  Get an image to use
            Image img = Image.FromFile(
                "Dan at Vernal Pool.gif");

            Label lblNormal = new Label();
            lblNormal.Parent = this;
            lblNormal.Location = new Point(0,20);
            lblNormal.Size = new Size(75,25);
            lblNormal.TextAlign = ContentAlignment.MiddleRight;
            lblNormal.Text = "Normal:";

            PictureBox pbNormalBig = new PictureBox();
            pbNormalBig.Parent = this;
            pbNormalBig.Size = new Size(200, 200);
            pbNormalBig.Location = new Point(75,20);
            pbNormalBig.BorderStyle = BorderStyle.FixedSingle;
            pbNormalBig.SizeMode = PictureBoxSizeMode.Normal;
            pbNormalBig.Image = img;

            PictureBox pbNormalSmall = new PictureBox();
            pbNormalSmall.Parent = this;
            pbNormalSmall.Size = new Size(100, 100);
            pbNormalSmall.Location = new Point(325,20);
            pbNormalSmall.BorderStyle = BorderStyle.FixedSingle;
            pbNormalSmall.SizeMode = PictureBoxSizeMode.Normal;
            pbNormalSmall.Image = img;

            Label lblAuto = new Label();
            lblAuto.Parent = this;
            lblAuto.Location = new Point(0, 250);
            lblAuto.Size = new Size(75,25);
```

Example 13-5. PictureBoxes in C# (PictureBoxes.cs) (continued)

```
        lblAuto.TextAlign = ContentAlignment.MiddleRight;
        lblAuto.Text = "AutoSize:";

        PictureBox pbAutoBig = new PictureBox( );
        pbAutoBig.Parent = this;
        pbAutoBig.Size = new Size(200, 200);
        pbAutoBig.Location = new Point(75, 250);
        pbAutoBig.BorderStyle = BorderStyle.FixedSingle;
        pbAutoBig.SizeMode = PictureBoxSizeMode.AutoSize;
        pbAutoBig.Image = img;

        PictureBox pbAutoSmall = new PictureBox( );
        pbAutoSmall.Parent = this;
        pbAutoSmall.Size = new Size(100, 100);
        pbAutoSmall.Location = new Point(325,250);
        pbAutoSmall.BorderStyle = BorderStyle.FixedSingle;
        pbAutoSmall.SizeMode = PictureBoxSizeMode.AutoSize;
        pbAutoSmall.Image = img;

        Label lblCenter = new Label( );
        lblCenter.Parent = this;
        lblCenter.Location = new Point(0,480);
        lblCenter.Size = new Size(75,25);
        lblCenter.TextAlign = ContentAlignment.MiddleRight;
        lblCenter.Text = "CenterImage:";

        PictureBox pbCenterBig = new PictureBox( );
        pbCenterBig.Parent = this;
        pbCenterBig.Size = new Size(200, 200);
        pbCenterBig.Location = new Point(75,480);
        pbCenterBig.BorderStyle = BorderStyle.FixedSingle;
        pbCenterBig.SizeMode = PictureBoxSizeMode.CenterImage;
        pbCenterBig.Image = img;

        PictureBox pbCenterSmall = new PictureBox( );
        pbCenterSmall.Parent = this;
        pbCenterSmall.Size = new Size(100, 100);
        pbCenterSmall.Location = new Point(325,480);
        pbCenterSmall.BorderStyle = BorderStyle.FixedSingle;
        pbCenterSmall.SizeMode = PictureBoxSizeMode.CenterImage;
        pbCenterSmall.Image = img;

        Label lblStretch = new Label( );
        lblStretch.Parent = this;
        lblStretch.Location = new Point(0,710);
        lblStretch.Size = new Size(75,25);
        lblStretch.TextAlign = ContentAlignment.MiddleRight;
        lblStretch.Text = "StretchImage:";

        PictureBox pbStretchBig = new PictureBox( );
        pbStretchBig.Parent = this;
        pbStretchBig.Size = new Size(200, 200);
```

Example 13-5. PictureBoxes in C# (PictureBoxes.cs) (continued)

```csharp
        pbStretchBig.Location = new Point(75,710);
        pbStretchBig.BorderStyle = BorderStyle.FixedSingle;
        pbStretchBig.SizeMode = PictureBoxSizeMode.StretchImage;
        pbStretchBig.Image = img;

        PictureBox pbStretchSmall = new PictureBox( );
        pbStretchSmall.Parent = this;
        pbStretchSmall.Size = new Size(100, 100);
        pbStretchSmall.Location = new Point(325,710);
        pbStretchSmall.BorderStyle = BorderStyle.FixedSingle;
        pbStretchSmall.SizeMode = PictureBoxSizeMode.StretchImage;
        pbStretchSmall.Image = img;
    } // close for constructor

    static void Main( )
    {
        Application.Run(new PictureBoxes( ));
    }

}       // close for form class
}       // close form namespace
```

Example 13-6. PictureBoxes in VB.NET (PictureBoxes.vb)

```vbnet
Option Strict On
imports System
imports System.Drawing
imports System.Windows.Forms

namespace ProgrammingWinApps
    public class PictureBoxes : inherits Form
        public sub New( )
            Text = "PictureBoxes"
            Size = new Size(550,500)
            AutoScroll = true

            ' Get an image to use
            dim img as Image = Image.FromFile( _
                "Dan at Vernal Pool.gif")

            dim lblNormal as new Label( )
            lblNormal.Parent = me
            lblNormal.Location = new Point(0,20)
            lblNormal.Size = new Size(75,25)
            lblNormal.TextAlign = ContentAlignment.MiddleRight
            lblNormal.Text = "Normal:"

            dim pbNormalBig as new PictureBox( )
            pbNormalBig.Parent = me
            pbNormalBig.Size = new Size(200, 200)
            pbNormalBig.Location = new Point(75,20)
            pbNormalBig.BorderStyle = BorderStyle.FixedSingle
```

Example 13-6. PictureBoxes in VB.NET (PictureBoxes.vb) (continued)

VB

```
        pbNormalBig.SizeMode = PictureBoxSizeMode.Normal
        pbNormalBig.Image = img

        dim pbNormalSmall as new PictureBox( )
        pbNormalSmall.Parent = me
        pbNormalSmall.Size = new Size(100, 100)
        pbNormalSmall.Location = new Point(325,20)
        pbNormalSmall.BorderStyle = BorderStyle.FixedSingle
        pbNormalSmall.SizeMode = PictureBoxSizeMode.Normal
        pbNormalSmall.Image = img

        dim lblAuto as new Label( )
        lblAuto.Parent = me
        lblAuto.Location = new Point(0, 250)
        lblAuto.Size = new Size(75,25)
        lblAuto.TextAlign = ContentAlignment.MiddleRight
        lblAuto.Text = "AutoSize:"

        dim pbAutoBig as new PictureBox( )
        pbAutoBig.Parent = me
        pbAutoBig.Size = new Size(200, 200)
        pbAutoBig.Location = new Point(75, 250)
        pbAutoBig.BorderStyle = BorderStyle.FixedSingle
        pbAutoBig.SizeMode = PictureBoxSizeMode.AutoSize
        pbAutoBig.Image = img

        dim pbAutoSmall as new PictureBox( )
        pbAutoSmall.Parent = me
        pbAutoSmall.Size = new Size(100, 100)
        pbAutoSmall.Location = new Point(325,250)
        pbAutoSmall.BorderStyle = BorderStyle.FixedSingle
        pbAutoSmall.SizeMode = PictureBoxSizeMode.AutoSize
        pbAutoSmall.Image = img

        dim lblCenter as new Label( )
        lblCenter.Parent = me
        lblCenter.Location = new Point(0,480)
        lblCenter.Size = new Size(75,25)
        lblCenter.TextAlign = ContentAlignment.MiddleRight
        lblCenter.Text = "CenterImage:"

        dim pbCenterBig as new PictureBox( )
        pbCenterBig.Parent = me
        pbCenterBig.Size = new Size(200, 200)
        pbCenterBig.Location = new Point(75,480)
        pbCenterBig.BorderStyle = BorderStyle.FixedSingle
        pbCenterBig.SizeMode = PictureBoxSizeMode.CenterImage
        pbCenterBig.Image = img

        dim pbCenterSmall as new PictureBox( )
        pbCenterSmall.Parent = me
        pbCenterSmall.Size = new Size(100, 100)
        pbCenterSmall.Location = new Point(325,480)
```

Example 13-6. PictureBoxes in VB.NET (PictureBoxes.vb) (continued)

```
pbCenterSmall.BorderStyle = BorderStyle.FixedSingle
pbCenterSmall.SizeMode = PictureBoxSizeMode.CenterImage
pbCenterSmall.Image = img

dim lblStretch as new Label( )
lblStretch.Parent = me
lblStretch.Location = new Point(0,710)
lblStretch.Size = new Size(75,25)
lblStretch.TextAlign = ContentAlignment.MiddleRight
lblStretch.Text = "StretchImage:"

dim pbStretchBig as new PictureBox( )
pbStretchBig.Parent = me
pbStretchBig.Size = new Size(200, 200)
pbStretchBig.Location = new Point(75,710)
pbStretchBig.BorderStyle = BorderStyle.FixedSingle
pbStretchBig.SizeMode = PictureBoxSizeMode.StretchImage
pbStretchBig.Image = img

dim pbStretchSmall as new PictureBox( )
pbStretchSmall.Parent = me
pbStretchSmall.Size = new Size(100, 100)
pbStretchSmall.Location = new Point(325,710)
pbStretchSmall.BorderStyle = BorderStyle.FixedSingle
pbStretchSmall.SizeMode = PictureBoxSizeMode.StretchImage
pbStretchSmall.Image = img
end sub    '   close for constructor

public shared sub Main( )
    Application.Run(new PictureBoxes( ))
end sub

end class
end namespace
```

The programs listed in Examples 13-5 and 13-6 start off by setting the AutoScroll property of the form to true so that a vertical scrollbar will automatically appear, since the eight picture boxes don't fit on the form as originally sized.

An image object is instantiated with the static Image.FromFile method:

```
Image img = Image.FromFile("Dan at Vernal Pool.gif");
```

```
dim img as Image = Image.FromFile("Dan at Vernal Pool.gif")
```

This example assumes that the file is located in the current directory. If it were not, then you would have to specify the full path.

The four sets of controls on the form each consist of a label and two picture boxes. Both picture boxes in each set use the same value of SizeMode; the label identifies which value of SizeMode is used. The first picture box is intentionally larger than the image (200,200 versus 151,140), and the second is intentionally too small (100,100). All picture boxes have their BorderStyle set to BorderStyle.FixedSingle, to make it easy to see how big the picture box is.

The first set has a SizeMode of PictureBoxSizeMode.Normal, the default value. In the large picture box, the image is in the upper-left corner, and in the small picture box, the image is clipped on the right and bottom edges, as shown in Figure 13-8.

Figure 13-8. PictureBox—SizeMode Normal

The next set has a SizeMode of PictureBoxSizeMode.AutoSize. This forces the picture box to be the same size as the image, as shown in Figure 13-9.

Figure 13-9. PictureBox—SizeMode AutoSize

The next set has a SizeMode of PictureBoxSizeMode.CenterImage. This setting centers the image in the picture box, as shown in Figure 13-10. If the picture box is too small for the image, the image is clipped on all four sides.

The final set has a SizeMode of PictureBoxSizeMode.StretchImage. This either stretches or shrinks the image as necessary to fit the picture box, as shown in Figure 13-11.

Figure 13-10. PictureBox—SizeMode CenterImage

Figure 13-11. PictureBox—SizeMode StretchImage

 This control is best for images that are relatively static. If the image changes frequently, resetting the Image property is inefficient. For these cases, a custom control is better.

ScrollBar

Scrollbars are everywhere in graphical user interfaces (GUIs). They can serve two different purposes: to shift the area of a graphical surface that is visible to the user (by far the most common usage) or to vary a parameter (similar to a TrackBar, described in the next section).

The ScrollableControl class, and all classes derived from it, can implement scrollbars for the purpose of moving around in a window or a region of a window by setting a single property:

```
AutoScroll = true
```

Controls that derive, directly or indirectly, from ScrollableControl include Form and Panel, so for many applications, this is all you need to know about scrollbars. With the AutoScroll property set to true, the form or panel will automatically include either horizontal and/or vertical scrollbars, as necessary, if the extent of controls drawn on the form or panel exceeds the visible client area. This is true at runtime either as a result of program action or user interaction.

In addition, most other controls that need scrollbars, such as the multiline TextBox, listbox, or combo box, already have them provided as part of the base functionality of those controls. As with the ScrollableControl objects, scrollbars appear as necessary with no effort required on the part of the developer.

However, automatically created scrollbars are mostly inaccessible to the developer. (There is some control of AutoScroll scrollbars through the use of the AutoScroll-Margin, AutoScrollMinSize, and AutoScrollPosition properties, but no events are exposed.) If you want to control the appearance or location of the scrollbars, apply them to a control that does not normally have them, or interact with them programmatically, then you must use the ScrollBar control.

The ScrollBar control is an abstract/MustInherit class derived directly from Control, as shown in Figure 13-1. Two classes are derived from it: HScrollBar for a horizontal scrollbar and VScrollBar for a vertical scrollbar.

With the ScrollBar control, you can

- Set the size and location of ScrollBar objects
- Control (indirectly) the size of the scroll box (sometimes called the thumb)
- Set the range of represented values
- Respond to events raised when the scrollbar is scrolled
- Retrieve a value from the control
- Set the increments by which the target is scrolled

The ScrollBar class inherits all the Control properties, including the size and positioning properties such as Size, Location, Length, and Width. Height and Width have intuitively opposite meanings when you consider the HScrollBar versus the VScrollBar. In either case, Height refers to the vertical distance and Width refers to the horizontal distance. Thus the Height of a horizontal scrollbar is its thickness (its short axis), while the Height of a vertical scrollbar is its length (its long axis).

The properties that are specific to the ScrollBar control and provide much of its functionality are listed in Table 13-11.

Table 13-11. ScrollBar properties

Property	Value type	Description
LargeChange	Integer	Read/write. The value to be added or subtracted from the Value property when the user clicks in the scrollbar track between the thumb and the scroll arrow, or presses the Page Up or Page Down key. Default value is 10. In proportion to the Maximum property, determines the width of thumb.
Maximum	Integer	Read/write. Maximum possible value of the Value property. Default value is 100.
Minimum	Integer	Read/write. Minimum possible value of the Value property. Default value is zero.
SmallChange	Integer	Read/write. The value to be added or subtracted from the Value property when the user clicks on the scroll arrow or presses the Up or Down arrow key. Default value is 1.
Value	Integer	Read/write. Numeric value representing the current position of the thumb in the scrollbar. The current position is indicated by the left edge of the thumb of a horizontal scrollbar or the top edge of the thumb of a vertical scrollbar. The smallest value of Value is the Minimum property. The largest value of Value is (Maximum − LargeChange + 1). Default value is zero.

Some of the standard Control properties are "missing" from the ScrollBar class—i.e., they are overridden and not available at design time. You can code against them, but they are ignored. These properties include BackColor, BackgroundImage, Fore-Color, and Text. In addition, the TabStop property is `false`, by default, unlike most controls, implying that scrollbars do not participate in the tab order.

There are two events raised by ScrollBar controls, listed in Table 13-12. The ValueChanged event is the most commonly used one: it is raised when the Value property is changed. At that point, the Value property reports the new value (after the change has occurred). If more granular information or higher performance is required, then the Scroll event can be trapped and handled.

Table 13-12. ScrollBar events

Event	Event data	Description
ValueChanged	EventArgs	Raised when the Value property has changed, either by a Scroll event or programmatically.
Scroll	ScrollEventArgs	Raised when the thumb has been moved, either by the mouse or the keyboard. Provides information about the event, including the new value and type of event.

As a Positioning Device

The programs listed in Example 13-7 (in C#) and Example 13-8 (in VB.NET) demonstrate the use of horizontal and vertical scrollbars to scroll a large image within a smaller panel. Since the image is too large to be visible all at once, the scrollbars allow the user to pan around the image, viewing a portion of the image through the "viewport" provided by the panel.

In these examples, the image used is the screenshot from Figure 13-6, which is 990 pixels wide by 380 pixels high. You can use any image you want, as long as it is larger than the panel size of 400 × 200 (unless you change the size of the panel control).

When the programs are compiled and run, the result is shown in Figure 13-12, after adjusting the scrollbars to show the top middle of the image.

An analysis follows the program listings.

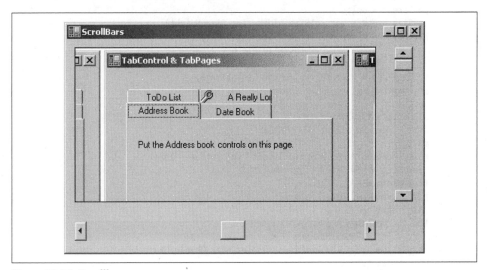

Figure 13-12. Scrollbars

Example 13-7. ScrollBars using C# (ScrollBars.cs)

```csharp
using System;
using System.Drawing;
using System.Windows.Forms;

namespace ProgrammingWinApps
{
    public class ScrollBars : Form
    {
        Panel pnl;
        PictureBox pb;
        HScrollBar hbar;
        VScrollBar vbar;
        Image img;

        public ScrollBars()
        {
            Text = "ScrollBars";
            Size = new Size(480,300);
```

Example 13-7. ScrollBars using C# (ScrollBars.cs) (continued)

```
        // Get an image to use
        img = Image.FromFile(
            "TabControlSizeMode.gif");

        pnl = new Panel( );
        pnl.Parent = this;
        pnl.Size = new Size(400,200);
        pnl.Location = new Point(10,10);
        pnl.BorderStyle = BorderStyle.FixedSingle;

        pb = new PictureBox( );
        pb.Parent = pnl;
        pb.Size = new Size(img.Size.Width, img.Size.Height);
        pb.Location = new Point((pnl.Size.Width / 2) -
                            (pb.Size.Width / 2),
                        (pnl.Size.Height / 2) - (pb.Size.Height / 2));
        pb.SizeMode = PictureBoxSizeMode.CenterImage;
        pb.Image = img;

        // Horizontal scrollbar
        hbar = new HScrollBar( );
        hbar.Parent = this;
        hbar.Location = new Point(pnl.Left, pnl.Bottom + 25);
        hbar.Size = new Size(pnl.Width, 25);
        hbar.Minimum = 0;
        hbar.Maximum = 100;
        hbar.SmallChange = 1;
        hbar.LargeChange = 10;
        hbar.Value = (hbar.Maximum - hbar.Minimum) / 2;
        hbar.ValueChanged += new EventHandler(hbar_OnValueChanged);

        // Vertical scrollbar
        vbar = new VScrollBar( );
        vbar.Parent = this;
        vbar.Location = new Point(pnl.Right + 25, pnl.Top);
        vbar.Size = new Size(25, pnl.Height);
        vbar.Minimum = 0;
        vbar.Maximum = 100 + vbar.LargeChange;
        vbar.SmallChange = 1;
        vbar.LargeChange = 10;
        vbar.Value = (vbar.Maximum - vbar.Minimum) / 2;
        vbar.ValueChanged += new EventHandler(vbar_OnValueChanged);
    } // close for constructor

    private void hbar_OnValueChanged(object sender, EventArgs e)
    {
        pb.Location = new Point((pnl.Size.Width - img.Size.Width) *
                        hbar.Value/( hbar.Maximum - hbar.LargeChange + 1),
                        pb.Top);
    }

    private void vbar_OnValueChanged(object sender, EventArgs e)
    {
```

Example 13-7. ScrollBars using C# (ScrollBars.cs) (continued)

```csharp
        pb.Location = new Point(pb.Left,
                    (pnl.Size.Height - img.Size.Height) *
                    vbar.Value / (vbar.Maximum- vbar.LargeChange + 1));
    }

    static void Main( )
    {
        Application.Run(new ScrollBars( ));
    }
}       //  close for form class
}       //  close form namespace
```

Example 13-8. ScrollBars using VB.NET (ScrollBars.vb)

```vb
Option Strict On
imports System
imports System.Drawing
imports System.Windows.Forms

namespace ProgrammingWinApps
    public class ScrollBars : inherits Form

        dim pnl as Panel
        dim pb as PictureBox
        dim hbar as HScrollBar
        dim vbar as VScrollBar
        dim img as Image

        public sub New( )
            Text = "ScrollBars"
          Size = new Size(480,300)

            '  Get an image
            img = Image.FromFile( _
              "TabControlSizeMode.gif")

            pnl = new Panel( )
            pnl.Parent = me
            pnl.Size = new Size(400,200)
            pnl.Location = new Point(10,10)
            pnl.BorderStyle = BorderStyle.FixedSingle

            pb = new PictureBox( )
            pb.Parent = pnl
            pb.Size = new Size(img.Size.Width, img.Size.Height)
            pb.Location = new Point( _
              CType((pnl.Size.Width / 2) - (pb.Size.Width / 2), integer), _
              CType((pnl.Size.Height / 2) - (pb.Size.Height /2), integer))
            pb.SizeMode = PictureBoxSizeMode.CenterImage
            pb.Image = img

            '  Horizontal scrollbar
            hbar = new HScrollBar( )
```

Example 13-8. ScrollBars using VB.NET (ScrollBars.vb) (continued)

```
VB
         hbar.Parent = me
         hbar.Location = new Point(pnl.Left, pnl.Bottom + 25)
         hbar.Size = new Size(pnl.Width, 25)
         hbar.Minimum = 0
         hbar.Maximum = 100
         hbar.SmallChange = 1
         hbar.LargeChange = 10
         hbar.Value = CType((hbar.Maximum - hbar.Minimum) / 2, integer)
         AddHandler hbar.ValueChanged, AddressOf hbar_OnValueChanged

         ' Vertical scrollbar
         vbar = new VScrollBar( )
         vbar.Parent = me
         vbar.Location = new Point(pnl.Right + 25, pnl.Top)
         vbar.Size = new Size(25, pnl.Height)
         vbar.Minimum = 0
         vbar.Maximum = 100
         vbar.SmallChange = 1
         vbar.LargeChange = 10
         vbar.Value = CType((vbar.Maximum - vbar.Minimum) / 2, integer)
         AddHandler vbar.ValueChanged, AddressOf vbar_OnValueChanged
      end sub  '  close for constructor

   private sub hbar_OnValueChanged(ByVal sender as object, _
                       ByVal e as EventArgs)
      pb.Location = new Point( _
         CType((pnl.Size.Width - img.Size.Width) * _
         hbar.Value /(hbar.Maximum - hbar.LargeChange + 1), integer), _
         pb.Top)
   end sub

   private sub vbar_OnValueChanged(ByVal sender as object, _
                    ByVal e as EventArgs)
      pb.Location = new Point(pb.Left, _
         CType((pnl.Size.Height - img.Size.Height) * _
         vbar.Value / (vbar.Maximum - vbar.LargeChange + 1), integer))
   end sub

   public shared sub Main( )
      Application.Run(new ScrollBars( ))
   end sub
  end class
end namespace
```

The programs in Examples 13-7 and 13-8 start by declaring several controls as member variables so they will be available to the event handler methods as well as the constructor.

In the constructor, the image is instantiated with the static Image.FromFile method. The syntax used here assumes that the image file is located in the current directory, but you can also include a full path to the image file if that is not the case.

The panel control is instantiated, sized to 400 pixels wide by 200 pixels high, and located 10 pixels down and to the right of the upper-left corner of the form client area in the next several lines of code. The border style of the panel is set to FixedSingle.

Next, the picture box control is instantiated. Its Parent property is set to be the panel: the picture box is contained by the panel.

C#
```
pb.Parent = pnl;
```

The Size property of the picture box is set by using the size of the image.

C#
```
pb.Size = new Size(img.Size.Width, img.Size.Height);
```

The initial location of the picture box is set to be centered about the panel so you initially see the middle of the image:

C#
```
pb.Location = new Point((pnl.Size.Width / 2) - (pb.Size.Width / 2),
                        (pnl.Size.Height / 2) - (pb.Size.Height / 2));
```

VB
```
pb.Location = new Point( _
    CType((pnl.Size.Width / 2) - (pb.Size.Width / 2), integer), _
    CType((pnl.Size.Height / 2) - (pb.Size.Height /2), integer))
```

Using the actual numbers from this example, where the panel is 400 × 200 and the image is 990 × 380, the Location property would calculate to:

C#
```
pb.Location = = new Point(-295, -90);
```

This puts the upper-left corner of the image up and to the left of the upper-left corner of the panel (out of the visible client area of the panel).

The SizeMode property of the panel is set to CenterImage to clip the image on all four sides and avoid distorting the image size.

Finally, the Image property of the panel is set to the previously instantiated image object.

The two scrollbars are instantiated and specified similarly to each other. The Parent property of both is set to the form. The Location property of the horizontal scrollbar is aligned with the left edge of the panel and 25 pixels below the bottom of the panel.

C#
```
hbar.Location = new Point(pnl.Left, pnl.Bottom + 25);
```

The vertical scrollbar is located 25 pixels to the right of the panel and aligned with the top of the panel.

C#
```
vbar.Location = new Point(pnl.Right + 25, pnl.Top);
```

Both scrollbars are sized equal to the appropriate edge of the panel and 25 pixels thick.

C#
```
hbar.Size = new Size(pnl.Width, 25);
vbar.Size = new Size(25, pnl.Height);
```

The minimum values are set to zero, and the maximum values are set to 100. Remember that the value of the scrollbar is the position of the left edge of the thumb on a horizontal scrollbar or the top edge of the thumb in a vertical scrollbar. This will be accounted for in the event handlers, which process the new location of the thumbs.

The SmallChange and LargeChange properties are set to 1 and 10, respectively. The SmallChange property is the change in Value if the user clicks on the scroll arrow or presses an arrow key on the keyboard. The LargeChange property is the change in Value if the user clicks on the scrollbar in the space between the thumb and the scroll arrow or presses the Page Up or Page Down key on the keyboard.

Using the these values for the Minimum, Maximum, SmallChange, and LargeChange properties makes a small change equal to 1 percent of the image size and a large change equal to 10 percent of the image size, results dictated by the choice of values of these properties. If the scrollbar were controlling a text document, on the other hand, you might want to set the Maximum property of a vertical scrollbar to the number of lines contained by the document, the SmallChange property equal to the space taken up by one line, and the LargeChange to the space taken up by one full screen.

The size of the thumb is controlled by the ratio of the LargeChange property to the Maximum property. It indicates the proportion of the image that is visible at one time.

The initial Value of each scrollbar is set to the midpoint between the Maximum value and Minimum value.

Finally, for each scrollbar, an event handler method is added to the delegate for the ValueChanged event. All the action takes place in the event handler.

The two event handler methods, hbar_OnValueChanged and vbar_OnValueChanged, are symmetrically similar. The ValueChanged event is fired every time the Value of the scrollbar is changed, either by user action or programmatically. Although the EventArgs event argument carries no additional information (unlike the Scroll event), the current ScrollBar properties reflect the post-change state. This allows the Location of the panel box to be reset based on the current Value of the scrollbar. The horizontal scrollbar is done with this line of code:

C#

```
pb.Location = new Point((pnl.Size.Width - img.Size.Width) *
                        hbar.Value/(hbar.Maximum - hbar.LargeChange + 1),
                        pb.Top);
```

VB

```
pb.Location = new Point( _
    CType((pnl.Size.Width - img.Size.Width) * _
    hbar.Value /(hbar.Maximum - hbar.LargeChange + 1), integer), _
    pb.Top)
```

For the vertical scrollbar, it is:

C#

```
pb.Location = new Point(pb.Left,
                        (pnl.Size.Height - img.Size.Height) *
                        vbar.Value / (vbar.Maximum- vbar.LargeChange + 1));
```

```
pb.Location = new Point(pb.Left, _
    CType((pnl.Size.Height - img.Size.Height) * _
    vbar.Value / (vbar.Maximum - vbar.LargeChange + 1), integer))
```

Any number of algorithms use the Value of the scrollbar in conjunction with other properties to achieve the desired goal of an application. In a text handling application, for example, the goal would be to position the document based on the total number of lines of text, the number of lines visible at one time, and the font.

In this image handling example, the goal is to set the picture box's Location property. In the horizontal event handler, the vertical dimension of the Location property is unchanged, but the horizontal dimension is calculated. Conversely, for the vertical scrollbar, the horizontal dimension is unchanged while the vertical dimension is calculated.

The calculation treats the difference between the relevant properties (Width or Height) as an offset from zero in each dimension of the Point structure that is the Location. This offset is multiplied by a scaling factor that is the relative position of the thumb. The relative position is the current position, or Value, divided by the total numeric length of the scrollbar. Although the Maximum property is the true total length of the scrollbar, it is not the highest value achievable by a user. The highest achievable value of the scrollbar is the Maximum value minus the thickness of the thumb, which is the LargeChange property, plus one to compensate for zero-based indexing.

In other words, the offset is multiplied by the relative position of the thumb, 0 percent to 100 percent. That is why the Minimum and Maximum value of the scrollbars were set to 0 and 100, respectively.

So instead of a scaling factor of the form:

```
hbar.Value/ hbar.Maximum
```

you have a scaling factor of the form:

```
hbar.Value/( hbar.Maximum- hbar.LargeChange + 1)
```

As a Parameter Adjuster

Scrollbars can be used to adjust parameters as well as adjust position, as the following example will demonstrate. The program listed in Example 13-9 (in C#, the VB. NET version is nearly identical) is a modified version of the program presented in the previous section in Examples 13-7 and 13-8. Instead of adjusting the position of a picture box in a panel, this example stretches or shrinks an image either horizontally or vertically.

When the programs are compiled and run, they look like the screenshot shown in Figure 13-13.

Figure 13-13. Scrollbars to adjust parameters

In this example, the image file has an original size of 151 by 140 pixels. It is centered in a picture box that is centered in a panel. As each scrollbar thumb is moved by the user, the image is stretched or shrunk in that direction.

The lines of code in Example 13-9 that differ from the version presented in the previous section (Example 13-7 in C# and Example 13-8 in VB.NET) are highlighted. An analysis follows the code listing.

Example 13-9. ScrollBar as parameter adjuster in C# (ScrollBars-param.cs)

```
using System;
using System.Drawing;
using System.Windows.Forms;

namespace ProgrammingWinApps
{
    public class ScrollBars : Form
    {
        Panel pnl;
        PictureBox pb;
```

```csharp
HScrollBar hbar;
VScrollBar vbar;

public ScrollBars()
{
    Text = "ScrollBars - Parameter Adjust";
    Size = new Size(480,500);

    // Get an image to use
    Image img = Image.FromFile(
        "Dan at Vernal Pool.gif");

    pnl = new Panel();
    pnl.Parent = this;
    pnl.BorderStyle = BorderStyle.FixedSingle;
    pnl.Size = new Size(400,400);
    pnl.Location = new Point(10,10);

    pb = new PictureBox();
    pb.Parent = pnl;
    pb.Size = new Size(200, 200);
    pb.Location = new Point((pnl.Size.Width / 2) -
                        (pb.Size.Width / 2),
                    (pnl.Size.Height / 2) - (pb.Size.Height /2));
    pb.BorderStyle = BorderStyle.FixedSingle;
    pb.SizeMode = PictureBoxSizeMode.StretchImage;
    pb.Image = img;

    // Horizontal scrollbar
    hbar = new HScrollBar();
    hbar.Parent = this;
    hbar.Location = new Point(pnl.Left, pnl.Bottom + 25);
    hbar.Size = new Size(pnl.Width, 25);
    hbar.Minimum = 25;
    hbar.Maximum = 400;
    hbar.SmallChange = 10;
    hbar.LargeChange = 100;
    hbar.Value = pb.Width - hbar.LargeChange;
    hbar.ValueChanged += new EventHandler(hbar_OnValueChanged);

    // Vertical scrollbar
    vbar = new VScrollBar();
    vbar.Parent = this;
    vbar.Location = new Point(pnl.Right + 25, pnl.Top);
    vbar.Size = new Size(25, pnl.Height);
    vbar.Minimum = 25;
    vbar.Maximum = 400;
    vbar.SmallChange = 10;
    vbar.LargeChange = 100;
    vbar.Value = pb.Height - vbar.LargeChange;
    vbar.ValueChanged += new EventHandler(vbar_OnValueChanged);
} // close for constructor
```

```
        private void hbar_OnValueChanged(object sender, EventArgs e)
        {
            pb.Size = new Size(hbar.Value + hbar.LargeChange - 1, pb.Height);
            SetLocation( );
        }

        private void vbar_OnValueChanged(object sender, EventArgs e)
        {
            pb.Size = new Size(pb.Width, vbar.Value + vbar.LargeChange - 1);
            SetLocation( );
        }

        private void SetLocation( )
        {
            pb.Location = new Point((pnl.Size.Width / 2) -
                                (pb.Size.Width / 2),
                        (pnl.Size.Height / 2) - (pb.Size.Height /2));
        }

        static void Main( )
        {
            Application.Run(new ScrollBars( ));
        }
    }        //  close for form class
}            //  close form namespace
```

This example starts off like the previous example, except the image object is not declared as a class member, since it is not referenced outside the constructor. The image instantiated and assigned to the picture box is smaller than the previous example, 151 by 140 pixels, but more importantly, it is smaller than the panel that holds the picture box that contains the image.

To keep the image centered at all times and force the four sides to be clipped evenly, the SizeMode property of the picture box is set to PictureBoxSizeMode.StretchImage.

The Minimum, Maximum, SmallChange, LargeChange, and initial Value properties of the scrollbars are all different from the previous example. In this example, the Maximum is set to 400 to correspond to the size of the panel. The Minimum is set to 25, only because it seemed that going any smaller was pointless. The initial Value property must consider the width of the thumb.

Again, all the action takes place in the event handlers. The Size property of the picture box is set by changing the dimension corresponding to the scrollbar only; the other dimension remains unchanged. A helper method, SetLocation, is then called to set the Location property of the picture box, centering it in the panel, based on the new dimensions of the picture box.

TrackBar

The TrackBar control resembles the ScrollBar because it provides a slider, analogous to the thumb of the scrollbar, for the user to position with the mouse or keyboard. The relative position of the slider is exposed as the Value of the control. Unlike the ScrollBar, there are no separate horizontal and vertical versions of the TrackBar control. Instead, an Orientation property can have the value of either Horizontal or Vertical. You can also change the background color using the BackColor property, unlike the ScrollBar control, although you still can't change the ForeColor or BackgroundImage properties or set the Text property.

A horizontal track bar is similar to a horizontal scrollbar in that the Value property increases as the slider is moved from left to right. In contrast, the vertical track bar is opposite the vertical scrollbar: the Value of a vertical scrollbar increases from top to bottom, but the value of a vertical track bar increases from bottom to top. This makes sense if you think about the primary use of the two controls: a scrollbar is usually used for positioning, but a track bar is generally used for setting a value.

Many of the TrackBar control's commonly used properties are listed in Table 13-13.

Table 13-13. TrackBar properties

Property	Value type	Description
AutoSize	Boolean	Read/write. If true (the default), the thickness of the control is sized automatically—the thickness (height or width for horizontal or vertical controls, respectively) is not affected by the Size property.
BackColor	Color	Read/write. The background color of the control.
LargeChange	Integer	Read/write. The value to be added or subtracted from the Value property when the user presses the Page Up or Page Down key. Default value is 5.
Maximum	Integer	Read/write. Maximum possible value of the Value property. Default value is 10. The SetRange method can set the Maximum and Minimum properties at the same time.
Minimum	Integer	Read/write. Minimum possible value of the Value property. Default value is zero. The SetRange method can set the Maximum and Minimum properties at the same time.
Orientation	Orientation	Read/write. Indicates the orientation of the control. Possible values are one of the two members of the Orientation enumeration: Horizontal or Vertical. Default is Orientation.Horizontal.
SmallChange	Integer	Read/write. The value to be added or subtracted from the Value property when the user presses one of the arrow keys. Default value is 1.
TickFrequency	Integer	Read/write. The delta between tick marks. Default is 1.
TickStyle	TickStyle	Read/write. Deer tick, Lone Star tick, or Dog tick. Oops, sorry, wrong book. Indicates the type of tick marks on a track bar. Valid values are members of the TickStyle enumeration, listed in Table 13-14. Default is TickStyle.BottomRight.

Table 13-13. TrackBar properties (continued)

Property	Value type	Description
Value	Integer	Read/write. Numeric value representing the current position of the slider in the track bar.
		The smallest value of Value is the Minimum property. The largest value of Value is the Maximum property.
		Default value is zero.

 The SDK documentation states that the slider will move a distance equal to the LargeChange property if the user clicks on the track bar on either side of the slider, analogous to the behavior of a scrollbar. However, this is not the case. If you click on the track bar, the slider will move to the multiple of LargeChange closest to where the mouse was clicked.

Table 13-14. TickStyle enumeration values

Value	Description
Both	Tick marks on both sides of the control.
BottomRight	Tick marks on the bottom of horizontal track bars or on the right side of vertical track bars.
None	No tick marks.
TopLeft	Tick marks on the top of horizontal track bars or on the left side of vertical track bars.

Although the TrackBar has the same named events as the ScrollBar control, listed in Table 13-15, they are somewhat different. Both TrackBar events take an event argument of type EventArgs. They occur together—first the Scroll event and then the ValueChanged event—unless the change is made programmatically, in which case only the ValueChanged event is raised.

Table 13-15. TrackBar events

Event	Event data	Description
ValueChanged	EventArgs	Raised when the Value property has changed, either by a Scroll event or programmatically.
Scroll	EventArgs	Raised when the slider has been moved, either by the mouse or the keyboard.

The program listed in Example 13-10 demonstrates track bar controls. This example is similar to the examples presented for the scrollbar control. The lines of code that differ are highlighted. (Only the C# version is presented here. The VB.NET version is identical to that listed in Example 13-8, except for the lines highlighted here, which are the same in both languages except for minor syntax differences.) An analysis follows the code listing.

Example 13-10. TrackBar in C# (TrackBars.cs)

```csharp
using System;
using System.Drawing;
using System.Windows.Forms;

namespace ProgrammingWinApps
{
    public class TrackBars : Form
    {
        Panel pnl;
        PictureBox pb;
        TrackBar htbar;
        TrackBar vtbar;

        public TrackBars()
        {
            Text = "TrackBars";
            Size = new Size(500,520);

            //  Get an image to use
            Image img = Image.FromFile(
                "Dan at Vernal Pool.gif");

            pnl = new Panel();
            pnl.Parent = this;
            pnl.BorderStyle = BorderStyle.FixedSingle;
            pnl.Size = new Size(400,400);
            pnl.Location = new Point(10,10);

            pb = new PictureBox();
            pb.Parent = pnl;
            pb.Size = new Size(200, 200);
            pb.Location = new Point((pnl.Size.Width / 2) -
                                    (pb.Size.Width / 2),
                            (pnl.Size.Height / 2) - (pb.Size.Height /2));
            pb.BorderStyle = BorderStyle.FixedSingle;
            pb.SizeMode = PictureBoxSizeMode.StretchImage;
            pb.Image = img;

            // Horizontal trackbar
            htbar = new TrackBar();
            htbar.Parent = this;
            htbar.Orientation = Orientation.Horizontal;
            htbar.Size = new Size(pnl.Width, 10);  //thickness doesn't matter
            htbar.Location = new Point(pnl.Left, pnl.Bottom + 25);
            htbar.TickStyle = TickStyle.BottomRight;
            htbar.TickFrequency = 25;
            htbar.Minimum = 25;
            htbar.Maximum = 400;
            htbar.SmallChange = 10;
            htbar.LargeChange = 25;
            htbar.BackColor = Color.Yellow;
```

Example 13-10. TrackBar in C# (TrackBars.cs) (continued)

```
htbar.Value = pb.Width;
htbar.ValueChanged += new EventHandler(htbar_OnValueChanged);

// Vertical scrollbar
vtbar = new TrackBar( );
vtbar.Parent = this;
vtbar.Orientation = Orientation.Vertical;
vtbar.Size = new Size(25,pnl.Height);  //thickness doesn't matter
vtbar.Location = new Point(pnl.Right + 25, pnl.Top);
vtbar.TickStyle = TickStyle.Both;
vtbar.SetRange(25,400);
vtbar.SmallChange = 10;
vtbar.LargeChange = 50;
vtbar.TickFrequency = vtbar.Maximum / 20;
vtbar.BackColor = Color.Pink;
vtbar.Value = pb.Height;
vtbar.ValueChanged += new EventHandler(vtbar_OnValueChanged);
} // close for constructor

private void htbar_OnValueChanged(object sender, EventArgs e)
{
    pb.Size = new Size(htbar.Value, pb.Height);
    SetLocation( );
}

private void vtbar_OnValueChanged(object sender, EventArgs e)
{
    pb.Size = new Size(pb.Width, vtbar.Value);
    SetLocation( );
}

private void SetLocation( )
{
    pb.Location = new Point((pnl.Size.Width / 2) -
                        (pb.Size.Width / 2),
                    (pnl.Size.Height / 2) - (pb.Size.Height /2));
}

static void Main( )
{
    Application.Run(new TrackBars( ));
}
} // close for form class
} // close form namespace
```

When this program is compiled and run, it looks like the screenshot in Figure 13-14. Although not visible in this monochrome book, the background color of the horizontal track bar is yellow, and pink for the vertical track bar. Notice the dotted line around the horizontal track bar, indicating that it has focus. Unlike scrollbars, track bars participate in the tab order and can receive focus.

Figure 13-14. Track bars

The first difference between the track bar example and the scrollbar examples is the declaration of the member variables for the controls: here you declare two TrackBar objects which will subsequently have an Orientation property applied to make them horizontal or vertical, rather than an HScroll object and a VScroll object.

Other than minor text and size differences, the next change relative to the scrollbar examples occurs when the track bar controls are instantiated in the constructor. Rather than separate horizontal and vertical versions of the control, both are instances of the TrackBar class, with the Orientation property set to Orientation. Horizontal or Orientation.Vertical, as appropriate.

The Size and Location properties are set as they were for the scrollbar examples. Note, however, that the thickness argument of the Size property (height of the horizontal control and width of the vertical control) has no effect, since the default Auto-Size value of true is in effect.

The next two lines for each control set the tick mark style and frequency. The horizontal control has the TickStyle property set to TickStyle.BottomRight, while the vertical control has it set to TickStyle.Both. The results are visible in Figure 13-14.

The TickFrequency property specifies how far apart the tick marks are. For the horizontal control, it is hardcoded to 25, while the vertical control has it set to a function of the Maximum property for the control. In the latter case, the TickFrequency is not set until after the line calling the SetRange method, which effectively sets the Maximum property for that control. If the TickFrequency line (which uses the Maximum property) comes before the Maximum property is set, the default value of Maximum, 10, is used. This does not have the desired effect.

The Minimum, Maximum, SmallChange, and LargeChange properties are set for the horizontal control just as they were for the scrollbars. For the vertical control, however, the SetRange method is used, and you do not set the Minimum and Maximum properties in two separate statements. The result is the same.

The initial Value properties are set to match the size of the image. Unlike the scrollbar example, there is no need to consider the size of the LargeChange property.

The BackColor properties are set for both controls—a feature that is not available to scrollbars.

The event handlers for the track bars are nearly the same as for the scrollbars, except that there is no need to deal with the thickness of the thumb as part of the calculation, greatly simplifying matters.

Up-Down Controls

Up-down controls consist of an edit box with an associated set of up and down arrows. The user can cycle through a range of values in the edit box by clicking on the arrows, or, if the ReadOnly property is not set to true, you can enter values in the edit box directly.

 Up-down controls used to be known in other languages as spin controls or spinners.

Most up-down control functionality comes from the UpDownBase class. This is an abstract/MustInherit class; it is not instantiated directly. The .NET Framework provides two classes derived from UpDownBase: NumericUpDown and DomainUpDown. The NumericUpDown control displays numeric values in the edit box, and the DomainUpDown control displays string values representing members of a collection of objects.

In addition to the properties inherited from Control and other base classes, such as ScrollableControl, UpDownBase has other properties, the most commonly used of which are listed in Table 13-16.

Table 13-16. UpDownBase properties

Property	Value type	Description
BorderStyle	BorderStyle	Read/write. Valid values are members of the BorderStyle enumeration, listed in Table 13-9.
InterceptArrowKeys	Boolean	Read/write. If true (the default), user can use up and down arrow keys to select values when the control has focus.
PreferredHeight	Integer	Read-only. Height of control in pixels, based on PreferredHeight property of the text box portion of the control, adjusted for border style.
ReadOnly	Boolean	Read/write. If false (the default), text in control can be edited by the user. If true, text can be changed using the up and down arrows only.
Text	String	Read/write. Text displayed in the control.
TextAlign	HorizontalAlignment	Read/write. Valid values are members of the HorizontalAlignment enumeration, listed in Table 13-17. Default is HorizontalAlignment.Left.
UpDownAlign	LeftRightAlignment	Read/write. The side of the edit box on which the up and down arrows are placed. Valid values are either LeftRightAlignment.Left or LeftRightAlignment.Right (the default).

Table 13-17. HorizontalAlignment enumeration values

Value	Description
Center	Aligned in the center of the control.
Left	Aligned to the left of the control.
Right	Aligned to the right of the control.

NumericUpDown

The NumericUpDown class displays a numeric value in the edit box. This number is incremented or decremented by the value of the Increment property every time the user clicks on one of the arrows or presses an arrow key on the keyboard (if the InterceptArrowKeys property is set to its default value of true).

If the user can enter values directly into the edit box, such as when the control is not set for ReadOnly, then validation automatically occurs when a new value is entered. The new value entered must be a number between the Minimum value and the Maximum value. If the entered value is outside the range of valid numbers, it will automatically be changed to either the Maximum or the Minimum value, depending on which property is exceeded.

Although this automatic validation saves you from writing your own validation code, it may lead to data-entry errors. Out of bounds values will be changed to another, still erroneous, value, and the user could easily miss this.

A ValueChanged event is raised every time the Value property of the numeric up-down is changed, either by user interaction or programmatically. This event, with its event argument of type EventArgs (which has no additional properties), can be trapped and handled, as will be demonstrated shortly.

The commonly used properties of the NumericUpDown control that are not derived from UpDownBase are listed in Table 13-18.

Table 13-18. NumericUpDown properties

Property	Value type	Description
DecimalPlaces	Integer	Read/write. Number of decimal places displayed. Default is zero.
Hexadecimal	Boolean	Read/write. If true, displays value in hexadecimal format. Default is false.
Increment	Decimal	Read/write. Value to increment or decrement the Value property when an arrow is clicked or an arrow key is pressed. Default is 1.
Maximum	Decimal	Read/write. The maximum value of the Value property. Default is 100. Use Decimal. MaxValue (equal to 2^{96} or approximately 7.9×10^{28}) to effectively remove the upper bound.
Minimum	Decimal	Read/write. The minimum value of the Value property. Default is zero. Use Decimal. MinValue (equal to -2^{96} or approximately -7.9×10^{28}) to effectively remove the lower bound.
ThousandsSeparator	Boolean	Read/write. If true, a thousands separator is displayed in the edit box, when appropriate. The separator to be used is determined by system settings. The default value is false.
Value	Decimal	Read/write. The numeric value displayed by the control.

The programs listed in Example 13-11 (in C#) and in Example 13-12 (in VB.NET) demonstrate the use of a numeric up-down to complement the scrollbars used in Example 13-9 for scaling an image. In this example, which is nearly identical to the previous scrollbar and track bar examples, a numeric up-down control is added to the form, which scales the image uniformly in both directions.

When the code in either example is compiled and run, it looks like the screenshot shown in Figure 13-15.

The lines of code that differ from the previous examples are highlighted. An analysis of the code follows the listings.

Figure 13-15. NumericUpDown control

Example 13-11. NumericUpDown control in C# (NumericUpDowns.cs)

```csharp
using System;
using System.Drawing;
using System.Windows.Forms;

namespace ProgrammingWinApps
{
   public class NumericUpDowns : Form
   {
      Panel pnl;
      PictureBox pb;
      HScrollBar hbar;
      VScrollBar vbar;
      NumericUpDown nupdwn;
      Image img;
```

Example 13-11. NumericUpDown control in C# (NumericUpDowns.cs) (continued)

```
public NumericUpDowns( )
{
    Text = "ScrollBars - NumericUpDowns";
    Size = new Size(480,580);

    //  Get an image to use
    img = Image.FromFile(
        "Dan at Vernal Pool.gif");

    pnl = new Panel( );
    pnl.Parent = this;
    pnl.BorderStyle = BorderStyle.FixedSingle;
    pnl.Size = new Size(400,400);
    pnl.Location = new Point(10,10);

    pb = new PictureBox( );
    pb.Parent = pnl;
    pb.Size = new Size(200, 200);
    pb.Location = new Point((pnl.Size.Width / 2) -
                                (pb.Size.Width / 2),
                        (pnl.Size.Height / 2) - (pb.Size.Height /2));
    pb.BorderStyle = BorderStyle.FixedSingle;
    pb.SizeMode = PictureBoxSizeMode.StretchImage;
    pb.Image = img;

    //  Horizontal scrollbar
    hbar = new HScrollBar( );
    hbar.Parent = this;
    hbar.Location = new Point(pnl.Left, pnl.Bottom + 25);
    hbar.Size = new Size(pnl.Width, 25);
    hbar.Minimum = 25;
    hbar.Maximum = 400;
    hbar.SmallChange = 10;
    hbar.LargeChange = 100;
    hbar.Value = pb.Width;
    hbar.ValueChanged += new EventHandler(hbar_OnValueChanged);

    //  Vertical scrollbar
    vbar = new VScrollBar( );
    vbar.Parent = this;
    vbar.Location = new Point(pnl.Right + 25, pnl.Top);
    vbar.Size = new Size(25, pnl.Height);
    vbar.Minimum = 25;
    vbar.Maximum = 400;
    vbar.SmallChange = 10;
    vbar.LargeChange = 100;
    vbar.Value = pb.Height;
    vbar.ValueChanged += new EventHandler(vbar_OnValueChanged);

    //  NumericUpDown & Label
    Label lbl = new Label( );
    lbl.Parent = this;
```

Example 13-11. NumericUpDown control in C# (NumericUpDowns.cs) (continued)

```csharp
        lbl.Text = "Scale Factor:";
        lbl.Location = new Point(
            (((pnl.Right - pnl.Left) / 2) - 75),hbar.Bottom + 25) ;
        lbl.AutoSize = true;

        nupdwn = new NumericUpDown( );
        nupdwn.Parent = this;
        nupdwn.Location = new Point(
            (pnl.Right - pnl.Left) / 2, hbar.Bottom + 25);
        nupdwn.Size = new Size(60,20);
        nupdwn.Value = 1;
        nupdwn.Minimum = -10;
        nupdwn.Maximum = 10;
        nupdwn.Increment = .25m;       //  decimal
        nupdwn.DecimalPlaces = 2;
        nupdwn.ReadOnly = true;
        nupdwn.TextAlign = HorizontalAlignment.Right;
        nupdwn.ValueChanged += new EventHandler(nupdwn_OnValueChanged);
    } // close for constructor

    private void hbar_OnValueChanged(object sender, EventArgs e)
    {
        pb.Size = new Size(hbar.Value + hbar.LargeChange - 1, pb.Height);
        SetLocation( );
    }

    private void vbar_OnValueChanged(object sender, EventArgs e)
    {
        pb.Size = new Size(pb.Width, vbar.Value + vbar.LargeChange - 1);
        SetLocation( );
    }

    private void SetLocation( )
    {
        pb.Location = new Point(
            (pnl.Size.Width / 2) - (pb.Size.Width / 2),
            (pnl.Size.Height / 2) - (pb.Size.Height /2));
    }

    private void nupdwn_OnValueChanged(object sender, EventArgs e)
    {
        hbar.Value = Math.Max(hbar.Minimum,
            img.Width + (int)(( nupdwn.Value / 10) *
                ((hbar.Maximum - hbar.Minimum) / 2) ));
        vbar.Value = Math.Max(vbar.Minimum,
            img.Height + (int)(( nupdwn.Value / 10) *
                ((vbar.Maximum - vbar.Minimum) / 2) ));
    }

    static void Main( )
    {
        Application.Run(new NumericUpDowns( ));
```

Example 13-11. NumericUpDown control in C# (NumericUpDowns.cs) (continued)

```
      }
   }      // close for form class
}         // close form namespace
```

Example 13-12. NumericUpDown control in VB.NET (NumericUpDowns.vb)

```
Option Strict On
imports System
imports System.Drawing
imports System.Windows.Forms

namespace ProgrammingWinApps
   public class NumericUpDowns : inherits Form

      dim pnl as Panel
      dim pb as PictureBox
      dim hbar as HScrollBar
      dim vbar as VScrollBar
      dim nupdwn as NumericUpDown
      dim img as Image

      public sub New( )
         Text = "ScrollBars - NumericUpDowns"
         Size = new Size(480,580)

         ' Get an image
         img = Image.FromFile( _
            "Dan at Vernal Pool.gif")

         pnl = new Panel( )
         pnl.Parent = me
         pnl.BorderStyle = BorderStyle.FixedSingle
         pnl.Size = new Size(400,400)
         pnl.Location = new Point(10,10)

         pb = new PictureBox( )
         pb.Parent = pnl
         pb.Size = new Size(200, 200)
         pb.Location = new Point( _
            CType((pnl.Size.Width / 2) - (pb.Size.Width / 2),integer), _
            CType((pnl.Size.Height / 2) - (pb.Size.Height /2),integer))
         pb.BorderStyle = BorderStyle.FixedSingle
         pb.SizeMode = PictureBoxSizeMode.StretchImage
         pb.Image = img

         ' Horizontal scrollbar
         hbar = new HScrollBar( )
         hbar.Parent = me
         hbar.Location = new Point(pnl.Left, pnl.Bottom + 25)
         hbar.Size = new Size(pnl.Width, 25)
         hbar.Minimum = 25
         hbar.Maximum = 400
         hbar.SmallChange = 10
```

```vb
        hbar.LargeChange = 100
        hbar.Value = pb.Width
        AddHandler hbar.ValueChanged, AddressOf hbar_OnValueChanged

        ' Vertical scrollbar
        vbar = new VScrollBar( )
        vbar.Parent = me
        vbar.Location = new Point(pnl.Right + 25, pnl.Top)
        vbar.Size = new Size(25, pnl.Height)
        vbar.Minimum = 25
        vbar.Maximum = 400
        vbar.SmallChange = 10
        vbar.LargeChange = 100
        vbar.Value = pb.Height
        AddHandler vbar.ValueChanged, AddressOf vbar_OnValueChanged

        ' NumericUpDown & Label
        dim lbl as new Label( )
        lbl.Parent = me
        lbl.Text = "Scale Factor:"
        lbl.Location = new Point( _
            CType((pnl.Right - pnl.Left) / 2, integer) - 75, _
            hbar.Bottom + 25)
        lbl.AutoSize = true

        nupdwn = new NumericUpDown( )
        nupdwn.Parent = me
        nupdwn.Location = new Point( _
            CType((pnl.Right - pnl.Left) / 2, integer), _
            hbar.Bottom + 25)
        nupdwn.Size = new Size(60,20)
        nupdwn.Value = 1
        nupdwn.Minimum = -10
        nupdwn.Maximum = 10
        nupdwn.Increment = .25d        ' decimal
        nupdwn.DecimalPlaces = 2
        nupdwn.ReadOnly = true
        nupdwn.TextAlign = HorizontalAlignment.Right
        AddHandler nupdwn.ValueChanged, AddressOf nupdwn_OnValueChanged
    end sub  ' close for constructor

    private sub hbar_OnValueChanged(ByVal sender as object, _
                    ByVal e as EventArgs)
        pb.Size = new Size(hbar.Value + hbar.LargeChange - 1, pb.Height)
        SetLocation( )
    end sub

    private sub vbar_OnValueChanged(ByVal sender as object, _
                    ByVal e as EventArgs)
        pb.Size = new Size(pb.Width, vbar.Value + vbar.LargeChange - 1)
        SetLocation( )
    end sub
```

```
private sub SetLocation( )
    pb.Location = new Point( _
        CType((pnl.Size.Width / 2) - (pb.Size.Width / 2), integer), _
        CType((pnl.Size.Height / 2) - (pb.Size.Height /2), integer))
end sub

private sub nupdwn_OnValueChanged(ByVal sender as object, _
                                  ByVal e as EventArgs)
    hbar.Value = Math.Max(hbar.Minimum, _
        img.Width + CType((nupdwn.Value / 10) * _
            ((hbar.Maximum - hbar.Minimum) / 2), integer))
    vbar.Value = Math.Max(vbar.Minimum, _
        img.Height + CType((nupdwn.Value / 10) * _
            ((vbar.Maximum - vbar.Minimum) / 2), integer))
end sub

public shared sub Main( )
    Application.Run(new NumericUpDowns( ))
end sub
    end class
end namespace
```

The programs listed in Examples 13-11 and 13-12 start off by declaring several controls as member variables. For these examples, the NumericUpDown and the Image variables are declared as member variables rather than in the constructor, because they are referenced throughout the code.

Inside the constructor, the form size is increased in the vertical direction and the Image object is instantiated from the file that was used before. The panel, picture box, and scrollbars are identical to those in Figure 13-13.

Two new controls are added to the constructor: a NumericUpDown, and an associated Label that acts as a caption. The Location property of both controls are calculated to center them below the horizontal scrollbar.

Several properties of the up-down control are set, including the initial Value, the Minimum and Maximum values, the Increment, and the DecimalPlaces. Notice the type character appended to the Increment property value, which is of type Decimal number. It is:

```
nupdwn.Increment = .25d;
```

```
nupdwn.Increment = .25m
```

The ReadOnly property of the up-down control is set to true so the user cannot enter or modify the value other than through arrows or an arrow key. In the screenshot in Figure 13-15, you can see that this makes the edit box portion of the control appear with a gray background. If the field were editable (if ReadOnly were set to false), then the edit box would be the default background color (typically white, unless the BackColor property were set otherwise).

The TextAlign property is set to a value of HorizontalAlignment.Right to align the text to the right edge of the edit box.

The last line of code in the constructor assigns an event handler method to the event delegate for the ValueChanged event. This event handler, nupdwn_OnValueChanged, is called every time the Value property of the control is changed.

The event handler method achieves the desired effect by setting the Value properties of the scrollbars. Since the picture box control has its SizeMode property set to PictureBoxSizeMode.StretchImage, the original display of the image stretches the 151 × 140 pixel image to 200 × 200, which is slightly distorted because it appears longer than it should. As soon as the up-down control value is changed, the scrollbars are set so that the image is correctly proportioned again.

DomainUpDown

The DomainUpDown control displays a collection of strings, which can represent objects. Items can be added or removed from the collection by using the Add or Remove methods, respectively. If the ReadOnly property is set to false (the default), then a string typed in the edit box must match the string representation of an item already in the collection in order to be accepted.

Like the NumericUpDown control, an event, SelectedItemChanged, is raised when a different item is selected. If the control's Items collection contains objects, then the SelectedItem property can be used as a reference to the selected object in the event handler method. If the Items collection contains strings, then the SelectedItem property will contain the selected string.

The commonly used properties of the DomainUpDown control that are not derived from UpDownBase are listed in Table 13-19.

Table 13-19. DomainUpDown properties

Property	Value type	Description
Items	DomainUpDown-ItemCollection	Read-only. Collection of objects assigned to the control. Items can be added by using the Add or Insert methods.
SelectedIndex	Integer	Read/write. Zero-based index of selected item. If the user has entered a value or if no item is selected, the value is −1. Default value is −1.
SelectedItem	Object	Read/write. Currently selected item.
Sorted	Boolean	Read/write. If false (the default), the item collection is not sorted. If true, the collection is sorted alphabetically.
Wrap	Boolean	Read/write. If true, the list appears to continuously loop from the bottom to the top, and vice versa. The default is false.

The code listings in Example 13-13 (in C#) and in Example 13-14 (in VB.NET) are an extension of the previous example, adding a domain up-down control to change the border style of the panel. They show only the additional code required in Examples 13-11 and 13-12 to add a DomainUpDown control. The additional control has its Items collection populated with the members of the BorderStyle enumeration (not with strings representing the members of the enumeration). Whenever the up-down control is changed, the SelectedItemChanged event is handled, which applies the currently displayed style to the panel control.

When these programs are compiled and run, they produce the form shown in Figure 13-16. An analysis follows the code listings.

Figure 13-16. DomainUpDown control

*Example 13-13. DomainUpDown code delta from Example 13-11 in C#
(DomainUpDowns.cs)*

```csharp
DomainUpDown dupdwn;

public DomainUpDowns( )
{

    //  DomainUpDown & Label
    lbl = new Label( );
    lbl.Parent = this;
    lbl.Text = "BorderStyle:";
    lbl.Location = new Point(
        (((pnl.Right - pnl.Left) / 2) - 75),hbar.Bottom + 50) ;
    lbl.AutoSize = true;

    dupdwn = new DomainUpDown( );
    dupdwn.Parent = this;
    dupdwn.Location = new Point(
        (pnl.Right - pnl.Left) / 2, hbar.Bottom + 50);
    dupdwn.Size = new Size(150,dupdwn.PreferredHeight);
    dupdwn.ReadOnly = true;
    dupdwn.TextAlign = HorizontalAlignment.Center;
    dupdwn.UpDownAlign = LeftRightAlignment.Left;
    dupdwn.Wrap = true;
    dupdwn.SelectedItemChanged +=
        new EventHandler(dupdwn_OnSelectedItemChanged);
    //  Create the collection of items
    dupdwn.Items.Add(BorderStyle.Fixed3D);
    dupdwn.Items.Add(BorderStyle.FixedSingle);
    dupdwn.Items.Add(BorderStyle.None);
    dupdwn.SelectedIndex = 0;        //  zero-based index
} //  close for constructor

private void dupdwn_OnSelectedItemChanged(object sender, EventArgs e)
{
    pnl.BorderStyle = (BorderStyle)dupdwn.SelectedItem;
}
```

*Example 13-14. DomainUpDown code delta from Example 13-12 in VB.NET
(DomainUpDowns.vb)*

```vb
dim dupdwn as DomainUpDown

public sub New( )
    Text = "ScrollBars - DomainUpDowns"

    '  DomainUpDown & Label
    lbl = new Label( )
    lbl.Parent = me
```

```vb
    lbl.Text = "BorderStyle:"
    lbl.Location = new Point( _
        (((pnl.Right - pnl.Left) / 2) - 75),hbar.Bottom + 50)
    lbl.AutoSize = true

    dupdwn = new DomainUpDown( )
    dupdwn.Parent = me
    dupdwn.Location = new Point( _
        CType(((pnl.Right - pnl.Left) / 2), integer), _
        hbar.Bottom + 50)
    dupdwn.Size = new Size(150,dupdwn.PreferredHeight)
    dupdwn.ReadOnly = true
    dupdwn.TextAlign = HorizontalAlignment.Center
    dupdwn.UpDownAlign = LeftRightAlignment.Left
    dupdwn.Wrap = true
    AddHandler dupdwn.SelectedItemChanged, _
        AddressOf dupdwn_OnSelectedItemChanged
    ' Create the collection of items
    dupdwn.Items.Add(BorderStyle.Fixed3D)
    dupdwn.Items.Add(BorderStyle.FixedSingle)
    dupdwn.Items.Add(BorderStyle.None)
    dupdwn.SelectedIndex = 0        '  zero-based index
end sub  '  close for constructor

private sub dupdwn_OnSelectedItemChanged(ByVal sender as object, _
                        ByVal e as EventArgs)
    pnl.BorderStyle = CType(dupdwn.SelectedItem, BorderStyle)
end sub
```

The programs excerpted in Examples 13-13 and 13-14 are built up from the Numeric-UpDown examples in Examples 13-11 and 13-12. They add a member variable for the DomainUpDown control inside the class declaration, but outside the constructor.

Inside the constructor, two controls are added: the domain up-down control is instantiated, and an accompanying label is declared and instantiated to identify the up-down to the user. The domain up-down resembles the numeric up-down used in the previous example, with some changes.

The size property of the domain up-down uses the PreferredHeight property to set the vertical size of the control, rather than hardcoding in a pixel height.

```csharp
    dupdwn.Size = new Size(150,dupdwn.PreferredHeight);
```

Again the ReadOnly property is set to true, so the user can change the value only by using the up-down arrows or keyboard arrow keys. This also grays the edit box.

If the ReadOnly property were set to false in these examples, with no other changes made to the code, it would work fine if you used the up-down arrows to change the selected item, but it would crash as soon as you changed the value in the edit box directly. This is because the SelectedIndex property becomes -1 if the user edits the edit box. When the SelectedIndex property is -1, then the Selected-Item property has a null value. However, in the dupdwn_OnSelected-ItemChanged method, the SelectedItem property is referenced. When the program tries to reference the null value, it throws an exception.

You can work around this problem by modifying the dupdwn_OnSelectedItemChanged method as follows:

```
if (dud.SelectedIndex != -1)
{
    pnl.BorderStyle = (BorderStyle)dud.SelectedItem;
}
```

However, doing so will ignore any changes made directly in the edit box, even if it results in a valid value. Use the ValidateEditText and UpdateEditText methods to validate and process the text entered by the user.

The TextAlign property is set to HorizontalAlignment.Center to align the displayed text in the center of the edit box, and the UpDownAlign property is set to LeftRight-Alignment.Left to put the up-down arrows to the left of the edit box rather than the default position on the right. The Wrap property is set to true so that the items in the collection will loop endlessly.

An event handler is added to the SelectedItemChanged event delegate so that the dupdwn_OnSelectedItemChanged method will be called every time the selection is changed. The dupdwn_OnSelectedItemChanged method itself is very simple, consisting of a single line of code. It casts the SelectedItem property back to an object of type BorderStyle and assigns that property to the BorderStyle property of the panel.

In the constructor, the final section of code adds three objects, of type BorderStyle, to the collection of Items that comprise the Items property of the domain up-down. It also sets the SelectedIndex property to 0, which causes the first item in the collection to be displayed. If you failed to set the SelectedIndex property, the control would display initially with nothing visible in the edit box and nothing selected, i.e., the SelectedIndex property would be –1.

Although objects are added to the collection, the control displays string representations of the objects. When the SelectedItem property is retrieved in the dupdwn_OnSelectedItemChanged method, these objects must be cast back to BorderStyle objects because it is a narrowing conversion. However, it is a safe cast because you know that the BorderStyle objects were put into the collection to begin with.

ProgressBar

A ProgressBar control visually indicates the progress of a time-consuming operation, especially one that does not provide any other indication that the machine is still processing. It might be used for file copy operations, attempts to make a network or internet connection, or a lengthy computation.

The ProgressBar class has just four commonly used properties that are not inherited from Control or some other base class, listed in Table 13-20.

Table 13-20. ProgressBar properties

Property	Value type	Description
Maximum	Integer	Read/write. The maximum value of the range displayed by the control. Default value is 100.
Minimum	Integer	Read/write. The minimum value of the range displayed by the control. Default value is 0.
Step	Integer	Read/write. The amount by which the progress bar is incremented when the PerformStep method is called. Default value is 10.
Value	Integer	Read/write. The current position of the progress bar. Default value is zero.

In addition to the properties listed in Table 13-20, two methods are commonly invoked. The Increment method takes an integer as an argument, incrementing the progress by that amount. The PerformStep method takes no arguments, but increments the progress bar by the amount specified by the Step property.

The programs listed in Example 13-15 (in C#) and Example 13-16 (in VB.NET) demonstrate a progress bar. In these examples, a button click triggers a counter to count up to 10,000. For every 100 counts, a label displays the current value of the counter and the progress bar is updated. The running program looks much like Figure 13-17.

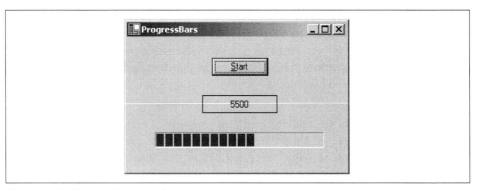

Figure 13-17. ProgressBar control

Example 13-15. ProgressBar in C# (ProgressBar.cs)

```
using System;
using System.Drawing;
using System.Windows.Forms;

namespace ProgrammingWinApps
{
    public class ProgressBars : Form
    {
        ProgressBar pb;
        Label lbl;

        public ProgressBars()
        {
            Text = "ProgressBars";
            Size = new Size(300,200);

            Button btn = new Button();
            btn.Parent = this;
            btn.Text = "&Start";
            btn.Location = new Point((Size.Width / 2) - (btn.Width / 2),
                            (Size.Height / 4) - btn.Height);
            btn.Click += new EventHandler(btn_OnClick);

            lbl = new Label();
            lbl.Parent = this;
            lbl.Size = new Size(100,23);
            lbl.Location = new Point((Size.Width / 2) - (lbl.Width / 2),
                            btn.Bottom + 25);
            lbl.BorderStyle = BorderStyle.FixedSingle;
            lbl.TextAlign = ContentAlignment.MiddleCenter;
            lbl.Text = "";

            pb = new ProgressBar();
            pb.Parent = this;
            pb.Location = new Point((Size.Width / 8), lbl.Bottom + 25);
            pb.Size = new Size((int)(Size.Width * 3 / 4), 20);
            pb.Minimum = 0;        //  the default value
            pb.Maximum = 100;      //  the default value
        } //  close for constructor

        private void btn_OnClick(object sender, EventArgs e)
        {
            int limit = 10000;
            int cntr = 0;
            pb.Value = 0;
            pb.Step = 1;
            for (int i = 0; i < limit; i++)
            {
                cntr ++;
                if (cntr % 100 == 0)
                {
                    lbl.Text = cntr.ToString();
```

Example 13-15. ProgressBar in C# (ProgressBar.cs) (continued)

```
C#
              pb.PerformStep( );
              Application.DoEvents( );
              System.Threading.Thread.Sleep(20);
          }
        }
      }

      static void Main( )
      {
        Application.Run(new ProgressBars( ));
      }
    }      //  close for form class
}          //  close form namespace
```

Example 13-16. ProgressBar in VB.NET (ProgressBar.vb)

```
VB
Option Strict On
imports System
imports System.Drawing
imports System.Windows.Forms

namespace ProgrammingWinApps
    public class ProgressBars : inherits Form

        dim pb as ProgressBar
        dim lbl as Label

        public sub New( )
            Text = "ProgressBars"
            Size = new Size(300,200)

            dim btn as new Button( )
            btn.Parent = me
            btn.Text = "&Start"
            btn.Location = new Point( _
                      CType((Size.Width / 2) - (btn.Width / 2), integer), _
                      CType((Size.Height / 4) - btn.Height, integer))
            AddHandler btn.Click, AddressOf btn_OnClick

            lbl = new Label( )
            lbl.Parent = me
            lbl.Size = new Size(100,23)
            lbl.Location = new Point( _
                      CType((Size.Width / 2) - (lbl.Width / 2), integer), _
                      btn.Bottom + 25)
            lbl.BorderStyle = BorderStyle.FixedSingle
            lbl.TextAlign = ContentAlignment.MiddleCenter
            lbl.Text = ""

            pb = new ProgressBar( )
            pb.Parent = me
            pb.Location = new Point( _
                      CType((Size.Width / 8), integer), lbl.Bottom + 25)
```

Example 13-16. ProgressBar in VB.NET (ProgressBar.vb) (continued)

```
VB        pb.Size = new Size(CType((Size.Width * 3 / 4), integer), 20)
          pb.Minimum = 0          '  the default value
          pb.Maximum = 100        '  the default value
       end sub '  close for constructor

       private sub btn_OnClick(ByVal sender as object, _
                       ByVal e as EventArgs)
          dim limit as integer = 10000
          dim cntr as integer = 0
          dim i as integer
          pb.Value = 0
          pb.Step = 1
          for i = 0 to limit
             cntr = cntr + 1
             if cntr mod 100 = 0 then
                lbl.Text = cntr.ToString()
                pb.PerformStep()
                Application.DoEvents()
                System.Threading.Thread.Sleep(40)
             end if
          next
       end sub

       public shared sub Main()
          Application.Run(new ProgressBars())
       end sub
    end class
end namespace
```

In these programs, two controls are declared as member variables: the progress bar and the label that will display the current value.

In the constructor, all three controls are instantiated and specified. The size and location of all controls, including the progress bar, are set based on the size of the form and the position of the control located above it on the form, as appropriate.

The progress bar has its Minimum and Maximum properties set to the default values of 0 and 100, respectively. In this example, these values lend themselves to easy calculation. However, other applications may call for different values. For example, if the progress bar indicates the time it takes to stream a number of lines to a file, it would make more sense to set the Maximum property to the total number of lines to be streamed.

In the button Click event handler, three integers are declared and instantiated for incrementing a counter. Also, the progress bar's Value property is reinitialized to 0 (necessary if the button is clicked a second or subsequent time) and the Step property is set to 1. This latter property is the amount by which the control is incremented when the PerformStep method is called.

Inside the for loop, which increments the counter, the modulo operator updates both the label and the progress bar every 100 counts.

C#
```
if (cntr % 100 == 0)
```

VB
```
if cntr mod 100 = 0 then
```

Within the loop, the label control's Text property is updated and the progress bar's PerformStep method is called. Then the static Application.DoEvents method is called to allow the form to repaint itself without having to wait until the Click event finishes its processing. If the DoEvents method is not called, you will not see the updated label, although the progress bar would still update properly.

The values used for the Step property and the modulo function are related. The modulo function updates the display every 100 counts, which is 1 percent of the limit. The Step property is also 1 percent of the Maximum value, so they correspond.

As an alternative to using the PerformStep method, you could omit the line that sets the Step property and replace the call to PerformStep with the appropriate following line:

C#
```
pb.Value = (int)((float)cntr/(float)limit * 100) ;
```

VB
```
pb.Value = _
    CType((CType(cntr, single) / CType(limit, single) * 100), integer)
```

As another alternative to using the PerformStep method, you could again omit the line that sets the Step property and replace the call to PerformStep with the following line (the same in both languages):

```
pb.Increment(1)
```

A 40 millisecond pause is introduced every 100 counts with a call to the static Thread.Sleep method. This slows things down so they can be observed.

CHAPTER 14

TreeView and ListView

The world is very confusing, with information everywhere—some related, some not. To survive, Homo sapiens have learned to organize: it is a survival trait. Two primary organization tools in .NET applications are lists and tree controls.

The essential character of a list is that it is linear, without branches or levels. The list can contain all the objects in a group or a subset, filtered according to an appropriate algorithm. It can be sorted: alphabetically, or by cost, color, or any number of other parameters, or not at all.

An alternative, and complementary, way to organize and classify is hierarchically. A hierarchical organization is comprised of parent/child relationships. Each object is at a specific level in the hierarchy, and each object can have a parent object, a child object, neither, or both. The best way to represent hierarchical organizations is with a tree structure, often drawn upside down, as shown in Figure 14-1.

The stereotypical, and most visible, use of list and tree controls in the Windows world is Windows Explorer, the file and directory management program that has been included with Windows since Windows 95. Files and directories (folders in the new parlance) lend themselves well to this blend of hierarchical and ListViews. Explorer uses a tree view control on the left to show the hierarchical nature of the directory tree structure, and a ListView on the right to show all the files and directories contained within a specific directory. The two main controls are separated by a splitter control to allow complementary resizing of the two adjacent controls.

In this chapter, you will learn about the classes provided by the .NET Framework to implement list and tree structures as part of the Windows Forms user interface. The next chapter will cover members of the ListControl class, including the ListBox, CheckedListBox, and ComboBox.

Class Hierarchy

The hierarchical structure (there's that concept again) of the classes discussed in this chapter is shown in Figure 14-2.

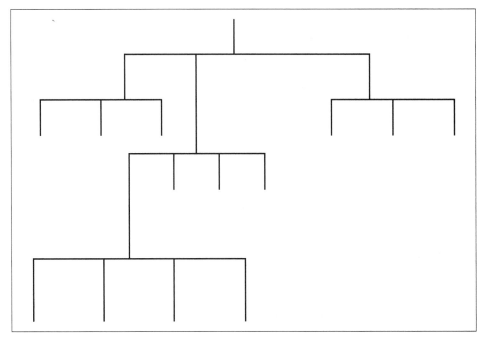

Figure 14-1. Tree structure

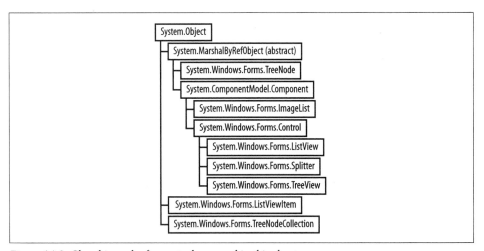

Figure 14-2. Class hierarchy for controls covered in this chapter

Splitter

Typically, complex controls that include treeview and/or list controls make use of a splitter control to separate the "panes" of the container. The splitter control is an unobtrusive, almost invisible control that allows the end user to resize other controls. It generally appears as a thin gray horizontal or vertical bar separating other resizable controls, such as panels, group boxes, ListViews, and tree views. When the mouse cursor hovers over the splitter, the cursor changes to either the Cursors.VSplit (↔) or Cursors.HSplit (↕) cursor to indicate that the adjacent control(s) can be resized. The user can then click and drag the splitter to resize the adjacent controls. There is no way to access a splitter from the keyboard.

Figure 14-3 shows a screenshot of Microsoft Outlook Express, an application that uses two splitters. The vertical splitter separates the tree view on the left from the two controls on the right, and the horizontal splitter separates the ListView and the text box on the right side. Either of the splitters can be moved by the user, changing the relative sizes of all three controls accordingly.

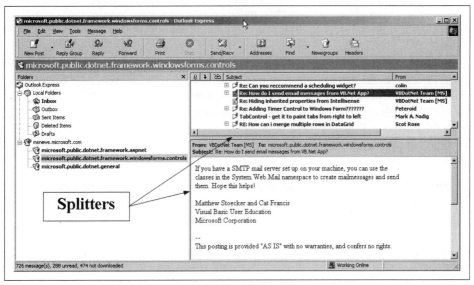

Figure 14-3. Splitter controls used in Outlook Express

The Splitter class is derived directly from Control, as shown in Figure 14-2. Although it has a few properties and methods of its own, the most commonly used of which are listed and discussed below, the splitter itself typically can be ignored by the developer once it is in place. It goes about resizing things without any explicit coding on your part.

Splitters work in conjunction with a control that is docked to one edge of the container—specifically, the control docked to the same edge as the splitter. (Docking was covered in Chapter 7.) This control is actually resized and is called the *target* control. Typically, the remainder of the container is filled with another control whose Dock property has been set to DockStyle.Fill so it will fill all the remaining space left after the target control was resized.

Correct usage of a splitter control depends on a number of factors:

- The splitter and the control(s) it affects must all have the same container.
- The target control, i.e., the control to be resized, must be docked against one edge of the container.
- The splitter must be docked against the same edge of the container as the target.
- The splitter must be higher in the z-order than the control it is resizing.

Z-order, covered in Chapter 7, represents the depth order of the controls (the order of the controls in the direction perpendicular to the plane of the screen). The control with a z-order of 0 is highest in the z-order (at the top of the z-order). The control with a z-order of Controls.Count-1 is lowest in the z-order—at the bottom.

The z-order of controls in a container is determined initially by the order in which they are added to the Controls collection of the container, which is generally the order in which the controls are created. The controls created earlier have a higher z-order—on top of those created later—although this appears to be reversed in Visual Studio .NET, as will be discussed shortly. (The z-order can also be modified with the BringToFront or SendToBack menu items in Visual Studio .NET, or with the BringToFront, SendToBack, or UpdateZOrder methods.)

Consider the sample programs listed in Example 14-1 (in C#) and in Example 14-2 (in VB.NET). These programs create a simple form comprised of two group boxes separated by a splitter, as shown in Figure 14-4, with the mouse cursor over the splitter. The group box on the left has its Dock property set to DockStyle.Left, as does the splitter control separating the two group boxes. The group box on the right has its Dock property set to DockStyle.Fill. When the splitter is moved by the user, the left group box, the target control, is resized; the right group box appears to change size as it fills the remaining space.

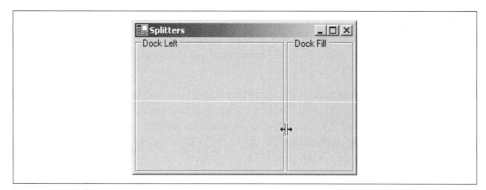

Figure 14-4. Splitter control

Example 14-1. Splitter control in C# (splitters.cs)

```csharp
using System;
using System.Drawing;
using System.Windows.Forms;

namespace ProgrammingWinApps
{
    public class Splitters : Form
    {
        public Splitters( )
        {
            Text = "Splitters";
            Size = new Size(300,200);

            GroupBox grpFill = new GroupBox( );
            grpFill.Parent = this;
            grpFill.Dock = DockStyle.Fill;
            grpFill.Text = "Dock Fill";

            Splitter s = new Splitter( );
            s.Parent = this;
            s.Dock = DockStyle.Left;

            GroupBox grpLeft = new GroupBox( );
            grpLeft.Parent = this;
            grpLeft.Dock = DockStyle.Left;
            grpLeft.Text = "Dock Left";
        }  //  close for constructor

        static void Main( )
        {
            Application.Run(new Splitters( ));
        }
    }        //  close for form class
}            //  close form namespace
```

Example 14-2. Splitter control in VB.NET (splitters.vb)

```vbnet
Option Strict On
imports System
imports System.Drawing
imports System.Windows.Forms

namespace ProgrammingWinApps
    public class Splitters : inherits Form

        public sub New( )
            Text = "Splitters"
            Size = new Size(300,200)

            dim grpFill as new GroupBox( )
            grpFill.Parent = me
            grpFill.Dock = DockStyle.Fill
            grpFill.Text = "Dock Fill"
```

Example 14-2. Splitter control in VB.NET (splitters.vb) (continued)

```
        dim s as new Splitter( )
        s.Parent = me
        s.Dock = DockStyle.Left

        dim grpLeft as new GroupBox( )
        grpLeft.Parent = me
        grpLeft.Dock = DockStyle.Left
        grpLeft.Text = "Dock Left"
    end sub  '  close for constructor

    public shared sub Main( )
        Application.Run(new Splitters( ))
    end sub
  end class
end namespace
```

In Examples 14-1 and 14-2, the controls are created in the following order:

1. grpFill

2. splitter

3. grpLeft

grpFill is created first, so it is at the top of the z-order. As each control is created, it goes to the bottom of the z-order. The splitter is created before the target, grpLeft, so the splitter is higher in the z-order than grpLeft.

grpLeft is docked to the left edge of the container. The splitter is also docked to the left edge, satisfying one of the requirements listed above for enabling a splitter to resize. When two different controls are docked to the same edge of a container, as is the case here, their relative positions are controlled by the z-order. The control with the higher z-order, in this case the splitter, is pushed toward the center of the container (away from the docking edge). This is the exact behavior you want: the splitter will be in the middle of the container rather than between the target and the edge of the container.

Suppose you had created grpFill after grpLeft in the above examples? The splitter still would have resized grpLeft, as before, since the criteria for the splitter would still be met. However, now grpLeft would be on top of grpFill. The Text displayed at the top left of the grpFill group box would not be visible until grpLeft was resized small enough to uncover most of the underlying grpFill.

Splitters in Visual Studio .NET

When using splitters in Visual Studio .NET, the order in which you create the controls is reversed from how the controls are created in a text editor:

1. grpLeft

2. splitter

3. grpFill

As controls are created in Visual Studio .NET, they go to the top of the z-order rather than the bottom. This is because Visual Studio .NET uses a technique for adding controls to the Controls collection that differs from that shown in Example 14-1 and Example 14-2. Whereas the Parent property of each control is set explicitly in these examples, Visual Studio .NET uses the AddRange method (inserting the arguments in reverse order) to add all controls to the Controls collection at once, with a syntax similar to the following:

```
this.Controls.AddRange(new System.Windows.Forms.Control[] {
        this.grpFill,
        this.splitter,
        this.grpLeft});
```

```
Me.Controls.AddRange(New System.Windows.Forms.Control() { _
        Me. grpFill, Me.splitter, Me. grpLeft })
```

The controls in the array, which is the argument to the AddRange method, are added to the Controls collection in order, so the first control in the array is at the top of the z-order, the next control is next in the z-order, and so on. However, Visual Studio .NET adds each new control to the beginning of the array, rather than to the end. Ultimately, the controls are pushed to the top of the z-order as they are created.

In addition to the Dock property described above, the splitter control has several potentially useful properties listed in Table 14-1.

Table 14-1. Splitter properties

Property	Value type	Description
BackColor	Color	Read/write. The color of the control. The default color is the container's background color.
BackgroundImage	Image	Read/write. Background image of the control. If the image is wider than the control, it will be truncated.
BorderStyle	BorderStyle	Read/write. The border style of the control. Valid values are members of the BorderStyle enumeration, listed in Table 14-2. Default is BorderStyle.None.
Dock	DockStyle	Read/write. The dock style of the control. Valid values are members of the DockStyle enumeration, listed in Table 14-3.
Height	Integer	Read/write. Overridden from Control. Thickness of horizontal splitter in pixels. Default is 3 pixels. Minimum value is 1.
MinExtra	Integer	Read/write. The minimum size, in pixels, of the control on the side of the splitter opposite the target. Default is 25.
MinSize	Integer	Read/write. The minimum size, in pixels, of the target control. Default is 25.
SplitPosition	Integer	Read/write. The distance, in pixels, between the splitter and the container edge to which it is docked. Can determine the splitter position after user interaction or set the splitter position programmatically. If the splitter is not docked to a target, then the value is -1.
Width	Integer	Read/write. Overridden from Control. Thickness of vertical splitter in pixels. Default is 3 pixels. Minimum value is 1.

Table 14-2. BorderStyle enumeration values

Value	Description
Fixed3D	3-D border.
FixedSingle	Single line border.
None	No border.

Table 14-3. DockStyle enumeration values

Value
Bottom
Fill
Left
None
Right
Top

Although it is generally not necessary for you to write event handlers for the splitter control, two events raised by the splitter control that might be useful are listed in Table 14-4. Both events provide an event argument of type SplitterEventArgs, which exposes the properties listed in Table 14-5.

Table 14-4. Splitter events

Event	Event argument	Description
SplitterMoved	SplitterEventArgs	Raised when the splitter is moved.
SplitterMoving	SplitterEventArgs	Raised while the splitter is being moved.

Table 14-5. SplitterEventArgs properties

Property	Description
SplitX	Read/write. X coordinate of the upper-left corner of the control, in client coordinates.
SplitY	Read/write. Y coordinate of the upper-left corner of the control, in client coordinates.
X	Read-only. X coordinate of the mouse cursor, in client coordinates.
Y	Read-only. Y coordinate of the mouse cursor, in client coordinates.

TreeView

A TreeView control displays a collection of items in a hierarchical view. Tree views are very common in the computer world, as seen in Windows Explorer, Microsoft Outlook, and Outlook Express, the Solution Explorer in Visual Studio .NET, and countless other applications.

Each item in a tree view is encapsulated within a TreeNode object. Each TreeNode can have zero, one, or many child nodes. The Nodes property of the tree view represents the collection of TreeNode objects that comprise the *root*, or top level, nodes in the hierarchy. Each node in turn has its own Nodes collection that contains all of that node's child nodes, and so on down the hierarchy. Your program can iterate through each of these collections, recursively if necessary, to walk the entire tree structure, as demonstrated shortly.

A tree view can have only a single node selected at any given time. The user can select a node either by clicking on the node with the mouse or using the arrow keys on the keyboard to move focus up and down the hierarchy. A node can be selected programmatically by setting the TreeView.SelectedNode property, and the currently selected node can be determined by getting the value of this property.

Since the SelectedNode property returns only the last node in the full path for that node in the hierarchy, which node in the tree is actually selected can be ambiguous if you rely only on the Text property of the TreeNode returned by the SelectedNode property. Use the FullPath property of the currently selected node to determine the entire hierarchy for the node. If necessary, the value of the FullPath property can be parsed by using the value of the TreeView.PathSeparator property in conjunction with the String.Split method. Each node also has a zero-based Index property that uniquely identifies that node's position within the Nodes collection of its parent node.

Your program can navigate the tree independent of user interaction (although some properties depend on previous user actions) through the use of several TreeNode properties, including Parent, FirstNode, LastNode, NextNode, NextVisibleNode, PrevNode, and PrevVisibleNode, all of which are described in Table 14-6.

If the ShowPlusMinus property of the tree view is set to true (the default value), then a plus sign is displayed next to nodes that have unexpanded child nodes, and a minus sign is displayed next to nodes that have their child nodes displayed. By clicking on successive plus signs, the user can expand the tree under a node and *drill down* through the hierarchy.

If there are no child nodes, then there will be no plus sign or minus sign. Irrespective of the value of the ShowPlusMinus property, the current node can also be expanded by double-clicking on the node or pressing the plus key on the numeric keypad. The current node can be collapsed by pressing the minus key on the numeric keypad.

 An undocumented feature: A node and all its child nodes can be expanded by pressing the asterisk on the numeric keypad. No keyboard shortcut collapses all the nodes.

The TreeView control has a CollapseAll method that collapses all the nodes in the entire hierarchy and an ExpandAll method that expands all the nodes in the entire hierarchy, both of which are listed along with other commonly used TreeView methods in Table 14-7. The ExpandAll method can take time to complete if there are a large number of nodes, such as in a reasonably complex directory structure, as demonstrated shortly.

You can expand and collapse individual nodes of a tree view programmatically, using several of the TreeNode methods listed in Table 14-9. The state of a node persists under certain circumstances, although it is not consistent between user interaction and programmatic control. For example, if a child node is expanded and a higher-level node is collapsed by clicking on its minus sign and then expanded by clicking on its plus sign, the original child node remains expanded. However, if the equivalent operations are performed by using the Collapse and Expand methods, the original node does not remain expanded.

Any node in a tree view can have an image associated with it. Unlike other controls that can use either a single image or an ImageList, the image(s) used in a tree view must be contained within a single ImageList object. (ImageLists are described fully in Chapter 7.) A default image can be specified for all the nodes in the tree view when you use the TreeView.ImageIndex property. A different image can be specified for the currently selected node with the TreeView.SelectedImageIndex property, which applies to the entire tree view. In addition, each node can have its own ImageIndex and SelectedImageIndex properties. As demonstrated in Example 14-3 and Example 14-4, this allows your application to have default images for all the nodes, such as directories, and then use different images for specific types of nodes, such as files.

All the properties and methods described above are listed, along with many other commonly used properties and methods of the TreeView, TreeNode, and TreeNode-Collection classes, in Tables 14-6 through 14-11. A sample program demonstrating a tree view and many of these properties and methods is shown in Example 14-3 (in C#) and in Example 14-4 (in VB.NET).

Table 14-6. TreeView properties

Property	Value type	Description
BorderStyle	BorderStyle	Read/write. The border style of the control. Valid values are members of the BorderStyle enumeration, listed in Table 14-2. Default is BorderStyle.None.
CheckBoxes	Boolean	If false (the default), nodes in the control are displayed without a checkbox. If true, a checkbox is displayed to the left of each node and image, if any. The AfterCheck event is raised when the state of a checkbox is changed.
FullRowSelect	Boolean	Read/write. If true, the entire width of the selection is highlighted. Default is false. Ignored if the ShowLines property is set to true.
HideSelection	Boolean	Read/write. If true (the default), the highlighting of the selected node disappears when the control does not have focus.
HotTracking	Boolean	Read/write. If true, the node appears as a hyperlink when the mouse passes over it. Default is false.

Table 14-6. TreeView properties (continued)

Property	Value type	Description
ImageIndex	Integer	Read/write. Zero-based index value of the Image object from the ImageList. Specifies the default image displayed by nodes not currently selected.
ImageList	ImageList	Read/write. The ImageList object that contains all the images is available for display with the nodes. Each node can display one image at a time, specified by the TreeView, TreeNode ImageIndex, or SelectedImageIndex properties. The ImageList component is described fully in Chapter 7.
Indent	Integer	Read/write. Distance, in pixels, each node level is indented. Default is 19.
ItemHeight	Integer	Read/write. Height, in pixels, of each node. By default, scales with the control's Font property.
LabelEdit	Boolean	Read/write. If `false` (the default), the node labels cannot be edited by the user.
Nodes	TreeNodeCollection	Read-only. The collection of root level nodes assigned to the tree view.
PathSeparator	String	Read/write. The delimiter string used by the TreeNode.FullPath property. The default is the backslash character (\).
Scrollable	Boolean	Read/write. If `true` (the default), the control displays vertical and/or horizontal scrollbars as necessary.
SelectedImageIndex	Integer	Read/write. Zero-based index value of the Image object from the ImageList. Specifies the image displayed by the currently selected node.
SelectedNode	TreeNode	Read/write. The currently selected TreeNode object.
ShowLines	Boolean	Read/write. If `true` (the default), lines are drawn between the nodes and the FullRowSelect property is ignored.
ShowPlusMinus	Boolean	Read/write. If `true` (the default), plus-sign and minus-sign buttons are displayed next to nodes that contain child nodes.
ShowRootLines	Boolean	Read/write. If `true` (the default), lines are drawn between root nodes. If `false`, plus or minus sign buttons will not appear next to root nodes, even if ShowPlusMinus is `true`.
Sorted	Boolean	Read/write. If `false` (the default), the nodes are not sorted. If `true`, the nodes are sorted alphabetically.
TopNode	TreeNode	Read-only. The first fully visible node in the control, taking into account scrolling performed by the user.
VisibleCount	Integer	Read-only. The number of potential nodes fully visible in the control, taking into account the height of the client area and the height of a node. Value may be greater than the actual number of nodes in the control.

Table 14-7. TreeView methods

Method	Description
BeginUpdate	Disables redrawing of the tree view control until the EndUpdate method is called. Improves performance when adding nodes one at a time.
CollapseAll	Collapses all the nodes in the tree view.

Table 14-7. TreeView methods (continued)

Method	Description
EndUpdate	Enables redrawing of the tree view control after BeginUpdate was called.
ExpandAll	Expands all the nodes in the tree view. If called on a large tree structure, it can take some time.
GetNodeAt	Returns the node at the specified point or coordinate pair. The MouseEventArgs.X and MouseEventArgs.Y coordinates of the MouseDown event can be passed as the coordinates.
GetNodeCount	Returns the number of nodes in the tree view. If the Boolean argument is true, it includes all the nodes in any subtrees.

Table 14-8. TreeNode properties

Property	Value type	Description
Checked	Boolean	Read/write. true if the node is checked. Only relevant if the TreeView.CheckBoxes property is true.
FirstNode	TreeNode	Read-only. The first child node in the Nodes collection of the current node. If the current node has no child nodes, it returns null/Nothing.
FullPath	String	Read-only. The path from the root node to the current node. Each node is represented by its Text property, separated by the string specified in the TreeView.PathSeparator property.
ImageIndex	Integer	Read/write. Zero-based index value of the Image object from the ImageList used as the image displayed by this node when not currently selected. Overrides the TreeView.ImageIndex property.
Index	Integer	Read-only. Zero-based value representing the position of this node within the Nodes collection of its parent node.
IsEditing	Boolean	Read-only. true if the node is editable, false otherwise.
IsExpanded	Boolean	Read-only. true if the node is expanded, false otherwise.
IsSelected	Boolean	Read-only. true if the node is selected, false otherwise.
IsVisible	Boolean	Read-only. true if the node is visible, false otherwise.
LastNode	TreeNode	Read-only. The last child node in the Nodes collection of the current node. If the current node has no child nodes, returns null/Nothing.
NextNode	TreeNode	Read-only. The next sibling node in the parent node's Nodes collection. If there is no next node, returns null/Nothing.
NextVisibleNode	TreeNode	Read-only. The next visible node, taking into account user interaction, the size of the client area, the font, and other visual properties. If there is no next visible node, returns null/Nothing.
NodeFont	Font	Read/write. The font used to display the text of the current node. Overrides the TreeView.Font property. If font is larger than that specified in the TreeView.Font property, text may be clipped.
Nodes	TreeNodeCollection	Read-only. The collection of nodes assigned to the current node. Properties and methods of the TreeNodeCollection class are listed in Table 14-10 and Table 14-11, respectively.

Table 14-8. TreeNode properties (continued)

Property	Value type	Description
Parent	TreeNode	Read-only. The parent node of the current node. Root level nodes return null/Nothing.
PrevNode	TreeNode	Read-only. The previous sibling node in the parent node's Nodes collection. If there is no previous node, returns null/Nothing.
PrevVisibleNode	TreeNode	Read-only. The previous visible node, taking into account user interaction, the size of the client area, the font, and other visual properties. If there is no previous node visible, returns null/Nothing.
SelectedImageIndex	Integer	Read/write. Zero-based index value of the Image object from the ImageList used as the image displayed by this node when currently selected. Overrides the TreeView.SelectedImageIndex property.
Tag	Object	Read/write. Object containing data about the node.
Text	String	Read/write. Text displayed as the label of the node. Can either be set explicitly or via one of the TreeNode methods, listed in Table 14-9.
TreeView	TreeView	Read-only. The parent tree view of the node.

Table 14-9. TreeNode methods

Method	Description
BeginEdit	Begins editing of node label. If TreeView.LabelEdit property is `false`, an exception will be thrown.
Clone	Copies the node and all its child nodes.
Collapse	Collapses the current node. Child nodes are not collapsed.
EndEdit	Ends editing of node label. If Boolean argument is `true`, editing is canceled without saving the changes.
EnsureVisible	Causes tree view to expand and scroll so that the current node is visible.
Expand	Expands the current node down to the next level of nodes.
ExpandAll	Expands all the nodes in the Nodes collection of the current node.
GetNodeCount	Returns number of child nodes. If Boolean argument is `true`, includes all child nodes and their child nodes.
Remove	Removes the current node and any child nodes from the tree view.
Toggle	If node is currently collapsed, it is expanded, and vice versa.

Table 14-10. TreeNodeCollection properties

Property	Value Type	Description
Count	Integer	Read-only. Total number of TreeNode objects in the collection.
IsReadOnly	Boolean	Read-only. If `false` (the default), the collection may be modified.
Item	TreeNode	Read/write. The node at the specified, zero-based index.

Table 14-11. *TreeNodeCollection methods*

Method	Description
Add	Overloaded. Adds new node to the end of current node collection. If string argument provided, returns TreeNode object representing the new node. If TreeNode argument provided, returns index of new node.
AddRange	Adds an array of previously created TreeNode objects to the end of current node collection.
Clear	Removes all the nodes from the current collection. Can be used to clear an entire tree view.
Contains	Returns true if the specified TreeNode is a member of the collection.
CopyTo	Copies entire collection to the specified array, starting at specified index.
IndexOf	Returns zero-based index of the specified TreeNode.
Insert	Inserts a previously created TreeNode into the collection at the location specified by the index. If TreeView.Sorted property is true, the index is ignored. An exception will be thrown if a node is added to a tree view while still a member of a different tree view. It must be either removed or cloned from the original tree view.
Remove	Removes the specified TreeNode from the collection. All subsequent nodes move up one position.
RemoveAt	Removes the TreeNode from the collection at the location specified by the zero-based index. All subsequent nodes move up one position.

A sample program using a tree view was presented in Chapter 5 to demonstrate an Explorer interface. That program, which was created using Visual Studio .NET, displayed a hierarchy of motor vehicles. It demonstrated the use of the TreeNode Editor for adding nodes to the tree view control, and the Image Collection Editor for adding images to the image list.

The sample programs listed here in Example 14-3 (in C#) and in Example 14-4 (in VB.NET) are more complex and fully featured than the example shown in Chapter 5. These new examples use a tree view control to display the logical drives on the local machine and the directories and (optionally) the files they contain. A checkbox is provided to toggle the display of the files: when it is checked, files are displayed; otherwise, only directories are displayed. There are also several buttons for displaying information about the currently selected node and for expanding and collapsing the tree.

When the example is compiled and run, it looks something like Figure 14-5. It may not be obvious in this monochrome book, but alternating directories are colored LightPink and alternating files are LightGreen.

A full analysis follows the code listings.

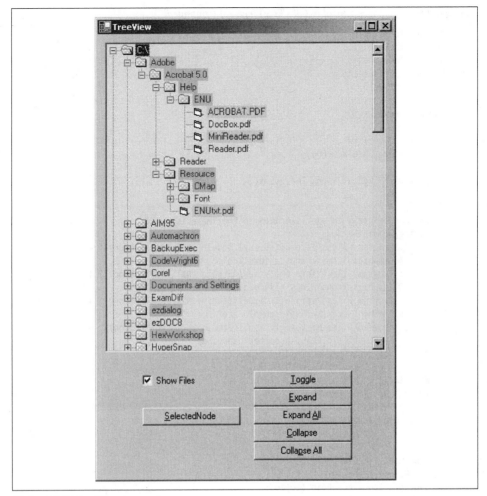

Figure 14-5. TreeViews program

Example 14-3. TreeView control in C# (TreeViews.cs)

```csharp
using System;
using System.Drawing;
using System.Windows.Forms;
using System.IO;                // necessary for Directory info

namespace ProgrammingWinApps
{
    public class TreeViews : Form
    {
        TreeView tvw;
        CheckBox cb;
        Button btnSelected;
```

Example 14-3. TreeView control in C# (TreeViews.cs) (continued)

```
Button btnExpand;
Button btnExpandAll;
Button btnCollapse;
Button btnCollapseAll;
Button btnToggle;

public TreeViews( )
{
    Text = "TreeView";
    Size = new Size(400,600);

    ImageList imgList = new ImageList( );
    Image img;

    // Use an array to add filenames to the ImageList
    String[ ] arFiles = {
        @"C:\Program Files\Microsoft Visual Studio .NET 2003\Common7\" +
            @"Graphics\icons\computer\form.ico",
        @"C:\Program Files\Microsoft Visual Studio .NET 2003\Common7\" +
            @"Graphics\icons\win95\clsdfold.ico",
        @"C:\Program Files\Microsoft Visual Studio .NET 2003\Common7\" +
            @"Graphics\icons\win95\openfold.ico",
        @"C:\Program Files\Microsoft Visual Studio .NET 2003\Common7\" +
            @"Graphics\bitmaps\assorted\happy.bmp"
        };

    for (int i = 0; i < arFiles.Length; i++)
    {
        img = Image.FromFile(arFiles[i]);
        imgList.Images.Add(img);
    }

    tvw = new TreeView( );
    tvw.Parent = this;
    tvw.Location = new Point(10,10);
    tvw.Size = new Size(ClientSize.Width - 20, Height - 200);
    tvw.Anchor = AnchorStyles.Top | AnchorStyles.Left |
            AnchorStyles.Right | AnchorStyles.Bottom;
    tvw.BackColor = Color.Moccasin;
    tvw.ForeColor = Color.DarkRed;
    tvw.BorderStyle = BorderStyle.Fixed3D;
    tvw.FullRowSelect = false;      // default
    tvw.ShowLines = true;           // default
    tvw.ShowPlusMinus = true;       // default
    tvw.Scrollable = true;          // default
    tvw.HideSelection = false;
    tvw.HotTracking = true;
    tvw.ImageList = imgList;
    tvw.ImageIndex = 1;
    tvw.SelectedImageIndex = 2;
//      tvw.Indent = 35;
//      tvw.Font = new Font("Times New Roman", 20f);
//      tvw.ItemHeight = tvw.Font.Height * 2;
```

Example 14-3. TreeView control in C# (TreeViews.cs) (continued)

```
C#    tvw.BeforeExpand += new
          TreeViewCancelEventHandler(tvw_BeforeExpand);

      cb = new CheckBox( );
      cb.Parent = this;
      cb.Location = new Point((Width - cb.Width) * 2 / 10,
                              tvw.Bottom + 25);
      cb.Text = "Show Files";
      cb.Anchor = AnchorStyles.Bottom;
      cb.CheckedChanged += new EventHandler(cb_CheckedChanged);

      btnSelected = new Button( );
      btnSelected.Parent = this;
      btnSelected.Text = "&SelectedNode";
      int xSize = ((int)(Font.Height * .75) * btnSelected.Text.Length);
      int ySize = Font.Height + 10;
      btnSelected.Size = new Size(xSize, ySize);
      btnSelected.Location = new Point(cb.Left, cb.Bottom + ySize);
      btnSelected.Anchor = AnchorStyles.Bottom;
      btnSelected.Click += new EventHandler(btnSelected_Click);

      btnToggle = new Button( );
      btnToggle.Parent = this;
      btnToggle.Location = new Point((Width - cb.Width) * 7 / 10,
                                     cb.Top);
      btnToggle.Text = "&Toggle";
      btnToggle.Size = new Size(btnSelected.Width, btnSelected.Height);
      btnToggle.Anchor = AnchorStyles.Bottom;
      btnToggle.Click += new EventHandler(btnToggle_Click);

      btnExpand = new Button( );
      btnExpand.Parent = this;
      btnExpand.Location = new Point(btnToggle.Left, btnToggle.Bottom);
      btnExpand.Text = "&Expand";
      btnExpand.Size = new Size(btnSelected.Width, btnSelected.Height);
      btnExpand.Anchor = AnchorStyles.Bottom;
      btnExpand.Click += new EventHandler(btnExpand_Click);

      btnExpandAll = new Button( );
      btnExpandAll.Parent = this;
      btnExpandAll.Location = new Point(btnExpand.Left,
                                        btnExpand.Bottom);
      btnExpandAll.Text = "Expand &All";
      btnExpandAll.Size = new Size(btnSelected.Width,
                                   btnSelected.Height);
      btnExpandAll.Anchor = AnchorStyles.Bottom;
      btnExpandAll.Click += new EventHandler(btnExpandAll_Click);

      btnCollapse = new Button( );
      btnCollapse.Parent = this;
      btnCollapse.Location = new Point(btnExpandAll.Left,
                                       btnExpandAll.Bottom);
```

Example 14-3. TreeView control in C# (TreeViews.cs) (continued)

```
C#          btnCollapse.Text = "&Collapse";
            btnCollapse.Size = new Size(btnSelected.Width,
                                    btnSelected.Height);
            btnCollapse.Anchor = AnchorStyles.Bottom;
            btnCollapse.Click += new EventHandler(btnCollapse_Click);

            btnCollapseAll = new Button( );
            btnCollapseAll.Parent = this;
            btnCollapseAll.Location = new Point(btnCollapse.Left,
                                        btnCollapse.Bottom);
            btnCollapseAll.Text = "Colla&pse All";
            btnCollapseAll.Size = new Size(btnSelected.Width,
                                    btnSelected.Height);
            btnCollapseAll.Anchor = AnchorStyles.Bottom;
            btnCollapseAll.Click += new EventHandler(btnCollapseAll_Click);

            FillDirectoryTree( );
        } // close for constructor

        static void Main( )
        {
            Application.Run(new TreeViews( ));
        }

        private void FillDirectoryTree( )
        {
            // Populate with the contents of the local hard drive.

            // Suppress redraw until tree view is complete
            tvw.BeginUpdate( );

               // First clear all the nodes.
            tvw.Nodes.Clear( );

            // Get the logical drives and put them into the root nodes.
            // Fill an array with all the logical drives on the machine.
            string[ ] strDrives = Environment.GetLogicalDrives( );

            // Iterate through the drives, adding them to the tree.
            // Use a try/catch block, so if a drive is not ready,
            // e.g. an empty floppy or CD, it will not be added to the tree.
            foreach (string rootDirectoryName in strDrives)
            {
              try
              {
                // Find all the first level subdirectories.
                // If the drive is not ready, this will throw an
                // exception, which will have the effect of
                // skipping that drive.
                Directory.GetDirectories(rootDirectoryName);
```

Example 14-3. TreeView control in C# (TreeViews.cs) (continued)

```
C#
                        // Create a node for each root directory
                        TreeNode ndRoot = new TreeNode(rootDirectoryName);

                        // Add the node to the tree
                        tvw.Nodes.Add(ndRoot);

                        // Set colors based on Index property.
                        // Index not set until after node added to collection.
                        if (ndRoot.Index % 2 == 0)
                        {
                            ndRoot.BackColor = Color.LightYellow;
                            ndRoot.ForeColor = Color.Green;
                        }

                        // Add subdirectory nodes.
                        // If Show Files checkbox checked, then also get
                        //    the filenames.
                        GetSubDirectoryNodes(ndRoot, cb.Checked);
                    }
                    catch (System.IO.IOException)
                    {
                        // let it through
                    }
                    catch (Exception e)
                    {
                        // Catch any other errors.
                        MessageBox.Show(e.Message);
                    }
                }
            tvw.EndUpdate( );
        }     // close FillDirectoryTree

        private void GetSubDirectoryNodes(TreeNode parentNode,
                                    bool getFileNames)
        {
            // Exit this method if the node is not a directory.
            DirectoryInfo di = new DirectoryInfo(parentNode.FullPath);
            if ((di.Attributes & FileAttributes.Directory) == 0)
            {
                return;
            }

            // Clear all the nodes in this node.
            parentNode.Nodes.Clear( );

            // Get an array of strings containing all the subdirectories
            //    in the parent node.
            string[ ] arSubs = Directory.GetDirectories(parentNode.FullPath);

            // Add a child node for each subdirectory.
            foreach (string subDir in arSubs)
            {
```

Example 14-3. TreeView control in C# (TreeViews.cs) (continued)

```csharp
                    DirectoryInfo dirInfo = new DirectoryInfo(subDir);
                    // do not show hidden folders
                    if ((dirInfo.Attributes & FileAttributes.Hidden)!= 0)
                    {
                        continue;
                    }

                TreeNode subNode = new TreeNode(dirInfo.Name);
                parentNode.Nodes.Add(subNode);

                //  Set colors based on Index property.
                if (subNode.Index % 2 == 0)
                    subNode.BackColor = Color.LightPink;
            }

        if (getFileNames)
        {
            //  Get any files for this node.
            string[ ] files = Directory.GetFiles(parentNode.FullPath);

            // After placing the nodes,
            // now place the files in that subdirectory.
            foreach (string str in files)
            {
                FileInfo fi = new FileInfo(str);
                TreeNode fileNode = new TreeNode(fi.Name);
                parentNode.Nodes.Add(fileNode);

                //  Set the icons
                fileNode.ImageIndex = 0;
                fileNode.SelectedImageIndex = 3;

                //  Set colors based on Index property.
                if (fileNode.Index % 2 == 0)
                    fileNode.BackColor = Color.LightGreen;
            }
        }
    }  // close GetSubDirectoryNodes

private void cb_CheckedChanged(object sender, EventArgs e)
{
    FillDirectoryTree( );
}

private void tvw_BeforeExpand(object sender,
                             TreeViewCancelEventArgs e)
{
    tvw.BeginUpdate( );

    foreach (TreeNode tn in e.Node.Nodes)
    {
        GetSubDirectoryNodes(tn, cb.Checked);
    }
```

Example 14-3. TreeView control in C# (TreeViews.cs) (continued)

```csharp
        tvw.EndUpdate( );
    }

    private void btnSelected_Click(object sender, EventArgs e)
    {
        MessageBox.Show(tvw.SelectedNode.ToString( ) + "\n" +
            "FullPath:\t" + tvw.SelectedNode.FullPath.ToString( ) + "\n" +
            "Index:\t" + tvw.SelectedNode.Index.ToString( ));
    }

    private void btnExpand_Click(object sender, EventArgs e)
    {
        tvw.SelectedNode.Expand( );
    }

    private void btnExpandAll_Click(object sender, EventArgs e)
    {
        tvw.SelectedNode.ExpandAll( );
    }

    private void btnCollapse_Click(object sender, EventArgs e)
    {
        tvw.SelectedNode.Collapse( );
    }

    private void btnCollapseAll_Click(object sender, EventArgs e)
    {
        tvw.CollapseAll( );
    }

    private void btnToggle_Click(object sender, EventArgs e)
    {
        tvw.SelectedNode.Toggle( );
    }
}        // close for form class
}        // close form namespace
```

Example 14-4. TreeView in VB.NET (TreeViews.vb)

```vbnet
Option Strict On
imports System
imports System.Drawing
imports System.Windows.Forms
imports System.IO                ' necessary for Directory info

namespace ProgrammingWinApps
    public class TreeViews : inherits Form

        dim tvw as TreeView
        dim cb as CheckBox
        dim btnSelected as Button
        dim btnExpand as Button
        dim btnExpandAll as Button
```

Example 14-4. TreeView in VB.NET (TreeViews.vb) (continued)

```
dim btnCollapse as Button
dim btnCollapseAll as Button
dim btnToggle as Button
dim i as integer

public sub New( )
    Text = "TreeView"
    Size = new Size(400,600)

    dim imgList as new ImageList( )
    dim img as Image

    '  Use an array to add filenames to the ImageList
    dim arFiles( ) as string = { _
      "C:\Program Files\Microsoft Visual Studio .NET 2003\Common7\" + _
              "Graphics\icons\computer\form.ico", _
        "C:\Program Files\Microsoft Visual Studio .NET 2003\Common7\" + _
              "Graphics\icons\win95\clsdfold.ico", _
        "C:\Program Files\Microsoft Visual Studio .NET 2003\Common7\" + _
              "Graphics\icons\win95\openfold.ico", _
        "C:\Program Files\Microsoft Visual Studio .NET 2003\Common7\" + _
              "Graphics\bitmaps\assorted\happy.bmp"}

    for i = 0 to arFiles.Length - 1
        img = Image.FromFile(arFiles(i))
        imgList.Images.Add(img)
    next

    tvw = new TreeView( )
    tvw.Parent = me
    tvw.Location = new Point(10,10)
    tvw.Size = new Size(ClientSize.Width - 20, Height - 200)
    tvw.Anchor = AnchorStyles.Top or AnchorStyles.Left or _
            AnchorStyles.Right or AnchorStyles.Bottom
    tvw.BackColor = Color.Moccasin
    tvw.ForeColor = Color.DarkRed
    tvw.BorderStyle = BorderStyle.Fixed3D
    tvw.FullRowSelect = false      ' default
    tvw.ShowLines = true         ' default
    tvw.ShowPlusMinus = true        ' default
    tvw.Scrollable = true         ' default
    tvw.HideSelection = false
    tvw.HotTracking = true
    tvw.ImageList = imgList
    tvw.ImageIndex = 1
    tvw.SelectedImageIndex = 2
'    tvw.Indent = 35
'    tvw.Font = new Font("Times New Roman", 20f)
'    tvw.ItemHeight = tvw.Font.Height * 2
    AddHandler tvw.BeforeExpand, AddressOf tvw_BeforeExpand

    cb = new CheckBox( )
    cb.Parent = me
```

Example 14-4. TreeView in VB.NET (TreeViews.vb) (continued)

```
cb.Location = new Point( _
        CType((Width - cb.Width) * 2 / 10, integer), _
        tvw.Bottom + 25)
cb.Text = "Show Files"
cb.Anchor = AnchorStyles.Bottom
AddHandler cb.CheckedChanged, AddressOf cb_CheckedChanged

btnSelected = new Button( )
btnSelected.Parent = me
btnSelected.Text = "&SelectedNode"
dim xSize as integer = CType(Font.Height * .75, integer) * _
                btnSelected.Text.Length
dim ySize as integer = Font.Height + 10
btnSelected.Size = new Size(xSize, ySize)
btnSelected.Location = new Point(cb.Left, cb.Bottom + ySize)
btnSelected.Anchor = AnchorStyles.Bottom
AddHandler btnSelected.Click, AddressOf btnSelected_Click

btnToggle = new Button( )
btnToggle.Parent = me
btnToggle.Location = new Point( _
        CType((Width - cb.Width) * 7 / 10, integer), _
        cb.Top)
btnToggle.Text = "&Toggle"
btnToggle.Size = new Size(btnSelected.Width, btnSelected.Height)
btnToggle.Anchor = AnchorStyles.Bottom
AddHandler btnToggle.Click, AddressOf btnToggle_Click

btnExpand = new Button( )
btnExpand.Parent = me
btnExpand.Location = new Point(btnToggle.Left, btnToggle.Bottom)
btnExpand.Text = "&Expand"
btnExpand.Size = new Size(btnSelected.Width, btnSelected.Height)
btnExpand.Anchor = AnchorStyles.Bottom
AddHandler btnExpand.Click, AddressOf btnExpand_Click

btnExpandAll = new Button( )
btnExpandAll.Parent = me
btnExpandAll.Location = new Point(btnExpand.Left, _
                                    btnExpand.Bottom)
btnExpandAll.Text = "Expand &All"
btnExpandAll.Size = new Size(btnSelected.Width, _
                    btnSelected.Height)
btnExpandAll.Anchor = AnchorStyles.Bottom
AddHandler btnExpandAll.Click, AddressOf btnExpandAll_Click

btnCollapse = new Button( )
btnCollapse.Parent = me
btnCollapse.Location = new Point(btnExpandAll.Left, _
                                    btnExpandAll.Bottom)
btnCollapse.Text = "&Collapse"
btnCollapse.Size = new Size(btnSelected.Width, _
```

Example 14-4. TreeView in VB.NET (TreeViews.vb) (continued)

VB

```
                        btnSelected.Height)
    btnCollapse.Anchor = AnchorStyles.Bottom
    AddHandler btnCollapse.Click, AddressOf btnCollapse_Click

    btnCollapseAll = new Button( )
    btnCollapseAll.Parent = me
    btnCollapseAll.Location = new Point(btnCollapse.Left, _
                                  btnCollapse.Bottom)
    btnCollapseAll.Text = "Colla&pse All"
    btnCollapseAll.Size = new Size(btnSelected.Width, _
                    btnSelected.Height)
    btnCollapseAll.Anchor = AnchorStyles.Bottom
    AddHandler btnCollapseAll.Click, AddressOf btnCollapseAll_Click

    FillDirectoryTree( )
end sub  '  close for constructor

private sub FillDirectoryTree( )
    '  Populate with the contents of the local hard drive.

    '  Suppress redraw until tree view is complete
    tvw.BeginUpdate( )

     '  First clear all the nodes.
    tvw.Nodes.Clear( )

    '  Get the logical drives and put them into the root nodes.
    '  Fill an array with all the logical drives on the machine.
    dim strDrives( ) as string = Environment.GetLogicalDrives( )

    '  Iterate through the drives, adding them to the tree.
    '  Use a try/catch block, so if a drive is not ready,
    '  e.g. an empty floppy or CD, it will not be added to the tree.
    dim rootDirectoryName as string
    for each rootDirectoryName in strDrives
        try
            '  Find all the first level subdirectories.
            '  If the drive is not ready, this will throw an exception,
            '  which will have the effect of skipping that drive.
            Directory.GetDirectories(rootDirectoryName)

            '  Create a node for each root directory
            dim ndRoot as TreeNode = new TreeNode(rootDirectoryName)

            '  Add the node to the tree
            tvw.Nodes.Add(ndRoot)

            '  Set colors based on Index property.
             '  Index not set until after node added to collection.
            if ndRoot.Index mod 2 = 0 then
                ndRoot.BackColor = Color.LightYellow
                ndRoot.ForeColor = Color.Green
```

Example 14-4. TreeView in VB.NET (TreeViews.vb) (continued)

```
VB                    end if

                      '  Add subdirectory nodes.
                      '  If Show Files checkbox checked, then also get
                      '  the filenames.
                      GetSubDirectoryNodes(ndRoot, cb.Checked)
                   catch e as System.IO.IOException
                      '  let it through
                   catch e as Exception
                       '  Catch any other errors.
                      MessageBox.Show(e.Message)
                   end try
               next
               tvw.EndUpdate( )
           end sub         '  close FillDirectoryTree

           private sub GetSubDirectoryNodes(parentNode as TreeNode, _
                                  getFileNames as Boolean)
              '  Exit this method if the node is not a directory.
              dim di as DirectoryInfo = new DirectoryInfo(parentNode.FullPath)
              if (di.Attributes and FileAttributes.Directory) = 0   then
                 return
              end if

              '  Clear all the nodes in this node.
              parentNode.Nodes.Clear( )

              '  Get an array of strings containing all the subdirectories
              '  in the parent node.
              dim arSubs( ) as string = _
                 Directory.GetDirectories(parentNode.FullPath)

              '  Add a child node for each subdirectory.
              dim subDir as string
              for each subDir in arSubs
                 dim dirInfo as DirectoryInfo = new DirectoryInfo(subDir)

                 ' do not show hidden folders
                 if (dirInfo.Attributes and FileAttributes.Hidden) = 0 then

                    dim subNode as TreeNode = new TreeNode(dirInfo.Name)
                    parentNode.Nodes.Add(subNode)

                    '  Set colors based on Index property.
                    if (subNode.Index mod 2 = 0) then
                       subNode.BackColor = Color.LightPink
                    end if
                 end if
              next

              if getFileNames then
                 '  Get any files for this node.
                 dim files( ) as string = _
```

Example 14-4. TreeView in VB.NET (TreeViews.vb) (continued)

```
VB
                 Directory.GetFiles(parentNode.FullPath)

            ' After placing the nodes,
            ' now place the files in that subdirectory.
            dim str as string
            for each str in files
               dim fi as FileInfo = new FileInfo(str)
               dim fileNode as TreeNode = new TreeNode(fi.Name)
               parentNode.Nodes.Add(fileNode)

               '  Set the icons
               fileNode.ImageIndex = 0
               fileNode.SelectedImageIndex = 3

               '  Set colors based on Index property.
               if fileNode.Index mod 2 = 0 then
                  fileNode.BackColor = Color.LightGreen
               end if
            next
         end if
      end sub    ' close GetSubDirectoryNodes

      private sub cb_CheckedChanged(ByVal sender as object, _
                           ByVal e as EventArgs)
         FillDirectoryTree( )
      end sub

      private sub tvw_BeforeExpand(ByVal sender as object, _
                           ByVal e as TreeViewCancelEventArgs)
         tvw.BeginUpdate( )
         dim tn as TreeNode
         for each tn in e.Node.Nodes
            GetSubDirectoryNodes(tn, cb.Checked)
         next
         tvw.EndUpdate( )
      end sub

      private sub btnSelected_Click(ByVal sender as object, _
                           ByVal e as EventArgs)
         MessageBox.Show(tvw.SelectedNode.ToString( ) + vbNewLine + _
            "FullPath:" + vbTab + tvw.SelectedNode.FullPath.ToString( ) + _
                vbNewLine + _
            "Index:" + vbTab + tvw.SelectedNode.Index.ToString( ))
      end sub

      private sub btnExpand_Click(ByVal sender as object, _
                           ByVal e as EventArgs)
         tvw.SelectedNode.Expand( )
      end sub

      private sub btnExpandAll_Click(ByVal sender as object, _
                           ByVal e as EventArgs)
         tvw.SelectedNode.ExpandAll( )
```

Example 14-4. TreeView in VB.NET (TreeViews.vb) (continued)

```vb
      end sub

      private sub btnCollapse_Click(ByVal sender as object, _
                         ByVal e as EventArgs)
         tvw.SelectedNode.Collapse( )
      end sub

      private sub btnCollapseAll_Click(ByVal sender as object, _
                         ByVal e as EventArgs)
         tvw.CollapseAll( )
      end sub

      private sub btnToggle_Click(ByVal sender as object, _
                         ByVal e as EventArgs)
         tvw.SelectedNode.Toggle( )
      end sub

      public shared sub Main( )
         Application.Run(new TreeViews( ))
      end sub
   end class
end namespace
```

Code Analysis

This is a large and complex program. The following analysis will break it down into manageable segments that illustrate the tree view and list controls.

The constructor

An image list is declared and populated in the constructor. This image list contains four images, all of which are taken from files that are included as part of the normal Visual Studio .NET installation. The ImageList property of the tree view is set to this image list, the default image for all the nodes is set to the second image (with a zero-based index of 1) in the image list using the TreeView.ImageIndex property, and the image to be displayed when a node is selected is set to the third image (index of 2), using the TreeView.SelectedImageIndex property:

```csharp
      String[ ] arFiles = {
         @"C:\Program Files\Microsoft Visual Studio .NET 2003\Common7\" +
            @"Graphics\icons\computer\form.ico",
         @"C:\Program Files\Microsoft Visual Studio .NET 2003\Common7\" +
            @"Graphics\icons\win95\clsdfold.ico",
         @"C:\Program Files\Microsoft Visual Studio .NET 2003\Common7\" +
            @"Graphics\icons\win95\openfold.ico",
         @"C:\Program Files\Microsoft Visual Studio .NET 2003\Common7\" +
               @"Graphics\bitmaps\assorted\happy.bmp"
         };

      for (int i = 0; i < arFiles.Length; i++)
```

```
C#          {
                img = Image.FromFile(arFiles[i]);
                imgList.Images.Add(img);
            }

            tvw.ImageList = imgList;
            tvw.ImageIndex = 1;
            tvw.SelectedImageIndex = 2;
```

```
VB          '  Use an array to add filenames to the ImageList
            dim arFiles() as string = { _
                "C:\Program Files\Microsoft Visual Studio .NET 2003\Common7\" + _
                    "Graphics\icons\computer\form.ico", _
                "C:\Program Files\Microsoft Visual Studio .NET 2003\Common7\" + _
                    "Graphics\icons\win95\clsdfold.ico", _
                "C:\Program Files\Microsoft Visual Studio .NET 2003\Common7\" + _
                    "Graphics\icons\win95\openfold.ico", _
                "C:\Program Files\Microsoft Visual Studio .NET 2003\Common7\" + _
                    "Graphics\bitmaps\assorted\happy.bmp"}

            for i = 0 to arFiles.Length - 1
                img = Image.FromFile(arFiles(i))
                imgList.Images.Add(img)
            next

            tvw.ImageList = imgList
            tvw.ImageIndex = 1
            tvw.SelectedImageIndex = 2
```

In the GetSubDirectoryNodes method, which is called to fill the nodes with subdirectories and files (if the Show Files checkbox is checked), the standard and selected images for files (as opposed to directories) are set differently from the default node images using the ImageIndex and SelectedImageIndex properties of the TreeNode class:

```
VB          fileNode.ImageIndex = 0
            fileNode.SelectedImageIndex = 3
```

Looking back at the constructor, the tree view's Size property set is based on the size of the parent form.

```
VB          tvw.Size = new Size(ClientSize.Width - 20, Height - 200)
```

The tree view width is calculated based on the Width subproperty of the form's ClientSize to allow the four pixels that are occupied by the form border on each edge. Since the Location of the tree view is offset 10 pixels in from the left edge of the form, sizing it 20 pixels less than the ClientSize.Width will center the control in the form. In the vertical direction, it is not centered, so there is no compelling need to account for the small difference between ClientSize.Height and Height.

Setting the Anchor property of the tree view to all four sides has the effect of automatically resizing the control correctly when the user resizes the form (see Chapter 7 for a complete discussion of anchoring):

C#

```
tvw.Anchor = AnchorStyles.Top | AnchorStyles.Left |
             AnchorStyles.Right | AnchorStyles.Bottom;
```

VB

```
tvw.Anchor = AnchorStyles.Top or AnchorStyles.Left or _
             AnchorStyles.Right or AnchorStyles.Bottom
```

Because the Scrollable property of the tree view is set to its default value of true, scrollbars will automatically appear in the tree view as the form and tree view are resized. This also occurs as the nodes of the tree are expanded.

Several other properties of the tree view, including FullRowSelect, ShowLines, and ShowPlusMinus, are set to their default values in the constructor to give you an opportunity to change the default values and observe the resulting behavior.

The HideSelection and HotTracking properties are set to nondefault values because they are commonly used to improve the clarity of the UI. With HideSelection set true, the selected node loses its highlighting when the form loses focus. Although this is the default value of the property, it is not the way either Windows Explorer or Outlook operate, and leaving this property true can confuse the user. Setting the HotTracking property to true causes a node to appear as a hyperlink when the mouse cursor passes over it. This is primarily a matter of personal preference.

Three other properties of the tree view are included in the constructor but commented out: Indent, Font, and ItemHeight. They are included to provide the opportunity to explore the different behavior that this control can exhibit, which is left as an exercise for the ambitious reader.

The final detail specified for the tree view in the constructor is to add an event handler for the BeforeExpand event:

C#

```
tvw.BeforeExpand += new TreeViewCancelEventHandler(tvw_BeforeExpand);
```

VB

```
AddHandler tvw.BeforeExpand, AddressOf tvw_BeforeExpand
```

This event and its handler will be discussed shortly.

The other controls on the form are straightforward: a checkbox to toggle the display of files in the tree view, a button to display information about the currently selected node, and several buttons to control expanding and collapsing of the nodes. Each control is placed and sized using techniques described in previous chapters. All are sized and placed to make them dependent upon the size of the form, the size and location of the tree view, and the size of the current font. There are no absolute sizes or positions used, so if the user changes the default Windows font or resizes the form, everything will retain its proper look.

The Location property of the checkbox control is based on the size of the form and the Bottom property of the tree view, as well as its own width:

C#

```
cb.Location = new Point((Width - cb.Width) * 2 / 10, tvw.Bottom + 25);
```

```vb
VB    cb.Location = new Point( _
              CType((Width - cb.Width) * 2 / 10, integer), tvw.Bottom + 25)
```

The size of the SelectedNode button is based on the length of its Text property and the current font and its location is based on the location of the checkbox control. It is then anchored to the bottom of the form:

```csharp
C#    int xSize = ((int)(Font.Height * .75) * btnSelected.Text.Length);
      int ySize = Font.Height + 10;
      btnSelected.Size = new Size(xSize, ySize);
      btnSelected.Location = new Point(cb.Left, cb.Bottom + ySize);
      btnSelected.Anchor = AnchorStyles.Bottom;
```

```vb
VB    dim xSize as integer = CType(Font.Height * .75, integer) * _
                      btnSelected.Text.Length
      dim ySize as integer = Font.Height + 10
      btnSelected.Size = new Size(xSize, ySize)
      btnSelected.Location = new Point(cb.Left, cb.Bottom + ySize)
      btnSelected.Anchor = AnchorStyles.Bottom
```

Since the SelectedNode button has the longest Text property, the Size property of all other buttons is set to be the same as the SelectedNode button, thereby achieving a uniform look. This is accomplished with a line of code such as the following:

```csharp
C#    btnToggle.Size = new Size(btnSelected.Width, btnSelected.Height);
```

The location of the Toggle button is set based on the width of the form and the checkbox control's width and location:

```csharp
C#    btnToggle.Location = new Point((Width - cb.Width) * 7 / 10, cb.Top);
```

```vb
VB    btnToggle.Location = new Point( _
              CType((Width - cb.Width) * 7 / 10, integer), cb.Top)
```

The locations of all other buttons are based on the Left and Bottom properties of the button above each. As with the checkbox control, all buttons are anchored to the bottom of the form, as in:

```vb
VB    btnExpand.Location = new Point(btnToggle.Left, btnToggle.Bottom)
      btnExpand.Anchor = AnchorStyles.Bottom
```

Each control has its own event handler added. These buttons demonstrate several of the commonly used TreeView and TreeNode properties and methods.

The SelectedNode button uses the TreeView.SelectedNode property and the Tree-Node FullPath and Index properties to display information about the currently selected node. Notice how the TreeNode properties are invoked by using the Select-edNode property of the TreeView instance, as in:

```vb
VB    tvw.SelectedNode.FullPath.ToString()
```

The Toggle, Expand, Expand All, and Collapse buttons all call the respective Tree-Node methods. Of these, only Expand All has an equivalent TreeView method, but it is not used here because it takes too long to run. As it is, if the current node is a root level node (the root of a hard drive), it may still take some time to expand all the nodes. The Collapse All button calls a TreeView method; there is no equivalent TreeNode method.

The final line of code in the constructor is a call to the FillDirectoryTree method, which actually populates the tree. This method, and the GetSubDirectoryNodes method that it calls, is where most of the action occurs.

Populating the Tree

FillDirectoryTree is a method that fills the root level of the tree view with the logical drives on the computer, plus all first-level subdirectories. Even though the first level subdirectories are not displayed initially, it is necessary to find them so that the plus signs can be displayed next to the root nodes that have child nodes available. This method is called in two places in the program: once in the constructor and in the CheckedChanged event handler every time the state of the checkbox is changed.

The FillDirectoryTree method begins by calling the BeginUpdate method on the tree view.

```C#
tvw.BeginUpdate( );
```

This suspends all redraws of the tree view until the EndUpdate method is called. If BeginUpdate/EndUpdate is not used, then the tree view will redraw itself every time a node is added, with a significant performance penalty.

 In FillDirectoryTree, the nodes are added one at a time by iterating through an array of strings representing the logical drives on the machine. An alternative would be to create an array of TreeNodes, and then add the entire array to the Nodes collection by using the AddRange method of the TreeNodeCollection class. In that case, there would be no benefit to using BeginUpdate and EndUpdate.

The next line calls the Clear method of the TreeNodeCollection class.

```C#
tvw.Nodes.Clear( );
```

Since this line is called against the Nodes collection of the tree view, it removes all the nodes and subnodes from the entire tree. If this step were omitted, then the tree would acquire a duplicate set of nodes every time the FillDirectoryTree method were called.

To create the root level nodes for this tree view, a call is made to the static (shared) GetLogicalDrives method of the Environment class. This method returns an array of strings of the form "C:\", each element of which represents one of the logical drives on the machine.

There are two different static (Shared in VB.NET) methods in the .NET Framework called GetLogicalDrives: one in the Environment class and one in the Directory class. They are equivalent and interchangeable.

Each logical drive is added to the tree view by iterating through the array of strings using a foreach (for each) loop. However, the array of strings representing the logical drives includes all the logical drives on the machine, including those not ready for reading, such as an empty floppy or CD drive.

To prevent not-ready drives from displaying in the tree (which is *not* how Windows Explorer behaves), wrap the entire contents of the foreach loop in a try/catch block. The first line within the try block is a call to the static (shared) method GetDirectories of the Directory class. This form of the overloaded method takes a string representing a directory and returns an array of strings representing all the directories contained within the specified directory. If the drive is not ready, it will throw an exception of type System.IO.IOException, which will be caught by the first catch block. Nothing happens in this first catch block: execution is allowed to pass through, but the drive that caused the exception to be thrown will be gracefully ignored. If any other errors occur, they are caught by the second catch block, which displays a message:

C#

```csharp
foreach (string rootDirectoryName in strDrives)
{
    try
    {
        Directory.GetDirectories(rootDirectoryName);
        TreeNode ndRoot = new TreeNode(rootDirectoryName);
        tvw.Nodes.Add(ndRoot);
        if (ndRoot.Index % 2 == 0)
        {
            ndRoot.BackColor = Color.LightYellow;
            ndRoot.ForeColor = Color.Green;
        }
        GetSubDirectoryNodes(ndRoot, cb.Checked);
    }
    catch (System.IO.IOException)
    {
        // let it through
    }
    catch (Exception e)
    {
        MessageBox.Show(e.Message);
    }
}
```

VB

```vbnet
dim rootDirectoryName as string
for each rootDirectoryName in strDrives
    try
        Directory.GetDirectories(rootDirectoryName)
```

```vb
        dim ndRoot as TreeNode = new TreeNode(rootDirectoryName)
        tvw.Nodes.Add(ndRoot)
        if ndRoot.Index mod 2 = 0 then
            ndRoot.BackColor = Color.LightYellow
            ndRoot.ForeColor = Color.Green
        end if
        GetSubDirectoryNodes(ndRoot, cb.Checked)
    catch e as System.IO.IOException
        ' let it through
    catch e as Exception
        MessageBox.Show(e.Message)
    end try
next
```

Back in the try block, a TreeNode object is instantiated for each logical drive that is ready to read, and that TreeNode object is then added to the Nodes collection of the tree view. As a final touch, the foreground and background colors of every other directory is changed from the default—i.e., if the Index property of the TreeNode object is an even value.

The final line of code inside the try block calls the method GetSubDirectoryNodes. This method, which gets called for every root node in the tree, takes two arguments: a Node object representing the current node for which it needs to get the subdirectories and a Boolean that is the value of the Show Files checkbox. Even though the subdirectories are not displayed at this point, it is necessary to get the subdirectories, if any, so that the tree view will know to display the plus sign next to each node indicating that there are subdirectories.

The first thing that happens inside GetSubDirectoryNodes is to verify that the node passed in as the argument parentNode is in fact a directory. It does this by instantiating a DirectoryInfo object on the full pathname of parentNode, using the TreeNode. FullPath property, in order to access the Attributes property of the DirectoryInfo object. The Attributes property is a bitwise combination of members of the File-Attributes enumeration, listed in Table 14-12. These attributes may pertain to either files or directories. The Attributes property of the current node is logically AND'ed with the Directory value of the FileAttributes enumeration: if the result is zero, then the node is not a directory. If it is not a directory, there can be no subdirectories to retrieve, so the method is exited immediately:

```csharp
DirectoryInfo di = new DirectoryInfo(parentNode.FullPath);
if ((di.Attributes & FileAttributes.Directory) == 0)
{
    return;
}
```

```vb
dim di as DirectoryInfo = new DirectoryInfo(parentNode.FullPath)
if (di.Attributes and FileAttributes.Directory) = 0   then
    return
end if
```

If the node is in fact a directory, then processing continues.

Table 14-12. FileAttributes enumeration

Attribute	Description
Archive	File's archive bit.
Compressed	File is compressed.
Device	Reserved for future use.
Directory	Directory.
Encrypted	If a file, it is encrypted. If a directory, the default for newly created files or directories.
Hidden	File is hidden.
Normal	File is normal and has no other set attributes. Only valid if used alone.
NotContentIndexed	Not indexed by operating system's indexing service.
Offline	File data not immediately available.
ReadOnly	Read-only.
ReparsePoint	File contains reparse point.
SparseFile	Sparse file, i.e., a large file comprised mostly of zeros.
System	System file.
Temporary	Temporary file. Should be deleted as soon as not needed.

All nodes of the parentNode are cleared with the TreeNodeCollection.Clear method and an array of strings representing all the subdirectories of the parentNode is obtained with the static (shared) GetDirectories method, as was done earlier in the FillDirectoryTree method:

C#
```
parentNode.Nodes.Clear( );
string[ ] arSubs = Directory.GetDirectories(parentNode.FullPath);
```

VB
```
parentNode.Nodes.Clear( )
dim arSubs( ) as string = Directory.GetDirectories(parentNode.FullPath)
```

Again, this array of directory strings is iterated, as was done in FillDirectoryTree, except this time there is no need to use a try/catch block, since you know that the only possible iterated contents of the array are directories.

However, some directories, specifically Hidden directories, are not readable. To avoid displaying hidden directories, instantiate a DirectoryInfo object on the directory being processed and test to see if it is a Hidden directory by logically AND'ing the DirectoryInfo Attributes with the Hidden attribute of the FileAttributes enumeration. If it is Hidden, then skip that directory.

In C#, this is achieved by using the continue keyword in the foreach loop, which causes execution to immediately start over at the top of the loop. Otherwise, instantiate a TreeNode for the subdirectory and add it to the Nodes collection of the parentNode. As before, the background color of the node is changed if its Index property is even.

```csharp
foreach (string subDir in arSubs)
{
    DirectoryInfo dirInfo = new DirectoryInfo(subDir);
    if ((dirInfo.Attributes & FileAttributes.Hidden)!= 0)
    {
        continue;
    }

    TreeNode subNode = new TreeNode(dirInfo.Name);
    parentNode.Nodes.Add(subNode);

    if (subNode.Index % 2 == 0)
        subNode.BackColor = Color.LightPink;
}
```

In VB.NET, the continue keyword does not exist, so the logic of the if statement must be slightly different:

```vbnet
dim subDir as string
for each subDir in arSubs
    dim dirInfo as DirectoryInfo = new DirectoryInfo(subDir)

    ' do not show hidden folders
    if (dirInfo.Attributes and FileAttributes.Hidden) = 0 then

        dim subNode as TreeNode = new TreeNode(dirInfo.Name)
        parentNode.Nodes.Add(subNode)

        ' Set colors based on Index property.
        if (subNode.Index mod 2 = 0) then
            subNode.BackColor = Color.LightPink
        end if
    end if
next
```

As you will recall, the second argument passed in to the GetSubDirectoryNodes method is the value of the ShowFiles checkbox. If that checkbox is checked, then files and directories will be displayed in the tree view. The next section of code is where that functionality is implemented:

```csharp
if (getFileNames)
{
```

```vbnet
if getFileNames then
```

Similarly to how directories were handled previously in this method, the static (shared) Directory.GetFiles method is called to fill an array of strings with all the files in the directory:

```csharp
string[ ] files = Directory.GetFiles(parentNode.FullPath);
```

```vbnet
dim files( ) as string = Directory.GetFiles(parentNode.FullPath)
```

The array of strings is iterated with a foreach (for each) loop. For each file in the directory, a FileInfo object is created and a TreeNode object is instantiated to encapsulate that FileInfo object and added to the Nodes collection. The image to use for each file is set with the TreeNode.ImageIndex property, and the image to use when the file is selected is set with the TreeNode.SelectedImageIndex property. Both image properties are set to the zero-based index of the image list created in the constructor. Finally, the background color of the file is set to LightGreen if the Index of the node is even:

C#

```csharp
foreach (string str in files)
{
    FileInfo fi = new FileInfo(str);
    TreeNode fileNode = new TreeNode(fi.Name);
    parentNode.Nodes.Add(fileNode);

    fileNode.ImageIndex = 0;
    fileNode.SelectedImageIndex = 3;

    if (fileNode.Index % 2 == 0)
        fileNode.BackColor = Color.LightGreen;
}
```

VB

```vbnet
dim str as string
for each str in files
    dim fi as FileInfo = new FileInfo(str)
    dim fileNode as TreeNode = new TreeNode(fi.Name)
    parentNode.Nodes.Add(fileNode)

    fileNode.ImageIndex = 0
    fileNode.SelectedImageIndex = 3

    if fileNode.Index mod 2 = 0 then
        fileNode.BackColor = Color.LightGreen
    end if
next
```

Look Ma, no recursion

Nowhere in the discussion so far have you seen the word "recursion." Yes, the Get-SubDirectoryNodes method was called back in the FillDirectoryTree method so the plus signs could be properly displayed next to nodes that have subdirectories. That only goes down one level from the root, though. Inside GetSubDirectoryNodes, no recursion takes place to determine the full tree structure. So how does the application get the full tree structure? Each deeper level of the tree is determined just before its parent node is expanded, by handling the BeforeExpand event raised by the Tree-View control. TreeView events will be discussed shortly.

You could implement a traditional recursive technique for filling the tree by commenting out the line of code in the constructor that adds an event handler to the BeforeExpand event delegate. That line looks like:

```
tvw.BeforeExpand += new TreeViewCancelEventHandler(tvw_BeforeExpand);
```

```
AddHandler tvw.BeforeExpand, AddressOf tvw_BeforeExpand
```

Then in the GetSubDirectoryNodes method, add a line of code that calls itself again, this time passing in the current node as the parent node. You would insert this line of code just before the close of the foreach (For Each in VB.NET) loop:

```
GetSubDirectoryNodes(subNode, getFileNames);
```

The problem with this approach becomes apparent when you run the program: it takes a long time.[*] As soon as the program is executed, and again whenever the Show Files checkbox is changed, the entire directory structure is searched to find all subdirectories and (if the Show Files checkbox is checked) all files. On my machine (a reasonably fast machine with a typically complex directory structure), this takes well over a minute—clearly too long to wait.

TreeView events

As just mentioned, the BeforeExpand event is trapped to fill each successive level of the tree hierarchy just in time (immediately before it is displayed). The TreeView class has many events, including several listed in Table 14-13 that are not inherited from Control. (For a general discussion of events, see Chapter 4) These events come in pairs: one before the action and one after.

All "before" events, with the exception of BeforeLabelEdit, take an event argument of type TreeViewCancelEventArgs. This event argument exposes the properties listed in Table 14-14. The Action property tells you the type of action that raised the event, such as keyboard action or mouse action. (All the possible values of this property are members of the TreeViewAction enumeration, listed in Table 14-15.) The Cancel property of TreeViewCancelEventArgs can be set to false if you want to cancel the operation. The Node property returns the node that raised the event. This is probably the most commonly used property because it provides access to all the TreeNode properties, including the Nodes collection, which is used in the tvw_BeforeExpand event handler Example 14-3 and Example 14-4.

All the "after" events, again with the exception of AfterLabelEdit, take an event argument of type TreeViewEventArgs. This event argument is virtually identical to the TreeViewCancelEventArgs event argument of the "before" events, except that there is no Cancel property. This makes sense: you cannot cancel an event after it has already occurred.

Both the BeforeLabelEdit and AfterLabelEdit events take the same event argument: NodeLabelEditEventArgs, whose properties are listed in Table 14-16. These

---

[*] This slower method was shown in *Programming C#*, by Jesse Liberty (O'Reilly). Live and learn.

properties let you edit the text associated with a node and cancel the editing process, discarding any changes made to the text.

Table 14-13. TreeView events

Event	Event argument	Description
BeforeCheck	TreeViewCancelEventArgs	Raised before node checkbox is checked. Only raised if the Check-Boxes property is true.
BeforeCollapse	TreeViewCancelEventArgs	Raised before the node is collapsed.
BeforeExpand	TreeViewCancelEventArgs	Raised before the node is expanded.
BeforeLabelEdit	NodeLabelEditEventArgs	Raised before the node label is edited.
BeforeSelect	TreeViewCancelEventArgs	Raised before the node is selected. Only raised if the CheckBoxes property is false.
AfterCheck	TreeViewEventArgs	Raised after node check box is checked. Only raised if the Check-Boxes property is true.
AfterCollapse	TreeViewEventArgs	Raised after the node is collapsed.
AfterExpand	TreeViewEventArgs	Raised after the node is expanded.
AfterLabelEdit	NodeLabelEditEventArgs	Raised after the node label is edited.
AfterSelect	TreeViewEventArgs	Raised after the node is selected. Only raised if the CheckBoxes property is false.

Table 14-14. TreeViewCancelEventArgs and TreeViewEventArgs properties

Property	Description
Action	Returns the type of action that raised the event. Possible values are members of the TreeViewAction enumeration, listed in Table 14-15.
Cancel	TreeViewCancelEventArgs only. Read-write Boolean value indicating if event should be canceled. Inherited from CancelEventArgs.
Node	Returns the node that is checked, collapsed, expanded, or selected.

Table 14-15. TreeViewAction enumeration

Value	Description
ByKeyboard	Event caused by keystroke.
ByMouse	Event caused by mouse operation.
Collapse	Event caused by collapsing TreeNode.
Expand	Event caused by expanding TreeNode.
Unknown	Event cause is unknown.

Table 14-16. NodeLabelEditEventArgs properties

Property	Description
CancelEdit	Read-write Boolean value indicating if the edit has been canceled.
Label	Returns the new text associated with the node.
Node	Returns the node whose text is to be edited.

Look at the tvw_BeforeExpand event handler from Examples 14-3 and 14-4, reproduced here:

```csharp
private void tvw_BeforeExpand(object sender,
                             TreeViewCancelEventArgs e)
{
   tvw.BeginUpdate();
   foreach (TreeNode tn in e.Node.Nodes)
   {
      GetSubDirectoryNodes(tn, cb.Checked);
   }
   tvw.EndUpdate();
}
```

```vbnet
private sub tvw_BeforeExpand(ByVal sender as object, _
                            ByVal e as TreeViewCancelEventArgs)
   tvw.BeginUpdate()
   dim tn as TreeNode
   for each tn in e.Node.Nodes
      GetSubDirectoryNodes(tn, cb.Checked)
   next
   tvw.EndUpdate()
end sub
```

You see that the two passed-in arguments are an object, named Sender, representing the source of the event and an event argument of type TreeViewCancelEventArgs. The contents of the method are bookended by BeginUpdate and an EndUpdate method calls so that performance will not suffer when the call to GetSubDirectory-Nodes adds nodes to the tree.

The Nodes collection of the node that is about to be expanded is iterated via e.Node. Nodes—i.e., the Nodes collection of the Node property of the event argument e. For each node in this collection, GetSubDirectoryNodes is called, passing to it the current node in the iteration, as well as the value of the Show Files checkbox. This expands the tree one level deep at a time, which occurs nearly instantaneously for all but the most extensive hierarchies or the slowest network connections.

ListView

The ListView control displays a list of items, with optional icons and subitems associated with each. A ListView is used as the right pane in Windows Explorer, displaying the files and directories contained within the directory currently selected in the tree view in the left pane. The ListView class contains a number of useful properties, methods, and events, listed in Tables 14-17, 14-22, and 14-23, respectively.

The ListView control contains a collection of objects of type ListViewItem: the Items property (listed in Table 14-17, along with other commonly used ListView properties). The Items property itself is of type ListViewItemCollection, which has methods (listed in Table 14-30) for adding, inserting, removing, and otherwise manipulating items in the collection.

The ListViewItemCollection class implements the ICollection interface, the IList interface that derives from it, and the IEnumerable interface. The first two interfaces provide access to individual items via a zero-based index, and the IEnumerable interface provides the capability to iterate over the collection. Both features are central to the capabilities of the ListView, as seen below.

The ListView control can be viewed in one of four ways, specified by the ListView. View property: large icon, small icon, list, and detail. Valid values of the View property, corresponding to each of these view modes, are members of the View enumeration, listed and described in Table 14-21.

When the View property is set to either View.SmallIcon or View.List, the image displayed with each item is obtained from the image list specified by the SmallImage-List property. When the View property is set to View.LargeIcon, the images are obtained from the image list specified by the LargeImageList property. Typically, small images are displayed at 16 × 16 pixels (which is the default image size for an ImageList), while large images are typically displayed at anywhere from 32 to 64 pixels square. In all three view modes, the only information displayed with each item, in addition to an image, is the item's Text property.

 ImageLists are covered in Chapter 7. Remember that all the images in a particular ImageList display at the same size, specified in pixels by the ImageList.ImageSize property, and not dictated by the original size of the image.

When the View property is set to View.Details, the ListView displays columns containing subitems (pieces of information related to the item). In Windows Explorer, these subitems typically include the size and type of file and the last modified date. Although the Explorer UI allows the user to specify the subitems and order of columns, this capability is not native to the ListView control, but must be added programmatically. What is native to the control, and comes for free if the AllowColumnReorder property is set to true, is the ability for the user to reorder the columns at runtime simply by dragging a column to a new location relative to the other columns in the ListView.

One or more items in a ListView can be *selected*. If the MultiSelect property is set to true (the default value), then multiple items can be selected using the standard Windows techniques of selecting contiguous items by holding down the Shift key or noncontiguous items by holding down the Ctrl key. (If the HoverSelection property is set to true, then simply hovering the mouse over an item selects it.) Selected items typically display as highlighted.

In any case, the selected item (or items) are accessible through the SelectedItems and SelectedIndices properties. The SelectedItems property contains a read-only collection of the selected items and the SelectedIndices property contains a read-only collection of indexes of the selected items, either of which can be iterated to process the selection. When the selected item in a single-selection ListView changes, or when an item is selected or deselected in a multiple-selection ListView, then the SelectedIndexChanged event (described in Table 14-23) is raised. You can then process either the SelectedItems or the SelectedIndices collections in the event handler.

 Be aware that the SelectedIndexChanged event may be raised twice when selecting an item—once when the first item is deselected and again when the new selection is selected. To avoid duplicate event handling, test the SelectedIndices.Count property of the ListView (see Table 14-17 for a list of ListView properties) inside the event handler and do only the desired processing when the count is nonzero. That way, it will not process when the first item is deselected. For example:

```
private void listView1_SelectedIndexChanged
                    (object sender, EventArgs e)
{
    if (listView1.SelectedIndices.Count != 0)
    {
        // Do some processing here
    }
}
```

Item *activation* is closely related to item selection. When an item is activated, the ItemActivate event (described in Table 14-23) is raised, and again, the SelectedItems or the SelectedIndices properties can be processed in the event handler. Activation lets your program respond to user action, such as by opening a file.

The user action required to initiate activation is controlled by the Activation property, valid values of which are members of the ItemActivation enumeration, listed in Table 14-18. The default value, ItemActivation.Standard, specifies that double-clicking on the item activates it, but there is no visual cue to that effect. If the Activation property is set to either OneClick or TwoClick, then the mouse cursor changes to a hand pointer and the item text changes color when the mouse cursor passes over. OneClick gives browser-like functionality (similar to clicking on a hyperlink), and TwoClick is similar to the standard behavior, but with the visual cue and, more significantly, with two single clicks (the first click selects the item and the second click activates it) rather than one double-click causing activation. Irrespective of the value of the Activation property, pressing Enter effectively activates all the currently selected items.

It is also possible to display checkboxes with each list item by setting the CheckBoxes property to true. If this is the case, then the user can select items by clicking on the checkbox next to that item, allowing the user to select multiple items without using either the Ctrl or Shift keys.

If the CheckBoxes property is set to true, then multiple items can be selected even if the MultiSelect property is set to false.

Processing items selected with checkboxes is analogous to the behavior when checkboxes are disabled. The ItemCheck event (listed in Table 14-23) is raised whenever the check state of an item changes. The checked items can be accessed via the CheckedItems or CheckedIndices properties, both of which are read-only collections of items or indexes, respectively.

Table 14-17. ListView properties

Property	Value type	Description
Activation	ItemActivation	Read/write. Specifies how the user activates an item. Valid values are members of the ItemActivation enumeration, listed in Table 14-18. Default value is ItemActivation.Standard. If value is non-default, label editing will be disallowed, regardless of LabelEdit property value.
Alignment	ListViewAlignment	Read/write. Specifies the alignment of items in the control. Valid values are members of the ListViewAlignment enumeration, listed in Table 14-19. Default is ListViewAlignment.Top.
AllowColumnReorder	Boolean	Read/write. If false (the default), drag-and-drop column reordering at runtime is not allowed. Only applicable if View property is set to View.Details.
AutoArrange	Boolean	Read/write. If true (the default), icons are automatically arranged and snapped to grid to not overlap at runtime. Only applicable if View property is set to View.LargeIcon or View.SmallIcon.
BorderStyle	BorderStyle	Read/write. The border style of the control. Valid values are members of the BorderStyle enumeration, listed in Table 14-2. Default is BorderStyle.Fixed3D.
CheckBoxes	Boolean	Read/write. If true, a checkbox appears next to each item. User can then select items by clicking on the checkbox. Allows multiselection without use of the Ctrl key and even if MultiSelect property is false. ItemCheck event is raised when an item is checked. Default is false.
CheckedIndices	ListView.CheckedIndex-Collection	Read-only. Collection of indexes of the currently checked items. Returns an empty collection if no items are checked. Only applicable if CheckBoxes property is set to true.
CheckedItems	ListView.CheckedList-ViewItemCollection	Read-only. Collection of the currently checked items. Returns an empty collection if no items are checked. Only applicable if CheckBoxes property is set to true.
Columns	ListView.ColumnHeader-Collection	Read-only. Collection of ColumnHeader objects, each of which represents the a column header when the View property is set to View.Details. If no column headers are specified and View property is set to View.Details, no items will be displayed.
FocusedItem	ListViewItem	Read-only. The item that currently has focus. If no item has focus, returns null (Nothing).
ForeColor	Color	Read/write. Foreground color of the control. This is the color used to display the text of the item.

Table 14-17. *ListView properties (continued)*

Property	Value type	Description
FullRowSelect	Boolean	Read/write. If `true`, clicking an item selects all of its subitems. Default is `false`. Only applicable if View property is set to View. Details.
GridLines	Boolean	Read/write. If `true`, gridlines are displayed around items and sub-items. Default is `false`. Only applicable if View property is set to View.Details. These gridlines do not give users resizing functionality, as is the case in Microsoft Excel.
HeaderStyle	ColumnHeaderStyle	Read/write. Valid values are the members of the ColumnHeaderStyle enumeration, listed in Table 14-20. If set to ColumnHeaderStyle.Clickable (the default), header can respond to clicks. If set to ColumnHeaderStyle.None, the header will not be displayed. Only applicable if View property set to View.Details and the ColumnHeaderCollection is not empty.
HideSelection	Boolean	Read/write. If `true` (the default), the highlighting of the selected item disappears when the control does not have focus.
HoverSelection	Boolean	Read/write. If `true`, hovering mouse cursor over an item automatically selects it. Default is `false`.
Items	ListView.ListViewItem-Collection	Read-only. The collection of items in the control. Items can be added, removed, and otherwise manipulated from the collection using methods of the ListViewItemCollection class, listed in Table 14-30.
LabelEdit	Boolean	Read/write. If `true`, users can edit the item labels at runtime. Default is `false`.
LabelWrap	Boolean	Read/write. If `true` (the default), item labels will wrap when necessary if icons are displayed. Only applicable if View property is set to View.LargeIcon or ViewSmallIcon.
LargeImageList	ImageList	Read/write. The ImageList to use when the View property is set to View.LargeIcon.
ListViewItemSorter	IComparer	Read/write. The IComparer object used to perform sorting on the items in the ListView. Setting the value of this property allows the Sort method (described in Table 14-22) to be called.
MultiSelect	Boolean	Read/write. If `true` (the default), multiple items in the ListView can be selected.
Scrollable	Boolean	Read/write. If `true` (the default), scrollbars are added to the control as necessary.
SelectedIndices	ListView.SelectedIndex-Collection	Read-only. A collection of indexes of selected items. If no items are selected, an empty collection is returned. If the MultiSelect property is `false`, the collection contains at most a single item.
SelectedItems	ListView.SelectedList-ViewItemCollection	Read-only. A collection of selected items. If no items are selected, an empty collection is returned. If the MultiSelect property is `false`, the collection contains at most a single item.
SmallImageList	ImageList	Read/write. The ImageList to use when the View property is set to View.SmallIcon.
Sorting	SortOrder	Read/write. The sort order for the items in the control. Valid values are members of the SortOrder enumeration: Ascending, Descending, or None (the default).

Table 14-17. ListView properties (continued)

Property	Value type	Description
StateImageList	ImageList	Read/write. The ImageList used to display an application-defined state of an item. The state image is displayed for all values of the View property, to the left of the icon for the item.
		If the CheckBoxes property is `true`, then the image at index 0 is displayed instead of an unchecked box and the image at index 1 is used instead of a checked box.
Text	String	Read/write. The text string displayed with an item in the control.
TopItem	ListViewItem	Read-only. The first item visible in the control.
View	View	Read/write. Specifies how items are displayed in the control. Valid values are members of the View enumeration, listed in Table 14-21. Default is View.LargeIcon.

Table 14-18. ItemActivation enumeration values

Value	Description
OneClick	User single-clicks to activate the item. Mouse cursor changes to hand pointer and item text changes color as mouse cursor passes over the item.
Standard	User double-clicks to activate the item. No visual changes to item as mouse cursor passes over.
TwoClick	User double-clicks to activate the item, but the two clicks can have any duration between them. Item text changes color as mouse cursor passes over.

Table 14-19. ListViewAlignment enumeration values

Value	Description
Default	Item remains where dropped when moved by user.
Left	Items in ListView aligned to the left.
SnapToGrid	Items aligned to invisible grid when moved by user.
Top	Items in ListView aligned to the top.

Table 14-20. ColumnHeaderStyle enumeration values

Value	Description
Clickable	Column headers behave like buttons and can perform an action when clicked.
Nonclickable	Column headers do not behave like buttons, ignoring clicks.
None	Column headers not displayed and do not respond to clicks.

Table 14-21. View enumeration values

Value	Description
Details	Each item appears on a separate line with subitems arranged in columns.
LargeIcon	Each item appears with the specified icon from the image list specified in the LargeImageList property. The item label appears below the icon.

Table 14-21. View enumeration values (continued)

Value	Description
List	Items are arranged in columns with no column headers. Each item appears with the specified icon from the image list specified in the SmallImageList property. The item label appears to the right of the icon.
SmallIcon	Each item appears with the specified icon from the image list specified in the SmallImageList property. The item label appears to the right of the icon.

Table 14-22. ListView methods

Method	Description
ArrangeIcons	Overloaded. Arranges icons using either the default or specified alignment setting (possible values are members of the ListViewAlignment enumeration listed in Table 14-19) when the View property is set to View.LargeIcon or View.SmallIcon.
BeginUpdate	Prevents the control from repainting until the EndUpdate method is called. This improves performance and prevents flickering when adding multiple items by using the Add method.
Clear	Removes all items and columns from the control.
EnsureVisible	Ensures that the item with the specified index is visible in the control, scrolling as necessary.
EndUpdate	Causes the control to repaint after the BeginUpdate method has been called.
EnsureVisible	Ensures that the item with the specified zero-based index is visible, scrolling the control as necessary.
GetItemAt	Gets the item at the point specified by the X and Y client coordinates. Typically these coordinates are determined by a mouseclick.
GetItemRect	Overloaded. Gets either the bounding rectangle or the specified portion of the bounding rectangle for the item specified by the zero-based index.
Sort	Sorts the items in the ListView using the IComparer specified in the ListViewItemSorter property.

Table 14-23. ListView events

Event	Event argument	Description
ColumnClick	ColumnClickEventArgs	Raised when the user clicks a column header and the View property is set to View.Details. This is typically used to sort the items in the ListView by the clicked column.
		The ColumnClickEventArgs has a single property, Column, which returns the zero-based index of the clicked column.
AfterLabelEdit	LabelEditEventArgs	Raised after the label of a ListViewItem has been edited. The LabelEditEventArgs returns the properties listed in Table 14-24.
BeforeLabelEdit	LabelEditEventArgs	Raised before the label of a ListViewItem is about to be edited. The LabelEditEventArgs event argument returns the properties listed in Table 14-24. The ListView.Activation property must be set to Standard in order for this event to be raised and label editing to be allowed.
ItemActivate	EventArgs	Raised when an item is activated.
ItemCheck	ItemCheckEventArgs	Raised when the check state of an item changes. The ItemCheckEventArgs event argument returns the properties listed in Table 14-25. The ListView.CheckBoxes property must be set to true for this event to be raised

Table 14-23. ListView events (continued)

Event	Event argument	Description
ItemDrag	ItemDragEventArgs	Raised when the user begins dragging an item.
SelectedIndex-Changed	EventArgs	If MultiSelect property is `false`, this event is raised when there is a change in the index of the selected item. If MultiSelect property is `true`, this event is raised when an item is either selected or deselected.

Table 14-24. LabelEditEventArgs properties

Property	Description
CancelEdit	Read-write Boolean value indicating if the edit has been canceled.
Item	Returns the zero-based index of the ListViewItem whose label is to be edited.
Label	Returns the new text associated with the ListViewItem.

Table 14-25. ItemCheckEventArgs properties

Property	Description
CurrentValue	Returns the current state of the item's checkbox. Valid values are members of the CheckState enumeration, listed in Table 14-26.
Index	Zero-based index of the current item.
NewValue	Read/write. The new value of the item after the change takes effect. Valid values are members of the CheckState enumeration, listed in Table 14-26. This value can be changed in the event handler to override the user action.

Table 14-26. CheckState enumeration values

Value	Description
Checked	Item is checked.
Unchecked	Item is not checked.
Indeterminate	Item is neither checked nor unchecked. Appears shaded.

As mentioned earlier, each item in a ListView, i.e., each element of the Items collection, is an object of type ListViewItem. The ListViewItem class has seven different constructors. The argument list for each constructor is listed in Table 14-27. As you can see, there are many different ways to instantiate a new list item, depending upon what objects are currently available and whether subitems go with the item.

Table 14-27. ListViewItem constructors

C# argument list	VB.NET argument list	Description
No parameters	No parameters	Initializes a new instance with default values.
string	String	Initializes a new instance with the text specified in the string.
string[ ]	String( )	Initializes a new instance with subitems represented by the array of strings.

Table 14-27. ListViewItem constructors (continued)

C# argument list	VB.NET argument list	Description
ListViewItem. ListViewSubItem[ ], int	ListViewItem. ListViewSubItem( ), Integer	Initializes a new instance with the array of ListViewSubItem objects representing the subitems and an icon represented by the specified index into the appropriate image list.
string, int	String, Integer	Initializes a new instance with text specified in the string and an icon represented by the specified index into the appropriate image list.
string[ ], int	String( ), Integer	Initializes a new instance with subitems represented by the array of strings and an icon represented by the specified index into the appropriate image list.
string[ ], int, Color, Color, Font	String( ), Integer, Color, Color, Font	Initializes a new instance with subitems represented by the array of strings, an icon represented by the specified index into the appropriate image list, the foreground color, the background color, and the item's font.

In addition to the ListView properties listed in Table 14-17 that apply to the List-View as a whole, each item in the ListView has its own set of properties, listed in Table 14-28, and methods, listed in Table 14-29. So, for example, you can set the foreground color of each item programmatically, depending on some feature of that item, such as whether it exceeds a certain numeric value.

Table 14-28. ListViewItem properties

Property	Value type	Description
BackColor	Color	Read/write. Specifies the item's background color.
Bounds	Rectangle	Read-only. The item's bounding rectangle, including any subitems.
Checked	Boolean	Read/write. If the CheckBoxes property is set to true, then this property is true if the checkbox is checked. Default is false.
Focused	Boolean	Read/write. If true, the item has focus.
Font	Font	Read/write. Specifies the font of the text associated with the item.
ForeColor	Color	Read/write. Specifies the color of the item's text.
ImageIndex	Integer	Read/write. The zero-based index of the image, from the appropriate image list, displayed with the item.
ImageList	ImageList	Read-only. The image list that contains the image displayed with the item.
Index	Integer	Read-only. The zero-based index of the item within the control's ListView.ListViewItemCollection. Returns -1 if the item is not associated with a ListView control.
ListView	ListView	Read-only. The ListView control that contains the item.
Selected	Boolean	Read/write. If true, the item is selected.
StateImageIndex	Integer	Read/write. The zero-based index of the state image in the image list specified by the ListView.StateImageList property. Typically used to display images representing checked and unchecked states. Maximum value of StateImageIndex property is 14, but only the images at index 0 and 1 can be displayed as state images.

Table 14-28. ListViewItem properties (continued)

Property	Value type	Description
SubItems	ListViewItem.ListViewSubItem-Collection	Read-only. The collection containing the subitems for the item. The List-ViewSubItemCollection class contains methods (listed in Table 14-32) for manipulating the collection.
Tag	Object	Read/write. An object containing data associated with the item.
Text	String	Read/write. Specifies the text associated with the item.
UseItemStyleForSub-Items	Boolean	Read/write. If `true` (the default), the Font, ForeColor, and BackColor properties of the item will also apply to the item's subitems and changes to the appropriate ListViewSubItem properties are ignored.

Table 14-29. ListViewItem methods

Method	Description
BeginEdit	Places the item in edit mode so that the text associated with the item can be modified by the user. Only relevant if the LabelEdit property is set to `true`.
Clone	Creates a new instance of a ListViewItem, which is an identical copy of the original, including sub-items. Implements IClonable.Clone.
EnsureVisible	Similar to the ListView.EnsureVisible method. Scrolls the list as necessary to ensure that the item is visible. Often used to make visible any item that fails validation.
Remove	Removes the item from the ListView.

All ListViewItems in the control are contained within a collection of type ListView-ItemCollection. This collection has several methods that allow you to programmatically manipulate the collection, such as by adding one or more ListViewItems, removing one or more items, or finding the index of a specific item in the collection. The commonly used ListViewItemCollection methods are listed in Table 14-30.

Table 14-30. ListViewItemCollection methods

Method	Description
Add	Overloaded. Adds either a string or an existing ListViewItem to the collection. Returns the List-ViewItem object that was added to the collection.
AddRange	Removes all existing items from the ListView control and adds an array of ListViewItem objects to the collection.
Clear	Removes all the items from the collection. Implements IList.Clear.
Contains	Returns `true` if the specified ListViewItem is contained within the collection.
CopyTo	Copies the entire collection to the specified array at the index specified by the index. Implements ICollection.CopyTo.
IndexOf	Returns the zero-based index of the specified ListViewItem. If not found, returns −1.
Insert	Overloaded. Inserts and returns a ListViewItem with the specified text into the collection at the specified index, optionally using the image at the specified index of the appropriate image list.
Remove	Removes the specified ListViewItem from the collection.
RemoveAt	Removes the ListViewItem with the specified zero-based index from the collection.

If the ListView.View property is set to View.Details, then each item can have sub-items associated with it. For example, the ListView in Windows Explorer has an Items collection consisting of files and directories. The subitems typically displayed with each item are size, file type, and the last modified date. Each subitem has a set of properties, listed in Table 14-31.

Table 14-31. ListViewSubItem properties

Property	Value type	Description
BackColor	Color	Read/write. Specifies the background color of the subitem.
Font	Font	Read/write. Specifies the font of the text associated with the subitem.
ForeColor	Color	Read/write. Specifies the color of the subitem's text.
Text	string	Read/write. Specifies the text associated with the subitem.

All of the subitems associated with a ListViewItem are contained in a collection of type ListViewSubItemCollection. Analogously to the ListViewItemCollection class, this class also has methods for manipulating the subitems in the collection. The commonly used ListViewSubItemCollection methods are listed in Table 14-32.

Table 14-32. ListViewItem.ListViewSubItemCollection methods

Method	Description
Add	Overloaded. Adds either an existing ListViewSubItem, a string, or a string with specified colors and font to the collection. Returns the ListViewSubItem that was added to the collection.
AddRange	Overloaded. Removes all existing subitems from the parent ListViewItem and adds either an array of ListViewSubItem objects, an array of strings, or an array of strings with specified colors and font to the collection.
Clear	Removes all the subitems from the collection. Implements IList.Clear.
Contains	Returns `true` if the specified ListViewSubItem is contained within the collection.
IndexOf	Returns the zero-based index of the specified ListViewSubItem. If not found, returns -1.
Insert	Inserts an existing ListViewSubItem into the collection at the specified zero-based index.
Remove	Removes the specified ListViewSubItem from the collection.
RemoveAt	Removes the ListViewSubItem with the specified zero-based index from the collection.

Windows Explorer Clone

The best way to put all this together is to look at an example that uses the ListView in a real-world way. The code built up over the next several pages and shown in its entirety in Example 14-5 (in C#) and in Example 14-6 (in VB.NET) creates a clone of Windows Explorer, with a TreeView on the left side of the window and ListView on the right, separated by a splitter. The code creating and handling the TreeView is borrowed essentially intact from Example 14-3 (in C#) and Example 14-4 (in VB.NET).

Creating the form

Unlike the previous examples in this chapter, these examples are created by using Visual Studio .NET. When you create an Explorer clone in Visual Studio .NET, you add the controls to the form in the opposite order from when hand coding in a text editor: add the TreeView first, set its Dock property to Left, add the splitter, and then add ListView with its Dock property set to Fill.

To create this example, open Visual Studio .NET and create a new project by using the Windows Application template in the language of your choice. Resize the form so it is approximately 600 square pixels.

Drag a TreeView control from the toolbox onto the form. Rename the TreeView to tvw. Set its Dock property to Left.

Next, drag a splitter control onto the form. It will glom onto the right edge of the TreeView and its Dock property will default to Left. Since you will not refer to the splitter anywhere in your code, there is no need to rename the splitter control.

Finally, drag a ListView control onto the form. Rename the control to lv. Set its Dock property to Fill.

If you now build and run the project, you will get a form similar to Windows Explorer, except with no content. However, the splitter is functional and will resize the two panes of the window. Next, add code to add the Explorer functionality.

Right-click on Form1.cs or Form1.vb in the Solution Explorer and click on View Code. The code will be displayed for editing. If you are working in C#, add the following two statements at the top of the code:

C#
```
using System.IO;
using System.Diagnostics;
```

If you are working in VB.NET, add the following import statement at the top of the code, above the Form1 class declaration:

VB
```
imports System.IO;
```

 VB.NET automatically imports the System.Diagnostics namespace, so it is not necessary to do so explicitly. The namespaces that are imported by default can be seen in the Project Property Pages by right-clicking on the project in Solution Explorer, selecting Properties, and clicking on Imports under Common Properties.

The three controls on the form are initialized in the InitializeComponent method created for you by Visual Studio .NET and called from within the constructor—Form1() in C# and New() in VB.NET. However, there is more work required on form initialization, so you will add code to the constructor to do that work after the call to InitializeComponent.

First create two image lists—one for small images and the other for large images. The ListView will use both image lists, and the TreeView will also use the small image list. The code to create these image lists resembles that used previously in Example 14-3 (in C#) and Example 14-4 (in VB.NET). Add the following code to the appropriate constructor:

C#
```csharp
String[ ] arFiles = {
    @"C:\Program Files\Microsoft Visual Studio .NET 2003\Common7\" +
        @"Graphics\icons\computer\form.ico",
    @"C:\Program Files\Microsoft Visual Studio .NET 2003\Common7\" +
        @"Graphics\icons\win95\clsdfold.ico",
    @"C:\Program Files\Microsoft Visual Studio .NET 2003\Common7\" +
        @"Graphics\icons\win95\openfold.ico",
    @"C:\Program Files\Microsoft Visual Studio .NET 2003\Common7\" +
        @"Graphics\bitmaps\assorted\happy.bmp",
    @"C:\Program Files\Microsoft Visual Studio .NET 2003\Common7\" +
        @"Graphics\bitmaps\outline\NoMask\doc.bmp",
    @"C:\Program Files\Microsoft Visual Studio .NET 2003\Common7\" +
        @"Graphics\bitmaps\outline\NoMask\exe.bmp",
    @"C:\Program Files\Microsoft Visual Studio .NET 2003\Common7\" +
        @"Graphics\bitmaps\outline\NoMask\txt.bmp",
    @"C:\Program Files\Microsoft Visual Studio .NET 2003\Common7\" +
        @"Graphics\bitmaps\outline\NoMask\windoc.bmp"
};
ImageList imgListSmall = new ImageList( );  // default size 16x16
ImageList imgListLarge = new ImageList( );
imgListLarge.ImageSize = new Size(32,32);
for (int i = 0; i < arFiles.Length; i++)
{
    imgListSmall.Images.Add(Image.FromFile(arFiles[i]));
    imgListLarge.Images.Add(Image.FromFile(arFiles[i]));
}
```

VB
```vbnet
dim arFiles( ) as string = { _
    "C:\Program Files\Microsoft Visual Studio .NET 2003\Common7\" + _
        "Graphics\icons\computer\form.ico", _
    "C:\Program Files\Microsoft Visual Studio .NET 2003\Common7\" + _
        "Graphics\icons\win95\clsdfold.ico", _
    "C:\Program Files\Microsoft Visual Studio .NET 2003\Common7\" + _
        "Graphics\icons\win95\openfold.ico", _
    "C:\Program Files\Microsoft Visual Studio .NET 2003\Common7\" + _
        "Graphics\bitmaps\assorted\happy.bmp", _
    "C:\Program Files\Microsoft Visual Studio .NET 2003\Common7\" + _
        "Graphics\bitmaps\outline\NoMask\doc.bmp", _
    "C:\Program Files\Microsoft Visual Studio .NET 2003\Common7\" + _
        "Graphics\bitmaps\outline\NoMask\exe.bmp", _
    "C:\Program Files\Microsoft Visual Studio .NET 2003\Common7\" + _
        "Graphics\bitmaps\outline\NoMask\txt.bmp", _
    "C:\Program Files\Microsoft Visual Studio .NET 2003\Common7\" + _
        "Graphics\bitmaps\outline\NoMask\windoc.bmp"}

dim imgListSmall as new ImageList( )        ' default size 16x16
```

```
dim imgListLarge as new ImageList( )
imgListLarge.ImageSize = new Size(32,32)

dim i as Integer
for i = 0 to arFiles.Length - 1
   imgListSmall.Images.Add(Image.FromFile(arFiles(i)))
   imgListLarge.Images.Add(Image.FromFile(arFiles(i)))
next
```

This code first creates an array of strings, with each string containing the full path and filename of an image file found as part of the standard Visual Studio .NET installation. It then instantiates and populates two image lists. imgListSmall retains the default size of 16 × 16 pixels, while the size of the images in imgListLarge is set to 32 square pixels.

Next, add several lines to set additional properties of the TreeView. Add these lines of code:

C#

```
tvw.Size = new Size(ClientSize.Width / 3, ClientSize.Height);
tvw.BackColor = Color.Moccasin;
tvw.HideSelection = false;
tvw.ImageList = imgListSmall;
tvw.ImageIndex = 1;
tvw.SelectedImageIndex = 2;
```

VB

```
tvw.Size = new Size(ClientSize.Width / 3, ClientSize.Height)
tvw.BackColor = Color.Moccasin
tvw.HideSelection = false
tvw.ImageList = imgListSmall
tvw.ImageIndex = 1
tvw.SelectedImageIndex = 2
```

You have previously dragged a ListView control onto the form in the design view and renamed it lv. Now you must add the following lines of code to set additional properties for that ListView. All of these properties are described in Table 14-17. Several of the properties are set to default values, primarily for self-documentation. This code is identical in both languages, except for the trailing semicolon in C# and different comment characters.

C#

```
lv.BackColor = Color.PaleTurquoise;
lv.ForeColor = Color.DarkBlue;
lv.HideSelection = false;
lv.SmallImageList = imgListSmall;
lv.LargeImageList = imgListLarge;
lv.View = View.SmallIcon;
lv.Activation = ItemActivation.TwoClick;
lv.MultiSelect = true;           // default
lv.HoverSelection = false;       // default
lv.Sorting = SortOrder.None;     // default
lv.AllowColumnReorder = true;
lv.FullRowSelect = true;
lv.GridLines = true;
lv.HeaderStyle = ColumnHeaderStyle.Clickable;        // default
```

The next line of code calls to the FillDirectoryTree method, which fills the TreeView control with the directory structure from the filesystem. This method is identical to that used in Examples 14-3 and 14-4, and described with those examples.

C#
```
FillDirectoryTree( );
```

The FillDirectoryTree method calls the GetSubDirectoryNodes method, which is also identical to that used in Examples 14-3 and 14-4. A third method borrowed from Examples 14-3 and 14-4 is tvw_BeforeExpand. The only difference between these methods in this example and in Examples 14-3 and 14-4 is that the TreeView example had a checkbox to indicate whether the GetSubDirectoryNodes would get filenames as well as directory names. The value of this checkbox is passed as a parameter to GetSubDirectoryNodes. In the current examples, that value is hard-coded to false, since the TreeView in the left pane never displays files and the check-box is not present in this program.

The previously mentioned method tvw_BeforeExpand handles the TreeView Before-Expand event. Visual Studio .NET eases the chore of creating the event handler and adding it to the event delegate.

Setting events

In C#, go to the design view of the form, click on the tree view (which has already been named tvw) on the form, and click on the yellow lightning bolt in the Properties window. All possible events for tvw will be listed in the Properties window. Find the BeforeExpand event and double-click on the empty field next to it. This will automatically fill in the event handler name as tvw_BeforeExpand, insert a line in the InitializeComponent method to add the event handler to the event delegate, and create an empty code skeleton for the event handler method. Then you can just copy the code from Example 14-3, with the minor change of hardcoding the second parameter to the GetSubDirectoryNodes method to false.

In VB.NET, the procedure is different. Go to the code page, click on the drop-down menu at the top left of the code window, and select tvw from the list of objects in the class. Then click on the drop-down menu at the top right of the code window, which displays a list of all the events for that control. Select BeforeExpand. This will automatically create the requisite code skeleton with the necessary Handles keyword to implement the event handling. Again, copy the code from Example 14-4 with the minor change of hard-coding the second parameter to the GetSubDirectoryNodes method to false.

Creating the menus

The next task is to create a simple menuing system for the application, consisting of a View menu item with four subitems: Small Icons, Large Icons, List, and Details, corresponding to the four values of the View property listed in Table 14-21. (Menus will be covered in detail in Chapter 18.)

To create the menu, go to design view and drag a MainMenu control onto the form. It will display at the bottom of the design window as MainMenu1, and a field will be visible in the form's menu area with the legend Type Here. Type in &View. The leading ampersand will cause the V to display underlined when the program runs and act as a shortcut key. When you press Enter, there will be two Type Here's displayed; click on the one below and type in &Small Icons. After pressing Enter, continue typing in the following submenu items: &Large Icons, Lis&t, and &Details. Click back on the each menu subitem, in turn, and change the name of each in the Properties window, respectively to mnuSmallIcons, mnuLargeIcons, mnuList, and mnuDetails.

The final step is clicking on the form itself, and then going to the Properties window and setting the Menu property of the form to MainMenu1.

You will now create a single event handler method to handle the Click event for all the subitems, called mnuView_Click.

> Events are discussed in detail in Chapter 4. In that chapter, the differences in implementing events in C# versus VB.NET is explained.

In C#, add the following code to the Form1 class:

```csharp
private void mnuView_Click(object sender, EventArgs e)
{
    MenuItem mnu = (MenuItem)sender;
    switch (mnu.Mnemonic.ToString())
    {
        case "L"  :      // Large Icons
            lv.View = View.LargeIcon;
            break;
        case "S"  :      // Small Icons
            lv.View = View.SmallIcon;
            break;
        case "T" :      // List view
            lv.View = View.List;
            break;
        case "D" :      // Detail view
            lv.View = View.Details;
            break;
    }
}
```

In VB.NET, the event handler looks like the following:

```vbnet
private sub mnuView_Click(ByVal sender As Object, ByVal e As EventArgs) _
    Handles mnuDetails.Click, mnuLargeIcons.Click, mnuList.Click, _
        mnuSmallIcons.Click
dim mnu as New MenuItem
mnu = CType(sender, MenuItem)
select case (mnu.Mnemonic.ToString())
    case "L"  :        ' Large Icons
```

```
                lv.View = View.LargeIcon
            case "S"  :      '  Small Icons
                lv.View = View.SmallIcon
            case "T" :       '  List view
                lv.View = View.List
            case "D" :        '  Detail view
                lv.View = View.Details
        end select
    end sub
```

Once the event handler is in place, you can now assign that event handler to each menu subitem. In C#, this is done with the following sequence of steps:

1. Click on the yellow lightning bolt in the Properties window.

2. Click on each menu subitem in turn.

3. For each menu subitem, click on the drop-down arrow next to the Click event.

4. Select mnuView_Click.

In VB.NET, these steps not necessary. Adding the Handles keyword to the event handler declaration and listing the events to be handled by the method is all that is necessary to hook the event handler to those events. Alternatively, you could omit the Handles keyword and instead add the following AddHandler statements back in the constructor:

```
AddHandler mnuSmallIcons.Click, AddressOf mnuView_Click
AddHandler mnuLargeIcons.Click, AddressOf mnuView_Click
AddHandler mnuList.Click, AddressOf mnuView_Click
AddHandler mnuDetails.Click, AddressOf mnuView_Click
```

Populating the ListView

If you run the program at this point, it will work well, except that the ListView on the right side will never be populated. To implement that functionality, the program must respond to a selection in the tree view on the left. This is done by handling the TreeView AfterSelect event.

In C#, go to the Design view, click on the TreeView control, and then the yellow lightning bolt in the Properties window. Click on the space next to the AfterSelect event. The default method name tvw_AfterSelect will be filled in, and you will be taken to a code skeleton for that event handler. Enter the following code in the method:

```
private void tvw_AfterSelect(object sender,
                            TreeViewEventArgs e)
{
    lv.Clear();
    lv.BeginUpdate();

    DirectoryInfo di = new DirectoryInfo(e.Node.FullPath);
    FileSystemInfo[] afsi = di.GetFileSystemInfos();
    foreach (FileSystemInfo fsi in afsi)
    {
```

```csharp
        ListViewItem lvi = new ListViewItem(fsi.Name);

        if ((fsi.Attributes & FileAttributes.Directory) != 0)
        {
           lvi.ImageIndex = 1;
           lvi.SubItems.Add("");           // Bytes subitem
        }
        else
        {
           switch(fsi.Extension.ToUpper())
           {
              case ".DOC" :
                 lvi.ImageIndex = 4;
                 break;
              case ".EXE" :
                 lvi.ImageIndex = 5;
                 break;
              case ".TXT" :
                 lvi.ImageIndex = 6;
                 break;
              default :
                 lvi.ImageIndex = 7;
                 break;
           }
           // Bytes subitem, w/ commas
           // Cast FileSystemInfo object to FileInfo object so the size
           //    can be obtained.
           lvi.SubItems.Add(((FileInfo)fsi).Length.ToString("N0"));
        }

        // Add the remaining subitems to the ListViewItem
        lvi.SubItems.Add(fsi.Extension);                    // type
        lvi.SubItems.Add(fsi.LastWriteTime.ToString());     // modified

        // Build up the Attributes string
        string strAtt = "";
        if ((fsi.Attributes & FileAttributes.ReadOnly) != 0)
           strAtt += "R";
        if ((fsi.Attributes & FileAttributes.Hidden) != 0)
           strAtt += "H";
        if ((fsi.Attributes & FileAttributes.System) != 0)
           strAtt += "S";
        if ((fsi.Attributes & FileAttributes.Archive) != 0)
           strAtt += "A";
        lvi.SubItems.Add(strAtt);                    // attributes

        lv.Items.Add(lvi);
     }  // end foreach

     lv.Columns.Add("Name", 150, HorizontalAlignment.Left);
     lv.Columns.Add("Bytes", 75, HorizontalAlignment.Right);
     lv.Columns.Add("Ext.", 50, HorizontalAlignment.Left);
```

```csharp
        lv.Columns.Add("Modified", 125, HorizontalAlignment.Left);
        lv.Columns.Add("Attrib.", 50, HorizontalAlignment.Left);

        lv.EndUpdate();
    }                           // close tvw_AfterSelect
```

In VB.NET, go to the code window. Click on the drop-down menu at the top left of the window, select tvw, then click on the drop-down menu at the top right of the window. Click on AfterSelect. It will take you to a code skeleton for the event handler. Here is the code for the tvw_AfterSelect method in VB.NET:

```vbnet
    Private Sub tvw_AfterSelect(ByVal sender As Object, _
                    ByVal e As System.Windows.Forms.TreeViewEventArgs) _
                    Handles tvw.AfterSelect
        lv.Clear()
        lv.BeginUpdate()

        dim di as new DirectoryInfo(e.Node.FullPath)
        dim afsi() as FileSystemInfo
        afsi = di.GetFileSystemInfos()    ' both files & directories

        dim fsi as FileSystemInfo
        for each fsi in afsi
            dim lvi as new ListViewItem(fsi.Name)

            if ((fsi.Attributes and FileAttributes.Directory) <> 0) then
                lvi.ImageIndex = 1
                lvi.SubItems.Add("")          ' Bytes subitem
            else
                select case (fsi.Extension.ToUpper())
                    case ".DOC" :
                        lvi.ImageIndex = 4
                    case ".EXE" :
                        lvi.ImageIndex = 5
                    case ".TXT" :
                        lvi.ImageIndex = 6
                    case else :
                        lvi.ImageIndex = 7
                end select
                '  Bytes subitem, w/ commas
                '  Cast FileSystemInfo object to FileInfo object so
                '     the size can be obtained.
                lvi.SubItems.Add(CType(fsi,FileInfo).Length.ToString("N0"))
            end if

            '  Add the remaining subitems to the ListViewItem
            lvi.SubItems.Add(fsi.Extension)                   ' type
            lvi.SubItems.Add(fsi.LastWriteTime.ToString())    ' modified

            '  Build up the Attributes string
            dim strAtt as String = ""
            if ((fsi.Attributes and FileAttributes.ReadOnly) <> 0) then
                strAtt += "R"
            end if
```

```
              if ((fsi.Attributes & FileAttributes.Hidden) <> 0) then
                  strAtt += "H"
              end if
              if ((fsi.Attributes & FileAttributes.System) <> 0) then
                  strAtt += "S"
              end if
              if ((fsi.Attributes & FileAttributes.Archive) <> 0) then
                  strAtt += "A"
              end if
              lvi.SubItems.Add(strAtt)                         ' attributes

              lv.Items.Add(lvi)
          next    '  end foreach

        lv.Columns.Add("Name", 150, HorizontalAlignment.Left)
        lv.Columns.Add("Bytes", 75, HorizontalAlignment.Right)
        lv.Columns.Add("Ext.", 50, HorizontalAlignment.Left)
        lv.Columns.Add("Modified", 125, HorizontalAlignment.Left)
        lv.Columns.Add("Attrib.", 50, HorizontalAlignment.Left)

        lv.EndUpdate( )
    End Sub
```

The tvw_AfterSelect method begins by calling the ListView.Clear method to remove all the preexisting items and columns from the control. It then calls the BeginUpdate method, which prevents the control from repainting until the EndUpdate method is called after all the ListViewItems have been added. This prevents flicker.

The goal of the AfterSelect event handler is to populate the right pane with all the directories and files contained in the directory currently selected in the left pane. To do this, a DirectoryInfo object called di is instantiated from the current TreeView node. The TreeViewEventArgs passed to the event handler has a Node property, of type TreeNode, that contains the node just selected. That TreeNode itself has a Full-Path property that returns the entire path from the root of the tree.

This DirectoryInfo object represented by the tree node calls the GetFileSystemInfos instance method to return an array of FileSystemInfo objects contained by the directory represented by that node. The key fact here is that the FileSystemInfo class is the base class for both FileInfo and DirectoryInfo objects, i.e., the array contains all the files and directories contained in the node.

Iterate through this array of FileSystemInfo objects, adding each directory or file in turn to the ListView. You also add the subitems for each object, used when the List-View is displayed in Details mode.

The processing of each FileSystemInfo object begins by instantiating a new ListVie-wItem object, given the Name property of the FileSystemInfo object. This will constitute the text displayed for that item. As shown in Table 14-27, ListViewItem has seven different constructors; this example uses the one that takes a single string as a parameter.

Next, assign the appropriate image for each item. This depends on whether the item is a directory or a file, and if a file, on the file extension.

The if statement tests to see if the object is a file or a directory, using the Attributes property of the FileSystemObject, similarly to how it was done in the TreeView examples in Example 14-3 and Example 14-4. The Attributes property is a bitwise combination of FileAttributes enumeration members, listed in Table 14-12. These attributes pertain to either files or directories. The current node's Attributes property is logically AND'ed with the Directory value of the FileAttributes enumeration: if the result is zero, then the node is not a file; otherwise, it is a directory:

C#
```
if ((fsi.Attributes & FileAttributes.Directory) != 0)
```

VB
```
if ((fsi.Attributes and FileAttributes.Directory) <> 0) then
```

If it is a directory, then the ImageIndex is set to 1—i.e., the second image in the current image list (either imgListSmall or imgListLarge, depending on the current View mode; both image lists should have corresponding images so itdisplays correctly). At the same time, the first subitem, representing the Bytes column, is set to an empty string, since Explorer does not display the byte size of directories.

On the other hand, if the object is a file, then the image is set according to the type of file, based on the file extension. This program uses a limited selection of file types, while a real-world application would obviously use a more extensive list.

Adding SubItems to the ListView

The size subitem is added by casting the FileSystemInfo object to a FileInfo object, and then calling the ToString method on the FileInfo.Length property. This usage of the ToString method passes in a formatting string, N0 (i.e., N followed by a zero) to format the Bytes column with commas (a feature that Windows Explorer ought to incorporate):

C#
```
lvi.SubItems.Add((((FileInfo)fsi).Length.ToString("N0"));
```

VB
```
lvi.SubItems.Add(CType(fsi,FileInfo).Length.ToString("N0"))
```

Irrespective of whether the FileSystemInfo object is a file or a directory, three more subitem columns are added: the file extension, the time stamp for when the file or directory was last modified, and an attribute string. The latter is built up by logically AND'ing the Attributes property with each relevant member of the FileAttributes enumeration (as was done initially to determine if the FileSystemInfo object was a file or a directory) and concatenating string values, if the attribute is present for the object.

Once the subitems are added for all the ListViewItems, only then can you add the ColumnHeader objects to the Columns property. This is done using the Add method of the ListView.ColumnHeaderCollection class. This method had two overloaded forms. The first adds a ColumnHeader object, specified as a parameter. The second, used here, takes three arguments: a string displaying as the column header text, an integer specifying the initial width of the column in pixels, and a member of the HorizontalAlignment enumeration, listed in Table 12-10 of Chapter 12. In both languages, except for the trailing semicolon, the code is as follows:

```
lv.Columns.Add("Name", 150, HorizontalAlignment.Left);
lv.Columns.Add("Bytes", 75, HorizontalAlignment.Right);
lv.Columns.Add("Ext.", 50, HorizontalAlignment.Left);
lv.Columns.Add("Modified", 125, HorizontalAlignment.Left);
lv.Columns.Add("Attrib.", 50, HorizontalAlignment.Left);
```

Notice that the first column is always the ListViewItem itself and the second column is the first added subitem.

The last line of code in the tvw_AfterSelect method is a call to the EndUpdate method, which allows the ListView to redraw itself.

The program is now getting close to the real Windows Explorer. When run, it displays the two panes with the tree on the left and the list on the right, separated by a splitter. The View menu lets you set the display mode of the ListView, and when viewed in Details mode, it displays the columns of subitems you would expect. The user can resize the columns by dragging the sides of the column headers or by double-clicking the side of a column header, and the columns can be dragged to a different order. However, the program is missing some of the functionality one expects, such as the ability to open a file by double-clicking on it and the ability to sort the items by clicking on a column header. This functionality will be added next.

Activation

As described earlier, activation lets your program respond to user action, such as by opening a file.

In the constructor, you included the following line of code that set the ListView Activation property to ItemActivation.TwoClick, which is not the default behavior.

```
lv.Activation = ItemActivation.TwoClick;
```

Creating the event handler in Visual Studio .NET is slightly different, depending on the language in use. In C#, go to the Design view, click on the ListView, and then click on the yellow lightning bolt in the Properties window. Scroll to and double-click on the ItemActivate item in the list. That will automatically fill in the default event handler name, lv_ItemActivate, and create a code skeleton for the method in the code window. Then enter the following highlighted code in the code skeleton:

```
private void lv_ItemActivate(object sender, EventArgs e)
{
    ListView lv = (ListView)sender;
    foreach (ListViewItem lvi in lv.SelectedItems)
    {
        try
```

```
        {
            Process.Start(tvw.SelectedNode.FullPath + "\\" + lvi.Text);
        }
        catch
        {
        }
    }
}
```

In VB.NET, go to the code window, click on the drop-down menu at the upper left of the window, and select the ListView object, lv. Then click on the drop-down menu at the upper right of the window and select the ItemActivate event. A code skeleton will be created for that event. Enter the following highlighted code in the code skeleton:

```
Private Sub lv_ItemActivate(ByVal sender As Object, _
                            ByVal e As System.EventArgs) _
                            Handles lv.ItemActivate
    lv = CType(sender, ListView)
    dim lvi as ListViewItem
    for each lvi in lv.SelectedItems
        try
            Process.Start(tvw.SelectedNode.FullPath + "\" + lvi.Text)
        catch
        end try
    next
End Sub
```

In either language, a ListView object is cast from the object sender passed in to the event handler. Then the SelectedItems collection of that ListView is iterated in a foreach (for each) loop. For each selected item, a fully qualified filename is constructed from the Node.FullPath property of the TreeView's SelectedNode property and the current ListViewItem's Text property. This filename used is a parameter for the static Process.Start method, which will open the default application for files with the specific extension. Files with an extension of *txt* will open with Notepad, files with an extension of *htm* will open in a browser, and files with extensions of *exe* will execute.

Sorting by Text property

The items in the ListView can be sorted automatically by setting the Sorting property. If the Sorting property is set to the default value of SortOrder.None, then no sorting occurs. The other two valid values are SortOrder.Ascending or SortOrder. Descending. The latter two values sort the items alphabetically by the item's Text property. In the example in this section, the Sorting property has been set to the default value of SortOrder.None.

```
    lv.Sorting = SortOrder.None;   // default
```

This is appropriate for a list of files and directories, since the order in which they appear in the list will be the order they are presented in the FileSystemInfo array (directories first, in alphabetical order followed by files in alphabetical order). If the Sorting property were to be set to either of the other two values, then the files and directories would be interspersed.

Sorting by clicking on a column

A common feature of ListViews is the ability to sort the list by any one of the columns in Details mode simply by clicking on the column header. Each time the column header is clicked again, the sort order toggles. In any case, the used sort algorithm is appropriate to the type of data in that subitem, whether it be a text string, a number, or a date. Although the ListView control provides several capabilities to the developer for free, this, unfortunately, is not one of them. However, it does provide the hooks that let you implement your own sorting.

Follow these steps to sort the items in a ListView by column:

1. Handle the ListView.ColumnClick event when the user clicks on the column header.

2. Set up for and call the ListView Sort method.

You will handle that second step first.

In Table 14-22, you see that the Sort method sorts the items in the ListView using the IComparer object specified in the ListViewItemSorter property. The IComparer interface provides a single method, Compare, which compares two objects and returns a value (listed in Table 14-33), depending upon how the objects compare. How the items are compared, and which is greater, is up to you to implement.

Table 14-33. IComparer.Compare return values

Comparison	Return value
First object less than second object	Less than zero
First object equals second object	Zero
First object greater than second object	Greater than zero

Before the Sort method can be called, an IComparer object must be created and the ListViewItemSorter property must be set to an instance of that IComparer object. To do this, you will create a nested class within the Form1 class that implements the IComparer interface:

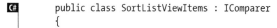

```
public class SortListViewItems : IComparer
{
```

VB

```
public class SortListViewItems
    implements IComparer
```

This class will have three private member variables that contain the index of the column being sorted, the type of data contained in the column (described shortly)—e.g., string data, DateTime data, or numeric data—and a Boolean that indicates whether the column should be sorted in ascending or descending order:

C#
```
int columnIndex;
ColumnType columnType;
bool isAscending;
```

VB
```
dim columnIndex as Integer
dim colType as ColumnType
dim isAscending as Boolean
```

The class will also have a number of public static (shared in VB.NET) Boolean variables to keep track of the current sort order for each column. These variables allow each successive click on a specific column header to toggle the sort order from ascending to descending and back:

C#
```
public static Boolean isNameAscending = true;
public static Boolean isBytesAscending = false;
public static Boolean isExtAscending = false;
public static Boolean isModifiedAscending = false;
public static Boolean isAttribAscending = false;
```

VB
```
public shared isNameAscending as Boolean = true
public shared isBytesAscending as Boolean = false
public shared isExtAscending as Boolean = false
public shared isModifiedAscending as Boolean = false
public shared isAttribAscending as Boolean = false
```

The constructor for the class takes three parameters and uses them to set the private member variables:

C#
```
public SortListViewItems(int columnIndex,
                         ColumnType columnType,
                         bool isAscending)
{
   this.columnIndex = columnIndex;
   this.columnType = columnType;
   this.isAscending = isAscending;
}
```

VB
```
public sub New(columnIndex as Integer, _
               colType as ColumnType, _
               isAscending as Boolean)
   me.columnIndex = columnIndex
   me.colType = colType
   me.isAscending = isAscending
End Sub
```

Now comes the meat of the matter—the Compare method, which compares two objects and returns a value that indicates their relative order, as listed in Table 14-33.

The criteria used to compare the two objects depends on the type of data in the column: e.g., a numeric value sorts differently from a text value. Consider the following literal values:

1
2
10

If they were sorted according to their numeric value, they would be in the order shown above. If they were to be sorted as text strings, then they would be in this order:

1
10
2

It is up to your Compare method to implement the correct sort algorithm. The type of data in the column must be passed as a parameter to the constructor and used by the Compare method to determine which sorting algorithm to use.

Three column types are possible in this application, and are specified in a public enumeration called ColumnType, declared in the Form1 class:

C#

```
public enum ColumnType
{
    Alpha,
    Numeric,
    DateTimeValue
}
```

VB

```
public enum ColumnType
    Alpha
    Numeric
    DateTimeValue
end enum
```

The Compare method is never explicitly called in the code. However, when the Sort method is called on the ListView after the ListViewItemSorter property is set to the IComparer object (as seen in more detail shortly), the Compare method is called implicitly to compare each successive pair of items in the list and place them in the proper order.

The SortListViewItems class's Compare method is declared with two parameters of type Object, as required by the IComparer interface:

C#

```
public int Compare(object x, object y)
{
```

VB

```
public function Compare(x as Object, y as Object) as Integer _
                        implements IComparer.Compare
```

A string representation of each object is obtained by first casting the object as a List-ViewItem, and then getting the Text property of the appropriate column (indexed by the columnIndex member variable, passed in via the constructor) from the SubItems collection:

C#
```
string strFirst = ((ListViewItem)x).SubItems[columnIndex].Text;
string strSecond = ((ListViewItem)y).SubItems[columnIndex].Text;
```

VB
```
dim strFirst as String = _
    (CType(x,ListViewItem)).SubItems(columnIndex).Text
dim strSecond as String = _
    (CType(y,ListViewItem)).SubItems(columnIndex).Text
```

The ColumnType, passed in via the constructor, is used in a switch block (select case in VB.NET) to return the correct value, depending on the type of data in the column:

C#
```
switch (columnType)
{
    case ColumnType.Alpha :
        if (isAscending)
            return strFirst.CompareTo(strSecond);
        else
            return strSecond.CompareTo(strFirst);
    case ColumnType.DateTimeValue :
        if (isAscending)
            return
                DateTime.Parse(strFirst).CompareTo(DateTime.Parse(strSecond));
        else
            return
                DateTime.Parse(strSecond).CompareTo(DateTime.Parse(strFirst));
    case ColumnType.Numeric :
        //  Special case blank byte values.
        if (strFirst == "")
            strFirst = "-1";
        if (strSecond == "")
            strSecond = "-1";

        if (isAscending)
            return Double.Parse(strFirst).CompareTo(Double.Parse(strSecond));
        else
            return
                Double.Parse(strSecond).CompareTo(Double.Parse(strFirst));
    default:
        return 0;
}
```

VB
```
select case colType
    case ColumnType.Alpha
        if isAscending then
            return strFirst.CompareTo(strSecond)
        else
```

```
                return strSecond.CompareTo(strFirst)
            end if
        case ColumnType.DateTimeValue
            if isAscending
                return _
                    DateTime.Parse(strFirst).CompareTo(DateTime.Parse(strSecond))
            else
                return _
                    DateTime.Parse(strSecond).CompareTo(DateTime.Parse(strFirst))
            end if
        case ColumnType.Numeric
            '   Special case blank byte values.
            if strFirst = "" then
                strFirst = "-1"
            end if
            if strSecond = "" then
                strSecond = "-1"
            end if
            if isAscending then
                return _
                    Double.Parse(strFirst).CompareTo(Double.Parse(strSecond))
            else
                return _
                    Double.Parse(strSecond).CompareTo(Double.Parse(strFirst))
            end if
        case else
            return 0
    End Select
```

In the case of the DateTimeValue column type, the DateTime.Parse method converts the string value to a DateTime value, and in the case of the Numeric column type, the Double.Parse method is used. In all cases, the native data types represented by the ColumnType enumeration—string, double, and DateTime—are .NET value types. All value types implement a CompareTo method that behaves the same as the Compare method, returning a value based on the relative value of the two operands, as listed in Table 14-33.

Now that the IComparer object is ready, you can implement the event handler for the ColumnClick event. This is done as it was for previous event handlers in Visual Studio .NET. In C#, click on the ListView in design view, and then the lightning bolt in the Properties window, and then double-click the ColumnClick event. In VB.NET, select lv from the left drop-down menu at the top of the code window, and then select the ColumnClick event from the right drop-down menu.

In either language, a code skeleton for the event handler will be created. Add the highlighted code shown here:

```
private void lv_ColumnClick(object sender, ColumnClickEventArgs e)
{
    ColumnType columnType;
    bool isAscending = true;
    string strName = ((ListView)sender).Columns[e.Column].Text;
    switch(strName)
```

```csharp
        {
            case "Name":
                columnType = ColumnType.Alpha;
                SortListViewItems.isNameAscending =
                        !SortListViewItems.isNameAscending;
                isAscending = SortListViewItems.isNameAscending;
                break;
            case "Bytes":
                columnType = ColumnType.Numeric;
                SortListViewItems.isBytesAscending =
                        !SortListViewItems.isBytesAscending;
                isAscending = SortListViewItems.isBytesAscending;
                break;
            case "Ext.":
                columnType = ColumnType.Alpha;
                SortListViewItems.isExtAscending =
                        !SortListViewItems.isExtAscending;
                isAscending = SortListViewItems.isExtAscending;
                break;
            case "Modified":
                columnType = ColumnType.DateTimeValue;
                SortListViewItems.isModifiedAscending =
                        !SortListViewItems.isModifiedAscending;
                isAscending = SortListViewItems.isModifiedAscending;
                break;
            case "Attrib.":
                columnType = ColumnType.Alpha;
                SortListViewItems.isAttribAscending =
                        !SortListViewItems.isAttribAscending;
                isAscending = SortListViewItems.isAttribAscending;
                break;
            default:
                columnType = ColumnType.Alpha;
                break;
        }
        lv.ListViewItemSorter = new SortListViewItems(e.Column,
                                                      columnType,
                                                      isAscending);

        lv.Sort();
}
```

```vbnet
Private Sub lv_ColumnClick(ByVal sender As Object, _
             ByVal e As System.Windows.Forms.ColumnClickEventArgs) _
             Handles lv.ColumnClick
    dim colType as ColumnType
    dim isAscending as Boolean = true
    dim strName as String = _
        CType(sender, ListView).Columns(e.Column).Text
    select case strName
        case "Name"
            colType = ColumnType.Alpha
            SortListViewItems.isNameAscending = _
                not (SortListViewItems.isNameAscending)
```

```
                isAscending = SortListViewItems.isNameAscending
            case "Bytes"
                colType = ColumnType.Numeric
                SortListViewItems.isBytesAscending = _
                    not (SortListViewItems.isBytesAscending)
                isAscending = SortListViewItems.isBytesAscending
            case "Ext."
                colType = ColumnType.Alpha
                SortListViewItems.isExtAscending = _
                    not (SortListViewItems.isExtAscending)
                isAscending = SortListViewItems.isExtAscending
            case "Modified"
                colType = ColumnType.DateTimeValue
                SortListViewItems.isModifiedAscending = _
                    not (SortListViewItems.isModifiedAscending)
                isAscending = SortListViewItems.isModifiedAscending
            case "Attrib."
                colType = ColumnType.Alpha
                SortListViewItems.isAttribAscending = _
                    not (SortListViewItems.isAttribAscending)
                isAscending = SortListViewItems.isAttribAscending
            case else
                colType = ColumnType.Alpha
        end select
        lv.ListViewItemSorter = _
            new SortListViewItems(e.Column, colType, isAscending)
        lv.Sort( )
    End Sub
```

This method first declares two local variables—one for the column type, which is of type ColumnType (i.e., the enumeration previously declared) and a Boolean to indicate the sort order.

Next, the name of the column that was clicked is extracted and stored. First the sender object is cast as a ListView. Then the ColumnClickEventArgs.Column property, which returns the zero-based index of the column within the ColumnHeaderCollection, is used as the index into the Columns collection of the ListView itself passed in as sender. Finally, the strName variable is set to the Text property of Column:

C#

```
string strName = ((ListView)sender).Columns[e.Column].Text;
```

VB

```
dim strName as String = CType(sender, ListView).Columns(e.Column).Text
```

Once the name of the column is in hand, a switch block (select case in VB.NET) sets the column type variable, toggles the value of the Boolean that controls the sort order, and sets the value of the isAscending flag:

C#

```
switch(strName)
{
    case "Name":
        columnType = ColumnType.Alpha;
        SortListViewItems.isNameAscending =
            !SortListViewItems.isNameAscending;
```

```
        isAscending = SortListViewItems.isNameAscending;
        break;
    case "Bytes":
        columnType = ColumnType.Numeric;
        SortListViewItems.isBytesAscending =
            !SortListViewItems.isBytesAscending;
        isAscending = SortListViewItems.isBytesAscending;
        break;
    case "Ext.":
        columnType = ColumnType.Alpha;
        SortListViewItems.isExtAscending =
            !SortListViewItems.isExtAscending;
        isAscending = SortListViewItems.isExtAscending;
        break;
    case "Modified":
        columnType = ColumnType.DateTimeValue;
        SortListViewItems.isModifiedAscending =
            !SortListViewItems.isModifiedAscending;
        isAscending = SortListViewItems.isModifiedAscending;
        break;
    case "Attrib.":
        columnType = ColumnType.Alpha;
        SortListViewItems.isAttribAscending =
            !SortListViewItems.isAttribAscending;
        isAscending = SortListViewItems.isAttribAscending;
        break;
    default:
        columnType = ColumnType.Alpha;
        break;
}
```

```
select case strName
    case "Name"
        colType = ColumnType.Alpha
        SortListViewItems.isNameAscending = _
            not (SortListViewItems.isNameAscending)
        isAscending = SortListViewItems.isNameAscending
    case "Bytes"
        colType = ColumnType.Numeric
        SortListViewItems.isBytesAscending = _
            not (SortListViewItems.isBytesAscending)
        isAscending = SortListViewItems.isBytesAscending
    case "Ext."
        colType = ColumnType.Alpha
        SortListViewItems.isExtAscending = _
            not (SortListViewItems.isExtAscending)
        isAscending = SortListViewItems.isExtAscending
    case "Modified"
        colType = ColumnType.DateTimeValue
        SortListViewItems.isModifiedAscending = _
            not (SortListViewItems.isModifiedAscending)
        isAscending = SortListViewItems.isModifiedAscending
```

```
  case "Attrib."
     colType = ColumnType.Alpha
     SortListViewItems.isAttribAscending = _
         not (SortListViewItems.isAttribAscending)
     isAscending = SortListViewItems.isAttribAscending
  case else
     colType = ColumnType.Alpha
end select
```

Once these variables are set, the ListView's ListViewItemSorter property can be set to a new instance of a SortListViewItems object and the called Sort method:

```
lv.ListViewItemSorter = new SortListViewItems(e.Column,
                                              columnType,
                                              isAscending);
lv.Sort();
```

```
lv.ListViewItemSorter = _
    new SortListViewItems(e.Column, colType, isAscending)
lv.Sort()
```

When the Sort method is called, the items of the ListView will magically sort themselves according to the algorithm specified in the SortListViewItems class. Unlike at Hogwarts, no Sorting Hat is required.

Editing the Labels

The end user can edit labels associated with ListView items at runtime if the LabelEdit property is set to true *and* the value of the Activation property is set to ItemActivation.Standard (the default).

 If the ListView.ItemActivation property is set to either nondefault value, then label editing will be disabled, regardless of the value of the LabelEdit property.

With these two properties set appropriately, double-clicking an item activates the item (discussed above), while clicking an item twice slowly puts it into edit mode. In actuality, the first click selects the item and the second click puts it into edit mode.

The ListViewItem.BeginEdit method (described in Table 14-29) allows you to put an item label into edit mode programmatically. This would be useful, for example, if a label fails validation after being edited by the user and you want it to remain in edit mode until it passes validation.

 Setting the LabelEdit property to true allows editing only of the text associated with the item itself, not of any subitems.

The ListView control provides two events that are useful for label editing, Before-LabelEdit and AfterLabelEdit, both of which are listed in Table 14-23. You can see how these events work by adding event handlers for them, using the same techniques used throughout this chapter. Once you have the code skeletons in place for each event, add the following highlighted code:

```csharp
private void lv_BeforeLabelEdit(object sender, LabelEditEventArgs e)
{
    MessageBox.Show("About to edit\n" +
        "Item:" + e.Item.ToString() + "\n" +
        "label:" + e.Label );
}

private void lv_AfterLabelEdit(object sender, LabelEditEventArgs e)
{
    MessageBox.Show("After edit\n" +
        "Item:" + e.Item.ToString() + "\n" +
        "label:" + e.Label );
}
```

```vbnet
Private Sub lv_BeforeLabelEdit(ByVal sender As Object, _
                ByVal e As System.Windows.Forms.LabelEditEventArgs) _
                Handles lv.BeforeLabelEdit
    MessageBox.Show("About to edit" & vbNewLine & _
        "Item:" & e.Item.ToString() & vbNewLine & _
        "label:" & e.Label )
End Sub

Private Sub lv_AfterLabelEdit(ByVal sender As Object, _
                ByVal e As System.Windows.Forms.LabelEditEventArgs) _
                Handles lv.AfterLabelEdit
    MessageBox.Show("After edit" & vbNewLine & _
        "Item:" & e.Item.ToString() & vbNewLine & _
        "label:" & e.Label )
End Sub
```

While these methods will show you the before and after results of editing a label, assuming the LabelEdit and Activation properties are properly set, this code will not actually change anything. If you change the name of a file, the actual name of that file will not be changed in the file system unless you add code to specifically rename the file. That is left as an exercise for the reader.

Complete Code Listings

Examples 14-5 and 14-6 list the entire code listing for the Windows Explorer clone in both C# and VB.NET. Methods that are borrowed unchanged from the TreeView examples listed in Example 14-3 (in C#) and Example 14-4 (in VB.NET) are indicated, but not listed to conserve space. Likewise, methods autogenerated by Visual Studio .NET, such as InitializeComponent, Dispose, and Main, are omitted.

Example 14-5. ListView control as part of Explorer clone in C# (csExplorerClone)

```csharp
using System;
using System.Drawing;
using System.Collections;
using System.ComponentModel;
using System.Windows.Forms;
using System.Data;
using System.IO;
using System.Diagnostics;        //  for Process.Start

namespace csExplorerClone
{
    public class Form1 : System.Windows.Forms.Form
    {
        private System.Windows.Forms.Splitter splitter1;
        private System.Windows.Forms.ListView lv;
        private System.Windows.Forms.TreeView tvw;
        private System.Windows.Forms.MainMenu mainMenu1;
        private System.Windows.Forms.MenuItem menuItem1;
        private System.Windows.Forms.MenuItem mnuSmallIcons;
        private System.Windows.Forms.MenuItem mnuLargeIcons;
        private System.Windows.Forms.MenuItem mnuList;
        private System.Windows.Forms.MenuItem mnuDetails;

        public enum ColumnType
        {
            Alpha,
            Numeric,
            DateTimeValue
        }

        private System.ComponentModel.Container components = null;

        public Form1()
        {
            InitializeComponent();

            //  Use an array to add filenames to the ImageLists
            String[] arFiles = {
              @"C:\Program Files\Microsoft Visual Studio .NET 2003\Common7\" +
                    @"Graphics\icons\computer\form.ico",
              @"C:\Program Files\Microsoft Visual Studio .NET 2003\Common7\" +
                    @"Graphics\icons\win95\clsdfold.ico",
              @"C:\Program Files\Microsoft Visual Studio .NET 2003\Common7\" +
                    @"Graphics\icons\win95\openfold.ico",
              @"C:\Program Files\Microsoft Visual Studio .NET 2003\Common7\" +
                    @"Graphics\bitmaps\assorted\happy.bmp",
              @"C:\Program Files\Microsoft Visual Studio .NET 2003\Common7\" +
                    @"Graphics\bitmaps\outline\NoMask\doc.bmp",
              @"C:\Program Files\Microsoft Visual Studio .NET 2003\Common7\" +
                    @"Graphics\bitmaps\outline\NoMask\exe.bmp",
              @"C:\Program Files\Microsoft Visual Studio .NET 2003\Common7\" +
                    @"Graphics\bitmaps\outline\NoMask\txt.bmp",
```

C#

```
        @"C:\Program Files\Microsoft Visual Studio .NET 2003\Common7\" +
            @"Graphics\bitmaps\outline\NoMask\windoc.bmp"
    };
ImageList imgListSmall = new ImageList();  // default size 16x16
ImageList imgListLarge = new ImageList();
imgListLarge.ImageSize = new Size(32,32);
for (int i = 0; i < arFiles.Length; i++)
{
    imgListSmall.Images.Add(Image.FromFile(arFiles[i]));
    imgListLarge.Images.Add(Image.FromFile(arFiles[i]));
}

tvw.Size = new Size(ClientSize.Width / 3, ClientSize.Height);
tvw.BackColor = Color.Moccasin;
tvw.HideSelection = false;
tvw.ImageList = imgListSmall;
tvw.ImageIndex = 1;
tvw.SelectedImageIndex = 2;

lv.BackColor = Color.PaleTurquoise;
lv.ForeColor = Color.DarkBlue;
lv.HideSelection = false;
lv.SmallImageList = imgListSmall;
lv.LargeImageList = imgListLarge;
lv.View = View.SmallIcon;
lv.Activation = ItemActivation.Standard;  // default
lv.MultiSelect = true;          // default
lv.HoverSelection = false;       // default
lv.Sorting = SortOrder.None;     // default
lv.AllowColumnReorder = true;
lv.FullRowSelect = true;
lv.GridLines = true;
lv.HeaderStyle = ColumnHeaderStyle.Clickable;        // default
lv.LabelEdit = true;

FillDirectoryTree();
}

// These 3 methods essentially same as in TreeViews program
private void FillDirectoryTree()
private void GetSubDirectoryNodes(TreeNode parentNode,
                                 bool getFileNames)
private void tvw_BeforeExpand(object sender,
                    TreeViewCancelEventArgs e)

// This populates the list view after a tree node is selected
private void tvw_AfterSelect(object sender,
                    TreeViewEventArgs e)
{
    lv.Clear();
    lv.BeginUpdate();
```

`C#`

```csharp
DirectoryInfo di = new DirectoryInfo(e.Node.FullPath);
FileSystemInfo[ ] afsi = di.GetFileSystemInfos( );
foreach (FileSystemInfo fsi in afsi)
{
    ListViewItem lvi = new ListViewItem(fsi.Name);

    if ((fsi.Attributes & FileAttributes.Directory) != 0)
    {
        lvi.ImageIndex = 1;
        lvi.SubItems.Add("");          // Bytes subitem
    }
    else
    {
        switch(fsi.Extension.ToUpper( ))
        {
            case ".DOC" :
                lvi.ImageIndex = 4;
                break;
            case ".EXE" :
                lvi.ImageIndex = 5;
                break;
            case ".TXT" :
                lvi.ImageIndex = 6;
                break;
            default :
                lvi.ImageIndex = 7;
                break;
        }
        //  Bytes subitem, w/ commas
        //  Cast FileSystemInfo object to FileInfo object so the
        //     size can be obtained.
        lvi.SubItems.Add((((FileInfo)fsi).Length.ToString("N0")));
    }

    //  Add the remaining subitems to the ListViewItem
    lvi.SubItems.Add(fsi.Extension);                // type
    lvi.SubItems.Add(fsi.LastWriteTime.ToString( ));  // modified

    //  Build up the Attributes string
    string strAtt = "";
    if ((fsi.Attributes & FileAttributes.ReadOnly) != 0)
        strAtt += "R";
    if ((fsi.Attributes & FileAttributes.Hidden) != 0)
        strAtt += "H";
    if ((fsi.Attributes & FileAttributes.System) != 0)
        strAtt += "S";
    if ((fsi.Attributes & FileAttributes.Archive) != 0)
        strAtt += "A";
    lvi.SubItems.Add(strAtt);                // attributes

    lv.Items.Add(lvi);
}  // end foreach
```

```
C#        lv.Columns.Add("Name", 150, HorizontalAlignment.Left);
          lv.Columns.Add("Bytes", 75, HorizontalAlignment.Right);
          lv.Columns.Add("Ext.", 50, HorizontalAlignment.Left);
          lv.Columns.Add("Modified", 125, HorizontalAlignment.Left);
          lv.Columns.Add("Attrib.", 50, HorizontalAlignment.Left);

          lv.EndUpdate( );
       }                       //  close tvw_AfterSelect

       private void mnuView_Click(object sender, EventArgs e)
       {
          MenuItem mnu = (MenuItem)sender;
          switch (mnu.Mnemonic.ToString( ))
          {
             case "L"  :      //  Large Icons
                lv.View = View.LargeIcon;
                break;
             case "S"  :      //  Small Icons
                lv.View = View.SmallIcon;
                break;
             case "T" :      //  List view
                lv.View = View.List;
                break;
             case "D" :      //  Detail view
                lv.View = View.Details;
                break;
          }
       }

       protected override void Dispose( bool disposing )

       #region Windows Form Designer generated code
       private void InitializeComponent( )
       #endregion

       static void Main( )

       private void lv_ItemActivate(object sender, EventArgs e)
       {
          ListView lv = (ListView)sender;
          foreach (ListViewItem lvi in lv.SelectedItems)
          {
             try
             {
                Process.Start(tvw.SelectedNode.FullPath + "\\" + lvi.Text);
             }
             catch
             {
             }
          }
       }
```

```
public class SortListViewItems : IComparer      //  nested class
{
    int columnIndex;
    ColumnType columnType;
    bool isAscending;
    public static Boolean isNameAscending = true;
    public static Boolean isBytesAscending = false;
    public static Boolean isExtAscending = false;
    public static Boolean isModifiedAscending = false;
    public static Boolean isAttribAscending = false;

    public SortListViewItems(int columnIndex,
                             ColumnType columnType,
                             bool isAscending)
    {
        this.columnIndex = columnIndex;
        this.columnType = columnType;
        this.isAscending = isAscending;
    }

    public int Compare(object x, object y)
    {
        string strFirst =
            ((ListViewItem)x).SubItems[columnIndex].Text;
        string strSecond =
            ((ListViewItem)y).SubItems[columnIndex].Text;

        switch (columnType)
        {
            case ColumnType.Alpha :
                if (isAscending)
                    return strFirst.CompareTo(strSecond);
                else
                    return strSecond.CompareTo(strFirst);
            case ColumnType.DateTimeValue :
                if (isAscending)
                    return DateTime.Parse(strFirst).
                        CompareTo(DateTime.Parse(strSecond));
                else
                    return DateTime.Parse(strSecond).
                        CompareTo(DateTime.Parse(strFirst));
            case ColumnType.Numeric :
                //  Special case blank byte values.
                if (strFirst == "")
                    strFirst = "-1";
                if (strSecond == "")
                    strSecond = "-1";
                if (isAscending)
                    return Double.Parse(strFirst).
                        CompareTo(Double.Parse(strSecond));
                else
                    return Double.Parse(strSecond).
```

```
                        CompareTo(Double.Parse(strFirst));
            default:
                return 0;
        }            //  close switch block
    }                //  close Compare method
}                    //  close nested SortListViewItems class

private void lv_ColumnClick(object sender, ColumnClickEventArgs e)
{
    ColumnType columnType;
    bool isAscending = true;
    string strName = ((ListView)sender).Columns[e.Column].Text;
    switch(strName)
    {
        case "Name":
            columnType = ColumnType.Alpha;
            SortListViewItems.isNameAscending =
                   !SortListViewItems.isNameAscending;
            isAscending = SortListViewItems.isNameAscending;
            break;
        case "Bytes":
            columnType = ColumnType.Numeric;
            SortListViewItems.isBytesAscending =
                   !SortListViewItems.isBytesAscending;
            isAscending = SortListViewItems.isBytesAscending;
            break;
        case "Ext.":
            columnType = ColumnType.Alpha;
            SortListViewItems.isExtAscending =
                   !SortListViewItems.isExtAscending;
            isAscending = SortListViewItems.isExtAscending;
            break;
        case "Modified":
            columnType = ColumnType.DateTimeValue;
            SortListViewItems.isModifiedAscending =
                   !SortListViewItems.isModifiedAscending;
            isAscending = SortListViewItems.isModifiedAscending;
            break;
        case "Attrib.":
            columnType = ColumnType.Alpha;
            SortListViewItems.isAttribAscending =
                   !SortListViewItems.isAttribAscending;
            isAscending = SortListViewItems.isAttribAscending;
            break;
        default:
            columnType = ColumnType.Alpha;
            break;
    }

    lv.ListViewItemSorter = new SortListViewItems(e.Column,
                                                  columnType,
                                                  isAscending);
```

C#

```
        lv.Sort( );
    }                       // close lv_ColumnClick

    private void lv_BeforeLabelEdit(object sender, LabelEditEventArgs e)
    {
        MessageBox.Show("About to edit\n" +
            "Item:" + e.Item.ToString( ) + "\n" +
            "label:" + e.Label );
    }

    private void lv_AfterLabelEdit(object sender, LabelEditEventArgs e)
    {
        MessageBox.Show("After edit\n" +
            "Item:" + e.Item.ToString( ) + "\n" +
            "label:" + e.Label );
    }
  }
}
```

Example 14-6. ListView control as part of Explorer clone in VB.NET (vbExplorerClone)

VB

```
imports System.IO
imports System.Collections

Public Class Form1
    Inherits System.Windows.Forms.Form

        public enum ColumnType
            Alpha
            Numeric
            DateTimeValue
        end enum

#Region " Windows Form Designer generated code "

    Public Sub New( )
        MyBase.New( )
        InitializeComponent( )

            ' Use an array to add filenames to the ImageList
            dim arFiles( ) as string = { _
            "C:\Program Files\Microsoft Visual Studio .NET 2003\Common7\" + _
                    "Graphics\icons\computer\form.ico", _
            "C:\Program Files\Microsoft Visual Studio .NET 2003\Common7\" + _
                    "Graphics\icons\win95\clsdfold.ico", _
            "C:\Program Files\Microsoft Visual Studio .NET 2003\Common7\" + _
                    "Graphics\icons\win95\openfold.ico", _
            "C:\Program Files\Microsoft Visual Studio .NET 2003\Common7\" + _
                    "Graphics\bitmaps\assorted\happy.bmp", _
            "C:\Program Files\Microsoft Visual Studio .NET 2003\Common7\" + _
                    "Graphics\bitmaps\outline\NoMask\doc.bmp", _
```

```
VB              "C:\Program Files\Microsoft Visual Studio .NET 2003\Common7\" + _
                    "Graphics\bitmaps\outline\NoMask\exe.bmp", _
                "C:\Program Files\Microsoft Visual Studio .NET 2003\Common7\" + _
                    "Graphics\bitmaps\outline\NoMask\txt.bmp", _
                "C:\Program Files\Microsoft Visual Studio .NET 2003\Common7\" + _
                    "Graphics\bitmaps\outline\NoMask\windoc.bmp"}

        dim imgListSmall as new ImageList( )      ' default size 16x16
        dim imgListLarge as new ImageList( )
        imgListLarge.ImageSize = new Size(32,32)

        dim i as Integer
        for i = 0 to arFiles.Length - 1
           imgListSmall.Images.Add(Image.FromFile(arFiles(i)))
           imgListLarge.Images.Add(Image.FromFile(arFiles(i)))
        next

        tvw.Size = new Size(ClientSize.Width / 3, ClientSize.Height)
        tvw.BackColor = Color.Moccasin
        tvw.HideSelection = false
        tvw.ImageList = imgListSmall
        tvw.ImageIndex = 1
        tvw.SelectedImageIndex = 2

        lv.BackColor = Color.PaleTurquoise
        lv.ForeColor = Color.DarkBlue
        lv.HideSelection = false
        lv.SmallImageList = imgListSmall
        lv.LargeImageList = imgListLarge
        lv.View = View.SmallIcon
        lv.Activation = ItemActivation.Standard       ' default
        lv.MultiSelect = true          ' default
        lv.HoverSelection = false        ' default
        lv.Sorting = SortOrder.None      ' default
        lv.AllowColumnReorder = true
        lv.FullRowSelect = true
        lv.GridLines = true
        lv.HeaderStyle = ColumnHeaderStyle.Clickable     ' default
        lv.LabelEdit = true


        FillDirectoryTree( )
    End Sub

    Protected Overloads Overrides Sub Dispose(ByVal disposing As Boolean)
#End Region

    '  These 3 methods essentially same as in TreeViews program
    private sub FillDirectoryTree( )
    private sub GetSubDirectoryNodes(parentNode as TreeNode, _
                            getFileNames as Boolean)
    Private Sub tvw_BeforeExpand(ByVal sender As Object, _
```

*Example 14-6. ListView control as part of Explorer clone in VB.NET
(vbExplorerClone) (continued)*

```
        ByVal e As System.Windows.Forms.TreeViewCancelEventArgs) _
        Handles tvw.BeforeExpand

private sub mnuView_Click(ByVal sender As Object, _
                         ByVal e As EventArgs) _
    Handles mnuDetails.Click, mnuLargeIcons.Click, mnuList.Click, _
        mnuSmallIcons.Click
    dim mnu as New MenuItem
    mnu = CType(sender, MenuItem)
    select case (mnu.Mnemonic.ToString())
        case "L"  :       ' Large Icons
            lv.View = View.LargeIcon
        case "S"  :       ' Small Icons
            lv.View = View.SmallIcon
        case "T" :        ' List view
            lv.View = View.List
        case "D" :        ' Detail view
            lv.View = View.Details
    end select
end sub

'  This populates the list view after a tree node is selected
Private Sub tvw_AfterSelect(ByVal sender As Object, _
        ByVal e As System.Windows.Forms.TreeViewEventArgs) _
        Handles tvw.AfterSelect
    lv.Clear()              ' remove all items & columns
    lv.BeginUpdate()

    dim di as new DirectoryInfo(e.Node.FullPath)
    dim afsi() as FileSystemInfo
    afsi = di.GetFileSystemInfos()   ' both files & directories

    dim fsi as FileSystemInfo
    for each fsi in afsi
        dim lvi as new ListViewItem(fsi.Name)

        if ((fsi.Attributes and FileAttributes.Directory) <> 0) then
            lvi.ImageIndex = 1
            lvi.SubItems.Add("")          ' Bytes subitem
        else
            select case (fsi.Extension.ToUpper())
                case ".DOC" :
                    lvi.ImageIndex = 4
                case ".EXE" :
                    lvi.ImageIndex = 5
                case ".TXT" :
                    lvi.ImageIndex = 6
                case else :
                    lvi.ImageIndex = 7
            end select
            ' Bytes subitem, w/ commas
```

```
VB                      ' Cast FileSystemInfo object to FileInfo object so
                        '   the size can be obtained.
                        lvi.SubItems.Add(CType(fsi,FileInfo).Length.ToString("NO"))
                    end if

                    ' Add the remaining subitems to the ListViewItem
                    lvi.SubItems.Add(fsi.Extension)                    ' type
                    lvi.SubItems.Add(fsi.LastWriteTime.ToString())     ' modified

                    ' Build up the Attributes string
                    dim strAtt as String = ""
                    if ((fsi.Attributes and FileAttributes.ReadOnly) <> 0) then
                        strAtt += "R"
                    end if
                    if ((fsi.Attributes & FileAttributes.Hidden) <> 0) then
                        strAtt += "H"
                    end if
                    if ((fsi.Attributes & FileAttributes.System) <> 0) then
                        strAtt += "S"
                    end if
                    if ((fsi.Attributes & FileAttributes.Archive) <> 0) then
                        strAtt += "A"
                    end if
                    lvi.SubItems.Add(strAtt)                           ' attributes
                    lv.Items.Add(lvi)
                next    ' end for each

            lv.Columns.Add("Name", 150, HorizontalAlignment.Left)
            lv.Columns.Add("Bytes", 75, HorizontalAlignment.Right)
            lv.Columns.Add("Ext.", 50, HorizontalAlignment.Left)
            lv.Columns.Add("Modified", 125, HorizontalAlignment.Left)
            lv.Columns.Add("Attrib.", 50, HorizontalAlignment.Left)

            lv.EndUpdate()
    End Sub

    Private Sub lv_ItemActivate(ByVal sender As Object, _
                    ByVal e As System.EventArgs) _
                    Handles lv.ItemActivate
        lv = CType(sender, ListView)
        dim lvi as ListViewItem
        for each lvi in lv.SelectedItems
            try
                Process.Start(tvw.SelectedNode.FullPath + "\" + lvi.Text)
            catch
            end try
        next
    End Sub

    public class SortListViewItems
        implements IComparer
```

```
VB    dim columnIndex as Integer
      dim colType as ColumnType
      dim isAscending as Boolean
      public shared isNameAscending as Boolean = true
      public shared isBytesAscending as Boolean = false
      public shared isExtAscending as Boolean = false
      public shared isModifiedAscending as Boolean = false
      public shared isAttribAscending as Boolean = false

      public sub New(columnIndex as Integer, _
                     colType as ColumnType, _
                     isAscending as Boolean)
         me.columnIndex = columnIndex
         me.colType = colType
         me.isAscending = isAscending
      End Sub

      public function Compare(x as Object, y as Object) as Integer _
                                    implements IComparer.Compare
         dim strFirst as String = _
            (CType(x,ListViewItem)).SubItems(columnIndex).Text
         dim strSecond as String = _
            (CType(y,ListViewItem)).SubItems(columnIndex).Text

         select case colType
            case ColumnType.Alpha
               if isAscending then
                  return strFirst.CompareTo(strSecond)
               else
                  return strSecond.CompareTo(strFirst)
               end if
            case ColumnType.DateTimeValue
               if isAscending
                  return _
                     DateTime.Parse(strFirst). _
                        CompareTo(DateTime.Parse(strSecond))
               else
                  return _
                     DateTime.Parse(strSecond). _
                        CompareTo(DateTime.Parse(strFirst))
               end if
            case ColumnType.Numeric
               ' Special case blank byte values.
               if strFirst = "" then
                  strFirst = "-1"
               end if
               if strSecond = "" then
                  strSecond = "-1"
               end if
               if isAscending then
                  return _
```

VB

```
                    Double.Parse(strFirst). _
                        CompareTo(Double.Parse(strSecond))
            else
                return _
                    Double.Parse(strSecond). _
                        CompareTo(Double.Parse(strFirst))
            end if
        case else
            return 0
     End Select
   End Function
end class      ' nested class

Private Sub lv_ColumnClick(ByVal sender As Object, _
             ByVal e As System.Windows.Forms.ColumnClickEventArgs) _
             Handles lv.ColumnClick
   dim colType as ColumnType
   dim isAscending as Boolean = true
   dim strName as String = _
        CType(sender, ListView).Columns(e.Column).Text

   select case strName
      case "Name"
         colType = ColumnType.Alpha
         SortListViewItems.isNameAscending = _
              not (SortListViewItems.isNameAscending)
         isAscending = SortListViewItems.isNameAscending
      case "Bytes"
         colType = ColumnType.Numeric
         SortListViewItems.isBytesAscending = _
              not (SortListViewItems.isBytesAscending)
         isAscending = SortListViewItems.isBytesAscending
      case "Ext."
         colType = ColumnType.Alpha
         SortListViewItems.isExtAscending = _
              not (SortListViewItems.isExtAscending)
         isAscending = SortListViewItems.isExtAscending
      case "Modified"
         colType = ColumnType.DateTimeValue
         SortListViewItems.isModifiedAscending = _
              not (SortListViewItems.isModifiedAscending)
         isAscending = SortListViewItems.isModifiedAscending
      case "Attrib."
         colType = ColumnType.Alpha
         SortListViewItems.isAttribAscending = _
              not (SortListViewItems.isAttribAscending)
         isAscending = SortListViewItems.isAttribAscending
      case else
         colType = ColumnType.Alpha
   end select
```

Example 14-6. ListView control as part of Explorer clone in VB.NET (vbExplorerClone) (continued)

```
        lv.ListViewItemSorter = _
            new SortListViewItems(e.Column, colType, isAscending)
        lv.Sort( )
    End Sub

    Private Sub lv_BeforeLabelEdit(ByVal sender As Object, _
                        ByVal e As System.Windows.Forms.LabelEditEventArgs) _
                        Handles lv.BeforeLabelEdit
        MessageBox.Show("About to edit" & vbNewLine & _
            "Item:" & e.Item.ToString( ) & vbNewLine & _
            "label:" & e.Label )
    End Sub

    Private Sub lv_AfterLabelEdit(ByVal sender As Object, _
                        ByVal e As System.Windows.Forms.LabelEditEventArgs) _
                        Handles lv.AfterLabelEdit
        MessageBox.Show("After edit" & vbNewLine & _
            "Item:" & e.Item.ToString( ) & vbNewLine & _
            "label:" & e.Label )
    End Sub
End Class
```

CHAPTER 15

List Controls

Many applications require the display of simple lists. Sometimes these lists are finite and static: the months of the year, product codes in a company catalogue, and so on. At other times, the list may be large and dynamic, allowing the user to add items as necessary: a list of organizations to which customers may belong or books read by students in a class, for example. The list controls described in this chapter—ListBox, CheckedListBox, and ComboBox—serve both these needs.

Class Hierarchy

The hierarchical structure of the classes discussed in this chapter is shown in Figure 15-1.

ListControls

In addition to the TreeView and ListView controls described in the previous chapter, the .NET Framework provides three other controls that display lists of items: the ListBox, the CheckedListBox, and the ComboBox. All derive from the ListControl base class shown in Figure 15-1. The ListControl class is abstract (MustInherit in VB. NET); it cannot be instantiated itself, but concrete classes derived from it can be instantiated.

The ListControl class provides much (although not all, as you will see) of the common functionality of these three controls. Table 15-1 lists the five native properties of the ListControl class that are inherited by derived classes. These properties include the DataSource property and several properties useful to a single-selection list. Table 15-2 lists properties that are not actually members of the ListControl class, but are members of all three derived classes. They include properties used to define the appearance of the control and properties related to the controls' Items collection, described next. Table 15-3 lists commonly used methods of the ListControl class.

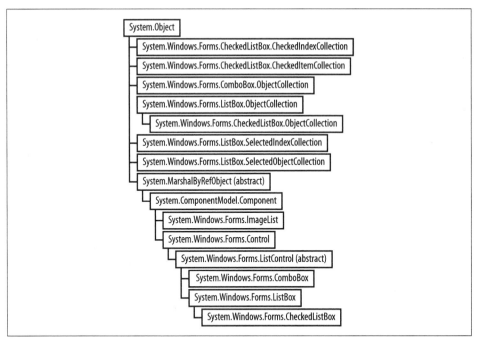

Figure 15-1. Class hierarchy for controls covered in this chapter

Table 15-1. ListControl properties

Property	Value type	Description
DataSource	Object	Read/write. Specifies the data source for the list control.
DisplayMember	String	Read/write. Specifies the property of the data source displayed by the list control.
SelectedValue	Object	Read/write. Contains the value of the currently selected item specified by the ValueMember property. If ValueMember is not specified, returns object. ToString( ).
ValueMember	String	Read/write. Specifies the property of the data source returned as the Selected-Value property. Can be cleared by setting to empty string ("") or null (Nothing) reference.
SelectedIndex	Integer	Read/write. The zero-based index of the currently selected item. A value of −1 corresponds to no item currently selected.

Table 15-2. Properties Common to all list controls

Property	Value type	Description
DrawMode	DrawMode	Read/write. Specifies the drawing mode for the control. Valid values are Draw-Mode.Normal (the default), DrawMode.OwnerDrawFixed, and DrawMode. OwnerDrawVariable. The latter two values indicate that application code handles drawing the control, as opposed to the operating system.
IntegralHeight	Boolean	Read/write. If `true` (the default), control resizes to avoid displaying partial items.

Table 15-2. Properties Common to all list controls (continued)

Property	Value type	Description
ItemHeight	Integer	Read/write. Height of an item in the control, in pixels.
Items	ObjectCollection	Read-only. Collection of items in the control.
PreferredHeight	Integer	Read-only. The height of all items in the control, in pixels. This is the height the control needs to be to display all the items without a vertical scrollbar.
SelectedItem	Object	Read/write. The item currently selected in the control.
Sorted	Boolean	Read/write. If false (the default), items in the control are not sorted and new items are added to the end of the list; otherwise they are sorted in an ascending, case-insensitive, alphabetical order. If true, the index of specific items may change as new items are added.
Text	String	Read/write. The text associated with the currently selected item.

Table 15-3. Methods common to all list controls

Method	Description
BeginUpdate	Prevents redrawing of control while items are added to the Items collection.
EndUpdate	Resumes drawing of the control after BeginUpdate was called.
FindString	Overloaded. Returns zero-based index of first item in Items collection that starts with the specified string, optionally starting at the specified index (−1 to search from beginning). Not case-sensitive. Returns ListBox.NoMatches if nothing found.
FindStringExact	Overloaded. Returns zero-based index of first item in Items collection that exactly matches the specified string, optionally starting at the specified index (−1 to search from beginning). Not case-sensitive. Returns ListBox.NoMatches if nothing found.

Filling a ListControl

There are two ways to fill a ListControl: via the Items property of the control or by data-binding the control to a data source.

Filling a ListControl via the Items collection

The Items property represents the collection of objects contained in the list. Like all collection objects, it implements the IList, ICollection, and IEnumerable interfaces, and provides methods for adding to, deleting from, and otherwise manipulating the collection. Table 15-4 lists the most commonly used methods.

Table 15-2 indicates that the Items collection is of type ObjectCollection, and Table 15-4 lists the commonly used ObjectCollection methods. This discussion now needs some clarification. There is no ObjectCollection class per se. Each of the three

controls derived from ListControl have their own ObjectCollection class: ListBox.
ObjectCollection, CheckedListBox.ObjectCollection, and ComboBox.Object-
Collection. However, all three classes contain essentially the same methods, with the
exceptions noted in the relevant sections following.

Table 15-4. Commonly used ObjectCollection methods

Method	Description
Add	Adds new object to the current Items collection. Returns the zero-based index of the item in the collection.
AddRange	Adds an array of objects to the collection.
Clear	Removes all the items from the collection.
Contains	Returns true if the specified object is found in the collection.
CopyTo	Copies the entire collection to the specified object array, starting at the specified index.
IndexOf	Returns zero-based index of the specified object within the collection. If object is not found, returns −1.
Insert	Inserts an object into the collection at the specified index. If the Sorted property is true, the index is ignored.
Remove	Removes the specified object from the collection. All subsequent objects move up one position.
RemoveAt	Removes the object from the collection at the location specified by the index. All subsequent items move up one position.

In addition to the methods listed in Table 15-4, the ObjectCollection classes contain
a read-only Count property that returns the number of items in the collection and a
read/write Item property that is an indexer into the collection. These properties will
be demonstrated in the examples below.

When using Visual Studio .NET, strings can be added to the Items collection at
design time by using the Strings Collection Editor. This is accessed in Design view by
clicking on the Build button (with three dots) next to the Items property in the Property window. Doing so will bring up the dialog box shown in Figure 15-2.

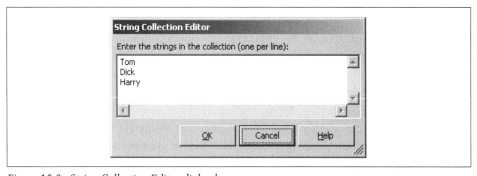

Figure 15-2. String Collection Editor dialog box

The String Collection Editor uses the AddRange method shown in Table 15-4 to add the strings to the Items collection. The code that does this is in the Initialize-Component method autogenerated by Visual Studio .NET. Your code can then further manipulate the collection, if necessary.

Filling a ListControl using a DataSource

The second way to fill a ListControl is to data bind the control to a data source using the DataSource property. The DataSource can be any object that implements the IList interface. The IList interface represents collections of objects that are individually accessible by index, including:

- ADO.NET classes such as DataTable, DataView, or DataSet
- Array or ArrayList
- Any strongly typed collection that derives from CollectionBase

Database access using ADO.NET is covered in Chapters 19 and 20.

The DataSource property binds the data in the DataSource to the control. Generally a DataSource has one or more members, such as DataColumns in a DataTable or member fields of a class that populates an array. You will often want to display one of these members in the user interface, but pass a different member to the program for processing when an item in the list is selected. For example, you might like to list a series of products, but when the user selects one product, your program might obtain the associated ProductID. The DisplayMember property specifies the member to display in the user interface (e.g., the Product Name) and the ValueMember property specifies the member to return to your program (e.g., the Product ID).

For example, suppose you have a database table that contains all the states in the United States. Further, suppose this table has two columns: StateName and Abbreviation. You would like to display the StateName in the list control, but pass the Abbreviation to the program for processing. Your code might look something like the following, where the highlighted lines are crucial for this discussion:

```
string connectionString =
    "server=YourServer; uid=sa; pwd=YourPassword; database=YourDB";
string commandString =
    "Select StateName, Abbreviation from States";
SqlDataAdapter dataAdapter =
    new SqlDataAdapter(commandString, connectionString);
DataSet dataSet = new DataSet( );
dataAdapter.Fill(dataSet,"States");
DataTable dataTable = dataSet.Tables[0];

// bind to the DataTable
```

```csharp
lb.DataSource= dataTable;
lb.DisplayMember = "StateName";
lb.ValueMember = "Abbreviation";
```

Then in the SelectedValueChanged event handler for the ListBox, the lines of code shown next would extract the value member for further processing (assuming that the string variable strState was previously declared).

```csharp
if (lb.SelectedIndex != -1)
    strState = lb.SelectedValue.ToString( );
```

```vb
if lb.SelectedIndex <> -1 then
    strState = CType(lb.SelectedValue, string)
end if
```

You must cast or convert the SelectedValue property to the correct type (in this case, string) because the property is inherently of type object, as is each item in the Items collection. This point is important when working with ListControls.

In Examples 19-6 (C#) and 19-7 (VB.NET), a ListBox is populated from a database table without using the DataSource property to data-bind the control. Instead, a DataTable is iterated and the Items.Add method are called for each record. The relevant C# code is shown here:

```csharp
foreach (DataRow dataRow in dataTable.Rows)
{
    lbBugs.Items.Add(
        dataRow["BugID"] + ": " + dataRow["Description"]  );
}
```

This technique offers two apparent benefits over data binding. The first is that it is a convenient way to display the concatenation of one or more member fields and text strings. The second benefit derives from the fact that if the DataSource property is used, then the Items collection of the list cannot be modified. This technique avoids that pitfall of not being able to modify the Items collection. However, it loses the ability to display one value in the list, represented by the DisplayMember property, and retrieve a different value for further processing, represented by the ValueMember.

You can use the DataSource property and data binding, thereby preserving the use of both the DisplayMember and ValueMember properties while still concatenating fields and text strings. Consider the code snippet in Example 15-1 for retrieving the author ID, last name, and first name from the authors table of the pubs database that is included with the default installations of Microsoft Access and SQL Server.

Example 15-1. Binding ListBox to database table

```csharp
string connectionString =
    "server= YourServer; uid=sa; pwd=YourPassword; database=pubs";
string commandString =
    "Select au_id, au_lname + ', ' + au_fname as name from authors";
SqlDataAdapter dataAdapter =
    new SqlDataAdapter(commandString, connectionString);
```

Example 15-1. Binding ListBox to database table (continued)

```csharp
DataSet dataSet = new DataSet( );
dataAdapter.Fill(dataSet,"Authors");
DataTable dataTable = dataSet.Tables[0];

// bind to the data table
lb.DataSource= dataTable;
lb.DisplayMember = "name";
lb.ValueMember = "au_id";
```

The SQL query contained in the command string retrieves the au_id column, plus a concatenation of the last name and first name columns with a comma separating the two, calling that field name. Then after setting the DataSource property, the DisplayMember property is set to the name member, and the ValueMember property is set to the au_id member.

Suppose this code were part of form that contains a listbox and a button for displaying the selected items, as shown in Figure 15-3.

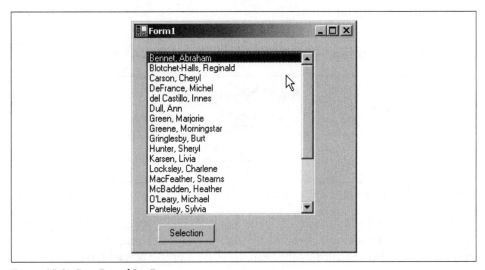

Figure 15-3. DataBound ListBox

The Click event handler for the button might look like Example 15-2, if the listbox were single selection—i.e., had its SelectionMode property (described in Table 15-8) set to 1.

Example 15-2. Click Event Handler for single selection ListBox (in C#)

```csharp
private void btnSelect_Click(object sender, System.EventArgs e)
{
    if (lb.SelectedIndex != -1)
    {
        string s = ((DataRowView)lb.SelectedItem)["name"].ToString( );
```

Example 15-2. Click Event Handler for single selection ListBox (in C#) (continued)

```
C#        MessageBox.Show("Value:  " + lb.SelectedValue.ToString() +
                      "\nDisplay:  " + s);
      }
      else
      {
         MessageBox.Show("Nothing selected");
      }
   }
}
```

The equivalent if block in VB.NET would look like Example 15-3.

Example 15-3. Click event handler if block for single selection ListBox (in VB.NET)

```
VB  if lb.SelectedIndex <> -1 then
       dim s as String = CType(lb.SelectedItem, DataRowView) _
                     ("name").ToString()
       MessageBox.Show("Value:  " + lb.SelectedValue.ToString() + vbCrLf + _
                   "Display:  " + s)
    else
       MessageBox.Show("Nothing selected")
    end if
```

The resulting message box will look like that shown in Figure 15-4.

Figure 15-4. MessageBox from single selection ListBox

Looking at Examples 15-2 and 15-3, the SelectedValue property and the ToString method display the member specified by the ValueMember property. However, displaying the member specified by the DisplayMember property is a bit convoluted.

You might expect that you could replace the argument to the MessageBox with the following code:

```
VB       MessageBox.Show("Value: " + lb.SelectedValue.ToString() + vbCrLf + _
                     "Display:" + lb.SelectedItem.ToString())
```

Doing so, however, results in the MessageBox shown in Figure 15-5. This result drives home the point, mentioned above, that the items in the Items collection are objects—in this case, DataRowView objects.

You might expect that the items in the Items Collection in this example would be DataRow objects, since the DataSource property is a DataTable, which is comprised of DataRows. However, whenever data is displayed in a Windows Forms control, it is displayed as a DataRowView object.

Figure 15-5. Erroneous MessageBox from single selection ListBox

Therefore, the highlighted lines of code in Examples 15-2 and 15-3 cast the Selected-Item to a DataRowView object, index into that object to get the member named name, and then call the ToString method on it to convert it to a string for display in the MessageBox.

This works fine, except for two shortcomings. First, it requires hardcoding the name of the member. Second, if the ListBox were multiselect, it would display only the first selected item.

Replacing the Click event handler with the code shown in Example 15-4 (in C#) and in Example 15-5 (in VB.NET) solves both issues.

Example 15-4. Click Event Handler for multiselection ListBox (in C#)

```
private void btnSelect_Click(object sender, System.EventArgs e)
{
    string strMsg = "";
    if (lb.SelectedIndex != -1)
    {
        foreach(object item in lb.SelectedItems)
        {
            string s1 = ((DataRowView) item)[lb.ValueMember].ToString( );
            string s2 = ((DataRowView) item)[lb.DisplayMember].ToString( );
            strMsg += "Value:  " + s1 + "\n" + "Display:   " + s2 + "\n\n";
        }
        MessageBox.Show(strMsg);
    }
    else
    {
        MessageBox.Show("Nothing selected");
    }
}
```

Example 15-5. Click Event Handler for multiselection ListBox (in VB.NET)

```
Private Sub btnSelect_Click(ByVal sender As System.Object, _
                            ByVal e As System.EventArgs) _
                            Handles btnSelect.Click
    dim strMsg as String = ""
    if lb.SelectedIndex <> -1 then
```

```
dim item as Object
for each item in lb.SelectedItems
    dim s1 as string = _
        CType(item, DataRowView)(lb.ValueMember).ToString( )
    dim s2 as String = _
        CType(item,DataRowView)(lb.DisplayMember).ToString( )
    strMsg += _
        "Value:  " + s1 + vbCrLf + "Display:  " + s2 + vbCrLf + vbCrLf
    next
    MessageBox.Show(strMsg)
else
    MessageBox.Show("Nothing selected")
end if
End Sub
```

The code in Examples 15-4 and 15-5 solves the multiple items selected issue by iterating through the SelectedItems collection of items, building up a string to display in the MessageBox. The member names are not hardcoded, but the ValueMember and DisplayMember properties are used directly to index into the DataRowView objects. The results of selecting several items from the ListBox are shown in Figure 15-6.

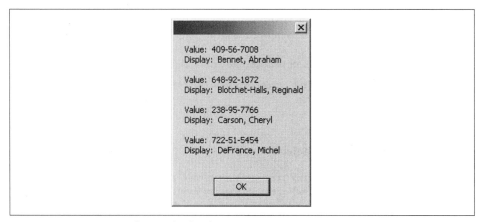

Figure 15-6. MessageBox from multiple selection ListBox

Many developers are not allowed direct access to the database layer of the application for practical reasons. They cannot write or embed ad hoc database queries in their code. Instead, there may be stored procedures they can call that return fixed columns of data. In these situations, you can create virtual columns in the DataSet based on an expression that concatenates other columns or applies any number of transformations to the data. The DataSet with the expression column(s) provides the same sort of capabilities as those shown in Example 15-1.

Retrieving Item Text

The examples above demonstrated different ways to retrieve the text associated with an item in the Items collection, such as by using the SelectedItem, SelectedItems, and SelectedValue properties. The ListControl class also provides the GetItemText method to simplify this task, which takes an item object as an argument and returns a text string.

Using the GetItemText method, you can rewrite and consolidate Examples 15-2 and 15-4 (in C#) and Examples 15-3 and 15-5 (in VB.NET) to demonstrate both single selection and multiselection techniques. Example 15-6 shows this concept in C# and Example 15-7 shows it in VB.NET.

Example 15-6. Click Event Handler using GetItemText (in C#)

```csharp
private void btnSelect_Click(object sender, System.EventArgs e)
{
    string strMsg = "";
    if (lb.SelectedIndex != -1)
    {
        //  for single selection listbox
        MessageBox.Show("ItemText:  " + lb.GetItemText(lb.SelectedItem));

        //  for multi selection listbox
        foreach(object item in lb.SelectedItems)
        {
            string s1 =  ((DataRowView) item)[lb.ValueMember].ToString( );
            string s2 = ((DataRowView) item)[lb.DisplayMember].ToString( );
            string s3 = lb.GetItemText(item);
            strMsg += "Value:  " + s1 + "\n" + "Display:  " + s2 + "\n" +
                      "ItemText:  " + s3 + "\n\n";
        }
    }
    MessageBox.Show(strMsg);
}
else
{
    MessageBox.Show("Nothing selected");
}
```

Example 15-7. Click Event Handler using GetItemText (in VB.NET)

```vbnet
Private Sub btnSelect_Click(ByVal sender As System.Object, _
                           ByVal e As System.EventArgs) _
                           Handles btnSelect.Click
    dim strMsg as String = ""
    if lb.SelectedIndex <> -1 then
        ' for single selection listbox
        MessageBox.Show("ItemText:  " + lb.GetItemText(lb.SelectedItem))

        ' for multi-selection listbox
        dim item as Object
        for each item in lb.SelectedItems
```

Example 15-7. Click Event Handler using GetItemText (in VB.NET) (continued)

```
            dim s1 as string = _
               CType(item, DataRowView)(lb.ValueMember).ToString( )
            dim s2 as String = _
               CType(item,DataRowView)(lb.DisplayMember).ToString( )
            dim s3 as String = lb.GetItemText(item)
            strMsg += "Value: " + s1 + vbCrLf + "Display: " + s2 + vbCrLf + _
                      "ItemText: " + s3 + vbCrLf + vbCrLf
        next
        MessageBox.Show(strMsg)
    else
        MessageBox.Show("Nothing selected")
    end if
End Sub
```

Finally, there is yet another, simpler way to retrieve the displayed item. The Text property of the classes derived from ListControl overrides the base Control.Text property. The Text property of ListBox, CheckedListBox, and ComboBox reflects not the text string associated with the control itself, but the currently selected item. In the case of the controls that support multiselection (ListBox and CheckedList-Box), it corresponds to the text of the first selected item.

So the lines of code in Examples 15-6 and 15-7 that display the value of the single selected value could be equivalently replaced with the following:

```
    MessageBox.Show("Text:   " + lb.Text);
```

ListControl Events

Two commonly used scenarios retrieve and process the currently selected items of a list control. The first, demonstrated in the ListControl examples above, uses an event external to the ListControl, such as a button click, to capture the current state of the list. The second scenario uses a ListControl event.

The ListControl class provides five events, listed in Table 15-5, that can be trapped and handled. These events allow your program to respond immediately to any change in selection made by the user, as well as changes to the DataSource, Display-Member, or ValueMember properties.

 The SelectedIndexChanged event is not actually a member of the List-Control class, but is included here because it is a member of all three derived controls.

Table 15-5. ListControl events

Event	Event argument	Description
DataSourceChanged	EventArgs	Raised when a new data source is set
DisplayMemberChanged	EventArgs	Raised when a new data member is set

Table 15-5. ListControl events (continued)

Event	Event argument	Description
SelectedIndexChanged	EventArgs	Raised when the SelectedIndex changes
SelectedValueChanged	EventArgs	Raised when the SelectedValue changes
ValueMemberChanged	EventArgs	Raised when a new ValueMember property is set

The following examples created in Visual Studio .NET (csListBoxEvents in C# and vbListBoxEvents in VB.NET) demonstrate the use of these events. As you will see, some events are not always raised when you would expect, and others are raised at times you would not expect. These examples consist of a form with a listbox and a pair of radio buttons for selecting the data source for the listbox. One data source will be the authors table from the pubs database, as demonstrated earlier in Example 15-1. The other data source will be an array of football quarterbacks who are members of a class called QB.

To create the list control events example, open Visual Studio .NET and create a new Windows Application project in the language of your choice. Drag a ListBox onto the form, and then a GroupBox, and then two radio buttons inside the GroupBox. Rename the controls as indicated in Table 15-6. Set the Checked property of the Authors radio button to True.

Table 15-6. Control Names in ListBox events example

Control	Name	Text
ListBox	lb	
GroupBox		DataSource
RadioButton	rbAuthors	Authors
RadioButton	rbQBs	QB's

The form in design view should look something like Figure 15-7.

Right-click on the form in design view and select View Code to open the source file in the code editor. To prepare for database access, add the following using statements to the C# version:

C#
```
using System.Data;
using System.Data.SqlClient;
```

or this imports statement to the VB.NET version:

VB
```
imports System.Data.SqlClient
```

Add the code from Example 15-8 to define the QB class in C#.

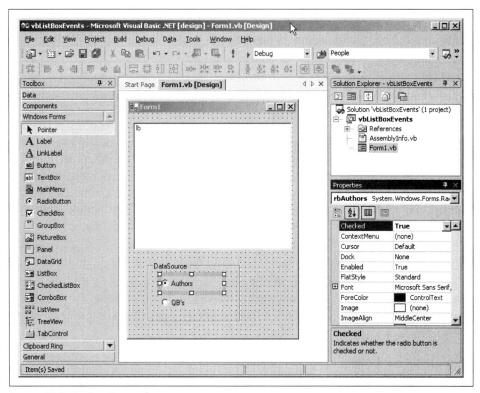

Figure 15-7. ListBoxEvents design view

Example 15-8. QB class in C#

```csharp
public class QB
{
   private string theID ;
   private string theName ;

   public  QB(string strName, string strID)
   {
      this.theID = strID;
      this.theName = strName;
   }
   public string ID
   {
      get
      {
         return theID;
      }
   }
   public string Name
   {
      get
      {
```

Example 15-8. QB class in C# (continued)

```csharp
            return theName ;
        }
    }
    public override string ToString( )
    {
        return this.theID + " : " + this.Name;
    }
}
```

And code from Example 15-9 to define the QB class in VB.NET.

Example 15-9. QB class in VB.NET

```vbnet
public class QB
    dim theID as string
    dim theName as string

    public sub New(strName as string, strID as string)
        me.theID = strID
        me.theName = strName
    end sub

    public readonly property ID as string
        get
            return theID
        end get
    end property

    public readonly property Name as string
        get
            return theName
        end get
    end property

    public overrides function ToString( ) as string
        return me.theID + " : " + me.Name
    end function
end class
```

The QB class has two read-only properties: ID and Name, both strings. It also over-rides the ToString method to return a concatenation of the two properties.

Now move your attention to the Form1 class. First, add the following declarations to the class outside the constructor:

```csharp
private DataTable dataTable;
private ArrayList QBs = new ArrayList( );
```

```vbnet
dim dt as DataTable
dim QBs as new ArrayList( )
```

Add the code from Example 15-10 to the C# constructor to connect to and query the pubs database and set the data source properties of the listbox. This code also populates the ArrayList of QB objects in C#.

Example 15-10. Constructor code in C#

```
string connectionString =
    "server= YourServer; uid=sa; pwd=YourPassword; database=pubs";
string commandString =
    "Select au_id, au_lname + ', ' + au_fname as name from authors";
SqlDataAdapter dataAdapter =
    new SqlDataAdapter(commandString, connectionString);
DataSet dataSet = new DataSet();
dataAdapter.Fill(dataSet,"Authors");
dataTable = dataSet.Tables[0];

// bind to the data table
lb.DataSource= dataTable;
lb.DisplayMember = "name";
lb.ValueMember = "au_id";

// populate the arraylist for later use.
QBs.Add(new QB("Joe Montana", "SF"));
QBs.Add(new QB("Joe Willie", "NYJ"));
QBs.Add(new QB("Tom Brady", "NE"));
QBs.Add(new QB("Drew Bledsoe", "Buf"));
QBs.Add(new QB("Johny Unitas", "Bal"));
QBs.Add(new QB("Troy Aikman", "Dal"));
QBs.Add(new QB("Brett Favre", "GB"));
```

It populates code from Example 15-11 in VB.NET as well.

Example 15-11. Constructor code in VB.NET

```
dim connectionString as String = _
    "server=YourServer; uid=sa; pwd=YourPassword; database=pubs"
dim commandString as String = _
    "Select au_id, au_lname + ', ' + au_fname as name from authors"
dim dataAdapter as new SqlDataAdapter(commandString, connectionString)
dim ds as new DataSet()
dataAdapter.Fill(ds,"Authors")
dt = ds.Tables(0)

' bind to the data table
lb.DataSource= dt
lb.DisplayMember = "name"
lb.ValueMember = "au_id"

' populate the arraylist for later use.
QBs.Add(new QB("Joe Montana", "SF"))
QBs.Add(new QB("Joe Willie", "NYJ"))
QBs.Add(new QB("Tom Brady", "NE"))
QBs.Add(new QB("Drew Bledsoe", "Buf"))
```

Example 15-11. Constructor code in VB.NET (continued)

```
QBs.Add(new QB("Johny Unitas", "Bal"))
QBs.Add(new QB("Troy Aikman", "Dal"))
QBs.Add(new QB("Brett Favre", "GB"))
```

You are now going to use Visual Studio .NET to create the event handlers. In the C# version, add an event handler by going to the design view of the form, clicking on the yellow lightning bolt in the Properties window, selecting the control whose event you wish to handle, and double-clicking in the Properties window next to the event name. In VB.NET, you can achieve the same result by going to the code editor, selecting the control from the drop-down menu at the top left of the code window, and then clicking on the desired event name in the drop-down menu at the top right of the code window.

In either language, a code skeleton will be opened, in the code window with the property declaration for an event handler method, with a default name for that control's default event, plus the code required to hook that event handler to the event.

This technique will not work directly for this example because you want to use the same event handler for multiple controls, i.e., both radio buttons, which is not how Visual Studio .NET does things by default. You can, however, accomplish this task directly.

To do so in C#, select both radio button controls in design view. Then click on the yellow lightning bolt in the Properties window, and enter the desired method name (rb_CheckedChanged) next to the CheckedChanged event. A code skeleton will be created in the code window for an event handler named rb_CheckedChanged and the cursor will be placed in the method, ready for typing. Enter the highlighted code shown in Example 15-12.

Example 15-12. Radio button event handler in C#

```
private void rb_CheckedChanged(object sender, System.EventArgs e)
{
    if (rbAuthors.Checked )
    {
        lb.DataSource= dataTable;
        lb.DisplayMember = "name";
        lb.ValueMember = "au_id";
    }
    else
    {
        lb.DataSource = QBs;
        lb.DisplayMember = "Name";
        lb.ValueMember = "ID";
    }
}
```

In VB.NET, the procedure is somewhat different. Create an event handler with the default name for the CheckedChanged event for one of the radio buttons. In the code window, change the name of the event handler to rb_CheckedChanged. Add the highlighted code shown in Example 15-13. Be sure to modify the Handles clause to list the CheckedChanged event for both radio button events.

Example 15-13. Radio button event handler in VB.NET

```
Private Sub rb_CheckedChanged(ByVal sender As Object, _
                    ByVal e As System.EventArgs) _
           Handles rbQBs.CheckedChanged, rbAuthors.CheckedChanged
    if rbAuthors.Checked then
       lb.DataSource= dt
       lb.DisplayMember = "name"
       lb.ValueMember = "au_id"
    else
       lb.DataSource = QBs
       lb.DisplayMember = "Name"
       lb.ValueMember = "ID"
    end if
End Sub
```

Now both rbAuthors and rbQBs use the same event handler for the Checked-Changed event in both languages.

Run the form. When you click on the radio buttons, the items displayed in the list-box will be populated from either the Authors table or the array of quarterbacks.

Next, add event handlers for the ListBox SelectedIndexChanged, SelectedValue-Changed, DataSourceChanged, DisplayMemberChanged, and ValueMemberChanged events, as described above. All of these event handlers do nothing more than display a MessageBox with the name of the event handler as a caption and relevant listbox properties as the body. The event handlers look like Examples 15-14 and 15-15.

Example 15-14. Event handlers in C#

```
private void lb_SelectedIndexChanged(object sender, System.EventArgs e)
{
    MessageBox.Show(lb.SelectedIndex.ToString( )+ "\n" +
                lb.GetItemText(lb.SelectedItem),
                "lb_SelectedIndexChanged");
}
private void lb_SelectedValueChanged(object sender, System.EventArgs e)
{
    MessageBox.Show(lb.GetItemText(lb.SelectedItem),
                "lb_SelectedValueChanged");
}
private void lb_DataSourceChanged(object sender, System.EventArgs e)
{
    MessageBox.Show(lb.DataSource.ToString( ), "lb_DataSourceChanged");
}
private void lb_DisplayMemberChanged(object sender, System.EventArgs e)
```

Example 15-14. Event handlers in C# (continued)

```C#
{
    MessageBox.Show(lb.DisplayMember.ToString(),
                    "lb_DisplayMemberChanged");
}
private void lb_ValueMemberChanged(object sender, System.EventArgs e)
{
    MessageBox.Show(lb.ValueMember.ToString(), "lb_ValueMemberChanged");
}
```

Example 15-15. Event handlers in VB.NET

```VB
Private Sub lb_SelectedIndexChanged(ByVal sender As Object, _
                                    ByVal e As System.EventArgs) _
                                    Handles lb.SelectedIndexChanged
    MessageBox.Show(lb.SelectedIndex.ToString()+ vbCrLf + _
                lb.GetItemText(lb.SelectedItem), _
                "lb_SelectedIndexChanged")
End Sub

Private Sub lb_SelectedValueChanged(ByVal sender As Object, _
                                    ByVal e As System.EventArgs) _
                                    Handles lb.SelectedValueChanged
    MessageBox.Show(lb.GetItemText(lb.SelectedItem), _
                "lb_SelectedValueChanged")
End Sub

Private Sub lb_DataSourceChanged(ByVal sender As Object, _
                                 ByVal e As System.EventArgs) _
                                 Handles lb.DataSourceChanged
    MessageBox.Show(lb.DataSource.ToString(), _
                "lb_DataSourceChanged")
End Sub

Private Sub lb_DisplayMemberChanged(ByVal sender As Object, _
                                    ByVal e As System.EventArgs) _
                                    Handles lb.DisplayMemberChanged
    MessageBox.Show(lb.DisplayMember.ToString(), _
                "lb_DisplayMemberChanged")
End Sub

Private Sub lb_ValueMemberChanged(ByVal sender As Object, _
                                  ByVal e As System.EventArgs) _
                                  Handles lb.ValueMemberChanged
    MessageBox.Show(lb.ValueMember.ToString(), _
                "lb_ValueMemberChanged")
End Sub
```

When you run this application now, you will see a surprising number of events being raised. First, the SelectedIndexChanged and SelectedValueChanged events always fire in pairs: they are redundant. You can comment out one of them to reduce clutter when this application runs.

Of more interest is the sheer number of times either event is raised. It turns out that when the DataSource, DisplayMember and ValueMember properties are set, the SelectedIndexChanged and SelectedValueChanged events are raised repeatedly, as well as twice more when the constructor completes. Notably, the pair of events is raised only once if you use Items.Add rather than data binding to populate the listbox.

This is not the behavior most applications want. Typically, you should raise the SelectedIndexChanged or SelectedValueChanged events only when a user interaction causes a change. To force this, you must undo a bit of the plumbing code inserted by Visual Studio .NET and replace it with some of your own.

Create an event handler for the form Load event by double-clicking on the form in design view. Then go to the code window.

In the C# version, find the two lines of code in InitializeComponent() that add the event handlers for the two events in question. They look like the following:

C#
```
this.lb.SelectedValueChanged +=
    new System.EventHandler(this.lb_SelectedValueChanged);
this.lb.SelectedIndexChanged +=
    new System.EventHandler(this.lb_SelectedIndexChanged);
```

Move those lines of code out of InitializeComponent() and into the Form1_Load event handler method.

In the VB.NET version, add the following lines of code to the Form1_Load event handler method:

VB
```
AddHandler lb.SelectedIndexChanged, AddressOf lb_SelectedIndexChanged
AddHandler lb.SelectedValueChanged, AddressOf lb_SelectedValueChanged
```

Then delete the Handles clause from the method declarations for each of the two event handlers.

Now when you run the application in either language, neither the SelectedIndex-Changed nor SelectedValueChanged events will be handled until after the form is loaded.

The DataSourceChanged event only seems to be raised in the constructor, not when DataSource is changed within the radio button CheckedChanged event handler, although clearly the data source is set correctly.

ListBox

As seen in the previous examples in this chapter and displayed in Figure 15-3, a ListBox presents a list of items to a user.

The items displayed in the list are members of an Items collection, which may be filled either by manipulating the Items collection directly or by data binding the control to a data source via the DataSource property. The Items property is of type

ListBox.ObjectCollection. Other commonly used ListBox methods are listed in Table 15-7. Table 15-4 lists commonly used methods available to all Object-Collections. In addition, the ListBox.ObjectCollection has an overloaded form of the AddRange method that lets you add the items from an existing ListBox.Object-Collection to the collection.

The programs listed in Example 15-16 (in C#) and Example 15-17 (in VB.NET) demonstrate the use of the Items.Add method to populate the Items collection. Note the call to the BeginUpdate method before any items are added to the collection, followed by a call to EndUpdate. When adding items individually, thi provides better performance and prevents screen flicker by suspending the redrawing of the control until EndUpdate is called.

Example 15-16. Adding Items to ListBox Items Collection in C# (ListBoxItems.cs)

```csharp
using System;
using System.Drawing;
using System.Windows.Forms;
using System.Data;
using System.Data.SqlClient;

namespace ProgrammingWinApps
{
    public class ListBoxItems : Form
    {
        ListBox lb;

        public ListBoxItems()
        {
            Text = "ListBox Items Collection";
            Size = new Size(300,400);

            lb = new ListBox();
            lb.Parent = this;
            lb.Location = new Point(10,10);
            lb.Size = new Size(ClientSize.Width - 20, Height - 200);
            lb.Anchor = AnchorStyles.Top | AnchorStyles.Left |
                    AnchorStyles.Right | AnchorStyles.Bottom;
            lb.BorderStyle = BorderStyle.Fixed3D;

            // get the data to populate the ListBox from pubs authors table
            string connectionString =
                "server=YourServer; uid=sa; pwd=YourPassword; database=pubs";
            string commandString =
                "Select au_id,au_lname +', ' + au_fname as name from authors";
            SqlDataAdapter dataAdapter =
                    new SqlDataAdapter(commandString, connectionString);
            DataSet dataSet = new DataSet();
            dataAdapter.Fill(dataSet,"Authors");
            DataTable dataTable = dataSet.Tables[0];
```

C#

```
        lb.BeginUpdate( );
        for (int i = 0; i < dataTable.Rows.Count; i++)
        {
           lb.Items.Add(
               dataTable.Rows[i]["au_id"] + "\t" +
               dataTable.Rows[i]["name"]);
        }

        lb.Items.Add("12345\tHurwitz, Dan");
        lb.Items.Add("67890\tLiberty, Jesse");
        lb.EndUpdate( );
     } //  close for constructor

     static void Main( )
     {
        Application.Run(new ListBoxItems( ));
     }
  }       //  close for form class
}         //  close form namespace
```

Example 15-17. Adding Items to ListBox Items Collection in VB.NET (ListBoxItems.vb)

VB

```
Option Strict On
imports System
imports System.Drawing
imports System.Windows.Forms
imports System.Data
imports System.Data.SqlClient
Imports System.Xml

namespace ProgrammingWinApps
   public class ListBoxItems : inherits Form

      dim lb as ListBox

      public sub New( )
         Text = "ListBox Items Collection"
         Size = new Size(300,400)

         lb = new ListBox( )
         lb.Parent = me
         lb.Location = new Point(10,10)
         lb.Size = new Size(ClientSize.Width - 20, Height - 200)
         lb.Anchor = AnchorStyles.Top or AnchorStyles.Left or _
                 AnchorStyles.Right or AnchorStyles.Bottom
         lb.BorderStyle = BorderStyle.Fixed3D

         '  get the data to populate the ListBox from pubs authors table
         dim connectionString as String = _
            "server=YourServer; uid=sa; pwd=YourPassword; database=pubs"
```

```vb
dim commandString as String = _
    "Select au_id,au_lname + ', ' + au_fname as name from authors"
dim dataAdapter as new SqlDataAdapter(commandString, _
                                      connectionString)
dim ds as new DataSet()
dataAdapter.Fill(ds,"Authors")
dim dt as new DataTable()
dt = ds.Tables(0)

lb.BeginUpdate()
dim i as integer
for i = 0 to dt.Rows.Count - 1
  lb.Items.Add( _
        dt.Rows(i)("au_id").ToString() + vbTab + _
        dt.Rows(i)("name").ToString())
next

lb.Items.Add("12345" + vbTab + "Hurwitz, Dan")
lb.Items.Add("67890" + vbTab + "Liberty, Jesse")
lb.EndUpdate()
end sub   '  close for constructor

public shared sub Main()
    Application.Run(new ListBoxItems())
    end sub
  end class
end namespace
```

In these examples, you are precluded from using data binding (i.e., the DataSource property) because items are added to the Items collection that are not in the database. (You could, if you wanted, add these extra items to the DataSet after populating from the database but before data binding occurs.) However, it is still more efficient to add the items from the database as a group, using the AddRange method rather than the Add method. To do this, replace the highlighted code in Example 15-16 with the following block of code:

```csharp
string[] arNames = new string[dataTable.Rows.Count];
lb.BeginUpdate();
for (int i = 0; i < dataTable.Rows.Count; i++)
{
   arNames[i] = dataTable.Rows[i]["au_id"] + "\t" +
       dataTable.Rows[i]["name"];
}
lb.Items.AddRange(arNames);

lb.Items.Add("12345\tHurwitz, Dan");
lb.Items.Add("67890\tLiberty, Jesse");
lb.EndUpdate();
```

and the highlighted code in Example 15-17 with the block of code shown next.

```
        dim arNames(dt.Rows.Count - 1) as string
        lb.BeginUpdate( )
        dim i as integer
        for i = 0 to dt.Rows.Count - 1
            arNames(i) = dt.Rows(i)("au_id").ToString( ) + vbTab + _
                dt.Rows(i)("name").ToString( )
        next
        lb.Items.AddRange(arNames)

        lb.Items.Add("12345" + vbTab + "Hurwitz, Dan")
        lb.Items.Add("67890" + vbTab + "Liberty, Jesse")
        lb.EndUpdate( )
```

In these code snippets, an array list is created to hold the database data. Since the overloaded version of the AddRange method used here takes an array of objects as an argument, the ArrayList.ToArray method converts the array list to the requisite array. If AddRange is used exclusively to add all the items to the collection, then using the BeginUpdate and EndUpdate methods is not beneficial. Table 15-7 lists common ListBox methods.

Table 15-7. ListBox methods

Method	Description
ClearSelected	Unselects all selected items. Equivalent to setting SelectedIndex property to −1.
GetSelected	Returns true if the item at the specified index is selected.
IndexFromPoint	Overloaded. Returns zero-based index of item at the specified point. Returns ListBox.NoMatches if nothing found.
SetSelected	Sets or clears the selection status of the item at the specified index, based on specified Boolean value.

The ListBox control has a number of properties, listed in Table 15-8, in addition to those derived from the ListControl class (listed in Table 15-1) and those in common with the other list controls (listed in Table 15-2).

The ListBox control (and the CheckedListBox that derives from it) can allow either no selections, a single selection, or multiple selections, depending on the value of the of the SelectionMode property. Valid values of the SelectionMode property are members of the SelectionMode enumeration, listed in Table 15-9. The default mode is single selection (i.e., a value of SelectionMode.One).

If the SelectionMode is set to SelectionMode.None, meaning that no selection is possible, then you cannot use data binding to populate the ListBox, since doing so implicitly sets the SelectedIndex to 0. Nor can you explicitly select an item in code, such as setting the SelectedIndex or SelectedItem properties or calling the SetSelected method. Any attempt to do so will not cause a compile error, but will cause a runtime error.

Table 15-8. ListBox properties

Property	Value type	Description
ColumnWidth	Integer	Read/write. The width, in pixels, of each column in a multicolumn listbox. If set to zero, the default width is assigned.
HorizontalExtent	Integer	Read/write. The width, in pixels, that the horizontal scrollbar can scroll the listbox if the HorizontalScrolling property is set to `true`.
HorizontalScrollbar	Boolean	Read/write. If `true`, a horizontal scrollbar is displayed when the width of the items exceeds the width of the control. Default value is `false`.
Items	ListBox.ObjectCollection	Collection of items in the listbox. ListBox.ObjectCollection class has the methods listed in Table 15-4 plus AddRange.
MultiColumn	Boolean	Read/write. If `true`, the listbox displays the items in multiple columns. Default value is `false`.
ScrollAlwaysVisible	Boolean	Read/write. If `true`, the vertical scrollbar is always visible in a listbox with MultiColumn set `false`. For multicolumn listboxes, this property controls the horizontal scrollbar. Default value is `false`.
SelectedIndices	ListBox.SelectedIndex-Collection	Read-only. The collection of zero-based indexes of all currently selected items.
SelectedItems	ListBox.SelectedObject-Collection	Read-only. The collection of all currently selected items.
SelectionMode	SelectionMode	Read/write. Specifies the selection mode of the ListBox. Valid values are members of the SelectionMode enumeration, listed in Table 15-9. The default value is SelectionMode.One.
TopIndex	Integer	Read/write. The zero-based index of the first visible item in the control.

Table 15-9. SelectionMode enumeration values

Value	Description
MultiExtended	Multiple items can be selected using the Shift, Ctrl, and arrow keys.
MultiSimple	Multiple items can be selected using the arrow keys and the spacebar.
None	No items can be selected.
One	A single item can be selected.

The application shown in Example 15-18 (in C#) and Example 15-19 (in VB.NET) demonstrates several properties, including SelectionMode and TopIndex. When run, it looks something like Figure 15-8. A set of radio buttons allows you to switch between the different selection modes. (SelectionMode.None is not supported because the listbox is data bound.) Clicking on the Update button displays the current value of TopIndex in the text box. This number will change as you resize the form and/or scroll the listbox.

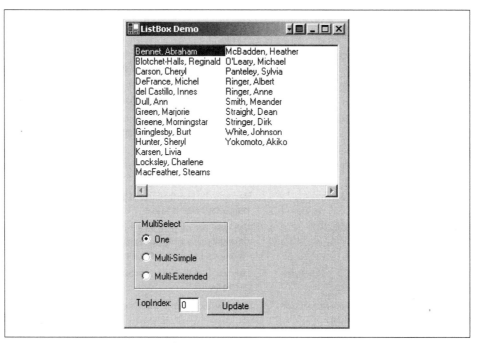

Figure 15-8. ListBox properties application

Example 15-18. ListBox properties in C# (ListBox.cs)

```csharp
using System;
using System.Drawing;
using System.Windows.Forms;
using System.Data;
using System.Data.SqlClient;

namespace ProgrammingWinApps
{
    public class ListBoxes : Form
    {
        ListBox lb;
        RadioButton rdoMultiExtended;
        RadioButton rdoMultiSimple;
        RadioButton rdoMultiOne;
        TextBox txtTop;
        Button btnTop;

        public ListBoxes( )
        {
            int xSize, ySize;

            Text = "ListBox Demo";
            Size = new Size(300,400);
```

Example 15-18. ListBox properties in C# (ListBox.cs) (continued)

```csharp
    lb = new ListBox( );
    lb.Parent = this;
    lb.Location = new Point(10,10);
    lb.Size = new Size(ClientSize.Width - 20, Height - 200);
    lb.Anchor = AnchorStyles.Top | AnchorStyles.Left |
            AnchorStyles.Right | AnchorStyles.Bottom;
    lb.BorderStyle = BorderStyle.Fixed3D;
    lb.MultiColumn = true;
    lb.ScrollAlwaysVisible = true;

    GroupBox grpMulti = new GroupBox( );
    grpMulti.Parent = this;
    grpMulti.Text = "MultiSelect";
    grpMulti.Location = new Point(lb.Left, lb.Bottom + 25);
    grpMulti.Anchor = AnchorStyles.Left | AnchorStyles.Bottom;

    rdoMultiOne = new RadioButton( );
    rdoMultiOne.Parent = grpMulti;
    rdoMultiOne.Text = "One";
    rdoMultiOne.Tag = SelectionMode.One;
    rdoMultiOne.Checked = true;
    rdoMultiOne.Location = new Point(10,15);
    rdoMultiOne.CheckedChanged +=
            new System.EventHandler(rdoMulti_CheckedChanged);

    rdoMultiSimple = new RadioButton( );
    rdoMultiSimple.Parent = grpMulti;
    rdoMultiSimple.Text = "Multi-Simple";
    rdoMultiSimple.Tag = SelectionMode.MultiSimple;
    rdoMultiSimple.Location = new Point(10, rdoMultiOne.Bottom);
    rdoMultiSimple.CheckedChanged +=
            new System.EventHandler(rdoMulti_CheckedChanged);

    rdoMultiExtended = new RadioButton( );
    rdoMultiExtended.Parent = grpMulti;
    rdoMultiExtended.Text = "Multi-Extended";
    rdoMultiExtended.Tag = SelectionMode.MultiExtended;
    rdoMultiExtended.Location = new Point(10, rdoMultiSimple.Bottom);
    rdoMultiExtended.CheckedChanged +=
            new System.EventHandler(rdoMulti_CheckedChanged);

    //  Set the size of the groupbox based on the child radio buttons
    xSize = (int)(Font.Height * .75) * rdoMultiExtended.Text.Length;
    ySize = ((int)rdoMultiOne.Height * 3) + 20;
    grpMulti.Size = new Size(xSize, ySize);

    //  3 controls to display TopIndex inside a panel
    Panel pnlTop = new Panel( );
    pnlTop.Parent = this;
    pnlTop.Location = new Point(lb.Left, grpMulti.Bottom + 10);
    pnlTop.Anchor = AnchorStyles.Left | AnchorStyles.Bottom;
```

Example 15-18. ListBox properties in C# (ListBox.cs) (continued)

```csharp
        Label lblTop = new Label( );
        lblTop.Parent = pnlTop;
        lblTop.Text = "TopIndex: ";
        xSize = ((int)(Font.Height * .5) * lblTop.Text.Length);
        lblTop.Size = new Size(xSize, Font.Height + 10);

        txtTop = new TextBox( );
        txtTop.Parent = pnlTop;
        txtTop.Location = new Point(lblTop.Right, lblTop.Top);
        txtTop.Text = lb.TopIndex.ToString( );
        txtTop.Size = new Size((int)(Font.Height * .75) * 3,
                               Font.Height + 10);

        btnTop = new Button( );
        btnTop.Parent = pnlTop;
        btnTop.Text = "Update";
        btnTop.Location = new Point(txtTop.Right + 10, txtTop.Top);
        btnTop.Click += new System.EventHandler(btnTop_Click);

        //  get the data to populate the ListBox from pubs authors table
        string connectionString =
           "server=YourServer; uid=sa; pwd=YourPassword; database=pubs";
        string commandString =
           "Select au_id,au_lname +', ' + au_fname as name from authors";
        SqlDataAdapter dataAdapter =
              new SqlDataAdapter(commandString, connectionString);
        DataSet dataSet = new DataSet( );
        dataAdapter.Fill(dataSet,"Authors");
        DataTable dataTable = dataSet.Tables[0];

        // bind to the data table
        lb.DataSource= dataTable;
        lb.DisplayMember = "name";
        lb.ValueMember = "au_id";
    } //  close for constructor

    static void Main( )
    {
        Application.Run(new ListBoxes( ));
    }

    private void rdoMulti_CheckedChanged(object sender, EventArgs e)
    {
        RadioButton rdo = (RadioButton)sender;
        lb.SelectionMode = (SelectionMode)rdo.Tag;
    }

    private void btnTop_Click(object sender, EventArgs e)
    {
        txtTop.Text = lb.TopIndex.ToString( );
    }
```

Example 15-18. ListBox properties in C# (ListBox.cs) (continued)

```
    }       //  close for form class
}           //  close form namespace
```

Example 15-19. ListBox properties in VB.NET (ListBox.vb)

```
Option Strict On
imports System
imports System.Drawing
imports System.Windows.Forms
imports System.Data
imports System.Data.SqlClient

namespace ProgrammingWinApps
    public class ListBoxes : inherits Form

        dim lb as ListBox
        dim rdoMultiExtended as RadioButton
        dim rdoMultiSimple as RadioButton
        dim rdoMultiOne as RadioButton
        dim txtTop as TextBox
        dim btnTop as Button

        public sub New( )
            dim xSize, ySize as integer

            Text = "ListBox Demo"
            Size = new Size(300,400)

            lb = new ListBox( )
            lb.Parent = me
            lb.Location = new Point(10,10)
            lb.Size = new Size(ClientSize.Width - 20, Height - 200)
            lb.Anchor = AnchorStyles.Top or AnchorStyles.Left or _
                    AnchorStyles.Right or AnchorStyles.Bottom
            lb.BorderStyle = BorderStyle.Fixed3D
            lb.MultiColumn = true
            lb.ScrollAlwaysVisible = true

            dim grpMulti as new GroupBox( )
            grpMulti.Parent = me
            grpMulti.Text = "MultiSelect"
            grpMulti.Location = new Point(lb.Left, lb.Bottom + 25)
            grpMulti.Anchor = AnchorStyles.Left or AnchorStyles.Bottom

            rdoMultiOne = new RadioButton( )
            rdoMultiOne.Parent = grpMulti
            rdoMultiOne.Text = "One"
            rdoMultiOne.Tag = SelectionMode.One
            rdoMultiOne.Checked = true
            rdoMultiOne.Location = new Point(10,15)
            AddHandler rdoMultiOne.CheckedChanged, _
                    AddressOf rdoMulti_CheckedChanged
```

Example 15-19. ListBox properties in VB.NET (ListBox.vb) (continued)

```vb
rdoMultiSimple = new RadioButton( )
rdoMultiSimple.Parent = grpMulti
rdoMultiSimple.Text = "Multi-Simple"
rdoMultiSimple.Tag = SelectionMode.MultiSimple
rdoMultiSimple.Location = new Point(10, rdoMultiOne.Bottom)
AddHandler rdoMultiSimple.CheckedChanged, _
        AddressOf rdoMulti_CheckedChanged

rdoMultiExtended = new RadioButton( )
rdoMultiExtended.Parent = grpMulti
rdoMultiExtended.Text = "Multi-Extended"
rdoMultiExtended.Tag = SelectionMode.MultiExtended
rdoMultiExtended.Location = new Point(10, rdoMultiSimple.Bottom)
AddHandler rdoMultiExtended.CheckedChanged, _
        AddressOf rdoMulti_CheckedChanged

'  Set the size of the groupbox based on the child radio buttons
xSize = CType(Font.Height * .75, integer) * _
            rdoMultiExtended.Text.Length
ySize = CType(rdoMultiOne.Height * 3, integer) + 20
grpMulti.Size = new Size(xSize, ySize)

'  3 controls to display TopIndex inside a panel
dim pnlTop as new Panel( )
pnlTop.Parent = me
pnlTop.Location = new Point(lb.Left, grpMulti.Bottom + 10)
pnlTop.Anchor = AnchorStyles.Left or AnchorStyles.Bottom

dim lblTop as new Label( )
lblTop.Parent = pnlTop
lblTop.Text = "TopIndex: "
xSize = CType(Font.Height * .5, integer) * lblTop.Text.Length
lblTop.Size = new Size(xSize, Font.Height + 10)

txtTop = new TextBox( )
txtTop.Parent = pnlTop
txtTop.Location = new Point(lblTop.Right, lblTop.Top)
txtTop.Text = lb.TopIndex.ToString( )
txtTop.Size = new Size(CType((Font.Height * .75) * 3, integer), _
                    Font.Height + 10)

btnTop = new Button( )
btnTop.Parent = pnlTop
btnTop.Text = "Update"
btnTop.Location = new Point(txtTop.Right + 10, txtTop.Top)
AddHandler btnTop.Click, _
        AddressOf btnTop_Click

'  get the data to populate the ListBox from pubs authors table
dim connectionString as String = _
   "server=YourServer; uid=sa; pwd=YourPassword; database=pubs"
dim commandString as String = _
   "Select au_id,au_lname + ', ' + au_fname as name from authors"
```

Example 15-19. ListBox properties in VB.NET (ListBox.vb) (continued)

```
        dim dataAdapter as new SqlDataAdapter(commandString, _
                                   connectionString)
        dim ds as new DataSet( )
        dataAdapter.Fill(ds,"Authors")
        dim dt as new DataTable( )
        dt = ds.Tables(0)

        ' bind to the data table
        lb.DataSource= dt
        lb.DisplayMember = "name"
        lb.ValueMember = "au_id"
    end sub  ' close for constructor

    public shared sub Main( )
        Application.Run(new ListBoxes( ))
    end sub

    private sub rdoMulti_CheckedChanged(ByVal sender as object, _
                        ByVal e as EventArgs)
        dim rdo as RadioButton = CType(sender, RadioButton)
        lb.SelectionMode = CType(rdo.Tag, SelectionMode)
    end sub

    private sub btnTop_Click(ByVal sender as object, _
                    ByVal e as EventArgs)
        txtTop.Text = lb.TopIndex.ToString( )
    end sub
  end class
end namespace
```

The listbox created in Examples 15-18 and 15-19 has the MultiColumn and ScrollAlwaysVisible properties set to true, neither of which is the default value. A MultiColumn listbox creates as many columns as are necessary to display the data. You can control the column width by setting the ColumnWidth property. A default width is used either by setting the property to zero or omitting the property altogether, as was done in these examples.

The radio buttons used to set the SelectionMode use the Tag property. This property lets the common radio button CheckedChanged event handler set the value of the SelectionMode property directly from the value of the Tag property. (For a complete discussion of radio buttons, refer to Chapter 11.)

CheckedListBox

The CheckedListBox derives from ListBox, so it inherits all the members and functionality of the ListBox class. The two controls have just a few differences. Table 15-10 lists the properties that are unique to the CheckedListBox control.

Table 15-10. CheckedListBox properties

Property	Value type	Description
CheckedIndices	CheckedListBox.Checked-IndexCollection	Read-only. The collection of indexes that are either checked or indeterminate.
CheckedItems	CheckedListBox.CheckedItemCollection	Read-only. The collection of items that are either checked or indeterminate.
CheckOnClick	Boolean	Read/write. If `true`, an item's checked status will be toggled immediately when it is clicked. The default, `false`, allows the user to select an item without changing its checked status. A second click then changes the checked status. Use of the arrow keys and the spacebar to toggle the checked status is unaffected by this property.
Items	CheckedListBox.ObjectCollection	Collection of items in the control.
SelectionMode	SelectionMode	Overridden from ListBox. Since multiple selection is not supported (other than by checking multiple checkboxes), the only legal values are SelectionMode.One and SelectionMode.None.
ThreeDCheckBoxes	Boolean	Read/write. If `true`, checkboxes have a 3-D appearance. If `false` (the default), checkboxes are flat squares.

The obvious visual difference between ListBoxes and CheckedListBoxes is that each item in the list of the CheckedListBox has a small square checkbox next to it. Checked items display a checkmark in the checkbox rather than display the item in a highlighted color. The ThreeDCheckBoxes property can be set true to force the checkboxes to display with a three-dimensional appearance; otherwise, they are flat squares.

The second significant difference between the two controls is that the CheckedListBox has a tri-state selection capability: each item can have one of the three CheckState enumeration values listed in Table 15-11. Only the Checked and Unchecked states can be set by the end user. No provision in the UI sets the checked state of an item to Indeterminate; this must be done in code. Typically the indeterminate state is used when the UI tries to convey mixed information. A common example would be a checkbox that indicates bold text. If some of the text is bold and some is not, then it is indeterminate.

Table 15-11. CheckState enumeration values

Value	Description
Checked	Item is checked.
Unchecked	Item is not checked.
Indeterminate	Item is indeterminate. Checkbox has a shaded appearance.

The SelectedItems and SelectedIndices collections are still available to the CheckedListBox control, but as seen in Examples 15-20 and 15-21, they contain only the currently selected item. In their places, you will usually use the analogous CheckedItems and CheckedIndices collections.

The Items property, of type CheckedListBox.ObjectCollection, contains the collection of items in the control. The CheckedListBox.ObjectCollection class has the methods common to all the list controls listed in Table 15-4, plus two additional overloaded forms of the Add method that take into account the checked status.

The CheckedListBox class has several methods, listed in Table 15-12, that allow your code to set and retrieve the checked status of an item in the control. The GetItem-Checked method treats Indeterminate items as though they are Checked, while the GetItemCheckState and SetItemCheckState methods explicitly take the trimodal CheckState into account.

Table 15-12. CheckedListBox methods

Method	Description
GetItemChecked	Returns `true` if the item at the specified index is Checked or Indeterminate; otherwise returns `false`.
GetItemCheckState	Returns the checked status of the item at the specified index. Return values are members of the CheckState enumeration, listed in Table 15-11.
SetItemChecked	Sets the item at the specified index to either CheckState.Checked or CheckState.Unchecked.
SetItemCheckState	Sets the item at the specified index to the specified CheckState value. Legal values of Check-State are members of the CheckState enumeration, listed in Table 15-11.

The CheckedListBox has a single event, ItemCheck, which is not inherited from the ListBox control. It takes an event argument of type ItemCheckEventArgs, which exposes the properties listed in Table 15-13. This event is raised before the change takes effect. The event argument exposes both the old and the new values, and your code can change the new value, but as demonstrated in Examples 15-20 and 15-21, if you need information about the CheckedIndices or CheckedItems collections that is current after the change takes effect, then you should trap the SelectedIndex-Changed event instead.

Table 15-13. ItemCheckEventArgs properties

Property	Description
CurrentValue	The current state, before the change takes effect, of the item's checkbox.
Index	The zero-based index of the item whose check state is about to change.
NewValue	Read/write. The new check state of the item after the change takes effect.

The application listed in Example 15-20 (in C#) and Example 15-21 (in VB.NET) demonstrates the usage of the CheckedListBox control. It is based on the ListBox examples seen previously in Figures 15-7 and 15-8, with the list items coming from the authors table of the pubs database. (Since the CheckedListBox control is data bound, the Items collection cannot be further manipulated, precluding a demonstration of the Add methods.)

When compiled and run, the example looks like Figure 15-9. The MultiColumn, ScrollAlwaysVisible, and ThreeDCheckBoxes properties are all true, resulting in a nondefault but intuitive appearance. The CheckOnClick property is also set to true, so the first click on an item toggles the check state between Checked and Unchecked.

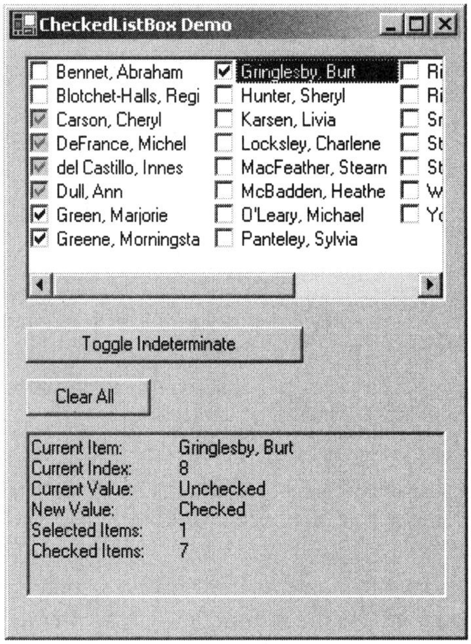

Figure 15-9. CheckedListBox application

The Toggle Indeterminate button toggles all the checked items to Indeterminate, and vice versa. In Figure 15-9, four items are Indeterminate, displayed as grayed check-marks in a gray checkbox. The Clear All button clears all the checkboxes. The gray text box displays information about the currently selected item as well as a count of the selected items and the checked items. As seen later, this last bit of information was tricky to get.

An analysis follows the code listings.

Example 15-20. CheckedListBox demo in C# (CheckedListBox.cs)

```
using System;
using System.Drawing;
using System.Windows.Forms;
using System.Data;
using System.Data.SqlClient;

namespace ProgrammingWinApps
{
```

Example 15-20. CheckedListBox demo in C# (CheckedListBox.cs) (continued)

```csharp
public class CheckedListBoxes : Form
{
    CheckedListBox clb;
    Button btnToggle;
    Button btnClear;
    TextBox txt;
    String str;

    public CheckedListBoxes( )
    {
        Text = "CheckedListBox Demo";
        Size = new Size(300,400);
        this.Load += new EventHandler(this_Load);

        clb = new CheckedListBox( );
        clb.Parent = this;
        clb.Location = new Point(10,10);
        clb.Size = new Size(ClientSize.Width - 20, Height - 240);
        clb.Anchor = AnchorStyles.Top | AnchorStyles.Left |
                AnchorStyles.Right | AnchorStyles.Bottom;
        clb.BorderStyle = BorderStyle.Fixed3D;
        clb.MultiColumn = true;
        clb.ScrollAlwaysVisible = true;
        clb.ThreeDCheckBoxes = true;
        clb.CheckOnClick = true;
        clb.ItemCheck += new ItemCheckEventHandler(clb_ItemCheck);

        // Toggle Indeterminate Button
        btnToggle = new Button( );
        btnToggle.Parent = this;
        btnToggle.Text = "Toggle Indeterminate";
        btnToggle.Size = new Size(
                        (int)(Font.Height * .75) * btnToggle.Text.Length,
                        Font.Height + 10);
        btnToggle.Location = new Point( clb.Left, clb.Bottom + 10);
        btnToggle.Anchor = AnchorStyles.Left | AnchorStyles.Bottom;
        btnToggle.Click += new System.EventHandler(btnToggle_Click);

        // Clear Button
        btnClear = new Button( );
        btnClear.Parent = this;
        btnClear.Text = "Clear All";
        btnClear.Size = new Size(
                        (int)(Font.Height * .75) * btnClear.Text.Length,
                        Font.Height + 10);
        btnClear.Location = new Point(btnToggle.Left,
                                        btnToggle.Bottom + 10);
        btnClear.Anchor = AnchorStyles.Left | AnchorStyles.Bottom;
        btnClear.Click += new System.EventHandler(btnClear_Click);

        // Selected Items TextBox
        txt = new TextBox( );
```

Example 15-20. CheckedListBox demo in C# (CheckedListBox.cs) (continued)

```csharp
txt.Parent = this;
txt.Multiline = true;
txt.ReadOnly = true;
txt.BackColor = Color.LightGray;
txt.Location = new Point(btnClear.Left, btnClear.Bottom + 10);
txt.Size = new Size(clb.Width, Font.Height * 8);
txt.Anchor = AnchorStyles.Left | AnchorStyles.Bottom |
             AnchorStyles.Right;

// get the data to populate the ListBox from pubs authors table
string connectionString =
   "server=YourServer; uid=sa; pwd=YourPassword; database=pubs";
string commandString =
    "Select au_id,au_lname+', ' + au_fname as name from authors";
SqlDataAdapter dataAdapter =
      new SqlDataAdapter(commandString, connectionString);
DataSet dataSet = new DataSet( );
dataAdapter.Fill(dataSet,"Authors");
DataTable dataTable = dataSet.Tables[0];

// bind to the data table
clb.DataSource= dataTable;
clb.DisplayMember = "name";
clb.ValueMember = "au_id";
}  // close for constructor

static void Main( )
{
   Application.Run(new CheckedListBoxes( ));
}

private void btnToggle_Click(object sender, EventArgs e)
{
   for (int i = 0; i <= (clb.Items.Count - 1); i++)
   {
      if (clb.GetItemCheckState(i) == CheckState.Checked)
      {
         clb.SetItemCheckState(i, CheckState.Indeterminate);
      }
      else if (clb.GetItemCheckState(i) == CheckState.Indeterminate)
      {
         clb.SetItemCheckState(i, CheckState.Checked);
      }
   }
}

private void btnClear_Click(object sender, EventArgs e)
{
   for (int i = 0; i <= (clb.Items.Count - 1); i++)
   {
      clb.SetItemChecked(i, false);
   }
```

Example 15-20. CheckedListBox demo in C# (CheckedListBox.cs) (continued)

```csharp
         txt.Text = "";
   }

   private void clb_ItemCheck(object sender, ItemCheckEventArgs e)
   {
      str = "";
      str += "Current Item:\t" +
            clb.GetItemText(clb.Items[e.Index]) + "\r\n";
      str += "Current Index:\t" + e.Index.ToString( ) + "\r\n";
      str += "Current Value:\t" + e.CurrentValue.ToString( ) + "\r\n";
      str += "New Value:\t" + e.NewValue.ToString( );
   }

   private void clb_SelectedIndexChanged(object sender, EventArgs e)
   {
      str += "\r\n";
      str += "Selected Items:\t" +
            clb.SelectedItems.Count.ToString( ) + "\r\n";
      str += "Checked Items:\t" + clb.CheckedItems.Count.ToString( );
      txt.Text = str;
   }

   private void this_Load(object sender, EventArgs e)
   {
      clb.SelectedIndexChanged +=
            new EventHandler(clb_SelectedIndexChanged);
   }
   }      //   close for form class
}        //   close form namespace
```

Example 15-21. CheckedListBox demo in VB.NET (CheckedListBox.vb)

```vbnet
Option Strict On
imports System
imports System.Drawing
imports System.Windows.Forms
imports System.Data
imports System.Data.SqlClient

namespace ProgrammingWinApps
   public class CheckedListBoxes : inherits Form

      dim clb as CheckedListBox
      dim txt as TextBox
      dim btnToggle as Button
      dim btnClear as Button
      dim str as string

      public sub New( )
         Text = "CheckedListBox Demo"
         Size = new Size(300,400)
         AddHandler me.Load, AddressOf me_Load
```

```
clb = new CheckedListBox( )
clb.Parent = me
clb.Location = new Point(10,10)
clb.Size = new Size(ClientSize.Width - 20, Height - 240)
clb.Anchor = AnchorStyles.Top or AnchorStyles.Left or _
        AnchorStyles.Right or AnchorStyles.Bottom
clb.BorderStyle = BorderStyle.Fixed3D
clb.MultiColumn = true
clb.ScrollAlwaysVisible = true
clb.ThreeDCheckBoxes = true
clb.CheckOnClick = true
AddHandler clb.ItemCheck, AddressOf clb_ItemCheck

' Toggle Indeterminate Button
btnToggle = new Button( )
btnToggle.Parent = me
btnToggle.Text = "Toggle Indeterminate"
btnToggle.Size = new Size(CType(Font.Height * .75, integer) * _
            btnToggle.Text.Length, Font.Height + 10)
btnToggle.Location = new Point( clb.Left, clb.Bottom + 10)
btnToggle.Anchor = AnchorStyles.Left or AnchorStyles.Bottom
AddHandler btnToggle.Click, AddressOf btnToggle_Click

' Clear Button
btnClear = new Button( )
btnClear.Parent = me
btnClear.Text = "Clear All"
btnClear.Size = new Size(CType(Font.Height * .75, integer) * _
            btnClear.Text.Length, Font.Height + 10)
btnClear.Location = new Point(btnToggle.Left, _
                            btnToggle.Bottom + 10)
btnClear.Anchor = AnchorStyles.Left or AnchorStyles.Bottom
AddHandler btnClear.Click, AddressOf btnClear_Click

' Selected Items TextBox
txt = new TextBox( )
txt.Parent = me
txt.Multiline = true
txt.ReadOnly = true
txt.BackColor = Color.LightGray
txt.Location = new Point(btnClear.Left, _
                txt.Bottom + 10)
txt.Size = new Size(clb.Width, Font.Height * 7)
txt.Anchor = AnchorStyles.Left or _
        AnchorStyles.Bottom or AnchorStyles.Right

' get the data to populate the ListBox from pubs authors table
dim connectionString as String = _
    "server=YourServer; uid=sa; pwd=YourPassword; database=pubs"
dim commandString as String = _
    "Select au_id,au_lname + ', ' + au_fname as name from authors"
dim dataAdapter as new SqlDataAdapter(commandString, _
                        connectionString)
```

```vb
       dim ds as new DataSet( )
       dataAdapter.Fill(ds,"Authors")
       dim dt as new DataTable( )
       dt = ds.Tables(0)

       ' bind to the data table
       clb.DataSource= dt
       clb.DisplayMember = "name"
       clb.ValueMember = "au_id"
    end sub  '  close for constructor

    public shared sub Main( )
       Application.Run(new CheckedListBoxes( ))
    end sub

    private sub btnToggle_Click(ByVal sender as object, _
                             ByVal e as EventArgs)
       dim i as integer
       for i = 0 to clb.Items.Count - 1
          if clb.GetItemCheckState(i) = CheckState.Checked then
             clb.SetItemCheckState(i, CheckState.Indeterminate)
          else if clb.GetItemCheckState(i)=CheckState.Indeterminate then
             clb.SetItemCheckState(i, CheckState.Checked)
          end if
       next
    end sub

    private sub btnClear_Click(ByVal sender as object, _
                             ByVal e as EventArgs)
       dim i as integer
       for i = 0 to clb.Items.Count - 1
          clb.SetItemChecked(i, false)
       next
       txt.Text = ""
    end sub

    private sub clb_ItemCheck(ByVal sender as object, _
                             ByVal e as ItemCheckEventArgs)
       str = ""
       str += "Current Item:" + vbTab + _
             clb.GetItemText(clb.Items(e.Index)) + vbCrLf
       str += "Current Index:" + vbTab + _
             e.Index.ToString( ) + vbCrLf
       str += "Current Value:" + vbTab + _
             e.CurrentValue.ToString( ) + vbCrLf
       str += "New Value:" + vbTab + e.NewValue.ToString( )
    end sub

    private sub clb_SelectedIndexChanged(ByVal sender as object, _
                                       ByVal e as EventArgs)
       str += vbCrLf
       str += "Selected Items:" + vbTab + _
                clb.SelectedItems.Count.ToString( ) + vbCrLf
```

Example 15-21. CheckedListBox demo in VB.NET (CheckedListBox.vb) (continued)

`C#`
```
        str += "Checked Items:" + vbTab + _
                    clb.CheckedItems.Count.ToString( )
        txt.Text = str
    end sub

    private sub me_Load(ByVal sender as object, _
                    ByVal e as EventArgs)
        AddHandler clb.SelectedIndexChanged, _
                    AddressOf clb_SelectedIndexChanged
    end sub
  end class
end namespace
```

Looking in the constructor, an event handler is installed for the Form Load event and an event handler is for the CheckedListBox ItemCheck event:

`C#`
```
    this.Load += new EventHandler(this_Load);
    clb.ItemCheck += new ItemCheckEventHandler(clb_ItemCheck);
```

`VB`
```
    AddHandler me.Load, AddressOf me_Load
    AddHandler clb.ItemCheck, AddressOf clb_ItemCheck
```

Looking ahead to the Form Load event handler, an event handler is installed for the CheckedListBox SelectedIndexChanged event:

`C#`
```
    private void this_Load(object sender, EventArgs e)
    {
        clb.SelectedIndexChanged +=
            new EventHandler(clb_SelectedIndexChanged);
    }
```

`VB`
```
    private sub me_Load(ByVal sender as object, _
                    ByVal e as EventArgs)
        AddHandler clb.SelectedIndexChanged, _
                    AddressOf clb_SelectedIndexChanged
    end sub
```

You must use the SelectedIndexChanged event to get the current count of checked items for display in the text box. Although you can retrieve the value of the CheckedListBox.CheckedItems.Count property in the ItemCheck event handler, it will lag the current value by one operation; the ItemCheck event is raised *before* the change takes place, while the SelectedIndexChanged event is raised *after* the change. The SelectedIndexChanged event handler is added to the event delegate in the Form Load event handler to avoid the SelectedIndexChanged event being handled during the data binding and form initialization, as discussed earlier in this chapter in the section "ListControl Events."

The Toggle Indeterminate button toggles all the checked items to Indeterminate and vice versa. This is accomplished by iterating through the CheckedListBox Items collection and using the GetItemCheckState method to test each item within an if/ else if construct. The advantage to this technique is that the index of the for loop corresponds to the index of each item within the collection. All the CheckedListBox methods listed in Table 15-12 require the index of the item it manipulates.

An alternative technique would iterate through the CheckedItems collection with a code snippet similar to the following:

C#
```
if (clb.CheckedItems.Count != 0)
{
    for (int i = 0; i <= clb.CheckedItems.Count - 1; i++)
    {
        // Do some processing here
    }
}
```

VB
```
if clb.CheckedItems.Count <> 0 then
    dim i as integer
    for i = 0 to clb.CheckedItems.Count - 1
        ' Do some processing here
    next i
end if
```

In this case, the loop index does not correspond to the index of the item in the Items collection, but to the index within the CheckedItems collection. The requirements of your application will determine which one is the appropriate technique.

The Clear All button clears all the checked items, whether the check state is Checked or Indeterminate. Similar to the btnToggle_Click event handler, it iterates through the Items collection and uses the CheckedListBox SetItemChecked method to unconditionally clear the checkbox. It also clears the contents of the text box used to display item information.

> The ListBox control has a ClearSelected method that should work for the CheckedListBox as well. Contrary to the documentation, the ClearSelected method does not work for CheckedListBox control at the time of this writing (.NET Framework Version 1.1.4322).

As mentioned above, the ItemCheck event is raised whenever the user changes the check status of one of the items, before the change takes effect, and the SelectedIndexChanged event is raised after the change takes effect. The two event handlers work in concert here to build up a text string for display in the text box.

You could also change the new value of the checkbox in the ItemCheck event handler with a line of code similar to the following:

```
e.NewValue = CheckState.Indeterminate
```

ComboBox

A ComboBox control, derived from the ListControl class, is essentially a single selection ListBox combined with an edit field that allows the user to modify existing values and enter values not currently included in the list. As with the other list controls, the contents of the list are contained in the Items collection. This collection may be populated either by manipulating the Items collection directly using the Object-Collection methods (listed in Table 15-4 and discussed in the earlier section "Filling a ListControl via the Items collection") or by data binding with the DataSource property (listed in Table 15-1 and discussed in the "Filling a ListControl using a Data-Source" section).

The list in a ComboBox is typically displayed as a drop-down menu with a user-editable text field, although this need not always be the case. Depending on the value of the DropDownStyle property, listed in Table 15-14 along with other commonly used ComboBox properties, the control may also be displayed as a simple list that is always visible or as a drop-down menu whose text field is not editable.

The default value for the DropDownStyle property, ComboBoxStyle.DropDown, is well suited to applications where there are a relatively large number of possible values, with the possibility of more being added by the user. ComboBoxStyle.Simple lends itself to applications where the form has enough screen real-estate to accommodate the 13 or so values that are always displayed. While these two editable styles don't totally preclude erroneous entries, the mere presence of pre-existing items tends to minimize the proliferation of similar, but misspelled, entries in the list. ComboBoxStyle.DropDownList is the value to use if the list of items is read-only—for example, a lookup of product codes or months of the year.

Table 15-14. ComboBox properties

Property	Value type	Description
DropDownStyle	ComboBoxStyle	Read/write. A member of the ComboBoxStyle enumeration, listed in Table 15-15, which controls the appearance and editability of the control. The default value is ComboBoxStyle.DropDown.
DropDownWidth	Integer	Read/write. Specifies the width of the drop-down box, in pixels. This property must be equal to or greater than the width of the control. Not relevant if Drop-DownStyle set to ComboBoxStyle.Simple.
DroppedDown	Boolean	Read/write. If `true`, the drop-down menu is displayed. Default is `false`.
Items	ComboBox.Object-Collection	Collection of items in the combo box. The ComboBox.ObjectCollection class has the methods listed in Table 15-4.
MaxDropDown-Items	Integer	Read/write. An integer between 1 and 100, inclusive, specifying the number of items in the drop-down menu. Default value is 8.
MaxLength	Integer	Read/write. The maximum number of characters allowed in an editable combo box.

Table 15-14. ComboBox properties (continued)

Property	Value type	Description
SelectedIndex	Integer	Read/write. The zero-based index of the currently selected item, unless the current item is being edited, in which case it returns −1.
SelectedText	String	Read/write. The text that is currently selected in the editable text field. Setting this property changes the text in the edit field. If no text is selected or if the DropDownStyle property is set to ComboBoxStyle.DropDownList, SelectedText returns a zero-length string.
SelectionLength	Integer	Read/write. The number of characters selected in the edit field.
SelectionStart	Integer	Read/write. The zero-based index of the first character in the selected text within the edit field. Setting this property when no text is selected specifies the insertion point.
Text	String	Read/write. The text that appears in the edit field.

Table 15-15. ComboBoxStyle enumeration values

Value	Description
DropDown	The user clicks the drop-down arrow to display the list. The text is editable.
DropDownList	The user clicks the drop-down arrow to display the list. The text is not editable. The TextChanged event is never raised.
Simple	The list is always visible and the text is editable. DropDownWidth and MaxDropDownItems properties are ignored.

Unlike the other ListControls, you cannot always depend on the SelectedIndex property to return the index of the currently selected item if the control is editable—i.e., if the DropDownStyle property is set to either ComboBoxStyle.DropDown or ComboBoxStyle.Simple. As soon as the edit field is edited, the value of the SelectedIndex property changes to −1. When the editing is complete, depending on the specific sequence of user actions, the SelectedIndex typically reverts to zero—i.e., the first item in the list becomes the currently selected item.

The Text property will always reflect the text contained in the edit field. This is true whether or not the contents of the field is edited. As the user selects different items from the list or edits the contents of the field, the Text property will change accordingly.

In addition to the list control methods listed in Table 15-3, the ComboBox has two commonly used methods listed in Table 15-16. The Select and SelectAll methods allow you to select either a range of text in the edit field or all the text in the edit field. As with all selected text in Windows, it displays in a highlighted color and may be manipulated with standard Windows features such as cutting and pasting and replacing with typing. The SelectedText property reflects the selected text, and may be manipulated programmatically.

Table 15-16. ComboBox text selection methods

Method	Description
Select	Selects a range of text in the edit field of the control, starting at the specified zero-based index, and of specified length.
SelectAll	Selects all the text in the control's edit field.

In addition to the ListControl events listed in Table 15-5, the ComboBox has several other events, the most commonly used of which are listed in Table 15-17. Among other things, these events allow your code to detect when a new item has been selected and when the user has edited the text in the edit field.

You can validate the new text character by character, for example, modify the value in the list, or add the new value to the list or a database, or both. As seen in the following example, however, retrieving the new value after editing is completed is not straightforward since no single event is raised when the editing is complete.

Table 15-17. ComboBox events

Event	Event argument	Description
DropDown	EventArgs	Raised when the drop-down menu is displayed.
DropDownStyleChanged	EventArgs	Raised when the DropDownStyle property has changed.
SelectedIndexChanged	EventArgs	Raised when the SelectedIndex property has changed.
SelectionChange-Committed	EventArgs	Raised when the selected index has changed and the change is committed.
TextChanged	EventArgs	Raised when the text in the edit field changes (with every keystroke) or the currently selected item changes. Never raised if the DropDownStyle property is set to ComboBoxStyle.DropDownList.

The sample application listed in Example 15-22 (in C#) and Example 15-23 (in VB.NET) demonstrates many of the properties, methods and events of the ComboBox. Similarly to the previous examples in this chapter, it populates the Items collection from the authors table of the pubs database.

The form has a label below the ComboBox that displays the currently selected item. If the user edits that text, that too is reflected in the label. When the user finishes editing the text, either by leaving the control or moving to the next item in the list, then the label displays:

```
Edited:  <the final edited value>
```

Clicking on the Insert Item button inserts the edited value into the list if it is neither a duplicate with an existing item nor an empty string.

The Display Items button displays the current contents of the entire list beneath a timestamp in the large text box. The Select 4 button selects four characters in the current item, starting with the second character (index 1).

The running application, after you select a name from the list and click the Display Items and Select 4 buttons, looks something like that shown in Figure 15-10. A full analysis follows the code listings.

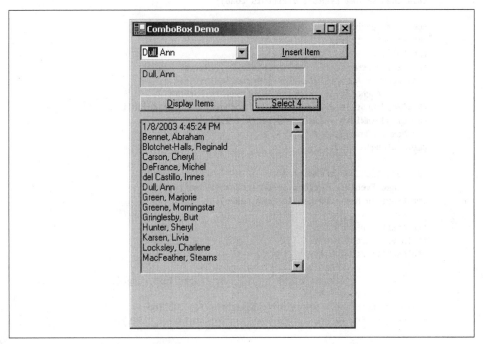

Figure 15-10. ComboBox application

Example 15-22. ComboBox demo in C# (ComboBox.cs)

```csharp
using System;
using System.Drawing;
using System.Windows.Forms;
using System.Data;
using System.Data.SqlClient;

namespace ProgrammingWinApps
{
   public class ComboBoxes : Form
   {
      ComboBox cmb;
      Button btnDisplay;
      Button btnInsert;
      Button btnSelect;
      Label lblEdit;
      TextBox txtDisplay;
      Boolean boolChange = false;
      Boolean boolProcessed = false;

      public ComboBoxes()
      {
```

Example 15-22. ComboBox demo in C# (ComboBox.cs) (continued)

```
                    Text = "ComboBox Demo";
                    Size = new Size(300,400);
                    this.Load += new EventHandler(this_Load);

                    cmb = new ComboBox( );
                    cmb.Parent = this;
                    cmb.Location = new Point(10,10);
                    cmb.Size = new Size(ClientSize.Width / 2, Height - 200);
                    cmb.Anchor = AnchorStyles.Top | AnchorStyles.Left |
                            AnchorStyles.Right | AnchorStyles.Bottom;
                    cmb.DropDownStyle = ComboBoxStyle.DropDown;       // default
                    cmb.DropDownWidth = (int)(cmb.Width * 1.5);
                    cmb.MaxDropDownItems = 12;
                    cmb.MaxLength = 20;

                    cmb.SelectionChangeCommitted +=
                            new EventHandler(cmb_SelectionChangeCommitted);
                    cmb.Leave += new EventHandler(cmb_Leave);

                    btnInsert = new Button( );
                    btnInsert.Parent = this;
                    btnInsert.Text = "&Insert Item";
                    btnInsert.Size = new Size(
                                (int)(Font.Height * .75) * btnInsert.Text.Length,
                                cmb.Height);
                    btnInsert.Location = new Point(cmb.Right + 10, cmb.Top);
                    btnInsert.Click += new System.EventHandler(btnInsert_Click);

                    lblEdit = new Label( );
                    lblEdit.Parent = this;
                    lblEdit.BorderStyle = BorderStyle.Fixed3D;
                    lblEdit.Location = new Point(cmb.Left, cmb.Bottom + 10);
                    lblEdit.BackColor = Color.LightGray;
                    lblEdit.Text = "";
                    lblEdit.Size = new Size(cmb.DropDownWidth, Font.Height * 2);

                    btnDisplay = new Button( );
                    btnDisplay.Parent = this;
                    btnDisplay.Text = "&Display Items";
                    btnDisplay.Size = new Size(
                                (int)(Font.Height * .75) * btnDisplay.Text.Length,
                                cmb.Height);
                    btnDisplay.Location = new Point(lblEdit.Left,
                                                lblEdit.Bottom + 10);
                    btnDisplay.Click += new System.EventHandler(btnDisplay_Click);

                    txtDisplay = new TextBox( );
                    txtDisplay.Parent = this;
                    txtDisplay.Location = new Point(btnDisplay.Left,
                                                btnDisplay.Bottom + 10);
                    txtDisplay.Multiline = true;
                    txtDisplay.ReadOnly = true;
                    txtDisplay.BackColor = Color.LightGray;
```

Example 15-22. ComboBox demo in C# (ComboBox.cs) (continued)

```
            txtDisplay.ScrollBars = ScrollBars.Vertical;
            txtDisplay.Text = "";
            txtDisplay.Size = new Size(cmb.DropDownWidth, 200);

            btnSelect = new Button( );
            btnSelect.Parent = this;
            btnSelect.Text = "&Select 4";
            btnSelect.Size = new Size(
                        (int)(Font.Height * .75) * btnSelect.Text.Length,
                        cmb.Height);
            btnSelect.Location = new Point(btnDisplay.Right + 10,
                                            btnDisplay.Top);
            btnSelect.Click += new System.EventHandler(btnSelect_Click);

            // get the data to populate the ListBox from pubs authors table
            string connectionString =
                "server=YourServer; uid=sa; pwd=YourPassword; database=pubs";
            string commandString =
                "Select au_id,au_lname+', ' + au_fname as name from authors";
            SqlDataAdapter dataAdapter =
                    new SqlDataAdapter(commandString, connectionString);
            DataSet dataSet = new DataSet( );
            dataAdapter.Fill(dataSet,"Authors");
            DataTable dataTable = dataSet.Tables[0];

            // Iterate the dataset and add the rows to the Items collection
            foreach (DataRow dataRow in dataTable.Rows)
            {
                cmb.Items.Add(dataRow["name"]);
            }
            cmb.SelectedIndex = 0;
        } // close for constructor

        static void Main( )
        {
            Application.Run(new ComboBoxes( ));
        }

        private void this_Load(object sender, EventArgs e)
        {
            cmb.TextChanged += new EventHandler(cmb_TextChanged);
            cmb.SelectedIndexChanged +=
                    new EventHandler(cmb_SelectedIndexChanged);
        }

        private void cmb_TextChanged(object sender, EventArgs e)
        {
            if (!boolProcessed)
                lblEdit.Text = cmb.Text;
            boolChange = true;
        }
        private void cmb_SelectedIndexChanged(object sender, EventArgs e)
        {
```

Example 15-22. ComboBox demo in C# (ComboBox.cs) (continued)

```csharp
      if (boolChange)
      {
         boolChange = false;
         boolProcessed = false;
      }
   }

   private void cmb_SelectionChangeCommitted(object sender,
                                               EventArgs e)
   {
      if (boolChange)
         ProcessChange( );
   }

   private void cmb_Leave(object sender, EventArgs e)
   {
      if (boolChange)
      {
         ProcessChange( );
         boolChange = false;
      }
   }

   private void ProcessChange( )
   {
      lblEdit.Text = "Edited: " + cmb.Text;
      boolProcessed = true;
   }

   private void btnDisplay_Click(object sender, EventArgs e)
   {
      string str = DateTime.Now.ToString( ) + "\r\n";
      foreach (object item in cmb.Items)
      {
         str += item.ToString( ) + "\r\n";
      }

      txtDisplay.Text = str;
   }

   private void btnSelect_Click(object sender, EventArgs e)
   {
      cmb.Select(1,4);
   }

   private void btnInsert_Click(object sender, EventArgs e)
   {
      // Determine if current item already in the list
      if (cmb.FindStringExact(cmb.Text) != -1)
      {
         MessageBox.Show("'" + cmb.Text +
               "' already exists in the list.\r\n" +
               "Will not be added again.",
```

Example 15-22. ComboBox demo in C# (ComboBox.cs) (continued)

```csharp
                    "Already Exists!");
        }
        else if (cmb.Text == "")
        {
            MessageBox.Show("There is nothing to add.","Nothing There");
        }
        else
        {
            cmb.Items.Add(cmb.Text);
        }
    }
}       // close for form class
}       // close form namespace
```

Example 15-23. ComboBox demo in VB.NET (ComboBox.vb)

```vb
Option Strict On
imports System
imports System.Drawing
imports System.Windows.Forms
imports System.Data
imports System.Data.SqlClient

namespace ProgrammingWinApps
    public class ComboBoxes : inherits Form

        dim cmb as ComboBox
        dim btnDisplay as Button
        dim btnInsert as Button
        dim btnSelect as Button
        dim lblEdit as Label
        dim txtDisplay as TextBox
        dim boolChange as Boolean = false
        dim boolProcessed as Boolean = false

        public sub New( )
            Text = "ComboBox Demo"
        Size = new Size(300,400)
        AddHandler me.Load, AddressOf me_Load

        cmb = new ComboBox( )
        cmb.Parent = me
        cmb.Location = new Point(10,10)
        cmb.Size = new Size(CInt(ClientSize.Width / 2), Height - 200)
        cmb.Anchor = AnchorStyles.Top or AnchorStyles.Left or _
                AnchorStyles.Right or AnchorStyles.Bottom
        cmb.DropDownStyle = ComboBoxStyle.DropDown        ' default
        cmb.DropDownWidth = CInt(cmb.Width * 1.5)
        cmb.MaxDropDownItems = 12
        cmb.MaxLength = 20

        AddHandler cmb.SelectionChangeCommitted, _
                AddressOf cmb_SelectionChangeCommitted
```

Example 15-23. ComboBox demo in VB.NET (ComboBox.vb) (continued)

VB

```
        AddHandler cmb.Leave, AddressOf cmb_Leave

        btnInsert = new Button()
        btnInsert.Parent = me
        btnInsert.Text = "&Insert Item"
        btnInsert.Size = new Size( _
            CInt(Font.Height * .75) * btnInsert.Text.Length, cmb.Height)
        btnInsert.Location = new Point(cmb.Right + 10, cmb.Top)
        AddHandler btnInsert.Click, AddressOf btnInsert_Click

        lblEdit = new Label()
        lblEdit.Parent = me
        lblEdit.BorderStyle = BorderStyle.Fixed3D
        lblEdit.Location = new Point(cmb.Left, cmb.Bottom + 10)
        lblEdit.BackColor = Color.LightGray
        lblEdit.Text = ""
        lblEdit.Size = new Size(cmb.DropDownWidth, Font.Height * 2)

        btnDisplay = new Button()
        btnDisplay.Parent = me
        btnDisplay.Text = "&Display Items"
        btnDisplay.Size = new Size( _
            CInt(Font.Height * .75) * btnDisplay.Text.Length, cmb.Height)
        btnDisplay.Location = new Point(lblEdit.Left, _
                                        lblEdit.Bottom + 10)
        AddHandler btnDisplay.Click, AddressOf btnDisplay_Click

        txtDisplay = new TextBox()
        txtDisplay.Parent = me
        txtDisplay.Location = new Point(btnDisplay.Left, _
                              btnDisplay.Bottom + 10)
        txtDisplay.Multiline = true
        txtDisplay.ReadOnly = true
        txtDisplay.BackColor = Color.LightGray
        txtDisplay.ScrollBars = ScrollBars.Vertical
        txtDisplay.Text = ""
        txtDisplay.Size = new Size(cmb.DropDownWidth, 200)

        btnSelect = new Button()
        btnSelect.Parent = me
        btnSelect.Text = "&Select 4"
        btnSelect.Size = new Size( _
            CInt(Font.Height * .75) * btnSelect.Text.Length, cmb.Height)
        btnSelect.Location = new Point(btnDisplay.Right + 10, _
                                       btnDisplay.Top)
        AddHandler btnSelect.Click, AddressOf btnSelect_Click

        ' get the data to populate the ComboBox from pubs authors table
        dim connectionString as String = _
            "server=YourServer; uid=sa; pwd=YourPassword; database=pubs"
        dim commandString as String = _
            "Select au_id,au_lname + ', ' + au_fname as name from authors"
        dim dataAdapter as new SqlDataAdapter(commandString, _
```

Example 15-23. ComboBox demo in VB.NET (ComboBox.vb) (continued)

```vb
                                 connectionString)
    dim ds as new DataSet( )
    dataAdapter.Fill(ds,"Authors")
    dim dt as new DataTable( )
    dt = ds.Tables(0)

    '  Iterate the dataset and add the rows to the Items collection
    dim dr as DataRow
    for each dr in dt.Rows
       cmb.Items.Add(dr("name"))
    next
    cmb.SelectedIndex = 0
end sub   '  close for constructor

public shared sub Main( )
    Application.Run(new ComboBoxes( ))
end sub

private sub me_Load(ByVal sender as object, _
               ByVal e as EventArgs)
    AddHandler cmb.TextChanged, AddressOf cmb_TextChanged
    AddHandler cmb.SelectedIndexChanged, _
           AddressOf cmb_SelectedIndexChanged
end sub

private sub cmb_TextChanged(ByVal sender as object, _
                       ByVal e as EventArgs)
    if not boolProcessed then
       lblEdit.Text = cmb.Text
    end if
    boolChange = true
end sub

private sub cmb_SelectedIndexChanged(ByVal sender as object, _
                            ByVal e as EventArgs)
    if boolChange then
       boolChange = false
       boolProcessed = false
    end if
end sub

private sub cmb_SelectionChangeCommitted(ByVal sender as object, _
                            ByVal e as EventArgs)
    if boolChange then
       ProcessChange( )
    end if
end sub

private sub cmb_Leave(ByVal sender as object, _
               ByVal e as EventArgs)
    if boolChange then
       ProcessChange( )
       boolChange = false
```

Example 15-23. ComboBox demo in VB.NET (ComboBox.vb) (continued)

```
      end if
   end sub

   private sub ProcessChange( )
      lblEdit.Text = "Edited: " + cmb.Text
      boolProcessed = true
   end sub

   private sub btnDisplay_Click(ByVal sender as object, _
                     ByVal e as EventArgs)
      dim str as string = DateTime.Now.ToString( ) + vbCrLf
      dim item as object
      for each item in cmb.Items
         str += item.ToString( ) + vbCrLf
      next

      txtDisplay.Text = str
   end sub

   private sub btnSelect_Click(ByVal sender as object, _
                     ByVal e as EventArgs)
      cmb.Select(1,4)
   end sub

   private sub btnInsert_Click(ByVal sender as object, _
                     ByVal e as EventArgs)
      '  Determine if current item already in the list
      if cmb.FindStringExact(cmb.Text) <> -1 then
         MessageBox.Show("'" + cmb.Text + _
              "' already exists in the list." + _
              vbCrLf + "Will not be added again.", _
              "Already Exists!")
      else if cmb.Text = "" then
         MessageBox.Show("There is nothing to add.","Nothing There")
      else
         cmb.Items.Add(cmb.Text)
      end if
   end sub

  end class
end namespace
```

Like the CheckedListBox examples shown in Examples 15-20 and 15-21, an event handler is loaded for the Form Load event in the constructor, and for the same reason: ComboBox event handlers are loaded in the Form Load event to prevent those events from being handled until after the form is fully initialized. In this case, two event handlers are installed in the Form Load event: TextChanged and SelectedIndexChanged.

Several properties of the ComboBox are then set. The DropDownStyle property is set to the default value of ComboBoxStyle.DropDown, which provides for a drop-down menu with an editable text field. You can easily change this property to one of the other values in Table 15-15 to see the effect.

The DropDownWidth property is set to one and half times the width of the ComboBox. This causes the drop-down menu to be wider than its parent control. The MaxDropDownItems property is increased from its default of 8 to 12 so that more of the list is visible at one time, and the MaxLength property is set to 20, the maximum number of characters a user can enter into the edit field.

 Isn't it irritating how often a ComboBox is too short by one or two items? For example, you often see a ComboBox containing the months of the year with a 10-item drop-down menu and a vertical scrollbar. How much more convenient that would be if the MaxDropDownItems property were set to 12.

Two event handlers are added for the ComboBox and discussed next: SelectionChangeCommitted and Leave.

Although this example populates the Items collection from the authors table in the pubs database, it does so using the Add method of the ComboBox.ObjectCollection class rather than the DataSource property, as was done in the previous examples in this chapter. This change occurs because the requirements of the application called for the Insert Item button to add an item to the Items collection. If the control were data bound, the Items collection could not be modified. Instead, you would need to either add the appropriate data to the database and rebind the data to the control or add the item to the DataTable directly without rebinding.

Handling the events in this application is less intuitive than might be expected. Let's review the design goals:

- The contents of the current item should be echoed in the label below the ComboBox, including edits made by the user.
- When the user is finished editing an item, the label will display the legend Edited: <edited item>.
- Clicking the Insert Item button will add the currently selected item to the list.
  - If the current item is identical to the pre-existing item, it will not be added, preventing duplicates.
  - If the edit field is empty, nothing will be added, preventing blanks in the Items collection.
- Clicking the Display Items button will display a time stamp, followed by the entire Items collection in the large text box.
- Clicking the Select 4 button will select the second through fifth characters in the edit field.

The design goals for the three buttons are easy to implement. The Insert Item button is implemented in the btnInsert_Click event handler. The Text property of the

ComboBox returns the current contents of the edit field. The FindExactString method determines whether that string already exists in the list: it returns −1 if it is not found. An if/else if/else construct tests whether the string already exists in the list or whether the edit field is empty. If neither of these conditions are met, then the string is added to the Items collection by using the Add method of the ComboBox. ObjectCollection class.

The Display Items button is implemented in the btnDisplay_Click event handler. It instantiates a string with the time stamp followed by a Carriage Return/Line Feed. Then the Items collection is iterated, concatenating each item, along with a the CR/LF characters, to the string. Finally, the text box Text property is set to the string.

 If performance were an issue here, it would be better to use the StringBuilder class to build up the string rather than simple concatenation.

The Select 4 button is even easier to implement. The btnSelect_Click event handler consists of a single line of code, a call to the ComboBox Select method. When running the application, if you click the button with the mouse and then try to do something with the highlighted characters, such as delete them, the selection changes when you click back on the ComboBox to give it focus. The solution here is to leave the focus on the ComboBox, and then use the Select 4 button shortcut key (Alt-S) to select the characters.

The first design goal, echoing the contents of the edit field in the label below the ComboBox, should be easy, since the TextChanged event is raised after every keystroke and whenever a new item is selected from the list. If the second design goal did not exist, i.e., if there were no need to determine when the user finished editing the item, then the contents of the cmb_TextChanged event handler would consist of a single line of code:

```
lblEdit.Text = cmb.Text
```

The second requirement, the need to determine when the user finished editing the item, throws a monkey wrench into the works. Unfortunately, this requirement is fairly typical: your program must be able to distinguish when to add the edited item to the database, for example, and what exactly should be added. However, the .NET Framework does not provide an intrinsic event to tell the program when the editing is complete.

For this application, you will consider the editing to be complete if either of two user actions occur: focus leaves the ComboBox control or a new item is selected from the list. The first action raises the Leave event, while the second action raises both the SelectionChangeCommitted and the SelectedIndexChanged events.

Whenever it is determined that editing has occurred and the editing is complete, the ProcessChange method is called. In this example, that processing consists only of updating the Text property of the appropriate label. In a production application, it may consist of a validation routine, a database update, adding the item to the list, or something similar.

To understand exactly what events are raised and in what sequence, run the example in Visual Studio .NET and trace the execution by using the debugger. Figure 15-11 shows this process, with set breakpoints and a Watch window displaying useful values. This snapshot was taken after moving from the first item in the list to the sixth (index = 5). In the code shown in Figure 15-11, the SelectedValueChanged event handler has been inserted with a line of dummy code to observe the role it plays in the event stream.

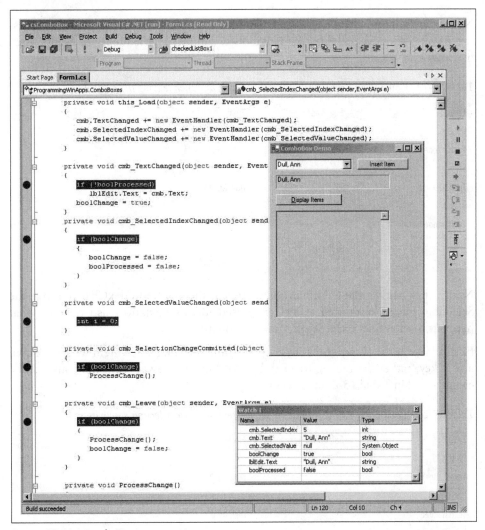

Figure 15-11. ComboBox event tracing

Now run the program and change the selected item from the first item (Bennet, Abraham) to the sixth (Dull, Ann) using either the down arrow key or the mouse. The sequence of events shown in Table 15-18 occurs with associated values.

Table 15-18. ComboBox events—changing selected item

Event	SelectedIndex	Text
SelectionChangeCommitted	5	Bennet, Abraham
TextChanged	5	Dull, Ann
SelectedValueChanged	5	Dull, Ann
SelectedIndexChanged	5	Dull, Ann

Now edit the text field, changing "Dull, Ann" to "Dull, AnnXXX," and then press the Tab key to move focus off the ComboBox control. The sequence of events listed in Table 15-19 occur.

Table 15-19. ComboBox events—editing selected item and then leaving the control

Event	SelectedIndex	Text
Press X		
TextChanged	5	Dull, AnnX
Press X		
TextChanged	-1	Dull, AnnXX
Press X		
TextChanged	-1	Dull, AnnXXX
Tab		
Leave	-1	Dull, AnnXXX

Notice that neither the SelectedValueChanged, the SelectedIndexChanged, nor the SelectionChangeCommitted events are raised in this scenario. Also observe what happens to the value of the SelectedIndex property.

Finally, repeat the above scenario, only this time selecting a new item with the down arrow key, rather than using the Tab key to shift focus away from the control. The events listed in Table 15-20 will occur.

Table 15-20. ComboBox events—editing selected item and then selecting a new item

Event	SelectedIndex	Text
Press X		
TextChanged	5	Dull, AnnX
Press X		
TextChanged	-1	Dull, AnnXX
Press X		

Table 15-20. ComboBox events—editing selected item and then selecting a new item (continued)

Event	SelectedIndex	Text
TextChanged	-1	Dull, AnnXXX
Down Arrow		
SelectionChangeCommitted	0	Dull, AnnXXX
TextChanged	0	Bennet, Abraham
SelectedValueChanged	0	Bennet, Abraham
SelectedIndexChanged	0	Bennet, Abraham

In this scenario, the SelectionChangeCommitted event is raised and the Text property contains the final edited value, although at that point, the SelectedIndex property has already changed to 0, even though you pressed the down arrow that would indicate the new index should have been 6. Setting aside for a moment the fact that the next item displayed after editing is always the first item in the list (index 0), this scenario demonstrates that although the Text property during the SelectionChangeCommitted event is the final, committed text, the SelectedIndex already points to the next item. It sort of makes sense that the next item will be the first item, since the SelectedIndex property changes to –1 during editing and the control has no way of knowing where in the list it was. This is true even if only a single character was added to the text field, contrary to what you might think by examining Table 15-20.

Interestingly, throughout all these scenarios, the value of the SelectedValue property was unchanged at null (Nothing in VB.NET).

With all this in mind, you can now go back to the code and understand what is going on. Remember, the goal is to determine when editing is complete and what is the final edited value.

A flag, boolChange, keeps track of whether editing has occurred, a so-called dirty bit. It is initialized to false, set true in the TextChanged event handler, and then reset to false either in the Leave event handler when focus leaves the control or in the SelectedIndexChanged event handler when a new item is selected.

A second flag, boolProcess, keeps track of whether or not the final value has been processed. This is necessary in this application to prevent the TextChanged event handler from overwriting the contents of the label after the SelectionChangeCommitted event handler has written the "Edited:" text string to it in the scenario outlined in Table 15-20.

CHAPTER 16

Date and Time Controls

> *Time flies like an arrow. Fruit flies like a banana.*
> —Anonymous

Dates and times are ubiquitous in our lives. So too in computer programs. Programs are commonly used to gather and display date and time information. While it is always possible to use simple text boxes and labels to gather and display these values, and to painstakingly format and validate text strings to appear as valid date and time values, the .NET Framework provides several controls and classes to ease this chore and make it more robust. As an added benefit, these classes automatically take into account the time zone and regional settings on the end user's machine. This chapter will cover those controls and classes.

Class Hierarchy

The hierarchical structure of the classes discussed in this chapter is shown in Figure 16-1.

Date and Time Values

Before you can fully understand date and time controls, you must first be familiar with how the .NET Framework deals with date and time values. Two different structures are provided for representing dates and times. The DateTime structure represents a specific point in time, while the TimeSpan structure represents a length of time. These structures are described in the next two sections.

DateTime Structure

Date and time values in the .NET Framework are typically represented with a *DateTime* structure. This structure is a value type representing a point in time, typically expressed with both a date and a time component. Like a class, it has

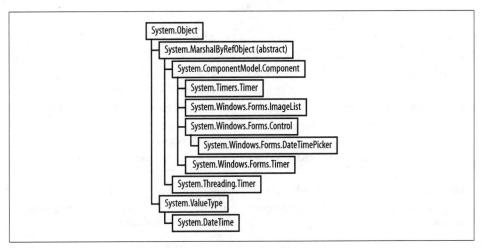

Figure 16-1. Class hierarchy for controls covered in this chapter

constructors, fields, properties and methods, plus several operators, all for the purpose of allowing your code to represent and manipulate date and time values.

Time values in the .NET Framework are measured in units of *ticks*, each 100 nanoseconds long. Dates are measured as the number of ticks since midnight, January 1, 1 C.E. in the Gregorian calendar, unless a different calendar is explicitly specified.

> The civil calendar in common use today is called the Gregorian calendar, named after Pope Gregory XIII. In 1582 he ordered changes to the calendar then in use to correct errors arising from the fact that a solar year is approximately 11 minutes short of 365 1/4 days. It is nominally based on the year of the birth of Jesus. Years prior to the birth of Jesus are referred to either as B.C. (Before Christ) or B.C.E. (Before the Common Era), and years after the birth of Jesus are referred to as A.D. (Latin abbreviation for Anno Domini, which translates to "in the year of the Lord") or C.E. (Common Era). The German astronomer Johannes Kepler (1571–1630) later showed that Jesus was actually born in the year 4 B.C.E.

Time values can be either positive or negative. They can be expressed in units of ticks, seconds, hours, or in instances of TimeSpan (described below). Time values can be added to or subtracted from DateTime objects. All DateTime calculations assume the same time zone, so your program must take differing time zones into account. All methods and properties of the DateTime class use the local time zone.

There are seven overloaded forms of the DateTime structure's constructor. Table 16-1 lists the arguments for each different constructor.

Table 16-1. DateTime constructors

Argument types	Description
Long	Number of ticks.
Integer, integer, integer	Year (1 through 9999), month (1 through 12), and day (1 through number of days in month).
Integer, integer, integer, Calendar	Year, month, and day using the specified calendar object.
Integer, integer, integer, integer, integer, integer	Year, month, day, hour (0 through 23), minute (0 through 59), and seconds (0 through 59).
Integer, integer, integer, integer, integer, integer, Calendar	Year, month, day, hour, minute, and seconds using the specified calendar object.
Integer, integer, integer, integer, integer, integer, integer	Year, month, day, hour, minute, seconds, and milliseconds.
Integer, integer, integer, integer, integer, integer, integer, Calendar	Year, month, day, hour, minute, seconds, and milliseconds using the specified calendar object.

The DateTime structure has two public read-only fields. MaxValue represents the largest possible value, corresponding to one tick before January 1, 10000, or 23:59: 59.9999999 December 31, 9999. MinValue represents the smallest possible value, corresponding to 00:00:00.0000000 January 1, 0001.

A number of read-only properties, some static (Shared in VB.NET), provide date-time functionality, listed in Table 16-2.

Table 16-2. DateTime properties

Property	Value type	Description
Date	DateTime	The date component of the DateTime instance, with the time set to 12:00 AM (midnight — 00:00:00).
Day	Integer	The day of the month of the DateTime instance. An integer between 1 and 31, inclusive.
DayOfWeek	DayOfWeek	The day of the week enumerated constant. Sunday corresponds to zero, Monday to one, and so forth.
DayOfYear	Integer	The day of the year, between 1 and 366, inclusive, of the DateTime instance.
Hour	Integer	The hour component of the DateTime instance. An integer between 0 and 23, inclusive.
Millisecond	Integer	The millisecond component of the DateTime instance. An integer between 0 and 999, inclusive.
Minute	Integer	The minute component of the DateTime instance. An integer between 0 and 59, inclusive.
Month	Integer	The month component of the DateTime instance. An integer between 1 and 12, inclusive.
Now	DateTime	Static. The current local date and time. The resolution depends on the OS: 55 milliseconds under Win98, 16 milliseconds under WinNT 3.1, and 10 milliseconds under WinNT 3.5 and later.
Second	Integer	The seconds component of the DateTime instance. An integer between 0 and 59, inclusive.

Table 16-2. DateTime properties (continued)

Property	Value type	Description
Ticks	Long	The number of 100 nanosecond ticks representing the DateTime instance. It is a number between MinValue and MaxValue.
TimeOfDay	TimeSpan	The span of time since midnight of the current day.
Today	DateTime	Static. The current local date. The time portion of the DateTime is 12:00 AM (midnight—00:00:00).
UtcNow	DateTime	Static. The current local date and time expressed as coordinated universal time (UTC), previously known as Greenwich Mean Time (GMT). The resolution is the same as for the Now property.
Year	Integer	The year component of the DateTime instance. An integer between 1 and 9999, inclusive.

The DateTime methods, the most commonly used of which are listed in Table 16-3, perform DateTime manipulation, such as adding and subtracting date-time values, comparing values, and converting from one format to another.

Table 16-3. DateTime methods

Method	Description
Add	Adds TimeSpan object to DateTime. Returns a new DateTime.
AddDays	Adds number of whole and fractional days, positive or negative, to DateTime. Returns a new DateTime.
AddHours	Adds number of whole and fractional hours, positive or negative, to DateTime. Returns a new DateTime.
AddMilliseconds	Adds number of whole and fractional milliseconds, positive or negative, to DateTime. Returns a new DateTime.
AddMinutes	Adds number of whole and fractional minutes, positive or negative, to DateTime. Returns a new DateTime.
AddMonths	Adds integer number of months, positive or negative, to DateTime. Returns a new DateTime.
AddSeconds	Adds number of whole and fractional seconds, positive or negative, to DateTime. Returns a new DateTime.
AddTicks	Adds number of ticks, positive or negative, to DateTime. Returns a new DateTime.
AddYears	Adds integer number of years, positive or negative, to DateTime. Returns a new DateTime.
Compare	Static. Compares two DateTime objects. Returns zero if they are equal, less then zero if the first is less than the second, and greater then zero if the first is greater than the second.
CompareTo	Compares this instance to a specified DateTime object. Returns same as Compare method, except it also returns greater than zero if specified DateTime object is null (Nothing).
DaysInMonth	Static. Returns number of days in specified year and month (number from 1 to 12). Takes leap year into account.
Equals	Overloaded. Static version returns `true` if two DateTimes represent the same date-time value. Instance version returns `true` if DateTime represents the same date-time value as the instance.
FromFileTime	Static. Returns DateTime object representing OS file timestamp.

Table 16-3. DateTime methods (continued)

Method	Description
GetDateTime-Formats	Overloaded. Returns string array containing all the representations supported by standard DateTime format specifiers.
IsLeapYear	Static. Returns `true` if specified year is leap year, `false` otherwise.
Parse	Static. Overloaded. Converts specified string to DateTime object.
ParseExact	Static. Overloaded. Converts specified string, which must precisely match a specified format, to DateTime object.
Subtract	Overloaded. Subtracts the specified DateTime or TimeSpan and returns a TimeSpan or DateTime object, respectively.
ToFileTime	Converts this instance to local system file time format, which is 64-bit unsigned value representing number of ticks since January 1, 1601 12:00 AM.
ToLocalTime	Returns local DateTime object equivalent to current UTC time adjusted for local time zone and daylight saving time.
ToLongDateString	Returns equivalent long date string representation, containing name of the day, name of the month, numeric day of month, and year. Equivalent to ToString or to using "D" format character from Table 16-10.
ToLongTimeString	Returns equivalent long time string representation. Equivalent to using "T" format character from Table 16-10.
ToShortDateString	Returns equivalent short date string representation, containing numeric month, numeric day of month, and year. Equivalent to using "d" format character from Table 16-10.
ToShortTimeString	Returns equivalent short time string representation. Equivalent to using "t" format character from Table 16-10.
ToString	Overloaded, overrides. Returns string representation, optionally using specified format and culture information.
ToUniversalTime	Returns UTC DateTime object equivalent to current local time.

The DateTime structure provides several arithmetic and logical operators, listed in Table 16-4. All of these operators have equivalent methods.

Table 16-4. DateTime operators

Operator	Description
Addition	Adds a DateTime and a TimeSpan, returning a DateTime. In C#, use the plus sign (+). In VB.NET, use DateTime.op_Addition. Equivalent to Add method.
Equality	Returns `true` if two DateTimes are equal. In C#, use two equal signs (==). In VB.NET, use DateTime.op_Equality. Equivalent to Equals method.
Greater Than	Returns `true` if first DateTime is greater than the second. In C#, use the greater-than sign (>). In VB.NET, use DateTime.op_GreaterThan. Equivalent to Compare method.
Greater Than or Equal	Returns `true` if first DateTime is greater than the second. In C#, use the greater than or equal signs (>=). In VB.NET, use DateTime.op_GreaterThanOrEqual. Equivalent to Compare method.
Inequality	Returns `true` if the two DateTimes do not represent the same date and time. In C#, use the inequality signs (!=). In VB.NET, use DateTime.op_Inequality. Equivalent to Equals method.

Table 16-4. DateTime operators (continued)

Operator	Description
Less Than	Returns true if first DateTime is less than the second. In C#, use the less-than sign (<). In VB.NET, use DateTime.op_LessThan. Equivalent to Compare method.
Less Than or Equal	Returns true if first DateTime is less than or equal to the second. In C#, use the less than or equal signs (<=). In VB.NET, use DateTime.op_LessThanOrEqual. Equivalent to Compare method.
Subtraction	Overloaded. Either subtracts one DateTime from another, returning a TimeSpan, or subtracts a TimeSpan from a DateTime, returning a DateTime. In C#, use the minus sign (-). In VB.NET, use DateTime.op_Subtraction. Equivalent to Subtract method.

TimeSpan Structure

The TimeSpan object, also a structure, represents a period of time, in number of ticks. TimeSpan values can be either positive or negative. It resembles the DateTime object in constructors, properties, methods and operators, with just enough differences to drive you crazy.

There are four overloaded forms of the constructor for the TimeSpan structure. Table 16-5 lists the arguments for each constructor.

Table 16-5. TimeSpan constructors

Argument types	Description
long	Number of ticks.
integer, integer, integer	Hours, minutes, and seconds.
integer, integer, integer, integer	Days, hours, minutes, and seconds.
integer, integer, integer, integer, integer	Days, hours, minutes, seconds, and milliseconds.

The string representation of TimeSpan objects includes components for the sign, days, hours, minutes, seconds, and fractional seconds to seven decimal places, of the form [-][d.]hh:mm:ss[.ff], where characters in brackets are optional. So, for example, you could create a new TimeSpan object with the following line of code:

```
TimeSpan ts = new TimeSpan(1,2,10,10,500)
```

This TimeSpan instance would represent a period of 1 day, 2 hours, 10 minutes, 10 seconds, and 500 milliseconds. The string representation of this object, obtained by using the ToString method listed in Table 16-7, would be:

```
1.02:10:10.5000000
```

Conversely, the Parse method, also listed in Table 16-7, can convert strings to TimeSpan objects. So for example, the following two lines of code:

```
TimeSpan ts = new TimeSpan( )
ts = TimeSpan.Parse("-1:15:15.1234")
```

result in a TimeSpan object representing negative one hour, 15 minutes, 15.1234 seconds, with the following string representation:

```
-01:15:15.1234000
```

The properties of the TimeSpan structure, all of which are read-only and apply to specific instances of the structure, are listed in Table 16-6.

Table 16-6. TimeSpan properties

Property	Value type	Description
Days	Integer	Read-only. The day component of the TimeSpan object.
Hours	Integer	Read-only. The hour component of the TimeSpan object.
Milliseconds	Integer	Read-only. The millisecond component of the TimeSpan object.
Minutes	Integer	Read-only. The minute component of the TimeSpan object.
Seconds	Integer	Read-only. The second component of the TimeSpan object.
Ticks	Long	Read-only. The number of 100 nanosecond ticks contained in the TimeSpan object.
TotalDays	Double	Read-only. The number of whole and fractional days contained in the TimeSpan object.
TotalHours	Double	Read-only. The number of whole and fractional hours contained in the TimeSpan object.
TotalMilliseconds	Double	Read-only. The number of whole and fractional milliseconds contained in the TimeSpan object.
TotalMinutes	Double	Read-only. The number of whole and fractional minutes contained in the TimeSpan object.
TotalSeconds	Double	Read-only. The number of whole and fractional seconds contained in the TimeSpan object.

The commonly used methods of the TimeSpan structure are listed in Table 16-7. Notice that some methods are static (shared in VB.NET).

Table 16-7. TimeSpan methods

Method	Description
Add	Adds TimeSpan object to TimeSpan. Returns a new TimeSpan.
Compare	Static. Compares two TimeSpan objects. Returns zero if they are equal, less then zero if the first is less than the second, and greater then zero if the first is greater than the second.
CompareTo	Compares this instance to a specified TimeSpan object. Returns the same as Compare method, except it also returns greater than zero if specified TimeSpan object is null (Nothing).
Duration	Returns a TimeSpan object that is the absolute value (i.e., always positive) of this TimeSpan instance.
Equals	Overloaded. Static version returns true if two TimeSpans represent the same value. Instance version returns true if the specified TimeSpan represents the same value as the instance.
FromDays	Static. Returns a TimeSpan representing the specified number of days, accurate to the nearest millisecond.
FromHours	Static. Returns a TimeSpan representing the specified number of hours, accurate to the nearest millisecond.

Table 16-7. TimeSpan methods (continued)

Method	Description
FromMilliseconds	Static. Returns a TimeSpan representing the specified number of milliseconds.
FromMinutes	Static. Returns a TimeSpan representing the specified number of minutes, accurate to the nearest millisecond.
FromSeconds	Static. Returns a TimeSpan representing the specified number of seconds, accurate to the nearest millisecond.
FromTicks	Static. Returns a TimeSpan representing the specified number of ticks.
Negate	Returns a TimeSpan object with the same value as the instance, but of the opposite sign.
Parse	Static. Converts specified string to TimeSpan object.
Subtract	Subtracts the specified TimeSpan and returns a TimeSpan object.
ToString	Returns a string representation of the TimeSpan instance in the form [-][d.]hh:mm:ss[.ff], where characters in brackets are optional. Does not accept any formatting strings as arguments.

The TimeSpan structure provides several arithmetic and logical operators, listed in Table 16-8. Except for the two unary operators, all of these operators have equivalent methods.

Table 16-8. TimeSpan operators

Operator	Description
Addition	Adds two TimeSpan objects, returning a TimeSpan. In C#, use the plus sign (+). In VB.NET, use TimeSpan.op_Addition. Equivalent to Add method.
Equality	Returns true if two TimeSpans are equal. In C#, use the two equal signs (==). In VB.NET, use TimeSpan.op_Equality. Equivalent to Equals method.
Greater Than	Returns true if first TimeSpan is greater than the second. In C#, use the greater-than sign (>). In VB.NET, use TimeSpan.op_GreaterThan. Equivalent to Compare method.
Greater Than or Equal	Returns true if first TimeSpan is greater than the second. In C#, use the greater than or equal signs (>=). In VB.NET, use TimeSpan.op_GreaterThanOrEqual. Equivalent to Compare method.
Inequality	Returns true if the two TimeSpans do not represent the same value. In C#, use the inequality signs (!=). In VB.NET, use TimeSpan.op_Inequality. Equivalent to Equals method returning the opposite value.
Less Than	Returns true if first TimeSpan is less than the second. In C#, use the less-than sign (<). In VB.NET, use TimeSpan.op_LessThan. Equivalent to Compare method.
Less Than or Equal	Returns true if first TimeSpan is less than or equal to the second. In C#, use the less-than or equal signs (<=). In VB.NET, use TimeSpan.op_LessThanOrEqual. Equivalent to Compare method.
Subtraction	Subtracts one TimeSpan from another, returning a TimeSpan. In C#, use the minus sign (-). In VB.NET, use TimeSpan.op_Subtraction. Equivalent to Subtract method.
Unary Negation	Returns a TimeSpan with the same numeric value as the specified TimeSpan but of opposite sign. In C#, use the minus sign (-). In VB.NET, use TimeSpan.op_UnaryNegation.
Unary Plus	Returns the specified TimeSpan. In C#, use the plus sign (+). In VB.NET, use TimeSpan.op_UnaryPlus.

You will see many of these DateTime and TimeSpan members used throughout this chapter, especially in the CountDownTimer application in Examples 16-6 and 16-7.

Date and Time Format Strings

There are an infinite number of ways to format text representations of date and time. Days and months can be expressed as single digits, two digits, abbreviations of names, or full names. Hours can be single digits or two digits in a 12-hour format, either followed by AM/PM, A/P, or nothing, or in 24-hour format. Years can be one, two, or four digits. Times can include seconds or milliseconds, or neither. This list doesn't even begin to include all the custom formats you or your clients can dream up: "Saturday, the 8th of January, '05 at 2:08 in the afternoon," for example.

Looking at the DateTime methods in Table 16-3, you see several methods that convert to long and short date and time strings. These and other methods and properties depend on the regional settings of the end-user machine.

The Regional settings for a machine are set via Regional Options in the Control Panel. In Windows 2000, the Locale is set in the General tab of the Regional Options dialog box. Time and Date tabs customize time formats and both short and long date formats. In Windows XP, the Locale is set in the Regional Options tab of the Regional and Language Options dialog box, and the time and date formats are customized by clicking the Customize button. Both operating systems use the formatting characters listed in Table 16-9.

In addition, the DateTime.ToString method listed in Table 16-3, which overrides Control.ToString, has overloaded forms that take format strings to allow you to customize the resulting string. Those format strings are comprised of the characters found in Tables 16-9 and 16-10. If a string contains characters contained in both Tables 16-9 and 16-10, the meaning listed in Table 16-10 will prevail.

As you will see in the next section, the DateTimePicker control has two properties that control how the date-time value is displayed in the control. The Format property determines if the display format is Short, Long, Time, or Custom. If it is set to DateTimePickerFormat.Custom, then the CustomFormat property must contain a text string comprised of the formatting characters contained in Table 16-9.

Literal string characters can be included in format strings. If there is any ambiguity about whether the characters will be interpreted as literal strings or formatting characters, they should be escaped using single quotes, as shown in examples later in the chapter.

Table 16-9. DateTime format strings

Format string	Description
d	One- or two-digit days.
dd	Two-digit days. Single-digit values are padded with a leading zero.
ddd	Three-character day of the week abbreviation—e.g., Mon.
dddd	Full day of the week name—e.g., Monday.

Table 16-9. DateTime format strings (continued)

Format string	Description
h	One- or two-digit hours in 12-hour format.
hh	Two-digit hours in 12-hour format. Single-digit values are padded with a leading zero.
H	One- or two-digit hours in 24-hour format.
HH	Two-digit hours in 24-hour format. Single-digit values are padded with a leading zero.
m	One- or two-digit minutes.
mm	Two-digit minutes. Single-digit values are padded with a leading zero.
M	One- or two-digit month.
MM	Two-digit month. Single-digit values are padded with a leading zero.
MMM	Three-character month abbreviation—e.g., Jan.
MMMM	Full month name—e.g., January.
s	One- or two-digit seconds.
ss	Two-digit seconds. Single-digit values are padded with a leading zero.
t	One-letter AM/PM abbreviation—e.g., A.
tt	Two-letter AM/PM abbreviation—e.g., AM.
y	One-digit year—e.g., 2001 is "1".
yy	Last two digits of the year.
yyyy	Full year.

Table 16-10. DateTimeFormatInfo format characters

Format string	Description
d	Short date—e.g., M/d/yyyy
D	Long date—e.g., dddd, dd MMMM yyyy
f	Full date—e.g., dddd, MMMM dd, yyyy hh:mm tt
F	Full date—e.g., dddd, MMMM dd, yyyy hh:mm:ss tt
g	General—e.g., M/d/yyyy hh:mm tt
G	General—e.g., M/d/yyyy hh:mm:ss tt
m, M	Month and day—e.g., MMMM dd
r, R	RFC1123—e.g., ddd,dd MMM yyyy HH':'mm':'ss 'GMT'
s	Sortable DateTime—e.g., yyyy'-'MM'-'dd'T'HH':'mm':'ss
t	Short time—e.g., hh:mm tt
T	Long time—e.g., hh:mm:ss tt
u	Universal sortable DateTime—e.g., yyyy'-'MM'-'dd HH':'mm':'ss'Z'
U	Full date and time using universal time—e.g., dddd, MMMM dd, yyyy hh:mm:ss tt
y,Y	YearMonth—e.g., MMMM, yyyy

DateTimePicker

The DateTimePicker control lets the user interactively pick a single date and time. It provides the developer lot of flexibility and assurance that any value it returns is a valid DateTime value, eliminating the need for extensive data validation. It also automatically considers the computer's regional settings when displaying various date and time formats.

The control uses a relatively small amount of screen real estate, being about the same size as a single line text box, as seen in Figure 16-2. By default, it displays the current date in the Long Date format currently in effect on the user's machine, although this is configurable with the Format and CustomFormat properties. Clicking on the drop-down arrow at the right end of the control drops down a graphical calendar that shows the selected month with both the selected date and today's date (DateTime.Today) indicated, as shown in Figure 16-3. The colors of the different parts of the calendar can be set, as demonstrated below.

Once the calendar is dropped down, the user can change months by clicking on scroll buttons to either side of the month and year in the title or by clicking on the month name in the title and selecting from the drop-down menu. If the user clicks on the year in the title, up-down scroll buttons appear, which enable scrolling to a new year.

Table 16-11 lists many of the most commonly used properties of the DateTimePicker class.

Table 16-11. DateTimePicker properties

Property	Value type	Description
CalendarFont	Font	Read/write. The font applied to the calendar.
CalendarForeColor	Color	Read/write. The color of the text used for the calendar dates and the Today legend.
CalendarMonthBackground	Color	Read/write. The background color of the calendar month.
CalendarTitleBackColor	Color	Read/write. The background color of the calendar title.
CalendarTitleForeColor	Color	Read/write. The color of the text used for the calendar title and the selected date.
CalendarTrailingForeColor	Color	Read/write. The color of the text used for the calendar trailing dates, which precede and follow the current month in the calendar.
Checked	Boolean	Read/write. If true (the default), the Value property has been set with a valid value and the displayed value can be updated.
CustomFormat	String	Read/write. A string comprised of format strings (listed in Table 16-9) and/or string literals (escaped with single quotes), representing custom DateTime formats. Default is null (Nothing). Format property must be set to DateTimePickerFormat.Custom for this property to have any effect.

Table 16-11. DateTimePicker properties (continued)

Property	Value type	Description
DropDownAlign	LeftRight-Alignment	Read/write. Specifies the left/right alignment of the calendar. Default is LeftRightAlignment.Left. Other possible value is LeftRightAlignment.Right.
Format	DateTimePicker-Format	Read/write. Specifies the format for date and time. Must be a member of the DateTimePickerFormat enumeration, listed in Table 16-12. Actual displayed formats are determined by the user's operating system and regional settings. Default is DateTimePickerFormat.Long.
MaxDate	DateTime	Read/write. The maximum date and time that can be selected by the control. The default is 12/31/9998 23:59:59.
MinDate	DateTime	Read/write. The minimum date and time that can be selected by the control. The default is 1/1/1753 00:00:00.
PreferredHeight	Integer	Read-only. Minimum height of the control, in pixels, to accommodate the displayed text.
ShowCheckBox	Boolean	Read/write. If true, a checkbox is displayed to the left of the date-time value in the control. When this checkbox is checked, the values in the control can be changed by the user at runtime by highlighting a portion of the date and pressing the arrow keys. When not checked, the date can only be changed by clicking the drop-down menu to display the calendar. Default is false.
ShowUpDown	Boolean	Read/write. If true, the calendar drop-down menu is disabled and up-down scroll buttons are displayed to the right of the date-time value in the control, which are used to increment/decrement the highlighted portion of the date-time value. Default is false.
Text	String	Read/write. Overridden. Equivalent to the Value property with the appropriate or custom formatting applied.
Value	DateTime	Read/write. The DateTime value assigned to the control. If Value has not yet been set, it returns the current date and time (DateTime.Now).

Table 16-12. DateTimePickerFormat enumeration

Value	Description
Custom	Date-time values displayed in a custom format
Long	Date-time values displayed in the long format set by the user's OS and regional settings
Short	Date-time values displayed in the short format set by the user's OS and regional settings
Time	Date-time values displayed in the time format set by the user's OS and regional settings

The DateTimePicker class has several events that are not inherited from base classes, all listed in Table 16-13. The most commonly used event is ValueChanged, which is raised whenever the Value property changes (i.e., whenever the user selects a new date or time).

Table 16-13. DateTimePicker events

Event	Event argument	Description
CloseUp	EventArgs	Raised when the drop-down calendar disappears
DropDown	EventArgs	Raised when the drop-down calendar is shown
FormatChanged	EventArgs	Raised when the Format property is changed
ValueChanged	EventArgs	Raised when the Value property changes

The programs listed in Example 16-1 (in C#) and Example 16-2 (in VB.NET) demonstrate the DateTimePicker control, along with several different formatting capabilities of the control and of the DateTime class. The programs consist of a form with a DateTimePicker control that displays the date by using a custom format. Below the control is the selected date in several different formats, including the generic ToString, long date and time, short date and time, and a custom format that reflects the custom string that the user enters in a text box.

The program looks like Figure 16-2 after a new date has been selected and a different custom string is entered in the text box.

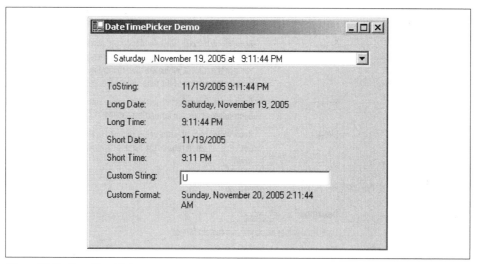

Figure 16-2. DateTimePicker program

Figure 16-3 shows what the calendar drop-down menu looks like. This monochrome book does not do justice to the vibrant color scheme applied to the calendar, but in real life the title text is blue, the title background is lime green, the calendar itself is yellow with red text, and the trailing dates are a shade of pink. (Hopefully you will not inflict such garish aesthetics on your users.) The code listings show how this color scheme was achieved.

Figure 16-3. DateTimePicker calendar

Today's date is circled on the calendar when the current month is displayed. Clicking on the Today circle at the bottom of every month will instantly select today's date. It is not possible to suppress the Today circle.

An analysis follows the code listings.

Example 16-1. DateTimePicker in C# (DateTimePicker.cs)

```csharp
using System;
using System.Drawing;
using System.Windows.Forms;

namespace ProgrammingWinApps
{
   public class DTPicker : Form
   {
      DateTimePicker dtp;
      Label lblToString;
      Label lblLongDate;
      Label lblLongTime;
      Label lblShortDate;
      Label lblShortTime;
      Label lblCustomFormat;
      TextBox txtCustomString;

      public DTPicker()
      {
         Text = "DateTimePicker Demo";
         Size = new Size(400,300);
         this.Load += new EventHandler(this_Load);
```

Example 16-1. DateTimePicker in C# (DateTimePicker.cs) (continued)

```csharp
        dtp = new DateTimePicker( );
        dtp.Parent = this;
        dtp.Location = new Point(20,20);
        dtp.Size = new Size(ClientSize.Width - 40, dtp.PreferredHeight);
        dtp.Anchor = AnchorStyles.Top | AnchorStyles.Left |
                AnchorStyles.Right;
        Font fnt = new Font("Times New Roman", 16);
        dtp.CalendarFont = new Font(fnt,
                                    FontStyle.Bold | FontStyle.Italic);
        dtp.CalendarForeColor = Color.Red;
        dtp.CalendarMonthBackground = Color.Yellow;
        dtp.CalendarTitleBackColor = Color.Lime;
        dtp.CalendarTitleForeColor = Color.Blue;
        dtp.CalendarTrailingForeColor = Color.FromArgb(255,192,192);
        dtp.CustomFormat = "dddd,MMMM d, yyyy 'at' h:mm:ss tt";
        dtp.Format = DateTimePickerFormat.Custom;
        dtp.DropDownAlign = LeftRightAlignment.Right;
        dtp.ShowUpDown = false;         // default
        dtp.ValueChanged +=
            new EventHandler(dtp_ValueChanged);

        Label lbl1 = new Label( );
        lbl1.Parent = this;
        lbl1.Text = "ToString:";
        lbl1.Location = new Point(dtp.Left, dtp.Bottom + 20);

        lblToString = new Label( );
        lblToString.Parent = this;
        lblToString.Size = new Size(200,
                            lblToString.PreferredHeight + 10);
        lblToString.Location = new Point(lbl1.Right, dtp.Bottom + 20);

        Label lbl2 = new Label( );
        lbl2.Parent = this;
        lbl2.Text = "Long Date:";
        lbl2.Location = new Point(dtp.Left, lblToString.Bottom);

        lblLongDate = new Label( );
        lblLongDate.Parent = this;
        lblLongDate.Size = new Size(200,
                            lblLongDate.PreferredHeight + 10);
        lblLongDate.Location = new Point(lbl1.Right,
                                    lblToString.Bottom );

        Label lbl3 = new Label( );
        lbl3.Parent = this;
        lbl3.Text = "Long Time:";
        lbl3.Location = new Point(dtp.Left, lblLongDate.Bottom);

        lblLongTime = new Label( );
        lblLongTime.Parent = this;
        lblLongTime.Size = lblLongDate.Size;
```

Example 16-1. DateTimePicker in C# (DateTimePicker.cs) (continued)

```
         lblLongTime.Location = new Point(lbl1.Right, lblLongDate.Bottom);

         Label lbl4 = new Label( );
         lbl4.Parent = this;
         lbl4.Text = "Short Date:";
         lbl4.Location = new Point(dtp.Left, lblLongTime.Bottom);

         lblShortDate = new Label( );
         lblShortDate.Parent = this;
         lblShortDate.Size = lblLongDate.Size;
         lblShortDate.Location = new Point(lbl1.Right,
                                           lblLongTime.Bottom);

         Label lbl5 = new Label( );
         lbl5.Parent = this;
         lbl5.Text = "Short Time:";
         lbl5.Location = new Point(dtp.Left, lblShortDate.Bottom);

         lblShortTime = new Label( );
         lblShortTime.Parent = this;
         lblShortTime.Size = lblLongDate.Size;
         lblShortTime.Location = new Point(lbl1.Right,
                                           lblShortDate.Bottom);

         Label lbl6 = new Label( );
         lbl6.Parent = this;
         lbl6.Text = "Custom String:";
         lbl6.Location = new Point(dtp.Left, lblShortTime.Bottom);

         txtCustomString = new TextBox( );
         txtCustomString.Parent = this;
         txtCustomString.Size = lblLongDate.Size;
         txtCustomString.Location = new Point(lbl1.Right,
                                              lblShortTime.Bottom);
         txtCustomString.Text = "D";
         txtCustomString.TextChanged +=
              new EventHandler(txtCustomString_TextChanged);

         Label lbl7 = new Label( );
         lbl7.Parent = this;
         lbl7.Text = "Custom Format:";
         lbl7.Location = new Point(dtp.Left, txtCustomString.Bottom + 5);

         lblCustomFormat = new Label( );
         lblCustomFormat.Parent = this;
         lblCustomFormat.Size = new Size(lblLongDate.Width,
                                         lblLongDate.Height * 3);
         lblCustomFormat.Location = new Point(lbl1.Right,
                                              txtCustomString.Bottom + 5);
     }  // close for constructor

     static void Main( )
```

Example 16-1. DateTimePicker in C# (DateTimePicker.cs) (continued)

```csharp
    {
        Application.Run(new DTPicker( ));
    }

    private void UpdateLabels( )
    {
        lblToString.Text = dtp.Value.ToString( );
        lblLongDate.Text = dtp.Value.ToLongDateString( );
        lblLongTime.Text = dtp.Value.ToLongTimeString( );
        lblShortDate.Text = dtp.Value.ToShortDateString( );
        lblShortTime.Text = dtp.Value.ToShortTimeString( );
        lblCustomFormat.Text = dtp.Value.ToString(txtCustomString.Text);
    }

    private void this_Load(object sender, EventArgs e)
    {
        UpdateLabels( );
    }

    private void dtp_ValueChanged(object sender, EventArgs e)
    {
        UpdateLabels( );
    }

    private void txtCustomString_TextChanged(object sender, EventArgs e)
    {
        UpdateLabels( );
    }
    }      //  close for form class
}          //  close form namespace
```

Example 16-2. DateTimePicker in VB.NET (DateTimePicker.vb)

```vbnet
Option Strict On
imports System
imports System.Drawing
imports System.Windows.Forms

namespace ProgrammingWinApps
    public class DTPicker : inherits Form

        dim dtp as DateTimePicker
        dim lblToString as Label
        dim lblLongDate as Label
        dim lblLongTime as Label
        dim lblShortDate as Label
        dim lblShortTime as Label
        dim lblCustomFormat as Label
        dim txtCustomString as TextBox

        public sub New( )
            Text = "DateTimePicker Demo"
```

Example 16-2. DateTimePicker in VB.NET (DateTimePicker.vb) (continued)

`VB`

```
        Size = new Size(400,300)
        AddHandler me.Load, AddressOf me_Load

        dtp = new DateTimePicker( )
        dtp.Parent = me
        dtp.Location = new Point(20,20)
        dtp.Size = new Size(ClientSize.Width - 40, dtp.PreferredHeight)
        dtp.Anchor = AnchorStyles.Top or AnchorStyles.Left or _
                AnchorStyles.Right
        dim fnt as new Font("Times New Roman", 16)
        dtp.CalendarFont = new Font(fnt, FontStyle.Bold or _
                                        FontStyle.Italic)
        dtp.CalendarForeColor = Color.Red
        dtp.CalendarMonthBackground = Color.Yellow
        dtp.CalendarTitleBackColor = Color.Lime
        dtp.CalendarTitleForeColor = Color.Blue
        dtp.CalendarTrailingForeColor = Color.FromArgb(255,192,192)
        dtp.CustomFormat = "dddd,MMMM d, yyyy 'at' h:mm:ss tt"
        dtp.Format = DateTimePickerFormat.Custom
        dtp.DropDownAlign = LeftRightAlignment.Right
        dtp.ShowUpDown = false            ' default
        AddHandler dtp.ValueChanged, AddressOf dtp_ValueChanged

        dim lbl1 as new Label( )
        lbl1.Parent = me
        lbl1.Text = "ToString:"
        lbl1.Location = new Point(dtp.Left, dtp.Bottom + 20)

        lblToString = new Label( )
        lblToString.Parent = me
        lblToString.Size = new Size(200, _
                                lblToString.PreferredHeight + 10)
        lblToString.Location = new Point(lbl1.Right, dtp.Bottom + 20)

        dim lbl2 as new Label( )
        lbl2.Parent = me
        lbl2.Text = "Long Date:"
        lbl2.Location = new Point(dtp.Left, lblToString.Bottom)

        lblLongDate = new Label( )
        lblLongDate.Parent = me
        lblLongDate.Size = new Size(200, _
                                lblLongDate.PreferredHeight + 10)
        lblLongDate.Location = new Point(lbl1.Right, lblToString.Bottom)

        dim lbl3 as new Label( )
        lbl3.Parent = me
        lbl3.Text = "Long Time:"
        lbl3.Location = new Point(dtp.Left, lblLongDate.Bottom)

        lblLongTime = new Label( )
        lblLongTime.Parent = me
```

Example 16-2. DateTimePicker in VB.NET (DateTimePicker.vb) (continued)

```
        lblLongTime.Size = lblLongDate.Size
        lblLongTime.Location = new Point(lbl1.Right, lblLongDate.Bottom)

        dim lbl4 as new Label( )
        lbl4.Parent = me
        lbl4.Text = "Short Date:"
        lbl4.Location = new Point(dtp.Left, lblLongTime.Bottom)

        lblShortDate = new Label( )
        lblShortDate.Parent = me
        lblShortDate.Size = lblLongDate.Size
        lblShortDate.Location = new Point(lbl1.Right, lblLongTime.Bottom)

        dim lbl5 as new Label( )
        lbl5.Parent = me
        lbl5.Text = "Short Time:"
        lbl5.Location = new Point(dtp.Left, lblShortDate.Bottom)

        lblShortTime = new Label( )
        lblShortTime.Parent = me
        lblShortTime.Size = lblLongDate.Size
        lblShortTime.Location = new Point(lbl1.Right, _
                                        lblShortDate.Bottom)

        dim lbl6 as new Label( )
        lbl6.Parent = me
        lbl6.Text = "Custom String:"
        lbl6.Location = new Point(dtp.Left, lblShortTime.Bottom)

        txtCustomString = new TextBox( )
        txtCustomString.Parent = me
        txtCustomString.Size = lblLongDate.Size
        txtCustomString.Location = new Point(lbl1.Right, _
                                    lblShortTime.Bottom)
        txtCustomString.Text = "D"
        AddHandler txtCustomString.TextChanged, _
                AddressOf txtCustomString_TextChanged

        dim lbl7 as new Label( )
        lbl7.Parent = me
        lbl7.Text = "Custom Format:"
        lbl7.Location = new Point(dtp.Left, txtCustomString.Bottom + 5)

        lblCustomFormat = new Label( )
        lblCustomFormat.Parent = me
        lblCustomFormat.Size = new Size(lblLongDate.Width, _
                            lblLongDate.Height * 3)
        lblCustomFormat.Location = new Point(lbl1.Right, _
                            txtCustomString.Bottom + 5)
    end sub   ' close for constructor

    public shared sub Main( )
        Application.Run(new DTPicker( ))
```

Example 16-2. DateTimePicker in VB.NET (DateTimePicker.vb) (continued)

VB
```
        end sub

        private sub UpdateLabels( )
            lblToString.Text = dtp.Value.ToString( )
            lblLongDate.Text = dtp.Value.ToLongDateString( )
            lblLongTime.Text = dtp.Value.ToLongTimeString( )
            lblShortDate.Text = dtp.Value.ToShortDateString( )
            lblShortTime.Text = dtp.Value.ToShortTimeString( )
            lblCustomFormat.Text = dtp.Value.ToString(txtCustomString.Text)
        end sub

        private sub me_Load(ByVal sender as object, _
                    ByVal e as EventArgs)
            UpdateLabels( )
        end sub

        private sub dtp_ValueChanged(ByVal sender as object, _
                        ByVal e as EventArgs)
            UpdateLabels( )
        end sub

        private sub txtCustomString_TextChanged(ByVal sender as object, _
                            ByVal e as EventArgs)
            UpdateLabels( )
        end sub
    end class
end namespace
```

The formatted contents of the labels are updated when the form first loads, every time the value of the DateTimePicker control changes, and whenever the contents of the custom string text box changes. In the constructor, event handlers are created for each event:

C#
```
    this.Load += new EventHandler(this_Load);
    dtp.ValueChanged += new EventHandler(dtp_ValueChanged);
    txtCustomString.TextChanged +=
            new EventHandler(txtCustomString_TextChanged);
```

VB
```
    AddHandler me.Load, AddressOf me_Load
    AddHandler dtp.ValueChanged, AddressOf dtp_ValueChanged
    AddHandler txtCustomString.TextChanged,
            AddressOf txtCustomString_TextChanged
```

To accomplish the update, a helper method, UpdateLabels, is created and then called in each of the event handlers. UpdateLabels sets the Text properties of the labels with the appropriate formatting method:

C#
```
    private void UpdateLabels( )
    {
        lblToString.Text = dtp.Value.ToString( );
        lblLongDate.Text = dtp.Value.ToLongDateString( );
```

DateTimePicker | 757

```
C#     lblLongTime.Text = dtp.Value.ToLongTimeString( );
       lblShortDate.Text = dtp.Value.ToShortDateString( );
       lblShortTime.Text = dtp.Value.ToShortTimeString( );
       lblCustomFormat.Text = dtp.Value.ToString(txtCustomString.Text);
}
```

```
VB    private sub UpdateLabels( )
         lblToString.Text = dtp.Value.ToString( )
         lblLongDate.Text = dtp.Value.ToLongDateString( )
         lblLongTime.Text = dtp.Value.ToLongTimeString( )
         lblShortDate.Text = dtp.Value.ToShortDateString( )
         lblShortTime.Text = dtp.Value.ToShortTimeString( )
         lblCustomFormat.Text = dtp.Value.ToString(txtCustomString.Text)
      end sub
```

Notice that the ToString method is called twice using different overloaded versions: once with no arguments and once with a formatting string provided by the contents of the Custom String text box.

Back in the constructor, the DateTimePicker control has its various properties set. The CalendarFont, CalendarForeColor, CalendarMonthBackground, CalendarTitle-BackColor, CalendarTitleForeColor, and CalendarTrailingForeColor properties are all set to control the appearance of the calendar. Notice how the last color property is set using an overloaded form of the static FromArgb method to pass in RGB values rather than a color name.

```
C#     dtp.CalendarTrailingForeColor = Color.FromArgb(255,192,192);
```

The CustomFormat and Format properties work in tandem to display the date in the custom format shown. The format string is comprised of the formatting characters in Table 16-9. The word "at" is escaped with single quotes. If that were not the case, then the "t" in "at" would have been interpreted as a formatting character corresponding to a one-letter abbreviation for AM/PM.

Also, the components of the string do not always fill the space allocated to that component in the control. For example, there are extra spaces between Monday and the comma in Figure 16-2, as well as extra spaces between the "at" and the 9. As you change the values, you will realize that the space allocated for each component is equal to the necessary maximum, and each component is then centered within that allocated space.

If the Format property were not specified, it would have defaulted to the long date format, as shown on the form in Figure 16-2. If the Format property were set to DateTimePickerFormat.Time, then the control could be used to set the time, although the drop-down calendar would be of little use in that case: the time would always be set to the current time.

The time can be set however, along with all the other date-time components, if the ShowUpDown property is set to true. Setting that property replaces the calendar

---

drop-down button with up-down scroll buttons. This disables the drop-down calendar. Each component can then be individually highlighted and scrolled either with the scroll buttons or the arrow keys. Figure 16-4 shows the control with the same custom formatting as Figure 16-2, but with both the ShowUpDown and ShowCheckBox properties set true. The latter property locks the displayed value if the checkbox is unchecked, preventing inadvertent changes.

Wednesday, January 14, 2004 at 11:49:26 PM

Figure 16-4. DateTimePicker with ShowUpDown and ShowCheckBox properties set

As you will see in Examples 16-6 and 16-7, a DateTimePicker can also set a TimeSpan value, although you must take a few extra steps to do so.

MonthCalendar

The MonthCalendar control allows the user to pick a date or a range of dates. Unlike the DateTimePicker, it does not offer any time component, nor does it provide extensive formatting capabilities. However, the DateTime objects it makes available in the SelectionStart, SelectionEnd, and SelectionRange properties can always be formatted after the fact.

By default, the control displays a single month, although you can display a rectangular array of up to 12 months by setting the CalendarDimensions property. This property is of type Size, where the first coordinate is the number of columns and the second is the number of rows.

 The product of the two coordinates must not exceed 12 or the greater of the two numbers will be reduced until the product is 12 or less.

Paradoxically, the size of the control cannot be set directly using the Size property as with most other controls (nor the Height nor Width properties, for that matter), even when creating a new Size object. The Size property instead effectively changes the CalendarDimensions property: if the new size is large enough to accommodate another row or column of months, then the size of the array of months increases; otherwise, no change in size occurs.

The actual size of the calendar can be changed by setting the Font property. Setting the Font property to a larger font increases the size of the control.

Several properties change the appearance of the control, including ShowTodayCircle, ShowWeekNumbers, TitleBackColor, TitleForeColor, and TrailingForeColor, all of which are described in Table 16-14.

By default, today's date (DateTime.Today) is displayed at the bottom of the control, as shown in Figure 16-5. It can be turned off by setting the ShowToday property to false. Clicking on today's date at any time will immediately scroll the control back to today's date and select today.

You can programmatically bold one or more dates, on an annual, monthly, or one-time basis, by adding DateTime objects to the arrays of DateTime objects referenced in the AnnuallyBoldedDates, MonthlyBoldedDates, or BoldedDates properties. Any-time you modify the contents of one of the bolded date arrays, you must call the UpdateBoldedDates method to force the calendar to repaint and reflect the new bolded dates.

You can also add dates to these arrays by using the AddAnnuallyBoldedDate, AddMonthlyBoldedDate, and AddBoldedDate methods described in Table 16-15. Likewise, you can clear a specific bolded date, using the RemoveAnnuallyBolded-Date, RemoveMonthlyBoldedDate, and RemoveBoldedDate methods, or clear all the bolded dates by using the RemoveAllAnnuallyBoldedDates, RemoveAllMonthly-BoldedDates, and RemoveAllBoldedDates methods.

Three properties retrieve the selected dates from the MonthCalendar control. The SelectionStart property contains the starting date, and the SelectionEnd property contains the ending date. If only a single date is selected, then these two properties will have the same value. The SelectionRange property, of type SelectionRange, con-tains both the starting and ending dates in SelectionRange.Start and SelectionRange. End, respectively.

By default, only seven days can be selected. This default can be overridden by setting the MaxSelectionCount property. If the range of selected days exceeds the value specified in the MaxSelectionCount property, the SelectionEnd property will be adjusted to conform automatically.

All properties mentioned above, as well as other commonly used properties of the MonthCalendar class, are listed in Table 16-14.

Table 16-14. MonthCalendar properties

Property	Value type	Description
AnnuallyBoldedDates	DateTime array	Read/write. An array of annual DateTime objects that are displayed in a bold font.
BoldedDates	DateTime array	Read/write. An array of dates displayed in a bold font.
CalendarDimensions	Size	Read/write. Specifies the number of columns and rows of displayed months. Maximum number of displayed months is 12. If product of x (columns) and y (rows) values is greater than 12, the greater of the two values is reduced until the product is 12 or less.
FirstDayOfWeek	Day	Read/write. Specifies the first day of the week to display in the con-trol. Default is Day.Default, which corresponds to Day.Sunday on sys-tems with the locale set to English (US) and to Day.Monday on systems with the locale set to most European countries.

Table 16-14. *MonthCalendar properties (continued)*

Property	Value type	Description
Font	Font	Read/write. The font used by the text displayed in the control. Use this property to change the size of the calendar.
MaxDate	DateTime	Read/write. The maximum allowable date that can be selected. The default is 12/31/9998.
MaxSelectionCount	Integer	Read/write. The maximum number of days that can be selected. Default is 7. The SelectionStart and SelectionEnd properties can be no more than MaxSelectionCount - 1 days apart.
MinDate	DateTime	Read/write. The minimum allowable date that can be selected. The default is 01/01/1753.
MonthlyBoldedDates	DateTime array	Read/write. An array of monthly DateTime objects that are displayed in a bold font.
ScrollChange	Integer	Read/write. A positive number representing the scroll rate, or number of months the calendar moves when the user clicks a scroll button. The default is the number of months currently displayed. The maximum value is 20,000. A value of zero resets the property to the default value.
SelectionEnd	DateTime	Read/write. The last date in the selection range. If the resulting number of selected days exceeds the value of MaxSelectionCount, the SelectionEnd property is automatically adjusted so the number of days selected is equal to MaxSelectionCount.
SelectionRange	SelectionRange	Read/write. The range of selected dates. The starting date is SelectionRange.Start and the ending date is SelectionRange.End. If only one day is selected, the two values are equal.
SelectionStart	DateTime	Read/write. The first date in the selection range. If the resulting number of selected days exceeds the value of MaxSelectionCount, the SelectionEnd property is automatically adjusted so the number of days selected is equal to MaxSelectionCount.
ShowToday	Boolean	Read/write. If `true` (the default), today's date (DateTime.Today) is displayed at the bottom of the control. Clicking on that date scrolls the calendar so today's date is visible.
ShowTodayCircle	Boolean	Read/write. If `true` (the default), today's date (DateTime.Today) is circled.
ShowWeekNumbers	Boolean	Read/write. If `true`, week numbers are displayed. The default is `false`.
SingleMonthSize	Size	Read-only. Returns the minimum size, in pixels, to display one month. The size depends on the font.
Size	Size	Read/write. Must declare new Size object for this to have any effect. Does not set the size of the control as it does for most controls, but effectively changes the CalendarDimensions property to fit as many months as possible into the specified size.
Text	String	Read/write. Always an empty string unless set otherwise in code. Does not display as part of the control.

Table 16-14. MonthCalendar properties (continued)

Property	Value type	Description
TitleBackColor	Color	Read/write. The color of the title background area, the days of the week, the highlighting of the currently selected date(s), and the week numbers (if ShowWeekNumbers is true). Default is the system color for active captions.
TitleForeColor	Color	Read/write. The color that the title text and currently selected date(s) display in. Default is the system color for active caption text.
TodayDate	DateTime	Read/write. The value used as today's date. By default, it is DateTime. Today and TodayDateSet is false. If TodayDate is set, then TodayDateSet becomes true.
TodayDateSet	Boolean	Read-only. Returns true if the TodayDate property has been set. Default is false.
TrailingForeColor	Color	Read/write. The color of the leading and trailing dates. The default is Color.Gray.

In addition to the MonthCalendar methods just described for setting and unsetting bolded dates, the control has other commonly used methods, all of which are listed and described in Table 16-15.

Table 16-15. MonthCalendar methods

Method	Description
AddAnnuallyBoldedDate	Adds the specified DateTime to the array of annually bolded dates specified by the AnnuallyBoldedDates property.
AddBoldedDate	Adds the specified DateTime to the array of bolded dates specified by the BoldedDates property.
AddMonthlyBoldedDate	Adds the specified DateTime to the array of monthly bolded dates specified by the MonthlyBoldedDates property.
GetDisplayRange	Returns a SelectionRange that contains the start and ending dates of dates displayed in the control.
HitTest	Overloaded. Returns a HitTestInfo object with information about the specified spot on the control.
RemoveAllAnnuallyBoldedDates	Clears the annually bolded dates array.
RemoveAllBoldedDates	Clears the bolded dates array.
RemoveAllMonthlyBoldedDates	Clears the monthly bolded dates array.
RemoveAnnuallyBoldedDate	Removes the specified date from the array of annually bolded dates.
RemoveBoldedDate	Removes the specified date from the array of bolded dates.
RemoveMonthlyBoldedDate	Removes the specified date from the array of monthly bolded dates.
SetCalendarDimension	Sets the number of columns and rows of months to display. Equivalent to setting the CalendarDimensions property.
SetDate	Sets the specified date as the currently selected date.

Table 16-15. MonthCalendar methods (continued)

Method	Description
SetSelectionRange	Sets the range specified by two dates as currently selected.
UpdateBoldedDates	Repaints the calendar to reflect any changes made to the bolded dates properties.

The MonthCalendar control has only two events, listed in Table 16-16, other than those inherited from the Control class. These two events are redundant. The DateChanged event is always raised when a new date is selected or the selection range is changed, either by clicking with the mouse or using the keyboard arrow keys. If the mouse is used to click on a date, then the DateSelected event is also raised before the DateChanged event. Both events take an event argument of type DateRangeEventArgs, which has the two properties listed in Table 16-17, for getting the start and end dates of the selection range.

Table 16-16. MonthCalendar events

Event	Event argument	Description
DateChanged	DateRangeEventArgs	Raised when the selected date range in the control is changed. The event argument returns the properties listed in Table 16-17.
DateSelected	DateRangeEventArgs	Raised before DateChanged when a date is selected in the control. The event argument returns the properties listed in Table 16-17.

Table 16-17. DateRangeEventArgs properties

Property	Description
End	Returns the last date-time value selected in the control.
Start	Returns the first date-time value selected in the control.

The examples listed in Example 16-3 (in C#) and in Example 16-4 (in VB.NET) demonstrate the use of the MonthCalendar control. The resulting application is shown in Figure 16-5 after changing the start and end dates and bolding some dates. The default color scheme is used.

The CalendarDimension property has been set to 2 × 1 so that two months display. Clicking on the scroll buttons at the top left and right corners of the control scroll the control two months at a time. The ScrollChange property could have been set to a non-default value to change the number of months the control scrolls when the scroll buttons are clicked.

Below the MonthCalendar control are two DateTimePickers: one labeled Start Date and the other End Date. Changing the selected dates in the MonthCalendar updates the dates displayed in the DateTimePickers, and vice versa: changing the values displayed in the DateTimePickers changes the selection in the MonthCalendar control.

Scrolling the months in the MonthCalendar control causes the selected dates range to scroll as well. For example, the selected date range in Figure 16-5 is 1/20 through 2/9. Scrolling the months so that March and April are displayed will result in a selected date range of 3/20 through 4/9.

Below the DateTimePicker controls is a read-only combo box that allows selection of a day of the week to be assigned to the FirstDayOfWeek property. This example initializes with the nondefault value (for English-US systems) of Monday.

Below the Start Day combo box is another DateTimePicker—this one configured to display the date in the Short format. When one of the three buttons next to that control are clicked, the displayed date is added to the respective bolded date array. In Figure 16-5, 1/15/03 is bolded and the 17th is bolded monthly. This example does not provide any means of clearing or otherwise manipulating the bolded dates, but that functionality would be easy to implement.

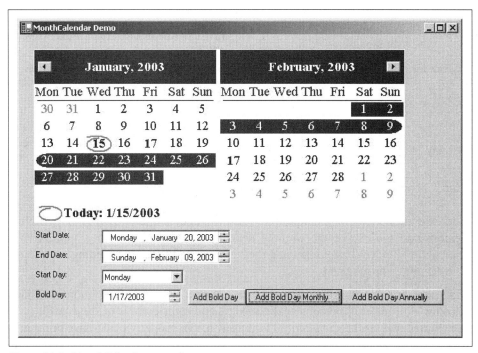

Figure 16-5. MonthCalendar control

A full analysis of the example follows the code listings.

Example 16-3. MonthCalendar application in C# (MonthCalendar.cs)

```csharp
using System;
using System.Drawing;
using System.Windows.Forms;

namespace ProgrammingWinApps
{
   public class Calendar : Form
   {
      MonthCalendar mc;
      DateTimePicker dtpStart;
      DateTimePicker dtpEnd;
      DateTimePicker dtpBold;
      Label lblStart;
      Label lblEnd;
      Label lblStartDay;
      Label lblBold;
      ComboBox cmbStart;
      Button btnBoldDay;
      Button btnBoldMonthly;
      Button btnBoldAnnually;

      public Calendar()
      {
         Text = "MonthCalendar Demo";
         Size = new Size(650,450);
         this.Load += new EventHandler(this_Load);

         mc = new MonthCalendar();
         mc.Parent = this;
         mc.Location = new Point(20,20);
         mc.Font = new Font("Times New Roman", 14);
         mc.CalendarDimensions = new Size(2,1);
         mc.FirstDayOfWeek = Day.Monday;
         mc.MaxSelectionCount = 45;
         mc.DateChanged += new DateRangeEventHandler(mc_DateChanged);
         mc.DateSelected += new DateRangeEventHandler(mc_DateSelected);

         lblStart = new Label();
         lblStart.Parent = this;
         lblStart.Text = "Start Date:";

         dtpStart = new DateTimePicker();
         dtpStart.Parent = this;
         dtpStart.Size = new Size((int)(Font.Height * .6) *
                        dtpStart.Value.ToString("D").Length,
                        dtpStart.PreferredHeight);
         dtpStart.Format = DateTimePickerFormat.Long;
         dtpStart.ShowUpDown = true;
         dtpStart.ValueChanged +=
               new EventHandler(dtpStart_ValueChanged);

         lblEnd = new Label();
         lblEnd.Parent = this;
```

Example 16-3. MonthCalendar application in C# (MonthCalendar.cs) (continued)

```csharp
                 lblEnd.Text = "End Date:";

                 dtpEnd = new DateTimePicker( );
                 dtpEnd.Parent = this;
                 dtpEnd.Size = new Size((int)(Font.Height * .6) *
                                  dtpEnd.Value.ToString("D").Length,
                                  dtpEnd.PreferredHeight);
                 dtpEnd.Format = DateTimePickerFormat.Long;
                 dtpEnd.ShowUpDown = true;
                 dtpEnd.ValueChanged +=
                      new EventHandler(dtpEnd_ValueChanged);

                 lblStartDay = new Label( );
                 lblStartDay.Parent = this;
                 lblStartDay.Text = "Start Day:";

                 cmbStart = new ComboBox( );
                 cmbStart.Parent = this;
                 cmbStart.DropDownStyle = ComboBoxStyle.DropDownList;
                 cmbStart.Items.AddRange(new object[] {"Monday",
                                             "Tuesday",
                                             "Wednesday",
                                             "Thursday",
                                             "Friday",
                                             "Saturday",
                                             "Sunday"});
                 cmbStart.SelectedIndex = 0;
                 cmbStart.SelectedIndexChanged +=
                         new EventHandler(cmbStart_SelectedIndexChanged);

                 lblBold = new Label( );
                 lblBold.Parent = this;
                 lblBold.Text = "Bold Day:";

                 dtpBold = new DateTimePicker( );
                 dtpBold.Parent = this;
                 dtpBold.Size = new Size((int)(Font.Height ) *
                                  dtpBold.Value.ToString("d").Length,
                                  dtpBold.PreferredHeight);
                 dtpBold.Format = DateTimePickerFormat.Short;
                 dtpBold.ShowUpDown = true;

                 btnBoldDay = new Button( );
                 btnBoldDay.Parent = this;
                 btnBoldDay.Text = "Add Bold Day";
                 btnBoldDay.Size = new Size((int)(Font.Height * .6) *
                                  btnBoldDay.Text.Length,
                                  (int)(Font.Height * 1.75));
                 btnBoldDay.Click += new EventHandler(btnBoldDay_Click);

                 btnBoldMonthly = new Button( );
                 btnBoldMonthly.Parent = this;
```

Example 16-3. MonthCalendar application in C# (MonthCalendar.cs) (continued)

```
        btnBoldMonthly.Text = "Add Bold Day Monthly";
        btnBoldMonthly.Size = new Size((int)(Font.Height * .6) *
                               btnBoldMonthly.Text.Length,
                               (int)(Font.Height * 1.75));
        btnBoldMonthly.Click += new EventHandler(btnBoldMonthly_Click);

        btnBoldAnnually = new Button( );
        btnBoldAnnually.Parent = this;
        btnBoldAnnually.Text = "Add Bold Day Annually";
        btnBoldAnnually.Size = new Size((int)(Font.Height * .6) *
                               btnBoldAnnually.Text.Length,
                               (int)(Font.Height * 1.75));
        btnBoldAnnually.Click += new EventHandler(btnBoldAnnually_Click);
    } // close for constructor

    static void Main( )
    {
        Application.Run(new Calendar( ));
    }

    private void this_Load(object sender, EventArgs e)
    {
        lblStart.Location = new Point(mc.Left, mc.Bottom + 10);
        dtpStart.Location = new Point(lblStart.Right, mc.Bottom + 10);

        lblEnd.Location = new Point(mc.Left, lblStart.Bottom + 5);
        dtpEnd.Location = new Point(lblStart.Right, lblStart.Bottom + 5);

        lblStartDay.Location = new Point(mc.Left, lblEnd.Bottom + 5);
        cmbStart.Location = new Point(lblStart.Right, lblEnd.Bottom + 5);

        lblBold.Location = new Point(mc.Left, lblStartDay.Bottom + 5);
        dtpBold.Location = new Point(lblBold.Right,
                                     lblStartDay.Bottom + 5);

        btnBoldDay.Location = new Point(dtpBold.Right + 10, dtpBold.Top);
        btnBoldMonthly.Location = new Point(btnBoldDay.Right,
                                            dtpBold.Top);
        btnBoldAnnually.Location = new Point(btnBoldMonthly.Right,
                                             dtpBold.Top);
    }

    private void dtpStart_ValueChanged(object sender, EventArgs e)
    {
        mc.SelectionStart = dtpStart.Value;
    }

    private void dtpEnd_ValueChanged(object sender, EventArgs e)
    {
        mc.SelectionEnd = dtpEnd.Value;
    }
```

Example 16-3. MonthCalendar application in C# (MonthCalendar.cs) (continued)

```
     private void mc_DateChanged(object sender, DateRangeEventArgs e)
     {
//        MessageBox.Show("DateChanged");
        dtpStart.Value = e.Start;
        dtpEnd.Value = e.End;
     }

     private void mc_DateSelected(object sender, DateRangeEventArgs e)
     {
//        MessageBox.Show("DateSelected");
     }

     private void cmbStart_SelectedIndexChanged(object sender,
                                                EventArgs e)
     {
        mc.FirstDayOfWeek = (Day)cmbStart.SelectedIndex;
     }

     private void btnBoldDay_Click(object sender, EventArgs e)
     {
        mc.AddBoldedDate(dtpBold.Value);
        mc.UpdateBoldedDates();
     }

     private void btnBoldMonthly_Click(object sender, EventArgs e)
     {
        mc.AddMonthlyBoldedDate(dtpBold.Value);
        mc.UpdateBoldedDates();
     }

     private void btnBoldAnnually_Click(object sender, EventArgs e)
     {
        mc.AddAnnuallyBoldedDate(dtpBold.Value);
        mc.UpdateBoldedDates();
     }
  }      //  close for form class
}         //  close form namespace
```

Example 16-4. MonthCalendar application in VB.NET (MonthCalendar.vb)

```
Option Strict On
imports System
imports System.Drawing
imports System.Windows.Forms

namespace ProgrammingWinApps
   public class Calendar : inherits Form

      dim mc as MonthCalendar
      dim dtpStart as DateTimePicker
      dim dtpEnd as DateTimePicker
      dim dtpBold as DateTimePicker
```

```
dim lblStart as Label
dim lblEnd as Label
dim lblStartDay as Label
dim lblBold as Label
dim cmbStart as ComboBox
dim btnBoldDay as Button
dim btnBoldMonthly as Button
dim btnBoldAnnually as Button

public sub New( )
    Text = "MonthCalendar Demo"
    Size = new Size(690,450)
    AddHandler me.Load, AddressOf me_Load

    mc = new MonthCalendar( )
    mc.Parent = me
    mc.Location = new Point(20,20)
    mc.Font = new Font("Times New Roman", 14)
    mc.CalendarDimensions = new Size(2,1)
    mc.FirstDayOfWeek = Day.Monday
    mc.MaxSelectionCount = 45
    AddHandler mc.DateChanged, AddressOf mc_DateChanged
    AddHandler mc.DateSelected, AddressOf mc_DateSelected

    lblStart = new Label( )
    lblStart.Parent = me
    lblStart.Text = "Start Date:"

    dtpStart = new DateTimePicker( )
    dtpStart.Parent = me
    dtpStart.Size = new Size(CInt(Font.Height * .6) * _
                    dtpStart.Value.ToString("D").Length, _
                    dtpStart.PreferredHeight)
    dtpStart.Format = DateTimePickerFormat.Long
    dtpStart.ShowUpDown = true
    AddHandler dtpStart.ValueChanged, _
                    AddressOf dtpStart_ValueChanged

    lblEnd = new Label( )
    lblEnd.Parent = me
    lblEnd.Text = "End Date:"

    dtpEnd = new DateTimePicker( )
    dtpEnd.Parent = me
    dtpEnd.Size = new Size(CInt(Font.Height * .6) * _
                    dtpEnd.Value.ToString("D").Length, _
                    dtpEnd.PreferredHeight)
    dtpEnd.Format = DateTimePickerFormat.Long
    dtpEnd.ShowUpDown = true
    AddHandler dtpEnd.ValueChanged, _
                    AddressOf dtpEnd_ValueChanged
```

```
lblStartDay = new Label()
lblStartDay.Parent = me
lblStartDay.Text = "Start Day:"

cmbStart = new ComboBox()
cmbStart.Parent = me
cmbStart.DropDownStyle = ComboBoxStyle.DropDownList
cmbStart.Items.AddRange(new object() { _
            "Monday", _
            "Tuesday", _
            "Wednesday", _
            "Thursday", _
            "Friday", _
            "Saturday", _
            "Sunday"})
cmbStart.SelectedIndex = 0
AddHandler cmbStart.SelectedIndexChanged, _
            AddressOf cmbStart_SelectedIndexChanged

lblBold = new Label()
lblBold.Parent = me
lblBold.Text = "Bold Day:"

dtpBold = new DateTimePicker()
dtpBold.Parent = me
dtpBold.Size = new Size(CInt(Font.Height) * _
            dtpBold.Value.ToString("d").Length, _
            dtpBold.PreferredHeight)
dtpBold.Format = DateTimePickerFormat.Short
dtpBold.ShowUpDown = true

btnBoldDay = new Button()
btnBoldDay.Parent = me
btnBoldDay.Text = "Add Bold Day"
btnBoldDay.Size = new Size(CInt(Font.Height * .6) * _
            btnBoldDay.Text.Length, _
            CInt(Font.Height * 1.75))
AddHandler btnBoldDay.Click, AddressOf btnBoldDay_Click

btnBoldMonthly = new Button()
btnBoldMonthly.Parent = me
btnBoldMonthly.Text = "Add Bold Day Monthly"
btnBoldMonthly.Size = new Size(CInt(Font.Height * .6) * _
            btnBoldMonthly.Text.Length, _
            CInt(Font.Height * 1.75))
AddHandler btnBoldMonthly.Click, AddressOf btnBoldMonthly_Click

btnBoldAnnually = new Button()
btnBoldAnnually.Parent = me
btnBoldAnnually.Text = "Add Bold Day Annually"
btnBoldAnnually.Size = new Size(CInt(Font.Height * .6) * _
            btnBoldAnnually.Text.Length, _
            CInt(Font.Height * 1.75))
```

```
        Addhandler btnBoldAnnually.Click, AddressOf btnBoldAnnually_Click
    end sub  '  close for constructor

    public shared sub Main( )
        Application.Run(new Calendar( ))
    end sub

    private sub me_Load(ByVal sender as object, _
                    ByVal e as EventArgs)
        lblStart.Location = new Point(mc.Left, mc.Bottom + 10)
        dtpStart.Location = new Point(lblStart.Right, mc.Bottom + 10)

        lblEnd.Location = new Point(mc.Left, lblStart.Bottom + 5)
        dtpEnd.Location = new Point(lblStart.Right, lblStart.Bottom + 5)

        lblStartDay.Location = new Point(mc.Left, lblEnd.Bottom + 5)
        cmbStart.Location = new Point(lblStart.Right, lblEnd.Bottom + 5)

        lblBold.Location = new Point(mc.Left, lblStartDay.Bottom + 5)
        dtpBold.Location = new Point(lblBold.Right, _
                                    lblStartDay.Bottom + 5)

        btnBoldDay.Location = new Point(dtpBold.Right + 10, dtpBold.Top)
        btnBoldMonthly.Location = new Point(btnBoldDay.Right, _
                                        dtpBold.Top)
        btnBoldAnnually.Location = new Point(btnBoldMonthly.Right, _
                                        dtpBold.Top)
    end sub

    private sub dtpStart_ValueChanged(ByVal sender as object, _
                                    ByVal e as EventArgs)
        mc.SelectionStart = dtpStart.Value
    end sub

    private sub dtpEnd_ValueChanged(ByVal sender as object, _
                                    ByVal e as EventArgs)
        mc.SelectionEnd = dtpEnd.Value
    end sub

    private sub mc_DateChanged(ByVal sender as object, _
                            ByVal e as DateRangeEventArgs)
'        MessageBox.Show("DateChanged")
        dtpStart.Value = e.Start
        dtpEnd.Value = e.End
    end sub

    private sub mc_DateSelected(ByVal sender as object, _
                            ByVal e as DateRangeEventArgs)
'        MessageBox.Show("DateSelected")
    end sub

    private sub cmbStart_SelectedIndexChanged(ByVal sender as object, _
                                    ByVal e as EventArgs)
```

```vb
        mc.FirstDayOfWeek = CType(cmbStart.SelectedIndex, Day)
    end sub

    private sub btnBoldDay_Click(ByVal sender as object, _
                                 ByVal e as EventArgs)
       mc.AddBoldedDate(dtpBold.Value)
       mc.UpdateBoldedDates()
    end sub

    private sub btnBoldMonthly_Click(ByVal sender as object, _
                                     ByVal e as EventArgs)
       mc.AddMonthlyBoldedDate(dtpBold.Value)
       mc.UpdateBoldedDates()
    end sub

    private sub btnBoldAnnually_Click(ByVal sender as object, _
                                      ByVal e as EventArgs)
       mc.AddAnnuallyBoldedDate(dtpBold.Value)
       mc.UpdateBoldedDates()
    end sub
  end class
end namespace
```

As with the previous examples in this chapter, an event handler for the Form Load event is added to the event delegate. In this example, this addition is necessary to achieve the correct positioning of the controls, as explained shortly.

The MonthCalendar control is instantiated and several properties are set. The Font property is changed to a 14-point Times New Roman. This enlarges the size of the control.

```vb
        mc.Font = new Font("Times New Roman", 14)
```

The CalendarDimensions property is set for 2 in the x direction and 1 in the y direction, or two columns and one row.

```vb
        mc.CalendarDimensions = new Size(2,1)
```

The FirstDayOfWeek property is set for Monday. This setting is the default for most European systems, but for US and many other systems, the default is Day.Sunday.

```vb
        mc.FirstDayOfWeek = Day.Monday
```

The MaxSelectionCount is increased from its default value of 7 to 45, allowing a date range to span 45 days.

```vb
        mc.MaxSelectionCount = 45
```

Finally, two event handlers are added for the MonthCalendar control: DateChanged and DateSelected:

```csharp
        mc.DateChanged += new DateRangeEventHandler(mc_DateChanged);
        mc.DateSelected += new DateRangeEventHandler(mc_DateSelected);
```

```VB
AddHandler mc.DateChanged, AddressOf mc_DateChanged
AddHandler mc.DateSelected, AddressOf mc_DateSelected
```

The event handler for the DateChanged event assigns the Start and End properties of
the DateRangeEventArgs event argument, which are equivalent to the MonthCalendar
control's SelectionStart and SelectionEnd properties, to the Start Date and End Date
DateTimePicker controls. Both event handlers also have a commented-out Message-
Box, which you can uncomment to observe under which circumstances these events
are raised:

```C#
private void mc_DateChanged(object sender, DateRangeEventArgs e)
{
    // MessageBox.Show("DateChanged");
    dtpStart.Value = e.Start;
    dtpEnd.Value = e.End;
}

private void mc_DateSelected(object sender, DateRangeEventArgs e)
{
    // MessageBox.Show("DateSelected");
}
```

```VB
private sub mc_DateChanged(ByVal sender as object, _
                    ByVal e as DateRangeEventArgs)
    ' MessageBox.Show("DateChanged")
    dtpStart.Value = e.Start
    dtpEnd.Value = e.End
end sub

private sub mc_DateSelected(ByVal sender as object, _
                    ByVal e as DateRangeEventArgs)
    ' MessageBox.Show("DateSelected")
end sub
```

The Size properties of the DateTimePickers are dynamically based on the Height of
the form Font property and the length of the displayed date as it is formatted, as well
as the control's PreferredHeight property. The .6 scale factor is arrived at empirically—the result looks good:

```C#
dtpStart.Size = new Size((int)(Font.Height * .6) *
                    dtpStart.Value.ToString("D").Length,
                    dtpStart.PreferredHeight);
```

```VB
dtpStart.Size = new Size(CInt(Font.Height * .6) * _
                    dtpStart.Value.ToString("D").Length, _
                    dtpStart.PreferredHeight)
```

The first two DateTimePickers, those for the Start Date and End Date, have event
handlers in place that change the selected dates in the MonthCalendar control.

```csharp
private void dtpStart_ValueChanged(object sender, EventArgs e)
{
   mc.SelectionStart = dtpStart.Value;
}

private void dtpEnd_ValueChanged(object sender, EventArgs e)
{
   mc.SelectionEnd = dtpEnd.Value;
}
```

```vb
private sub dtpStart_ValueChanged(ByVal sender as object, _
                                  ByVal e as EventArgs)
   mc.SelectionStart = dtpStart.Value
end sub

private sub dtpEnd_ValueChanged(ByVal sender as object, _
                                ByVal e as EventArgs)
   mc.SelectionEnd = dtpEnd.Value
end sub
```

The Combo box has its DropDownStyle set to DropDownList so it will be read-only. It displays the days of the week and provides an event handler to change the First-DayOfWeek property of the MonthCalendar control:

```csharp
cmbStart.DropDownStyle = ComboBoxStyle.DropDownList;
cmbStart.Items.AddRange(new object[] {"Monday",
                                      "Tuesday",
                                      "Wednesday",
                                      "Thursday",
                                      "Friday",
                                      "Saturday",
                                      "Sunday"});
cmbStart.SelectedIndex = 0;
cmbStart.SelectedIndexChanged +=
        new EventHandler(cmbStart_SelectedIndexChanged);


private void cmbStart_SelectedIndexChanged(object sender,
                                           EventArgs e)
{
   mc.FirstDayOfWeek = (Day)cmbStart.SelectedIndex;
}
```

```vb
cmbStart.DropDownStyle = ComboBoxStyle.DropDownList
cmbStart.Items.AddRange(new object() { _
                "Monday", _
                "Tuesday", _
                "Wednesday", _
                "Thursday", _
                "Friday", _
                "Saturday", _
                "Sunday"})
```

```
        cmbStart.SelectedIndex = 0
        AddHandler cmbStart.SelectedIndexChanged, _
                        AddressOf cmbStart_SelectedIndexChanged


    private sub cmbStart_SelectedIndexChanged(ByVal sender as object, _
                            ByVal e as EventArgs)
        mc.FirstDayOfWeek = CType(cmbStart.SelectedIndex, Day)
    end sub
```

Notice how the event handler method casts the SelectedIndex property of the Combo box to a Day object before assigning it to the FirstDayOfWeek property.

The third DateTimePicker, labeled Bold Day, has no event handler associated with it. Instead, each of the three bolding buttons reads the value of the control and calls the appropriate method for bolding the date, followed by a call to UpdateBoldedDates that ensures their proper display:

```csharp
    private void btnBoldDay_Click(object sender, EventArgs e)
    {
        mc.AddBoldedDate(dtpBold.Value);
        mc.UpdateBoldedDates();
    }

    private void btnBoldMonthly_Click(object sender, EventArgs e)
    {
        mc.AddMonthlyBoldedDate(dtpBold.Value);
        mc.UpdateBoldedDates();
    }

    private void btnBoldAnnually_Click(object sender, EventArgs e)
    {
        mc.AddAnnuallyBoldedDate(dtpBold.Value);
        mc.UpdateBoldedDates();
    }
```

(The VB.NET code is essentially the same.)

You will notice that all controls on the form, other than the MonthCalendar control, have their location properties set in the Form Load event handler rather than in the constructor. The Location properties are all based on the size and location of the control immediately above it, so ultimately all the controls are based on the size of the MonthCalendar control. The size of that control depends on the font used in the control. The final size of the MonthCalendar control with non-default font size is not known until after the form initializes. Setting the Location properties of the subsequent controls in the Form Load event handler allows them to accurately know the final size of the MonthCalendar control.

You may have noticed that the Size property of the form in the two languages is slightly different. This was necessary to accommodate one of the rare differences between equivalent C# and VB.NET programs. The bolding buttons at the bottom of the form displayed slightly larger in VB.NET than in C#, although the sizing code is identical in both languages.

Comparing the two executables in ILDASM, the two language versions are very similar. However, the VB.NET version of the button constructors had a call to the Math.Round method that was not in the C# IL code. The difference in button size results from a difference in rounding techniques.

Timer Component

The Timer component raises a Tick event at specified time intervals. The Tick event handler can then process a regularly occurring event, such as repainting the screen for animation or a clock display, updating a status report, or terminating a program based on elapsed time.

The interval between Tick events, specified by the Interval property, is measured in milliseconds, with valid values between 1 and 2,147,483,647, inclusive. The maximum value corresponds to approximately 597 hours, or a little over 24 days.

If there are heavy demands on the system running the application, either from the current or other applications, the Tick events may not be raised as often as specified by the Interval property, especially if the Interval is very short. Under any circumstances, the interval is not guaranteed to be accurate. If accuracy is required, the system clock should be checked as needed, especially for long intervals.

Although the Interval property is in milliseconds, the system clock generates only 18 ticks per second. Therefore, the true precision of the Timer is no better than one-eighteenth of a second, which is about 55 milliseconds.

Three types of timers are provided in the .NET Framework. The first is a member of the System.Threading namespace. It is used primarily for multi-threaded applications and will not be covered in this book. It is not represented in any Visual Studio .NET Toolbox.

The second is a member of the System.Timers namespace. It is primarily intended for server applications and also is designed for multithreaded applications. It is found on the Components tab of the Visual Studio .NET Toolbox. It too will not be covered in this book.

The third type of timer component, described in this book, is a member of the System.Windows.Form namespace. It is designed for the single-threaded environment of Windows Forms, where the UI thread controls processing. This single-threaded timer is available from the Windows Forms tab of the Visual Studio .NET Toolbox.

The Timer component is not a control, since it does not have a visual aspect. Because it is not a control, it does not have a Parent property and is not part of the Controls collection.

In Visual Studio .NET, a Timer component is added to the form by dragging it from the Toolbox onto the form. However, it doesn't stay or appear on the form, but displays in the component tray at the bottom of the design window, as shown in Figure 16-6.

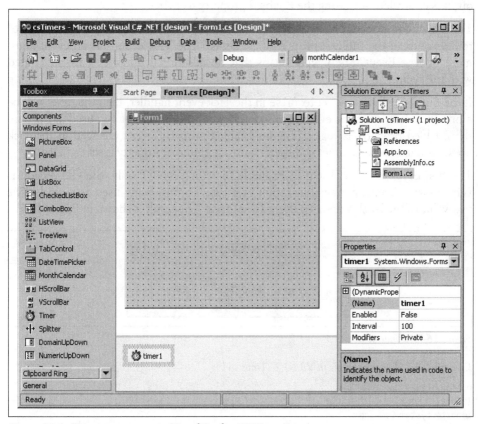

Figure 16-6. Timer component in Visual Studio .NET

The Timer component has only two properties, listed in Table 16-18. The Enabled property must be set to true in order to turn the timer function on. This can be done in the Properties window of Visual Studio .NET, in the code in the constructor (which is effectively the same), or in some other part of the program, in the event handler for a button Click. Setting the Enabled property false turns the timer off.

Table 16-18. Timer properties

Property	Value type	Description
Enabled	Boolean	Read/write. If `true`, the time is enabled. The default is `false`.
Interval	Integer	Read/write. The number of milliseconds between timer ticks.

The Timer component has two methods. The Start method starts the timer; it is equivalent to setting the Enabled property to true. The Stop method turns the timer off; it is equivalent to setting the Enabled property to false.

The Timer component has a single event, Tick. It is raised every time the number of milliseconds in the Interval property has passed. The Tick event has an event argument of type EventArgs, which means that no additional properties are associated with the event.

If the Enabled property is set to false in the Tick event handler, then the timer will be a one-shot deal: once the event is raised and handled, it will not be raised again until the Enabled property is toggled. If the Enabled property is not changed in the Tick event handler, then the timer will keep recurring until the property is set to false.

The first timer example, listed in Example 16-5 (in VB.NET only; the C# version is very similar) is a simple demonstration of a label control being used as a clock. The text value of the label is updated every 10 seconds. The result is shown in Figure 16-7.

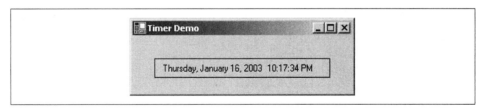

Figure 16-7. Timer demo

Example 16-5. Timer example in VB.NET (Timers.vb)

```
Option Strict On
imports System
imports System.Drawing
imports System.Windows.Forms

namespace ProgrammingWinApps
   public class Timers : inherits Form

      dim lblTime as Label
      dim strFormat as String

      public sub New( )
         Text = "Timer Demo"
         Size = new Size(300,100)

         strFormat = "dddd, MMMM d, yyyy  h:mm:ss tt"
```

Example 16-5. Timer example in VB.NET (Timers.vb) (continued)

```vb
        lblTime = new Label( )
        lblTime.Parent = me
        lblTime.Size = new Size(CInt(ClientSize.Width * .8), 25)
        lblTime.Location = new Point(CInt(ClientSize.Width * .1), _
                              CInt(ClientSize.Height * .4))
        lblTime.BorderStyle = BorderStyle.FixedSingle
        lblTime.Text = DateTime.Now.ToString(strFormat)
        lblTime.TextAlign = ContentAlignment.MiddleCenter

        dim t as new Timer( )
        t.Interval = 10000        ' 10 seconds
        t.Start( )
        AddHandler t.Tick, AddressOf t_Tick
    end sub  '  close for constructor

    public shared sub Main( )
        Application.Run(new Timers( ))
    end sub

    private sub t_Tick(ByVal sender as object, _
                    ByVal e as EventArgs)
        lblTime.Text = DateTime.Now.ToString(strFormat)
    end sub
  end class
end namespace
```

In this example, the Timer is instantiated in the constructor with an Interval property of 10,000 milliseconds, which is equivalent to 10 seconds. The Timer Start method is called so the timer will run as soon as the form is loaded.

In the Tick event handler, t_Tick, the Text property of the label is updated to display the current time, DateTime.Now, using the ToString method. The format of the label is controlled by an argument to the ToString method, a formatting string instantiated back in the constructor.

The next example is a countdown timer. It is similar to the previous example in that it displays a text string with the time—in this case, updated every second. It also provides a DateTimePicker control for the user to enter a time interval to count down. The countdown begins when the user clicks the Start button, with the remaining time displayed. When the specified time elapses, a message is displayed in a label control. The resulting application looks like Figure 16-8 during countdown.

In addition to using a different technique for displaying updated text strings, this example also demonstrates the use of TimeSpan objects, described earlier in this chapter.

The C# version of the CountDownTimer application is listed in Example 16-6, and the VB.NET version is listed in Example 16-7. As you will see in the analysis that follows the code listings, it was necessary to jump through some DateTime and TimeSpan hoops to get the times to display properly.

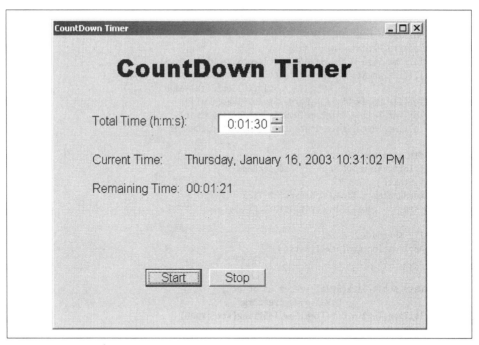

Figure 16-8. Countdown timer

Example 16-6. CountDownTimer in C# (CountDownTimer.cs)

```csharp
using System;
using System.Drawing;
using System.Windows.Forms;

namespace ProgrammingWinApps
{
    public class CountDownTimer : Form
    {
        DateTimePicker dtpTotalTime;
        Button btnStart;
        Button btnStop;
        bool boolStart = false;
        DateTime dtEndTime;
        Label lblTimesUp;
        Label lblTitle;

        public CountDownTimer()
        {
            Text = "CountDown Timer";
            Size = new Size(500,400);
            FormBorderStyle = FormBorderStyle.FixedDialog;
            Font = new Font("Arial", 12);

            Timer t = new Timer();
            t.Interval = 1000;
```

Example 16-6. CountDownTimer in C# (CountDownTimer.cs) (continued)

```csharp
        t.Start();
        t.Tick += new EventHandler(t_Tick);

        lblTitle = new Label();
        lblTitle.Parent = this;
        lblTitle.Font = new Font("Arial Black", 24);
        lblTitle.Text = "CountDown Timer";
        lblTitle.TextAlign = ContentAlignment.MiddleCenter;
        lblTitle.Size = new Size((int)(lblTitle.Font.Height * .7) *
                                    lblTitle.Text.Length, 35);
        lblTitle.Location = new Point(ClientSize.Width / 2 -
                                        lblTitle.Width / 2, 25);

        Label lblTotalTime = new Label();
        lblTotalTime.Parent = this;
        lblTotalTime.Text = "Total Time (h:m:s):";
        lblTotalTime.Size = new Size((int)(Font.Height * .5) *
                                        lblTotalTime.Text.Length, 25);
        lblTotalTime.Location = new Point(ClientSize.Width / 10, 100);

        dtpTotalTime = new DateTimePicker();
        dtpTotalTime.Parent = this;
        dtpTotalTime.Format = DateTimePickerFormat.Custom;
        dtpTotalTime.CustomFormat = "H:mm:ss";
        dtpTotalTime.Value = DateTime.Parse("00:00:00");
        dtpTotalTime.ShowUpDown = true;
        dtpTotalTime.Size = new Size((int)(Font.Height * .6) *
                                        dtpTotalTime.Value.ToString("t").Length,
                                        dtpTotalTime.PreferredHeight);
        dtpTotalTime.Location = new Point(lblTotalTime.Right, 100);

        btnStart = new Button();
        btnStart.Parent = this;
        btnStart.Text = "Start";
        btnStart.Location = new Point(ClientSize.Width / 4, 300);
        btnStart.Click += new EventHandler(btnStart_Click);

        btnStop = new Button();
        btnStop.Parent = this;
        btnStop.Text = "Stop";
        btnStop.Location = new Point(btnStart.Right + 10, 300);
        btnStop.Click += new EventHandler(btnStop_Click);

        lblTimesUp = new Label();
        lblTimesUp.Parent = this;
        lblTimesUp.Size = new Size(200, 35);
        lblTimesUp.Location = new Point(btnStart.Left,
                                    btnStart.Top - 75);
        lblTimesUp.Text = "";
        lblTimesUp.Font = new Font("Times New Roman Bold", 20);
    } // close for constructor
```

Example 16-6. CountDownTimer in C# (CountDownTimer.cs) (continued)

```csharp
static void Main( )
{
   Application.Run(new CountDownTimer( ));
}

private void t_Tick(object sender, EventArgs e)
{
   Invalidate( );
}

protected override void OnPaint(PaintEventArgs e)
{
   base.OnPaint(e);
   Graphics g = e.Graphics;
   Brush b = new SolidBrush(ForeColor);
   StringFormat fmt = new StringFormat( );
   fmt.Alignment = StringAlignment.Near;
   PointF pt = new PointF(ClientSize.Width / 10, 150);
   Font fnt = new Font("Arial", 12);
   String str = "Current Time:       " +
            DateTime.Now.ToString("F") + "\n\n";

   if (boolStart)
   {
      TimeSpan ts = new TimeSpan( );
      ts = dtEndTime - DateTime.Now;
      DateTime dt = new DateTime( );
      dt = DateTime.Parse(ts.ToString( ));
      str += "Remaining Time:   " + dt.ToString("HH:mm:ss");
   }
   else
   {
      str += "Remaining Time:";
   }
   g.DrawString(str, fnt, b, pt, fmt);

   if (boolStart && (dtEndTime - DateTime.Now) <= TimeSpan.Zero)
   {
      TimesUp( );
   }
}

private void btnStart_Click(object sender, EventArgs e)
{
   lblTimesUp.Text = "";
   boolStart = true;
   TimeSpan ts = new TimeSpan( );
   ts = TimeSpan.Parse(dtpTotalTime.Value.Hour.ToString( ) + ":" +
                  dtpTotalTime.Value.Minute.ToString( ) + ":" +
                  dtpTotalTime.Value.Second.ToString( ));
   dtEndTime = DateTime.Now + ts;
}
```

Example 16-6. CountDownTimer in C# (CountDownTimer.cs) (continued)

```
private void btnStop_Click(object sender, EventArgs e)
{
    boolStart = false;
}

private void TimesUp()
{
    lblTimesUp.Text = "Times Up!";
    boolStart = false;
}
    }       //  close for form class
}           //  close form namespace
```

Example 16-7. CountDownTimer in VB.NET (CountDownTimer.vb)

```
Option Strict On
imports System
imports System.Drawing
imports System.Windows.Forms

namespace ProgrammingWinApps
   public class CountDownTimer : inherits Form

      dim dtpTotalTime as DateTimePicker
      dim btnStart as Button
      dim btnStop as Button
      dim boolStart as Boolean = false
      dim dtEndTime as DateTime
      dim lblTimesUp as Label
      dim lblTitle as Label

      public sub New()
         Text = "CountDown Timer"
         Size = new Size(500,400)

         FormBorderStyle = FormBorderStyle.FixedDialog
         Font = new Font("Arial", 12)

         dim t as new Timer()
         t.Interval = 1000
         t.Start()
         AddHandler t.Tick, AddressOf t_Tick

         lblTitle = new Label()
         lblTitle.Parent = me
         lblTitle.Font = new Font("Arial Black", 24)
         lblTitle.Text = "CountDown Timer"
         lblTitle.TextAlign = ContentAlignment.MiddleCenter
         lblTitle.Size = new Size(CInt(lblTitle.Font.Height * .7) * _
                               lblTitle.Text.Length, 35)
         lblTitle.Location = new Point(CInt(ClientSize.Width / 2 - _
                               lblTitle.Width / 2), 25)
```

Example 16-7. CountDownTimer in VB.NET (CountDownTimer.vb) (continued)

```vb.net
    dim lblTotalTime as new Label( )
    lblTotalTime.Parent = me
    lblTotalTime.Text = "Total Time (h:m:s):"
    lblTotalTime.Size = new Size(CInt(Font.Height * .5) * _
                                  lblTotalTime.Text.Length, 25)
    lblTotalTime.Location = new Point( _
                             CInt(ClientSize.Width / 10), 100)

    dtpTotalTime = new DateTimePicker( )
    dtpTotalTime.Parent = me
    dtpTotalTime.Format = DateTimePickerFormat.Custom
    dtpTotalTime.CustomFormat = "H:mm:ss"
    dtpTotalTime.Value = DateTime.Parse("00:00:00")
    dtpTotalTime.ShowUpDown = true
    dtpTotalTime.Size = new Size(CInt(Font.Height * .6) * _
                    dtpTotalTime.Value.ToString("t").Length, _
                    dtpTotalTime.PreferredHeight)
    dtpTotalTime.Location = new Point(lblTotalTime.Right, 100)

    btnStart = new Button( )
    btnStart.Parent = me
    btnStart.Text = "Start"
    btnStart.Location = new Point(CInt(ClientSize.Width / 4), 300)
    AddHandler btnStart.Click, AddressOf btnStart_Click

    btnStop = new Button( )
    btnStop.Parent = me
    btnStop.Text = "Stop"
    btnStop.Location = new Point(btnStart.Right + 10, 300)
    AddHandler btnStop.Click, AddressOf btnStop_Click

    lblTimesUp = new Label( )
    lblTimesUp.Parent = me
    lblTimesUp.Size = new Size(200, 35)
    lblTimesUp.Location = new Point(btnStart.Left, _
                                   btnStart.Top - 75)
    lblTimesUp.Text = ""
    lblTimesUp.Font = new Font("Times New Roman Bold", 20)
end sub  '  close for constructor

public shared sub Main( )
    Application.Run(new CountDownTimer( ))
end sub

private sub t_Tick(ByVal sender as object, _
            ByVal e as EventArgs)
    Invalidate( )
end sub

protected overrides sub OnPaint(ByVal e as PaintEventArgs)
    myBase.OnPaint(e)
```

Example 16-7. CountDownTimer in VB.NET (CountDownTimer.vb) (continued)

```
dim g as Graphics = e.Graphics
dim b as new SolidBrush(ForeColor)
dim fmt as new StringFormat( )
fmt.Alignment = StringAlignment.Near
dim pt as new PointF(CInt(ClientSize.Width / 10), 150)
dim fnt as new Font("Arial", 12)
dim str as string = "Current Time:      " + _
        DateTime.Now.ToString("F") + vbCrLf + vbCrLf

if boolStart then
    dim ts as new TimeSpan( )
    ts = DateTime.op_Subtraction(dtEndTime, DateTime.Now)
    dim dt as new DateTime( )
    dt = DateTime.Parse(ts.ToString( ))
    str += "Remaining Time:  " + dt.ToString("HH:mm:ss")
else
    str += "Remaining Time:"
end if
g.DrawString(str, fnt, b, pt, fmt)

if (boolStart and _
    (TimeSpan.op_LessThanOrEqual(DateTime.op_Subtraction( _
        dtEndTime, DateTime.Now), TimeSpan.Zero))) then
    TimesUp( )
end if
end sub

private sub btnStart_Click(ByVal sender as object, _
                    ByVal e as EventArgs)
    lblTimesUp.Text = ""
    boolStart = true
    dim ts as new TimeSpan( )
    ts = TimeSpan.Parse(dtpTotalTime.Value.Hour.ToString( ) + ":" + _
                dtpTotalTime.Value.Minute.ToString( ) + ":" + _
                dtpTotalTime.Value.Second.ToString( ))
    dtEndTime = DateTime.op_Addition(DateTime.Now, ts)
end sub

private sub btnStop_Click(ByVal sender as object, _
                    ByVal e as EventArgs)
    boolStart = false
end sub

private sub TimesUp( )
    lblTimesUp.Text = "Times Up!"
    boolStart = false
end sub

end class
end namespace
```

The FormBorderStyle is set in the constructor to FormBorderStyle.FixedDialog, which prevents the user from resizing the form. By doing so, there is no need to anchor any of the controls or otherwise worry about how the look of the form will be affected by user interaction. Also in the constructor, the default font for the form is set to 12-point Arial.

```
FormBorderStyle = FormBorderStyle.FixedDialog
Font = new Font("Arial", 12)
```

The Timer is declared and instantiated in the constructor, with the Interval property set to one second (1,000 milliseconds) and the Start method called to enable the timer. An event handler is added for the Tick event:

```
Timer t = new Timer( );
t.Interval = 1000;
t.Start( );
t.Tick += new EventHandler(t_Tick);
```

```
dim t as new Timer( )
t.Interval = 1000
t.Start( )
AddHandler t.Tick, AddressOf t_Tick
```

The DateTimePicker control is used here as a convenient way for the user to enter the time to count down in hours, minutes, and seconds. This use requires that the value initially be set to "00:00:00" (which is cast from a string to a DateTime object using the static DateTime.Parse method) and displayed using a custom format, "H:mm:ss." As you recall from Table 16-9, the leading uppercase H in that format string specifies a one- or two-digit hour in a 24-hour format.

```
dtpTotalTime.Format = DateTimePickerFormat.Custom
dtpTotalTime.CustomFormat = "H:mm:ss"
dtpTotalTime.Value = DateTime.Parse("00:00:00")
```

At first, this custom formatting may seem unnecessary, since the DateTimePicker-Format.Time format should provide what you are looking for. However, if the Time format is used, the DateTimePicker control displays 12:00:00, rather than the desired 00:00:00.

Notice that the horizontal component of the Size property of the DateTimePicker control is calculated using the Value property of the control in conjunction with the ToString method, taking a formatting argument to retrieve the number of characters. From Table 16-10, you saw that the "t" formatting string corresponds to a short time display, which is effectively how the custom format used by the control appears. As with all the Size calculations based on the Font.Height property, the ".6" factor is arrived at empirically:

```
dtpTotalTime.Size = new Size((int)(Font.Height * .6) *
                        dtpTotalTime.Value.ToString("t").Length,
                        dtpTotalTime.PreferredHeight);
```

```vb
dtpTotalTime.Size = new Size(CInt(Font.Height * .6) * _
            dtpTotalTime.Value.ToString("t").Length, _
            dtpTotalTime.PreferredHeight)
```

The TimesUp label is positioned, sized, and given a nice bold 20-point font, but the Text property is initially set to an empty string. The Text property will be set appropriately as necessary, as you will see in a moment.

Now turn your attention to the Start button. The Click event handler for the Start button first clears the TimesUp label.

```vb
lblTimesUp.Text = ""
```

Next it sets a flag, boolStart, to true. This flag was initialized to false as a class member variable.

```vb
boolStart = true
```

Now comes a tricky part. The value in the DateTimePicker control is a DateTime object. It must be converted to a TimeSpan object so that the ending time, dtEnd-Time, which is a DateTime object, can be calculated. This is necessary because the DateTime Addition operator (and the DateTime Add method, as well) can only add a TimeSpan to a DateTime, not add together two DateTimes.

The conversion of the DateTimePicker value to a TimeSpan is accomplished by using the static TimeSpan.Parse method, which takes a string argument. That string argument is built up by calling the ToString method against the Hour, Minute, and Second components of the DateTimePicker control's Value property.

Then the ending time can be calculated by adding the resulting TimeSpan object to the current time:

```csharp
TimeSpan ts = new TimeSpan();
ts = TimeSpan.Parse(dtpTotalTime.Value.Hour.ToString() + ":" +
            dtpTotalTime.Value.Minute.ToString() + ":" +
            dtpTotalTime.Value.Second.ToString());
dtEndTime = DateTime.Now + ts;
```

```vb
dim ts as new TimeSpan()
ts = TimeSpan.Parse(dtpTotalTime.Value.Hour.ToString() + ":" + _
            dtpTotalTime.Value.Minute.ToString() + ":" + _
            dtpTotalTime.Value.Second.ToString())
dtEndTime = DateTime.op_Addition(DateTime.Now, ts)
```

Notice that the C# version allows the use of the + DateTime operator, and the VB. NET version does not. Instead, it uses the shared DateTime method DateTime.op_ Addition.

You could get the correct value for ts, the TimeSpan object with the following line of code:

C#

```
TimeSpan ts = dtpTotalTime.TimeOfDay;
```

VB

```
dim ts as new TimeSpan( ) = _
        dtpTotalTime.TimeOfDay
```

However, doing so this way would not allow a demonstration of the TimeSpan.Parse method.

Now that you have the boolStart flag and the ending time, dtEndTime, you can handle the Tick event.

The Tick event handler consists of a single line of code, which invalidates the form and causes the OnPaint method to be invoked. This OnPaint method has been overridden, so it draws the text strings containing the current time of day and the remaining time being counted down.

Chapter 10 covers the technique of using the Invalidate method to repaint the form or part of the form.

The overridden OnPaint method first chains up to the base class:

C#

```
base.OnPaint(e);
```

VB

```
myBase.OnPaint(e)
```

Next it declares and instantiates several objects, which will be used shortly in the Graphics DrawString method:

- A Graphics object.
- A Brush object with the foreground color (which defaults to black on most systems).
- A StringFormat object used to set the Alignment property. (StringAlignment. Near corresponds to Left in a Left-to-Right language—see Tables 9-8 and 9-9 for a description of the StringAlignment enumeration.)
- A PointF object.
- A Font object specifying 12-point Arial.
- A string object containing the current time, formatted with the "F" formatting string:

C#

```
Graphics g = e.Graphics;
Brush b = new SolidBrush(ForeColor);
StringFormat fmt = new StringFormat( );
fmt.Alignment = StringAlignment.Near;
```

```csharp
    PointF pt = new PointF(ClientSize.Width / 10, 150);
    Font fnt = new Font("Arial", 12);
    String str = "Current Time:        " +
            DateTime.Now.ToString("F") + "\n\n";
```

```vbnet
    dim g as Graphics = e.Graphics
    dim b as new SolidBrush(ForeColor)
    dim fmt as new StringFormat()
    fmt.Alignment = StringAlignment.Near
    dim pt as new PointF(CInt(ClientSize.Width / 10), 150)
    Font fnt = new Font("Arial", 12)
    dim str as string = "Current Time:        " + _
            DateTime.Now.ToString("F") + vbCrLf + vbCrLf
```

The specified string will be drawn with every timer tick—i.e., every second. The contents of the next string, however, depend on whether the application is counting down. For this, it tests the boolStart flag, which was set in the Start button Click event handler.

If the boolStart flag is true, then another string is built up by subtracting the current time, DateTime.Now, from the ending time, dtEndTime, which was calculated in the Start Button event handler. This process is surprisingly tricky. You might think you could use the following code to display the remaining time, where the TimeSpan is calculated and then displayed using the TimeSpan ToString method.

```csharp
    TimeSpan ts = new TimeSpan();
    ts = dtEndTime - DateTime.Now;
    str += "Remaining Time:  " + ts.ToString();
```

This works, but it displays the time with hours, minutes, and fractional seconds, as in 01:01:01.1234567, with the seconds displaying seven decimal digits. You should, however, display only hours, minutes, and whole seconds, as in 01:01:01.

No problem, you think: I'll just add a formatting argument to the ToString method. However, this causes a compiler error. The DateTime.ToString method accepts a formatting argument, but the TimeSpan.ToString does not. So you need to convert the TimeSpan to a DateTime, using the static DateTime.Parse method. This method takes a string argument, so you give it the TimeSpan object converted to a string with ToString. Then the string for display can be built up using the DateTime ToString, which accepts the formatting argument.

The complete code section for testing the boolStart flag, constructing the line that displays the remaining time and drawing the two lines of text, is reproduced here:

```csharp
    if (boolStart)
    {
        TimeSpan ts = new TimeSpan();
        ts = dtEndTime - DateTime.Now;
        DateTime dt = new DateTime();
        dt = DateTime.Parse(ts.ToString());
        str += "Remaining Time:   " + dt.ToString("HH:mm:ss");
```

```
    }
    else
    {
        str += "Remaining Time:";
    }
    g.DrawString(str, fnt, b, pt, fmt);
```

```
    if boolStart then
        dim ts as new TimeSpan()
        ts = DateTime.op_Subtraction(dtEndTime, DateTime.Now)
        dim dt as new DateTime()
        dt = DateTime.Parse(ts.ToString())
        str += "Remaining Time:   " + dt.ToString("HH:mm:ss")
    else
        str += "Remaining Time:"
    end if
    g.DrawString(str, fnt, b, pt, fmt)
```

The final piece of the OnPaint method tests to see if time has expired. If so, it calls the TimesUp helper method:

```
    if (boolStart && (dtEndTime - DateTime.Now) <= TimeSpan.Zero)
    {
        TimesUp();
    }
```

```
    if (boolStart and _
        (TimeSpan.op_LessThanOrEqual(DateTime.op_Subtraction( _
            dtEndTime, DateTime.Now), TimeSpan.Zero))) then
        TimesUp()
    end if
```

Again, as with the TimeSpan and DateTime operators used previously, the C# version uses the <= operator, while the VB.NET version must use the shared TimeSpan. op_LessThanOrEqual method.

The TimesUp method is simple. It sets the Text property of the lblTimesUp label and resets the boolStart flag to false.

The Stop button Click event handler is also simple—it just sets the boolStart flag to false. The next time the Tick event fires and the OnPaint method is called, the form will correctly display with the count down stopped.

CHAPTER 17

Custom Controls

Much of this book focuses on demonstrating how to use the cornucopia of controls provided by the .NET framework. Chapter 7 and Chapters 11 through 16 explain each control in detail, including the methods, properties, and events that make your program act the way you want.

Sometimes, however, even this incredible variety of controls is inadequate. You need a different kind of control, one not offered by the .NET Framework. In that case, you are free to create your own custom control.

In fact, there are three ways to create your own controls. Perhaps the easiest alternative is to specialize an existing control. To do so, you derive from an existing control class and then override methods or add your own properties, as you would when deriving from any existing class. Thus, you might derive from Button to make a button that counts how many times it has been clicked, or you might derive from a text box to create a phone number text box that accepts only numerals in the correct format.

A second, more powerful, alternative derives from UserControl. A UserControl is a composite control, created by combining one or more existing control types into a new control, with its own properties and methods. Thus, you might combine various text and label controls to create an address control that captures user input, or combine a button and a timer to create a button whose message changes every minute.

 Do not confuse Windows Forms user controls with ASP.NET user controls. Windows Forms user controls are composite custom controls.

Finally, if you need an even more powerful alternative, you can derive from the base Control class and create a custom control from scratch. In this case, you'll be responsible for drawing your own control, but you can decide on the exact look, feel, and behavior of it. Thus, you might create a pop-up button that allows you to set its behavior, or you might create an analog alarm-clock control that displays the time as a 24-hour clock.

This chapter shows you how to create each type of custom control.

Specializing an Existing Control

You'll create a customized button class that keeps track of how often it has been clicked. To begin, open a new project in Visual Studio .NET. In the Project Type window, choose your language of choice, and in the Templates window, choose Windows Control Library. Be sure to set an appropriate location, and name the library CountedControl.

 This example is similar to a custom control demonstrated in *Programming ASP.NET*, but there are significant differences in how custom controls are created for use with Windows Forms.

You are placed in the designer for a user control. That isn't quite what you want (you'll be creating a user control in the next example), but it isn't a problem. Right-click on the form and choose View Code. Modify the class name to CountedButton and the base class from UserControl to Button:

C#
```
public class CountedButton : System.Windows.Forms.Button
```

VB
```
Public Class CountedButton
    Inherits System.Windows.Forms.Button
```

In C#, you must also modify the constructor so it has the same name as the class:

C#
```
public CountedButton( )
```

While you are at it, change the filename from *UserControl1* to *CountedButton.cs* or *CountedButton.vb*.

 When you change the base type from UserControl to Button, Visual Studio .NET will no longer use the Forms Designer in Design view. You'll add to the new derived button type entirely through code.

Override the OnPaint method to draw the number of times the button was clicked:

C#
```
protected override void OnPaint (PaintEventArgs e)
{
   if ( numClicks == 0 )
      this.Text = "Never been clicked";
   else
      this.Text = "Clicked " + numClicks + " times";

   base.OnPaint(e);
}
```

```
Protected Overrides Sub OnPaint(ByVal e As PaintEventArgs)
    If numClicks = 0 Then
        Me.Text = "Never been clicked"
        Else
            Me.Text = "Clicked " & numClicks & " times"
    End If
    MyBase.OnPaint(e)
End Sub
```

Finally, override the on-click method to update the number of clicks, and invalidate the button so it will be repainted.

```
protected override void OnClick( EventArgs e )
{
    numClicks++;
    Invalidate( );
    base.OnClick(e);
}
```

```
Protected Overrides Sub OnClick(ByVal e As EventArgs)
    numClicks = numClicks + 1
    Invalidate( )
    MyBase.OnClick(e)
End Sub
```

That's all there is to it! Build your control, and you are ready to test it. The complete source code for the custom control in C# is shown in Example 17-1 and the VB.NET version is shown in Example 17-2.

Example 17-1. Custom derived control (C#)

```
using System;
using System.Collections;
using System.ComponentModel;
using System.Drawing;
using System.Data;
using System.Windows.Forms;

namespace CountedButtonCS1
{
    // change the base class to button
    public class CountedButton : System.Windows.Forms.Button
    {
        private System.ComponentModel.Container components = null;
        private int numClicks = 0; // keep track of number of clicks

        public CountedButton( )
        {
            InitializeComponent( );
        }

        // override OnPaint to display the number of clicks
        protected override void OnPaint (PaintEventArgs e)
```

Example 17-1. Custom derived control (C#) (continued)

```csharp
        {
            if ( numClicks == 0 )
                this.Text = "Never been clicked";
            else
                this.Text = "Clicked " + numClicks + " times";

            base.OnPaint(e);
        }

        // when the button is clicked update the counter
        // and invalidate the control
        protected override void OnClick( EventArgs e )
        {
            numClicks++;
            Invalidate( );
            base.OnClick(e);
        }


        /// <summary>
        /// Clean up any resources being used.
        /// </summary>
        protected override void Dispose( bool disposing )
        {
            if( disposing )
            {
                if( components != null )
                    components.Dispose( );
            }
            base.Dispose( disposing );
        }
        #region Component Designer generated code
        #endregion
    }
}
```

Example 17-2. Custom derived control (VB.NET)

```vbnet
' change the base class to button
Public Class CountedButton
    Inherits System.Windows.Forms.Button


    ' keep track of number of clicks
    Private numClicks As Integer = 0

    Public Sub New( )
        MyBase.New( )
        InitializeComponent( )
    End Sub

    ' override OnPaint to display the number of clicks
    Protected Overrides Sub OnPaint(ByVal e As PaintEventArgs)
```

Example 17-2. Custom derived control (VB.NET) (continued)

```
        If numClicks = 0 Then
            Me.Text = "Never been clicked"
        Else
            Me.Text = "Clicked " & numClicks & " times"
        End If
        MyBase.OnPaint(e)
    End Sub

    ' when the button is clicked update the counter
    ' and invalidate the control
    Protected Overrides Sub OnClick(ByVal e As EventArgs)
        numClicks = numClicks + 1
        Invalidate()
        MyBase.OnClick(e)
    End Sub

#Region " Windows Form Designer generated code "
#End Region
End Class
```

Testing the Control

Of course, you can't just "run" a control; you need a container, such as a form, within which to test the control. Create a new Windows project in your language of choice and add a reference to the control project. To do so from within Visual Studio .NET, right-click on References and choose Add Reference. Click on the Projects tab, and then click the Browse button. Navigate to the dll you created for your control, and double-click on it. Then click OK to close the Add Reference dialog.

You can add your control to your toolbox by right-clicking on the toolbox and choosing Customize Toolbox. Choose the .NET Framework Components tab, and then click the Browse button. Navigate to and double-click on your dll; the control appears at the bottom of your toolbox.

 You can create your control in one language (e.g., C# or VB.NET) and your test program in another.

Double-click on the control to add it to the form, and size it to display the full message. Run the test program and click on the button. The result, shown in Figure 17-1, is that the button keeps track of how often it is clicked.

Adding Properties

One powerful use for custom controls is to expose custom properties. You might derive from the Button class only to expose new and interesting properties to your clients. In the next example, you'll modify your CountedButton class to add a property that reveals how often the button has been clicked.

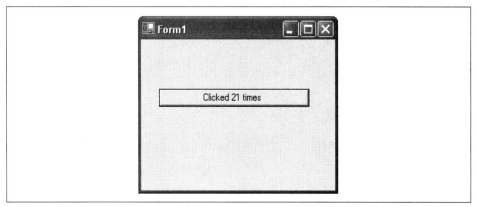

Figure 17-1. The CountedButton control

The change to the control is almost trivial. Just add a property to the control to provide access to the number of times the button was clicked:

```csharp
public int NumClicks
{
    get { return numClicks; }
    set { numClicks = value; }
}
```

```vb
Public Property numClicks() As Integer
    Get
        Return _numClicks
    End Get
    Set(ByVal Value As Integer)
        _numClicks = Value
    End Set
End Property
```

 Because I wanted the property to be named numClicks, I had to change the private field to _numClicks (note the underscore). VB.NET is case insensitive, so you can't use the idiom common in C# of naming the field with a lowercase letter and the property with an uppercase letter.

You can use this property in your test program. Add a label (named lblOut) and a button (named btnUpdate) to your form. Add an event handler for the button to update the label based on the numClicks property:

```csharp
private void btnUpdate_Click(object sender, System.EventArgs e)
{
    lblOut.Text =
        "The button was clicked " +
        countedButton1.NumClicks.ToString() +
        " times.";
}
```

```vb
Private Sub btnUpdate_Click( _
    ByVal sender As System.Object, _
    ByVal e As System.EventArgs) Handles btnUpdate.Click
    lblOut.Text = _
      "The button was clicked " & _
      CountedButton1.numClicks.ToString( ) & _
      " times."
End Sub
```

The key line of code is shown in bold. Determine how many times the button was pressed by accessing its numClicks property.

Creating a User Control

For some designs, deriving from an existing control is insufficient. One common alternative is to create a new control by combining two or more existing controls. This is such a common idiom that Visual Studio .NET provides extensive support for it.

In the next exercise, you'll create a Teeter Totter, as shown in Figure 17-2.

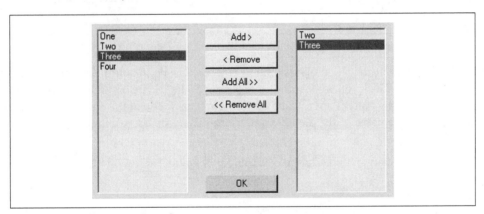

Figure 17-2. Teeter Totter control

In a Teeter Totter, you have a list on the left side (source), and you selectively add from that list to the list on the right side. When you press OK, the list on the right is processed.

This example will not implement all the possible functionality of an industrial-strength Teeter Totter, but it focuses on the key issues in creating user controls: adding the constituent controls, handling internal events, publishing events, and publishing properties.

To get started, create a new Windows Control Library, shown in Figure 17-3, using your preference of VB.NET or C#.

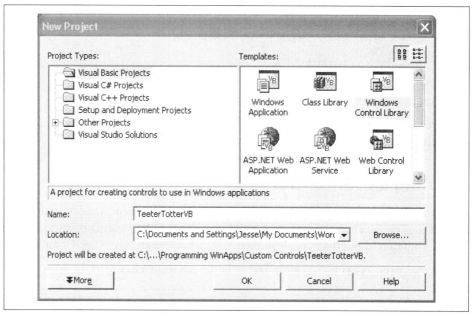

Figure 17-3. Creating the Windows control library

Windows will create a UserControl and provide a UserControl to add the constituent controls. Click on the form, and change the name of the control from UserControl1 to TeeterTotter. Click on the source code file in the Solution Explorer, and change the name of the file from *UserControl1.vb* (or *UserControl1.cs*) to *Teeter-Totter.vb/cs*.

Make the form larger, and add the controls as shown in Table 17-1.

Table 17-1. Controls for Teeter Totter user control

Control name	Type	Control text
lbSource	ListBox	
lbDestination	ListBox	
btnAdd	Button	Add >
btnRemove	Button	< Remove
btnAddAll	Button	Add All >>
btnRemoveAll	Button	<< Remove All
btnOK	Button	OK

Resize the form to fit all the controls, as shown in Figure 17-4.

The complete code is shown in Example 17-3 (in C#) and in Example 17-4 (in VB. NET), and is analyzed in the following pages.

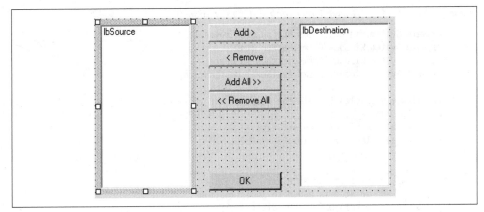

Figure 17-4. Designing the Teeter Totter

Example 17-3. Code for Teeter Totter control (C#)

```csharp
using System;
using System.Collections;
using System.ComponentModel;
using System.Drawing;
using System.Data;
using System.Windows.Forms;

namespace TeeterTotter
{
   // Specialized EventArgs class to provide
   // the items collection of the destination list box
   public class TeeterTotterEventArgs : EventArgs
   {
      private ListBox.ObjectCollection items;

      public TeeterTotterEventArgs (ListBox.ObjectCollection items)
      {
         this.items = items;
      }

      // cleaner than just making items public
      public ListBox.ObjectCollection Items
      {
         get { return items; }
      }
   }


   // the teeter totter user control
   public class TeeterTotter : System.Windows.Forms.UserControl
   {
      // the constituent controls
      private System.Windows.Forms.Button btnAdd;
      private System.Windows.Forms.Button btnRemove;
      private System.Windows.Forms.Button btnAddAll;
```

Example 17-3. Code for Teeter Totter control (C#) (continued)

```
C#    private System.Windows.Forms.Button btnRemoveAll;
      private System.Windows.Forms.Button btnOK;
      private System.Windows.Forms.ListBox lbSource;
      private System.Windows.Forms.ListBox lbDestination;

      // private variables to hold the color of the
      // buttons and list boxes
      private Color btnColor = Color.Beige;
      private Color lbColor = Color.PapayaWhip;


      // declare a delegate and an event
      // fired when an item is added to lbDestination
      public delegate void OKButtonHandler(
         object sender, TeeterTotterEventArgs e);
      public event OKButtonHandler OKButtonEvent;

      private System.ComponentModel.Container components = null;

      // constructor sets the colors
      public TeeterTotter( )
      {
         InitializeComponent( );
         SetColors( );
      }

      // helper method to factor out setting colors
      private void SetColors( )
      {
         btnAdd.BackColor = btnColor;
         btnRemove.BackColor = btnColor;
         btnAddAll.BackColor = btnColor;
         btnRemoveAll.BackColor = btnColor;

         lbSource.BackColor = lbColor;
         lbDestination.BackColor = lbColor;
      }

      // raise the event
      protected virtual void OnOK(TeeterTotterEventArgs e)
      {
         if ( OKButtonEvent != null )
            OKButtonEvent(this,e);
      }

      // add items from the client to the source list box
      public void AddSource(string s)
      {
         lbSource.Items.Add(s);
      }

      // properties for button and listbox background color
```

Example 17-3. Code for Teeter Totter control (C#) (continued)

```csharp
public Color BtnBackColor
{
   get { return btnColor; }
   set { btnColor = value; SetColors(); }
}

public Color ListBoxBackColor
{
   get { return lbColor; }
   set { lbColor = value; SetColors(); }
}


/// <summary>
/// Clean up any resources being used.
/// </summary>
protected override void Dispose( bool disposing )
{
   if( disposing )
   {
      if( components != null )
         components.Dispose( );
   }
   base.Dispose( disposing );
}

#region Component Designer generated code
#endregion

// internal event handlers
private void btnRemove_Click(object sender, System.EventArgs e)
{
   lbDestination.Items.Remove(lbDestination.SelectedItem);

}

private void btnAdd_Click(object sender, System.EventArgs e)
{
   lbDestination.Items.Add(lbSource.SelectedItem);
}

private void btnAddAll_Click(object sender, System.EventArgs e)
{
   lbDestination.Items.Clear( );
   foreach (object o in lbSource.Items)
   {
      lbDestination.Items.Add(o);
   }
}

private void btnRemoveAll_Click(
         object sender, System.EventArgs e)
```

Example 17-3. Code for Teeter Totter control (C#) (continued)

```csharp
        {
            lbDestination.Items.Clear( );
        }

        // they clicked ok, raise the event
        private void btnOK_Click(object sender, System.EventArgs e)
        {
            TeeterTotterEventArgs tte =
                new TeeterTotterEventArgs(lbDestination.Items);
            OnOK(tte);
        }
    }
}
```

Example 17-4. Code for Teeter Totter control (VB.NET)

```vbnet
' Specialized EventArgs class to provide
' the items collection of the destination list box
Public Class TeeterTotterEventArgs
    Inherits EventArgs

    Private _items As ListBox.ObjectCollection

    Public Sub New(ByVal items As ListBox.ObjectCollection)
        _items = items
    End Sub

    ' cleaner than making _items public
    ReadOnly Property Item( ) As ListBox.ObjectCollection
        Get
            Return _items
        End Get
    End Property
End Class ' TeeterTotterEventArgs

' the teeter totter control
Public Class TeeterTotter
    Inherits System.Windows.Forms.UserControl

    ' declare the delegate and event for handling the
    ' okay button event
    Public Delegate Sub OKButtonHandler( _
    ByVal sender As Object, ByVal e As TeeterTotterEventArgs)

    Public Event OKButtonEvent As OKButtonHandler

    ' private variables to hold the color for the buttons and
    ' list boxes
    Private btnColor As Color = Color.Beige
    Private lbColor As Color = Color.PapayaWhip
```

Example 17-4. Code for Teeter Totter control (VB.NET) (continued)

```vb
Public Sub New( )
    MyBase.New( )

    'This call is required by the Windows Form Designer.
    InitializeComponent( )
    SetColors( )

    'Add any initialization after the InitializeComponent( ) call

End Sub

#Region " Windows Form Designer generated code "
#End Region

    ' internal event handlers
    Public Sub AddSource(ByVal s As String)
        lbSource.Items.Add(s)
    End Sub

    Private Sub btnAdd_Click( _
        ByVal sender As System.Object, ByVal e As System.EventArgs) _
        Handles btnAdd.Click
        lbDestination.Items.Add(lbSource.SelectedItem)
    End Sub

    Private Sub btnRemove_Click( _
        ByVal sender As System.Object, ByVal e As System.EventArgs) _
        Handles btnRemove.Click
        lbDestination.Items.Remove(lbDestination.SelectedItem)
    End Sub

    Private Sub btnAddAll_Click( _
        ByVal sender As System.Object, ByVal e As System.EventArgs) _
        Handles btnAddAll.Click

        lbDestination.Items.Clear( )

        Dim o As Object
        For Each o In lbSource.Items
            lbDestination.Items.Add(o)
        Next

    End Sub


    Private Sub btnRemoveAll_Click( _
        ByVal sender As System.Object, ByVal e As System.EventArgs) _
        Handles btnRemoveAll.Click

        lbDestination.Items.Clear( )

    End Sub
```

Example 17-4. Code for Teeter Totter control (VB.NET) (continued)

VB

```
    ' helper method to factor out setting the colors
    Private Sub SetColors()
        btnAdd.BackColor = btnColor
        btnRemove.BackColor = btnColor
        btnAddAll.BackColor = btnColor
        btnRemoveAll.BackColor = btnColor

        lbSource.BackColor = lbColor
        lbDestination.BackColor = lbColor
    End Sub

    ' properties for setting the background colors
    ' for the buttons and list boxes
    Public Property BtnBackColor() As Color
        Get
            Return btnColor
        End Get
        Set(ByVal Value As Color)
            btnColor = Value
            SetColors()
        End Set
    End Property

    Public Property ListBoxBackColor() As Color
        Get
            Return lbColor
        End Get
        Set(ByVal Value As Color)
            lbColor = Value
            SetColors()
        End Set
    End Property


    ' handle the click of the ok button
    Private Sub btnOK_Click( _
        ByVal sender As System.Object, ByVal e As System.EventArgs) _
        Handles btnOK.Click

        Dim tte As New TeeterTotterEventArgs(lbDestination.Items)
        OnOK(tte)

    End Sub

    ' raise the event
    Public Overridable Sub OnOK(ByVal e As TeeterTotterEventArgs)
        RaiseEvent OKButtonEvent(Me, e)
    End Sub

End Class
```

Teeter Totter Analysis

There is a great deal of code here, but none of it is terribly complex. The code's key aspects are as follows:

- Properties that allow users to set colors within the Teeter Totter
- Internal events handled by the Teeter Totter itself
- External events raised for the client to handle

Properties

You'll provide your Teeter Totter with a couple of properties to show that the client code can set properties on the new user control. In this example, you'll provide a Btn-BackColor property that will get or set the background color of the buttons, and a ListBoxBackColor property that will get or set the background color of the listboxes.

To facilitate this, first create private member variables to hold the respective colors:

```csharp
private Color btnColor = Color.Beige;
private Color lbColor = Color.PapayaWhip;
```

```vb
Private btnColor As Color = Color.Beige
Private lbColor As Color = Color.PapayaWhip
```

Set the colors for the buttons and the listbox when you first start the application; again, each time a property is set. To manage this, factor out this code into a method:

```csharp
private void SetColors()
{
    btnAdd.BackColor = btnColor;
    btnRemove.BackColor = btnColor;
    btnAddAll.BackColor = btnColor;
    btnRemoveAll.BackColor = btnColor;

    lbSource.BackColor = lbColor;
    lbDestination.BackColor = lbColor;
}
```

```vb
Private Sub SetColors()
    btnAdd.BackColor = btnColor
    btnRemove.BackColor = btnColor
    btnAddAll.BackColor = btnColor
    btnRemoveAll.BackColor = btnColor

    lbSource.BackColor = lbColor
    lbDestination.BackColor = lbColor
End Sub
```

Modify the constructor to invoke the SetColors method when the control is initialized:

C#
```csharp
public TeeterTotter( )
{
    InitializeComponent( );
    SetColors( );
}
```

VB
```vb
Public Sub New( )
    MyBase.New( )
    InitializeComponent( )
    SetColors( )
End Sub
```

You are now ready to implement the properties. The only tricky part is that the set accessor must not only set the color, but also invoke SetColors( ):

C#
```csharp
public Color BtnBackColor
{
    get { return btnColor; }
    set { btnColor = value; SetColors( ); }
}

public Color ListBoxBackColor
{
    get { return lbColor; }
    set { lbColor = value; SetColors( ); }
}
```

VB
```vb
Public Property BtnBackColor( ) As Color
    Get
        Return btnColor
    End Get
    Set(ByVal Value As Color)
        btnColor = Value
        SetColors( )
    End Set
End Property

Public Property ListBoxBackColor( ) As Color
    Get
        Return lbColor
    End Get
    Set(ByVal Value As Color)
        lbColor = Value
        SetColors( )
    End Set
End Property
```

Handling Internal Events

Many events handled by the Teeter Totter will not be made available to the client; they will be handled internally by the Teeter Totter itself. For example, if the user clicks on Add, Remove, Add All, or Remove All, you will not raise an event to the client application; instead, the Teeter Totter will take the appropriate action.

 In some Teeter Totters, when an item is added to the destination list, it is removed from the source list. You may want to make this behavior depend on a property of the Teeter Totter. This is, as they say, left as an exercise for the reader.

As a further enhancement, you may want to add the ability to double-click on an item in the source list to add that item or in the destination list to remove that item, or implement drag-and-drop.

Implement custom control event handlers just as you would any other event handler. Visual Studio .NET makes it simple; double-click on the buttons and Visual Studio .NET will create the event handlers; you only have to fill in the event-handling code.

The Add button simply adds the selected item from the source list to the destination list:

```
private void btnAdd_Click(object sender, System.EventArgs e)
{
    lbDestination.Items.Add(lbSource.SelectedItem);
}
```

```
Private Sub btnAdd_Click( _
    ByVal sender As System.Object, ByVal e As System.EventArgs) _
    Handles btnAdd.Click
        lbDestination.Items.Add(lbSource.SelectedItem)
End Sub
```

The Remove button removes the currently selected item from the destination list.

```
private void btnRemove_Click(object sender, System.EventArgs e)
{
    lbDestination.Items.Remove(lbDestination.SelectedItem);
}
```

```
Private Sub btnRemove_Click( _
    ByVal sender As System.Object, ByVal e As System.EventArgs) _
    Handles btnRemove.Click
        lbDestination.Items.Remove(lbDestination.SelectedItem)
End Sub
```

The Add All button's event handler iterates through the items list in the source and adds each one to the destination list. To avoid the problem of duplicating items that were already in the destination list, clear the destination list first:

C#
```csharp
private void btnAddAll_Click(object sender, System.EventArgs e)
{
    lbDestination.Items.Clear();
    foreach (object o in lbSource.Items)
    {
        lbDestination.Items.Add(o);
    }
}
```

VB
```vb
Private Sub btnAddAll_Click( _
    ByVal sender As System.Object, ByVal e As System.EventArgs) _
    Handles btnAddAll.Click

    lbDestination.Items.Clear()

    Dim o As Object
    For Each o In lbSource.Items
        lbDestination.Items.Add(o)
    Next

End Sub
```

Finally, the Remove All button clears the destination listbox:

C#
```csharp
private void btnRemoveAll_Click(object sender, System.EventArgs e)
{
    lbDestination.Items.Clear();
}
```

VB
```vb
Private Sub btnRemoveAll_Click( _
    ByVal sender As System.Object, ByVal e As System.EventArgs) _
    Handles btnRemoveAll.Click

    lbDestination.Items.Clear()

End Sub
```

Publishing Events

Some events, however, should be made available to the client application. In this example, you will add an OK button to the Teeter Totter. When the user clicks this button, the Teeter Totter will raise the OKButtonEvent event, giving the client application an opportunity to process the items in the destination list. To facilitate this process, you'll create a custom EventArgs type named TeeterTotterEventArgs, which will provide a collection of all the strings in the destination listbox.

```csharp
public class TeeterTotterEventArgs : EventArgs
{
    private ListBox.ObjectCollection items;

    public TeeterTotterEventArgs (ListBox.ObjectCollection items)
    {
        this.items = items;
    }

    public ListBox.ObjectCollection Items
    {
        get { return items; }
    }
}
```

```vbnet
Public Class TeeterTotterEventArgs
    Inherits EventArgs

    Private _items As ListBox.ObjectCollection

    Public Sub New(ByVal items As ListBox.ObjectCollection)
        _items = items
    End Sub

    ReadOnly Property Item( ) As ListBox.ObjectCollection
        Get
            Return _items
        End Get
    End Property

End Class
```

The TeeterTotterEventArgs class has only one member: an object of type ListBox. ObjectCollection; which is the type returned by the List Box's items property. Create a TeeterTotterEventArgs by passing in to the TeeterTotterEventArgs constructor an object of type ListBox.ObjectCollection, which is stashed in the private member variable. The TeeterTotterEventArgs class also provides a public read-only property to return this value on demand.

When the user clicks OK, you'll call OnOK, passing in a TeeterTotterEventArgs object that was initialized with the items collection from the destination listbox:

```csharp
private void btnOK_Click(object sender, System.EventArgs e)
{
    TeeterTotterEventArgs tte =
        new TeeterTotterEventArgs(lbDestination.Items);
    OnOK(tte);
}
```

```vbnet
Private Sub btnOK_Click( _
    ByVal sender As System.Object, ByVal e As System.EventArgs) _
```

```
        Handles btnOK.Click

            Dim tte As New TeeterTotterEVentArgs(lbDestination.Items)
            OnOK(tte)

    End Sub
```

The OnOK method takes a TeeterTotterEventArgs object as a parameter, and then raises the OKButtonEvent, passing in a reference to the Teeter Totter itself, along with the TeeterTotterEventArgs object:

```
    protected virtual void OnOK(TeeterTotterEventArgs e)
    {
        if ( OKButtonEvent != null )
            OKButtonEvent(this,e);
    }
```

```
    Public Overridable Sub OnOK(ByVal e As TeeterTotterEVentArgs)
        RaiseEvent OKButtonEvent(Me, e)
    End Sub
```

To make this work, first create the appropriate delegate for the Event Handler.

```
    public delegate void OKButtonHandler(
        object sender, TeeterTotterEventArgs e);

    public event OKButtonHandler OKButtonEvent;
```

```
    Public Delegate Sub OKButtonHandler( _
    ByVal sender As Object, ByVal e As TeeterTotterEVentArgs)
```

Then create an instance of the delegate:

```
    Public Event OKButtonEvent As OKButtonHandler
```

The net effect is that when the user clicks the OK button, the client receives an event, with a TeeterTotterEventArgs object that contains the items collection from the destination listbox.

To see how this works, you'll need to create the client.

Testing the User Control

Your test program will be very simple: just a Windows Form on which you will place a Teeter Totter and a single button to trigger code to set the properties, as shown in Figure 17-5.

When you click the Modify Colors button, the colors of the buttons and the listbox will change, as shown in Figure 17-6.

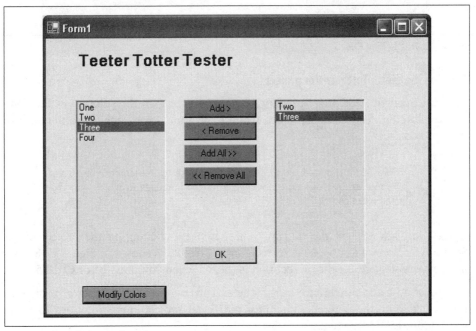

Figure 17-5. Teeter Totter tester

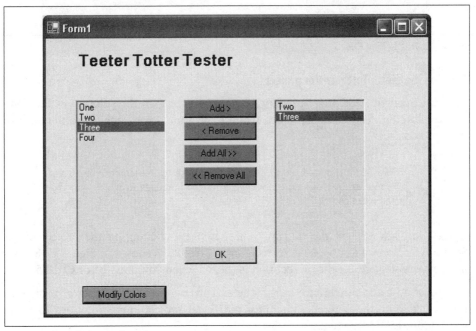

Figure 17-6. Changing the colors

When you click OK on the control, the test form will catch the event, uncork the TeeterTotterEventArgs object, and take out the list of strings, which it will then display in a MessageBox, as shown in Figure 17-7.

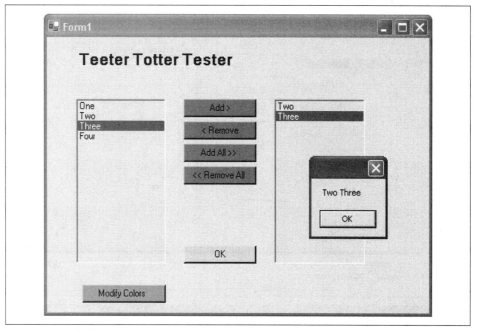

Figure 17-7. Clicking OK

Creating the Teeter Totter tester project

To implement the test program shown here, right-click on the solution in the Solution Explorer, and add a new project. Choose the appropriate language and name for your project.

 To make this interesting, you might choose to implement your tester program in a different language from the language in which you created the control.

Make your new project the startup project by right-clicking on the project in the Solution Explorer and choosing Set as Startup Project, as shown in Figure 17-8. This makes the tester project the project that is started when you press F5 or Ctrl-F5.

You must now add a reference to the Teeter Totter control to your tester project by right-clicking on the References item for the Tester project in the Solutions Explorer and choosing Add Reference, as shown in Figure 17-9.

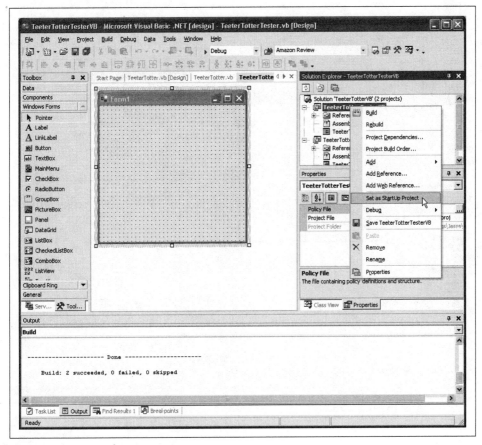

Figure 17-8. Setting the startup project

Within the Add Reference dialog, click on Projects. You will see the project, which you can double-click to add it to the list of selected components, as shown in Figure 17-10.

This will also add the Teeter Totter to your toolbox. Drag a Teeter Totter from the toolbox onto the form, and resize the form to fit. Rename the Teeter Totter from TeeterTotter1 to teeter.

While you are at it, drag a button onto the form, name it *btnColors*, set its Back-Color property to a pleasant shade of orange, and set its text to Modify Colors. Your form should now look like the form shown in Figure 17-11.

Interacting with properties

The Teeter Totter exposes the BtnBackColor and ListBoxBackColor properties. You'll test interacting with these properties from your test program by setting the properties in response to a click on the ModifyColors button.

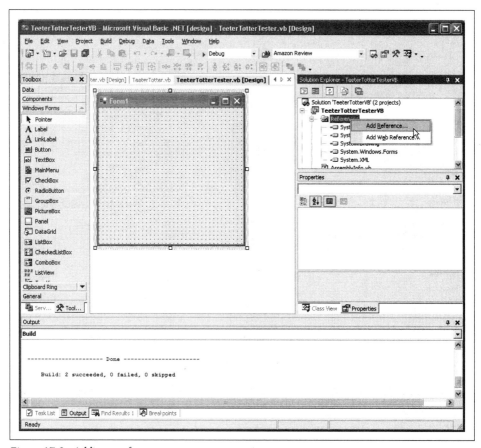

Figure 17-9. Adding a reference

To make this work, implement a click-event handler for the button. The easiest way to do so is by double-clicking on the button in the Visual Studio .NET designer window. Visual Studio .NET will create the event handler for you and place your cursor in the event handler. Fill in the handler as follows:

```csharp
private void btnColors_Click(object sender, System.EventArgs e)
{
    if ( teeter.BtnBackColor != Color.Red )
        teeter.BtnBackColor = Color.Red;
    else
        teeter.BtnBackColor = Color.Beige;

    if ( teeter.ListBoxBackColor != Color.PapayaWhip )
        teeter.ListBoxBackColor = Color.PapayaWhip;
    else
        teeter.ListBoxBackColor = Color.Aquamarine;
}
```

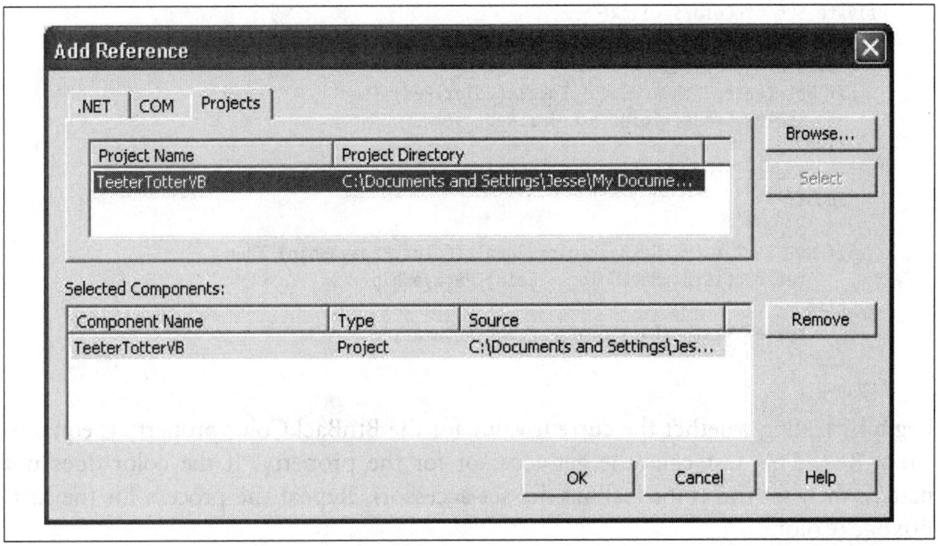

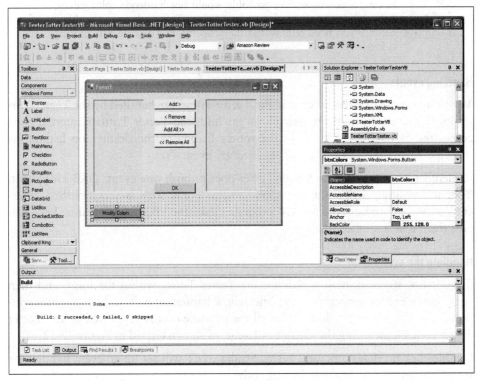

Figure 17-10. Adding the project

Figure 17-11. The test form

```
Private Sub btnColors_Click( _
  ByVal sender As System.Object, ByVal e As System.EventArgs) _
  Handles btnColors.Click
    If Not teeter.BtnBackColor.Equals(Color.Red) Then
        teeter.BtnBackColor = Color.Red
    Else
        teeter.BtnBackColor = Color.Beige
    End If

    If Not teeter.ListBoxBackColor.Equals(Color.PapayaWhip) Then
        teeter.ListBoxBackColor = Color.PapayaWhip
    Else
        teeter.ListBoxBackColor = Color.Aquamarine
    End If
End Sub
```

Begin by testing whether the current value for the BtnBackColor property is equal to Color.Red. This test calls the get-accessor for the property. If the color does not match, then set the color (calling the set-accessor). Repeat the process for the ListBoxBackColor.

> In production code, you probably would not hardcode color values, but would invoke a color picker dialog. This code was simplified because you need only to test the property, not demonstrate picking colors.

Handling events

Most events raised by the buttons in the Teeter Totter are handled by the Teeter Totter itself. For example, if the user clicks on Add, the Teeter Totter's internal code copies the highlighted value from the source listbox to the destination listbox (as shown earlier in the section "Handling Internal Events").

Remember, though, that the Teeter Totter does publish one event: OKButtonEvent. Your test program will want to respond to this event. This is accomplished differently in Visual Studio .NET for C# programs than for VB.NET programs. Let's discuss them one at a time.

Handling the event in C#

In your C# application, you click on the Teeter Totter within the form, and then click on the Events property button (the yellow lightening bolt in the Properties window). The Properties window shows all the possible events supported by the Teeter Totter control, including the OKButtonEvent, as shown circled in Figure 17-12.

Double-click on that event, and Visual Studio .NET will set up an event handler for you. You can then fill in the following code:

```
private void teeter_OKButtonEvent(object sender,
    TeeterTotter.TeeterTotterEventArgs e)
{
```

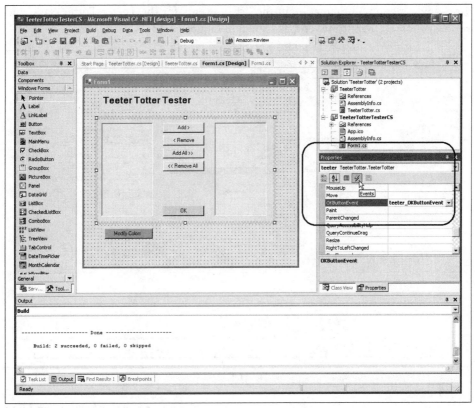

Figure 17-12. Clicking on the events button

```
StringBuilder sb = new StringBuilder();
foreach (string s in e.Items)
{
    sb.Append(s);
    sb.Append(" ");
}

MessageBox.Show(sb.ToString());
}
```

For this test program, you'll assemble a string (using the StringBuilder class) based on the string items in the TeeterTotterEventArgs object passed in to the event handler. (Notice that Visual Studio .NET was able to set the method with the correct argument type defined in the control itself.) Then display that string in a message box to validate that you've responded to the event and extracted the relevant information from the TeeterTotterEventArgs object.

Handling the event In Visual Basic .NET

To create the event handler in VB.NET, go to the code-editing window and use the class-name drop-down menu to locate the Teeter Totter class. The Declarations drop-down menu will then contain the list of events for the Teeter Totter class, and you can choose OKButtonEvent, as shown in Figure 17-13.

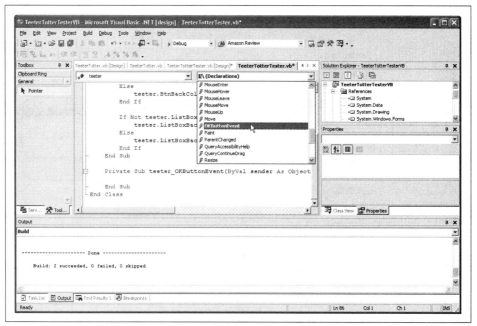

Figure 17-13. Setting the event handler in VB.NET

Choosing this event will cause VB.NET to create the event handler for you, and you can fill in the code, as shown here:

```
Private Sub teeter_OKButtonEvent( _
  ByVal sender As Object, _
  ByVal e As TeeterTotterVB.TeeterTotterEventArgs) _
  Handles teeter.OKButtonEvent
    Dim sb As New StringBuilder( )
    Dim s As String
    For Each s In e.Item
        sb.Append(s)
        sb.Append(" ")
    Next
    MessageBox.Show(sb.ToString( ))
End Sub
```

For this test program, as in the C# example, you'll assemble a string (using the StringBuilder class) based on the string items in the TeeterTotterEventArgs object passed in to the event handler. (Notice that Visual Studio .NET was able to set the method with the correct argument type defined in the control itself.) You then display that string in a message box to validate that you've responded to the event and extracted the relevant information from the TeeterTotterEventArgs object.

You'll need to add an imports (using) statement for System.Text to use StringBuilder.

Populating the listbox

Before you can test the program, you must populate the source listbox with test strings. You'll do so in the constructor for the TeeterTotterTester form, using the AddSource public method of the Teeter Totter:

```csharp
public Form1()
{
    InitializeComponent();
    teeter.AddSource("One");
    teeter.AddSource("Two");
    teeter.AddSource("Three");
    teeter.AddSource("Four");
}
```

```vb
Public Sub New()
    MyBase.New()

    InitializeComponent()
    teeter.AddSource("One")
    teeter.AddSource("Two")
    teeter.AddSource("Three")
    teeter.AddSource("Four")
End Sub
```

You may now start the test program by pressing F5. Highlight a string (e.g., "Two") in the source box and press Add—it should be added to the destination. Add and remove a few strings, and click OK—you should see the strings in the destination box shown in the message box. Before you exit, be sure to click Modify Colors a few times to see the properties at work.

Creating Custom Controls from Scratch

Sooner or later, the Betty Crocker cookies just aren't exactly what you had in mind, and it is time to bake up a new control from scratch. In the previous examples, you derived first from an existing control type (e.g., Button) and then from UserControl. In the next example, you will derive from the base control type: Control.

Creating your control from scratch lets you manage the look and feel of your new control with precision. However, it also requires that you implement every aspect of the control, including painting it—that is, you get power, but at the cost of greater responsibility, a lesson to us all.

You'll create a control that provides the analog clock functionality you implemented in Chapter 10, but makes that functionality available to any program as a control—as easy to use as a button.

Begin by creating a new Windows Control Library project in Visual Studio .NET in your language of choice. Call it ClockFaceControl. When you first create the project, you'll be put into the design mode. Right-click on the form and choose View Code. Change the name of the source file from *UserControl1.cs* or *.vb* to *ClockFaceControl.cs* or *.vb*

Next, change the name of the class from UserControl1 to ClockFaceCtrl, and change the base class from UserControl to Control.

C#
```
public class ClockFaceCtrl : System.Windows.Forms.Control
```

VB
```
Public Class ClockFaceCtrl
    Inherits System.Windows.Forms.Control
```

After you make this change to the base class, go back to the designer. You'll find that there is no longer a visible form. The Control class does not provide the form functionality that UserControl provides, but this is fine; you'll add the UI explicitly in the OnPaint method.

The code for this control is nearly identical to that shown in Chapter 10. Here are the changes:

- The ClockFaceControl derives from Control rather than Form.
- None of the *form* code (e.g., Dispose or InitializeComponent) is needed.
- Remove the mouse-down event handler (the control will not respond to this event). Thus, there is no need for the xCenter and yCenter member variables, and the center is set to the width and height divided by 2 and then left alone.
- Expose TwentyFourHours as a Boolean property so the client can set a 24- or 12- hour format.

You can create the ClockFaceControl by lifting the code from Chapter 10 and dropping it into a new Control class. The complete source for the control is shown in Examples 17-5 and 17-6.

Example 17-5. The ClockFace control (C#)

C#
```
using System;
using System.Collections;
using System.Drawing;
using System.Drawing.Drawing2D;    // for LineCap enumerations
using System.Timers;               // for onTimer event
using System.Windows.Forms;

namespace ClockFace
{
```

Example 17-5. The ClockFace control (C#) (continued)

```csharp
public class ClockFaceCtrl : System.Windows.Forms.Control
{
    private int FaceRadius = 700;
    private bool b24Hours = false;
    private DateTime currentTime;
    private static int DateRadius = 900;
    private static int offset = 0;
    Font font = new Font("Arial", 80);
    private StringDraw sdToday;

    public ClockFaceCtrl( )
    {

        BackColor = SystemColors.Window;
        ForeColor = SystemColors.WindowText;

        string today = System.DateTime.Now.ToLongDateString( );
        today = " " + today.Replace(",","");
        sdToday = new StringDraw(today,this);


        currentTime = DateTime.Now;

        System.Timers.Timer timer = new System.Timers.Timer( );
        timer.Elapsed +=
                    new System.Timers.ElapsedEventHandler(OnTimer);
        timer.Interval = 50;
        timer.Enabled = true;

    }

    public bool TwentyFourHours
    {
        get { return b24Hours; }
        set { b24Hours = value; }
    }


    public void OnTimer(Object source, ElapsedEventArgs e)
    {

        Graphics g = this.CreateGraphics( );
        SetScale(g);
        DrawFace(g);
        DrawTime(g,false);
        DrawDate(g);
        g.Dispose( );
    }

    protected override void OnPaint ( PaintEventArgs e )
    {
        base.OnPaint(e);
```

Example 17-5. The ClockFace control (C#) (continued)

```
C#          Graphics g = e.Graphics;
            SetScale(g);
            DrawFace(g);
            DrawTime(g,true);
        }

        private void SetScale(Graphics g)
        {
            if ( Width == 0 || Height == 0 )
                return;

            // set the origin at the center
            g.TranslateTransform(Width / 2, Height / 2);
            // set inches to the minimum of the
            // width or height divided
            // by the dots per inch
            float inches = Math.Min(Width / g.DpiX, Height / g.DpiX);

            g.ScaleTransform(inches * g.DpiX / 2000,
                        inches * g.DpiY / 2000);
        }


        private static float GetSin(float degAngle)
        {
            return (float) Math.Sin(Math.PI * degAngle / 180f);
        }

        private static float GetCos(float degAngle)
        {
            return (float) Math.Cos(Math.PI * degAngle / 180f);
        }

        private void DrawFace(Graphics g)
        {

            Brush brush = new SolidBrush(ForeColor);
            Brush greenBrush = new SolidBrush(Color.Green);

            float x, y;

            int numHours = b24Hours ? 24 : 12;
            int deg = 360 / numHours;

            for (int i = 1; i <= numHours; i++)
            {
                SizeF stringSize = g.MeasureString(
                            i.ToString( ),font);
                x = GetCos(i*deg + 90) * FaceRadius;
                y = GetSin(i*deg + 90) * FaceRadius;

                StringFormat format = new StringFormat( );
```

Example 17-5. The ClockFace control (C#) (continued)

```csharp
            format.Alignment = StringAlignment.Center;
            format.LineAlignment = StringAlignment.Center;

            if ( currentTime.Second  == i * 5)
               g.DrawString(i.ToString( ), font,
                                    greenBrush, -x, -y,format);
            else
               g.DrawString(i.ToString( ), font, brush, -x,
                                    -y,format);
         }
      }


      private void DrawTime(Graphics g, bool forceDraw)
      {

         float hourLength = FaceRadius * 0.5f;
         float minuteLength = FaceRadius * 0.7f;
         float secondLength = FaceRadius * 0.9f;

         Pen hourPen = new Pen(BackColor);
         Pen minutePen = new Pen(BackColor);
         Pen secondPen = new Pen(BackColor);

         hourPen.EndCap = LineCap.ArrowAnchor;
         minutePen.EndCap = LineCap.ArrowAnchor;

         hourPen.Width = 30;
         minutePen.Width = 20;

         Brush secondBrush = new SolidBrush(Color.Green);
         Brush blankBrush = new SolidBrush(BackColor);


         float rotation;
         GraphicsState state;

         DateTime newTime = DateTime.Now;
         bool newMin = false;

         if ( newTime.Minute != currentTime.Minute )
            newMin = true;

         rotation = GetSecondRotation( );
         state = g.Save( );
         g.RotateTransform(rotation);
         g.FillEllipse(blankBrush,-25,-secondLength,50,50);
         g.Restore(state);

         if ( newMin  || forceDraw )
         {
            rotation = GetMinuteRotation( );
```

Example 17-5. The ClockFace control (C#) (continued)

```
C#              state = g.Save( );
                g.RotateTransform(rotation);
                g.DrawLine(minutePen,0,0,0,-minuteLength);
                g.Restore(state);

                rotation = GetHourRotation( );
                state = g.Save( );
                g.RotateTransform(rotation);
                g.DrawLine(hourPen,0,0,0,-hourLength);
                g.Restore(state);
            }


            currentTime = newTime;

            hourPen.Color = Color.Red;
            minutePen.Color = Color.Blue;
            secondPen.Color = Color.Green;

            state = g.Save( );
            rotation = GetSecondRotation( );
            g.RotateTransform(rotation);
            g.FillEllipse(secondBrush,-25,-secondLength,50,50);
            g.Restore(state);

            if ( newMin || forceDraw )
            {

                state = g.Save( );
                rotation = GetMinuteRotation( );
                g.RotateTransform(rotation);
                g.DrawLine(minutePen,0,0,0,-minuteLength);
                g.Restore(state);

                state = g.Save( );
                rotation = GetHourRotation( );
                g.RotateTransform(rotation);
                g.DrawLine(hourPen,0,0,0,-hourLength);
                g.Restore(state);
            }
        }


        // determine the rotation to draw the hour hand
        private float GetHourRotation( )
        {
            // degrees depend on 24 vs. 12 hour clock
            float deg = b24Hours ? 15 : 30;
            float numHours = b24Hours ? 24 : 12;
            return( 360f * currentTime.Hour / numHours +
                deg * currentTime.Minute / 60f);
        }
```

Example 17-5. The ClockFace control (C#) (continued)

```
private float GetMinuteRotation()
{
    return( 360f * currentTime.Minute / 60f ); //+
    // 6f * currentTime.Second / 60f);
}

private float GetSecondRotation()
{
    return(360f * currentTime.Second / 60f);

}

private class LtrDraw
{
    char myChar;
    float x;
    float y;
    float oldx;
    float oldy;


    public LtrDraw(char c)
    {
        myChar = c;
    }

    public float X
    {
        get { return x; }
        set { oldx = x; x = value; }
    }

    public float Y
    {
        get { return y; }
        set { oldy = y; y = value; }
    }

    public float GetWidth(Graphics g, Font font)
    {
        SizeF stringSize =
            g.MeasureString(myChar.ToString(),font);
        return stringSize.Width;
    }

    public float GetHeight(Graphics g, Font font)
    {
        SizeF stringSize =
            g.MeasureString(myChar.ToString(),font);
        return stringSize.Height;
    }
```

Example 17-5. The ClockFace control (C#) (continued)

```csharp
C#        public void DrawString(
                    Graphics g, Brush brush, ClockFaceCtrl ctrl)
          {
             // Font font = new Font("Arial", 40);
             Font font = ctrl.font;
             Brush blankBrush =
                new SolidBrush(ctrl.BackColor);
             g.DrawString(
                 myChar.ToString( ),font,blankBrush,oldx,oldy);
             g.DrawString(myChar.ToString( ),font,brush,x,y);
          }
       }   //  close for nested class LtrDraw

       private class StringDraw
       {
          ArrayList theString = new ArrayList( );
          LtrDraw l;
          ClockFaceCtrl theControl;

          public StringDraw(string s, ClockFaceCtrl theControl)
          {
             this.theControl = theControl;
             foreach (char c in s)
             {
                l = new LtrDraw(c);
                theString.Add(l);
             }
          }

          public void DrawString(Graphics g, Brush brush)
          {
             int angle = 360 / theString.Count;
             int counter = 0;

             foreach (LtrDraw theLtr in theString)
             {
                float newX = GetCos(angle  * counter + 90 -
                  ClockFaceCtrl.offset) * ClockFaceCtrl.DateRadius ;
                float newY = GetSin(angle * counter + 90 -
                  ClockFaceCtrl.offset) * ClockFaceCtrl.DateRadius ;
                theLtr.X = newX - (theLtr.GetWidth(g,theControl.font) / 2);
                theLtr.Y = newY - (theLtr.GetHeight(g,theControl.font) / 2);
                counter++;
                theLtr.DrawString(g,brush,theControl);
             }
             ClockFaceCtrl.offset += 1;
          }
       }   //  close for nested class StringDraw

       private void DrawDate(Graphics g)
       {
          Brush brush = new SolidBrush(ForeColor);
```

Example 17-5. The ClockFace control (C#) (continued)

```
        sdToday.DrawString(g,brush);
    }

  }
}
```

Example 17-6. The ClockFace control (VB.NET)

```
Imports System
Imports System.Collections
Imports System.Drawing
Imports System.Drawing.Drawing2D
Imports System.Timers
Imports System.Windows.Forms


Namespace ClockFace

    Public Class ClockFaceCtrl
        Inherits System.Windows.Forms.Control
        Private FaceRadius As Integer = 700
        Private b24Hours As Boolean = False
        Private currentTime As DateTime
        Private Shared DateRadius As Integer = 900
        Private Shared offset As Integer = 0
        Private font As New font("Arial", 80)
        Private sdToday As StringDraw

        Public Sub New()

            BackColor = SystemColors.Window
            ForeColor = SystemColors.WindowText

            Dim today As String = System.DateTime.Now.ToLongDateString()
            today = " " + today.Replace(",", "")
            sdToday = New StringDraw(today, Me)


            currentTime = DateTime.Now
            Dim timer As New System.Timers.Timer()
            AddHandler timer.Elapsed, AddressOf OnTimer
            timer.Interval = 50
            timer.Enabled = True
        End Sub 'New


        Public Property TwentyFourHours() As Boolean
            Get
                Return b24Hours
            End Get
            Set(ByVal Value As Boolean)
```

Example 17-6. The ClockFace control (VB.NET) (continued)

```
                b24Hours = Value
        End Set
    End Property

    Public Sub OnTimer( _
      ByVal [source] As [Object], _
      ByVal e As ElapsedEventArgs)

        Dim g As Graphics = Me.CreateGraphics( )
        'Brush brush = new SolidBrush(ForeColor);
        SetScale(g)
        DrawFace(g)
        DrawTime(g, False)
        DrawDate(g)
        g.Dispose( )
    End Sub 'OnTimer
    ' DrawDate(g,brush);

    Protected Overrides Sub OnPaint(ByVal e As PaintEventArgs)
        MyBase.OnPaint(e)
        Dim g As Graphics = e.Graphics
        SetScale(g)
        DrawFace(g)
        DrawTime(g, True)
    End Sub 'OnPaint


    Private Sub SetScale(ByVal g As Graphics)
        If Width = 0 Or Height = 0 Then
            Return
        End If
        ' set the origin at the center
        g.TranslateTransform(Width / 2, Height / 2)

        Dim inches As Single = _
            Math.Min(Width / g.DpiX, Height / g.DpiX)

        g.ScaleTransform( _
            inches * g.DpiX / 2000, inches * g.DpiY / 2000)
    End Sub 'SetScale


    Private Shared Function _
        GetSin(ByVal degAngle As Single) As Single
        Return CSng(Math.Sin((Math.PI * degAngle / 180.0F)))
    End Function 'GetSin


    Private Shared Function _
        GetCos(ByVal degAngle As Single) As Single
        Return CSng(Math.Cos((Math.PI * degAngle / 180.0F)))
    End Function 'GetCos
```

Example 17-6. The ClockFace control (VB.NET) (continued)

```
VB    Private Sub DrawFace(ByVal g As Graphics)

          Dim brush = New SolidBrush(ForeColor)
          Dim greenBrush = New SolidBrush(Color.Green)

          Dim x, y As Single

          Dim numHours As Integer
          If b24Hours Then
              numHours = 24
          Else
              numHours = 12
          End If

          Dim deg As Integer = 360 / numHours

          Dim i As Integer
          For i = 1 To numHours
              Dim stringSize As SizeF = _
                g.MeasureString(i.ToString(), font)
              x = GetCos((i * deg + 90)) * FaceRadius
              y = GetSin((i * deg + 90)) * FaceRadius

              Dim format As New StringFormat()
              format.Alignment = StringAlignment.Center
              format.LineAlignment = StringAlignment.Center

              If currentTime.Second = i * 5 Then
                  g.DrawString(i.ToString(), font, _
                    greenBrush, -x, -y, format)
              Else
                  g.DrawString(i.ToString(), font, _
                    brush, -x, -y, format)
              End If
          Next i
      End Sub 'DrawFace

      Private Sub DrawTime( _
        ByVal g As Graphics, ByVal forceDraw As Boolean)

          Dim hourLength As Single = FaceRadius * 0.5F
          Dim minuteLength As Single = FaceRadius * 0.7F
          Dim secondLength As Single = FaceRadius * 0.9F

          Dim hourPen As New Pen(BackColor)
          Dim minutePen As New Pen(BackColor)
          Dim secondPen As New Pen(BackColor)

          hourPen.EndCap = LineCap.ArrowAnchor
          minutePen.EndCap = LineCap.ArrowAnchor

          hourPen.Width = 30
```

Example 17-6. The ClockFace control (VB.NET) (continued)

```
minutePen.Width = 20

Dim secondBrush = New SolidBrush(Color.Green)
Dim blankBrush = New SolidBrush(BackColor)


Dim rotation As Single
Dim state As GraphicsState

Dim newTime As DateTime = DateTime.Now
Dim newMin As Boolean = False

If newTime.Minute <> currentTime.Minute Then
    newMin = True
End If

rotation = GetSecondRotation( )
state = g.Save( )
g.RotateTransform(rotation)
g.FillEllipse(blankBrush, -25, -secondLength, 50, 50)
g.Restore(state)

If newMin Or forceDraw Then

    rotation = GetMinuteRotation( )
    state = g.Save( )
    g.RotateTransform(rotation)
    g.DrawLine(minutePen, 0, 0, 0, -minuteLength)
    g.Restore(state)

    rotation = GetHourRotation( )
    state = g.Save( )
    g.RotateTransform(rotation)
    g.DrawLine(hourPen, 0, 0, 0, -hourLength)
    g.Restore(state)
End If

currentTime = newTime

hourPen.Color = Color.Red
minutePen.Color = Color.Blue
secondPen.Color = Color.Green

state = g.Save( )
rotation = GetSecondRotation( )
g.RotateTransform(rotation)
g.FillEllipse(secondBrush, -25, -secondLength, 50, 50)
g.Restore(state)

If newMin Or forceDraw Then

    state = g.Save( )
```

Example 17-6. The ClockFace control (VB.NET) (continued)

```
                rotation = GetMinuteRotation( )
                g.RotateTransform(rotation)
                g.DrawLine(minutePen, 0, 0, 0, -minuteLength)
                g.Restore(state)

                state = g.Save( )
                rotation = GetHourRotation( )
                g.RotateTransform(rotation)
                g.DrawLine(hourPen, 0, 0, 0, -hourLength)
                g.Restore(state)
            End If
        End Sub 'DrawTime


        ' determine the rotation to draw the hour hand
        Private Function GetHourRotation( ) As Single
            ' degrees depend on 24 vs. 12 hour clock
            Dim deg As Single
            Dim numHours As Single
            If b24Hours Then
                deg = 15
                numHours = 24
            Else
                deg = 30
                numHours = 12
            End If

            Return 360.0F * currentTime.Hour / numHours + deg * _
                currentTime.Minute / 60.0F
        End Function 'GetHourRotation


        Private Function GetMinuteRotation( ) As Single
            Return 360.0F * currentTime.Minute / 60.0F '+
        End Function 'GetMinuteRotation
        ' 6f * currentTime.Second / 60f);

        Private Function GetSecondRotation( ) As Single
            Return 360.0F * currentTime.Second / 60.0F
        End Function 'GetSecondRotation
        _

        Private Class LtrDraw
            Private myChar As Char
            Private _x As Single
            Private _y As Single
            Private oldx As Single
            Private oldy As Single


            Public Sub New(ByVal c As Char)
                myChar = c
```

Example 17-6. The ClockFace control (VB.NET) (continued)

```
            End Sub 'New

            Public Property X( ) As Single
                Get
                    Return _x
                End Get
                Set(ByVal Value As Single)
                    oldx = _x
                    _x = Value
                End Set
            End Property

            Public Property Y( ) As Single
                Get
                    Return _y
                End Get
                Set(ByVal Value As Single)
                    oldy = _y
                    _y = Value
                End Set
            End Property

            Public Function GetWidth( _
              ByVal g As Graphics, ByVal font As font) _
              As Single
                Dim stringSize As SizeF = _
                  g.MeasureString(myChar.ToString( ), font)
                Return stringSize.Width
            End Function 'GetWidth


            Public Function GetHeight( _
              ByVal g As Graphics, ByVal font As font) _
              As Single
                Dim stringSize As SizeF = _
                  g.MeasureString(myChar.ToString( ), font)
                Return stringSize.Height
            End Function 'GetHeight


            Public Sub DrawString( _
              ByVal g As Graphics, ByVal brush As Brush, _
              ByVal ctrl As ClockFaceCtrl)
                ' Font font = new Font("Arial", 40);
                Dim font As Font = ctrl.font
                Dim blankBrush = New SolidBrush(ctrl.BackColor)
                g.DrawString(myChar.ToString( ), font, _
                  blankBrush, oldx, oldy)
                g.DrawString(myChar.ToString( ), _
                  font, brush, X, Y)
            End Sub 'DrawString
        End Class 'LtrDraw

        _
```

Example 17-6. The ClockFace control (VB.NET) (continued)

VB
```
        Private Class StringDraw
            Private theString As New ArrayList()
            Private l As LtrDraw
            Private theControl As ClockFaceCtrl


            Public Sub New(ByVal s As String, _
              ByVal theControl As ClockFaceCtrl)
                Me.theControl = theControl
                Dim c As Char
                For Each c In s
                    l = New LtrDraw(c)
                    theString.Add(l)
                Next c
            End Sub 'New


            Public Sub DrawString( _
              ByVal g As Graphics, ByVal brush As Brush)
                Dim angle As Integer = 360 / theString.Count
                Dim counter As Integer = 0

                Dim theLtr As LtrDraw
                For Each theLtr In theString
                    Dim newX As Single = _
                      GetCos((angle * counter + 90 - _
                      ClockFaceCtrl.offset)) * _
                      ClockFaceCtrl.DateRadius

                    Dim newY As Single = _
                      GetSin((angle * counter + 90 - _
                      ClockFaceCtrl.offset)) * _
                      ClockFaceCtrl.DateRadius
                    theLtr.X = newX - theLtr.GetWidth( _
                      g, theControl.font) / 2
                    theLtr.Y = newY - theLtr.GetHeight( _
                      g, theControl.font) / 2
                    counter += 1
                    theLtr.DrawString(g, brush, theControl)
                Next theLtr
                ClockFaceCtrl.offset += 1
            End Sub 'DrawString
        End Class 'StringDraw


        Private Sub DrawDate(ByVal g As Graphics)
            Dim brush = New SolidBrush(ForeColor)
            sdToday.DrawString(g, brush)
        End Sub 'DrawDate
    End Class 'ClockFaceCtrl
End Namespace 'ClockFace
```

Testing the custom control

As you did with the UserControl, you'll test the custom control by creating a testing project in the same solution as the control. Call the new test project ClockFace-Tester. Add a reference to your control, and then update the toolbar to include the control (you may need to browse to the dll for the control). Drag the control onto the form, name it clockFace, and then resize the form to fit.

Finally, drag a button onto the form, set its text to 24 Hours, and set its name to btn24. Your form should now look like Figure 17-14.

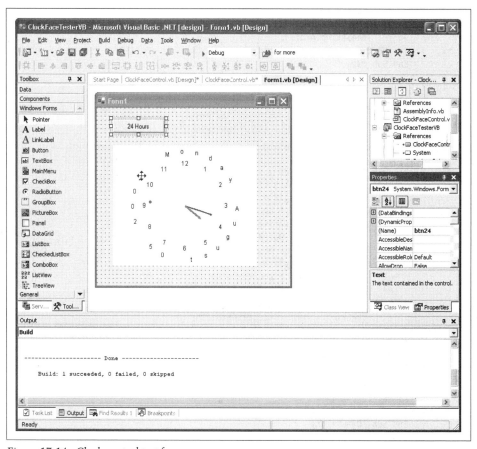

Figure 17-14. Clock control test form

You can see already that the clock control is working, but you'll want to set the 24-hour property programmatically. Double-click on the button to create its event handler:

```csharp
private void btn24_Click(object sender, System.EventArgs e)
{
    if ( clockFace.TwentyFourHours )
```

```csharp
{
    btn24.Text = "24 Hours";
    clockFace.TwentyFourHours = false;
    clockFace.Invalidate();
}
else
{
    btn24.Text = "12 Hours";
    clockFace.TwentyFourHours = true;
    clockFace.Invalidate();
}
}
```

```vb
Private Sub btn24_Click( _
    ByVal sender As System.Object, ByVal e As System.EventArgs) _
    Handles btn24.Click
        If clockFace.TwentyFourHours Then
            btn24.Text = "24 Hours"
            clockFace.TwentyFourHours = False
            clockFace.Invalidate()
        Else
            btn24.Text = "12 Hours"
            clockFace.TwentyFourHours = True
            clockFace.Invalidate()
        End If
End Sub
```

That's it! Set the tester program as the startup project and run it—you'll see the control executing on the form much as it did in Chapter 10, but this time it is a custom control you can drop on any form.

CHAPTER 18

Menus and Bars

None but the most rudimentary Windows application is complete without a set of menus listed at the top of the window. In addition, most modern Windows applications include pop-up context-sensitive menus, toolbars, and a status bar. A toolbar is a set of buttons that act as menu shortcuts, and the status bar provides information about the current state of the application, as illustrated in Figure 18-1.

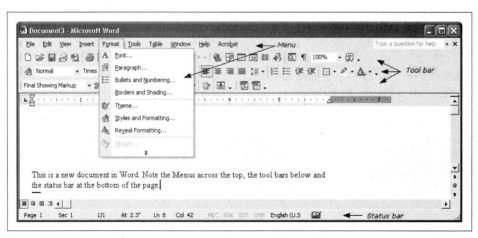

Figure 18-1. Menus and bars

Creating Your First Menu

There are two ways to create a menu in .NET. Using Visual Studio .NET is by far the easiest. However, it can obscure some of the internal workings, and so later in this chapter you will see a simple menu that uses Notepad.

To get started, fire up Visual Studio .NET and start a new project. Drag a Main-Menu item from the Toolbox onto your Form, as shown in Figure 18-2.

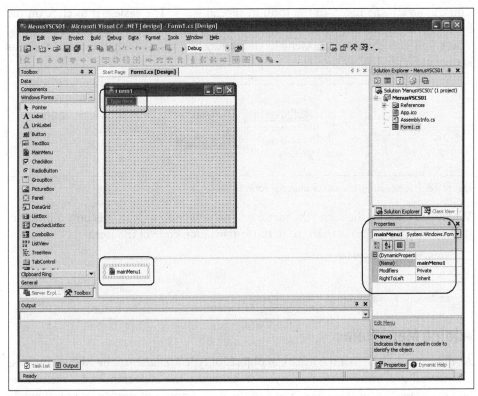

Figure 18-2. New menu item

There are a few things to notice in Figure 18-2. First, in the upper-lefthand corner is the new menu item, ready for you to add text. This placement makes adding the menu items incredibly easy. Second, in the lower-lefthand corner, a non-UI element, mainMenu1, has been added. Its properties are visible in the properties window.

The MainMenu Object

Your control, mainMenu1, is of type System.Windows.Forms.MainMenu. This class represents the container for the entire menu structure within a form. While the MainMenu class has a number of properties, the one you will use most often is the MenuItems property, which returns a collection of MenuItem objects. A menu consists of these MenuItem objects, each of which represents one choice on the menu.

You will find that when you click on the form, the menu disappears! When you click on mainMenu1, the menu reappears, in place, ready for you to edit. The menu is actually independent of the form; it is shown in its place as a convenience for you. However, if you run the application now, the menu will not appear—it is not yet attached to the form.

You can attach the menu to the form in several ways. The easiest is to click on the form to bring up its Properties window, and then scroll down to the Menu property. There you can choose mainMenu1, associating the menu with the form itself, as shown in Figure 18-3.

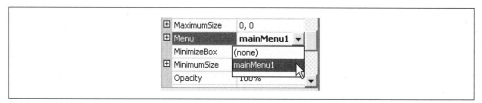

Figure 18-3. Associating the menu with the form

When you click on the form, the menu will no longer disappear; it is now a property of the form itself. This is reflected in the initialization code of the form:

C#
```
this.Menu = this.mainMenu1;
```

VB
```
me.Menu = me.mainMenu1
```

Adding Menu Items

As noted above, the menu consists of objects of type *MenuItem*. The MenuItem class has several properties that enable you to configure the appearance of a menu item and determine its functionality. Some of the most important properties are shown in Table 18-1.

Table 18-1. MenuItem properties

Property	Type	Description
Checked	Boolean	Read/write. Specifies whether a checkmark appears next to the menu item. The default is false.
DefaultItem	Boolean	Read/write. Is this the default item on the menu? The default is false.
Enabled	Boolean	Is this menu item enabled? The default is true.
Index	Integer	Read/Write. Indicates the position within the parent menu (zero based).
IsParent	Boolean	Read-only. Does this item have child items?
MdiList	Boolean	Read/Write. Indicates whether the menu item will have a list of MDI Child windows. The default is false.
MergeOrder	Integer	Read/write. Relative zero-based position of this item when merged with other menus. The default is zero.
MergeType	MenuMerge	Read/write. Behavior of this menu item when it is merged into another menu. Valid values are members of the MenuMerge enumeration: Add, MergeItems, Remove, and Replace.
OwnerDraw	Boolean	Read/write. Do you provide the code to draw the menu item, or does Windows? The default is false.

Table 18-1. MenuItem properties (continued)

Property	Type	Description
Parent	Menu	Read-only. The menu in which this item appears.
RadioCheck	Boolean	Read/write. Should the checkmark be a radio button instead of a checkmark? The default is false.
ShowShortCut	Boolean	Read/write. Should the associated shortcut key be displayed? The default is true.
Text	String	Read/write. The caption for the menu item.
Visible	Boolean	Read/write. Is this item visible? The default is true.

If you examine a typical menu (in Word, Visual Studio .NET, or another application), you'll find that most menus consist of words (or short phrases) strung horizontally across the top of the window. When you click on each, a submenu (sometimes referred to as a child menu) appears.

 The Visual Studio .NET menu editor makes it very easy to add new menu and child menu items, but it names each item with sequential numbering. Be careful to rename these items so that you can refer to them in code with meaningful names. Doing so makes your code self-documenting and easier to maintain.

To get started, create a few simple menu items that correspond to some of the menu items available in a typical application. Enter the first menu item as File, by replacing the text "Type Here" with "File". As you do, you will note that the menu editor opens two new typing areas, one to the right of your menu item and one below it, as shown in Figure 18-4.

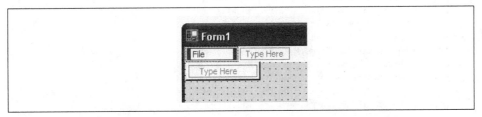

Figure 18-4. Entering a menu item

Also note that the properties window refers to your new menu item as menuItem1. Rename your menu item to mnuFile. Next, you will do one of a number of things:

- Add more items to the main menu.
- Add items to the submenus.
- Set properties on each of the items within the menu.
- Set event handlers for items in the menu.

Add the usual child menu items to File (Open, Close, Save, or SaveAs). Once this is done, add an Edit menu with Copy and Paste, as shown in Figure 18-5.

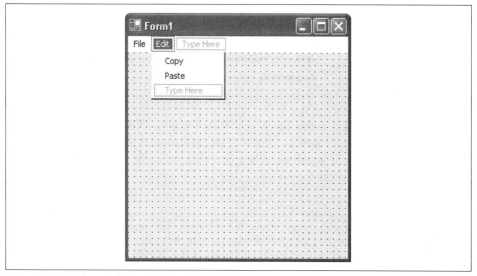

Figure 18-5. Adding child menus

This menu creates a total of eight Menu items. Click on each and provide a meaningful name, such as mnuFileOpen or mnuFileClose. After doing so, you can examine the Windows Form Designer generated code in the code window (*Form1.cs* or *Form1.vb*), where you will find the renamed menu items:

```csharp
private System.Windows.Forms.MainMenu mainMenu1;
private System.Windows.Forms.MenuItem mnuFile;
private System.Windows.Forms.MenuItem mnuFileOpen;
private System.Windows.Forms.MenuItem mnuFileClose;
private System.Windows.Forms.MenuItem mnuFileSave;
private System.Windows.Forms.MenuItem mnuFileSaveAs;
private System.Windows.Forms.MenuItem mnuEdit;
private System.Windows.Forms.MenuItem mnuEditCopy;
private System.Windows.Forms.MenuItem mnuEditPaste;
```

```vb
Friend WithEvents MainMenu1 As System.Windows.Forms.MainMenu
Friend WithEvents mnuFile As System.Windows.Forms.MenuItem
Friend WithEvents mnuEdit As System.Windows.Forms.MenuItem
Friend WithEvents mnuFileOpen As System.Windows.Forms.MenuItem
Friend WithEvents mnuFileClose As System.Windows.Forms.MenuItem
Friend WithEvents mnuFileSave As System.Windows.Forms.MenuItem
Friend WithEvents mnuFileSaveAs As System.Windows.Forms.MenuItem
Friend WithEvents mnuEditCopy As System.Windows.Forms.MenuItem
Friend WithEvents mnuEditPaste As System.Windows.Forms.MenuItem
```

Responding to Events

Menu items exist to be clicked. How your program responds to these events is determined by how you architect your code. One simple approach is to create independent event handlers for each click event. Visual Studio .NET makes this very easy; double-click on the menu item and an event handler is created for you.

For example, switch to the form view and double-click on mnuFileOpen in the File submenu. Visual Studio .NET switches back to code view and places your cursor within an event handler named mnuFileOpen_Click.

Each menu item has a default event; in this case, the Click event. To test this event handler, add a simple message box to pop up when the user clicks File → Open:

```csharp
private void mnuFileOpen_Click(object sender, System.EventArgs e)
{
    MessageBox.Show ("You clicked File Open", "Menu Event Tester",
        MessageBoxButtons.OK, MessageBoxIcon.Asterisk);
}
```

```vb
Private Sub mnuFileOpen_Click(ByVal sender As System.Object, ByVal e As System.
EventArgs) _
Handles mnuFileOpen.Click
    MessageBox.Show("You clicked file open!", _
    "Menu event tester", _
    MessageBoxButtons.OK, _
    MessageBoxIcon.Information)
End Sub
```

When you run the application and click on File → Open, the message box appears, as shown in Figure 18-6.

Figure 18-6. Testing the event handler

The MenuItem object provides a number of other events as well, the most important of which are shown in Table 18-2.

Table 18-2. *MenuItem events*

Event	Event argument	Description
Click	EventArgs	Default event, occurs when the item is selected or when a shortcut key is used.
DrawItem	DrawItemEventArgs	Used when the OwnerDraw property of a menu item is set to `true` and it is time to draw the menu item. Covered later in this chapter.
MeasureItem	MeasureItemEventArgs	Used by the menu to determine the size of the menu item before drawing it (used with OwnerDraw items).
Popup	EventArgs	Occurs just before the menuItem's list of child menu items is displayed.
Select	EventArgs	Raised when the user places the cursor over a menu item or the menu item is highlighted using the keyboard arrow keys. This event is not raised if the MenuItem has any child items.

Adding MDI Windows

You can flesh out the File menu with a New command, which will create a new MDI Child window. To do so, first create a new form, MDIChild.cs or MDIChild.vb, which will serve as the child window. Fill that form with a rich text control so it will look like a standard text window that you might open from your application.

Prepare your first form to be an MDI container by setting the IsMDIContainer property to true (as described in Chapter 5). You are now ready to add code to respond to the menu choice:

C#
```csharp
private void mnuNew_Click(object sender, System.EventArgs e)
{
    MDIChild newMDIChild = new MDIChild( );
    newMDIChild.MdiParent = this;
    newMDIChild.Show( );
}
```

VB
```vb
Private Sub mnuNew_Click(ByVal sender As System.Object, ByVal e As System.EventArgs) _
Handles mnuNew.Click
    Dim newMDIChild As New MDIChild( )
    newMDIChild.MdiParent = Me
    newMDIChild.Show( )
End Sub
```

You can see that creating the new MDI Child window is as simple as instantiating your new form, assigning its MdiParent property to the current form, and then showing the child. What is particularly sweet about this is that you can now add a Window menu item, which will track your MDI Windows for you. You need only set a single property on the menu item: MdiList to true.

If you open several MDI Child windows (by repeatedly clicking File → New), and then click on the Window menu item, it will display all the MDI Child windows with a checkmark next to the one that is current. You can change which child window is current by clicking on any of the listed child windows, as shown in Figure 18-7.

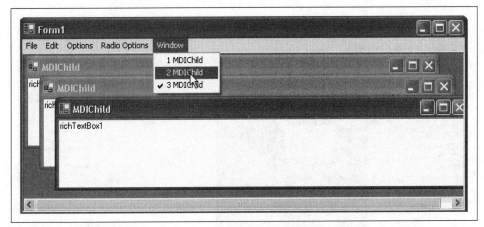

Figure 18-7. Managing MDI Child windows

Option Menu Items

Menu items can be added to indicate whether or not the user has selected various options. They come in two flavors: *check options* and *radio button options*. Check options let the user select one or more of a series of options, while radio button options are mutually exclusive.

The only difference between a check option and a radio button option is the value of the MenuItem's RadioCheck property. If set to true, the checkmark will be drawn as a filled-in dot. The framework does not, however, enforce that the options are mutually exclusive, and so you must do so in code, as shown next.

Shared Event Handlers

Both radio button options and check options cry out for shared event handlers. There is no point in having separate event handlers for each selectable option within one submenu; all will do the same thing (set or clear the checkmark).

You set up shared event handlers somewhat differently in C# than you do in VB.NET. In C#, you begin by creating the single (shared) event handler in code. Then set the event handler for each menu item from the properties window. Click on the yellow lightening bolt in the Properties window and choose the shared event handler for each item's click event, as shown in Figure 18-8.

The shared event-handling code itself is straightforward:

```csharp
private void Option_Click(object sender, System.EventArgs e)
{
    MenuItem item = sender as MenuItem;

    if ( item != null )
    {
```

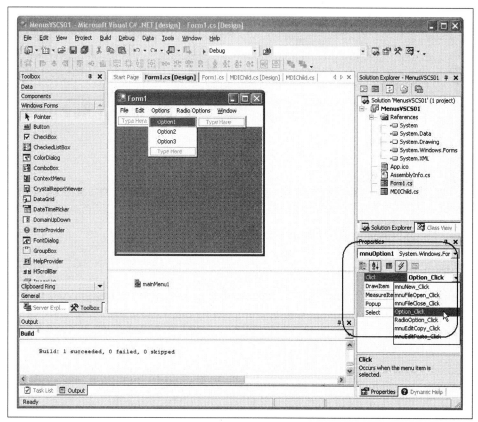

Figure 18-8. Setting the event handler

```csharp
            item.Checked = ! item.Checked;
        }
    }
```

Cast the sender object to be of type MenuItem, and then set the Checked property of the MenuItem to the opposite of its current state.

In VB.NET, you must create the event handler and then mark that event handler in the code to indicate that it handles the events for all the various options (remember to provide the options with meaningful names before implementing the handler):

```vbnet
    Private Sub Option_Click(ByVal sender As System.Object, ByVal e As System.EventArgs)

    Handles mnuOption1.Click, mnuOption2.Click, mnuOption3.Click
        Dim item As MenuItem = CType(sender, MenuItem)
        item.Checked = Not item.Checked
    End Sub
```

Once set up, however, the logic is the same as for C#: you cast the sender object to be of type MenuItem, and then you set the Checked property to the opposite of its current state.

Handling radio button options

Radio button options are handled with code that is nearly identical to that used to handle checkmarks, except that you must be sure to first clear all the checkmarks to ensure that only one is ever checked at a time. To accomplish this, ask the radio button item for its parent so you can get the parent's collection of MenuItems and iterate through that collection setting each MenuItem's Checked property to false. You can then set the current (chosen) item's Checked property to true:

```csharp
private void RadioOption_Click(object sender, System.EventArgs e)
{
    MenuItem item = sender as MenuItem;
    Menu parent = item.Parent;
    if ( item != null )
    {
        foreach ( MenuItem mi in parent.MenuItems )
        mi.Checked = false;
        item.Checked = true;
    }
}
```

```vbnet
Private Sub RadioOption_Click(ByVal sender As System.Object, ByVal e As System.EventArgs) _
Handles mnuRadioOption1.Click, mnuRadioOption2.Click, mnuRadioOption3.Click
    Dim item As MenuItem = CType(sender, MenuItem)
    Dim parent As Menu = item.Parent
    Dim tempMi As MenuItem
    For Each tempMi In parent.MenuItems
    tempMi.Checked = False
    Next
    item.Checked = True
End Sub
```

Menu Navigation

There are several easy ways to enhance the user's navigation of your menu items. The first is to provide an access key by placing an ampersand (&) before the character to be used as the access key. This causes the access key to be underlined (in XP, it is underlined when the user taps the Alt key).

The default for navigating menus is to access the various menu choices using the Alt key and the first letter of the menu item. For example, Alt-F will open the File menu. If you have two items with the same first letter (e.g., Save and SaveAs), you may want to add an access key for the A in SaveAs, so that pressing S will invoke Save and pressing A will invoke SaveAs, as shown in Figure 18-9.

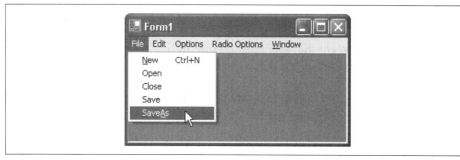

Figure 18-9. Using the access key

Shortcut keys

The second way to enhance keyboard usage of your menus is to provide shortcuts. Notice that in Figure 18-9, the File → New menu choice has a shortcut of Ctrl+N. Holding the control key and pressing N will invoke this menu choice even if the File menu is not open.

You can add shortcuts programmatically, or through Visual Studio .NET, by setting the ShortCut property of the MenuItem. When you use the Properties dialog in Visual Studio .NET, all potential shortcut keys are displayed in a drop-down menu, as shown in Figure 18-10.

You must also make sure that the ShowShortCut property of the MenuItem is set to true, or else the shortcut key combination will not be displayed in the menu (though the shortcut will continue to work).

Creating Menus by Hand

While creating menus in Visual Studio .NET is quick, easy, and painless, there is an advantage (at least once) in writing your menus by hand in Notepad. The code produced by Visual Studio .NET can hide some of the intimate details of the relationship among the various MenuItems, the Menu, and the Form. In addition, writing it by hand gives you the opportunity to explore some of the overloaded constructors for MenuItems, and is generally a good way to gain insight into what Visual Studio .NET is actually doing for you. This is illustrated in C# in Example 18-1 and in VB.NET in Example 18-2. A detailed analysis follows the listings.

For the code in Examples 18-1 or 18-2 to compile, you must add a reference in the compiler command line to the DLL that contains the MDI Child form. Example 18-3 (in C#) and Example 18-4 (in VB.NET) list the code for this form.

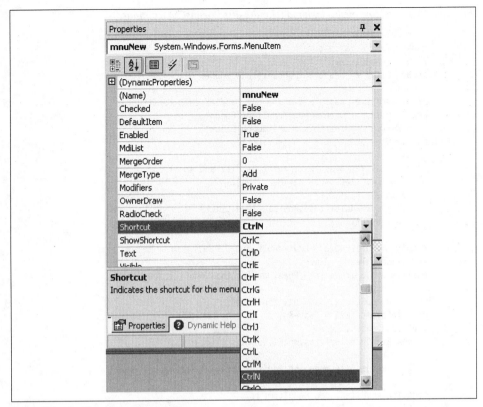

Figure 18-10. Choosing a shortcut key

Example 18-1. Creating menus by hand (HandCraftedMenusCS)

```csharp
using System;
using System.Windows.Forms;

namespace MenuByHand
{
    public class MenuForm : Form
    {
        // run the app
        public static void Main()
        {
            Application.Run(new MenuForm());
        }

        // constructor
        public MenuForm()
        {
            // build the menu inside out
            MenuItem mnuNew = new MenuItem();
            // short cut
            mnuNew.Shortcut = Shortcut.CtrlN;
```

Example 18-1. Creating menus by hand (HandCraftedMenusCS) (continued)

`C#`

```
        // accelerator
        mnuNew.Text = "&New";
        // event handler
        mnuNew.Click += new EventHandler(this.mnuNew_Click);

        // alternative, pass text and event handler into constructor
        MenuItem mnuFileOpen = new MenuItem("&Open",
            new EventHandler(this.mnuFileOpen_Click));
        mnuFileOpen.Shortcut = Shortcut.Ctrl0;

        // alternative, pass text, event handler and short cut
        MenuItem mnuFileClose = new MenuItem(
            "&Close",
            new EventHandler(this.mnuFileClose_Click),
            Shortcut.CtrlC);

        MenuItem mnuFileSave = new MenuItem( );
        mnuFileSave.Text = "Save";
        mnuFileSave.Click += new EventHandler(this.mnuFileSave_Click);

        MenuItem mnuFileSaveAs = new MenuItem( );
        mnuFileSaveAs.Text = "Save&As";
        mnuFileSaveAs.Click +=
            new EventHandler(this.mnuFileSaveAs_Click);

        // Create the file menu and add the array of sub-menu items
        // to its MenuItems collection
        MenuItem mnuFile = new MenuItem( );
        mnuFile.Text = "File";
        mnuFile.MenuItems.AddRange(new MenuItem[ ] {
                mnuNew,
                mnuFileOpen,
                mnuFileClose,
                mnuFileSave,
                mnuFileSaveAs});

        // create submenus for Edit menu
        MenuItem mnuEditCopy = new MenuItem( );
        mnuEditCopy.Text = "&Copy";
        mnuEditCopy.Click += new EventHandler(this.mnuEditCopy_Click);

        MenuItem mnuEditPaste = new MenuItem( );
        mnuEditPaste.Text = "Paste";
        mnuEditPaste.Click += new EventHandler(this.mnuEditPaste_Click);

        // Add the edit menu
        MenuItem mnuEdit = new MenuItem( );
        mnuEdit.Text = "Edit";
        mnuEdit.MenuItems.AddRange(new MenuItem[ ]
            { mnuEditCopy, mnuEditPaste } );

        // options sub-menu
        MenuItem mnuOption1 = new MenuItem( );
```

Example 18-1. Creating menus by hand (HandCraftedMenusCS) (continued)

```
mnuOption1.Text = "Option1";
mnuOption1.Click += new EventHandler(this.Option_Click);

MenuItem mnuOption2 = new MenuItem( );
mnuOption2.Text = "Option2";
mnuOption2.Click += new EventHandler(this.Option_Click);

MenuItem mnuOption3 = new MenuItem( );
mnuOption3.Text = "Option3";
mnuOption3.Click += new EventHandler(this.Option_Click);

// Add the options menu
MenuItem mnuOptions = new MenuItem( );
mnuOptions.Text = "Options";
mnuOptions.MenuItems.AddRange(new MenuItem[ ]
    { mnuOption1, mnuOption2, mnuOption3 } );


// radio options sub-menu
MenuItem mnuROption1 = new MenuItem( );
mnuROption1.Text = "Radio Option1";
mnuROption1.RadioCheck = true;
mnuROption1.Click += new EventHandler(this.RadioOption_Click);


MenuItem mnuROption2 = new MenuItem( );
mnuROption2.Text = "Radio Option2";
mnuROption2.RadioCheck = true;
mnuROption2.Click += new EventHandler(this.RadioOption_Click);

MenuItem mnuROption3 = new MenuItem( );
mnuROption3.Text = "Radio Option3";
mnuROption3.RadioCheck = true;
mnuROption3.Click += new EventHandler(this.RadioOption_Click);

// Add the radio options menu
MenuItem mnuRadioOptions = new MenuItem( );
mnuRadioOptions.Text = "Radio Options";

mnuRadioOptions.MenuItems.AddRange(
    new MenuItem[ ]
    { mnuROption1, mnuROption2, mnuROption3 } );

// Add the window menu
MenuItem mnuWindow = new MenuItem( );
mnuWindow.MdiList = true;
mnuWindow.Text = "&Window";

MainMenu mainMenu1 = new MainMenu(
    new MenuItem[ ]
    {mnuFile, mnuEdit, mnuOptions, mnuRadioOptions, mnuWindow} );
```

Example 18-1. Creating menus by hand (HandCraftedMenusCS) (continued)

```
        Text = "Menu Form Demonstration (by hand)";
        AutoScaleBaseSize = new System.Drawing.Size(5, 13);
        ClientSize = new System.Drawing.Size(292, 186);
        IsMdiContainer = true;
        Menu = mainMenu1;
    }

    private void mnuNew_Click(object sender, EventArgs e)
    {
        MDIChild newMDIChild = new MDIChild( );
        newMDIChild.MdiParent = this;
        newMDIChild.Show( );
    }

    private void mnuFileOpen_Click(object sender, EventArgs e)
    {
        MessageBox.Show ("You clicked File Open", "Menu Event Tester",
            MessageBoxButtons.OK, MessageBoxIcon.Asterisk);
    }

    private void mnuFileClose_Click(object sender, EventArgs e)
    {
        MessageBox.Show ("You clicked File Close", "Menu Event Tester",
            MessageBoxButtons.OK, MessageBoxIcon.Asterisk);

    }
    private void Option_Click(object sender, EventArgs e)
    {
        MenuItem item = sender as MenuItem;

        if ( item != null )
        {
            item.Checked = ! item.Checked;
        }
    }

    private void RadioOption_Click(object sender, EventArgs e)
    {
        MenuItem item = sender as MenuItem;

        if ( item != null )
        {
            Menu parent = item.Parent;
            foreach ( MenuItem mi in parent.MenuItems )
                mi.Checked = false;
            item.Checked = true;
        }
    }

    private void mnuEditCopy_Click(object sender, EventArgs e)
    {
        MessageBox.Show ("You clicked Edit Copy", "Menu Event Tester",
```

Example 18-1. Creating menus by hand (HandCraftedMenusCS) (continued)

```csharp
        MessageBoxButtons.OK, MessageBoxIcon.Asterisk);
    }

    private void mnuEditPaste_Click(object sender, EventArgs e)
    {
        MessageBox.Show ("You clicked Edit Paste", "Menu Event Tester",
            MessageBoxButtons.OK, MessageBoxIcon.Asterisk);
    }

    private void mnuFileSave_Click(object sender, EventArgs e)
    {
        MessageBox.Show ("You clicked Save", "Menu Event Tester",
            MessageBoxButtons.OK, MessageBoxIcon.Asterisk);
    }

    private void mnuFileSaveAs_Click(object sender, EventArgs e)
    {
        MessageBox.Show ("You clicked SaveAs", "Menu Event Tester",
            MessageBoxButtons.OK, MessageBoxIcon.Asterisk);
    }
  }
}
```

Example 18-2. Creating menus by hand (HandCraftedMenusVB)

```vb
Imports System
Imports System.Windows.Forms

Namespace MenuByHand
    Public Class MenuForm
        Inherits Form

        ' run the app
        Public Shared Sub Main()
            Application.Run(New MenuForm())
        End Sub 'Main


        ' constructor - create the menu
        Public Sub New()
            ' build the menu inside out
            Dim mnuNew As New MenuItem()
            ' short cut
            mnuNew.Shortcut = Shortcut.CtrlN
            ' accelerator
            mnuNew.Text = "&New"
            ' event handler
            AddHandler mnuNew.Click, AddressOf Me.mnuNew_Click


            ' alternative, pass text and event handler into constructor
            Dim mnuFileOpen As New MenuItem( _
```

Example 18-2. Creating menus by hand (HandCraftedMenusVB) (continued)

VB

```
                    "&Open", New EventHandler(AddressOf Me.mnuFileOpen_Click))
            mnuFileOpen.Shortcut = Shortcut.CtrlO

            ' alternative, pass text, event handler and short cut
            Dim mnuFileClose As New MenuItem( _
                "&Close", New EventHandler( _
                    AddressOf Me.mnuFileClose_Click), Shortcut.CtrlC)


            ' remaining items use default constructor and add
            ' properties individually
            Dim mnuFileSave As New MenuItem( )
            mnuFileSave.Text = "Save"
            AddHandler mnuFileSave.Click, AddressOf Me.mnuFileSave_Click

            Dim mnuFileSaveAs As New MenuItem( )
            mnuFileSaveAs.Text = "Save&As"
            AddHandler mnuFileSaveAs.Click, _
                AddressOf Me.mnuFileSaveAs_Click


            ' Create the file menu and add the array
            ' of sub-menu items to its
            ' MenuItems collection
            Dim mnuFile As New MenuItem( )
            mnuFile.Text = "File"
            mnuFile.MenuItems.AddRange( _
                New MenuItem( ) _
                {  mnuNew, mnuFileOpen, mnuFileClose, _
                    mnuFileSave, mnuFileSaveAs } )


            ' create submenus for Edit menu
            Dim mnuEditCopy As New MenuItem( )
            mnuEditCopy.Text = "&Copy"
            AddHandler mnuEditCopy.Click, AddressOf Me.mnuEditCopy_Click

            Dim mnuEditPaste As New MenuItem( )
            mnuEditPaste.Text = "Paste"
            AddHandler mnuEditPaste.Click, AddressOf Me.mnuEditPaste_Click

            ' Add the edit menu
            Dim mnuEdit As New MenuItem( )
            mnuEdit.Text = "Edit"
            mnuEdit.MenuItems.AddRange( _
                New MenuItem( ) _
                { mnuEditCopy, mnuEditPaste } )

            ' options sub-menu
            Dim mnuOption1 As New MenuItem( )
            mnuOption1.Text = "Option1"
            AddHandler mnuOption1.Click, AddressOf Me.Option_Click
```

Example 18-2. Creating menus by hand (HandCraftedMenusVB) (continued)

```
Dim mnuOption2 As New MenuItem( )
mnuOption2.Text = "Option2"
AddHandler mnuOption2.Click, AddressOf Me.Option_Click


Dim mnuOption3 As New MenuItem( )
mnuOption3.Text = "Option3"
AddHandler mnuOption3.Click, AddressOf Me.Option_Click

' Add the options menu
Dim mnuOptions As New MenuItem( )
mnuOptions.Text = "Options"
mnuOptions.MenuItems.AddRange( _
   New MenuItem( ) _
   { mnuOption1, mnuOption2, mnuOption3 } )


' radio options sub-menu
Dim mnuROption1 As New MenuItem( )
mnuROption1.Text = "Radio Option1"
mnuROption1.RadioCheck = True
AddHandler mnuROption1.Click, AddressOf Me.RadioOption_Click


Dim mnuROption2 As New MenuItem( )
mnuROption2.Text = "Radio Option2"
mnuROption2.RadioCheck = True
AddHandler mnuROption2.Click, AddressOf Me.RadioOption_Click


Dim mnuROption3 As New MenuItem( )
mnuROption3.Text = "Radio Option3"
mnuROption3.RadioCheck = True
AddHandler mnuROption3.Click, AddressOf Me.RadioOption_Click


' Add the radio options menu
Dim mnuRadioOptions As New MenuItem( )
mnuRadioOptions.Text = "Radio Options"

mnuRadioOptions.MenuItems.AddRange( _
   New MenuItem( ) _
   { mnuROption1, mnuROption2, mnuROption3 } )

' Add the window menu
Dim mnuWindow As New MenuItem( )
mnuWindow.MdiList = True
mnuWindow.Text = "&Window"

' create an instance of MainMenu and add the sub-menus
Dim mainMenu1 As New MainMenu( _
    New MenuItem( ) _
```

Example 18-2. Creating menus by hand (HandCraftedMenusVB) (continued)

`VB`

```
                {mnuFile, mnuEdit, mnuOptions, mnuRadioOptions, mnuWindow} )

      ' set the menu property of the form to the menu
      ' you just created
      Menu = mainMenu1

      ' set other form properties
      [Text] = "Menu Form Demonstration (by hand)"
      AutoScaleBaseSize = New System.Drawing.Size(5, 13)
      ClientSize = New System.Drawing.Size(292, 186)
      IsMdiContainer = true
   End Sub 'New

   ' implement the event handlers for the menus
   Private Sub mnuNew_Click( _
     ByVal sender As Object, ByVal e As EventArgs)
      Dim newMDIChild As New MDIChild( )
      newMDIChild.MdiParent = Me
      newMDIChild.Show( )
   End Sub 'mnuNew_Click

   Private Sub mnuFileOpen_Click( _
      ByVal sender As Object, ByVal e As EventArgs)
      MessageBox.Show("You clicked File Open", _
      "Menu Event Tester", _
      MessageBoxButtons.OK, _
      MessageBoxIcon.Asterisk)
   End Sub 'mnuFileOpen_Click

   Private Sub mnuFileClose_Click( _
     ByVal sender As Object, ByVal e As EventArgs)
      MessageBox.Show( _
        "You clicked File Close", _
        "Menu Event Tester", _
        MessageBoxButtons.OK, _
        MessageBoxIcon.Asterisk)
   End Sub 'mnuFileClose_Click

   Private Sub Option_Click( _
      ByVal sender As Object, ByVal e As EventArgs)
      Dim item As MenuItem = sender
      If Not (item Is Nothing) Then
          item.Checked = Not item.Checked
      End If
   End Sub 'Option_Click

   Private Sub RadioOption_Click( _
     ByVal sender As Object, ByVal e As EventArgs)

      Dim item As MenuItem = sender

      If Not (item Is Nothing) Then
```

Example 18-2. Creating menus by hand (HandCraftedMenusVB) (continued)

```vb
            Dim parent As Menu = item.Parent
                Dim mi As MenuItem
                For Each mi In parent.MenuItems
                    mi.Checked = False
                Next mi
                item.Checked = True
            End If
    End Sub 'RadioOption_Click

    Private Sub mnuEditCopy_Click( _
      ByVal sender As Object, ByVal e As EventArgs)
        MessageBox.Show( _
            "You clicked Edit Copy", _
            "Menu Event Tester", _
            MessageBoxButtons.OK, _
            MessageBoxIcon.Asterisk)
    End Sub 'mnuEditCopy_Click

    Private Sub mnuEditPaste_Click( _
      ByVal sender As Object, ByVal e As EventArgs)
        MessageBox.Show( _
            "You clicked Edit Paste", _
            "Menu Event Tester", _
            MessageBoxButtons.OK, _
            MessageBoxIcon.Asterisk)
    End Sub 'mnuEditPaste_Click

    Private Sub mnuFileSave_Click( _
        ByVal sender As Object, ByVal e As EventArgs)
        MessageBox.Show( _
            "You clicked Save", _
            "Menu Event Tester", _
            MessageBoxButtons.OK, _
            MessageBoxIcon.Asterisk)
    End Sub 'mnuFileSave_Click

    Private Sub mnuFileSaveAs_Click( _
        ByVal sender As Object, ByVal e As EventArgs)
        MessageBox.Show( _
            "You clicked SaveAs", _
            "Menu Event Tester", _
            MessageBoxButtons.OK, _
            MessageBoxIcon.Asterisk)
    End Sub 'mnuFileSaveAs_Click
  End Class 'MenuForm
End Namespace 'MenuByHand
```

Analysis

In this hand-coded example, you begin by creating your form and setting up your Main( ) method to start the application.

```csharp
namespace MenuByHand
{
    public class MenuForm : Form
    {
        // run the app
        public static void Main( )
        {
            Application.Run(new MenuForm( ));
        }
```

```vbnet
Namespace MenuByHand
    Public Class MenuForm
        Inherits Form

        ' run the app
        Public Shared Sub Main( )
            Application.Run(New MenuForm( ))
        End Sub 'Main
```

Adding imports statements in C# and using statements in VB.NET allows you to avoid prepending object references with System or System.Windows.Forms. You will notice, however, that Visual Studio .NET ignores this convenience.

This code is immediately followed by the constructor, in which you will create your menus and submenus. The process is somewhat inside-out. First you create the submenu MenuItems (e.g., New, Open, Close, Save, or SaveAs) and set their properties. You then create the outer MenuItem (File) and add the submenu items to the outer menu item's collection of MenuItems collection. Continue adding inner menus to outer menus until you reach the MainMenu, which you then add to the form.

There are a number of ways to create each MenuItem. The simplest is to use the default constructor:

```csharp
MenuItem mnuNew = new MenuItem( );
```

```vbnet
Dim mnuNew As New MenuItem( )
```

You can then set the various properties of this MenuItem, such as its shortcut key, its text, and its event handler:

```csharp
mnuNew.Shortcut = Shortcut.CtrlN;
mnuNew.Text = "&New";
mnuNew.Click += new EventHandler(this.mnuNew_Click);
```

```vbnet
mnuNew.Shortcut = Shortcut.CtrlN
mnuNew.Text = "&New"
AddHandler mnuNew.Click, AddressOf Me.mnuNew_Click
```

An alternative is to use one of the overloaded constructors, such as the constructor that takes the text and event handler as arguments:

```C#
MenuItem mnuFileOpen =
    new MenuItem("&Open",
    new EventHandler(this.mnuFileOpen_Click));
```

You are then free to add more properties to that MenuItem, as needed:

```C#
mnuFileOpen.Shortcut = Shortcut.CtrlO;
```

```VB
Dim mnuFileOpen As New MenuItem( _
    "&Open", New EventHandler(AddressOf Me.mnuFileOpen_Click))

mnuFileOpen.Shortcut = Shortcut.CtrlO
```

As a third alternative, you can pass the text, the event handler, and the shortcut all at one go:

```C#
MenuItem mnuFileClose=
    new MenuItem(
    "&Close",
    new EventHandler(this.mnuFileClose_Click),
    Shortcut.CtrlC);
```

```VB
Dim mnuFileClose As New MenuItem( _
    "&Close", New EventHandler( _
        AddressOf Me.mnuFileClose_Click), Shortcut.CtrlC)
```

In any case, once all the submenu items are added, you can add subitems to the menu item. Your first step is to create the File menu item.

```C#
MenuItem mnuFile = new MenuItem( );
mnuFile.Text = "File";
```

```VB
Dim mnuFile As New MenuItem( )
mnuFile.Text = "File"
```

You are then ready to create an array of the submenus and add it to the File menu's MenuItems collection:

```C#
MenuItem[ ] theSubMenus = new MenuItem[ ]
    { mnuNew, mnuFileOpen, mnuFileClose, mnuFileSave, mnuFileSaveAs };
mnuFile.MenuItems.AddRange ( theSubMenus );
```

```VB
Dim theSubMenus As MenuItem( ) = _
    {mnuNew, mnuFileOpen, mnuFileClose, mnuFileSave, mnuFileSaveAs}

mnuFile.MenuItems.AddRange(theSubMenus)
```

Your next step is to create the submenus for the Edit menu, and then add the submenus to the Edit menus MenuItems collection. You can combine the steps of creating the array and adding it to the collection into a single statement, if you prefer:

C#
```csharp
mnuEdit.MenuItems.AddRange(new MenuItem[ ] {mnuEditCopy, mnuEditPaste});
```

VB
```vb
mnuEdit.MenuItems.AddRange(New MenuItem( ) {mnuEditCopy, mnuEditPaste})
```

Creating the options menu

Options menus require special attention because each option wants to share a common event handler. In C#, you accomplish this by creating an EventHandler for the specific event handler method, and then you assign that event handler to the event for each of the three MenuItems:

C#
```csharp
EventHandler optionHandler = new EventHandler(this.Option_Click);

MenuItem mnuOption1 =  new MenuItem( );
mnuOption1.Text = "Option1";
mnuOption1.Click += optionHandler;

MenuItem mnuOption2 =  new MenuItem( );
mnuOption2.Text = "Option2";
mnuOption2.Click += optionHandler;

MenuItem mnuOption3 =  new MenuItem( );
mnuOption3.Text = "Option3";
mnuOption3.Click += optionHandler;
```

The syntax is a bit different in VB.NET, where you use the AddHandler command for each MenuItem to set the event handler:

VB
```vb
Dim mnuOption1 As New MenuItem( )
mnuOption1.Text = "Option1"
AddHandler mnuOption1.Click, AddressOf Me.Option_Click

Dim mnuOption2 As New MenuItem( )
mnuOption2.Text = "Option2"
AddHandler mnuOption2.Click, AddressOf Me.Option_Click

Dim mnuOption3 As New MenuItem( )
mnuOption3.Text = "Option3"
AddHandler mnuOption3.Click, AddressOf Me.Option_Click
```

Creating the RadioButton options is identical to creating the checkmark options, except that you must remember to set the RadioCheck property to true:

C#
```csharp
MenuItem mnuROption1 =  new MenuItem( );
mnuROption1.Text = "Radio Option1";
mnuROption1.RadioCheck = true;
mnuROption1.Click += radioOptionHandler;
```

```vb
Dim mnuROption1 As New MenuItem( )
mnuROption1.Text = "Radio Option1"
mnuROption1.RadioCheck = True
AddHandler mnuROption1.Click, AddressOf Me.RadioOption_Click
```

The Window MenuItem must have its MdiList property set to true so it can manage the MDI menus:

```csharp
MenuItem mnuWindow= new MenuItem( );
mnuWindow.MdiList = true;
mnuWindow.Text = "&Window";
```

```vb
Dim mnuWindow As New MenuItem( )
mnuWindow.MdiList = True
mnuWindow.Text = "&Window"
```

You are now ready to create the instance of MainMenu: mainMenu1. There are two constructors: the default (that takes no arguments) and the one you'll use that takes an array of MenuItem objects. You'll pass in an array that consists of the topmost menu items.

```csharp
MenuItem[ ] theTopMenus = new MenuItem[ ]
    {mnuFile, mnuEdit, mnuOptions, mnuRadioOptions, mnuWindow};

MainMenu mainMenu1 = new MainMenu( theTopMenus );
```

```vb
Dim theTopMenus As MenuItem( ) = _
    {mnuFile, mnuEdit, mnuOptions, mnuRadioOptions, mnuWindow}

Dim mainMenu1 As New MainMenu(theTopMenus)
```

When this is done, you are ready to attach the newly created MainMenu to the form itself by setting the Menu property of the form.

```csharp
Menu = mainMenu1;
```

While you are at it, you can set the Text property and the scale of the form, and set the ClientSize property:

```csharp
Text = "Menu Form Demonstration (by hand)";
AutoScaleBaseSize = new System.Drawing.Size(5, 13);
ClientSize = new System.Drawing.Size(292, 186);
```

Finally, you will set the IsMdiContainer property of the form to true to make the form an MDI container (required by your FileNew event handler):

```csharp
IsMdiContainer = true;
```

All you need to do now is implement the various event handlers. The first is the New submenu on the File menu, in which you will create a new instance of MDIChild(). This is a class you must create yourself. It consists of nothing but a form with a rich text control on it. The complete source code is shown in Example 18-3 for C# and Example 18-4 for VB.NET.

Example 18-3. MDI Child (HandCraftedMenusCS—MDIChild.cs)

```csharp
using System;
using System.Windows.Forms;

namespace MenuByHand
{
    public class MDIChild : Form
    {
        private RichTextBox richTextBox1;

        public MDIChild( )
        {
            richTextBox1 = new RichTextBox( );
            this.SuspendLayout( );

            // set the rich text box properties
            this.richTextBox1.Name = "richTextBox1";
            this.richTextBox1.Size = new System.Drawing.Size(296, 264);
            this.richTextBox1.TabIndex = 0;
            this.richTextBox1.Text = "richTextBox1";

            // set the form properties
            this.AutoScaleBaseSize = new System.Drawing.Size(5, 13);
            this.ClientSize = new System.Drawing.Size(292, 266);
            this.Controls.AddRange(new Control[ ] {this.richTextBox1});
            this.Name = "MDIChild";
            this.Text = "MDIChild";
            this.ResumeLayout(false);
        }

    }
}
```

Example 18-4. MDI Child (HandCraftedMenusVB—MDIChild.vb)

```vbnet
Imports System
Imports System.Windows.Forms

Namespace MenuByHand

    Public Class MDIChild : Inherits Form
        Private richTextBox1 As RichTextBox

        Public Sub New( )
            richTextBox1 = New RichTextBox( )
            Me.SuspendLayout( )

            ' set the rich text box properties
            Me.richTextBox1.Name = "richTextBox1"
            Me.richTextBox1.Size = New System.Drawing.Size(296, 264)
            Me.richTextBox1.TabIndex = 0
            Me.richTextBox1.Text = "richTextBox1"
```

Example 18-4. MDI Child (HandCraftedMenusVB—MDIChild.vb) (continued)

`VB`
```
            ' set the form properties
            Me.AutoScaleBaseSize = New System.Drawing.Size(5, 13)
            Me.ClientSize = New System.Drawing.Size(292, 266)
            Me.Controls.AddRange(New Control( ) {Me.richTextBox1})
            Me.Name = "MDIChild"
            Me.Text = "MDIChild"
            Me.ResumeLayout(False)
        End Sub 'New
    End Class 'MDIChild
End Namespace 'MenuByHand
```

Returning to Examples 18-1 and 18-2, the event handler for the New menu choice on the File menu creates an instance of this MDIChild class, sets its parent to the current form, and shows the window.

`C#`
```
    private void mnuNew_Click(object sender, System.EventArgs e)
    {
        MDIChild newMDIChild = new MDIChild( );
        newMDIChild.MdiParent = this;
        newMDIChild.Show( );
    }
```

`VB`
```
    Private Sub mnuNew_Click( _
        ByVal sender As Object, ByVal e As System.EventArgs)
        Dim newMDIChild As New MDIChild( )
        newMDIChild.MdiParent = Me
        newMDIChild.Show( )
    End Sub 'mnuNew_Click
```

The File Open and File Close menu choices open a MessageBox indicating the action you've taken. For example, the event handler for File Open calls the Show method of MessageBox, passing in the message to be displayed ("You clicked File Open"), the title of the MessageBox ("MenuEventTester"), the button to display (using the MessageBoxButtons enumeration), and the icon to display (using the MessageBox-Icon enumeration):

`C#`
```
    private void mnuFileOpen_Click(object sender, EventArgs e)
    {
        MessageBox.Show ("You clicked File Open", "Menu Event Tester",
            MessageBoxButtons.OK, MessageBoxIcon.Asterisk);
    }
```

`VB`
```
    Private Sub mnuFileOpen_Click( _
        ByVal sender As Object, ByVal e As EventArgs)
        MessageBox.Show("You clicked File Open", _
        "Menu Event Tester", _
        MessageBoxButtons.OK, _
        MessageBoxIcon.Asterisk)
    End Sub 'mnuFileOpen_Click
```

The options menu item event handler

You've already seen how to wire up the event handler for the Options menu. The implementation is straightforward:

```csharp
private void Option_Click(object sender, EventArgs e)
{
    MenuItem item = sender as MenuItem;

    if ( item != null )
    {
        item.Checked = ! item.Checked;
    }
}
```

```vbnet
Private Sub Option_Click(sender As Object, e As EventArgs)
    Dim item As MenuItem = sender
    If Not (item Is Nothing) Then
        item.Checked = Not item.Checked
    End If
End Sub 'Option_Click
```

For this method, cast the sender to be of type MenuItem, and assuming the cast is successful, toggle the value of the Checked property.

The RadioButton's Click handler is different. Here you will take two actions. First, set all the RadioButtons to unchecked, and then set the chosen one to checked.

This process can get a bit confusing, so let's take it step by step. The sender argument to the event handler is the MenuItem that was clicked on by the user. Begin by casting that item to type MenuItem:

```csharp
private void RadioOption_Click(object sender, EventArgs e)
{
    MenuItem item = sender as MenuItem;
```

This MenuItem is part of a submenu, and you want to set all the RadioButtons in this submenu to unchecked. This submenu can be retrieved as the MenuItems property of the current item's parent menu. Thus, to uncheck all these RadioButtons, you need that parent menu item:

```csharp
Menu parent = item.Parent;
```

This code gets the parent menu to which the sender belongs. That parent menu has a collection, MenuItems, in which all the RadioButton menu items appear. You can iterate through that collection, setting all the RadioButtons to unchecked:

```csharp
foreach ( MenuItem mi in parent.MenuItems )
    mi.Checked = false;
```

```vbnet
For Each mi In parent.MenuItems
    mi.Checked = False
Next mi
```

You are now ready for the second step: setting the RadioButton menu item that the user clicked on to true. You return to the variable item (which you'll remember you cast to type MenuItem from the sender argument to the event handler) and set its Checked property to true:

C#

```
item.Checked = true;
```

Merging Menus

MDI Child windows can have menus just like any other form. When you create a menu on an MDI Child from within an MDI Container (as you do in the previous example with the modified code that runs when you choose File New), the menu of the child window is merged with the parent menu by default.

Two properties control how the items in the two menus are merged: MergeOrder and MergeType. The MergeOrder sets the relative order of the items in the two menus. If two items have the same MergeOrder, then the outcome of the merge is determined by the MergeType property of the merged menu.

The MergeType is an enumeration, as shown in Table 18-3.

Table 18-3. MenuMerge enumeration

Member	Description
Add	The default for MDI Children. The MenuItem is added to the collection of existing MenuItem objects.
MergeItems	All submenu items are merged with those of the existing MenuItem objects at the same position in a merged menu.
Remove	The MenuItem is not included in the merged menu.
Replace	The MenuItem replaces an existing MenuItem at the same position.

In the following example, you'll modify the MDIChild class you created in Examples 18-3 and 18-4 to add a menu, as shown in Figure 18-11. Notice that the MergeOrder is set to 1, as shown circled in the properties window.

The MDIChild class is unchanged, except the event handler:

C#

```
private void Option_Click(object sender, System.EventArgs e)
{
    MenuItem item = sender as MenuItem;

    if ( item != null )
    {
        item.Checked = ! item.Checked;
    }
}
```

VB

```
Private Sub Option_Click( _
    ByVal sender As System.Object, _
    ByVal e As System.EventArgs) _
```

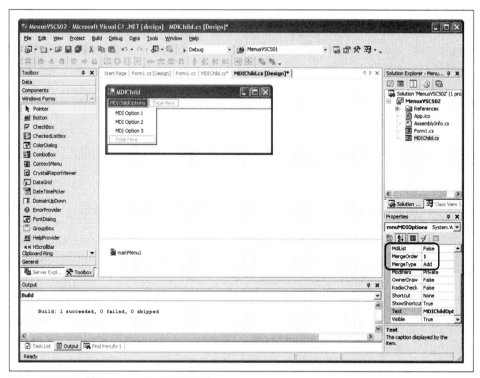

Figure 18-11. Adding a menu to MDIChild

```
    Handles mnuMDIOption1.Click, mnuMDIOption2.Click, mnuMDIOption3.Click
        Dim item As MenuItem = CType(sender, MenuItem)
        item.Checked = Not item.Checked
    End Sub
```

With this in place, return to Form1 and ensure that all items on the menu have a MergeOrder of 0 *except* for Window, which you'll give a MergeOrder of 99. This will force the new MDIChild menu to merge between the Radio Options and the Window option. You can assign each item in the menu its own MergeOrder to gain even finer control of the outcome. When you run the application and open an MDI Child (e.g., click on File → New), the MDI Child's merged menu is inserted just before the Window Menu item, as shown in Figure 18-12.

If you set MDI Option 2 in this MDI Child window, and then create a second child, you'll find that the MDIChildOption menu reflects the state of the *current* MDI Child Windows. As you change what is current (using the Window menu choice), the options will reflect the current window's state.

Merging menus by hand

Under some exceptional circumstances, you may want to manually merge two or more menus. Do so by calling the MenuMerge method on the menu you are merging

---

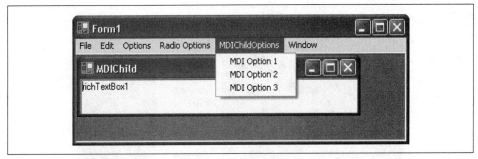

Figure 18-12. The MDIChild menu inserted

into and passing the menu you wish to merge. The same rules of MergeOrder and MergeType apply.

For an artificial example, return to the main form and add two menus: Menu1 and Menu2. In Menu1, add five items, as shown in Table 18-4.

Table 18-4. Items to add to Menu1

Text	Name	Merge order
Menu 1.1	mnuMenu11	1
Menu 1.2	mnuMenu12	2
Menu 1.3	mnuMenu13	3
Menu 1.4	mnuMenu14	4
Merge!	mnuMerge	99

For Menu2, add four items, as shown in Table 18-5.

Table 18-5. Items to add to Menu2

Text	Name	Merge order	MergeType
Menu 2.1	mnuMenu21	1	Add
Menu2.2	mnuMenu22	2	Replace
Menu2.3	mnuMenu23	3	Remove
Menu2.4	mnuMenu24	5	Add

To see the results of these various settings, you must press Merge (to merge the menus) and then press it again (to merge a second time). It takes a moment to sort through the results, which are illustrated in Figure 18-13.

Notice that Menu 2.1 was added twice, just as you'd expect because it was set to Add. Menu 2.2 is added only once because it was set to replace, so when it found 2.2 on the menu, it replaced the original. Menu 2.3 doesn't appear at all! Its MergeType was set to Remove, so it does not appear in the merged menu. Finally, Menu 2.4 appears twice because it had no conflict (its MergeOrder was set to 5 and no other item had that MergeOrder).

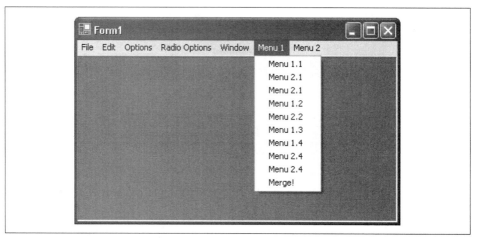

Figure 18-13. Merged twice

Once again, the code is unchanged, except to add the event handler for the Merge! menu command.

Remember to add the event handler either by editing the Initialize-Component method directly, or, more easily, by double-clicking on the Merge! menu item in Visual Studio .NET.

C#

```csharp
private void mnuMerge_Click(object sender, System.EventArgs e)
{
    MenuItem item = sender as MenuItem;
    if ( item != null )
    {
        item.Parent.MergeMenu(mnuMenu2);

    }
}
```

VB

```vb
Private Sub mnuMerge_Click(ByVal sender As System.Object, _
                    ByVal e As System.EventArgs)
    Dim item As MenuItem = CType(sender, MenuItem)
    item.Parent.MergeMenu(mnuMenu2)
End Sub
```

Because the changes are small, and because all the changes are shown in the text, the complete listing for this example is provided for download, but not shown here.

OwnerDraw Menus

Until now, all menus have been simple text. There are times, however, when you'd like to draw your own menu items, perhaps to use fancy graphics. This task is simple, and even with very little graphical talent (and it is hard to have less than I do), you can create snazzy menus, as shown in Figure 18-14.

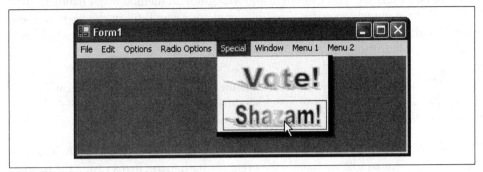

Figure 18-14. OwnerDraw menu

Here are the (incredibly easy) steps for creating this menu:

1. Create the bitmaps (this is the hard part).
2. Set the OwnerDraw property for your OwnerDraw menu items to true.
3. Implement two event handlers for each OwnerDraw MenuItem: DrawItem and MeasureItem.

That's it! Let's take it step by step.

Create the bitmaps

We created these two bitmaps by opening Microsoft Word, using WordArt to make the picture. We then captured the picture to a bitmap using one of our favorite desktop utilities: Hypersnap DX.[*] We saved these files to our temp directory to make it easy to find and load them.

You'll see later in this chapter (in the section "Toolbars") that Visual Studio .NET comes complete with dozens of bitmaps you can use. Also, you can always create your own, with programs as simple as Paint or as complex as Photoshop.

Set the OwnerDraw property

The second step is to create a new menu (in this case marked Special) with two submenu items (Vote and Shazam). Enter them like any other menu item (normal text—nothing special), but set their OwnerDraw property to true.

---

[*] Found at *http://www.hypersnap.com*.

To make things interesting, you may drag the new menu along the menu bar to any position you like. In Figure 18-14, it has been dragged to the left of the Windows menu.

Click on the lightening bolt (if you are doing this in C#) for each menu item (Vote and Shazam), and set their DrawItem and MeasureItem method event handlers. You may call these methods anything you like, and soon you'll fill in the body of these event handlers. While you're at it, set the Click event handler as well, (OnODDraw_Click).

For consistency, you might call the event handler for the DrawItem event "OnDrawItem" and the event handler for the MeasureItem method "OnMeasureItem."

VB.NET programmers create these event handlers in the drop-down menu, and then modify the event handler to handle the event for both menu items (using the handles keyword). For example:

```
Private Sub mnuODVote_DrawItem( _
ByVal sender As Object, _
ByVal e As System.Windows.Forms.DrawItemEventArgs) _
    Handles mnuODVote.DrawItem, mnuODShazam.DrawItem
```

In either case, you end up with three event handlers (OnDrawItem, OnMeasure-Item, and OnODDraw_Click), which you must now implement.

Implement the event handlers

Making these MenuItems OwnerDraw: MeasureItem and DrawItem requires only two event handlers. The third, Click, allows you to respond to the menu items (a useful idea), though this one is no different from any other MenuItem event handler.

MeasureItem is called before the owner draw menu item is displayed. The event handler receives a MeasureItemEventArgs object, which you can use to set the Item-Height and ItemWidth:

```
private void OnMeasureItem(
    object sender, System.Windows.Forms.MeasureItemEventArgs e)
{
    Image img = Image.FromFile(files[e.Index]);
    e.ItemHeight = img.Height;
    e.ItemWidth = img.Width;
}
```

```
Private Sub mnuODVote_MeasureItem( _
    ByVal sender As Object, _
    ByVal e As System.Windows.Forms.MeasureItemEventArgs) _
```

```vb
        Handles mnuODVote.MeasureItem, mnuODShazam.MeasureItem

        Dim img As Image
        img = Image.FromFile(files(e.Index))
        e.ItemHeight = img.Height
        e.ItemWidth = img.Width

    End Sub
```

All you are doing is getting the image from the file and setting the Measure-ItemEventArgs ItemHeight and ItemWidth to the images Height and Width properties. Easy as pie.

The call to Image.FromFile calls a static method of the Image class. You'll pass in an array of strings. To make this work, return to the top of the class and define the string array files as a member variable:

```csharp
    private string[ ] files = { @"c:\temp\vote.bmp", @"c:\temp\shazam.bmp" };
```

```vb
    Private files( ) As String = {"c:\temp\vote.bmp", "c:\temp\shazam.bmp"}
```

> The tricky thing about MeasureItem is that you are not guaranteed that your images will be drawn with the size you indicate. The .NET framework gathers information about how much room you need, but all owner-drawn menu items get the same size rectangle.

The second required event handler is DrawItem. This is raised when it is time to draw the item. Here, *you* are responsible for drawing your MenuItem. This event handler receives a DrawItemEventArgs object. A few of its most useful properties are shown in Table 18-6.

Table 18-6. DrawItemEventArgs properties

Property	Type	Description
BackColor	Color	Read only. Gets the background color for the item being drawn.
Bounds	Rectangle	Read only. The bounding rectangle to be drawn.
Font	Font	Read only. The font of the item being drawn.
ForeColor	Color	Read only. The foreground color of item being drawn.
Graphics	Graphics	Read only. The graphics surface to draw on.

Since you use are using a bitmap for the menu item, the code is fairly straightforward. Start by getting the bitmap from the file, as you did in OnMeasureItem:

```csharp
    private void OnDrawItem(object sender, System.Windows.Forms.DrawItemEventArgs e)
    {
        Image img = Image.FromFile(files[e.Index]);
```

```
VB    Dim img As Image
      img = Image.FromFile(files(e.Index))
```

Next, create a rectangle based on the property Bounds.rectangle of the Draw-
ItemEventArgs parameter:

```
C#    Rectangle r = e.Bounds;
```

```
VB    Dim r As Rectangle
      r = e.Bounds
```

Create a pen to draw the rectangle, and deflate the rectangle by six pixels in both
width and height to leave room for the border. Draw the rectangle, and then draw
the bitmap image:

```
C#    Pen pen = new Pen(e.BackColor,2);
      r.Inflate(-6,-6);
      e.Graphics.DrawRectangle(pen,r);
      e.Graphics.DrawImage(img,r);
```

```
VB    Dim p As Pen = New Pen(e.BackColor, 2)
      r.Inflate(-6, -6)
      e.Graphics.DrawRectangle(p, r)
      e.Graphics.DrawImage(img, r)
```

All of the information you need is in either the bitmap itself or in the DrawItemEvent-
Args parameter.

Finally, you can implement the click event handler, much as you have other event
handlers:

```
C#    private void mnuODDraw_Click(object sender, System.EventArgs e)
      {
         MenuItem item = sender as MenuItem;
         if ( item != null )
         {
            string choice = item.Text;

            MessageBox.Show ("You clicked " + choice, "Menu Event Tester",
               MessageBoxButtons.OK, MessageBoxIcon.Asterisk);
         }
      }
```

```
VB    Private Sub mnuODDraw_Click( _
         ByVal sender As System.Object, _
         ByVal e As System.EventArgs) _
         Handles mnuODVote.Click, mnuODShazam.Click
         Dim item As MenuItem = CType(sender, MenuItem)
         Dim choice As String = item.Text
         MessageBox.Show("You clicked " & choice, _
            "Menu Event Tester", MessageBoxButtons.OK, _
            MessageBoxIcon.Asterisk)
      End Sub
```

Don't forget to add the event handlers for both menu items for all these events.

Because the changes are small and all the changes are shown in the text, the complete listing for this example is provided for download as OwnerDrawnCS/OwnerDrawnVB.

Context Menus

Modern Windows applications are filled with context menus. Whenever you need to accomplish a task or find out what is possible, right-click on a control, and up pops a context menu.

Creating these menus is simple. Begin by creating a menu as you would for your form (this time dragging a context menu), but rather than attaching it to the form, attach it to one or more controls. That's all there is to it.

In the next simplified example, create a form with four controls as listed in Table 18-7 and shown in Figure 18-15.

Table 18-7. Controls on the form

Control	Name	Text	Description
ListBox	listBox1	None	A simple, small listbox
Textbox	textBox1	None	A simple text box
Button	btnAdd	Add	
Button	btnDone	Done	

Drag a ContextMenu from the Toolbox onto the form. Name it mnuContext. Add four subitems below it, labeled Move Down, Move Up, Delete, and Duplicate. Name those menu items mnuDown, mnuUp, mnuDelete, and mnuDuplicate.

To associate this context menu with the listbox control, click on the listbox control, and click on the ContextMenu property in the Properties window. Set the property value to mnuContext. If you now run the form and right-click on the listbox, the context menu will pop up. None of the event handlers are in place yet, so nothing will happen, but you see where this is headed.

The user will enter text in the text box and then click on the Add button to add it to the listbox. This will invoke the event handler, as shown here (the VB.NET is nearly identical):

```
private void btnAdd_Click(object sender, System.EventArgs e)
{
    listBox1.Items.Add(textBox1.Text);
    textBox1.Text = "";
}
```

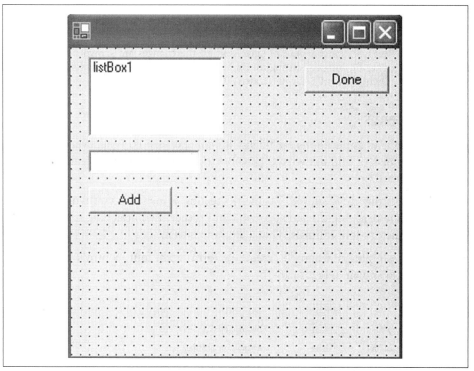

Figure 18-15. Simple form for the context menu

Once the listbox is populated, the user can right-click on the it to bring up a Context menu for manipulating the listbox, as shown in Figure 18-16.

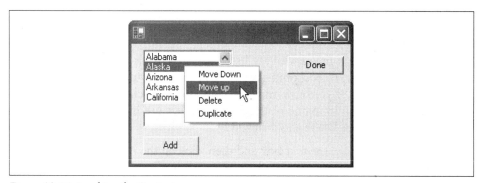

Figure 18-16. Invoking the Context menu

The implementation for the click event on a Context menu is accomplished much like the implementation for any other menu. You have a choice of creating separate event handlers for each menu item or combining them into a single event handler.

Enter the following code snippet to implement a single event handler for all context menus.

```csharp
private void ctxtMenuClick(object sender, System.EventArgs e)
{
    if ( listBox1.SelectedIndex != -1 )
    {
        MenuItem mi = (MenuItem) sender;
        MessageBox.Show("You asked to " + mi.Text + " on "
            + listBox1.SelectedItem,
            "Context Menu Tester",
            MessageBoxButtons.OK,
            MessageBoxIcon.Asterisk);
    }
    else
    {
        MessageBox.Show("Please select an item",
            "Context Menu Tester",
            MessageBoxButtons.OK,
            MessageBoxIcon.Asterisk);
    }
}
```

```vbnet
Private Sub mnuDown_Click( _
    ByVal sender As System.Object, _
    ByVal e As System.EventArgs) _
    Handles mnuDown.Click, mnuUp.Click, _
    mnuDelete.Click, mnuDuplicate.Click
    If Not listBox1.SelectedIndex = -1 Then
        Dim mi As MenuItem = CType(sender, MenuItem)
        MessageBox.Show("You asked to " & mi.Text + " on " + _
            listBox1.SelectedItem, "Context Menu Tester", _
            MessageBoxButtons.OK, MessageBoxIcon.Asterisk)
    Else
        MessageBox.Show("Please select an item", _
                        "Context Menu Tester", _
            MessageBoxButtons.OK, MessageBoxIcon.Asterisk)

    End If
End Sub
```

The complete listing for C# is shown in Example 18-5 and in Example 18-6 for VB.NET.

Example 18-5. Context menu in C# (ContextCS01)

```csharp
using System;
using System.Drawing;
using System.Collections;
using System.ComponentModel;
using System.Windows.Forms;
using System.Data;
```

Example 18-5. Context menu in C# (ContextCS01) (continued)

```csharp
namespace ContextCS01
{
    public class Form1 : System.Windows.Forms.Form
    {
        private System.Windows.Forms.Button btnDone;
        private System.Windows.Forms.TextBox textBox1;
        private System.Windows.Forms.Button btnAdd;
        private System.Windows.Forms.ListBox listBox1;
        private System.Windows.Forms.ContextMenu contextMenu1;
        private System.Windows.Forms.MenuItem mnuDown;
        private System.Windows.Forms.MenuItem mnuUp;
        private System.Windows.Forms.MenuItem mnuDelete;
        private System.Windows.Forms.MenuItem mnuDuplicate;

        private System.ComponentModel.Container components = null;

        public Form1( )
        {
            InitializeComponent( );
        }

        protected override void Dispose( bool disposing )
        {
            if( disposing )
            {
                if (components != null)
                {
                    components.Dispose( );
                }
            }
            base.Dispose( disposing );
        }

        #region Windows Form Designer generated code
        private void InitializeComponent( )
        {
            this.btnDone = new System.Windows.Forms.Button( );
            this.textBox1 = new System.Windows.Forms.TextBox( );
            this.btnAdd = new System.Windows.Forms.Button( );
            this.listBox1 = new System.Windows.Forms.ListBox( );
            this.contextMenu1 =
                        new System.Windows.Forms.ContextMenu( );
            this.mnuDown = new System.Windows.Forms.MenuItem( );
            this.mnuUp = new System.Windows.Forms.MenuItem( );
            this.mnuDelete = new System.Windows.Forms.MenuItem( );
            this.mnuDuplicate = new System.Windows.Forms.MenuItem( );
            this.SuspendLayout( );
            //
            // btnDone
            //
            this.btnDone.Location =
                        new System.Drawing.Point(208, 16);
```

Example 18-5. Context menu in C# (ContextCS01) (continued)

```
this.btnDone.Name = "btnDone";
this.btnDone.TabIndex = 3;
this.btnDone.Text = "Done";
this.btnDone.Click +=
            new System.EventHandler(this.btnDone_Click);
//
// textBox1
//
this.textBox1.Location =
              new System.Drawing.Point(16, 88);
this.textBox1.Name = "textBox1";
this.textBox1.TabIndex = 5;
this.textBox1.Text = "";
//
// btnAdd
//
this.btnAdd.Location = new System.Drawing.Point(16, 120);
this.btnAdd.Name = "btnAdd";
this.btnAdd.TabIndex = 6;
this.btnAdd.Text = "Add";
this.btnAdd.Click +=
            new System.EventHandler(this.btnAdd_Click);
//
// listBox1
//
this.listBox1.ContextMenu = this.contextMenu1;
this.listBox1.Location = new System.Drawing.Point(16, 8);
this.listBox1.Name = "listBox1";
this.listBox1.Size = new System.Drawing.Size(120, 69);
this.listBox1.TabIndex = 7;
//
// contextMenu1
//
this.contextMenu1.MenuItems.AddRange(
              new System.Windows.Forms.MenuItem[ ] {
    this.mnuDown,
    this.mnuUp,
    this.mnuDelete,
    this.mnuDuplicate});
//
// mnuDown
//
this.mnuDown.Index = 0;
this.mnuDown.Text = "Move Down";
this.mnuDown.Click +=
            new System.EventHandler(this.ctxtMenuClick);
//
// mnuUp
//
this.mnuUp.Index = 1;
this.mnuUp.Text = "Move up";
this.mnuUp.Click +=
            new System.EventHandler(this.ctxtMenuClick);
```

Example 18-5. Context menu in C# (ContextCS01) (continued)

C#

```
        //
        // mnuDelete
        //
        this.mnuDelete.Index = 2;
        this.mnuDelete.Text = "Delete";
        this.mnuDelete.Click +=
                    new System.EventHandler(this.ctxtMenuClick);
        //
        // mnuDuplicate
        //
        this.mnuDuplicate.Index = 3;
        this.mnuDuplicate.Text = "Duplicate";
        this.mnuDuplicate.Click +=
                    new System.EventHandler(this.ctxtMenuClick);
        //
        // Form1
        //
        this.AutoScaleBaseSize = new System.Drawing.Size(5, 13);
        this.ClientSize = new System.Drawing.Size(292, 266);
        this.Controls.AddRange(new System.Windows.Forms.Control[ ] {
            this.listBox1,
            this.btnAdd,
            this.textBox1,
            this.btnDone});
        this.Name = "Form1";
        this.ResumeLayout(false);

    }
    #endregion

    [STAThread]
    static void Main( )
    {
        Application.Run(new Form1( ));
    }

    private void btnDone_Click(object sender, System.EventArgs e)
    {
        Application.Exit( );
    }

    private void btnAdd_Click(object sender, System.EventArgs e)
    {
        listBox1.Items.Add(textBox1.Text);
        textBox1.Text = "";
    }

    private void ctxtMenuClick(object sender, System.EventArgs e)
    {
        if ( listBox1.SelectedIndex != -1 )
        {
            MenuItem mi = (MenuItem) sender;
```

Example 18-5. Context menu in C# (ContextCS01) (continued)

```csharp
            MessageBox.Show("You asked to " + mi.Text + " on "
                + listBox1.SelectedItem,
                "Context Menu Tester",
                MessageBoxButtons.OK,
                MessageBoxIcon.Asterisk);
        }
        else
        {
            MessageBox.Show("Please select an item",
                "Context Menu Tester",
                MessageBoxButtons.OK,
                MessageBoxIcon.Asterisk);

        }
    }
  }
}
```

Example 18-6. Context menu in VB.NET (ContextVB01)

```vbnet
Public Class Form1
    Inherits System.Windows.Forms.Form

#Region " Windows Form Designer generated code "

    Public Sub New()
        MyBase.New()
        InitializeComponent()
    End Sub

    Protected Overloads Overrides Sub Dispose(ByVal disposing As Boolean)
        If disposing Then
            If Not (components Is Nothing) Then
                components.Dispose()
            End If
        End If
        MyBase.Dispose(disposing)
    End Sub

    Private components As System.ComponentModel.IContainer

    Friend WithEvents listBox1 As System.Windows.Forms.ListBox
    Friend WithEvents btnAdd As System.Windows.Forms.Button
    Friend WithEvents textBox1 As System.Windows.Forms.TextBox
    Friend WithEvents btnDone As System.Windows.Forms.Button
    Friend WithEvents contextMenu1 As System.Windows.Forms.ContextMenu
    Friend WithEvents mnuDown As System.Windows.Forms.MenuItem
    Friend WithEvents mnuUp As System.Windows.Forms.MenuItem
    Friend WithEvents mnuDelete As System.Windows.Forms.MenuItem
    Friend WithEvents mnuDuplicate As System.Windows.Forms.MenuItem
    <System.Diagnostics.DebuggerStepThrough()> Private Sub InitializeComponent()
        Me.listBox1 = New System.Windows.Forms.ListBox()
```

Example 18-6. Context menu in VB.NET (ContextVB01) (continued)

```vb
        Me.btnAdd = New System.Windows.Forms.Button( )
        Me.textBox1 = New System.Windows.Forms.TextBox( )
        Me.btnDone = New System.Windows.Forms.Button( )
        Me.contextMenu1 = New System.Windows.Forms.ContextMenu( )
        Me.mnuDown = New System.Windows.Forms.MenuItem( )
        Me.mnuUp = New System.Windows.Forms.MenuItem( )
        Me.mnuDelete = New System.Windows.Forms.MenuItem( )
        Me.mnuDuplicate = New System.Windows.Forms.MenuItem( )
        Me.SuspendLayout( )
        '
        'listBox1
        '
        Me.listBox1.ContextMenu = Me.contextMenu1
        Me.listBox1.Location = New System.Drawing.Point(13, 8)
        Me.listBox1.Name = "listBox1"
        Me.listBox1.Size = New System.Drawing.Size(120, 69)
        Me.listBox1.TabIndex = 11
        '
        'btnAdd
        '
        Me.btnAdd.Location = New System.Drawing.Point(16, 120)
        Me.btnAdd.Name = "btnAdd"
        Me.btnAdd.TabIndex = 10
        Me.btnAdd.Text = "Add"
        '
        'textBox1
        '
        Me.textBox1.Location = New System.Drawing.Point(16, 88)
        Me.textBox1.Name = "textBox1"
        Me.textBox1.TabIndex = 9
        Me.textBox1.Text = ""
        '
        'btnDone
        '
        Me.btnDone.Location = New System.Drawing.Point(216, 8)
        Me.btnDone.Name = "btnDone"
        Me.btnDone.TabIndex = 8
        Me.btnDone.Text = "Done"
        '
        'contextMenu1
        '
        Me.contextMenu1.MenuItems.AddRange( _
          New System.Windows.Forms.MenuItem( ) _
             {Me.mnuDown, Me.mnuUp, Me.mnuDelete, Me.mnuDuplicate})
        '
        'mnuDown
        '
        Me.mnuDown.Index = 0
        Me.mnuDown.Text = "Move Down"
        '
        'mnuUp
        '
```

Example 18-6. Context menu in VB.NET (ContextVB01) (continued)

```
Me.mnuUp.Index = 1
Me.mnuUp.Text = "Move up"
'
'mnuDelete
'
Me.mnuDelete.Index = 2
Me.mnuDelete.Text = "Delete"
'
'mnuDuplicate
'
Me.mnuDuplicate.Index = 3
Me.mnuDuplicate.Text = "Duplicate"
'
'Form1
'
Me.AutoScaleBaseSize = New System.Drawing.Size(5, 13)
Me.ClientSize = New System.Drawing.Size(292, 266)
Me.Controls.AddRange(New System.Windows.Forms.Control( ) _
    {Me.listBox1, Me.btnAdd, Me.textBox1, Me.btnDone})
Me.Name = "Form1"
Me.Text = "Form1"
Me.ResumeLayout(False)

    End Sub

#End Region

    Private Sub btnAdd_Click( _
        ByVal sender As System.Object, ByVal e As System.EventArgs) _
        Handles btnAdd.Click
        listBox1.Items.Add(textBox1.Text)
        textBox1.Text = ""
    End Sub


    Private Sub mnuDown_Click( _
        ByVal sender As System.Object, _
        ByVal e As System.EventArgs) _
        Handles mnuDown.Click, mnuUp.Click, _
        mnuDelete.Click, mnuDuplicate.Click
        If Not listBox1.SelectedIndex = -1 Then
            Dim mi As MenuItem = CType(sender, MenuItem)
            MessageBox.Show("You asked to " & mi.Text + " on " + _
                listBox1.SelectedItem, "Context Menu Tester", _
                MessageBoxButtons.OK, MessageBoxIcon.Asterisk)
        Else
            MessageBox.Show("Please select an item", "Context Menu Tester", _
            MessageBoxButtons.OK, MessageBoxIcon.Asterisk)

        End If

    End Sub
End Class
```

Toolbars

Modern Windows applications come complete with extensive toolbars that serve as quick access to various menu choices. In the early days of Windows, these toolbars were nothing but buttons, but today they may include drop downs, combo boxes, and other advanced controls.

Visual Studio .NET makes creating toolbars for your application very easy. The steps are as follows:

1. Create an image list.
2. Create a toolbar and associate the image list with the toolbar.
3. Set up event handlers for the buttons on the toolbar.
4. Optionally, add additional controls programmatically.

To keep the example simple, start with the OwnerDraw menu you completed earlier and add a simple toolbar.

Creating the ImageList

Begin by dragging an ImageList onto the form. Notice that one of the properties, Images, is marked as a collection. Click on the ellipsis (...) to open the image list. This opens the Image Collection Editor. Click the Add button.

This step opens a dialog for identifying the image you want to add from images you may have stored on disk. Navigate to *Program Files\Microsoft Visual Studio .NET 2003\Common7\Graphics\Bitmaps*. In this directory, there are two directories with useful icons: *OffCtlBr* and *Assorted*. For this example, navigate into *OffCtlBr*, into *Large*, and then *Color*.

Choose the *New.bmp* file, which adds the bitmap to your collection. Notice that the righthand side of the dialog, with the bitmap properties, is read-only. Add a few more bitmaps, as shown in Figure 18-17.

Adding the toolbar

You now have a collection of bitmaps, and you are ready to create your toolbar. Drag a Toolbar control onto the form. It docks under your menu, although you will be free to change that later.

Navigate to the ImageList property of the new toolbar and set the property to the ImageList you've just created.

Click on the Buttons property of the Toolbar to open the ToolBarButton Collection Editor. Click on the Add button to add a button. In the Properties window of the ToolBarButton Collection Editor, set the Button name to btnNew, and set the ImageIndex to the index for the New file icon (index 0). Set the Text to New and set the ToolTip text to "Create new File." Finally, set the Tag property to New as well.

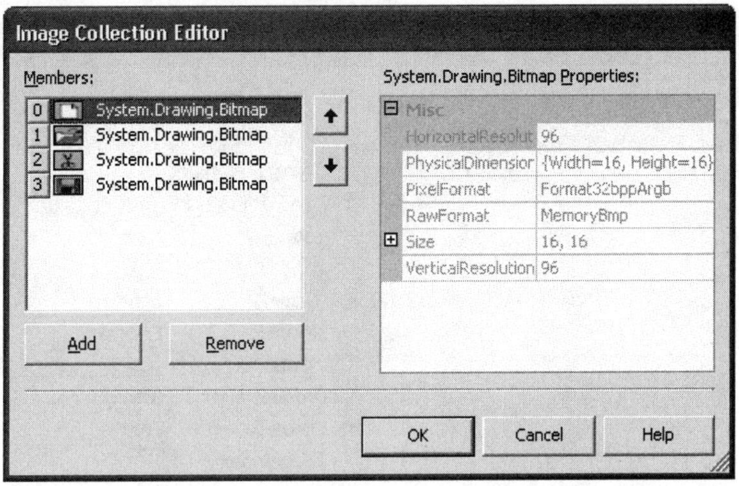

Figure 18-17. Image collection editor

The Tag property does not affect the display of the menu, but it helps identify which button was pressed, as all buttons on a toolbar share a common event handler.

Your ToolBarButton Collection Editor should look like Figure 18-18.

Go ahead and add an Open button and a Save button. You do not have to use all the images in your image list; which one you use is up to you.

Adding event handlers

If you double-click on one of the buttons, Visual Studio .NET will create an event handler for the toolbar. Notice that the event handler is not per button. You'll have to figure out which button was pressed, but this task is simplified when the ToolBar-ButtonClickEventArgs parameter is passed in to the event handler.

```csharp
private void toolBar1_ButtonClick(
    object sender,
    System.Windows.Forms.ToolBarButtonClickEventArgs e)
{
    switch ( e.Button.Tag.ToString() )
    {
        case "New":
            mnuNew.PerformClick();
            break;
        case "Open":
            mnuFileOpen.PerformClick();
                break;
        case "Save":
            mnuFileSave.PerformClick();
            break;
    }

}
```

Figure 18-18. Adding buttons to the toolbar

```vb
Private Sub ToolBar1_ButtonClick( _
    ByVal sender As System.Object, _
    ByVal e As System.Windows.Forms.ToolBarButtonClickEventArgs) _
    Handles ToolBar1.ButtonClick

    Dim tag As String = e.Button.Tag

    Select Case tag
        Case "New"
            mnuNew.PerformClick( )
        Case "Open"
            mnuFileOpen.PerformClick( )
        Case "Save:"
            mnuFileSave.PerformClick( )
    End Select
End Sub
```

Clicking on the New button now opens an MDI window, and clicking on Open or Save evokes the same event handler as the menu choices, as shown in Figure 18-19.

Figure 18-19. Implementing toolbar events

Tool tips

Notice that one of the properties you set on your toolbar was the ToolTipText property. If the user hovers over one of your buttons, the tool tip will appear to provide additional information about the button, as shown in Figure 18-20.

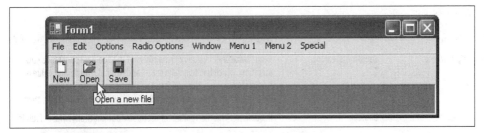

Figure 18-20. Using tool tips

Altering the appearance

Several toolbar properties can help you tailor the appearance of your buttons. For example, you can change the TextAlign property from Underneath to Right, and put the text next to the icon to make wider, but shorter buttons, as shown in Figure 18-21.

Another example is the Appearance property, which can be set to either Flat or Normal. If you change the appearance to Flat, the buttons look flat except when you hold the cursor over the button, as shown in Figure 18-22. You have to look closely and compare the New button (for example) in Figure 18-22 with the New button shown in Figure 18-20.

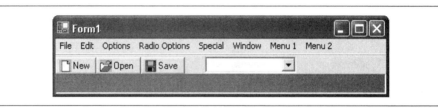

Figure 18-21. Setting the TextAlign property

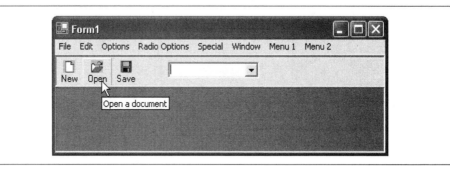

Figure 18-22. Appearance set to flat

Dozens of properties can set the appearance of the Toolbar. Some of the most important and common properties are listed in Table 18-8.

Table 18-8. Toolbar properties

Property	Type	Description
Appearance	ToolBarAppearance	Read/Write. Valid values are members of the ToolBarAppearance enumeration, which has two values: Flat and Normal. The default value is ToolBarAppearance.Normal. If the appearance is set to ToolBar-Appearance.Flat, the buttons are flat until the mouse is held over them.
AutoSize	Boolean	Read/write. Will the Toolbar adjust its size automatically? The default is true.
BorderStyle	BorderStyle	Read/write. Specifies the style of border around the toolbar. Valid values are members of the BorderStyle enumeration, which has three values: Fixed3D, FixedSingle, and None. The default value is BorderStyle.None.
Buttons	ToolBarButtonCollection	Read-only. The collection of ToolBarButton objects contained by the Toolbar.
ButtonSize	Size	Read/write. The size of the buttons on the toolbar (typically 16 x 16).
Divider	Boolean	Read/write. If true (the default), a raised edge is displayed along the top of the Toolbar to separate it from the menus.
DropDownArrows	Boolean	Read/write. If true, drop-down Toolbar buttons display down arrows. The default value is false.
ImageList	ImageList	Read/write. The image list containing the images to be displayed by the buttons on the Toolbar.

Table 18-8. Toolbar properties (continued)

Property	Type	Description
ShowToolTips	Boolean	Read/write. If true, tool tips are displayed for each button. The default value is false.
TextAlign	ToolBarTextAlign	Read/write. Specifies the alignment of the text associated with a Toolbar button. Valid values are members of the ToolBarTextAlign enumeration: Right and Underneath. The default is ToolBarTextAlign. Underneath.
Wrappable	Boolean	Read/write. If true (the default), the Toolbar buttons wrap to the next line if there is insufficient space for all the buttons on a single line.

Adding a combo box to the Toolbar

You can do much more with toolbars. For example, while the IDE will not help you add more complex controls, you are free to add them programmatically.

To add a combo box to the Toolbar, add code to the constructor of the form that creates a combo box, initializes its members, and then adds it to the Toolbar:

C#
```csharp
public Form1( )
{
    InitializeComponent( );

    ComboBox cb = new ComboBox( );
    cb.Left = 150;
    cb.Top = 5;
    cb.Items.Add("Alabama");
    cb.Items.Add("Alaska");
    cb.Items.Add("Arizona");
    cb.Items.Add("Arkansas");
    toolBar1.Controls.Add(cb);
}
```

VB
```vb
Public Sub New( )
    MyBase.New( )

    InitializeComponent( )

    Dim cb As New ComboBox( )
    cb.Left = 150
    cb.Top = 5
    cb.Items.Add("Alabama")
    cb.Items.Add("Alaska")
    cb.Items.Add("Arizona")
    cb.Items.Add("Arkansas")
    ToolBar1.Controls.Add(cb)
End Sub
```

The Combo box is added to the Toolbar, as shown in Figure 18-23.

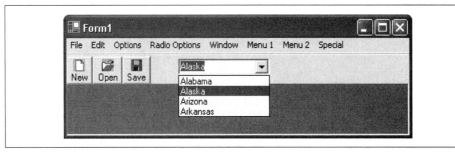

Figure 18-23. Adding a combo box to the Toolbar

 You can find this entire example in the downloadable source files *ToolBarsCS* and *ToolBarsVB*, respectively.

Writing It by Hand

While wizards and property windows make creating toolbars easy, they do limit you in some interesting, if subtle ways. In the previous code, you set the Button's Tag property to a string (e.g., "New"), and in the event handler, you switched on that string:

```C#
private void toolBar1_ButtonClick(
    object sender,
    System.Windows.Forms.ToolBarButtonClickEventArgs e)
{
    switch ( e.Button.Tag.ToString( ) )
    {
       case "New":
          mnuNew.PerformClick( );
          break;
       case "Open":
          mnuFileOpen.PerformClick( );
             break;
       case "Save":
          mnuFileSave.PerformClick( );
          break;
    }

}
```

A tag, however, can be any type of object. It would be nice to put a reference to the MenuItem itself into the tag; this would greatly simplify the event handler:

```C#
private void toolBar1_ButtonClick(
    object sender,
    System.Windows.Forms.ToolBarButtonClickEventArgs e)
{
    ToolBarButton btn = e.Button;
    MenuItem mi = (MenuItem) btn.Tag;
    mi.PerformClick( );
}
```

Creating the toolbar by hand is not much more difficult than creating it with Visual Studio .NET, as illustrated in Example 18-7 in C# and in Example 18-8 in VB.NET. In these examples, the modified code from the previous examples is highlighted. An analysis follows the code listings.

Example 18-7. Creating toolbars by hand in C# (ToolBarsByHandCS)

```csharp
using System;
using System.Drawing;
using System.Collections;
using System.ComponentModel;
using System.Windows.Forms;
using System.Data;

namespace MenusVSCS05
{
    public class Form1 : System.Windows.Forms.Form
    {
        private System.Windows.Forms.MainMenu mainMenu1;
        private System.Windows.Forms.MenuItem mnuNew;
        private System.Windows.Forms.MenuItem mnuFile;
        private System.Windows.Forms.MenuItem mnuFileOpen;
        private System.Windows.Forms.MenuItem mnuFileClose;
        private System.Windows.Forms.MenuItem mnuFileSave;
        private System.Windows.Forms.MenuItem mnuFileSaveAs;
        private System.Windows.Forms.MenuItem mnuEdit;
        private System.Windows.Forms.MenuItem mnuEditCopy;
        private System.Windows.Forms.MenuItem mnuEditPaste;
        private System.Windows.Forms.MenuItem mnuOption1;
        private System.Windows.Forms.MenuItem mnuOption2;
        private System.Windows.Forms.MenuItem mnuOption3;
        private System.Windows.Forms.MenuItem mnuROption1;
        private System.Windows.Forms.MenuItem mnuROption2;
        private System.Windows.Forms.MenuItem mnuROption3;
        private System.Windows.Forms.MenuItem mnuWindow;
        private System.Windows.Forms.MenuItem mnuOptions;
        private System.Windows.Forms.MenuItem mnuRadioOptions;
        private System.Windows.Forms.MenuItem mnuMenu1;
        private System.Windows.Forms.MenuItem mnuMenu11;
        private System.Windows.Forms.MenuItem mnuMenu12;
        private System.Windows.Forms.MenuItem mnuMenu13;
        private System.Windows.Forms.MenuItem mnuMenu14;
        private System.Windows.Forms.MenuItem mnuMenu2;
        private System.Windows.Forms.MenuItem mnuMenu21;
        private System.Windows.Forms.MenuItem mnuMenu22;
        private System.Windows.Forms.MenuItem mnuMenu23;
        private System.Windows.Forms.MenuItem mnuMenu24;
        private System.Windows.Forms.MenuItem mnuMerge;
        private System.Windows.Forms.MenuItem mnuODShazam;

        private string[] files ={@"c:\temp\vote.bmp",
                                 @"c:\temp\shazam.bmp"};
        private System.Windows.Forms.MenuItem mnuODVote;
```

Example 18-7. Creating toolbars by hand in C# (ToolBarsByHandCS) (continued)

```csharp
private System.Windows.Forms.MenuItem mnuSpecial;

private System.Windows.Forms.ToolBar toolBar1;
private System.Windows.Forms.ImageList imgListFileButtons;

private System.ComponentModel.Container components = null;

public Form1( )
{
   InitializeComponent( );
   CreateImageList( );
   InitializeToolbar( );
}

private void InitializeToolbar( )
{
   toolBar1 = new ToolBar( );
   toolBar1.ImageList = imgListFileButtons;

   ToolBarButton btnNew = new ToolBarButton( );
   btnNew.Tag = mnuNew;
   btnNew.Enabled = true;
   btnNew.ImageIndex = 0; // new file
   btnNew.Pushed = false;
   btnNew.Style = ToolBarButtonStyle.PushButton;
   btnNew.Text= "New";
   btnNew.ToolTipText = "New document";
   btnNew.Visible = true;
   toolBar1.Buttons.Add(btnNew);

   ToolBarButton btnOpen = new ToolBarButton( );
   btnOpen.Tag = mnuFileOpen;
   btnOpen.Enabled = true;
   btnOpen.ImageIndex = 1; // open file
   btnOpen.Pushed = false;
   btnOpen.Style = ToolBarButtonStyle.PushButton;
   btnOpen.Text = "Open";
   btnOpen.ToolTipText = "Open a document";
   btnOpen.Visible = true;
   toolBar1.Buttons.Add(btnOpen);

   ToolBarButton btnSave = new ToolBarButton( );
   btnSave.Tag = mnuFileSave;
   btnSave.Enabled = true;
   btnSave.ImageIndex = 3; // save file
   btnSave.Pushed = false;
   btnSave.Style = ToolBarButtonStyle.PushButton;
   btnSave.Text = "Save";
   btnSave.ToolTipText = "Save document";
   btnSave.Visible = true;
   toolBar1.Buttons.Add(btnSave);
```

Example 18-7. Creating toolbars by hand in C# (ToolBarsByHandCS) (continued)

```
        ComboBox cb = new ComboBox( );
        cb.Left = 150;
        cb.Top = 5;
        cb.Items.Add("Alabama");
        cb.Items.Add("Alaska");
        cb.Items.Add("Arizona");
        cb.Items.Add("Arkansas");
        ToolTip tip = new ToolTip( );
        tip.AutomaticDelay = 500; // sets the next three automatically
        // tip.AutoPopDelay = 10 times AutomaticDelay
        // tip.InitialDelay = AutomaticDelay
        //tip.ReshowDelay = 1/5 AutomaticDelay
        tip.ShowAlways = true; // display even if control is disabled
        tip.SetToolTip(cb,"Pick a state");
        toolBar1.Controls.Add(cb);

        toolBar1.Parent = this;
        toolBar1.BorderStyle = System.Windows.Forms.BorderStyle.Fixed3D;
        toolBar1.DropDownArrows = true;
        toolBar1.Name = "toolBar1";
        toolBar1.ShowToolTips = true;
        toolBar1.Size = new System.Drawing.Size(440, 41);
        toolBar1.TabIndex = 1;
        toolBar1.ButtonClick += new System.Windows.Forms.
ToolBarButtonClickEventHandler(toolBar1_ButtonClick);

    }

    private void CreateImageList( )
    {
        imgListFileButtons = new ImageList( );
        Image img;

        // Use an array to add filenames to the ImageList
        String[ ] arFiles = { @"C:\Program Files\Microsoft Visual Studio .NET 2003\
Common7\Graphics\bitmaps\OffCtlBr\Large\Color\New.bmp",
            @"C:\Program Files\Microsoft Visual Studio .NET 2003\Common7\Graphics\
bitmaps\OffCtlBr\Large\Color\Open.bmp",
            @"C:\Program Files\Microsoft Visual Studio .NET 2003\Common7\Graphics\
bitmaps\OffCtlBr\Large\Color\Cut.bmp",
            @"C:\Program Files\Microsoft Visual Studio .NET 2003\Common7\Graphics\
bitmaps\OffCtlBr\Large\Color\Save.bmp" };

        for (int i = 0; i < arFiles.Length; i++)
        {
            img = Image.FromFile(arFiles[i]);
            imgListFileButtons.Images.Add(img);
        }
    }
```

Example 18-7. Creating toolbars by hand in C# (ToolBarsByHandCS) (continued)

```
protected override void Dispose( bool disposing )
{
   if( disposing )
   {
      if (components != null)
      {
         components.Dispose( );
      }
   }
   base.Dispose( disposing );
}

#region Windows Form Designer generated code
#endregion

[STAThread]
static void Main( )
{
   Application.Run(new Form1( ));
}


private void mnuNew_Click(object sender, System.EventArgs e)
{
   MDIChild newMDIChild = new MDIChild( );
   newMDIChild.MdiParent = this;
   newMDIChild.Show( );
}

private void mnuFileOpen_Click(object sender, System.EventArgs e)
{
   MessageBox.Show ("You clicked File Open", "Menu Event Tester",
      MessageBoxButtons.OK, MessageBoxIcon.Asterisk);
}

private void mnuFileClose_Click(object sender, System.EventArgs e)
{
   MessageBox.Show ("You clicked File Close", "Menu Event Tester",
      MessageBoxButtons.OK, MessageBoxIcon.Asterisk);
}

private void Option_Click(object sender, System.EventArgs e)
{
   MenuItem item = sender as MenuItem;

   if ( item != null )
   {
      item.Checked = ! item.Checked;
   }
}

private void RadioOption_Click(object sender, System.EventArgs e)
```

Example 18-7. Creating toolbars by hand in C# (ToolBarsByHandCS) (continued)

```csharp
    {
        MenuItem item = sender as MenuItem;

        if ( item != null )
        {
            Menu parent = item.Parent;
            foreach ( MenuItem mi in parent.MenuItems )
                mi.Checked = false;
            item.Checked = true;
        }
    }

    private void mnuEditCopy_Click(object sender, System.EventArgs e)
    {
        MessageBox.Show ("You clicked Edit Copy", "Menu Event Tester",
            MessageBoxButtons.OK, MessageBoxIcon.Asterisk);
    }

    private void mnuEditPaste_Click(object sender, System.EventArgs e)
    {
        MessageBox.Show ("You clicked Edit Paste", "Menu Event Tester",
            MessageBoxButtons.OK, MessageBoxIcon.Asterisk);
    }

    private void mnuFileSave_Click(object sender, System.EventArgs e)
    {
        MessageBox.Show ("You clicked Save", "Menu Event Tester",
            MessageBoxButtons.OK, MessageBoxIcon.Asterisk);
    }

    private void mnuFileSaveAs_Click(object sender, System.EventArgs e)
    {
        MessageBox.Show ("You clicked SaveAs", "Menu Event Tester",
            MessageBoxButtons.OK, MessageBoxIcon.Asterisk);
    }

    private void mnuMerge_Click(object sender, System.EventArgs e)
    {
        MenuItem item = sender as MenuItem;
        if ( item != null )
        {
            item.Parent.MergeMenu(mnuMenu2);
        }
    }

    private void OnDrawItem(object sender, System.Windows.Forms.DrawItemEventArgs e)
    {
        Image img = Image.FromFile(files[e.Index]);
        Rectangle r = e.Bounds;
        Pen pen = new Pen(e.BackColor,2);
        r.Inflate(-6,-6);
        e.Graphics.DrawRectangle(pen,r);
        e.Graphics.DrawImage(img,r);
```

Example 18-7. Creating toolbars by hand in C# (ToolBarsByHandCS) (continued)

```csharp
        }

        private void OnMeasureItem(
            object sender, System.Windows.Forms.MeasureItemEventArgs e)
        {
            Image img = Image.FromFile(files[e.Index]);
            e.ItemHeight = img.Height;
            e.ItemWidth = img.Width;
        }

        private void mnuODDraw_Click(object sender, System.EventArgs e)
        {
            MenuItem item = sender as MenuItem;
            if ( item != null )
            {
                string choice = item.Text;

                MessageBox.Show ("You clicked " + choice, "Menu Event Tester",
                    MessageBoxButtons.OK, MessageBoxIcon.Asterisk);
            }
        }

        private void toolBar1_ButtonClick(
            object sender,
            System.Windows.Forms.ToolBarButtonClickEventArgs e)
        {
            ToolBarButton btn = e.Button;
            MenuItem mi = (MenuItem) btn.Tag;
            mi.PerformClick( );
        }
    }
}
```

Example 18-8. Creating toolbars by hand in VB.NET (ToolBarsByHandVB)

```vbnet
Public Class Form1
    Inherits System.Windows.Forms.Form

    Private files( ) As String = {"c:\temp\vote.bmp", "c:\temp\shazam.bmp"}
    Friend WithEvents toolBar1 As ToolBar
    Private imgListFileButtons As ImageList

#Region " Windows Form Designer generated code "

    Public Sub New( )
        MyBase.New( )

        'This call is required by the Windows Form Designer.
        InitializeComponent( )
        CreateImageList( )
        InitializeToolbar( )
    End Sub
```

VB

```vb
#End Region

    Private Sub InitializeToolbar()
        toolBar1 = New ToolBar()
        toolBar1.ImageList = imgListFileButtons

        Dim btnNew As New ToolBarButton()
        btnNew.Tag = mnuNew
        btnNew.Enabled = True
        btnNew.ImageIndex = 0 ' new file
        btnNew.Pushed = False
        btnNew.Style = ToolBarButtonStyle.PushButton
        btnNew.Text = "New"
        btnNew.ToolTipText = "New document"
        btnNew.Visible = True
        toolBar1.Buttons.Add(btnNew)

        Dim btnOpen As New ToolBarButton()
        btnOpen.Tag = mnuFileOpen
        btnOpen.Enabled = True
        btnOpen.ImageIndex = 1 ' open file
        btnOpen.Pushed = False
        btnOpen.Style = ToolBarButtonStyle.PushButton
        btnOpen.Text = "Open"
        btnOpen.ToolTipText = "Open a document"
        btnOpen.Visible = True
        toolBar1.Buttons.Add(btnOpen)


        Dim btnSave As New ToolBarButton()
        btnSave.Tag = mnuFileSave
        btnSave.Enabled = True
        btnSave.ImageIndex = 3 ' save file
        btnSave.Pushed = False
        btnSave.Style = ToolBarButtonStyle.PushButton
        btnSave.Text = "Save"
        btnSave.ToolTipText = "Save document"
        btnSave.Visible = True
        toolBar1.Buttons.Add(btnSave)

        Dim cb As New ComboBox()
        cb.Left = 150
        cb.Top = 5
        cb.Items.Add("Alabama")
        cb.Items.Add("Alaska")
        cb.Items.Add("Arizona")
        cb.Items.Add("Arkansas")
        Dim tip As New ToolTip()
        tip.AutomaticDelay = 500 ' sets the next three automatically
        ' tip.AutoPopDelay = 10 times AutomaticDelay
        ' tip.InitialDelay = AutomaticDelay
        'tip.ReshowDelay = 1/5 AutomaticDelay
```

```vb
        tip.ShowAlways = True ' display even if control is disabled
        tip.SetToolTip(cb, "Pick a state")
        toolBar1.Controls.Add(cb)

        toolBar1.Parent = Me
        toolBar1.BorderStyle = System.Windows.Forms.BorderStyle.Fixed3D
        toolBar1.DropDownArrows = True
        toolBar1.Name = "toolBar1"
        toolBar1.ShowToolTips = True
        toolBar1.Size = New System.Drawing.Size(440, 41)
        toolBar1.TabIndex = 1
    End Sub

    Private Sub CreateImageList( )
        imgListFileButtons = New ImageList( )
        Dim img As Image
        Dim arFiles( ) As String = {"C:\Program Files\Microsoft Visual Studio .NET 2003\
Common7\Graphics\bitmaps\OffCtlBr\Large\Color\New.bmp", _
            "C:\Program Files\Microsoft Visual Studio .NET 2003\Common7\Graphics\bitmaps\
OffCtlBr\Large\Color\Open.bmp", _
            "C:\Program Files\Microsoft Visual Studio .NET 2003\Common7\Graphics\bitmaps\
OffCtlBr\Large\Color\Cut.bmp", _
            "C:\Program Files\Microsoft Visual Studio .NET 2003\Common7\Graphics\bitmaps\
OffCtlBr\Large\Color\Save.bmp"}

        Dim i As Integer
        For i = 0 To arFiles.Length - 1
            img = Image.FromFile(arFiles(i))
            imgListFileButtons.Images.Add(img)
        Next
    End Sub

    Private Sub mnuNew_Click(ByVal sender As System.Object, ByVal e As System.EventArgs) _
    Handles mnuNew.Click
        Dim newMDIChild As New MDIChild( )
        newMDIChild.MdiParent = Me
        newMDIChild.Show( )
    End Sub

    Private Sub mnuFileOpen_Click(ByVal sender As System.Object, ByVal e As System.
EventArgs) _
    Handles mnuFileOpen.Click
        MessageBox.Show("You clicked file open!", _
        "Menu event tester", _
        MessageBoxButtons.OK, _
        MessageBoxIcon.Information)
    End Sub

    Private Sub mnuFileClose_Click(ByVal sender As System.Object, ByVal e As System.
EventArgs) _
```

```
    Handles mnuFileClose.Click
        MessageBox.Show("You clicked file close!", "Menu event tester", MessageBoxButtons.
OK, MessageBoxIcon.Information)
    End Sub

    Private Sub mnuEditCopy_Click(ByVal sender As System.Object, ByVal e As System.
EventArgs) _
    Handles mnuEditCopy.Click
        MessageBox.Show("You clicked Edit copy!", "Menu event tester", MessageBoxButtons.
OK, MessageBoxIcon.Information)
    End Sub

    Private Sub mnuEditPaste_Click(ByVal sender As System.Object, ByVal e As System.
EventArgs) _
    Handles mnuEditPaste.Click
        MessageBox.Show("You clicked Edit paste!", "Menu event tester", MessageBoxButtons.
OK, MessageBoxIcon.Information)
    End Sub

    Private Sub Option_Click(ByVal sender As System.Object, ByVal e As System.EventArgs) _
    Handles mnuOption1.Click, mnuOption2.Click, mnuOption3.Click
        Dim item As MenuItem = CType(sender, MenuItem)
        item.Checked = Not item.Checked
    End Sub

    Private Sub RadioOption_Click(ByVal sender As System.Object, ByVal e As System.
EventArgs) _
    Handles mnuRadioOption1.Click, mnuRadioOption2.Click, mnuRadioOption3.Click
        Dim item As MenuItem = CType(sender, MenuItem)
        Dim parent As Menu = item.Parent
        Dim tempMi As MenuItem
        For Each tempMi In parent.MenuItems
            tempMi.Checked = False
        Next
        item.Checked = True
    End Sub

    Private Sub mnuMerge_Click(ByVal sender As System.Object, ByVal e As System.EventArgs)
        Dim item As MenuItem = CType(sender, MenuItem)
        item.Parent.MergeMenu(mnuMenu2)
    End Sub

    Private Sub mnuODVote_DrawItem(ByVal sender As Object, ByVal e As System.Windows.
Forms.DrawItemEventArgs) _
        Handles mnuODVote.DrawItem, mnuODShazam.DrawItem

        Dim img As Image
        img = Image.FromFile(files(e.Index))
        Dim r As Rectangle
        r = e.Bounds
        Dim p As Pen = New Pen(e.BackColor, 2)
        r.Inflate(-6, -6)
```

VB

```
            e.Graphics.DrawRectangle(p, r)
            e.Graphics.DrawImage(img, r)
        End Sub

    Private Sub mnuODVote_MeasureItem( _
        ByVal sender As Object, _
        ByVal e As System.Windows.Forms.MeasureItemEventArgs) _
        Handles mnuODVote.MeasureItem, mnuODShazam.MeasureItem

        Dim img As Image
        img = Image.FromFile(files(e.Index))
        e.ItemHeight = img.Height
        e.ItemWidth = img.Width
    End Sub

    Private Sub mnuODDraw_Click( _
        ByVal sender As System.Object, _
        ByVal e As System.EventArgs) _
        Handles mnuODVote.Click, mnuODShazam.Click
        Dim item As MenuItem = CType(sender, MenuItem)
        Dim choice As String = item.Text
        MessageBox.Show("You clicked " & choice, _
            "Menu Event Tester", MessageBoxButtons.OK, _
            MessageBoxIcon.Asterisk)
    End Sub

    Private Sub toolBar1_ButtonClick( _
        ByVal sender As Object, _
        ByVal e As ToolBarButtonClickEventArgs) _
        Handles toolBar1.ButtonClick

        Dim btn As ToolBarButton = e.Button
        Dim mi As MenuItem = CType(btn.Tag, MenuItem)
        mi.PerformClick( )
    End Sub
End Class
```

 To save space, the region of code generated by Visual Studio .NET was elided from these listings (with the exception of the constructor in the VB.NET code).

Creating the Toolbar by Hand: Analysis

You begin by creating two private member variables of the Form class: a toolbar, and an ImageList to attach to that toolbar:

C#

```
    private System.Windows.Forms.ToolBar toolBar1;
    private System.Windows.Forms.ImageList imgListFileButtons;
```

(Hidden inside the Windows Form Designer generated code, along with other member variables):

```
Friend WithEvents imgListFileButtons As System.Windows.Forms.ImageList
Friend WithEvents ToolBar1 As System.Windows.Forms.ToolBar
```

You add two method calls to the constructor: one to create the ImageList and the other to initialize the ToolBar:

```
public Form1( )
{
    InitializeComponent( );
    CreateImageList( );
    InitializeToolbar( );
}
```

```
Public Sub New( )
    MyBase.New( )
    InitializeComponent( )
    CreateImageList( )
    InitializeToolbar( )
End Sub
```

Creating the ImageList is straightforward. Initialize a new empty image list and create a local variable to hold an Image object.

```
imgListFileButtons = new ImageList( );
Image img;
```

Then create an array to hold the four filenames for the bitmaps supplied by Microsoft:

```
String[ ] arFiles = { @"C:\Program Files\Microsoft Visual Studio .NET 2003\Common7\
Graphics\bitmaps\OffCtlBr\Large\Color\New.bmp", @"C:\Program Files\Microsoft Visual
Studio .NET 2003\Common7\Graphics\bitmaps\OffCtlBr\Large\Color\Open.bmp", @"C:\
Program Files\Microsoft Visual Studio .NET 2003\Common7\Graphics\bitmaps\OffCtlBr\
Large\Color\Cut.bmp",  @"C:\Program Files\Microsoft Visual Studio .NET 2003\Common7\
Graphics\bitmaps\OffCtlBr\Large\Color\Save.bmp" };
```

```
Dim arFiles( ) As String = {"C:\Program Files\Microsoft Visual Studio .NET 2003\
Common7\Graphics\bitmaps\OffCtlBr\Large\Color\New.bmp", _
    "C:\Program Files\Microsoft Visual Studio .NET 2003\Common7\Graphics\bitmaps\
OffCtlBr\Large\Color\Open.bmp", _
    "C:\Program Files\Microsoft Visual Studio .NET 2003\Common7\Graphics\bitmaps\
OffCtlBr\Large\Color\Cut.bmp", _
    "C:\Program Files\Microsoft Visual Studio .NET 2003\Common7\Graphics\bitmaps\
OffCtlBr\Large\Color\Save.bmp"}
```

Finally, create a reference to an image from each of the filenames, and add that image to the ImageList's collection of images:

```
for (int i = 0; i < arFiles.Length; i++)
{
```

```
C#       img = Image.FromFile(arFiles[i]);
         imgListFileButtons.Images.Add(img);
       }
```

Initializing the toolbar is more tedious, but not terribly difficult. Begin by instantiating the toolbar and setting its ImageList property to the ImageList you just created:

```
C#     toolBar1 = new ToolBar( );
       toolBar1.ImageList = imgListFileButtons;
```

Next, create a button and set its properties:

```
C#     ToolBarButton btnNew = new ToolBarButton( );
       btnNew.Tag = mnuNew;
       btnNew.Enabled = true;
       btnNew.ImageIndex = 0; // new file
       btnNew.Pushed = false;
       btnNew.Style = ToolBarButtonStyle.PushButton;
       btnNew.Text= "New";
       btnNew.ToolTipText = "New document";
       btnNew.Visible = true;
```

Notice that the ImageIndex property is set to the appropriate index into the ImageList that you assigned to the ToolBar'sImageList property. Also notice that in this example you are not setting the Tag property to a string, but you are setting the Tag property to a reference to a MenuItem.

Once all properties are set, you can add the button to the ToolBar's Buttons collection:

```
C#     toolBar1.Buttons.Add(btnNew);
```

Repeat these steps for the next two buttons, changing only which MenuItem and ImageIndex you must use, along with the appropriate changes to the Text and the ToolTip text.

```
C#     ToolBarButton btnOpen = new ToolBarButton( );
       btnOpen.Tag = mnuFileOpen;
       btnOpen.Enabled = true;
       btnOpen.ImageIndex = 1; // open file
       btnOpen.Pushed = false;
       btnOpen.Style = ToolBarButtonStyle.PushButton;
       btnOpen.Text = "Open";
       btnOpen.ToolTipText = "Open a document";
       btnOpen.Visible = true;
       toolBar1.Buttons.Add(btnOpen);

       ToolBarButton btnSave = new ToolBarButton( );
       btnSave.Tag = mnuFileSave;
       btnSave.Enabled = true;
       btnSave.ImageIndex = 3; // save file
       btnSave.Pushed = false;
       btnSave.Style = ToolBarButtonStyle.PushButton;
       btnSave.Text = "Save";
       btnSave.ToolTipText = "Save document";
       btnSave.Visible = true;
       toolBar1.Buttons.Add(btnSave);
```

Adding ToolTips and setting their properties

You are now ready to add the Combo box. This is unchanged from the previous examples, except this time you'll add a ToolTip to the Combo box as well:

```
ComboBox cb = new ComboBox( );
cb.Left = 150;
cb.Top = 5;
cb.Items.Add("Alabama");
cb.Items.Add("Alaska");
cb.Items.Add("Arizona");
cb.Items.Add("Arkansas");
ToolTip tip = new ToolTip( );
```

The ToolTip object itself has many useful properties. You can set the InitialDelay (how long the system waits before displaying the tip—500 milliseconds by default), the AutoPopDelay (how long the tip is displayed), and the ReshowDelay (how long before the tip is redisplayed when you return to the button). Alternatively, you can just set the AutomaticDelay, and the other delays are set for you. The AutoPopDelay is set to 10 times the AutomaticDelay, while the ReshowDelay is set to 1/5 of the AutomaticDelay, and the InitialDelay is set to the same value as the AutomaticDelay.

```
tip.AutomaticDelay = 500; // sets the next three automatically (milliseconds)
// tip.AutoPopDelay = 10 times AutomaticDelay (5 seconds)
// tip.InitialDelay = AutomaticDelay (1/2 second)
//tip.ReshowDelay = 1/5 AutomaticDelay (1/10 second)
```

Setting the ShowAlways property to true instructs the tip to be displayed whether or not the control is disabled.

```
tip.ShowAlways = true; // display even if control is disabled
```

Finally, you are ready to attach the ToolTip to the Combo box. Surprisingly, you do so by calling the SetToolTip method on the ToolTip itself, passing in two arguments—the control to set the ToolTip on and the text to display:

```
tip.SetToolTip(cb,"Pick a state");
```

You are now ready to add the Combo box to the ToolBar:

```
toolBar1.Controls.Add(cb);
```

Setting properties of the Toolbar

Once the controls have been added to the ToolBar, you can set properties of the Toolbar itself. Begin by setting the Parent control of the Toolbar to the form:

```
toolBar1.Parent = this;
```

```
toolBar1.Parent = Me
```

You are now ready to set the border style, how DropDownArrows will be handled, and so forth:

```
toolBar1.Parent = this;
toolBar1.BorderStyle = System.Windows.Forms.BorderStyle.Fixed3D;
toolBar1.DropDownArrows = true;
toolBar1.Name = "toolBar1";
toolBar1.ShowToolTips = true;
toolBar1.Size = new System.Drawing.Size(440, 41);
toolBar1.TabIndex = 1;
```

Finally, if you are doing this in C#, you must set up the event handler:

```
toolBar1.ButtonClick +=
    new System.Windows.Forms.ToolBarButtonClickEventHandler(
        toolBar1_ButtonClick);
```

Handling ToolBar button clicks

Now that you've stashed the appropriate MenuItem into the Button's Tag property, your event handler is much simpler. First extract the Button itself from the ToolBar-ButtonClickEventArgs argument:

```
private void toolBar1_ButtonClick(
    object sender,
    System.Windows.Forms.ToolBarButtonClickEventArgs e)
{
    ToolBarButton btn = e.Button;
```

```
Private Sub toolBar1_ButtonClick( _
    ByVal sender As Object, _
    ByVal e As ToolBarButtonClickEventArgs) _
    Handles toolBar1.ButtonClick
    Dim btn As ToolBarButton = e.Button
```

With the Button in hand, extract the Tag, which you are free to cast to a MenuItem:

```
MenuItem mi = (MenuItem) btn.Tag;
```

```
Dim mi As MenuItem = CType(btn.Tag, MenuItem)
```

You can now tell that MenuItem to act as if it were clicked:

```
mi.PerformClick();
```

Status Bars

Status bars can provide additional information about your program, as well as to add controls to the bottom of your form for informational display. A status bar consists of a number of Panels (each of which may contain other controls), and you can display information directly on the status bar itself.

In the next example, you will modify the previous example to add a status bar that will display both the current time and the amount of time the application has been running, as shown in Figure 18-24.

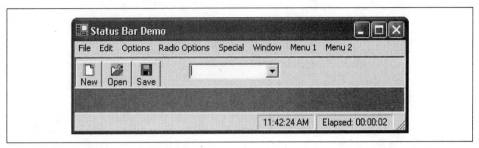

Figure 18-24. Status bar demonstration

In addition, when you click on or hover over menu choices, the time panels will disappear and information about the menu choice will be displayed, as shown in Figure 18-25.

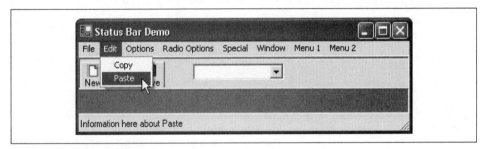

Figure 18-25. Hiding the panels

To add some spice to this application, when you left-click on the status bar, the elapsed timer will be reset to zero, and when you right-click on the status bar, a context menu will pop up, offering to reset, suspend, or resume the timer as shown in Figure 18-26.

The complete source code is greatly duplicative of the previous example, so it will not be shown here, but it can be downloaded as StatusBarsCS or StatusBarsVB. The relevant changes are detailed in the coming pages.

To get started, copy the ToolBarsCS or ToolBarsVB solution and change all the relevant filenames and text from ToolBars to StatusBars, as described in Chapter 1. Open your new StatusBarsVB or StatusBarsCS program and double-click on Form1 to display the form.

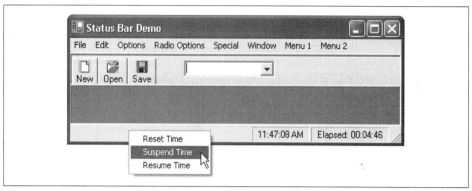

Figure 18-26. Pop-up menu

Analysis

First, add a StatusBar object to your form. Notice that when you drag this object onto your form, it adheres to the form (unlike the Menu, which must be set as a property of the form). This is just Visual Studio .NET's way of keeping life interesting.

The StatusBar object itself has a great many properties, methods, and events, most inherited from Control. Some of the most important properties are shown in Table 18-9.

Table 18-9. Status bar properties

Property	Type	Description
Dock	DockStyle	Read/Write. DockStyle is an Enumeration (Bottom, Fill, Left, None, Right, Top) that determines how the status bar is docked to the form.
Panels	StatusPanelCollection	Read-only. The collection of Panels in the status bar.
ShowPanels	Boolean	Read/Write. If `true`, the panels are displayed: otherwise, the Text property is displayed. The default is `false`.
SizingGrip	Boolean	Read/Write. If `true` (the default), a sizing grip is displayed in the lower-right corner of the status bar.
Text	String	Text that is displayed if the ShowPanels property is set to `false`.

Your first task is to add a couple of panels to the status bar. In this case, you'll want three. One will hold the place for the menu information, and the other two will be for the time and elapsed time, respectively.

Status bar panels are encapsulated in the StatusBarPanel class, which also has several useful properties. These properties will be discussed next when you create the Panels.

Navigate to the Panels (Collection) property and click on the button to open the StatusBarPanel Collection Editor. Click Add to add your first panel, which you will name pnlMenuHelp. Set the AutoSize property of this panel to Spring. This property is an enumeration of type StatusBarPanelAutoSize, whose three possible values are shown in Table 18-10.

Table 18-10. StatusBarAutoSize enumeration

Value	Description
Contents	The width is determined by the contents.
None	The panel does not change size when the status bar control resizes.
Spring	The panel shares available space within the status bar with other properties set to Spring.

The complete set of properties to set is shown in Figure 18-27.

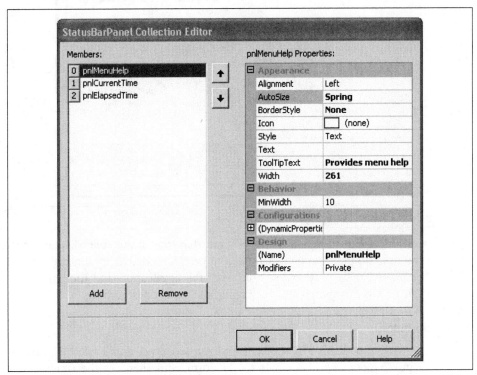

Figure 18-27. Properties for pnlMenuHelp

The second panel you need to add is for the current time. Its properties are shown in Figure 18-28.

Notice that this panel has its Alignment set to Center (so that the time is centered) and its Border style set to Sunken. In addition, the AutoSize property is set to Contents so that the panel will be sized to the display string.

Finally, add a third panel for the Elapsed time, as shown in Figure 18-29, noting the minor differences from the CurrentTime panel. Notice that the ToolTipText for this panel is "Time you've had this application open".

Figure 18-28. pnlCurrentTime properties

If you run the application now, you'll find that the status bar displays only "StatusBar1" and no panels are visible. Back in design mode, click on the status bar and set the ShowPanels property to true. Run the application and the panels display, but the time is not shown and clicking on the panel does nothing.

Setting the timer

To get the panels to display the current and elapsed time, you'll need a timer, as described in Chapter 1. Add a timer to the form, and then set the timer in the +constructor:

```
timer1.Interval = 1000;
timer1.Start( );
```

This creates a timer that will fire an event every second (the Interval property is in milliseconds).

You'll also need a private member variable to keep track of the starting time (to display elapsed time):

```
private DateTime startTime;
```

```
Private startTime As DateTime
```

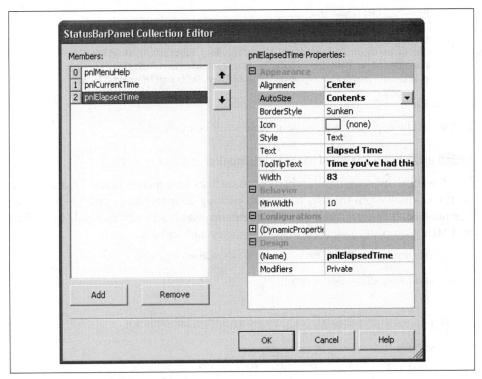

Figure 18-29. Elapsed time panel

In your constructor, you'll initialize the startTime member variable with the current time:

C#
```
startTime = DateTime.Now;
```

The Timer will fire the Tick event. Double-click on the timer in your designer to set up the event handler. In the event handler, you'll want to do two things. First, set the panel for the current time to the current time:

C#
```
private void timer1_Tick(object sender, System.EventArgs e)
{
    pnlCurrentTime.Text = DateTime.Now.ToLongTimeString( );
```

Second, compute the elapsed time, and then display it in the panel for the elapsed time:

C#
```
    TimeSpan elapsedSpan = DateTime.Now - this.startTime;
    DateTime elapsed = DateTime.Parse(elapsedSpan.ToString( ));
    pnlElapsedTime.Text = "Elapsed: " + elapsed.ToString("HH:mm:ss");
}
```

VB
```
Private Sub Timer1_Tick( _
    ByVal sender As System.Object, _
    ByVal e As System.EventArgs) _
```

```
Handles Timer1.Tick

    pnlCurrentTime.Text = DateTime.Now.ToLongTimeString( )
    Dim elapsedSpan As TimeSpan = (DateTime.Now).Subtract(Me.startTime)
    Dim elapsed As DateTime = DateTime.Parse(elapsedSpan.ToString( ))
    pnlElapsedTime.Text = "Elapsed: " + elapsed.ToString("HH:mm:ss")

End Sub
```

If you run the application now, your panels will be updated.

Updating the status bar based on menu information

You'll want to hide the panels when the user clicks on a menu choice. That is easy to do if you know when the user has begun clicking on menu items and when the user has finished. The form itself has two events to which you can respond: MenuStart and MenuComplete. You need write only the event handlers:

```
private void OnMenuStart(object sender, System.EventArgs e)
{
    statusBar1.ShowPanels = false;
}

private void OnMenuComplete(object sender, System.EventArgs e)
{
    statusBar1.ShowPanels = true;
}
```

```
Private Sub Form1_MenuStart( _
    ByVal sender As Object, _
    ByVal e As System.EventArgs) _
    Handles MyBase.MenuStart

    StatusBar1.ShowPanels = False

End Sub

Private Sub Form1_MenuComplete( _
    ByVal sender As Object, _
    ByVal e As System.EventArgs) _
    Handles MyBase.MenuComplete

    StatusBar1.ShowPanels = True
End Sub
```

 VB.NET programmers note: the events MenuStart and MenuComplete are listed under BaseClassEvents.

When the user actually does highlight on a menu choice, update the information in the status bar for that MenuItem. Each MenuItem has a Select event, and there is no reason not to use a common event handler for this event. In a sophisticated program, you will want to determine which menu choice the user is considering and provide meaningful help, but for now you can stub out the event handler:

C#

```csharp
private void OnMenuSelect(object sender, System.EventArgs e)
{
    MenuItem mi = (MenuItem) sender;
    statusBar1.Text = "Information here about " + mi.Text;
}
```

VB

```vb
Private Sub OnMenuSelect( _
    ByVal sender As Object, _
    ByVal e As System.EventArgs) _
    Handles mnuFile.Select, mnuFileOpen.Select, mnuFileClose.Select, _
    mnuFileSave.Select, mnuFileSaveAs.Select, mnuEdit.Select, _
    mnuEditCopy.Select, mnuEditPaste.Select, mnuOption1.Select, _
    mnuOption2.Select, mnuOption3.Select, mnuOptions.Select, _
    mnuRadioOptions.Select, mnuRadioOption1.Select, _
    mnuRadioOption2.Select, mnuRadioOption3.Select, mnuSpecial.Select, _
    mnuODVote.Select, mnuODShazam.Select, mnuMerge.Select, _
    mnuMenu1.Select, mnuMenu11.Select, mnuMenu12.Select, _
    mnuMenu13.Select, mnuMenu14.Select, mnuMenu2.Select, _
    mnuMenu21.Select, mnuMenu22.Select, _
    mnuMenu23.Select, mnuMenu24.Select, mnuWindow.Select

    Dim mi As MenuItem = CType(sender, MenuItem)
    StatusBar1.Text = "Information here about " + mi.Text

End Sub
```

Handling status bar events

The status bar itself has several events to which you might want to respond. The default event is PanelClick. In this example, you'll implement an event handler to test which button the user has pressed—if it is the right button, you'll zero the elapsed timer. This is facilitated by the StatusBarPanelClickEventArgs parameter passed into the event handler, which can, among other things, provide access to the mouse button that was clicked:

C#

```csharp
private void statusBar1_PanelClick(
    object sender,
    System.Windows.Forms.StatusBarPanelClickEventArgs e)
{
    if ( e.Button. == MouseButtons.Left)
    {
        startTime = DateTime.Now;
    }
}
```

```
Private Sub StatusBar1_PanelClick( _
    ByVal sender As System.Object, _
    ByVal e As System.Windows.Forms.StatusBarPanelClickEventArgs) _
    Handles StatusBar1.PanelClick

    If e.Button = MouseButton.Left Then
        startTime = DateTime.Now
    End If

End Sub
```

Adding a context menu

Finally, to handle the right mouse button, you'll add a context menu. Do so as described earlier in the section "Context Menus," by adding three entries: Reset Time, Suspend Time, and Resume Time. Name the context menu pnlContextMenu, and assign it to the ContextMenu property of the status bar, either in the properties window as shown in Figure 18-30 or, if you prefer, programmatically in the constructor.

```
public Form1( )
{
    InitializeComponent( );
    timer1.Interval = 1000;
    timer1.Start( );
    startTime = DateTime.Now;
    statusBar1.ContextMenu = pnlContextMenu;
```

Add three menu items to the context menu: Reset Time, Suspend Time, and Resume Time.

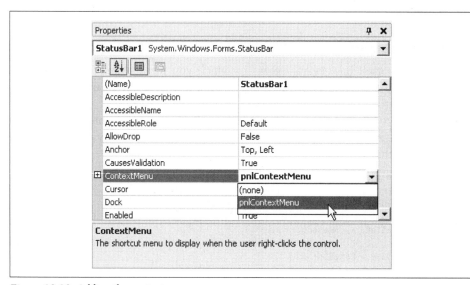

Figure 18-30. Adding the context menu

The Resume Time option should not be visible (or it should be disabled) when the timer is running, and the Suspend Time option should not be visible, or it should be disabled when the timer is suspended. In addition, when the time is resumed, the elapsed time (between suspension and resumption) should be subtracted out. All of this is left as an exercise for the reader to keep the example simple and prevent this book from weighing more than it already does.

In either case, you now must implement the three event handlers:

C#

```csharp
private void MnuResetTime_Click(object sender, System.EventArgs e)
{
    startTime = DateTime.Now;
}

private void mnuSuspendTime_Click(object sender, System.EventArgs e)
{
    timer1.Stop();
}

private void mnuResumeTime_Click(object sender, System.EventArgs e)
{
    timer1.Start();
}
```

VB

```vb
Private Sub mnuResetTime_Click( _
    ByVal sender As System.Object, _
    ByVal e As System.EventArgs) _
    Handles mnuResetTime.Click

    startTime = DateTime.Now

End Sub

Private Sub mnuSuspendTime_Click( _
    ByVal sender As System.Object, _
    ByVal e As System.EventArgs) _
    Handles mnuSuspendTime.Click

    Timer1.Stop()

End Sub

Private Sub mnuResumeTime_Click( _
    ByVal sender As System.Object, _
    ByVal e As System.EventArgs) _
    Handles mnuResumeTime.Click

    Timer1.Start()

End Sub
```

CHAPTER 19

ADO.NET

The heart of many serious commercial software products is data, stored in a database. If you are going to interact with a database, however, you must match the object-oriented perspective of .NET to the relational perspective of your backend database.

An inherent "impedance-mismatch" between the object-oriented and the relational world has been a problem for object-oriented programmers for many years. Microsoft attempts to overcome this obstacle by offering a complete set of classes for interacting with your database within an object-oriented hierarchy of classes. This set of classes is called ADO.NET.

ADO.NET looks, at first, very similar to ADO, its predecessor technology. The key difference between ADO and ADO.NET is that ADO is built around a recordset, while ADO.NET has as one of its key elements a DataSet that models the entire database, including tables, relationships among tables, and constraints added to interactions to maintain referential integrity. ADO.NET goes beyond the DataSet to include objects that serve as abstractions for the connection to your database, commands, connected fire-hose cursors, and so forth, all of which will be covered in this chapter.

The DataSet represents a *disconnected* data architecture, which is ideal for Windows (WinForm) applications. A disconnected architecture is database resource–frugal. Connections are used only briefly. Of course, ADO.NET does connect to the database to retrieve data, and connects again to update data when you've made changes. When not updating data to or from the database, the connection is broken. Most applications spend most of their time simply reading through data and displaying it, and ADO.NET provides a disconnected subset of the data for your use while reading and displaying.

As you might imagine, disconnected DataSets can have scale and performance problems of their own. There is overhead in creating and tearing down connections, and if you drop the connection each time you fill the DataSet and then must reestablish it each time you update the data, you will find that performance degrades quickly. This problem is mitigated by the use of connection pooling. While it looks to your application like you are creating and destroying connections, you are actually borrowing and returning connections from a pool that ADO.NET manages on your behalf.

Bug Database: A Windows Application

In our earlier book, *Programming ASP.NET*, we created a web-based bug-tracking application. ADO.NET does such a good job of abstracting the data from the implementing technology that much of the design of that application can easily be ported to Windows programming; recreating the bug tracking database as a rich-client desktop application.

 You do *not* have to have read *Programming ASP.NET* to follow this discussion, though if you have read it, many of its design considerations will be familiar.

To build an application to track software bugs, you'll need a form for entering bugs and a form for reviewing and editing bugs. To support this, you will design a relational database to hold the data about each bug. ADO.NET supports any database technology that has an ODBC driver (Access, Oracle, etc.), but this book focuses on SQL Server because many ADO.NET classes are optimized for Microsoft's chosen database technology.

Preliminary Design Considerations

Begin by thinking about the kinds of information you want to capture in the database and how that information will be used. You will allow any user of the system to create a bug report. You'll also want certain users (e.g., developers and a quality assurance team) to be able to update bug reports. Developers will want to be able to record progress in fixing a bug or to mark a bug as fixed. QA will want to check the fix and either close the bug or reopen it for further investigation. The original reporter of the bug will want to find out who is working on the bug and track progress.

One requirement imposed early in the design process is that the bug database ought to provide an "audit trail." If the bug is modified, you'll want to be able to say who modified it and when they did so. In fact, you'll want to track changes to the bug so you can generate a report like the excerpt shown in Example 19-1.

Example 19-1. Excerpt from a bug report

```
Bug 101 - System crashes on login
101.1 - Reporter: Osborn
Date: 1/1/2002  Original bug filed
Description: When I login I crash.
```

Example 19-1. Excerpt from a bug report (continued)

```
Status: Open
Owner: QA

101.2 - Modified by: Smith
Date: 1/2/2002 Changed Status, Owner
Action: Confirmed bug.
Status: Assigned
Owner: Hurwitz

101.3 - Modified by Hurwitz
Date 1/2/2002 Changed Status
Action: I'll look into this but I don't think it is my code.
Status: Accepted
Owner: Hurwitz

101.4 - Modified by Hurwitz
Date 1/3/2002 Changed Status, Owner
Action: Fault lies in login code. Reassigned to Liberty
Status: Assigned
Owner: Liberty

101.5 - Modified by Liberty
Date: 1/3/2002 Changed Status
Action: Yup, this is mine.
Status: Accepted
Owner: Liberty

101.6 - Modified by Liberty
Date 1/4/2002 Changed Status, Owner
Action: Added test for null loginID in DoLogin( )
Status: Fixed
Owner: QA

101.7 - Modified by Smith
Date: 1/4/2002 Changed Status
Action: Tested and confirmed
Status: Closed
Owner: QA
```

To track this information, you'll need to know the date and time of each modification, as well as who made the modification and what was done. There will probably be other information you'll want to capture as well, though this may become more obvious as you build the application (and use it).

It is quickly becoming clear that you'll need two different tables to represent the bug itself. Each record in the Bug table will represent a single bug, but you'll need an additional table to track the revisions. Call this second table BugHistory.

A Bug record will have a bugID and include the information that is constant for the bug throughout its history. A BugHistory record will have the information specific to each revision.

The Bug Database Design

The bug database design described in this section includes three significant tables: Bugs, BugHistory, and People. Bugs and BugHistory work together to track the progress of a bug. For any given bug, a single record is created in the Bugs table, and a record is created in BugHistory each time the bug is revised. The People table tracks the developers, QA, and other personnel who might be referred to in a Bug report.

> This simplified design meets the detailed specifications but focuses on key technologies; a robust professional design would necessarily be more complex. The complete database design used in this book is shown in the Appendix. The Appendix also provides a crash course on relational database design.

Figure 19-1 shows a snapshot of the Bugs table, and Figure 19-2 shows a snapshot of the BugHistory table.

Data in Table 'Bugs' in 'Bugs' on '(LOCAL)'

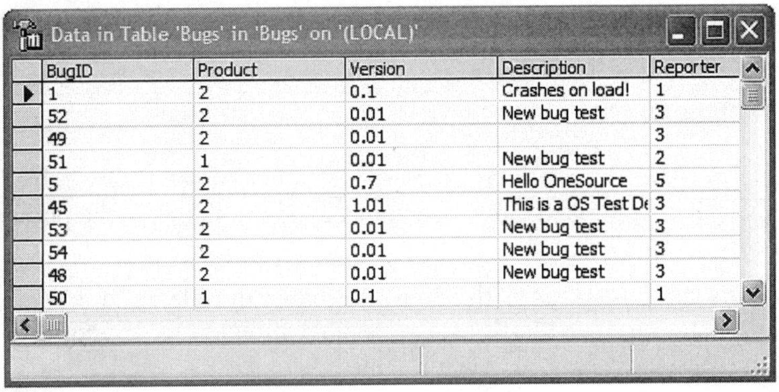

BugID	Product	Version	Description	Reporter
1	2	0.1	Crashes on load!	1
52	2	0.01	New bug test	3
49	2	0.01		3
51	1	0.01	New bug test	2
5	2	0.7	Hello OneSource	5
45	2	1.01	This is a OS Test De	3
53	2	0.01	New bug test	3
54	2	0.01	New bug test	3
48	2	0.01	New bug test	3
50	1	0.1		1

Figure 19-1. The Bug table

Data in Table 'BugHistory' in 'Bugs' on '(LOCAL)'

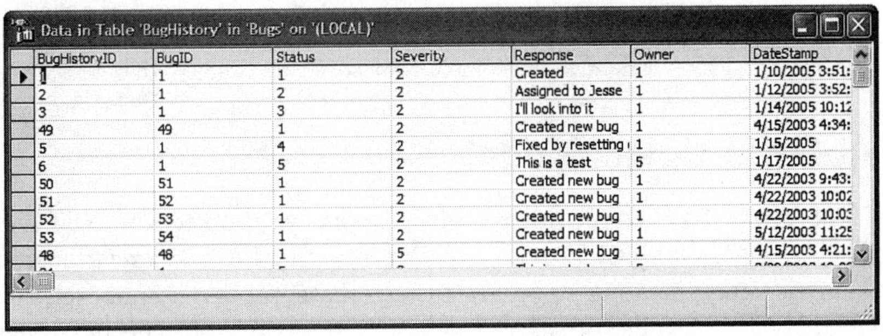

BugHistoryID	BugID	Status	Severity	Response	Owner	DateStamp
1	1	1	2	Created	1	1/10/2005 3:51:
2	1	2	2	Assigned to Jesse	1	1/12/2005 3:52:
3	1	3	2	I'll look into it	1	1/14/2005 10:12
49	49	1	2	Created new bug	1	4/15/2003 4:34:
5	1	4	2	Fixed by resetting	1	1/15/2005
6	1	5	2	This is a test	5	1/17/2005
50	51	1	2	Created new bug	1	4/22/2003 9:43:
51	52	1	2	Created new bug	1	4/22/2003 10:02
52	53	1	2	Created new bug	1	4/22/2003 10:03
53	54	1	2	Created new bug	1	5/12/2003 11:25
48	48	1	5	Created new bug	1	4/15/2003 4:21:

Figure 19-2. The BugHistory table

When a bug is first entered, a record is created in the Bug and BugHistory tables. Each time the bug is updated, a record is added to BugHistory. During the evolution of a bug, the status, severity, and owner of a bug may change, but the initial description and reporter will not. The items that are consistent for the entire life of the bug are in the Bugs table; those that are updated as the bug is fixed are in the BugHistory table.

The reporter, for example, is the ID of the person who reported the bug. This ID is unchanged for the life of the bug, so it is recorded in the Bugs table. The owner may be adjusted from time to time, so it is recorded in the BugHistory table. In both cases, however, what is actually recorded is just a personID, which acts as a foreign key into the People table. An excerpt from the People table is shown in Figure 19-3.

PersonID	FullName	eMail	Phone	Role
1	Jesse Liberty	jliberty@libertyassociates.cor	617-555-1212	1
2	Dan Hurwitz	dhurwitz@stersol.com	978-555-5432	1
3	John Osborn	josborn@oreilly.com	617-555-3232	4
5	Val Quericia	vq@oreily.com	617-555-9876	2
6	Tatiana Diaz	tatiana@oreilly.com	617-555-4523	2

Data in Table 'People' in 'Windform_Bugs' on '(LOCAL)'

Figure 19-3. The People table

In addition to these three primary tables, a number of secondary tables serve as lookup tables. For example, lkStatus serves as a lookup table for the possible values of BugHistory's status column.

The format for all lookup tables (lkStatus, lkProduct, lkRoles, and lkSeverity) is the same: the ID followed by a text field. Each table will hold one row for each possible value. Figure 19-4 shows various lookup tables.

Figure 19-5 illustrates the tables in their various relationships graphically.

 SQL server generated Figure 19-5. The Enterprise Manager has a diagramming tool used to create this diagram, though you can create similar diagrams right within some versions of Visual Studio .NET.

The ADO.NET Object Model

The goal of ADO.NET is to provide a bridge between your objects in .NET and your backend database. ADO.NET provides an object-oriented API to a relational view of your database, encapsulating many of the database properties and relationships within ADO.NET objects. More importantly, the ADO.NET objects encapsulate and hide the details of database access; your objects can interact with ADO.NET objects without knowing or worrying about the details of how the data is moved to and from the database.

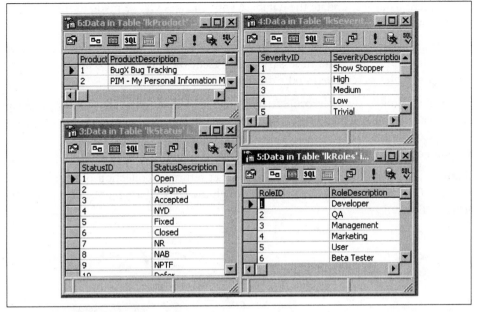

Figure 19-4. The lookup tables

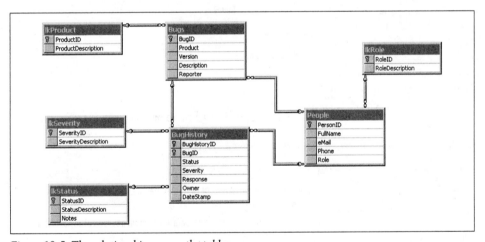

Figure 19-5. The relationship among the tables

The DataSet Class

The ADO.NET object model is rich, but at its heart is a fairly straightforward set of classes. One very powerful class, key to the disconnected architecture, is the DataSet, which is located in the System.Data namespace.

The DataSet represents a subset of the entire database, cached on your machine without a continuous connection to the database. Periodically, you'll reconnect the DataSet to its parent database, update the database with changes you've made to the DataSet, and update the DataSet with changes in the database made by other processes.

The DataSet captures not just a few rows from a single table, but represents a set of tables with all the metadata necessary to represent the relationships and constraints among the tables as recorded in the original database.

The DataSet offers two key properties: Tables and Relations. The Tables property returns a collection of DataTables. Each DataTable, in turn, has two important properties: Columns and Rows. The Columns property returns a collection of DataColumn objects, while the Rows property returns a collection of DataRows.

Similarly, the Relations property of the DataSet returns a collection of DataRelation objects. The principal objects available through the DataSet are represented schematically in Figure 19-6.

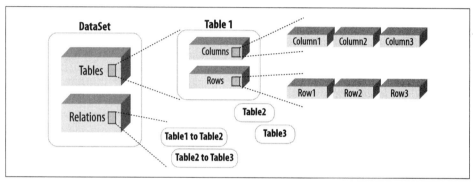

Figure 19-6. The DataSet objects

Table 19-1 shows the most important methods and properties of the DataSet class.

Table 19-1. The most important DataSet properties and methods

Class Member	Description
DefaultViewManager property	Gets a view manager that provides a view of the data in the DataSet that allows filtering, searching, and navigation.
HasErrors property	Gets a value indicating whether there are any errors in any rows of any of tables.
Relations property	Gets the relations collection.
Tables property	Gets the tables collection.
AcceptChanges method	Accepts all the changes made since loaded or since last time AcceptChanges was called (see GetChanges).
Clear method	Clears the DataSet of any data.
GetChanges method	Returns a copy of the DataSet containing all the changes made to the DataSet since it was loaded or since AcceptChanges was called.
GetXML method	Gets the XML representation of the data in the DataSet.
GetXMLSchema method	Gets the XSD schema for the XML representation of the data in the DataSet.

Class Member	Description
Merge method	Merges the data in this DataSet with another DataSet.
ReadXML method	Reads an XML schema and data into the DataSet.
ReadXMLSchema method	Reads an XML schema into the DataSet.
RejectChanges method	Rolls back to the state since the last AcceptChanges (see AcceptChanges).
WriteXML method	Writes out the XML schema and data from the DataSet.
WrixteXMLSchema method	Writes the structure of the DataSet as an XML schema.

The DataTable class

The DataSet object's Tables property returns a DataTableCollection collection, which contains tables in the DataSet. For example, the following line of code (in C#) creates a reference to the first DataTable in the Tables collection of a DataSet object named myDataSet:

```C#
DataTable dataTable = myDataSet.Tables[0];
```

```VB
dim dataTable as DataTable = myDataSet.Tables(0)
```

The DataTable has several public properties, including the Columns property, which returns the ColumnsCollection object, which consists of DataColumn objects. Each DataColumn object represents a column in a table.

The Relations property returns a DataRelationCollection object, which contains DataRelation objects. Each DataRelation object represents a relationship between two tables through DataColumn objects. For example, in the Bugs database, the Bug table is in a relationship with the People table through the PersonID column. The nature of this relationship is many to one—for any given Bug, there will be exactly one owner, but any given person may be represented in any number of Bugs. The Bugs and BugHistory collection actually establish an even tighter relationship: that of parent/child. The Bug acts as a parent record for all of its history records (that is, for all the history records with the same BugID as the Bug).

DataTables, DataColumns, and DataRelations are explored in more detail later in this chapter.

The most important methods and properties of the DataTable class are shown in Table 19-2.

Table 19-2. The most important DataTable properties and methods

Class Member	Type	Description
ChildRelations	Property	Gets the collection of child relations (see Relations object).
Columns	Property	Gets the Columns collection.

Table 19-2. The most important DataTable properties and methods (continued)

Class Member	Type	Description
Constraints	Property	Gets the Constraints collection.
DataSet	Property	Gets the DataSet to which this table belongs.
DefaultView	Property	Gets a view of the table for filtering.
ParentRelations	Property	Gets the ParentRelations collection.
PrimaryKey	Property	Gets or sets an array of columns as the primary key for this table.
Rows	Property	Gets the Rows collection.
AcceptChanges	Method	Commits all the changes since the last AcceptChanges.
Clear	Method	Clears the table of all data.
GetChanges	Method	Gets a copy of the DataTable with all the changes since the last AcceptChanges (see AcceptChanges).
NewRow	Method	Create a new DataRow with the same schema as the table.
RejectChanges	Method	Rolls back changes since the last AcceptChanges (see AcceptChanges).
Select	Method	Gets an array of DataRow objects.

The DataRow class

The Rows collection contains DataRow objects, one for each row in the table. Use this collection to examine the results of queries against the database, iterating through the rows to examine each record in turn. Programmers experienced with ADO are often confused by the absence of the RecordSet with its moveNext and movePrevious commands. With ADO.NET, you do not iterate through the DataSet; instead you access the table you need, and then you can iterate through the rows collection, typically with a foreach loop. You'll see this process in Example 19-2.

The most important methods and properties of the DataRow class are shown in Table 19-3.

Table 19-3. The most important DataRow properties and methods

Class Member	Type	Description
Item	Property	Get or set the data stored in a specific column (in C#, this is the indexer).
ItemArray	Property	Get or set all the values for the row using an array,
Table	Property	Get the table that owns this row.
AcceptChanges	Method	Accept all the changes since the last time AcceptChanges was called.
GetChildRows	Method	Get the child rows for this row.
GetParentRow	Method	Get the parent row of this row.
RejectChanges	Method	Reject all the changes since the last time AcceptChanges was called (see AcceptChanges).

DBCommand and DBConnection

The DBConnection object represents a connection to a data source. This connection may be shared among different command objects.

The DBCommand object allows you to send a command (typically a SQL statement or the name of a stored procedure) to the database. Often these objects are created implicitly when you create your DataSet, but you can explicitly access these objects, as you'll see in Examples 19-4 and 19-5.

The DataAdapter Object

Rather than tie the DataSet object too closely to your database architecture, ADO. NET uses a DataAdapter object to mediate between the DataSet object and the database. This decouples the DataSet from the database, and allows a single DataSet to represent more than one database or other data source.

.NET provides versions of the DataAdapter object; one for each data provider (e.g., SQL Server). If you are connecting to a SQL Server database, you will increase the performance of your application by using SqlDataAdapter (from System.Data.SqlClient) along with SqlCommand and SqlConnection. If you are using another database, you will often use OleDbDataAdapter (from System.Data.OleDb) along with OleDb-Command and OleDbConnection.

 As of this writing, there are also ODBC and Oracle providers, with more providers being written all the time. Check with your database provider to see whether there is an ADO.NET provider for your technology.

The most important methods and properties of the DataAdapter class are shown in Table 19-4.

Table 19-4. The most important DataAdapter properties and methods

Class Member	Description
AcceptChangesDuringFill property	Indicates whether to call AcceptChanges on a DataRow after adding it to a DataTable.
Fill method	Fills a DataTable by adding or updating rows in the DataSet.
FillSchema method	Adds a DataTable object to the specified DataSet. Configures the schema to the specified SchemaType.
Update method	Updates all the modified rows in the specified table of the DataSet.

Getting Started with ADO.NET

In the coming examples, you'll create a more complex display with a DataGrid, and you'll display data from multiple tables—but to get started, you'll keep it as simple as possible. In this first example, you'll create a simple Windows Form with a single ListBox called lbBugs. You'll populate this ListBox with bits of information from the Bugs table in the WindForms_Bugs database.

To get started, you need to create the WindForm_Bugs database based on the description provided previously, or you may download it from our web site. In addition, you may find it convenient to create an ODBC connection known as a Data Source Name (DSN).

To create the DSN, click Start → Settings → Control Panel. Within the Control Panel, click on Administrative Tools and then on Data Sources (ODBC). The ODBC Data Source Administrator dialog box will open, as shown in Figure 19-7.

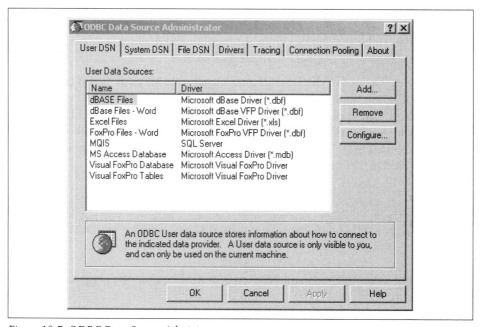

Figure 19-7. ODBC Data Source Administrator

Click on the System DSN tab, and then click on the Add button. The dialog to select a data source will open as shown in Figure 19-8. Scroll to the bottom and choose SQL Server.

Enter the name WindForm_bugs and choose your server from the drop-down menu in the next dialog. You will be prompted to identify how SQL Server should verify the authenticity of the login ID. Choose "With SQL Server authentication using a login ID and password entered by the user." In the Login ID, choose sa (the system administrator) and enter the sa password, as shown in Figure 19-9.

On the next dialog box, change the default database to WindForm_Bugs, as shown in Figure 19-10.

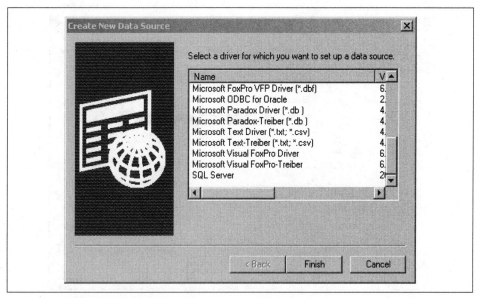

Figure 19-8. Create a data source

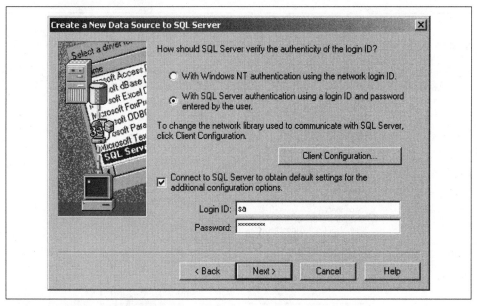

Figure 19-9. Entering the login ID

Accept the defaults on the following dialog and then test the data source you've created on the final dialog, as shown in Figure 19-11. You can now use this DSN in your application.

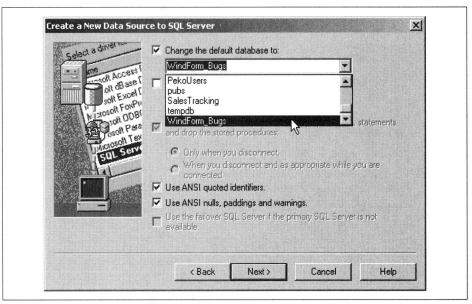

Figure 19-10. Changing the default database

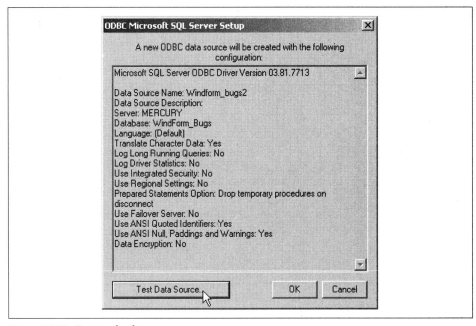

Figure 19-11. Testing the data source

To test your DSN and see how you place data in a Windows application, you'll create a new Windows Application project named SimpleBugListBox. You can create it in either C# or in VB.NET.

Drag a ListBox onto the form and name it lbBugs (that is, change the value of its (Name) property to lbBugs). Stretch the ListBox to fill the form, as shown in Figure 19-12.

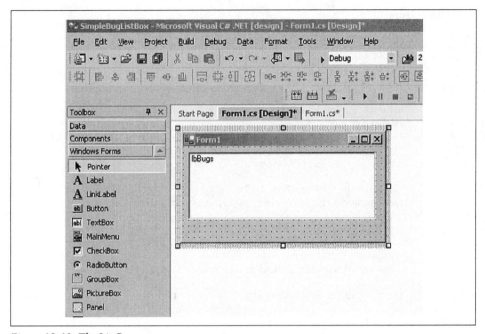

Figure 19-12. The ListBox

Example 19-2 is the complete source code from the code window.

Example 19-2. A Simple ADO.NET in C#

```
using System;
using System.Drawing;
using System.Collections;
using System.ComponentModel;
using System.Windows.Forms;
using System.Data;
using System.Data.SqlClient;

namespace SimpleBugListBox
{
    /// <summary>
    /// Summary description for Form1.
    /// </summary>
    public class Form1 : System.Windows.Forms.Form
    {
        private System.Windows.Forms.ListBox lbBugs;
        /// <summary>
        /// Required designer variable.
```

Example 19-2. A Simple ADO.NET in C# (continued)

```csharp
        /// </summary>
        private System.ComponentModel.Container components = null;

        public Form1( )
        {
           //
           // Required for Windows Form Designer support
           //
           InitializeComponent( );

              // connect to the Bugs database
              string connectionString =
              "server=YourServer; uid=sa; pwd=YourPassword;            database=WindForm_
Bugs";

              // get records from the Bugs table
              string commandString =  "Select BugID, Description from Bugs";

              // create the data set command object
              // and the DataSet
              SqlDataAdapter dataAdapter =
                  new SqlDataAdapter(commandString, connectionString);

              DataSet dataSet = new DataSet( );

              // fill the data set object
              dataAdapter.Fill(dataSet,"Bugs");

              // Get the one table from the DataSet
              DataTable dataTable = dataSet.Tables[0];

              // for each row in the table, display the info
              foreach (DataRow dataRow in dataTable.Rows)
              {
                  lbBugs.Items.Add(
                      dataRow["BugID"] +
                      ": " + dataRow["Description"]  );
              }
        }

        /// <summary>
        /// Clean up any resources being used.
        /// </summary>
        protected override void Dispose( bool disposing )
        {
           if( disposing )
           {
              if (components != null)
              {
                  components.Dispose( );
              }
```

Example 19-2. A Simple ADO.NET in C# (continued)

```csharp
        }
        base.Dispose( disposing );
    }

    #region Windows Form Designer generated code
    /// <summary>
    /// Required method for Designer support - do not modify
    /// the contents of this method with the code editor.
    /// </summary>
    private void InitializeComponent( )
    {
        this.lbBugs = new System.Windows.Forms.ListBox( );
        this.SuspendLayout( );
        //
        // lbBugs
        //
        this.lbBugs.Location = new System.Drawing.Point(24, 16);
        this.lbBugs.Name = "lbBugs";
        this.lbBugs.Size = new System.Drawing.Size(240, 95);
        this.lbBugs.TabIndex = 0;
        //
        // Form1
        //
        this.AutoScaleBaseSize = new System.Drawing.Size(5, 13);
        this.ClientSize = new System.Drawing.Size(292, 273);
        this.Controls.AddRange(new System.Windows.Forms.Control[ ] {
                                                    this.lbBugs});
        this.Name = "Form1";
        this.Text = "Form1";
        this.ResumeLayout(false);

    }
    #endregion

    /// <summary>
    /// The main entry point for the application.
    /// </summary>
    [STAThread]
    static void Main( )
    {
        Application.Run(new Form1( ));
    }
}
}
```

The VB.NET example is nearly identical, except for the constructor, which is shown in Example 19-3.

Example 19-3. Constructor in VB.NET

```vbnet
Public Sub New( )
    MyBase.New( )
```

Example 19-3. Constructor in VB.NET (continued)

```
    'This call is required by the Windows Form Designer.
    InitializeComponent( )

    Dim connectionString As String
    connectionString = _
    "Server=YourServer; uid=sa; pwd=YourPassword; " & _
      database=WindForm_Bugs"

    Dim commandString As String
    commandString = "Select BugID, Description from Bugs"

    Dim myDataAdapter As New System.Data.SqlClient.SqlDataAdapter(_
        commandString, connectionString)

    Dim myDataSet As New DataSet( )

    myDataAdapter.Fill(myDataSet, "Bugs")

    Dim myDataTable As DataTable
    myDataTable = myDataSet.Tables(0)

    Dim theRow As DataRow
    For Each theRow In myDataTable.Rows
        lbBugs.Items.Add(theRow("BugID") & ": " & _
          theRow("Description"))
    Next
End Sub
```

With just about eight lines of code in the form's constructor, you have extracted a set of data from the database and displayed it in the ListBox, as shown in Figure 19-13

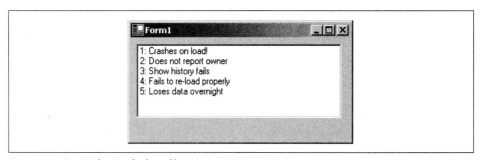

Figure 19-13. Displaying the list of bugs

The eight lines accomplished the following tasks:

1. Created the string for the connection. The connection string is whatever string is needed to connect to the database. In the case of our example:

```
    string connectionString =
        "server=YourServer; uid=sa;
          pwd=YourPassword; database=WindForms_Bugs";
```

```vb
VB    Dim connectionString As String
      connectionString = _
      "Server=YourServer; uid=sa; pwd=YourPassword; " & _
        database=WindForm_Bugs"
```

2. Created the string for the select statement, which generates a table containing bug IDs and their descriptions:

```csharp
C#    string commandString =
        "Select BugID, Description from Bugs";
```

```vb
VB    Dim commandString As String
      commandString = "Select BugID, Description from Bugs"
```

3. Created the DataAdapter to extract the data from the SQL Server database and pass in the selection and connection strings:

```csharp
C#    SqlDataAdapter dataAdapter =
      new SqlDataAdapter(
      commandString, connectionString);
```

```vb
VB    Dim myDataAdapter As New System.Data.SqlClient.SqlDataAdapter(_
          commandString, connectionString)
```

4. Created a new DataSet object:

```csharp
C#    DataSet dataSet = new DataSet();
```

```vb
VB    Dim myDataSet As New DataSet()
```

5. Filled the DataSet with the data obtained from the SQL select statement using the DataAdapter:

```csharp
C#    dataAdapter.Fill(dataSet,"Bugs");
```

```vb
VB    myDataAdapter.Fill(myDataSet, "Bugs")
```

6. Extracted the DataTable from the DataTableCollection object:

```csharp
C#    DataTable dataTable = dataSet.Tables[0];
```

```vb
VB    Dim myDataTable As DataTable
      myDataTable = myDataSet.Tables(0)
```

7. Iterated the rows in the data table to fill the ListBox:

```csharp
C#    foreach (DataRow dataRow in dataTable.Rows)
      {
         lbBugs.Items.Add(
           dataRow["BugID"] +
           ": " + dataRow["Description"] );
      }
```

```vb
VB    Dim theRow As DataRow
      For Each theRow In myDataTable.Rows
```

```
        lbBugs.Items.Add(theRow("BugID") & ": " & _
        theRow("Description"))
Next
```

Using the Wizards

Visual Studio .NET provides extensive wizard support for automating the interaction with the DataBase. The advantage of using wizards is that it can simplify the development process and shield you from the details of database interaction. The disadvantage is that it shields you from the details of database interaction, and thus can leave you vulnerable when things don't work as expected.

This book does not focus on using the wizards; frankly we prefer to write code by hand. However, a quick review will give you a sense of the power of this level of automation. Create a new Windows application and drag a ListBox in place as you have in previous examples. Next, drag a SqlConnection control onto the form. (The SqlConnection control can be found under the Data tab of the Toolbox.) The Sql-Connection control will appear in the "tray" below the form, as shown circled in Figure 19-14.

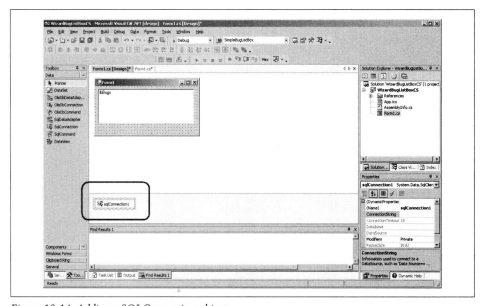

Figure 19-14. Adding a SQLConnection object

> SQL is pronounced "see-quill" or "ess-que-ell." In this book, we pronounce it as "see-quill" and so write "a SQLConnection" (a see-quillConnection) rather than "an SQLConnection" (an ess-que-ellConnection).

Select the SQLConnection control on the form and click on the connectionString property in the properties window (highlighted in the lower-righthand corner of Figure 19-14) and drop down the list. Click on New Connection and a new connection dialog box appears, as shown in Figure 19-15. You can use the same values used in your ODBC connection.

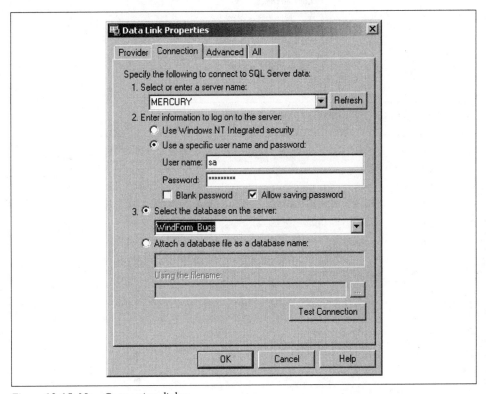

Figure 19-15. New Connection dialog

Drag an SqlCommand control (again from the Data tab of the Toolbox) onto the tray. Drop its Connection property and set it to the existing connection you just created, as shown in Figure 19-16.

Click on the CommandText property. Click on the button with three dots. This brings up the Query Builder, as shown in Figure 19-17. Click on Bugs to choose the Bugs table, click Add, and then close. You will select only from the Bugs table for now.

Within the Query Builder, you can select the columns you want to display and control sorting and filtering. Check BugID and Description to include these columns in the query results (as you did manually in the previous example), as shown in Figure 19-18.

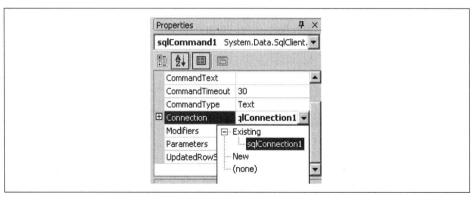

Figure 19-16. Hooking the command to the connection

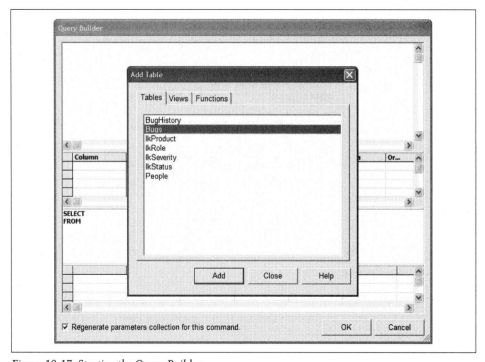

Figure 19-17. Starting the Query Builder

You are ready now to return to your code to use the command and connection objects. Enter the code-editing window, and you'll find that Visual Studio .NET has added two member variables to your class:

```csharp
private System.Data.SqlClient.SqlConnection sqlConnection1;
private System.Data.SqlClient.SqlCommand sqlCommand1;
```

These components are initialized in the InitializeComponent section of the code (normally collapsed). Click the + sign next to this block of code to expand it. You'll

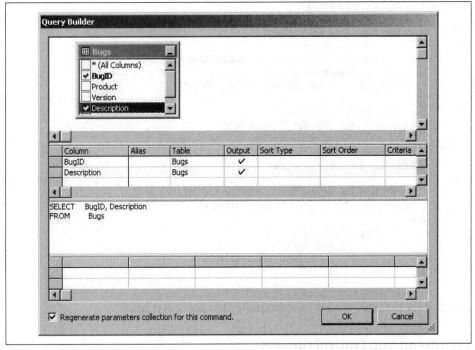

Figure 19-18. Building the query

find that the Connection and Command objects are instantiated and initialized, as shown in this excerpt:

```
this.sqlConnection1 = new System.Data.SqlClient.SqlConnection();
this.sqlCommand1 = new System.Data.SqlClient.SqlCommand();
this.sqlConnection1.ConnectionString = "data source=YourServer;initial
catalog=WindForm_Bugs;password=YourPassword;persist security info=True;user
id=sa;workstation id=YOURSERVER;packet size=4096";
this.sqlCommand1.CommandText = "SELECT BugID, Description FROM Bugs";
this.sqlCommand1.Connection = this.sqlConnection1;
```

Associate the command object with the data adapter explicitly:

```
SqlDataAdapter dataAdapter = new SqlDataAdapter();
dataAdapter.SelectCommand = sqlCommand1;
dataAdapter.TableMappings.Add("Table", "Bugs");
```

Don't forget to add:

```
using System.Data.SqlClient;
```

to the top of the file.

The complete constructor is shown in:

```
public Form1()
{
```

```
        InitializeComponent( );

        DataSet DataSet = new DataSet( );

        SqlDataAdapter dataAdapter = new SqlDataAdapter( );
        dataAdapter.SelectCommand = sqlCommand1;
        dataAdapter.TableMappings.Add("Table", "Bugs");

        // fill the data set object
        dataAdapter.Fill(DataSet,"Customers");

        // Get the one table from the DataSet
        DataTable dataTable = DataSet.Tables[0];

        // for each row in the table, display the info
        foreach (DataRow dataRow in dataTable.Rows)
        {
            lbBugs.Items.Add(
                dataRow["BugID"] +
                ": " + dataRow["Description"]  );
        }
    }
```

You can see that the wizards have simplified the process considerably.

Command and Control Objects

Rather than using the wizards, you can create the command and control objects programmatically as shown in Example 19-4 in C# and in Example 19-5 in VB.NET.

 Much of the code generated by Visual Studio .NET is left out of this listing to save space.

Example 19-4. Explicit command and connection objects (C#)

```
using System;
using System.Drawing;
using System.Collections;
using System.ComponentModel;
using System.Windows.Forms;
using System.Data;
using System.Data.SqlClient;

namespace CommandObjectCS
{
    public class Form1 : System.Windows.Forms.Form
    {
        private System.Data.SqlClient.SqlConnection myConnection;
        private System.Data.DataSet myDataSet;
        private System.Data.SqlClient.SqlCommand myCommand;
        private System.Data.SqlClient.SqlDataAdapter myDataAdapter;
```

Example 19-4. Explicit command and connection objects (C#) (continued)

```
      private System.Windows.Forms.ListBox lbBugs;
   /// <summary>
   /// Required designer variable.
   /// </summary>
   private System.ComponentModel.Container components = null;

   public Form1( )
   {
      //
      // Required for Windows Form Designer support
      //
      InitializeComponent( );
         string connectionString =
            "server=YourServer; uid=sa; pwd=YourPW; database=WindForm_Bugs";

         // create and open the myConnection object
         myConnection =
           new System.Data.SqlClient.SqlConnection(connectionString);
         myConnection.Open( );

         // create the dataset, set property
         myDataSet = new System.Data.DataSet( );
         myDataSet.CaseSensitive=true;

         // get records from the Bugs table
         string commandString = "Select BugID, Description from Bugs";

         myCommand = new System.Data.SqlClient.SqlCommand( );
         myCommand.Connection=myConnection;
         myCommand.CommandText= commandString;

         myDataAdapter = new SqlDataAdapter( );
         myDataAdapter.SelectCommand = myCommand;
         myDataAdapter.TableMappings.Add("Table", "Bugs");
         myDataAdapter.Fill(myDataSet);


         // Get the one table from the DataSet
         DataTable myDataTable = myDataSet.Tables[0];

         // for each row in the table, display the info
         foreach (DataRow dataRow in myDataTable.Rows)
         {
            lbBugs.Items.Add(
               dataRow["BugID"] +
               ": " + dataRow["Description"]  );
         }
      }

   }
}
```

Example 19-5. Explicit command and connection objects (VB.NET)

VB
```vb
Imports System.Data
Imports System.Data.SqlClient

Public Class Form1
    Inherits System.Windows.Forms.Form

    Private myConnection As System.Data.SqlClient.SqlConnection
    Private myDataSet As System.Data.DataSet
    Private myCommand As System.Data.SqlClient.SqlCommand
    Private myDataAdapter As System.Data.SqlClient.SqlDataAdapter

#Region " Windows Form Designer generated code "
#End Region

    Public Sub New()
        MyBase.New()

        'This call is required by the Windows Form Designer.
        InitializeComponent()

        Dim connectionString As String
        connectionString = _
        "Server=YourServer; uid=sa; pwd=YourPW; database=WindForm_Bugs"

        myConnection = _
         New System.Data.SqlClient.SqlConnection(connectionString)
        myConnection.Open()

        myDataSet = New System.Data.DataSet()
        myDataSet.CaseSensitive = True


        Dim commandString As String
        commandString = "Select BugID, Description from Bugs "

        myCommand = New System.Data.SqlClient.SqlCommand()
        myCommand.Connection = myConnection
        myCommand.CommandText = commandString

        myDataAdapter = New SqlDataAdapter()
        myDataAdapter.SelectCommand = myCommand
        myDataAdapter.TableMappings.Add("Table", "Bugs")
        myDataAdapter.Fill(myDataSet)

        Dim myDataTable As DataTable
        myDataTable = myDataSet.Tables(0)

        Dim dataRow As DataRow
        For Each dataRow In myDataTable.Rows
            lbBugs.Items.Add(dataRow("BugID") & ": " & _
```

Example 19-5. Explicit command and connection objects (VB.NET) (continued)

```
VB              dataRow("Description"))
          Next
      End Sub
End Class
```

In Examples 19-4 and 19-5, start by creating four new instance members for the Form class:

```
C#   private System.Data.SqlClient.SqlConnection myConnection;
     private System.Data.DataSet myDataSet;
     private System.Data.SqlClient.SqlCommand myCommand;
     private System.Data.SqlClient.SqlDataAdapter myDataAdapter;
```

```
VB   Private myConnection As System.Data.SqlClient.SqlConnection
     Private myDataSet As System.Data.DataSet
     Private myCommand As System.Data.SqlClient.SqlCommand
     Private myDataAdapter As System.Data.SqlClient.SqlDataAdapter
```

The connection is created by instantiating a SQLConnection object with the connection string:

```
VB   myConnection = new System.Data.SqlClient.SqlConnection(connectionString);
```

The VB.NET is identical, except that you leave off the semicolon.

The connection is explicitly opened:

```
VB   myConnection.Open( )
```

You can hang on to this connection object and reuse it, as you'll see in later examples. This connection can also be used for transactions, as described in Chapter 20.

Next, create the DataSet object and set its CaseSensitive property to true to indicate that string comparisons within DataTable objects are case sensitive:

```
VB   myDataSet = New System.Data.DataSet( )
     myDataSet.CaseSensitive = True
```

Create the SqlCommand object and give that new command object the connection object and the text for the command:

```
VB   myCommand = New System.Data.SqlClient.SqlCommand( )
     myCommand.Connection = myConnection
     myCommand.CommandText = commandString
```

Finally, create the SqlDataAdapter object and assign to it the SqlCommand object you just created. Then tell the DataSet how to map the table columns and instruct the SqlDataAdapter to fill the DataSet:

```
VB   myDataAdapter = New SqlDataAdapter( )
     myDataAdapter.SelectCommand = myCommand
     myDataAdapter.TableMappings.Add("Table", "Bugs")
     myDataAdapter.Fill(myDataSet)
```

Managed Providers

The previous examples used one of the managed providers initially available with ADO.NET: the SQL managed provider. The SQL managed provider is optimized for Microsoft SQL Server, but it is restricted to working with SQL Server databases. The more general solution is the OLE DB managed provider, which connects to any OLE DB provider, including Microsoft Access and MSDE (which is provided for free).

You can rewrite Example 19-1 to work with the Bugs database using Microsoft Access rather than Microsoft SQL Server with just a few small changes. First, you need to create a new Access database. Name the new database SimpleBugListBox-AccessDB. Example 19-6 assumes you will save your database to the root directory on your C drive, but you may save it anywhere else that is convenient for you as long as you adjust the connection string accordingly.

Use the File → Get External Data → Import menu option in Access to import the data from the SQL database. This will create tables in Access that reflect the structure and content of the data in the SQL database. Notice that the Bugs database is now named dbo_Bugs in Access.

Create a new ASP Application project named SimpleBugListboxAccessCS, and once again drag a ListBox onto the form, resize it, and name it lbBugs. Copy the code from Example 19-2, but make the following changes:

1. Change the connection string to:

   C#
   ```
   string connectionString =
       "provider=Microsoft.JET.OLEDB.4.0; "
       + "data source = c:\\simpleBugListBoxAccessDB.mdb";
   ```

   This will connect to the database you just created. Note the space between data and source in the connection string. Be sure to substitute the correct path for the *mdb* file on your machine.

2. Change the DataAdapter object to be an OleDbDataAdapter rather than a Sql-DataAdapter:

   C#
   ```
   OleDbDataAdapter DataAdapter =
       new OleDbDataAdapter (commandString, connectionString);
   ```

3. Replace the using statement (in C#) or the imports statement (in VB.NET) System.Data.SqlClient with the corresponding statement for the OleDb namespace:

   C#
   ```
   using System.Data.OleDb;
   ```

   VB
   ```
   imports System.Data.OleDb
   ```

This design pattern continues while you work with the two managed providers; for every object whose class name begins with Sql, a corresponding class begins with OleDb. Example 19-6 is the complete OLE DB version of Example 19-2 in C#, while Example 19-7 is the complete OLE DB version in VB.NET.

Example 19-6. Using ADO.NET with Access (in C#)

```
using System;
using System.Data;
using System.Data.OleDb;
using System.Drawing;
using System.Collections;
using System.ComponentModel;
using System.Windows.Forms;


namespace SimpleBugListboxAccessCS
{
    /// <summary>
    /// Summary description for Form1.
    /// </summary>
    public class Form1 : System.Windows.Forms.Form
    {
        private System.Windows.Forms.ListBox lbBugs;
        /// <summary>
        /// Required designer variable.
        /// </summary>
        private System.ComponentModel.Container components = null;

        public Form1( )
        {
            //
            // Required for Windows Form Designer support
            //
            InitializeComponent( );

            // connect to the Bugs database
            string connectionString =
                "provider=Microsoft.JET.OLEDB.4.0; "
                + "data source = c:\\simpleBugListBoxAccessDB.mdb";

            // get records from the Bugs table
            string commandString =
                "Select BugID, Description from dbo_Bugs";

            // create the data set command object
            // and the DataSet
            OleDbDataAdapter dataAdapter =
                new OleDbDataAdapter (commandString, connectionString);

            DataSet DataSet = new DataSet( );

            // fill the data set object
```

Example 19-6. Using ADO.NET with Access (in C#) (continued)

```csharp
        dataAdapter.Fill(DataSet,"Customers");

        // Get the one table from the DataSet
        DataTable dataTable = DataSet.Tables[0];

        // for each row in the table, display the info
        foreach (DataRow dataRow in dataTable.Rows)
        {
           lbBugs.Items.Add(
             dataRow["BugID"] +
             ": " + dataRow["Description"]  );
        }
     }

     /// <summary>
     /// Clean up any resources being used.
     /// </summary>
     protected override void Dispose( bool disposing )
     {
        if( disposing )
        {
           if (components != null)
           {
              components.Dispose( );
           }
        }
        base.Dispose( disposing );
     }

     #region Windows Form Designer generated code
     #endregion

     /// <summary>
     /// The main entry point for the application.
     /// </summary>
     [STAThread]
     static void Main( )
     {
        Application.Run(new Form1( ));
     }
  }
}
```

Example 19-7. Using ADO.NET with Access (in VB.NET)

```vbnet
Public Class Form1
    Inherits System.Windows.Forms.Form

#Region " Windows Form Designer generated code "

    Public Sub New( )
        MyBase.New( )
```

Example 19-7. Using ADO.NET with Access (in VB.NET) (continued)

```
VB          'This call is required by the Windows Form Designer.
            InitializeComponent( )

            Dim connectionString As String
            connectionString = _
            "provider=Microsoft.JET.OLEDB.4.0; data source = _
                c:\\simpleBugListBoxAccessDB.mdb"

            Dim commandString As String
            commandString = "Select BugID, Description from dbo_Bugs"

            Dim myDataAdapter As New _
                System.Data.OleDb.OleDbDataAdapter( _
                    commandString, connectionString)

            Dim myDataSet As New DataSet( )

            myDataAdapter.Fill(myDataSet, "Bugs")

            Dim myDataTable As DataTable
            myDataTable = myDataSet.Tables(0)

            Dim theRow As DataRow
            For Each theRow In myDataTable.Rows
                lbBugs.Items.Add(theRow("BugID") & ": " & _
                    theRow("Description"))
            Next
        End Sub


    #End Region

    End Class
```

Before you run this program, edit the description of the first bug to include the word
Access; this will help you ensure that you are looking at the correct data. The output, shown in Figure 19-19, is identical to that from the previous example (except for
the change you've made to the description of the first bug).

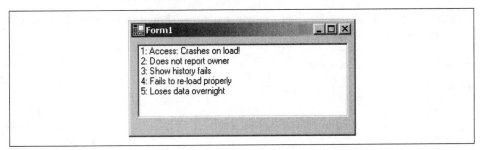

Figure 19-19. Using the ADO provider

The OLE DB managed provider is more general than the SQL managed provider and can, in fact, be used to connect to Microsoft SQL Server as well as to any other OLE DB object. Because the SQL Server provider is optimized for SQL Server, it will be more efficient to use the SQL Server–specific provider when working with SQL Server.

Binding Data

Rather than iterating through the table and loading each record individually, you can *bind* the ListBox control to the database table. In general, data binding lets you create a relationship between a control (such as a ListBox) and a source of data (such as a DataSet whose backing store is SQL Server).

Virtually any object can act as a data source, including such simple sources as properties, expressions, or the result of a method call, and such complex sources as arrays, collections, and DataSets. For controls that display a collection, such as a listbox or a DataGrid, you must bind to a source that implements one of the binding interfaces such as ICollection, IBindingList, or IListSource. This allows the control to iterate over the collection and display each member in turn.

For example, you can modify the previous examples to remove the foreach loop:

```
// for each row in the table, display the info
foreach (DataRow dataRow in dataTable.Rows)
{
    lbBugs.Items.Add(
        dataRow["BugID"] +
        ": " + dataRow["Description"] );
}
```

and replace it with these two statements:

```
lbBugs.DataSource= dataTable;
lbBugs.DisplayMember = "Description";
```

The first statement instructs the control to bind to a dataTable and populate itself based on that table's data. The second sets the DisplayMember property, which tells the ListBox which field within the table the ListBox will display.

The complete source code for the form constructor is shown in Example 19-8 for C# and Example 19-9 for VB.NET.

Example 19-8. Binding data in C#

```
public Form1( )
{
    //
    // Required for Windows Form Designer support
    //
    InitializeComponent( );
```

Example 19-8. Binding data in C# (continued)

```csharp
    // connect to the Bugs database
    string connectionString =
        "server=YourServer; uid=sa; pwd=YourPassword; database=WindForm_Bugs";

    // get records from the Bugs table
    string commandString =
        "Select BugID, Description from Bugs";

    // create the data set command object
    // and the DataSet
    SqlDataAdapter dataAdapter =
        new SqlDataAdapter(
        commandString, connectionString);

    DataSet DataSet = new DataSet( );

    // fill the data set object
    dataAdapter.Fill(DataSet,"Customers");

    // Get the one table from the DataSet
    DataTable dataTable = DataSet.Tables[0];

    // bind to the data table
    lbBugs.DataSource= dataTable;
    lbBugs.DisplayMember = "Description";
}
```

Example 19-9. Binding data in VB.NET

```vbnet
Public Sub New( )
    MyBase.New( )

    'This call is required by the Windows Form Designer.
    InitializeComponent( )

    Dim connectionString As String
    connectionString = _
    "Server=YourServer; uid=sa; pwd=YourPassword; database=WindForm_Bugs"

    Dim commandString As String
    commandString = "Select BugID, Description from Bugs"

    Dim myDataAdapter As New System.Data.SqlClient.SqlDataAdapter( _
        commandString, connectionString)

    Dim myDataSet As New DataSet( )

    myDataAdapter.Fill(myDataSet, "Bugs")

    Dim myDataTable As DataTable
    myDataTable = myDataSet.Tables(0)
```

Example 19-9. Binding data in VB.NET (continued)

VB
```
' bind to the data table
lbBugs.DataSource = myDataTable
lbBugs.DisplayMember = "Description"

End Sub
```

Data Reader

An alternative to creating a DataSet is to create an instance of DataReader. The DataReader provides connected, forward-only, read-only access to a collection of tables, by, for example, executing a SQL statement or a stored procedure. Data-Readers are lightweight objects ideally suited for filling a control or a form with data and then breaking the connection to the backend database.

> Like DataAdapter, the DataReader class comes in two flavors: Sql-DataReader for use with SQL Server and OleDbDataReader for use with other databases.

Table 19-5 shows the most important methods and properties of the DataReader class.

Table 19-5. The most important DataReader methods

Class member	Description
Close	Closes the DataReader.
NextResult	When reading the results of a batch SQL statement, advances to the next result set (set of records).
Read	Read a record and advance the iterator. Returns `true` if there are more records to read, otherwise `false`.

The DataReader is a very powerful object, but you won't use many of its methods or properties often. Most of the time, you'll simply use the DataReader to retrieve and iterate through the records that represent the result of your query.

> Note to ADO programmers: you do not issue a MoveNext command to the DataReader. By reading a record, you automatically move to the next record. This eliminates one of the most common bugs with recordsets—forgetting to move to the next record.

Do not try to create a DataReader by instantiating it with the keyword new. The constructors for the DataReader class are public internal; they are created only by the helper methods of related objects. As a client of the ADO.NET framework, you create a DataReader by calling ExecuteReader on your command object.

The next example modifies Example 19-4 (in C#) and Example 19-5 (VB.NET) to use a DataReader rather than a DataSet. The source code for C# is provided in Example 19-10, and the source for VB.NET is provided in Example 19-11, followed by a detailed analysis.

Example 19-10. Data reader in C#

```
using System;
using System.Drawing;
using System.Collections;
using System.ComponentModel;
using System.Windows.Forms;
using System.Data;
using System.Data.SqlClient;

namespace DataReaderCS
{
    public class Form1 : System.Windows.Forms.Form
    {
        private System.Data.SqlClient.SqlConnection connection;
        private System.Data.DataSet dataSet;
        private System.Data.SqlClient.SqlCommand command;
        private System.Data.SqlClient.SqlDataAdapter dataAdapter;
        private System.Windows.Forms.ListBox lbBugs;
        private System.ComponentModel.Container components = null;

        public Form1()
        {
            InitializeComponent();
            string connectionString =
                "server=YourServer; uid=sa; pwd=YourPwd; database=WindForm_Bugs";

            // create and open the connection object
            using (connection = new System.Data.SqlClient.SqlConnection(
                connectionString))
            {

                connection.Open();

                // create the dataset, set property
                using(dataSet = new System.Data.DataSet())
                {
                    dataSet.CaseSensitive=true;


                    // get records from the Bugs table
                    string commandString =
                "Select BugID, Description from Bugs";


                    command = new System.Data.SqlClient.SqlCommand();
                    command.Connection=connection;
                    command.CommandText= commandString;
```

Example 19-10. Data reader in C# (continued)

```C#
            using (SqlDataReader dataReader = command.ExecuteReader())
            {
               while (dataReader.Read())
               {
                  object bugID = dataReader["bugID"];
                  object description = dataReader["description"];

                  lbBugs.Items.Add(bugID.ToString() + ": "
            + description.ToString());
               }
            }    // end using datareader
         }       // end using dataset
      }          // end using connection
   }

   /// <summary>
   /// Clean up any resources being used.
   /// </summary>
   protected override void Dispose( bool disposing )
   {
      if( disposing )
      {
         if (components != null)
         {
            components.Dispose();
         }
      }
      base.Dispose( disposing );
   }

   #region Windows Form Designer generated code
   #endregion

   /// <summary>
   /// The main entry point for the application.
   /// </summary>
   [STAThread]
   static void Main()
   {
      Application.Run(new Form1());
   }
  }
}
```

Example 19-11. Data reader in VB.NET

```VB
Public Sub New()
    MyBase.New()

    'This call is required by the Windows Form Designer.
    InitializeComponent()
```

Example 19-11. Data reader in VB.NET (continued)

```vb
    Try
        Dim connectionString As String
        connectionString = _
            "Server=YourServer; uid=sa; pwd=YourPW; database=WindForm_Bugs"

        myConnection = _
            New System.Data.SqlClient.SqlConnection(connectionString)
        myConnection.Open( )

        myDataSet = New System.Data.DataSet( )
        myDataSet.CaseSensitive = True


        Dim commandString As String
        commandString = "Select BugID, Description from Bugs "

        myCommand = New System.Data.SqlClient.SqlCommand( )
        myCommand.Connection = myConnection
        myCommand.CommandText = commandString

        myDataReader = myCommand.ExecuteReader( )

        While myDataReader.Read
            lbBugs.Items.Add(myDataReader("bugID") & _
                ": " & myDataReader("Description"))
        End While
    Finally
        myConnection.Dispose( )
        myCommand.Dispose( )
        myDataReader.Close( )
    End Try
End Sub
```

Create the command object as you did in Examples 19-4 and 19-5, but this time you do not create a DataAdapter or DataSet. Instead, you invoke ExecuteReader( ) on the command object:

```vb
    myDataReader = myCommand.ExecuteReader( )
```

Iterate through the recordset in the DataReader within a while loop. Each time you call Read( ), a new record is provided. Access that record in a number of ways. Assign interim objects as shown in Example 19-10:

```csharp
    object bugID = dataReader["bugID"];
    object description = dataReader["description"];

    lbBugs.Items.Add(bugID.ToString( ) + ": " + description.ToString( ));
```

Alternatively, you can use unnamed temporary variables, as shown in Example 19-11:

```vb
    lbBugs.Items.Add(dataReader("bugID") & ": " & dataReader("Description"))
```

You can also access each column by using the zero-based ordinal value of the column:

VB
```
lbBugs.Items.Add(dataReader(0) & ": " & dataReader(1))
```

It is somewhat more efficient to use the accessors based on the native type of the underlying data (GetDateTime, GetDouble, GetInt32, and GetString):

VB
```
lbBugs.Items.Add(dataReader.GetInt32(0).ToString( ) & ": " _
    & dataReader.GetString(1))
```

 In C#, you use the using statement, and in VB.NET, you use a finally block to ensure that the DataReader is closed (and that the connection and command objects are disposed). For large-scale projects, this is vital, though to keep the code simple we may eschew this practice in some of the sample code.

Creating a DataGrid

The Visual Studio .NET development environment provides a very powerful control for displaying tabular data: the DataGrid. You can display a great deal of information from a table just by binding the table to the DataGrid.

Create a new C# or VB.NET project called SimpleADODataGrid. Drag a DataGrid control onto the form. Visual Studio will name it DataGrid1. Rename the DataGrid dgBugs and widen the grid to the width of the form.

In the constructor, retrieve the Bugs table from the database, much as you did in Example 19-2, except that this time you'll modify the select statement to retrieve all the fields from the bugs table:

C#
```
string connectionString =
    "server=YourServer; uid=sa;
    pwd=YourPassword; database=WindForms_Bugs";

// get records from the Bugs table
string commandString =
    "Select * from Bugs";

// create the data set command object
// and the DataSet
SqlDataAdapter dataAdapter =
    new SqlDataAdapter(
    commandString, connectionString);

DataSet DataSet = new DataSet( );

// fill the data set object
dataAdapter.Fill(DataSet,"Bugs");

// Get the one table from the DataSet
DataTable dataTable = DataSet.Tables[0];
```

```
Public Sub New( )
        MyBase.New( )

        'This call is required by the Windows Form Designer.
        InitializeComponent( )

        Dim connectionString As String
        connectionString = _
        "Server=YourServer; uid=sa; pwd=YourPassword; database=WindForm_Bugs"

        Dim commandString As String
        commandString = "Select * from Bugs"

        Dim myDataAdapter As New System.Data.SqlClient.SqlDataAdapter(_
            commandString, connectionString)

        Dim myDataSet As New DataSet( )

        myDataAdapter.Fill(myDataSet, "Bugs")

        Dim myDataTable As DataTable
        myDataTable = myDataSet.Tables(0)

    End Sub
```

In this example, rather than binding to a ListBox, you'll bind to the DataGrid control. To do so, set the DataGrid control's DataSource property to dataTable, the DataTable object you get from the DataSet:

```
dgBugs.DataSource=dataTable;
```

```
dgBugs.DataSource=myDataTable
```

When you run the program, the DataGrid is populated, as shown in Figure 19-20.

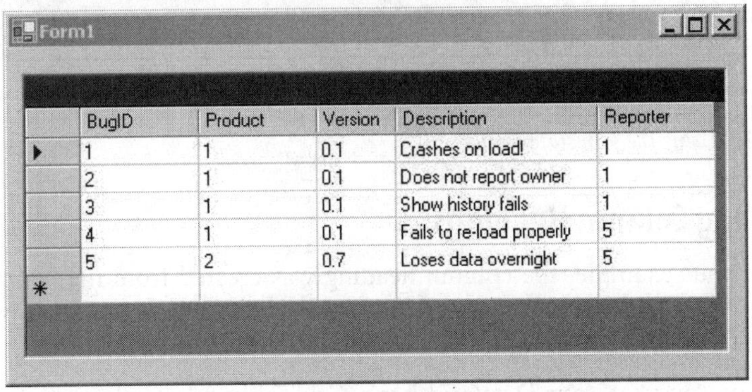

	BugID	Product	Version	Description	Reporter
▶	1	1	0.1	Crashes on load!	1
	2	1	0.1	Does not report owner	1
	3	1	0.1	Show history fails	1
	4	1	0.1	Fails to re-load properly	5
	5	2	0.7	Loses data overnight	5
*					

Figure 19-20. A simple DataGrid

Notice that the columns in the DataGrid have titles. These are the titles of the columns from the Bug table. Unless you tell it otherwise, the DataGrid picks up the titles from the columns in the database. You'll see how to modify this later.

Some columns have numeric field IDs that do not convey a lot of information to the user. It would be better to substitute the name of the product (rather than Product 1 or Product 2) and the name of the person filing the report (rather than Reporter 1 or 5). Accomplish this by using a more sophisticated SQL select statement in the command string:

```
string commandString =
"Select b.BugID, b.Description, p.ProductDescription,
peo.FullName from Bugs b join lkProduct p on b.Product = p.ProductID
join People peo on b.Reporter = peo.PersonID ";
```

In this select statement, you draw fields from three tables: Bugs, Product, and People. Join the Product table to the Bugs table on the ProductID in the Bugs record, and join the People table on the PersonID of the Reporter field in Bugs.

The results are shown in Figure 19-21.

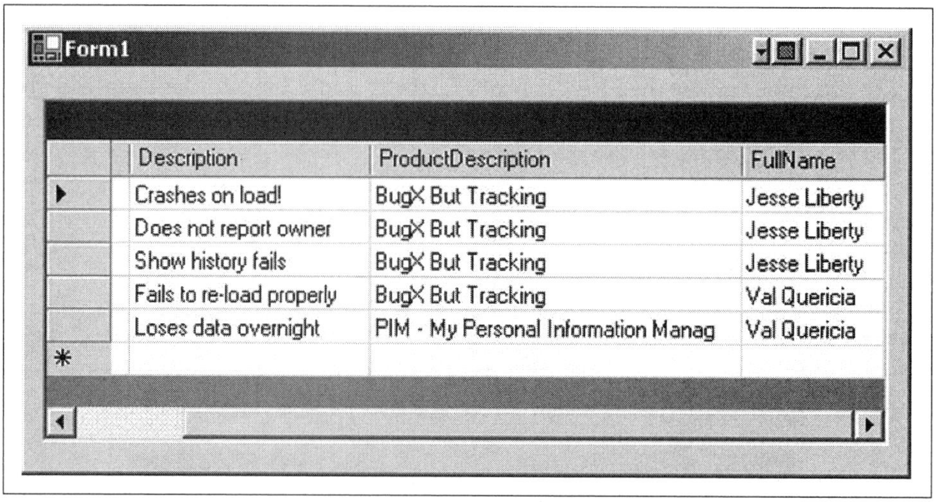

Figure 19-21. Using the join statement

Controlling Column Headings

In the previous example, the column heading was created from the columns in the database. While this is convenient, it is not quite ready for prime time. If you want to control the names of the columns, you can do so, but it is tricky.

Here's how it works. Your DataGrid has a GridTableStylesCollection that contains DataGridTableStyle objects. Each DataGridTableStyle object represents the style for one table represented in the grid.

Within each DataGridTableStyle object is a GridColumnStylesCollection, which contains instances of type DataGridColumnStyle. To control the presentation of your columns, you'll create a DataGridColumnStyle object for each column and set its HeaderText to the text you want to display. You'll also map the DataGridColumnStyle object to the appropriate column in your data table.

Here are the steps:

1. Create an instance of a DataTable and assign to it a table from your DataSet.

`C#`
```
DataTable dataTable = DataSet.Tables[0];
```

`VB`
```
Dim myDataTable As DataTable
myDataTable = myDataSet.Tables(0)
```

2. For each table you will display in the grid you must create a DataGridTableStyle object.

`C#`
```
DataGridTableStyle tableStyle = new DataGridTableStyle( );
```

`VB`
```
Dim tableStyle As New DataGridTableStyle( )
```

3. Set the DataGridTableStyle object's MappingName to the TableName property you get from your DataTable obtained in Step 1:

`C#`
```
tableStyle.MappingName = dataTable.TableName;
```

`VB`
```
tableStyle.MappingName = myDataTable.TableName
```

4. Create an instance of GridColumnStylesCollection and initialize it with the collection returned by the GridColumnStyles property of the DataGridTableStyle object you created in Step 2:

`C#`
```
GridColumnStylesCollection columnStyles = tableStyle.GridColumnStyles;
```

5. Create a DataGridColumnStyle object for each column you want to add to the grid.

`C#`
```
DataGridColumnStyle columnStyle = new DataGridTextBoxColumn( );
```

`VB`
```
Dim columnStyles As GridColumnStylesCollection = _ tableStyle.GridColumnStyles
```

6. For each DataGridColumnStyle, set the Mapping name to a column name from the data, and set the HeaderText to the text you want to appear in the header of the column.

`C#`
```
columnStyle.MappingName="BugID";
columnStyle.HeaderText = "Bug ID";
```

7. Add each DataGridColumnStyle object to the GridColumnStyles Collection:

`C#`
```
columnStyles.Add(columnStyle);
```

8. When all the DataGridColumnStyle objects are in the GridColumnStyles collection, create an instance of GridTableStylesCollection by obtaining the Table-Styles property from the DataGrid.

C#
```
GridTableStylesCollection tableStyles = dgBugs.TableStyles;
```

VB
```
Dim tableStyles As GridTableStylesCollection = _
    dgBugs.TableStyles()
```

9. Add the DataGridTableStyle object you created in Step 2 to the GridTableStyles-Collection you obtained in Step 8.

C#
```
tableStyles.Add(tableStyle);
```

Piece of cake. The code in Example 19-12 illustrates these steps in action. Example 19-13 shows the same code in VB.NET:

Example 19-12. Adding column styles in C#

C#
```
public Form1()
{
  //
  // Required for Windows Form Designer support
  //
  InitializeComponent();
   string connectionString =
       "server=YourServer; uid=sa; pwd=YourPassword; database=WindForm_Bugs";

   // get records from the Bugs table
       string commandString =
       "Select b.BugID, b.Description, p.ProductDescription, ";
       commandString += "peo.FullName from Bugs b ";
       commandString += "join lkProduct p on b.Product = p.ProductID ";
       commandString += "join People peo on b.Reporter = peo.PersonID ";

   // create the data set command object
   // and the DataSet
   SqlDataAdapter dataAdapter =
       new SqlDataAdapter(
       commandString, connectionString);

   DataSet DataSet = new DataSet();

   // fill the data set object
   dataAdapter.Fill(DataSet,"Bugs");

   // Get the one table from the DataSet
   DataTable dataTable = DataSet.Tables[0];

   // create a DataGridTableStyle object and initialize
   // based on the dataTable's TableName.
   DataGridTableStyle tableStyle = new DataGridTableStyle();
   tableStyle.MappingName = dataTable.TableName;
```

Example 19-12. Adding column styles in C# (continued)

```csharp
    // Get the GridColumnsStylesCollection
    // from the table style's GridColumnStyles collection
    GridColumnStylesCollection columnStyles = tableStyle.GridColumnStyles;

    // Make a columnStyle object and add column info to it
    // then add the columnStyle to the columnStyles collection
    DataGridColumnStyle columnStyle = new DataGridTextBoxColumn();
    columnStyle.MappingName="BugID";
    columnStyle.HeaderText = "Bug ID";
    columnStyles.Add(columnStyle);

    columnStyle = new DataGridTextBoxColumn();
    columnStyle.MappingName = "ProductDescription";
    columnStyle.HeaderText="Product";
    columnStyles.Add(columnStyle);

    columnStyle = new DataGridTextBoxColumn();
    columnStyle.MappingName = "Description";
    columnStyle.HeaderText="Description";
    columnStyles.Add(columnStyle);

    columnStyle = new DataGridTextBoxColumn();
    columnStyle.MappingName = "FullName";
    columnStyle.HeaderText="Reporter";
    columnStyles.Add(columnStyle);

    // Get the table Styles collection from the gird
    // Add the tableStyle object just created
    GridTableStylesCollection tableStyles =  dgBugs.TableStyles;
    tableStyles.Add(tableStyle);

    dgBugs.DataSource=dataTable;
}
```

Example 19-13. Column headings in VB.NET

```vbnet
    Public Sub New()
        MyBase.New()

        InitializeComponent()

        Dim connectionString As String
        connectionString = _
            "Server=YourServer; uid=sa; pwd=YourPW; database=Bugs"


        Dim commandString As String
        commandString = _
            "Select b.BugID, b.Description, p.ProductDescription, "
        commandString += "peo.FullName from Bugs b "
        commandString += "join lkProduct p on b.Product = p.ProductID "
        commandString += "join People peo on b.Reporter = peo.PersonID "
```

Example 19-13. Column headings in VB.NET (continued)

```
        Dim myDataAdapter As New _
            System.Data.SqlClient.SqlDataAdapter( _
                commandString, connectionString)

        Dim myDataSet As New DataSet( )

        myDataAdapter.Fill(myDataSet, "Bugs")

        Dim myDataTable As DataTable
        myDataTable = myDataSet.Tables(0)

' create a DataGridTableStyle object and initialize
' based on the dataTable's TableName.
Dim tableStyle As New DataGridTableStyle( )
tableStyle.MappingName = myDataTable.TableName

' Get the GridColumnsStylesCollection
' from the table style's GridColumnStyles collection
Dim columnStyles As GridColumnStylesCollection = tableStyle.GridColumnStyles

' Make a columnStyle object and add column info to it
' then add the columnStyle to the columnStyles collection
Dim columnStyle As New DataGridTextBoxColumn( )
columnStyle.MappingName = "BugID"
columnStyle.HeaderText = "Bug ID"
columnStyles.Add(columnStyle)

columnStyle = New DataGridTextBoxColumn( )
columnStyle.MappingName = "ProductDescription"
columnStyle.HeaderText = "Product"
columnStyles.Add(columnStyle)

columnStyle = New DataGridTextBoxColumn( )
columnStyle.MappingName = "Description"
columnStyle.HeaderText = "Description"
columnStyles.Add(columnStyle)

columnStyle = New DataGridTextBoxColumn( )
columnStyle.MappingName = "FullName"
columnStyle.HeaderText = "Reporter"
columnStyles.Add(columnStyle)

' Get the table Styles collection from the gird
' Add the tableStyle object just created
Dim tableStyles As GridTableStylesCollection = dgBugs.TableStyles( )
tableStyles.Add(tableStyle)
  dgBugs.DataSource = myDataTable
End Sub
```

The result is that the columns are displayed with the column heading you asked for in the order you've added them to the collection, as shown in Figure 19-22.

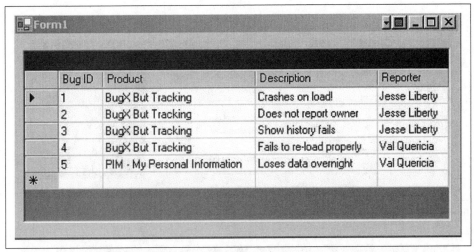

Figure 19-22. Using column styles

Displaying Parent/Child Relationships

The relationship between Bugs and BugHistory is that every Bug includes a BugID, which is a *primary key* in Bugs and a *foreign key* in BugHistory. Thus, you have a one-to-many relationship in which one Bug relates to many BugHistory records, but each BugHistory relates to exactly one Bug order. This is also known as a parent/ child relationship, with the Bug record as parent and the BugHistory records as children.

You can model that relationship in your DataSet and use a DataGrid to display the relationship. The DataGrid is designed to reflect the parent/child relationship by putting a plus mark next to each Bug record. When the user clicks on the plus mark, a link is displayed. Clicking on the link brings up a DataGrid with the child records (the bug history entries for that bug), as shown in Figures 19-23 and 19-24.

Notice in Figure 19-23 that the Bug for which you are seeing the History records is shown in a row across the top. You can navigate back to the bug record by clicking on the white left-pointing arrow in the upper-righthand corner.

To model the relationship between the Bugs table and the BugHistory table, you will need two command objects and two DataAdapter objects. Use them to fill two tables within the DataSet.

Once your two tables are filled, you'll create references to two DataColumn objects that represent the Bugs column in each table, and you'll use these DataColumn objects to create a DataRelation object that will encapsulate the relationship between the two tables.

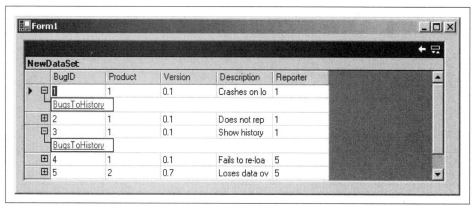

Figure 19-23. DataGrid with child records

BugHistoryID	BugID	Status	Severity	Response	Owner	DateStamp
1	1	1	2	Created	1	1/10/2005
2	1	2	2	Assigned to J	1	1/12/2005
3	1	3	2	I'll look into it	1	1/14/2005
5	1	4	2	Fixed by rese	1	1/15/2005
6	1	5	2	Fixed sproc c	5	1/17/2005

Figure 19-24. BugHistory child records

The complete listing is shown in Examples 19-14 and 19-15, and is followed by a detailed analysis.

Example 19-14. Parent/child grid (C#)

```
public class Form1 : System.Windows.Forms.Form
{
    private System.Data.SqlClient.SqlConnection connection;
    private System.Data.DataSet DataSet;
    private System.Data.SqlClient.SqlCommand bugCommand;
    private System.Data.SqlClient.SqlCommand historyCommand;
    private System.Data.SqlClient.SqlDataAdapter bugDataAdapter;
    private System.Data.SqlClient.SqlDataAdapter historyDataAdapter;
    private System.Windows.Forms.DataGrid dgBugs;
    private System.ComponentModel.Container components = null;

    public Form1( )
    {
        InitializeComponent( );
```

Example 19-14. Parent/child grid (C#) (continued)

```
C#
```

```csharp
      string connectionString =
         "server=YourServer; uid=sa; pwd=YourPassword; database=WindForm_Bugs";

      // create the connection, open it, and create the DataSet
      connection = new
         System.Data.SqlClient.SqlConnection(connectionString);
      connection.Open();
      DataSet = new System.Data.DataSet();
      DataSet.CaseSensitive=true;

      //The first command gets the bugs table
      string bugsCommandString = "Select * from bugs";
      bugCommand = new System.Data.SqlClient.SqlCommand();
      bugCommand.Connection=connection;
      bugCommand.CommandText= bugsCommandString;

      // the second command gets the history table
      string historyCommandString = "Select * from bugHistory";
      historyCommand = new System.Data.SqlClient.SqlCommand();
      historyCommand.Connection=connection;
      historyCommand.CommandText= historyCommandString;

      // create a dataAdapter to get the Bugs table and use it
      // to populate the dataset
      bugDataAdapter = new SqlDataAdapter();
      bugDataAdapter.SelectCommand = bugCommand;
      bugDataAdapter.TableMappings.Add("Table", "Bugs");
      bugDataAdapter.Fill(DataSet);

      // create a dataAdapter to get the history table and use it
      // to populate the dataset
      historyDataAdapter = new SqlDataAdapter();
      historyDataAdapter.SelectCommand = historyCommand;
      historyDataAdapter.TableMappings.Add("Table", "BugHistory");
      historyDataAdapter.Fill(DataSet);

      // create a DataRelation object and references to two
      // dataColumn objects
      System.Data.DataColumn dataColumn1;
      System.Data.DataColumn dataColumn2;

      // Use the dataColumns to represent the Bugs field in both tables
      dataColumn1 = DataSet.Tables["Bugs"].Columns["BugID"];
      dataColumn2 = DataSet.Tables["BugHistory"].Columns["BugID"];

      // Instantiate the DataRelation object with the two columns
      // name the relationship BugsToHistory
      DataRelation bugsToHistory = new System.Data.DataRelation(
         "BugsToHistory",dataColumn1, dataColumn2);

      // Add the DataRelation object to the Relations table in
      //   the dataset
```

Example 19-14. Parent/child grid (C#) (continued)

```csharp
        DataSet.Relations.Add(bugsToHistory);

        // Bind the DataSet to the DataGrid
        DataViewManager dataView = DataSet.DefaultViewManager;
        dgBugs.DataSource= dataView;

    }
```

Example 19-15. Parent/child relationships (VB.NET)

```vbnet
Public Class Form1
    Inherits System.Windows.Forms.Form

    Private myConnection As System.Data.SqlClient.SqlConnection
    Private myDataSet As System.Data.DataSet
    Private bugCommand As System.Data.SqlClient.SqlCommand
    Private historyCommand As System.Data.SqlClient.SqlCommand
    Private bugDataAdapter As System.Data.SqlClient.SqlDataAdapter
    Private historyDataAdapter As System.Data.SqlClient.SqlDataAdapter
#Region " Windows Form Designer generated code "
#End Region

    Public Sub New()
        MyBase.New()

        'This call is required by the Windows Form Designer.
        InitializeComponent()

        Dim connectionString As String
        connectionString = _
        "Server=YourServer; uid=sa; pwd=YourPassword; database=WindForm_Bugs"

        ' create the connection, open it, and create the DataSet
        myConnection = New _
            System.Data.SqlClient.SqlConnection(connectionString)
        myConnection.Open()
        myDataSet = New System.Data.DataSet()
        myDataSet.CaseSensitive = True

        'The first command gets the bugs table
        Dim bugCommandString As String
        bugCommandString = "Select * from bugs"
        bugCommand = New System.Data.SqlClient.SqlCommand()
        bugCommand.Connection = myConnection
        bugCommand.CommandText = bugCommandString

        'the second command gets the history table
        Dim historyCommandString As String
        historyCommandString = "Select * from bugHistory"
        historyCommand = New System.Data.SqlClient.SqlCommand()
        historyCommand.Connection = myConnection
        historyCommand.CommandText = historyCommandString
```

Example 19-15. Parent/child relationships (VB.NET) (continued)

```vb
' create the dataAdapter to get the Bugs table and use
' it to populate the dataset
bugDataAdapter = New SqlDataAdapter()
bugDataAdapter.SelectCommand = bugCommand
bugDataAdapter.TableMappings.Add("Table", "Bugs")
bugDataAdapter.Fill(myDataSet)


' create the dataAdapter to get the history table and
' use it to populate the dataset
historyDataAdapter = New SqlDataAdapter()
historyDataAdapter.SelectCommand = historyCommand
historyDataAdapter.TableMappings.Add("Table", "BugHistory")
historyDataAdapter.Fill(myDataSet)

Dim dataColumn1 As DataColumn
Dim dataColumn2 As DataColumn
dataColumn1 = myDataSet.Tables("Bugs").Columns("BugID")
dataColumn2 = myDataSet.Tables("BugHistory").Columns("BugID")

Dim bugHistory As New DataRelation("BugsToHistory", dataColumn1, dataColumn2)

myDataSet.Relations.Add(bugHistory)

Dim dataView As DataViewManager = myDataSet.DefaultViewManager
dgBugs.DataSource = dataView

End Sub

End Class
```

Begin by creating a command and dataAdapter objects as member variables:

```csharp
private System.Data.SqlClient.SqlCommand bugCommand;
private System.Data.SqlClient.SqlCommand historyCommand;
private System.Data.SqlClient.SqlDataAdapter bugDataAdapter;
private System.Data.SqlClient.SqlDataAdapter historyDataAdapter;
```

```vb
Private bugCommand As System.Data.SqlClient.SqlCommand
Private historyCommand As System.Data.SqlClient.SqlCommand
Private bugDataAdapter As System.Data.SqlClient.SqlDataAdapter
Private historyDataAdapter As System.Data.SqlClient.SqlDataAdapter
```

Within the constructor, create the connection, and then create the command objects, using select statements to retrieve all the fields in the two tables—Bugs and BugHistory:

```csharp
string bugsCommandString = "Select * from bugs";
bugCommand = new System.Data.SqlClient.SqlCommand();
bugCommand.Connection=connection;
bugCommand.CommandText= bugsCommandString;
```

```C#
string historyCommandString = "Select * from bugHistory";
historyCommand = new System.Data.SqlClient.SqlCommand( );
historyCommand.Connection=connection;
historyCommand.CommandText= historyCommandString;
```

```VB
Dim bugCommandString As String
bugCommandString = "Select * from bugs"
bugCommand = New System.Data.SqlClient.SqlCommand( )
bugCommand.Connection = myConnection
bugCommand.CommandText = bugCommandString

Dim historyCommandString As String
historyCommandString = "Select * from bugHistory"
historyCommand = New System.Data.SqlClient.SqlCommand( )
historyCommand.Connection = myConnection
historyCommand.CommandText = historyCommandString
```

Create a DataAdapter for the Bugs table, and use that adapter to create a Bugs table within the DataSet. Then do the same for the BugHistory table (in C#; the VB.NET version is nearly identical):

```C#
bugDataAdapter = new SqlDataAdapter( );
bugDataAdapter.SelectCommand = bugCommand;
bugDataAdapter.TableMappings.Add("Table", "Bugs");
bugDataAdapter.Fill(DataSet);

historyDataAdapter = new SqlDataAdapter( );
historyDataAdapter.SelectCommand = historyCommand;
historyDataAdapter.TableMappings.Add("Table", "BugHistory");
historyDataAdapter.Fill(DataSet);
```

Your DataSet now has two tables: Bugs and BugHistory. You are ready to create the relationship between the tables. Each DataSet has a Relations collection that consists of DataRelation objects. A DataRelation object maps the relationship between two columns through DataColumn objects. Each DataColumn object represents a column in a table. A DataRelation encapsulates the primary/foreign key relationship through those columns:

```C#
System.Data.DataColumn dataColumn1;
System.Data.DataColumn dataColumn2;
```

```VB
Dim dataColumn1 As DataColumn
Dim dataColumn2 As DataColumn
```

Start by creating DataColumn objects for the two data columns in Bugs and BugHistory, respectively (in C#; the VB.NET version is identical except for the semicolon):

```C#
dataColumn1 = DataSet.Tables["Bugs"].Columns["BugID"];
dataColumn2 = DataSet.Tables["BugHistory"].Columns["BugID"];
```

Instantiate the DataRelation object, passing in the two DataColumn objects and a string representing the name of the relationship ("BugsToHistory"):

```
C#
DataRelation bugsToHistory = new System.Data.DataRelation(
    "BugsToHistory",dataColumn1, dataColumn2);
```

```
VB
Dim bugsToHistory As New DataRelation("BugsToHistory", _
    dataColumn1, dataColumn2)
```

Add the new DataRelation object to the Relations collection in your DataSet:

```
VB
myDataSet.Relations.Add(bugsToHistory)
```

Extract the default view from the DataSet and bind the grid to that view:

```
C#
DataViewManager dataView = DataSet.DefaultViewManager;
dgBugs.DataSource= dataView;
```

```
VB
Dim dataView As DataViewManager = myDataSet.DefaultViewManager
dgBugs.DataSource = dataView
```

The DataGrid will display the Bugs table members, recognize the relationship, and automatically put in the links for the BugHistory records.

Creating Data Objects by Hand

In all of the examples so far, you have created the DataSet object and its DataTable and DataRow objects by selecting data from the database. There are, however, occasions when you will want to fill a DataSet or a table by hand.

For example, you may want to gather data from a user and then push that data into the database. It can be convenient to add records to a table manually, and then update the database from that table.

The DataSet is also an excellent transport mechanism for data. You may even want to create a DataSet by hand, only to pass it to another tier in your application, where it will be used as a data source.

In the next example, you will create a DataSet and populate three tables by hand. You'll start by creating the Bugs table and specifying its data structure. You'll then fill that table with records. You'll do the same for the lkProducts table and the People table.

Once the tables are created, you'll set constraints on a number of columns, set default values, establish identity columns, and create keys. In addition, you'll establish a foreign key relationship between two tables, and create a data relation tying two tables together. It sounds like more work than it really is.

The complete source is shown in Example 19-16 for C# and in Example 19-17 for VB.NET, followed by a detailed analysis. Create a new Windows project and name it

DataSetByHand. Add a DataGrid to the form, and size it large enough to display a few records, as shown in Figure 19-25.

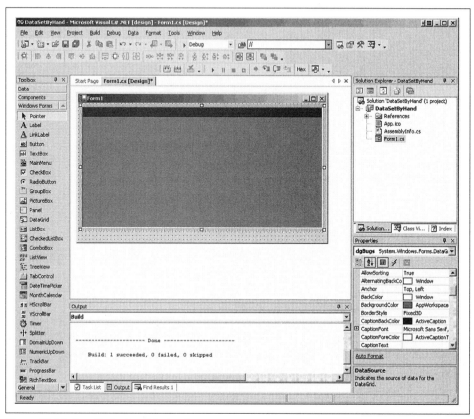

Figure 19-25. DataSet by hand design form

Example 19-16. DataSet built by hand in C#

```csharp
private DataSet CreateDataSet( )
{
    // instantiate a new DataSet object that
    // you will fill with tables and relations
    DataSet DataSet = new DataSet( );

    // make the bug table and its columns
    // mimic the attributes from the SQL database
    DataTable tblBugs = new DataTable("Bugs");

    DataColumn newColumn; // hold the new columns as you create them

    newColumn =
        tblBugs.Columns.Add(
        "BugID", Type.GetType("System.Int32"));
```

Example 19-16. DataSet built by hand in C# (continued)

```csharp
newColumn.AutoIncrement = true;      // autoincrementing
newColumn.AutoIncrementSeed=1;       // starts at 1
newColumn.AutoIncrementStep=1;       // increments by 1
newColumn.AllowDBNull=false;         // nulls not allowed

UniqueConstraint constraint =
    new UniqueConstraint("UniqueBugID",newColumn);
tblBugs.Constraints.Add(constraint);

// create an array of columns for the primary key
DataColumn[ ] columnArray = new DataColumn[1];
columnArray[0] = newColumn;

// add the array to the Primary key property
tblBugs.PrimaryKey=columnArray;

// The Product column
newColumn = tblBugs.Columns.Add(
    "Product", Type.GetType("System.Int32"));
newColumn.AllowDBNull=false;
newColumn.DefaultValue = 1;

// save for foreign key creation
DataColumn bugProductColumn = newColumn;

// The Version column
newColumn = tblBugs.Columns.Add(
    "Version", Type.GetType("System.String"));
newColumn.AllowDBNull=false;
newColumn.MaxLength=50;
newColumn.DefaultValue = "0.1";

// The Description column
newColumn = tblBugs.Columns.Add(
    "Description", Type.GetType("System.String"));
newColumn.AllowDBNull=false;
newColumn.MaxLength=8000;
newColumn.DefaultValue = "";

// The Reporter column
newColumn = tblBugs.Columns.Add(
    "Reporter", Type.GetType("System.Int32"));
newColumn.AllowDBNull=false;

// save for foreign key creation
DataColumn bugReporterColumn = newColumn;

// Add rows based on the db schema you just created
DataRow newRow;       // holds the new row

newRow = tblBugs.NewRow( );
newRow["Product"] = 1;
```

Example 19-16. DataSet built by hand in C# (continued)

```
C#    newRow["Version"] = "0.1";
      newRow["Description"] = "Crashes on load";
      newRow["Reporter"] = 5;
      tblBugs.Rows.Add(newRow);

      newRow = tblBugs.NewRow( );
      newRow["Product"] = 1;
      newRow["Version"] = "0.1";
      newRow["Description"] =
          "Does not report correct owner of bug";
      newRow["Reporter"] = 5;
      tblBugs.Rows.Add(newRow);

      newRow = tblBugs.NewRow( );
      newRow["Product"] = 1;
      newRow["Version"] = "0.1";
      newRow["Description"] =
          "Does not show history of previous action";
      newRow["Reporter"] = 6;
      tblBugs.Rows.Add(newRow);

      newRow = tblBugs.NewRow( );
      newRow["Product"] = 1;
      newRow["Version"] = "0.1";
      newRow["Description"] =
          "Fails to reload properly";
      newRow["Reporter"] = 5;
      tblBugs.Rows.Add(newRow);

      newRow = tblBugs.NewRow( );
      newRow["Product"] = 2;
      newRow["Version"] = "0.1";
      newRow["Description"] = "Loses data overnight";
      newRow["Reporter"] = 5;
      tblBugs.Rows.Add(newRow);

      newRow = tblBugs.NewRow( );
      newRow["Product"] = 2;
      newRow["Version"] = "0.1";
      newRow["Description"] = "HTML is not shown properly";
      newRow["Reporter"] = 6;
      tblBugs.Rows.Add(newRow);

      // add the table to the dataset
      DataSet.Tables.Add(tblBugs);


      DataTable tblBugHistory = new DataTable("BugHistory");


      newColumn =
          tblBugHistory.Columns.Add(
          "BugHistoryID", Type.GetType("System.Int32"));
```

Example 19-16. DataSet built by hand in C# (continued)

```
newColumn.AutoIncrement = true;     // autoincrementing
newColumn.AutoIncrementSeed=1;      // starts at 1
newColumn.AutoIncrementStep=1;      // increments by 1
newColumn.AllowDBNull=false;        // nulls not allowed


constraint = new UniqueConstraint("UniqueBugHistoryID",newColumn);
tblBugHistory.Constraints.Add(constraint);


DataColumn secondColumn;
secondColumn = tblBugHistory.Columns.Add(
    "BugID", Type.GetType("System.Int32"));
secondColumn.AllowDBNull=false;
secondColumn.DefaultValue = 1;

// create an array of columns for the primary keys
columnArray = new DataColumn[2];
columnArray[0] = newColumn;
columnArray[1] = secondColumn;

// add the array to the Primary key property
tblBugHistory.PrimaryKey=columnArray;

// The Status column
newColumn = tblBugHistory.Columns.Add(
    "Status", Type.GetType("System.Int32"));
newColumn.AllowDBNull=false;
newColumn.DefaultValue = 1;

// The Severity column
newColumn = tblBugHistory.Columns.Add(
    "Severity", Type.GetType("System.Int32"));
newColumn.AllowDBNull=false;
newColumn.DefaultValue = 1;

// The Response column
newColumn = tblBugHistory.Columns.Add(
    "Response", Type.GetType("System.String"));
newColumn.AllowDBNull=false;
newColumn.MaxLength=8000;
newColumn.DefaultValue = "";

// The Owner column
newColumn = tblBugHistory.Columns.Add(
    "Owner", Type.GetType("System.Int32"));
newColumn.AllowDBNull=false;
newColumn.DefaultValue = 1;

// The DateStamp column
newColumn = tblBugHistory.Columns.Add(
    "DateStamp", Type.GetType("System.DateTime"));
```

Example 19-16. DataSet built by hand in C# (continued)

```
                newColumn.AllowDBNull=false;
                newColumn.DefaultValue = System.DateTime.Now;


                // Add rows based on the db schema you just created
                newRow = tblBugHistory.NewRow( );
                newRow["bugID"] = 1;
                newRow["Status"] = "1";
                newRow["Severity"] = "2";
                newRow["Response"] = "Created";
                newRow["Owner"] = 1;
                newRow["DateStamp"] = System.DateTime.Now;
                tblBugHistory.Rows.Add(newRow);

                newRow = tblBugHistory.NewRow( );
                newRow["bugID"] = 1;
                newRow["Status"] = "2";
                newRow["Severity"] = "2";
                newRow["Response"] = "Assigned to Jesse";
                newRow["Owner"] = 1;
                newRow["DateStamp"] = System.DateTime.Now;
                tblBugHistory.Rows.Add(newRow);

                newRow = tblBugHistory.NewRow( );
                newRow["bugID"] = 1;
                newRow["Status"] = "3";
                newRow["Severity"] = "2";
                newRow["Response"] = "I'll Look into it";
                newRow["Owner"] = 1;
                newRow["DateStamp"] = System.DateTime.Now;
                tblBugHistory.Rows.Add(newRow);

                newRow = tblBugHistory.NewRow( );
                newRow["bugID"] = 1;
                newRow["Status"] = "4";
                newRow["Severity"] = "2";
                newRow["Response"] = "Fixed by resetting initial values";
                newRow["Owner"] = 1;
                newRow["DateStamp"] = System.DateTime.Now;
                tblBugHistory.Rows.Add(newRow);

                newRow = tblBugHistory.NewRow( );
                newRow["bugID"] = 2;
                newRow["Status"] = "1";
                newRow["Severity"] = "3";
                newRow["Response"] = "Created";
                newRow["Owner"] = 1;
                newRow["DateStamp"] = System.DateTime.Now;
                tblBugHistory.Rows.Add(newRow);


                newRow = tblBugHistory.NewRow( );
                newRow["bugID"] = 2;
```

Example 19-16. DataSet built by hand in C# (continued)

```
newRow["Status"] = "2";
newRow["Severity"] = "3";
newRow["Response"] = "Assigned to Jesse";
newRow["Owner"] = 1;
newRow["DateStamp"] = System.DateTime.Now;
tblBugHistory.Rows.Add(newRow);

// add the table to the dataset
DataSet.Tables.Add(tblBugHistory);



// Product Table

// make the Products table and add the columns
DataTable tblProduct = new DataTable("lkProduct");
newColumn = tblProduct.Columns.Add(
    "ProductID", Type.GetType("System.Int32"));
newColumn.AutoIncrement = true;      // autoincrementing
newColumn.AutoIncrementSeed=1;       // starts at 1
newColumn.AutoIncrementStep=1;       // increments by 1
newColumn.AllowDBNull=false;         // nulls not allowed
newColumn.Unique=true;               // each value must be unique

newColumn = tblProduct.Columns.Add(
    "ProductDescription", Type.GetType("System.String"));
newColumn.AllowDBNull=false;
newColumn.MaxLength=8000;
newColumn.DefaultValue = "";

newRow = tblProduct.NewRow( );
newRow["ProductDescription"] = "BugX Bug Tracking";
tblProduct.Rows.Add(newRow);

newRow = tblProduct.NewRow( );
newRow["ProductDescription"] =
    "PIM - My Personal Information Manager";
tblProduct.Rows.Add(newRow);

// add the products table to the data set
DataSet.Tables.Add(tblProduct);



// People


// make the People table and add the columns
DataTable tblPeople = new DataTable("People");
newColumn = tblPeople.Columns.Add(
    "PersonID", Type.GetType("System.Int32"));
newColumn.AutoIncrement = true;      // autoincrementing
newColumn.AutoIncrementSeed=1;       // starts at 1
```

Example 19-16. DataSet built by hand in C# (continued)

```C#
    newColumn.AutoIncrementStep=1;         // increments by 1
    newColumn.AllowDBNull=false;           // nulls not allowed

    UniqueConstraint uniqueConstraint =
        new UniqueConstraint(
        "UniquePersonID",newColumn);
    tblPeople.Constraints.Add(uniqueConstraint);

    // stash away the PersonID column for the foreign
    // key constraint
    DataColumn PersonIDColumn = newColumn;

    columnArray = new DataColumn[1];
    columnArray[0] = newColumn;
    tblPeople.PrimaryKey=columnArray;


    newColumn = tblPeople.Columns.Add(
        "FullName", Type.GetType("System.String"));
    newColumn.AllowDBNull=false;
    newColumn.MaxLength=8000;
    newColumn.DefaultValue = "";

    newColumn = tblPeople.Columns.Add(
        "eMail", Type.GetType("System.String"));
    newColumn.AllowDBNull=false;
    newColumn.MaxLength=100;
    newColumn.DefaultValue = "";

    newColumn = tblPeople.Columns.Add(
        "Phone", Type.GetType("System.String"));
    newColumn.AllowDBNull=false;
    newColumn.MaxLength=20;
    newColumn.DefaultValue = "";

    newColumn = tblPeople.Columns.Add(
        "Role", Type.GetType("System.Int32"));
    newColumn.DefaultValue = 0;
    newColumn.AllowDBNull=false;

    newRow = tblPeople.NewRow( );
    newRow["FullName"] = "Jesse Liberty";
    newRow["email"] = "jliberty@libertyassociates.com";
    newRow["Phone"] = "617-555-7301";
    newRow["Role"] = 1;
    tblPeople.Rows.Add(newRow);

    newRow = tblPeople.NewRow( );
    newRow["FullName"] = "Dan Hurwitz";
    newRow["email"] = "dhurwitz@stersol.com";
    newRow["Phone"] = "781-555-3375";
    newRow["Role"] = 1;
```

Example 19-16. DataSet built by hand in C# (continued)

```
tblPeople.Rows.Add(newRow);

newRow = tblPeople.NewRow( );
newRow["FullName"] = "John Galt";
newRow["email"] = "jGalt@franconia.com";
newRow["Phone"] = "617-555-9876";
newRow["Role"] = 1;
tblPeople.Rows.Add(newRow);

newRow = tblPeople.NewRow( );
newRow["FullName"] = "John Osborn";
newRow["email"] = "jOsborn@oreilly.com";
newRow["Phone"] = "617-555-3232";
newRow["Role"] = 3;
tblPeople.Rows.Add(newRow);

newRow = tblPeople.NewRow( );
newRow["FullName"] = "Ron Petrusha";
newRow["email"] = "ron@oreilly.com";
newRow["Phone"] = "707-555-0515";
newRow["Role"] = 2;
tblPeople.Rows.Add(newRow);

newRow = tblPeople.NewRow( );
newRow["FullName"] = "Tatiana Diaz";
newRow["email"] = "tatiana@oreilly.com";
newRow["Phone"] = "617-555-1234";
newRow["Role"] = 2;
tblPeople.Rows.Add(newRow);

// add the People table to the dataset
DataSet.Tables.Add(tblPeople);

// create the Foreign Key constraint
// pass in the parent column from people
// and the child column from Bugs
ForeignKeyConstraint fk =
    new ForeignKeyConstraint(
    "FK_BugToPeople",PersonIDColumn,bugReporterColumn);
fk.DeleteRule=Rule.Cascade;    // like father like son
fk.UpdateRule=Rule.Cascade;
tblBugs.Constraints.Add(fk);  // add the new constraint


// declare the DataRelation and DataColumn objects
System.Data.DataRelation dataRelation;
System.Data.DataColumn dataColumn1;
System.Data.DataColumn dataColumn2;

// set the dataColumns to create the relationship
// between Bug and BugHistory on the BugID key
dataColumn1 =
```

Example 19-16. DataSet built by hand in C# (continued)

```csharp
            DataSet.Tables["Bugs"].Columns["BugID"];
        dataColumn2 =
            DataSet.Tables["BugHistory"].Columns["BugID"];

        dataRelation =
            new System.Data.DataRelation(
            "BugsToHistory",
            dataColumn1,
            dataColumn2);

        // add the new DataRelation to the dataset
        DataSet.Relations.Add(dataRelation);

        return DataSet;

    }
    public Form1()
    {
        //
        // Required for Windows Form Designer support
        //
        InitializeComponent();

        DataSet ds = CreateDataSet();
        dgBugs.DataSource = ds.Tables[0];
    }
```

Example 19-17. DataSet built by hand in VB.NET

```vbnet
Public Class Form1
    Inherits System.Windows.Forms.Form

#Region " Windows Form Designer generated code "

    Public Sub New()
        MyBase.New()

        'This call is required by the Windows Form Designer.
        InitializeComponent()
        Dim ds As DataSet = CreateDataSet()
        dgBugs.DataSource = ds.Tables(0)


        'Add any initialization after the InitializeComponent() call

    End Sub


#End Region
    Private Function CreateDataSet() As DataSet

        ' instantiate a new DataSet object that
        ' you will fill with tables and relations
```

Example 19-17. DataSet built by hand in VB.NET (continued)

```
Dim myDataSet As New DataSet( )

' make the bug table and its columns
' mimic the attributes from the SQL database
Dim tblBugs As New DataTable("Bugs")

Dim newColumn As DataColumn ' hold the new columns as you
                            ' create them

newColumn = tblBugs.Columns.Add( _
   "BugID", Type.GetType("System.Int32"))

newColumn.AutoIncrement = True      ' autoincrementing
newColumn.AutoIncrementSeed = 1     ' starts at 1
newColumn.AutoIncrementStep = 1     ' increments by 1
newColumn.AllowDBNull = False       ' nulls not allowed

Dim constraint As _
        New UniqueConstraint("UniqueBugID", newColumn)
tblBugs.Constraints.Add(Constraint)

' create an array of columns for the primary key
Dim columnArray(1) As DataColumn
columnArray(0) = newColumn

' add the array to the Primary key property
tblBugs.PrimaryKey = columnArray

' The Product column
newColumn = tblBugs.Columns.Add( _
   "Product", Type.GetType("System.Int32"))
newColumn.AllowDBNull = False
newColumn.DefaultValue = 1

' save for foreign key creation
Dim bugProductColumn As DataColumn = newColumn

' The Version column
newColumn = tblBugs.Columns.Add( _
        "Version", Type.GetType("System.String"))
newColumn.AllowDBNull = False
newColumn.MaxLength = 50
newColumn.DefaultValue = "0.1"

' The Description column
newColumn = tblBugs.Columns.Add( _
        "Description", Type.GetType("System.String"))
newColumn.AllowDBNull = False
newColumn.MaxLength = 8000
newColumn.DefaultValue = ""

' The Reporter column
newColumn = tblBugs.Columns.Add( _
```

Example 19-17. DataSet built by hand in VB.NET (continued)

```
VB                      "Reporter", Type.GetType("System.Int32"))
         newColumn.AllowDBNull = False

         ' save for foreign key creation
         Dim bugReporterColumn As DataColumn = newColumn

         ' Add rows based on the db schema you just created
         Dim newRow As DataRow     ' holds the new row

         newRow = tblBugs.NewRow( )
         newRow("Product") = 1
         newRow("Version") = "0.1"
         newRow("Description") = "Crashes on load"
         newRow("Reporter") = 5
         tblBugs.Rows.Add(newRow)

         newRow = tblBugs.NewRow( )
         newRow("Product") = 1
         newRow("Version") = "0.1"
         newRow("Description") = _
                  "Does not report correct owner of bug"
         newRow("Reporter") = 5
         tblBugs.Rows.Add(newRow)

         newRow = tblBugs.NewRow( )
         newRow("Product") = 1
         newRow("Version") = "0.1"
         newRow("Description") = _
                  "Does not show history of previous action"
         newRow("Reporter") = 6
         tblBugs.Rows.Add(newRow)

         newRow = tblBugs.NewRow( )
         newRow("Product") = 1
         newRow("Version") = "0.1"
         newRow("Description") = _
                  "Fails to reload properly"
         newRow("Reporter") = 5
         tblBugs.Rows.Add(newRow)

         newRow = tblBugs.NewRow( )
         newRow("Product") = 2
         newRow("Version") = "0.1"
         newRow("Description") = "Loses data overnight"
         newRow("Reporter") = 5
         tblBugs.Rows.Add(newRow)

         newRow = tblBugs.NewRow( )
         newRow("Product") = 2
         newRow("Version") = "0.1"
         newRow("Description") = "HTML is not shown properly"
         newRow("Reporter") = 6
```

Example 19-17. DataSet built by hand in VB.NET (continued)

VB

```
tblBugs.Rows.Add(newRow)

' add the table to the dataset
myDataSet.Tables.Add(tblBugs)


Dim tblBugHistory As New DataTable("BugHistory")


newColumn = tblBugHistory.Columns.Add( _
        "BugHistoryID", Type.GetType("System.Int32"))
newColumn.AutoIncrement = True      ' autoincrementing
newColumn.AutoIncrementSeed = 1     ' starts at 1
newColumn.AutoIncrementStep = 1     ' increments by 1
newColumn.AllowDBNull = False       ' nulls not allowed


constraint = New UniqueConstraint("UniqueBugHistoryID", newColumn)
tblBugHistory.Constraints.Add(constraint)


Dim secondColumn As New DataColumn( )
secondColumn = tblBugHistory.Columns.Add( _
        "BugID", Type.GetType("System.Int32"))
secondColumn.AllowDBNull = False
secondColumn.DefaultValue = 1

' create an array of columns for the primary keys

Dim secondColumnArray(2) As DataColumn
secondColumnArray(0) = newColumn
secondColumnArray(1) = secondColumn

' add the array to the Primary key property
tblBugHistory.PrimaryKey = secondColumnArray

' The Status column
newColumn = tblBugHistory.Columns.Add( _
        "Status", Type.GetType("System.Int32"))
newColumn.AllowDBNull = False
newColumn.DefaultValue = 1

' The Severity column
newColumn = tblBugHistory.Columns.Add( _
        "Severity", Type.GetType("System.Int32"))
newColumn.AllowDBNull = False
newColumn.DefaultValue = 1

' The Response column
newColumn = tblBugHistory.Columns.Add( _
    "Response", Type.GetType("System.String"))
newColumn.AllowDBNull = False
```

Example 19-17. DataSet built by hand in VB.NET (continued)

```
newColumn.MaxLength = 8000
newColumn.DefaultValue = ""

' The Owner column
newColumn = tblBugHistory.Columns.Add( _
    "Owner", Type.GetType("System.Int32"))
newColumn.AllowDBNull = False
newColumn.DefaultValue = 1

' The DateStamp column
newColumn = tblBugHistory.Columns.Add( _
        "DateStamp", Type.GetType("System.DateTime"))
newColumn.AllowDBNull = False
newColumn.DefaultValue = System.DateTime.Now


' Add rows based on the db schema you just created
newRow = tblBugHistory.NewRow( )
newRow("bugID") = 1
newRow("Status") = "1"
newRow("Severity") = "2"
newRow("Response") = "Created"
newRow("Owner") = 1
newRow("DateStamp") = System.DateTime.Now
tblBugHistory.Rows.Add(newRow)

newRow = tblBugHistory.NewRow( )
newRow("bugID") = 1
newRow("Status") = "2"
newRow("Severity") = "2"
newRow("Response") = "Assigned to Jesse"
newRow("Owner") = 1
newRow("DateStamp") = System.DateTime.Now
tblBugHistory.Rows.Add(newRow)

newRow = tblBugHistory.NewRow( )
newRow("bugID") = 1
newRow("Status") = "3"
newRow("Severity") = "2"
newRow("Response") = "I'll Look into it"
newRow("Owner") = 1
newRow("DateStamp") = System.DateTime.Now
tblBugHistory.Rows.Add(newRow)

newRow = tblBugHistory.NewRow( )
newRow("bugID") = 1
newRow("Status") = "4"
newRow("Severity") = "2"
newRow("Response") = "Fixed by resetting initial values"
newRow("Owner") = 1
newRow("DateStamp") = System.DateTime.Now
tblBugHistory.Rows.Add(newRow)
```

Example 19-17. DataSet built by hand in VB.NET (continued)

```
VB    newRow = tblBugHistory.NewRow( )
      newRow("bugID") = 2
      newRow("Status") = "1"
      newRow("Severity") = "3"
      newRow("Response") = "Created"
      newRow("Owner") = 1
      newRow("DateStamp") = System.DateTime.Now
      tblBugHistory.Rows.Add(newRow)


      newRow = tblBugHistory.NewRow( )
      newRow("bugID") = 2
      newRow("Status") = "2"
      newRow("Severity") = "3"
      newRow("Response") = "Assigned to Jesse"
      newRow("Owner") = 1
      newRow("DateStamp") = System.DateTime.Now
      tblBugHistory.Rows.Add(newRow)

      ' add the table to the dataset
      myDataSet.Tables.Add(tblBugHistory)


      ' Product Table

      ' make the Products table and add the columns
      Dim tblProduct As New DataTable("lkProduct")
      newColumn = tblProduct.Columns.Add( _
            "ProductID", Type.GetType("System.Int32"))
      newColumn.AutoIncrement = True        ' autoincrementing
      newColumn.AutoIncrementSeed = 1       ' starts at 1
      newColumn.AutoIncrementStep = 1       ' increments by 1
      newColumn.AllowDBNull = False         ' nulls not allowed
      newColumn.Unique = True               ' each value must be unique

      newColumn = tblProduct.Columns.Add( _
            "ProductDescription", Type.GetType("System.String"))
      newColumn.AllowDBNull = False
      newColumn.MaxLength = 8000
      newColumn.DefaultValue = ""

      newRow = tblProduct.NewRow( )
      newRow("ProductDescription") = "BugX Bug Tracking"
      tblProduct.Rows.Add(newRow)

      newRow = tblProduct.NewRow( )
      newRow("ProductDescription") = _
            "PIM - My Personal Information Manager"
      tblProduct.Rows.Add(newRow)
```

Example 19-17. DataSet built by hand in VB.NET (continued)

```vbnet
' add the products table to the data set
myDataSet.Tables.Add(tblProduct)


' People


' make the People table and add the columns
Dim tblPeople As New DataTable("People")
newColumn = tblPeople.Columns.Add( _
        "PersonID", Type.GetType("System.Int32"))
newColumn.AutoIncrement = True       ' autoincrementing
newColumn.AutoIncrementSeed = 1      ' starts at 1
newColumn.AutoIncrementStep = 1      ' increments by 1
newColumn.AllowDBNull = False        ' nulls not allowed

Dim myUniqueConstraint As New UniqueConstraint( _
    "UniquePersonID", newColumn)
tblPeople.Constraints.Add(myUniqueConstraint)

' stash away the PersonID column for the foreign
' key constraint
Dim PersonIDColumn As DataColumn = newColumn

Dim thirdColumnArray(1) As DataColumn
thirdColumnArray(0) = newColumn
tblPeople.PrimaryKey = thirdColumnArray


newColumn = tblPeople.Columns.Add( _
        "FullName", Type.GetType("System.String"))
newColumn.AllowDBNull = False
newColumn.MaxLength = 8000
newColumn.DefaultValue = ""

newColumn = tblPeople.Columns.Add( _
        "eMail", Type.GetType("System.String"))
newColumn.AllowDBNull = False
newColumn.MaxLength = 100
newColumn.DefaultValue = ""

newColumn = tblPeople.Columns.Add( _
        "Phone", Type.GetType("System.String"))
newColumn.AllowDBNull = False
newColumn.MaxLength = 20
newColumn.DefaultValue = ""

newColumn = tblPeople.Columns.Add( _
        "Role", Type.GetType("System.Int32"))
newColumn.DefaultValue = 0
newColumn.AllowDBNull = False
```

Example 19-17. DataSet built by hand in VB.NET (continued)

```
VB
        newRow = tblPeople.NewRow( )
        newRow("FullName") = "Jesse Liberty"
        newRow("email") = "jliberty@libertyassociates.com"
        newRow("Phone") = "617-555-7301"
        newRow("Role") = 1
        tblPeople.Rows.Add(newRow)

        newRow = tblPeople.NewRow( )
        newRow("FullName") = "Dan Hurwitz"
        newRow("email") = "dhurwitz@stersol.com"
        newRow("Phone") = "781-555-3375"
        newRow("Role") = 1
        tblPeople.Rows.Add(newRow)

        newRow = tblPeople.NewRow( )
        newRow("FullName") = "John Galt"
        newRow("email") = "jGalt@franconia.com"
        newRow("Phone") = "617-555-9876"
        newRow("Role") = 1
        tblPeople.Rows.Add(newRow)

        newRow = tblPeople.NewRow( )
        newRow("FullName") = "John Osborn"
        newRow("email") = "jOsborn@oreilly.com"
        newRow("Phone") = "617-555-3232"
        newRow("Role") = 3
        tblPeople.Rows.Add(newRow)

        newRow = tblPeople.NewRow( )
        newRow("FullName") = "Ron Petrusha"
        newRow("email") = "ron@oreilly.com"
        newRow("Phone") = "707-555-0515"
        newRow("Role") = 2
        tblPeople.Rows.Add(newRow)

        newRow = tblPeople.NewRow( )
        newRow("FullName") = "Tatiana Diaz"
        newRow("email") = "tatiana@oreilly.com"
        newRow("Phone") = "617-555-1234"
        newRow("Role") = 2
        tblPeople.Rows.Add(newRow)

        ' add the People table to the dataset
        myDataSet.Tables.Add(tblPeople)

        ' create the Foreign Key constraint
        ' pass in the parent column from people
        ' and the child column from Bugs
        Dim fk As New ForeignKeyConstraint( _
            "FK_BugToPeople", PersonIDColumn, bugReporterColumn)
        fk.DeleteRule = Rule.Cascade ' like father like son
```

Example 19-17. DataSet built by hand in VB.NET (continued)

```
VB                fk.UpdateRule = Rule.Cascade
                  tblBugs.Constraints.Add(fk)  ' add the new constraint


                  ' declare the DataRelation and DataColumn objects
                  Dim myDataRelation As System.Data.DataRelation
                  Dim dataColumn1 As System.Data.DataColumn
                  Dim dataColumn2 As System.Data.DataColumn

                  ' set the dataColumns to create the relationship
                  ' between Bug and BugHistory on the BugID key
                  dataColumn1 = myDataSet.Tables("Bugs").Columns("BugID")
                  dataColumn2 = myDataSet.Tables("BugHistory").Columns("BugID")

                  myDataRelation = New System.Data.DataRelation( _
                      "BugsToHistory", dataColumn1, dataColumn2)

                  ' add the new DataRelation to the dataset
                  myDataSet.Relations.Add(myDataRelation)

                  Return myDataSet

              End Function

      End Class
```

This code centers on a method named CreateDataSet that will be responsible for creating the DataSet and returning it to the constructor. You will create this DataSet by hand (not from a DataBase), so you must fill it with DataTables. Each DataTable must be created by hand, and you are responsible for adding each column to the table and then establishing any constraints or key fields, again by hand. Finally, you will fill the table with rows of data.

Once you've created the DataSet in the CreateDataSet method, return to the form's constructor where you assign the returned value to a reference to a DataSet. You can then extract the first table and set it as the DataGrid's DataSource.

```
C#    DataSet ds = CreateDataSet();
      dgBugs.DataSource = ds.Tables[0];
```

Creating the DataSet by Hand

CreateDataSet begins by instantiating a new DataTable object, passing in the name of the table as a parameter to the constructor.

```
C#    DataTable tblBugs = new DataTable("Bugs");
```

```
VB    Dim tblBugs As New DataTable("Bugs")
```

The new table you are creating should mimic the data structure of the Bugs table in the SQL Server. Figure 19-26 shows that structure.

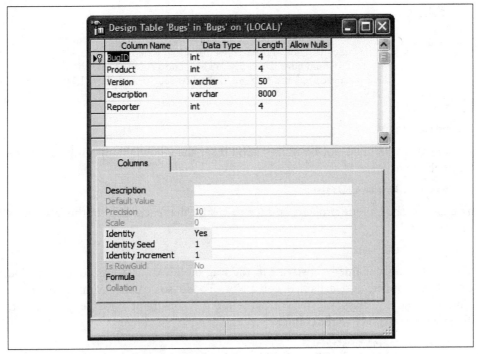

Figure 19-26. The structure of the Bugs table in SQL Server

To add a column to this DataTable object, do not call a constructor. Instead, call the Add method of the DataTable object's Columns collection. The Add method takes two parameters—the name of the column and its data type:

```
DataColumn newColumn;
newColumn =
    tblBugs.Columns.Add("BugID", Type.GetType("System.Int32"));
```

```
dim newColumn as DataColumn
newColumn = _
    tblBugs.Columns.Add("BugID", Type.GetType("System.Int32"))
```

Setting column properties

The Add method creates the new column and returns a reference to it, which you may now manipulate. Since it will be an identity column (see the highlighted area of Figure 19-26), you'll want to set its AutoIncrement property to true and set the AutoIncrementSeed and AutoIncrementStep properties to set the seed and step values of the identity, respectively. The following code fragment does this:

```
newColumn.AutoIncrement = true;
newColumn.AutoIncrementSeed=1;
newColumn.AutoIncrementStep=1;
```

The AutoIncrementSeed property sets the initial value for the identity column, and the AutoIncrementStep property sets the increment for each new record. Thus, if the seed were 5 and the step were 3, the first five records would have IDs of 5, 8, 11, 14, and 17. In the case shown, where both the seed and step are 1, the first four records have IDs of 1,2,3,4.

Setting constraints

Identity columns must not be null, so you'll set the AllowDBNull property of the new column to `false`:

C#
```
newColumn.AllowDBNull=false;
```

You can set the Unique property to `true` to ensure that each entry in this column is unique:

C#
```
newColumn.Unique=true;
```

This creates an unnamed constraint in the Bug table's Constraints collection. You can, if you prefer, add a named constraint. To do so, create an instance of the UniqueConstraint class and pass a name for the constraint into the constructor, along with a reference to the column:

C#
```
UniqueConstraint constraint =
    new UniqueConstraint("UniqueBugID",newColumn);
```

VB
```
Dim constraint As _
        New UniqueConstraint("UniqueBugID", newColumn)
```

Then manually add that constraint to the table's Constraints collection:

C#
```
tblBugs.Constraints.Add(constraint);
```

You may call your constraint anything you like. It is good programming practice to call it something that identifies the constraint clearly. If you do add a named constraint, be sure to comment out the Unique property. Creating a primary key is covered later in this chapter, in the section "Creating Primary Keys."

This completes the first column in the table. The second column is the Product column. Notice that this column is of type integer, with no nulls and a default value of 1 (see the highlighted property in Figure 19-27). Create the Product column by calling the Add method of the Columns collection of the tblBugs table, this time passing in the type for an integer. Then set the AllowDBNull property as you did with the earlier column, and set the DefaultValue property to set the default value for the column. This is illustrated in the code fragment shown next.

```csharp
newColumn = tblBugs.Columns.Add(
    "Product", Type.GetType("System.Int32"));
newColumn.AllowDBNull=false;
newColumn.DefaultValue = 1;
```

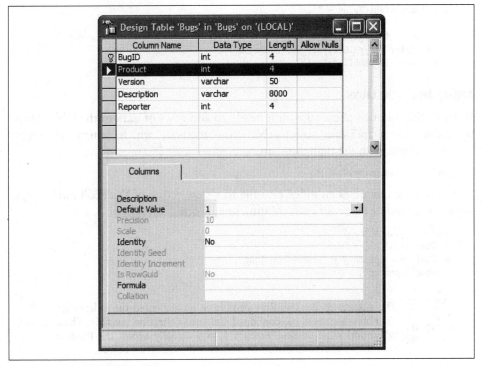

Figure 19-27. The Product column

Looking at Figure 19-27 again, you can see that the third column is Version, with a type of varChar.

 A varChar is a variable length character string. A varChar can be declared to be any length between 1 and 8000 bytes. Typically, you will limit the length of the string as a form of documentation about the largest string you expect in the field.

Declare the column type to be string for a varchar and set the length of the string with the MaxLength property, as shown in the following code fragment:

```csharp
newColumn = tblBugs.Columns.Add(
    "Version", Type.GetType("System.String"));
newColumn.AllowDBNull=false;
newColumn.MaxLength=50;
newColumn.DefaultValue = "0.1";
```

Declare the Description and Reporter columns similarly:

```csharp
newColumn = tblBugs.Columns.Add("Description", Type.GetType("System.String"));
newColumn.AllowDBNull=false;
newColumn.MaxLength=8000;
newColumn.DefaultValue = "";

newColumn = tblBugs.Columns.Add(
    "Reporter", Type.GetType("System.Int32"));
newColumn.AllowDBNull=false;
```

Adding data to the table

With all the columns declared, you're ready to add rows of data to the table. Do so by calling the DataTable object's NewRow method, which returns an empty DataRow object with the right structure:

```csharp
newRow = tblBugs.NewRow( );
```

Use the column name as an index into the row's collection of DataColumns, assigning the appropriate value for each column, one by one.

```csharp
newRow["Product"] = 1;
newRow["Version"] = "0.1";
newRow["Description"] = "Crashes on load";
newRow["Reporter"] = 5;
```

 The authors of the DataRow class have implemented the indexer for their class to access the contained Columns collection invisibly. Thus, when you write newRow["Product"], you actually access the Product column within the Columns collection of the DataRow object.

When the columns are complete, add the row to the table's Rows collection by calling the Add method and pass in the row you just created:

```csharp
tblBugs.Rows.Add(newRow);
```

You are now ready to create another new row:

```csharp
newRow = tblBugs.NewRow( );
newRow["Product"] = 1;
newRow["Version"] = "0.1";
newRow["Description"] = "Does not report correct owner of bug";
newRow["Reporter"] = 5;
tblBugs.Rows.Add(newRow);
```

When all the rows are created, you can create an instance of a DataSet object and add the table:

```csharp
DataSet DataSet = new DataSet( );
DataSet.Tables.Add(tblBugs);
```

Adding additional tables to the DataSet

With the Bugs table added to the new DataSet, you are ready to create a new table for the BugHistory:

```
DataTable tblBugHistory = new DataTable("BugHistory");
```

Once again, you'll define the columns and then add data. You'll then go on to add a new table for Products and People. In theory, you could also add all the other tables from the previous example, but to keep things simple, stop with these four.

Adding rows with an array of objects

The DataRowCollection object's Add method is overloaded. In the code shown earlier, you created a new DataRow object, populated its columns, and added the row. You can also create an array of Objects, fill the array, and pass the array to the Add method. For example, rather than writing:

```
newRow = tblPeople.NewRow( );
newRow["FullName"] = "Jesse Liberty";
newRow["email"] = "jliberty@libertyassociates.com";
newRow["Phone"] = "617-555-7301";
newRow["Role"] = 1;
tblPeople.Rows.Add(newRow);
```

you can instead create an array of five objects and fill that array with the values you would have added to the columns in the row:

```
Object[ ] PersonArray = new Object[5];
PersonArray[0] = 1;
PersonArray[1] = "Jesse Liberty";
PersonArray[2] = "jliberty@libertyassociates.com";
PersonArray[3] = "617-555-7301";
PersonArray[4] = 1;
tblPeople.Rows.Add(PersonArray);
```

In this case, you must manually add a value for the identity column, BugID. When you created the row object, the identity column value was automatically created for you with the right increment from the previous row, but since you are now creating an array of objects, you must do it by hand.

Creating Primary Keys

The Bugs table uses the PersonID as a foreign key into the People table. To recreate this, first create a primary key in the People table.

Start by declaring the PersonID column as a unique non-null identity column, just as you did earlier for the BugID column in bugs:

```
newColumn = tblPeople.Columns.Add("PersonID", Type.GetType("System.Int32"));
newColumn.AutoIncrement = true;      // autoincrementing
newColumn.AutoIncrementSeed=1;       // starts at 1
```

```
newColumn.AutoIncrementStep=1;      // increments by 1
newColumn.AllowDBNull=false;        // nulls not allowed

// add the unique constraint
UniqueConstraint uniqueConstraint =
  new UniqueConstraint("UniquePersonID",newColumn);
tblPeople.Constraints.Add(uniqueConstraint);
```

To create the primary key, set the table's PrimaryKey property. This property takes
an array of DataColumn objects.

 In many tables, the primary key is not a single column, but rather two
or more columns. For example, you might keep track of orders for a
customer. A given order might be order number 17. Your database
may have many orders whose order number is 17. What uniquely
identifies a given order is the order number combined with the customer number. Thus, that table would use a compound key of the
order number and the customer number.

The primary key for the Bugs table is a single column: BugID. To set the primary key,
create an array (in this case, with one member), and assign to that member the col-
umn(s) you want to make the primary key.

```
DataColumn[ ] columnArray = new DataColumn[1]
columnArray[0] = newColumn;
```

The newColumn object contains a reference to the BugID column returned from calling Add. Assign the array to the PrimaryKey property of the table:

```
tblBugs.PrimaryKey=columnArray;
```

The BugHistory table has a more complex Primary Key, consisting of the BugID and
the BugHistoryID. Create the Primary Key by holding a reference to the two columns and creating an array with two members:

```
columnArray = new DataColumn[2];
columnArray[0] = newColumn;
columnArray[1] = secondColumn;
tblBugHistory.PrimaryKey=columnArray;
```

Creating Foreign Keys

The PersonID acts as a primary key in People and as a foreign key in Bugs. To create
the foreign key relationship, instantiate a new object of type ForeignKeyConstraint,
passing in the name of the constraint ("FK_BugToPeople") as well as a reference to
the two columns.

To facilitate passing references to the key fields to the ForeignKeyConstraint constructor, squirrel away a reference to the PersonID column in People and the
Reporter column in Bugs. Immediately after you create the columns, save a reference.

```C#
newColumn =
    tblBugs.Columns.Add("Reporter", Type.GetType("System.Int32"));
newColumn.AllowDBNull=false;
DataColumn bugReporterColumn =
    newColumn; // save for foreign key creation
```

Assuming you've saved the Reporter column in bugReporterColumn and the PersonID column from People in PersonIDColumn, you are ready to create the ForeignKeyConstraint object:

```C#
ForeignKeyConstraint fk =
    New ForeignKeyConstraint(
        "FK_BugToPeople",PersonIDColumn,bugReporterColumn);
```

This creates a ForeignKeyConstraint named fk. Before you add it to the Bugs table, set two properties:

```C#
fk.DeleteRule=Rule.Cascade;
fk.UpdateRule=Rule.Cascade;
```

The DeleteRule determines the action that will occur when a row is deleted from the parent table. Similarly, the UpdateRule determines what will happen when a row is updated in the parent column. The potential values are enumerated by the Rule enumeration, as shown in Table 19-6.

Table 19-6. The rows enumeration

Member name	Description
Cascade	Delete or update related rows (default).
None	Take no action on related rows.
SetDefault	Set the values in the related rows to the value contained in the DefaultValue property.
SetNull	Set the related rows to null.

In the case shown, the value is set to Rule.Cascade; if a record is deleted from the parent table, all child records will be deleted as well. You are now ready to add the foreign key constraint to the Bugs table:

```C#
tblBugs.Constraints.Add(fk);
```

Creating Data Relations

As you saw earlier in the chapter, you can encapsulate the relationship among tables in a DataRelation object. The code for building relationships among handcrafted DataTables is just like the code you saw earlier when you pulled the data structure from the database itself:

```C#
System.Data.DataRelation dataRelation;
System.Data.DataColumn dataColumn1;
System.Data.DataColumn dataColumn2;
```

```
dataColumn1 =
    DataSet.Tables["Bugs"].Columns["BugID"];
dataColumn2 =
    DataSet.Tables["BugHistory"].Columns["BugID"];

dataRelation =
    new System.Data.DataRelation(
    "BugsToHistory",
    dataColumn1,
    dataColumn2);
DataSet.Relations.Add(dataRelation);
```

The DataGrid can now display the data from the DataSet, complete with the relationships between the Bug table and the BugHistory table, as shown in Figure 19-28.

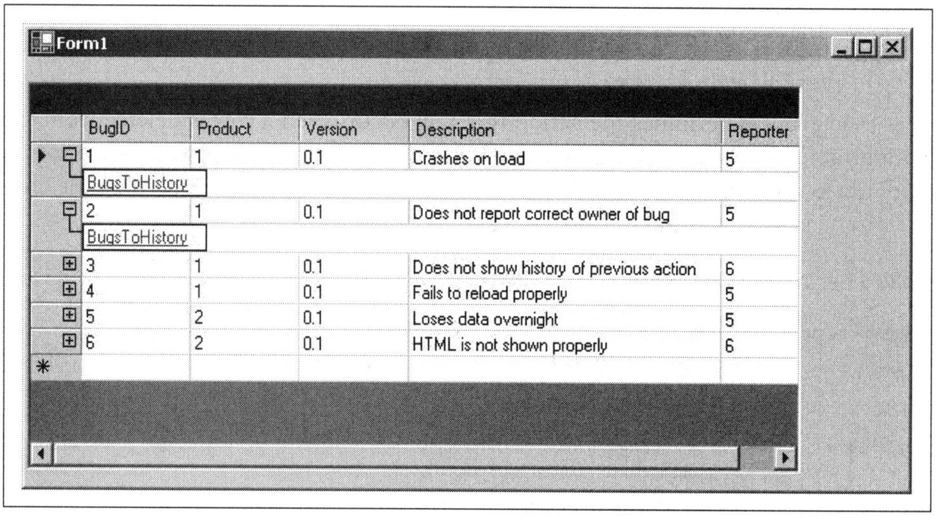

Figure 19-28. Displaying handcrafted DataSet

CHAPTER 20

Updating ADO.NET

Chapter 19 demonstrated how to retrieve data from a database and display it in various ways. In many cases, you will also want to allow the user to interact with your application to modify the data, and you must write these changes back to the database.

Two aspects to writing applications allow users to update data. The first is to provide the user with controls to modify the data. Methods to enter the proposed changes include the use of controls such as listboxes and radio buttons for making selections and text boxes for editing text entries. You'll find extensive coverage of these controls in Chapters 5 through 9.

Once you know what changes the user wants to make, your program must then provide code for updating the database. To keep the focus on the database issues, the examples in this chapter show very little of the user interface. Many examples use hard-coded data changes; others use a quick and dirty form for updating the data tables.

Updating data in a database is simple if you update only a single table, but things can be more complicated once you update related tables. This chapter explores how transactions ensure your data's integrity.

Since your program may be used by more than one user at a time, you will encounter issues with concurrency: is it possible for one user's changes to overwrite the changes of another user? This chapter explores how to manage concurrency issues and shows some of the powerful support available in the .NET Framework that simplifies this difficult task.

Updating with SQL

The simplest way to update the database is to generate a SQL insert, update, or delete statement, and execute it using the Command object's ExecuteNonQuery method. For example, you can insert a few records into one or more tables, edit existing rows, and delete rows, all with the appropriate SQL statements.

To illustrate the use of the ExecuteNonQuery statement, you'll use Visual Studio .NET to create a simple form that will display the current records in a listbox. This will be a very simple user interface to keep the focus on SQL rather than on interaction with the control.

Choose whichever language you feel most comfortable using, and name the project BugHistoryHandEdits. Drag a listbox onto the form and make it wide. Add a text-box below and three buttons to the right, as shown in Figure 20-1.

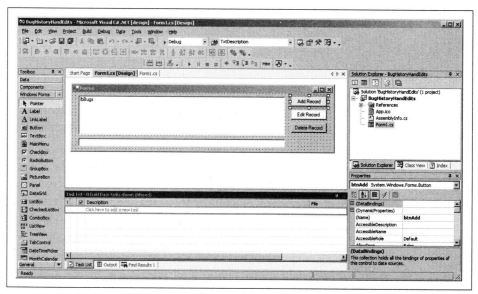

Figure 20-1. Hand-edits form

Name the ListBox lbBugs and the textbox txtDescription. Clear the Text property of the TextBox. Name the three buttons btnAdd, btnEdit, and btnDelete. Stretch the three buttons and modify their text fields to say Add Record, Edit Record, and Delete Record, respectively. You may want to set their backColor to pale green, yellow, and red. Add a textbox and be sure to set its text field to blank.

Fill the listbox with a stored procedure: spBugsNoHistory, as shown in Example 20-1. (See the sidebar "Stored Procedures.")

Example 20-1. SpBugsNoHistory

```
CREATE PROCEDURE spBugsNoHistory as
Select b.BugID, b.Description,p.ProductDescription,
r.FullName as reporter
from
bugs b
join lkProduct p on b.Product = p.ProductID
join People r on b.Reporter = r.PersonID
```

Double-click on each button in turn to create skeleton Click event handlers. In these handlers, you will interact with the database, executing the SQL statements needed to add a record, edit a record, or delete a record. To simplify the user interface even further, always edit or delete the last record in the table. (In a real application, the user would indicate which record to modify.) The complete C# source code is shown in Example 20-2, and the complete VB.NET equivalent is shown in Example 20-3. Be certain to add the requisite using statements in C# or the imports statement in VB.NET.

 The Windows Form Designer generated code was cut from the listing to save space.

Example 20-2. Hand-edited code (C#)

```
using System;
using System.Drawing;
using System.Collections;
using System.ComponentModel;
using System.Windows.Forms;
using System.Data;
using System.Data.SqlClient;

namespace BugHistoryHandEdits
{
    public class Form1 : System.Windows.Forms.Form
    {
        private System.Windows.Forms.Button btnAdd;
        private System.Windows.Forms.Button btnEdit;
        private System.Windows.Forms.Button btnDelete;
        private System.Windows.Forms.TextBox txtDescription;
        private System.Windows.Forms.ListBox lbBugs;
        private System.ComponentModel.Container components = null;

        public Form1( )
        {
            InitializeComponent( );
            PopulateListBox( );
        }
        // return a DataReader object based on the sproc
        private void PopulateListBox( )
        {

            lbBugs.Items.Clear( );
            // connection string to connect to the Bugs Database
            string connectionString =
                "server=YourServer; uid=sa; pwd=YourPW; " +
                    " database=WindForm_Bugs";

            // Create connection object, initialize with
            // connection string. Open it.
            System.Data.SqlClient.SqlConnection connection =
```

Example 20-2. Hand-edited code (C#) (continued)

```
              new System.Data.SqlClient.SqlConnection(
              connectionString);
          connection.Open( );

          // Create a SqlCommand object and assign the connection
          System.Data.SqlClient.SqlCommand command =
              new System.Data.SqlClient.SqlCommand( );
          command.Connection=connection;

          // set the stored procedure to get the bug records
          command.CommandText="spBugsNoHistory";                command.
CommandType=CommandType.StoredProcedure;

          DataSet bugDataSet = new DataSet( );
          SqlDataAdapter bugDataAdapter = new SqlDataAdapter( );
          bugDataAdapter.SelectCommand = command;
          bugDataAdapter.TableMappings.Add("Table","Bugs");
          bugDataAdapter.Fill(bugDataSet);
          DataTable bugTable = bugDataSet.Tables[0];

          foreach (DataRow row in bugTable.Rows)
          {
              lbBugs.Items.Add(row["BugID"] + ") " +
                  row["Description"] + " [ " +
                  row["ProductDescription"] +
                  " ]. Reported by: " + row["reporter"]);
          }
      }


      protected override void Dispose( bool disposing )
      {
         if( disposing )
         {
            if (components != null)
            {
               components.Dispose( );
            }
         }
         base.Dispose( disposing );
      }

      #region Windows Form Designer generated code
      #endregion

      /// <summary>
      /// The main entry point for the application.
      /// </summary>
      [STAThread]
      static void Main( )
```

Example 20-2. Hand-edited code (C#) (continued)

```
C#
        {
           Application.Run(new Form1( ));
        }

      private void btnEdit_Click(object sender, System.EventArgs e)
      {
          string cmd = @"Update bugs set description = '" +
              txtDescription.Text +
              @"' where bugid = (select max(BugID) from bugs)";

          UpdateDB(cmd);
      }

      private void btnAdd_Click(object sender, System.EventArgs e)
      {
          string cmd = @"Insert into bugs values (1,'0.1', '" +
              txtDescription.Text + @"',1)";

          UpdateDB(cmd);
      }

      private void btnDelete_Click(object sender, System.EventArgs e)
      {
          string cmd =
              @"delete from bugs where bugid =
       (select max(BugID) from bugs)";

          UpdateDB(cmd);
      }

      // common routine for all database updates
      private void UpdateDB(string cmd)
      {
          // connection string to connect to the Bugs Database
          string connectionString =
              "server=YourServer; uid=sa; pwd=YourPW;" +
                  " database=WindForm_Bugs";

          // Create connection object, initialize with
          // connection string. Open it.
          System.Data.SqlClient.SqlConnection connection =
              new System.Data.SqlClient.SqlConnection(connectionString);
          connection.Open( );

          // Create a SqlCommand object and assign the connection
          System.Data.SqlClient.SqlCommand command =
              new System.Data.SqlClient.SqlCommand( );
          command.Connection=connection;
          command.CommandText=cmd;
          command.ExecuteNonQuery( );

          // clear the text box
```

Example 20-2. Hand-edited code (C#) (continued)

```
            txtDescription.Text = "";
            PopulateListBox( );
            return;
        }
    }
}
```

Example 20-3. Hand-edited code (VB.NET)

```
Imports System.Data.SqlClient

Public Class Form1
    Inherits System.Windows.Forms.Form

#Region " Windows Form Designer generated code "

    Public Sub New( )
        MyBase.New( )

        'This call is required by the Windows Form Designer.
        InitializeComponent( )
        PopulateListBox( )

        'Add any initialization after the InitializeComponent( ) call

    End Sub

#End Region
    Private Sub PopulateListBox( )
        lbBugs.Items.Clear( )
        ' connection string to connect to the Bugs Database
        Dim connectionString As String = "server=YourServer; uid=sa; " + _
                " pwd=YourPW; database=WindForm_Bugs"

        ' Create connection object, initialize with
        ' connection string. Open it.
        Dim connection As New _
            System.Data.SqlClient.SqlConnection(connectionString)
        connection.Open( )

        ' Create a SqlCommand object and assign the connection
        Dim command As New System.Data.SqlClient.SqlCommand( )
        command.Connection = connection

        ' set the stored procedure to get the bug records
        command.CommandText = "spBugsNoHistory"
        command.CommandType = CommandType.StoredProcedure

        Dim bugDataSet As New DataSet( )
        Dim bugDataAdapter As New SqlDataAdapter( )
        bugDataAdapter.SelectCommand = command
        bugDataAdapter.TableMappings.Add("Table", "Bugs")
```

Example 20-3. Hand-edited code (VB.NET) (continued)

```
VB        bugDataAdapter.Fill(bugDataSet)
          Dim bugTable As DataTable = bugDataSet.Tables(0)

          Dim row As DataRow
          For Each row In bugTable.Rows
              lbBugs.Items.Add(row("BugID") & " " & _
              row("Description") & " [ " & row("ProductDescription") & _
              " ]. Reported by: " & row("reporter"))
          Next
      End Sub


      Private Sub btnAdd_Click(ByVal sender As System.Object, _
                          ByVal e As System.EventArgs) _
                          Handles btnAdd.Click
          Dim cmd As String = "Insert into bugs values (1,'0.1', '" & _
              txtDescription.Text & "',1)"
          UpdateDB(cmd)
      End Sub

      Private Sub btnEdit_Click(ByVal sender As System.Object, _
                          ByVal e As System.EventArgs) _
                          Handles btnEdit.Click
          Dim cmd As String = "Update bugs set description = '" & _
              txtDescription.Text & "' where bugID = " & _
              "(select max(bugID) from bugs)"
          UpdateDB(cmd)
      End Sub

      Private Sub btnDelete_Click(ByVal sender As System.Object, _
                          ByVal e As System.EventArgs) _
                          Handles btnDelete.Click
          Dim cmd As String = "delete from bugs where bugid = " & _
              "(select max(BugID) from bugs)"
          UpdateDB(cmd)
      End Sub

      Private Sub UpdateDB(ByVal cmd As String)
          ' connection string to connect to the Bugs Database
          Dim connectionString As String = "server=YourServer; uid=sa; " + _
                  " pwd=YourPW; database=WindForm_Bugs"

          ' Create connection object, initialize with
          ' connection string. Open it.
          Dim connection As New _
              System.Data.SqlClient.SqlConnection(connectionString)
          connection.Open()

          ' Create a SqlCommand object and assign the connection
          Dim command As New System.Data.SqlClient.SqlCommand()
          command.Connection = connection
          command.CommandText = cmd
```

Example 20-3. Hand-edited code (VB.NET) (continued)

```
            command.ExecuteNonQuery( )

            ' clear the text box
            txtDescription.Text = ""
            PopulateListBox( )
            Return
        End Sub
    End Class
```

For each of the three buttons, execute the same steps in the Click event handler:

1. Create the SQL string.
2. Create a Connection object and a Command object.
3. Set the Command object's CommandText property to the SQL statement you've created.
4. Execute the SQL statement.
5. Rebind the data to update the display.

All three event handlers require identical steps 2 through 5, so this work is factored out into a common method, UpdateDB, to which you pass the command string you want executed. The syntax of the UpdateDB method is as follows:

[C#]

```
        private void UpdateDB(string cmd)
```

[VB]

```
        Private Sub UpdateDB(cmd As String)
```

Create your connection string and Connection object as you have in the examples in the previous chapter. Then set the Command object's CommandText property to the string passed in as a parameter and execute the query with the ExecuteNonQuery method:

[C#]

```
        command.CommandText=cmd;
        command.ExecuteNonQuery( );
```

Remember that ExecuteNonQuery, as you saw in Chapter 19, is used when you do not expect to get back a result set. The return value is the number of records affected, which you pass back to the calling program.

The SQL statement for adding a record is a simple insert statement. In this example, you'll hardwire the values for the Product, Version, and Reporter fields, but you'll pick up the text for the Description field from the TextBox:

[C#]

```
        string cmd = @"Insert into bugs values (1,'0.1', '" +
            TxtDescription.Text + @"',1)";
```

[VB]

```
        Dim cmd As String = "Insert into bugs values (1,'0.1', '" & _
            txtDescription.Text & "',1)"
```

C# tip: The @ symbol creates a verbatim string, allowing you to pass in single quotation marks without escaping them.

Pass this cmd string to the UpdateDB method, where you create a connection to the database, and execute the passed-in command by calling ExecuteNonQuery.

VB
```
Dim connection As New
    System.Data.SqlClient.SqlConnection(connectionString)
connection.Open( )

Dim command As New System.Data.SqlClient.SqlCommand( )
command.Connection = connection
command.CommandText = cmd

command.ExecuteNonQuery( )
```

Finally, empty the contents of the TextBox update the ListBox to reflect the change:

C#
```
PopulateListBox( );
```

The three event handlers are identical except for the particular SQL statement executed. Note that the Edit and Delete buttons are hardwired to operate on the record with the highest BugID. This was done only to keep the example very simple.

Stored Procedures

A stored procedure is, essentially, a SQL method. Like a method, stored procedures have a name and, optionally, parameters. There is no return type for a stored procedure, though it is possible to get back values by either using parameters (like passing by reference in VB.NET or C#) or returning a recordset.

Stored procedure parameters are prepended with the at-sign (@) and marked with their type, each separated from the next by a comma, as shown here:

```
spAddBugWithTransactions
    @ProductID int,
    @Version varChar(50),
    @Description varChar(8000)
```

The value in parentheses is the size of the parameter. In the code shown, Version is a parameter of type varChar, which will hold up to 50 characters. For more information on stored procedures and SQL programming, see *Transact-SQL Programming*, by Kevin E. Kline, Lee Gould, and Andrew Zanevsky (O'Reilly).

Updating Data with Transactions

An important feature of most industrial-strength databases is support for transactions. A *transaction* is a set of database operations that must all complete or fail together. That is, either all operations must complete successfully (commit the transaction), or all must be undone (roll back the transaction) to leave the database in the state it was in before the transaction began.

The canonical transaction is depositing a check. If you receive a check for $50 and you deposit it, you and the check writer both expect that once the bank transaction is completed, your account will have increased by $50 and the check writer's will have decreased by $50. Presumably the bank computer accomplishes this transaction in two steps:

1. Reduce the check writer's account by $50.
2. Increase your account by $50.

If the system fails between steps 1 and 2, or for any reason your account cannot be increased by $50, the transaction should be rolled back; that is, it should fail as a whole (neither account should be affected).

If the check writer's account is reduced by $50 and your account is not increased, then the database has become corrupted. This should never be allowed, and it is the job of transactions to ensure that either both actions are taken or neither is.

The remaining alternative, in which the check writer's account is not decreased but yours is increased, may be a happy outcome for you ("Bank Error In Your Favor—Collect $50"), but the bank would not be pleased.

The ACID Test

Database designers define the requirements of a transaction in the so-called Atomic, Consistent, Isolated, and Durable (ACID) test. Here's a brief summary of what each of these terms means:

Atomic

An atomic interaction is indivisible (i.e., it cannot be partially implemented). Every transaction must be atomic. For instance, in the previous banking example, it must not be possible to decrement the check writer's account but fail to increment yours. If the transaction fails, it must return the database to the state it would have been in without the transaction.

All transactions, even failed ones, affect the database in trivial ways (e.g., resources are expended, performance is affected, or an entry is made in the log). The atomic requirement implies only that if a transaction is rolled back, all tables and data (except the log) will be in the state they would have been in had the transaction not been attempted at all.

Consistent

The database is presumed to be in a consistent state before the transaction begins, and the transaction must leave it in a consistent state when it completes. While the transaction is being processed, however, the database need not be in a consistent state. To continue with our example of depositing a check, the database need not be consistent during the transaction (e.g., it is okay to decrement the check writer's account before incrementing your account), but it must end in a consistent state (i.e., when the transaction completes, the books must balance).

Isolated

Transactions are not processed one at a time. Typically, a database may process many transactions at once, switching its attention back and forth among various operations. This creates the possibility that a transaction can view and act upon data that reflects intermediate changes from another transaction that is still in progress and that therefore currently has its data in an inconsistent state. Transaction isolation is designed to prevent this problem. For a transaction to be isolated, the effects of the transaction must be exactly as if the transaction were acted on alone; there can be no effects on or dependencies on other database activities. For more information, see the sidebar "Data Isolation" in this chapter.

Durable

Once a transaction is committed, the effect on the database is permanent.

Implementing Transactions

There are two ways to implement transactions when building a Windows application. You can allow the database to manage the transaction by using transactions within your stored procedure, or you can use connection-based transactions. In the latter case, the transaction is created and enforced outside the database and allows your transaction to span multiple interactions between the client and the database.

You will remember from Chapter 19 that the Bug database is designed to record each bug event as one record in Bugs and one or more records in BugHistory. In the next example, you will elicit information from the user about a new bug (e.g., the description, severity, etc.), and you will update both the Bug table and the BugHistory table.

If the update to the BugHistory table fails for any reason, make sure that the update to the Bug table rolls back as well. To ensure this, wrap these updates in a transaction.

In this example, you will offer the user the option to have the transaction implemented by either the database or the connection.

If the user selects DB Transaction, you will call a stored procedure that implements the transaction semantics. If the user selects Connection Transaction, you will manage the transaction yourself, using an instance of the System.Data.SqlClient. SqlTransaction class.

Data Isolation

Creating fully isolated transactions in a multithreaded environment is a nontrivial exercise. There are three ways isolation can be violated:

Lost update

One thread reads a record, a second thread updates the record, and then the first thread overwrites the second thread's update.

Dirty read

Thread one writes data; thread two reads what thread one wrote. Thread one then overwrites the data, thus leaving thread two with old data.

Unrepeatable read

Thread one reads data and the data is then overwritten by thread two. Thread one tries to re-read the data, but it has changed.

Database experts identify four degrees of isolation:

- Degree 0 is limited only to preventing the overwriting of data by any other transaction that is of degree 1 or greater.
- Degree 1 isolation has no lost updates.
- Degree 2 isolation has no lost updates and no dirty reads, but may have unrepeatable reads.
- Degree 3 isolation has no lost updates, no dirty reads, and no unrepeatable reads.

While details about transaction isolation is beyond the scope of this book, the section "Multiuser Updates," later in this chapter, discusses issues related to avoiding violation of isolation.

The very simple user interface you'll use is shown in Figure 20-2. At the bottom of the form are two radio buttons: Data Base Transaction and Connection Transaction. The user will choose which type of transaction to use to update the database.

Database transactions

To implement the DB Transaction option, you need a stored procedure (or *sproc*) that adds a record to the Bugs table and to the BugsHistory table, using SQL transaction support.

To decide which parameters to provide this sproc, examine the two tables you will update, as shown in Figure 20-3.

Twelve fields must be filled in for the two tables. For Bugs, the required fields are BugID, Product, Version, Description, and Reporter. However, you don't need to provide a BugID, since it is an identity column provided by the database.

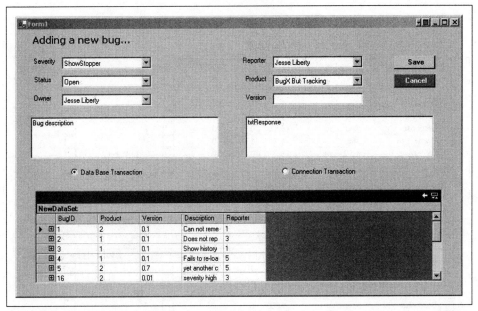

Figure 20-2. Adding a new bug with transactions

For BugHistory, the obligatory fields are BugHistoryID, BugID, Status, Severity, Response, Owner, and DateStamp. BugID must match the BugID generated by Bugs. So, rather than passing the BugID into the stored procedure, you'll get it back from the database when you add the Bug record

The BugHistoryID numbers are specific to each bug. Bug 1 corresponds to BugHistory records numbered 1 through n, and Bug 2 has its own BugHistory records numbered 1 through x. Thus, the BugHistoryID starts over at 1 for each new bug. Since this is a new Bug, you'll set the BugHistoryID to 1. The DateStamp need not be passed as a parameter, since by default the database gets the current date. You therefore need only pass in eight parameters. See the sidebar "Stored Procedures" in this chapter.

```
CREATE PROCEDURE spAddBugWithTransactions
@ProductID int,
@Version varChar(50),
@Description varChar(8000),
@Response varChar(8000),
@Reporter int,
@Owner int,
@Status int,
@Severity int
```

The core of the procedure is a pair of insert statements. First, you will insert values into the Bugs table:

```
Insert into Bugs values (@ProductID, @Version, @Description, @Reporter)
```

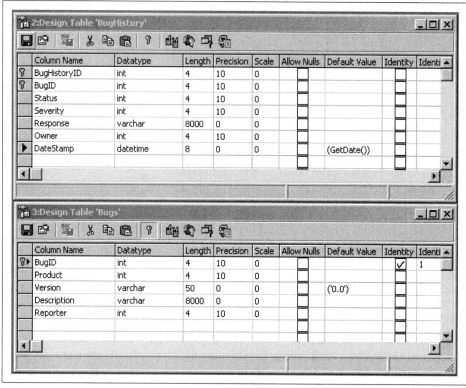

Figure 20-3. Bugs and bug history

 SQL statements and sprocs are not case sensitive.

The Bugs table has an identity column, which you can retrieve with the SQL keyword @@identity:

```
declare @bugID int
select @bugID = @@identity
```

With that bugID in hand, you are ready to insert a record into BugHistory:

```
Insert into BugHistory
   (bugHistoryID, bugID, status, severity, response, owner)
   values
   (
      1,              -- BugHistoryID
      @bugID,
      @Status,
      @Severity,
      @Response,
      @Owner
   )
```

To make this all work with database transactions, before the Insert statement that adds a record to the first table, you need to begin with the line:

```
Begin Transaction
```

After the insert, check the @@error value, which should be 0 if the insert succeeded:

```
if @@Error <> 0 goto ErrorHandler
```

If there is an error, jump to the error handler, where you'll call Rollback Transaction:

```
ErrorHandler:
rollback transaction
```

If there is no error, continue on to the second Insert statement. If there is no error after that insert, you are ready to commit the transaction and exit the sproc:

```
if @@Error <> 0 goto ErrorHandler
commit transaction
return
```

The net effect is that either both insert statements are acted on, or neither is. The complete sproc is shown in Example 20-4.

Example 20-4. Stored procedure spAddBugWithTransactions

```
CREATE PROCEDURE spAddBugWithTransactions
@ProductID int,
@Version varChar(50),
@Description varChar(8000),
@Response varChar(8000),
@Reporter int,
@Owner int,
@Status int,
@Severity int
 AS
Begin Transaction
    declare @bugID int
    Insert into Bugs values (@ProductID, @Version, @Description, @Reporter)
    select @bugID = @@identity
    if @@Error <> 0 goto ErrorHandler

    Insert into BugHistory
    (bugHistoryID, bugID, status, severity, response, owner)
    values
    (
        1,
        @bugID,
        @Status,          -- status
        @Severity,
        @Response,
        @Owner
    )
    if @@Error <> 0 goto ErrorHandler
    commit transaction
    return
```

Example 20-4. Stored procedure spAddBugWithTransactions (continued)

```
ErrorHandler:
  rollback transaction
  return
```

With the stored procedure in hand, you are ready to create the form that allows the user to choose a database transaction or a connection-based transaction. Create a new VB.NET or C# project named AddBugWithTransactions and add the controls shown in Figure 20-4, and described in Table 20-1.

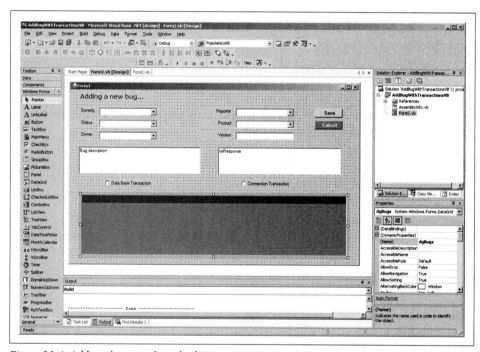

Figure 20-4. Adding the controls to the form

Table 20-1. Controls for the form

Control type	Name	Value
Label	label1	Adding a new bug
Label	label2	Severity
Label	label3	Owner
Label	label4	Reporter
Label	label5	Product
Label	label6	Version
ComboBox	cbSeverity	DropDownStyle: DropDownList
ComboBox	cbSeverity	DropDownStyle: DropDownList

Table 20-1. Controls for the form (continued)

Control type	Name	Value
ComboBox	cbStatus	DropDownStyle: DropDownList
ComboBox	cbOwner	DropDownStyle: DropDownList
ComboBox	cbReporter	DropDownStyle: DropDownList
ComboBox	cbProduct	DropDownStyle: DropDownList
TextBox	txtVersion	
TextBox	txtDescription	AcceptReturn: true
		AcceptTab: true
		Multiline: true
		Text: bug description
TextBox	txtResponse	AcceptReturn: true
		AcceptTab: true
		Multiline: true
		Text: txtResponse
RadioButton	rbDBTransaction	Database Transaction
RadioButton	rbConnection-Transaction	Connection Transaction
Button	btnSave	BackColor: Lime
		Font: Bold
		Text: Save
Button	btnCancel	BackColor: Red
		Font: Bold
		Text: Cancel
DataGrid	dgBugs	

The complete listing in C# is shown in Example 20-5, and the complete VB.NET listing is shown in Example 20-6. Detailed analysis follows.

Example 20-5. DB and connection transactions in C#

```
using System;
using System.Drawing;
using System.Collections;
using System.ComponentModel;
using System.Windows.Forms;
using System.Data;
using System.Data.SqlClient;

namespace AddBugWithTransactionsCS
{
    public class Form1 : System.Windows.Forms.Form
    {
        private System.Windows.Forms.RadioButton rbDBTransaction;
        private System.Windows.Forms.RadioButton rbConnectionTransaction;
```

Example 20-5. DB and connection transactions in C# (continued)

```
private System.Windows.Forms.Button btnCancel;
private System.Windows.Forms.Button btnSave;
private System.Windows.Forms.Label label5;
private System.Windows.Forms.Label label4;
private System.Windows.Forms.Label label3;
private System.Windows.Forms.Label label2;
private System.Windows.Forms.Label label1;
private System.Windows.Forms.ComboBox cbProduct;
private System.Windows.Forms.ComboBox cbOwner;
private System.Windows.Forms.ComboBox cbReporter;
private System.Windows.Forms.ComboBox cbStatus;
private System.Windows.Forms.ComboBox cbSeverity;
private System.Windows.Forms.TextBox txtResponse;
private System.Windows.Forms.TextBox txtDescription;
private System.Windows.Forms.Label label6;
private System.Windows.Forms.Label label7;
private System.Windows.Forms.TextBox txtVersion;
private System.Windows.Forms.DataGrid dgBugs;
private System.ComponentModel.Container components = null;

public Form1( )
{
   InitializeComponent( );
   PopulateListBoxes( );
   FillDataGrid( );
}

protected override void Dispose( bool disposing )
{
   if( disposing )
   {
      if (components != null)
      {
         components.Dispose( );
      }
   }
   base.Dispose( disposing );
}

private void PopulateListBoxes( )
{
   // creat the dataset
   DataSet dataSet = new System.Data.DataSet( );
   dataSet.CaseSensitive=true;

   // connect to the database
   string connectionString =
      "server=YourServer; uid=sa; pwd=YourPW; " +
      " database=WindForm_Bugs";

   SqlConnection connection = new
      System.Data.SqlClient.SqlConnection(connectionString);
```

Example 20-5. DB and connection transactions in C# (continued)

```csharp
connection.Open( );

SqlCommand command1 = new System.Data.SqlClient.SqlCommand( );
command1.Connection=connection;

// fill the various tables

command1.CommandText = "Select * from lkProduct";
SqlDataAdapter dataAdapter =
    new System.Data.SqlClient.SqlDataAdapter( );
dataAdapter.SelectCommand= command1;
dataAdapter.TableMappings.Add("Table","Products");
dataAdapter.Fill(dataSet);

command1.CommandText = "Select * from lkSeverity";
dataAdapter = new System.Data.SqlClient.SqlDataAdapter( );
dataAdapter.SelectCommand= command1;
dataAdapter.TableMappings.Add("Table","Severity");
dataAdapter.Fill(dataSet);

command1.CommandText = "Select * from lkStatus";
dataAdapter = new System.Data.SqlClient.SqlDataAdapter( );
dataAdapter.SelectCommand= command1;
dataAdapter.TableMappings.Add("Table","Status");
dataAdapter.Fill(dataSet);

command1.CommandText = "Select * from People";
dataAdapter = new System.Data.SqlClient.SqlDataAdapter( );
dataAdapter.SelectCommand= command1;
dataAdapter.TableMappings.Add("Table","Reporter");
dataAdapter.Fill(dataSet);

command1.CommandText = "Select * from People";
dataAdapter = new System.Data.SqlClient.SqlDataAdapter( );
dataAdapter.SelectCommand= command1;
dataAdapter.TableMappings.Add("Table","Owner");
dataAdapter.Fill(dataSet);

connection.Close( );

// bind the controls to the tables

DataTable theTable = dataSet.Tables["Products"];
cbProduct.DataSource = theTable.DefaultView;
cbProduct.DisplayMember = "ProductDescription";
cbProduct.ValueMember = "ProductID";

theTable = dataSet.Tables["Severity"];
cbSeverity.DataSource = theTable.DefaultView;
cbSeverity.DisplayMember = "SeverityDescription";
cbSeverity.ValueMember = "SeverityID";
```

Example 20-5. DB and connection transactions in C# (continued)

```csharp
        theTable = dataSet.Tables["Status"];
        cbStatus.DataSource = theTable.DefaultView;
        cbStatus.DisplayMember = "StatusDescription";
        cbStatus.ValueMember = "StatusID";

        theTable = dataSet.Tables["Owner"];
        cbOwner.DataSource = theTable.DefaultView;
        cbOwner.DisplayMember = "FullName";
        cbOwner.ValueMember = "PersonID";

        theTable = dataSet.Tables["Reporter"];
        cbReporter.DataSource = theTable.DefaultView;
        cbReporter.DisplayMember = "FullName";
        cbReporter.ValueMember = "PersonID";

        rbDBTransaction.Checked = true;  // pick a radio button
    }   //  close PopulateListBoxes


    #region Windows Form Designer generated code
    #endregion

    /// <summary>
    /// The main entry point for the application.
    /// </summary>
    [STAThread]
    static void Main( )
    {
        Application.Run(new Form1( ));
    }

    private void btnSave_Click(object sender, System.EventArgs e)
    {
        if (rbDBTransaction.Checked)
        {
            UpdateDBTransaction( );
        }
        else
        {
            UpdateConnectionTransaction( );
        }
        MessageBox.Show("Bug added!");
        PopulateListBoxes( );
        FillDataGrid( );
    }

    private void UpdateConnectionTransaction( )
    {
        string connectionString =
            "server=YourServer; uid=sa; pwd=YourPW; " +
                " database=WindForm_Bugs";
```

Example 20-5. DB and connection transactions in C# (continued)

```
// Create connection object, initialize with
// connection string. Open it.
System.Data.SqlClient.SqlConnection connection =
   new System.Data.SqlClient.SqlConnection(connectionString);

// declare the command object for the sql statements
System.Data.SqlClient.SqlCommand command =
   new System.Data.SqlClient.SqlCommand( );

// connection string to connect to the Bugs Database
connection.Open( );

// declare an instance of SqlTransaction
SqlTransaction transaction;

// begin the transaction
transaction = connection.BeginTransaction( );

// attach the transaction to the command
command.Transaction = transaction;

// attach connection to the command
command.Connection = connection;

try
{
   command.CommandText = "spAddBug";
   command.CommandType = CommandType.StoredProcedure;

   // declare the parameter object
   System.Data.SqlClient.SqlParameter param;

   int productID =
     Convert.ToInt32(cbProduct.SelectedValue.ToString( ));
   int reporterID =
     Convert.ToInt32(cbReporter.SelectedValue.ToString( ));

   // add each parameter and set its direciton and value
   param = command.Parameters.Add("@ProductID",SqlDbType.Int);
   param.Direction = ParameterDirection.Input;
   param.Value = productID;

   param =
       command.Parameters.Add("@Version",SqlDbType.VarChar,50);
   param.Direction = ParameterDirection.Input;
   param.Value = txtVersion.Text;

   param =
     command.Parameters.Add("@Description",
                            SqlDbType.VarChar,8000);
   param.Direction = ParameterDirection.Input;
   param.Value = txtDescription.Text;
```

Example 20-5. DB and connection transactions in C# (continued)

```
    param = command.Parameters.Add("@Reporter",SqlDbType.Int);
    param.Direction = ParameterDirection.Input;
    param.Value = reporterID;

    param = command.Parameters.Add("@BugID",SqlDbType.Int);
    param.Direction = ParameterDirection.Output;

    command.ExecuteNonQuery(); // execute the sproc

    // retrieve the identity column
    int BugID =
        Convert.ToInt32(command.Parameters["@BugID"].Value);

    int ownerID =
        Convert.ToInt32(cbOwner.SelectedValue.ToString());
    int statusID =
        Convert.ToInt32(cbStatus.SelectedValue.ToString());
    int severityID =
        Convert.ToInt32(cbSeverity.SelectedValue.ToString());

    // formulate the string to update the bug history
    string strAddBugHistory = "Insert into BugHistory " +
        "(bugHistoryID, bugID, status, severity, response, owner)"+
        " values (1, " + BugID + ", " +
        statusID + ", " + severityID + ", '" + txtResponse.Text +
        "', " + ownerID + ")";

    // set up the command object to update the bug history
    command.CommandType = CommandType.Text;
    command.CommandText = strAddBugHistory;

    // execute the insert statement
    command.ExecuteNonQuery();

    // commit the transaction
    transaction.Commit();

}
catch (Exception e)
{
    MessageBox.Show("Exception caught! " + e.Message);
    transaction.Rollback();
}
}   //close UpdateConnectionTransaction

private void UpdateDBTransaction()
{
    // connection string to connect to the Bugs Database
    string connectionString =
        "server=YourServer; uid=sa; pwd=YourPW; " +
            " database=WindForm_Bugs";
```

Example 20-5. DB and connection transactions in C# (continued)

```
// Create connection object, initialize with
// connection string. Open it.
System.Data.SqlClient.SqlConnection connection =
    new System.Data.SqlClient.SqlConnection(connectionString);
connection.Open( );

System.Data.SqlClient.SqlCommand command =
    new System.Data.SqlClient.SqlCommand( );
command.Connection = connection;

command.CommandText= "spAddBugWithTransactions";
command.CommandType = CommandType.StoredProcedure;


int productID =
    Convert.ToInt32(cbProduct.SelectedValue.ToString( ));
int reporterID =
    Convert.ToInt32(cbReporter.SelectedValue.ToString( ));
int ownerID = Convert.ToInt32(cbOwner.SelectedValue.ToString( ));
int statusID = Convert.ToInt32(cbStatus.SelectedValue.ToString( ));
int severityID =
    Convert.ToInt32(cbSeverity.SelectedValue.ToString( ));

// declare the parameter object
System.Data.SqlClient.SqlParameter param;

// add each parameter and set its direciton and value
param = command.Parameters.Add("@ProductID",SqlDbType.Int);
param.Direction = ParameterDirection.Input;
param.Value = productID;

param = command.Parameters.Add("@Version",SqlDbType.VarChar,50);
param.Direction = ParameterDirection.Input;
param.Value = txtVersion.Text;

param =
    command.Parameters.Add("@Description",SqlDbType.VarChar,8000);
param.Direction = ParameterDirection.Input;
param.Value = txtDescription.Text;

param =
    command.Parameters.Add("@Response",SqlDbType.VarChar,8000);
param.Direction = ParameterDirection.Input;
param.Value = txtResponse.Text;

param = command.Parameters.Add("@Reporter",SqlDbType.Int);
param.Direction = ParameterDirection.Input;
param.Value = reporterID;

param = command.Parameters.Add("@Owner",SqlDbType.Int);
param.Direction = ParameterDirection.Input;
param.Value = ownerID;
```

Example 20-5. DB and connection transactions in C# (continued)

```
C#       param = command.Parameters.Add("@Status",SqlDbType.Int);
         param.Direction = ParameterDirection.Input;
         param.Value = statusID;

         param = command.Parameters.Add("@Severity",SqlDbType.Int);
         param.Direction = ParameterDirection.Input;
         param.Value = severityID;

         command.ExecuteNonQuery( ); // execute the sproc
      }   //  close UpdateDBTransaction

      private void FillDataGrid( )
      {
         string connectionString =
            "server=YourServer; uid=sa; pwd=YourPW; " +
               " database=WindForm_Bugs";

         // create the connection, open it, and create the DataSet
         SqlConnection connection = new
            System.Data.SqlClient.SqlConnection(connectionString);
         connection.Open( );
         DataSet dataSet = new System.Data.DataSet( );
         dataSet.CaseSensitive=true;

         //The first command gets the bugs table
         string bugsCommandString = "Select * from bugs";
         SqlCommand bugCommand = new System.Data.SqlClient.SqlCommand( );
         bugCommand.Connection=connection;
         bugCommand.CommandText= bugsCommandString;

         // the second command gets the history table
         string historyCommandString = "Select * from bugHistory";
         SqlCommand historyCommand =
             new System.Data.SqlClient.SqlCommand( );
         historyCommand.Connection=connection;
         historyCommand.CommandText= historyCommandString;

         // create a dataAdapter to get the Bugs table and use it
         // to populate the dataset
         SqlDataAdapter bugDataAdapter = new SqlDataAdapter( );
         bugDataAdapter.SelectCommand = bugCommand;
         bugDataAdapter.TableMappings.Add("Table", "Bugs");
         bugDataAdapter.Fill(dataSet);

         // create a dataAdapter to get the history table and use it
         // to populate the dataset
         SqlDataAdapter historyDataAdapter = new SqlDataAdapter( );
         historyDataAdapter.SelectCommand = historyCommand;
         historyDataAdapter.TableMappings.Add("Table", "BugHistory");
         historyDataAdapter.Fill(dataSet);

         // create a DataRelation object and two dataColumn objects
```

Example 20-5. DB and connection transactions in C# (continued)

```
C#
        System.Data.DataColumn dataColumn1;
        System.Data.DataColumn dataColumn2;

        // Use the dataColumns to represent the Bugs field in both tables
        dataColumn1 = dataSet.Tables["Bugs"].Columns["BugID"];
        dataColumn2 = dataSet.Tables["BugHistory"].Columns["BugID"];

        // Instantiate the DataRelation object with the two columns
        // name the relationship BugsToHistory
        DataRelation bugsToHistory = new System.Data.DataRelation(
            "BugsToHistory",dataColumn1, dataColumn2);

        // Add the DataRelation object to the Relations table in
        //    the dataset
        dataSet.Relations.Add(bugsToHistory);

        // Bind the DataSet to the DataGrid
        DataViewManager dataView = dataSet.DefaultViewManager;
        dgBugs.DataSource= dataView;
    }    //  close FillDataGrid
  }      //  close Form1
}
```

Example 20-6. DB and connection transactions in VB.NET

```
VB
Imports System.Data.SqlClient

Public Class Form1
    Inherits System.Windows.Forms.Form

#Region " Windows Form Designer generated code "

    Public Sub New( )
        MyBase.New( )

        'This call is required by the Windows Form Designer.
        InitializeComponent( )
        PopulateListBoxes( )
        FillDataGrid( )

    End Sub


#End Region
    Private Sub PopulateListBoxes( )
        ' creat the dataset
        Dim myDataSet As New System.Data.DataSet( )
        myDataSet.CaseSensitive = True

        ' connect to the database
        Dim connectionString As String = _
            "server=YourServer; uid=sa; pwd=YourPW; database=WindForm_Bugs"
```

Example 20-6. DB and connection transactions in VB.NET (continued)

```vbnet
Dim myConnection As New System.Data.SqlClient.SqlConnection(connectionString)
myConnection.Open()

Dim command1 As New System.Data.SqlClient.SqlCommand()
command1.Connection = myConnection

' fill the various tables

command1.CommandText = "Select * from lkProduct"
Dim dataAdapter As New System.Data.SqlClient.SqlDataAdapter()
dataAdapter.SelectCommand = command1
dataAdapter.TableMappings.Add("Table", "Products")
dataAdapter.Fill(myDataSet)

command1.CommandText = "Select * from lkSeverity"
dataAdapter = New System.Data.SqlClient.SqlDataAdapter()
dataAdapter.SelectCommand = command1
dataAdapter.TableMappings.Add("Table", "Severity")
dataAdapter.Fill(myDataSet)

command1.CommandText = "Select * from lkStatus"
dataAdapter = New System.Data.SqlClient.SqlDataAdapter()
dataAdapter.SelectCommand = command1
dataAdapter.TableMappings.Add("Table", "Status")
dataAdapter.Fill(myDataSet)

command1.CommandText = "Select * from People"
dataAdapter = New System.Data.SqlClient.SqlDataAdapter()
dataAdapter.SelectCommand = command1
dataAdapter.TableMappings.Add("Table", "Reporter")
dataAdapter.Fill(myDataSet)

command1.CommandText = "Select * from People"
dataAdapter = New System.Data.SqlClient.SqlDataAdapter()
dataAdapter.SelectCommand = command1
dataAdapter.TableMappings.Add("Table", "Owner")
dataAdapter.Fill(myDataSet)

myConnection.Close()

' bind the controls to the tables

Dim theTable As DataTable = myDataSet.Tables("Products")
cbProduct.DataSource = theTable.DefaultView
cbProduct.DisplayMember = "ProductDescription"
cbProduct.ValueMember = "ProductID"

theTable = myDataSet.Tables("Severity")
cbSeverity.DataSource = theTable.DefaultView
cbSeverity.DisplayMember = "SeverityDescription"
cbSeverity.ValueMember = "SeverityID"
```

Example 20-6. DB and connection transactions in VB.NET (continued)

```
VB          theTable = myDataSet.Tables("Status")
            cbStatus.DataSource = theTable.DefaultView
            cbStatus.DisplayMember = "StatusDescription"
            cbStatus.ValueMember = "StatusID"

            theTable = myDataSet.Tables("Owner")
            cbOwner.DataSource = theTable.DefaultView
            cbOwner.DisplayMember = "FullName"
            cbOwner.ValueMember = "PersonID"

            theTable = myDataSet.Tables("Reporter")
            cbReporter.DataSource = theTable.DefaultView
            cbReporter.DisplayMember = "FullName"
            cbReporter.ValueMember = "PersonID"

            rbDBTransaction.Checked = True   ' pick a radio button
        End Sub    '   close PopulateListBoxes

    Private Sub btnSave_Click( _
        ByVal sender As System.Object, ByVal e As System.EventArgs) _
        Handles btnSave.Click

        If rbDBTransaction.Checked = True Then
            UpdateDBTransaction( )
        Else
            UpdateConnectionTransaction( )
        End If
        MessageBox.Show("Bug added!")
        PopulateListBoxes( )
        FillDataGrid( )
    End Sub

    Private Sub UpdateDBTransaction( )
        ' connection string to connect to the Bugs Database
        Dim connectionString As String = _
            "server=YourServer; uid=sa; pwd=YourPW; database=WindForm_Bugs"

        ' Create connection object, initialize with
        ' connection string. Open it.
        Dim myConnection As New System.Data.SqlClient.SqlConnection(connectionString)
        myConnection.Open( )

        Dim myCommand As New System.Data.SqlClient.SqlCommand( )
        myCommand.Connection = myConnection

        myCommand.CommandText = "spAddBugWithTransactions"
        myCommand.CommandType = CommandType.StoredProcedure


        Dim productID As Int32 = CInt(cbProduct.SelectedValue)
        Dim reporterID As Int32 = CInt(cbReporter.SelectedValue)
        Dim ownerID As Int32 = CInt(cbOwner.SelectedValue)
```

Example 20-6. DB and connection transactions in VB.NET (continued)

```vb
    Dim statusID As Int32 = CInt(cbStatus.SelectedValue)
    Dim severityID As Int32 = CInt(cbSeverity.SelectedValue)

    ' declare the parameter object
    Dim param As New System.Data.SqlClient.SqlParameter()

    ' add each parameter and set its direciton and value
    param = myCommand.Parameters.Add("@ProductID", SqlDbType.Int)
    param.Direction = ParameterDirection.Input
    param.Value = productID

    param = myCommand.Parameters.Add("@Version", SqlDbType.VarChar, 50)
    param.Direction = ParameterDirection.Input
    param.Value = txtVersion.Text

    param = myCommand.Parameters.Add("@Description", _
                                 SqlDbType.VarChar, 8000)
    param.Direction = ParameterDirection.Input
    param.Value = txtDescription.Text

    param = myCommand.Parameters.Add("@Response", SqlDbType.VarChar, _
                                 8000)
    param.Direction = ParameterDirection.Input
    param.Value = txtResponse.Text

    param = myCommand.Parameters.Add("@Reporter", SqlDbType.Int)
    param.Direction = ParameterDirection.Input
    param.Value = reporterID

    param = myCommand.Parameters.Add("@Owner", SqlDbType.Int)
    param.Direction = ParameterDirection.Input
    param.Value = ownerID

    param = myCommand.Parameters.Add("@Status", SqlDbType.Int)
    param.Direction = ParameterDirection.Input
    param.Value = statusID

    param = myCommand.Parameters.Add("@Severity", SqlDbType.Int)
    param.Direction = ParameterDirection.Input
    param.Value = severityID

    myCommand.ExecuteNonQuery() ' execute the sproc
    MessageBox.Show("Bug added!")
    PopulateListBoxes()
    FillDataGrid()
End Sub    '  close UpdateDBTransaction

Private Sub FillDataGrid()
    Dim connectionString As String
    connectionString = _
    "Server=YourServer; uid=sa; pwd=YourPW; database=WindForm_Bugs"
```

Example 20-6. DB and connection transactions in VB.NET (continued)

```vb
Dim myConnection As New _
            System.Data.SqlClient.SqlConnection(connectionString)
myConnection.Open( )
Dim myDataSet As New System.Data.DataSet( )
myDataSet.CaseSensitive = True

'The first command gets the bugs table
Dim bugCommandString As String
bugCommandString = "Select * from bugs"
Dim bugCommand As New System.Data.SqlClient.SqlCommand( )
bugCommand.Connection = myConnection
bugCommand.CommandText = bugCommandString

'the second command gets the history table
Dim historyCommandString As String
historyCommandString = "Select * from bugHistory"
Dim historyCommand As New System.Data.SqlClient.SqlCommand( )
historyCommand.Connection = myConnection
historyCommand.CommandText = historyCommandString

' create the dataAdapter to get the Bugs table and use
' it to populate the dataset
Dim bugDataAdapter As New SqlDataAdapter( )
bugDataAdapter.SelectCommand = bugCommand
bugDataAdapter.TableMappings.Add("Table", "Bugs")
bugDataAdapter.Fill(myDataSet)


' create the dataAdapter to get the history table and
' use it to populate the dataset
Dim historyDataAdapter As New SqlDataAdapter( )
historyDataAdapter.SelectCommand = historyCommand
historyDataAdapter.TableMappings.Add("Table", "BugHistory")
historyDataAdapter.Fill(myDataSet)

Dim dataColumn1 As DataColumn
Dim dataColumn2 As DataColumn
dataColumn1 = myDataSet.Tables("Bugs").Columns("BugID")
dataColumn2 = myDataSet.Tables("BugHistory").Columns("BugID")

Dim bugHistory As New DataRelation("BugsToHistory", dataColumn1, _
                                   dataColumn2)

myDataSet.Relations.Add(bugHistory)

Dim dataView As DataViewManager = myDataSet.DefaultViewManager
dgBugs.DataSource = dataView

End Sub    '  close FillDataGrid

Private Sub UpdateConnectionTransaction( )
    Dim connectionString As String = _
```

Example 20-6. DB and connection transactions in VB.NET (continued)

```
            "server=YourServer; uid=sa; pwd=YourPW; database=WindForm_Bugs"

    ' Create connection object, initialize with
    ' connection string. Open it.
    Dim myConnection As New System.Data.SqlClient.SqlConnection(connectionString)

    ' declare the command object for the sql statements
    Dim myCommand As New System.Data.SqlClient.SqlCommand( )

    ' connection string to connect to the Bugs Database
    myConnection.Open( )

    ' declare an instance of SqlTransaction
    Dim transaction As SqlTransaction

    ' begin the transaction
    transaction = myConnection.BeginTransaction( )

    ' attach the transaction to the command
    myCommand.Transaction = transaction

    ' attach connection to the command
    myCommand.Connection = myConnection

    Try
        myCommand.CommandText = "spAddBug"
        myCommand.CommandType = CommandType.StoredProcedure

        ' declare the parameter object
        Dim param As System.Data.SqlClient.SqlParameter

        Dim productID As Int32 = CInt(cbProduct.SelectedValue)
        Dim reporterID As Int32 = CInt(cbReporter.SelectedValue)
        Dim ownerID As Int32 = CInt(cbOwner.SelectedValue)
        Dim statusID As Int32 = CInt(cbStatus.SelectedValue)
        Dim severityID As Int32 = CInt(cbSeverity.SelectedValue)

        ' add each parameter and set its direciton and value
        param = myCommand.Parameters.Add("@ProductID", SqlDbType.Int)
        param.Direction = ParameterDirection.Input
        param.Value = productID

        param = myCommand.Parameters.Add("@Version", SqlDbType.VarChar, 50)
        param.Direction = ParameterDirection.Input
        param.Value = txtVersion.Text

        param = myCommand.Parameters.Add("@Description", SqlDbType.VarChar, 8000)
        param.Direction = ParameterDirection.Input
        param.Value = txtDescription.Text

        param = myCommand.Parameters.Add("@Reporter", SqlDbType.Int)
        param.Direction = ParameterDirection.Input
```

Example 20-6. DB and connection transactions in VB.NET (continued)

```vbnet
            param.Value = reporterID

            param = myCommand.Parameters.Add("@BugID", SqlDbType.Int)
            param.Direction = ParameterDirection.Output

            myCommand.ExecuteNonQuery( ) ' execute the sproc
            ' retrieve the identity column
            Dim BugID As Integer = _
                Convert.ToInt32(myCommand.Parameters("@BugID").Value)


            ' formulate the string to update the bug history
            Dim strAddBugHistory As String = _
            "Insert into BugHistory " & _
            "(bugHistoryID, bugID, status, severity, response, owner)" + _
            " values (1, " & _
            BugID & ", " & statusID & ", " & severityID & ", '" & _
            txtResponse.Text & "', " & ownerID & ")"

            ' set up the command object to update the bug hsitory
            myCommand.CommandType = CommandType.Text
            myCommand.CommandText = strAddBugHistory

            ' execute the insert statement
            myCommand.ExecuteNonQuery( )

            ' commit the transaction
            transaction.Commit( )

        Catch e As Exception
            MessageBox.Show(("Exception caught! " + e.Message))
            transaction.Rollback( )
        End Try
    End Sub '  close UpdateConnectionTransaction
End Class
```

Filling in the ListBoxes

The first method you create will be the helper method called PopulateListBoxes that will fill your combo boxes:

```csharp
private void PopulateListBoxes( )
{
```

```vbnet
private Sub PopulateListBoxes( )
```

You'll create a DataSet to hold the tables representing the various lookup tables (e.g., Severity, Status, etc.). Begin by creating the DataSet and Connection objects:

```csharp
// create the dataset
DataSet dataSet = new System.Data.DataSet( );
dataSet.CaseSensitive=true;
```

```
// connect to the database
string connectionString =
   "server=YourServer; uid=sa; pwd=YourPW; database=WindForm_Bugs";

SqlConnection connection = new
   System.Data.SqlClient.SqlConnection(connectionString);
connection.Open( );
```

```
' create the dataset
Dim myDataSet As New System.Data.DataSet( )
myDataSet.CaseSensitive = True

' connect to the database
Dim connectionString As String = _
   "server=YourServer; uid=sa; pwd=YourPW; database=WindForm_Bugs"

Dim myConnection As New System.Data.SqlClient.SqlConnection(connectionString)
myConnection.Open( )
```

Create a Command object to assign to the DataAdapter. The Text property of the Command object will hold the select statement. You will then fill a table in the DataSet using the DataAdapter:

```
SqlCommand command1 = new System.Data.SqlClient.SqlCommand( );
command1.Connection=connection;

// fill the various tables

command1.CommandText = "Select * from lkProduct";
SqlDataAdapter dataAdapter = new System.Data.SqlClient.SqlDataAdapt
dataAdapter.SelectCommand= command1;
dataAdapter.TableMappings.Add("Table","Products");
dataAdapter.Fill(dataSet);
```

```
Dim command1 As New System.Data.SqlClient.SqlCommand( )
command1.Connection = myConnection

' fill the various tables

command1.CommandText = "Select * from lkProduct"
Dim dataAdapter As New System.Data.SqlClient.SqlDataAdapter( )
dataAdapter.SelectCommand = command1
dataAdapter.TableMappings.Add("Table", "Products")
dataAdapter.Fill(myDataSet)
```

You can now modify the text in the Select statement and reuse it to fill the next table:

```
command1.CommandText = "Select * from lkSeverity";
dataAdapter = new System.Data.SqlClient.SqlDataAdapter( );
dataAdapter.SelectCommand= command1;
dataAdapter.TableMappings.Add("Table","Severity");
dataAdapter.Fill(dataSet);
```

Do this repeatedly for each lookup table. For convenience, you'll create a table called Reporter and one called Owner, both based on the lookup table People:

```
command1.CommandText = "Select * from People";
dataAdapter = new System.Data.SqlClient.SqlDataAdapter( );
dataAdapter.SelectCommand= command1;
dataAdapter.TableMappings.Add("Table","Reporter");
dataAdapter.Fill(dataSet);

command1.CommandText = "Select * from People";
dataAdapter = new System.Data.SqlClient.SqlDataAdapter( );
dataAdapter.SelectCommand= command1;
dataAdapter.TableMappings.Add("Table","Owner");
dataAdapter.Fill(dataSet);
```

Once all the tables are created, you can close the connection:

```
connection.Close( );
```

You are now ready to bind the tables to the controls. Start by creating a reference to the table you want to bind to the control:

```
DataTable theTable = dataSet.Tables["Products"];
```

```
Dim theTable As DataTable = myDataSet.Tables("Products")
```

Set the DataSource property of the control to the DefaultView property of the table.

```
cbProduct.DataSource = theTable.DefaultView;
```

This binds the control to the table, but you must tell the control which field holds the value to display.

```
cbProduct.DisplayMember = "ProductDescription";
```

The listbox will now display the description of the product, but when it is time to update the database, you don't want the description—you want the product ID. You can tell the listbox to hold the associated ProductID in its ValueMember property.

```
cbProduct.ValueMember = "ProductID";
```

You can do the same for each of the other ListBoxes. For example, you can set the severity ListBox with this code:

```
theTable = dataSet.Tables["Severity"];
cbSeverity.DataSource = theTable.DefaultView;
cbSeverity.DisplayMember = "SeverityDescription";
cbSeverity.ValueMember = "SeverityID";
```

```
theTable = myDataSet.Tables("Severity")
cbSeverity.DataSource = theTable.DefaultView
cbSeverity.DisplayMember = "SeverityDescription"
cbSeverity.ValueMember = "SeverityID"
```

Once all the listboxes are set, set the first of the two radio buttons to be the default selection.

```
rbDBTransaction.Checked = true;
```

With that in place, you can test the application. The various listboxes should be populated, although the application will not do anything as of yet.

The job of the button handler is to determine which of the two radio buttons is selected and invoke the appropriate method. If the user chooses a database transaction, invoke the private UpdateDBTransaction helper method, which in turn invokes the spAddBugWithTransactions stored procedure (described earlier).

Double-click on the Save button and add this C# code to the event handler:

```
private void btnSave_Click(object sender, System.EventArgs e)
{
    if (rbDBTransaction.Checked)
    {
        UpdateDBTransaction();
    }
    else
    {
        UpdateConnectionTransaction();
    }
}
```

```
Private Sub btnSave_Click( _
    ByVal sender As System.Object, ByVal e As System.EventArgs) _
    Handles btnSave.Click

    If rbDBTransaction.Checked = True Then
        UpdateDBTransaction()
    Else
        UpdateConnectionTransaction()
    End If
End Sub
```

DataBase Transactions

In the UpdateDBTransaction method, you create a connection and a Command object in the normal way, setting the Command object's CommandType property to CommandType.StoredProcedure:

```
string connectionString =
    "server=YourServer; uid=sa; pwd=YourPW; database=WindForm_Bugs";

System.Data.SqlClient.SqlConnection connection =
    new System.Data.SqlClient.SqlConnection(connectionString);
connection.Open();

System.Data.SqlClient.SqlCommand command =
```

```
C#    new System.Data.SqlClient.SqlCommand( );
      command.Connection = connection;

      command.CommandText= "spAddBugWithTransactions";
      command.CommandType = CommandType.StoredProcedure;
```

```
VB    Dim connectionString As String = _
         "server=YourServer; uid=sa; pwd=YourPW; database=WindForm_Bugs"

      Dim myConnection As New _
         System.Data.SqlClient.SqlConnection(connectionString)
      myConnection.Open( )

      Dim myCommand As New System.Data.SqlClient.SqlCommand( )
      myCommand.Connection = myConnection

      myCommand.CommandText = "spAddBugWithTransactions"
      myCommand.CommandType = CommandType.StoredProcedure
```

Before creating the parameters, you'll create interim integer variables to hold the choices in the ListBoxes. You must extract each selected value as a string and then convert it to an integer:

```
C#    int productID = Convert.ToInt32(cbProduct.SelectedValue.ToString( ));
      int reporterID = Convert.ToInt32(cbReporter.SelectedValue.ToString( ));
      int ownerID = Convert.ToInt32(cbOwner.SelectedValue.ToString( ));
      int statusID = Convert.ToInt32(cbStatus.SelectedValue.ToString( ));
      int severityID = Convert.ToInt32(cbSeverity.SelectedValue.ToString( ));
```

```
VB    Dim productID As Int32 = CInt(cbProduct.SelectedValue)
      Dim reporterID As Int32 = CInt(cbReporter.SelectedValue)
      Dim ownerID As Int32 = CInt(cbOwner.SelectedValue)
      Dim statusID As Int32 = CInt(cbStatus.SelectedValue)
      Dim severityID As Int32 = CInt(cbSeverity.SelectedValue)
```

Add parameters to the Command object's parameters collection by calling the Add method.

```
C#    command.Parameters.Add("@ProductID",SqlDbType.Int);
```

What you get back is a reference to the new parameter. To hold that reference, you'll create a local variable:

```
C#    System.Data.SqlClient.SqlParameter param;
```

```
VB    Dim param As System.Data.SqlClient.SqlParameter( )
```

Set the Direction property on the parameter to input (rather than output) and set its value to the value for the parameter:

```
C#    param.Direction = ParameterDirection.Input;
      param.Value = productID;
```

You can then go on and add each of the other parameters in turn. For example, to add the @Version parameter, you will write:

```C#
param = command.Parameters.Add("@Version",SqlDbType.VarChar,50);
param.Direction = ParameterDirection.Input;
param.Value = txtVersion.Text;
```

Invoke the stored procedure by calling the ExecuteNonQuery method:

```C#
command.ExecuteNonQuery();
```

Once you update the database, return to btnSave_Click, where you display a message—in this case using a MessageBox object (supplied by the .NET Framework), resetting the ListBoxes to their default settings, and updating the DataGrid:

```C#
MessageBox.Show("Bug added!");
PopulateListBoxes();
FillDataGrid();
```

The call to FillDataGrid queries the database again and binds the DataGrid to the new returned tables. This is similar to the code shown in the previous chapter. In fact, there is nothing new or surprising in any of this code so far; all the work that supports the transaction is actually done in the stored procedure itself.

Connection Transaction

The user may choose to use a Connection Transaction rather than a DB Transaction.

> Normally, of course, you would simply choose the optimal technique for transactions and not offer this as a choice to the user. You might choose SQL transactions to simplify your code, or you might choose .NET transactions if you want direct programmatic control of the transaction or if your transaction will transcend a single stored procedure.

With a Connection transaction, there is no transaction support provided by the stored procedure. Instead, add the transaction support by creating an SQLTransaction object.

In Examples 20-5 and 20-6, the user had the option of choosing either a database connection or a connection transaction. If the connection transaction radio button is chosen, the btnSave_Click event handler will invoke UpdateConnectionTransaction:

```C#
private void btnSave_Click(object sender, System.EventArgs e)
{
    if (rbDBTransaction.Checked)
    {
        UpdateDBTransaction();
    }
    else
    {
        UpdateConnectionTransaction();
    }
```

To learn how Connection Transactions work, you'll update the Bug and BugHistory tables in two steps. In Step 1, you'll call a stored procedure spAddBug, shown in Example 20-7.

Example 20-7. SpAddBug stored procedure

```
CREATE PROCEDURE spAddBug
@ProductID int,
@Version varChar(50),
@Description varChar(8000),
@Reporter int,
@BugID int output
 AS
Insert into Bugs values (@ProductID, @Version, @Description, @Reporter)
select @BugID = @@identity
```

This stored procedure takes five parameters and updates the Bugs table. The final parameter, BugID, is marked output. You do not pass a BugID into the procedure (BugID is an identity column), but you should retrieve this value. The output parameter returns the BugID after the bug is added.

Once the bug is added, you'll update the BugHistory table with a SQL statement that you'll create based on the values in various UI components.

```
string strAddBugHistory = "Insert into BugHistory " +
    "(bugHistoryID, bugID, status, severity, response, owner) values (1, " + BugID +
", " +
    statusID + ", " + severityID + ", '" + txtResponse.Text +  "', " + ownerID + ")";
```

Execute the SQL statement by calling ExecuteNonQuery.

```
command.CommandType = CommandType.Text;
command.CommandText = strAddBugHistory;
command.ExecuteNonQuery( );
```

Either event could fail. That is, the stored procedure might generate an error, or the query might fail to properly add a record to the database. If either fails, you do not want any part of the effort to succeed. In short, you need to wrap both steps within a transaction. By using a transaction, if either step fails, the entire transaction is rolled back and the database is left in the exact state it was before you began the transaction.

The job of the UpdateConnectionTransaction method, shown in Examples 20-5 and 20-6, invokes both the stored procedure and the SQL update statement by using a Connection transaction. The steps are as follows:

1. Create the connection string and the SqlConnection object:

```
string connectionString =
    "server=YourServer; uid=sa; pwd=YourPW; database=WindForm_Bugs";
System.Data.SqlClient.SqlConnection connection =
    new System.Data.SqlClient.SqlConnection(connectionString);
```

```vb
VB    Dim connectionString As String = _
          "server=YourServer; uid=sa; pwd=YourPW; database=WindForm_Bugs"

      Dim myConnection As New _
          System.Data.SqlClient.SqlConnection(connectionString)
```

2. Create the SqlCommand object:

```csharp
C#    System.Data.SqlClient.SqlCommand command =
          new System.Data.SqlClient.SqlCommand( );
```

```vb
VB    Dim myCommand As New System.Data.SqlClient.SqlCommand( )
```

3. Open the connection:

```csharp
C#    connection.Open( );
```

```vb
VB    myConnection.Open( )
```

4. Instantiate a SqlTransaction object by calling the BeginTransaction method of the SqlConnection object:

```csharp
C#    SqlTransaction transaction;
      transaction = connection.BeginTransaction( );
```

```vb
VB    Dim transaction As SqlTransaction
      transaction = myConnection.BeginTransaction( )
```

5. Set the SqlCommand object's Transaction property to the SqlTransaction object you've instantiated, and set the SqlCommand object's Connection property to the SqlConnection object you've created.

```csharp
C#    command.Transaction = transaction;
      command.Connection = connection;
```

```vb
VB    myCommand.Transaction = transaction
      myCommand.Connection = myConnection
```

6. Open a try block, in which you will try to update the two tables. Set the SQL Command object's CommandText property to the name of the stored procedure, and set the CommandType property to CommandType.StoredProcedure:

```csharp
C#    try
      {
         command.CommandText = "spAddBug";
         command.CommandType = CommandType.StoredProcedure;
```

```vb
VB    Try
         myCommand.CommandText = "spAddBug"
         myCommand.CommandType = CommandType.StoredProcedure
```

7. Add all the parameters, including the output parameters:

```csharp
C#    System.Data.SqlClient.SqlParameter param;

      int productID = Convert.ToInt32(cbProduct.SelectedValue.ToString( ));
```

```csharp
int reporterID = Convert.ToInt32(cbReporter.SelectedValue.ToString());

// add each parameter and set its direciton and value
param = command.Parameters.Add("@ProductID",SqlDbType.Int);
param.Direction = ParameterDirection.Input;
param.Value = productID;

param = command.Parameters.Add("@Version",SqlDbType.VarChar,50);
param.Direction = ParameterDirection.Input;
param.Value = txtVersion.Text;

param = command.Parameters.Add("@Description",SqlDbType.VarChar,8000);
param.Direction = ParameterDirection.Input;
param.Value = txtDescription.Text;

param = command.Parameters.Add("@Reporter",SqlDbType.Int);
param.Direction = ParameterDirection.Input;
param.Value = reporterID;

param = command.Parameters.Add("@BugID",SqlDbType.Int);
param.Direction = ParameterDirection.Output;
```

```vb
Dim param As System.Data.SqlClient.SqlParameter

Dim productID As Int32 = CInt(cbProduct.SelectedValue)
Dim reporterID As Int32 = CInt(cbReporter.SelectedValue)
Dim ownerID As Int32 = CInt(cbOwner.SelectedValue)
Dim statusID As Int32 = CInt(cbStatus.SelectedValue)
Dim severityID As Int32 = CInt(cbSeverity.SelectedValue)

' add each parameter and set its direciton and value
param = myCommand.Parameters.Add("@ProductID", SqlDbType.Int)
param.Direction = ParameterDirection.Input
param.Value = productID

param = myCommand.Parameters.Add("@Version", SqlDbType.VarChar, 50)
param.Direction = ParameterDirection.Input
param.Value = txtVersion.Text

param = myCommand.Parameters.Add("@Description", SqlDbType.VarChar, 8000)
param.Direction = ParameterDirection.Input
param.Value = txtDescription.Text

param = myCommand.Parameters.Add("@Reporter", SqlDbType.Int)
param.Direction = ParameterDirection.Input
param.Value = reporterID

param = myCommand.Parameters.Add("@BugID", SqlDbType.Int)
param.Direction = ParameterDirection.Output
```

8. Invoke the query:

```
command.ExecuteNonQuery( );
```

```
myCommand.ExecuteNonQuery( )
```

9. Get back the BugID:

```
int BugID =   Convert.ToInt32(command.Parameters["@BugID"].Value);
```

```
Dim BugID As Integer = _
    Convert.ToInt32(myCommand.Parameters("@BugID").Value)
```

10. Create a SQL statement from the controls:

```
int ownerID = Convert.ToInt32(cbOwner.SelectedValue.ToString( ));
int statusID = Convert.ToInt32(cbStatus.SelectedValue.ToString( ));
int severityID = Convert.ToInt32(cbSeverity.SelectedValue.ToString( ));

string strAddBugHistory = "Insert into BugHistory " +
    "(bugHistoryID, bugID, status, severity, response, owner) values (1, " + BugID
+ ", " +
    statusID + ", " + severityID + ", '" + txtResponse.Text +  "', " + ownerID +
")";
```

```
Dim ownerID As Int32 = CInt(cbOwner.SelectedValue)
Dim statusID As Int32 = CInt(cbStatus.SelectedValue)
Dim severityID As Int32 = CInt(cbSeverity.SelectedValue)
Dim strAddBugHistory As String = _
"Insert into BugHistory " & _
"(bugHistoryID, bugID, status, severity, response, owner) values (1, " & _
BugID & ", " & statusID & ", " & severityID & ", '" & _
txtResponse.Text & "', " & ownerID & ")"
```

11. Execute the query:

```
command.CommandType = CommandType.Text;
command.CommandText = strAddBugHistory;
command.ExecuteNonQuery( );
```

```
myCommand.CommandType = CommandType.Text
myCommand.CommandText = strAddBugHistory

' execute the insert statement
myCommand.ExecuteNonQuery( )
```

12. Commit the transaction:

```
transaction.Commit( );
```

```
transaction.Commit( )
```

13. If an exception is thrown, catch the exception and roll back the transaction:

```csharp
catch (Exception e)
{
    transaction.Rollback();
    MessageBox.Show("Exception caught! " + e.Message);
}
```

```vbnet
Catch e As Exception
    MessageBox.Show(("Exception caught! " + e.Message))
    transaction.Rollback()
End Try
```

Updating Data Using DataSets

So far in this chapter, you have seen how to update a database and add transactions to ensure data integrity. All of that is fine, but nothing you've done so far to update the database uses the DataSet object

If you are using the DataSet object to retrieve data and pass it from tier to tier within your application, you can also manipulate that data within the DataSet and push the changes back to the database. To make this more sophisticated model of data updating work, you need to take advantage of the advanced capabilities of the DataSet and the DataAdapter classes and understand how they in turn use the Command and Connection objects to mediate between the DataSet and the database itself.

In the next application, UpdatingDataSets, shown in Figure 20-5, you will retrieve the contents of the Bug and Bug History databases in a DataSet and display the DataSet in a grid. You will then update the DataSet, and optionally update the database from the updated DataSet.

To create this application, start a new WinForm project and add the following four controls to the form, as shown in Table 20-2.

Table 20-2. Controls for updating through the DataSet

Control	Name	Text
Button	btnUpdateDS	Update DataSet
Button	btnRefreshDS	Refresh DataSet
Button	btnUpdateDB	Update Database
DataGrid	dgBugs	

The complete listing in C# is shown in Example 20-8 and in VB.NET in Example 20-9. An analysis follows.

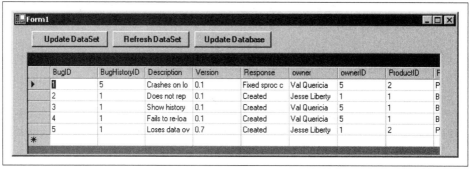

Figure 20-5. DataSet update of database

Example 20-8. Updating with the DataSet (C#)

```
using System;
using System.Drawing;
using System.Collections;
using System.ComponentModel;
using System.Windows.Forms;
using System.Data;
using System.Data.SqlClient;

namespace UpdatingDataSets
{
    public class Form1 : System.Windows.Forms.Form
    {
        private System.Windows.Forms.DataGrid dgBugs;
        private System.Windows.Forms.Button btnUpdateDS;
        private System.Windows.Forms.Button btnRefreshDS;
        private System.Windows.Forms.Button btnUpdateDB;
        private DataSet bugDS;

        private System.ComponentModel.Container components = null;

        public Form1()
        {
            InitializeComponent();
            RefreshDataSet();
        }

        protected override void Dispose( bool disposing )
        {
            if( disposing )
            {
                if (components != null)
                {
                    components.Dispose();
                }
            }
            base.Dispose( disposing );
        }
```

Example 20-8. Updating with the DataSet (C#) (continued)

```
#region Windows Form Designer generated code
#endregion

[STAThread]
static void Main( )
{
    Application.Run(new Form1( ));
}

private DataSet CreateBugDataSet( )
{
    // connection string to connect to the Bugs Database
    string connectionString =
        "server=YourServer; uid=sa; pwd=YourPW; " +
            " database=WindForm_Bugs";

    // Create connection object, initialize with
    // connection string. Open it.
    System.Data.SqlClient.SqlConnection connection =
        new System.Data.SqlClient.SqlConnection(connectionString);


    // Create a SqlCommand object and assign the connection
    System.Data.SqlClient.SqlCommand command =
        new System.Data.SqlClient.SqlCommand( );
    command.Connection=connection;
    command.CommandText="spBugsWithIDs";
    command.CommandType=CommandType.StoredProcedure;

    // create a data adapter and assign the command object
    // and add the table mapping for bugs
    SqlDataAdapter dataAdapter = new SqlDataAdapter( );
    dataAdapter.SelectCommand=command;
    dataAdapter.TableMappings.Add("Table","BugInfo");

    // Create the data set and use the data adapter to fill it
    DataSet dataSet = new DataSet( );
    dataAdapter.Fill(dataSet);
    return dataSet;
}   //  close CreateBugDataSet

// Update the dataset with bogus data
private void btnUpdateDS_Click(object sender, System.EventArgs e)
{
    DataTable bugTable = bugDS.Tables["BugInfo"];
    bugTable.Rows[0]["Response"] = "This is a test";
    bugTable.Rows[1].Delete( );
    DataRow newRow = bugTable.NewRow( );
    newRow["BugHistoryID"] = 1;
    newRow["Description"] = "New bug test";
    newRow["Response"] = "Created new bug";
    newRow["Owner"] = "Jesse Liberty";
```

Example 20-8. Updating with the DataSet (C#) (continued)

```
    newRow["OwnerID"] = 1;
    newRow["ProductID"] = 2;
    newRow["ProductDescription"] = "PIM - My Personal Infomation Manager";
    newRow["Version"] = "0.01";
    newRow["ReporterID"] = 3;
    newRow["Reporter"] = "John Galt";
    newRow["StatusID"] = 1;
    newRow["StatusDescription"] = "open";
    newRow["SeverityID"] = 2;
    newRow["SeverityDescription"] = "High";
    newRow["DateStamp"] = "07-27-2005";
    bugTable.Rows.Add(newRow);

}   // close btnUpdateDS_Click

private void btnRefreshDS_Click(object sender, System.EventArgs e)
{
    RefreshDataSet();
}

private void RefreshDataSet()
{
    bugDS = CreateBugDataSet();
    dgBugs.DataSource = bugDS.Tables[0];
}

private void btnUpdateDB_Click(object sender, System.EventArgs e)
{
    SqlDataAdapter dataAdapter = new SqlDataAdapter();

    string connectionString =
        "server=YourServer; uid=sa; pwd=YourPW; " +
            " database=WindForm_Bugs";

    // Create connection object, initialize with
    // connection string. Open it.
    System.Data.SqlClient.SqlConnection connection =
        new System.Data.SqlClient.SqlConnection(connectionString);

    SqlTransaction transaction;
    connection.Open();
    transaction = connection.BeginTransaction();

    // *** create the update command object
    SqlCommand updateCmd =
        new SqlCommand("spUpdateBugFromDataSet",connection);
    updateCmd.CommandType=CommandType.StoredProcedure;

    // declare the parameter object
    System.Data.SqlClient.SqlParameter param;

    // Add new parameters, get back a reference
    // set the parameters' direction and value
```

Example 20-8. Updating with the DataSet (C#) (continued)

```
C#
         param =
             updateCmd.Parameters.Add("@ProductID",SqlDbType.Int);
         param.Direction = ParameterDirection.Input;
         param.SourceColumn="ProductID";
         param.SourceVersion=DataRowVersion.Current;

         param =
             updateCmd.Parameters.Add("@Description",SqlDbType.Text,8000);
         param.Direction = ParameterDirection.Input;
         param.SourceColumn="Description";
         param.SourceVersion=DataRowVersion.Current;

         param =
             updateCmd.Parameters.Add("@Response",SqlDbType.Text,8000);
         param.Direction = ParameterDirection.Input;
         param.SourceColumn="Response";
         param.SourceVersion=DataRowVersion.Current;

         param =
             updateCmd.Parameters.Add("@Reporter",SqlDbType.Int);
         param.Direction = ParameterDirection.Input;
         param.SourceColumn="ReporterID";
         param.SourceVersion=DataRowVersion.Current;

         param =
             updateCmd.Parameters.Add("@Owner",SqlDbType.Int);
         param.Direction = ParameterDirection.Input;
         param.SourceColumn="OwnerID";
         param.SourceVersion=DataRowVersion.Current;

         param =
             updateCmd.Parameters.Add("@Status",SqlDbType.Int);
         param.Direction = ParameterDirection.Input;
         param.SourceColumn="StatusID";
         param.SourceVersion=DataRowVersion.Current;

         param =
             updateCmd.Parameters.Add("@Severity",SqlDbType.Int);
         param.Direction = ParameterDirection.Input;
         param.SourceColumn="SeverityID";
         param.SourceVersion=DataRowVersion.Current;

         param =
             updateCmd.Parameters.Add("@bugID",SqlDbType.Int);
         param.Direction = ParameterDirection.Input;
         param.SourceColumn="bugID";
         param.SourceVersion=DataRowVersion.Original; // note Original

         param =
             updateCmd.Parameters.Add("@BugHistoryID",SqlDbType.Int);
         param.Direction = ParameterDirection.Input;
         param.SourceColumn="BugHistoryID";
```

Example 20-8. Updating with the DataSet (C#) (continued)

```
                    param.SourceVersion=DataRowVersion.Original; // note Original

                    dataAdapter.UpdateCommand=updateCmd;

                    // *** the delete command
                    SqlCommand deleteCmd =
                       new SqlCommand("spDeleteBugFromDataSet",connection);
                    deleteCmd.CommandType=CommandType.StoredProcedure;

                    param = deleteCmd.Parameters.Add("@bugID",SqlDbType.Int);
                    param.Direction = ParameterDirection.Input;
                    param.SourceColumn="bugID";
                    param.SourceVersion=DataRowVersion.Original;  // note Original

                    param = deleteCmd.Parameters.Add("@BugHistoryID",SqlDbType.Int);
                    param.Direction = ParameterDirection.Input;
                    param.SourceColumn="BugHistoryID";
                    param.SourceVersion=DataRowVersion.Original;  // note Original

                    dataAdapter.DeleteCommand=deleteCmd;

                    // *** insert command
                    SqlCommand insertCmd =
                       new SqlCommand("spInsertBugFromDataSet",connection);
                    insertCmd.CommandType=CommandType.StoredProcedure;

                    param = insertCmd.Parameters.Add("@ProductID",SqlDbType.Int);
                    param.Direction = ParameterDirection.Input;
                    param.SourceColumn="ProductID";
                    param.SourceVersion=DataRowVersion.Current;

                    param =
                       insertCmd.Parameters.Add("@Version",SqlDbType.Text,50);
                    param.Direction = ParameterDirection.Input;
                    param.SourceColumn="Version";
                    param.SourceVersion=DataRowVersion.Current;

                    param =
                       insertCmd.Parameters.Add("@Description",SqlDbType.Text,8000);
                    param.Direction = ParameterDirection.Input;
                    param.SourceColumn="Description";
                    param.SourceVersion=DataRowVersion.Current;

                    param =
                       insertCmd.Parameters.Add("@Response",SqlDbType.Text,8000);
                    param.Direction = ParameterDirection.Input;
                    param.SourceColumn="Response";
                    param.SourceVersion=DataRowVersion.Current;

                    param = insertCmd.Parameters.Add("@Reporter",SqlDbType.Int);
                    param.Direction = ParameterDirection.Input;
                    param.SourceColumn="ReporterID";
```

Example 20-8. Updating with the DataSet (C#) (continued)

```csharp
        param.SourceVersion=DataRowVersion.Current;

        param = insertCmd.Parameters.Add("@Owner",SqlDbType.Int);
        param.Direction = ParameterDirection.Input;
        param.SourceColumn="OwnerID";
        param.SourceVersion=DataRowVersion.Current;

        param = insertCmd.Parameters.Add("@Status",SqlDbType.Int);
        param.Direction = ParameterDirection.Input;
        param.SourceColumn="StatusID";
        param.SourceVersion=DataRowVersion.Current;

        param = insertCmd.Parameters.Add("@Severity",SqlDbType.Int);
        param.Direction = ParameterDirection.Input;
        param.SourceColumn="SeverityID";
        param.SourceVersion=DataRowVersion.Current;

        dataAdapter.InsertCommand=insertCmd;

        // add transaction support for each command
        dataAdapter.UpdateCommand.Transaction = transaction;
        dataAdapter.DeleteCommand.Transaction = transaction;
        dataAdapter.InsertCommand.Transaction = transaction;

        // try to update, if all succeed commit
        // otherwise roll back
        try
        {
            int rowsUpdated = dataAdapter.Update(bugDS,"BugInfo");
            transaction.Commit();
            MessageBox.Show(rowsUpdated.ToString() + " rows Updated.");
            RefreshDataSet();
        }
        catch (Exception ex)
        {
            MessageBox.Show("Unable to update db!" + ex.Message);
            transaction.Rollback();
        }

        // rebind the grid to show the results
        // grid should be unchanged
        dgBugs.DataSource = bugDS.Tables["BugInfo"];
    }   //  close btnUpdateDB_Click
  }
}
```

Example 20-9. Updating with the DataSet (VB.NET)

```vbnet
Imports System.Data.SqlClient
Public Class Form1
    Inherits System.Windows.Forms.Form
```

Example 20-9. Updating with the DataSet (VB.NET) (continued)

```vb
    Dim bugDS As DataSet

#Region " Windows Form Designer generated code "

    Public Sub New( )
       MyBase.New( )

        'This call is required by the Windows Form Designer.
        InitializeComponent( )
        RefreshDataSet( )
#End Region

    Private Function CreateBugDataSet( ) As DataSet
        ' myConnection string to connect to the Bugs Database
       Dim connectionString As String = "server=YourServer; uid=sa; " + _
                " pwd=YourPW; database=WindForm_Bugs"

        ' Create myConnection object, initialize with
        ' myConnection string. Open it.
        Dim myConnection As New _
           System.Data.SqlClient.SqlConnection(connectionString)
        myConnection.Open( )


        ' Create a SqlCommand object and assign the myConnection
        Dim command As New System.Data.SqlClient.SqlCommand( )
        command.Connection = myConnection
        command.CommandText = "spBugsWithIDs"
        command.CommandType = CommandType.StoredProcedure

        ' create a data adapter and assign the command object
        ' and add the table mapping for bugs
        Dim myDataAdapter As New SqlDataAdapter( )
        myDataAdapter.SelectCommand = command
        myDataAdapter.TableMappings.Add("Table", "BugInfo")

        ' Create the data set and use the data adapter to fill it
        Dim myDataSet As New DataSet( )
        myDataAdapter.Fill(myDataSet)
        Return myDataSet
    End Function    ' close CreateBugDataSet

    Private Sub RefreshDataSet( )
       bugDS = CreateBugDataSet( )
       dgBugs.DataSource = bugDS.Tables(0)
    End Sub

    ' Update the dataset with bogus data
    Private Sub btnUpdateDS_Click(ByVal sender As System.Object, _
                                  ByVal e As System.EventArgs) _
                                  Handles btnUpdateDS.Click
        Dim bugTable As DataTable = bugDS.Tables("BugInfo")
```

Example 20-9. Updating with the DataSet (VB.NET) (continued)

VB

```
        bugTable.Rows(0)("Response") = "This is a test"
        bugTable.Rows(1).Delete()

        Dim newRow As DataRow = bugTable.NewRow()
        newRow("BugHistoryID") = 1
        newRow("Description") = "New bug test"
        newRow("Response") = "Created new bug"
        newRow("Owner") = "Jesse Liberty"
        newRow("OwnerID") = 1
        newRow("ProductID") = 2
        newRow("ProductDescription") = "PIM - My Personal Infomation Manager"
        newRow("Version") = "0.01"
        newRow("ReporterID") = 3
        newRow("Reporter") = "John Galt"
        newRow("StatusID") = 1
        newRow("StatusDescription") = "open"
        newRow("SeverityID") = 2
        newRow("SeverityDescription") = "High"
        newRow("DateStamp") = "07-27-2005"
        bugTable.Rows.Add(newRow)

End Sub

Private Sub btnRefreshDS_Click(ByVal sender As System.Object, _
                            ByVal e As System.EventArgs) _
                            Handles btnRefreshDS.Click
    RefreshDataSet()
End Sub
Private Sub btnUpdateDB_Click(ByVal sender As System.Object, _
                            ByVal e As System.EventArgs) _
                            Handles btnUpdateDB.Click
    Dim myDataAdapter As New SqlDataAdapter()

  Dim connectionString As String = "server=YourServer; uid=sa; " + _
          " pwd=YourPW; database=WindForm_Bugs"

    ' Create myConnection object, initialize with
    ' myConnection string. Open it.
    Dim myConnection As New SqlConnection(connectionString)
    Dim transaction As SqlTransaction

    myConnection.Open()
    transaction = myConnection.BeginTransaction()

    ' *** create the update command object
    Dim updateCmd As New SqlCommand("spUpdateBugFromDataSet", _
                                    myConnection)
    updateCmd.CommandType = CommandType.StoredProcedure

    ' declare the parameter object
    Dim param As System.Data.SqlClient.SqlParameter
```

Example 20-9. Updating with the DataSet (VB.NET) (continued)

```
' Add new parameters, get back a reference
' set the parameters' direction and value
param = updateCmd.Parameters.Add("@ProductID", SqlDbType.Int)
param.Direction = ParameterDirection.Input
param.SourceColumn = "ProductID"
param.SourceVersion = DataRowVersion.Current


param = updateCmd.Parameters.Add("@Description", SqlDbType.Text, 8000)
param.Direction = ParameterDirection.Input
param.SourceColumn = "Description"
param.SourceVersion = DataRowVersion.Current

param = updateCmd.Parameters.Add("@Response", SqlDbType.Text, 8000)
param.Direction = ParameterDirection.Input
param.SourceColumn = "Response"
param.SourceVersion = DataRowVersion.Current

param = updateCmd.Parameters.Add("@Reporter", SqlDbType.Int)
param.Direction = ParameterDirection.Input
param.SourceColumn = "ReporterID"
param.SourceVersion = DataRowVersion.Current

param = updateCmd.Parameters.Add("@Owner", SqlDbType.Int)
param.Direction = ParameterDirection.Input
param.SourceColumn = "OwnerID"
param.SourceVersion = DataRowVersion.Current

param = updateCmd.Parameters.Add("@Status", SqlDbType.Int)
param.Direction = ParameterDirection.Input
param.SourceColumn = "StatusID"
param.SourceVersion = DataRowVersion.Current

param = updateCmd.Parameters.Add("@Severity", SqlDbType.Int)
param.Direction = ParameterDirection.Input
param.SourceColumn = "SeverityID"
param.SourceVersion = DataRowVersion.Current

param = updateCmd.Parameters.Add("@bugID", SqlDbType.Int)
param.Direction = ParameterDirection.Input
param.SourceColumn = "bugID"
param.SourceVersion = DataRowVersion.Original ' note Original

param = updateCmd.Parameters.Add("@BugHistoryID", SqlDbType.Int)
param.Direction = ParameterDirection.Input
param.SourceColumn = "BugHistoryID"
param.SourceVersion = DataRowVersion.Original ' note Original

myDataAdapter.UpdateCommand = updateCmd

' *** the delete command
Dim deleteCmd As New SqlCommand("spDeleteBugFromDataSet", myConnection)
```

Example 20-9. Updating with the DataSet (VB.NET) (continued)

```
    deleteCmd.CommandType = CommandType.StoredProcedure

    param = deleteCmd.Parameters.Add("@bugID", SqlDbType.Int)
    param.Direction = ParameterDirection.Input
    param.SourceColumn = "bugID"
    param.SourceVersion = DataRowVersion.Original ' note Original

    param = deleteCmd.Parameters.Add("@BugHistoryID", SqlDbType.Int)
    param.Direction = ParameterDirection.Input
    param.SourceColumn = "BugHistoryID"
    param.SourceVersion = DataRowVersion.Original ' note Original

    myDataAdapter.DeleteCommand = deleteCmd

    ' *** insert command
    Dim insertCmd As New SqlCommand("spInsertBugFromDataSet", myConnection)
    insertCmd.CommandType = CommandType.StoredProcedure

    param = insertCmd.Parameters.Add("@ProductID", SqlDbType.Int)
    param.Direction = ParameterDirection.Input
    param.SourceColumn = "ProductID"
    param.SourceVersion = DataRowVersion.Current

    param = insertCmd.Parameters.Add("@Version", SqlDbType.Text, 50)
    param.Direction = ParameterDirection.Input
    param.SourceColumn = "Version"
    param.SourceVersion = DataRowVersion.Current

    param = insertCmd.Parameters.Add("@Description", SqlDbType.Text, 8000)
    param.Direction = ParameterDirection.Input
    param.SourceColumn = "Description"
    param.SourceVersion = DataRowVersion.Current

    param = insertCmd.Parameters.Add("@Response", SqlDbType.Text, 8000)
    param.Direction = ParameterDirection.Input
    param.SourceColumn = "Response"
    param.SourceVersion = DataRowVersion.Current

    param = insertCmd.Parameters.Add("@Reporter", SqlDbType.Int)
    param.Direction = ParameterDirection.Input
    param.SourceColumn = "ReporterID"
    param.SourceVersion = DataRowVersion.Current

    param = insertCmd.Parameters.Add("@Owner", SqlDbType.Int)
    param.Direction = ParameterDirection.Input
    param.SourceColumn = "OwnerID"
    param.SourceVersion = DataRowVersion.Current

    param = insertCmd.Parameters.Add("@Status", SqlDbType.Int)
    param.Direction = ParameterDirection.Input
    param.SourceColumn = "StatusID"
    param.SourceVersion = DataRowVersion.Current
```

Example 20-9. Updating with the DataSet (VB.NET) (continued)

VB

```
        param = insertCmd.Parameters.Add("@Severity", SqlDbType.Int)
        param.Direction = ParameterDirection.Input
        param.SourceColumn = "SeverityID"
        param.SourceVersion = DataRowVersion.Current

        myDataAdapter.InsertCommand = insertCmd

        ' add transaction support for each command
        myDataAdapter.UpdateCommand.Transaction = transaction
        myDataAdapter.DeleteCommand.Transaction = transaction
        myDataAdapter.InsertCommand.Transaction = transaction

        ' try to update, if all succeed commit
        ' otherwise roll back
        Try
            Dim rowsUpdated As Int16 = myDataAdapter.Update(bugDS, "BugInfo")
            transaction.Commit( )
            MessageBox.Show(rowsUpdated.ToString( ) + " rows Updated.")
            RefreshDataSet( )
        Catch ex As Exception
            MessageBox.Show("Unable to update db!" + ex.Message)
            transaction.Rollback( )
        End Try

        ' rebind the grid to show the results
        ' grid should be unchanged
        dgBugs.DataSource = bugDS.Tables("BugInfo")

    End Sub   '  close btnUpdateDB_Click
End Class
```

The DataSet and the DataAdapter

As explained in Chapter 19, the DataSet object interacts with the database through a DataAdapter object. The job of the DataAdapter is to decouple the DataSet from the underlying database (e.g., SqlServer or Oracle). The DataSet is a standalone representation of a subset of the database, including multiple tables and their relationships. The DataAdapter knows how to fill a DataSet from a given database.

Until now, you've created the DataAdapter by passing in a command string and a connection string to the DataAdapter's constructor and then calling the Fill( ) method.

The Fill( ) method does a lot of work on your behalf. The DataAdapter has, as properties, four SqlCommand objects at its disposal: DeleteCommand, InsertCommand, SelectCommand, and UpdateCommand. The job of the SelectCommand, for example, is to manage the selection statement. When you pass a selection command string in to the constructor, the DataAdapter's SelectCommand property is initialized to a SqlCommand object using that select string.

To update the database with the changes you'll make to your DataSet, you'll need to explicitly set the other three properties: UpdateCommand, DeleteCommand, and InsertCommand. You will fill these three properties with either SQL statements, or, more commonly, the names of stored procedures. When the DataAdapter is told to update the database, it examines the changes to the DataSet and calls the appropriate Command objects to update, delete, or insert records. Often, a single request to a DataSet to update the database causes each command to be called repeatedly, once for each modified row.

Steps for Updating the Database

The steps for updating a database using a DataSet are as follows:

1. Create and display a DataSet by retrieving data from the database.
2. Update the records in the DataSet. This task might include adding new records, deleting records, and updating existing records.
3. Optionally, create stored procedures in the database to manage the select, update, insert, and delete commands.
4. Create Command objects to invoke the stored procedures or to pass in SQL commands. Add parameters to the Command objects as needed.
5. Add transaction support to ensure that either all or no updates are done.
6. Call the Update method on the data adapter. The data adapter examines the changes in the DataSet and calls the appropriate Command objects, which will update the database on your behalf.

Creating and displaying a DataSet

As you have done in many previous examples, start by retrieving data from the database using a stored procedure and displaying that data in a grid.

This DataGrid is created again by calling the CreateBugDataSet method:

```csharp
private DataSet CreateBugDataSet()
{
    string connectionString =
        "server=YourServer; uid=sa; pwd=YourPW; database=WindForm_Bugs";

    System.Data.SqlClient.SqlConnection connection =
        new System.Data.SqlClient.SqlConnection(connectionString);

    System.Data.SqlClient.SqlCommand command =
        new System.Data.SqlClient.SqlCommand();
    command.Connection=connection;
    command.CommandText="spBugsWithIDs";
    command.CommandType=CommandType.StoredProcedure;

    SqlDataAdapter dataAdapter = new SqlDataAdapter();
```

C#

```csharp
        dataAdapter.SelectCommand=command;
        dataAdapter.TableMappings.Add("Table","BugInfo");

        DataSet dataSet = new DataSet();
        dataAdapter.Fill(dataSet);
        return dataSet;
    }
```

VB

```vb
    Private Function CreateBugDataSet() As DataSet
        Dim connectionString As String = _
            "server=YourServer; uid=sa; pwd=YourPW; database=WindForm_Bugs"

        Dim myConnection As New System.Data.SqlClient.SqlConnection(connectionString)
        myConnection.Open()


        Dim command As New System.Data.SqlClient.SqlCommand()
        command.Connection = myConnection
        command.CommandText = "spBugsWithIDs"
        command.CommandType = CommandType.StoredProcedure

        Dim myDataAdapter As New SqlDataAdapter()
        myDataAdapter.SelectCommand = command
        myDataAdapter.TableMappings.Add("Table", "BugInfo")

        Dim myDataSet As New DataSet()
        myDataAdapter.Fill(myDataSet)
        Return myDataSet
    End Function
```

The DataSet is created with a SqlCommand object, which in turn invokes the stored procedure spBugsWithIDs, shown in Example 20-10. You should note two important things in this stored procedure. First, the data displayed in the grid is drawn from a number of different tables. The Description field is from the Bugs table. The Response field (used to populate the Most Recent Action column on the grid) is taken from the last BugHistory record for each Bug. The Owner is drawn from the People table based on the Owner value in the latest BugHistory record (described in the sidebar "Finding the Last BugHistory").

Example 20-10. The stored procedure spBugsWithIDs

```
CREATE PROCEDURE spBugsWithIDs  AS
select b.BugID, h.BugHistoryID, b.Description, b.Version, h.Response,
o.FullName as owner, h.owner as ownerID,
b.Product as ProductID, p.ProductDescription,
b.Reporter as ReporterID, r.FullName as reporter,
h.status as statusID, s.StatusDescription,
h.severity as severityID, sev.SeverityDescription, h.DateStamp
from
(select bugID, max(bugHistoryID) as maxHistoryID from BugHistory group by bugID) t
join bugs b on b.bugid = t.bugid
```

Example 20-10. The stored procedure spBugsWithIDs (continued)

```
join BugHistory h on h.bugHistoryID = t.maxHistoryID
join lkProduct p on b.Product = p.ProductID
join People r on b.Reporter = r.PersonID
join People o on h.Owner = o.PersonID
join lkStatus s on s.statusid = h.status
join lkSeverity sev on sev.SeverityID = h.severity
GO
```

Finding the Last BugHistory

Your goal is to get information about the latest entry in the BugHistory table for each bug. You know that each entry in the BugHistory table has its own BugHistoryID, but how do you find the highest BugHistoryID for each bug? Use the group by clause in SQL. You can find the maximum entry for each BugID per BugID with this query:

```
select bugID, max(bugHistoryID) as maxHistoryID from BugHistory group by bugID
```

Save the results of this query into a temporary table (t), and then join the other tables on t to get the data you need from the appropriate records. Thus, in the stored procedure shown above, you get the Description, Version, etc., for the appropriate records that match the BugID and bugHistoryID from the temporary table.

Second, this stored procedure both retrieves the values to be displayed and carefully retrieves the IDs of the fields as they appear in Bugs and BugHistory.

That is, not only do you retrieve the severity description (High, Medium, or Low) to display in the grid, but you also retrieve the corresponding severity ID values (5, 4, or 3) as they are stored in the underlying records. This is important because in this example, you will update these records, and you'll need the IDs to appear in the table you have created in the dataset. If users indicate that they want to change the severity from High to Medium, your update will change the value from 5 to 4.

Once a Command object that can invoke the new stored procedure is created, as shown in the previous code fragment, a new data adapter is created and the Select-Command property is set manually to that Command object, as shown in the following code fragment:

[C#]
```
SqlDataAdapter dataAdapter = new SqlDataAdapter();
dataAdapter.SelectCommand=command;
```

[VB]
```
Dim myDataAdapter As New SqlDataAdapter()
myDataAdapter.SelectCommand = command
```

Then add a new TableMapping object to the TableMappings collection to map the results of the stored procedure to a table within the BugInfo DataSet named BugInfo:

[C#]
```
dataAdapter.TableMappings.Add("Table","BugInfo");
```

```vb
VB    myDataAdapter.TableMappings.Add("Table", "BugInfo")
```

Understand that to the DataSet, BugInfo appears as a single table, consisting of the fields and values returned by the stored procedure. The DataSet, in this example, is oblivious to the underlying data structure of multiple interrelated tables.

Finally, a new DataSet is created and filled using the DataAdapter you've crafted:

```csharp
C#    DataSet dataSet = new Data
      dataAdapter.Fill(dataSet);
```

```vb
VB    Dim myDataSet As New DataSet()
      myDataAdapter.Fill(myDataSet)
```

Updating the records in the DataSet

There are many ways to allow the user to indicate how the data should be modified. This example ignores all user interface issues and focuses on interacting with the data. To keep things simple, you'll have only three buttons: Update DataSet, Refresh DataSet, and Update Database.

The event handler for the first button, UpdateDataSet, implements hardwired changes to the data in the data. This has no effect on the underlying database. If you close the form after updating and displaying these changes, the database tables will be unaffected. The second button, Refresh DataSet, restores the DataSet to the data in the database. Finally, the third button, Update Database, writes the changes you make to the DataSet back to the database.

Updating the DataSet

When a user clicks on the Update DataSet button, the btnUpdateDS_Click event handler is called. Extract the table from the bugDS DataSet, and you are ready to modify the table:

```csharp
C#    DataTable bugTable = bugDS.Tables["BugInfo"];
```

```vb
VB    Dim bugTable As DataTable = bugDS.Tables("BugInfo")
```

The DataTable contains a collection of DataRows. The DataRow class has an Item property that returns the data stored in a specified column. Because this is implemented as the *indexer* in C# and as the default property in VB.NET, you can access the value for a particular field in a given row by providing the row offset and the field name. For example, the following line of C# code changes the Response value in the first row (remember that in C#, arrays are zero-indexed) to the value This is a test:

```csharp
C#    bugTable.Rows[0]["Response"] = "This is a test";
```

In VB.NET, this code is nearly identical:

```vb
VB    bugTable.Rows(0)("Response") = "This is a test"
```

Delete a row by calling the Delete method on the row itself:

`C#`
```
bugTable.Rows[1].Delete( );
```

Add a new row by using exactly the same syntax you saw for creating new data rows by hand in Chapter 19:

`C#`
```
DataRow newRow = bugTable.NewRow( );
newRow["BugHistoryID"] = 1;
newRow["Description"] = "New bug test";
newRow["Response"] = "Created new bug";
newRow["Owner"] = "Jesse Liberty";
newRow["OwnerID"] = 1;
newRow["ProductID"] = 2;
newRow["ProductDescription"] = "PIM - My Personal Infomation Manager";
newRow["Version"] = "0.01";
newRow["ReporterID"] = 3;
newRow["Reporter"] = "John Galt";
newRow["StatusID"] = 1;
newRow["StatusDescription"] = "open";
newRow["SeverityID"] = 2;
newRow["SeverityDescription"] = "High";
newRow["DateStamp"] = "07-27-2005";
bugTable.Rows.Add(newRow);
```

`VB`
```
Dim newRow As DataRow = bugTable.NewRow( )
newRow("BugHistoryID") = 1
newRow("Description") = "New bug test"
newRow("Response") = "Created new bug"
newRow("Owner") = "Jesse Liberty"
newRow("OwnerID") = 1
newRow("ProductID") = 2
newRow("ProductDescription") = "PIM - My Personal Infomation Manager"
newRow("Version") = "0.01"
newRow("ReporterID") = 3
newRow("Reporter") = "John Galt"
newRow("StatusID") = 1
newRow("StatusDescription") = "open"
newRow("SeverityID") = 2
newRow("SeverityDescription") = "High"
newRow("DateStamp") = "07-27-2005"
bugTable.Rows.Add(newRow)
```

Remember that you're filling the BugInfo table in the DataSet that was created by calling the spBugsWithIDs stored procedure. You must add a field for every field in the resulting set returned by that sproc.

> It is up to you to ensure the data integrity of the hand-created rows. For example, nothing stops you from adding a SeverityID of 4 (normally Low) with a SeverityDescription of High, except that if you do, you will display a value to the user that will not correspond to the value with which you'll update the database!

Your changes are immediately visible in the datagrid, as shown in Figure 20-6.

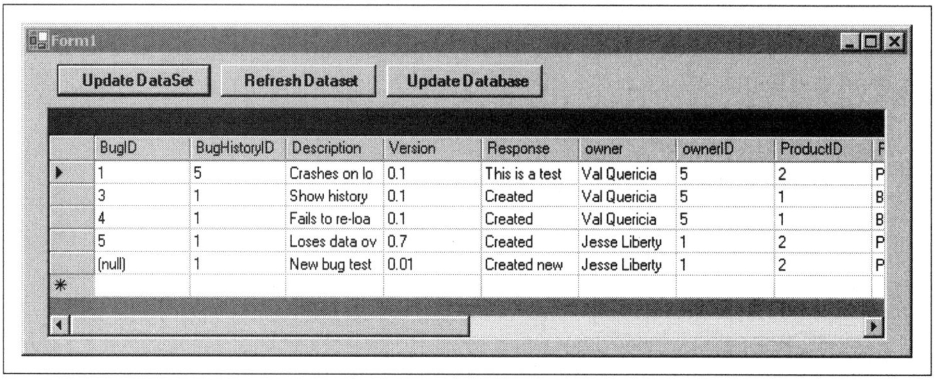

	BugID	BugHistoryID	Description	Version	Response	owner	ownerID	ProductID	F
▶	1	5	Crashes on lo	0.1	This is a test	Val Quericia	5	2	P
	3	1	Show history	0.1	Created	Val Quericia	5	1	B
	4	1	Fails to re-loa	0.1	Created	Val Quericia	5	1	B
	5	1	Loses data ov	0.7	Created	Jesse Liberty	1	2	P
	(null)	1	New bug test	0.01	Created new	Jesse Liberty	1	2	P
*									

Figure 20-6. After updating the DataSet

Notice that the first record has been updated in Figure 20-6. This new value is reflected in a change to the Response field:

```
bugTable.Rows[0]["Response"] = "This is a test";
```

BugID 2, which was the second record (bugTable.Rows[1]), appears to have been deleted. In fact, it was marked for deletion, but the datagrid is smart enough not to display records marked for deletion.

A new record has been added, as shown on the final line in the grid. Notice that there is no BugID. (When looking at the example, you will note that you did not provide a BugID.) The BugID field is an identity column, which is provided by the database when you write this data back to the database.

The absence of a BugID illustrates that while you've updated the DataSet, you have not yet written these changes back to the database. You can prove this to yourself by examining the tables in the database directly, as shown in Figure 20-7.

Updating the Database from the Dataset

When the user clicks on the third button, Update Database, the btnUpdateDB_Click event handler is invoked. Your goal in this method is to update the database with the changes in the DataSet.

The DataSet keeps track of the changes to its data. You can update the database with all the changes just by calling the Update method on the DataAdapter, and passing in a reference to the DataSet object and the name of the table you want to update.

That said, there is a bit of preparation work. For the update to work, you first need to provide Command objects to DataAdapter's InsertCommand, UpdateCommand, and DeleteCommand properties. You'll learn more about these preparatory steps in the following sections.

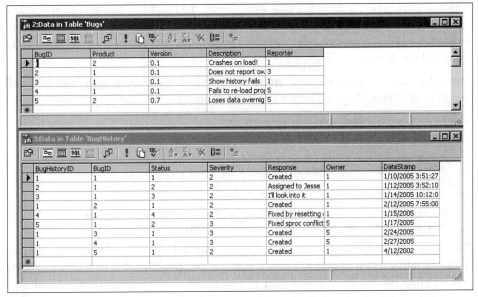

Figure 20-7. Bug and history table after the DataSet update, but before the database update

The delete command

As indicated earlier, you must begin by creating the appropriate stored procedures. Example 20-11 shows the spDeleteBugFromDataSet stored procedure for deleting bug records.

When the user deletes a record from the grid, delete the entire bug and all of its history. Because of referential integrity, *first* remove all records from that bug within BugHistory, and then remove the record from the Bugs table.

Example 20-11. Delete bugs stored procedure

```
CREATE PROCEDURE spDeleteBugFromDataSet
@bugID int,
@BugHistoryID int
as
Begin Transaction
        Delete from BugHistory where
                bugID = @BugID and BugHistoryID = @BugHistoryID
if @@Error <> 0 goto ErrorHandler
        Delete from Bugs where bugID = @BugID
if @@Error <> 0 goto ErrorHandler
   commit transaction
   return
ErrorHandler:
   rollback transaction
   return
```

You will pass in two parameters that will identify the record to delete. You will delete from BugHistory and Bugs as part of a transaction. That way, if the delete from either table fails, the entire delete will be rolled back, protecting your database from potential corruption.

With this stored procedure, you are ready to create the Command object you will assign to the DataAdapters DeleteCommand property.

Begin by creating a new SqlCommand object:

C#

```
SqlCommand deleteCmd =
    new SqlCommand("spDeleteBugFromDataSet",connection);
deleteCmd.CommandType=CommandType.StoredProcedure;
```

VB

```
Dim deleteCmd As New SqlCommand("spDeleteBugFromDataSet", myConnection)
deleteCmd.CommandType = CommandType.StoredProcedure
```

This SqlCommand object is just like every Command object you've created to date. You will name it deleteCmd to make it easy to identify, but it is just a garden-variety SqlCommand object, like all the others you've used so far to invoke stored procedures.

Add two parameters, BugID and BugHistoryID. These are input parameters, but rather than assigning a value to them, this time you must set two new properties of the Parameter object, SourceColumn, and SourceVersion. The SourceColumn property identifies the column within the table in the dataset from which this parameter will get its value. That is, when you invoke the stored procedure, the parameter (@BugID) will draw its value from this column in the record to be deleted. The column you want, of course, is BugID:

C#

```
param.SourceColumn="bugID";
```

The second property of the parameter is the SourceVersion, which must be set to one of the DataRowVersion enumerated values (Current, Default, Original, or Proposed).

The Default value is used only when you wish to use a default value, which does not apply to this example.

The Original value is the value the field had when the DataSet was created. The original value is compared to the value in the database when the update is performed to see if the database was changed by another process. This topic is covered later in the section "Multiuser Updates."

The Current value holds the changes to the column you've made since the DataSet was created. That is, as you update columns, the Current value holds the changes you've made, while the Original value has the value as you originally obtained it from the database.

In the case of the BugID, you'll tell the Param to use the Original value (though, of course, since you have not changed the value, you can use the Current value as well):

C#

```
param.SourceVersion=DataRowVersion.Original;
```

Create a Parameter object for the BugHistory in exactly the same way:

```
param = deleteCmd.Parameters.Add("@BugHistoryID",SqlDbType.Int);
param.Direction = ParameterDirection.Input;
param.SourceColumn="BugHistoryID";
param.SourceVersion=DataRowVersion.Original;
```

You are now ready to assign the Command object to the data adapter's Delete-Command property:

```
dataAdapter.DeleteCommand=deleteCmd;
```

The Update command

The stored procedure for updating the database is more complicated than the procedure for deleting records. This time, pass in parameters for each field that may be changed. Also pass in the BugID and BugHistory ID to uniquely identify the bug you wish to alter. The complete code for the spUpdateBugFromDataSet stored procedure is shown in Example 20-12.

The word Description is a keyword for SQL, so you must bracket the Description field as shown in Example 20-12.

Example 20-12. The stored procedure for updating a bug

```
CREATE PROCEDURE spUpdateBugFromDataSet
@ProductID int,
@Description varChar(8000),
@Response varChar(8000),
@Reporter int,
@Owner int,
@Status int,
@Severity int,
@bugID int,
@BugHistoryID int
as
Begin Transaction
Update Bugs
set
        Product = @productID,
        [Description] = @Description,
        Reporter = @Reporter
        where bugID = @BugID
if @@Error <> 0 goto ErrorHandler

Update BugHistory
Set
        status = @Status,
        severity = @Severity,
        response = @Response,
        owner = @Owner
```

Example 20-12. The stored procedure for updating a bug (continued)

```
where BugHistoryID = @bugHistoryID and bugID = @bugID
if @@Error <> 0 goto ErrorHandler
commit transaction
return
ErrorHandler:
rollback transaction
return
```

Once again, you create a Command object, this time to hold the Update command stored procedure:

```
SqlCommand updateCmd =
    new SqlCommand("spUpdateBugFromDataSet",connection);
updateCmd.CommandType=CommandType.StoredProcedure;
```

```
Dim updateCmd As New SqlCommand("spUpdateBugFromDataSet", myConnection)
updateCmd.CommandType = CommandType.StoredProcedure
```

Add a SqlParameter object for each parameter to the stored procedure:

```
param = updateCmd.Parameters.Add("@ProductID",SqlDbType.Int);
param.Direction = ParameterDirection.Input;
param.SourceColumn="ProductID";
param.SourceVersion=DataRowVersion.Current;
```

The ProductID parameter is like the BugID parameter, except now you use the enumerated value DataRowVersion.Current for the SourceVersion property. Use Current for any value that may have been changed in the DataSet; this instructs the DataAdapter to update the DataSet with the value current in the DataSet, rather than with the value that may reside back in the database.

When you create the parameters for the Reporter, Owner, Status, and Severity fields, be careful to use the ReporterID, OwnerID, StatusID, and SeverityID Source-Columns, respectively. Remember that while you display the full names of the reporter and owner and the text value of the status and severity, the records you update in the Bugs and BugHistory tables use the ID.

The Insert command

The final command you'll need to implement is the Insert command. Start, once again, by creating the necessary stored procedure, spInsertBugFromDataSet, as shown in Example 20-13.

Example 20-13. The stored procedure for inserting a bug

```
CREATE PROCEDURE spInsertBugFromDataSet
@ProductID int,
@Version varChar(50),
@Description varChar(8000),
@Response varChar(8000),
```

Example 20-13. The stored procedure for inserting a bug (continued)

```
@Reporter int,
@Owner int,
@Status int,
@Severity int
as
Begin Transaction
    declare @bugID int
    Insert into Bugs values (@ProductID, @Version, @Description, @Reporter)
    if @@Error <> 0 goto ErrorHandler
    select @bugID = @@identity
    Insert into BugHistory
    (bugHistoryID, bugID, status, severity, response, owner)
    values
    (
     1,        -- bug history id
    @bugID,
    @status,
    @Severity,
    @response,
    @owner
    )
    if @@Error <> 0 goto ErrorHandler
    commit transaction
    return
ErrorHandler:
    rollBack transaction
    return
```

Remember to insert into the Bugs table before inserting into the BugHistory table, since referential integrity constraints require that the BugID exist in Bugs before it can be inserted into BugHistory.

Do not pass in either the BugID or the BugHistoryID. The bugID is created by the database, and for new records, the BugHistoryID is always 1. The BugHistory table requires that the BugID be generated by adding a record to Bugs; obtain this value from @@identity.

This stored procedure will be called to insert the record you created by hand in the btnUpdateDS_Click event procedure. You must create a Command object, this time for the DataAdapter object's InsertCommand property:

```
param = insertCmd.Parameters.Add("@ProductID",SqlDbType.Int);
```

Once again, you create all the parameters and set their values. Then assign the Command object to the DataAdapter object's InsertCommand property:

```
dataAdapter.InsertCommand=insertCmd;
```

Adding transaction support

It is possible for one of the updates to fail, and if they do not all fail, returning the database to a valid state can be difficult. Therefore, wrap connection transaction

support around all the updates. Start, as last time, by obtaining a reference to a Sql-
Transaction object by calling BeginTransaction on the Connection object:

C#

```csharp
SqlTransaction transaction;
connection.Open();
transaction = connection.BeginTransaction();
```

VB

```vb
Dim transaction As SqlTransaction
myConnection.Open()
transaction = myConnection.BeginTransaction()
```

With all three Command properties set, you can add the transaction to each command's Transaction property:

C#

```csharp
dataAdapter.UpdateCommand.Transaction = transaction;
dataAdapter.DeleteCommand.Transaction = transaction;
dataAdapter.InsertCommand.Transaction = transaction;
```

 There is no need to provide database transaction support if you are
providing a connection transaction, but there is no harm either. You
may find that you want the connection transaction to ensure that all
the updates succeed or fail together, but that the sprocs want their
own transactions so they can be reused in other circumstances.

Calling the Update method

You are now ready to call the Update method of the SqlDataAdapter object, which
you will do from within a try block. The Update method will return the number of
rows that are updated, which you will use to fill in the text of a label at the bottom of
the DataGrid. The code is as follows:

C#

```csharp
try
{
    int rowsUpdated = dataAdapter.Update(bugDS,"BugInfo");
    transaction.Commit();
    MessageBox.Show(rowsUpdated.ToString() + " rows Updated.");
    RefreshDataSet();
}
catch (Exception ex)
{
    MessageBox.Show("Unable to update db!" + ex.Message);
    transaction.Rollback();
}
```

VB

```vb
Try
    Dim rowsUpdated As Int16 = myDataAdapter.Update(bugDS, "BugInfo")
    transaction.Commit()
    MessageBox.Show(rowsUpdated.ToString() + " rows Updated.")
    RefreshDataSet()
```

```
Catch ex As Exception
    MessageBox.Show("Unable to update db!" + ex.Message)
    transaction.Rollback( )
End Try
```

If no exception is thrown, commit the transactions; otherwise, roll them back. If all goes well, you will see a message box indicating that the records were updated and the updates are reflected in the DataGrid, as shown in Figure 20-8.

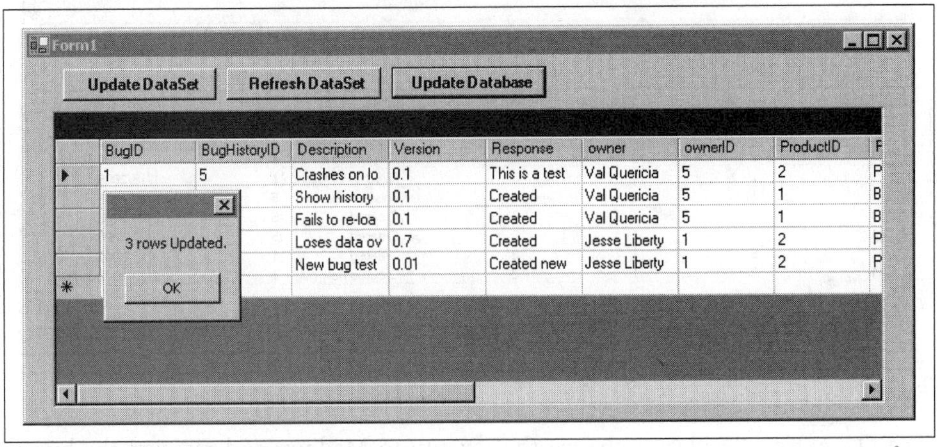

Figure 20-8. After updating the database

If you examine the Bugs and BugHistory tables, you should now see that the data has been updated, as shown in Figure 20-9.

Multiuser Updates

In the previous section, you read data from the database into a DataSet, updated the data in the DataSet, and then wrote the changes back to the database. In a real-world application, it would be possible for other people to read the same data into DataSets of their own, edit *their* data, and write *their* changes back to the database.

You can easily imagine that this possibility could possibly cause tremendous data corruption. Imagine, for example, that a quality assurance person downloads the current open bugs with an eye toward updating some of the information. Meanwhile, across the office (or across town) a developer has downloaded and is reviewing a few open bugs. Both of them are reading bug 17, which looks like this:

```
BugID 17
Reporter: John Galt
Severity: High
Status: Assigned
Owner: Jesse Liberty
```

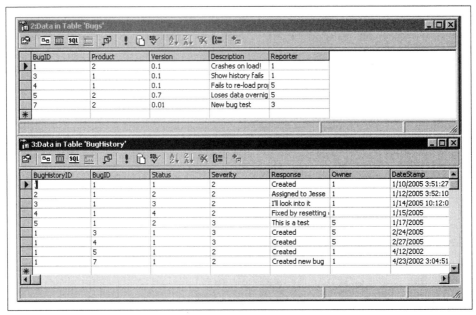

Figure 20-9. Bug and history table after the database update

The QA person decides to change the severity to Medium and reassign the bug to Dan Hurwitz. Meanwhile, the developer is updating the DataSet to change the action taken on the bug. The QA person writes back the changed DataSet, and the database now thinks the Owner is Dan and the Severity is Medium. The record now appears as follows:

```
BugID 17
Reporter: John Galt
Severity: Medium
Status: Assigned
Owner: Dan Hurwitz
```

Then the developer writes back *his* DataSet, in which the Owner was Jesse and the Severity was High. These earlier values are written over the values updated by QA, and the QA edits are lost. The technical term for this is *bad*.

To prevent this kind of problem, use any of the following strategies:

1. Lock the records. When one user works with a record, other users can read the records but cannot update them.

2. Update only the columns you change. In the previous example, QA would have changed only the owner and the status, while the developer would have changed only the description.

3. Preview whether the database has changed before you make your updates. If so, notify the user.

4. Attempt the change and handle the error, if any.

The following sections explore each of these possible strategies.

Lock the Records

Many databases provide *pessimistic record locking*. When a user opens a record, it is locked, and no other user may write to that record. For database efficiency, most databases also implement pessimistic page locking; not only is the particular record locked, but many surrounding records are locked as well.

While record and page locking is not uncommon in some database environments, it is generally undesirable. It's possible for a record to be locked, and the user never to return to the database to unlock it (if the user goes to lunch or her computer crashes). In that case, you would need to write monitoring processes that keep track of how long records have been locked, and unlock records after a time-out period.

As you saw in the previous example, a single query may touch many records in many tables. If you were to lock all those records for each user, it wouldn't take long before the entire database was locked. In addition, it often isn't necessary. While each user may look at dozens of records, each user usually updates only a very few. Locking is a very big, blunt weapon; what is needed is a small, delicate surgical tool.

Compare Original Against New

To understand how to compare the DataSet against the database, consider three possible values for each field:

- The value currently in the database
- The value that was in the database when you first filled the DataSet
- The value that is now in the DataSet because you have changed it

The DataSet provides support for this approach even though it is not an efficient way to manage data updates. This approach involves creating an event handler for the RowUpdating event. The event handler examines the original value of each field and queries the database for the value currently in the database. If these values are different, then someone has changed the database since the DataSet was filled, and you can take corrective action.

You will find two significant problems with this approach. First, you must query the database for the current values before each update. Second, there is no guarantee that you have solved the problem. It is certainly possible that someone will update a record after you have queried the database, but before you write back your changes. In any case, this approach is inefficient and won't be demonstrated here.

Handle the Errors

Odd as it may seem at first, the best approach to managing concurrency is to try the update, and then respond to errors as they arise. For this approach to be effective, however, you must craft your update statement so it will be guaranteed to fail if someone else updates the records.

This approach is very efficient. In most cases, your update will succeed, and you will not have bothered with extra reads of the database. If your update succeeds, there is no lag between checking the data and the update, so there is no chance of someone sneaking in another write. Finally, if your update fails, you know why, and you can take corrective action.

For this approach to work, your stored procedure for updates must fail if the data has changed in the database since the time you retrieved the DataSet. Since the DataSet can tell you the original values it received from the database, you can pass those values back into the stored procedure as parameters, and then add them to the Where clause in your update statement, as shown in the spUpdateBugFrom-DataSetWithConcurrency stored procedure listed in Example 20-14.

Example 20-14. Updating with concurrency

```
CREATE PROCEDURE spUpdateBugFromDataSetWithConcurrency
@ProductID int,
@OldProductID int,
@Description varChar(8000),
@OldDescription varChar(8000),
@Response varChar(8000),
@OldResponse varChar(8000),
@Reporter int,
@OldReporter int,
@Owner int,
@OldOwner int,
@Status int,
@OldStatus int,
@Severity int,
@OldSeverity int,
@bugID int,
@BugHistoryID int
as
Begin transaction
      Update Bugs
      set
      Product = @productID,
      [Description] = @Description,
      Reporter = @Reporter
      where bugID = @BugID and Product = @OldProductID
            and [Description] = @OldDescription
            and Reporter = @OldReporter
if @@Error <> 0 goto ErrorHandler
if @@RowCount > 0
```

Example 20-14. Updating with concurrency (continued)

```
begin

        Update BugHistory
        Set
        status = @Status,
        severity = @Severity,
        response = @Response,
        owner = @Owner
        where BugHistoryID = @bugHistoryID and bugID = @bugID
        and status = @oldStatus and severity = @OldSeverity
        and response = @oldResponse and owner = @OldOwner
end
if @@Error <> 0 goto ErrorHandler
    commit transaction
    return
ErrorHandler:
    rollBack transaction
    return
```

When you update the record, the original values will now be checked against the values in the database. If they have changed, no records will match, and you will not update any records. After you attempt to update the BugsTable, check the @@RowCount to see if any rows were successfully added. If so, add these lines to the BugHistory table:

```
if @@RowCount > 0
begin

Update BugHistory
```

The result of this test of @@RowCount is that if no records are added to the Bugs table, then no records will be added to the BugHistory table.

> The transaction tests for errors. If no rows match, there is no error and the transaction will continue. You must make sure that at least one row was added to Bugs before updating the BugHistory.

You can test for how many rows were added altogether in the RowUpdated event handler. If no row was updated, you can assume that it was because the original row was changed, and you can take appropriate corrective action.

> It is possible for the update to Bugs to work, yet the update to Bug-History fails. The program will return one updated record. For simplicity, this example does not handle that permutation. A well-crafted update statement could catch this problem, but at the cost of making the code more difficult to understand.

The complete listing is shown in Example 20-15 for C# and Example 20-16 for VB.
NET. A detailed analysis follows the listing.

Example 20-15. Updating the DataSet with concurrency (C#)

```csharp
using System;
using System.Drawing;
using System.Collections;
using System.ComponentModel;
using System.Windows.Forms;
using System.Data;
using System.Data.SqlClient;

namespace UpdatingDataSetsWithConcurrencyCS
{
    public class Form1 : System.Windows.Forms.Form
    {
        private System.Windows.Forms.DataGrid dgBugs;
        private System.Windows.Forms.Button btnUpdateDS;
        private System.Windows.Forms.Button btnRefreshDS;
        private System.Windows.Forms.Button btnUpdateDB;
        private DataSet bugDS;

        private System.ComponentModel.Container components = null;

        public Form1()
        {
            InitializeComponent();
            RefreshDataSet();
        }

        protected override void Dispose( bool disposing )
        {
            if( disposing )
            {
                if (components != null)
                {
                    components.Dispose();
                }
            }
            base.Dispose( disposing );
        }

        #region Windows Form Designer generated code
        #endregion

        [STAThread]
        static void Main()
        {
            Application.Run(new Form1());
        }

        private DataSet CreateBugDataSet()
        {
```

Example 20-15. Updating the DataSet with concurrency (C#) (continued)

```
// connection string to connect to the Bugs Database
string connectionString =
    "server=YourServer; uid=sa; pwd=YourPW; "+
    "database=WindForm_Bugs";

// Create connection object, initialize with
// connection string. Open it.
System.Data.SqlClient.SqlConnection connection =
    new System.Data.SqlClient.SqlConnection(connectionString);
connection.Open( );


// Create a SqlCommand object and assign the connection
System.Data.SqlClient.SqlCommand command =
    new System.Data.SqlClient.SqlCommand( );
command.Connection=connection;
command.CommandText="spBugsWithIDs";
command.CommandType=CommandType.StoredProcedure;

// create a data adapter and assign the command object
// and add the table mapping for bugs
SqlDataAdapter dataAdapter = new SqlDataAdapter( );
dataAdapter.SelectCommand=command;
dataAdapter.TableMappings.Add("Table","BugInfo");

// Create the data set and use the data adapter to fill it
DataSet dataSet = new DataSet( );
dataAdapter.Fill(dataSet);
return dataSet;
}

private void btnUpdateDS_Click(object sender, System.EventArgs e)
{
    DataTable bugTable = bugDS.Tables["BugInfo"];
    bugTable.Rows[0]["Response"] = "This is a test";
    bugTable.Rows[1].Delete( );
    DataRow newRow = bugTable.NewRow( );
    newRow["BugHistoryID"] = 1;
    newRow["Description"] = "New bug test";
    newRow["Response"] = "Created new bug";
    newRow["Owner"] = "Jesse Liberty";
    newRow["OwnerID"] = 1;
    newRow["ProductID"] = 2;
    newRow["ProductDescription"] = "PIM - My Personal Infomation Manager";
    newRow["Version"] = "0.01";
    newRow["ReporterID"] = 3;
    newRow["Reporter"] = "John Galt";
    newRow["StatusID"] = 1;
    newRow["StatusDescription"] = "open";
    newRow["SeverityID"] = 2;
    newRow["SeverityDescription"] = "High";
    newRow["DateStamp"] = "07-27-2005";
```

Example 20-15. Updating the DataSet with concurrency (C#) (continued)

```csharp
      bugTable.Rows.Add(newRow);

}

private void btnRefreshDS_Click(object sender, System.EventArgs e)
{
   RefreshDataSet( );
}

private void RefreshDataSet( )
{
   bugDS = CreateBugDataSet( );
   dgBugs.DataSource = bugDS.Tables[0];
}

private void btnUpdateDB_Click(object sender, System.EventArgs e)
{
   SqlDataAdapter dataAdapter = new SqlDataAdapter( );

   string connectionString =
      "server=YourServer; uid=sa; pwd=YourPW; "+
      "database=WindForm_Bugs";


   // mimic another user writing to your data after
   // you have retrieved the data from the database
   System.Data.SqlClient.SqlConnection connection2 =
      new System.Data.SqlClient.SqlConnection(connectionString);
   connection2.Open( );
   string cmd = "Update Bugs set Product = 2 where BugID = 1";
   SqlCommand cmd1 = new SqlCommand(cmd,connection2);
   cmd1.ExecuteNonQuery( );


   // Create connection object, initialize with
   // connection string. Open it.
   System.Data.SqlClient.SqlConnection connection =
      new System.Data.SqlClient.SqlConnection(connectionString);

   SqlTransaction transaction;
   connection.Open( );
   transaction = connection.BeginTransaction( );

   // *** create the update command object
   SqlCommand updateCmd = new SqlCommand(
         "spUpdateBugFromDataSetWithConcurrency",connection);
   updateCmd.CommandType=CommandType.StoredProcedure;

   // declare the parameter object
   System.Data.SqlClient.SqlParameter param;

   // Add new parameters, get back a reference
```

Example 20-15. Updating the DataSet with concurrency (C#) (continued)

```
// set the parameters' direction and value
param =
   updateCmd.Parameters.Add("@ProductID",SqlDbType.Int);
param.Direction = ParameterDirection.Input;
param.SourceColumn="ProductID";
param.SourceVersion=DataRowVersion.Current;

// pass in the original value for the where statement
param =
   updateCmd.Parameters.Add("@OldProductID",SqlDbType.Int);
param.Direction = ParameterDirection.Input;
param.SourceColumn="ProductID";
param.SourceVersion=DataRowVersion.Original;

param =
   updateCmd.Parameters.Add("@Description",SqlDbType.Text,8000);
param.Direction = ParameterDirection.Input;
param.SourceColumn="Description";
param.SourceVersion=DataRowVersion.Current;

param =
   updateCmd.Parameters.Add("@OldDescription",SqlDbType.Text,8000);
param.Direction = ParameterDirection.Input;
param.SourceColumn="Description";
param.SourceVersion=DataRowVersion.Original;

param =
   updateCmd.Parameters.Add("@Response",SqlDbType.Text,8000);
param.Direction = ParameterDirection.Input;
param.SourceColumn="Response";
param.SourceVersion=DataRowVersion.Current;

param =
   updateCmd.Parameters.Add("@OldResponse",SqlDbType.Text,8000);
param.Direction = ParameterDirection.Input;
param.SourceColumn="Response";
param.SourceVersion=DataRowVersion.Original;

param =
   updateCmd.Parameters.Add("@Reporter",SqlDbType.Int);
param.Direction = ParameterDirection.Input;
param.SourceColumn="ReporterID";
param.SourceVersion=DataRowVersion.Current;

param =
   updateCmd.Parameters.Add("@OldReporter",SqlDbType.Int);
param.Direction = ParameterDirection.Input;
param.SourceColumn="ReporterID";
param.SourceVersion=DataRowVersion.Original;

param =
   updateCmd.Parameters.Add("@Owner",SqlDbType.Int);
```

Example 20-15. Updating the DataSet with concurrency (C#) (continued)

```
param.Direction = ParameterDirection.Input;
param.SourceColumn="OwnerID";
param.SourceVersion=DataRowVersion.Current;

param =
    updateCmd.Parameters.Add("@OldOwner",SqlDbType.Int);
param.Direction = ParameterDirection.Input;
param.SourceColumn="OwnerID";
param.SourceVersion=DataRowVersion.Original;

param =
    updateCmd.Parameters.Add("@Status",SqlDbType.Int);
param.Direction = ParameterDirection.Input;
param.SourceColumn="StatusID";
param.SourceVersion=DataRowVersion.Current;

param =
    updateCmd.Parameters.Add("@OldStatus",SqlDbType.Int);
param.Direction = ParameterDirection.Input;
param.SourceColumn="StatusID";
param.SourceVersion=DataRowVersion.Original;

param =
    updateCmd.Parameters.Add("@Severity",SqlDbType.Int);
param.Direction = ParameterDirection.Input;
param.SourceColumn="SeverityID";
param.SourceVersion=DataRowVersion.Current;

param =
    updateCmd.Parameters.Add("@OldSeverity",SqlDbType.Int);
param.Direction = ParameterDirection.Input;
param.SourceColumn="SeverityID";
param.SourceVersion=DataRowVersion.Original;

param =
    updateCmd.Parameters.Add("@bugID",SqlDbType.Int);
param.Direction = ParameterDirection.Input;
param.SourceColumn="bugID";
param.SourceVersion=DataRowVersion.Original; // note Original

param =
    updateCmd.Parameters.Add("@BugHistoryID",SqlDbType.Int);
param.Direction = ParameterDirection.Input;
param.SourceColumn="BugHistoryID";
param.SourceVersion=DataRowVersion.Original; // note Original

dataAdapter.UpdateCommand=updateCmd;

// *** the delete command
SqlCommand deleteCmd =
    new SqlCommand("spDeleteBugFromDataSet",connection);
deleteCmd.CommandType=CommandType.StoredProcedure;
```

Example 20-15. Updating the DataSet with concurrency (C#) (continued)

```csharp
param = deleteCmd.Parameters.Add("@bugID",SqlDbType.Int);
param.Direction = ParameterDirection.Input;
param.SourceColumn="bugID";
param.SourceVersion=DataRowVersion.Original;  // note Original

param = deleteCmd.Parameters.Add("@BugHistoryID",SqlDbType.Int);
param.Direction = ParameterDirection.Input;
param.SourceColumn="BugHistoryID";
param.SourceVersion=DataRowVersion.Original;  // note Original

dataAdapter.DeleteCommand=deleteCmd;

// *** insert command
SqlCommand insertCmd =
    new SqlCommand("spInsertBugFromDataSet",connection);
insertCmd.CommandType=CommandType.StoredProcedure;

// Add new parameters, get back a reference
// set the parameters' direction and value
param = insertCmd.Parameters.Add("@ProductID",SqlDbType.Int);
param.Direction = ParameterDirection.Input;
param.SourceColumn="ProductID";
param.SourceVersion=DataRowVersion.Current;

param =
    insertCmd.Parameters.Add("@Version",SqlDbType.Text,50);
param.Direction = ParameterDirection.Input;
param.SourceColumn="Version";
param.SourceVersion=DataRowVersion.Current;

param =
    insertCmd.Parameters.Add("@Description",SqlDbType.Text,8000);
param.Direction = ParameterDirection.Input;
param.SourceColumn="Description";
param.SourceVersion=DataRowVersion.Current;

param =
    insertCmd.Parameters.Add("@Response",SqlDbType.Text,8000);
param.Direction = ParameterDirection.Input;
param.SourceColumn="Response";
param.SourceVersion=DataRowVersion.Current;

param = insertCmd.Parameters.Add("@Reporter",SqlDbType.Int);
param.Direction = ParameterDirection.Input;
param.SourceColumn="ReporterID";
param.SourceVersion=DataRowVersion.Current;

param = insertCmd.Parameters.Add("@Owner",SqlDbType.Int);
param.Direction = ParameterDirection.Input;
param.SourceColumn="OwnerID";
param.SourceVersion=DataRowVersion.Current;
```

Example 20-15. Updating the DataSet with concurrency (C#) (continued)

```csharp
      param = insertCmd.Parameters.Add("@Status",SqlDbType.Int);
      param.Direction = ParameterDirection.Input;
      param.SourceColumn="StatusID";
      param.SourceVersion=DataRowVersion.Current;

      param = insertCmd.Parameters.Add("@Severity",SqlDbType.Int);
      param.Direction = ParameterDirection.Input;
      param.SourceColumn="SeverityID";
      param.SourceVersion=DataRowVersion.Current;

      dataAdapter.InsertCommand=insertCmd;

      // add transaction support for each command
      dataAdapter.UpdateCommand.Transaction = transaction;
      dataAdapter.DeleteCommand.Transaction = transaction;
      dataAdapter.InsertCommand.Transaction = transaction;

      // try to update, if all succeed commit
      // otherwise roll back
      try
      {
         dataAdapter.RowUpdated +=
            new SqlRowUpdatedEventHandler(OnRowUpdate);
         int rowsUpdated = dataAdapter.Update(bugDS,"BugInfo");
         transaction.Commit();
         MessageBox.Show(rowsUpdated.ToString() + " rows Updated.");
         RefreshDataSet();
      }
      catch
      {
         transaction.Rollback();
      }

      // rebind the grid to show the results
      // grid should be unchanged
      dgBugs.DataSource = bugDS.Tables["BugInfo"];
   }
   // handle the Row Updated event
   public void OnRowUpdate(object sender, SqlRowUpdatedEventArgs e)
   {
      // get the type of update (update, insert, delete)
      // as a string
      string s = "Attempted " +
         System.Enum.GetName(
         e.StatementType.GetType(),e.StatementType) + ". ";

      // if the update failed
      if (e.RecordsAffected < 1)
      {
         MessageBox.Show(s + "Concurrency error! Unable to update BugID: " +
            e.Row["BugID",DataRowVersion.Original].ToString());
```

Example 20-15. Updating the DataSet with concurrency (C#) (continued)

```csharp
                // skip over this row, continue with the next
                e.Status = UpdateStatus.SkipCurrentRow;
        }
        else // the update succeeded
        {
            MessageBox.Show(s + " Row updated, BugID: " +
                e.Row["BugID",DataRowVersion.Original].ToString( ));
        }
    }   // close OnRowUpdate
    }
}
```

Example 20-16. Updating DataSet with concurrency (VB.NET)

```vbnet
Imports System.Data.SqlClient
Public Class Form1
    Inherits System.Windows.Forms.Form

    Dim bugDS As DataSet

#Region " Windows Form Designer generated code "

    Public Sub New( )
        MyBase.New( )

        'This call is required by the Windows Form Designer.
        InitializeComponent( )
        RefreshDataSet( )

#End Region

    Private Function CreateBugDataSet( ) As DataSet
        ' myConnection string to connect to the Bugs Database
        Dim connectionString As String = _
            "server=YourServer; uid=sa; pwd=YourPW; database=WindForm_Bugs"

        ' Create myConnection object, initialize with
        ' myConnection string. Open it.
        Dim myConnection As New System.Data.SqlClient.SqlConnection(connectionString)
        myConnection.Open( )


        ' Create a SqlCommand object and assign the myConnection
        Dim command As New System.Data.SqlClient.SqlCommand( )
        command.Connection = myConnection
        command.CommandText = "spBugsWithIDs"
        command.CommandType = CommandType.StoredProcedure

        ' create a data adapter and assign the command object
        ' and add the table mapping for bugs
        Dim myDataAdapter As New SqlDataAdapter( )
        myDataAdapter.SelectCommand = command
```

Example 20-16. Updating DataSet with concurrency (VB.NET) (continued)

```
    myDataAdapter.TableMappings.Add("Table", "BugInfo")

    ' Create the data set and use the data adapter to fill it
    Dim myDataSet As New DataSet()
    myDataAdapter.Fill(myDataSet)
    Return myDataSet
End Function    ' close CreateBugDataSet

Private Sub RefreshDataSet()
    bugDS = CreateBugDataSet()
    dgBugs.DataSource = bugDS.Tables(0)
End Sub

' Update the dataset with bogus data
Private Sub btnUpdateDS_Click(ByVal sender As System.Object, _
                              ByVal e As System.EventArgs) _
                              Handles btnUpdateDS.Click
    Dim bugTable As DataTable = bugDS.Tables("BugInfo")
    bugTable.Rows(0)("Response") = "This is a test"
    bugTable.Rows(1).Delete()

    Dim newRow As DataRow = bugTable.NewRow()
    newRow("BugHistoryID") = 1
    newRow("Description") = "New bug test"
    newRow("Response") = "Created new bug"
    newRow("Owner") = "Jesse Liberty"
    newRow("OwnerID") = 1
    newRow("ProductID") = 2
    newRow("ProductDescription") = "PIM - My Personal Infomation Manager"
    newRow("Version") = "0.01"
    newRow("ReporterID") = 3
    newRow("Reporter") = "John Galt"
    newRow("StatusID") = 1
    newRow("StatusDescription") = "open"
    newRow("SeverityID") = 2
    newRow("SeverityDescription") = "High"
    newRow("DateStamp") = "07-27-2005"
    bugTable.Rows.Add(newRow)

End Sub    '  close btnUpdateDS_Click

Private Sub btnRefreshDS_Click(ByVal sender As System.Object, _
                               ByVal e As System.EventArgs) _
                               Handles btnRefreshDS.Click
    RefreshDataSet()
End Sub

Private Sub btnUpdateDB_Click(ByVal sender As System.Object, _
                              ByVal e As System.EventArgs) _
                              Handles btnUpdateDB.Click
    Dim myDataAdapter As New SqlDataAdapter()
```

Example 20-16. Updating DataSet with concurrency (VB.NET) (continued)

```
     Dim connectionString As String = "server=YourServer; uid=sa; pwd=YourPW;
database=WindForm_Bugs"

     ' Create myConnection object, initialize with
     ' myConnection string. Open it.
     Dim myConnection As New SqlConnection(connectionString)
     Dim myConnection2 As New SqlConnection(connectionString)

     Dim transaction As SqlTransaction

     myConnection.Open( )
     myConnection2.Open( )
     transaction = myConnection.BeginTransaction( )

     ' mimic concurrent user
     Dim cmd As String = "Update Bugs set Product = 1 where BugID = 1"
     Dim cmd1 As New SqlCommand(cmd, myConnection2)
     cmd1.ExecuteNonQuery( )


     ' *** create the update command object
     Dim updateCmd As _
     New SqlCommand("spUpdateBugFromDataSetWithConcurrency", _
                    myConnection)
     updateCmd.CommandType = CommandType.StoredProcedure

     ' declare the parameter object
     Dim param As System.Data.SqlClient.SqlParameter

     ' Add new parameters, get back a reference
     ' set the parameters' direction and value
     param = updateCmd.Parameters.Add("@ProductID", SqlDbType.Int)
     param.Direction = ParameterDirection.Input
     param.SourceColumn = "ProductID"
     param.SourceVersion = DataRowVersion.Current

     ' pass in the original value for the where statement
     param = updateCmd.Parameters.Add("@OldProductID", SqlDbType.Int)
     param.Direction = ParameterDirection.Input
     param.SourceColumn = "ProductID"
     param.SourceVersion = DataRowVersion.Original

     param = updateCmd.Parameters.Add("@Description", _
                                 SqlDbType.Text, 8000)
     param.Direction = ParameterDirection.Input
     param.SourceColumn = "Description"
     param.SourceVersion = DataRowVersion.Current

     param = updateCmd.Parameters.Add( _
        "@OldDescription", SqlDbType.Text, 8000)
     param.Direction = ParameterDirection.Input
     param.SourceColumn = "Description"
```

Example 20-16. Updating DataSet with concurrency (VB.NET) (continued)

```
param.SourceVersion = DataRowVersion.Original

param = updateCmd.Parameters.Add("@Response", SqlDbType.Text, 8000)
param.Direction = ParameterDirection.Input
param.SourceColumn = "Response"
param.SourceVersion = DataRowVersion.Current

param = updateCmd.Parameters.Add("@OldResponse", _
                              SqlDbType.Text, 8000)
param.Direction = ParameterDirection.Input
param.SourceColumn = "Response"
param.SourceVersion = DataRowVersion.Original

param = updateCmd.Parameters.Add("@Reporter", SqlDbType.Int)
param.Direction = ParameterDirection.Input
param.SourceColumn = "ReporterID"
param.SourceVersion = DataRowVersion.Current

param = updateCmd.Parameters.Add("@OldReporter", SqlDbType.Int)
param.Direction = ParameterDirection.Input
param.SourceColumn = "ReporterID"
param.SourceVersion = DataRowVersion.Original

param = updateCmd.Parameters.Add("@Owner", SqlDbType.Int)
param.Direction = ParameterDirection.Input
param.SourceColumn = "OwnerID"
param.SourceVersion = DataRowVersion.Current

param = updateCmd.Parameters.Add("@OldOwner", SqlDbType.Int)
param.Direction = ParameterDirection.Input
param.SourceColumn = "OwnerID"
param.SourceVersion = DataRowVersion.Original

param = updateCmd.Parameters.Add("@Status", SqlDbType.Int)
param.Direction = ParameterDirection.Input
param.SourceColumn = "StatusID"
param.SourceVersion = DataRowVersion.Current

param = updateCmd.Parameters.Add("@OldStatus", SqlDbType.Int)
param.Direction = ParameterDirection.Input
param.SourceColumn = "StatusID"
param.SourceVersion = DataRowVersion.Original

param = updateCmd.Parameters.Add("@Severity", SqlDbType.Int)
param.Direction = ParameterDirection.Input
param.SourceColumn = "SeverityID"
param.SourceVersion = DataRowVersion.Current

param = updateCmd.Parameters.Add("@OldSeverity", SqlDbType.Int)
param.Direction = ParameterDirection.Input
param.SourceColumn = "SeverityID"
param.SourceVersion = DataRowVersion.Original
```

Example 20-16. Updating DataSet with concurrency (VB.NET) (continued)

```vb
param = updateCmd.Parameters.Add("@bugID", SqlDbType.Int)
param.Direction = ParameterDirection.Input
param.SourceColumn = "bugID"
param.SourceVersion = DataRowVersion.Original ' note Original

param = updateCmd.Parameters.Add("@BugHistoryID", SqlDbType.Int)
param.Direction = ParameterDirection.Input
param.SourceColumn = "BugHistoryID"
param.SourceVersion = DataRowVersion.Original ' note Original

myDataAdapter.UpdateCommand = updateCmd


' *** the delete command
Dim deleteCmd As New SqlCommand("spDeleteBugFromDataSet", _
                                myConnection)
deleteCmd.CommandType = CommandType.StoredProcedure

param = deleteCmd.Parameters.Add("@bugID", SqlDbType.Int)
param.Direction = ParameterDirection.Input
param.SourceColumn = "bugID"
param.SourceVersion = DataRowVersion.Original ' note Original

param = deleteCmd.Parameters.Add("@BugHistoryID", SqlDbType.Int)
param.Direction = ParameterDirection.Input
param.SourceColumn = "BugHistoryID"
param.SourceVersion = DataRowVersion.Original ' note Original

myDataAdapter.DeleteCommand = deleteCmd

' *** insert command
Dim insertCmd As New SqlCommand("spInsertBugFromDataSet", _
                                myConnection)
insertCmd.CommandType = CommandType.StoredProcedure

' Add new parameters, get back a reference
' set the parameters' direction and value
param = insertCmd.Parameters.Add("@ProductID", SqlDbType.Int)
param.Direction = ParameterDirection.Input
param.SourceColumn = "ProductID"
param.SourceVersion = DataRowVersion.Current

param = insertCmd.Parameters.Add("@Version", SqlDbType.Text, 50)
param.Direction = ParameterDirection.Input
param.SourceColumn = "Version"
param.SourceVersion = DataRowVersion.Current

param = insertCmd.Parameters.Add("@Description", _
                                 SqlDbType.Text, 8000)
param.Direction = ParameterDirection.Input
param.SourceColumn = "Description"
param.SourceVersion = DataRowVersion.Current
```

Example 20-16. Updating DataSet with concurrency (VB.NET) (continued)

```
    param = insertCmd.Parameters.Add("@Response", SqlDbType.Text, 8000)
    param.Direction = ParameterDirection.Input
    param.SourceColumn = "Response"
    param.SourceVersion = DataRowVersion.Current

    param = insertCmd.Parameters.Add("@Reporter", SqlDbType.Int)
    param.Direction = ParameterDirection.Input
    param.SourceColumn = "ReporterID"
    param.SourceVersion = DataRowVersion.Current

    param = insertCmd.Parameters.Add("@Owner", SqlDbType.Int)
    param.Direction = ParameterDirection.Input
    param.SourceColumn = "OwnerID"
    param.SourceVersion = DataRowVersion.Current

    param = insertCmd.Parameters.Add("@Status", SqlDbType.Int)
    param.Direction = ParameterDirection.Input
    param.SourceColumn = "StatusID"
    param.SourceVersion = DataRowVersion.Current

    param = insertCmd.Parameters.Add("@Severity", SqlDbType.Int)
    param.Direction = ParameterDirection.Input
    param.SourceColumn = "SeverityID"
    param.SourceVersion = DataRowVersion.Current

    myDataAdapter.InsertCommand = insertCmd

    ' add transaction support for each command
    myDataAdapter.UpdateCommand.Transaction = transaction
    myDataAdapter.DeleteCommand.Transaction = transaction
    myDataAdapter.InsertCommand.Transaction = transaction

    ' try to update, if all succeed commit
    ' otherwise roll back
    Try
       AddHandler myDataAdapter.RowUpdated, AddressOf OnRowUpdate
       Dim rowsUpdated As Int16 = myDataAdapter.Update(bugDS, "BugInfo")
       transaction.Commit()
       MessageBox.Show(rowsUpdated.ToString() + " rows Updated.")
       RefreshDataSet()
    Catch ex As Exception
       MessageBox.Show("Unable to update db!" + ex.Message)
       transaction.Rollback()
    End Try


    ' rebind the grid to show the results
    ' grid should be unchanged
    dgBugs.DataSource = bugDS.Tables("BugInfo")
End Sub    '  close btnUpdateDB_Click

Public Sub OnRowUpdate(ByVal sender As Object, _
                       ByVal e As SqlRowUpdatedEventArgs)
```

Example 20-16. Updating DataSet with concurrency (VB.NET) (continued)

```
      ' get the type of update (update, insert, delete)
      ' as a string
      Dim s As String = _
         "Attempted " & _
         System.Enum.GetName(e.StatementType.GetType( ), e.StatementType) & _
         ". "

      ' if the update failed
      If (e.RecordsAffected < 1) Then
         ' write to the trace log
         MessageBox.Show(s & "Concurrency error updating BugID: " & _
         e.Row("BugID", DataRowVersion.Original))

         ' skip over this row, continue with the next
         e.Status = UpdateStatus.SkipCurrentRow
      Else ' the update succeeded
         ' write a success message to the trace log
         MessageBox.Show(s & " Row updated, BugID: " & _
               e.Row("BugID", DataRowVersion.Original))
      End If
   End Sub

End Class
```

The key change in this listing is in the btnUpdateDB_Click method, in which you must add additional parameters for the original values, such as the highlighted lines in the code snippet below.

```
@ProductID int,
@OldProductID int,
@Description varChar(8000),
@OldDescription varChar(8000)
```

Both the ProductID and the OldProductID are drawn from the same field in the DataSet: ProductID. For ProductID, you will use the Current version of the field; for OldProductID, you'll use the Original version:

```
param =
    updateCmd.Parameters.Add("@ProductID",SqlDbType.Int);
param.Direction = ParameterDirection.Input;
param.SourceColumn="ProductID";
param.SourceVersion=DataRowVersion.Current;

// pass in the original value for the where statement
param =
updateCmd.Parameters.Add("@OldProductID",SqlDbType.Int);
param.Direction = ParameterDirection.Input;
param.SourceColumn="ProductID";
param.SourceVersion=DataRowVersion.Original;

param =
    updateCmd.Parameters.Add("@Description",SqlDbType.Text,8000);
```

```
C#    param.Direction = ParameterDirection.Input;
      param.SourceColumn="Description";
      param.SourceVersion=DataRowVersion.Current;

      param =
         updateCmd.Parameters.Add("@OldDescription",SqlDbType.Text,8000);
      param.Direction = ParameterDirection.Input;
      param.SourceColumn="Description";
      param.SourceVersion=DataRowVersion.Original;
```

Other than setting the new parameters for the Update command, the only other change to btnUpdateDB_Click comes just before you call Update on the data adapter. You will add an event handler for the RowUpdated event:

```
C#    dataAdapter.RowUpdated +=
         new SqlRowUpdatedEventHandler(OnRowUpdate);
```

```
VB    AddHandler myDataAdapter.RowUpdated, AddressOf OnRowUpdate
```

The RowUpdate event is called each time a row is updated and offers you an opportunity to examine the updated row. In the event handler, you will get the statement type, which will be one of the StatementTypeEnumeration values: Delete, Insert, Select, or Update. You can turn the enumerated value into a string by calling the static GetName method on the System.Enum class, passing in the type and the value:

```
C#    string s =
         System.Enum.GetName(
               e.StatementType.GetType( ),e.StatementType);
```

```
VB    Dim s As String = _
         "Attempted " & _
         System.Enum.GetName(e.StatementType.GetType( ), e.StatementType) & ". "
```

Use the type to inform the user of the success or failure of updating (or inserting or deleting) each row. You can now examine the number of rows affected by the update:

```
C#    if (e.RecordsAffected < 1)
```

Each update action affects zero or more rows. However, a single update might affect two or more rows, as you saw in the update stored procedure, which updates a row in Bugs and also a row in BugsHistory. If this procedure succeeds, e.RecordsAffected will be 2 (one record each in Bugs and BugHistory). You have crafted the update procedure so that if the update fails, no rows are affected and you can catch the error:

```
C#    if (e.RecordsAffected < 1)
      {
         MessageBox.Show(s + "Concurrency error! Unable to update BugID: " +
            e.Row["BugID",DataRowVersion.Original].ToString( ));
```

VB
```
If (e.RecordsAffected < 1) Then
    MessageBox.Show(s & "Concurrency error updating BugID: " & _
    e.Row("BugID", DataRowVersion.Original))
```

In this example, you handle the error by opening a message box with the error message. You could, in a real-world application, determine which row update had the problem and display that row (perhaps along with the current contents of the database) to the user for resolution.

The Status property is a property of the SqlRowUpdatedEventArgs object that was passed into your RowUpdated event handler. This will be one of the UpdateStatus enumerated values: Continue, ErrorsOccurred, SkipAllRemainingRows, or Skip-CurrentRow. If an error was found (e.g., the update failed), this value will be set to ErrorsOccurred, and if you do not change it, an exception will be thrown. Since you have now handled the error (by displaying it to the user or in whatever way you've chosen), you will want to change the value to SkipCurrentRow, which will allow the update command to continue, skipping over the row whose update failed:

C#
```
e.Status = UpdateStatus.SkipCurrentRow;
```

To test whether the update will be protected against concurrency issues, you will hand-update one field in one record before attempting the automated update. To do so, just before you begin the transaction, create a new connection in btnUpdateDB_ Click, open it, and execute a SQL statement to update the Bugs table; you will also set the Product value to 1 where the BugID equals 1:

C#
```
System.Data.SqlClient.SqlConnection connection2 =
    new System.Data.SqlClient.SqlConnection(connectionString);
connection2.Open();
string cmd = "Update Bugs set Product = 2 where BugID = 1";
SqlCommand cmd1 = new SqlCommand(cmd,connection2);
cmd1.ExecuteNonQuery();
```

VB
```
Dim myConnection2 As _
    New System.Data.SqlClient.SqlConnection(connectionString)
myConnection2.Open()
Dim cmd As String = _
    "Update Bugs set Product = 1 where BugID = 1"
Dim cmd1 As New SqlCommand(cmd, myConnection2)
cmd1.ExecuteNonQuery()
```

The sequence of events is now:

1. Fill the DataSet from the database and display it in a grid.

2. When the user clicks Update DataSet, modify the DataSet and display the changes.

3. When the user clicks Update Database, hand-modify one record in the database and then tell the DataSet to update the database. The record you modified (for BugID =1) should make the update from the DataSet for that bug fail.

4. Catch the failure by noting that for one record, RecordsAffected is zero, and handle the error.

5. Report on the remaining updates, deletes, and inserts. (They should all work well.)

 You must make one change to the btnUpdateDataSet_Click method for this test to be meaningful. The field you update in BugID1 should be a field in Bugs rather than in BugHistory. In previous examples, you wrote:

```
bugTable.Rows[0]["Response"] =
    "This is a test";
```

In this example, you will modify it to:

```
bugTable.Rows[0]["ReporterID"] = "1";
```

Command Builder

In the previous section, you painstakingly created the Update, Insert, and Delete commands. You first created stored procedures, and then you created Command objects for each procedure, passing in the necessary parameters. The .NET Framework does a lot of this work for you, if the update, insert, and delete commands are simple enough.

The framework provides a Command Builder (SqlCommandBuilder and OleDb-CommandBuilder) to generate the necessary Delete, Update, and Insert commands without your writing stored procedures. To take advantage of these objects, the following conditions must be met:

- The rows in the table you generate must come from a single table (or view) in the database.

- The table must have a primary key or a field with values guaranteed to be unique.

- The unique value column must be returned by the query used to fill the DataSet (the select command).

- The name of the table must not have spaces, periods, quotation marks, or other special characters.

To see how using the Command Builder classes simplifies the task when these conditions are met, you'll modify the program to build the DataSet only from the Bugs table. Your user interface will be much simpler because you'll use a simple Select statement: "Select * from Bugs".

Create a new application called UpdatingDataSetsCommandBuilder with a form like that shown in Figure 20-10. Add three buttons and a DataGrid, as described in Table 20-3.

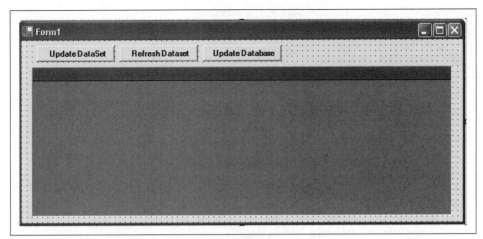

Figure 20-10. Updating DataSets Command Builder form

Table 20-3. Controls for UpdatingDataSetsCommandBuilder

Control	ID	Text
Button	btnUpdateDS	Update DataSet
Button	btnRefreshDS	Refresh DataSet
Button	btnUpdateDB	Update Database
DataGrid	dgBugs	

Example 20-17 shows the complete listing in C# and Example 20-18 shows the complete listing in VB.NET. A detailed analysis follows.

Example 20-17. Using Command Builder (C#)

```
using System;
using System.Drawing;
using System.Collections;
using System.ComponentModel;
using System.Windows.Forms;
using System.Data;
using System.Data.SqlClient;

namespace UpdatingDataSetsCommandBuilderCS
{
    public class Form1 : System.Windows.Forms.Form
    {
        private System.Windows.Forms.DataGrid dgBugs;
        private System.Windows.Forms.Button btnUpdateDS;
        private System.Windows.Forms.Button btnRefreshDS;
        private System.Windows.Forms.Button btnUpdateDB;
        private DataSet bugDS;

        private System.ComponentModel.Container components = null;
```

Example 20-17. Using Command Builder (C#) (continued)

```
[C#]    public Form1( )
        {
           InitializeComponent( );
           RefreshDataSet( );
        }

        protected override void Dispose( bool disposing )
        {
           if( disposing )
           {
              if (components != null)
              {
                 components.Dispose( );
              }
           }
           base.Dispose( disposing );
        }

        #region Windows Form Designer generated code
        #endregion

        [STAThread]
        static void Main( )
        {
           Application.Run(new Form1( ));
        }

        private DataSet CreateBugDataSet( )
        {
           // connection string to connect to the Bugs Database
           string connectionString =
              "server=YourServer; uid=sa; pwd=YourPW; " +
              "database=WindForm_Bugs";

           // Create connection object, initialize with
           // connection string. Open it.
           System.Data.SqlClient.SqlConnection connection =
              new System.Data.SqlClient.SqlConnection(connectionString);


           // Create a SqlCommand object and assign the connection
           System.Data.SqlClient.SqlCommand command =
              new System.Data.SqlClient.SqlCommand( );
           command.Connection=connection;
           command.CommandText="select * from bugs";
           command.CommandType=CommandType.Text;

           // create a data adapter and assign the command object
           // and add the table mapping for bugs
           SqlDataAdapter dataAdapter = new SqlDataAdapter( );
           dataAdapter.SelectCommand=command;
           dataAdapter.TableMappings.Add("Table","BugInfo");
```

Example 20-17. Using Command Builder (C#) (continued)

```
        // Create the data set and use the data adapter to fill it
        DataSet dataSet = new DataSet( );
        dataAdapter.Fill(dataSet);
        return dataSet;
    }   //  close CreateBugDataSet

    // Update the dataset with bogus data
    private void btnUpdateDS_Click(object sender, System.EventArgs e)
    {
        DataTable bugTable = bugDS.Tables["BugInfo"];
        bugTable.Rows[0]["Description"] = "This is a test";
        DataRow newRow = bugTable.NewRow( );
        newRow["Description"] = "New bug test";
        newRow["Product"] = 2;
        newRow["Version"] = "0.01";
        newRow["Reporter"] = 3;
        bugTable.Rows.Add(newRow);
    }

    private void btnRefreshDS_Click(object sender, System.EventArgs e)
    {
        RefreshDataSet( );
    }

    private void RefreshDataSet( )
    {
        bugDS = CreateBugDataSet( );
        dgBugs.DataSource = bugDS.Tables[0];
    }

    private void btnUpdateDB_Click(object sender, System.EventArgs e)
    {
        string connectionString =
            "server=YourServer; uid=sa; pwd=YourPW; " +
            "database=WindForm_Bugs";


        // Create connection object, initialize with
        // connection string. Open it.
        System.Data.SqlClient.SqlConnection connection =
            new System.Data.SqlClient.SqlConnection(connectionString);

        connection.Open( );

        SqlDataAdapter dataAdapter =
            new SqlDataAdapter("select * from Bugs", connection);
        SqlCommandBuilder bldr = new SqlCommandBuilder(dataAdapter);
        dataAdapter.DeleteCommand = bldr.GetDeleteCommand( );
        dataAdapter.UpdateCommand = bldr.GetUpdateCommand( );
        dataAdapter.InsertCommand = bldr.GetInsertCommand( );

        SqlTransaction transaction;
```

Example 20-17. Using Command Builder (C#) (continued)

```csharp
            transaction = connection.BeginTransaction();
            dataAdapter.DeleteCommand.Transaction = transaction;
            dataAdapter.UpdateCommand.Transaction = transaction;
            dataAdapter.InsertCommand.Transaction = transaction;


            // try to update, if all succeed commit
            // otherwise roll back
            try
            {
               int rowsUpdated = dataAdapter.Update(bugDS,"BugInfo");
               transaction.Commit();
               MessageBox.Show(rowsUpdated.ToString() + " rows Updated.");
               RefreshDataSet();
            }
            catch (Exception ex)
            {
               MessageBox.Show("Unable to update: " + ex.Message);
               transaction.Rollback();
            }

            // rebind the grid to show the results
            // grid should be unchanged
            dgBugs.DataSource = bugDS.Tables["BugInfo"];
        }   //  close btnUpdateDB_Click
    }
}
```

Example 20-18. Using Command Builder (VB.NET)

```vb
Imports System.Data.SqlClient
Public Class Form1
    Inherits System.Windows.Forms.Form

    Dim bugDS As DataSet



#Region " Windows Form Designer generated code "

    Public Sub New()
        MyBase.New()

        'This call is required by the Windows Form Designer.
        InitializeComponent()
        RefreshDataSet()

#End Region

    Private Function CreateBugDataSet() As DataSet
        ' myConnection string to connect to the Bugs Database
        Dim connectionString As String = _
```

Example 20-18. Using Command Builder (VB.NET) (continued)

```
        "server=YourServer; uid=sa; pwd=YourPW; " + _
        "database=WindForm_Bugs"

    ' Create myConnection object, initialize with
    ' myConnection string. Open it.
    Dim myConnection As New _
        System.Data.SqlClient.SqlConnection(connectionString)
    myConnection.Open( )


    ' Create a SqlCommand object and assign the myConnection
    Dim command As New System.Data.SqlClient.SqlCommand( )
    command.Connection = myConnection
    command.CommandText = "Select * from Bugs"
    command.CommandType = CommandType.Text

    ' create a data adapter and assign the command object
    ' and add the table mapping for bugs
    Dim myDataAdapter As New SqlDataAdapter( )
    myDataAdapter.SelectCommand = command
    myDataAdapter.TableMappings.Add("Table", "BugInfo")

    ' Create the data set and use the data adapter to fill it
    Dim myDataSet As New DataSet( )
    myDataAdapter.Fill(myDataSet)
    Return myDataSet
End Function    '  close CreateBugDataSet

Private Sub RefreshDataSet( )
    bugDS = CreateBugDataSet( )
    dgBugs.DataSource = bugDS.Tables(0)
End Sub

' Update the dataset with bogus data
Private Sub btnUpdateDS_Click(ByVal sender As System.Object,
                             ByVal e As System.EventArgs)
                             Handles btnUpdateDS.Click
    Dim bugTable As DataTable = bugDS.Tables("BugInfo")
    bugTable.Rows(0)("Description") = "This is a test"

    Dim newRow As DataRow = bugTable.NewRow( )
    newRow("Description") = "New bug test"
    newRow("Product") = 2
    newRow("Version") = "0.01"
    newRow("Reporter") = 3
    bugTable.Rows.Add(newRow)

End Sub

Private Sub btnRefreshDS_Click(ByVal sender As System.Object,
                             ByVal e As System.EventArgs)
                             Handles btnRefreshDS.Click
```

Example 20-18. Using Command Builder (VB.NET) (continued)

```vb
        RefreshDataSet()
    End Sub

    Private Sub btnUpdateDB_Click(ByVal sender As System.Object,
                                  ByVal e As System.EventArgs)
                                  Handles btnUpdateDB.Click

        Dim connectionString As String = "server=YourServer; uid=sa; " + _
           "pwd=YourPW; database=WindForm_Bugs"

        ' Create myConnection object, initialize with
        ' myConnection string. Open it.
        Dim myConnection As New SqlConnection(connectionString)

        Dim transaction As SqlTransaction

        myConnection.Open()

        Dim myDataAdapter As New SqlDataAdapter( _
           "Select * from Bugs", myConnection)
        Dim bldr As New SqlCommandBuilder(myDataAdapter)
        myDataAdapter.DeleteCommand = bldr.GetDeleteCommand()
        myDataAdapter.UpdateCommand = bldr.GetUpdateCommand()
        myDataAdapter.InsertCommand = bldr.GetInsertCommand()

        transaction = myConnection.BeginTransaction()
        myDataAdapter.DeleteCommand.Transaction = transaction
        myDataAdapter.UpdateCommand.Transaction = transaction
        myDataAdapter.InsertCommand.Transaction = transaction


        ' try to update, if all succeed commit
        ' otherwise roll back
        Try
           Dim rowsUpdated As Int16 = myDataAdapter.Update(bugDS, "BugInfo")
           transaction.Commit()
           MessageBox.Show(rowsUpdated.ToString() + " rows Updated.")
           RefreshDataSet()
        Catch ex As Exception
           MessageBox.Show("Unable to update db!" + ex.Message)
           transaction.Rollback()
        End Try


        ' rebind the grid to show the results
        ' grid should be unchanged
        dgBugs.DataSource = bugDS.Tables("BugInfo")
    End Sub    '  close btnUpdateDB_Click
End Class
```

Because you can use the Command Builder only with very simple queries, toss out all the code that deals with the BugHistory table. Modify btnUpdateDS_Click so that you update and add fields only in Bugs:

```
DataRow newRow = bugTable.NewRow( );
newRow["Product"] = 2;
newRow["Version"] = "0.01";
newRow["Description"] = "New bug test";
newRow["Reporter"] = 3;
bugTable.Rows.Add(newRow);
```

```
Dim newRow As DataRow = bugTable.NewRow( )
newRow("Description") = "New bug test"
newRow("Product") = 2
newRow("Version") = "0.01"
newRow("Reporter") = 3
bugTable.Rows.Add(newRow)
```

Notice that you no longer delete a row. Because of referential integrity, you cannot delete the row without deleting from BugHistory, and because the Command Builder can work only with a single table at a time, you cannot delete from BugHistory. To keep this example simple, you'll just update and insert.

The important change is in btnUpdateDB_Click, which is now far easier. Simply retrieve the DataSet and set up the Connection object, just as you did previously:

```
string connectionString =
    "server=YourServer; uid=sa;
            pwd=YourPassword; database=ProgASPDotNetBugs";

System.Data.SqlClient.SqlConnection connection =
    new System.Data.SqlClient.SqlConnection(connectionString);

connection.Open( );
```

```
Dim connectionString As String = "server=YourServer; uid=sa; " + _
    "pwd=YourPW; database=WindForm_Bugs"

Dim myConnection As New SqlConnection(connectionString)
myConnection.Open( )
```

Then create a DataAdapter and a SqlCommandBuilder:

```
SqlDataAdapter dataAdapter =
    new SqlDataAdapter("select * from Bugs", connection);
SqlCommandBuilder bldr = new SqlCommandBuilder(dataAdapter);
```

```
Dim myDataAdapter As New SqlDataAdapter( _
    "Select * from Bugs", myConnection)
Dim bldr As New SqlCommandBuilder(myDataAdapter)
```

Use the Command Builder to build the DeleteCommand, UpdateCommand, and InsertCommand objects required by the DataAdapter, which you previously built by hand:

C#
```
dataAdapter.DeleteCommand = bldr.GetDeleteCommand( );
dataAdapter.UpdateCommand = bldr.GetUpdateCommand( );
dataAdapter.InsertCommand = bldr.GetInsertCommand( );
```

VB
```
myDataAdapter.DeleteCommand = bldr.GetDeleteCommand( )
myDataAdapter.UpdateCommand = bldr.GetUpdateCommand( )
myDataAdapter.InsertCommand = bldr.GetInsertCommand( )
```

That's it! You are ready to enlist the commands in the transaction:

C#
```
SqlTransaction transaction;
transaction = connection.BeginTransaction( );
dataAdapter.DeleteCommand.Transaction = transaction;
dataAdapter.UpdateCommand.Transaction = transaction;
dataAdapter.InsertCommand.Transaction = transaction;
```

VB
```
Dim transaction As SqlTransaction
transaction = myConnection.BeginTransaction( )
myDataAdapter.DeleteCommand.Transaction = transaction
myDataAdapter.UpdateCommand.Transaction = transaction
myDataAdapter.InsertCommand.Transaction = transaction
```

With that done, you are ready to call Update on the DataAdapter, as you did previously:

C#
```
int rowsUpdated = dataAdapter.Update(ds,"Bugs");
```

VB
```
Dim rowsUpdated As Int16 = myDataAdapter.Update(bugDS, "BugInfo")
```

The CommandBuilder object has created the necessary commands on your behalf.

That's all there is to it; the Command Builder does all the work of updating the database and ensuring concurrency integrity. You can see what the Command builder has done by adding this code to the try block:

C#
```
MessageBox.Show(dataAdapter.InsertCommand.CommandText);
MessageBox.Show(dataAdapter.UpdateCommand.CommandText);
```

The result is that the Update command is displayed in a message box, as shown in Figures 20-11 and 20-12.

Pay particular attention to the Update command; you can see that the Where clause is similar to the one you built earlier (this more complex command considers null fields).

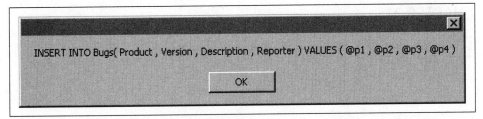

Figure 20-11. Command Builder insert command

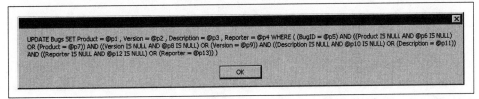

Figure 20-12. Command Builder update command

CHAPTER 21

Exceptions and Debugging

In 1992, Jesse Liberty worked for Pat Johnson, who used to say "Save time—don't put the bugs into your code in the first place." Good advice.

It turns out, however, that bugs do creep into your code. But here is what we know: the earlier you find a bug, the cheaper it is to fix. Bugs found just as you are entering the code are the cheapest: just hit delete and fix the code. Bugs found during compilation are next cheapest: compiler bugs fail every time, and if you are careful you can squish them all before you show your code to anyone else.

Bugs that make it to Quality Assurance (QA) are more expensive than bugs you find when you compile the code, but they are a heck of a lot cheaper to fix than bugs that make it all the way to your customer—the most expensive bugs of all. The bugs you want to avoid are the embarrassing ones that show up when you demo your new product to your prospective customer, or that show up months (or years) after you've sold the product. Fixing those bugs require you to do something that every programmer hates: go back to code you're done with to reopen it and see all the dopey things you did when you were young and stupid.

Bugs Versus Exceptions

This chapter shows what tools will help you avoid bugs, find them early, and squish them when they are found. There are some conditions, however, that appear to the user as an error but are not bugs—exceptional and unavoidable circumstances that you can not eliminate. Circumstances such as running out of memory, running out of disk space, or dropping a network connection. Not your fault, but they'll bring your program to its knees just as quickly as dividing by zero. You have to handle these problems.

The traditional approach to managing these problems is to crash, but that is frowned upon these days. Better yet, allow the user to fix the problem and continue. Better still is to fix the problem yourself (assuming you will do no harm) and not make the user aware of the problem.

In any case, these situations are not bugs, but exceptions. Before looking at how to find and eliminate the bugs in your program, let's look at exceptions.

Exceptions

When your [program encounters an exceptional circumstance, such as running out of memory, it *throws* (or "raises") an exception. You might throw an exception in your own methods (for example, if you realize that an invalid parameter was provided) or an exception might be thrown in a class provided by the Framework Class Library (for example, if you try to write to a read-only file). Many exceptions are thrown at runtime when the program can no longer continue due to an operating system problem (such as a security violation). Exceptions must be handled before the program can continue.

Provide for the possibility of exceptions by adding try/catch blocks in your program. The catch blocks are also called *exception handlers*. The idea is that you *try* potentially dangerous code, and if an exception is thrown, you *catch* (or *handle*) the exception in your catch block.

Ideally, if the exception is caught and handled, the program can fix the problem and continue. Even if your program can't continue, by catching the exception you have an opportunity to print a meaningful error message and terminate gracefully.

When an exception is thrown, execution of the current function halts and the Common Language Runtime (CLR) searches back through the stack until an appropriate exception handler is found. The search for an exception handler can "unwind the stack." This means that if the currently running function does not handle the exception, the current function terminates and the calling function gets a chance to handle the exception. If none of the calling functions handle it, the exception is ultimately handled by the CLR, which will terminate your program abruptly.

If Function A calls Function B and Function B calls Function C, these function calls are all placed on the *stack* (an area of memory set aside for local variables). When a programmer talks about "unwinding the stack," you back up from C to B to A, as illustrated in Figure 21-1.

If you must unwind the stack from C to B to A to handle the exception, when you are done, you are in A—there is no automatic return to C.

If you return all the way to the first method and no exception handler is found, the *default* exception handler (provided by the Windows Form's Application Run method) wraps all calls to event handlers in a try block and manages uncaught exceptions. Program termination is the default behavior.

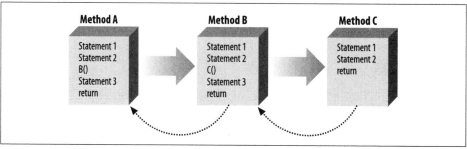

Figure 21-1. Unwinding the stack

Throwing and Catching Exceptions

In .NET languages such as C# and VB.NET, all exceptions will be of either type System.Exception or types derived from System.Exception. The CLR System namespace includes a number of exception types that can use your program. These exception types include ArgumentNullException and InvalidCastException. You can guess their use based on their name. For example, an ArgumentNullException is thrown when an argument to a method is null when null is not an expected (or acceptable) value.

The Throw Statement

To signal an abnormal condition in a .NET program, throw an exception. To do this, use the keyword throw. The following line of code creates a new instance of System. Exception and throws it:

C#
```
throw new System.Exception();
```

VB
```
Throw New System.Exception()
```

If you throw an exception and no try/catch block can handle it, your program will come to a grinding halt and display an ugly message, as shown in Figure 21-2.

 To reproduce this ugly situation for yourself, create the form as shown, and in the click event handler for the Throw button, add the code:

C#
```
throw new System.Exception();
```
or download the program NoTryCatch from the web site.

The Try and Catch Statements

To handle exceptions, take the following steps:

1. Execute any code that you suspect might throw an exception (such as code that opens a file or allocates memory) in a try block.

2. Catch any exceptions thrown in a catch block.

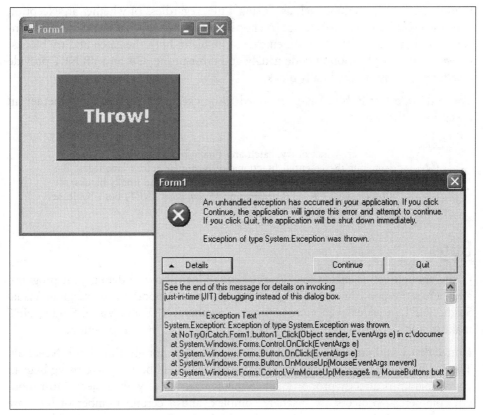

Figure 21-2. Throwing an uncaught exception

In C#, a try block is created with the keyword try, and the block is enclosed in braces.

In VB.NET, a try block is created with the keyword Try and ended with the keywords End Try.

In C#, a catch block is created using the keyword catch, and is also enclosed within braces.

In VB.NET, a catch block begins with the keyword Catch and can be terminated by either the next use of the Catch keyword or the End Try statement. Catch statements can be written to catch either specific types of exceptions or all thrown exceptions.

The finally statement

In some instances, throwing an exception and unwinding the stack can create a problem. For example, if you have opened a file or otherwise committed a resource, you might need an opportunity to close the file or flush the buffer.

If you want to take action, such as closing a file, regardless of whether an exception is thrown, you have two strategies to choose from. One approach encloses the dangerous action in a try block and then closes the file in both the catch and try blocks. However, this duplication of code is ugly and error prone. C# and VB.NET provide a better alternative in the finally block.

The code in a finally block is guaranteed to be executed regardless of whether an exception is thrown.

 The exact syntax of try, catch and finally blocks are language dependent, but the essential functionality is similar across languages. For further details on creating and using try, catch, and finally blocks, see *Programming C#* or *Programming Visual Basic .NET*, both by Jesse Liberty (O'Reilly).

Bugs

Okay, enough about exceptions. You're here to learn how to debug your program, and here's the good news: .NET provides *extensive* support for debugging. Visual Studio .NET provides even more support. Together, .NET and Visual Studio .NET make it much easier to find and remove most of the bugs in your program.

Notice that I said *most*. I'll go further, *nearly all*—but not all, I'm afraid. Never all. The sad but honest state of the industry is that the likelihood of there being bugs in your program is directly proportional to the complexity of your project. Most modern commercial projects are insanely complex, and a certain number of bugs are (nearly) inevitable in any real project. In addition, software attracts bugs like bread crumbs attract insects. Spray all you want, and you'll still find an ant or two in the pantry.

Debugging in Visual Studio .NET

The easiest and best way to avoid bugs is to let Visual Studio .NET help you find and remove them.

When you run your code in the debugger, you can literally watch your code progress, step by step. As you walk through the code, you can see the variables change values and watch as objects are created and destroyed. A good symbolic debugger is like a full motion CAT scan of your program.

The debugger is one of the most powerful tools at your disposal for learning Windows programming. This section provides a brief introduction to the most important parts of the debugger within Visual Studio .NET. For complete coverage of the Visual Studio .NET debugger, please see *Mastering Visual Studio .NET* by Ian Griffiths (O'Reilly).

Finding Syntax Errors

Your eye tends to see what it expects. For example, read the sentence in Figure 21-3.

Figure 21-3. Seeing what you expect

Many readers will see this as "Paris in the spring" even after reading it a few times. Some readers will see the mistake only when they actually place their index fingers on the page and mark off each word. The brain tends to see what it expects to see, and finding syntax errors can be terribly difficult. Fortunately, this is the easiest kind of error for Visual Studio .NET to find.

Consider the following C# code that will not compile:

```C#
private void mnuStartLoop_Click(object sender, System.EventArgs e)
{
   for (int i = 1; i < 10; i++);
   {
      if ( i == 10 )
      {
         MessageBox.Show("Counted 10!",
            "MessageBoxCounter",MessageBoxButtons.OK,
            MessageBoxIcon.Information);
      }

      Application.DoEvents();

   }
}
```

Can you spot the error? Now take a look at it in Visual Studio .NET—the error is highlighted by Visual Studio .NET (with a red, squiggly line) before you even try to compile, as shown in Figure 21-4.

Notice the underlined semicolon at the end of the for statement and note that the Task list also flags that line as a potential problem. In fact, if you double-click on the line in the task list, you are taken directly to the semicolon for easy deletion.

Syntax errors are easy as pie; runtime errors, though, can be tricky, which is where the debugger can really help you out.

Debug Versus Release Mode

To use Visual Studio .NET for debugging, you must set up to run your program in Debug mode (this is the default, so you really don't have to do very much).

You can compile your program in either Debug or Release mode (or in a custom mode you create for yourself). The Release configuration mode is designed to strip out all the debugging information (which might otherwise bloat your program) and turn on optimizations (which will make your program run faster). The debug mode turns off optimizations (which can otherwise make debugging tricky) and adds back the symbolic information (the C# or VB.NET code) that helps you to figure out what is going wrong.

Look at the top of the Toolbar in the Visual Studio .NET editor. You'll find a drop-down menu that lets you switch between Debug and Release and invoke the Configuration Manager, as shown in Figure 21-5.

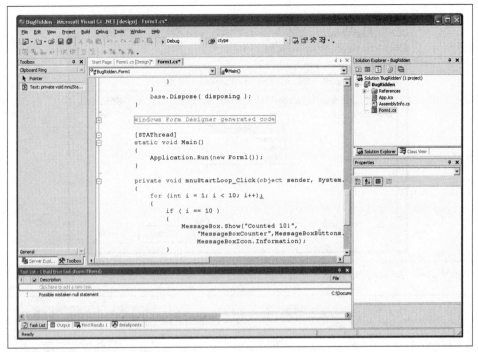

Figure 21-4. Syntax error highlighting

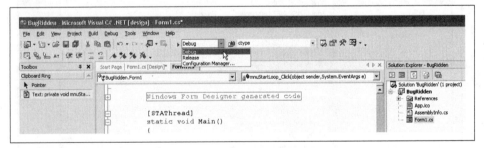

Figure 21-5. Setting Debug mode

The Configuration Manager option brings up the Configuration Manager dialog box, shown in Figure 21-6.

The Configuration Manager lets you modify the configuration (e.g., for Debug builds) or create new configurations for special requirements. These options are limited, however. The most powerful way to control the configuration for debugging is to bring up the properties window for the project itself by right-clicking on the project in the Solution Explorer window and then choosing the Configuration Properties/Debugging option in the left pane, as shown in Figure 21-7.

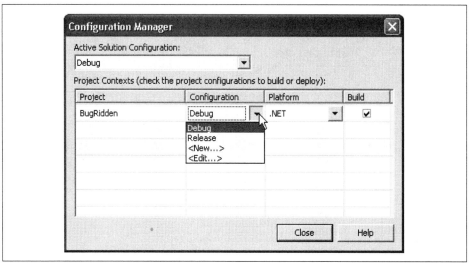

Figure 21-6. The Configuration Manager

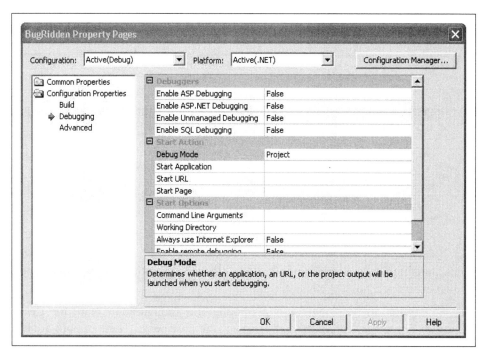

Figure 21-7. Project Properties

The Debug Toolbar

A *Debug toolbar* is available in the IDE. To make it visible, click on the View/Toolbars menu commands, and then click on Debug, if it is not already checked. Table 21-1 shows the icons that appear on the Debug toolbar (unless you customize it to your own needs).

Table 21-1. Debug toolbar icons

Icon	Debug menu equivalent	Keyboard shortcut	Description
			Toolbar handle. Click and drag to move the toolbar to a new location.
	Start / Continue	F5	Start or continue executing the program.
	Break All	Ctrl+Alt+Break	Stop program execution at the currently executing line.
	Stop Debugging	Shift+F5	Stop debugging.
	Restart	Ctrl+Shift+F5	Stop the run currently being debugged and immediately begin a new run.
			Show the next statement.
	Step Into	F11	If the current line contains a call to a method or function, this icon will single step the debugger into that method or function.
	Step Over	F10	If the current line contains a call to a method or function, this icon will not step into that method or function, but go to the next line after the call.
	Step Out	Shift+F11	If the current line is in a method or function, that method or function will complete and the debugger will next stop on the line after the method or function call.
Statement			A unit of debugger stepping. Possible values are Line, Statement, and Instruction.
Hex			A hexadecimal display toggle.
	Windows		A debug window selector.
			Toolbar options. Offer options for adding and removing buttons from the Debug, Text Editor, and all other toolbars.

Breakpoints

Breakpoints are at the heart of debugging. A breakpoint is an instruction to .NET to stop at a specific line in your code if that line is about to be executed. While the execution is paused, you can perform one of the actions from the list shown next.

- Examine and modify values of variables and expressions.
- Single step through the code.
- Move into and out of methods and functions, even stepping into classes written in other CLR-compliant languages.
- Perform any number of other debugging and analysis tasks.

Setting a breakpoint

A breakpoint is set in the Source window (any Source window—page file, control file, code-behind, etc.) by single-clicking on the gray vertical bar along the left margin of the window (or by pressing F9). A red dot will appear in the left margin, and the line of code will be highlighted, as shown in Figure 21-8.

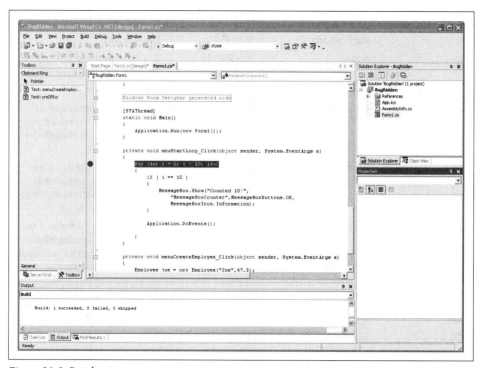

Figure 21-8. Breakpoint

An alternative to clicking in the left margin is selecting the Debug/New Breakpoint... menu command (Ctrl+B). Clicking on the File tab brings up the dialog shown in Figure 21-9. The text boxes will already be filled in with the current location of the cursor.

The four tabs in the dialog box in Figure 21-9 correspond to the four types of breakpoints, described in Table 21-2.

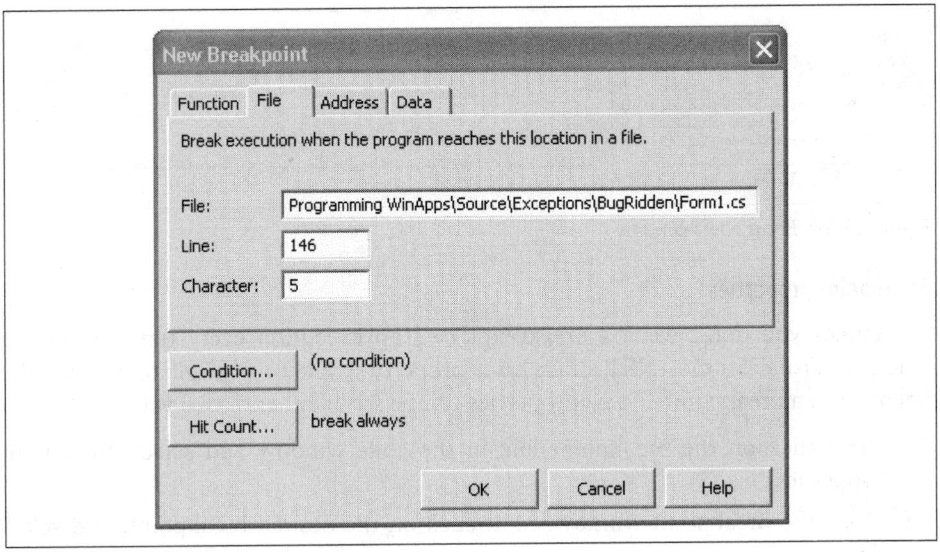

Figure 21-9. New Breakpoint dialog box

Table 21-2. Four types of breakpoints

Type	Description
Function	Allows you to specify where, in which language, and in which method or function the break will occur.
File	Sets a breakpoint at a specific point in a source file. When you set a breakpoint by clicking in the left margin (or pressing F9), a file breakpoint is set.
Address	Sets a breakpoint at a specified memory address.
Data	Sets a breakpoint when the value of a variable changes.

Breakpoint window

You can see all the currently set breakpoints by looking at the Breakpoint window. To display the Breakpoint window, perform any one of the following actions:

- Press Ctrl+Alt+B.
- Select Breakpoints from the Debug/Windows menu command.
- Click on Windows icon of the Debug toolbar and select Breakpoints.

A Breakpoint window is shown in Figure 21-10.

You can toggle a breakpoint between Enabled and Disabled by clicking on the corresponding CheckBox in the Breakpoint window.

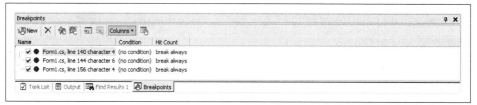

Figure 21-10. Breakpoint window

Breakpoint properties

Sometimes you don't want a breakpoint to stop execution every time the line is reached. Visual Studio .NET offers two properties that can be set to modify the behavior of a breakpoint. These properties can be set in either of two ways:

- Right-click on the breakpoint line in the code window and select Breakpoint Properties.

- Open the Breakpoint window, right-click on the desired breakpoint, and select Properties.

In either case, you will see the dialog box shown previously in Figure 21-9.

The fields at the top of the Breakpoint Properties dialog box will default to the current breakpoint's location. The two buttons allow access to the Condition and Hit Count properties.

Condition. The Condition button brings up the dialog shown in Figure 21-11.

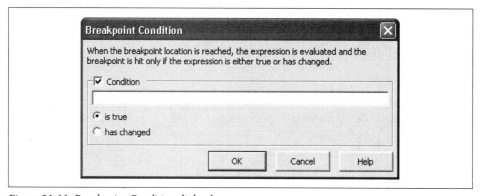

Figure 21-11. Breakpoint Condition dialog box

You can enter any valid expression in the edit field. This expression is evaluated when program execution reaches the breakpoint. Depending on which radio button is selected and how the Condition expression evaluates, the program execution will either pause or move on. The two radio buttons are labeled as described next.

is true

If the entered Condition evaluates to a Boolean true, then the program will pause.

has changed

If the entered Condition has changed, then the program will pause. On the first pass through the piece of code being debugged, the breakpoint will never pause execution because there is nothing to compare against. On the second and subsequent passes, the expression will have been initialized and the comparison will take place.

Hit count. *Hit count* is the number of times that spot in the code has been executed since either the run began or the Reset Hit Count button was pressed. The Hit Count button brings up the dialog shown in Figure 21-12.

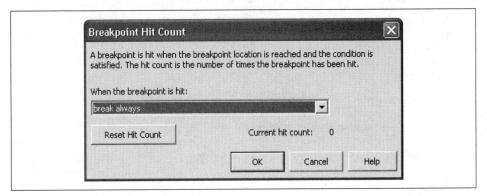

Figure 21-12. Breakpoint hit count dialog box

Clicking on the drop-down list presents the following options:

- Break always.
- Break always when the hit count is equal to.
- Break always when the hit count is a multiple of.
- Break always when the hit count is greater than or equal to.

Click on any option other than "break always," the default, and the dialog box will add an edit field for you to enter a target hit count.

Suppose that this breakpoint is set in a loop of some sort. You selected "break when the hit count is a multiple of" and entered 5 in the edit field. Then the program pauses execution every fifth time through.

Breakpoint icons

There are several different breakpoint symbols, or glyphs, each conveying a different type of breakpoint. These glyphs appear in Table 21-3.

Table 21-3. Breakpoint symbols

Glyph	Type	Description
●	Enabled	A normal, active breakpoint. If breakpoint conditions or hit count settings are met, execution will pause at this line.
○	Disabled	Execution will not pause at this line until the breakpoint is re-enabled.
◐	Error	The location or condition is not valid.
❷	Warning	The code at this line is not yet loaded, so a breakpoint can't be set. If the code is subsequently loaded, then the breakpoint will become enabled.

Stepping through code

The Start Loop menu choice invokes the method mnuStartLoop_Click. The idea of this method is to count from 1 to 10 and display a message box, but this method has a bug: the message box is never displayed. Here's the code:

```csharp
private void mnuStartLoop_Click(object sender, System.EventArgs e)
{
    for (int i = 1; i < 10; i++)
    {
        if ( i == 10 )
        {
            MessageBox.Show("Counted 10!",
                "MessageBoxCounter",MessageBoxButtons.OK,
                MessageBoxIcon.Information);
        }
        Application.DoEvents();
    }
}
```

You may be able to find the bug on inspection (without a debugger) but let's assume that this one has you stumped. Place a breakpoint on the first line of the method, as shown in Figure 21-13.

> For the examples in this chapter, I've created a simple program that has two menu choices: Start Loop and Create Employee (menu creation is discussed in Chapter 18). You can download this program from the web site as *BugRidden.sln*, or create your own simple version from the code shown here. To save space, only the relevant event handlers are shown.

Click on Debug → Start (or press F5) to run to the breakpoint. Click on the first menu choice to invoke the method. Your program will break at the first line of the event handler, as shown in Figure 21-14.

Examining variables and objects

Once the program is stopped, you can examine the value of objects and variables currently in scope. This process is incredibly intuitive and easy. Just place the mouse

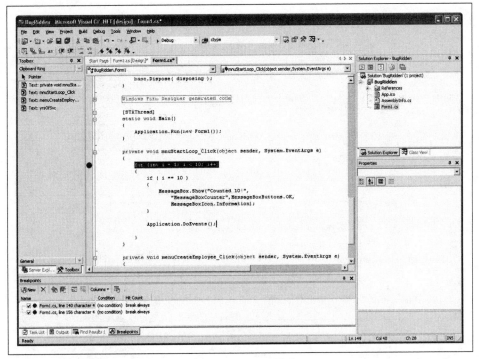

```
                                 base.Dispose( disposing );


                        Windows Form Designer generated code


                        [STAThread]
                        static void Main()
                        {
                                 Application.Run(new Form1());
                        }

                        private void mnuStartLoop_Click(object sender, System.EventArgs e)
                        {
                                 for (int i = 1; i < 10; i++)
                                 {
                                         if ( i == 10 )
                                         {
                                                 MessageBox.Show("Counted 10!",
                                                     "MessageBoxCounter",MessageBoxButtons.OK,
                                                     MessageBoxIcon.Information);
                                         }

                                         Application.DoEvents();
                                 }
                        }

                        private void menuCreateEmployee_Click(object sender, System.EventArgs e)
                        {
```

Figure 21-13. Breakpoint on first line of mnuStartLoop_Click

cursor over the top of any variable or object in the code, wait a moment, and a little pop-up window will appear with its current value

If the cursor hovers over a variable, the pop-up window will contain the type of variable, its value (if relevant), and any other properties it may have.

If the cursor hovers over some other object, the pop-up window will contain information relevant to its type, including its full namespace, its syntax, and a descriptive line of help.

Press F10 to step into the loop and ensure that the variable i has a meaningful value.

Immediate window

The Immediate window lets you type almost any variable, property, or expression and immediately see its value. To open the Immediate window, do any of the following:

- Press Ctrl+Alt+I.
- Select Immediate from the Debug/Windows menu commands.
- Click on the Windows icon of the Debug toolbar and select Immediate.

You can enter expressions for immediate execution in the Immediate window. If you want to see the value of an expression, prepend it with a question mark. For

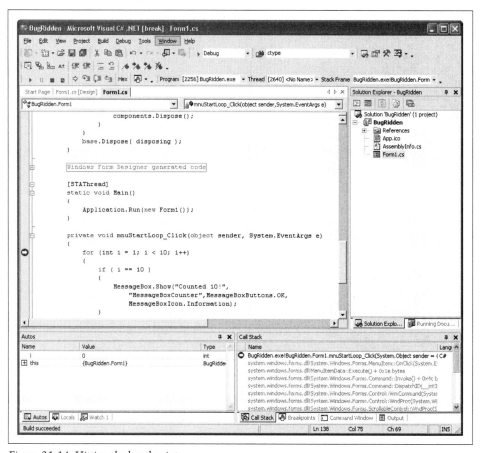

Figure 21-14. Hitting the breakpoint

instance, if the breakpoint is on the line shown in Figure 21-14, you can see the value of the integer i by entering:

```
?i
```

in the Immediate window and pressing Enter. Figure 21-15 shows the result of that exercise; additionally, this figure shows how to assign a new value to the variable i and then view its value again.

You can clear the contents of the Immediate window by right-clicking anywhere in the window and selecting Clear All. Close the window by clicking on the X in the upper-righthand corner. If you close the window and subsequently bring it back up in the same session, it will still have all the previous contents.

As you step through this example, you can see that the variable i never reaches the value 10. That is because you've asked the for loop to count only as long as i is less than 10. Changing the for loop instruction fixes the problem.

```
for (int i = 1; i <= 10; i++)
```

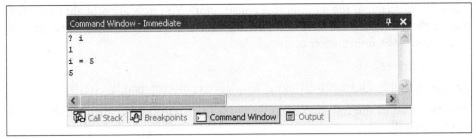

Figure 21-15. Immediate window

Examining Objects

Try a somewhat more complicated example. Create a breakpoint in the first line of the mnuCreateEmployee_Click method. Run the program and choose the second menu choice, "Create Employee." Stop on the breakpoint as shown in Figure 21-16.

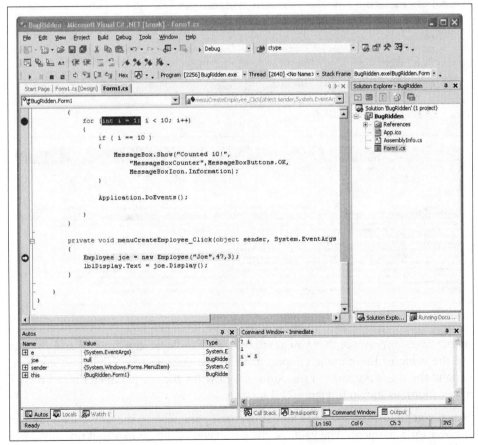

Figure 21-16. Breaking in the event handler

Press F11 to step *into* the method (the constructor). You now are brought to the first line of the Employee constructor. There is much to examine. First, open the call stack window by doing either of the following:

- Press Ctrl+Alt+C.
- Select Call Stack from the Debug/Windows menu commands.

You can examine the call stack from the Stack Frame drop-down menu in the Debug toolbar as well.

Both the Call Stack window (shown in Figure 21-17) and the Stack Frame drop-down menu (shown in Figure 21-18), show the same information: the list of method calls that brought you to this point in the program.

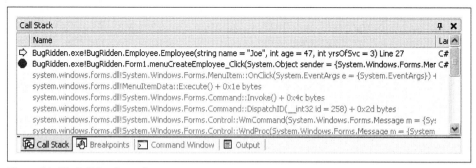

Figure 21-17. Call Stack window

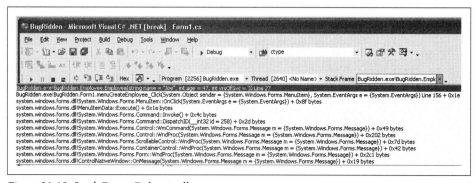

Figure 21-18. Stack Frame Debug toolbar

In any case, you can see that you are now in the Employee constructor, and you can see the value of the parameters passed in to the constructor. While you are here, expand the this parameter in the Autos window (or the me parameter in a VB.NET application), as shown in Figure 21-19.

Before you go further, place the mouse over any parameter to the constructor, and let it hover for a moment. The value of the parameter is shown in a tool tip, illustrated in Figure 21-20.

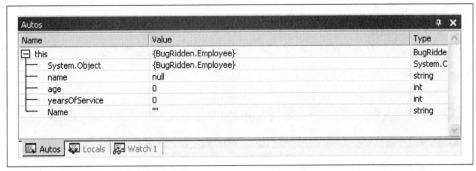

Figure 21-19. Autos window initial values

Press F10 to step into the constructor, and continue to press F10 two more times to set the member variable name and age.

Figure 21-20. Tool tip shows values

Autos window

The *Autos window* shows all the variables used in the current statement and the previous statement, displayed in a hierarchical table. To open the Autos window, do any of the actions described in the list shown next.

- Press Ctrl+Alt+V, followed by A.
- Select Autos from the Debug/Windows menu commands.
- Click on the Windows icon of the Debug toolbar and select Autos.

The Autos window is shown in Figure 21-21.

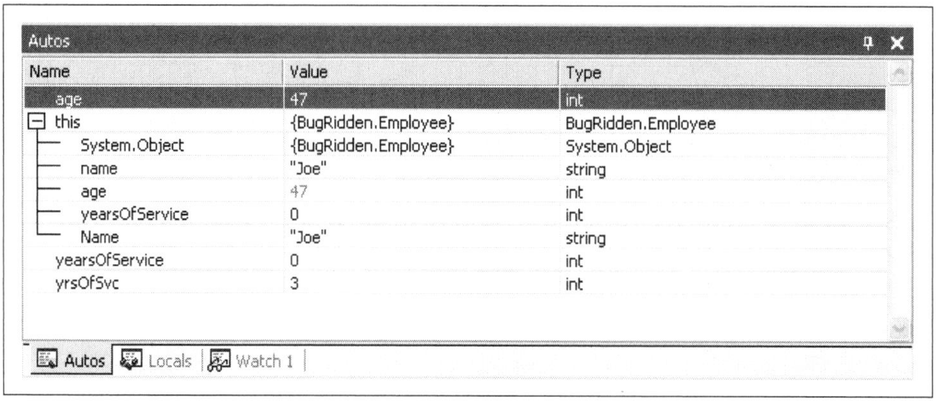

Figure 21-21. Autos window

You will find columns for the Name of the object, its Value, and its Type. A plus sign next to an object indicates that it has child objects that are not displayed; a minus sign indicates that its child objects are visible. Clicking on a plus symbol expands the tree and shows all children, while clicking on a minus symbol contracts the tree and displays only the parent.

You can select and edit the value of any variable. Any changed value displays as red in the Autos window. Any changes to values take effect immediately.

Locals window

The *Locals window* is the same as the Autos window, except that it shows variables local to the current context. By default, the current context is the method or function containing the current execution location.

To open a Locals window, do any of the following:

- Press Ctrl+Alt+V, L. (Press and hold Ctrl+Alt+V, release all three keys, and then press L.)
- Select Locals from the Debug/Windows menu commands.
- Click on Windows icon of the Debug toolbar and select Locals.

This/Me window

The C# *This window* and the VB.NET *Me window* are exactly the same as the Autos window, except that they show all objects pointed to by this in C# and Managed C++ and by Me in VB.NET.

To open a This/Me window, do any of the following:

- Press Ctrl+Alt+V, T.(Press and hold Ctrl+Alt+V, release all three keys, then press T.)
- Select This or Me from the Debug/Windows menu commands.
- Click on the Windows icon of the Debug toolbar; select This or Me.

Watch window

The *Watch window* is the same as the Autos window, except that it shows only variables, properties, or expressions that you enter into the Name field in the window or drag from another window. The advantage to using a Watch window is that it lets you watch objects from several different source windows simultaneously and watch objects that might otherwise not be displayed (e.g., expressions, etc.). This overcomes the inability to add object types other than the specified type to any other debug window.

To open a Watch window, do any of the following:

- Press Ctrl+Alt+W, followed by n, where n is either 1, 2, 3, or 4.
- Select Watch from the Debug/Windows menu commands.
- Click on the Windows icon of the Debug toolbar and select Watch.

In addition to typing in the name of the object you want to watch, you can drag-and-drop variables, properties, or expressions from a Code window. Select the object in the code that you want to put in the Watch window, and then drag it to the Name field in the open Watch window.

You can also drag-and-drop objects from any of the following windows into the Watch window:

- Locals
- Autos
- This/Me
- Disassembly

To drag something from one of these windows to the Watch window, both the source window and the Watch window must be open. Highlight a line in the source window, and then drag it down over the Watch tab. The Watch window will come to the foreground. Continue dragging the object to an empty line in the Watch window.

Threads window

The *Threads window* lets you examine and control threads in the program you are debugging. Threads are sequences of executable instructions. Programs can be either single-threaded or multithreaded. The topic of threading and multiprocess programming is beyond the scope of this book. For a complete discussion of threading, see *Programming C#*, Third Edition, or *Programming Visual Basic .NET*, Second Edition, both by Jesse Liberty (O'Reilly).

To open a Threads window, do any of the following:

- Press Ctrl+Alt+H.
- Select Threads from the Debug/Windows menu commands.
- Click on the Windows icon of the Debug toolbar and select Threads.

Modules window

The *Modules window* lets you examine the *.exe* and *.dll* files that are used by the program being debugged. To open a Modules window, do any of the following:

- Press Ctrl+Alt+U.
- Select Modules from the Debug/Windows menu commands.
- Click on the Windows icon of the Debug toolbar and select Modules.

A modules window is shown in Figure 21-22.

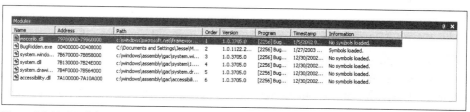

Figure 21-22. Modules window

By default, the modules are shown in the order in which they were loaded. You can resort the table by clicking on any column header.

Disassembly window

The *Disassembly window* shows the current program in assembly code. If you are debugging managed code, such as code from VB.NET, C#, or Managed C++, this window will correspond to the Just In Time compiled code.

A Disassembly window is shown in Figure 21-23.

Unlike the previous several windows, the Disassembly window displays as a tabbed item and as part of the main Source code window. You can set breakpoints anywhere

---

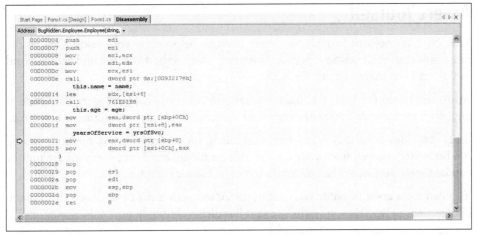

Figure 21-23. Disassembly window

in the window, as you can for any other Source code window. To open a Disassembly window, do any of the following:

- Press Ctrl+Alt+D.
- Select Disassembly from the Debug/Windows menu commands.
- Click on the Windows icon of the Debug toolbar and select Disassembly.

Registers window

The *Registers window* lets you examine the contents of the microprocessor's registers. Values that have recently changed are displayed in red. To open a Registers window, do any of the following:

- Press Ctrl+Alt+G.
- Select Registers from the Debug/Windows menu commands.
- Click on Windows icon of the Debug toolbar and select Registers.

You can select which pieces of information to view by right-clicking anywhere in the Registers window and clicking on the information you would like displayed.

Memory windows

Four *Memory windows* are available for viewing memory dumps of large buffers, strings, and other data that will not display well in any other window. To open a Memory window, do any of the following:

- Press Ctrl+Alt+M followed by n, where n is either 1, 2, 3, or 4.
- Select Memory from the Debug/Windows menu commands.
- Click on the Windows icon of the Debug toolbar and select Memory.

Assert Yourself

The .NET framework provides a Debug class to help debug your code. One of the most powerful methods in this class is Assert. This method is static and returns void in C#, and is a shared sub in VB.NET.

An Assert statement both documents what you believe is happening in your code at any given moment and forces an error and notification if that assumption is incorrect.

.NET provides both a Debug.Assert statement and a Trace.Assert method. Debug methods are removed from your code in release mode, but Trace methods are not (or can be toggled on and off from configuration files (see Chapter 22).

You can see a good (if contrived) use of the Assert statement by adding a third menu choice, "menuTestDivsion," whose event handler is shown here:

```
private void menuTestDivision_Click(
    object sender, System.EventArgs e)
{
    Employee joe = new Employee("Joe",47,5);
    Double pctgOfLife = joe.Age / joe.YearsOfService;
    lblDisplay.Text =
        joe.Name +
        " has worked here for " +
        pctgOfLife + "% of his life!";
}
```

When you run this code and choose the Test Division menu choice, you learn that Joe has worked at the company for 9 percent of his life. What happens, however, if the value passed in as years of service is 0. You will then divide 47 by 0, which is illegal, and your program will crash.

The right approach is to test for zero years of service, and if it is found, to skip the division. Assume for a moment, however, that you have other code that prohibits creating a user with zero years of service. Is it now safe to proceed with the division? In theory, yes. But to quote Pat Johnson one more time, "In theory, theory and practice are the same, but in practice they never are."

To ensure that your assumptions are correct, you may want to assert that the years of service cannot be zero. Do so by using the Debug.Assert method with up to three arguments. The first argument is mandatory: the condition you wish to assert:

```
private void menuTestDivision_Click(
    object sender, System.EventArgs e)
{
    Employee joe = new Employee("Joe",47,0);
    Debug.Assert(joe.YearsOfService != 0);
```

If you run this code, when the Assert fails (as it will in this case), you are presented with an Assertion failure window, shown in Figure 21-24, which provides a stack trace and the ability to ignore the failure, retry the condition, or abort the program.

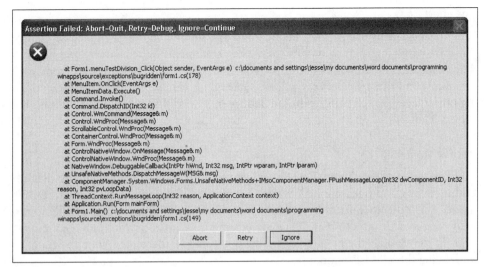

Figure 21-24. Assertion failure

You are free to add two more parameters: a short string and a longer description:

```csharp
Debug.Assert(joe.YearsOfService != 0,
    "Age can not be zero!",
    "It was expected that the age of an employee could never be zero");
```

If you do, the Assert window will display this additional information, as shown circled in Figure 21-25.

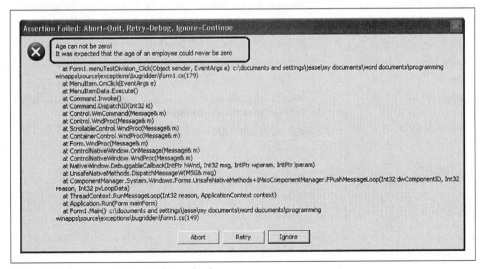

Figure 21-25. Assert failed—additional information

Side effects

When using Debug statements, take care to not set any values or otherwise change the state of your program within the Assert statement. When you recompile into Release mode, the Debug Assertions and other statements are removed from your programs, and these side effects will be removed as well, which can result in confusing bugs ("every time I put this in the debugger, it works fine, but when I release the code...").

Trace versus Debug

The key difference between Trace and Debug is that Trace is enabled (by default) both in debug and release mode, while Debug is enabled (by default) only in Debug mode. This difference allows you to decide what debugging statements make it into your release code. (Note that Trace statements take up room in your release code even if you disable them, unless you do not compile them into your program by undefining the TRACE symbol.)

Trace and Debug methods

The Trace and Debug classes have many useful methods in addition to Assert. Each method is static and void (in C#) or shared sub in VB.NET. The most important methods are listed in Table 21-4.

Table 21-4. Trace and Debug methods

Method	Description
Assert	Overloaded. Tests a condition and displays a message.
Fail	Like Assert but doesn't test a condition—just displays a message.
Indent	Increases the indentation level in the output by one (for organizing output).
Unindent	Decreases the indentation level by one.
Write/WriteLine	Overloaded method that writes extensive debug information to the listeners in the Listeners collection. WriteLine version adds a new line at the end.
WriteIf/WriteLineIf	Like Write, but writes only if a condition is met.

Listeners

A powerful alternative to displaying error messages isl capturing errors to log files. To do this you will need to add a Listener to your program.

Listeners can listen to both Debug and Trace classes. You will find three types of predefined listeners:

TextWriterListener
> Redirects its output to an instance of the TextWriter class or to any Stream class. This listener can also write to the console or to a file because both are Stream objects.

EventLogListener

Emits Write/WriteLine messages to an Event log.

DefaultTraceListener

Emits Write and WriteLine messages to the OutputDebugString and to the Debugger.Log method. If you want a listener besides (or instead of) the Default-TraceListener to receive Debug and Trace output, you must explicitly add it to the Listeners collection.

For example, you can change the Test Division code to write to a custom log with these lines of code:

```csharp
private void menuTestDivision_Click(
    object sender, System.EventArgs e)
{
    Employee joe = new Employee("Joe",47,0);

    Trace.Listeners.Clear( ); // clear all listeners
    Trace.Listeners.Add(new EventLogTraceListener("BugRiddenLog"));

    Debug.Assert(joe.YearsOfService != 0,
        "Age can not be zero!",
        "It was expected that the age of an employee could never be zero");
    if ( joe.YearsOfService != 0 )
    {
        Double pctgOfLife = joe.Age / joe.YearsOfService;
        lblDisplay.Text =
            joe.Name +
            " has worked here for " +
            pctgOfLife + "% of his life!";
    }
}
```

Notice that you've encased the actual division in a test so you do not fire an exception. When you run this code, nothing appears to happen. To see the actual log, go to Start → AdministrativeTools → EventViewer and click on ApplicationLog. You'll find an entry with a source of BugRiddenLog, and if you double-click on it, you'll find your log entry, as shown in Figure 21-26.

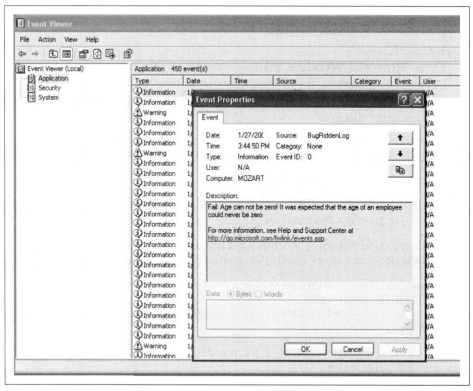

Figure 21-26. Event log

CHAPTER 22

Configuration and Deployment

No software project is complete until it is properly configured and deployed on the end user's machine. Deploying and configuring Windows applications has, historically, been very difficult. One of .NET's great strengths is its easy configuration and deployment.

Configuration of .NET applications involves XML configuration files that provide a flexible and hierarchical configuration scheme. Configuration settings can apply to every application on the machine or to specific applications.

.NET's deployment is perhaps its greatest improvement over previous generations of development environments:

- DLL's only need be located in a specific directory to be visible to an application (XCOPY installation).
- No registration of objects is required for an application to use the contents of a DLL, either in the Registry or elsewhere. Installation does not require the registration of components with *regsvr32* or any other utility, though some globally available components may be placed in the Global Assembly Cache.
- There are no versioning issues with conflicting DLLs.

All these improvements are discussed in this chapter. In the meantime, shout it from the rooftops: "No more DLL Hell!"

Class Hierarchy

Figure 22-1 shows the hierarchical structure of the classes discussed in this chapter.

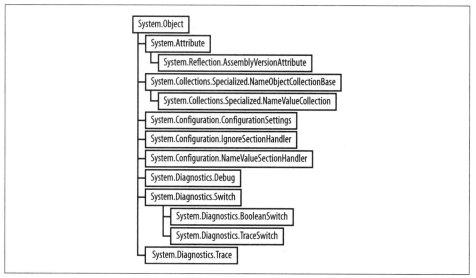

Figure 22-1. Class hierarchy for controls covered in this chapter

Configuration

The .NET Framework provides a powerful and flexible means of configuring applications. This configuration is accomplished by using text-based XML configuration files. The machine-wide configuration file is called *machine.config* (described later). This file is supplemented by application-specific configuration files, also described shortly.

This configuration scheme offers the following advantages:

- The XML files that control the configuration can be edited with any standard text editor or XML parser. It is not necessary to use special configuration tools, although the .NET Framework does include a graphical configuration tool.

- Since the configuration is accomplished with text files, it is easy to administer remotely. Files can be created or edited on a development machine, and then copied into place via FTP or remote network access by anyone with security clearance.

- The system is *hierarchical*. Each application inherits a baseline configuration from *machine.config*. The application configuration file then applies successive configuration attributes and parameters.

- A corollary of the hierarchical nature of the system is that each application can have its own independent configuration. Applications do not need to share a machine-wide configuration.

- The system is *extensible*. The baseline system provides configurability to a large number of standard program areas. In addition, you can add custom parameters, attributes, and section handlers, as required by your application.

- The configuration settings for each application are computed at load time, using all the relevant hierarchical configuration files, if they exist. Changes made to any configuration files after the program begins execution will not take effect until the program is terminated and restarted.

 This last point is distinctly different from the way that ASP.NET web applications are configured. ASP.NET automatically detects whether any configuration files anywhere in the hierarchy are modified, recomputes and re-caches the configuration settings accordingly, and transparently starts a new application domain. For a complete discussion of configuration of ASP.NET applications, see our book *Programming ASP.NET* (O'Reilly).

Hierarchical Configuration

The configuration system is hierarchical—configuration files are applied in successive order. Unlike many hierarchies, and unlike ASP.NET configuration, this hierarchy does not have any parallel branches—only levels.

A file called *machine.config* is at the top of the hierarchy. This file is contained in the subdirectory:

```
c:\windows\Microsoft.NET\Framework\version number\CONFIG
```

where *version number* will be replaced with the version of the .NET runtime installed on your machine, such as v1.1.4322.

The next level in the configuration hierarchy has publisher policy files. These files are provided by the publisher of an assembly and are associated with a specific version of a specific assembly. They apply to all managed applications that call that assembly's version. Their purpose is to redirect requests for older versions of an assembly to the new version. The creation and use of publisher configuration policy files is obscure and beyond the scope of this book (see the integrated documentation from Microsoft for details).

The bottom level of the configuration hierarchy is the application-specific configuration file, named after the application executable with an additional extension of *.config*, and located in the same directory as the executable file. For example, if an application executable file is called *SomeApp.exe*, the configuration file associated with that application will be *SomeApp.exe.config*.

As discussed in the section "Deployment," later in this chapter, Visual Studio .NET can build either a Debug or a Release version of an application (or a custom version). If you build a debug or release version in C#, VS.NET will output to a subdirectory of the project called *bin\Debug* or *bin\Release*, respectively. (When using VB.NET, both Debug and Release versions of the output go to the *bin* directory.) Since the application configuration file must be in the same directory as the executable, and with the correct name corresponding to the name of the executable, you must manually create copies of the application configuration file and place one in each output directory.

To avoid this tedious requirement, create a single application configuration file named *app.config* and place it in the project's root directory. In Solution Explorer, add the file *app.config* to the project by right-clicking on the project, selecting Add → Add New Item, and then selecting Application Configuration File. When the project is built, the configuration file will be correctly renamed automatically and copied to the output directory (such as *Debug* or *Release*).

The application configuration files are optional. If there are none for a given application, then the configuration settings contained in *machine.config* will apply to that application without any modification.

Each application executable can have at most a single configuration file. The configuration settings contained in an application configuration file apply only to that application. If an application configuration file contains a setting that is in conflict with a setting higher up in the configuration hierarchy (i.e., in *machine.config*), then the lower-level setting will override and apply to its application.

Security Configuration Files

Hierarchical configuration files also apply security policy. At the top of the security hierarchy is an enterprise security policy file, called *enterprisesec.config*, which applies to all managed code in an enterprise setting. Next in the hierarchy is a file called *security.config*, which contains the machine-wide security policy. Both files are in the same location as *machine.config*. Next are configuration files applicable to specific users of the machine, also called *security.config*, located in:

```
c:\Documents and Settings\user name\Application Data\Microsoft\CLR Security
Config\version number
```

When an application runs, it uses the intersection of permissions granted in all the security configuration files. Successive configuration files cannot increase the permissions granted at another level, but they can decrease the permissions.

These security configuration policy files are best administered by using the .NET Framework Configuration Tool, described later, or the command-line Code Access Security Policy tool (*caspol.exe*).

The application configuration files described here don't meet all the configuration requirements an application may have. For example, you cannot store user settings for multiuser applications here because the config files are per application and not per user. In addition, updating a config file as an application runs requires write access to Program Files, which is normally granted only to users with Administrative privileges. If you want to store per-user configuration settings, use some other technique, such as writing a custom XML file or making a Registry entry.

Configuration File Format

The configuration files are XML files. As such, they must be well formed. (For a description of well-formed XML files, see the sidebar "Well-Formed XML.")

Typically, tag and attribute names consist of one or more words using camel case. Attribute values are *usually* Pascal cased.

> *Camel casing* means that you combine multiple words, with each word except the first capitalized. For example, you might have a tag named myNewTag.
>
> *Pascal casing* is exactly like camel casing, except the first letter is uppercase as well: MyNewAttribute.

Note that not all attributes use Pascal casing:

- true and false are always lowercase.
- Literal strings do not adhere to either camel or Pascal casing—for example, a database connection string, may be specified as `"SERVER=Zeus;DATABASE=Pubs;UID=sa;PWD=secret;"`.
- If the value is the name of another tag in a configuration file, then it will be camel-cased.

The first line in the configuration files declares the file an XML file, with attributes specifying the version of the XML specification to which the file adheres and the character encoding used.

```
<?xml version="1.0" encoding="UTF-8" ?>
```

The character encoding specified here is UTF-8, which is a superset of ASCII. The character-encoding parameter may be omitted only if the XML document is written in either UTF-8 or UTF-32. Therefore, if the XML file is written in pure ASCII, the encoding parameter may be omitted, although including the attribute contributes to self-documentation.

> This first line is an exception to the rule and does *not* have a corresponding closing tag.

Well-Formed XML

XML files must be well-formed, meaning that they must conform to a very specific set of formatting rules to avoid rejection by the XML parser. The rules of well-formed XML include:

- Close All Tags. In well-formed XML, there will always be a closing tag, such as `</appSettings>`. Many tags can be made self-closing by putting the closing forward slash within the tag itself. This makes it well formed. For example:

```
<add key="appTitle"
    value="Programming .NET Windows Applications" />
```

- No Overlapping Tags. Well-formed XML requires that tags do not overlap. For example, the tags in the following line of code overlap the `<i>` tag within the `<b>` tag:

```
<b>This is <i>the year</b>for the Red Sox.</i>
```

This line can be made well formed by avoiding the overlap:

```
<b>This is</b> <i><b>the year</b>for the Red Sox.</i>
```

- Case Sensitivity. XML files are case sensitive.
- Start- and end-tags must have matching cases.
- All attributes are enclosed in either single or double quotation marks.
- All XML files must have a single top-level root. The top-level element in a configuration file must be `<configuration>`. Remember to close it at the end with `</configuration>`.
- Reserved Characters. The only five built-in character entities in XML are:

```
&lt;     <
&gt;     >
&amp;    &
&quot;   "
&apos;   '
```

If any of these characters is used in script, then it must be "escaped" by using the character entity above, or by enclosing the entire script block in a CDATA section. (CDATA is an XML type.)

For more information on well formed XML see *XML in a Nutshell* by Elliotte Rusty Harold and W. Scott Means (O'Reilly).

The next line in the configuration files is the opening <configuration> tag:

```
<configuration>
```

The entire contents of the configuration file, except the initial XML declaration, is contained between the opening <configuration> tag and the closing </configuration> tag.

Comments can bec contained within the file by using the standard HTML comment:

```
<!-- Your comments here -->
```

Comments may be located anywhere within the file except prior to the first line that declares the XML file.

Within the <configuration> tags are two broad categories of entries. They are, in the order in which they appear in the configuration files:

- Configuration Section Handler Declarations
- Configuration Sections

Configuration Section Handler Declarations

The first part of the *machine.config* file consists of handler declarations that are contained between an opening <configSections> tag and a closing </configSections> tag. Each handler declaration specifies the name of a configuration section, contained elsewhere in the file, that provides specific configuration data. Each declaration also contains the name of the .NET class that will process the configuration data in that section.

> This terminology can be very confusing. The first part of the file is enclosed in <configSections> tags, but contains only a list of the configuration sections and their handlers, not the configuration sections themselves. And as you will see shortly, the configuration sections are each contained within tags, but no grouping tag contains all the separate configuration sections, analogous to <configSections>.

The *machine.config* file contains, in the default installation, many configuration section handler declarations that cover the areas subject to configuration by default. (Since this system is extensible, you can also create your own, as described next.)

A typical entry containing a handler declaration is shown in Example 22-1.

> In the original *machine.config* file, the contents of Example 22-1 were all contained in a single line. That line is broken here only for readability.

Example 22-1. A typical configuration section handler declaration

```
<section name="system.diagnostics"
        type="System.Diagnostics.DiagnosticsConfigurationHandler,
        System,
        Version=1.0.5000.0,
        Culture=neutral,
        PublicKeyToken=b77a5c561934e089"/>
```

Despite appearances to the contrary, this <section> tag has only two attributes: name and type. The name is system.diagnostics. This name implies that somewhere else in the configuration file lies a configuration section called system.diagnostics.

That configuration section contains the actual configuration settings, which typically are name/value pairs contained within XML elements, to be used by the application(s). It will be described in detail shortly.

The type attribute has a lengthy value enclosed in quotation marks. It contains:

- The class that handles the named configuration section
- The assembly file (DLL) that contains that class
- Version and culture information to coordinate with the assembly file
- A public key token used to verify that the DLL being called is secure

Each handler need only be declared once, either in the base-level *machine.config* file or in an application configuration file further down the configuration hierarchy. The configuration section it refers to can then be specified as often as desired in other configuration files.

Example 22-2 shows a truncated version of the default *machine.config*.

 Only a small subset of the actual entries in *machine.config* are included in Example 22-2. Also, the type attribute of each entry was edited to remove all but the class, and lines have been broken to enhance the readability.

Example 22-2. Truncated machine.config file

```
<?xml version="1.0" encoding="UTF-8"?>
<configuration>

   <configSections>
      <section name="runtime"
               type="System.Configuration.IgnoreSectionHandler"/>
      <section name="mscorlib"
               type="System.Configuration.IgnoreSectionHandler"/>
      <section name="startup"
               type="System.Configuration.IgnoreSectionHandler"/>
      <section name="system.runtime.remoting"
               type="System.Configuration.IgnoreSectionHandler"/>

      <section name="system.diagnostics"
               type="System.Diagnostics.DiagnosticsConfigurationHandler"/>
      <section name="appSettings"
               type="System.Configuration.NameValueFileSectionHandler"/>

      <sectionGroup name="system.net">
        <section name="authenticationModules"
         type="System.Net.Configuration.NetAuthenticationModuleHandler"/>
        <section name="defaultProxy"
                 type="System.Net.Configuration.DefaultProxyHandler"/>
        <section name="webRequestModules"
                 type="System.Net.Configuration.WebRequestModuleHandler"/>
      </sectionGroup>
```

Example 22-2. Truncated machine.config file (continued)

```
        <section name="system.windows.forms"
                type="System.Windows.Forms.WindowsFormsSectionHandler"/>
    </configSections>

    <!-- use this section to add application specific configuration
         example:
    <appSettings>
        <add key="XML File Name" value="myXmlFileName.xml" />
    </appSettings>
    -->

    <system.diagnostics>
        <switches>
            <!-- <add name="SwitchName" value="4"/>  -->
        </switches>
        <trace autoflush="false" indentsize="4"/>
    </system.diagnostics>

    <system.net>
        <defaultProxy>
            <proxy usesystemdefault="true"/>
        </defaultProxy>
        <webRequestModules>
            <add prefix="http" type="System.Net.HttpRequestCreator"/>
            <add prefix="https" type="System.Net.HttpRequestCreator"/>
            <add prefix="file" type="System.Net.FileWebRequestCreator"/>
        </webRequestModules>
    </system.net>

    <!-- <system.windows.forms jitDebugging="false" /> -->

    <system.runtime.remoting>
        <application>
            <channels>
                <channel ref="http client"
                        displayName="http client (delay loaded)"
                        delayLoadAsClientChannel="true"/>
                <channel ref="tcp client"
                        displayName="tcp client (delay loaded)"
                        delayLoadAsClientChannel="true"/>
            </channels>
        </application>
    </system.runtime.remoting>
</configuration>
```

The first three declarations in *machine.config* are runtime, mscorlib, and startup. They are special because they are the only declarations that do not have corresponding configuration sections in the file.

In Example 22-2, many handler declarations are contained within <sectionGroup> tags, which allows nesting of elements. By loose convention, the name attribute of these tags corresponds to the namespace that contains the handlers. This groups all configuration sections that are handled out of the same namespace.

Configuration Sections

The configuration sections contain the actual configuration data. They each are contained within an element corresponding to the name of the section specified in the configuration section handler declaration. The following two configuration sections are equivalent:

```
<globalization requestEncoding="utf-8" responseEncoding="utf-8" />
```

and:

```
<globalization>
    requestEncoding="utf-8"
    responseEncoding="utf-8"
</globalization>
```

Configuration sections typically contain name/value pairs that hold the configuration data. They may also contain subsections.

machine.config contains, at most, one configuration section for each handler declaration. (Not all handler declarations have a configuration section actually associated with it.) If the handler declaration is contained within a <sectionGroup> tag, then its corresponding configuration section will be contained within a tag containing the name of the <sectionGroup>. This can be seen in Example 22-2 for system.net.

The sections that follow provide a description of each configuration section relevant to Windows Forms contained in the default *machine.config*. Other configuration sections are outside the scope of this book, including system.net, system.web, and system.runtime.remoting.

appSettings

appSettings allow you to store application-wide name/value pairs for read-only access.

The handler declaration for appSettings, shown in Example 22-2 and reproduced here (minus the Culture and PublicKeyToken portions of the type attribute):

```
<section name="appSettings"
        type="System.Configuration.NameValueFileSectionHandler, System" />
```

indicates that the NameValueFileSectionHandler class handles appSettings. This class provides name/value pair configuration handling for a specific configuration section.

As seen in Example 22-2, the appSettings section in the default *machine.config* file is commented out. If it were uncommented, any setting placed here would apply to every application on this machine. More typically, you would add an appSettings section to an application configuration file that would be in the directory of the application you wish to affect.

Example 22-3 shows an application configuration file for a specific application with an appSettings section added to provide two application-wide values. The appSettings section is not contained within any higher-level tag other than <configuration>.

Example 22-3. Application configuration file containing appSettings section

```xml
<?xml version="1.0" encoding="utf-8" ?>
<configuration>
    <appSettings>
        <add key="PubsConnection"
            value="server=YourSrvr; uid=YourID; pwd=YourPW; database=pubs" />
        <add key="Title" value="Programming .NET Windows Applications" />
    </appSettings>
</configuration>
```

This appSettings section would be saved in a configuration file in the same directory as the executable for a given application, and these values could then be accessed anywhere within that application by referring to the static (shared, in VB.NET) App-Settings property of the System.Configuration.ConfigurationSettings class. This App-Settings property is of type NameValueCollection: give it the name of the key and it returns the value associated with that key.

For example, all the sample programs listed in Chapter 15 query the pubs database included with the default installations of SQL Server and Microsoft Access. Each program has the connection string hardcoded into the program, including the SQL Server user ID and password. This is a bad idea for two reasons:

- If either the server or the password is changed, you must locate and update all the code lines in all the applications that use that connection string, and then you must recompile.

- Hardcoding the connection string makes it very unwieldy to do development against a test server and then to deploy the live application against a production server.

Rather than hardcoding these connection strings, the application configuration file shown in Example 22-3 can be included in the application directory, or the high-lighted code from Example 22-3 can be included in *machine.config*. In either case, your code could then refer to the appSettings in lieu of the actual connection string. In C#, you would replace this line of code:

```csharp
string connectionString =
        "server=YourSrvr; uid=YourID; pwd=YourPW; database=pubs";
```

with this line:

```csharp
string connectionString = ConfigurationSettings.AppSettings["PubsConnection"];
```

In VB.NET, you would replace this line of code:

```
dim connectionString as String = _
    "server=YourSrvr; uid=YourID; pwd=YourPW; database=pubs"
```

with this line:

```
dim connectionString as String = _
    ConfigurationSettings.AppSettings("PubsConnection")
```

> Any data included in a configuration file is in plain text, clearly visible to anyone who looks at the config file. Therefore, depending on the projected distribution of your application, it may be a bad idea to use appSettings to hold passwords, unless you encrypt the string in the config file and decrypt it in your application. (Of course, any encryption scheme is potentially breakable to someone with enough time and motivation.)
>
> appSettings work well for secure storage of passwords in ASP.NET applications because the application is hosted on a remote server, and browsers—and hence, users—are blocked from retrieving the config files.

The System.Configuration.ConfigurationSettings class is part of the System.Configuration namespace. Therefore, to use appSettings, you must reference that namespace in your code. Include the appropriate using or imports statement, respectively:

```
using System.Configuration;
```

```
imports System.Configuration
```

system.diagnostics

The system.diagnostics configuration section contains settings relating to the use of the System.Diagnostics Trace and Debug classes in your applications. These classes let you instrument your application for tracing and debugging without having to recompile the code.

To use tracing or debugging, compile the application with the appropriate flag. This process is discussed in the later section "Build Configurations."

The default system.diagnostics configuration section from *machine.config* is shown in Example 22-2; you can also add additional system.diagnostics sections to application configuration files.

The <switches> tags allow you to add switches and set their values, remove a specific switch, and clear all switches. The value of a switch can be tested using the properties of the TraceSwitch and BooleanSwitch classes, and depending on the result, appropriate action will be taken.

The <trace> tag in the default *machine.config* file has attributes to set the values of the AutoFlush and IndentSize properties of the Trace class:

```
<trace autoflush="false" indentsize="4"/>
```

system.net

The system.net configuration section contains subsections that deal with the .NET runtime. These subsections include authenticationModules, defaultProxy, connection-Management, and webRequestModules. These subsections are outside the scope of this book.

system.web

The system.web configuration section contains subsections that configure ASP.NET. For a complete description of these sections, please refer to our book *Programming ASP.NET* (O'Reilly).

system.windows.forms

The default *machine.config* file contains only a single attribute in the system.windows.forms configuration section, and even then the entire single-line section is commented out. It is reproduced here from Example 22-2.

```
<!-- <system.windows.forms jitDebugging="false" /> -->
```

The jitDebugging attribute controls just-in-time debugging, which is disabled by default. Uncommenting this line and setting this value to true enables just-in-time debugging. When just-in-time debugging is enabled, a special dialog box appears when the program crashes, offering the user the opportunity to start one of the installed debuggers.

Visual Studio .NET controls just-in-time debugging independently of the configuration files. Click on Tools → Options → Debugging → Just-In-Time. Two checkboxes enable just-in-time debugging for CLR programs and script programs. By default, these checkboxes are checked.

 For a more complete discussion of JIT debugging, see *Mastering Visual Studio .NET* by Chris Sells, Jon Flanders, and Ian Griffiths (O'Reilly).

system.runtime.remoting

The system.runtime.remoting configuration section contains subsections that control remoting, which is the process of using an object residing in a different process or on a different machine. The details of this configuration section are beyond the scope of this book.

Custom Configuration

In addition to all the predefined configuration sections, you can add your own custom configuration sections. You might wish to add two different types of custom configuration sections:

- Sections that provide access to a collection of name/value pairs, similar to appSettings.
- Sections that return any type of object.

Name/Value pairs

In Example 22-3, you added an <appSettings> tag to store the database connection string. Suppose you wanted to store connection strings for multiple databases, say one called Test (for testing purposes) and one called Content (to hold the production content). A custom configuration section returning a name/value pair would be one way to handle this situation.

The lines of code inserted into a configuration file to accomplish this task are shown in Example 22-4. Adding a custom configuration section that returns a name/value pair requires the following steps:

1. Determine which configuration file you will use to hold the custom section. This file determines the scope, or visibility, of the custom section.

   Adding the section to *machine.config* will make it available to every application on that machine. Adding it to an application configuration file will make the section visible only to that application.

2. Declare the section handler by adding a line to the <configSections> section of the designated configuration file. This tells the CLR to expect a configuration section with the specified name and which class and assembly file to use to process the section.

   Add the highlighted lines between the <configSections> tags in Example 22-4 to the designated configuration file. If the file you are editing does not already have the opening XML declaration line, the <configuration> tags, or the <configSections> tags, then you will need to add them as well.

   The PublicKeyToken is part of the strong name of the file that contains the NameValueFileSectionHandler class, *System.dll*, supplied as part of the .NET Framework. The value of the PublicKeyToken is copied from a reference to that file in *machine.config*. For a complete discussion of strong names, please refer to the "Strong Names" section later in this chapter.

3. Add the custom section itself to the configuration file. This section consists of the highlighted lines in Example 22-4 containing the <altDB> tags. This custom configuration section contains two entries, one named Test and the other named Content, each with its own value attribute.

Example 22-4. Custom sections in configuration files

```xml
<?xml version="1.0" encoding="UTF-8"?>
<configuration>
   <configSections>
      <section name="altDB"
              type="System.Configuration.NameValueSectionHandler,
                  System, Version=1.0.5000.0, Culture=neutral,
                  PublicKeyToken=b77a5c561934e089"/>
   </configSections>

   <altDB>
      <add key="Test"
           value="SERVER=Server1;DATABASE=Test;UID=YourID;PWD=secret;" />
      <add key="Content"
           value="SERVER=Server2;DATABASE=Content;UID=YourID;PWD=secret;" />
   </altDB>
</configuration>
```

> The lines of code in Example 22-4 are wrapped for readability. The configuration files are sensitive to new line characters, so it is safest to make each line contiguous.

Note that the type in the <section> tag is nearly the same as that provided for app-Settings in the *machine.config* file. It specifies the NameValueSectionHandler class in the *System.dll* assembly file

> The appSettings section handler specified in the *machine.config* file refers to the NameValueFileSectionHandler class, while the altDB section handler created in Example 22-4 refers to the NameValueSection-Handler class, both of which are contained in *System.dll*. The classes seem interchangeable. Only the latter is documented in the SDK as being a member of the System.Configuration namespace hierarchy.

To read the contents of this custom configuration section, use the GetConfig method from the ConfigurationSettings class, as demonstrated in Example 22-5 in C# and in Example 22-6 in VB.NET. These examples create a very simple form with two buttons: one labeled Test and one labeled Content. Clicking on either button displays the appropriate connection string from the configuration file listed in Example 22-4.

> Remember that if the code from Example 22-4 is contained in a stand-alone application configuration file rather than *machine.config*, then that configuration file must have the same name as the program executable with the added extension of *.config*. For example, if the C# version of the program is compiled to *CustomConfigCS.exe*, then the config file should be called *CustomConfigCS.exe.config*.

Example 22-5. Using custom configuration in C# (CustomConfig.cs)

```csharp
using System;
using System.Drawing;
using System.Windows.Forms;
using System.Configuration;              //necessary for appSettings
using System.Collections.Specialized;   //necessary for NameValueCollection

namespace ProgrammingWinApps
{
    public class CustomConfig : Form
    {
        Button btnTest;
        Button btnContent;

        public CustomConfig()
        {
            Text = "Custom Configuration Demo";
            Size = new Size(300,200);

            btnTest = new Button();
            btnTest.Parent = this;
            btnTest.Text = "Test DB";
            btnTest.Location = new Point(100, 50);
            btnTest.Click += new System.EventHandler(btnTest_Click);

            btnContent = new Button();
            btnContent.Parent = this;
            btnContent.Text = "Content DB";
            btnContent.Location = new Point(btnTest.Left,
                                            btnTest.Bottom + 25);
            btnContent.Click += new System.EventHandler(btnContent_Click);
        } //  close for constructor

        static void Main()
        {
            Application.Run(new CustomConfig());
        }

        private void btnTest_Click(object sender, EventArgs e)
        {
            string strMSg = ((NameValueCollection)
                    ConfigurationSettings.GetConfig("altDB"))["Test"];
            MessageBox.Show(strMSg,   "Test Connection String");
        }

        private void btnContent_Click(object sender, EventArgs e)
        {
            string strMSg = ((NameValueCollection)
                    ConfigurationSettings.GetConfig("altDB"))["Content"];
            MessageBox.Show(strMSg,   "Content Connection String");
        }
    }   //  close for form class
}       //  close form namespace
```

Example 22-6. Using custom configuration in VB.NET (CustomConfig.vb)

```vb
Option Strict On
imports System
imports System.Drawing
imports System.Windows.Forms
imports System.Configuration           'necessary for appSettings
imports System.Collections.Specialized 'necessary for NameValueCollection

namespace ProgrammingWinApps
   public class CustomConfig : inherits Form

      dim btnTest as Button
      dim btnContent as Button

      public sub New( )
            Text = "Custom Configuration Demo"
         Size = new Size(300,200)

         btnTest = new Button( )
         btnTest.Parent = me
         btnTest.Text = "Test DB"
         btnTest.Location = new Point(100, 50)
         AddHandler btnTest.Click, AddressOf btnTest_Click

         btnContent = new Button( )
         btnContent.Parent = me
         btnContent.Text = "Content DB"
         btnContent.Location = new Point(btnTest.Left, _
                                    btnTest.Bottom + 25)
      AddHandler btnContent.Click, AddressOf btnContent_Click
      end sub  '  close for constructor

      public shared sub Main( )
         Application.Run(new CustomConfig( ))
      end sub

      private sub btnTest_Click(ByVal sender as object, _
                     ByVal e as EventArgs)
         dim strMsg as string
         strMsg = CType(ConfigurationSettings.GetConfig("altDB"), _
               NameValueCollection)("Test")
         MessageBox.Show(strMSg,  "Test Connection String")
      end sub

      private sub btnContent_Click(ByVal sender as object, _
                     ByVal e as EventArgs)
         dim strMsg as string
         strMsg = CType(ConfigurationSettings.GetConfig("altDB"), _
               NameValueCollection)("Content")
         MessageBox.Show(strMSg,   "Content Connection String")
      end sub
   end class
end namespace
```

The highlighted lines of code in Example 22-5 and Example 22-6 are the calls to the GetConfig method. They are different for VB.NET and C#, and a bit confusing in both.

The GetConfig method takes a configuration section name as a parameter and returns an object of type NameValueCollection. The desired value in the collection is retrieved by using the key as an offset into the collection, using the get property syntax. In VB.NET, a property is retrieved by enclosing the property name in parenthesis, and in C#, the property is retrieved by using square brackets.

In both languages, the code first casts the value returned by GetConfig to type NamedValueCollection. In C#, this is required since that language does not support late binding. In VB.NET, late binding is supported by default, but since Option Strict is turned On in the first line of code in the program (almost always a good idea), this VB.NET program also disallows late binding.

> In Visual Studio .NET, the default for Option Strict is Off. You can change this default by right-clicking on the project in the Solution Explorer and selecting Properties to view the Property Pages (not to be confused with the Properties window). Then go to Common Properties → Build. There are drop-down menus for Option Explicit, Option Strict, and Option Compare. You can also change these for all projects by clicking on Tools → Options → Projects → VB Defaults and setting the values in the drop-down menus.

If Option Strict were not turned on in VB.NET, thereby allowing late binding, you could forego the cast by substituting the following line of code for the equivalent highlighted line in Example 22-6:

```
strMsg = ConfigurationSettings.GetConfig("altDB")("Test")
```

Objects

appSettings and custom configuration sections are very useful. However, they both suffer from the same limitation: they can return only a name/value pair. Sometimes returning an object would be very useful.

For example, suppose you have a standard query into a database. You could store the query string in an appSettings tag, then open a database connection after retrieving the string. However, it might be more convenient to store the query string in a configuration file and then have the configuration system return a DataSet directly.

To do this, add a <section> tag and a configuration section to the designated configuration file, as with the custom section returning name/value pairs, described in the previous section.

> This example is presented only in VB.NET. The C# implementation is essentially the same, with only language syntax differences.

Edit the configuration file used in the previous example and shown in Example 22-4, adding the lines of code highlighted in Example 22-7.

Example 22-7. Returning objects from custom sections in a configuration file

```
<?xml version="1.0" encoding="UTF-8"?>
<configuration>

    <configSections>
        <section name="altDB"
                type="System.Configuration.NameValueSectionHandler,
                      System, Version=1.0.3300.0, Culture=neutral,
                      PublicKeyToken=b77a5c561934e089"/>

        <section name="DataSetSectionHandler"
                type="ProgWinApps.Handlers.DataSetSectionHandler,
                      vbSectionHandlers">
        </section>
    </configSections>

    <altDB>
        <add key="Test"
            value="SERVER=Server1;DATABASE=Test;UID=sa;PWD=secret;" />
        <add key="Content"
            value="SERVER=Server2;DATABASE=Content;UID=sa;PWD=secret;" />
    </altDB>

    <!-- Custom config section returning an object -->
    <DataSetSectionHandler
      str="Select au_id,au_lname + ', ' + au_fname as name from authors" />

</configuration>
```

In a <section> section within the <configSections> section, a handler declaration is created for the DataSetSectionHandler. This declaration specifies that elsewhere within the file, there will be a custom configuration section called DataSetSectionHandler. Furthermore, it specifies that the class handling that configuration section is called ProgWinApps.Handlers.DataSetSectionHandler, and that the class will be found in an assembly file called *vbSectionHandlers.dll*.

The two <section> sections in Example 22-7 differ in that one is self-closing while the other has a closing tag. They are equivalent and you can choose the one you prefer. As a rule, the self-closing tag is self-documenting in that you intend the element to have no contents (nothing between the open and close tags) while the paired tags indicate the opposite. If the element has children, of course, you have no choice but to use a pair of tags.

Further down in the configuration file, you will find a section called DataSetSection-Handler. It has a single attribute, str. This string contains the SQL statement you wish to pass to the database.

Next you must create the ProgWinApps.Handlers.DataSetSectionHandler class and place it in a source file called *DataSetSectionHandler.vb*, which will subsequently be compiled to vbSectionHandlers.dll. To do this, create a VB.NET source code file as shown in Example 22-8.

Example 22-8. Source code for section handler in VB.NET (DataSetSectionHandler.vb)

```
Imports System
Imports System.Data
Imports System.Data.SqlClient
Imports System.XML
Imports System.Configuration

Namespace ProgWinApps.Handlers
    public class DataSetSectionHandler : _
        Implements IConfigurationSectionHandler

    public Function Create(parent as Object, _
                           configContext as Object, _
                           section as XmlNode) as Object _
        Implements IConfigurationSectionHandler.Create

        dim strSql as string
        strSql = section.Attributes.Item(0).Value

        dim connectionString as string = "server=YourServer; " & _
            "uid=YourID; pwd=YourPassword; database=pubs"

        ' create the data set command object and the DataSet
        dim da as SqlDataAdapter = new SqlDataAdapter(strSql, _
                        connectionString)
        dim dsData as DataSet = new DataSet( )

        ' fill the data set object
        da.Fill(dsData,"Authors")

        return dsData
    end Function
    end class
end NameSpace
```

 Be sure to set the connection string to match your specific database.

The database aspects of the code in this example are covered thoroughly in Chapter 19 and won't be discussed here in detail.

At the beginning of the Example 22-8 are several Imports statements (if written in C#, they would be using statements). Next, a namespace is declared to contain the class (to prevent ambiguity when calling the class).

For a class to be used as a configuration section handler, it must be derived from the IConfigurationSectionHandler interface. In VB.NET, this is implemented by using the Implements keyword. (In C#, this would be indicated with a colon between the class name and the inherited interface.)

> A full discussion of the object-oriented concepts such as inheritance, base classes, and interfaces is beyond the scope of this book. For now, you remember that an interface acts as a contract that the implementing class must fulfill. The interface may, for example, dictate the signature of methods the implementing class must implement, or it may dictate which properties the class must provide. For a complete discussion of object-oriented concepts, see *Programming C#* or *Programming Visual Basic .NET*, both by Jesse Liberty (O'Reilly).

The IConfigurationSectionHandler interface has only a single method, Create. Therefore, your implementing class must implement the Create method with the specified signature. The three parameters are dictated by the interface. The first two parameters are rarely used and will not be discussed further. The third parameter is the XML data from the configuration file.

The XML node is parsed and the value of the first item in the Attributes collection of the <DataSetSectionHandler> tag (the str attribute) is assigned to a string variable in this line:

VB
```
strSql = section.Attributes.Item(0).Value
```

Once the SQL string is in hand, the connection string is coded, a SqlDataAdapter object is instantiated and executed, and the DataSet is filled. Then the DataSet is returned.

> You could have also obtained the connection string in Example 22-8 from the configuration file, as demonstrated in Examples 22-3 and 22-4. Leaving the connection string in this class (which will be compiled) has the benefit of hiding it from prying eyes a bit more securely (although nothing is totally secure from dedicated snoops), but it sacrifices the advantages of configuration files mentioned in previous sections.

Before this class can be used, it must be compiled. Open a command prompt by clicking on the Start button, and then Programs → Microsoft Visual Studio .NET 2003 → Visual Studio .NET Tools → Visual Studio .NET 2003 Command Prompt.

Use the cd command to make current the directory that will contain the application. Then enter the following command line:

```
vbc /t:library /out:vbSectionHandlers.dll /r:system.dll,System.data.dll,System.xml.
dll DataSetSectionHandler.vb
```

Chapter 2 explains how to use command-line compilers. Here the target type of the output is set to be library (a DLL). The name of the output file will be *vbSection-Handlers.dll*. Notice that three DLL files are referenced. The input source file is *DataSetSectionHandler.vb*. When the source file is compiled, you will have the output DLL in the current directory, where the classes it contains will be available to the application automatically.

 Rather than creating this DataSetSectionHandler class as a separate source code file and DLL, you could embed the class directly in the application that uses it, obviating the need for the compilation step. Doing so, however, prevents you from reusing the code in multiple applications.

The application shown in Example 22-9 (in VB.NET) shows how to use this configuration section. This is similar to the application seen in Example 15-17 in Chapter 15, modified to get the dataset from the configuration file.

Example 22-9. Section handler demonstration in VB.NET (ListBoxItems-CustomConfig.vb)

```
Option Strict On
imports System
imports System.Drawing
imports System.Windows.Forms
imports System.Data
imports System.Data.SqlClient
Imports System.Xml
imports System.Collections       ' necessary for ArrayList
imports System.Configuration     ' necessary for ConfigurationSettings

namespace ProgrammingWinApps
   public class ListBoxItems : inherits Form

      dim lb as ListBox

      public sub New( )
         Text = "ListBox Items Collection"
         Size = new Size(300,400)

         lb = new ListBox( )
         lb.Parent = me
         lb.Location = new Point(10,10)
         lb.Size = new Size(ClientSize.Width - 20, Height - 200)
         lb.Anchor = AnchorStyles.Top or AnchorStyles.Left or _
                  AnchorStyles.Right or AnchorStyles.Bottom
         lb.BorderStyle = BorderStyle.Fixed3D
```

Example 22-9. Section handler demonstration in VB.NET
(ListBoxItems-CustomConfig.vb) (continued)

```
' get the data to populate the ListBox from pubs authors table
dim ds as new DataSet( )
ds = CType(ConfigurationSettings.GetConfig( _
           "DataSetSectionHandler"),DataSet)

dim dt as new DataTable( )
dt = ds.Tables(0)

dim arlstNames as new ArrayList( )
dim arNames( ) as object
dim dr as DataRow
lb.BeginUpdate( )
for each dr in dt.Rows
  lb.Items.Add( _
        CType(dr("au_id"), string) + vbTab + _
        CType(dr("name"), string))
next

lb.Items.Add("12345" + vbTab + "Hurwitz, Dan")
lb.Items.Add("67890" + vbTab + "Liberty, Jesse")
lb.EndUpdate( )
end sub ' close for constructor

public shared sub Main( )
   Application.Run(new ListBoxItems( ))
end sub

  end class
end namespace
```

The lines of code in Example 22-9 that differ from the original version of the program in Example 15-17 in Chapter 15 are highlighted. An additional namespace, System. Configuration, is imported. Several lines of code from the original program, reproduced here:

```
dim connectionString as String = _
   "server=YourServer; uid=sa; pwd=YourPassword; database=pubs"
dim commandString as String = _
   "Select au_id,au_lname + ', ' + au_fname as name from authors"
dim dataAdapter as new SqlDataAdapter(commandString, _
                                    connectionString)
dim ds as new DataSet( )
dataAdapter.Fill(ds,"Authors")
```

are replaced with the highlighted lines from Example 22-9, reproduced here:

```
dim ds as new DataSet( )
ds = CType(ConfigurationSettings.GetConfig( _
           "DataSetSectionHandler"),DataSet)
```

Rather than supply a connection string and SQL query string, a call is made to the static GetConfig method of the ConfigurationSettings class, which returns a DataSet object directly. Then the DataTable object is extracted from the DataSet. The parameter of the GetConfig method is a string containing the name of the section containing the configuration settings.

.NET Framework Configuration Tool (mscorcfg.msc)

This discussion about configuration has shown the actual configuration files that you can edit with any text editor or from within Visual Studio .NET. You can avoid some of the manual editing of standard config sections within configuration files by using the .NET Framework Configuration tool, *mscorcfg.msc*.

The .NET Framework Configuration tool, shown in Figure 22-2, is a Microsoft Management Console snap-in. It can be accessed by going to Control Panel and selecting Administrative Tools, and then Microsoft .NET Framework Configuration.

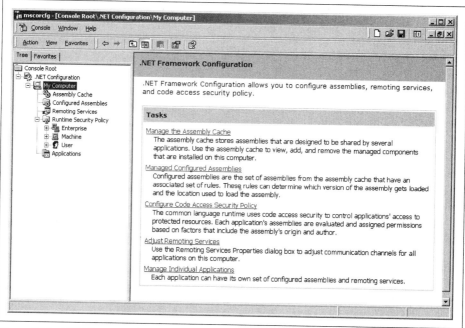

Figure 22-2. .NET Framework Configuration tool (mscorcfg.msc)

 Having the .NET Configuration Tool available from within Visual Studio .NET is often convenient. It is easy to add it to the Tools menu. In Visual Studio .NET, click on Tools → External Tools. Click on the Add button of the External Tools dialog box. Change the default tool name from [New Tool 1] to .NET Config Tool. In the Command field, enter mmc.exe. In the Arguments field, enter:

```
c:\windows\microsoft.net\framework\version number\mscorcfg.
msc.
```

where *version number* is the version directory on your machine.

Most configuration handled by this tool involves assemblies.

Assemblies

All files that comprise a .NET application are gathered into one or more *assemblies*. Assemblies are the basic unit of .NET programming. They appear to the user as dynamic link library (DLL) files or an executable (EXE) file. (DLLs contain classes and methods that are linked into an application at runtime as needed.)

Assemblies also contain versioning information. An assembly is the minimum unit for a single version of a piece of code. Multiple versions of the same code can run side by side in different applications, with no conflicts, by packaging the different versions into separate assemblies and specifying which version is allowed in the configuration files.

Assemblies can contain one or more files. The constituent files in an assembly are portable executable files such as EXEs or DLLs.

Microsoft Intermediate Language (MSIL)

When a .NET application is compiled into an executable file, that file does not contain machine code (unless it was compiled with the Managed C++ compiler), as is the case with most other language compilers. Instead, the compiler output is a language known as Microsoft Intermediate Language (MSIL), or IL for short. When the program is run, the .NET Framework calls a Just-In-Time (JIT) compiler to compile the IL into machine code, which is then executed. The JITed machine code is cached on the machine, so there is no need to recompile with every execution.

In theory, a program will produce the same IL code if written with any .NET compliant language. While this is not always true in practice, it is fair to say that for all practical purposes, all the .NET languages are equivalent. This is evident from the examples in this book that are presented in both C# and VB.NET.

Using IL offers several advantages. First, it allows the JIT compiler to optimize the output for the platform. As of this writing, the .NET platform is supported on Windows environments running on Intel Pentium-compatible processors, and the .NET Compact Framework runs on ARM processors. It is not a stretch to imagine the Framework being ported to other operating environments, such as Linux or Mac OS, or other hardware platforms. Even more likely, as new generations of processor chips become available, Microsoft could release new JIT compilers that detect the specific target processor and optimize the output accordingly.

The second major advantage of an IL architecture is that it enables the language-neutral nature of the .NET Framework. Language choice is no longer dictated by the capabilities of one language over another, but by the preferences of the developer or the team. It is even possible to mix languages in a single application. A class written in C# can be derived from a VB.NET class, and an exception thrown in a C# method can be caught in a VB.NET method.

A third advantage is that the CLR can analyze code to determine compliance with requirements such as type safety. Things like buffer overflows and unsafe casts can be caught and disallowed, greatly enhancing security and stability.

ILDASM

It is possible to examine the contents of a compiled .NET EXE or DLL by using Intermediate Language Disassembler (ILDASM), a tool provided as part of the .NET SDK. ILDASM parses the contents of the file, displaying its contents in human-readable format. It shows the IL code, as well as namespaces, classes, methods, and interfaces.

 Although it is often useful to look at the IL code generated by a .NET compiler, IL code is beyond the scope of this book. For details on IL programming, we recommend *CIL Programming: Under the Hood of .NET* by Jason Bock (APress).

This useful tool is not installed as part of any menu, either on the Start menu or inside Visual Studio .NET, although it can be added to either. To run ILDASM, open a .NET command line by clicking the Start button, and then Programs → Microsoft Visual Studio .NET 2003 → Visual Studio .NET Tools → Visual Studio .NET 2003 Command Prompt. Then enter:

```
ildasm
```

to open the program. Click on File → Open to open the file you wish to look at or drag the file from Windows Explorer onto the ILDASM window. Alternatively, enter:

```
ildasm <full path>\<appname>
```

where the full path (optional if the *exe* or *dll* is in the current directory) and name of the *exe* or *dll* is given as an argument. In either case, you will get something similar to that shown in Figure 22-3. You can click on the plus sign next to each node in the tree to expand that node, and then drill down through the file.

In Figure 22-3, the examined file is called *csConfigDeploy.exe*. You can see that it has a Manifest (described later in the section "Manifests"), there is a namespace called csConfigDeploy containing a class called Form1, and Form1 contains several fields and methods.

The icons used in ILDASM are listed in Table 22-1. The colors in which the icons are displayed are also listed.

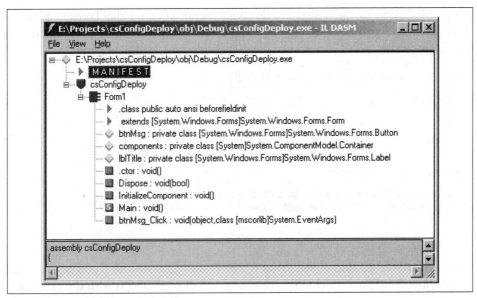

Figure 22-3. ILDASM

Table 22-1. ILDASM icons

Icon	Description
	Namespace (blue icon with red top edge)
	Class (blue icon)
	Interface (blue icon with yellow letter I)
	Value class (yellow icon)
	Enum (yellow icon with purple letter E)
	Method (pink icon)
	Static method (pink icon with yellow letter S)
	Field (aqua icon)
	Static field (aqua icon with dark blue letter S)
	Event (green icon)
	Property (red icon)
	Manifest or class info item (red icon)

To add ILDASM to the Visual Studio .NET menu, click on the Tools → External Tools menu item. You will get the External Tools dialog box. Click on the Add button, fill in the fields with the values shown in Table 22-2, and then click OK.

Table 22-2. Adding ILDASM to Visual Studio .NET

Field	Value
Title	ILDASM
Command	C:\Program Files\Microsoft Visual Studio .NET 2003\SDK\v1.1\Bin\ildasm.exe[a]
Arguments	$(TargetPath)

[a]The exact location of *ILDASM.exe* may vary from installation to installation. It may be necessary to search for the file on your specific machine.

The Initial Directory field can be left blank.

Now when you go into Visual Studio .NET and click on the Tools menu item, ILDASM will be listed. Clicking on that item will open ILDASM with the executable from the current project. If you also want to open ILDASM without any file, add another external tool entry with a different Title (say "ILDASM - No file"), and leave the Arguments field blank.

Modules

A module is a unit of code that can be loaded and run by the CLR. All assemblies contain at least one, although it is possible for an assembly to contain multiple modules. Modules are compiled from your source code, by using the language-specific command-line compiler or the Build command in Visual Studio .NET. To be deployed, a module must be contained within an assembly.

 Assemblies created in Visual Studio .NET always contain only a single module, unless you are using Managed C++. To create multimodule assemblies in C# or VB.NET, you must compile from the command line. Multimodule assemblies will be discussed more fully in the later section "Single- and Multimodule Assemblies."

Modules use a format that is an extension of the Windows Portable Executable (PE) format. This format applies to DLLs and EXEs, files that may be linked together at runtime to form an executable program. All PE files contain a field that is the location of the code to jump to when the operating system loads the executable. .NET modules don't actually contain any executable code, but contain intermediate language (IL) code, described previously. This IL code must be compiled at runtime by the CLR just-in-time (JIT) compiler. Hence, the location of the code to jump to is inside the CLR, which calls the JIT compiler, and then that JITed code is executed.

Manifests

Assemblies in .NET are self-describing: they contain *metadata*, which describe the files contained in the assembly and how they relate to one another (references to types, for example), version and security information relevant to the assembly, and dependencies on other assemblies. This metadata is contained in the *assembly manifest*. Each assembly must have exactly one assembly manifest. Each module has its own *module manifest*, which contains the metadata pertaining only to that module.

Looking back at Figure 22-3, you can see that a manifest in the file. Double-clicking on the manifest in ILDASM brings up a window that displays the contents of the manifest, as shown in Figure 22-4.

Looking at the manifest displayed in Figure 22-4, you can see that several external assemblies are referenced, including System.Windows.Forms, System, mscorlib, System.Drawing, and csConfigDeployLibrary. All except the last one are part of the .NET Framework. This assembly itself is referred to with the following section:

```
.assembly csConfigDeploy
{
    ...
}
```

All of these assemblies have version attributes, and the Framework assemblies also have public key token attributes. Both attributes will be discussed shortly.

Single- and Multimodule Assemblies

Assemblies created by Visual Studio .NET are always single modules contained in a single file with an extension of either EXE for a directly executable file or DLL for a library file. In either case, the manifest is contained within the file.

You can create an assembly that consists of multiple modules, but (at least for now) they must be created from the command line.

> Multimodule assemblies *can* be created in Visual Studio .NET when using Managed C++.

A multimodule assembly might be desirable for several reasons:

- To combine modules written in different languages into a single assembly
- To combine code written by different developers into a single assembly
- To package multiple modules that will always be used together and that must increment version number as a unit

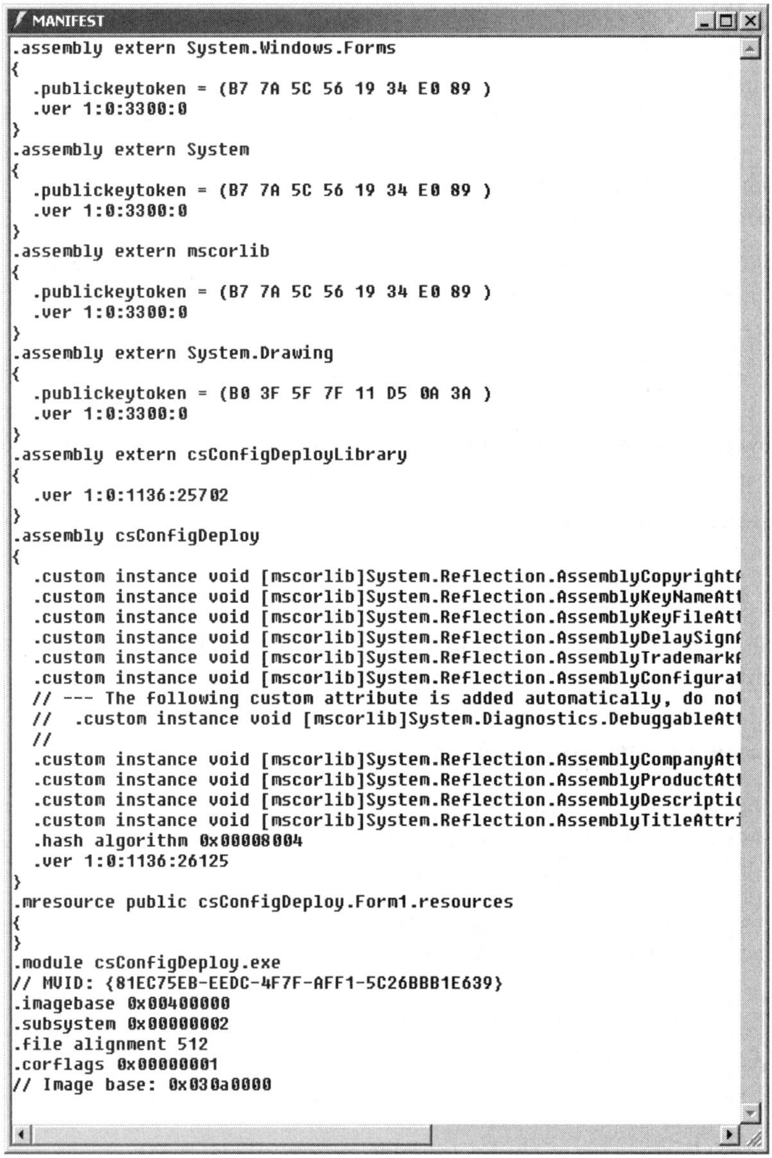

```
MANIFEST                                                        _ □ ×
.assembly extern System.Windows.Forms
{
  .publickeytoken = (B7 7A 5C 56 19 34 E0 89 )
  .ver 1:0:3300:0
}
.assembly extern System
{
  .publickeytoken = (B7 7A 5C 56 19 34 E0 89 )
  .ver 1:0:3300:0
}
.assembly extern mscorlib
{
  .publickeytoken = (B7 7A 5C 56 19 34 E0 89 )
  .ver 1:0:3300:0
}
.assembly extern System.Drawing
{
  .publickeytoken = (B0 3F 5F 7F 11 D5 0A 3A )
  .ver 1:0:3300:0
}
.assembly extern csConfigDeployLibrary
{
  .ver 1:0:1136:25702
}
.assembly csConfigDeploy
{
  .custom instance void [mscorlib]System.Reflection.AssemblyCopyright
  .custom instance void [mscorlib]System.Reflection.AssemblyKeyNameAtt
  .custom instance void [mscorlib]System.Reflection.AssemblyKeyFileAtt
  .custom instance void [mscorlib]System.Reflection.AssemblyDelaySign
  .custom instance void [mscorlib]System.Reflection.AssemblyTrademark
  .custom instance void [mscorlib]System.Reflection.AssemblyConfigura
  // --- The following custom attribute is added automatically, do not
  //   .custom instance void [mscorlib]System.Diagnostics.DebuggableAtt
  //
  .custom instance void [mscorlib]System.Reflection.AssemblyCompanyAtt
  .custom instance void [mscorlib]System.Reflection.AssemblyProductAtt
  .custom instance void [mscorlib]System.Reflection.AssemblyDescriptio
  .custom instance void [mscorlib]System.Reflection.AssemblyTitleAttri
  .hash algorithm 0x00008004
  .ver 1:0:1136:26125
}
.mresource public csConfigDeploy.Form1.resources
{
}
.module csConfigDeploy.exe
// MVID: {81EC75EB-EEDC-4F7F-AFF1-5C26BBB1E639}
.imagebase 0x00400000
.subsystem 0x00000002
.file alignment 512
.corflags 0x00000001
// Image base: 0x030a0000
```

Figure 22-4. Manifest in ILDASM

- To allow the assembly to be updated by updating only a few of the modules as well as the assembly manifest
- To allow the CLR to load only the necessary modules, minimizing impact on resources

On the other hand, it is advantageous to have a single module assembly in other circumstances:

- To provide versioning flexibility, since an assembly is the smallest deployable unit of a single version of code, although each module within a multimodule assembly can also have its own version assigned to it (see the later section "Versioning").
- To optimize deployment performance when deploying the application over the LAN or WAN (see the later section "Deployment").
- For greater simplicity in deployment

To demonstrate both single- and multimodule assemblies, you will create a simple application in Visual Studio .NET comprised of a main EXE and a class library contained in a DLL. Both the EXE and the DLL will be in their own single-module assembly, and the EXE will reference the assembly containing the DLL. Then you will compile the same application from the command line as a monolithic multimodule assembly.

Single-file assemblies

Open Visual Studio .NET and create a new Windows Application in the language of your choice. Name it Deploy.

 Since both C# and VB.NET examples are included, the projects here will be named csDeploy and vbDeploy, respectively. Likewise, the library projects will be named csDeployLibrary and vbDeployLibrary.

Right-click on the Solution in Solution Explorer and select Add and then New Project..., which will bring up the Add New Project dialog box. Click on the Class Library template and name the new project DeployLibrary. You should look at the code window for *Class1.cs* or *Class1.vb*.

In the Solution Explorer, right-click on References in the DeployLibrary project and select Add Reference, bringing up the Add Reference dialog box. In the .NET tab, slide down to locate System.Windows.Forms and double-click on it, which will add it to the Selected Components grid at the bottom of the dialog box. Click OK.

At the top of the code window for *Class1.cs/vb*, add a reference to the System. Windows.Forms namespace. In C#:

x

C#
```
using System.Windows.Forms;
```
and in VB.NET:

VB
```
imports System.Windows.Forms
```

Now add a method to the Class1 class in DeployLibrary called SayHi. This method will be static (shared in VB.NET) and return nothing (void in C# and a sub in VB.NET) and take a single string argument. This method will put up a message box displaying the string argument.

Assemblies | **1139**

```csharp
public static void SayHi(string strMsg)
{
    MessageBox.Show(strMsg, "csConfigDeploy.Class1");
}
```

```vb
public shared sub SayHi(strMsg as String)
    MessageBox.Show(strMsg, "vbConfigDeploy.Class1")
end sub
```

Notice that the MessageBox.Show has a second argument, the message box title, which is hardwired to the name of the class.

The VB.NET version of the project so far should look something like in Figure 22-5.

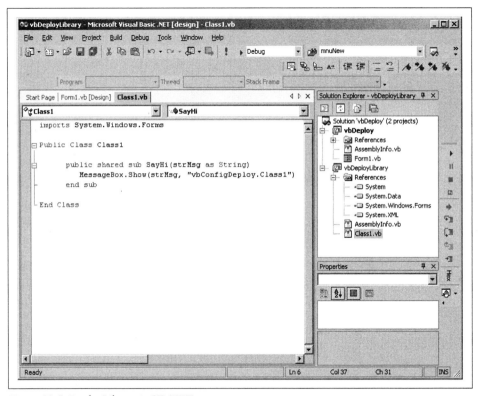

Figure 22-5. DeployLibrary in VB.NET

The C# version will look very similar to the VB.NET code shown in Figure 22-5. The complete C# code listing for DeployLibrary is shown in Example 22-10.

Example 22-10. DeployLibrary in C#

```csharp
using System;
using System.Windows.Forms;
```

Example 22-10. DeployLibrary in C# (continued)

```csharp
namespace csDeployLibrary
{
    /// <summary>
    /// Summary description for Class1.
    /// </summary>
    public class Class1
    {
        public Class1()
        {
        }

        public static void SayHi(string strMsg)
        {
            MessageBox.Show(strMsg, "csConfigDeploy.Class1");
        }
    }
}
```

You can build the DeployLibrary project at this point to verify that there are no build errors.

Now go back to the design view of the first project, Deploy. Drag a button from the Toolbox onto the form. Change the Text property of the button to Message and rename the button btnMsg.

In Solution Explorer, right-click on the References in the Deploy project and click on Add Reference. In the Add Reference dialog box, click on the Projects tab. The DeployLibrary project should be listed in the top half of the dialog. Double-click on it to add it to the bottom half of the dialog, and then click OK.

Double-click on the button on the form, which will create a skeleton for the button click event handler and bring you to the code window. Inside the event handler, enter a single line of code (identical for both languages, except the trailing semicolon in C#):

```csharp
csDeployLibrary.Class1.SayHi("Is this cool or what?");
```

Notice as you type that when you enter the first period, IntelliSense pops up all the classes in the library (there is only one), and as you type the next period, IntelliSense again pops up all the methods, including SayHi.

Now when you run the project, a form displays with a single button. Clicking the button pops up a dialog box with your message, as shown in Figure 22-6.

The complete code listing from Visual Studio .NET (minus the autogenerated comments) for the Deploy project is listed in Example 22-11 in C# and in Example 22-12 in VB.NET.

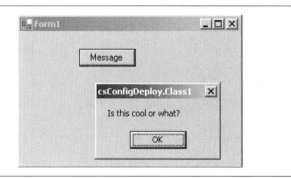

Figure 22-6. Deploy application with message box

Example 22-11. Deploy project in C# (Form1.cs)

```csharp
using System;
using System.Drawing;
using System.Collections;
using System.ComponentModel;
using System.Windows.Forms;
using System.Data;

namespace csDeploy
{
    public class Form1 : System.Windows.Forms.Form
    {
        private System.Windows.Forms.Button btnMsg;
        private System.ComponentModel.Container components = null;

        public Form1( )
        {
            InitializeComponent( );
        }

        protected override void Dispose( bool disposing )
        {
            if( disposing )
            {
                if (components != null)
                {
                    components.Dispose( );
                }
            }
            base.Dispose( disposing );
        }

        #region Windows Form Designer generated code
        private void InitializeComponent( )
        {
            this.btnMsg = new System.Windows.Forms.Button( );
```

Example 22-11. Deploy project in C# (Form1.cs) (continued)

```csharp
            this.SuspendLayout( );
            //
            // btnMsg
            //
            this.btnMsg.Location = new System.Drawing.Point(80, 80);
            this.btnMsg.Name = "btnMsg";
            this.btnMsg.TabIndex = 0;
            this.btnMsg.Text = "Message";
            this.btnMsg.Click += new System.EventHandler(this.btnMsg_Click);
            //
            // Form1
            //
            this.AutoScaleBaseSize = new System.Drawing.Size(5, 13);
            this.ClientSize = new System.Drawing.Size(292, 273);
            this.Controls.AddRange(new System.Windows.Forms.Control[ ] {
                                                this.btnMsg});
            this.Name = "Form1";
            this.Text = "Form1";
            this.ResumeLayout(false);
        }
        #endregion

        [STAThread]
        static void Main( )
        {
            Application.Run(new Form1( ));
        }

        private void btnMsg_Click(object sender, System.EventArgs e)
        {
            csDeployLibrary.Class1.SayHi("Is this cool or what?");
        }
    }
}
```

Example 22-12. Deploy project in VB.NET (Form1.vb)

```vbnet
Public Class Form1
    Inherits System.Windows.Forms.Form

#Region " Windows Form Designer generated code "

    Public Sub New( )
        MyBase.New( )
        InitializeComponent( )
    End Sub

    Protected Overloads Overrides Sub Dispose(ByVal disposing As Boolean)
        If disposing Then
            If Not (components Is Nothing) Then
                components.Dispose( )
```

Example 22-12. Deploy project in VB.NET (Form1.vb) (continued)

```
            End If
        End If
        MyBase.Dispose(disposing)
    End Sub

    Private components As System.ComponentModel.IContainer

    Friend WithEvents btnMsg As System.Windows.Forms.Button
        <System.Diagnostics.DebuggerStepThrough()> Private Sub InitializeComponent()
Me.btnMsg = New System.Windows.Forms.Button()
Me.SuspendLayout()
'

'btnMsg
'
Me.btnMsg.Location = New System.Drawing.Point(96, 88)
Me.btnMsg.Name = "btnMsg"
Me.btnMsg.TabIndex = 0
Me.btnMsg.Text = "Message"
'
'Form1
'
Me.AutoScaleBaseSize = New System.Drawing.Size(5, 13)
Me.ClientSize = New System.Drawing.Size(292, 273)
Me.Controls.AddRange(New System.Windows.Forms.Control() {Me.btnMsg})
Me.Name = "Form1"
Me.Text = "Form1"
Me.ResumeLayout(False)

    End Sub

#End Region

    Private Sub btnMsg_Click(ByVal sender As System.Object, _
                         ByVal e As System.EventArgs) _
                         Handles btnMsg.Click
        vbDeployLibrary.Class1.SayHi("Is this cool or what?")
    End Sub
End Class
```

When this application is run in Visual Studio .NET, the DeployLibrary project is compiled into a DLL and placed in the *bin\debug* directory (for C#; for VB.NET, all outputs go in the single *bin* directory) under the project directory. Looking at that DLL in ILDASM (Figure 22-7), you can see the manifest, Class1, the constructor (.ctor), and the static (Shared in VB.NET) method SayHi.

Drilling down into the manifest, you will see the code listed in Example 22-13, with some of the lines truncated or omitted for clarity. The first two highlighted lines indicate references to external assemblies that are part of the .NET Framework. The third highlighted line indicates that this DLL is an assembly, as you would expect from the way it was built.

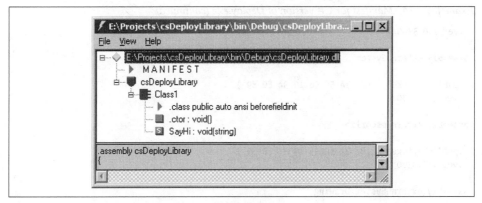

Figure 22-7. C# version of DeployLibrary.dll in ILDASM

Example 22-13. Manifest for C# version of DeployLibrary.dll

```
.assembly extern mscorlib
{
  .publickeytoken = (B7 7A 5C 56 19 34 E0 89 )
  .ver 1:0:3300:0
}
.assembly extern System.Windows.Forms
{
  .publickeytoken = (B7 7A 5C 56 19 34 E0 89 )
  .ver 1:0:3300:0
}
.assembly csDeployLibrary
{
  // lines omitted for brevity
  .hash algorithm 0x00008004
  .ver 1:0:1137:20914
}
.module csDeployLibrary.dll
// MVID: {AB7ACB6E-17F9-4BF1-94BF-0E4DDF9EE8D9}
.imagebase 0x11000000
.subsystem 0x00000003
.file alignment 512
.corflags 0x00000001
// Image base: 0x03090000
```

Likewise, opening *Deploy.exe* in ILDASM and drilling into the manifest reveals the code shown in Example 22-14. This manifest also references several external assemblies, all but one of which are part of the .NET Framework. The exception, csDeploy-Library, is the class library project you created as part of the solution. Again, the last highlighted line of code indicates that *csDeploy.exe* is itself an assembly.

Example 22-14. Manifest for C# version of Deploy.exe

```
.assembly extern System.Windows.Forms
{
  .publickeytoken = (B7 7A 5C 56 19 34 E0 89 )
```

Example 22-14. Manifest for C# version of Deploy.exe (continued)

```
   .ver 1:0:3300:0
}
.assembly extern System
{
   .publickeytoken = (B7 7A 5C 56 19 34 E0 89 )
   .ver 1:0:3300:0
}
.assembly extern mscorlib
{
   .publickeytoken = (B7 7A 5C 56 19 34 E0 89 )
   .ver 1:0:3300:0
}
.assembly extern System.Drawing
{
   .publickeytoken = (B0 3F 5F 7F 11 D5 0A 3A )
   .ver 1:0:3300:0
}
.assembly extern csDeployLibrary
{
   .ver 1:0:1137:20914
}
.assembly csDeploy
{
   // lines omitted for brevity
   .hash algorithm 0x00008004
   .ver 1:0:1137:21381
}
.mresource public csDeploy.Form1.resources
{
}
.module csDeploy.exe
// MVID: {CC84A390-869D-4DD1-91FF-E323812D19EF}
.imagebase 0x00400000
.subsystem 0x00000002
.file alignment 512
.corflags 0x00000001
// Image base: 0x03090000
```

From the foregoing example, you see that Visual Studio .NET creates one single-module assembly for each DLL or EXE, and then references the assemblies in the manifests as necessary. *Deploy.exe* knows to reference *DeployLibrary.dll* because you added a reference in Solution Explorer.

You can verify that the CLR will load the modules only as necessary by running the application in the debugger with the Modules window displayed. (Open the Modules window in the running program by selecting Debug → Windows → Modules.) In Figure 22-8, the module *csDeployLibrary.dll* has not yet been loaded because the button was not yet clicked. As soon as the button is clicked and the code in the event handler is executed, that module will appear in the modules window.

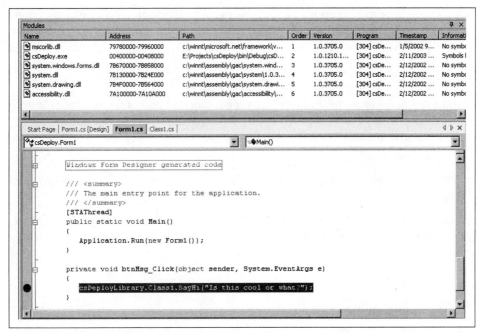

Figure 22-8. Modules window in running application

Multimodule assemblies

Now you will compile the same application as a single assembly containing multiple modules. This cannot be done from within Visual Studio .NET (except when using Managed C++, which will not be covered in this book), but from the command line. It is a multistep process.

> Though multimodule assemblies are rarely used, we've included this section for completeness.

First, you compile each source file into individual modules. (Remember, a module is a unit of code that can be included in an assembly.) Then use the *Assembly Linker* tool (*al.exe*) to combine all the modules into a single assembly, which can be either a DLL or an EXE. To deploy this assembly, you must include all the constituent module files as well as the assembly file.

Preparing the source files. Before you begin, create a new directory to hold all the source code and output files. (It doesn't matter what you call it.) Copy *Form1.cs* or *Form1.vb* from the Deploy project directory and *Class1.cs* or *Class1.vb* from the DeployLibrary project directory to this new directory.

Now some slight modifications need to be made to the source code, which is done easily in a text editor. (All modifications, with one exception, can be made in Visual Studio .NET before you copy the files, since they will not affect the build process in Visual Studio .NET. The exception is the manner in which the SayHi method is called in VB.NET.)

If you work in C#, you must make a very slight modification to the source code from the Deploy project, *Form1.cs*, adding the keyword public to the declaration for the Main method, which is the entry point for the program.

`C#`
```
public static void Main( )
```

In VB.NET, this is not necessary because the entry point, New( ), is already declared as public by default.

If you are working in VB.NET, you must enclose the library class in a namespace. Edit *class1.vb*, adding the highlighted lines from Example 22-15 to the code originally shown in Figure 22-5.

Example 22-15. DeployLibrary with added namespace in VB.NET

`VB`
```
imports System.Windows.Forms

namespace vbDeployLibraryNS
   Public Class Class1
         public shared sub SayHi(strMsg as String)
            MessageBox.Show(strMsg, "vbConfigDeploy.Class1")
         end sub
   End Class
End NameSpace
```

None of the modifications made so far will affect the build of the application in Visual Studio .NET. This next modification will work only when compiling from the command line.

Modify the call to the SayHi method made from the button click event handler within the Deploy project (*Form1.vb*), originally shown in Example 22-12, replacing it with the highlighted code shown in Example 22-16.

Example 22-16. Modified call to library in Deploy project (Form1.vb)

`VB`
```
Private Sub btnMsg_Click(ByVal sender As System.Object, _
                       ByVal e As System.EventArgs) _
                       Handles btnMsg.Click
   vbDeployLibraryNS.Class1.SayHi("Is this cool or what?")
End Sub
```

You must also explicitly add an entry point to the VB.NET form. (In Visual Studio .NET, this is done for you behind the scenes.) Add the Main method listed in Example 22-17 to *Form1.vb*, somewhere inside the class.

Example 22-17. Entry point in Deploy project (Form1.vb)

VB
```
public shared sub Main( )
    System.Windows.Forms.Application.Run(new Form1( ))
end sub
```

Compiling the modules. The source files must be compiled into modules by using the language-specific command-line compilers. The /target: argument (/t: for short) to the compiler specifies the type of output file that will be created. The valid values of this argument were listed in Table 2-1 in Chapter 2. For your purposes here, you will use the /target:module argument to output a module that can be added to an assembly later.

You can specify the name of the output file by using the /out: argument. If the target type is module and the /out: argument is omitted, then the output filename will default to the same name as the source file with an extension of *.netmodule*.

First, compile the library file into a module, and then use the output from that operation to compile the main part of the application into another module. The second module will refer to the library module.

To compile the library file, *Class1.cs* or *Class1.vb*, use the following command line:

C#
```
csc /t:module class1.cs
```

VB
```
vbc /r:system.windows.forms.dll /t:module class1.vb
```

> The C# compiler does not need the references to Framework DLLs in the command-line compile because a file called *csc.rsp* contains "default" references for the C# compiler. There is no equivalent in VB. NET, so the references must be included in the command line.

The result of either command will be a module file with the name *class1.netmodule*.

If you open *class1.netmodule* in ILDASM and drill down to the manifest, you will see that there are no references to itself as an assembly of the form:

```
.assembly class1
```

This verifies that you have created a module that is not yet an assembly. In comparison, if you were to compile the same source code as a library with the following command line:

C#
```
csc /t:library /out:class1.dll class1.cs
```

then open *class1.dll* in ILDASM and look at the manifest—you will see the following section (with some lines truncated or omitted):

```
.assembly class1
{
  .hash algorithm 0x00008004
```

```
    .ver 0:0:0:0
  }
```

which indicates that the DLL is a self-contained assembly.

Drilling down through Class1, you will see the static method (Shared in VB.NET) SayHi, which is present in *Class1.cs* or *Class1.vb*.

Next, compile *Form1.cs* or *Form1.vb* into a module. The command for doing so is similar to the previous command, with the addition of an /addmodule: argument that brings *class1.netmodule* into the picture. Use this command:

```
csc /addmodule:class1.netmodule /t:module form1.cs
```

```
vbc /r:system.dll,system.windows.forms.dll,system.drawing.dll /addmodule:class1.
netmodule /t:module form1.vb
```

 Each command-line command shown here should be entered as a single line without pressing the Enter key until the end.

If you wanted to refer to a pre-existing PE file, such as a DLL or EXE, you would use the /reference: argument. However, *class1.netmodule* is not a PE file. The /addmodule: argument performs the same function for a module. It is necessary here because *form1.cs/form1.vb* makes calls to a method contained in class1.

Again, the output from this command in either language will be a module file called *form1.netmodule*.

Linking the modules into an assembly. The modules created so far can be linked into an assembly using the Assembly Linker tool, *al.exe*. This command has the generic form:

```
al <module name> <module name> ... /main:<method name> /out:<file name> /target:
<assembly type>
```

The module names constitute the source modules that will be linked to the assembly. You can also embed or link resource files as additional source files. The /main: argument specifies the fully qualified method that is the entry point when creating an executable file. The /out: argument specifies the name of the output file. It is the only argument that is actually required. The /target: argument (/t: for short) specifies the type of output file. Valid values are analogous to, but slightly different from, the target values used in the compilers: lib for library file (i.e., a DLL), exe for a console application, and win for a windows application.

For example, enter the following command line (in either language):

```
al class1.netmodule form1.netmodule /main:csDeploy.Form1.Main /out:Deploy.exe /
target:win
```

The /main argument in *al.exe* is case sensitive for both C# and VB. NET. For instance, in the VB.NET example, /main:Form1.Main works, but /main:Form1.main does not.

The result is an executable called *Deploy.exe*, which will be a Windows application. Looking at the output file in ILDASM, you will see only a manifest and a static method called _EntryPoint. The actual IL code comprising the application is contained in the two *.netmodule* files. Looking into the manifest, you will see, among other things, the following lines:

```
.module extern Form1.netmodule
.assembly Deploy
.file Class1.netmodule
.file Form1.netmodule
.class extern public csDeployLibrary.Class1
.class extern public csDeploy.Form1
```

From these lines, you can see that this assembly references an external file called *Form1.netmodule* (which itself references *Class1.netmodule*), *Deploy* is itself an assembly, the two files *Class1.netmodule* and *Form1.netmodule* are required, and the two external classes Class1 and Form1 are referenced. To deploy this application, you must deploy three files: *Deploy.exe*, *Class1.netmodule*, and *Form1.netmodule*.

 If you create an application requiring command-line building and linking, you will find it much easier to put all the commands into either a batch file or a make file.

Versioning

Every assembly can have a four-part version number assigned to it, of the form:

```
<major version>.<minor version>.<build number>.<revision number>
```

Each part of the version can have any meaning you wish to assign. There is no enforced meaning to the first number as opposed to the second, for example. The generally recommended meanings are that the major version represents a distinctly new release that may not be backward compatible with previous versions, the minor version represents a significant feature enhancement that probably is backward compatible, the build number represents a bug fix or patch level, and the revision number represents a specific compilation. Your marketing department may have other ideas, and you can assign any versioning meaning you wish to the parts of the version number.

 Although there is no enforced meaning to the four parts of the version number, the fact that they are ordered from most to least significant is used in the assembly-binding process if you specify a range of versions to redirect. Assembly binding is detailed later.

In Figure 22-4, every assembly has a version associated with it. For example, System. Windows.Forms has the following version attribute:

```
.ver 1:0:3300:0
```

corresponding to a major version of 1, a minor version of 0, a build number of 3300, and a revision number of 0.

Version numbers are part of the assembly's identity. The CLR considers two assemblies that differ only in version number as two distinctly different assemblies. This consideration allows multiple versions of the same assembly to reside side by side in the same application, and even on the same machine.

 Although it is possible to have side-by-side versions of the same assembly in the same application, this is rarely a good idea as a practical matter. You must go out of your way to make it happen.

As you will see shortly, the CLR differentiates between two different types of assemblies: private and shared. The CLR ignores the version number of private assemblies. Adding a version number to a private assembly is for self-documentation (only for the benefit of people perusing the source code or the manifest). However, if an assembly is shared (explained in the later section "Private Versus Shared Assemblies"), then the CLR is cognizant of the version and can use it to allow or disallow the assembly to load, depending on which version is needed.

Versions are assigned to an assembly with assembly *attributes*, either at the top of your main source file or at the top of a separate source file compiled into the assembly.

 Visual Studio .NET automatically includes a file called *AssemblyInfo.cs* or *AssemblyInfo.vb* with every project. This file provides a convenient means of adding or modifying attributes.

Any source file that will include attributes must make reference to the System.Reflection namespace (unless you type in fully qualified attribute names). Include the following using statement:

C#
```
using System.Reflection;
```

VB
```
imports System.Reflection
```

The attribute, or attributes, must be at the top of the source file, after the using/imports statements, but before any class definitions. It looks something like the following:

C#
```
[assembly: AssemblyVersion("1.1.*")]
```

VB
```
<assembly: AssemblyVersion("1.1.*")>
```

Version syntax in manifests uses colons to separate the numbers, while attributes in source code use periods.

The argument provided to the attribute is a string. Although the four parts of the version number have the meanings just described (major, minor, build, and revision), you can use any values you want. To the extent that the CLR checks the version number, it does not enforce any meaning, but compares whether the total version number is equal to, greater than, or less than a specified value, or whether it falls within a specified range.

That said, the Framework does impose some rules, and it provides shortcuts for automatically generating meaningful version numbers.

- If you specify the version, you must specify at least the major revision number—e.g., "1" will result in Version 1.0.0.0.
- You can specify all four parts of the version. If you specify fewer than four parts, the remaining parts will default to zero—e.g., "1.2" will result in Version 1.2.0.0.
- You can specify the major and minor numbers, plus an asterisk for the build. This will result in the specified major and minor numbers, the build will be equal to the number of days since January 1, 2000, and the revision will be equal to the number of seconds since midnight local time, divided by 2 and truncated to the nearest integer. For example, "1.2.*" will result in Version 1.2.1138.28933 if the file was compiled on February 12, 2003 at 4:04:27 PM.
- You can specify the major, minor, and build numbers, plus an asterisk for the revision. This will result in the specified major, minor, and build numbers, plus the revision will be equal to the number of seconds since midnight local time, divided by 2 and truncated to the nearest integer. For example, "1.2.3.*" will result in Version 1.2.3.28933 if the file was compiled at 4:04:27 PM.

Visual Studio .NET defaults the version number in *AssemblyInfo.cs/.vb* with the following line of code:

```
[assembly: AssemblyVersion("1.0.*")]
```

and this line in *AssemblyInfo.vb*:

```
<Assembly: AssemblyVersion("1.0.*")>
```

Private Versus Shared Assemblies

Broadly speaking, there are two types of assemblies: private and shared. A private assembly is used only by a single application, while a shared assembly can be used by more than one application.

A private assembly is located in the application directory (the same directory as the program executable and all the other private assemblies associated with the application). This directory is also known as the *AppBase*, or the application base directory.

Any public member (method, field, or property) contained in a private assembly will be available to any application in that directory, just by virtue of its presence in the directory. There is no need to register the assembly with the Registry, for example, as is the case with COM.

Private assemblies make no provision for versioning. The CLR does not check the version of private assemblies and cannot make load decisions based on version number. From this, it follows that it is not possible to have multiple versions of the same assembly in the same directory. However, different directories can each have their own copy of a given assembly, which may or may not include different versions. The intent here is to allow different applications to have different versions of the same assembly.

COM allows only a single copy of a given DLL on a machine, to be used by all applications requiring that DLL. (Actually, support for side-by-side COM DLL's has been added to Windows XP, but this is a relatively new feature.) When hard disk space was a precious commodity, single copies of each DLL was a laudable, if imperfectly implemented, goal. Now, with very large hard drives making disk space a virtually unlimited resource, it makes sense to allow multiple copies of DLL's, one for each application that needs it. The benefit of this approach is the elimination of DLL Hell, as well as vastly simplified installation and management. The deployment ramifications of private assemblies are discussed later in this chapter in the section "Private (XCOPY) Installations."

DLL Hell is a phenomenon in which the user installs a new program (A), and suddenly a different program (B) stops working. As far as the user is concerned, A has nothing to do with B, but unbeknownst to the user, both A and B share a DLL; unfortunately, they require different versions of that same DLL. This problem disappears with .NET: each application can have its own private version of the DLL, or the application specifies which version of the DLL it requires.

In contrast, a shared assembly can be made available to multiple applications on the machine. Typically, (although this is not a requirement; you can specify an alternative location with a <CodeBase> element in a configuration file, as described shortly) shared assemblies are located in a special area of the drive called the Global Assembly Cache (GAC). The GAC will be discussed in more detail shortly.

There are often reasons for creating a shared assembly other than to share an assembly between applications. For example, to take advantage of Code Access Security (CAS), an assembly must have a strong name (described in the next section), which effectively makes it shared.

Shared assemblies also eliminate DLL Hell because the version of the assembly is part of its identity. An application will either use the version of the assembly it was originally compiled with or the version specified by the version policy contained in a controlling configuration file.

 Of course, nothing prevents a developer from releasing a new assembly with the same version numbers as a previous release. In this circumstance, you will have replaced DLL Hell with Assembly Hell.

Shared assemblies in the GAC offer some benefits over shared assemblies not in the GAC, and shared assemblies generally offer several benefits over private assemblies, although they are much more of a bother to prepare, install, and administer. These benefits include:

- Performance
  - The CLR first looks for an assembly in the GAC, and then in the application's directory.
  - Assemblies stored in the GAC do not need to have their public key signature verified every time they are loaded, while shared assemblies not in the GAC do. However, private assemblies never have their signature verified because they do not have a strong name (described in the next section).
  - The files in a shared assembly in the GAC are verified to be present and neither tampered with nor corrupt when the assembly is installed in the GAC. For shared assemblies not in the GAC, this verification step is performed every time the assembly is loaded.
- Versioning
  - Side-by-side execution, in which an application, or different applications, can use different versions of the same assembly. Remember that private assemblies in different application directories can also be different versions.
  - An application uses the same version of an assembly that it was originally compiled with unless overridden by a binding policy specified in a configuration policy.
  - Applications can be redirected to use a different version of an assembly (allowing easy updating).
- Robustness
  - Files cannot be deleted except by an administrator.
  - All files in a shared assembly are verified to be present and neither tampered with nor corrupted.
  - The shared assembly itself, whether in the GAC or another location, is signed with a public key to ensure that it was not tampered with.

Strong Names

For an assembly to be shared, it must have a *strong name*. A strong name uniquely identifies a particular assembly. It is comprised of a concatenation of:

- The text name of the assembly (without any file extension)
- The version
- The culture
- A public key token

A typical fully qualified name might look like:

```
myAssembly,Version=1.0.0.1,Culture=en-US,PublicKeyToken=9e9ddef18d355781
```

A strong name with all four parts is *fully qualified*, while one with fewer than all four components is *partially qualified*. If the culture is omitted, it can be specified as neutral. If the public key is omitted, it can be specified as null.

The public key identifies the developer or organization responsible for the assembly. Functionally, it replaces the role of GUIDs in COM, guaranteeing that the name is unique. It is the public half of a public key encryption scheme. The token listed as part of the strong name is a hash of the public key.

A public key encryption scheme, also called asymmetric encryption, relies on two numbers: a public key and a private key. They are mathematically related in such a way that if one key is used to encrypt a message, that message can be decrypted only by the other key, and vice versa. Furthermore, it is computationally infeasible, although not totally impossible, to determine one key, given only the other. (Given enough time with a supercomputer, any encryption scheme can be broken.)

Many algorithms are available for calculating hashes. The only two supported by the .NET Framework at this time are the MD5 and SHA1 algorithms. The algorithm used for an assembly is indicated in the manifest by the keywords .hash algorithm, followed by 0x00008003 for MD5 or 0x00008004 for SHA1.

The general principle is this: you generate a pair of keys, designating one as private and one as public. Keep your private key safe and secret.

A hash code is generated for the assembly using the specified encryption algorithm, typically SHA1. That hash code is then encrypted using RSA encryption and the private key. The encrypted hash code is embedded in the assembly manifest along with the public key. (The spaces where the encrypted hash code and the public key go in the manifest are set to zeros before the encryption and taken into account by the encryption program.)

The CLR decrypts the hash code included in the manifest using the public key. The CLR also uses the algorithm indicated in the manifest, again typically SHA1, to hash the assembly. The decrypted hash code is compared to the just-generated hash code. If they match, the CLR can be sure that the assembly has not been altered since it was signed.

Creating a strong name, step by step

Two steps are required to generate a strong name for an assembly.

The first step creates the public/private pair of keys. The .NET Framework provides a command-line tool for this purpose, *sn.exe*. Generate a pair of keys by executing sn with the -k option and the name of the file to hold the keys.

```
sn -k KeyPair.snk
```

 The options passed to *sn.exe* are case sensitive.

Save this file and guard it carefully if you are going to use the keys for providing proof of origin. Make a copy (on diskette or CD) and put it in a secure place, such as a safe deposit box. (If you are just using the keys for testing or as a guaranteed unique identifier, then there is no need for this level of paranoia.) This file contains the private key that you should use for all assemblies created by your organization.

In a large organization where it is not feasible for all the developers to access the private key, you can use a procedure known as delayed signing, explained in the next section.

The second step is to either compile the source code, including the key file, into an assembly, or compile the source code into a module and then link that module (or modules) into an assembly along with the key file.

The most common way to include the key file as part of the compile is to use an AssemblyKeyFile attribute inserted into the source code, similar to the way an attribute was used previously in this chapter to set the version number.

When working with C# in Visual Studio .NET, this attribute is present by default in *AssemblyInfo.cs*, although with an empty string where the key filename would go. Whether in *AssemblyInfo.cs* or in another source file, the following line specifies the location of the key file:

C#
```
[assembly: AssemblyKeyFile("c:\\projects\\KeyPair.snk")]
```

In VB.NET, the AssemblyKeyFile attribute is not included by default in *AssemblyFile. vb*. Add the following line to that file or to the top your source code file if working outside Visual Studio .NET:

VB
```
<assembly: AssemblyKeyFile("c:\projects\KeyPair.snk")>
```

The specified filename should have a fully qualified path so that you can use the same key file for all your projects. If the file does not contain a path, it assumes the current directory.

You can also specify a key file if compiling from the command line in VB.NET (but not in C#) with the /keyfile: option (/keyf: for short). For example:

```
vbc /out:myAssembly.dll /keyfile:keyfile.snk /target:library myAssembly.vb
```

Finally, you can compile modules without specifying a key file, and then include the key file as part of the linking process using the /keyfile: option (/keyf: for short). For example:

```
al myDLL.netmodule /keyfile:"c:\projects\KeyPair.snk" /out:myDLL.dll /target:library
```

If a fully qualified path is not provided for the key file in either the VB.NET compiler or the Assembly Linker, the current directory will be assumed.

> Some software development shops choose not to store the private/
> public key file on disk, deeming it too great a risk. Instead, they store
> the key pair in a hardware device. In this case, everything is done the
> same way as with a normal key file, except you substitute the /key-
> name option for the /keyfile option in the command-line tools, and
> substitute the AssemblyKeyName attribute for the AssemblyKeyFile
> attribute in your source code, where the keyname value refers to the
> name of the device.

Delayed signing

As mentioned earlier, it is imperative that the private key be a closely guarded item. However, this presents a quandary: access to the private key is necessary to create a strong name for an assembly. Creating a strong name is necessary to properly develop and test a shared assembly. However, it may not be prudent to provide the firm's private key to all developers working on the project who legitimately need to create strong names.

To get around this quandary, use *delayed signing*, sometimes called *partial signing*. In this scenario, you create the strong-named assembly using only the public key, which is safe to disseminate to anybody who wants it. Do all your development and testing. Then when you are ready to do the final build, sign it properly with both the private and public keys.

The first step in delayed signing extracts the public key from the key file that contains both the private and public key. This is done from the command line using the sn tool again, passing it the -p option, the name of the key file, and the name of a file that holds the public key. In the following command, only the public key is contained in *PublicKey.snk*.

```
sn -p KeyPair.snk PublicKey.snk
```

If linking from the command line, link the assembly as you normally would, except using the public key file, *PublicKey.snk*, instead of the private/public key file, *Key-Pair.snk*. In addition, add the /delaysign+ option.

```
al class1.netmodule /out:MyAssembly.dll /keyfile:PublicKey.snk /delaysign+
```

The more common way of implementing delayed signing is to add the Assembly-DelaySign attribute to your source code (typically in *AssemblyInfo.cs/vb* if working in Visual Studio .NET), giving it a value of true. Use the following lines of code:

```
[assembly: AssemblyKeyFile("c:\\projects\\PublicKey.snk")]
[assembly: AssemblyDelaySign(true)]
```

```
<assembly: AssemblyKeyFile("c:\projects\PublicKey.snk")>
<assembly: AssemblyDelaySign(true)>
```

In any case, before you can work further with the assembly, you must disable signature verification, again using the sn tool.

```
sn -Vr MyAssembly.dll
```

After your development, testing, and debugging is complete and you are ready to ship the DLL, sign the assembly with the correct private key. This step is usually performed by someone other than the normal developer—someone with access to the private key.

```
sn -R MyAssembly.dll KeyPair.snk
```

The final step is to then re-enable signature verification.

```
sn -Vu MyAssembly.dll
```

One additional useful option of the sn tool is -v, which allows you to verify the assembly, as in:

```
sn -vf MyAssembly.dll
```

This option will tell you whether the assembly is valid.

Global Assembly Cache (GAC)

The Global Assembly Cache (GAC) stores assemblies that need to be available to multiple applications on a machine (i.e., shared assemblies). The GAC is a special area of the directory structure, accessible only to administrators and typically located at *c:\windows\assembly\GAC*.

The contents of the GAC can be seen and manipulated through either a command-line utility, *GacUtil.exe* (described shortly) or a special extension in Windows Explorer, shown in Figure 22-9.

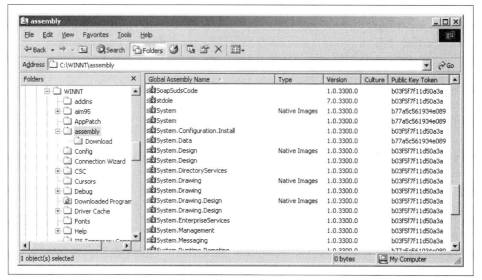

Figure 22-9. Global Assembly Cache in Windows Explorer

Although the contents of the GAC are displayed in Windows Explorer as "normal" files, they are in fact each physically present as a directory.

You can verify this by opening a command window and navigating to *c:\windows\assembly\GAC*. Executing a dir command will show one subdirectory for each assembly contained in the GAC. Drilling further down into one of those subdirectories with the cd command will reveal another subdirectory, this one named after a concatenation of the version, an empty string representing a neutral culture (the culture would go between the two underscores), and the assembly's public key token.

Assuming that an assembly has a strong name, you can add it to the GAC by dragging it from one Explorer window into the GAC Explorer window. Likewise, you can delete assemblies from the GAC in Windows Explorer by selecting it and pressing Delete or by right-clicking and selecting Delete.

Right-clicking on an assembly and selecting Properties brings up the Properties dialog box shown in Figure 22-10 for *System.dll*.

The CodeBase property is the physical location where the assembly came from. For assemblies you create yourself, it would have a value such as *file:///c:/projects/MyApp/MyDll.dll*.

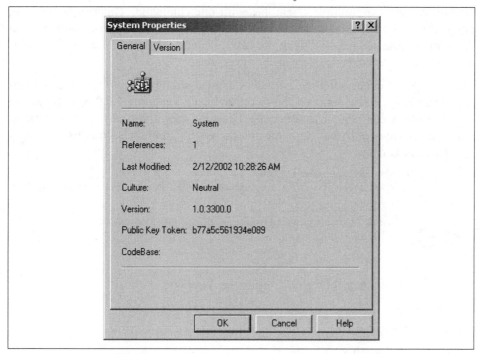

Figure 22-10. System.dll properties in GAC

 You will notice that some entries in Figure 22-9 are of type Native Image. These are assemblies that were pre-JITed into machine code, rather than IL code, using the *Ngen.exe* command-line tool. Native image assemblies may load and execute faster than IL assemblies, although benchmarking is needed in specific cases to verify this. These native image files are contained within the native image cache. For more information about *Ngen.exe*, refer to the SDK documentation.

GacUtil.exe

Assemblies can be added and removed from the GAC by using Windows Explorer, as just described. A command-line utility called *GacUtil.exe* allows the same functionality.

To add an assembly to the GAC with GacUtil, use the /i option.

```
gacutil /i myAssembly.dll
```

To remove an assembly, use the /u option.

```
gacutil /u myAssembly
```

Note that when installing files, the file extension must be included, but when removing the assembly, no extension is used.

GacUtil can remove multiple assemblies with one command. This can be a strong point, if it is your intent, but it can be a disaster if it is not. Suppose you have two different versions of myAssembly in the GAC, Version 1.1.0.0 and 1.2.0.0. The command line shown above would delete both versions.

You can specify either a fully or partially qualified strong name to specifically identify the assembly to be removed. So to remove only Version 1.1.0.0, you could use either of the following two commands. The first uses a partially qualified strong name consisting of only the text name and the version, and the second uses the fully qualified strong name.

```
gacutil /u myAssembly,version=1.1.0.0
gacutil /u myAssembly,version=1.1.0.0,culture=neutral,PublicKeyToken=9e9ddef18d355781
```

 The strong name provided to GacUtil must contain no spaces.

You can list the contents of the GAC using the /l option.

```
gacutil /l
```

Alternatively, you can list a specific assembly by including its name.

```
gacutil /l myAssembly
```

Resolving and Binding Assemblies

When the CLR receives a reference to an object, the assembly containing the object is either already present in memory and bound to the calling application or it must be loaded. *Resolving* an assembly is the process of figuring out whether it needs to be loaded into memory, and if so, which version and from what location. Once an assembly is resolved, the calling application can *bind* to it.

References to an assembly can be either static or dynamic. Static references are hardcoded into an assembly manifest. Dynamic references are constructed at runtime by calling methods such as those from the System.Reflection namespace. For example, a call to the static (Shared in VB.NET) method System.Reflection.Assembly.Load returns an instance of an assembly.

Regardless of whether it is static or dynamic, the CLR goes through the same steps for resolving the assembly reference if it has a fully qualified strong name. These steps are described below. If only the simple name is made available to the calling method, then only the application directory is searched for the assembly, and none of the other steps are performed to try to locate the assembly.

For example, the following line of code loads Version 1.2.10.507 of myNamespace. myAssembly with the French culture and the specified public key token.

```
System.Reflection.Assembly.Load("myNamespace.myAssembly, Culture=fr,
PublicKeyToken=a5d015c7d5a0b012, Version=1.2.10.507")
```

The CLR uses the steps described below to locate this specific assembly. On the other hand, this line of code:

```
System.Reflection.Assembly.Load("myNamespace.myAssembly")
```

causes the CLR to look in the application directory and no further.

 If you want to use a partially qualified name and still have the CLR look in the GAC, then use the System.Reflection.Assembly.LoadWith-PartialName method. Alternatively, use the Load method in conjunction with the <qualifyAssembly> tag in the application configuration file. This allows you to provide the full reference information in a config file rather hardcoded in the application.

The CLR takes the following steps to resolve a strongly named assembly:

1. Use the version policy in the configuration files to determine the correct version to load. A sample version policy is shown in Example 22-18.

   The CLR attempts to bind to the same version of an assembly as the calling application was built with, unless this default behavior is overridden by configuration files imposing a different version policy.

   The CLR first looks at the version policy specified machine-wide in *machine.config*, then at the policy specified in the publisher configuration file (unless the application configuration file specifically says to ignore publisher policy), and then finally in the application configuration file. Each successive configuration file builds on the settings of the previous one.

   Each configuration file can have an <assemblyBinding> element that in turn contains one or more <dependentAssembly> sections, one for each assembly that requires specification.

   Within each <dependentAssembly> section, there is:

   - One <assemblyIdentity> section that specifies each available segment of the strong name

   - One or more <bindingRedirect> sections, which specify which old version, or range of versions, of the assembly should be redirected to use which new version

   - A <publisherPolicy> section that allows publisher policy configuration to be disabled for this assembly

   - A <codeBase> section, described shortly

2. Check to see whether the assembly is already loaded in memory. If it is, that copy is used and no further steps are taken. If the assembly was originally called by another application, then that same copy in memory can be bound to the current application, as with any other Win32 DLL, if it is the correct version and the other parts of the strong name correspond.

3. Look in the GAC for the assembly. If the assembly is found in the GAC, it is used and no further steps are taken.

4. Probe the directory structure using the following substeps:

   a. Look at the location specified by the *codebase* hint. Codebase hints are contained in <codeBase> elements in the configuration files, which specify the URL (which may refer to a location on the Web or to a file on the local or network filesystem) where a specific version of the assembly can be found. A <codeBase> element is the only way to share an assembly other than installing it to the GAC. A strong name is required in either case.

   If a <codeBase> element is used and the assembly is not found at the specified location, an exception is raised and the search stops.

   b. If there is no matching <codeBase> element in any configuration file, then it uses the directories specified in the <privatePath> attribute of the <probing> element of the configuration file to build the tree of subdirectories to search. The directories specified are all subdirectories of the application directory, or AppBase. Only subdirectories specified in the <privatePath> attribute are searched, not the entire subdirectory tree of the AppBase. Both DLLs and EXEs are searched for until the assembly is found. Cultures specified as part of the strong name are taken into account when building the search tree.

5. If it still is not found, then the Windows Installer is run, requesting the missing assembly, acting as an install-on-demand feature. (The Windows Installer will be covered in a subsequent section.)

Example 22-18. Sample version policy in configuration file

```
<configuration>
  <runtime>
    <assemblyBinding xmlns="urn:schemas-microsoft-com:asm.v1">
      <dependentAssembly>
        <assemblyIdentity name="myAssembly"
                          publicKeyToken="a5d015c7d5a0b012"
                          culture="fr" />
        <bindingRedirect OldVersion="1.2.0.0"
                         NewVersion="1.5.0.0" />
        <bindingRedirect OldVersion="1.3.0.0-1.4.65535.65535"
                         NewVersion="1.5.0.0" />
        <publisherPolicy apply="no" />
        <codeBase version="1.5.0.0"
                  href="http://www.software.com/myAssembly.dll" />
      </dependentAssembly>
      <probing privatePath="bin;bin2" />
    </assemblyBinding>
  </runtime>
</configuration>
```

Build Configurations

The .NET Framework provides two classes in the System.Diagnostics namespace, Debug and Trace, which help debug your application. These classes, mentioned in the earlier section "system.diagnostics" and described in Chapter 21, enable several debugging techniques, such as assertions, conditional error messages, and capturing errors to a log file. The Debug and Trace classes have identical methods and properties.

To use tracing or debugging, you must compile the application with the appropriate flag. To include Debug statements in a C# program, include /d:DEBUG in the compile command line or add #define DEBUG as the first line in the source code file. To include Trace statements in a C# program, include /d:TRACE in the compile command line or add #define TRACE as the first line in the source code file.

To include Debug statements in a VB.NET program, include /d:DEBUG=True in the compile command line. To include Trace statements in a VB.NET program, include /d:TRACE=True in the compile command line.

The /d command-line compile switch is the short form of /define, used to define conditional compilation symbols.

In Visual Studio .NET, these flags are set by default by the Configuration Manager, described shortly. They can also be set explicitly. In C#, this is done by right-clicking on the project in the Solution Explorer and viewing the Property Pages dialog box for the project (not to be confused with the Properties window), and then going to the Configuration Properties → Build page. The Conditional Compilation Constants are listed under Code Generation. In VB.NET, the procedure is the same, except that two checkboxes are on the Configuration Properties → Build page, labeled Define DEBUG constant and Define TRACE constant.

The Configuration Manager in Visual Studio .NET provides an easy way to control the build process. By default, the Configuration Manager contains two different configurations: Debug and Release. You can quickly select between the two using the Configuration Manager drop-down menu shown in Figure 22-11.

The main difference between the two configurations is that Debug statements are included only in compiled Debug builds, not Release builds, while Trace statements are included in both. All the differences between Debug and Release builds are listed in Table 22-3.

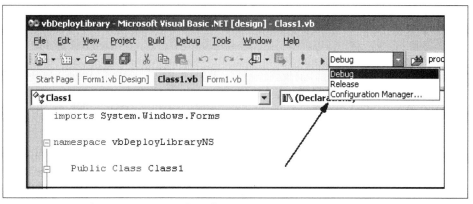

Figure 22-11. Configuration Manager drop-down menu

Table 22-3. Configuration build differences

Debug	Release
Debug and Trace statements included in compiled build.	Only Trace statements included in compiled build.
Not optimized for speed.	Optimized for speed.
Enables incremental build.	Disables incremental build.
C# output goes into *bin\Debug* directory.	C# output goes into *bin\Release* directory.
VB.NET output goes into *bin* directory.	VB.NET output goes into *bin* directory.
Breakpoints enabled.	Breakpoints disabled.

Notice that in C# projects, Debug and Release builds go into separate *bin* directories, while in VB.NET, both go into the same *bin* directory. You can change the output path in either language for any specific configuration by right-clicking on the project in the Solution Explorer and selecting Properties. This opens the Property Pages dialog box, shown in Figure 22-12 for C#. The VB.NET version of the dialog box is formatted somewhat differently but is functionally the same. Any changes made to a configuration apply only to this project.

The settings for each Visual Studio .NET project are stored in a file named after the project with an extension of either *.csproj* or *.vbproj*, depending on the language, in the project directory.

You can specify which projects within a solution will be built for any specific configuration by opening the Configuration Manager dialog box, shown in Figure 22-13. This dialog box can be accessed from the configuration drop-down menu shown in Figure 22-11, from the Property Pages dialog box shown in Figure 22-12, or from the Build menu.

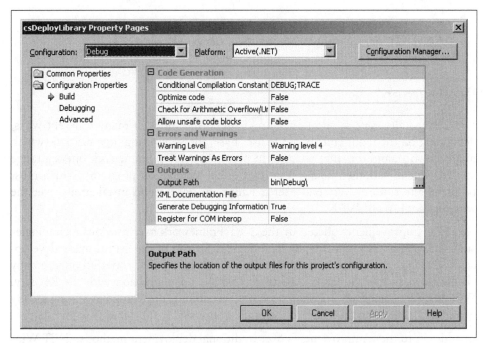

Figure 22-12. Project Property pages dialog box for C#

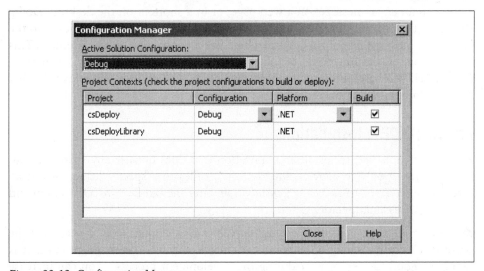

Figure 22-13. Configuration Manager

The Active Solution Configuration drop-down menu lets you select the active configuration and create new configurations or edit existing configurations. You can control which projects get built for each configuration by checking or unchecking the boxes in the Build column.

As of this writing, the only available platforms are .NET and Pocket PC (for applications using the .NET Compact Framework).

Deployment

You can install ayour application on end users' machines in many different ways, depending on the requirements of the user base, the supporting organization (which might be you), and the infrastructure in place. The .NET Framework offers a range of deployment options, ranging from traditional installation programs, which must be physically run on every end user machine, to on-demand installations over the wire—either LAN or WAN.

Of all the improvements offered by the .NET Framework over previous technologies such as COM and DCOM, deployment is near the top of the list for many developers. If the application does not require any shared assemblies, you need only to copy all files to a specific directory structure. There is no interaction with the Registry. Whether the assemblies are shared or not, versioning problems have been mostly eliminated, relegating DLL Hell to the unpleasant past.

In addition to these improvements over traditional deployment methods, .NET Windows Forms applications can be deployed over the wire, via a URL in a browser or as a link—in an email message, on a web page, or in a shortcut on the desktop. Doing so automatically brings the most current version of any required assemblies onto the end user's machine (as long as that machine has a connection to the Internet). This model offers all the functional benefits of Windows Forms (especially when compared to HTML based browser applications), along with an ease of deployment that rivals traditional web applications.

Private (XCOPY) Installations

As mentioned earlier, to install an application that does not use any shared assemblies, you need only to copy all the application files to a specified directory structure. This is referred to as *XCOPY installation*, after the old DOS XCOPY command that copies files and directories.

XCOPY deployment is well suited to relatively simple applications, especially if the person doing the installation is technically proficient at a command prompt. It is especially good for deployment during the development process. (You can increase the sophistication of the installation process a bit and simultaneously make it easier to use, if a series of DOS commands are grouped within a batch or scripting file.) To uninstall the application, you need only to delete the application directory.

The directory containing the program executable is called the *AppBase*. All files that comprise the application are contained either in the AppBase or in a subdirectory of the AppBase. (Any assemblies shared with other applications would typically be found in the GAC, as described in previous sections of this chapter.)

XCOPY installations do not create such niceties as program shortcuts and entries in the Start → Programs menu, unless you get very creative with your command-line commands. For that and other functionality, you must use either the Windows Installer (described in the next section) or a third-party tool. XCOPY installations are not appropriate if any of the following situations apply:

- A service needs to be installed.
- A file being updated is exclusively locked—e.g., by a service.
- COM components must be installed and registered.
- Assemblies must be installed to the GAC or other shared location.
- Shortcuts and Start menu entries need to be created.

The syntax of the XCOPY command is as follows:

```
xcopy <source> <target> [switches]
```

where <source> is the file or directory (directories) to be copied, <target> is the destination for the copied stuff, and a series of optional switches control the copy process. As with most DOS commands, /? displays a help file for the command.

A typical use of XCOPY would be:

```
xcopy \\myServer\Apps\myApp c:\"Program Files"\myApp /e /k /r /i
```

where the source directory is *myApp* in a directory named *Apps* on myServer, the target directory is *c:\Program Files\myApp* on the local machine, and the switches have the meanings listed in Table 22-4. Switches are not case sensitive.

Table 22-4. Commonly used XCOPY switches

Switch	Description
/?	Displays help.
/e	Copies directories and subdirectories, including empty ones.
/i	Assumes that the destination is a directory and creates it if necessary.
/k	Copies attributes as-is. Omitting this switch resets the read-only attribute.
/r	Forces overwrite of read-only files.
/s	Copies directories and subdirectories, excepting empty ones.
/t	Creates a directory structure without copying any files or empty directories. /t /e copies empty directories.

Windows Installer

For most real-world deployment situations, XCOPY deployment simply cannot do the job, and an installation tool with more robust capabilities is required. Several third-party installation tools are available, such as InstallShield, InstallAnywhere, and ActiveInstall.

Windows has its own installation technology, known as *Windows Installer*, which is included with all the Windows operating systems starting with Windows 2000.

 You can download Windows Installer for Windows 95, 98, and Me, as well as the latest version for Windows 2000, from *http://msdn. microsoft.com/downloads*.

Windows Installer runs as a service, providing installation, removal, and management of applications. It also supports features such as automatic repair of existing installations, transactional operations (any operation performed by the installer can be undone if it does not complete successfully), installation on demand (where application features are not installed until the first time a user tries to use that feature), and installation in locked-down environments if an administrator approves an installation package by means of group policy.

The Windows Installer is based on a relational database. Each application to be installed has a file associated with it, with an extension of *.msi*, which contains the data for that application, including rules for controlling the installation.

There are several ways of opening an *.msi* file. Double-clicking on the file opens the Windows Installer for that application. If the application is not currently installed on the machine, you will be presented with a series of dialog boxes for installing the application. Depending upon how the installation package was customized, these dialogs allow the user to select a target destination, select installation for the current user or all users, present software license information, and so on. If the application is already installed on the machine, you are presented with a dialog box offering the choice to either repair or remove the installation.

If you right-click on an *.msi* file in Windows Explorer, the context menu includes three relevant menu items: Install, Repair, and Uninstall. These options perform the same operations you might access by double-clicking on the file.

You can execute the Windows Installer from a command prompt. To install an application, use the following command:

```
msiexec /i MyApp.msi
```

To uninstall the application, use the following command:

```
msiexec /x MyApp.msi
```

To repair an installation, use this line:

```
msiexec /f MyApp.msi
```

 msiexec.exe is one of the few command-line tools provided by Microsoft that does not display a list of parameters when executed with the /? switch.

Probably the easiest way to run the Installer is to execute *setup.exe*, the Installer Bootstrapper that is created by Visual Studio .NET, along with an associated *.ini* file, in a process described later.

The Windows Installer automatically logs installations and removals in the Application Log of the Event Viewer found in Control Panel → Administrative Tools. Each entry in the log has a value for Source of MsiInstaller.

Using Visual Studio .NET

The Windows Installer is integrated into Visual Studio .NET. Create installation packages for your application by adding one or more setup projects to the solution. Each setup project sets up a specific configuration (Debug or Release). By having more than one setup project as part of a solution, the same application can be deployed easily with different configurations.

To demonstrate how to use Visual Studio .NET to build deployment packages, you will add setup projects to the Deploy application created previously in this chapter in the section "Single- and Multimodule Assemblies" (the applications are named csDeploy for the C# version and vbDeploy for the VB.NET version). The design of this application (and the source code for the class file in VB.NET) is shown in Figure 22-5 and the C# source code for the class file is listed in Example 22-10. The source code for the main project is listed in Example 22-11 in C# and in Example 22-12 in VB.NET.

Using the wizard to create a debug version

Open the Deploy solution (csDeploy or vbDeploy) in Visual Studio .NET so that it looks similar to Figure 22-5. (Make sure the active configuration is set to Debug.) Right-click on the solution in Solution Explorer and select Add → New Project.... When the Add New Project dialog box comes up, select Setup and Deployment Projects from the list of Project Types on the left and Setup Wizard from the Templates on the right. Enter a suitable name, as shown in Figure 22-14.

 You can tell from the name assigned to this project that it will deploy a debug configuration. If you deduce that there will also be a release configuration deployed, you are correct.

The wizard takes you through five screens. The first is a splash screen. The second screen asks you to choose a Project Type. Leave the default selection of Create a setup for a Windows application.

The third screen asks you to select the outputs from all the projects in the solution. Click on the primary output from both projects—Deploy and DeployLibrary—so that the screen looks like Figure 22-15. Click the Next button.

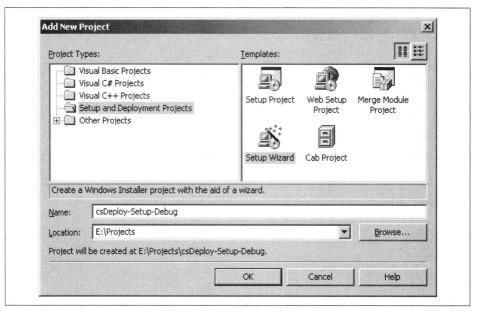

Figure 22-14. Add New Project dialog box

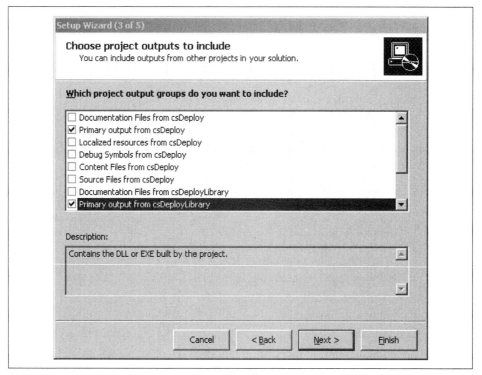

Figure 22-15. Project outputs screen in Setup Wizard

The next screen lets you include other files, such as readmes. The final screen displays a summary of all the settings for this setup project. Click Finish.

A project is added to Solution Explorer and the main design window now shows a File System editor for the setup project, similar to the screenshot shown in Figure 22-16.

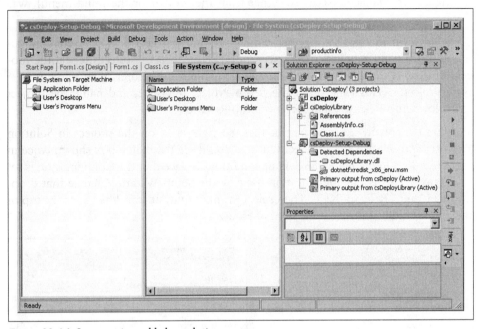

Figure 22-16. Setup project added to solution

Build the setup project by right-clicking on the project name in Solution Explorer and selecting the Build menu item.

Build will build the application, taking all dependencies into account, but not building components that are up to date. In a large solution where current development work is only done on one or two projects, it results in a faster build process.

The Rebuild menu item first deletes all intermediary files and previous build outputs, and then it builds the entire application from scratch. It may take longer, but it is smart to do a Rebuild before testing the final build.

You can open the Output window to view a log of the build process by clicking on View → Other Windows → Output. At the end of the build process, it should say:

```
Build: 3 succeeded, 0 failed, 0 skipped
```

The number 3 refers to the three projects in this solution.

Creating a release version

This section of the chapter should be more properly titled "Creating a version using a configuration different from the Current Active Configuration," but that would be a bit too wordy. In the previous section, you used the Setup Wizard to create a Debug version. It was Debug only because the current active configuration, as set in the Configuration Manager (accessed either from the toolbar or the Build menu), was Debug.

To create a version using a specified configuration, regardless of the current configuration, use a plain vanilla Setup Project, not a Setup Wizard project. Repeat the process of right-clicking on the solution name in Solution Explorer, then select Add → New Project.... This time select the Setup Project template, and name the project csDeploy-Setup-Release (or vbDeploy-Setup-Release).

You must manually add the output files, so right-click on the project in Solution Explorer and select Add → Project Output. You'll see the dialog box shown twice in Figure 22-17. On the left is the default condition. Notice that the Configuration is set to (Active). This is the configuration used by the Setup Wizard. Change that drop-down menu to Release .NET. Then select Primary Output from the list at the top of the dialog box, as shown on the right of Figure 22-17.

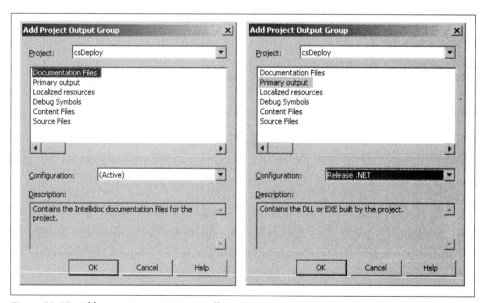

Figure 22-17. Adding project output manually

You can select multiple outputs by using standard Windows techniques with the Ctrl or Shift keys.

Although it would not hurt anything, it is not necessary to repeat the Add → Project Output for csDeployLibrary. As soon as the primary output from csDeploy (or vbDeploy) is added, the dependency of that EXE on *csDeployLibrary.dll* (*vbDeploy-Library.dll*) is detected and the class library is automatically included in the build.

The new project with that name displays in Solution Explorer with the primary outputs, similar to that shown in Figure 22-18.

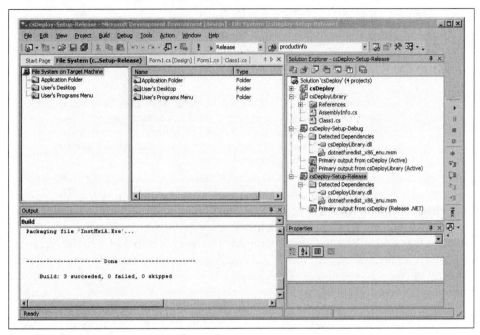

Figure 22-18. Adding project output manually

 For a C# project, the default location for a Debug build is in the *bin/Debug* directory, while a Release build goes to *bin/Release*. (All VB. NET builds will go to the *bin* directory.) Even though, in this example, you have added the primary outputs as Release builds, the output still goes to *Debug* if the current configuration is left as Debug at the time the setup project is built.

Further customizations

Whether the setup project came from the wizard or not, several customizations are available to you. Specifically, right-clicking on a setup project in Solution Explorer and selecting View or clicking on the View → Editor menu item brings up six different editor choices.

Clicking on any editor will display that editor for that project in the main pane. (When you first added a setup project, the File System editor is what you are looking at.)

File System. This editor, displayed in Figure 22-18, allows you to control where files are added to the end user's machine. The items in the left-most pane are named folders on the target machine (e.g., the Application folder—the directory where the application is installed), the user's desktop, or the user's program menu. Clicking on any of them displays their contents in the right pane.

Right-clicking on an item displays a context menu. Select Add to add either a folder, a file, an assembly, or a project output. You can add shortcuts to either the desktop or the Start → Programs menu by right-clicking on the appropriate item.

 Before adding any files to a named folder, first set the AlwaysCreate property of that folder to true before building the setup project. To do so, click on the relevant named folder under the root entry File System on Target Machine in the left-most pane, and set the Always-Create property in the Properties window.

Use this editor to add shared assemblies to the GAC on the target machine. To do so, right-click on the root of the left pane, File System on Target Machine, and select Add Special Folder. You will see a plethora of special folders, many of which should be familiar to you. Click on Global Assembly Cache Folder to add it to the left pane. Right-click on it and select Add → Assembly... to add an assembly to the GAC. Remember: for an assembly to be added to the GAC, it must first have a strong name.

Registry. The Registry editor allows your setup program to make entries in the Registry of the target machine. The screenshot in Figure 22-19 shows a new key called TestValue inserted in *HKEY_LOCAL_MACHINE\Software\[Manufacturer]*, where [Manufacturer] will be replaced with the value of the Manufacturer property of the setup project. (It defaults to the organization entered when Visual Studio .NET was installed.)

Get to the Registry editor, shown in Figure 22-19, by right-clicking on the right pane, selecting New, and then clicking on one of the following:

- String Value
- Environment String Value
- Binary Value
- DWORD Value

Set the name of the new key and its value in the Property window.

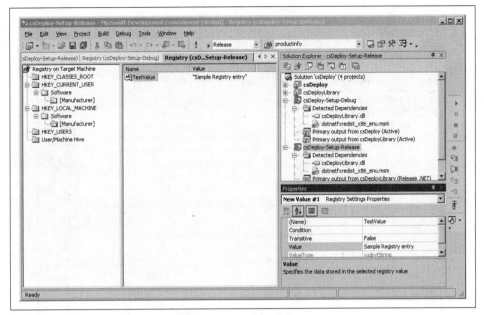

Figure 22-19. Registry editor

File Types. The File Types editor lets you associate file extensions with the application. If an associated file type is double-clicked in Windows Explorer, the application will open with that filename passed in as an argument.

To add a file type to the project, right-click on File Types on Target Machine and select Add File Type. A default document type will appear with the &Open command below it. In the Properties window, change the name to something meaningful, say MyApp Data File, and enter the extension in the Extensions property, such as abc, as shown in Figure 22-20.

Now if a file on the target machine with an extension of *.abc*, such as *SomeData.abc*, is double-clicked in Windows Explorer, the application will open with that file.

User Interface. The User Interface editor allows you to customize the dialog boxes that are displayed during the installation process. The process is divided into two categories: Install and Administrative Install. The first is for normal installation by users on their local machine, and the latter is for installation to a network for use by members of a workgroup.

Within each category, the editor is further divided into three phases: Start, Progress, and End. The default configuration looks like Figure 22-21.

Right-clicking on any item in the window and selecting the Add Dialog menu item brings up a selection of standard dialog boxes that can be added and further customized, such as dialogs with radio buttons, checkboxes or textboxes, a customer information screen, a splash screen, and a license agreement.

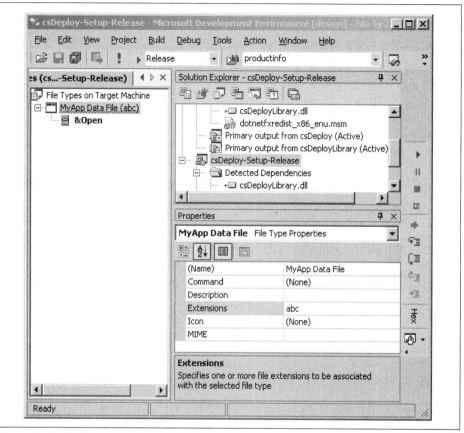

Figure 22-20. File Types editor

Any dialog box added this way will have properties for text files or bitmaps to display and executables to run.

Custom Actions. The Custom Actions editor displays four phases of the installation process: Install, Commit, Rollback, and Uninstall. You can assign an executable or script file to execute at the conclusion of any phase.

Launch Conditions. The Launch Conditions editor lets you create conditional installs. For example, you can specify that a certain version of Windows be installed, a certain file be present, or a certain Registry entry have the correct value.

Internet Deployment

If you want to deploy shared assemblies, add shortcuts to the user's desktop or Start → Programs menu, make Registry entries, or add other customizations, then Windows

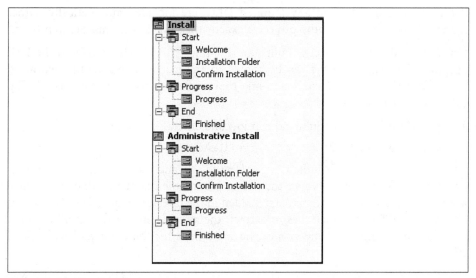

Figure 22-21. User Interface editor

Installer is the way to go. However, one of the major shortcomings of this approach is that Windows Installer must be run on each target machine.

On the other hand, you often do not need any of these features, or can give them up in exchange for incredibly easy deployment over the Internet or Intranet. There are several ways to accomplish this, as discussed next.

Auto deployment via Cabinet (CAB) files

You learned in the previous section how to add a Setup project to your application in Visual Studio .NET so that a Windows Installer file was created. That file could then be installed on a local machine.

In an analogous manner, you can add a Visual Studio .NET project to your solution that will create a Cabinet (CAB) file. CAB files are a means of including multiple installation files in a compressed format. CAB files can be either distributed on CDs or over the LAN or included as part of a Windows Installer package, but more significantly, they can also be downloaded over the Internet via a browser.

To demonstrate how to create a CAB file, open the csDeploy or vbDeploy solution in Visual Studio .NET. Right-click on the solution in Solution Explorer and add a new project, similar to what was shown earlier in Figure 22-14, except this time select a Cab Project, rather than a Setup Wizard or Setup Project. Name the project appropriately.

You must explicitly add the Primary Outputs for both the main executable and the DLL, unlike the situation with a normal Setup Project, where dependencies are detected automatically and any required DLLs are included automatically. Other than this, creating a CAB setup project is exactly the same as a normal Setup project.

Once the CAB setup project is built, the resulting CAB file contains both the EXE and the DLL. This CAB file can be copied to any machine and the files extracted either with the EXPAND command-line tool or third-party tools such as WinZip (*http://www.winzip.com*).

To use EXPAND, open a command window and enter:

```
expand csDeploy-cab.cab -f:* "c:\Program Files\csDeploy"
```

where the name of the CAB file is *csDeploy-cab.cab* and the destination directory is *c:\Program Files\csDeploy*. Notice the quotes around the destination directory, which are necessary because of the space embedded in the directory name. The -f argument allows you to specify which files to extract; the asterisk says to extract all the files. You can see all the available syntax and arguments for the command with the /? switch.

The useful part comes when you copy the CAB file to a virtual directory on a web server, accessible over the Intranet or Internet. Entering the CAB file as a URI in a browser lets you copy the file to the end user machine, where the files can then be extracted.

Auto deployment via URL

One of the most interesting models enabled by the .NET Framework is *auto deployment*, the direct distribution and execution of applications over the Net: Intra- or Inter-. The user accomplishes this by calling an executable as part of a URL, either in a browser or as a link, such as in an email or in a shortcut on a user's desktop.

To a first approximation, you need only to place the executable and any required assemblies in a virtual directory on a web server. However, as enticing as this approach is, it has some serious limitations arising from security issues, discussed shortly.

As a quick demonstration of this capability, return to the application shown earlier in Figure 22-6. Either copy both the EXE and DLL from that application to an existing virtual directory on your machine or virtualize the directory containing the EXE, using one of the techniques described in the sidebar "Virtual Directories."

Suppose you made a virtual directory called MultiModuleAssy. Open a browser and enter the following URL:

```
localhost/MultiModuleAssy/csDeploy.exe
```

The application will appear on your desktop, with no browser window around it, exactly as if it had been started from the Start button. Hoo hah!

To demonstrate this and other internet deployment strategies, you will need to have Internet Information Server (IIS) installed on your development machine or otherwise have access to a web server.

Assuming you have IIS installed on your local machine, the file to be deployed must be copied to a virtual directory, which is a directory that logically can be referred to as part of a browser URL. The easiest way to create a virtual directory on your local machine is to right-click on the directory in Windows Explorer, click on Sharing, and go to the Web Sharing tab. Click the Share this folder radio button. Then click the Add... button to add an alias, which is the name the virtual directory will be known as.

You can also create a virtual directory by going to Computer Management in Control Panel → Administrative Tools, drilling down to Services and Applications → Internet Information Services → Default Web Site, then right-clicking and adding a new virtual directory.

The default root virtual directory in IIS is located at *c:\inetpub\wwwroot*. If the CAB file is copied to that directory, it can be accessed from a browser on the local machine with either of the following URLs:

```
localhost/MyCabFile.cab
127.0.0.1/MyCabFile.cab
```

Likewise, if the domain name registered for the web server is MyDomain.com, then the following URL will access the CAB file:

```
www.MyDomain.com/MyCabFile.cab
```

You would typically place the CAB file in another virtual directory, not the virtual root. In that case, the URL would be something like:

```
localhost/MyVirtualDir/MyCabFile.cab
```

or:

```
www.MyDomain.com/MyVirtualDir/MyCabFile.cab
```

.NET applications can be deployed this way to any client machine that has the .NET Framework installed. (Installing the .NET Redistributable on end users' machines will be covered shortly.) It is not necessary for the web server to have the .NET Framework installed, nor must it be running either IIS or Windows.

The CLR on the client machine downloads the executable from the web server and caches it in two different locations: the browser download cache (typically located at *c:\Documents and Settings\username\Local Settings\Temporary Internet Files*) and the .NET download cache. This latter cache is part of the GAC and can be managed by using the GacUtil tool. To list the contents of the .NET download cache, use the following command:

```
gacutil /ldl
```

To empty the .NET download cache, use this command:

```
gacutil /cdl
```

To clear the browser download cache in Internet Explorer, go to Tools → Internet Options, and click on the Delete Files button on the General tab.

The next time this same application is executed from the same URL, the CLR first checks to see if it is present in the cache. If not, it is downloaded and cached. If it is, then the last-modified date on the cached copy is compared with the last-modified date on the server copy. If the server has a more recent copy, it is downloaded and the cached copy is replaced.

If the executable references another assembly, i.e., if a class, method, or property from another assembly is invoked, then the CLR checks the download cache to see if the referenced assembly is present. As with all assembly references, if the required assembly is not present, it is downloaded from the same location as the original assembly (the AppBase) and cached. If it is present in the download cache, then its last-modified date is compared with the copy on the web server and the more recent copy is used.

Notice that the version, as known to a strongly named assembly, is not part of this picture. If an older version of an assembly has been built more recently, and hence has a more recent last-modified date, then it will be downloaded and will replace the newer version in the download cache.

Versions do play a role if an assembly being downloaded from the server references a specific version of another assembly.

This trickle-down approach to deployment can minimize the delay the first time an application is run. By splitting rarely invoked classes, or groups of classes generally called together, into separate assemblies, you can minimize load times if those assemblies are never referenced by the user. (This strategy may also promote more efficient code reuse.) In any event, several smaller downloads may seem more palatable to the user than one large download. To front-load the download time, reference all the assemblies you will use in the form constructor.

Now to get a hint of the problems that auto deployment can raise, call the application in a browser again. This time use the standard IP address for localhost, as in:

```
127.0.0.1/MultiModuleAssy/csDeploy.exe
```

The application will run again, but this time a prominently displayed message will say:

Microsoft .NET Security Information
This application is running in a partially trusted context. Some functionality in the application may be disabled due to security restriction.

The difference is that localhost is interpreted as an Intranet address, while its equivalent 127.0.0.1, or any IP address or dotted domain name, is considered an Internet address.

In the old days, code downloaded over the Internet—say a script or an ActiveX component on a web page—executed with the permissions of the user. This meant, as a practical matter, that a lot of code from unknown sources was executing, often with Administrative privileges. To add insult to the very real possibility of injury, the user was presented with an inscrutable dialog box asking if this code was to be trusted. Even if you could vouch for the morals of the software developer, who can guarantee that an application will be perfectly well behaved and bug-free?

The .NET Framework corrects this security gap with the introduction of *Code Access Security* (CAS). CAS assigns permissions to assemblies based on *evidence*. One of the prime pieces of evidence is the originating location of the code.

Several predefined *security zones* are listed in Table 22-5. All assemblies come from one of these zones. The system imposes a set of restrictions based, in part, on the individual zones, as defined by the security policy set by the administrator on that machine (or network). Data can only be transferred from less trusted to more trusted zones. This allows Intranet applications to access data on the Internet, but not vice versa.

Table 22-5. Security zones

Zone	Permission Set	Description
Internet	Internet (Framework Version 1 & 1.1.) Nothing (Framework Version 1 SP1 & SP2)	Internet permission set: Access to open file dialog only, isolated storage (10 KB maximum quota), code execution, safe windowing and own clipboard, and safe printing. Nothing permission set: no access to any restricted resources.
Intranet	LocalIntranet	Access to isolated storage (effectively unlimited quota), full UI, reflection emit, limited environment variables, file dialogs, code execution, DNS, and default printing.
MyComputer	FullTrust	Full access to all resources.
Trusted	Internet	Access to open file dialog only, isolated storage, code execution, safe windowing and own clipboard, and safe printing.
Untrusted	Nothing	Corresponds to Restricted sites in IE. No access to any restricted resources.

The CLR determines which security zone an assembly is from by the form of the path to its originating location, as shown in Table 22-6.

Table 22-6. Security zone paths

Zone	Path	Examples
Internet	Numeric IP Address	*http://207.46.134.190/AppDir/MyApp.exe*
	Dotted URL	*http://127.0.0.1/AppDir/MyApp.exe*
		http://www.MyDomain.com/AppDir/MyApp.exe
Intranet	UNC Name	*\\serverName\AppDir\MyApp.exe*
	Non-dotted URL	*http://localhost/AppDir/MyApp.exe*
	Network Share	*z:\AppDir\MyApp.exe*
MyComputer	local file	*c:\AppDir\MyApp.exe*

As you can see from Table 22-5, depending on the zone from which an assembly originates, it may not have access to much of the functionality you have come to expect. Operations that are especially restricted include file access, interaction with the Registry, accessing environment variables, and printing.

 Applications deployed via a URL are unable to read application configuration files, but they can read the *machine.config* file from the originating machine.

Test your application under all the zones in which it might be deployed. Any operation that might fail in a given security zone should be wrapped in a try block. Then if an operation fails, the application can handle the situation gracefully, rather than present the user with an error message and then crash.

An alternative strategy is to test which zone the assembly is in, and then disable the features that might cause a problem, although some organizations modify the security policy so that certain zones may have more or less access than would normally be expected. Your code can determine the zone it is from by using the static Zone. CreateFromUrl method in the System.Security.Policy namespace.

 Several good books and articles provide in-depth coverage of Code Access Security. One such book is *.NET Framework Security* by Brian A. LaMacchia (Addison Wesley). Two good articles in *MSDN Magazine* on the security aspects of deploying applications via URL are "Code Access Security and Distribution Features in .NET Enhance Client-Side Apps" by Jason Clark, June 2002, and "Security and Versioning Models in Windows Forms Engine Help You Create and Deploy Smart Clients" by Chris Sells, July 2002.

Auto deployment via calling program

Deploying via a URL is fine for a single application, but such an approach may be too cumbersome for multiple applications. Suppose you want to provide a programmatic way of allowing the user to choose the application to run, such as by selecting from a drop-down list populated from a database.

In this situation, you need a stub, or calling, program. Typically the stub is a very simple program that does nothing other than call the real application. The name and URL of the assembly containing the application to run is captured as a string by the stub program. For example:

```csharp
string strUrl = "http" + "://localhost/MultiModuleAssy/csDeploy.exe";
```

```vbnet
dim strUrl as String = "http" & _
"://localhost/MultiModuleAssy/vbDeploy.exe"
```

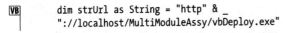

> These strings are built up from two substrings to avoid Visual Studio .NET's annoying default behavior that make hyperlinks active links, even in source code string literals. In Visual Studio .NET 2003, this is much less of an issue because you must Ctrl-click to follow a link in source code. In either version of Visual Studio .NET, you can disable this behavior by going to Tools → Options → Text Editor and unchecking "Enable single-click URL navigation" under either All Languages or the language(s) of your choice.

Then an assembly is instantiated by making a call to the static (Shared in VB.NET) Assembly.LoadFrom( ) method, passing in the name and URL of the assembly:

```csharp
Assembly a = Assembly.LoadFrom(strUrl);
```

```vbnet
dim a as [Assembly] = [Assembly].LoadFrom(strUrl)
```

> The word Assembly is enclosed in square brackets in the VB.NET code because it is a keyword in VB.NET, although it is not in C#.

Once you have an instance of the assembly, the form can be instantiated in a three-step process: a Type object is obtained for the form using the Assembly.GetType method, an Object is instantiated from that Type object, and that Object is cast to a Form:

```csharp
Type t = a.GetType("csDeploy.Form1");
Object o = Activator.CreateInstance(t);
Form frm = (Form)o;
```

```vbnet
dim t as Type = a.GetType("Form1")
dim o as Object = Activator.CreateInstance(t)
dim frm as Form = CType(o, Form)
```

Finally, you show the form:

```csharp
frm.Show( );
```

The whole thing is wrapped inside a try block, so if there are any problems along the way, e.g., the connection to the net is lost, they will be handled gracefully.

For this code to run, you must reference the System.Reflection namespace. Include the following line of code in the project:

C#
```
using System.Reflection;
```

VB
```
imports System.Reflection
```

The complete code for implementing the stub code in a button click event handler is shown in Example 22-19 in C# and in Example 22-20 in VB.NET.

Example 22-19. Programmatic auto deployment in C#

C#
```csharp
private void button1_Click(object sender, System.EventArgs e)
{
    try
    {
        string strUrl = "http" +  "://localhost/MultiFileAssy/csDeploy.exe";
        Assembly a = Assembly.LoadFrom(strUrl);
        Type t = a.GetType("csDeploy.Form1");
        Object o = Activator.CreateInstance(t);
        Form frm = (Form)o;
        frm.Show();
    }
    catch (Exception ex)
    {
        MessageBox.Show(ex.ToString());
    }
}
```

Example 22-20. Programmatic auto deployment in VB.NET

VB
```vbnet
Private Sub Button1_Click(ByVal sender As System.Object, _
                        ByVal e As System.EventArgs) _
                        Handles Button1.Click
    try
        dim strUrl as String = "http" & _
                        "://localhost/MultiFileAssy/csDeploy.exe"
        dim a as [Assembly] = [Assembly].LoadFrom(strUrl)
        dim t as Type = a.GetType("Form1")
        dim o as Object = Activator.CreateInstance(t)
        dim frm as Form = CType(o, Form)
        frm.Show()
    catch ex as Exception
        MessageBox.Show(ex.ToString)
    End Try
End Sub
```

When an application is deployed this way, the assembly containing the form is downloaded automatically, as described earlier in the section "Auto deployment via

URL." The download cache is checked to see if it contains a copy of the assembly and, if so, the last-modified date of that copy is compared with the copy on the server. Any referenced assemblies are automatically trickled down to the client machine.

All security issues pertaining to Internet deployment via URL's apply to programmatic deployment as well. This means that deployment over the Internet may be problematic beyond practicality for many applications, but deployment over the Intranet or LAN is a real possibility in many cases.

.NET Runtime Redistributable

The .NET Framework must be installed on a client machine before any .NET application will run. For a developer's machine, this is not an issue. However, for deployment of .NET applications to most end user machines, the Framework must first be installed. If the Framework has been installed on a machine for one application, it does not need to be installed again for the next.

The .NET Framework is included in Windows 2003 Server and as an optional installation from Windows XP Service Pack 1. Presumably it will be either an optional or standard part of every future Microsoft operating system. It is also likely to become part of the standard installation for major .NET-enabled applications from Microsoft, including Internet Explorer (IE) and Office XP. Any machine with the Framework installed, from any source, can run .NET applications.

A virgin machine can get the.NET Framework by installing the .NET Framework *Redistributable*, available either on a Visual Studio .NET installation disk or from the Microsoft web site.

 The URL of the Microsoft web page for downloading the Redistributable has sometimes been difficult to find. The easiest way to find it is to go to *http://www.msdn.Microsoft.com/downloads* and search for Redistributable.

The Redistributable file is called *Dotnetfx.exe*. When executed, it installs the Framework, unless it is already installed. If the Framework is already installed, *Dotnetfx.exe* tells you before quitting harmlessly.

 You need administrative privileges to run *Dotnetfx.exe* and install the Redistributable.

As of this writing, the .NET Redistributable can be installed on the following operating systems:

- Windows 98
- Windows 98 SE
- Windows NT 4.0 (SP 6a required)
- Windows Me
- Windows 2000 (SP2 recommended)
- Windows XP Home
- Windows XP Professional

 The .NET Runtime cannot be installed on Windows 95. Time to upgrade.

The system must have IE 5.01 installed, although you might want to upgrade to at least IE 6.0.

The minimum hardware configuration for installing the .NET Redistributable is a 90 MHz Pentium or faster, and 32 MB of RAM for a client machine or 128 MB of RAM for a server. The recommended hardware is 96 MB of RAM for a client and 256 MB of RAM for a server.

If any of the .NET applications to be run on the machine require data access, then MDAC needs to be present. (.NET runs with MDAC 2.6, but 2.7 is recommended.) If MDAC is not already on the machine, it can be downloaded from Microsoft.com and installed.

If you look at a deployment project in Solution Explorer, you will notice that a node called Detected Dependencies always has the subnode *dotnetfxredist_x86_xxx.msm*, where xxx is replaced with the language code. (This can best be seen in Figure 22-18.) The Framework uses this node to prevent individual Framework assemblies from being listed as dependencies. It is intentionally excluded from the project; do not include it. In any case, the presence of this dependency will not cause the Framework redistributable to be installed if the Framework is missing from the machine.

This point bears emphasis. The only way to install a .NET application on a machine that has never had the .NET Framework installed is to first install the .NET Redistributable, and then run the deployment package for the application itself. You would think that a Visual Studio .NET deployment project would allow you to install the Framework if it were missing, but that assumption is problematic. The .NET installer requires the Framework to run, and vice versa. The easiest solution is have the user run the Redistributable and then install your application. Several third-party installation tools on the market can automate the installation of the Framework, MDAC, and an application.

An administrator can push the .NET Framework Redistributable across the network onto end-user machines by using either Systems Management Server (SMS) or Active Directory. The details are beyond the scope of this book. For more information, check out Microsoft Knowledgebase articles 318434 (for SMS) or 329191 (for Active Directory), or search the Framework SDK documentation for the article "Redistributing the .NET Framework."

Characters and Keys

Table A-1 lists the low-order ASCII (American Standards Committee for Information Interchange) characters, i.e., decimal value 0 through 127, including both the decimal and hexadecimal equivalents, plus a description if the meaning of the character is not unambiguous.

Table A-1. ASCII characters

Decimal code	Hex code	Character	Description
0	00	NUL	Null
1	01	SOH	Start of heading
2	02	STX	Start of text
3	03	ETX	End of text
4	04	EOT	End of transmit
5	05	ENQ	Enquiry
6	06	ACK	Acknowledge
7	07	BEL	Audible bell
8	08	BS	Backspace
9	09	HT	Horizontal tab
10	0A	LF	Line feed
11	0B	VT	Vertical tab
12	0C	FF	Form feed
13	0D	CR	Carriage return
14	0E	SO	Shift out
15	0F	SI	Shift in
16	10	DLE	Data link escape
17	11	DC1	Device control 1
18	12	DC2	Device control 2
19	13	DC3	Device control 3

Decimal code	Hex code	Character	Description
20	14	DC4	Device control 4
21	15	NAK	Negative acknowledge
22	16	SYM	Synchronous idle
23	17	ETB	End transmission block
24	18	CAN	Cancel
25	19	EM	End of medium
26	1A	SUB	Substitution
27	1B	ESC	Escape
28	1C	FS	File separator
29	1D	GS	Group separator
30	1E	RS	Record separator
31	1F	US	Unit separator
32	20	Space	Space in text
33	21	!	Exclamation point
34	22	"	Double quote
35	23	#	Number or pound sign, hash, octothorp
36	24	$	Dollar sign
37	25	%	Percent sign
38	26	&	Ampersand
39	27	'	Single close-quote, apostrophe
40	28	(	Left parenthesis
41	29	)	Right parenthesis
42	2A	*	Asterisk
43	2B	+	Plus sign
44	2C	,	Comma
45	2D	-	Hyphen / minus
46	2E	.	Period
47	2F	/	Slash
48	30	0	The number zero
49	31	1	The number one
50	32	2	The number two
51	33	3	The number three
52	34	4	The number four
53	35	5	The number five
54	36	6	The number six

Table A-1. *ASCII characters (continued)*

Decimal code	Hex code	Character	Description
55	37	7	The number seven
56	38	8	The number eight
57	39	9	The number nine
58	3A	:	Colon
59	3B	;	Semicolon
60	3C	<	Less-than sign, left angle bracket
61	3D	=	Equals sign
62	3E	>	Greater-than sign, right angle bracket
63	3F	?	Question mark
64	40	@	At sign
65	41	A	Uppercase letter A
66	42	B	Uppercase letter B
67	43	C	Uppercase letter C
68	44	D	Uppercase letter D
69	45	E	Uppercase letter E
70	46	F	Uppercase letter F
71	47	G	Uppercase letter G
72	48	H	Uppercase letter H
73	49	I	Uppercase letter I
74	4A	J	Uppercase letter J
75	4B	K	Uppercase letter K
76	4C	L	Uppercase letter L
77	4D	M	Uppercase letter M
78	4E	N	Uppercase letter N
79	4F	O	Uppercase letter O
80	50	P	Uppercase letter P
81	51	Q	Uppercase letter Q
82	52	R	Uppercase letter R
83	53	S	Uppercase letter S
84	54	T	Uppercase letter T
85	55	U	Uppercase letter U
86	56	V	Uppercase letter V
87	57	W	Uppercase letter W
88	58	X	Uppercase letter X
89	59	Y	Uppercase letter Y

Decimal code	Hex code	Character	Description
90	5A	Z	Uppercase letter Z
91	5B	[	Left square bracket
92	5C	\	Backslash
93	5D	]	Right square bracket
94	5E	^	Caret, circumflex accent
95	5F	_	Underscore
96	60	`	Single open-quote, grave accent
97	61	a	Lowercase letter a
98	62	b	Lowercase letter b
99	63	c	Lowercase letter c
100	64	d	Lowercase letter d
101	65	e	Lowercase letter e
102	66	f	Lowercase letter f
103	67	g	Lowercase letter g
104	68	h	Lowercase letter h
105	69	i	Lowercase letter i
106	6A	j	Lowercase letter j
107	6B	k	Lowercase letter k
108	6C	l	Lowercase letter l
109	6D	m	Lowercase letter m
110	6E	n	Lowercase letter n
111	6F	o	Lowercase letter o
112	70	p	Lowercase letter p
113	71	q	Lowercase letter q
114	72	r	Lowercase letter r
115	73	s	Lowercase letter s
116	74	t	Lowercase letter t
117	75	u	Lowercase letter u
118	76	v	Lowercase letter v
119	77	w	Lowercase letter w
120	78	x	Lowercase letter x
121	79	y	Lowercase letter y
122	7A	z	Lowercase letter z
123	7B	{	Left brace
124	7C	|	Pipe
125	7D	}	Right brace

Decimal code	Hex code	Character	Description
126	7E	~	Tilde
127	7F	DEL	Delete

Table A-2 lists the members of the Keys enumeration provided by the .NET Framework for specifying keyboard key codes and modifiers.

Table A-2. Keys enumeration members

Name	Key code (decimal)	Description
A	65	A key
Add	107	Add key (numeric keypad +)
Alt	18	Alt modifier key—sometimes called Menu because it often is used for menu selection
Apps	93	Application key (Microsoft Natural Keyboard)
Attn	246	Attn key
B	66	B key
Back	8	Backspace key
BrowserBack	166	Browser Back key (Windows 2000 or later)
BrowserFavorites	171	Browser Favorites key (Windows 2000 or later)
BrowserForward	167	Browser Forward key (Windows 2000 or later)
BrowserHome	172	Browser Home key (Windows 2000 or later)
BrowserRefresh	168	Browser Refresh key (Windows 2000 or later)
BrowserSearch	170	Browser Search key (Windows 2000 or later)
BrowserStop	169	Browser Stop key (Windows 2000 or later)
C	67	C key
Cancel	3	Cancel key
Capital	20	Caps Lock key
CapsLock	20	Caps Lock key
Clear	254	Clear key
Control	17	Ctrl modifier key
ControlKey	17	Ctrl key
Crsel	247	Crsel key
D	68	D key
D0	48	0 key
D1	49	1 key
D2	50	2 key
D3	51	3 key
D4	52	4 key

Name	Key code (decimal)	Description
D5	53	5 key
D6	54	6 key
D7	55	7 key
D8	56	8 key
D9	57	9 key
Decimal	110	Decimal key
Delete	46	Del key
Divide	111	Divide key (numeric keypad /)
Down	40	Down Arrow key
E	69	E key
End	35	End key
Enter	13	Enter key
EraseEof	249	Erase Eof key
Escape	27	Esc key
Execute	43	Execute key
Exsel	248	Excel key
F	70	F key
F1	112	F1 key
F2	113	F2 key
F3	114	F3 key
F4	115	F4 key
F5	116	F5 key
F6	117	F6 key
F7	118	F7 key
F8	119	F8 key
F9	120	F9 key
F10	121	F10 key
F11	122	F11 key
F12	123	F12 key
F13	124	F13 key
F14	125	F14 key
F15	126	F15 key
F16	127	F16 key
F17	128	F17 key
F18	129	F18 key
F19	130	F19 key

Name	Key code (decimal)	Description
F20	131	F20 key
F21	132	F21 key
F22	133	F22 key
F23	134	F23 key
F24	135	F24 key
FinalMode	24	IME final mode key
G	71	G key
H	72	H key
HanguelMode	21	IME Hanguel mode key. Maintained for compatibility; use HangulMode
HangulMode	21	IME Hangul mode key
HanjaMode	25	IME Hanja mode key
Help	47	Help key
Home	36	Home key
I	73	I key
IMEAceept	30	IME Accept key—note apparent misspelling of member name
IMEConvert	28	IME Convert key
IMEModeChange	31	IME Mode Change key
IMENonconvert	29	IME Nonconvert key
Insert	45	INS key
J	74	J key
JunjaMode	23	IME Junja mode key
K	75	K key
KanaMode	21	IME Kana mode key
KanjiMode	25	IME Kanji mode key
KeyCode		Bitmask to extract a key code from a key value
L	76	L key
LaunchApplication1	182	Start Application one key (Windows 2000 or later)
LaunchApplication2	183	Start Application two key (Windows 2000 or later)
LaunchMail	180	Launch Mail key (Windows 2000 or later)
LButton	1	Left mouse button
LControlKey	162	Left Ctrl key
Left	37	Left Arrow key
LineFeed	10	Linefeed key
LMenu	164	Left Alt key
LShiftKey	161	Left Shift key

Table A-2. Keys enumeration members (continued)

Name	Key code (decimal)	Description
LWin	91	Left Windows logo key (Microsoft Natural Keyboard)
M	77	M key
MButton	4	Middle mouse button (three-button mouse)
MediaNextTrack	176	Media Next Track key (Windows 2000 or later)
MediaPlayPause	179	Media Play Pause key (Windows 2000 or later)
MediaPreviousTrack	177	Media Previous Track key (Windows 2000 or later)
MediaStop	178	Media Stop key (Windows 2000 or later)
Menu	18	Alt key—called Menu because it often is used for menu selection
Modifiers		Bitmask to extract modifiers from a key value
Multiply	106	Multiply key (numeric keypad *)
N	78	N key
Next	34	Page Down key
NoName	252	A constant reserved for future use
None		No key pressed
NumLock	144	Num Lock key
NumPad0	96	0 key on the numeric keypad
NumPad1	97	1 key on the numeric keypad
NumPad2	98	2 key on the numeric keypad
NumPad3	99	3 key on the numeric keypad
NumPad4	100	4 key on the numeric keypad
NumPad5	101	5 key on the numeric keypad
NumPad6	102	6 key on the numeric keypad
NumPad7	103	7 key on the numeric keypad
NumPad8	104	8 key on the numeric keypad
NumPad9	105	9 key on the numeric keypad
O	79	O key
Oem8	223	OEM specific
OemBackslash	226	OEM Angle bracket or Backslash key on the RT 102 key keyboard (Windows 2000 or later)
OemClear	254	Clear key
OemCloseBrackets	221	OEM Close Bracket key on a US standard keyboard (Windows 2000 or later)
Oemcomma	188	OEM Comma key on any country/region keyboard (Windows 2000 or later)
OemMinus	189	OEM Minus key on any country/region keyboard (Windows 2000 or later)

Name	Key code (decimal)	Description
OemOpenBrackets	219	OEM OpenBracket key on a US standard keyboard (Windows 2000 or later)
OemPeriod	190	OEM Period key on any country/region keyboard (Windows 2000 or later)
OemPipe	220	OEM Pipe key on a US standard keyboard (Windows 2000 or later)
Oemplus	187	OEM Plus key on any country/region keyboard (Windows 2000 or later)
OemQuestion	191	OEM Question Mark key on a US standard keyboard (Windows 2000 or later)
OemQuotes	222	OEM Singled/Double Quote key on a US standard keyboard (Windows 2000 or later)
OemSemicolon	186	OEM Semicolon key on a US standard keyboard (Windows 2000 or later)
Oemtilde	192	OEM Tilde key on a US standard keyboard (Windows 2000 or later)
P	80	P key
Pa1	253	PA1 key
PageDown	34	Page Down key (Next)
PageUp	33	Page Up key
Pause	19	Pause key
Play	250	Play key
Print	42	Print key
PrintScreen	44	Print Screen key
Prior	33	Page Up key
ProcessKey	229	Process Key key
Q	81	Q key
R	82	R key
RButton	2	Right mouse button
RControlKey	163	Right Ctrl key
Return	13	Return key
Right	39	Right Arrow key
RMenu	165	Right Alt key. (Alt key referred to because it is often used for menu selection.)
RShiftKey	161	Right Shift key
RWin	92	Right Windows logo key (Microsoft Natural Keyboard)
S	83	S key
Scroll	145	Scroll Lock key
Select	41	Select key
SelectMedia	181	Select Media key (Windows 2000 or later)

Name	Key code (decimal)	Description
Separator	108	Separator key
Shift	16	Shift modifier key
ShiftKey	16	Shift key
Snapshot	44	Print Screen key
Space	32	Spacebar key
Subtract	109	Subtract key (numeric keypad -)
T	84	T key
Tab	9	Tab key
U	85	U key
Up	38	Up Arrow key
V	86	V key
VolumeDown	174	Volume Down key (Windows 2000 or later)
VolumeMute	173	Volume Mute key (Windows 2000 or later)
VolumeUp	175	Volume Up key (Windows 2000 or later)
W	87	W key
X	88	X key
XButton1	5	First X mouse button (five-button mouse)
XButton2	6	Second X mouse button (five-button mouse)
Y	89	Y key
Z	90	Z key
Zoom	251	Zoom key

Table A-3 lists the standard system-defined colors provided by the .NET Framework as properties of the Color structure.

Table A-3. Standard colors

AliceBlue	AntiqueWhite	Aqua
Aquamarine	Azure	Beige
Bisque	Black	BlanchedAlmond
Blue	BlueViolet	Brown
BurlyWood	CadetBlue	Chartreuse
Chocolate	Coral	CornflowerBlue
Cornsilk	Crimson	Cyan
DarkBlue	DarkCyan	DarkGoldenrod
DarkGray	DarkGreen	DarkKhaki
DarkMagenta	DarkOliveGreen	DarkOrange
DarkOrchid	DarkRed	DarkSalmon

Table A-3. Standard colors (continued)

DarkSeaGreen	DarkSlateBlue	DarkSlateGray
DarkTurquoise	DarkViolet	DeepPink
DeepSkyBlue	DimGray	DodgerBlue
Firebrick	FloralWhite	ForestGreen
Fuchsia	Gainsboro	GhostWhite
Gold	Goldenrod	Gray
Green	GreenYellow	Honeydew
HotPink	IndianRed	Indigo
Ivory	Khaki	Lavender
LavenderBlush	LawnGreen	LemonChiffon
LightBlue	LightCoral	LightCyan
LightGoldenrodYel-low	LightGray	LightGreen
LightPink	LightSalmon	LightSeaGreen
LightSkyBlue	LightSlateGray	LightSteelBlue
LightYellow	Lime	LimeGreen
Linen	Magenta	Maroon
MediumAquamarine	MediumBlue	MediumOrchid
MediumPurple	MediumSeaGreen	MediumSlateBlue
MediumSpringGreen	MediumTurquoise	MediumVioletRed
MidnightBlue	MintCream	MistyRose
Moccasin	NavajoWhite	Navy
OldLace	Olive	OliveDrab
Orange	OrangeRed	Orchid
PaleGoldenrod	PaleGreen	PaleTurquoise
PaleVioletRed	PapayaWhip	PeachPuff
Peru	Pink	Plum
PowderBlue	Purple	Red
RosyBrown	RoyalBlue	SaddleBrown
Salmon	SandyBrown	SeaGreen
SeaShell	Sienna	Silver
SkyBlue	SlateBlue	SlateGray
Snow	SpringGreen	SteelBlue
Tan	Teal	Thistle
Tomato	Transparent	Turquoise
Violet	Wheat	White
WhiteSmoke	Yellow	YellowGreen

Table A-4 lists the properties of the SystemColors class provided by the .NET Framework.

Table A-4. SystemColors properties

ActiveBorder	ActiveCaption
ActiveCaptionText	AppWorkspace
Control	ControlDark
ControlDarkDark	ControlLight
ControlLightLight	ControlText
Desktop	GrayText
Highlight	HighlightText
HotTrack	InactiveBorder
InactiveCaption	InactiveCaptionText
Info	InfoText
Menu	MenuText
ScrollBar	Window
WindowFrame	WindowText

Index

We'd like to hear your suggestions for improving our indexes. Send email to *index@oreilly.com*.

O

object icons, IntelliSense, 49
ObjectCollection, methods, 683
objects
    ADO.NET object model, 914
        DataSet class, 915
    command objects (ADO.NET), creating
        programmatically, 932
    control objects (ADO.NET), creating
        programmatically, 932
    data objects, creating by hand, 976
    debugging example, 1097–1103
    examining debugging code, 1094
    Form, 117
    Graphics, 326
OleDbCommandBuilder, 1070
    (see also Command Builder,
        SqlCommandBuilder)
Online Community, Visual Studio .NET Start
        Page, 33
OnPaint method
    Analog Clock project, 369
    Control class, definition in, 356
    overriding, 356–358
    SystemInformation class, 275
OnTimer event handler, Analog Clock
        project, 386
Open menu item, Visual Studio .NET File
        menu, 41
Open/Open With... menu item, Visual
        Studio .NET View menu, 51
OpenType fonts
    icons, 309
    (see also TrueType fonts)
operators
    DateTime structure, 742
    TimeSpan structure, 745
Option Strict, configuration files and, 1126
options
    menu items, 843
    radio buttons, 845
options menu, 858
    event handler, 862
Options... menu item, Visual Studio .NET
        Tools menu, 68
ordered pairs, geometric structures,
        System.Drawing namespace, 349
Outlining menu item, Visual Studio .NET
        Edit menu, 47
output console, 8

overriding methods
    OnPaint method, 356–358
    specializing controls and, 792
OwnerDraw menus, 867
    bitmaps, 867
    event handlers, 868
    OwnerDraw property, 867

P

Padding property, TabControl, 543
page transforms, coordinates, 344
PageSetupDialog properties, 207
PageUnit property, Graphics object, 344
Paint event, 353–361
    controls, 253
    forcing, 358
    Graphics objects, 347–348
    Invalidate method, 358
Paint method, OnPaint method
        invoking, 282
PaintDemo.cs, 353
PaintDemo.vb, 354
PaintEventArgs parameter, Graphics objects
        and, 347
PaintInvalidate.cs, 358
PaintOverride.cs, 356
PaintOverride.vb, 357
Palatino font, 308
Panel control, 462, 530
    properties, Enabled, 531
parameters
    /arget, 12
    scrollbars as adjusters, 569
        C#, 570
parent relationships, ADO.NET
        databases, 953
    C#, 954
    VB.NET, 956
Pascal casing, 1113
passwords, configuration files and, 1120
Paste, Clipboard and, 494
Paste menu item, event handler, 494
Pen class, 351
    Analog Clock project, 387
    properties, 352
Pen object
    Analog Clock project, 387
    instantiation, 351
PenAlignment enumeration, 352
pens
    disposal, 351
    properties, 352

X

x coordinate
    Analog Clock project float variables, 373
    computing, 371
XCOPY application installation, 1168
XCopy deployment, 118
XML
    configuration files, 1113–1115
    well-formed, 1114
XML Web Services, Visual Studio .NET Start
        Page, 33

Y

y coordinate, computing, 371
yPosition variable, Location property, 242

Z

z-order, Splitter control, 600

About the Authors

Jesse Liberty is the author of a dozen books, including the best-selling *Programming C#* from O'Reilly, now in its third edition. Jesse is the president of Liberty Associates, Inc. (*http://www.LibertyAssociates.com*), where he provides .NET training, contract programming, and consulting. He is a former vice president of electronic delivery for Citibank and a former Distinguished Software Engineer and architect for AT&T, Ziff Davis, Xerox, and PBS.

Dan Hurwitz has been a software entrepreneur, developer, and trainer specializing in database applications for more than fifteen years. He is the principal in Sterling Solutions, a provider of database and PC consulting services, now focusing on .NET web and Windows training and application development. When not working on software projects or books or spending time with his family, he loves riding his mountain bike.

Colophon

Our look is the result of reader comments, our own experimentation, and feedback from distribution channels. Distinctive covers complement our distinctive approach to technical topics, breathing personality and life into potentially dry subjects.

The animal on the cover of *Programming .NET Windows Applications* is a darter. The darter is so named because it attacks its prey with a quick thrust of its long neck and sharp beak (effectively stabbing its victim), moving in a "darting" motion. The darter is also sometimes known as the snake bird, because its swimming style consists of submerging its entire body, except for its head and long neck, under water. This behavior gives the darter the appearance of a snake.

The darter is native to the southern United States, as well as to parts of Asia, Africa, and Australia. It lives alone or in groups of two or three near freshwater lakes, rivers, ponds, and swamps. Its main food is fish, and it supplements this diet with insects and reptiles.

Mary Brady was the production editor, and Ann Schirmer was the copyeditor for *Programming .NET Windows Applications*. Mary Brady, Phil Dangler, and Sarah Sherman proofread the book. Matt Hutchinson, Colleen Gorman, and Claire Cloutier provided quality control. Tom Dinse and Johnna Van Hoose Dinse wrote the index. Jamie Peppard, James Quill, Marlowe Shaeffer, and Derek Di Matteo provided production support.

Ellie Volckhausen designed the cover of this book, based on a series design by Edie Freedman. The cover image is a 19th-century engraving from the Dover Pictorial Archive. Emma Colby produced the cover layout with QuarkXPress 4.1 using Adobe's ITC Garamond font.

David Futato designed the interior layout. This book was converted by Andrew Savikas to FrameMaker 5.5.6 with a format conversion tool created by Erik Ray, Jason McIntosh, Neil Walls, and Mike Sierra that uses Perl and XML technologies. The text font is Linotype Birka; the heading font is Adobe Myriad Condensed; and the code font is LucasFont's TheSans Mono Condensed. The illustrations that appear in the book were produced by Robert Romano and Jessamyn Read using Macromedia FreeHand 9 and Adobe Photoshop 6. The tip and warning icons were drawn by Christopher Bing. This colophon was written by Mary Brady.

Related Titles Available from O'Reilly

.NET

.NET and XML
.NET Framework Essentials, *3rd Edition*
.NET Windows Forms in a Nutshell
ADO.NET in a Nutshell
ADO.NET Cookbook
ASP.NET in a Nutshell, *2nd Edition*
ASP.NET Cookbook
C# Essentials, *2nd Edition*
C# in a Nutshell, *2nd Edition*
C# Cookbook
C# Language Pocket Guide
Learning C#
Learning Visual Basic.NET
Mastering Visual Studio.NET
Object Oriented Programming with Visual Basic .NET
Programming .NET Components
Programming .NET Security
Programming .NET Web Services
Programming ASP.NET, *2nd Edition*
Programming C#, *3rd Edition*
Programming Visual Basic .NET, *2nd Edition*
VB.NET Core Classes in a Nutshell
VB.NET Language in a Nutshell, *2nd Edition*
VB.NET Language Pocket Reference

O'REILLY®

Our books are available at most retail and online bookstores.
To order direct: 1-800-998-9938 • *order@oreilly.com* • *www.oreilly.com*
Online editions of most O'Reilly titles are available by subscription at *safari.oreilly.com*

Keep in touch with O'Reilly

1. Download examples from our books

To find example files for a book, go to:

www.oreilly.com/catalog

select the book, and follow the "Examples" link.

2. Register your O'Reilly books

Register your book at *register.oreilly.com*

Why register your books?
Once you've registered your O'Reilly books you can:

* Win O'Reilly books, T-shirts or discount coupons in our monthly drawing.
* Get special offers available only to registered O'Reilly customers.
* Get catalogs announcing new books (US and UK only).
* Get email notification of new editions of the O'Reilly books you own.

3. Join our email lists

Sign up to get topic-specific email announcements of new books and conferences, special offers, and O'Reilly Network technology newsletters at:

elists.oreilly.com

It's easy to customize your free elists subscription so you'll get exactly the O'Reilly news you want.

4. Get the latest news, tips, and tools

www.oreilly.com

* "Top 100 Sites on the Web"—PC Magazine
* CIO Magazine's Web Business 50 Awards

Our web site contains a library of comprehensive product information (including book excerpts and tables of contents), downloadable software, background articles, interviews with technology leaders, links to relevant sites, book cover art, and more.

5. Work for O'Reilly

Check out our web site for current employment opportunities:

jobs.oreilly.com

6. Contact us

O'Reilly & Associates, Inc.
1005 Gravenstein Hwy North
Sebastopol, CA 95472 USA

TEL: 707-827-7000 or 800-998-9938
      (6am to 5pm PST)

FAX: 707-829-0104

order@oreilly.com
For answers to problems regarding your order or our products. To place a book order online, visit:

www.oreilly.com/order_new

catalog@oreilly.com
To request a copy of our latest catalog.

booktech@oreilly.com
For book content technical questions or corrections.

corporate@oreilly.com
For educational, library, government, and corporate sales.

proposals@oreilly.com
To submit new book proposals to our editors and product managers.

international@oreilly.com
For information about our international distributors or translation queries. For a list of our distributors outside of North America check out:

international.oreilly.com/distributors.html

adoption@oreilly.com
For information about academic use of O'Reilly books, visit:

academic.oreilly.com

O'REILLY®

Our books are available at most retail and online bookstores.
To order direct: 1-800-998-9938 • *order@oreilly.com* • *www.oreilly.com*
Online editions of most O'Reilly titles are available by subscription at *safari.oreilly.com*